BURNS

INDIANA STATUTES

ANNOTATED

CODE EDITION

TITLE 35
Articles 44–50

2009 REPLACEMENT VOLUME

Original Edition by
HARRISON BURNS

LexisNexis®

(Pub.42605)

PREFACE

This 2009 replacement includes acts of the 2009 First Regular Session and the 2009 Special Session of the 116th General Assembly. This volume is conformed to the Indiana Code as enacted by the 1976 Regular Session of the General Assembly, as amended. For the convenience of the user, the complete Code number, indicating title, article, chapter, and section of the Code, appears at the beginning of each section.

To better serve our customers, by making our annotations more current, LexisNexis has changed the sources that are read to create annotations for this publication. Rather than waiting for cases to appear in printed reporters, we now read court decisions as they are released by the courts. A consequence of this more current reading of cases, as they are posted online on LEXIS, is that the most recent cases annotated may not yet have print reporter citations. These will be provided, as they become available, through later publications.

This publication contains annotations taken from the decisions of the Supreme Court of Indiana as of May 21, 2009, the Court of Appeals of Indiana as of June 12, 2009 and the Indiana Tax Court posted as of May 14, 2009. These cases will be printed in the North Eastern 2d Reporter series. Also included in this volume are annotations taken from the opinions of federal courts for cases arising in Indiana, appearing on LexisNexis, and issued through May 15, 2009. Where available, citations have been provided to the Supreme Court Reporter (S.Ct.), Federal Reporter, 3d Series (F.3d), Federal Supplement, 2d Series (F. Supp. 2d), and Bankruptcy Reporter (Bankr.).

The annotations include references to the Indiana Law Journal, Indiana Law Review, Notre Dame Law Review, Res Gestae, Valparaiso University Law Review. These and other helpful notes and references have been reviewed, updated, and relocated where necessary. Cross reference notes providing directions to statutory material of similar and/or related subject matter located elsewhere in the Code are provided. Where a law has been repealed, the compiler's notes to that section contain a reference to any new or present provision on a similar subject, where applicable.

Additional information on the use of Burns Statutes is included in the User's Guide, published in the volume containing Titles 1, 2, 3 (Arts. 1-7). The User's Guide should be consulted for a basic understanding of the features available in Burns Statutes.

If you have questions or suggestions concerning Burns' Indiana Statutes, please write, call toll free 1-800-833-9844, fax toll free 1-800-643-1280, visit our website at www.lexis.com, or email us at customer.support@bender.com. Direct written inquiries to:

LexisNexis
Attn: Customer Service
    Burns Indiana Statutes Annotated
1275 Broadway
Albany, NY 12204-2694

Please note that, for your convenience, there are postpaid cards at the back of each index volume for your suggestions.

LexisNexis®

September 2009

_____

Prepared by the Editorial Staff of the Publisher:

Robert W. Gibson   Senior Legal Analyst
Florence McCowin   Coordinating Editor
Stephen White   Indexing Legal Analyst
Andrea Stinnie   Indexing Coordinating Editor

USER'S GUIDE

In order to assist both the legal profession and the layman in obtaining the maximum benefit from Burns' Indiana Statutes Annotated, a User's Guide is included with the set. The Guide contains comments and information on the many features found in the Burns' Statutes volumes, which are intended to increase the usefulness of the set. See the volume containing Titles 1, 2, 3 (Arts. 1-7), for the complete User's Guide.

History of Burns' Statutes Annotated

For over one hundred years, the Bench and Bar of Indiana have relied on Burns' Indiana Statutes Annotated, published first by The Bobbs-Merrill Company and now by LexisNexis. Bobbs-Merrill first became involved in 1889 with the publication of Elliott's Supplement to the Revised Statutes of 1881 by the Bowen-Merrill Company, a predecessor company. (The Revised Statutes of 1881 are an unenacted compilation sanctioned by the state of Indiana.)

From that time until the publication of the official Indiana Code, Burns' Indiana Statutes Annotated was the sole organized and indexed source of the official statute law of Indiana with the exception of Revised Statutes of Indiana published by E.D. Myers & Co., Chicago, Illinois in 1896, and Baldwin's 1934 Indiana Statutes published by the Baldwin Law Publishing Company, Cleveland, Ohio.

On November 3, 1892, Harrison Burns of Vincennes, Indiana, entered into an agreement which led to the publication of Burns' Annotated Indiana Statutes in three volumes in 1894. This work followed the organization of the Revised Statutes of 1881 but the sections were all assigned numbers continuously through the three volumes and it was completely annotated and fully indexed. Supplements were published in 1895 and 1897. Additional revisions by Judge Burns were required in 1908 and 1914 and the 1914 revision was supplemented in 1918 and 1921. A complete revision edited by Benjamin F. Watson was published in 1926 and supplemented in 1929.

In 1933 Bobbs-Merrill began publication of a new and improved edition of Burns' Annotated Indiana Statutes in 12 volumes, completely annotated, indexed and edited by the publisher's editorial staff. This edition contained a new section numbering system, provided for annual supplementation of each volume and for individual volume revision to keep the work current and up-to-date at all times. This edition was kept current by supplementation and revision and was the standard reference for Indiana Statutes until it was replaced by the present Burns' Code Edition beginning in 1972. The Burns' Code Edition, also completely annotated and indexed, was necessary to conform to the organization and numbering system of the Indiana Code of 1971 which was carried into the official Indiana Code of 1976.

In 1976, the Law Division of the Bobbs-Merrill Company was acquired by The Michie Company, and for a number of years the Burns' Code was published under the name Michie/Bobbs-Merrill. While there has been a continuity of editorial personnel working on Burns' Indiana Statutes Annotated, beginning in 1985 the Burns' Code was published under the name of The Michie Company, and, following subsequent acquisitions, is now published under the name of LexisNexis. It is the desire and goal of the Publishers to continue to provide an authoritative, useful and convenient edition of Indiana Statutes Annotated.

EFFECTIVE DATES OF ACTS AND STATUTES WITHOUT
EFFECTIVE DATE PROVISIONS

Between 1979 and 1987, under IC 1-1-3-3, each act passed at a regular session of the general assembly took effect on September 1 next following its enactment, unless a different time was specified in the act. In 1987, IC 1-1-3-3 was amended to change the date to July 1. Prior to the adoption of IC 1-1-3-3, the effective date of acts which did not contain an emergency clause was the date of the last filing in the counties as shown by the proclamation of the governor under IC 1-1-3-2. The table below lists the effective dates for acts and statutes which did not contain other effective date provisions.

[R. = Regular Session; S. = Special Session]

1842-1843 Revised Statutes	Approved Feb. 11, 1843—no effective date record
1851-1852 Special Acts	November 6, 1852
1851-1852 Revised Statutes	May 6, 1853
1853	July 24, 1853
1855	August 17, 1855
1857	August 24, 1857
1858 S.	August 6, 1859
1859	August 6, 1859
1861	July 5, 1861
1861 S.	September 7, 1861
1863	October 10, 1863
1865	September 2, 1865
1865 S.	April 13, 1866
1867	June 6, 1867
1869 R. and S.	August 16, 1869
1871	July 10, 1871
1872 S.	July 7, 1873
1873	July 7, 1873
1875 R. and S.	August 24, 1875
1877 R. and S.	July 2, 1877
1879 R. and S.	May 31, 1879
1881 R. and S.	September 19, 1881
1883	June 5, 1883
1885 R. and S.	July 18, 1885
1887	May 21, 1887
1889	May 10, 1889
1891	June 3, 1891
1893	May 18, 1893
1895	June 28, 1895
1897	April 14, 1897
1899	April 27, 1899
1901	May 15, 1901
1903	April 23, 1903
1905	April 15, 1905
1907	April 10, 1907
1908 S.	November 20, 1908
1909	April 5, 1909
1911	April 21, 1911
1913	April 30, 1913
1915	April 26, 1915
1917	May 31, 1917
1919	May 15, 1919
1920 S.	January 16, 1920

TABLE OF TITLES AND ARTICLES

TABLE OF CONTENTS

TITLE 35

CRIMINAL LAW AND PROCEDURE

Indiana Code

———

TITLE 35

CRIMINAL LAW AND PROCEDURE

ARTICLE 44

OFFENSES AGAINST PUBLIC ADMINISTRATION

CHAPTER 1

BRIBERY — OFFICIAL MISCONDUCT

35-44-1-1. Bribery.

(a) A person who:

(1) confers, offers, or agrees to confer on a public servant, either before or after the public servant becomes appointed, elected, or qualified, any property except property the public servant is authorized by law to accept, with intent to control the performance of an act related to the employment or function of the public servant or because of any official act performed or to be performed by the public servant, former public servant, or person selected to be a public servant;

(2) being a public servant, solicits, accepts, or agrees to accept, either before or after the person becomes appointed, elected, or qualified, any property, except property the person is authorized by law to accept, with intent to control the performance of an act related to the person's employment or function as a public servant;

(3) confers, offers, or agrees to confer on a person any property, except property the person is authorized by law to accept, with intent to cause that person to control the performance of an act related to the employment or function of a public servant;

1

(4) solicits, accepts, or agrees to accept any property, except property the person is authorized by law to accept, with intent to control the performance of an act related to the employment or function of a public servant;

(5) confers, offers, or agrees to confer any property on a person participating or officiating in, or connected with, an athletic contest, sporting event, or exhibition, with intent that the person will fail to use the person's best efforts in connection with that contest, event, or exhibition;

(6) being a person participating or officiating in, or connected with, an athletic contest, sporting event, or exhibition, solicits, accepts, or agrees to accept any property with intent that the person will fail to use the person's best efforts in connection with that contest, event, or exhibition;

(7) being a witness or informant in an official proceeding or investigation, solicits, accepts, or agrees to accept any property, with intent to:

(A) withhold any testimony, information, document, or thing;

(B) avoid legal process summoning the person to testify or supply evidence; or

(C) absent the person from the proceeding or investigation to which the person has been legally summoned;

(8) confers, offers, or agrees to confer any property on a witness or informant in an official proceeding or investigation, with intent that the witness or informant:

(A) withhold any testimony, information, document, or thing;

(B) avoid legal process summoning the witness or informant to testify or supply evidence; or

(C) absent himself or herself from any proceeding or investigation to which the witness or informant has been legally summoned; or

(9) confers or offers or agrees to confer any property on an individual for:

(A) casting a ballot or refraining from casting a ballot; or

(B) voting for a political party, for a candidate, or for or against a public question;

in an election described in IC 3-5-1-2 or at a convention of a political party authorized under IC 3;

commits bribery, a Class C felony.

(b) It is no defense that the person whom the accused person sought to control was not qualified to act in the desired way.

History.
IC 35-44-1-1, as added by Acts 1976, P.L.148, § 4; 1977, P.L.340, § 53; P.L.103-2005, § 41; P.L.222-2005, § 47; P.L.1-2006, § 532.

Compiler's Notes.
P.L.222-2005, § 51, effective May 11, 2005, provides:
"(a) IC 4-2-6-13, IC 4-2-6-14, IC 4-15-10-4, IC 35-44-1-2, and IC 35-44-1-7, all as amended by this act, apply only to crimes committed after passage of this act.

"(b) IC 35-44-1-1, as amended by this act, applies only crimes committed after June 30, 2005."

Cross References.
Giving or offering financial inducement to vote or refrain from voting, IC 3-14-3-19.
Defenses relating to culpability, IC 35-41-3-1 — IC 35-41-3-10.
Penalties for felonies, IC 35-50-1, IC 35-50-2, IC 35-50-5-2.

NOTES TO DECISIONS

—Conspiracy.
—Duplicity.
—Insufficient.
—Joinder of Counts.
—Knowledge.
—Sufficient.
—Variance.
Instructions.
Intent.
—Rebuttal of Guilt.
Money.
Prosecuting Attorney.
Retrial.
Sheriff.
Single Transaction.
Time of Payment.
Township Trustees.
Value of Bribe.

City Council.

An indictment against a member of a city council for soliciting pay for voting for an ordinance did not need to allege that the defendant intended to vote for the ordinance because of the money solicited. Higgins v. State, 157 Ind. 57, 60 N.E. 685, 1901 Ind. LEXIS 122 (1901).

Compounding Felonies.

—Note and Mortgage.

In a suit on a promissory note and to foreclose a mortgage, the question whether the note and the mortgage were given in consideration of the plaintiff's promise to dismiss a criminal prosecution against the maker, in violation of former section punishing the compounding of felonies, was a question of fact for the jury. Kosiba v. Gary Wholesale Grocery Co., 91 Ind. App. 71, 170 N.E. 105, 1930 Ind. App. LEXIS 40 (1930).

Conspiracy.

Where an indictment charged a conspiracy and also an overt act which was itself felonious under a former section punishing bribery of public officers, the conspiracy was not merged in the felony, where defendant was put on trial on the charge of conspiracy only. Williams v. State, 188 Ind. 283, 123 N.E. 209, 1919 Ind. LEXIS 44 (1919).

Under former statutes, a conspiracy by a prosecuting officer and other officers to solicit bribes was a crime, and the conspirators did not need to have been charged and tried singly under the bribery statutes. Williams v. State, 188 Ind. 283, 123 N.E. 209, 1919 Ind. LEXIS 44 (1919).

In order to sustain a conviction for conspiracy to bribe a state official it was not necessary to prove that a bribery had been committed. Hutcheson v. State, 244 Ind. 345, 192 N.E.2d 748, 1963 Ind. LEXIS 199 (1963).

Where circumstantial evidence raised a mere suspicion of guilt and a series of inferences had to be drawn from such evidence to sustain the theory of guilt, a conviction for conspiracy to bribe a state official could not be sustained. Hutcheson v. State, 244 Ind. 345, 192 N.E.2d 748, 1963 Ind. LEXIS 199 (1963).

Where the evidence supported defendant's conviction of conspiring to commit bribery, his acquittal on a bribery charge did not necessarily constitute a determination that the charged overt act was not committed, and his conviction on a conspiracy count was not contrary to law. Sawyer v. State, 583 N.E.2d 795, 1991 Ind. App. LEXIS 2211 (1991).

Defendant's entrance into an agreement with another company to form a working relationship and subsequent payment to the principals of the other company so they would utilize their official positions to provide special treatment and financial opportunities to defendant through his company supported a conviction for conspiracy to commit bribery. Hightower v. State, 866 N.E.2d 356, 2007 Ind. App. LEXIS 1015 (2007).

Election Judge.

In charging a person with an attempt to bribe an election judge, it was necessary to allege under and by what authority such judge was designated or appointed. Banks v. State, 157 Ind. 190, 60 N.E. 1087, 1901 Ind. LEXIS 143 (1901).

Elements.

—Date of Offense.

In bribery cases, like most felonies in which time is not of the essence, where a specific date is charged for the offense, the state may prove any date prior to the indictment and within the statute of limitations. This doctrine is limited, and reversal is required only where it is shown that the defendant was misled in his defense, or when the evidence may not preclude second jeopardy. Moritz v. State, 465 N.E.2d 748, 1984 Ind. App. LEXIS 2750 (1984).

—Influence.

In a prosecution of an officer for soliciting a bribe, it was not a necessary element of the offense that a person soliciting money or other valuable things should in fact be influenced in his official conduct as a result of the solicitation; it was only essential that there should have been an offer made by the officer to be influenced by money or other valuable things in his official action in a matter pending or that might legally come before him. Vehling v. State, 210 Ind. 17, 196 N.E. 107, 1935 Ind. LEXIS 229 (1935).

An accused cannot raise as a defense to a charge of bribery the fact that the person whom the accused sought to bribe could not act in the desired way. Winn v. State, 722 N.E.2d 345, 1999 Ind. App. LEXIS 2223 (1999).

Defendant could not argue that, because his video game machines were not illegal, he could not have attempted to influence the actions of the county prosecutor by sending the county prosecutor cash-filled envelopes. Winn v. State, 722 N.E.2d 345, 1999 Ind. App. LEXIS 2223 (1999).

Evidence.

—Other Offenses.

In a prosecution under former section punishing bribery of a public officer to procure a public contract, evidence of other offenses could be considered as bearing on purpose of payment only.

Evidence. (Cont'd)

—Other Offenses. (Cont'd)
Clevenger v. State, 188 Ind. 592, 125 N.E. 41, 1919 Ind. LEXIS 86 (1919).

It was not error to permit testimony of other alleged acts of bribery on the part of the defendant where such testimony tended to show both intent and guilty knowledge, and a common scheme or plan by establishing a course of conduct in soliciting bribes from others. Van Deveer v. State, 256 Ind. 509, 269 N.E.2d 865, 1971 Ind. LEXIS 667 (1971).

—Sufficient.
Evidence was sufficient to convict forest ranger of bribery where he sold trees from state forest for cash although standard procedure in selling such trees was by public bidding and placing the funds in accounts available only to department officials even though such ranger told the purchasers that the money would be used to purchase a back hoe for use on state land. Martin v. State, 419 N.E.2d 256, 1981 Ind. App. LEXIS 1348 (1981).

Where the probative evidence and reasonable inferences favorable to the verdict show that the defendant offered sums of money, ranging from $100 to $500, to complaining witness in exchange for her "dropping the charges," a reasonable trier of fact could conclude therefrom that defendant was guilty of bribery beyond a reasonable doubt. Minniefield v. State, 512 N.E.2d 1103, 1987 Ind. LEXIS 1067 (1987).

Gravamen of Offense.
In Indiana it is the soliciting or the receiving of money by an official to influence him with respect to his official duties that is the gravamen of the offense of bribery. United States v. Forszt, 655 F.2d 101, 1981 U.S. App. LEXIS 11072 (7th Cir. Ind. 1981).

The gravamen of the offense of bribery is the soliciting or receiving of money by an official to influence him with respect to his official duties. It is the receiving or soliciting of the payment which is prohibited, not the use of corrupted or influenced discretion, and therefore, it is the payment which triggers the beginning of the limitations period within which prosecution must be commenced. Stuckey v. State, 560 N.E.2d 88, 1990 Ind. App. LEXIS 1271 (1990).

Whether the public servant was actually controlled or influenced is irrelevant, so long as the payment was accepted or solicited with the intent to control the public servant. Stuckey v. State, 560 N.E.2d 88, 1990 Ind. App. LEXIS 1271 (1990).

This section requires that the act intended to be controlled relate to the employment or function of the public servant. Sawyer v. State, 583 N.E.2d 795, 1991 Ind. App. LEXIS 2211 (1991).

Payments from poker machine vendors to a county sheriff and chief deputy were not political contributions but were intended to influence the sheriff and chief deputy in the execution of their duties, all parties understanding that buying tickets to the sheriff's fundraiser also meant buying favors, such as raiding the competition's machines

and protecting the "friendly" vendors. United States v. Mokol, 957 F.2d 1410, 1992 U.S. App. LEXIS 4728 (7th Cir. Ind. 1992), cert. denied, 506 U.S. 899, 113 S. Ct. 284, 121 L. Ed. 2d 210, 1992 U.S. LEXIS 6246 (1992).

Highway Engineer.
A gravel road engineer appointed by county commissioners to superintend work on free gravel roads could be indicted for soliciting bribes. State v. Duncan, 153 Ind. 318, 54 N.E. 1066, 1899 Ind. LEXIS 45 (1899).

Persons could be indicted for conspiring to bribe a civil engineer appointed by county commissioners to superintend work on free gravel roads. State v. Ray, 153 Ind. 334, 54 N.E. 1067, 1899 Ind. LEXIS 47 (1899).

Indictment or Information.

—Conspiracy.
An indictment for conspiracy to solicit bribes did not need to directly allege that the money was the property of the persons to be solicited for bribes, in view of the well understood meaning of the word "bribe." Williams v. State, 188 Ind. 283, 123 N.E. 209, 1919 Ind. LEXIS 44 (1919).

If the names of persons soliciting bribes were known or were reasonably ascertainable by a grand jury, they should be pleaded in the indictment. Williams v. State, 188 Ind. 283, 123 N.E. 209, 1919 Ind. LEXIS 44 (1919).

In an indictment under prior statutes charging a conspiracy to solicit bribes from law violators, it was unnecessary to allege that the conspirators, at the time of the conspiracy, knew of specific violations or names of persons so engaged and from whom they could solicit bribes. Williams v. State, 188 Ind. 283, 123 N.E. 209, 1919 Ind. LEXIS 44 (1919).

An indictment for soliciting bribes by prosecuting attorney did not need to show overt acts done in pursuance of conspiracy. Williams v. State, 188 Ind. 283, 123 N.E. 209, 1919 Ind. LEXIS 44 (1919).

—Duplicity.
An indictment for conspiracy to commit a felony for soliciting bribes from persons conducting various illegal businesses, so classified as to bring them within the prohibition of the criminal statute, was not bad for duplicity. Williams v. State, 188 Ind. 283, 123 N.E. 209, 1919 Ind. LEXIS 44 (1919).

—Insufficient.
Where the defendant was charged with unlawful solicitation of a bribe, the looseness with which the indictment was drafted did not meet the test that an accused was entitled to have the charge against him stated with such certainty as would enable him to distinguish it from any other violation of the same statute, and to know not only that he was charged with a public offense, but also the particulars thereof so that he could be able to anticipate the proof and make defense, if he has one. State v. Jarboe, 240 Ind. 371, 165 N.E.2d 765, 1960 Ind. LEXIS 195 (1960).

Where an indictment was silent as to the par-

Indictment or Information. (Cont'd)

—Insufficient. (Cont'd)

ticular act of alleged bribery of the defendant, but was based on the so-called "generalized bribe" theory, it did not pass the specificity test allowing the defendant to anticipate the evidence to be adduced at trial, since the bribery statute specifically exempts property a public servant is authorized by law to accept, and the defendant was authorized by statute to accept compensation for part-time employment. Wurster v. State, 708 N.E.2d 587, 1999 Ind. App. LEXIS 426 (1999), transfer granted, 726 N.E.2d 298, 1999 Ind. LEXIS 550 (1999), aff'd in part, vacated in part, 715 N.E.2d 341, 1999 Ind. LEXIS 546 (1999).

—Joinder of Counts.

The separate acts of soliciting payment of the crime of burglary in the promise of a bribe and the subsequent payment of such bribe, as contemplated by the accused, were transactions consummated within the time contemplated by the character of the transaction involved and it was proper to join the charge of such acts in single counts. Smith v. State, 241 Ind. 1, 168 N.E.2d 199, 1960 Ind. LEXIS 134 (1960).

—Knowledge.

An allegation of knowledge of the official character of the person to whom the bribe was offered was necessary. Banks v. State, 157 Ind. 190, 60 N.E. 1087, 1901 Ind. LEXIS 143 (1901).

—Sufficient.

An affidavit (predecessor to information) for attempted bribery of a prosecuting attorney was held to allege sufficiently that accused knew that the person to whom the bribe was offered was the prosecuting attorney when she offered the bribe. Robinson v. State, 185 Ind. 119, 113 N.E. 306, 1916 Ind. LEXIS 23 (1916).

Under prior statutes, the allegation of an indictment that a prosecuting attorney had received a certain amount of bribes did not necessarily show that the grand jurors knew the names of those paying bribes or that evidence before them was satisfactory, so that omission to allege their names was not fatal. Williams v. State, 188 Ind. 283, 123 N.E. 209, 1919 Ind. LEXIS 44 (1919).

An indictment which was sufficient to enable the court and jury to distinctly understand the issue to be tried and to fully inform defendant of the nature of the charge was not uncertain. Williams v. State, 188 Ind. 283, 123 N.E. 209, 1919 Ind. LEXIS 44 (1919).

An affidavit (predecessor to information) under former statute punishing bribery of a public officer to procure a public contract was sufficient, although failing to allege that defendant knew party paid was public officer, where all allegations of the affidavit made that knowledge apparent. Clevenger v. State, 188 Ind. 592, 125 N.E. 41, 1919 Ind. LEXIS 86 (1919).

In a prosecution for attempted bribery of a sheriff in the selection of a jury, the failure of the affidavit (predecessor to information) to state that

accused was on trial did not render the affidavit defective, since the gist of the offense was the corrupt purpose of the defendants. Fenwick v. State, 200 Ind. 460, 164 N.E. 632, 1929 Ind. LEXIS 74 (1929).

An affidavit (predecessor to information) charging a coroner with an offer to take a bribe of money and thereby influence his official action by returning a verdict of "accidental death" of certain decedents was held sufficient as against a motion to quash for uncertainty. Vehling v. State, 210 Ind. 17, 196 N.E. 107, 1935 Ind. LEXIS 229 (1935).

The indictment was sufficient for a man of common intelligence to be able to ascertain that he was being charged with bribery and therefore apprise him of the nature of the charges that he was to defend. Thomas v. State, 251 Ind. 76, 238 N.E.2d 20, 1968 Ind. LEXIS 539 (1968).

—Variance.

The general rule relating to variance between the date of an alleged offense and the proof of the actual event is: (1) was the defendant misled by the variance from the allegations and specifications in the charge in the preparation and maintenance of his defense, and was he harmed or prejudiced thereby; (2) will the defendant be protected in the future criminal proceeding covering the same event, facts, and evidence against double jeopardy. Smith v. State, 241 Ind. 1, 168 N.E.2d 199, 1960 Ind. LEXIS 134 (1960).

Defendant could not have been misled in the preparation of his defense because of a variance between the alleged offense and the proof of the amount of the bribe, where the indictment charged bribery with respect to a certain number of specifically described unit of equipment manufactured by a named corporation for which bids were accepted on the date recited in the indictment and for which defendant received payment of a definite sum. Smith v. State, 241 Ind. 1, 168 N.E.2d 199, 1960 Ind. LEXIS 134 (1960).

Variance between indictments charging defendant with receiving United States currency and evidence establishing that he received three checks was immaterial, where defendant was not misled in the preparation of his defense. Stuckey v. State, 560 N.E.2d 88, 1990 Ind. App. LEXIS 1271 (1990).

Instructions.

In a prosecution for attempted bribery of a sheriff in the selection of a jury, it was not error for the court to refuse to give a tendered instruction authorizing assessment of the penalty fixed by former section relating to influencing, intimidating, or impeding jurors, witnesses, or court officers. Fenwick v. State, 200 Ind. 460, 164 N.E. 632, 1929 Ind. LEXIS 74 (1929).

In a prosecution for attempt to bribe a sheriff in the selection of a jury, an instruction that it is the province of the court to fix and assess the punishment was not erroneous. Fenwick v. State, 200 Ind. 460, 164 N.E. 632, 1929 Ind. LEXIS 74 (1929).

Where neither the specific time nor the physical circumstances under which the offense was committed were indispensable to the offense, the in-

Instructions. (Cont'd)
struction was proper where it was stated that the precise time of the commission of the offense did not need to be stated in the indictment, and the variance in time, if any, was immaterial since the alleged offense was stated as being within the statute of limitations. Smith v. State, 241 Ind. 1, 168 N.E.2d 199, 1960 Ind. LEXIS 134 (1960).

Intent.

—Rebuttal of Guilt.
Facts could be proved to rebut a guilty intent under an indictment for attempting to bribe an officer. Banks v. State, 157 Ind. 190, 60 N.E. 1087, 1901 Ind. LEXIS 143 (1901).

Money.
In a prosecution for attempted bribery of a sheriff in the selection of a jury, failure in the prosecution to allege or prove actual tender of money was immaterial. Fenwick v. State, 200 Ind. 460, 164 N.E. 632, 1929 Ind. LEXIS 74 (1929).

In a prosecution for attempted bribery of a sheriff, the jury was warranted in concluding that the offer by defendant to the sheriff of "fifty" meant $50.00 in money. Fenwick v. State, 200 Ind. 460, 164 N.E. 632, 1929 Ind. LEXIS 74 (1929).

Prosecuting Attorney.
A prosecuting attorney was held to be an officer entrusted with the administration of justice under the statute of 1852. State v. Henning, 33 Ind. 189, 1870 Ind. LEXIS 75 (1870).

Retrial.
Retrial was not barred where there was sufficient evidence to sustain convictions for bribery and official misconduct, where the evidence demonstrated that the defendant accepted money from an individual he believed to be a drug dealer in exchange for the names of several police informants and the descriptions of several police undercover vehicles, and that the defendant believed that the individual would loan him more money in exchange for more information at a later date. Geiger v. State, 721 N.E.2d 891, 1999 Ind. App. LEXIS 2218 (1999).

Sheriff.
In a prosecution under this section for attempted bribery of a sheriff in the selection of a petit jury, the sheriff was not disqualified by Ind. Const., Art. 1, § 13, to call talesmen in the trial of defendant so as to require the coroner to select the talesmen. Fenwick v. State, 200 Ind. 460, 164 N.E. 632, 1929 Ind. LEXIS 74 (1929).

Single Transaction.
Where there was one transaction between a chemical salesman and the defendant, a city mayor, for which the defendant was paid a single lump sum of $2,900 in exchange for five orders of supplies for the city, there was a single intent and design — a bribe in exchange for the purchase of material — and the fact that it was separated into five orders for the same city at the same time did not alter that result. One offense was committed; conviction on a single count was therefore affirmed, and judgment was vacated on the duplicitous counts in the indictment. Moritz v. State, 465 N.E.2d 748, 1984 Ind. App. LEXIS 2750 (1984).

Since a prosecution for professional gambling contemplated prosecution for a single act, and since the offense of bribery requires the conferring of a benefit with intent to control the performance of an act related to the employment of an official, the defendant could not be convicted of bribing a county prosecutor seven times when the intent was to induce the official not to prosecute him a single time. Winn v. State, 722 N.E.2d 345, 1999 Ind. App. LEXIS 2223 (1999).

Time of Payment.
It is unlawful for a public official to sell his public trust while in office even though the last installment for the services rendered is to come after he leaves office. United States v. Forszt, 655 F.2d 101, 1981 U.S. App. LEXIS 11072 (7th Cir. Ind. 1981).

Indiana bribery is a continuing offense so that payments made as part of an arrangement to influence a public official in the discharge of his duties are violations of Indiana law regardless of whether the money is paid before or after the bargained-for acts are performed. United States v. Forszt, 655 F.2d 101, 1981 U.S. App. LEXIS 11072 (7th Cir. Ind. 1981).

Township Trustees.
The offering to township trustees of money or property to induce them to purchase school supplies was bribery. State v. McDonald, 106 Ind. 233, 6 N.E. 607, 1886 Ind. LEXIS 97 (1886); Glover v. State, 109 Ind. 391, 10 N.E. 282, 1887 Ind. LEXIS 165 (1887).

Value of Bribe.
It was held that the receiving of a promissory note by an officer to influence his action was not bribery, as the note was worthless. State v. Walls, 54 Ind. 561, 1876 Ind. LEXIS 358 (1876).

An indictment for bribery should have distinctly stated and charged that the officer charged with being bribed accepted, or agreed to accept, for his official action, some amount of money or article of value. State v. Stephenson, 83 Ind. 246, 1882 Ind. LEXIS 264 (1882).

Cited:
State v. Pickett, 423 N.E.2d 717, 1981 Ind. App. LEXIS 1538 (1981); United States v. Allen, 10 F.3d 405, 1993 U.S. App. LEXIS 28022 (7th Cir. Ind. 1993); United States v. Stephens, 46 F.3d 587, 1995 U.S. App. LEXIS 1604 (7th Cir. Ind. 1995); Ingram v. State, 760 N.E.2d 615, 2001 Ind. App. LEXIS 2146 (2001).

OPINIONS OF ATTORNEY GENERAL

A city officer or employee who accepts additional emolument from private sources to perform a pre-existing public duty may run the risk of being charged with the crime of bribery. 1970, No. 17, p. 43.

RESEARCH REFERENCES

Valparaiso University Law Review.
Bribery as a "Real" Defense Against a Holder in Due Course, 19 Val. U.L. Rev. 397 (1985).

Collateral References.
Criminal liability of corporation for bribery or conspiracy to bribe public official. 52 A.L.R.3d 1274.
Furnishing public official with meals lodging, or travel, or receipt of such benefits, as bribery. 67 A.L.R.3d 1231.
Criminal offense of bribery as affected by lack of authority of state public officer or employee. 73 A.L.R.3d 374.
Venue in bribery cases where crime is committed partly in one county and partly in another. 11 A.L.R.4th 704.

Federal regulation of competitive practices in liquor industry under § 5 of Federal Alcohol Administration Act (27 U.S.C.S. § 205). 58 A.L.R. Fed. 797.
Propriety of lesser-included-offense charge to jury in federal bribery prosecution. 107 A.L.R. Fed. 427.
Construction and application of § 2C1.1 of United States Sentencing Guidelines (18 U.S.C.S. APPX § 2C1.1) pertaining to offenses involving public officials offering, giving, soliciting, or receiving bribes, or extortion under color of official right. 144 A.L.R. Fed. 615.
Who is public official within meaning of federal statute punishing bribery of public official (18 U.S.C.A. § 201). 161 A.L.R. Fed. 491.

35-44-1-2. Official misconduct.

A public servant who:

(1) knowingly or intentionally performs an act that the public servant is forbidden by law to perform;

(2) performs an act the public servant is not authorized by law to perform, with intent to obtain any property for himself or herself;

(3) knowingly or intentionally solicits, accepts, or agrees to accept from an appointee or employee any property other than what the public servant is authorized by law to accept as a condition of continued employment;

(4) knowingly or intentionally acquires or divests himself or herself of a pecuniary interest in any property, transaction, or enterprise or aids another person to do so based on information obtained by virtue of the public servant's office that official action that has not been made public is contemplated;

(5) knowingly or intentionally fails to deliver public records and property in the public servant's custody to the public servant's successor in office when that successor qualifies; or

(6) knowingly or intentionally violates IC 36-6-4-17(b);

commits official misconduct, a Class D felony.

History.
IC 35-44-1-2, as added by Acts 1976, P.L.148, § 4; 1977, P.L.340, § 54; 1980, P.L.73, § 2; P.L.34-1992, § 2; P.L.222-2005, § 48.

Compiler's Notes.
P.L.222-2005, § 51, effective May 11, 2005, provides:
"(a) IC 4-2-6-13, IC 4-2-6-14, IC 4-15-10-4, IC 35-44-1-2, and IC 35-44-1-7, all as amended by this act, apply only to crimes committed after passage of this act.
"(b) IC 35-44-1-1, as amended by this act, applies only crimes committed after June 30, 2005."

Cross References.
Escape, IC 35-44-3-5.
Fees, taxing illegal, IC 5-7-2-8.
Impeachment of local officers, IC 5-8-1-21 — IC 5-8-1-31.
Penalties for felonies, IC 35-50-1, IC 35-50-2, IC 35-50-5-2.
Removal from office for intoxication, IC 5-8-2-1.
Removal from office upon conviction of official misconduct, IC 35-50-5-1.1.

NOTES TO DECISIONS

In General.

This section does not impose a duty to act. State v. Pickett, 423 N.E.2d 717, 1981 Ind. App. LEXIS 1538 (1981).

No language in this section restricts the forbidden offenses to those acts which only public officials are forbidden to commit. Daugherty v. State, 466 N.E.2d 46, 1984 Ind. App. LEXIS 2788 (1984).

Applicability.

State had discretion to charge state excise police officer, who violated IC 7.1-5-5-2 by accepting gratuities from alcoholic beverage permit holder, under either IC 7.1-5-1-8, which applies to violations of IC Title 7.1 for which no other penalty is provided, or under official misconduct statute, IC 35-44-1-2(1). State v. Dugan, 793 N.E.2d 1034, 2003 Ind. LEXIS 692 (2003).

Confessions Obtained by Force.

The fact that acts of police officers may have constituted a violation of former section prohibiting obtaining a confession from a prisoner by force did not prevent a trial and conviction of assault and battery. Bonahoon v. State, 203 Ind. 51, 178 N.E. 570, 1931 Ind. LEXIS 51, 79 A.L.R. 453 (1931).

Confessions by prisoners obtained by force were useless because they were not admissible in evidence, and the prior statute prohibiting obtaining

such confessions applied with equal force whether formal charges had been filed, or the arrested person was being held for investigation. Suter v. State, 227 Ind. 648, 88 N.E.2d 386, 1949 Ind. LEXIS 176 (1949).

Construction With Other Laws.

Defendant was improperly charged under IC 35-44-1-2 for professional misconduct in receiving gratuities from companies licensed to sell alcoholic beverages and in receiving the payment of wages for the performance of duties not related to his position as a public servant; IC 7.1-5-1-8 was intended to cover such misconduct and defendant could only be charged with a Class B misdemeanor under IC 7.1-5-1-8. State v. Dugan, 769 N.E.2d 235, 2002 Ind. App. LEXIS 891 (2002), transfer granted, — N.E.2d —, 2002 Ind. LEXIS 951 (2002), superseded, 793 N.E.2d 1034, 2003 Ind. LEXIS 692 (2003).

County Officers.

A county treasurer who received illegal fees in the collection of taxes by distress and sale was liable. State v. Burton, 3 Ind. 93 (1851).

County officers could only charge such fees as were provided by law for preparing instruments connected with their official duties. Eley v. Miller, 7 Ind. App. 529, 34 N.E. 836, 1893 Ind. App. LEXIS 286 (1893).

County commissioners could not be prosecuted for allowing illegal claims after the passage of an act legalizing their action. State v. Trueblood, 23 Ind. App. 31, 54 N.E. 822, 1899 Ind. App. LEXIS 7 (1899).

As a result of an inmate's substantial dependency and the extraordinary control jailers wield over their prisoners, inmates are not precluded from recovering damages from a sheriff for injuries suffered by intentional wrongful acts of jail employees, and a service provider may not claim consent as a defense for sexual misconduct with a detainee. Robins v. Harris, 740 N.E.2d 914, 2000 Ind. App. LEXIS 2035 (2000), clarified, 743 N.E.2d 1142, 2001 Ind. App. LEXIS 204 (2001), transfer granted, 753 N.E.2d 17, 2001 Ind. LEXIS 599 (2001), aff'd, appeal dismissed, 769 N.E.2d 586, 2002 Ind. LEXIS 478 (Ind. 2002).

De Facto Officers.

The fact that jury commissioners failed to take oath to support the federal constitution and the constitution of Indiana, prior to entering upon their duties as such commissioners, did not render their authority to act subject to collateral attack by application for writ of error coram nobis (since abolished), since the commissioners acted as de facto officers. Steinbarger v. State, 214 Ind. 36, 14 N.E.2d 533, 1938 Ind. LEXIS 138 (1938).

Evidence.

—False Certification by Notary.

Evidence was sufficient to sustain conviction for commanding notary to certify falsely to swearing

Evidence. (Cont'd)

—False Certification by Notary. (Cont'd)
person to affidavit. Klink v. State, 203 Ind. 647, 179 N.E. 549, 1932 Ind. LEXIS 87, 79 A.L.R. 272 (1932).

The mere fact that an owner of a retail store, who was charged with conspiracy with a township trustee, his bookkeeper, and notary public, to have the notary feloniously and falsely certify that defendant had been sworn to an affidavit affixed to and forming a part of a claim filed with the trustee, had conversations with the trustee, would not justify an inference that they entered into an unlawful conspiracy. Shonfeld v. State, 219 Ind. 654, 40 N.E.2d 700, 1942 Ind. LEXIS 177 (1942).

In a prosecution charging a conspiracy between defendant, his bookkeeper, a township trustee, and a notary public, to have the notary public feloniously and falsely certify that defendant had been sworn to an affidavit affixed to and forming a part of a claim filed with the trustee, whereas the affidavit had not been subscribed and sworn to by the defendant, a conviction could not be sustained by evidence from which an inference might be drawn that there was a conspiracy to have the notary falsely certify that defendant's bookkeeper had subscribed and sworn to the affidavit. Shonfeld v. State, 219 Ind. 654, 40 N.E.2d 700, 1942 Ind. LEXIS 177 (1942).

In order to sustain a conviction under an indictment charging defendant, his bookkeeper, a township trustee, and a notary public, with having the notary public feloniously and falsely certify that defendant had been sworn to an affidavit, whereas the affidavit had not been subscribed and sworn to by defendant, there must have been evidence from which an agreement between at least two persons named in the indictment could have been legally inferred. Shonfeld v. State, 219 Ind. 654, 40 N.E.2d 700, 1942 Ind. LEXIS 177 (1942).

In a prosecution for unlawfully and feloniously counseling and procuring a notary public to falsely certify that defendant had subscribed his name and was sworn to an affidavit affixed to and forming a part of a claim filed with a township trustee against poor relief funds, the evidence was insufficient to sustain a conviction, where it could not be reasonably inferred that the notary intended to, or did, certify that defendant had subscribed and sworn to the affidavit. Shonfeld v. State, 219 Ind. 654, 40 N.E.2d 700, 1942 Ind. LEXIS 177 (1942).

Where the evidence showed that the employees of a license branch had the custom of waiting until closing hours before notarizing certificates obtained during the day's business, there was insufficient proof of false attestation, since prior statute punishing false attestation required knowledge on the part of the notary public that the person certified to have sworn before the notary was not present. Kyser v. State, 247 Ind. 482, 217 N.E.2d 585, 1966 Ind. LEXIS 450 (1966).

—Insufficient.
Evidence was insufficient to support defendant's convictions for official misconduct as to the first victim, because there was no evidence that defendant was performing "official duties" when the offenses were committed against the first victim; defendant interacted with the first victim's family as a county case worker for about a week and there was no evidence that defendant still had such a responsibility at the time the offenses were committed. Heinzman v. State, 895 N.E.2d 716, 2008 Ind. App. LEXIS 2444 (2008).

—Sufficient.
Evidence sufficient to establish official misconduct. Flick v. State, 455 N.E.2d 339, 1983 Ind. LEXIS 1000 (1983).

Fictitious Name.
The jury had the duty to determine whether the use of a fictitious name was to commit a fraud, from all the evidence. In so doing the members of the jury could use their own personal experiences and knowledge in everyday matters of affairs of this sort. Peak v. State, 240 Ind. 334, 163 N.E.2d 584, 1960 Ind. LEXIS 191 (1960).

The law does not permit the use of a fictitious name to perpetrate a fraud. Peak v. State, 240 Ind. 334, 163 N.E.2d 584, 1960 Ind. LEXIS 191 (1960).

Indictment.

—Illegal Collection of Fees.
An indictment for collecting more than was due should have stated how much was due, and if nothing was due, that fact should have been stated. State v. Coggswell, 1832 Ind. LEXIS 18 (1832).

When it was alleged that the officer received more than was due, the amount illegally received did not need to have been stated. State v. Stotts, 1840 Ind. LEXIS 128 (1840).

An indictment showing the receipt by an officer of more fees than was due was sufficient. Emory v. State, 1842 Ind. LEXIS 4 (1842).

An indictment should have properly described the writ or execution under which it was alleged money was illegally collected. Seany v. State, 1843 Ind. LEXIS 46 (1843).

An indictment would lie for obtaining money by extortion from a county. State v. Moore, 1 Ind. 548, Smith Ind. 316 (1849).

It must have been alleged that the fees were taxed and received by the officer in his official capacity. State v. Oden, 10 Ind. App. 136, 37 N.E. 731, 1894 Ind. App. LEXIS 123 (1894).

—Neglect of Roads.
In an indictment it was not necessary for the highway to have been established by law. Tate v. State, 1839 Ind. LEXIS 7 (1839).

If the road was described as one within the jurisdiction of the officer, it was sufficient. State v. Harsh, 1843 Ind. LEXIS 15 (1843).

The particular roads or parts of roads suffered to be out of repair should have been named in the indictment. State v. McMurrin, 1 Ind. 44 (1848).

—Notaries.
In a prosecution for unlawfully and feloniously counseling and procuring a notary public to falsely

Indictment. (Cont'd)

—Notaries. (Cont'd)
certify that defendant had subscribed his name and was sworn to an affidavit affixed to and forming a part of a claim filed with a township trustee and for conspiring with the trustee and the notary to have the notary so certify, the indictment was not bad because it failed to show that the notary public affixed her seal to the jurat. Shonfeld v. State, 219 Ind. 654, 40 N.E.2d 700, 1942 Ind. LEXIS 177 (1942).

A count of an indictment charging that defendant and a township trustee unlawfully and feloniously united, conspired, combined, confederated, and agreed to and with each other and to and with a notary public and another for the unlawful and felonious purpose and with the felonious intent to have the notary falsely certify that defendant had been sworn by the notary to an affidavit, whereas the affidavit had not been subscribed and sworn to by the defendant, sufficiently alleged a conspiracy for the purpose and with the object of committing a felony. Shonfeld v. State, 219 Ind. 654, 40 N.E.2d 700, 1942 Ind. LEXIS 177 (1942).

A count of an indictment alleging that accused and another "did then and there unlawfully and feloniously counsel, encourage, and procure" a notary public to make a false certificate, sufficiently alleged that the crime charged was committed, since the word "procure" means "to bring about by contrivance," "to effect," or "to cause." Shonfeld v. State, 219 Ind. 654, 40 N.E.2d 700, 1942 Ind. LEXIS 177 (1942).

In the prosecution of defendant for making a false certificate as a notary public to deed purporting to be executed by one person to the defendant's parents, the indictment did not need allege that the notary did not see the party execute the document and that the party failed to acknowledge the execution. Peak v. State, 240 Ind. 334, 163 N.E.2d 584, 1960 Ind. LEXIS 191 (1960).

Where a notary public attested an affidavit purportedly signed in the notary's presence by an affiant he had known for a substantial period of time, even though the purported affiant had been dead for over five months at the time of execution of the affidavit, guilty knowledge required by proof of mens rea was established. Nor was the requirement any different if the notary attested an affidavit which was blank when he signed it for he could not possibly assure himself that the signature of a purported affiant would be validly placed on the document. Johnson v. State, 251 Ind. 17, 238 N.E.2d 651, 1968 Ind. LEXIS 536 (1968).

—Official Negligence.
An indictment alleging that the members of a board of county commissioners allowed a claim against the county which they knew to have been illegal did not charge a crime under the provisions of the statute that "any officer under the constitution or laws of this state who fails to perform any duty in the manner and within the time prescribed by law, shall upon conviction thereof be fined," etc. State v. Robertson, 23 Ind. App. 424, 55 N.E. 491, 1899 Ind. App. LEXIS 70 (1899).

—Suffering Escape.
An indictment did not need to allege that the prisoner was held by a sufficient warrant nor was it necessary that a copy of the warrant have been set out. State v. Sparks, 78 Ind. 166, 1881 Ind. LEXIS 482 (1881).

Instructions.
In a prosecution of a peace officer for assault and battery with intent to kill, based on the act of the officer in shooting a man whom he was trying to arrest for a misdemeanor, and who was resisting such attempted arrest, and trying to escape from it, an instruction that such officer would not be authorized to use force and instruments which would imperil life was erroneous in view of defendant's duties to enforce fish and game laws. Durham v. State, 199 Ind. 567, 159 N.E. 145, 1927 Ind. LEXIS 61 (1927).

Judges.
The legislature could prohibit judges from practicing law. McCracken v. State, 27 Ind. 491, 1867 Ind. LEXIS 146 (1867); Justice v. Lairy, 19 Ind. App. 272, 49 N.E. 459, 1898 Ind. App. LEXIS 30 (1898).

Lesser Included Offense.
Where a sheriff was prosecuted for battery and official misconduct, the jury's failure to return a verdict on battery charge was not inconsistent with its guilty verdict on official misconduct count because the battery count is analogous to a lesser included offense. Daugherty v. State, 466 N.E.2d 46, 1984 Ind. App. LEXIS 2788 (1984).

Municipal Officers.
Policemen were formerly liable to prosecution for failure to discharge official duties. Hopewell v. State, 22 Ind. App. 489, 54 N.E. 127, 1899 Ind. App. LEXIS 211 (1899).

Until modified by the Municipal Code of 1905, prior statutes punishing extortion and official negligence included municipal officers, such as patrolmen. Gaughan v. State, 187 Ind. 334, 118 N.E. 565, 1918 Ind. LEXIS 36 (1918).

Since the enactment of the statute regulating municipal corporations in 1905, municipal officers had to be prosecuted under section 240 (former IC 18-1-20-4) of that act, and the statute punishing extortion and official negligence was no longer applicable to them. Gaughan v. State, 187 Ind. 334, 118 N.E. 565, 1918 Ind. LEXIS 36 (1918).

Omission to Act.
This section does not make the omission to perform an act an offense but merely specifies under what circumstances an omission to act may be made punishable. State v. Pickett, 423 N.E.2d 717, 1981 Ind. App. LEXIS 1538 (1981).

Performance of Act Forbidden by Law.
The allegation that a public servant failed to enforce or cause to be enforced an ordinance would not state a crime under this section because such failure would not constitute the performance of an

Performance of Act Forbidden by Law. (Cont'd)
act forbidden by law. State v. Pickett, 423 N.E.2d 717, 1981 Ind. App. LEXIS 1538 (1981).

The act, by a prison guard, of permitting a prisoner to have a conjugal visit is highly irregular and irresponsible, but is not illegal, and a conviction for official misconduct is not supported by sufficient evidence and must be reversed. Thomas v. State, 515 N.E.2d 880, 1987 Ind. App. LEXIS 3247 (1987).

State had discretion to charge state excise police officer, who violated IC 7.1-5-5-2 by accepting gratuities from alcoholic beverage permit holder, under either IC 7.1-5-1-8, which applies to violations of IC Title 7.1 for which no other penalty is provided, or under official misconduct statute, IC 35-44-1-2(1). State v. Dugan, 793 N.E.2d 1034, 2003 Ind. LEXIS 692 (2003).

Permitting Lynching.
If a sheriff permitted a prisoner to be taken from his custody and lynched, the coroner of the county could not, on his own relation, sue to have the sheriff removed from office. State ex rel. Maxwell v. Dudley, 161 Ind. 431, 68 N.E. 899, 1903 Ind. LEXIS 188 (1903).

Prosecuting Attorney.
An agreement by a prosecuting attorney to delay or discontinue a prosecution was void. Gray v. State, 107 Ind. 177, 8 N.E. 16, 1886 Ind. LEXIS 316 (1886); State v. Bain, 112 Ind. 335, 14 N.E. 232, 1887 Ind. LEXIS 412 (1887).

Former statutes relating to penalties for usurpation of office and acting as an officer without qualifying did not affect the legality of a criminal trial conducted by a prosecuting attorney who was not qualified to act. Bruce v. State, 199 Ind. 489, 158 N.E. 480, 1927 Ind. LEXIS 53 (1927).

Public Servant.
A store security officer employed by a private security firm, who was also an appointed sheriff's special deputy, was a "public servant," and could be convicted of official misconduct. Robey v. State, 481 N.E.2d 138, 1985 Ind. App. LEXIS 2668 (1985).

—Off Duty.
Act of off-duty special deputy, who at time of act was acting as the employee of a private security firm, in accepting money to forego arresting and prosecuting a person who had left a store without paying for merchandise constituted official misconduct. Bell v. Bingham, 484 N.E.2d 624, 1985 Ind. App. LEXIS 2891 (1985).

Removal for Intoxication.
The legislature had power to provide for the removal of an officer on account of intoxication. McComas v. Krug, 81 Ind. 327, 1882 Ind. LEXIS 9 (1882).

Repair of Roads.
If the officer had no means to keep the roads in repair, he should have set the fact up as a defense. Tate v. State, 1839 Ind. LEXIS 7 (1839); State v. Harsh, 1843 Ind. LEXIS 15 (1843); State v. Brown, 8 Blackf. 69, 1846 Ind. LEXIS 38 (1846).

A prosecution could be maintained for not keeping roads in repair before the expiration of the time limited for expending moneys thereon in each year. State v. Hogg, 5 Ind. 515 (1854).

—Civil Actions.
Statutes providing a civil liability for failure to keep roads in repair did not prohibit a criminal prosecution for such failure. State v. Virt, 3 Ind. 447 (1852).

Persons were not deprived of the right to maintain civil actions for the obstruction of highways. Martin v. Marks, 154 Ind. 549, 57 N.E. 249, 1900 Ind. LEXIS 70 (1900).

—Mandamus.
The statutes requiring the road supervisor to keep the roads in good repair did not prevent a road supervisor from being compelled by mandate to repair highways. State ex rel. Cutter v. Kamman, 151 Ind. 407, 51 N.E. 483, 1898 Ind. LEXIS 110 (1898).

The duty of a supervisor to keep highways in good repair was a public duty, imperative and not discretionary, and he could be compelled by mandate to perform such duty. Lamphier v. Karch, 59 Ind. App. 661, 109 N.E. 938, 1915 Ind. App. LEXIS 241 (1915).

Retrial.
Retrial was not barred where there was sufficient evidence to sustain convictions for bribery and official misconduct, where the evidence demonstrated that the defendant accepted money from an individual he believed to be a drug dealer in exchange for the names of several police informants and the descriptions of several police undercover vehicles, and that the defendant believed that the individual would loan him more money in exchange for more information at a later date. Geiger v. State, 721 N.E.2d 891, 1999 Ind. App. LEXIS 2218 (1999).

Cited:
State v. Pickett, 424 N.E.2d 452, 1981 Ind. App. LEXIS 1541 (1981).

OPINIONS OF ATTORNEY GENERAL

Attorney who was also justice of peace was not prohibited from practicing law in city courts. 1949, No. 96, p. 360.

Inasmuch as the auditor of state was charged with the responsibility of safeguarding blank warrants, together with the fact that the nature of such warrants required utmost care in handling and custody, the auditor was not required to release blank warrants from the jurisdiction and control of his office. 1963, No. 20, p. 90.

A member of a county council would appear to be in violation of this chapter, concerning official misconduct and conflict of interest, in an instance where the county council let a county contract with a business which in turn offered a portion of the work to a company in which the member of the county council owns a substantial interest. 1980, No. 80-38, p. 122.

RESEARCH REFERENCES

Collateral References.

Construction and application of § 2C1.1 of United States Sentencing Guidelines (18 U.S.C.S. APPX § 2C1.1) pertaining to offenses involving public officials offering, giving, soliciting, or receiving bribes, or extortion under color of official right. 144 A.L.R. Fed. 615.

35-44-1-3. Conflicts of interest — Public servants.

(a) A public servant who knowingly or intentionally:
(1) has a pecuniary interest in; or
(2) derives a profit from;
a contract or purchase connected with an action by the governmental entity served by the public servant commits conflict of interest, a Class D felony.

(b) This section does not prohibit a public servant from receiving compensation for:
(1) services provided as a public servant; or
(2) expenses incurred by the public servant as provided by law.

(c) This section does not prohibit a public servant from having a pecuniary interest in or deriving a profit from a contract or purchase connected with the governmental entity served under any of the following conditions:
(1) If the:
(A) public servant is not a member or on the staff of the governing body empowered to contract or purchase on behalf of the governmental entity;
(B) functions and duties performed by the public servant for the governmental entity are unrelated to the contract or purchase; and
(C) public servant makes a disclosure under subsection (d)(1) through (d)(6).
(2) If the contract or purchase involves utility services from a utility whose rate structure is regulated by the state or federal government.
(3) If the public servant:
(A) is an elected public servant or a member of the board of trustees of a state supported college or university; and
(B) makes a disclosure under subsection (d)(1) through (d)(6).
(4) If the public servant:
(A) was appointed by an elected public servant or the board of trustees of a state supported college or university; and
(B) makes a disclosure under subsection (d)(1) through (d)(7).
(5) If the public servant:
(A) acts in only an advisory capacity for a state supported college or university; and
(B) does not have authority to act on behalf of the college or university in a matter involving a contract or purchase.
(6) If the public servant:
(A) is employed by the governing body of a school corporation and the contract or purchase involves the employment of a dependent or the payment of fees to a dependent; and
(B) makes a disclosure under subsection (d)(1) through (d)(6).
(7) If the public servant is under the jurisdiction of the state ethics commission as provided in IC 4-2-6-2.5 and obtains from the state ethics commission, following full and truthful disclosure, written approval that the public servant will not or does not have a conflict of interest in connection with the contract or purchase under IC 4-2-6 and this section. The approval required under this subdivision must be:

(A) granted to the public servant before action is taken in connection with the contract or purchase by the governmental entity served; or

(B) sought by the public servant as soon after the contract or purchase as the public servant becomes aware of the facts that give rise to a question of conflict of interest.

(d) A disclosure required by this section must:

(1) be in writing;

(2) describe the contract or purchase to be made by the governmental entity;

(3) describe the pecuniary interest that the public servant has in the contract or purchase;

(4) be affirmed under penalty of perjury;

(5) be submitted to the governmental entity and be accepted by the governmental entity in a public meeting of the governmental entity prior to final action on the contract or purchase;

(6) be filed within fifteen (15) days after final action on the contract or purchase with:

(A) the state board of accounts; and

(B) if the governmental entity is a governmental entity other than the state or a state supported college or university, the clerk of the circuit court in the county where the governmental entity takes final action on the contract or purchase; and

(7) contain, if the public servant is appointed, the written approval of the elected public servant (if any) or the board of trustees of a state supported college or university (if any) that appointed the public servant.

(e) The state board of accounts shall forward to the state ethics commission a copy of all disclosures filed with the board under IC 16-22-2 through IC 16-22-5, IC 16-23-1, or this section.

(f) The state ethics commission shall maintain an index of all disclosures received by the commission. The index must contain a listing of each public servant, setting forth the disclosures received by the commission made by that public servant.

(g) A public servant has a pecuniary interest in a contract or purchase if the contract or purchase will result or is intended to result in an ascertainable increase in the income or net worth of:

(1) the public servant; or

(2) a dependent of the public servant who:

(A) is under the direct or indirect administrative control of the public servant; or

(B) receives a contract or purchase order that is reviewed, approved, or directly or indirectly administered by the public servant.

(h) It is a defense in a prosecution under this section that the public servant's interest in the contract or purchase and all other contracts and purchases made by the governmental entity during the twelve (12) months before the date of the contract or purchase was two hundred fifty dollars ($250) or less.

(i) Notwithstanding subsection (d), a member of the board of trustees of a state supported college or university, or a person appointed by such a board of trustees, complies with the disclosure requirements of this chapter with respect to the member's or person's pecuniary interest in a particular type of contract or purchase which is made on a regular basis from a particular vendor if the member or person files with the state board of accounts and the board of trustees a statement of pecuniary interest in that particular type of contract or purchase made with that particular vendor. The statement required by this subsection must be made on an annual basis.

(j) This section does not apply to members of the governing board of a hospital organized or operated under IC 16-22-1 through IC 16-22-5 or IC 16-23-1.

(k) As used in this section, "dependent" means any of the following:

(1) The spouse of a public servant.

(2) A child, stepchild, or adoptee (as defined in IC 31-9-2-2) of a public servant who is:

(A) unemancipated; and

(B) less than eighteen (18) years of age.

(3) Any individual more than one-half (½) of whose support is provided during a year by the public servant.

History.
IC 35-44-1-3, as added by Acts 1978, P.L.144, § 7; 1981, P.L.304, § 1; P.L.329-1983, § 1; P.L.13-1987, § 16; P.L.66-1987, § 28; P.L.109-1988, § 3; P.L.183-1988, § 1; P.L.197-1989, § 3; P.L.2-1993, § 185; P.L.22-1995, § 3; P.L.1-1997, § 149.

Cross References.
Penalties for felonies, IC 35-50-1, IC 35-50-2, IC 35-50-5-2.
Public contracts, collusive bidding prohibited, IC 24-1-2-3, IC 24-1-2-4.

NOTES TO DECISIONS

ANALYSIS

In General.
Contracts Void.
Councilman.
Eligibility for Office.
Health Officers.
Indictment and Information.
Land in Trust.
Public Contracts.
Purchase of Supplies.
Purpose.
Recovery of Amount Paid.
Relation by Marriage.
Room of Township Trustee.
Time of Becoming Public Servant.

In General.
Cities could not make contracts with any officer thereof that would create any liability against the city. Brazil v. McBride, 69 Ind. 244, 1879 Ind. LEXIS 61 (1879); Ft. Wayne v. Rosenthal, 75 Ind. 156, 1881 Ind. LEXIS 236 (1881); McGregor v. City of Logansport, 79 Ind. 166, 1881 Ind. LEXIS 746 (1881); Case v. Johnson, 91 Ind. 477, 1883 Ind. LEXIS 401 (1883); Benton v. Hamilton, 110 Ind. 294, 11 N.E. 238, 1887 Ind. LEXIS 53 (1887).

No officer of a municipal corporation can have any interest in a contract which would create an indebtedness or liability against the corporation. Mogul v. Garvey, 54 Ind. App. 547, 103 N.E. 118, 1913 Ind. App. LEXIS 134 (1913).

Public officers are prohibited by law from receiving any percentage or profit or money whatever on, or being interested directly or indirectly in public contracts passed upon and entered into under their jurisdiction and authority. State ex rel. Steers v. Holovachka, 236 Ind. 565, 142 N.E.2d 593, 1957 Ind. LEXIS 208 (1957).

Contracts Void.
All contracts executed in contravention of the provisions of a statute prohibiting state and other public officers to have interest in certain contracts for public works were void. Wingate v. Harrison School Township, 59 Ind. 520, 1877 Ind. LEXIS 755 (1877); Ft. Wayne v. Rosenthal, 75 Ind. 156, 1881 Ind. LEXIS 236 (1881); Case v. Johnson, 91 Ind. 477, 1883 Ind. LEXIS 401 (1883); Benton v. Hamilton, 110 Ind. 294, 11 N.E. 238, 1887 Ind. LEXIS 53 (1887).

Councilman.
Where councilman did not become a member of the council officially until after the resolution was passed by the common council approving the off-street parking project, the fact that he owned property the legal title of which was in his name while the equitable title was in the name of another, did not establish a conflict of interest between him acting individually and as a council member. Keener v. Kendallville, 244 Ind. 87, 191 N.E.2d 6, 1963 Ind. LEXIS 163 (1963).

Eligibility for Office.
Persons interested in franchises granted by a city, or in a contract with a city, were ineligible to hold office in the city and the ineligibility refers to the time when the term of office began and not to the time of the election to such office. Hoy v. State, 168 Ind. 506, 81 N.E. 509, 1907 Ind. LEXIS 132 (1907).

Health Officers.
A member of the board of health appointed by a city council was prohibited from making a contract with the city. Ft. Wayne v. Rosenthal, 75 Ind. 156, 1881 Ind. LEXIS 236 (1881).

A secretary of a city board of health could not contract with the city to render medical aid to diseased persons. Greenfield v. Black, 42 Ind. App. 645, 82 N.E. 797, 1907 Ind. App. LEXIS 9 (1908).

A contract made by the board of trustees of a town with the secretary of the town's board of health to care for smallpox patients was not illegal under the statute, but could be contrary to public policy. New Carlisle v. Tullar, 61 Ind. App. 230, 110 N.E. 1001, 1916 Ind. App. LEXIS 51 (1916).

A contract by a health officer of a town with the board of health to treat smallpox patients for a consideration did not come within the prohibition of former section. New Carlisle v. Tullar, 61 Ind.

Health Officers. (Cont'd)
App. 230, 110 N.E. 1001, 1916 Ind. App. LEXIS 51 (1916).

Indictment and Information.
Affidavit charging city councilman with being interested in a contract entered into between the city and a third person for painting fire stations was held insufficient for failure to state manner in which defendant became interested in contract after it was entered into. State v. Green, 207 Ind. 583, 194 N.E. 182, 1935 Ind. LEXIS 175 (1935).

Land in Trust.
A city cannot contract to buy land which is owned in trust by the mayor's father even though the mayor himself may not have actually pursued the contract. Blinn v. Marion, 181 Ind. App. 87, 390 N.E.2d 1066, 1979 Ind. App. LEXIS 1223 (1979).

Public Contracts.
Since a special or local assessment was justified and authorized only by, and would be unconstitutional and invalid without, a special benefit to the property assessed, resulting from a special or local public improvement and since the city acts as a statutory agent for the affected property owners, the contracts for the construction of the sewers must be public contracts within the meaning of former section. State ex rel. Steers v. Holovachka, 236 Ind. 565, 142 N.E.2d 593, 1957 Ind. LEXIS 208 (1957).

Purchase of Supplies.
A public officer could not contract with himself for the supply of articles which he could be authorized by law to purchase. Miller v. Jackson Tp., 178 Ind. 503, 99 N.E. 102, 1912 Ind. LEXIS 117 (1912).

Purpose.
The intent of the law was not to outlaw a primary contract of employment between the town board and an employee but to prevent a board

member or employee of a municipal corporation from using his existing position of public trust to further his own private gain. Crider v. State, 258 Ind. 541, 282 N.E.2d 819, 1972 Ind. LEXIS 601 (1972).

Recovery of Amount Paid.
If an officer of a municipal corporation sold articles to the corporation and received pay therefor, the corporation could recover the amount paid without returning such articles. McNay v. Lowell, 41 Ind. App. 627, 84 N.E. 778, 1908 Ind. App. LEXIS 206 (1908).

Relation by Marriage.
A contract entered into for street improvements was not rendered invalid by reason of the fact that the deputy civil engineer of the city was the father-in-law of one of the contractors. Cason v. Lebanon, 153 Ind. 567, 55 N.E. 768, 1899 Ind. LEXIS 84 (1899).

Room of Township Trustee.
A township trustee was not prohibited by former section from appropriating the money appropriated for office rent, for the use of a room in his dwelling for the conduct of township business, where there was no other available room in the township for such purpose, and the township was of the eighth class. Marion Tp. of Boone County v. Howard, 196 Ind. 167, 147 N.E. 619, 1925 Ind. LEXIS 29 (1925).

Time of Becoming Public Servant.
Where councilman did not become a member of the council officially until after the resolution was passed by the common council approving the off-street parking project, the fact that he owned property, the legal title of which was in his name while the equitable title was in the name of another, did not establish a conflict of interest between him acting individually and as a council member. Keener v. Kendallville, 244 Ind. 87, 191 N.E.2d 6, 1963 Ind. LEXIS 163 (1963).

OPINIONS OF ATTORNEY GENERAL

A county attorney was prohibited from entering into a contract with the board of county commissioners for the furnishing of insurance on county property. 1935, p. 304.

Both the common law and statute law prohibit a firm or corporation, of which a member of the park board of a city is a member, a stockholder, or officer, from selling supplies or materials or otherwise entering into a contract with the park board or the city acting through the agency of the park board, but do not prohibit such firm or corporation from bona fide selling supplies or materials or otherwise entering into contracts with some other independent department of the city. 1943, p. 340.

Former section might be construed to prohibit board of trustees of Northern Indiana Children's Hospital from appointing one of themselves as member of the active staff. 1949, No. 98, p. 373.

A member of the parole board was not permitted legally to enter into contracts for purchases made

with the correctional institution on which he was serving. 1958, No. 9, p. 38.

A member of a county board of public welfare, being the holder of a lucrative office, could not be in a position where he could receive profit or money through a contract entered into by the board of county commissioners, with a firm of which he was a member. 1958, No. 21, p. 92.

In an absence of fraud, a member of the board of public works who was employed by a company which supplied materials to contractors who had contracts with said board of public works did not have a direct or indirect interest in such contract so as to render it void or illegal either in violation of the statutes of this state or as contrary to public policy. 1959, No. 18, p. 85.

In order for a justice of the peace to rent a part of his premises for courtroom facilities it would have been necessary for him, a township officer, to enter into a contract with the township in which he exercised official jurisdiction and received "profit or money" for such contract. It was not permissible for the township trustee to pay rent for a part of the premises owned by a justice of the peace for use by said justice in conducting his court. 1959, No. 40, p. 190.

A member of a city or town board of zoning appeals or plan commission was an officer so that any contract between said official and the unit of government in which he exercises his official jurisdiction was absolutely void. 1961, No. 45, p. 287.

A contract between a member of a city or town board of zoning appeals or plan commission and some other unit of government, outside the official's normal sphere of authority, probably would not have violated former sections, although such contracts should have been avoided by any public official. 1961, No. 45, p. 287.

Any allowances made for sheriff's house rent and fuel pursuant to former IC 17-3-8-1, would not have violated provisions of former section prohibiting officers from being interested in public contracts. 1961, No. 68, p. 394.

Neither the secretary to the mayor of a city nor the airport manager were employees within the prohibition of former section. 1962, No. 14, p. 62.

A contract between an individual serving as a member of an "independent administrative board of a municipality" who was directly or indirectly interested in such contract, with some other department of the same municipality including some other "independent administrative board" of which the individual was not a member, was void as against public policy and as being contrary to the provisions of former section, and the character of the board on which the contracting officer served and the character of the board with which he contracted was immaterial, providing the contract created a liability against the municipality. 1962, No. 44, p. 233.

There is no statutory or constitutional prohibition against a city fireman of the city of New Castle being employed to do additional work under the city engineer in laying curbs, gutters, and sewers in parts of the city. Responsibility for a determination of whether such employment would be against public policy rests with the appointing authority. 1964, No. 56, p. 304.

A member of the state fair board was a "state officer" within the meaning of former statute. 1966, No. 25, p. 168.

While it was true that the members of the police force in a fifth-class city were appointees of the mayor, it would seem unreasonable to conclude that such police officers were "appointees" as that term was employed in the former criminal statute, but it would seem more reasonable to assume the legislature intended that statute to have applied only to those "appointees" who would have been officers exercising some of the sovereign authority of the governmental unit and not to police officer appointees who were mere "employees" and not "officers" in the legal connotation of that term. 1966, No. 39, p. 268.

A member of the county board of public welfare

could not be hired as an attorney for such board or be put in any other governmental position whereby he would receive a pecuniary benefit from the welfare department's business. 1973, No. 1, p. 1.

It was illegal for a state official owning or having an interest in real estate to enter into a lease contract with the state of Indiana for the rental of such property to a state agency; and the courts of Indiana held further that any such contracts made and entered into by public officials under which such officials might have received a benefit were void and could not be enforced. 1973, No. 10, p. 43.

A sheriff who appoints special deputies under IC 36-8-10-6 and receives a pecuniary interest from their appointment may be in violation of this section. 1982, No. 82-14, p. 167.

Since the four local individual grantees (the attorney for the city plan commission, a member of the city housing authority, the daughter of a city redevelopment commission member, and the secretary to the city economic development commission director) would be receiving grants from the federal government Rental Rehabilitation Program through the state and city redevelopment commission, all city employees and their families and persons with whom the city employees have business ties may be prohibited by Federal Regulation 24 CFR 511.11 from receiving grants to rehabilitate private property owned by them which will be rented to persons under the Federal Rule 8 Rental Assistance Program unless the federal Department of HUD, which is the ultimate authority, grants an exception on a case-by-case basis, after disclosure and an opinion of the grantees' attorney that the interest for which the exception is sought would not violate state or local law, as provided by 24 CFR 511.11. 1985, No. 85-22, p. 117.

Disclosures under this section are by subsections (d)(2) and (d)(5) required to be submitted to the governmental entity and accepted by the governmental entity in a public meeting of the governmental entity prior to final action on the contract or purchase. 1988, No. 88-14, p. 210.

All school officers and employees are considered to be "public servants" as that term is used in this section. 1988, No. 88-14, p. 210.

A "disclosure" under this section does not necessarily permit a public servant to have a pecuniary interest in or derive a profit from a contract or purchase connected with a governmental entity he serves. Whether a civil conflict of interest exists or whether an action is against public policy is a question of fact. 1989, No. 89-3.

Although a city councilman may not necessarily violate this section by bidding on real property put up for auction by the city redevelopment commission, bidding on or contracting to purchase real estate from the city redevelopment commission should be avoided by a city councilman. 1989, No. 89-3.

The vote of a co-speaker of the house of representatives to approve payment of attorney fees for private legal counsel to defend the Indiana house apportionment statute did not constitute a conflict of interest under this section. 1990, No. 90-22.

RESEARCH REFERENCES

Indiana Law Review.
2006 Survey on Recent Developments in Indiana Law: Access to Justice for People Who Do Not Speak English, 40 Ind. L. Rev. 643 (2007).

Res Gestae.
Warning: Multiple Representation Where Public Interest Is Involved May Be Hazardous to Your Professional Standing, 26 Res Gestae 434.

Collateral References.
Validity and construction of orders and enactment requiring public officers and employees, or candidates for office, to disclose financial condition, interests, or relationships. 22 A.L.R.4th 237.

35-44-1-4. [Repealed.]

Compiler's Notes.
This section, concerning the illegality of contracts or agreements between county or city-county council members in the county, was repealed by P.L.329-1983, § 2.

35-44-1-5. Sexual relations between service provider and detainee.

(a) As used in this section, "service provider" means a public servant or other person employed by a governmental entity or another person who provides goods or services to a person who is subject to lawful detention.

(b) A service provider who knowingly or intentionally engages in sexual intercourse or deviate sexual conduct with a person who is subject to lawful detention commits sexual misconduct, a Class C felony.

(c) A service provider at least eighteen (18) years of age who knowingly or intentionally engages in sexual intercourse or deviate sexual conduct with a person who is:
(1) less than eighteen (18) years of age; and
(2) subject to lawful detention;
commits sexual misconduct, a Class B felony.

(d) It is not a defense that an act described in subsection (b) or (c) was consensual.

(e) This section does not apply to sexual intercourse or deviate sexual conduct between spouses.

History.
P.L.324-1987, § 1; P.L.69-2007, § 1, eff. July 1, 2007.

Compiler's Notes.
P.L.69-2007, § 2, effective July 1, 2007, provides:

"IC 35-44-1-5, as amended by this act, applies to offenses committed after June 30, 2007."

Cross References.
Penalties for felonies, IC 35-50-1, IC 35-50-2, IC 35-50-5-2.

NOTES TO DECISIONS

Constitutionality.
Off-duty civilian employee of a work-release center was a "service provider" under IC 35-44-1-5(a)-(d), an inmate on an 8-hour pass was subject to lawful detention, prosecution of employee for consensual sex with inmate did not violate the employee's due process or liberty interest protections, and as applied to the employee, the statute was therefore not unconstitutional. Hubbard v. State, 849 N.E.2d 1165, 2006 Ind. App. LEXIS 1262 (2006).

Cited:
Robins v. Harris, 740 N.E.2d 914, 2000 Ind. App. LEXIS 2035 (2000).

RESEARCH REFERENCES

Res Gestae.
Appellate civil law case update, 46 (No. 2) Res Gestae 13 (2002).

35-44-1-7. Profiteering from public service.

(a) As used in this section, "pecuniary interest" has the meaning set forth in section 3(g) [IC 35-44-1-3(g)] of this chapter.

(b) A person who knowingly or intentionally:

(1) obtains a pecuniary interest in a contract or purchase with an agency within one (1) year after separation from employment or other service with the agency; and

(2) is not a public servant for the agency but who as a public servant approved, negotiated, or prepared on behalf of the agency the terms or specifications of:

(A) the contract; or

(B) the purchase;

commits profiteering from public service, a Class D felony.

(c) This section does not apply to negotiations or other activities related to an economic development grant, loan, or loan guarantee.

(d) This section does not apply if the person receives less than two hundred fifty dollars ($250) of the profits from the contract or purchase.

(e) It is a defense to a prosecution under this section that:

(1) the person was screened from any participation in the contract or purchase;

(2) the person has not received a part of the profits of the contract or purchase; and

(3) notice was promptly given to the agency of the person's interest in the contract or purchase.

History.
P.L.13-1987, § 17; P.L.9-1990, § 5; P.L.222-2005, § 49.

Compiler's Notes.
This chapter does not contain a section 6 (IC 35-44-1-6).
P.L.222-2005, § 51, effective May 11, 2005, provides:
"(a) IC 4-2-6-13, IC 4-2-6-14, IC 4-15-10-4, IC

35-44-1-2, and IC 35-44-1-7, all as amended by this act, apply only to crimes committed after passage of this act.
"(b) IC 35-44-1-1, as amended by this act, applies only crimes committed after June 30, 2005."

Cross References.
Penalties for felonies, IC 35-50-1, IC 35-50-2, IC 35-50-5-2.

CHAPTER 2

PERJURY AND OTHER FALSIFICATIONS

35-44-2-1. Perjury.

(a) A person who:

(1) Makes a false, material statement under oath or affirmation, knowing the statement to be false or not believing it to be true; or

(2) Has knowingly made two (2) or more material statements, in a proceeding before a court or grand jury, which are inconsistent to the degree that one (1) of them is necessarily false;

commits perjury, a Class D felony.

(b) In a prosecution under subsection (a)(2) of this section:

(1) The indictment or information need not specify which statement is actually false; and

(2) The falsity of a statement may be established sufficient for conviction, by proof that the defendant made irreconcilably contradictory statements which are material to the point in question.

History.
IC 35-44-2-1, as added by Acts 1976, P.L.148, § 4; 1977, P.L.340, § 55; 1981, P.L.281, § 4.

Cross References.
Defenses relating to culpability, IC 35-41-3-1 — IC 35-41-3-10.

Penalties for felonies, IC 35-50-1, IC 35-50-2, IC 35-50-5-2.
Verification by affirmation, Rule TR. 11(B).

NOTES TO DECISIONS

ANALYSIS

In General.
Affidavits.
—Interpretation.
—Not Shown.
—Test of Sufficiency.
Comparable Offenses.
Defendant in Criminal Action.
Distinct Offense.
Elements.
—Unlawfully Issuing Sales Tax Exemption Certificates Distinguished.
Evidence.
—In General.
—Admissibility.
—Corroboration.
—Insufficient.
—Number of Witnesses.
—Officer Administering Oath.
—Sufficient.
False Informations.
Federal Statutes.
Grand Jury Proceeding.
—Notice to Defendant of Additional Subjects Investigated.
Indictment or Information.
—Continuance.
—Elements.
—Insufficient.
—Joint Indictment.
—Officer Administering Oath.
—Sufficient.
—Tax Matters.
—Words Used.
—Written Instruments.
Intent.
Jurors.
Materiality of Testimony.
—In General.
—Burden of Proof.
—Not Shown.
—Pleading.
—Required.
Recantation.
Self-Incrimination.
Special Statutes.
"Trial Proceeding."
What Constitutes Perjury.
—In General.
—Affidavit.

—Belief.
—Confusion.
—Intentional False Impression.
—Mistake or Inadvertence.
—Opinion.
—Unequivocal Acts.
—Unsworn Contradictory Statements.

In General.
A conviction for perjury may not lie when a person truthfully answers a question subject to more than one reasonable interpretation or signs an ambiguous statement. Griepenstroh v. State, 629 N.E.2d 887, 1994 Ind. App. LEXIS 175 (1994).

Affidavits.

—Interpretation.
In a charge for perjury, the questions and answers in a sworn statement must be interpreted in their context. Daniels v. State, 658 N.E.2d 121, 1995 Ind. App. LEXIS 1570 (1995).

—Not Shown.
Affidavit which did not contain a statement under oath or affirmation as contemplated by subsection (a) of this section would not serve as a predicate for a perjury prosecution and was neither an affidavit under Rule TR. 56(E) nor a verification by affirmation or representation under Rule TR. 11(B). Tannehill by Podgorski v. Reddy, 633 N.E.2d 318, 1994 Ind. App. LEXIS 480 (1994).

—Test of Sufficiency.
The chief test of the sufficiency of an affidavit is its ability to serve as a predicate for a perjury prosecution. Tannehill by Podgorski v. Reddy, 633 N.E.2d 318, 1994 Ind. App. LEXIS 480 (1994).

Comparable Offenses.
Since perjury and obstruction of justice are offenses comparable to criminal contempt, in that they are Class D felonies, and the possible sentence for a Class D felony ranges from a minimum of six months to a maximum of three years, a trial court's sentence of eleven and one-half years for contempt of court was manifestly unreasonable, and remand for imposition of a sentence of three years was required. State v. MacWilliams (In re Gardner), 713 N.E.2d 346, 1999 Ind. App. LEXIS 1017 (1999).

Defendant in Criminal Action.

If a defendant in a criminal action was acquitted, he could be convicted of perjury in giving false testimony on the trial. State v. Carey, 159 Ind. 504, 65 N.E. 527, 1902 Ind. LEXIS 66 (1902).

Distinct Offense.

Perjury is a distinct offense which can be committed only by an individual in his individual capacity. Lynn v. State, 207 Ind. 393, 193 N.E. 380, 1934 Ind. LEXIS 284 (1934).

Elements.

—Unlawfully Issuing Sales Tax Exemption Certificates Distinguished.

This section and IC 6-2.5-9-1 providing the penalty for a violation of the sales tax do not cover the same subject matter or conduct; only the mens rea elements, "knowing" and "with the intention," may be in common between them. Kibbey v. State, 733 N.E.2d 991, 2000 Ind. App. LEXIS 1303 (2000).

Evidence.

—In General.

The evidence in a prosecution for perjury in a voluntary affidavit (predecessor to information) must not only show the defendant swore falsely in fact, but also that he did so wilfully, corruptly and knowingly. Pendleton v. State, 239 Ind. 341, 156 N.E.2d 782, 1959 Ind. LEXIS 169 (1959).

—Admissibility.

In the prosecution of accused for giving false testimony before the grand jury, namely, that he did not state to the sheriff that certain persons did the shooting at his place when the deceased was shot and killed, which testimony was shown to have been false, the court properly admitted testimony that the accused did make such statement to the sheriff, since such testimony might have been the deciding factor as to the return of an indictment against the accused. Maddox v. State, 213 Ind. 537, 12 N.E.2d 947 (1938).

In a prosecution on the charge of conspiracy to commit perjury in order to establish the validity of a certain promissory note, evidence that the note was genuine was admissible as a circumstance tending to establish that there was no rational motive for the defendant to conspire to produce perjured testimony to that effect. Pollard v. State, 218 Ind. 56, 29 N.E.2d 956, 1940 Ind. LEXIS 232 (1940).

—Corroboration.

If there was the positive testimony of one witness to the charge of false swearing, the corroborating evidence did not need to be equivalent to the testimony of a positive witness. Hendricks v. State, 26 Ind. 493, 1866 Ind. LEXIS 223 (1866); Galloway v. State, 29 Ind. 442, 1868 Ind. LEXIS 68 (1868).

In order to sustain a conviction of perjury, the evidence must be such as to satisfy the jury to the exclusion of a rational doubt of the falsity of the matter sworn to by the accused, but the evidence must be no less than the direct and positive testimony of two witnesses or one witness and corrobo-

rating facts and circumstances. Pendleton v. State, 239 Ind. 341, 156 N.E.2d 782, 1959 Ind. LEXIS 169 (1959).

The detailed rule pertaining to the nature of the corroboration of the testimony of a single witness applied only to the fact of false swearing and not to every detail or act surrounding the fact alleged as falsely sworn. Pendleton v. State, 239 Ind. 341, 156 N.E.2d 782, 1959 Ind. LEXIS 169 (1959).

In a prosecution for perjury it is necessary that the evidence for conviction be supported by the direct testimony of at least two witnesses, or one witness and corroborating facts and circumstances. Cassorla v. State, 251 Ind. 390, 241 N.E.2d 365, 1968 Ind. LEXIS 585 (1968).

—Insufficient.

Evidence was insufficient to support defendant's conviction for perjury because the state failed to prove that he knowingly signed a false statement. Griepenstroh v. State, 629 N.E.2d 887, 1994 Ind. App. LEXIS 175 (1994).

—Number of Witnesses.

Except for the existence of irreconcilable or inconsistent statements given under oath, as provided in this section, it is well settled in Indiana that to warrant a conviction of perjury, the evidence must be no less than the direct and positive evidence of two witnesses, or one witness and corroborating facts and circumstances. There is no detailed rule prescribing the nature of the testimony of a single witness, and the corroboration may be furnished by circumstantial evidence. Richardson v. State, 496 N.E.2d 620, 1986 Ind. App. LEXIS 2854 (1986).

—Officer Administering Oath.

On a trial for perjury, it had to be proven that the defendant was sworn, as charged in the indictment, by an officer authorized to administer the oath. Muir v. State, 1846 Ind. LEXIS 87 (1846); Hitesman v. State, 48 Ind. 473, 1874 Ind. LEXIS 412 (1874).

Where the affidavit (predecessor of information) or indictment alleged that the oath was taken before a designated city clerk, proof that it was taken before his deputy was a fatal variance. Davis v. State, 193 Ind. 650, 141 N.E. 458, 1923 Ind. LEXIS 131 (1923).

It had to be proven that defendant was sworn by the officer alleged in the affidavit (predecessor to information) or indictment to be the one before whom the oath was taken. Davis v. State, 193 Ind. 650, 141 N.E. 458, 1923 Ind. LEXIS 131 (1923).

In a prosecution for false swearing, three different witnesses testified that the bill for the roofing had not been paid at the time accused signed the affidavit. This was sufficient to meet the requirements of the rule as to the proof of the false swearing. Pendleton v. State, 239 Ind. 341, 156 N.E.2d 782, 1959 Ind. LEXIS 169 (1959).

Where defendant was convicted of perjury for making false statements on the questionnaire prescribed by the state board of accounts pursuant to IC 5-16-1-2, it was unnecessary to establish that the board indeed scrutinized the documents or relied upon the false statements in awarding the

Evidence. (Cont'd)

—Officer Administering Oath. (Cont'd)
contract, since it is sufficient that a false statement was made regarding a material matter and that the false statement was reasonably calculated to mislead the board in determining who was the best bidder. Zordani v. State, 175 Ind. App. 297, 371 N.E.2d 396, 1978 Ind. App. LEXIS 786 (1978).

—Sufficient.
Defendant's conviction for perjury was affirmed where he made false statements at rape trial that undermined the credibility of the victims and a key prosecution witness. Daniels v. State, 658 N.E.2d 121, 1995 Ind. App. LEXIS 1570 (1995).

False Informations.
Perjury committed in making false affidavits (predecessor of information) required by law fell within the provisions of the statute. State v. Hopper, 133 Ind. 460, 32 N.E. 878, 1892 Ind. LEXIS 288 (1892).

Federal Statutes.
State courts had no jurisdiction to punish perjury committed where the oath was taken pursuant to an act of congress. State v. Adams, 1836 Ind. LEXIS 1 (1836).

Grand Jury Proceeding.
Perjury could be committed in testifying before a grand jury. State v. McCormick, 52 Ind. 169, 1875 Ind. LEXIS 423 (1875); State v. Turley, 153 Ind. 345, 55 N.E. 30, 1899 Ind. LEXIS 49 (1899).

Because grand jury is not limited to actions on the particular purposes for which it was called, but can investigate a wide range of subjects or crimes within its jurisdiction, false statements made to it concerning the additional subjects it chooses to pursue may be punished by a charge of perjury. However, in order for such false statements to constitute perjury, the state must make some indication on the record that it is pursuing such additional lines of inquiry. State v. Fields, 527 N.E.2d 218, 1988 Ind. App. LEXIS 599 (1988).

—Notice to Defendant of Additional Subjects Investigated.
The defendant must be advised prior to testifying of the additional subjects the grand jury will choose to pursue in order for false statements made to it concerning those subjects to be punishable by a charge of perjury. State v. Crecelius, 531 N.E.2d 540, 1988 Ind. App. LEXIS 1032 (1988).

Indictment or Information.

—Continuance.
An affidavit (predecessor to information) for a continuance is one required by law and not voluntary and therefore an indictment for false swearing to an affidavit for continuance must show that the swearing touched a matter material to the point in question. State v. Flagg, 25 Ind. 243, 1865 Ind. LEXIS 197 (1865); State v. Anderson, 103 Ind. 170, 2 N.E. 332, 1885 Ind. LEXIS 498 (1885).

—Elements.
In charging the commission of perjury by making a voluntary affidavit (predecessor to information), it was sufficient to set out the affidavit and allege that it was falsely made. State v. Malone, 174 Ind. 746, 93 N.E. 170, 1910 Ind. LEXIS 171 (1910).

In a prosecution for a conspiracy to commit the felony of perjury defined by statute, the indictment, in addition to the charge of conspiracy to commit the felony, must fully and specifically set out in the indictment or affidavit (predecessor to information) the felony which defendants conspired to commit. Genett v. State, 197 Ind. 105, 149 N.E. 894, 1925 Ind. LEXIS 129 (1925).

—Insufficient.
An affidavit (predecessor to information) made by the seller stating that there were no liens against the property sold, was not sufficient to warrant a conviction for perjury where, at the time of the making of the affidavit, there was an unsatisfied judgment against the affiant, but no execution therefor in the hands of an officer. Rothchild v. State, 200 Ind. 501, 165 N.E. 60, 1929 Ind. LEXIS 79 (1929).

—Joint Indictment.
Where two persons joined in an affidavit (predecessor to information) for a continuance, signing the affidavit together, being sworn together, and one certificate of oath being attached, such persons could be indicted jointly. State v. Winstandley, 151 Ind. 316, 51 N.E. 92, 1898 Ind. LEXIS 92 (1898).

Two or more persons cannot be joined in a single charge of perjury except where the offense consists of swearing to one joint affidavit by two or more persons at the same time or where one makes a false affidavit while another is standing by instigating him. Lynn v. State, 207 Ind. 393, 193 N.E. 380, 1934 Ind. LEXIS 284 (1934).

Defendant charged with perjury was held improperly joined with others charged with having committed a similar, though separate and distinct, offense of perjury where it was not alleged that one of the defendants committed the offense of perjury at the instigation of the others nor that all joined in swearing to a single joint affidavit (predecessor to information). Lynn v. State, 207 Ind. 393, 193 N.E. 380, 1934 Ind. LEXIS 284 (1934).

—Officer Administering Oath.
The indictment had to show that the officer administering the oath had legal authority to do so. McGragor v. State, 1 Ind. 232, Smith Ind. 179 (1848).

An indictment for perjury should have named the officer administering the oath. Hitesman v. State, 48 Ind. 473, 1874 Ind. LEXIS 412 (1874).

An indictment or information for perjury did not need to expressly allege authority in the officer who administered the oath to defendant to administer the same, where the facts alleged showed that he had such authority. Hall v. State, 178 Ind. 448, 99 N.E. 732, 1912 Ind. LEXIS 108 (1912).

—Sufficient.
In prosecution for perjury by giving false testi-

Indictment or Information. (Cont'd)

—Sufficient. (Cont'd)

mony, it was sufficient to charge in the indictment generally that the false statement was material, without setting out the facts from which such a materiality appeared. Maddox v. State, 213 Ind. 537, 12 N.E.2d 947 (1938).

An indictment for perjury in testifying before the grand jury, which failed to use the word "falsely," stated a public offense where it charged in substance that the testimony given before the grand jury was unlawful, felonious, wilful, and corrupt. Maddox v. State, 213 Ind. 537, 12 N.E.2d 947 (1938).

In order to constitute perjury, it is not necessary that statements be false in all respects. Therefore, indictment which alleged that defendant had sworn that he had received only $500 from the sale of certain lots while trustee of court while in fact he had received $1,500 therefor charged a public offense. Harrison v. State, 231 Ind. 147, 106 N.E.2d 912, 1952 Ind. LEXIS 137, 32 A.L.R.2d 875 (1952).

—Tax Matters.

An indictment for perjury, based on testimony before a board of equalization relating to property not returned for taxation, had to state all the facts necessary to show that the property was subject to taxation. State v. Wood, 110 Ind. 82, 10 N.E. 639, 1887 Ind. LEXIS 11 (1887).

—Words Used.

The word "falsely" did not need to be used in an indictment if equivalent words were used. State v. Anderson, 103 Ind. 170, 2 N.E. 332, 1885 Ind. LEXIS 498 (1885).

In charging perjury, it is essential that the indictment allege that the testimony upon which it is predicated is false, but it is not necessary that the charge follow the exact language of the statute. Maddox v. State, 213 Ind. 537, 12 N.E.2d 947 (1938).

Charge of perjury does not need to follow exact language of the statute; substantial compliance with the statute is sufficient. Porter v. State, 246 Ind. 701, 210 N.E.2d 657, 1965 Ind. LEXIS 420 (1965).

—Written Instruments.

When the charge of perjury was based on a false oath to a written instrument, so much of the instrument as was alleged to be false should have been set forth in the indictment. Coppack v. State, 36 Ind. 513, 1871 Ind. LEXIS 190 (1871); State v. Blackstone, 74 Ind. 592, 1881 Ind. LEXIS 202 (1881).

Intent.

In determining materiality of false testimony which was the basis of a prosecution for perjury, there must have been criminal intent, although such an intention could be inferred from the giving of wilfully false testimony reasonably calculated to mislead the trier of facts upon a material question. Davis v. State, 218 Ind. 506, 34 N.E.2d 23, 1941 Ind. LEXIS 179 (1941).

Jurors.

Jurors could commit perjury in making false answers to questions touching their qualifications. State v. Howard, 63 Ind. 502, 1878 Ind. LEXIS 402 (1878).

Materiality of Testimony.

—In General.

An indictment for perjury, in cases where an oath was required by law, had to allege that the false testimony was concerning a matter material to the point in question. State v. Flagg, 25 Ind. 243, 1865 Ind. LEXIS 197 (1865); State v. Flagg, 27 Ind. 24, 1866 Ind. LEXIS 238 (1866); State v. Anderson, 103 Ind. 170, 2 N.E. 332, 1885 Ind. LEXIS 498 (1885); State v. Cunningham, 116 Ind. 209, 18 N.E. 613, 1888 Ind. LEXIS 124 (1888); State v. Sutton, 147 Ind. 158, 46 N.E. 468, 1897 Ind. LEXIS 22 (1897); State v. Turley, 153 Ind. 345, 55 N.E. 30, 1899 Ind. LEXIS 49 (1899); State v. Wilson, 156 Ind. 343, 59 N.E. 932, 1901 Ind. LEXIS 50 (1901).

Where an oath is made voluntarily, it is not necessary that the matter falsely sworn to should be material to any question involved in order to constitute perjury. State v. Flagg, 25 Ind. 243, 1865 Ind. LEXIS 197 (1865).

If the facts stated showed the materiality of the false testimony, a direct averment of materiality was not necessary. Hendricks v. State, 26 Ind. 493, 1866 Ind. LEXIS 223 (1866); Galloway v. State, 29 Ind. 442, 1868 Ind. LEXIS 68 (1868); Burk v. State, 81 Ind. 128, 1881 Ind. LEXIS 1014 (1881); State v. Cunningham, 116 Ind. 209, 18 N.E. 613, 1888 Ind. LEXIS 124 (1888); State v. Sutton, 147 Ind. 158, 46 N.E. 468, 1897 Ind. LEXIS 22 (1897).

Perjury cannot be predicated on immaterial matter. State v. Reynolds, 108 Ind. 353, 9 N.E. 287, 1886 Ind. LEXIS 241 (1886); State v. Cunningham, 116 Ind. 209, 18 N.E. 613, 1888 Ind. LEXIS 124 (1888).

Falsely testifying is not perjury unless it is "touching a matter material to the point in question." Davis v. State, 218 Ind. 506, 34 N.E.2d 23, 1941 Ind. LEXIS 179 (1941).

In a prosecution for perjury based on the giving of false testimony, the materiality of testimony upon a subject material in itself must be determined from the facts and circumstances of each case. Davis v. State, 218 Ind. 506, 34 N.E.2d 23, 1941 Ind. LEXIS 179 (1941).

Where defendant was convicted of perjury for falsely swearing to a material fact based upon his answers to the questionnaire required by IC 5-16-1-2, that section established the materiality of the questions presented since the extent and type of a contract bidder's prior experience are material to the determination of whether he is the best bidder for the award of a contract. Zordani v. State, 175 Ind. App. 297, 371 N.E.2d 396, 1978 Ind. App. LEXIS 786 (1978).

In the context of perjury, Indiana courts define "materiality" to mean that which is reasonably calculated to mislead an investigation. The state is not required to prove actual impairment of the investigation. Mere potential influence with a line of inquiry is sufficient to establish materiality.

Materiality of Testimony. (Cont'd)

—In General. (Cont'd)
Wilke v. State, 496 N.E.2d 616, 1986 Ind. App. LEXIS 2858 (1986).

The issue of materiality is an issue for the court to decide as a matter of law. Wilke v. State, 496 N.E.2d 616, 1986 Ind. App. LEXIS 2858 (1986).

Because defendant's false statements to grand jury as to use of marijuana were not material to the investigation of the alleged receipt of stolen property, an information charging him with perjury in making those false statements was properly dismissed. State v. Fields, 527 N.E.2d 218, 1988 Ind. App. LEXIS 599 (1988).

Within the context of a grand jury investigation, in order for a statement to be material it must be related to the stated purpose for which the grand jury was called to investigate. State v. Crecelius, 531 N.E.2d 540, 1988 Ind. App. LEXIS 1032 (1988).

Knowledge of prostitution was not material to a grand jury investigation into allegations of the receipt of stolen property. State v. Crecelius, 531 N.E.2d 540, 1988 Ind. App. LEXIS 1032 (1988).

Materiality has been defined as that which is reasonably calculated to mislead an investigation. Daniels v. State, 658 N.E.2d 121, 1995 Ind. App. LEXIS 1570 (1995).

—Burden of Proof.
Where testimony upon a matter in itself collateral was assigned as perjury, the state was charged with the burden of alleging that the particular facts falsely sworn to were material, and of proving sufficient of the surrounding circumstances to show their materiality. Davis v. State, 218 Ind. 506, 34 N.E.2d 23, 1941 Ind. LEXIS 179 (1941).

—Not Shown.
Where, in a prosecution for perjury based upon the giving of false testimony, it appeared, and the affidavit (predecessor to information) alleged, that the material question in the case in which the testimony was given was whether accused and a woman were in fact husband and wife, but there was neither a general allegation that the testimony claimed to be false related to a matter material to the point in question, nor were particular facts alleged showing the materiality of the testimony which was charged to be false, it was error to overrule a motion to quash the affidavit. Davis v. State, 218 Ind. 506, 34 N.E.2d 23, 1941 Ind. LEXIS 179 (1941).

—Pleading.
The materiality of defendant's false swearing could be pleaded by a general averment to that effect or it could appear from the facts alleged. State v. Dunn, 203 Ind. 265, 180 N.E. 5, 1932 Ind. LEXIS 45, 80 A.L.R. 1437 (1932).

Materiality may be pleaded by a general averment unless the facts alleged show as a matter of law that the false statement was not material to the issue. Porter v. State, 246 Ind. 701, 210 N.E.2d 657, 1965 Ind. LEXIS 420 (1965).

—Required.
If the testimony alleged to have been false was of no consequence, it could not be made the basis for a charge of perjury however false, for it would not touch the point in question under the statute. State v. Kellis, 193 Ind. 619, 141 N.E. 337, 1923 Ind. LEXIS 126 (1923).

One of the essential elements of the crime of perjury based upon the giving of false testimony is that the testimony was material to the issue. Pollard v. State, 218 Ind. 56, 29 N.E.2d 956, 1940 Ind. LEXIS 232 (1940).

While in a prosecution for perjury based on false testimony there could be cases in which a mere statement of the testimony said to have been false showed that it was material to the issue in the case in which it was given, yet where the facts sworn to involved a collateral matter not appearing on its face to be material, materiality must have been alleged and proved. Davis v. State, 218 Ind. 506, 34 N.E.2d 23, 1941 Ind. LEXIS 179 (1941).

Recantation.
Evidence of recantation by the defendant would be admissible for the jury to consider in its deliberation and determination of guilt or innocence, but it would not follow, as a matter of law, that he would be entitled to acquittal. Adams v. State, 249 Ind. 346, 232 N.E.2d 608, 1968 Ind. LEXIS 718 (1968).

Self-Incrimination.
Witnesses giving false testimony could be convicted of perjury although they might have declined to testify because of self-incrimination. State v. Turley, 153 Ind. 345, 55 N.E. 30, 1899 Ind. LEXIS 49 (1899); State v. Carey, 159 Ind. 504, 65 N.E. 527, 1902 Ind. LEXIS 66 (1902).

Special Statutes.
Whenever punishment was provided for false swearing by any particular statute, the prosecution had to be under such statute. State v. Runyan, 130 Ind. 208, 29 N.E. 779, 1892 Ind. LEXIS 320 (1892).

"Trial Proceeding."
Where information charged defendant with perjury concerning testimony "in a trial proceeding", and evidence in the perjury trial showed that when defendant gave the testimony complained of, he had been sworn by the court reporter in the courtroom in the presence of the prosecutor, the defendant in the case, and the defense attorney and was questioned by the prosecutor in the absence of the judge and before the jury had been selected and sworn, there was a fatal variance since such testimony was not given in a "trial proceeding." Waye v. State, 181 Ind. App. 66, 390 N.E.2d 700, 1979 Ind. App. LEXIS 1219 (1979).

What Constitutes Perjury.

—In General.
Representation by a lender's counsel that the lender "just discovered" that the automatic stay in the borrower's bankruptcy was in effect was not perjury because it was made by counsel, not by the lender under oath, and was not a material statement. Brown v. JPMorgan Chase Bank, — F. Supp. 2d —, 2008 U.S. Dist. LEXIS 20464 (2008).

—Affidavit.

Perjury could be committed in making an affidavit (predecessor to information) to institute a prosecution. Shell v. State, 148 Ind. 50, 47 N.E. 144, 1897 Ind. LEXIS 171 (1897).

It is essential in crime of perjury in voluntary affidavit (predecessor to information) that affidavit was "wilfully, corruptly and falsely" made. Mere inadvertence in signing such affidavit is not sufficient to prove perjury. Gardner v. State, 229 Ind. 368, 97 N.E.2d 921, 1951 Ind. LEXIS 165 (1951).

Affidavit which did not show that it was a written statement of fact "which is sworn to as the truth before an authorized officer" did not show that it contained a "statement under oath," as required by the applicable portion of the perjury statute, and would not subject the subscriber to the penalties for perjury. Tannehill by Podgorski v. Reddy, 633 N.E.2d 318, 1994 Ind. App. LEXIS 480 (1994).

—Belief.

Perjury may be committed by swearing that a fact is true when the witness believes it to be untrue, although the fact actually existed. Indianapolis Traction & Terminal Co. v. Henby, 178 Ind. 239, 97 N.E. 313, 1912 Ind. LEXIS 95 (1912).

—Confusion.

Confusion of witness concerning technical questions, such as legal consequences of conviction of shoplifting, could not be interpreted as perjury. Barnett v. State, 256 Ind. 303, 268 N.E.2d 615, 1971 Ind. LEXIS 629 (1971).

The state failed to prove statements made by defendant, county attorney, and chairman of board of supervisors of construction project to grand jury were perjurious where the evidence most favorable to the state showed defendant may have been confused about his pre-bid communications with vendors participating in public bid under IC 36-1-9-3, but his statements were not false. Dunnuck v. State, 644 N.E.2d 1275, 1994 Ind. App. LEXIS 1794 (1994).

Confusion or inconsistency alone is not enough to prove perjury. Daniels v. State, 658 N.E.2d 121, 1995 Ind. App. LEXIS 1570 (1995).

—Intentional False Impression.

Intentionally creating a false impression as to known existing facts could constitute perjury. State v. Wilson, 156 Ind. 343, 59 N.E. 932, 1901 Ind. LEXIS 50 (1901).

If a witness so testified as to create a false impression as to the existence of material facts, he could be guilty of perjury. State v. Wilson, 156 Ind. 343, 59 N.E. 932, 1901 Ind. LEXIS 50 (1901).

—Mistake or Inadvertence.

Perjury consists in knowingly and purposely making a false statement under oath, and if such a statement is made through mistake or inadvertence, it is not perjury. Indianapolis Traction & Terminal Co. v. Henby, 178 Ind. 239, 97 N.E. 313, 1912 Ind. LEXIS 95 (1912).

An individual who negligently fails to provide accurate information or inadvertently provides incorrect information does not commit perjury. Benjamin v. City of W. Lafayette, 701 N.E.2d 1268, 1998 Ind. App. LEXIS 2082 (1998).

Although the witness testified that he had suffered two gunshot wounds, and the medical records purportedly showed that he suffered a single gunshot wound, it was clear there was some confusion as to what was meant by "wounds" in the testimony, but confused or mistaken testimony is not perjury. Carter v. State, 738 N.E.2d 665, 2000 Ind. LEXIS 1108 (2000).

—Opinion.

When statements were matters of opinion, perjury could not be based thereon. State v. Henderson, 90 Ind. 406, 1883 Ind. LEXIS 260 (1883).

—Unequivocal Acts.

Defendants' signatures on applications for food stamps constituted "unequivocal acts" affirming they had disclosed all other sources of income, which they had not, and this evidence was sufficient to establish violations of this perjury statute. Cunningham v. State, 469 N.E.2d 1, 1984 Ind. App. LEXIS 2976 (1984).

Perjury must be clear and direct, and not implied or suggested. Barker v. State, 681 N.E.2d 727, 1997 Ind. App. LEXIS 541 (1997).

—Unsworn Contradictory Statements.

There is no ambiguity on the face of subsection (a)(2). Falsity is proven by the irreconcilable contradiction, and the legislature has evidently concluded that such a false statement before a court or grand jury, whether or not the declarant is formally sworn, constitutes the functional equivalent of perjury under subsection (a)(1). Blackburn v. State, 495 N.E.2d 806, 1986 Ind. App. LEXIS 2786 (1986).

Cited:

Warthan v. State, 440 N.E.2d 657, 1982 Ind. LEXIS 977 (1982); Fadell v. State, 450 N.E.2d 109, 1983 Ind. App. LEXIS 3023 (1983); In re Barratt, 663 N.E.2d 536, 1996 Ind. LEXIS 27 (1996); Paschall v. State, 717 N.E.2d 1273, 1999 Ind. App. LEXIS 1920 (1999); Stephens v. Irvin, 730 N.E.2d 1271, 2000 Ind. App. LEXIS 1007 (2000); Myers v. State, 848 N.E.2d 1108, 2006 Ind. App. LEXIS 1102 (2006).

RESEARCH REFERENCES

Res Gestae.

Rules, rulings for the trial lawyer, 38 (No. 5) Res Gestae 27 (1994).

Collateral References.

Actionability of conspiracy to give or to procure false testimony or other evidence. 31 A.L.R.3d 1423.

Dismissal of action of party's perjury or suppressing of evidence. 11 A.L.R.3d 1153.

Invalidity of statute or ordinance giving rise to proceedings in which false testimony was received as defense for prosecution for perjury. 34 A.L.R.3d 413.

Offense of perjury as affected by questions relating to jurisdiction of court or government agency before which testimony was given. 36 A.L.R.3d 1038.

Perjury or wilfully false testimony of expert witness as basis for new trial on ground of newly discovered evidence. 38 A.L.R.3d 812.

Recantation as defense in perjury prosecution. 64 A.L.R.2d 276.

Incomplete, misleading, or unresponsive but literally true statement as perjury. 69 A.L.R.3d 993.

Acquittal as bar to a prosecution of accused for perjury committed at trial. 89 A.L.R.3d 1098.

Right of defendant in prosecution for perjury to have the "two witnesses, or one witness and corroborating circumstances," rule included in charge to jury — state cases. 41 A.L.R.5th 1.

35-44-2-2. False informing.

(a) As used in this section, "consumer product" has the meaning set forth in IC 35-45-8-1.

(b) As used in this section, "misconduct" means a violation of a departmental rule or procedure of a law enforcement agency.

(c) A person who reports, by telephone, telegraph, mail, or other written or oral communication, that:

(1) the person or another person has placed or intends to place an explosive, a destructive device, or other destructive substance in a building or transportation facility;

(2) there has been or there will be tampering with a consumer product introduced into commerce; or

(3) there has been or will be placed or introduced a weapon of mass destruction in a building or a place of assembly;

knowing the report to be false commits false reporting, a Class D felony.

(d) A person who:

(1) gives a false report of the commission of a crime or gives false information in the official investigation of the commission of a crime, knowing the report or information to be false;

(2) gives a false alarm of fire to the fire department of a governmental entity, knowing the alarm to be false;

(3) makes a false request for ambulance service to an ambulance service provider, knowing the request to be false;

(4) gives a false report concerning a missing child (as defined in IC 10-13-5-4) or missing endangered adult (as defined in IC 12-7-2-131.3) or gives false information in the official investigation of a missing child or missing endangered adult knowing the report or information to be false;

(5) makes a complaint against a law enforcement officer to the state or municipality (as defined in IC 8-1-13-3) that employs the officer:

(A) alleging the officer engaged in misconduct while performing the officer's duties; and

(B) knowing the complaint to be false; or

(6) makes a false report of a missing person, knowing the report or information is false;

commits false informing, a Class B misdemeanor. However, the offense is a Class A misdemeanor if it substantially hinders any law enforcement process or if it results in harm to an innocent person.

History.

IC 35-44-2-2, as added by Acts 1976, P.L.148, § 4; 1977, P.L.340, § 56; 1977, P.L.341, § 1; P.L.326-1987, § 3; P.L.49-1989, § 23; P.L.156-2001, § 12; P.L.123-2002, § 39; P.L.2-2003, § 96; P.L.232-2003, § 1; P.L.140-2005, § 7; P.L.92-2007, § 5, eff. July 1, 2007.

Compiler's Notes.

P.L.140-2005, § 10, effective July 1, 2005, provides:

"IC 35-44-2-2, as amended by this act, and IC 35-45-17-2, as added by this act, apply only to crimes committed after June 30, 2005."

Cross References.

Obstructing firemen, IC 35-44-4.

Penalties for felonies, IC 35-50-1, IC 35-50-2, IC 35-50-5-2.

Penalties for misdemeanors, IC 35-50-1, IC 35-50-3, IC 35-50-5-2.

NOTES TO DECISIONS

ANALYSIS

Double Jeopardy.
Evidence.
—Insufficient.
—Sufficient.
False Reporting.
Investigation of Crime.
Lesser Included Offense.
Probable Cause.

Double Jeopardy.

Convictions for false reporting and intimidation were vacated due to double jeopardy violation because they were based on acts that were so compressed in terms of time, place, singleness of purpose, and continuation of action as to constitute a single transaction; the false reporting and intimidation charges were based on diversionary tactics used to facilitate robbery. Buchanan v. State, — N.E.2d —, 2009 Ind. App. LEXIS 72 (2009).

Evidence.

—Insufficient.

Given the severity of an accident and evidence that defendant had crossed the center line, the police had a reasonable belief that a crime might have been committed; thus, defendant was required to answer their questions truthfully regarding who was driving the truck. It is immaterial to the false informing charge that there ultimately was insufficient evidence to convict defendant of criminal recklessness with respect to the accident. Clancy v. State, 829 N.E.2d 203, 2005 Ind. App. LEXIS 1100 (2005).

The evidence was insufficient to support the defendant's conviction for false reporting for telephoning a bomb threat to a hospital, where the state's case presented no more than conjecture that the defendant was the caller. Gootee v. State, 588 N.E.2d 584, 1992 Ind. App. LEXIS 348 (1992).

—Sufficient.

Where defendant knew that he had outstanding warrants against him when he was questioned by officer, and presumably lied about his name and birth date to conceal his fugitive status, the evidence was sufficient to establish that the false answers were both intentional and material. Smith v. State, 660 N.E.2d 357, 1996 Ind. App. LEXIS 18 (1996).

While no documentary evidence was introduced at trial to establish defendant's forename and birth date, where officer testified that defendant's I.D. card indicated that defendant had given him an incorrect forename and birth date, and defendant admitted giving officer his brother's birth date, the evidence was sufficient to sustain conviction. Smith v. State, 660 N.E.2d 357, 1996 Ind. App. LEXIS 18 (1996).

The passenger in the vehicle had a duty to truthfully and accurately report the events surrounding the collision, including providing authorities with the driver's name, and when the passenger purposefully misled investigating officers at the scene by falsing telling them that he did not know who the driver of the vehicle was and that he had only met her that evening, the passenger committed the offense of false informing. Stephens v. Irvin, 730 N.E.2d 1271, 2000 Ind. App. LEXIS 1007 (2000), clarified, 734 N.E.2d 1133, 2000 Ind. App. LEXIS 1476 (Ind. App. 2000).

Although the police officer testified that he was driving at a high rate of speed to "pace" a speeder, the state presented several witnesses who testified that, although they observed an Indiana State Police vehicle speed by, they did not see a speeding vehicle in front of it. Therefore, based on this conflicting testimony, the jury could have reasonably inferred that the officer's statement was false, providing sufficient evidence to support his false informing conviction. Anderson v. State, 743 N.E.2d 1273, 2001 Ind. App. LEXIS 492 (2001).

Defendant committed the act of false reporting where defendant gave conflicting reports as to what occurred during an altercation with two automobiles. Jones v. State, 775 N.E.2d 322, 2002 Ind. App. LEXIS 1494 (2002).

Sufficient evidence supported convictions for violating IC 35-44-3-2 and IC 35-44-2-2: (1) the defendant's spouse told defendant that he had hurt a few people when he came home covered in blood and demanded that she pack their things so that they could quickly leave; (2) defendant learned from her mother that several people had been murdered; (3) defendant admitted to a detective that she told her spouse's stepmother to tell everyone, including the authorities, that she last saw them in Memphis, although they were not in Memphis; (4) defendant and her spouse returned to Indiana and hid in the woods until they ran out of food; and (5) the spouse remained in hiding while defendant returned to her home and spoke with detectives. Davis v. State, 892 N.E.2d 156, 2008 Ind. App. LEXIS 1682 (2008).

False Reporting.

Where the evidence showed that defendant's wife and a friend reported the alleged holdup to the police after defendant told them to do so, it failed to prove that the defendant made a fictitious report of a crime, and a conviction under former section could not stand. Streeval v. State, 251 Ind. 349, 241 N.E.2d 255, 1968 Ind. LEXIS 578, 1969 Ind. LEXIS 394 (1968).

A conviction for false reporting under subsection (b)(1) [now (c)(1)] can be predicated only upon a false statement of a past or existing fact, and cannot be based upon promised future conduct. Wilke v. State, 496 N.E.2d 1310, 1986 Ind. App. LEXIS 2886 (1986).

Trial court did not err in sentencing defendant on his convictions on two counts of being a serious violent felon in possession of a firearm and a count of false informing to 20 years on each possession count, to be served consecutively, and 180 days suspended on the false informing count to be

False Reporting. (Cont'd)
served concurrently to the sentences on the possession counts in a case where he purchased assault weapons that he gave to a known felon who could not possess them, the known felon was involved in a police chase in which the weapons were used to shoot a police officer to death and wound a bystander permanently, and defendant falsely reported that the weapons had been stolen; the sentence was justified in light of the nature of the crime and defendant's character. Meadows v. State, 853 N.E.2d 1032, 2006 Ind. App. LEXIS 1888 (2006).

Investigation of Crime.
Police officer was engaged in the investigation of a crime, even though the suspected crime might not actually have been committed, where officer pulled over a car in which defendant was a passenger, defendant stated that he and the driver had been drinking, and the officer suspected that defendant may have been underage; evidence was thus sufficient to support defendant's conviction where he gave false identification to the officer. Howell v. State, 684 N.E.2d 576, 1997 Ind. App. LEXIS 1260 (1997).

Willingness of an informant to give her name, address, and birthdate, in conjunction with the penalties for knowingly giving a false statement was sufficient, under the totality of the circumstances, to find that the informant's tip gave the police reasonable suspicion to stop defendant. Kellems v. State, 842 N.E.2d 352, 2006 Ind. LEXIS 130 (2006).

Lesser Included Offense.
False informing is not a lesser included offense

of obstruction of justice. Kingston v. State, 479 N.E.2d 1356, 1985 Ind. App. LEXIS 2586 (1985).

Probable Cause.
Admission of evidence found during a search incident to an arrest was proper under Ind. Const., art. 1, § 11 as: (1) the encounter between defendant and two officers remained consensual even after the officers reinitiated their questioning of defendant; (2) the encounter was minimally intrusive until defendant gave the wrong phone number of defendant's parents; and (3) once the officers ascertained that defendant was lying, they had probable cause to arrest defendant for false informing under IC 35-44-2-2(d)(1) and to search defendant. Taylor v. State, 891 N.E.2d 155, 2008 Ind. App. LEXIS 1678 (2008).

Evidence found during a search incident to defendant's arrest did not violate the Fourth Amendment as: (1) the initial encounter between defendant and two police officers did not lose its consensual nature when the officers reinitiated their questioning of defendant; and (2) the officers had probable cause to arrest defendant for false informing under IC 35-44-2-2(d)(1) after defendant gave them a wrong phone number for defendant's parents. Taylor v. State, 891 N.E.2d 155, 2008 Ind. App. LEXIS 1678 (2008).

Cited:
Schmidt v. State, 746 N.E.2d 369, 2001 Ind. App. LEXIS 559 (2001); Edwards v. State, 750 N.E.2d 377, 2001 Ind. App. LEXIS 757 (2001); Parker v. State, 754 N.E.2d 614, 2001 Ind. App. LEXIS 1502 (2001); State v. Spillers, 816 N.E.2d 67, 2004 Ind. App. LEXIS 2010 (2004); Kelley v. State, 825 N.E.2d 420, 2005 Ind. App. LEXIS 599 (2005).

RESEARCH REFERENCES

Collateral References.
Imposition of state or local penalties for threatening to use explosive devices at schools or other buildings. 79 A.L.R.5th 1.

Validity, construction, and application of 18 U.S.C.A. § 844(e), prohibiting use of mail, telephone, telegraph, or other instrument of commerce to convey bomb threat. 160 A.L.R. Fed. 625.

35-44-2-3. Impersonation of a public servant.

A person who falsely represents that the person is a public servant, with intent to mislead and induce another person to submit to false official authority or otherwise to act to the other person's detriment in reliance on the false representation, commits impersonation of a public servant, a Class A misdemeanor. However, a person who falsely represents that the person is:

(1) a law enforcement officer; or

(2) an agent or employee of the department of state revenue, and collects any property from another person;

commits a Class D felony.

History.
IC 35-44-2-3, as added by Acts 1976, P.L.148, § 4; 1977, P.L.340, § 57; P.L.6-1987, § 21; P.L.214-1997, § 1.

Penalties for misdemeanors, IC 35-50-1, IC 35-50-3, IC 35-50-5-2.

Cross References.
Penalties for felonies, IC 35-50-1, IC 35-50-2, IC 35-50-5-2.

NOTES TO DECISIONS

Evidence.

—Sufficient.

Evidence was sufficient to support defendant's conviction for impersonating a police officer where he appeared at a hospital, seeking treatment for injuries, and told a nurse that he was a city police officer and supplied the nurse with the identification numbers for his badge, unit, supervisor, vehicle, and district. Poole v. State, 559 N.E.2d 1214, 1990 Ind. App. LEXIS 1279 (1990).

Defendant's inappropriate body searches combined with a law enforcement officer's testimony that he recognized defendant as a security guard provided the jury with sufficient evidence to find that defendant did not have actual law enforcement authority to conduct the offensive and invasive search of the juvenile. Rogers v. State, 741 N.E.2d 395, 2000 Ind. App. LEXIS 2122 (2000).

Proportionality of Penalty.

Defendant's proportionality claim under Ind. Const. art. 1, § 16 was properly denied because the penalty for identity deception under IC 35-43-5-3.5 was not unconstitutionally disproportionate as compared with the penalty for impersonating a public servant under IC 35-44-2-3. Identity deception required that a person knowingly or intentionally obtained, possessed, transferred, or used the identifying information of another, which was not required for impersonating a public servant, and the fact that no person was harmed was not a defense to identity deception. Brown v. State, 856 N.E.2d 739, 2006 Ind. App. LEXIS 2332 (2006).

As drafted, IC 35-44-2-3 was a conduct-oriented statute that focused on the defendant's act of impersonating a public servant and his intent to mislead another person; the statute did not require the victim to actually believe or be induced by the misrepresentation to act to his detriment, and a defendant's conviction for impersonating a public servant could be sustained regardless of whether the victim actually believed the misrepresentation. Therefore, because a defendant could not be convicted of more than one count of impersonating a public servant pursuant to IC 35-44-2-3 based on the same occurrence, even if there were multiple victims, the appellate court directed the trial court to vacate defendant's conviction on the second count of impersonating a public servant. Geiger v. State, 866 N.E.2d 830, 2007 Ind. App. LEXIS 1081 (2007), aff'd, transfer granted, — N.E.2d —, 2007 Ind. LEXIS 655 (2007).

Cited:

State v. Dodson, 733 N.E.2d 968, 2000 Ind. App. LEXIS 1206 (2000).

35-44-2-4. Ghost employment.

(a) A public servant who knowingly or intentionally:

(1) hires an employee for the governmental entity that he serves; and

(2) fails to assign to the employee any duties, or assigns to the employee any duties not related to the operation of the governmental entity;

commits ghost employment, a Class D felony.

(b) A public servant who knowingly or intentionally assigns to an employee under his supervision any duties not related to the operation of the governmental entity that he serves commits ghost employment, a Class D felony.

(c) A person employed by a governmental entity who, knowing that he has not been assigned any duties to perform for the entity, accepts property from the entity commits ghost employment, a Class D felony.

(d) A person employed by a governmental entity who knowingly or intentionally accepts property from the entity for the performance of duties not related to the operation of the entity commits ghost employment, a Class D felony.

(e) Any person who accepts property from a governmental entity in violation of this section and any public servant who permits the payment of property in violation of this section are jointly and severally liable to the governmental entity for that property. The attorney general may bring a civil action to recover that property in the county where the governmental entity is located or the person or public servant resides.

(f) For the purposes of this section, an employee of a governmental entity who voluntarily performs services:

(1) that do not:

(A) promote religion;

(B) attempt to influence legislation or governmental policy; or

(C) attempt to influence elections to public office;
(2) for the benefit of:
(A) another governmental entity; or
(B) an organization that is exempt from federal income taxation under Section 501(c)(3) of the Internal Revenue Code;
(3) with the approval of the employee's supervisor; and
(4) in compliance with a policy or regulation that:
(A) is in writing;
(B) is issued by the executive officer of the governmental entity; and
(C) contains a limitation on the total time during any calendar year that the employee may spend performing the services during normal hours of employment;
is considered to be performing duties related to the operation of the governmental entity.

History.
IC 35-44-2-4, as added by Acts 1977, P.L.340, § 58; P.L.68-1998, § 1.

Cross References.
Penalties for felonies, IC 35-50-1, IC 35-50-2, IC 35-50-5-2.

NOTES TO DECISIONS

ANALYSIS

County Prosecutor.
Evidence.
—Other Acts.
—Sufficient.
Sentence.

County Prosecutor.
When the elected county prosecutor knowingly hired another attorney as chief deputy prosecutor, and failed to assign to him any duties, but instead employed him in the county prosecutor's private law firm, the crime of ghost employment was committed, which reflected adversely on the county prosecutor's honesty, trustworthiness, and fitness as a lawyer. In re Riddle, 700 N.E.2d 788, 1998 Ind. LEXIS 500 (1998).

Evidence.

—Other Acts.
Where former clerk of Supreme Court, Court of Appeals, and Tax Court was charged with ghost employment for using state employees to work on his political campaign, evidence of his other acts of misconduct which could have constituted ghost employment was admissible to rebut his claim that his conduct was the result of innocent mistake. Brown v. State, 684 N.E.2d 529, 1997 Ind. App.

LEXIS 1161 (1997), cert. denied, 523 U.S. 1027, 118 S. Ct. 1316, 140 L. Ed. 2d 479, 1998 U.S. LEXIS 1956 (1998).

—Sufficient.
Evidence was sufficient to sustain convictions of former clerk of Supreme Court, Court of Appeals, and Tax Court on charges of ghost employment where he used state employees to work on his political campaign. Brown v. State, 684 N.E.2d 529, 1997 Ind. App. LEXIS 1161 (1997), cert. denied, 523 U.S. 1027, 118 S. Ct. 1316, 140 L. Ed. 2d 479, 1998 U.S. LEXIS 1956 (1998).

Sentence.
Imposition of three-year, concurrent, suspended sentences upon seven felony convictions was not unreasonable. Brown v. State, 684 N.E.2d 529, 1997 Ind. App. LEXIS 1161 (1997), cert. denied, 523 U.S. 1027, 118 S. Ct. 1316, 140 L. Ed. 2d 479, 1998 U.S. LEXIS 1956 (1998).

Cited:
In re Hampton, 533 N.E.2d 122, 1989 Ind. LEXIS 20 (1989); Demos v. City of Indianapolis, 139 F. Supp. 2d 1026, 2001 U.S. Dist. LEXIS 5606 (S.D. Ind. 2001); Demos v. City of Indianapolis, 302 F.3d 698, 2002 U.S. App. LEXIS 17934 (7th Cir. Ind. 2002).

OPINIONS OF ATTORNEY GENERAL

Any city employee who, in a partisan or nonpartisan election, solicits contributions from anyone during working hours for which the employee is compensated would be committing ghost employment. 1992, No. 92-6.

35-44-2-5. Unlawful manufacture or sale of police or fire insignia.

(a) A person who knowingly or intentionally manufactures and sells or manufactures and offers for sale:

(1) an official badge or a replica of an official badge that is currently used by a law enforcement agency or fire department of the state or of a political subdivision of the state; or

(2) a document that purports to be an official employment identification that is used by a law enforcement agency or fire department of the state or of a political subdivision of the state;

without the written permission of the chief executive officer of the law enforcement agency commits unlawful manufacture or sale of a police or fire insignia, a Class A misdemeanor.

(b) However, the offense described in subsection (a) is:

(1) a Class D felony if the person commits the offense with the knowledge or intent that the badge or employment identification will be used to further the commission of an offense under IC 35-44-2-3; and

(2) a Class B felony if the person commits the offense with the knowledge or intent that the badge or employment identification will be used to further the commission of an offense under IC 35-47-12.

(c) It is a defense to a prosecution under subsection (a)(1) if the area of the badge or replica that is manufactured and sold or manufactured and offered for sale as measured by multiplying the greatest length of the badge by the greatest width of the badge is:

(1) less than fifty percent (50%); or

(2) more than one hundred fifty percent (150%);

of the area of an official badge that is used by a law enforcement agency or fire department of the state or a political subdivision of the state as measured by multiplying the greatest length of the official badge by the greatest width of the official badge.

History.
P.L.110-2009, § 16, emergency eff. July 1, 2009.

Compiler's Notes.
P.L.110-2009, § 19, effective July 1, 2009, provides:
"IC 35-44-2-5, as added by this act, applies only to offenses committed after June 30, 2009."

Cross References.
Penalties for felonies, IC 35-50-1, IC 35-50-2, IC 35-50-5-2.
Penalties for misdemeanors, IC 35-50-1, IC 35-50-3, IC 35-50-5-2.

CHAPTER 3

INTERFERENCE WITH GOVERNMENTAL OPERATIONS

35-44-3-1. [Repealed.]

Compiler's Notes.
This section, defining "lawful detention," was repealed by Acts 1978, P.L. 144, § 13. For present similar provisions, see IC 35-41-1-18.

35-44-3-2. Assisting a criminal.

(a) A person not standing in the relation of parent, child, or spouse to another person who has committed a crime or is a fugitive from justice who, with intent to hinder the apprehension or punishment of the other person, harbors, conceals, or otherwise assists the person commits assisting a criminal, a Class A misdemeanor. However, the offense is:

(1) a Class D felony if the person assisted has committed a Class B, Class C, or Class D felony; and

(2) a Class C felony if the person assisted has committed murder or a Class A felony, or if the assistance was providing a deadly weapon.

(b) It is not a defense to a prosecution under this section that the person assisted:

(1) has not been prosecuted for the offense;

(2) has not been convicted of the offense; or

(3) has been acquitted of the offense by reason of insanity.

However, the acquittal of the person assisted for other reasons may be a defense.

History.
IC 35-44-3-2, as added by Acts 1976, P.L.148, § 4; 1977, P.L.340, § 60; P.L.159-2009, § 1, eff. July 1, 2009.

Compiler's Notes.
P.L.159-2009, § 2, effective July 1, 2009, provides:
"IC 35-44-3-2, as amended by this act, applies only to crimes committed after June 30, 2009."

Amendments.
The 2009 amendment added the (a) designation and added (b).

Cross References.
Aiding or abetting criminal, IC 35-41-2-4.
Penalties for felonies, IC 35-50-1, IC 35-50-2, IC 35-50-5-2.
Penalties for misdemeanors, IC 35-50-1, IC 35-50-3, IC 35-50-5-2.

NOTES TO DECISIONS

In General.
This section was obviously intended to cover the situation where a person did not actively participate in the crime itself, but after the commission of the crime aided the criminal. Smith v. State, 429 N.E.2d 956, 1982 Ind. LEXIS 717 (1982), overruled, Wright v. State, 690 N.E.2d 1098, 1997 Ind. LEXIS 245 (1997).

Where it is clear on the face of the information that whatever assistance was given by the defendant to a criminal was given prior to or during the commission of the offense in question, the offense does not fit this statute. State v. Fields, 527 N.E.2d 218, 1988 Ind. App. LEXIS 599 (1988).

"Harbor" means to shelter, to give refuge, to lodge, care for and protect any person guilty of a

In General. (Cont'd)

felony. Clements v. State, 808 N.E.2d 198, 2004 Ind. App. LEXIS 895 (2004).

"Conceal" means to hide, secrete, to keep out of sight, or prevent the discovery of one guilty of a felony. Clements v. State, 808 N.E.2d 198, 2004 Ind. App. LEXIS 895 (2004).

Accessory After the Fact.

Where defendant was granted a new trial after being convicted of robbery, it was not error to file additional charges against defendant as an accessory after the fact. Thomas v. State, 275 Ind. 499, 417 N.E.2d 1124, 1981 Ind. LEXIS 703 (1981).

Acquittal of Principal.

When an accessory after the fact is found guilty after the alleged principal is acquitted in a separate trial, the conviction of the accessory must be reversed. McKnight v. State, 658 N.E.2d 559, 1995 Ind. LEXIS 160 (1995).

Felony assisting a criminal charge against defendant had to be dismissed after the dismissal of charges against the principal following a hung jury, since there was insufficient evidence to convict defendant as no crime had been proven. Myers v. State, 765 N.E.2d 663, 2002 Ind. App. LEXIS 468 (2002).

Aid to Escaping Prisoners.

Aid innocently given to an escaping prisoner was not a violation of former statute punishing aiding in the escape of prisoners. State v. Sutton, 170 Ind. 473, 170 Ind. 573, 84 N.E. 824, 1908 Ind. LEXIS 45 (1908).

Where two prisoners overpowered prison guard in prison automobile and were later driven away by defendant in another automobile, such person could be guilty of aiding in their escape as against contention that escape was complete when prisoners grabbed guard and took control of the prison automobile. Collins v. State, 174 Ind. App. 116, 366 N.E.2d 229, 1977 Ind. App. LEXIS 939 (1977).

Applicability.

Where defendant took part in same crimes as person she was convicted of assisting, crime of assisting criminal did not apply, and defendant's conviction for that crime had to be reversed. Kelly v. State, 813 N.E.2d 1179, 2004 Ind. App. LEXIS 1709 (2004).

Although a person who was the spouse of a person who committed an underlying offense could not be held liable for assisting a criminal under IC 35-44-3-2, defendant did not fall within the statute's exemption from Indiana's aiding a criminal liability; marriage of defendant and the person who committed the underlying offense was not recognized by Indiana under IC 31-11-8-6 since the parties entered Kentucky to get married while defendant was underage and without her parent's consent in order to purposely evade Indiana law. Davis v. State, 892 N.E.2d 156, 2008 Ind. App. LEXIS 1682 (2008).

"Assist."

This section makes it a crime to "assist" a fugitive from justice. "Assist" means "some positive, affirmative act intended to help or aid someone to escape arrest, capture, or punishment." Taylor v. State, 445 N.E.2d 1025, 1983 Ind. App. LEXIS 2655 (1983).

"Assist" contemplates some positive, affirmative act intended to help or aid someone to escape arrest, capture or punishment. Clements v. State, 808 N.E.2d 198, 2004 Ind. App. LEXIS 895 (2004).

Assisting Juvenile Offender.

Defendant's conviction for aiding or assisting a criminal or a fugitive was erroneous because the person aided was a juvenile charged with burglary who had not been waived to a court having criminal jurisdiction, and a juvenile cannot be charged with a crime and therefore is not a criminal, unless he has been so waived. Frost v. State, 527 N.E.2d 228, 1988 Ind. App. LEXIS 613 (1988).

Compounding Felonies.

The defendant must have had knowledge of the actual commission of the crime which it was alleged he agreed to compound or conceal. State v. Henning, 33 Ind. 189, 1870 Ind. LEXIS 75 (1870).

Conviction of Principal.

Conviction of the principal could be shown in the trial of a person charged as accessory after the fact. Walker v. State, 246 Ind. 386, 204 N.E.2d 850, 1965 Ind. LEXIS 364 (1965), cert. denied, 382 U.S. 991, 86 S. Ct. 569, 15 L. Ed. 2d 478, 1966 U.S. LEXIS 2658 (1966).

Evidence.

—In General.

If there is evidence from which the jury could conclude that the crime had been committed by the principal and that defendant was connected therewith judgment would not be disturbed. Murphy v. State, 184 Ind. 15, 110 N.E. 198, 1915 Ind. LEXIS 129 (1915).

Where the evidence showed only that defendant fled the crime scene with other participants and did not show he made any attempt to conceal or assist the others in their escape the evidence was insufficient to support a conviction. Overton v. State, 161 Ind. App. 650, 317 N.E.2d 467, 1974 Ind. App. LEXIS 992 (1974).

The evidence need not establish beyond a reasonable doubt that defendant hid a criminal either as a principal or accessory, to be convicted of the offense of assisting a criminal. Taylor v. State, 445 N.E.2d 1025, 1983 Ind. App. LEXIS 2655 (1983).

—Abortion.

Where testimony identified defendant as person through whom some arrangements were made and as having been present during the abortion, evidence was sufficient to convict defendant as an accessory. Rhim v. State, 264 Ind. 682, 348 N.E.2d 620, 1976 Ind. LEXIS 503 (1976).

—Concealing Felon.

Evidence that defendant transported the escapee in his car and had him in his home a few days after the escape without evidence that the

Evidence. (Cont'd)

—Concealing Felon. (Cont'd)
defendant knew the escapee had been in jail and had escaped was insufficient to sustain a conviction under former section punishing the concealment of a felon. Deering v. State, 249 Ind. 354, 232 N.E.2d 604, 1968 Ind. LEXIS 720 (1968).

—Concealing Stolen Goods.
Where there was evidence that a building had been broken into and a number of articles were taken and some of the articles were found in defendant's possession the state had met its burden of establishing the corpus delicti for second-degree burglary and defendant's accessorial acts of concealing and disposing of the stolen property. Collison v. State, 165 Ind. App. 596, 333 N.E.2d 787, 1975 Ind. App. LEXIS 1289 (1975).

—Criminal's Presence.
Where the evidence consists exclusively of defendant's possessory interest in a house and her presence there when the police entered, but her possessory interest and presence were nonexclusive, it was unreasonable under that circumstance to infer knowledge of a criminal's presence within the residence without other indicia of knowledge. Taylor v. State, 445 N.E.2d 1025, 1983 Ind. App. LEXIS 2655 (1983).

It was reasonable for the trial court to view defendant's statement that she neither knew a criminal nor his whereabouts as an affirmative act constituting assistance to a fugitive but only if the trial court could also reasonably infer defendant knew of the criminal's presence in the house at the time she denied knowledge of his whereabouts. Taylor v. State, 445 N.E.2d 1025, 1983 Ind. App. LEXIS 2655 (1983).

—Disposing of Evidence.
Where the defendant clearly intended to assist a co-conspirator and hinder his apprehension by helping to dispose of the gun used to commit murder, there was sufficient evidence to sustain a conviction for assisting a criminal. Shane v. State, 716 N.E.2d 391, 1999 Ind. LEXIS 799 (1999).

—False Certification by Notary.
In a prosecution for commanding a notary to certify falsely to the swearing of a certain person to an affidavit, where the testimony showed that the jury had ample grounds for finding accused guilty as charged, it was sufficient to sustain conviction. Klink v. State, 203 Ind. 647, 179 N.E. 549, 1932 Ind. LEXIS 87, 79 A.L.R. 272 (1932).

—Family Relationship.
Where evidence showed that two prisoners, after leaving hospital, overpowered prison guard and drove around in prison automobile, that one made a telephone call, came back and said, "they'll get us a car," after which they parked in an alley, walked down the street to another car and were driven away by defendant, there was no evidence to show that defendant knew these persons were escaped convicts, and an inference that she had such knowledge would not arise from the fact that she was a sister of one of the prisoners, where the facts of such relationship were not in evidence, and mere fact that defense attorney referred to defendant as the sister of one of them in his argument could not supply the deficiency of the evidence. Collins v. State, 174 Ind. App. 116, 366 N.E.2d 229, 1977 Ind. App. LEXIS 939 (1977).

Evidence was insufficient to convict the defendant of assisting a criminal, where the state relied on evidence that the assisted criminal had a significant other who was not the defendant to prove the assisted criminal and the defendant were not married, when that fact could have been easily proven through direct evidence. Jaunese v. State, 701 N.E.2d 1282, 1998 Ind. App. LEXIS 2080 (1998).

—Forgery.
The burning of stolen payroll check blanks which were part of a supply used in forgery of checks purporting to be drawn by the business establishment from which the blanks were stolen was an affirmative act intended to aid the forger of such checks escape punishment within the meaning of accessory after the fact section. Arterbery v. State, 249 Ind. 541, 233 N.E.2d 489, 1968 Ind. LEXIS 740 (1968).

—Insufficient.
Conviction of defendant restaurant owner for assisting criminal, who was being searched by police in parking lot of restaurant, was improper, where defendant's wife interfered with police search but defendant's only involvement was failure to follow officer's command to get his wife and leave, since defendant was not responsible for actions of wife. Clements v. State, 808 N.E.2d 198, 2004 Ind. App. LEXIS 895 (2004).

Because defendant was charged with harboring, concealing, or assisting a fugitive from justice under IC 35-44-3-2, but no evidence was presented that the fugitive had fled from one state to another, there was a failure of proof; accordingly, trial court erred in failing to give defendant's requested jury instruction defining a fugitive from justice. Lafferty v. State, 899 N.E.2d 683, 2009 Ind. App. LEXIS 1 (2009).

—Murder.
In order to sustain conviction as accessory after the fact to murder, it was necessary to show that defendant harbored, concealed or assisted his brother for the purpose of evading capture for the crime which such brother committed. Dennis v. State, 230 Ind. 210, 102 N.E.2d 650, 1952 Ind. LEXIS 184 (1952).

Where codefendant gave someone a shotgun knowing that the recipient planned to kill a person with it, and the gun was in fact used to kill that person, evidence was sufficient to link codefendant with defendant and to convict codefendant as accessory. Ortiz v. State, 265 Ind. 549, 356 N.E.2d 1188, 1976 Ind. LEXIS 424 (1976), overruled, Smith v. State, 689 N.E.2d 1238, 1997 Ind. LEXIS 243 (Ind. 1997).

—Robbery.
Where there was evidence that defendant drove a getaway car and made threatening phone calls to

Evidence. (Cont'd)

—Robbery. (Cont'd)
discourage the robbery victim from calling the police, the evidence was sufficient to support a conviction as accessory. Caine v. State, 160 Ind. App. 695, 313 N.E.2d 719, 1974 Ind. App. LEXIS 1100 (1974).

Where the defendants acted in unison with the confederate in committing the robbery, the confederate's actions which placed the victim in fear could be attributed to the defendants, making the evidence sufficient to support the jury's verdict. Moses v. State, 170 Ind. App. 451, 352 N.E.2d 851, 1976 Ind. App. LEXIS 1015 (1976).

Where defendant was convicted of accessory after the fact to infliction of an injury during a robbery, evidence which showed that before leaving the residence which was the scene of the crime defendant started a fire and that defendant concealed the means by which he obtained the stolen property was sufficient to support the conviction. Tessely v. State, 267 Ind. 445, 370 N.E.2d 907, 1978 Ind. LEXIS 580 (1978).

—Sufficient.
Where defendant drove the car which twice signaled the victim to stop, a shotgun was on the front seat of defendant's car, while a passenger in defendant's car was shooting the victims, defendant waited, upon the gunman's return to the car, defendant drove away and later the car defendant had been driving shortly before pulled into the inn with the gunman still in the passenger's seat, the jury could have inferred defendant assisted gunman in leaving the scene of the crime and followed the victims to the inn; there was sufficient evidence to sustain the conviction. Moore v. State, 445 N.E.2d 576, 1983 Ind. App. LEXIS 2663 (1983), overruled, Wright v. State, 690 N.E.2d 1098, 1997 Ind. LEXIS 245 (1997).

Sufficient evidence supported convictions for violating IC 35-44-3-2 and IC 35-44-2-2: (1) the defendant's spouse told defendant that he had hurt a few people when he came home covered in blood and demanded that she pack their things so that they could quickly leave; (2) defendant learned from her mother that several people had been murdered; (3) defendant admitted to a detective that she told her spouse's stepmother to tell everyone, including the authorities, that she last saw them in Memphis, although they were not in Memphis; (4) defendant and her spouse returned to Indiana and hid in the woods until they ran out of food; and (5) the spouse remained in hiding while defendant returned to her home and spoke with detectives. Davis v. State, 892 N.E.2d 156, 2008 Ind. App. LEXIS 1682 (2008).

Indictment or Information.
An indictment for aiding the escape of a prisoner did not need to set out the indictment against the prisoner, as it was sufficient to set out the substance of the felony which he was held to answer. Gunyon v. State, 68 Ind. 79, 1879 Ind. LEXIS 548 (1879).

The charge would be good against a motion in arrest of judgment although the manner of giving aid was not stated. Campton v. State, 140 Ind. 442, 39 N.E. 916, 1895 Ind. LEXIS 49 (1895).

When it was charged that an accused aided or accomplished the escape of the prisoner, it did not need to be alleged that the accused knew that the escaped person was a prisoner, when the facts stated showed that the accused knew that the person escaping was in the custody of an officer. State v. Sutton, 170 Ind. 473, 170 Ind. 573, 84 N.E. 824, 1908 Ind. LEXIS 45 (1908).

Indictment substantially in words of accessory after the fact statute was sufficient to charge crime of being such accessory. Dennis v. State, 230 Ind. 210, 102 N.E.2d 650, 1952 Ind. LEXIS 184 (1952).

The state may charge a defendant as a principal and then prove that he was an accessory. Wallace v. State, 426 N.E.2d 34, 1981 Ind. LEXIS 845 (1981).

Implicating Others.
Although many criminals will involve their confederate when they are questioned by police, they certainly are not required to do so, and their failure to involve a confederate cannot be considered to be a separate crime of aiding a criminal. Harris v. State, 617 N.E.2d 912, 1993 Ind. LEXIS 101 (1993), overruled, Wright v. State, 690 N.E.2d 1098, 1997 Ind. LEXIS 245 (1997).

Intent.
Under former accessory after the fact statute, intent was essential to make one "accessory after the fact" and required knowledge of the crime. Bielich v. State, 189 Ind. 127, 126 N.E. 220, 1920 Ind. LEXIS 10 (1920).

Lesser Included Offense.
Verdict of guilty as accessory after fact to second-degree murder was not contrary to law although principal was found guilty of murder in first degree since second-degree murder was an included offense of first-degree murder. The court further held, however, appellant waived any consideration on this point by failing to make objections to court's instructions regarding principal crime of which accessory could be found guilty. Walker v. State, 246 Ind. 386, 204 N.E.2d 850, 1965 Ind. LEXIS 364 (1965), cert. denied, 382 U.S. 991, 86 S. Ct. 569, 15 L. Ed. 2d 478, 1966 U.S. LEXIS 2658 (1966).

Assisting a criminal is not, in every instance, a lesser included offense of murder. Reynolds v. State, 460 N.E.2d 506, 1984 Ind. LEXIS 771 (1984).

Assisting a criminal is not an "inherently included" offense of robbery as an aider, etc. Assisting a criminal contains the element of an "intent to hinder the apprehension or punishment" of a person who has committed a crime, whereas robbery as an aider requires aiding, inducing or causing another to commit a robbery. Horn v. State, 503 N.E.2d 1235, 1987 Ind. App. LEXIS 2400 (1987).

One who aids, induces or causes another to commit murder has not necessarily assisted any person in avoiding detection and arrest, and the latter is not a necessary lesser and included offense within the former, from the statutory view-

Lesser Included Offense. (Cont'd)
point. Thacker v. State, 556 N.E.2d 1315, 1990 Ind. LEXIS 142 (1990).

Crime of assisting a criminal is neither inherently nor factually included as a lesser offense of murder. Wright v. State, 690 N.E.2d 1098, 1997 Ind. LEXIS 245 (1997), overruled in part, Fuller v. State, 875 N.E.2d 326, 2007 Ind. App. LEXIS 2359 (2007).

—Conspirary.
Because it is possible to conspire to commit murder without an intent to hinder the apprehension of a criminal or a fugitive from justice, assisting a criminal is not inherently a lesser included offense of conspiracy. Lahr v. State, 640 N.E.2d 756, 1994 Ind. App. LEXIS 1350 (1994).

In the charging information, assisting a criminal was not factually included within the charged crime of conspiracy to commit murder, so that the defendant was entitled to an instruction on the lesser included offense, where no act was done to hinder the apprehension or punishment of a person other than the actor. Lahr v. State, 640 N.E.2d 756, 1994 Ind. App. LEXIS 1350 (1994).

Misdemeanors.
There could be no accessories in misdemeanors, either before or after the fact. Stratton v. State, 45 Ind. 468, 1874 Ind. LEXIS 8 (1874); Lay v. State, 12 Ind. App. 362, 39 N.E. 768, 1895 Ind. App. LEXIS 108 (1895).

All who aided or abetted in the commission of a misdemeanor were indictable and punishable as principals. Merrill v. State, 175 Ind. 139, 93 N.E. 857, 1911 Ind. LEXIS 27, 44 L.R.A. (n.s.) 439 (1911).

In a misdemeanor there could be no accessories either before or after the fact, but all concerned in its commission were liable as principals. McDaniels v. State, 185 Ind. 245, 113 N.E. 1004, 1916 Ind. LEXIS 44 (1916).

Participation in Crime.
It was not necessary that the appellant actively engage in the homicide itself to be found guilty and the jury could well have found that the activity of the defendant in holding the victim while he was being shot, was within the range of active participation in the murder. Parks v. State, 264 Ind. 538, 348 N.E.2d 21, 1976 Ind. LEXIS 488 (1976).

Where the facts reveal that defendant's acts of aiding theft made her an active participant in the crime, and the fact that she assisted others in evading police after the theft was nothing more than an example of her attempt to hide her involvement in the crime, the facts were insufficient to show she committed the separate and distinct offense of assisting a criminal after the commission of the theft itself, so that her conviction for assisting a criminal was reversed. Joseph v. State, 659 N.E.2d 676, 1996 Ind. App. LEXIS 2 (1996).

Presence at Commission of Crime.
It was not necessary that defendant charged with being an accessory after the fact be absent at the commission of the crime. Walker v. State, 246 Ind. 386, 204 N.E.2d 850, 1965 Ind. LEXIS 364 (1965), cert. denied, 382 U.S. 991, 86 S. Ct. 569, 15 L. Ed. 2d 478, 1966 U.S. LEXIS 2658 (1966).

Receiving Stolen Goods.
Mother who was not charged with being an accessory after the fact or with concealing a felon could be convicted of receiving goods stolen by son notwithstanding statutes providing that persons in family relationship to principal or felon could not be convicted as accessory or of concealing felon. McCoy v. State, 241 Ind. 104, 170 N.E.2d 43, 1960 Ind. LEXIS 143 (1960).

Sentence.
The offenses of rape and accessory after the fact of rape are separate and distinct and the penalty for one need not be proportional to the penalty for the other. Clark v. State, 160 Ind. App. 206, 311 N.E.2d 439, 1974 Ind. App. LEXIS 1032 (1974).

Where defendant was sentenced on convictions of being both an accessory before and after the fact, the sentence for being an accessory after the fact was vacated. Tessely v. State, 267 Ind. 445, 370 N.E.2d 907, 1978 Ind. LEXIS 580 (1978).

Where murder defendant had her sister turn up volume on stereo while she shot her stepfather twice and then attempted to conceal murder by burning the body, any error in accepting defendant's jury trial waiver without advising defendant that she had right to have jury determine beyond reasonable doubt all facts legally essential to her sentence was deemed harmless. Averitte v. State, 824 N.E.2d 1283, 2005 Ind. App. LEXIS 563 (2005).

Venue.
Where defendant was convicted of being accessory after the fact, the fact that after the commission of the principal crime defendant accompanied others in automobile and while in Michigan defendant replaced the license plate on the automobile did not make the venue of the crime in Michigan instead of Indiana. Thomas v. State, 275 Ind. 499, 417 N.E.2d 1124, 1981 Ind. LEXIS 703 (1981).

Witness.

—Impeachment.
A witness's conviction for assisting a criminal is not an impeachable offense under Rule, Evid. R. 609(a). Cason v. State, 672 N.E.2d 74, 1996 Ind. LEXIS 143 (1996).

Cited:
Prophet v. Duckworth, 580 F.2d 926, 1978 U.S. App. LEXIS 9595 (7th Cir. Ind. 1978); Moore v. State, 426 N.E.2d 86, 1981 Ind. App. LEXIS 1653 (1981); Evans v. State, 489 N.E.2d 942, 1986 Ind. LEXIS 1039 (1986); Peck v. State, 563 N.E.2d 554, 1990 Ind. LEXIS 246 (1990); Sturgeon v. State, 719 N.E.2d 1173, 1999 Ind. LEXIS 1073 (1999); Hauk v. State, 729 N.E.2d 994, 2000 Ind. LEXIS 534 (2000); Williams v. State, 759 N.E.2d 661, 2001 Ind. App. LEXIS 2111 (2001).

OPINIONS OF ATTORNEY GENERAL

A determinate sentence of three years under former section punishing the concealment of felons was valid. 1936, p. 141.

RESEARCH REFERENCES

Collateral References.
Minor's entry into home of parent as sufficient to sustain burglary charge. 17 A.L.R.5th 111.

35-44-3-3. Resisting law enforcement.

(a) A person who knowingly or intentionally:

(1) forcibly resists, obstructs, or interferes with a law enforcement officer or a person assisting the officer while the officer is lawfully engaged in the execution of the officer's duties;

(2) forcibly resists, obstructs, or interferes with the authorized service or execution of a civil or criminal process or order of a court; or

(3) flees from a law enforcement officer after the officer has, by visible or audible means, including operation of the law enforcement officer's siren or emergency lights, identified himself or herself and ordered the person to stop;

commits resisting law enforcement, a Class A misdemeanor, except as provided in subsection (b).

(b) The offense under subsection (a) is a:

(1) Class D felony if:

(A) the offense is described in subsection (a)(3) and the person uses a vehicle to commit the offense; or

(B) while committing any offense described in subsection (a), the person draws or uses a deadly weapon, inflicts bodily injury on or otherwise causes bodily injury to another person, or operates a vehicle in a manner that creates a substantial risk of bodily injury to another person;

(2) Class C felony if, while committing any offense described in subsection (a), the person operates a vehicle in a manner that causes serious bodily injury to another person; and

(3) Class B felony if, while committing any offense described in subsection (a), the person operates a vehicle in a manner that causes the death of another person.

(c) For purposes of this section, a law enforcement officer includes an enforcement officer of the alcohol and tobacco commission and a conservation officer of the department of natural resources.

(d) If a person uses a vehicle to commit a felony offense under subsection (b)(1)(B), (b)(2), or (b)(3), as part of the criminal penalty imposed for the offense, the court shall impose a minimum executed sentence of at least:

(1) thirty (30) days, if the person does not have a prior unrelated conviction under this section;

(2) one hundred eighty (180) days, if the person has one (1) prior unrelated conviction under this section; or

(3) one (1) year, if the person has two (2) or more prior unrelated convictions under this section.

(e) Notwithstanding IC 35-50-2-2 and IC 35-50-3-1, the mandatory minimum sentence imposed under subsection (d) may not be suspended.

History.
IC 35-44-3-3, as added by Acts 1976, P.L.148, § 4; 1977, P.L.340, § 61; 1979, P.L.83, § 11; P.L.188-1984, § 1; P.L.325-1987, § 1; P.L.248-1993, § 1; P.L.13-1998, § 1; P.L.143-2006, § 2.

Compiler's Notes.
P.L.143-2006, § 3, effective July 1, 2006, provides:
"IC 35-44-3-3, as amended by this act, applies only to acts committed after June 30, 2006."

Cross References.

Contempt for not obeying process, IC 34-47-3-1. Penalties for felonies, IC 35-50-1, IC 35-50-2, IC 35-50-5-2.

Penalties for misdemeanors, IC 35-50-1, IC 35-50-3, IC 35-50-5-2.

NOTES TO DECISIONS

ANALYSIS

Arrest.
—Freeing Prisoner.
—Legality.
—Warrantless Arrest.
Assault.
Construction.
—"Drawing a Deadly Weapon."
—Forcibly.
—Forcibly Resists.
—With Other Laws.
Conviction Upheld.
Defenses.
Double Jeopardy.
Duties as an Officer.
Elements.
—Force.
—Knowledge.
—Substantial Risk of Bodily Injury.
Evidence.
—Admissibility.
—Force.
—Inferences.
—Insufficient.
—Intent.
—Sufficient.
False Arrest.
Felony.
Included Offenses.
Indictment or Information.
—Forcibly.
Instructions.
Law Enforcement Officer.
Misdemeanor Committed in Officer's Presence.
Number of Officers Irrelevant.
Officer Acting Unlawfully.
Other Offenses Distinguished.
—Battery.
Privilege to Resist.
—Excessive Force.
—Unlawful Entry.
Sentence.
Single Incident.
Verdict.

Arrest.

—Freeing Prisoner.

If, in freeing a prisoner from arrest, an assault and battery was committed, there could be a conviction of assault and battery and an acquittal of the freeing from arrest when the assault and battery was properly charged. Rose v. State, 33 Ind. 167, 1870 Ind. LEXIS 66 (1870).

—Legality.

The use of a deadly weapon against a uniformed police officer was not justified although the at-

tempted arrest may have been illegal. Williams v. State, 160 Ind. App. 294, 311 N.E.2d 619, 1974 Ind. App. LEXIS 1044 (1974), superseded by statute as stated in, Shoultz v. State, 735 N.E.2d 818, 2000 Ind. App. LEXIS 1483 (2000).

Where owner's vehicle was improperly registered but properly parked, police removal of the vehicle contravened the requirements of former IC 9-9-1.6-8; owner's attempt to interfere with the police removal by removing the vehicle himself did not constitute interference with the execution of the police officers' legal duties, and hence his arrest for resisting law enforcement was improper. Fields v. State, 178 Ind. App. 350, 382 N.E.2d 972, 1978 Ind. App. LEXIS 1156 (1978), superseded by statute as stated in, Shoultz v. State, 735 N.E.2d 818, 2000 Ind. App. LEXIS 1483 (2000).

Notwithstanding the outmoded common law rule that permitted resistance to unlawful arrests, a private citizen may not use force to resist peaceful arrest by one he knows or has good reason to believe is an authorized peace officer performing his duties, regardless of whether the arrest is illegal in the circumstances of the occasion. Fields v. State, 178 Ind. App. 350, 382 N.E.2d 972, 1978 Ind. App. LEXIS 1156 (1978), superseded by statute as stated in, Shoultz v. State, 735 N.E.2d 818, 2000 Ind. App. LEXIS 1483 (2000).

For factual analysis as to legality of arrest for resisting law enforcement, see Bovey v. Lafayette, 586 F. Supp. 1460, 1984 U.S. Dist. LEXIS 16459 (N.D. Ind. 1984), aff'd without op., 774 F.2d 1166, 1985 U.S. App. LEXIS 22854 (7th Cir. Ind. 1985).

An officer has a right to enforce a lawful order even if that means arresting a person who verbally refuses to obey the order and then makes a movement in furtherance of his goal of disobedience. Potts v. City of Lafayette, 121 F.3d 1106, 1997 U.S. App. LEXIS 20515 (7th Cir. Ind. 1997).

Defendant was not permitted to flee from the officer's show of authority, regardless of whether that authority was, in defendant's subjective view, unlawful, because a citizen may not resist arrest by a police officer performing his duties whether the officer's actions later turn out to be lawful or unlawful. Lashley v. State, 745 N.E.2d 254, 2001 Ind. App. LEXIS 505 (2001).

Officer had probable cause to arrest plaintiff where plaintiff continued driving despite officer's attempt to stop him for traffic violation since, in fleeing from officer, plaintiff committed felony of resisting arrest under IC 35-44-3-3(b)(1)(A). Tilson v. City of Elkhart, 317 F. Supp. 2d 861, 2003 U.S. Dist. LEXIS 25382 (N.D. Ind. 2003), aff'd, — F.3d —, 2004 U.S. App. LEXIS 8193 (7th Cir. Ind. 2004).

Court improperly granted defendant's motion to suppress all evidence of any events which occurred after sheriff's deputy served defendant with invalid prejudgment order of possession since defen-

Arrest. (Cont'd)

—Legality. (Cont'd)
dant could not use force in resisting peaceful arrest by police officer performing his duties even if arrest was unlawful. State v. Moriarity, 832 N.E.2d 555, 2005 Ind. App. LEXIS 1439 (2005).

—Warrantless Arrest.
Police officer's pursuit of defendant into his home in order to arrest him without a warrant was justified by probable cause where defendant had refused to stop upon police officer's request prior to entering home and thus was engaging in the offense of resisting arrest. State v. Blake, 468 N.E.2d 548, 1984 Ind. App. LEXIS 2941 (1984).

Assault.
Where shots were fired at pursuing police officers, from automobile in which defendant was riding, the jury could reasonably infer that defendant was guilty of assault with intent to kill. Bradberry v. State, 266 Ind. 530, 364 N.E.2d 1183, 1977 Ind. LEXIS 428 (1977).

Construction.
For purposes of a conviction for resisting law enforcement, "flight" should be understood to mean a knowing attempt to escape law enforcement when the defendant is aware that a law enforcement officer has ordered him to stop or remain, and it is enough that a defendant disobey a command to remain, by walking away from a law enforcement officer into the defendant's own house and locking the door behind him. Wellman v. State, 703 N.E.2d 1061, 1998 Ind. App. LEXIS 2091 (1998).
Police officer was entitled to qualified immunity on a citizen's Fourth Amendment claim against the officer arising out of officer's arrest of citizen for violating IC 35-44-3-3, resisting arrest, because state law was not entirely clear with respect to whether non violent, non-forcible behavior amounted to a violation of IC 35-44-3-3(a). Bowden v. Town of Speedway, 539 F. Supp. 2d 1092, 2008 U.S. Dist. LEXIS 10974 (2008).
In a 42 U.S.C.S. § 1983 suit in which a sheriff's deputy allegedly used excessive force in violation of the Fourth Amendment by smashing the windshield of an arrestee's car when lunging at it for failing to turn as directed at a roadblock, the officer had probable cause to forcefully handcuff the arrestee because it appeared that he had interfered with a officer performing his duties under IC 35-44-3-3(a)(1). Vandewalle v. Moffa, — F. Supp. 2d —, 2009 U.S. Dist. LEXIS 19303 (2009).

—"Drawing a Deadly Weapon."
"Drawing" a deadly weapon constitutes a separate and distinct offense from "pointing" or "aiming" a deadly weapon. Burk v. State, 716 N.E.2d 39, 1999 Ind. App. LEXIS 1470 (1999).

—Forcibly.
In order to sustain a conviction under this section, the state must prove not only that defendant resisted, but that he forcibly resisted, because the modifying word "forcibly" is within that section of the statute; "forcibly" is a required element of the crime, and it is error to find that mere action to resist service of process falls within the statute, absent a showing of use of force. Spangler v. State, 607 N.E.2d 720, 1993 Ind. LEXIS 13 (1993).
The word "forcibly" modifies the entire string of verbs in the particular sections of the statute where it is used, due to the placement of the adverb before the string of verbs in the particular clauses. Spangler v. State, 607 N.E.2d 720, 1993 Ind. LEXIS 13 (1993).
A defendant who physically resists arrest by placing his hands against a door frame, forcing a law enforcement officer to shove him through the doorway and to lift him onto his feet acts with the requisite force in resisting the officer in the performance of his duties to sustain a conviction for resisting arrest. Wellman v. State, 703 N.E.2d 1061, 1998 Ind. App. LEXIS 2091 (1998).

—Forcibly Resists.
A person "forcibly resists" law enforcement when strong, powerful, violent means are used to evade a law enforcement official's rightful exercise of his or her duties. Spangler v. State, 607 N.E.2d 720, 1993 Ind. LEXIS 13 (1993).
Any action to resist must be done with force in order to violate this section; it is error as a matter of law to conclude that "forcibly resists" includes all actions that are not passive. Spangler v. State, 607 N.E.2d 720, 1993 Ind. LEXIS 13 (1993).
Individual "forcibly resists" law enforcement when strong, powerful, violent means are used to evade law enforcement official's rightful exercise of his or her duties and word "force" means something more than mere action; accordingly, defendant's conviction for resisting law enforcement was reversed where evidence merely demonstrated that defendant hid in woods and trunk of vehicle to avoid capture. Atkinson v. State, 810 N.E.2d 1190, 2004 Ind. App. LEXIS 1269 (2004).
Officers did not have probable cause to arrest protestor for resisting law enforcement under IC 35-44-3-3 and protestor's rights under U.S. Const., Amend. 4, were therefore violated; protestor refused to move but put up no forcible resistance. Blair v. City of Evansville, 361 F. Supp. 2d 846, 2005 U.S. Dist. LEXIS 4833 (S.D. Ind. 2005).

—With Other Laws.
Fleeing from an officer, in a vehicle, in violation of IC 35-44-3-3(b)(1)(A), constituted a "violent felony" for purposes of the federal Armed Career Criminal Act. United States v. Spells, 537 F.3d 743, 2008 U.S. App. LEXIS 16861 (2008).

Conviction Upheld.
A conviction for resisting arrest by a railroad policeman while on duty, on property not identified as railroad property, was upheld, as by statute the railroad policeman has the general duty to enforce the laws of the state. Mazziotti v. State, 168 Ind. App. 511, 343 N.E.2d 816, 1976 Ind. App. LEXIS 840 (1976).
Defendant who fled from police after they identified themselves and who later resisted police while they were conducting a lawful strip search following arrest was properly convicted of resisting

Conviction Upheld. (Cont'd)
law enforcement. Frye v. State, 757 N.E.2d 684, 2001 Ind. App. LEXIS 1763 (2001), cert. denied, 535 U.S. 1103, 122 S. Ct. 2308, 152 L. Ed. 2d 1063, 2002 U.S. LEXIS 3956 (2002).

Defenses.
Defendant's assertion that his conduct in running from a police officer who had ordered defendant to stop should be excused under an outrageous conduct by law enforcement defense failed as the defense was not recognized in Indiana; moreover, under Indiana precedent, defendant had a duty to stop regardless of the apparent or ultimate lawfulness of the officer's order. Yowler v. State, 894 N.E.2d 1000, 2008 Ind. App. LEXIS 2222 (2008).

Double Jeopardy.
Sentencing defendant for both criminal confinement and resisting law enforcement did not constitute double jeopardy since they did not constitute the same offense. Inman v. State, 271 Ind. 491, 393 N.E.2d 767, 1979 Ind. LEXIS 707 (1979).

The double jeopardy clause did not bar defendant's convictions for resisting arrest and disorderly conduct, where both offenses required the proof of additional facts. Whitley v. State, 553 N.E.2d 511, 1990 Ind. App. LEXIS 495 (1990).

The elements of the offenses of resisting law enforcement and battery on a police officer are not identical. Battery requires the knowing or intentional touching of another person, whereas a resisting charge could be sustained on mere interference or obstruction of an arrest without any physical contact with the arresting officer. Guilty verdicts on the two offenses are, therefore, not inconsistent or illogical. Jackson v. State, 576 N.E.2d 607, 1991 Ind. App. LEXIS 1314 (1991).

Resisting law enforcement and battery by body waste each require proof of an element which the other does not, and, therefore, are not the same for double jeopardy purposes. Newman v. State, 677 N.E.2d 590, 1997 Ind. App. LEXIS 92 (1997).

Convictions for the offenses of resisting law enforcement and battery by body waste did not violate double jeopardy, where the facts revealed that defendant engaged in separate and distinct conduct to support each of the charged offenses, though the offenses arose from the same operative circumstances. Newman v. State, 677 N.E.2d 590, 1997 Ind. App. LEXIS 92 (1997).

Because the offense of resisting law enforcement involves drawing a handgun while fleeing from a law enforcement officer, which the offense of carrying a handgun without a license does not, and because the latter offense involves the absence of a valid license, which resisting law enforcement does not, there is no double jeopardy violation in convicting a defendant of both offenses. Burk v. State, 716 N.E.2d 39, 1999 Ind. App. LEXIS 1470 (1999).

There was a reasonable possibility that the same evidentiary facts used by the jury to establish the injury for aggravated battery may have also been used to establish the injury for the resisting law enforcement conviction where the injury alleged by State for both charges was the same; thus, there

was a double jeopardy violation which required reversal of the conviction for resisting law enforcement. James v. State, 755 N.E.2d 226, 2001 Ind. App. LEXIS 1605 (2001).

Where evidence that defendant bit officer twice was relied upon to convict defendant of both battery and resisting law enforcement, no double jeopardy violation was committed, since one bite was used to prove battery and other bite was used to prove resisting law enforcement, and defendant's appellate counsel was therefore not ineffective for failing to present that issue. Haggard v. State, 810 N.E.2d 751, 2004 Ind. App. LEXIS 1154 (2004).

Defendant's convictions of resisting law enforcement both as Class D felony and as Class A misdemeanor, IC 35-44-3-3(b)(1) and IC 35-44-3-3(a)(3), respectively, violated double jeopardy; defendant's flight from police, involving flight in car and on foot, constituted one continuous flight. Nevel v. State, 818 N.E.2d 1, 2004 Ind. App. LEXIS 2185 (2004).

Defendant's convictions of Class D felony resisting law enforcement in violation of IC 35-44-3-3(b)(1) and auto theft in violation of IC 35-43-4-2.5(a) did not violate double jeopardy since proof of elements of one offense did not necessarily prove other offense; use of vehicle, but not use of vehicle obtained without permission of owner, was essential element of resisting offense. Nevel v. State, 818 N.E.2d 1, 2004 Ind. App. LEXIS 2185 (2004).

Defendant's resisting law enforcement convictions were more than simply offenses against lawful authority because, although both of the resisting law enforcement as class D felonies involved a single incident of resisting, two people were injured as a result of defendant's resisting; each conviction required proof of at least one unique evidentiary fact, which in the present case were the different injuries to the two deputies involved in the arrest. Because each conviction involved separate victims, defendant's two convictions for resisting law enforcement as class D felonies did not violate double jeopardy. Whaley v. State, 843 N.E.2d 1, 2006 Ind. App. LEXIS 164 (2006).

When defendant was charged with resisting law enforcement both by fleeing in a truck and by forcibly ramming the truck into police vehicles, in violation of IC 35-44-3-3(a)(1) and (3), there was no double jeopardy violation. Resisting law enforcement by fleeing was different from resisting law enforcement by force. Shouse v. State, 849 N.E.2d 650, 2006 Ind. App. LEXIS 1154 (2006).

Defendant's convictions on two counts of resisting law enforcement did not violate defendant's double jeopardy rights since the two convictions involved discrete elements and were proved by discrete evidence; one conviction was based on defendant's resistance of the police officer and punching the officer in the face while the other conviction was based on knowingly fleeing from the officer after the officer had identified himself and ordered defendant to stop. Deshazier v. State, 877 N.E.2d 200, 2007 Ind. App. LEXIS 2724 (2007).

Duties as an Officer.
When a police officer, whether in uniform or not,

Duties as an Officer. (Cont'd)
takes it upon himself to enforce the law in order to maintain peace and order for the benefit of the public, the officer is performing official duties as a police officer. Nieto v. State, 499 N.E.2d 280, 1986 Ind. App. LEXIS 3117 (1986).

Elements.
In order to be guilty of the offense of resisting law enforcement, a defendant must engage in the prohibited conduct "knowingly" or "intentionally." Vickers v. State, 653 N.E.2d 110, 1995 Ind. App. LEXIS 736 (1995).

Where vehicle is involved in fleeing law enforcement, it is not necessary that person drive vehicle to be convicted of resisting law enforcement; it is enough that person used vehicle, even as passenger, to flee. Davis v. State, 835 N.E.2d 1102, 2005 Ind. App. LEXIS 1996 (2005).

—Force.
The use of force is an essential element of resisting law enforcement as that offense is defined in subsection (a)(1). White v. State, 545 N.E.2d 1124, 1989 Ind. App. LEXIS 1024 (1989).

Whether force has been used is a question for the jury. O'Connor v. State, 590 N.E.2d 145, 1992 Ind. App. LEXIS 486 (1992).

The use of force is an essential element of resisting law enforcement. Young v. State, 626 N.E.2d 474, 1993 Ind. App. LEXIS 1507 (1993).

One forcibly resists law enforcement when strong, powerful, and/or violent means are used to evade a law enforcement official's rightful exercise of his or her duties. Young v. State, 626 N.E.2d 474, 1993 Ind. App. LEXIS 1507 (1993).

An act of violence toward an officer is not constitutionally required before the officer may effect an arrest for forcible obstruction of his duties. Potts v. City of Lafayette, 121 F.3d 1106, 1997 U.S. App. LEXIS 20515 (7th Cir. Ind. 1997).

Although defendant showed an obnoxious disrespect for authority, refusing to present defendant's arms for cuffing did not constitute the use of force required by IC 35-44-3-3; therefore, it was error to convict defendant of the misdemeanor of resisting arrest. Graham v. State, — N.E.2d —, 2009 Ind. LEXIS 341 (2009).

—Knowledge.
To convict under this section, the evidence must show that the defendant knew or had reason to know that the person resisted is a police officer. Sayles v. State, 513 N.E.2d 183, 1987 Ind. App. LEXIS 3087 (1987).

Defendant's conviction for resisting law enforcement was reversed where he had no reason to believe that the person who arrested him was an officer, the evidence having shown that the officer was dressed as a civilian with his badge and gun hidden from view. Stack v. State, 534 N.E.2d 253, 1989 Ind. App. LEXIS 111 (1989).

—Substantial Risk of Bodily Injury.
Defendant's vehicle's speed as he fled from the police and his failure to observe seven red traffic lights sustained the inference that his operation of the vehicle posed a substantial risk of injury to others. Garner v. State, 646 N.E.2d 349, 1995 Ind. App. LEXIS 90 (1995).

Evidence.

—Admissibility.
A rifle and cartridges were properly admitted into evidence as connected with defendant where the items were found in the immediate vicinity of the place where defendant and his companions abandoned their escape vehicle, exchanged gunfire with police, and fled. Coleman v. State, 264 Ind. 64, 339 N.E.2d 51, 1975 Ind. LEXIS 263 (1975).

A rifle and cartridges were properly admitted into evidence with sufficient proof of chain of custody where the exhibits remained in custody of the police department from the time they were found until introduced at trial and where the rifle was marked, identified, and sent with one cartridge to a police laboratory. Coleman v. State, 264 Ind. 64, 339 N.E.2d 51, 1975 Ind. LEXIS 263 (1975).

Where defendant's truck was impounded after defendant crashed the truck in a parking lot while attempting to flee from an arrest, and the truck's contents were inventoried pursuant to the community care taking function and established police procedures, the inventory search exception to the warrant requirement of U.S. Const. amend. IV applied to money that was found in a suitcase inside the truck, and, accordingly, the money was not subject to suppression. Ratliff v. State, 770 N.E.2d 807, 2002 Ind. LEXIS 544 (2002).

Trial court did not abuse its discretion in refusing to admit a video of a police chase where the video's probative value would have been to show the jury a possible explanation for defendant's lengthy flight from the officers after initially fleeing; why defendant decided to lead the officers on a forty-five minute high-speed chase, rather than a shorter one, was irrelevant to the question of whether he resisted law enforcement as a Class D felony, a violation of IC 35-44-3-3(a)(3), (b)(1)(A); defendant resisted law enforcement when he began intentionally fleeing in his truck from officers who were visibly and audibly ordering him to stop. Hape v. State, 903 N.E.2d 977, 2009 Ind. App. LEXIS 637 (2009).

—Force.
The defendant's failure to obey the police officer's demand to lie on the floor was a definite resistance, obstruction, and interference with a law enforcement officer, but since there was no force involved on the defendant's part, the state failed to prove an essential element of resisting a law enforcement officer. Braster v. State, 596 N.E.2d 278, 1992 Ind. App. LEXIS 1138 (1992).

The defendant's actions were not a mere passive refusal to act since he refused to get up and walk after repeated requests to do so even after being told he was under arrest, and continued to refuse to leave the squad car or to put his feet under him to stand. McCaffrey v. State, 605 N.E.2d 241, 1992 Ind. App. LEXIS 1963 (1992).

Where person, while at his place of employment, abruptly discontinued his telephone conversation

Evidence. (Cont'd)

—Force. (Cont'd)

with a deputy, refused to accept court documents from the deputy and demanded that the deputy and the sheriff's department not bother him at work, he continued to express dissatisfaction with the deputy and the sheriff's department and turned and walked away from the deputy three times, in order to avoid service and to resume working, the record failed to disclose the presence of evidence from which a reasonable trier of fact could conclude with the required level of certainty that defendant acted forcibly, as forcibly is defined in this section; there was no strength, power, or violence directed towards the law enforcement official, there was no movement or threatening gesture made in the direction of the official, defendant repeatedly and firmly refused to accept service of process, then walked away, and thus there was no evidence of any "forcible" actions that the charged crime prohibited. Spangler v. State, 607 N.E.2d 720, 1993 Ind. LEXIS 13 (1993).

Evidence was sufficient to convict defendant where he refused to comply with the officers' repeated demands to put down his weapon by not only threatening to kill himself, but also by approaching officers with a loaded weapon, and by firing a shotgun in the direction of the officers when they attempted to unarm him. Young v. State, 626 N.E.2d 474, 1993 Ind. App. LEXIS 1507 (1993).

Where defendant resisted being handcuffed, he fought being put into the police car, and during the entire episode he tried to headbutt and kick the officers, this evidence, together with the officers' further testimony that he continued to struggle and fight until he was put into a cell was sufficient evidence of forcible resistance to support his conviction. Miller v. State, 634 N.E.2d 57, 1994 Ind. App. LEXIS 468 (1994).

Where the evidence showed that the defendant resisted a police officer by claiming ownership of a flag and holding on to it, but that he did not make threatening or violent actions toward the police, it was insufficient to support a conviction for resisting, obstructing or interfering with a law enforcement officer by force. Ajabu v. State, 704 N.E.2d 494, 1998 Ind. App. LEXIS 2098 (1998).

Where plaintiff election board mechanic sued defendant city, mayor, police chief, officers, and mayor's son for alleged constitutional violations resulting from his arrest and detention during an election investigation, grant of summary judgment to arresting officers on mechanic's Fourth Amendment false arrest claim was error since events leading to arrest were in dispute, thereby raising issue of fact as to whether there was probable cause to arrest mechanic for interfering with law enforcement under IC 35-44-3-3(a)(1). Morfin v. City of E. Chicago, 349 F.3d 989, 2003 U.S. App. LEXIS 23450 (7th Cir. Ind. 2003).

—Inferences.

Where a police officer driving a marked police car identified himself to defendant who was running near the scene of a robbery and called upon him to halt and flashed his headlights, whereupon the defendant looked at the officer and his car and immediately resumed his flight, the evidence permitted the inference that when defendant resumed his flight he did so knowing he had been ordered to stop by a police officer. Jones v. State, 164 Ind. App. 252, 328 N.E.2d 221, 1975 Ind. App. LEXIS 1139 (1975).

—Insufficient.

Conviction for resisting a law enforcement officer was reversed where there was no evidence that the officer identified himself when he approached defendant, who allegedly struck the officer and ran away. McCombs v. State, 536 N.E.2d 277, 1989 Ind. LEXIS 86 (1989).

The defendant's conviction was reversed since, although the charging information alleged that he knowingly and forcibly resisted one police officer, the only evidence of force was the use of a car to attempt to push another officer off the road. O'Connor v. State, 590 N.E.2d 145, 1992 Ind. App. LEXIS 486 (1992).

Absent a court order authorizing such action, deputies acted beyond the scope of their official duties when they used the consent of a third person who lacked authority to consent to assist the third person in entering a premises against the defendant's wishes. S. E. v. State, 744 N.E.2d 536, 2001 Ind. App. LEXIS 306 (2001).

In a case alleging that defendant fled from several different officers in several different ways, since multiple resisting convictions were permissible if each conviction arose from a separate offense, the names of the particular officers from whom defendant fled were essential to the description of the two separate resisting charges, and the State had to specifically identify in the information the officer or officers whose arrest efforts defendant resisted; since there was no evidence that defendant did anything to resist the arresting officer's efforts to arrest him, the conviction was not supported by sufficient evidence and was reversed. Bonner v. State, 789 N.E.2d 491, 2003 Ind. App. LEXIS 862 (2003).

There was not sufficient evidence to establish that defendant forcibly resisted the officer by strong, violent, or powerful means to evade an officers rightful exercise of the officer's duties and thus, defendant could not be retried on the resisting law enforcement charge. Sapen v. State, 869 N.E.2d 1273, 2007 Ind. App. LEXIS 1590 (2007).

Reversal of defendant's conviction for resisting law enforcement was required because the arresting officers, who were assisting defendant's former roommate in retrieving his belongings from defendant's apartment, were not lawfully engaged in the execution of their duties when they tried to restrict defendant's movement. Defendant was not under arrest, in custody, or under suspicion; thus, the encounter was a consensual one, and under the Fourth Amendment defendant was free to disregard the officers, to walk away, or even to order the officers to leave the apartment. Briggs v. State, 873 N.E.2d 129, 2007 Ind. App. LEXIS 2073 (2007).

—Intent.

In a trial for robbery and resisting law enforcement, the element of intent can be proven by the

Evidence. (Cont'd)

—Intent. (Cont'd)

surrounding circumstances. White v. State, 495 N.E.2d 725, 1986 Ind. LEXIS 1213 (1986).

Evidence that the defendant was able to walk and run, exert considerable physical force and resistance, and intelligibly communicate comments and opinions, some indicating comprehension of his circumstances, was sufficient to support a finding of requisite intent despite the defendant's intoxication. McCaffrey v. State, 523 N.E.2d 435, 1988 Ind. App. LEXIS 374 (1988).

In prosecution for resisting law enforcement, operating a vehicle while intoxicated, and public intoxication, there was ample evidence that defendant was not so intoxicated as to be unable to knowingly or intentionally flee from the police officers; defendant was aware that the police were following him and requesting that he stop, and he perceived that he was in trouble and decided to flee. Vickers v. State, 653 N.E.2d 110, 1995 Ind. App. LEXIS 736 (1995).

In an action brought by plaintiff, a diabetic, against defendants, a sheriff's department, two of its officers, and the sheriff, arising out of the officers' arrest of plaintiff after he sideswiped another car before lodging his own car on a curb during a hypoglycemic episode, the court denied summary judgment to the first officer on plaintiff's Fourth Amendment claim that the first officer unconstitutionally seized him by arresting him for resisting arrest under IC 35-44-3-3 and for fleeing the scene of an accident under IC 9-26-1-2 after learning that he was diabetic and had become hypoglycemic because although the undisputed evidence showed that until the medical personnel arrived and discovered plaintiff's low blood sugar, the first officer had probable cause to believe that plaintiff had knowingly resisted arrest and had knowingly fled an accident scene, once the first officer knew that plaintiff was diabetic and had low blood sugar, the existence of probable cause became much more questionable and presented a triable issue as those new facts required the first officer to reevaluate the reasonableness of his initial probable cause determination, and a reasonable jury could find that the first officer knew that plaintiff's hypoglycemia diminished his capacity to knowingly resist arrest and flee an accident scene. Overton v. Hicks, — F. Supp. 2d —, 2008 U.S. Dist. LEXIS 47186 (2008).

—Sufficient.

In the prosecution for resisting arrest, the evidence was sufficient to sustain a conviction, where it was shown that accused, who was placed under arrest and ordered to get out of a truck, refused to do so, and resisted the officers, who attempted to remove him, by fighting and kicking and clinging to the steering wheel of the truck, so that force was necessary. Inman v. State, 223 Ind. 500, 62 N.E.2d 627, 1945 Ind. LEXIS 133 (1945).

Where three officers, including the victim, testified that defendant hit victim four or five times and victim was hospitalized for two weeks, there was sufficient evidence to support conviction. Neeley v. State, 156 Ind. App. 489, 297 N.E.2d 847, 1973 Ind. App. LEXIS 1156 (1973).

Where the officer stopped his car near defendant and defendant took a shotgun from behind his back, pointed it at the officer and said he was going to kill him, there was sufficient evidence to support conviction. Dunbar v. State, 162 Ind. App. 375, 319 N.E.2d 630, 1974 Ind. App. LEXIS 844 (1974).

Where defendant took his unlicensed trailer from garage without paying storage and towing charges and while doing so struck a parked vehicle on his way out of garage and sheriff went to take the trailer back, there was sufficient evidence that the jury could find the sheriff was acting in the scope of his official duties (investigating the towing of an unlicensed vehicle on the highway and a hit and run accident) and not merely trying to resolve a civil dispute. Fields v. State, 179 Ind. App. 194, 384 N.E.2d 1127, 1979 Ind. App. LEXIS 1063 (1979).

Where police officer stood at corner with rifle in an attempt to stop car believed to contain three robbers and being driven by defendant and when car approached it swerved toward officer and one of the men in the car fired a shotgun at the officer, there was sufficient evidence to find that defendant aided in the commission of the crime of resisting law enforcement. Brady v. State, 275 Ind. 475, 417 N.E.2d 1108, 1981 Ind. LEXIS 706 (1981).

Evidence that police officers tried to talk defendant into surrendering, tried to box him in, and pursued him with lights and sirens on was sufficient to support conviction for fleeing a police officer, even though the officers allegedly did not order defendant to stop. Pettit v. State, 439 N.E.2d 1175, 1982 Ind. App. LEXIS 1396 (1982).

Evidence held sufficient to prove that the defendant was under a visual command to stop when he fired a weapon and fled. Cole v. State, 475 N.E.2d 306, 1985 Ind. LEXIS 744 (1985).

Evidence that the defendant jumped from a second story window after the police effected a forced entry into his apartment, and continued to proceed up the street after a police officer identified himself and ordered him to stop, was sufficient to sustain his conviction. Lewis v. State, 482 N.E.2d 487, 1985 Ind. App. LEXIS 2730 (1985).

Evidence held sufficient to support conviction. Hyde v. State, 531 N.E.2d 472, 1988 Ind. LEXIS 331 (1988); Bernard v. State, 540 N.E.2d 23, 1989 Ind. LEXIS 183 (1989); Gamble v. State, 591 N.E.2d 142, 1992 Ind. App. LEXIS 637 (1992).

Evidence of flight following a police officer's order to stop is admissible in a prosecution for resisting law enforcement regardless of the lawfulness of the officer's order. Corbin v. State, 568 N.E.2d 1064, 1991 Ind. App. LEXIS 453 (1991).

Where defendant necessarily engaged in force in order to pull away from police officer's grasp and did not merely refuse to be placed under arrest or simply walk away, but rather he used power and strength to evade the officer's attempt to effectuate a lawful arrest, the evidence was sufficient to support his conviction for resisting law enforcement. Small v. State, 632 N.E.2d 779, 1994 Ind. App. LEXIS 465 (1994).

Where the evidence established that deputy had identified himself as a law enforcement officer, defendant knew deputy to be a law enforcement

Evidence. (Cont'd)

—Sufficient. (Cont'd)

officer when he fled, deputy had ordered defendant to stop by audible means, and defendant knew the officer had ordered him to stop, the evidence was sufficient to support the conviction of resisting law enforcement. Staley v. State, 633 N.E.2d 314, 1994 Ind. App. LEXIS 479 (1994).

Evidence was sufficient to justify trial court's determination that defendant was guilty of resisting law enforcement, where defendant fled after firing shots at victim, police officers gave chase, and one officer repeatedly shouted at defendant to stop, was clad in his police uniform and was engaged in the execution of his duties as an officer when he ordered defendant to stop. Meriweather v. State, 659 N.E.2d 133, 1995 Ind. App. LEXIS 1572 (1995).

Evidence was sufficient to support a conviction, where upon arrival at the county lockup defendant refused to get out of the jail wagon and was forcefully removed and placed on the ground, and when asked to get up, he refused and had to be carried to the central receiving area. Guthrie v. State, 720 N.E.2d 7, 1999 Ind. App. LEXIS 2000 (1999).

The evidence was sufficient to convict defendant of resisting arrest where defendant applied pressure to his vehicle's lock button to keep the deputies from effectuating a lawful arrest, gripped the steering wheel and refused to let go when the deputies tried to remove him from his vehicle, and tried to keep his wrists from the deputies as they attempted to place handcuffs on him. Bringle v. State, 745 N.E.2d 821, 2001 Ind. App. LEXIS 372 (2001).

There was sufficient evidence to support defendant's conviction for resisting law enforcement where defendant was standing in the doorway in plain view interfering with the officer's attempt to issue and explain a citation, the officer initiated the arrest while defendant was still in the doorway, and when the officer entered the home, he was in hot pursuit of defendant, following him from a public space to a private space. Johnson v. State, 747 N.E.2d 623, 2001 Ind. App. LEXIS 750 (2001).

Items found in defendant's purse and defendant's flight provided independent evidence supporting her convictions for dealing in methamphetamine, conspiracy to deal in methamphetamine and resisting law enforcement, and existence of such evidence made incredible dubiosity rule inapplicable to defendant. Jacobs v. State, 802 N.E.2d 995, 2004 Ind. App. LEXIS 203 (2004).

Evidence that defendant passenger in car being chased by police took license plate out of car's rear window so that police could not identify car and that defendant did not tell driver to slow down or stop was sufficient to support conviction of defendant for resisting law enforcement. Smith v. State, 809 N.E.2d 938, 2004 Ind. App. LEXIS 1100 (2004).

Evidence was sufficient to support conviction of defendant for resisting law enforcement where defendant ignored order by police officer, who was dressed in civilian clothes, to stop, notwithstanding that officer stated that she was police officer and displayed her badge. Battle v. State, 818 N.E.2d 56, 2004 Ind. App. LEXIS 2298 (2004).

Sufficient evidence supported defendant's misdemeanor conviction of resisting law enforcement in violation of IC 35-44-3-3(a)(1); defendant forcibly resisted officers by pushing officers away with his shoulders as he was being searched and by stiffening his body while being placed in transport vehicle. Johnson v. State, 833 N.E.2d 516, 2005 Ind. App. LEXIS 1586 (2005).

Evidence was sufficient to convict defendant as principal to resisting law enforcement for his involvement in bank robbery; evidence showed that defendant and another planned to rob bank together, drove to bank together to carry out plan, and then instructed accomplice to wait in vehicle until robbery was complete, and It was unnecessary for defendant to have actually driven vehicle used to flee from police for conviction to be upheld. Davis v. State, 835 N.E.2d 1102, 2005 Ind. App. LEXIS 1996 (2005).

Defendant argued that he did not inflict bodily injury on two deputies, but that the deputies inflicted injury upon themselves by hitting defendant's arms while he was resisting arrest; defendant asked that the convictions be reduced to class A misdemeanors. The two different deputies' injuries were directly related to and caused by defendant's resisting arrest; thus, the evidence was sufficient to sustain defendant's convictions for two counts of resisting law enforcement as class D felonies. Whaley v. State, 843 N.E.2d 1, 2006 Ind. App. LEXIS 164 (2006).

Given the evidence that defendant juvenile flailed her arms, pulled, jerked, and yanked away from a police officer, there was sufficient evidence to uphold defendant's adjudication based upon the crime of resisting law enforcement. J.S. v. State, 843 N.E.2d 1013, 2006 Ind. App. LEXIS 474 (2006).

Defendant's conviction for resisting law enforcement pursuant to IC 35-44-3-3, which had been vacated when the trial court granted defendant's motion for judgment on the evidence, had to be reinstated; although no fugitive drug task force member who assisted in serving the warrant upon defendant expressly commanded defendant to stop as defendant tried to flee, the evidence showed that defendant had been visibly and audibly ordered not to flee, and did so anyway. Fowler v. State, 878 N.E.2d 889, 2008 Ind. App. LEXIS 370 (2008).

Defendant's conduct in fighting law enforcement officers and refusing to be handcuffed by them as they lawfully tried to arrest defendant after defendant fired shots at another man's truck sufficiently supported defendant's conviction for resisting law enforcement in violation of IC 35-44-3-3(a). Graham v. State, 889 N.E.2d 1283, 2008 Ind. App. LEXIS 1600 (2008).

Evidence that after twice being told to stop, defendant ran from a police officer who had come to defendant's home to serve a letter that banned defendant from the property of a public school, supported defendant's conviction for resisting law

Evidence. (Cont'd)

—Sufficient. (Cont'd)
enforcement by fleeing conviction. Yowler v. State, 894 N.E.2d 1000, 2008 Ind. App. LEXIS 2222 (2008).

False Arrest.
Where officers apprehended an arrestee following a reported suicide attempt, defendants were entitled to summary judgment as to the arrestee's false arrest claim and battery claim because the officers had probable cause to apprehend the arrestee under Indiana's Immediate Detention Statute. Jordan v. City of Indianapolis, — F. Supp. 2d —, 2002 U.S. Dist. LEXIS 26011 (S.D. Ind. 2002).

Felony.
Where statute made it an offense to commit a felony while armed, the word felony in such statute included the felony of possession of a controlled substance. Walton v. State, 272 Ind. 398, 398 N.E.2d 667, 1980 Ind. LEXIS 570 (1980).

Included Offenses.
Examination of the statutory elements of escape shows that resisting law enforcement is not an inherently included offense of attempted escape, because to commit the offense of resisting law enforcement, a person need not have been under detention. Taylor v. State, 659 N.E.2d 1054, 1995 Ind. App. LEXIS 1637 (1995).

Indictment or Information.
An indictment for obstructing legal process had to set forth facts showing the process to have been legally issued. State v. Tuell, 1843 Ind. LEXIS 12 (1843).

It must have been charged, when the offense was for freeing a prisoner from arrest, that the prisoner was forcibly freed from arrest, and that the accused knew he was under arrest. Brunson v. State, 97 Ind. 95, 1884 Ind. LEXIS 379 (1884).

Where an affidavit (predecessor to information) charged defendant in the first count with assaulting and resisting a police officer while such officer was engaged in the execution of his duties, and the second count was the same as the first, but in addition charged that defendant had been theretofore convicted of a felony three times and had been duly sentenced, imprisoned, and served time under each conviction, which affidavit followed the language of the statute defining the offense, it was sufficient. Grazer v. State, 219 Ind. 4, 36 N.E.2d 279, 1941 Ind. LEXIS 197 (1941).

An indictment in the language of the statute charging defendants with resisting and obstructing peace officers by use of dangerous and deadly weapons was sufficient although it did not allege that the peace officers were known by defendants to be such, since the statute did not embrace the element of knowledge. Appelby v. State, 221 Ind. 544, 48 N.E.2d 646, 1943 Ind. LEXIS 222 (1943).

State charged defendant with injuring a detective while fleeing from two deputies, but the evidence presented at trial revealed that defendant was fleeing a sergeant when he injured the detective; the state had to specifically identify the officer or officers that defendant resisted. Given the number of officers involved in arresting defendant and the number of ways he was alleged to have fled, the correct names of the officers involved were essential to a proper description of the offense charged in the information; thus, the evidence was insufficient to sustain defendant's conviction for resisting law enforcement as a class C felony. Whaley v. State, 843 N.E.2d 1, 2006 Ind. App. LEXIS 164 (2006).

—Forcibly.
Omission of the word "forcibly" from the information did not constitute fundamental error where defendant did not object to testimony by the state that his resistance was forcible, but instead, he contended that he had not resisted at all; on appeal, he did not demonstrate that he was misled or unable to prepare a defense, he was aware of the events constituting the crime and was able to defend against the accusation, and therefore, although an essential element of the crime was omitted from the information, that omission did not prevent him from presenting a defense to the charge and was not fundamental error. Miller v. State, 634 N.E.2d 57, 1994 Ind. App. LEXIS 468 (1994).

Instructions.
An instruction that was an attempt to advise the jury that if it found that the officer had malice towards the defendant, it could have taken that fact into account was properly refused, for the defendant had no right to resist arrest regardless of his assessment of the arresting officer's personal feelings and motives. Heichelbech v. State, 258 Ind. 334, 281 N.E.2d 102, 1972 Ind. LEXIS 566 (1972).

In defendant's trial on charge of resisting law enforcement, trial court's failure to instruct jury on elements of offense did not deprive defendant of fair trial where record indicated that trial court read charging information to jury during both preliminary and final instructions and prosecuting attorney recited elements of offense during closing argument. Davis v. State, 835 N.E.2d 1102, 2005 Ind. App. LEXIS 1996 (2005).

When defendant screamed at officers arresting a man, claiming that they were "doing him wrong," her speech was political in nature as an expression of her disagreement regarding the police actions toward the man. Thus, at her trial for resisting law enforcement and disorderly conduct, it was error to refuse her proffered jury instructions on protected speech under Ind. Const., art. 1, § 9. Snell v. State, 866 N.E.2d 392, 2007 Ind. App. LEXIS 1021 (2007).

Law Enforcement Officer.
For purposes of resisting law enforcement, a law enforcement officer includes an alcoholic beverage enforcement officer and a conservation officer of the department of natural resources. Taylor v. State, 659 N.E.2d 1054, 1995 Ind. App. LEXIS 1637 (1995).

Evidence was sufficient to support conviction of

Law Enforcement Officer. (Cont'd)
resisting law enforcement where defendant, who admitted to knowing that the police officer wished to effectuate the traffic stop, continued in defendant's vehicle for a lengthy period before stopping for the officer. Woodward v. State, 770 N.E.2d 897, 2002 Ind. App. LEXIS 1059 (2002).

Where defendant was arrested by park ranger, his conviction for resisting law enforcement was vacated because IC 9-13-2-92, IC 35-41-1-17 and IC 14-9-8-1, all of which define law enforcement officer, do not include park ranger, indicating that park ranger is not law enforcement officer as matter of law. Walker v. State, 813 N.E.2d 339, 2004 Ind. App. LEXIS 1599 (2004).

There was sufficient evidence that officer was police officer to support conviction of defendant for resisting law enforcement; although officer was working off-duty security at time of incident, officer was trained as police officer and had been police officer for 10 years. Harris v. State, 831 N.E.2d 848, 2005 Ind. App. LEXIS 1372 (2005).

Misdemeanor Committed in Officer's Presence.
Where police observed events which allowed them to conclude misdemeanor was committed in their presence, defendant had no right to use force to avoid arrest when such police waited for brief interval to quickly investigate situation before placing defendant under arrest. Branham v. State, 256 Ind. 145, 267 N.E.2d 160, 1971 Ind. LEXIS 602 (1971).

School security guard's defense was problematic because while the arrestee may have breached the peace (justifying the guard's citizen's arrest) by fighting, no fighting occurred in the guard's presence as required by IC 35-44-3-3(a)(3); there was also no evidence that the arrest was necessary to prevent the continuance of a breach of peace since the other alleged participant in the fight had left the scene. Pinkney v. Thomas, 583 F. Supp. 2d 970, 2008 U.S. Dist. LEXIS 70217 (2008).

Number of Officers Irrelevant.
In the context of resisting law enforcement, only one entity is harmed as a result of a single incident, regardless of the number of law enforcement officers involved. Armstead v. State, 549 N.E.2d 400, 1990 Ind. App. LEXIS 118 (1990).

A person who violates this section harms the peace and dignity of the State of Indiana and its law enforcement authority. The harm caused by one incident is the same regardless of the number of police officers resisted. Armstead v. State, 549 N.E.2d 400, 1990 Ind. App. LEXIS 118 (1990).

Officer Acting Unlawfully.
Because the arrest was not initiated in a public place and because no exigent circumstances existed, the deputy acted unlawfully when he forcibly entered defendant's residence to arrest her; therefore, because the deputy was not lawfully engaged in the execution of his duties as a law enforcement officer, the evidence was insufficient to support defendant's conviction for resisting law enforce-

ment. Adkisson v. State, 728 N.E.2d 175, 2000 Ind. App. LEXIS 744 (2000).

Revocation of defendant's probation based on charges of resisting law enforcement and possession of drug paraphernalia was reversed where officer's stop of defendant was illegal; while the officer may have had a "hunch" that something was amiss, a hunch was not sufficient to authorize an investigatory stop. Bovie v. State, 760 N.E.2d 1195, 2002 Ind. App. LEXIS 28 (2002).

Where the police officer attempted to stop defendant under the allegedly mistaken belief that defendant had committed a traffic violation, and defendant's attempt to avoid being stopped resulted in defendant being charged with resisting law enforcement under IC 35-44-3-3, reckless driving under IC 9-21-8-52, and operating a vehicle as a habitual traffic violator under IC 9-30-10-16, defendant was not entitled to dismissal of the remaining charges due to any unlawfulness of the initial stop; regardless of whether the initial stop was justified, the officer's affidavit established probable cause that defendant committed the above offenses supported the state's right to charge the defendant. State v. Howell, 782 N.E.2d 1066, 2003 Ind. App. LEXIS 168 (2003).

Police detention of a citizen in handcuffs in a locked police car exceeded the bounds of a proper Terry stop and violated the citizen's Fourth Amendment rights because, by the time the officer handcuffed the citizen and put him in the police car, he had no reason to believe that the citizen was dangerous or that he had been committing a crime; officer's later arrest of the citizen under IC 35-44-3-3(a) did not justify the initial detention because IC 35-44-3-3(a) would apply only while the officer was lawfully engaged in the execution of the officer's duties and the citizen's actions here, which at most involved removing his hands from the police car and wriggling out of one handcuff, were not the type of actions that constituted forcible resistance, obstruction, or interference for purposes of Indiana's resisting arrest statute. Bowden v. Town of Speedway, 539 F. Supp. 2d 1092, 2008 U.S. Dist. LEXIS 10974 (2008).

Other Offenses Distinguished.

—Battery.
Conviction of felony resisting law enforcement and felony battery was proper because the statutes require proof of additional facts. Felony resisting law enforcement contemplates harm to anyone, and felony battery contemplates harm specifically to a law enforcement officer. Armstead v. State, 549 N.E.2d 400, 1990 Ind. App. LEXIS 118 (1990).

Where police officer tried to enter defendant's residence after telemarketer reported that he could not get hold of defendant's wife and was therefore concerned for her safety, and where defendant then pushed officer off porch of defendant's house, police officer was acting unlawfully since there were no exigent circumstances to justify warrantless entry; accordingly, defendant was not guilty of crime of resisting law enforcement but was guilty of battery on law enforcement officer,

Other Offenses Distinguished. (Cont'd)

—Battery. (Cont'd)
and verdict was not inconsistent. Robinson v. State, 814 N.E.2d 704, 2004 Ind. App. LEXIS 1780 (2004).

Privilege to Resist.

—Excessive Force.
Defendant had a privilege to resist the officer where the force the officer used against defendant was objectively unreasonable and unconstitutionally excessive. Shoultz v. State, 735 N.E.2d 818, 2000 Ind. App. LEXIS 1483 (2000).

—Unlawful Entry.
There are circumstances where unlawful warrantless intrusion into the home creates a privilege to resist, and punishment of such resistance is therefore improper. Casselman v. State, 472 N.E.2d 1310, 1985 Ind. App. LEXIS 2097 (1985).

Although the common law right to resist arrests in public places has been abrogated, the right to offer reasonable resistance to an unlawful entry has not. Casselman v. State, 472 N.E.2d 1310, 1985 Ind. App. LEXIS 2097 (1985).

Although a citizen had the right to resist an unlawful entry by police into his home, the warrantless entry by deputy was justified by exigent circumstances. Alspach v. State, 755 N.E.2d 209, 2001 Ind. App. LEXIS 1594 (2001).

Sentence.
Trial court's imposition of an eight year sentence on defendant for his attempted escape conviction was not unreasonable and insufficiently based on balancing of aggravating and mitigating circumstances. Taylor v. State, 659 N.E.2d 1054, 1995 Ind. App. LEXIS 1637 (1995).

Because defendant's felony offenses, which included possession of cocaine, resisting law enforcement, and pointing firearm, constituted single episode of criminal conduct, IC 35-50-1-2(b) permitted trial court to impose consecutive sentences totaling 30 years for felonies; accordingly, trial court's imposition of consecutive sentences totaling 26 years did not violate IC 35-50-1-2. Johnican v. State, 804 N.E.2d 211, 2004 Ind. App. LEXIS 324 (2004).

For purposes of federal sentencing guidelines, defendant's conviction under IC 35-44-3-3 constituted a crime of violence because he endangered the lives of other drivers in fleeing from police officers. United States v. Jennings, 544 F.3d 815, 2008 U.S. App. LEXIS 19560 (2008).

Single Incident.
Only one charge of resisting law enforcement could be lodged against defendant, and where his acts in resisting law enforcement after he exited bank and during the ensuing chase arose from a single incident. Miller v. State, 726 N.E.2d 349, 2000 Ind. App. LEXIS 439 (2000), transfer granted, 741 N.E.2d 1250, 2000 Ind. LEXIS 792 (2000), aff'd in part, vacated in part, 753 N.E.2d 1284, 2001 Ind. LEXIS 779 (Ind. 2001).

Where defendant fled from officers after being told to stop and then forcibly resisted officers when they caught him, inflicting injury, he perpetrated two separate offenses of resisting law enforcement and conviction on two counts was proper. Williams v. State, 755 N.E.2d 1183, 2001 Ind. App. LEXIS 1743 (2001).

Verdict.
A verdict finding the defendant guilty of "resisting or interfering with an officer, and that he be imprisoned for 180 days" was not void because no fine was fixed. Under the former statute the jury had the option of imposing three separate punishments: (1) imprisonment in jail or the state farm; (2) a fine; (3) or both imprisonment and a fine. Ezzell v. State, 246 Ind. 268, 205 N.E.2d 145, 1965 Ind. LEXIS 161 (1965).

Defendant could not complain of the use of the word "or" in a verdict of guilty of "restricting or interfering with an officer" where he failed to show that he was harmed. Ezzell v. State, 246 Ind. 268, 205 N.E.2d 145, 1965 Ind. LEXIS 161 (1965).

Where verdict found defendant guilty of "drawing a weapon or committing injury upon an officer" he could not be guilty of "drawing" a weapon where the police officer drew the weapon himself but defendant thereafter obtained control of it, but he could be convicted of committing injury when he bit officer's thumb in obtaining control of the gun. Wise v. State, 272 Ind. 498, 400 N.E.2d 114, 1980 Ind. LEXIS 592 (1980).

Verdict of guilty of resisting law enforcement was not inconsistent with verdict of not guilty on count of attempted murder of the same police officer. Brady v. State, 275 Ind. 475, 417 N.E.2d 1108, 1981 Ind. LEXIS 706 (1981).

Cited:
Tapp v. State, 406 N.E.2d 296, 1980 Ind. App. LEXIS 1536 (1980); Westmoreland v. State, 424 N.E.2d 1062, 1981 Ind. App. LEXIS 1619 (1981); Cronk v. State, 443 N.E.2d 882, 1983 Ind. App. LEXIS 2509 (1983); Swingle v. State Employees' Appeal Com., 452 N.E.2d 178, 1983 Ind. App. LEXIS 3220 (1983); Gomez v. Adams, 462 N.E.2d 212, 1984 Ind. App. LEXIS 2497 (1984); Massey v. State, 473 N.E.2d 146, 1985 Ind. LEXIS 737 (1985); Prentice v. State, 474 N.E.2d 496, 1985 Ind. LEXIS 750 (1985); Decker v. State, 515 N.E.2d 1129, 1987 Ind. App. LEXIS 3251 (1987); Adams v. State, 542 N.E.2d 1362, 1989 Ind. App. LEXIS 833 (1989); Hazzard v. State, 642 N.E.2d 1368, 1994 Ind. LEXIS 151 (1994); Tom v. Voida, 654 N.E.2d 776, 1995 Ind. App. LEXIS 962 (1995); Hazzard v. State, 694 N.E.2d 283, 1998 Ind. LEXIS 56 (1998); Ross v. State, 729 N.E.2d 113, 2000 Ind. LEXIS 484 (2000); Cade v. State, 734 N.E.2d 575, 2000 Ind. LEXIS 720 (2000); State v. Straub, 749 N.E.2d 593, 2001 Ind. App. LEXIS 881 (2001); Lark v. State, 755 N.E.2d 1153, 2001 Ind. App. LEXIS 1703 (2001); Gonzalez v. Kokot, 314 F.3d 311, 2002 U.S. App. LEXIS 26843 (7th Cir. Ind. 2002); Thornton v. State, 792 N.E.2d 94, 2003 Ind. App. LEXIS 1357 (2003); Phelps v. City of Indianapolis, — F. Supp. 2d —, 2004 U.S. Dist. LEXIS 9151 (S.D. Ind. 2004); United States v. Hardy, — F. Supp. 2d —, 2005

U.S. Dist. LEXIS 6176 (N.D. Ind. 2005); Stokes v. State, 828 N.E.2d 937, 2005 Ind. App. LEXIS 1056 (2005); United States v. Hagenow, 423 F.3d 638, 2005 U.S. App. LEXIS 18821 (7th Cir. Ind. 2005); McMahon v. State, 856 N.E.2d 743, 2006 Ind. App. LEXIS 2333 (2006); Corbin v. State, 840 N.E.2d 424, 2006 Ind. App. LEXIS 31 (2006); J.D. v. State, — N.E.2d —, 2009 Ind. App. LEXIS 429 (2009).

RESEARCH REFERENCES

Indiana Law Review.

Recent Developments in Criminal Law and Procedure, 27 Ind. L. Rev. 959 (1994).

Recent Developments Under the Indiana Constitution, 28 Ind. L. Rev. 1067 (1995).

Survey: Criminal Law and Procedure: Recent Developments in Indiana, 32 Ind. L. Rev. 789 (1999).

Res Gestae.

Rules, rulings for the trial lawyer, 37 Res Gestae 122 (1993).

Criminal Justice Notes # 2: Vehicle stops, 46 (No. 9) Res Gestae 22 (2003).

Criminal Justice Notes 9/07: Resisting law enforcement - police not lawfully engaed in execution of their duties, 51 (No. 5) Res Gestae 38 (2007).

Collateral References.

Criminal liability for obstructing process as affected by invalidity or irregularity of the process. 10 A.L.R.3d 1146.

Right to resist excessive force used in accomplishing lawful arrest. 77 A.L.R.3d 281.

What constitutes obstructing or resisting officer, in absence of actual force. 66 A.L.R.5th 397.

35-44-3-3.5. Disarming law enforcement officer.

(a) As used in this section, "officer" includes the following:

(1) A person employed by:

(A) the department of correction;

(B) a law enforcement agency;

(C) a probation department;

(D) a county jail; or

(E) a circuit, superior, county, probate, city, or town court;

who is required to carry a firearm in performance of the person's official duties.

(2) A law enforcement officer.

(b) A person who:

(1) knows that another person is an officer; and

(2) knowingly or intentionally takes or attempts to take a firearm (as defined in IC 35-47-1-5) or weapon that the officer is authorized to carry from the officer or from the immediate proximity of the officer:

(A) without the consent of the officer; and

(B) while the officer is engaged in the performance of his or her official duties; commits disarming a law enforcement officer, a Class C felony. However, the offense is a Class B felony if it results in serious bodily injury to the officer, and the offense is a Class A felony if it results in death to the officer or if a firearm (as defined in IC 35-47-1-5) was taken and the offense results in serious bodily injury to the officer.

History.

P.L.64-2008, § 1, eff. July 1, 2008.

Cross References.

Penalties for felonies, IC 35-50-1, IC 35-50-2, IC 35-50-5-2.

35-44-3-4. Tampering — Obstruction of justice — Special privileges.

(a) A person who:

(1) knowingly or intentionally induces, by threat, coercion, or false statement, a witness or informant in an official proceeding or investigation to:

(A) withhold or unreasonably delay in producing any testimony, information, document, or thing;

(B) avoid legal process summoning him to testify or supply evidence; or

(C) absent himself from a proceeding or investigation to which he has been legally summoned;

(2) knowingly or intentionally in an official criminal proceeding or investigation:

(A) withholds or unreasonably delays in producing any testimony, information, document, or thing after a court orders him to produce the testimony, information, document, or thing;

(B) avoids legal process summoning him to testify or supply evidence; or

(C) absents himself from a proceeding or investigation to which he has been legally summoned;

(3) alters, damages, or removes any record, document, or thing, with intent to prevent it from being produced or used as evidence in any official proceeding or investigation;

(4) makes, presents, or uses a false record, document, or thing with intent that the record, document, or thing, material to the point in question, appear in evidence in an official proceeding or investigation to mislead a public servant; or

(5) communicates, directly or indirectly, with a juror otherwise than as authorized by law, with intent to influence the juror regarding any matter that is or may be brought before the juror;

commits obstruction of justice, a Class D felony.

(b) Subdivision (a)(2)(A) does not apply to:

(1) a person who qualifies for a special privilege under IC 34-46-4 with respect to the testimony, information, document, or thing; or

(2) a person who, as an:

(A) attorney;

(B) physician;

(C) member of the clergy; or

(D) husband or wife;

is not required to testify under IC 34-46-3-1.

History.

IC 35-44-3-4, as added by Acts 1976, P.L.148, § 4; 1977, P.L.340, § 62; 1981, P.L.301, § 2; 1982, P.L.195, § 3; P.L.1-1998, § 197.

Cross References.

Destruction of local public records, IC 5-15-6-8.

Penalties for felonies, IC 35-50-1, IC 35-50-2, IC 35-50-5-2.

NOTES TO DECISIONS

In General.

Trial court's refusal to dismiss decedent's representative's suit against decedent's employer for spoliation of evidence was proper where employer's owner removed and disposed of items from scene of explosion that killed decedent, including electrical pump that may have caused explosion, despite instructions by state investigator not to discard such items. Glotzbach v. Froman, 827 N.E.2d 105, 2005 Ind. App. LEXIS 797 (2005), transfer granted and vacated, 841 N.E.2d 189, 2005 Ind. LEXIS 1003, superseded, 854 N.E.2d 337, 2006 Ind. LEXIS 863 (2006).

Civil Order to Destroy Evidence.

Order finding a wife in civil contempt of a provision in her marriage dissolution decree requiring her to burn child pornographic photographs belonging to her husband was affirmed; the wife contended that the provision was void ab initio since the couple was under a police investigation, even though she had knowingly agreed to the provision. Evans v. Evans, 766 N.E.2d 1240, 2002 Ind. App. LEXIS 654 (2002).

Coercion.

The term "coercion" carries with it, at a minimum, the sense of some form of pressure or influence being exerted on the will or choice of another.

Coercion. (Cont'd)

The form that the pressure or influence may take may vary widely as long as it is exerted knowingly or intentionally to induce conduct by a witness or informant that is proscribed by this section. Sheppard v. State, 484 N.E.2d 984, 1985 Ind. App. LEXIS 2932 (1985).

Comparable Offenses.

Since perjury and obstruction of justice are offenses comparable to criminal contempt, in that they are Class D felonies, and the possible sentence for a Class D felony ranges from a minimum of six months to a maximum of three years, a trial court's sentence of eleven and one-half years for contempt of court was manifestly unreasonable, and remand for imposition of a sentence of three years was required. State v. MacWilliams (In re Gardner), 713 N.E.2d 346, 1999 Ind. App. LEXIS 1017 (1999).

Double Jeopardy.

Where the actual evidence the state used to prove forgery also proved that defendant was guilty of obstruction of justice, defendant's convictions for both forgery and obstruction of justice violated the double jeopardy clause of the Indiana Constitution. Lahr v. State, 731 N.E.2d 479, 2000 Ind. App. LEXIS 1068 (2000).

Entry of Satisfaction.

Entry of satisfaction of a judgment was a record within the meaning of the statute making it a crime to alter or deface records. State v. Henning, 158 Ind. 196, 63 N.E. 207, 1902 Ind. LEXIS 125 (1902).

Evidence.

—Insufficient.

A single telephone call to a witness, where there is no use of physical force, intimidation or threats against the witness in attempting to induce her to withhold testimony, is insufficient to prove coercion and, therefore, insufficient to support a conviction under this section. Sheppard v. State, 484 N.E.2d 984, 1985 Ind. App. LEXIS 2932 (1985).

Where plaintiff election board mechanic sued defendant city, mayor, police chief, officers, and mayor's son for alleged constitutional violations resulting from his arrest and detention during an election investigation, grant of summary judgment to arresting officers on mechanic's Fourth Amendment false arrest claim was error since events leading to arrest were in dispute, thereby raising issue of fact as to whether there was probable cause to arrest mechanic for obstruction of justice pursuant to IC 35-44-3-4. Morfin v. City of E. Chicago, 349 F.3d 989, 2003 U.S. App. LEXIS 23450 (7th Cir. Ind. 2003).

When defendant, who was a caseworker with a child protection agency, was charged with obstruction of justice, under IC 35-44-3-4, for preparing a report which inaccurately stated that no criminal records were found for people who wanted to adopt children on her caseload, and that these people had no prior contact with the agency defendant worked for, insufficient evidence supported her conviction because there was no evidence that she intended to mislead, as she did not want to place the children with these people, but was told she had to consider them. Moore v. State, 845 N.E.2d 225, 2006 Ind. App. LEXIS 635 (2006).

When defendant, who was a caseworker with a child protection agency, was charged with obstruction of justice, under IC 35-44-3-4, for preparing a report which inaccurately stated that no criminal records were found for people who wanted to adopt children on her caseload, and that these people had no prior contact with the agency defendant worked for, insufficient evidence supported her conviction because she was told she had to consider these individuals for adoptive placement and that it was her employer's policy to ignore misdemeanors and felony theft, of which one of the adopting individuals had been convicted, for purposes of such placement, so her report was not inaccurate because there was no material criminal history to report. Moore v. State, 845 N.E.2d 225, 2006 Ind. App. LEXIS 635 (2006).

When defendant, who was a caseworker with a child protection agency, was charged with obstruction of justice, under IC 35-44-3-4, for preparing a report which inaccurately stated that no criminal records were found for people who wanted to adopt children on her caseload, and that these people had no prior contact with the agency defendant worked for, insufficient evidence supported her conviction because, if she was negligent in not obtaining information about the individuals' prior contact with her agency, her negligence was not a crime. Moore v. State, 845 N.E.2d 225, 2006 Ind. App. LEXIS 635 (2006).

Because defendant's statements to his fiance asking her not to testify contained no declaration of consequences or threats that would follow for failure to comply with his request as required by IC 35-44-3-4, the evidence was not sufficient to support his conviction for attempted obstruction of justice. Brown v. State, 859 N.E.2d 1269, 2007 Ind. App. LEXIS 26 (2007).

—Sufficient.

Evidence that defendant threatened to tie a woman up and to force her to perform or submit to various forms of deviate sexual conduct, and that he told her that if he ever found out that she signed statements against his brother "there would be trouble" and she "would be sorry," was sufficient to support his convictions for attempted obstruction of justice and intimidation. Long v. State, 492 N.E.2d 700, 1986 Ind. App. LEXIS 2579 (1986).

Evidence was sufficient to sustain a conviction for obstruction of justice where the defendant, when approached by a police officer, put what appeared to be crack cocaine in his mouth, refused to spit it out, pushed the officer away to prevent him from recovering the crack cocaine, and swallowed it. Mullins v. State, 717 N.E.2d 902, 1999 Ind. App. LEXIS 1799 (1999).

Testimony of accomplice that defendant handed him two baggies of crushed pseudoephedrine and jar of lithium strips soaking in camp fuel from backseat of car as car was being chased by police

Evidence. (Cont'd)

—Sufficient. (Cont'd)
and that accomplice then threw baggies and jar out of car window was sufficient to support conviction of defendant for obstruction of justice. Smith v. State, 809 N.E.2d 938, 2004 Ind. App. LEXIS 1100 (2004).

Defendant was properly convicted as accomplice to obstruction of justice for asking friend, for purpose of custody proceeding, to lie to police by stating that defendant's wife falsely accused defendant of breaking into her house; friend's statement was relevant admissible evidence in criminal trial for obstruction even if statement would have been ruled hearsay in custody case. Vandivier v. State, 822 N.E.2d 1047, 2005 Ind. App. LEXIS 273 (2005).

Defendant's conviction for obstruction of justice under IC 35-44-3-4(a)(4) for assisting a friend in concealing the friend's urine sample from law enforcement was supported by sufficient evidence because: (1) the fact that the friend's blood sample also revealed the presence of drugs in the friend's system did not make the urine sample immaterial because materiality, for purposes of an obstruction of justice conviction, did not depend on the state's ability to convict the friend, as materiality was only that which was reasonably calculated to mislead an investigation; and (2) as defendant did not dispute that urine samples in question were switched or that defendant filled out forms in which defendant stated that a co-defendant's urine was in fact the friend's, facts were sufficient to find defendant made a false record that was reasonably calculated to mislead an investigation. Roush v. State, 875 N.E.2d 801, 2007 Ind. App. LEXIS 2404 (2007).

Indictment or Information.
In a prosecution for attempted bribery of a sheriff in the selection of a jury, the failure of the affidavit (predecessor to information) to state that accused was on trial did not render the affidavit defective, since the gist of the offense was the corrupt purpose of the defendant. Fenwick v. State, 200 Ind. 460, 164 N.E. 632, 1929 Ind. LEXIS 74 (1929).

An indictment in three counts, each charging the defendant with compounding a prosecution by accepting $50.00 from parties then under arrest, the first count charging an understanding and agreement that he should encourage the absence from the trial of a certain material and competent witness, therein named, the second charging an agreement to procure the absence of the witness, and the third charging that the agreement was to delay the trial, was held valid, especially against the contention that each count was defective in not alleging that the three elements of the agreement were unlawful. Sanders v. State, 89 Ind. App. 113, 165 N.E. 784, 1929 Ind. App. LEXIS 103 (1929).

When defendant, who was a caseworker with a child protection agency, was charged with obstruction of justice, under IC 35-44-3-4, for preparing a report which inaccurately stated that no criminal records were found for people who wanted to adopt children on her caseload, and that these people had no prior contact with the agency defendant worked for, the applicable limitations period, under IC 35-41-4-2, was five years from the commission of the crime, so her prosecution was barred because she prepared the inaccurate report five years and three months before her indictment for this crime was filed. Moore v. State, 845 N.E.2d 225, 2006 Ind. App. LEXIS 635 (2006).

It was not an abuse of discretion to allow the state to amend an information charging defendant with obstruction of justice under IC 35-44-3-4(a)(3) to charge defendant with obstruction of justice under IC 35-44-3-4(a)(4) because: (1) the amendment did not satisfy the prerequisite definition of an amendment of substance, under IC 35-34-1-5(b), as either information presented a valid felony obstruction of justice charge; and (2) defendant's substantial rights were not prejudiced because, under either version of the information, defendant's evidence and defense of lack of intent were equally available. Roush v. State, 875 N.E.2d 801, 2007 Ind. App. LEXIS 2404 (2007).

Intentional Withholding of Testimony.
Probation revocation was justified where a defendant refused to identify the name of an inmate who told him his life was threatened, refused to give the name of his own gang, and stated that he would not testify even if his safety could be insured and in spite of an offer of immunity, since he knowingly and intentionally withheld testimony, and thus could not utilize fifth amendment protection. Goonen v. State, 705 N.E.2d 209, 1999 Ind. App. LEXIS 73 (1999).

Defendant's refusal to testify at murder trial, where testimony was part of plea agreement with regard to his own criminal convictions arising out of murder at issue, constituted direct criminal contempt for which defendant's probation was properly revoked; two-year prison sentence for criminal contempt was upheld on appeal as reasonable. Downs v. State, 827 N.E.2d 646, 2005 Ind. App. LEXIS 897 (2005), dismissed, Downs v. Knight, — F. Supp. 2d —, 2006 U.S. Dist. LEXIS 74436 (S.D. Ind. 2006).

Obstruction of Justice.

—False Informing Distinguished.
The defendants were charged with obstruction of justice, the information not alleging that the false report filed by the defendants following an accident was made in the official investigation of the commission of a crime. Therefore, they could not be convicted of false informing, which is neither an inherently included lesser offense nor a possibly included lesser offense. Kingston v. State, 479 N.E.2d 1356, 1985 Ind. App. LEXIS 2586 (1985).

Sentence.
Defendant's 18-month sentence for obstruction of justice under IC 35-44-3-4(a)(4) was not an abuse of discretion because: (1) defendant presented no evidence supporting the special circumstances required to find an undue hardship on defendant's stepchildren due to defendant's incar-

Sentence. (Cont'd)
ceration; (2) the trial court considered defendant's lack of a criminal history as a mitigator; and (3) the trial court's finding of aggravators did not violate the Sixth Amendment as defendant received a presumptive sentence under IC 35-50-2-7. Roush v. State, 875 N.E.2d 801, 2007 Ind. App. LEXIS 2404 (2007).

Defendant's 18-month sentence for obstruction of justice under IC 35-44-3-4(a)(4) was not inappropriate under AP. 7(B) because: (1) the sentence was not inappropriate in light of the nature of the offense, as defendant committed the crime in an attempt to help a friend avoid criminal prosecution for an incident that left two small children dead and a third child seriously injured, and defendant schemed with others over a period of time in an attempt to commit the crime; and (2) the sentence

was not inappropriate in light of defendant's character as defendant abused position of authority and trust as a hospital employee to gain the access necessary to commit the crime, and in so doing, put defendant's career in jeopardy while defendant was partially responsible for the care of two young children, showing a complete lack of reasoned judgment and a serious lack of character. Roush v. State, 875 N.E.2d 801, 2007 Ind. App. LEXIS 2404 (2007).

Cited:
DesRosiers v. State, 528 N.E.2d 816, 1988 Ind. App. LEXIS 715 (1988); Loomis v. Ameritech Corp., 764 N.E.2d 658, 2002 Ind. App. LEXIS 290 (2002); Bryant v. State, 802 N.E.2d 486, 2004 Ind. App. LEXIS 150 (2004).

OPINIONS OF ATTORNEY GENERAL

Every coroner in a "coroner's case" shall before the scene is disturbed notify a police agency with proper jurisdiction to assist him in his investigation. However, before any dead body is moved or the scene of the death is disturbed, the coroner shall cause photographs to be taken of the body or scene unless the position or location of the dead body interferes unduly with activities carried on in the immediate area. If there is such interference, the coroner or any police officer may order the body

to be moved before the photographs are taken, providing it is not moved from the immediate area and providing it can be moved without substantially altering or destroying the evidence. It is a class A misdemeanor, pursuant to IC 35-44-3-4(a)(3), for any person to alter, damage or remove any record, document, or thing with intent to prevent it from being produced or used as evidence in any official proceeding or investigation. 1979, No. 79-27, p. 86.

RESEARCH REFERENCES

Notre Dame Law Review.
Document Retention and Destruction: Practical, Legal and Ethical Considerations (John M. Fedders and Lauryn H. Guttenplan), 56 Notre Dame L. Rev. 7.

Collateral References.
Actionability of conspiracy to give or to procure false testimony or other evidence. 31 A.L.R.3d 1423.

Admissibility in criminal case, on issue if defendant's guilt, of evidence that third person has attempted to influence a witness not to testify or to testify falsely. 79 A.L.R.3d 1156.

Admissibility and effect, on issue of party's credibility or merits of his case, of evidence of attempts to intimidate or influence witness in civil action. 4 A.L.R.4th 829.

Validity, construction, and application of state statutes imposing criminal penalties for influencing, intimidating, or tampering with witness. 8 A.L.R.4th 769.

Juror's reading of newspaper account of trial in federal criminal case during its progress as ground for mistrial, new trial, or reversal. 85 A.L.R. Fed. 13.

Intentional spoilation of evidence, interfering with prospective civil action as actionable. 70 A.L.R.4th 984.

Threats of violence against juror in criminal trial as ground for mistrial or dismissal of juror. 3 A.L.R.5th 963.

Criminal liability of attorney for tampering with evidence. 49 A.L.R.5th 619.

Defenses to state obstruction of justice charge relating to interfering with criminal investigation or judicial proceeding. 87 A.L.R.5th 597.

Negligent spoilation of evidence, interfering with prospective civil action, as actionable. 101 A.L.R.5th 61.

Effect of spoilation of evidence in products liability action. 102 A.L.R.5th 99.

Validity, construction, and application of federal witness tampering statute, 18 U.S.C.S. § 1512(b). 183 A.L.R. Fed. 611.

35-44-3-5. Escape — Violation of home detention order — Failure to return to lawful detention.

(a) A person, except as provided in subsection (b), who intentionally flees from lawful detention commits escape, a Class C felony. However, the offense is a Class B felony if, while committing it, the person draws or uses a deadly weapon or inflicts bodily injury on another person.

(b) A person who knowingly or intentionally violates a home detention order or intentionally removes an electronic monitoring device or GPS tracking device commits escape, a Class D felony.

(c) A person who knowingly or intentionally fails to return to lawful detention following temporary leave granted for a specified purpose or limited period commits failure to return to lawful detention, a Class D felony. However, the offense is a Class C felony if, while committing it, the person draws or uses a deadly weapon or inflicts bodily injury on another person.

History.
IC 35-44-3-5, as added by Acts 1976, P.L.148, § 4; 1977, P.L.340, § 63; P.L.207-1986, § 1; P.L.17-1998, § 2; P.L.137-2001, § 11; P.L.116-2009, § 16, eff. July 1, 2009.

Amendments.
The 2009 amendment added ""or GPS tracking device"" in (b).

Cross References.
Penalties for felonies, IC 35-50-1, IC 35-50-2, IC 35-50-5-2.

NOTES TO DECISIONS

ANALYSIS

Constitutionality.
Applicability.
Bodily Injury.
Defenses.
—Necessity.
Distinct Crime.
Elements of Attempted Escape.
Escape Construed.
Escape from Psychiatric Institution.
Evidence.
—Admissibility.
—Attempt.
— —Specific Intent.
—Subsequent Escape.
—Sufficiency.
Extension of Original Period.
Included Offenses.
Instructions.
Juvenile Detention.
Lawful Detention.
—Evidence.
—Public Highways.
Punishment.
Taking Deputy's Gun.
Use of Deadly Weapon.

Constitutionality.
Statute punishing escape from prison was not class legislation, and applied equally to all persons who committed the same offense under the same or similar circumstances, and was in accord with the spirit and letter of the state constitution. State v. Rardon, 221 Ind. 154, 46 N.E.2d 605, 1943 Ind. LEXIS 162 (1943).

Applicability.
Attempted escape statute applied only to escapes from lawful confinement but that did not entitle all who might question the legality of the proceedings leading to their confinement to resort to self-help. Johnson v. State, 258 Ind. 515, 282 N.E.2d 802, 1972 Ind. LEXIS 596 (1972).

Bodily Injury.
The crime of Class C felony escape does not require a showing that bodily injury was inflicted at the time the defendant gained his momentary freedom or during the events leading up to that point. Bodily injury may be inflicted when the defendant is fleeing from lawful detention. Isom v. State, 479 N.E.2d 61, 1985 Ind. App. LEXIS 2500 (1985), overruled, Schwass v. State, 554 N.E.2d 1127, 1990 Ind. LEXIS 121 (1990).

Defenses.

—Necessity.
Although a few cases have applied the necessity defense to prison escape, e.g., escape from homosexual assault or escape from prison fire, the escapee has a duty to surrender himself as soon as the immediate harm is avoided. Walker v. State, 269 Ind. 346, 381 N.E.2d 88, 1978 Ind. LEXIS 790 (1978).

Unsanitary, unhealthful or inhuman conditions of confinement are not a justification for escape. Walker v. State, 269 Ind. 346, 381 N.E.2d 88, 1978 Ind. LEXIS 790 (1978).

Where defendant justified his escape on the grounds of necessity, his kidnapping of hostages was evidence that he had no intention of surrendering once the conditions "necessitating" his escape had passed. Walker v. State, 269 Ind. 346, 381 N.E.2d 88, 1978 Ind. LEXIS 790 (1978).

Distinct Crime.
The statute punishing escape from prison defined a new crime, which was separate and distinct from the crime for which the prisoner was originally sentenced to prison. Ex parte Clifford, 29 Ind. 106, 1867 Ind. LEXIS 372 (1867).

Elements of Attempted Escape.
Attempted escape statute created a crime having the elements of: (1) the intent to escape from lawful confinement in any penal institution, prison

Elements of Attempted Escape. (Cont'd)
or jail; (2) the performance of some overt act or acts which were a step or steps toward the commission of the crime of escape; and (3) the failure of the escape. Fisher v. State, 156 Ind. App. 18, 294 N.E.2d 632, 1973 Ind. App. LEXIS 1076 (1973).

Escape Construed.

The word "escape" as used in former section meant to go away from or enjoy immunity from imprisonment without permission of someone in authority. So, if prisoners left the Indiana State Farm voluntarily before their sentences expired, without such permission, it was immaterial whether they intended to return the same day. Wiggins v. State, 194 Ind. 118, 141 N.E. 56, 1923 Ind. LEXIS 23 (1924).

When a person was ordered confined to a given prison, the order of confinement did not mean that that person had to be kept within a given four walls, but it did mean that he was confined for restraint upon his freedom by the authorities of that institution, and if they determined that he could leave the four walls of the institution for the purpose of performing some duty or accomplishing some task given him, and while outside the prison wall he escaped, he was guilty of escape from the correctional institution to which he was committed. State v. Rardon, 221 Ind. 154, 46 N.E.2d 605, 1943 Ind. LEXIS 162 (1943).

Escape from Psychiatric Institution.

Where party sentenced to women's prison was transferred to Central State Hospital for treatment and escaped therefrom, she was deemed to have escaped from the women's prison. Zimmer v. State, 17 Ind. Dec. 476, 247 N.E.2d 195 (Ind. 1969).

Evidence.

Where there was testimony that defendant, while a prison inmate, slashed a prison employee on her hands and under her arm with a pair of scissors after confronting the employee and taking a set of keys from her there was evidence of both the use of a deadly weapon and bodily injury in an attempted escape. Johnson v. State, 409 N.E.2d 699, 1980 Ind. App. LEXIS 1650 (1980).

Evidence was sufficient to sustain a conviction where it established that the defendant was under lawful detention at the Indiana State Prison, that he had chiseled a hole in his jail cell and had exited via that hole to the building's roof, that a dummy had been hidden under the blankets of the defendant's cell bed, that the defendant was apprehended on the building's roof with a 75-foot home-made rope in his possession, and that the defendant stated he intended to flee. Lyons v. State, 475 N.E.2d 719, 1985 Ind. App. LEXIS 2270 (1985).

—Admissibility.

Since a material element of the offense of jail breaking was that the defendant be lawfully confined at the time of such escape, it was proper for sheriff to testify that defendant was convicted of a prior offense, such conviction being the basis for

his lawful confinement. Gulley v. State, 156 Ind. App. 15, 294 N.E.2d 630, 1973 Ind. App. LEXIS 1075 (1973).

—Attempt.

Acts of prisoners in barricading themselves in a cell do not indicate an attempt to escape. Liston v. State, 252 Ind. 502, 250 N.E.2d 739, 1969 Ind. LEXIS 376 (1969).

— —Specific Intent.

Where defendant managed to unbuckle the seat belt, although his hands were handcuffed behind him, which was an act requiring physical skill, and when asked why he had run defendant responded that the officer would have run, too, if he were going to jail, the evidence was sufficient to support the determination that defendant entertained the specific intent to flee from lawful detention. Taylor v. State, 659 N.E.2d 1054, 1995 Ind. App. LEXIS 1637 (1995).

—Subsequent Escape.

Evidence of an escape, subsequent to the escape episode for which the defendant is standing trial, is admissible where it discloses conduct almost identical to that for which the defendant claims no responsibility by reason of diminished mental capacity, and where it evidences a conscious and intelligent choice and determination to escape. Eubank v. State, 456 N.E.2d 1012, 1983 Ind. LEXIS 1062 (1983).

—Sufficiency.

Where there was insufficient evidence of the mens rea or intent required to prove escape under former jail-breaking statute, the judgment was reversed and appellant ordered discharged. Utley v. State, 258 Ind. 443, 281 N.E.2d 888, 1972 Ind. LEXIS 586 (1972).

Evidence was sufficient to support jury finding that defendant intentionally left custody of his jailer where jailer testified that he and defendant were disposing of trash behind the jail when jailer was called to telephone, that jailer instructed defendant to dispose of trash in his absence, that defendant had disappeared when jailer returned, that defendant did not have permission to leave the premises, and that defendant was not seen again by the jailer for 22 days, which was upon his apprehension in Georgia. Gulley v. State, 156 Ind. App. 15, 294 N.E.2d 630, 1973 Ind. App. LEXIS 1075 (1973).

Where, while police officers were distracted searching for jewelry allegedly stolen, defendant fled from the police car where he had been placed following his arrest, the evidence clearly supported the finding of the trial court that he had been under lawful arrest at the time he fled from the police car and that he was therefore guilty of escape. Johnson v. State, 512 N.E.2d 1090, 1987 Ind. LEXIS 1055 (1987).

Where, when defendant arrived at the police station, he was informed that he was under arrest for rape, his action in leaving the building would indicate that he believed himself to be in custody since he did not simply attempt to walk out the door but jumped over a chair and attempted to run,

Evidence. (Cont'd)

—Sufficiency. (Cont'd)

he physically broke loose from the police officer who grabbed him in an attempt to keep him from leaving, and when he left the building, he did not quietly walk away but ran until he was out of breath and could run no more; thus, there was clearly an abundance of evidence to support the conviction of the escape under subsection (a) of this section and IC 35-41-1-18, which defines "lawful detention." Settle v. State, 526 N.E.2d 974, 1988 Ind. LEXIS 223 (1988).

Escape conviction was upheld where the prisoner did not make it outside the detention facility, but defendant fled cottage where he had been lawfully detained by breaking a lock off of a door, forcing open a second door, and removing a board covering a window, and defendant admitted that he had intended to leave the facility's property. Huffman v. State, 659 N.E.2d 214, 1995 Ind. App. LEXIS 1640 (1995).

Where officer pulled defendant driver over and informed defendant that he was under arrest, but officer then gave defendant permission to drive defendant's passenger home in defendant's own vehicle with officer following one car length behind, and defendant fled, there was insufficient evidence of lawful detainment or arrest to convict defendant of escape under IC 35-44-3-5; although defendant was lawfully detained pursuant to IC 35-41-1-18(a) when officer informed defendant of his arrest, lawful detainment ceased when defendant was permitted to drive passenger home. Mesarosh v. State, 801 N.E.2d 200, 2004 Ind. App. LEXIS 6 (2004).

Although there was insufficient evidence of arrest to convict defendant driver of escape under IC 35-44-3-5(a) where officer, after informing defendant that he was under arrest, allowed defendant to drive defendant's passenger home with officer following, and defendant then fled, there was sufficient evidence to convict defendant of failure to return to lawful detention in violation of IC 35-44-3-5(c). Mesarosh v. State, 801 N.E.2d 200, 2004 Ind. App. LEXIS 6 (2004).

To the extent that defendant argued that the state failed to prove beyond a reasonable doubt that he knowingly or intentionally violated his home detention order, the state met its burden: officer attempting to serve a warrant on another person in defendant's home saw defendant walking in an alley at about 3:40 p.m. and defendant was authorized to be out of his house only from 11:00 a.m. to 1:00 p.m. that day. Brown v. State, 894 N.E.2d 598, 2008 Ind. App. LEXIS 2263 (2008).

IC 35-44-3-5(b) does not require proof that a defendant was attempting to leave the jurisdiction or go anywhere in particular to sustain a conviction for escape, but, rather, requires only proof that the defendant knowingly or intentionally violated a home detention order or intentionally removed an electronic monitoring device. Brown v. State, 894 N.E.2d 598, 2008 Ind. App. LEXIS 2263 (2008).

Extension of Original Period.

Defendant who escaped from reformatory while serving a one to five year sentence could not have the period during which he was an escapee credited toward service of his sentence even though he had not been convicted of the separate and distinct crime of escape. Phend v. Thais, 154 Ind. App. 498, 290 N.E.2d 128, 1972 Ind. App. LEXIS 927 (1972).

The state was not estopped, in habeas corpus action, from relying upon escape period as extending the original period scheduled for prisoner's confinement because it dismissed "escape" charge against him. Phend v. Thais, 154 Ind. App. 498, 290 N.E.2d 128, 1972 Ind. App. LEXIS 927 (1972).

Included Offenses.

Examination of the statutory elements of escape shows that resisting law enforcement is not an inherently included offense of attempted escape, because to commit the offense of resisting law enforcement, a person need not have been under detention. Taylor v. State, 659 N.E.2d 1054, 1995 Ind. App. LEXIS 1637 (1995).

Where the information charged that defendant attempted to flee from detention, not from a law enforcement officer, resisting law enforcement was not a factually included offense of the crime of attempted escape. Taylor v. State, 659 N.E.2d 1054, 1995 Ind. App. LEXIS 1637 (1995).

Instructions.

Where the evidence was uncontradicted that the escape occurred, and the only dispute was whether defendant acted in concert with another escapee, an instruction on attempted escape was wholly harmless surplusage, and thus did not warrant reversal of defendant's conviction. Underhill v. State, 428 N.E.2d 759, 1981 Ind. LEXIS 918 (1981).

In a trial for escape under IC 35-44-3-5, the trial court did not err in failing to instruct about the offense of unauthorized absence from home detention under IC 35-38-2.5-13; latter offense applied only when a defendant was on home detention as a condition of probation whereas here home detention was part of an executed sentence. Brown v. State, 894 N.E.2d 598, 2008 Ind. App. LEXIS 2263 (2008).

Juvenile Detention.

Where defendant was in jail on a juvenile detention, and reached eighteenth birthday prior to escape, defendant was not imprisoned or in custody for a felony at time of escape. Renfroe v. State, 161 Ind. App. 519, 316 N.E.2d 405, 1974 Ind. App. LEXIS 970 (1974).

Defendant's adjudication for escape under IC 35-44-3-5(a) failed as defendant was not under lawful detention under IC 31-37-19-6(b)(2)(A) when he escaped; state did not show that academy in which defendant juvenile was detained was a juvenile detention facility under IC 31-31-8-2, a secure private facility under IC 31-9-2-115(a), or a shelter care facility under IC 31-9-2-117(a), or that the academy was a facility for custody of persons alleged or found to be delinquent children under IC 35-41-1-18(a)(4) since academy was a non-secure

Juvenile Detention. (Cont'd)
facility. T.D. v. State, 896 N.E.2d 547, 2008 Ind. App. LEXIS 2528 (2008).

Lawful Detention.

Where arrest warrant of defendant was valid on its face defendant was lawfully confined within the meaning of the law against jailbreaking notwithstanding there may have been defects which would have required his release under proper procedure. Carpenter v. State, 178 Ind. App. 446, 382 N.E.2d 1026, 1978 Ind. App. LEXIS 1137 (1978).

The title of a prior criminal cause, the fact that it had a criminal cause number, that bond was set in the cause, and that a bench warrant was issued for the arrest of the defendant when he failed to appear in court as ordered clearly demonstrated that the defendant was under arrest and had been charged with a criminal offense and, hence, was in "lawful detention." Dillbeck v. Duckworth, 585 F. Supp. 1074, 1984 U.S. Dist. LEXIS 17263 (N.D. Ind. 1984).

The definition of "lawful detention" in IC 35-41-1-18 is applicable to that phrase as used in this section defining escape. Triplett v. State, 669 N.E.2d 993, 1996 Ind. App. LEXIS 942 (1996).

Where a police officer places a person in handcuffs pursuant to a writ of body attachment, the person is "lawfully detained" within the meaning of the escape statute even though the writ later proves to be defective. Leshore v. State, 755 N.E.2d 164, 2001 Ind. LEXIS 832 (2001).

Evidence was sufficient to support defendant's conviction for escape as the law enforcement purpose for which defendant was ordered to wait in the hallway was for transportation to the jail and incarceration to serve the sentence which he had just been ordered to serve and thus, defendant was "detained" by the trial court in that he was not free to leave the building as soon as he was informed that the sheriff's department would pick him up at the designated location in the courthouse; that defendant was not in the physical custody of the transport officer at the time that he fled did not exclude the conclusion that he was in detention for law enforcement purposes. Anglin v. State, 787 N.E.2d 1012, 2003 Ind. App. LEXIS 800 (2003).

Conviction for failure to return to lawful detention, IC 35-44-3-5(c), was affirmed where defendant was initially granted stay of sentence and ordered to report to jail on future date but failed to do so; defendant's presence in trial court for sentencing, before being told that he was released until later report date, constituted "detention for law enforcement purposes" to which defendant was required to return on report date. Rowe v. State, 813 N.E.2d 1232, 2004 Ind. App. LEXIS 1713 (2004).

—Evidence.

Where there is no evidence as to the precise reasons underlying a defendant's detainment at the time he fled, such is not necessarily required if the lawful detention element can otherwise be inferred from evidence before the trier of fact. Triplett v. State, 669 N.E.2d 993, 1996 Ind. App. LEXIS 942 (1996).

—Public Highways.

Where evidence showed that defendant was apprehended on an entry ramp to Interstate 70, contention of defendant that there was no evidence of escape since there was no evidence that Interstate 70 was outside the confines of the Indiana State Farm was without effect since an interstate public highway cannot be viewed as part of a state penal institution. Pine v. State, 274 Ind. 78, 408 N.E.2d 1271, 1980 Ind. LEXIS 737 (1980).

Punishment.

The legislature, in determining the punishment for escape, has the right to take into account the fact that the man who escapes is not intent upon reform, and if he escapes from a sentence of 20 years he is committing a crime higher in degree than if he were to escape from a sentence of a single year. State v. Rardon, 221 Ind. 154, 46 N.E.2d 605, 1943 Ind. LEXIS 162 (1943).

It is for the legislature to determine what the punishment shall be for escape, and, in the creation of a statute concerning such crime, that body is not held to narrow limits. State v. Rardon, 221 Ind. 154, 46 N.E.2d 605, 1943 Ind. LEXIS 162 (1943).

Taking Deputy's Gun.

Although purpose of defendant was to escape when defendant took deputy's gun, he could be convicted of robbery. Ard v. State, 238 Ind. 222, 149 N.E.2d 825, 1958 Ind. LEXIS 224 (1958).

Use of Deadly Weapon.

Where defendant drew a weapon and pointed it at deputy marshal, forcing him to take cover in a ditch, then defendant sped away in his truck, and hid from police, the evidence was sufficient to show that defendant fled from lawful detention by use of a deadly weapon. Hart v. State, 671 N.E.2d 420, 1996 Ind. App. LEXIS 1091 (1996).

Cited:

Pearson v. State, 428 N.E.2d 808, 1981 Ind. App. LEXIS 1769 (1981); Powers v. State, 431 N.E.2d 799, 1982 Ind. LEXIS 759 (1982); Grimes v. State, 454 N.E.2d 388, 1983 Ind. LEXIS 986 (1983); Pier v. State, 446 N.E.2d 985, 1983 Ind. App. LEXIS 2750 (1983); Jaske v. State, 553 N.E.2d 181, 1990 Ind. App. LEXIS 488 (1990); Chanley v. State, 583 N.E.2d 126, 1991 Ind. LEXIS 256 (1991); Corbin v. State, 840 N.E.2d 424, 2006 Ind. App. LEXIS 31 (2006).

OPINIONS OF ATTORNEY GENERAL

The auditor of state has the authority to pay expense of transporting a prisoner to the state reformatory who has been found guilty of escaping from the state farm. 1943, p. 119.

Indiana State Farm has no authority to offer or pay any reward for the return of escaped prisoners. 1949, No. 113, p. 429.

In the absence of enabling legislation, the department of correction has no authority to offer and pay awards or rewards, to either peace officers or private citizens, for the return of an escapee to a school or other institution which is a part of the department of correction. 1953, No. 107, p. 494.

RESEARCH REFERENCES

Indiana Law Journal.
Escapes from Permissive Release Programs: Proposals for Reform, 53 Ind. L.J. 779.

Indiana Law Review.
Survey: Criminal Law and Procedure: Recent Developments in Indiana, 32 Ind. L. Rev. 789 (1999).

Collateral References.
Escape or prison breach as affected by means employed to effect it. 96 A.L.R.2d 520.

Liability of public officer or body for harm done by prisoner permitted to escape. 44 A.L.R.3d 899.

Escape from public employee or institution other than correctional or law enforcement employee or institution as criminal offense. 69 A.L.R.3d 625.

Escape from custody of private person as criminal offense. 69 A.L.R.3d 664.

Duress, necessity, or conditions of confinement as justification for escape from prison. 69 A.L.R.3d 678.

Failure of prisoner to return at expiration of work furlough or other permissive release period as crime of escape. 76 A.L.R.3d 658.

Temporary unauthorized absence of prisoner as escape or attempted escape. 76 A.L.R.3d 695.

Admissibility of evidence that defendant escaped or attempted to escape while being detained for offense in addition to that or those presently being prosecuted. 3 A.L.R.4th 1085.

Conviction for escape where prisoner fails to leave confines of prison or institution. 79 A.L.R.4th 1060.

Validity, construction, and application of juvenile escape statutes. 46 A.L.R.5th 523.

Duress, necessity, or conditions of confinement as justification for escape from prison. 54 A.L.R.5th 141.

35-44-3-6. Failure to appear.

(a) A person who, having been released from lawful detention on condition that he appear at a specified time and place in connection with a charge of a crime, intentionally fails to appear at that time and place commits failure to appear, a Class A misdemeanor. However, the offense is a Class D felony if the charge was a felony charge.

(b) It is no defense that the accused person was not convicted of the crime with which he was originally charged.

(c) This section does not apply to obligations to appear incident to release under suspended sentence or on probation or parole.

History.
IC 35-44-3-6, as added by Acts 1976, P.L.148, § 4; 1977, P.L.340, § 64.

Penalties for misdemeanors, IC 35-50-1, IC 35-50-3, IC 35-50-5-2.

Cross References.
Penalties for felonies, IC 35-50-1, IC 35-50-2, IC 35-50-5-2.

NOTES TO DECISIONS

ANALYSIS

Appearance Incident to Release.
Applicability.
Elements.
Intent.

Appearance Incident to Release.
The exemption in subsection (c) applies only to those cases wherein the criminal adjudicatory process has been completed and the defendant has been conditionally released from physical restraint and does not exempt a defendant who is on bail pending sentencing. Haskett v. State, 179 Ind. App. 655, 386 N.E.2d 1012, 1979 Ind. App. LEXIS 1095 (1979); Cleff v. State, 562 N.E.2d 456, 1990 Ind. App. LEXIS 1449 (Ind. App. 1990).

Applicability.
This section applies to defendants who are released on bail as well as to those who are released on their own recognizance. Korff v. State, 567 N.E.2d 1146, 1991 Ind. LEXIS 48 (1991), cert. denied, 502 U.S. 871, 112 S. Ct. 206, 116 L. Ed. 2d 164, 1991 U.S. LEXIS 5379 (1991).

Elements.

The elements of the crime of failure to appear are: (1) a person released from lawful detention; (2) on condition he appear at a specific time and place; (3) in connection with a charge of a crime; (4) who intentionally fails to appear at the time and place specified. Pennington v. State, 426 N.E.2d 408, 1981 Ind. LEXIS 865 (1981); Abdul-Musawwir v. State, 483 N.E.2d 464, 1985 Ind. App. LEXIS 2819 (1985); Cleff v. State, 562 N.E.2d 456, 1990 Ind. App. LEXIS 1449 (Ind. App. 1990).

Intent.

In the absence of extenuating circumstances or lack of adequate notice an intent to fail to appear may be presumed. Haskett v. State, 179 Ind. App. 655, 386 N.E.2d 1012, 1979 Ind. App. LEXIS 1095 (1979).

Cited:

Johnson v. Trigg, 28 F.3d 639, 1994 U.S. App. LEXIS 16432 (7th Cir. Ind. 1994).

RESEARCH REFERENCES

Collateral References.

State statutes making default on bail a separate criminal offense. 63 A.L.R.4th 1064.

35-44-3-6.5. Failure to respond to summons — Penalty.

(a) A person who, having been issued:

(1) A complaint and summons in connection with an infraction or ordinance violation; or

(2) A summons, or summons and promise to appear, in connection with a misdemeanor violation;

notifying him to appear at a specific time and place, intentionally fails to appear at the specified time and place commits failure to respond to a summons, a Class C misdemeanor.

(b) It is no defense that judgment was entered in favor of the person in the infraction or ordinance proceeding or that the person was acquitted of the misdemeanor for which he was summoned to appear.

History.

IC 35-44-3-6.5, as added by Acts 1981, P.L.108, § 38; 1982, P.L.204, § 37.

Cross References.

Penalties for misdemeanors, IC 35-50-1, IC 35-50-3, IC 35-50-5-2.

35-44-3-7. Refusal to aid officer.

A person who, when ordered by a law enforcement officer to assist the officer in the execution of the officer's duties, knowingly or intentionally, and without a reasonable cause, refuses to assist commits refusal to aid an officer, a Class B misdemeanor.

History.

IC 35-44-3-7, as added by Acts 1976, P.L.148, § 4; 1977, P.L.340, § 65.

Cross References.

Penalties for misdemeanors, IC 35-50-1, IC 35-50-3, IC 35-50-5-2.

NOTES TO DECISIONS

ANALYSIS

Evidence.
Indictment.
Justifying Aid.
Liability for Assisting.

Evidence.

Escort service employee's use of code words over the telephone to alert her employer to the presence of police officers was substantial evidence of probative value to support the jury's verdict on a charge of refusal to assist an officer. Low v. State,

580 N.E.2d 737, 1991 Ind. App. LEXIS 1881 (1991).

Indictment.

An indictment for refusing to aid an officer should have alleged that the accused knew of the official character of the officer. State v. Deniston, 1842 Ind. LEXIS 103 (1842).

Justifying Aid.

If the law under which process was issued was unconstitutional, the arrest could not be justified

Justifying Aid. (Cont'd)
under such process. Sumner v. Beeler, 50 Ind. 341, 1875 Ind. LEXIS 134 (1875).

Persons who were summoned to aid an officer in executing a warrant could justify under the warrant though it was informal. Goodwine v. Stephens, 63 Ind. 112, 1878 Ind. LEXIS 319 (1878).

Liability for Assisting.
Officers arresting persons on process invalid on its face, and persons assisting in making such arrests, were liable in actions of false imprisonment. Dietrichs v. Schaw, 43 Ind. 175, 1873 Ind. LEXIS 204 (1873).

Persons summoned to assist an officer in serving process could not be held liable for trespass if the process was of such a character as warranted the officer in serving same. Goodwine v. Stephens, 63 Ind. 112, 1878 Ind. LEXIS 319 (1878).

If an officer, holding a warrant for the arrest of a person, summoned a citizen to aid in making the arrest, such citizen was not liable for the unlawful acts of the officer when he did not aid or encourage the commission of such acts. Stuck v. Yates, 30 Ind. App. 441, 66 N.E. 177, 1903 Ind. App. LEXIS 31 (1903).

35-44-3-8. [Repealed.]

Compiler's Notes.
This section, concerning obstructing a fireman, was repealed by P.L.191-2001, § 2, effective July 1,

2001. For present similar provisions see IC 35-44-4.

35-44-3-8.5. Obstructing an emergency medical person.

(a) A person who knowingly or intentionally obstructs or interferes with an emergency medical person performing or attempting to perform his emergency functions or duties as an emergency medical person commits obstructing an emergency medical person, a Class B misdemeanor.

(b) "Emergency medical person" means a person who holds a certificate issued by the Indiana emergency medical services commission to provide emergency medical services.

History.
IC 35-44-3-8.5, as added by Acts 1977, P.L.341, § 2.

Cross References.
Penalties for misdemeanors, IC 35-50-1, IC 35-50-3, IC 35-50-5-2.

35-44-3-9. Trafficking with an inmate.

(a) As used in this section, "juvenile facility" means the following:

(1) A secure facility (as defined in IC 31-9-2-114) in which a child is detained under IC 31 or used for a child awaiting adjudication or adjudicated under IC 31 as a child in need of services or a delinquent child.

(2) A shelter care facility (as defined in IC 31-9-2-117) in which a child is detained under IC 31 or used for a child awaiting adjudication or adjudicated under IC 31 as a child in need of services or a delinquent child.

(b) Except as provided in subsection (d), a person who, without the prior authorization of the person in charge of a penal facility or juvenile facility knowingly or intentionally:

(1) delivers, or carries into the penal facility or juvenile facility with intent to deliver, an article to an inmate or child of the facility;

(2) carries, or receives with intent to carry out of the penal facility or juvenile facility, an article from an inmate or child of the facility;

(3) delivers, or carries to a worksite with the intent to deliver, alcoholic beverages to an inmate or child of a jail work crew or community work crew; or

(4) possesses in or carries into a penal facility or a juvenile facility:

(A) a controlled substance; or

(B) a deadly weapon;

commits trafficking with an inmate, a Class A misdemeanor.

(c) If the person who committed the offense under subsection (b) is an employee of:

(1) the department of correction; or
(2) a penal facility;

and the article is a cigarette or tobacco product (as defined in IC 6-7-2-5), the court shall impose a mandatory five thousand dollar ($5,000) fine under IC 35-50-3-2, in addition to any term of imprisonment imposed under IC 35-50-3-2.

(d) The offense under subsection (b) is a Class C felony if the article is:
(1) a controlled substance;
(2) a deadly weapon; or
(3) a cellular telephone or other wireless or cellular communications device.

History.
IC 35-44-3-9, as added by Acts 1976, P.L.148, § 4; 1977, P.L.340, § 67; 1981, P.L.300, § 2; P.L.223-1996, § 1; P.L.183-1999, § 2; P.L.243-1999, § 2; P.L.30-2004, § 1; P.L.128-2009, § 2, emergency eff. July 1, 2009.

Amendments.
The 2009 amendment added (b)(4) and (d)(3) and made related changes.

Cross References.
Penalties for felonies, IC 35-50-1, IC 35-50-2, IC 35-50-5-2.
Penalties for misdemeanors, IC 35-50-1, IC 35-50-3, IC 35-50-5-2.

NOTES TO DECISIONS

ANALYSIS

In General.
Halfway House.
Instructions.

In General.
"Trafficking" is a crime that involves delivering an article to a prisoner or carrying an article from a prisoner outside the prison without the prison administration's permission; for example, a nurse passing letters and eight-track tapes to a prisoner, and a prisoner passing a legal brief and an eight-track tape to a nurse. Lockert v. Faulkner, 843 F.2d 1015, 1988 U.S. App. LEXIS 5082 (7th Cir. Ind. 1988).

When a lawyer provided a cellular telephone to an incarcerated former client, resulting in the lawyer being charged with trafficking with an inmate, a class A misdemeanor, to which the lawyer pled guilty, the lawyer's criminal act reflected adversely on her honesty, trustworthiness, or fitness as a lawyer in other respects, in violation of

Ind. R. Prof. Conduct 8.4(b). In re Wagoner, 787 N.E.2d 377, 2003 Ind. LEXIS 384 (2003).

Halfway House.
The Second Chance Halfway House is a "penal facility." Sureeporn Roll v. State, 473 N.E.2d 161, 1985 Ind. App. LEXIS 2119 (1985).

Instructions.
Defendant waived error regarding instructions given and not given when she failed to tender any written instructions covering the areas in question. Sureeporn Roll v. State, 473 N.E.2d 161, 1985 Ind. App. LEXIS 2119 (1985).

Cited:
Perkins v. State, 483 N.E.2d 1379, 1985 Ind. LEXIS 1004 (1985); Huffman v. McBride, 853 F. Supp. 1095, 1994 U.S. Dist. LEXIS 5392 (N.D. Ind. 1994); Evans v. McBride, 94 F.3d 1062, 1996 U.S. App. LEXIS 22668 (7th Cir. Ind. 1996).

RESEARCH REFERENCES

Collateral References.
Nature and elements of offense of conveying contraband to state prisoner. 64 A.L.R.4th 902.

35-44-3-9.3. Trafficking with an inmate outside a facility — Class A misdemeanor — When offense is Class D felony — When offense is Class C felony.

(a) As used in this section, "contraband" means the following:
(1) Alcohol.
(2) A cigarette or tobacco product.
(3) A controlled substance.
(4) An item that may be used as a weapon.

(b) As used in this section, "inmate outside a facility" means a person who is incarcerated in a penal facility or detained in a juvenile facility on a full-time basis as the result of a conviction or a juvenile adjudication but who has been or is being transported to another location to participate in or prepare for a judicial proceeding. The term does not include the following:

(1) An adult or juvenile pretrial detainee.

(2) A person serving an intermittent term of imprisonment or detention.

(3) A person serving a term of imprisonment or detention as:

(A) a condition of probation;

(B) a condition of a community corrections program;

(C) part of a community transition program;

(D) part of a reentry court program;

(E) part of a work release program; or

(F) part of a community based program that is similar to a program described in clauses (A) through (E).

(4) A person who has escaped from incarceration or walked away from secure detention.

(5) A person on temporary leave (as described in IC 11-10-9) or temporary release (as described in IC 11-10-10).

(c) A person who, with the intent of providing contraband to an inmate outside a facility:

(1) delivers contraband to an inmate outside a facility; or

(2) places contraband in a location where an inmate outside a facility could obtain the contraband;

commits trafficking with an inmate outside a facility, a Class A misdemeanor. However, the offense is a Class D felony if the contraband is an item described in subsection (a)(3), and a Class C felony if the contraband is an item described in subsection (a)(4).

History.

P.L.173-2006, § 33.

Cross References.

Penalties for misdemeanors, IC 35-50-1, IC 35-50-3, IC 35-50-5-2.

35-44-3-9.5. Possession by incarcerated person of device capable of causing bodily injury — Possession by incarcerated person of deadly weapon.

A person who knowingly or intentionally while incarcerated in a penal facility possesses a device, equipment, a chemical substance, or other material that:

(1) is used; or

(2) is intended to be used;

in a manner that is readily capable of causing bodily injury commits a Class C felony. However, the offense is a Class B felony if the device, equipment, chemical substance, or other material is a deadly weapon.

History.

P.L.224-1996, § 1.

Cross References.

Penalties for felonies, IC 35-50-1, IC 35-50-2, IC 35-50-5-2.

NOTES TO DECISIONS

ANALYSIS

Evidence.
—Sufficient.
Sentence Enhancement.

Evidence.

—Sufficient.

Sufficient evidence was produced to convict inmate of possessing material capable of causing

Evidence. (Cont'd)

—Sufficient. (Cont'd)
bodily injury in violation of IC 35-44-3-9.5; in particular, evidence indicated that shank made of steel and sharpened to a point was discovered in inmate's cell and that inmate was sole occupant of cell. Abney v. State, 822 N.E.2d 260, 2005 Ind. App. LEXIS 214 (2005), overruled in part, Ryle v. State, 842 N.E.2d 320, 2005 Ind. LEXIS 1112 (2005).

Sentence Enhancement.
Defendant's incarceration, which was material element of offense for which he was charged, namely, possession of material capable of causing bodily injury by an inmate, could nevertheless be used as sentence aggravator since defendant committed offense while on probation for different offense; aggravator was derivative of defendant's criminal history and therefore did not violate

Blakely case prohibitions. Abney v. State, 822 N.E.2d 260, 2005 Ind. App. LEXIS 214 (2005), overruled in part, Ryle v. State, 842 N.E.2d 320, 2005 Ind. LEXIS 1112 (2005).

Two-year sentencing enhancement for possessing material capable of causing bodily injury by an inmate, under IC 35-44-3-9.5, was not inappropriate because: (1) while defendant had been previously attacked, the evidence did not clearly establish that defendant needed a shank to protect himself; (2) defendant had a prior conviction of battery with a deadly weapon; (3) defendant committed several drug and driving offenses prior to his final release date; and (4) the similarity of defendant's previous felony conviction to the present offense and the numerous misdemeanors committed before his first sentence was completed did not reflect favorably on defendant's character. Phillips v. State, 875 N.E.2d 480, 2007 Ind. App. LEXIS 2390 (2007).

35-44-3-10. Jury service — Intimidation or dismissal by employer prohibited — Penalty.

A person who knowingly or intentionally:
(1) Dismisses his employee;
(2) Deprives his employee of employment benefits; or
(3) Threatens such a dismissal or deprivation;
because the employee has received or responded to a summons, served as a juror, or attended court for prospective jury service commits interference with jury service, a Class B misdemeanor.

History.
IC 35-44-3-10, as added by Acts 1977, P.L.26, § 20.

Cross References.
Penalties for misdemeanors, IC 35-50-1, IC 35-50-3, IC 35-50-5-2.

35-44-3-11. [Repealed.]

Compiler's Notes.
This section, concerning use of a police radio in an automobile, was repealed by Acts 1977, P.L.

342, § 2. For present similar provisions, see IC 35-44-3-12.

35-44-3-11.1. Interference with witness service.

A person who knowingly or intentionally:
(1) Dismisses an employee;
(2) Deprives an employee of employment benefits; or
(3) Threatens such a dismissal or deprivation;
because the employee has received or responded to a subpoena in a criminal proceeding commits interference with witness service, a Class B misdemeanor.

History.
P.L.131-1985, § 18.

Cross References.
Penalties for misdemeanors, IC 35-50-1, IC 35-50-3, IC 35-50-5-2.

35-44-3-12. Possession of police radios.

(a) A person who knowingly or intentionally:
(1) Possesses a police radio;
(2) Transmits over a frequency assigned for police emergency purposes; or
(3) Possesses or uses a police radio:

(A) While committing a crime;

(B) To further the commission of a crime; or

(C) To avoid detection by a law enforcement agency;

commits unlawful use of a police radio, a Class B misdemeanor.

(b) Subsection (a)(1) and (a)(2) do not apply to:

(1) A governmental entity;

(2) A regularly employed law enforcement officer;

(3) A common carrier of persons for hire whose vehicles are used in emergency service;

(4) A public service or utility company whose vehicles are used in emergency service;

(5) A person who has written permission from the chief executive officer of a law enforcement agency to possess a police radio;

(6) A person who holds an amateur radio license issued by the Federal Communications Commission if the person is not transmitting over a frequency assigned for police emergency purposes;

(7) A person who uses a police radio only in the person's dwelling or place of business;

(8) A person:

(A) Who is regularly engaged in newsgathering activities;

(B) Who is employed by a newspaper qualified to receive legal advertisements under IC 5-3-1, a wire service, or a licensed commercial or public radio or television station; and

(C) Whose name is furnished by his employer to the chief executive officer of a law enforcement agency in the county in which the employer's principal office is located;

(9) A person engaged in the business of manufacturing or selling police radios; or

(10) A person who possesses or uses a police radio during the normal course of the person's lawful business.

(c) As used in this section, "police radio" means a radio that is capable of sending or receiving signals transmitted on frequencies assigned by the Federal Communications Commission for police emergency purposes and that:

(1) Can be installed, maintained, or operated in a vehicle; or

(2) Can be operated while it is being carried by an individual.

The term does not include a radio designed for use only in a dwelling.

History.

IC 35-44-3-12, as added by Acts 1977, P.L.342, § 1; P.L.162-1994, § 1.

Cross References.

Penalties for misdemeanors, IC 35-50-1, IC 35-50-3, IC 35-50-5-2.

NOTES TO DECISIONS

ANALYSIS

In General.
Evidence.
—Sufficient.
Radar Detection Devices.
Search and Seizure.
Sentencing.

In General.

This section is sufficiently clear and definite to prohibit, at the very least, possession of portable radios capable of receiving vocal police radio communications. Wallman v. State, 419 N.E.2d 1346, 1981 Ind. App. LEXIS 1401 (1981).

Evidence.

—Sufficient.

Evidence was sufficient to affirm defendant's conviction for knowingly or intentionally using police radio in violation of IC 35-44-3-12 where defendant did not deny possessing police radio and did not claim to be within statutory exception of IC 35-44-3-12(b). Grim v. State, 797 N.E.2d 825, 2003 Ind. App. LEXIS 1978 (2003).

Radar Detection Devices.

This section does not prohibit the possession of a portable radar detection device. Wallman v. State, 419 N.E.2d 1346, 1981 Ind. App. LEXIS 1401 (1981).

Search and Seizure.

The facts articulated by the officer for detaining the juvenile after giving him a verbal warning for traffic offenses consisted of no more than unparticularized suspicions and did not form the basis for *Terry v. Ohio,* 392 U.S. 1, 88 S. Ct. 1868, 20 L. Ed. 2d 889, 911 (1968)-level reasonable suspicion to detain the juvenile further in order to conduct a canine sniff of his vehicle; therefore, the sniff of the

vehicle was unreasonable and the motion to suppress admission of the police scanner found as a result of the sniff should have been granted. D.K. v. State, 736 N.E.2d 758, 2000 Ind. App. LEXIS 1533 (2000).

Sentencing.

Defendant should not have received criminal history point under U.S. Sentencing Guidelines Manual § 4A1.2(c) for misdemeanor conviction under IC 35-44-3-12 of possession of police scanner; crime of possession of police scanner is similar to offenses listed in U.S. Sentencing Guidelines Manual § 4A1.2(c)(2). United States v. Hagenow, 423 F.3d 638, 2005 U.S. App. LEXIS 18821 (7th Cir. Ind. 2005).

OPINIONS OF ATTORNEY GENERAL

Privately-owned wrecker services are not "common carriers of persons for hire." 1974, No. 5, p. 13.

RESEARCH REFERENCES

Res Gestae.

Criminal Justice Notes 10/03: Constructive pos-

session — handgun, drugs and paraphernalia in vehicle. 47 (No. 6) Res Gestae 43 (2004).

35-44-3-13. Violation of lifetime parole involving contact with child — Felony.

(a) A person who is being supervised on lifetime parole (as described in IC 35-50-6-1) and who knowingly or intentionally violates a condition of lifetime parole that involves direct or indirect contact with a child less than sixteen (16) years of age or with the victim of a crime that was committed by the person commits a Class D felony if, at the time of the violation:

(1) the person's lifetime parole has been revoked two (2) or more times; or

(2) the person has completed the person's sentence, including any credit time the person may have earned.

(b) The offense described in subsection (a) is a Class C felony if the person has a prior unrelated conviction under this section.

History.

P.L.139-2006, § 5; P.L.140-2006, § 34; P.L.173-2006, § 35; P.L.1-2007, § 233, emergency eff. March 30, 2007; P.L.216-2007, § 49, emergency eff. July 1, 2007.

Compiler's Notes.

P.L.216-2007, § 57, effective July 1, 2007, provides:

"IC 35-38-1-29, as added by this act, and IC 11-8-8-17, IC 11-8-8-18, IC 35-42-4-3, IC 35-42-4-6, IC 35-42-4-9, IC 35-42-4-10, IC 35-42-4-11, IC 35-44-3-13, IC 35-50-6-1(e), and IC 35-50-6-1(i), all as amended by this act, apply only to offenses committed after June 30, 2007."

CHAPTER 4

INTERFERENCE WITH A FIREFIGHTER

35-44-4-1. "Dispatched firefighter" defined.

As used in this chapter, "dispatched firefighter" means a member of:
(1) the fire company having jurisdiction over an emergency incident area; or
(2) a fire company that has entered into a mutual aid agreement with the fire company having jurisdiction over an emergency incident area;
who has been dispatched by the local fire department having jurisdiction over the particular emergency incident area.

History.
P.L.191-2001, § 1.

RESEARCH REFERENCES

Indiana Law Review.
Survey: Criminal Law and Procedure: Recent

Developments in Indiana Criminal Law and Procedure, 35 Ind. L. Rev. 1347 (2002).

35-44-4-2. "Emergency incident area" defined.

As used in this chapter, "emergency incident area" means the area surrounding a structure, vehicle, property, or area that is:
(1) defined by police or firefighters with flags, barricades, barrier tape, or other markers; or
(2) one hundred and fifty (150) feet in all directions from the perimeter of the emergency incident;
whichever is greater.

History.
P.L.191-2001, § 1.

35-44-4-3. "Firefighter" defined.

As used in this chapter, "firefighter" has the meaning set forth in IC 9-18-34-1.

History.
P.L.191-2001, § 1.

NOTES TO DECISIONS

Cited:
Moffitt v. State, 817 N.E.2d 239, 2004 Ind. App. LEXIS 2194 (2004).

35-44-4-4. "Fire protective clothing and fire protective gear" defined.

As used in this chapter, "fire protective clothing and fire protective gear" includes any of the following items generally used by firefighters:
(1) Outer fire retardant clothing and headgear.
(2) Fire gloves.
(3) Selfcontained breathing apparatus.
(4) Emergency medical services protective gear.
(5) Hazardous materials protective gear.

History.
P.L.191-2001, § 1.

35-44-4-5. Refusal to leave an emergency incident area by person not a firefighter.

A person who is not a firefighter who knowingly or intentionally refuses to leave an emergency incident area immediately after being requested to do so by a firefighter or law enforcement officer commits a Class A misdemeanor.

History.
P.L.191-2001, § 1.

Cross References.
Penalties for misdemeanors, IC 35-50-1, IC 35-50-3, IC 35-50-5-2.

35-44-4-6. Refusal to leave an emergency incident area by a firefighter not dispatched.

A firefighter who:
(1) has not been dispatched to an emergency incident area;
(2) enters an emergency incident area; and
(3) refuses to leave an emergency incident area immediately after being requested to do so by a dispatched firefighter or law enforcement officer;
commits a Class C infraction.

History.
P.L.191-2001, § 1.

Cross References.
Infraction and ordinance violation enforcement proceedings, IC 34-28-5.

35-44-4-7. Impersonating a firefighter.

A person other than a firefighter who, with intent to mislead a firefighter or law enforcement officer as to the person's status as a dispatched firefighter, knowingly or intentionally enters an emergency incident area while wearing, transporting, or otherwise possessing a uniform, fire protective clothing, or fire protective gear commits a Class A misdemeanor. However, the offense is a Class D felony if, as a proximate result of the person entering the emergency incident area, a person or firefighter suffers bodily injury (as defined in IC 35-41-1-4).

History.
P.L.191-2001, § 1.

Penalties for misdemeanors, IC 35-50-1, IC 35-50-3, IC 35-50-5-2.

Cross References.
Penalties for felonies, IC 35-50-1, IC 35-50-2, IC 35-50-5-2.

35-44-4-8. Obstructing a firefighter.

A person who knowingly or intentionally obstructs or interferes with a firefighter performing or attempting to perform the firefighter's emergency functions or duties as a firefighter commits obstructing a firefighter, a Class A misdemeanor.

History.
P.L.191-2001, § 1.

Penalties for misdemeanors, IC 35-50-1, IC 35-50-3, IC 35-50-5-2.

Cross References.
False fire alarm, IC 35-44-2-2.

NOTES TO DECISIONS

Strikers.
Striking city fire fighters who engaged in affirmative acts intended to prevent others from fighting a fire violated former IC 35-44-3-8. Boyle v. Anderson Fire Fighters Asso. Local 1262, 497 N.E.2d 1073, 1986 Ind. App. LEXIS 2996 (1986).

ARTICLE 45

OFFENSES AGAINST PUBLIC HEALTH, ORDER AND DECENCY

CHAPTER 1

OFFENSES AGAINST PUBLIC ORDER

35-45-1-1. Definitions.

As used in this chapter:

"Tumultuous conduct" means conduct that results in, or is likely to result in, serious bodily injury to a person or substantial damage to property.

"Unlawful assembly" means an assembly of five (5) or more persons whose common object is to commit an unlawful act, or a lawful act by unlawful means. Prior concert is not necessary to form an unlawful assembly.

History.
IC 35-45-1-1, as added by Acts 1976, P.L.148, § 5; 1977, P.L.340, § 68.

Cross References.
Defenses relating to culpability, IC 35-41-3-1 — IC 35-41-3-10.

NOTES TO DECISIONS

ANALYSIS

Tumultuous Conduct.
—Evidence Insufficient.

Tumultuous Conduct.

Walking in an empty hall with a pistol is not tumultuous conduct because it does not rise to the level that persons are immediately likely to be seriously injured. Gebhard v. State, 484 N.E.2d 45, 1985 Ind. App. LEXIS 2881 (1985).

Evidence was sufficient to support a finding that defendant engaged in "tumultuous conduct" by continuing to yell, scream, and curse after police had arrived at an apartment complex to investigate a neighborhood disturbance involving black women and white women. Whitley v. State, 553 N.E.2d 511, 1990 Ind. App. LEXIS 495 (1990).

Business owner's "picketing" of a union's booth at a convention after the union's business agent filed an unfair labor practice charge against the business was not "tumultuous conduct" as defined by IC 35-45-1-1 and therefore did not qualify as disorderly conduct under IC 35-45-1-3. Lovings v. Thomas, 805 N.E.2d 442, 2004 Ind. App. LEXIS 488 (2004).

Sufficient evidence supported determination that juvenile committed disorderly conduct by engaging in tumultuous conduct within meaning of IC 35-45-1-1 when he pulled out knife during argument with fellow student and pointed knife at

Tumultuous Conduct. (Cont'd)
student. B.R. v. State, 823 N.E.2d 301, 2005 Ind. App. LEXIS 315 (2005).

Because a reasonable jury could only conclude that the property owner's conduct of attempting to strike city employees with a board and failure to comply with the police officers' orders to put the board down was tumultuous conduct for purposes of IC 35-45-1-1, the officers were entitled to summary judgment on the owner's false arrest claim which he brought after he was arrested for disorderly conduct pursuant to IC 35-45-1-3; because the owner could have employed other and more peaceful methods to protest the officers' actions, he was not entitled to a defense under IC 35-41-3-2(b). McConnell v. McKillip, 573 F. Supp. 2d 1090, 2008 U.S. Dist. LEXIS 59015 (2008).

Police officers did not have probable cause to arrest the student for disorderly conduct for "tumultuous conduct" after a report was made that the student was fighting on a bus and the police officers responded to the report; police officers could not have believed after reviewing a bus videotape that there was any indication that serious bodily injury or substantial property damage was likely to occur, although a genuine issue of material fact remained about probable cause to arrest for disorderly conduct based on the student

making unreasonable noise. N.J. v. Metro. Sch. Dist. of Wash. Twp., 879 N.E.2d 1192, 2008 Ind. App. LEXIS 130 (2008).

—Evidence Insufficient.
There was insufficient evidence to support defendant's conviction for disorderly conduct where defendant failed to remove his hand from inside an automobile window after police requested defendant and his companions to clear the street during the third day of a riot in the area, because defendant's allegedly "tumultuous conduct" was not likely to result in personal injury or property damage. Davis v. State, 672 N.E.2d 1365, 1996 Ind. App. LEXIS 1514 (1996).

As the evidence was insufficient to demonstrate conduct likely to result in serious bodily injury or property damage as one could not reasonably expect the dean of students would respond to student defendant's tirade with physical aggression, defendant's behavior was not tumultuous under IC 35-45-1-1. Bailey v. State, 893 N.E.2d 749, 2008 Ind. App. LEXIS 2033 (2008).

Cited:
Gebhard v. State, 459 N.E.2d 58, 1984 Ind. App. LEXIS 2287 (1984).

35-45-1-2. Rioting.

A person who, being a member of an unlawful assembly, recklessly, knowingly, or intentionally engages in tumultuous conduct commits rioting, a Class A misdemeanor. However, the offense is a Class D felony if it is committed while armed with a deadly weapon.

History.
IC 35-45-1-2, as added by Acts 1976, P.L.148, § 5; 1977, P.L.340, § 69.

Cross References.
Penalties for felonies, IC 35-50-1, IC 35-50-2, IC 35-50-5-2.

Penalties for misdemeanors, IC 35-50-1, IC 35-50-3, IC 35-50-5-2.
Refusal to aid officer, IC 35-44-3-7.
Resisting law enforcement, IC 35-44-3-3.

NOTES TO DECISIONS

ANALYSIS

In General.
Constitutionality.
Declarations of Defendants.
Indictment.
Offenses Incidental to Riot.
Presence at Riot.

In General.
One person could not be found guilty of a riot when all the others charged were acquitted. Turpin v. State, 1835 Ind. LEXIS 36 (1835); Hardebeck v. State, 10 Ind. 349, 1858 Ind. LEXIS 929 (1858).

If three or more persons, acting in concert, made a great noise, tumultuously, in the hearing of others, it constituted a riot. State v. Dillard, 1840 Ind. LEXIS 72 (1840); State v. Scaggs, 6 Blackf. 37, 1841 Ind. LEXIS 92 (1841); Bankus v. State, 4 Ind.

114, 1853 Ind. LEXIS 26 (1853); State v. Voshall, 4 Ind. 589, 1853 Ind. LEXIS 227 (1853); State v. Acra, 2 Ind. App. 384, 28 N.E. 570, 1891 Ind. App. LEXIS 182 (1891).

The doing of a lawful act could constitute a riot. Kiphart v. State, 42 Ind. 273, 1873 Ind. LEXIS 72 (1873).

Tumultuous conduct of large crowd going to home of mine superintendent, shouting their demands, frightening his family and driving them away was a violation of prior statute. Bolin v. State, 193 Ind. 302, 139 N.E. 659, 1923 Ind. LEXIS 80 (1923).

Conduct of parties in uniting in the nighttime to distribute literature that was objectionable to many persons in the community, and to discuss the doctrines contained in the literature, was not made unlawful by conspiracy statute contained in Acts 1905, ch. 169, § 439 before the 1971 amend-

In General. (Cont'd)
ment. McKee v. State, 219 Ind. 247, 37 N.E.2d 940, 1941 Ind. LEXIS 234 (1941).

Constitutionality.
A federal court would not enjoin the prosecution of members of a religious sect known as "Jehovah's Witnesses" under prior section, the constitutionality of which was attacked in the absence of any showing of "exceptional circumstances" and "great and immediate danger of irreparable loss." Trent v. Hunt, 39 F. Supp. 373, 1941 U.S. Dist. LEXIS 3217 (D. Ind. 1941), aff'd, 314 U.S. 573, 62 S. Ct. 115, 86 L. Ed. 465, 1941 U.S. LEXIS 259 (1941).

Declarations of Defendants.
The acts and declarations of the defendants were admissible against them, though the commission of another crime might be shown thereby. Gallaher v. State, 101 Ind. 411, — N.E. —, 1885 Ind. LEXIS 336 (1885).

Indictment.
An indictment could charge the doing of all the acts mentioned in the statute without being bad

for duplicity. Hobbs v. State, 133 Ind. 404, 32 N.E. 1019, 1893 Ind. LEXIS 25, 18 L.R.A. 774 (1893).
Prior to the 1971 amendment of prior statute, in charging the commission of a riot, it was not necessary to allege that the acts constituting the offense were done in a public place. Carmody v. State, 178 Ind. 158, 98 N.E. 870, 1912 Ind. LEXIS 83 (1912).

Offenses Incidental to Riot.
The conviction for a riot could not be a bar to a conviction for another offense which was merely incidental to the riot. Wininger v. State, 13 Ind. 460, 13 Ind. 540, 1879 Ind. LEXIS 1 (1859).
Unlawful assemblage, before commission of the rioting, was no part of the offense under the statute. Bolin v. State, 193 Ind. 302, 139 N.E. 659, 1923 Ind. LEXIS 80 (1923).

Presence at Riot.
The separate and independent acts of a person committed just at the close of a riot would not make him guilty of a riot. Sloan v. State, 9 Ind. 537, 9 Ind. 565, 1857 Ind. LEXIS 670 (1857).

RESEARCH REFERENCES

Collateral References.
Participation of student in demonstration on or near campus as warranting imposition of criminal

liability for breach of peace, disorderly conduct, trespass, unlawful assembly, or similar offense. 32 A.L.R.3d 551.

35-45-1-3. Disorderly conduct.

(a) A person who recklessly, knowingly, or intentionally:
(1) engages in fighting or in tumultuous conduct;
(2) makes unreasonable noise and continues to do so after being asked to stop; or
(3) disrupts a lawful assembly of persons;
commits disorderly conduct, a Class B misdemeanor.
(b) The offense described in subsection (a) is a Class D felony if it:
(1) adversely affects airport security; and
(2) is committed in an airport (as defined in IC 8-21-1-1) or on the premises of an airport, including in a parking area, a maintenance bay, or an aircraft hangar.
(c) The offense described in subsection (a) is a Class D felony if it:
(1) is committed within five hundred (500) feet of:
(A) the location where a burial is being performed;
(B) a funeral procession, if the person described in subsection (a) knows that the funeral procession is taking place; or
(C) a building in which:
(i) a funeral or memorial service; or
(ii) the viewing of a deceased person;
is being conducted; and
(2) adversely affects the funeral, burial, viewing, funeral procession, or memorial service.

History.
IC 35-45-1-3, as added by Acts 1976, P.L.148, § 5, p. 718; 1977, P.L.340, § 70, p. 1533; P.L.92-1988, § 8; P.L.123-2002, § 40; P.L.3-2006, § 1.

Compiler's Notes.
P.L.3-2006, § 3, effective March 2, 2006, provides:
"IC 35-45-1-3 and IC 35-45-2-1, both as amended

by this act, apply only to crimes committed after the effective date of this act."

Cross References.

Interference with police or firemen, IC 35-44-2-2, IC 35-44-3-3, IC 35-44-4.

Obstruction of traffic, IC 35-42-2-4.

Penalties for felonies, IC 35-50-1, IC 35-50-2, IC 35-50-5-2.

Penalties for misdemeanors, IC 35-50-1, IC 35-50-3, IC 35-50-5-2.

NOTES TO DECISIONS

Constitutionality.

Where words spoken by defendant, although loud, did not appear to be addressed to any particular person or group and did not appear to be exhorting the crowd to go back into the street after police cleared it, and it did not appear that the words were likely to produce imminent disorder an arrest of defendant violated his right to freedom of speech. Hess v. Indiana, 414 U.S. 105, 38 L. Ed. 2d 303, 94 S. Ct. 326, 1973 U.S. LEXIS 177 (1973); Communist Workers Party v. City of E. Chicago, 556 F. Supp. 47, 1982 U.S. Dist. LEXIS 17058 (N.D. Ind. 1982).

Abating excessive noise is an objective the legislature may legitimately pursue. Price v. State, 622 N.E.2d 954, 1993 Ind. LEXIS 183 (1993), overruled in part, Blackman v. State, 868 N.E.2d 579, 2007 Ind. App. LEXIS 1323 (2007).

Treating as an abuse of this section political speech which does not harm any particular individual ("public nuisance") does amount to a material burden on the speaker's rights, but sanction-ing expression which inflicts upon determinable parties harm of a gravity analogous to that required under tort law does not. Price v. State, 622 N.E.2d 954, 1993 Ind. LEXIS 183 (1993), overruled in part, Blackman v. State, 868 N.E.2d 579, 2007 Ind. App. LEXIS 1323 (2007).

Political expression becomes "unreasonable noise" for purposes of subdivision (2) of this section when and only when it inflicts upon determinant parties harm analogous to that which would sustain tort liability against the speaker. Price v. State, 622 N.E.2d 954, 1993 Ind. LEXIS 183 (1993), overruled in part, Blackman v. State, 868 N.E.2d 579, 2007 Ind. App. LEXIS 1323 (2007).

Defendant could not be punished, consistent with the Ind. Const., art. 1, § 9, for her particular speech when she protested the arrest of someone noisily in an alley on New Year's Eve, which caused the neighbors to come out and look. Price v. State, 622 N.E.2d 954, 1993 Ind. LEXIS 183 (1993), overruled in part, Blackman v. State, 868 N.E.2d 579, 2007 Ind. App. LEXIS 1323 (2007).

IC 35-45-1-3(2) is content-neutral. Price v. State, 622 N.E.2d 954, 1993 Ind. LEXIS 183 (1993), overruled in part, Blackman v. State, 868 N.E.2d 579, 2007 Ind. App. LEXIS 1323 (2007).

Any application of IC 35-45-1-3(2) aimed at the content of expression is impermissible; the disorderly conduct statute also provides fair notice. Price v. State, 622 N.E.2d 954, 1993 Ind. LEXIS 183 (1993), overruled in part, Blackman v. State, 868 N.E.2d 579, 2007 Ind. App. LEXIS 1323 (2007).

IC 35-45-1-3(2)'s reasonableness standard provides a constraining and intelligible enforcement guideline for police and prosecutors. Price v. State, 622 N.E.2d 954, 1993 Ind. LEXIS 183 (1993), overruled in part, Blackman v. State, 868 N.E.2d 579, 2007 Ind. App. LEXIS 1323 (2007).

IC 35-45-1-3(2) is not overbroad or vague in violation of the First and Fourteenth Amendments. Price v. State, 622 N.E.2d 954, 1993 Ind. LEXIS 183 (1993), overruled in part, Blackman v. State, 868 N.E.2d 579, 2007 Ind. App. LEXIS 1323 (2007).

Even assuming a defendant's speech was protected under the Constitution, his conviction for disorderly conduct would be affirmed where the evidence presented showed that the complained-of speech infringed upon the right to peace and tranquility enjoyed by others; the prohibition against unreasonable noise in Indiana's disorderly conduct statute, subdivision (2) of this section, is aimed at the intrusiveness and loudness of expression, not whether the content of the language is obscene or provocative. Hooks v. State, 660 N.E.2d 1076, 1996 Ind. App. LEXIS 38 (1996).

Constitutionality. (Cont'd)

When reviewing the constitutionality of an application of the disorderly conduct statute a reviewing court must first determine whether state action has restricted a claimant's expressive activity, and second, if it has, whether the restricted activity constituted an "abuse" of the right to speak. Whittington v. State, 669 N.E.2d 1363, 1996 Ind. LEXIS 125 (1996).

An adjudication as a delinquent child based upon the commission of disorderly conduct was not unconstitutional, notwithstanding the assertion that the child's right to free speech was violated when he was arrested for arguing in a loud voice and interfering with a police investigation. Johnson v. State, 719 N.E.2d 445, 1999 Ind. App. LEXIS 1998 (1999).

The court applies a two-step inquiry when reviewing the constitutionality of an application of the disorderly conduct statute; first, to determine whether state action has restricted a claimant's expressive activity; and second, to determine whether the restricted activity constituted an abuse of the right to speak. Shoultz v. State, 735 N.E.2d 818, 2000 Ind. App. LEXIS 1483 (2000).

Since the disorderly conduct statute, IC 35-45-1-3, restricted a juvenile's expressive activity under Ind. Const., art. 1, § 9, and the content of the juvenile's speech was a commentary on government action, since her comments were, on the whole, largely an objection to the rules and living conditions of the county guardian home in which she lived, she should not have been adjudicated a delinquent child for committing disorderly conduct, a Class B misdemeanor if committed by an adult. J.D. v. State, 841 N.E.2d 204, 2006 Ind. App. LEXIS 122 (2006), superseded, 859 N.E.2d 341, 2007 Ind. LEXIS 2 (2007), transfer granted and vacated, 869 N.E.2d 446, 2007 Ind. LEXIS 6 (2007).

Actions of Defendant.

It was defendant's acts themselves and not those at whom they were directed that formed basis of disorderly conduct conviction. Whited v. State, 256 Ind. 386, 269 N.E.2d 149, 1971 Ind. LEXIS 643 (1971), clarified, 256 Ind. 618, 271 N.E.2d 513, 1971 Ind. LEXIS 685 (1971).

Assault and Battery Merged.

A conviction for an affray merged an assault and battery committed in the commission of the affray. Fritz v. State, 40 Ind. 18, 1872 Ind. LEXIS 191 (1872); Woodworth v. State, 185 Ind. 582, 114 N.E. 86, 1916 Ind. LEXIS 70 (1916).

Conspiracy to Incite Against Government.

A conviction of conspiracy to incite people in a given locality against all forms of organized government and to disrespect the flag of the United States could not be sustained under the portion of prior section pertaining to publication of literature, where it was not contended that the literature distributed advocated "physical injury to personal property" or "general cessation of industry" of any government, and the literature, although advocating the overthrow of all human government, did not advocate or incite such overthrow by the use of force or violence. McKee v. State, 219 Ind. 247, 37 N.E.2d 940, 1941 Ind. LEXIS 234 (1941).

Disturbing Meetings Generally.

The protection of the statute prohibiting disturbing meetings extended to meetings until an actual dispersion took place. State v. Snyder, 14 Ind. 352, 14 Ind. 429, 1860 Ind. LEXIS 176 (1860); State v. Lusk, 68 Ind. 264, 1879 Ind. LEXIS 598 (1879).

One who entered a room where the "Salvation Army" was conducting a service and with his hat on and a cigar in his mouth, persisted in conducting himself in an offensive manner, and so diverted attention from religious services then in progress was guilty of disturbing a meeting, within the meaning of prior statute. Hull v. State, 120 Ind. 153, 22 N.E. 117, 1889 Ind. LEXIS 377 (1889).

Double Jeopardy.

Under the same offense test of *Elmore v. State,* 269 Ind. 532, 382 N.E.2d 893, 1978 Ind. LEXIS 809 (1978), defendant's conviction on the two charges of assault and battery and disorderly conduct was proper, even though the two charges both arose from the same incident, since defendant's kicking a police officer was one offense and his yelling and cursing another. Fields v. State, 178 Ind. App. 350, 382 N.E.2d 972, 1978 Ind. App. LEXIS 1156 (1978), superseded by statute as stated in, Shoultz v. State, 735 N.E.2d 818, 2000 Ind. App. LEXIS 1483 (2000).

The double jeopardy clause did not bar defendant's convictions for resisting arrest and disorderly conduct, where both offenses required the proof of additional facts. Whitley v. State, 553 N.E.2d 511, 1990 Ind. App. LEXIS 495 (1990).

Elements.

While fact that crowd gathered was of some considerable evidentiary weight, it was not requisite to conviction of disorderly conduct. Whited v. State, 256 Ind. 386, 269 N.E.2d 149, 1971 Ind. LEXIS 643 (1971), clarified, 256 Ind. 618, 271 N.E.2d 513, 1971 Ind. LEXIS 685 (1971).

Enjoining Prosecution.

A federal court would not enjoin the prosecution of members of a religious sect known as "Jehovah's Witnesses" under statute prohibiting inciting of violence against the government, the constitutionality of which was attacked in the absence of any showing of "exceptional circumstances" and "great and immediate danger of irreparable loss." Trent v. Hunt, 39 F. Supp. 373, 1941 U.S. Dist. LEXIS 3217 (D. Ind. 1941), aff'd, 314 U.S. 573, 62 S. Ct. 115, 86 L. Ed. 465, 1941 U.S. LEXIS 259 (1941).

Evidence.

—In General.

Conduct which by its nature was offensive in context in which it was committed, only was required to support conviction of disorderly conduct,

Evidence. (Cont'd)

—In General. (Cont'd)
and such state of facts could as well be established by testimony of police officers as by any other testimony. Whited v. State, 256 Ind. 386, 269 N.E.2d 149, 1971 Ind. LEXIS 643 (1971), clarified, 256 Ind. 618, 271 N.E.2d 513, 1971 Ind. LEXIS 685 (1971).

—Insufficient.
Where teacher testified that he was the only person standing near the juvenile at the time of their encounter when the juvenile muttered an expletive at the teacher, the court determined the evidence was insufficient to support the trial court's finding that the juvenile committed the offense of disorderly conduct by disrupting a lawful assembly of persons. D.R. v. State, 729 N.E.2d 597, 2000 Ind. App. LEXIS 858 (2000).

Where defendant was engaged in political speech at the time of his arrest and his speech was protected by Ind. Const., art. 1, § 9, the state was required to produce evidence that defendant's speech inflicted particularized harm analogous to tortious injury to readily identifiable private interests, and the state failed to present such evidence, there was insufficient evidence of disorderly conduct to support the conviction. Johnson v. State, 747 N.E.2d 623, 2001 Ind. App. LEXIS 750 (2001).

Where plaintiff election board mechanic sued defendant city, mayor, police chief, officers, and mayor's son for alleged constitutional violations resulting from his arrest and detention during an election investigation, grant of summary judgment to arresting officers on mechanic's Fourth Amendment false arrest claim was error since events leading to arrest were in dispute, thereby raising issue of fact as to whether there was probable cause to arrest mechanic for disorderly conduct under IC 35-45-1-3(a)(1) and (2). Morfin v. City of E. Chicago, 349 F.3d 989, 2003 U.S. App. LEXIS 23450 (7th Cir. Ind. 2003).

Act of obstructing pedestrian traffic no longer constituted disorderly conduct, and an assembly of persons referred to a group that was already assembled, as opposed to one that was in the process of assembling; a conviction for disorderly conduct was reversed as based on insufficient evidence where defendant was standing on a sidewalk, carrying a sign, obstructing pedestrian traffic going to a professional football game. Oliver v. State, 789 N.E.2d 1003, 2003 Ind. App. LEXIS 995 (2003).

Officers did not have probable cause to arrest protestor for disorderly conduct under IC 35-45-1-3 and protestor's rights under U.S. Const., Amend. 4, were violated where no facts supported allegation that protestor's conduct was likely to result in serious personal injury or property damage, where no facts supported allegation that protestor made unreasonable noise and continued to do so after being asked to stop, and where small crowd that gathered during protestor's verbal exchange with officer dispersed quickly when told to do so. Blair v. City of Evansville, 361 F. Supp. 2d 846, 2005 U.S. Dist. LEXIS 4833 (S.D. Ind. 2005).

Evidence did not demonstrate beyond a reasonable doubt that defendant juvenile, who was observed in a crowded school hallway grabbing a boy's hair and smacking him with an open hand three times across his face, was "fighting" and thus committed disorderly conduct, where there was scant evidence in the record that defendant's actions were hostile and a great deal of evidence that her actions were, in fact, not hostile. J.S. v. State, 843 N.E.2d 1013, 2006 Ind. App. LEXIS 474 (2006).

As the evidence was insufficient to demonstrate conduct likely to result in serious bodily injury or property damage as one could not reasonably expect the dean of students would respond to student defendant's tirade with physical aggression, defendant's behavior was not tumultuous under IC 35-45-1-1. Bailey v. State, 893 N.E.2d 749, 2008 Ind. App. LEXIS 2033 (2008).

—Intent.
Evidence that defendant was able to walk and run; exert considerable physical force and resistance; and intelligibly communicate comments and opinions, some indicating comprehension of his circumstances, was sufficient to support finding of requisite intent despite defendant's intoxication. McCaffrey v. State, 523 N.E.2d 435, 1988 Ind. App. LEXIS 374 (1988).

—Sufficient.
In a prosecution for horse racing on a public highway, proof that the road used ran between two towns of the county was sufficient to show that it was a public highway. Watson v. State, 3 Ind. 123 (1851).

In a prosecution for horse racing on a public highway, it was not necessary to make out the charge that a bet or wager was made on the race, or that any distance was agreed on, or that judges were selected to decide on the result. Watson v. State, 3 Ind. 123 (1851).

In a prosecution for advocating, advising, and inciting the overthrow of the government of the United States and the state of Indiana, by force and violence, the evidence, when taken most strongly against the accused, which disclosed only the accused's opinion upon the economic or political questions of the times, and a possible partial solution for them, was insufficient to sustain a verdict of guilty. Butash v. State, 212 Ind. 492, 9 N.E.2d 88, 1937 Ind. LEXIS 337 (1937).

Evidence that the conduct of defendants in a front yard in a designated city at 2:35 a.m. was libidinous and sensual, that their language was boisterous, loud and profane, and that there were a number of beer bottles near them, and that a neighbor woman and her children were up with lights on in the house and policemen were attracted to the scene by such conduct, was sufficient to sustain a conviction of defendants for disorderly conduct. Romary v. State, 223 Ind. 667, 64 N.E.2d 22, 1945 Ind. LEXIS 159 (1945).

Evidence that as police officers approached the porch on which defendant sat, defendant yelled obscenities at such officers in loud and disorderly

Evidence. (Cont'd)

—Sufficient. (Cont'd)
manner, and that a large crowd gathered, was sufficient to support conviction of disorderly conduct. Whited v. State, 256 Ind. 386, 269 N.E.2d 149, 1971 Ind. LEXIS 643 (1971), clarified, 256 Ind. 618, 271 N.E.2d 513, 1971 Ind. LEXIS 685 (1971).

Where defendant, detained for suspected shoplifting, became loud, profane, and abusive, thereby causing a crowd to gather while protesting her detention, such speech was not constitutionally protected and under the circumstances defendant was guilty of disorderly conduct. Stults v. State, 166 Ind. App. 461, 336 N.E.2d 669, 1975 Ind. App. LEXIS 1378 (1975).

Where defendant was arguing with sheriff and jumping up and down and cursing, which language could be distinctly heard 200 feet away, there was sufficient evidence for jury to find disorderly conduct. Fields v. State, 179 Ind. App. 194, 384 N.E.2d 1127, 1979 Ind. App. LEXIS 1063 (1979).

Evidence was sufficient to support defendant's conviction for disorderly conduct, where his insults and provocations, including threats to kill an arresting officer, clearly fell within the "fighting words" category of unprotected speech. Brown v. State, 576 N.E.2d 605, 1991 Ind. App. LEXIS 1323 (1991).

The state established that defendant made unreasonable noise and continued to do so after being asked to stop; her disorderly conduct conviction was supported by sufficient evidence and was affirmed on rehearing. Radford v. State, 640 N.E.2d 90, 1994 Ind. App. LEXIS 1260 (1994).

Jury could reasonably have concluded from evidence that defendant's screaming was heard by neighbors across the street from his mother's house, that defendant's speech infringed upon the peace and tranquility of others. Hooks v. State, 660 N.E.2d 1076, 1996 Ind. App. LEXIS 38 (1996).

Evidence was sufficient to support an adjudication as a delinquent child based upon the commission of disorderly conduct where the child argued in a voice louder than the voices of others in the room and his volume disrupted a police investigation. Johnson v. State, 719 N.E.2d 445, 1999 Ind. App. LEXIS 1998 (1999).

There was sufficient evidence to support defendant's conviction for disorderly conduct, under IC 35-45-1-3, because defendant produced decibels of sound that were too loud for the circumstances because: (1) the sheer volume of defendant's outbursts disrupted police officers' investigation and attracted unwanted attention; (2) the officers repeatedly asked defendant to lower her voice and to leave the scene of their investigation; (3) defendant defiantly ignored their requests and shouted even louder; and (4) the ensuing commotion drew a crowd. Blackman v. State, 868 N.E.2d 579, 2007 Ind. App. LEXIS 1323 (2007).

State presented sufficient evidence to support defendant's conviction for Class B misdemeanor disorderly conduct arising out of defendant's refusal to leave a business establishment when asked to do so several times and defendant's resulting verbally disruptive conduct. The evidence showed that defendant recklessly, knowingly, or intentionally made unreasonable noise and continued to do so after being asked to stop. Anderson v. State, 881 N.E.2d 86, 2008 Ind. App. LEXIS 262 (2008).

Evidence that when a police officer came to defendant's home to serve a letter that barred defendant from the property of a public school, defendant exited his home, flailed his arms and yelled, used profanity, directed vulgar names at the officer, continued to yell after being asked to stop, and created a disturbance sufficient to cause his neighbors to come out of their homes, was sufficient to support defendant's conviction for disorderly conduct. Yowler v. State, 894 N.E.2d 1000, 2008 Ind. App. LEXIS 2222 (2008).

—Sufficient to Raise Issue.
Testimony by police officers that defendant shouted obscenities to them several times, and that his heated shouting, yelling, and cursing continued throughout the time he was placed under arrest, was sufficient evidence to send the issue of whether defendant was guilty of disorderly conduct to the jury. Lepard v. State, 542 N.E.2d 1347, 1989 Ind. App. LEXIS 1357 (1989).

Free Speech.
As there is no doubt that a citizen who is stopped by a police officer for a violation of a speeding ordinance or statute may exercise the right of free speech by inquiring as to the basis of the alleged offense, the following statements made by the defendant who was stopped for speeding did not violate this section: "What's the matter, Officer?", "I couldn't have been going that fast", "What are you accusing me of?", "Don't talk to my wife in that tone of voice!", "I already gave you my driver's license", and "I am a lawyer and I know my rights". Bovey v. Lafayette, 586 F. Supp. 1460, 1984 U.S. Dist. LEXIS 16459 (N.D. Ind. 1984), aff'd without op., 774 F.2d 1166, 1985 U.S. App. LEXIS 22854 (7th Cir. Ind. 1985).

Defendant's conviction for disorderly conduct under IC 35-45-1-3 for criticizing officer's conduct was improper since speech was political and was protected under Ind. Const., art. 1, § 9. U.M. v. State, 827 N.E.2d 1190, 2005 Ind. App. LEXIS 931 (2005).

When defendant screamed at officers arresting a man, claiming that they were "doing him wrong," her speech was political in nature as an expression of her disagreement regarding the police actions toward the man. Thus, at her trial for resisting law enforcement and disorderly conduct, it was error to refuse her proffered jury instructions on protected speech under Ind. Const., art. I, § 9. Snell v. State, 866 N.E.2d 392, 2007 Ind. App. LEXIS 1021 (2007).

Defendant's arrest for disorderly conduct, under IC 35-45-1-3, did not violate Ind. Const. art. 1, § 9 because, although defendant established that the state restricted her expressive activity because the record indicated that defendant was arrested for disorderly conduct after she shouted and swore at police officers: (1) defendant's expression was not

Free Speech. (Cont'd)
political and was therefore subject to rational review; (2) in filing the charges, the state could have reasonably concluded that defendant's expressive activity because of its volume, the attention that it attracted, the potential threat to officer safety, and the ensuing interference with the officers' investigation, was a threat to peace, safety, and well-being, and therefore, was an abuse of defendant's right to speak; (3) due to defendant's conduct, the officers' attention was diverted from conducting their investigation to monitoring and managing the scene that defendant had created; and (4) the state could have rationally concluded that where defendant obstructed and interfered with the officers' attempts to function as law enforcement officers, her conduct constituted an abuse of the right to speak and fell within the state's police power. Blackman v. State, 868 N.E.2d 579, 2007 Ind. App. LEXIS 1323 (2007).

Indictment or Information.
Where defendant threatened to shoot his wife, information charging that he "did and then and there act in a disorderly manner so as to disturb the family of" his wife "by threatening to kill" her, such information was sufficient so that the nature of the offense could be ascertained by the defendant. Gilman v. State, 180 Ind. App. 483, 389 N.E.2d 327, 1979 Ind. App. LEXIS 1100 (1979).

Unless the court can find that speech was obscene, that it could be characterized as "fighting words," that it amounted to a public nuisance infringing on anyone's privacy, or that it was a clear incitement to any violence or obvious lawless action, then, the court must find that the federal constitution requires that the indictment charging violation of this section be quashed. State v. New, 421 N.E.2d 626, 1981 Ind. LEXIS 759 (1981).

Where information charged defendant simply with "tumultuous conduct," and did not state any facts or circumstances in which to fully apprise the defendant of the nature of the offense with which the defendant was charged, the trial court erred in denying defendant's motion to dismiss for failure to apprise defendant of the charge against him. Gebhard v. State, 459 N.E.2d 58, 1984 Ind. App. LEXIS 2287 (1984).

—Disturbing Meeting.
An indictment in the same count could charge a disturbance of a meeting and the members thereof. The name of the society did not have to be stated. State v. Ringer, 1842 Ind. LEXIS 6 (1842).

An information charging defendants with disturbing a meeting by forcing their way against rules, and making a great noise by loud and boisterous talking, was good. State v. Oskins, 28 Ind. 364, 1867 Ind. LEXIS 281 (1867).

It should be alleged in the indictment that the meeting was held for a lawful purpose, but the particular purpose need not be stated. State v. Zimmerman, 53 Ind. 360, 1876 Ind. LEXIS 186 (1876); Howard v. State, 87 Ind. 68, 1882 Ind. LEXIS 755 (1882); Blake v. State, 18 Ind. App. 280, 47 N.E. 942, 1897 Ind. App. LEXIS 204 (1897).

In a prosecution for unlawfully disturbing an assemblage, an indictment charging defendant with disturbing a church meeting by talking in a loud and boisterous manner was sufficient on motion to quash. Kidder v. State, 58 Ind. 68, 1877 Ind. LEXIS 141 (1877).

When the charge was for disturbing a meeting, the persons disturbed did not need to be named, and if named, it was not necessary to prove that they were disturbed. Hull v. State, 120 Ind. 153, 22 N.E. 117, 1889 Ind. LEXIS 377 (1889).

An affidavit charging a person with disturbing the peace at a certain church did not charge the disturbance of a public meeting. State v. Bogard, 25 Ind. App. 123, 57 N.E. 722, 1900 Ind. App. LEXIS 61 (1900).

An affidavit in a prosecution under prior section charging that the defendant unlawfully disturbed a certain collection of inhabitants meeting for a lawful purpose, and fully stating the manner of such disturbance, and the county and state where the offense occurred and the date thereof, was sufficient as against motion to quash. Kirschbaum v. State, 196 Ind. 512, 149 N.E. 77, 1925 Ind. LEXIS 77 (1925).

—Evidence.
In a prosecution for disorderly conduct, any defect in the affidavit as to an allegation that certain conduct was such as to disturb the peace and quiet of the neighborhood where it took place, was cured by the evidence as against a motion in arrest of judgment, where the evidence disclosed that such conduct attracted the attention of policemen and that a neighbor woman and her children were up and had lights on at 2:35 a.m., the time the disturbance occurred, from which an inference was justifiable that they were disturbed thereby. Romary v. State, 223 Ind. 667, 64 N.E.2d 22, 1945 Ind. LEXIS 159 (1945).

—Sufficient.
An indictment charging horse racing on a public highway did not need to give a description of the highway. State v. Burgett, 1 Ind. 479 (1849); State v. Armstrong, 3 Ind. 139 (1851).

A charge that the defendant acted as "rider in a certain horse race which was then and there run along a public highway, in said county, between animals of the horse kind in a trial of speed," was sufficient. State v. New, 165 Ind. 571, 76 N.E. 400, 1905 Ind. LEXIS 174 (1905).

Neighborhood.
A tavern is a part of a neighborhood as well as any other business to which the public is invited, and proof of conduct, either inside or outside such establishment, which justified a finding that the peace of the neighborhood was disturbed, warranted a conviction of disorderly conduct. Morris v. State, 227 Ind. 630, 88 N.E.2d 328, 1949 Ind. LEXIS 173 (1949).

The word "neighborhood," as used in prior section included both residential and business sections. Morris v. State, 227 Ind. 630, 88 N.E.2d 328, 1949 Ind. LEXIS 173 (1949).

Political Speech.

—Not Found.

Defendant was properly convicted of disorderly conduct where the record did not indicate that she was protesting the appropriateness of police conduct, but she was arguing with her ex-boyfriend and his companions in a loud, screaming voice; the mere presence of a police officer did not convert her speech into political expression. Stites v. State, 627 N.E.2d 1343, 1994 Ind. App. LEXIS 37 (1994).

Defendant's expression, which resulted in her arrest for disorderly conduct, under IC 35-45-1-3, was not political and was therefore subject to rational review because: (1) defendant's speech was ultimately ambiguous as to whether she was commenting on her own conduct or that of police officers; (2) the dual nature of defendant's outbursts, coupled with her unreasonable noise levels, her refusal to comply with the officers' instructions, and the resulting disruption of a police investigation, led to the conclusion that although defendant's expressive activity began as political speech, it did not end as such; and (3) the court was particularly sensitive to attending policy considerations regarding the extent to which police officers had to endure defendant's insults, threats to their personal safety, and the disruption of their investigations, in the name of preserving defendant's right to free speech. Blackman v. State, 868 N.E.2d 579, 2007 Ind. App. LEXIS 1323 (2007).

Probable Cause.

Where police sought to question person about the fall of his wife from second floor but he refused to answer their questions but came out on porch and in a loud voice ordered them off the property and shouted obscenities at them and police efforts to calm him proved futile, there was probable cause for the arrest. South Bend v. Fleming, 397 N.E.2d 1075, 1979 Ind. App. LEXIS 1494 (1979).

Police had probable cause to arrest defendant for disorderly conduct where defendant was involved in a multi-person altercation and an officer saw defendant strike a woman; thus, the search of defendant's person, as well as a rag that had been in defendant's immediate control, was lawful as a search incident to an arrest and a motion to suppress was properly denied. Moffitt v. State, 817 N.E.2d 239, 2004 Ind. App. LEXIS 2194 (2004).

District court erred when it granted summary judgment to a police officer as to an arrestee's U.S. Const. amends. 4 and 14 civil rights claims because the officer did not have probable cause to arrest the arrestee for disorderly conduct under former IC 35-45-1-3 and material factual disputes existed as to whether the officer had probable cause to arrest the arrestee for criminal trespassing under IC 35-43-2-2(a)(2). There was no evidence that the arrestee had raised his voice, had engaged in tumultuous conduct, or had disrupted any assembly of persons, one of which is required for a disorderly conduct violation. Pourghoraishi v. Flying J, Inc., 449 F.3d 751, 2006 U.S. App. LEXIS 9875 (7th Cir. Ind. 2006), corrected, — F.3d —, 2006 U.S. App. LEXIS 13604 (7th Cir. Ind. 2006).

Public Policy.

Free speech and assembly must yield in some instances to the more important right of self-preservation of a government against its overthrow by violence. State v. Levitt, 246 Ind. 275, 203 N.E.2d 821, 1965 Ind. LEXIS 350 (1965).

Racing.

If the charge was for suffering a mare to be run in a race, proof that a horse was so run would not support the charge. Thrasher v. State, 1843 Ind. LEXIS 81 (1843); Conway v. State, 4 Ind. 94, 1853 Ind. LEXIS 19 (1853).

Suffering a horse to be run in a race, and acting as rider, were separate offenses. State v. Ness, 1 Ind. 64 (1848).

Proof of riding a horse in a race would not support a charge of suffering a horse to have been run in a race. Robb v. State, 52 Ind. 216, 1875 Ind. LEXIS 432 (1875).

Reasonable Reaction.

Disorderly conduct was not excused as reasonable reaction to any illegal police activity when defendant became disorderly without even inquiring into legal status of police officers. Whited v. State, 256 Ind. 386, 269 N.E.2d 149, 1971 Ind. LEXIS 643 (1971), clarified, 256 Ind. 618, 271 N.E.2d 513, 1971 Ind. LEXIS 685 (1971).

Recovery for Injuries.

One who attended as a spectator a race held in violation of prior section, and during the race went upon the street and was struck by one of the horses and injured, could not recover upon the sole ground of illegality of the race. Frazure v. Ruckles, 63 Ind. App. 538, 113 N.E. 730, 1916 Ind. App. LEXIS 216 (1916).

Separation of Witnesses.

In a prosecution for disorderly conduct, it was not error to refuse to exclude the prosecuting witness from the courtroom during the trial, nor to permit him to testify as a witness thereafter, notwithstanding defendant's motion for separation of witnesses. Romary v. State, 223 Ind. 667, 64 N.E.2d 22, 1945 Ind. LEXIS 159 (1945).

Tumultuous Conduct.

Walking in an empty hall with a pistol is not tumultuous conduct because it does not rise to the level that persons are immediately likely to be seriously injured. Gebhard v. State, 484 N.E.2d 45, 1985 Ind. App. LEXIS 2881 (1985).

The words "engages in" obviously require present, completed conduct which is likely to injure persons. Gebhard v. State, 484 N.E.2d 45, 1985 Ind. App. LEXIS 2881 (1985).

Evidence was sufficient to support a finding that defendant engaged in "tumultuous conduct" by continuing to yell, scream, and curse after police had arrived at an apartment complex to investigate a neighborhood disturbance involving black women and white women. Whitley v. State, 553 N.E.2d 511, 1990 Ind. App. LEXIS 495 (1990).

Business owner's "picketing" of a union's booth at a convention after the union's business agent

Tumultuous Conduct. (Cont'd)

filed an unfair labor practice charge against the business was not "tumultuous conduct" as defined by IC 35-45-1-1 and therefore did not qualify as disorderly conduct under IC 35-45-1-3. Lovings v. Thomas, 805 N.E.2d 442, 2004 Ind. App. LEXIS 488 (2004).

Because a reasonable jury could only conclude that the property owner's conduct of attempting to strike city employees with a board and failure to comply with the police officers' orders to put the board down was tumultuous conduct for purposes of IC 35-45-1-1, the officers were entitled to summary judgment on the owner's false arrest claim which he brought after he was arrested for disorderly conduct pursuant to IC 35-45-1-3; because the owner could have employed other and more peaceful methods to protest the officers' actions, he was not entitled to a defense under IC 35-41-3-2(b). McConnell v. McKillip, 573 F. Supp. 2d 1090, 2008 U.S. Dist. LEXIS 59015 (2008).

Unreasonable Noise.

Shouting or yelling that is not perceived as loud by a person standing across the street would not constitute unreasonable noise. Bailey v. Andrews, 811 F.2d 366, 1987 U.S. App. LEXIS 1968 (7th Cir. Ind. 1987).

A police officer's inadmissible conclusory statements as to the manner in which the defendant was exercising his free speech rights at the time of his arrest supported the defendant's conviction for disorderly conduct, since the evidence was admitted without objection and indicated that the defendant was making "unreasonable noise" at the time he was arrested. Humphries v. State, 568 N.E.2d 1033, 1991 Ind. App. LEXIS 438 (1991).

Loud speaking inside a private apartment could be found unreasonable if it threatened the safety of injured parties by aggravating their trauma or by distracting the medical personnel tending them, or agitated witnesses and disrupted police investigations, and was annoying to others present at the scene. Whittington v. State, 669 N.E.2d 1363, 1996 Ind. LEXIS 125 (1996).

Request by hospital security officers that defendant stop making unreasonable noise was sufficient to support disorderly conduct conviction; IC 35-45-1-3 does not require that person making unreasonable noise be asked to stop by law enforcement officer. Mitchell v. State, 813 N.E.2d 422, 2004 Ind. App. LEXIS 1631 (2004).

Police officers did not have probable cause to arrest the student for disorderly conduct for "tumultuous conduct" after a report was made that the student was fighting on a bus and the police officers responded to the report; police officers could not have believed after reviewing a bus videotape that there was any indication that serious bodily injury or substantial property damage was likely to occur, although a genuine issue of material fact remained about probable cause to arrest for disorderly conduct based on the student making unreasonable noise. N.J. v. Metro. Sch. Dist. of Wash. Twp., 879 N.E.2d 1192, 2008 Ind. App. LEXIS 130 (2008).

—Standard of Review.

Where defendant's remarks were not directed toward police officer but toward a private party, defendant protested that he had not done anything and other witnesses were lying, and his statements involved the conduct of private individuals, not state action, rationality review was applied by the court in determining whether the state could reasonably conclude that defendant's expressive activity, because of its volume, was an "abuse" of the right to speak. Whittington v. State, 669 N.E.2d 1363, 1996 Ind. LEXIS 125 (1996).

—Speech.

Application of a disorderly conduct statute such as this section to speech must be limited to unprotected classes of speech, e.g. obscenity, fighting words, public nuisance speech, and incitement to imminent lawless action. Cavazos v. State, 455 N.E.2d 618, 1983 Ind. App. LEXIS 3500 (1983).

There was insufficient evidence to support a finding that defendant's telling the police officer he had a grudge and had no right to arrest her brother, calling the officer an "asshole," and continuing to debate the arrest of her brother constituted "unreasonable noise." Cavazos v. State, 455 N.E.2d 618, 1983 Ind. App. LEXIS 3500 (1983).

Defendant's obscene language directed to police officers after the arrest of his companion was of sufficient intensity to provoke a violent reaction, and therefore, the "fighting words" exception to the right to freedom of speech applied. Mesarosh v. State, 459 N.E.2d 426, 1984 Ind. App. LEXIS 2295 (1984).

Evidence supported a disorderly conduct conviction where defendant, despite requests that he cease, intentionally used constitutionally unprotected "fighting words" in referring to crowd of revellers as "fuckers", "whores", "queers", and "AIDS people", and stated that they were condemned to hell. Gilles v. State, 531 N.E.2d 220, 1988 Ind. App. LEXIS 994 (1988), cert. denied, 493 U.S. 939, 110 S. Ct. 337, 107 L. Ed. 2d 325, 1989 U.S. LEXIS 5149 (1989); Gamble v. State, 591 N.E.2d 142, 1992 Ind. App. LEXIS 637 (1992).

The language used in epithets hurled toward police constituted fighting words undeserving of constitutional protection and may constitute disorderly conduct regardless of the fact that the abusive language was not overheard by others. Brittain v. State, 565 N.E.2d 757, 1990 Ind. App. LEXIS 1762 (1990).

The defendant's conviction for disorderly conduct was supported by sufficient evidence since the words he screamed at a police officer constituted "fighting words" undeserving of constitutional protection. Robinson v. State, 588 N.E.2d 533, 1992 Ind. App. LEXIS 328 (1992).

To the extent that the "unreasonable noise" provision of subdivision (2) prohibits unreasonable noise which emanates from speech, the statute may constitutionally do so with respect to: 1) "fighting words," 2) speech inciting imminent lawless action, and 3) public nuisance speech. Of course, the unprotected speech in these categories must also constitute "unreasonable noise" before

Unreasonable Noise. (Cont'd)

—Speech. (Cont'd)
conviction is authorized under this statute. Price v. State, 600 N.E.2d 103, 1992 Ind. App. LEXIS 1434 (1992), superseded, 622 N.E.2d 954, 1993 Ind. LEXIS 183 (1993).

The "unreasonable noise" provision of subdivision (2) prohibits noise, including speech, which constitutes a public nuisance or breach of the peace. This definition encompasses noise, including unprotected speech, which is unreasonably loud under the circumstances and adequately puts citizens on notice as to what noise and speech are prohibited. It does not vest the police with unwarranted discretion to suppress speech protected by the First Amendment. The statute therefore is not unconstitutionally vague. Price v. State, 600 N.E.2d 103, 1992 Ind. App. LEXIS 1434 (1992), superseded, 622 N.E.2d 954, 1993 Ind. LEXIS 183 (1993).

Defendant's prosecution for disorderly conduct did not violate his constitutional right of free speech; evidence was sufficient to support a finding that defendant's shouting outside of clinic was unreasonably loud despite his being asked to lower his voice, and the court properly admitted the testimony of a police officer as to the volume of the defendant's speech. Borchert v. State, 621 N.E.2d 657, 1993 Ind. App. LEXIS 1225 (1993).

Cited:
Census Federal Credit Union v. Wann, 403 N.E.2d 348, 1980 Ind. App. LEXIS 1407 (1980); State v. Culp, 433 N.E.2d 823, 1982 Ind. App. LEXIS 1137 (1982); Cronk v. State, 443 N.E.2d 882, 1983 Ind. App. LEXIS 2509 (1983); Gomez v. Adams, 462 N.E.2d 212, 1984 Ind. App. LEXIS 2497 (1984); Martin v. State, 499 N.E.2d 273, 1986 Ind. App. LEXIS 3084 (1986); Committee for Sane Nuclear Policy/Indianapolis Chapter v. Indianapolis, 668 F. Supp. 1211, 1987 U.S. Dist. LEXIS 8003 (S.D. Ind. 1987); Fox v. Hawkins, 594 N.E.2d 493, 1992 Ind. App. LEXIS 1010 (1992); Hanna v. State, 726 N.E.2d 384, 2000 Ind. App. LEXIS 511 (2000); Dennis v. State, 736 N.E.2d 300, 2000 Ind. App. LEXIS 1576 (2000); State v. Bilbrey, 743 N.E.2d 796, 2001 Ind. App. LEXIS 370 (2001); A.E.B. v. State, 756 N.E.2d 536, 2001 Ind. App. LEXIS 1742 (2001); Gonzalez v. Kokot, 314 F.3d 311, 2002 U.S. App. LEXIS 26843 (7th Cir. Ind. 2002); Lutz v. City of Indianapolis, 820 N.E.2d 766, 2005 Ind. App. LEXIS 34 (2005).

RESEARCH REFERENCES

Indiana Law Review.
Recent Developments in Criminal Law and Procedure, 27 Ind. L. Rev. 959 (1994).
Recent Developments Under the Indiana Constitution, 28 Ind. L. Rev. 1067 (1995).
Finding Rest in Peace and Not in Speech:The Government's Interest in Privacy Protection in and Around Funerals, 41 Ind. L. Rev. 383 (2008).

Res Gestae.
Criminal Justice Notes, 37 Res Gestae 333 (1994).

Collateral References.
Participation of student in demonstration on or near campus as warranting imposition of criminal liability for breach of peace, disorderly conduct, trespass, unlawful assembly, or similar offense. 32 A.L.R.3d 551.
Vagueness as invalidating statutes or ordinances dealing with disorderly persons or conduct. 12 A.L.R.3d 1448.
Validity, construction, and operation of Federal disorderly conduct regulation (36 C.F.R. § 2.34). 180 A.L.R. Fed. 637.

35-45-1-4. Desecration of flag of United States.

(a) A person who knowingly or intentionally mutilates, defaces, burns, or tramples any United States flag, standard, or ensign commits flag desecration, a Class A misdemeanor.

(b) This section does not apply to a person who disposes of a flag in accordance with 36 U.S.C. 176(k).

History.
IC 35-45-1-4, as added by Acts 1977, P.L.26, § 22; P.L.163-1990, § 1.

Cross References.
Code of rules and patriotic customs pertaining to the display and use of the flag of the United States, the playing of the national anthem, and the pledge of allegiance. 36 U.S.C.S. §§ 170-186.
Penalties for misdemeanors, IC 35-50-1, IC 35-50-3, IC 35-50-5-2.

NOTES TO DECISIONS

ANALYSIS

Enjoining Prosecution.
Sentence.

Enjoining Prosecution.
A federal court would not enjoin the prosecution of members of a religious sect known as "Jehovah's Witnesses" under prior section, the constitutionality of which had been attacked in the absence of any showing of "exceptional circumstances" and "great and immediate danger of irreparable loss." Trent v. Hunt, 39 F. Supp. 373, 1941 U.S. Dist.

Enjoining Prosecution. (Cont'd)
LEXIS 3217 (D. Ind. 1941), aff'd, 314 U.S. 573, 62 S. Ct. 115, 86 L. Ed. 465, 1941 U.S. LEXIS 259 (1941).

Demonstrator who had painted peace symbol on American flag she owned lacked standing to seek injunctive relief from possible prosecution under Indiana's flag desecration statute, IC 35-45-1-4, since mere existence of flag desecration statute did not establish threat of prosecution sufficiently great to allow her to sue. Lawson v. Hill, 368 F.3d 955, 2004 U.S. App. LEXIS 10158 (7th Cir. Ind. 2004).

Sentence.
Since the former flag desecration statute had a misdemeanor penalty, a verdict of guilty in a prosecution thereunder assessing the penalty of a felony was contrary to law. McKee v. State, 219 Ind. 247, 37 N.E.2d 940, 1941 Ind. LEXIS 234 (1941).

CHAPTER 2

OFFENSES RELATING TO COMMUNICATIONS

35-45-2-1. Intimidation.

(a) A person who communicates a threat to another person, with the intent:
  (1) that the other person engage in conduct against the other person's will;
  (2) that the other person be placed in fear of retaliation for a prior lawful act; or
  (3) of causing:
    (A) a dwelling, a building, or another structure; or
    (B) a vehicle;
  to be evacuated;
commits intimidation, a Class A misdemeanor.
(b) However, the offense is a:
  (1) Class D felony if:
    (A) the threat is to commit a forcible felony;
    (B) the person to whom the threat is communicated:
      (i) is a law enforcement officer;
      (ii) is a judge or bailiff of any court;
      (iii) is a witness (or the spouse or child of a witness) in any pending criminal proceeding against the person making the threat;
      (iv) is an employee of a school corporation;
      (v) is a community policing volunteer;
      (vi) is an employee of a court;
      (vii) is an employee of a probation department; or
      (viii) is an employee of a community corrections program.
    (C) the person has a prior unrelated conviction for an offense under this section concerning the same victim; or
    (D) the threat is communicated using property, including electronic equipment or systems, of a school corporation or other governmental entity; and
  (2) Class C felony if, while committing it, the person draws or uses a deadly weapon.
(c) "Threat" means an expression, by words or action, of an intention to:
  (1) unlawfully injure the person threatened or another person, or damage property;
  (2) unlawfully subject a person to physical confinement or restraint;
  (3) commit a crime;
  (4) unlawfully withhold official action, or cause such withholding;

(5) unlawfully withhold testimony or information with respect to another person's legal claim or defense, except for a reasonable claim for witness fees or expenses;

(6) expose the person threatened to hatred, contempt, disgrace, or ridicule;

(7) falsely harm the credit or business reputation of the person threatened; or

(8) cause the evacuation of a dwelling, a building, another structure, or a vehicle.

History.
IC 35-45-2-1, as added by Acts 1976, P.L.148, § 5; 1977, P.L.340, § 71; 1981, P.L.300, § 3; P.L.183-1984, § 6; P.L.325-1985, § 1; P.L.164-1993, § 12; P.L.242-1993, § 3; P.L.1-1994, § 169; P.L.241-2001, § 3; P.L.175-2003, § 3; P.L.3-2006, § 2.

Cross References.
Defenses relating to culpability, IC 35-41-3-1 — IC 35-41-3-10.
Penalties for felonies, IC 35-50-1, IC 35-50-2, IC 35-50-5-2.
Penalties for misdemeanors, IC 35-50-1, IC 35-50-3, IC 35-50-5-2.

NOTES TO DECISIONS

ANALYSIS

Action Constituting Blackmail.
Defense of Provocation.
Distinguished from Harassment.
Double Jeopardy.
Elements.
—Blackmail.
—Intimidation.
—Retaliation for Prior Lawful Act.
Evidence.
—Admissibility.
—Defendant's Testimony.
—Insufficient.
—Intent.
—Prejudice.
—Sufficient.
Harmless Error.
Indictment or Information.
—Conspiracy.
Instructions.
Intimidation.
Jurisdiction.
Lesser Included Offenses.
Racketeering.
—Civil Liability.
Right to Bear Arms.
Sentence.
Threats.
Use of Deadly Weapon.

Action Constituting Blackmail.
Threats to prosecute for a crime in order to coerce the payment of a just debt was not within the statute. State v. Hammond, 80 Ind. 80, 1881 Ind. LEXIS 863 (1881).

Threat of injury to person or property included any threat to invade any right for invasion of which an action in damages would have lain for injury to person or property. Meek v. State, 205 Ind. 102, 185 N.E. 899, 1933 Ind. LEXIS 71 (1933).

Where accused wrote a letter to a widow threatening to remove the body of her deceased husband from its grave unless money was given to the writer, such act constituted blackmail. Meek v. State, 205 Ind. 102, 185 N.E. 899, 1933 Ind. LEXIS 71 (1933).

Where person knowingly demanded by threat, control over property of owner, a crime was committed, even if person did not carry out threat. Vawter v. State, 258 Ind. 168, 279 N.E.2d 805, 1972 Ind. LEXIS 540 (1972), cert. denied, 410 U.S. 969, 93 S. Ct. 1449, 35 L. Ed. 2d 705, 1973 U.S. LEXIS 3181 (1973).

Defense of Provocation.
Even though the victim's police report was "probably actionable" as a false report, her exaggeration of the facts did not excuse defendant from threatening to kill her in retaliation for petitioning the authorities for protection from him, and the evidence was sufficient to sustain his conviction for intimidation. Johnson v. State, 544 N.E.2d 164, 1989 Ind. App. LEXIS 1163 (1989).

Distinguished from Harassment.
A comparison of this section and IC 35-45-2-2 shows that intimidation requires proof of an additional fact which harassment does not, that is, the perpetrator entertains the intent that the other person be placed in fear of retaliation for a prior lawful act. A comparison further shows that harassment requires proof of an additional fact which intimidation does not, that is, the perpetrator entertains the intent to harass, annoy, or alarm the other person. Intimidation and harassment are two offenses under the same elements test, and the legislature intended that cumulative punishments be allowed for convictions under those statutes in a single trial. Haynes v. State, 656 N.E.2d 505, 1995 Ind. App. LEXIS 1318 (1995).

Double Jeopardy.
Enhanced charges for intimidation and battery violated the double jeopardy prohibition, where the same use of a knife was utilized to enhance both charges. Lyles v. State, 576 N.E.2d 1344, 1991 Ind. App. LEXIS 1400 (1991).

Defendant who committed four distinct acts of intimidation against three victims was not subjected to double jeopardy by being convicted and sentenced for each separate act. Owens v. State, 659 N.E.2d 466, 1995 Ind. LEXIS 181 (1995).

Double Jeopardy. (Cont'd)

Where the defendant demonstrated a reasonable possibility that the jury used the same evidentiary facts to establish criminal confinement as a Class B felony as it did to establish the essential elements of intimidation as a Class C felony, the resulting violation of the state double jeopardy clause required the vacation of the conviction and sentence for intimidation. McIntire v. State, 717 N.E.2d 96, 1999 Ind. LEXIS 874 (1999).

Double jeopardy protections were not implicated by an intimidation conviction because the evidence that supported the charge and conviction of intimidation, which was threatening the victim while drawing a deadly weapon, was not the same evidence that supported the charges and convictions of confinement and battery, which was the act of placing the rope around the victim's neck. Stafford v. State, 736 N.E.2d 326, 2000 Ind. App. LEXIS 1585 (2000).

There was no double jeopardy under Ind. Const. art. 1, § 14 when defendant was convicted of Class B felony attempted aggravated battery, Class C felony intimidation, and Class D felony criminal recklessness. The intimidation charge involved defendant brandishing a gun while threatening to kill his neighbor; the battery charge involved the separate and distinct act of defendant firing at the neighbor; and the recklessness charge was based on defendant's shooting in the direction of the neighbor's home, endangering its occupants. Rawson v. State, 865 N.E.2d 1049, 2007 Ind. App. LEXIS 948 (2007).

Convictions for false reporting and intimidation were vacated due to double jeopardy violation because they were based on acts that were so compressed in terms of time, place, singleness of purpose, and continuation of action as to constitute a single transaction; the false reporting and intimidation charges were based on diversionary tactics used to facilitate robbery. Buchanan v. State, — N.E.2d —, 2009 Ind. App. LEXIS 72 (2009).

Elements.

—Blackmail.

The crime of blackmail consists in extorting money or valuables from a person by threatening to expose his crimes or immoralities. Green v. State, 157 Ind. 101, 60 N.E. 941, 1901 Ind. LEXIS 128 (1901); Eacock v. State, 169 Ind. 488, 82 N.E. 1039, 1907 Ind. LEXIS 81 (1907).

The thing intended to be extorted or gained is an essential element of the crime of blackmail. McNamara v. State, 203 Ind. 596, 181 N.E. 512, 1932 Ind. LEXIS 83 (1932).

—Intimidation.

The elements of the offense of intimidation are: (1) communicating a threat, (2) to another person, (3) with the intent that the other person engage in conduct against his will. Bolen v. State, 430 N.E.2d 398, 1982 Ind. App. LEXIS 1056 (1982).

The elements of the offense of intimidation are: (1) communicating a threat, (2) to another person, (3) with the intent that the other person either engage in conduct against his will or be placed in

fear of retaliation for a prior lawful act. Hyde v. State, 525 N.E.2d 627, 1988 Ind. App. LEXIS 497 (1988), superseded, 531 N.E.2d 472, 1988 Ind. LEXIS 331 (1988).

The victim's state of mind is not an element of the crime of intimidation. Hyde v. State, 525 N.E.2d 627, 1988 Ind. App. LEXIS 497 (1988), superseded, 531 N.E.2d 472, 1988 Ind. LEXIS 331 (1988).

Threatening someone with harm unless that person remains silent constitutes a threat to that person with the intent that he or she engage in conduct against his or her will. Johnson v. State, 717 N.E.2d 887, 1999 Ind. App. LEXIS 1791 (1999).

Defendant's threatening to "get" the police officer and his family after being arrested, could reasonably be concluded to be a threat with the intent to place the officer in fear of retaliation for arresting the defendant. Townsend v. State, 753 N.E.2d 88, 2001 Ind. App. LEXIS 1330 (2001).

—Retaliation for Prior Lawful Act.

In order to sustain a conviction under the intimidation statute, IC 35-45-2-1, the state must prove beyond a reasonable doubt that the accused intended to place the victim in fear of retaliation for a prior lawful act, and when the state seeks to have a juvenile adjudicated a delinquent for committing an act that would be a crime if committed by an adult, the state must prove every element of that crime beyond a reasonable doubt. H.J. v. State, 746 N.E.2d 400, 2001 Ind. App. LEXIS 636 (2001).

Evidence.

—Admissibility.

In a prosecution for blackmail under former Acts 1905, ch. 169, § 370, permitting the sheriff to name the person who came with defendant to the place where the money was deposited was held not error, where the sheriff stated that he did not know the other person's name at the time, but later found out who he was. Meek v. State, 205 Ind. 102, 185 N.E. 899, 1933 Ind. LEXIS 71 (1933).

In prosecution for conspiracy to blackmail a person named, evidence of conversations in which defendant participated, tending to prove threats against other persons, was admissible as showing part of a general scheme or plan, although such evidence incidentally tended to prove other crimes. Webster v. State, 206 Ind. 431, 190 N.E. 52, 1934 Ind. LEXIS 187 (1934).

Exhibits containing informations and statement of person who witnessed offenses charged in the informations were relevant to the prosecution of defendant for intimidation of the person who witnessed the other offenses, to show intent and motive. Williams v. State, 677 N.E.2d 1077, 1997 Ind. App. LEXIS 176 (1997).

At defendant's trial for intimidation under IC 35-45-2-1, testimony by defendant's wife and another man that they were afraid of defendant was admissible and did not violate Evid. R. 404(b); testimony did not concern evidence of defendant's prior crimes, wrongs, or acts but at most showed that defendant had emotionally, though not physi-

Evidence. (Cont'd)

—Admissibility. (Cont'd)
cally, abused his wife. Earlywine v. State, 847 N.E.2d 1011, 2006 Ind. App. LEXIS 926 (2006).

Defendant's statement to the victim that defendant had committed several murders in the past and that defendant was going to kill the victim was properly admitted as to the intimidation charge where the trial court admonished the jury that the evidence was only to show whether the victim was in fear. Frye v. State, 850 N.E.2d 951, 2006 Ind. App. LEXIS 1357 (2006).

—Defendant's Testimony.
Although the defendant testified that his actions were in jest, the jury was entitled to reject his testimony. Sayles v. State, 513 N.E.2d 183, 1987 Ind. App. LEXIS 3087 (1987).

—Insufficient.
Where state failed to allege or prove that defendant threatened victim in order to place her in fear of retaliation for a prior lawful act, defendant's conviction and sentence for intimidation was vacated. Casey v. State, 676 N.E.2d 1069, 1997 Ind. App. LEXIS 50 (1997).

Facts, which showed defendant raised his handgun to the window of his automobile for another driver to view, but the weapon was not pointed at the other driver or his vehicle, were insufficient to convict defendant of intimidation. Gaddis v. State, 680 N.E.2d 860, 1997 Ind. App. LEXIS 529 (1997).

Where no evidence on the record or any reasonable inference drawn therefrom supported the assertion that the defendant threatened a police officer with a revolver with an intent to place that officer in fear of retaliation for preparing to arrest the defendant, but rather supported the inference that the officer did not intend to arrest him, the evidence was insufficient to support a conviction for intimidation. VanMatre v. State, 714 N.E.2d 655, 1999 Ind. App. LEXIS 730 (1999).

Evidence was insufficient to support a conviction under this section, where the defendant student authored a document which described violent acts to be inflicted upon another student, and was intercepted by school personnel and eventually delivered to the student named in the document, since the defendant did not know that the document would be intercepted and transmitted through various intermediaries to the other student. J.T. v. State, 718 N.E.2d 1119, 1999 Ind. App. LEXIS 1840 (1999).

Defendant did not communicate a "threat" within the meaning of the intimidation statute by merely lifting his jacket to show the off-duty police officer that he was in possession of a handgun. Johnson v. State, 725 N.E.2d 984, 2000 Ind. App. LEXIS 436 (2000), transfer granted, 741 N.E.2d 1254, 2000 Ind. LEXIS 910 (2000), superseded, 743 N.E.2d 755, 2001 Ind. LEXIS 211 (2001).

Insufficient evidence supported defendant's Class C felony conviction of intimidation since there was no evidence that defendant threatened victim while actually possessing knife as required by IC 35-45-2-1(b)(2); testimony indicated that defendant picked up knife after threatening victim. Hall v. State, 831 N.E.2d 823, 2005 Ind. App. LEXIS 1363 (2005), vacated in part, 837 N.E.2d 159, 2005 Ind. App. LEXIS 2135 (2005).

There was insufficient evidence for an intimidation conviction under IC 35-45-2-1. Defendant's threat to shoot his neighbor's son-in-law if he came onto defendant's property was aimed at a future trespass, not a prior lawful act; furthermore, there was insufficient evidence that defendant threatened the son-in-law for the prior lawful act of arguing, as defendant remained on his property, the jury had acquitted him of pointing a gun, the son-in-law was the first to engage in the yelling, and defendant was the first to call the police. Ransley v. State, 850 N.E.2d 443, 2006 Ind. App. LEXIS 1341 (2006).

—Intent.
Where defendant communicated with the police officers and followed their directions to leave the premises, he also struggled with the two officers before being handcuffed and exerted considerable physical force while doing so, he did not dispute that he made threats to both officers or that he was intoxicated, and he repeatedly threatened to kill them after being arrested, and then described in great detail how he would kill them, sufficient evidence existed for the trier of fact to determine that his mental faculties were not impaired by his intoxication when he made the threats, and that he intended to place the officers in fear of retaliation for arresting him; sufficient evidence of probative value, therefore, existed to support the conviction for two counts of intimidation. Hendrix v. State, 615 N.E.2d 483, 1993 Ind. App. LEXIS 659 (1993).

—Prejudice.
In prosecution of defendant for intimidation, admission of informations for other offenses witnessed by person defendant was accused of intimidating was error, and focused the jury's attention on defendant's character rather than the conduct for which he was being prosecuted, warranting reversal of his conviction for intimidation. Williams v. State, 677 N.E.2d 1077, 1997 Ind. App. LEXIS 176 (1997).

—Sufficient.
Evidence was sufficient to support defendant's conviction for intimidation, where the victim viewed his telephoned statements as a true threat after the defendant had damaged her car, tried to drive her off the road, and threatened to kill her. Brehm v. State, 558 N.E.2d 906, 588 N.E.2d 906, 1990 Ind. App. LEXIS 1119 (1990).

Where the evidence revealed that defendant communicated a threat to victim with the intent that victim engage in conduct against her will, allowing defendant into restaurant, and victim testified at trial that defendant's threats put her in fear for her life, the state presented sufficient evidence to support every material element of intimidation, as a Class A misdemeanor, beyond a reasonable doubt. Crose v. State, 650 N.E.2d 1187, 1995 Ind. App. LEXIS 603 (1995).

Evidence supported conviction for intimidation, where defendant used print, radio and television

Evidence. (Cont'd)

—Sufficient. (Cont'd)
media to communicate threats that he knew or had good reason to believe would reach county prosecutor and another person, with the intent to influence the prosecutor's conduct as a law enforcement officer against his will and to place the other person in fear of retaliation for having supported prosecutor's request for death penalty against murder suspects, including defendant's son. Ajabu v. State, 677 N.E.2d 1035, 1997 Ind. App. LEXIS 80 (1997).

Evidence presented by state that defendant approached witness and warned him that he better not testify in prosecution of defendant for other offenses was sufficient to allow jury to conclude defendant was guilty of intimidation, and for case to be remanded for retrial without violation of the protections afforded by the double jeopardy clause. Williams v. State, 677 N.E.2d 1077, 1997 Ind. App. LEXIS 176 (1997).

Where the record supported the state's contention that the defendant threatened to retaliate against a witness for that witness' prior and continuing legal act of participating as a witness against the defendant with regard to an alleged battery, there was sufficient evidence for the trier of fact to infer, beyond a reasonable doubt, that the defendant was guilty of the offense of intimidation. Graham v. State, 713 N.E.2d 309, 1999 Ind. App. LEXIS 950 (1999).

The trial court's conclusion that the state failed to prove an element of the offense of public intoxication did not render the arrest an unlawful act within the meaning of this section, and the evidence was sufficient to support the conviction. Dennis v. State, 736 N.E.2d 300, 2000 Ind. App. LEXIS 1576 (2000).

Where defendant made two obscene remarks and then displayed a firearm and told the off-duty, out-of-uniform police officer, "don't even think it," the evidence was sufficient for a trier of fact to conclude that defendant communicated a threat within the meaning of the intimidation statute. Johnson v. State, 743 N.E.2d 755, 2001 Ind. LEXIS 211 (2001).

There was sufficient evidence for the trier of fact to infer, beyond a reasonable doubt, that the high school juvenile threatened a second juvenile with the intent of placing her in fear due to the second juvenile's report of the alleged existence of a list of people at the school that the first juvenile and a friend were to kill on the anniversary of the Columbine High School shooting. H.J. v. State, 746 N.E.2d 400, 2001 Ind. App. LEXIS 636 (2001).

Evidence was sufficient to convict defendant of Class D felony intimidation where the State proved that the defendant communicated a threat to the victim with the intent to place the victim in fear of retaliation for a prior lawful act and where the defendant's threat was to commit a forcible felony, i.e., that he was going to "get" the victim. Norris v. State, 755 N.E.2d 190, 2001 Ind. App. LEXIS 1285 (2001).

Evidence was sufficient to convict defendant of Class C felony intimidation where the State proved that the defendant communicated a threat to the victim with the intent to make the victim engage in conduct against his will by threatening to take his children from the care of their mother, who was staying with the victim, and that during the incident the defendant drew a gun. Norris v. State, 755 N.E.2d 190, 2001 Ind. App. LEXIS 1285 (2001).

Evidence that a defendant resisted a deputy who was transporting him to jail and that the defendant repeatedly told the deputy that he "was going to get" him and that the deputy had "better watch his back" was sufficient to establish the crime of intimidation because it showed that the defendant intended to place the deputy in fear due to his lawful act of transporting the defendant to jail; appellate court nevertheless reversed defendant's in absentia conviction because the record did not show that the defendant made a knowing and intelligent waiver of his right to counsel. Slayton v. State, 755 N.E.2d 232, 2001 Ind. App. LEXIS 1613 (2001).

Defendant committed the act of intimidation where defendant and the victim's former wife drove up beside the victim and defendant brandished a gun while threatening the victim regarding the victim's child visitation rights. Jones v. State, 775 N.E.2d 322, 2002 Ind. App. LEXIS 1494 (2002).

Evidence was sufficient to convict defendant of offenses of intimidation and stalking based on messages sent by defendant where jury could have reasonably concluded that more than one of messages was threatening and that messages amounted to impermissible contact that would cause a reasonable person emotional distress. Smith v. State, 802 N.E.2d 948, 2004 Ind. App. LEXIS 160 (2004).

Where defendant's wife had obtained protective order against him, defendant's statement to domestic violence advocate that "things were not going to be real pretty" if she continued to work with his wife was sufficient to support intimidation conviction. Huber v. State, 805 N.E.2d 887, 2004 Ind. App. LEXIS 573 (2004).

Where there was insufficient evidence to convict defendant of Class C felony intimidation, conviction of lesser included offense of Class A misdemeanor intimidation was appropriate; evidence indicated that defendant communicated threat with intent that victim fear retaliation for prior lawful act, which prior lawful act was that victim told defendant to leave her residence. Hall v. State, 831 N.E.2d 823, 2005 Ind. App. LEXIS 1363 (2005), vacated in part, 837 N.E.2d 159, 2005 Ind. App. LEXIS 2135 (2005).

Because defendant drew a knife immediately after he threatened to kill the victim, without any break in the chain of events, the threat and the wielding of the knife were part of one continuous transaction. Thus, the evidence was sufficient to prove that defendant drew a knife while committing intimidation against the victim, which supported his conviction as a Class C felony. Hall v. State, 837 N.E.2d 159, 2005 Ind. App. LEXIS 2135 (2005).

There was sufficient evidence that defendant, a

Evidence. (Cont'd)

—Sufficient. (Cont'd)
juvenile, communicated the threat to kill the teacher and to damage the school to find that defendant committed intimidation in violation of IC 35-45-2-1; it was reasonably probable that the threat would be brought to the threatened teacher's attention by the teacher who heard the threat, and defendant made a threat in front of a class of students. S.D. v. State, 847 N.E.2d 255, 2006 Ind. App. LEXIS 915 (2006).

Sufficient evidence existed to show that defendant communicated a threat to another man with the intent that the other man engage in conduct against his will, a violation of IC 35-45-2-1(a)(1), when defendant placed numerous phone calls to the other man's house where defendant's wife was located and told him that if defendant's wife did not come home, anyone in defendant's way would "get it." Earlywine v. State, 847 N.E.2d 1011, 2006 Ind. App. LEXIS 926 (2006).

Presiding judge appointed commissioner, in part, to hear jury trials and court trials, which was the equivalent of hearing and deciding legal matters in court; accordingly, commissioner was a "judge" withing meaning of IC 35-45-2-1 and defendant was properly convicted of intimidation for sending letters to the commissioner notifying her that he knew where she lived. Montgomery v. State, 878 N.E.2d 262, 2007 Ind. App. LEXIS 2742 (2007).

Evidence was sufficient to support defendant's intimidation as a Class D felony conviction under IC 35-45-2-1 where, although there was contradictory evidence, victim testified that she was placed in fear of retaliation for a prior lawful act. Griffith v. State, 898 N.E.2d 412, 2008 Ind. App. LEXIS 2599 (2008).

Harmless Error.
Although incorrect, references by the prosecutor and the trial court to the offense of intimidation while armed with a deadly weapon did not constitute fundamental error, where the defendant's conviction and sentence for intimidation as a Class C felony fell within the express statutory authority granted by this section and where, while the label applied to the charges may have been facially incorrect, the substance of the intimidation charges was proper. Funk v. State, 714 N.E.2d 746, 1999 Ind. App. LEXIS 1286 (1999).

Indictment or Information.
The indictment should aver to whom the threats were made. Kessler v. State, 50 Ind. 229, 1875 Ind. LEXIS 99 (1875).

The indictment need not aver that the person to whom the threats were made was innocent of the act threatened to be exposed. Kessler v. State, 50 Ind. 229, 1875 Ind. LEXIS 99 (1875); Motsinger v. State, 123 Ind. 498, 24 N.E. 342, 1890 Ind. LEXIS 234 (1890).

The thing sought to be extorted or gained cannot be pleaded in the language of the statute, where the statute is general, but the averment must descend to particulars. McNamara v. State, 203 Ind. 596, 181 N.E. 512, 1932 Ind. LEXIS 83 (1932).

—Conspiracy.
An indictment for conspiracy to levy blackmail must allege the ownership of the money or property which it was intended to extort by such conspiracy, or a sufficient excuse given for omitting such allegation. Green v. State, 157 Ind. 101, 60 N.E. 941, 1901 Ind. LEXIS 128 (1901).

Instructions.
Although it was error to instruct the jury that voluntary intoxication is a defense only for crimes that use the phrases "with intent to" or "with intention to," quoting verbatim the language of former IC 35-41-3-5(b) which has been declared void, the error was harmless, because it was clear the jury did not think defendant had been so intoxicated that he could not intend his actions because the jury also convicted the defendant of four counts of intimidation. Owens v. State, 659 N.E.2d 466, 1995 Ind. LEXIS 181 (1995).

Intimidation.
Evidence that defendant threatened to tie a woman up and to force her to perform or submit to various forms of deviate sexual conduct, and that he told her that if he ever found out that she signed statements against his brother "there would be trouble" and she "would be sorry," was sufficient to support his convictions for attempted obstruction of justice and intimidation. Long v. State, 492 N.E.2d 700, 1986 Ind. App. LEXIS 2579 (1986).

Only the defendant's intent that the plaintiff change his course of conduct is necessary to establish "intimidation." Evidence that defendant's "intimidation" or "pattern" of "intimidation" in some way damaged plaintiff would suffice to establish a submissible case under the Indiana Racketeer Influenced and Corrupt Organization statute. Raybestos Prods. Co. v. Younger, 54 F.3d 1234, 1995 U.S. App. LEXIS 7689 (7th Cir. Ind. 1995).

Employer's interference with employee's effort to obtain a position with another company was not intimidation under this section since the employer did not threaten the other company and there was no evidence of its intent to harm that company. Butts v. OCE-USA, Inc., 9 F. Supp. 2d 1007, 1998 U.S. Dist. LEXIS 8660 (S.D. Ind. 1998).

By the nature of the position, a police officer's duty includes some degree of intimidation as it is described in this section; police officers actions did not amount to intimidation, even if intimidation were a civil cause of action. Jones v. Sweeney, — F. Supp. 2d —, 2000 U.S. Dist. LEXIS 15702 (N.D. Ind. 2000).

Jurisdiction.
Indiana court had jurisdiction over a prosecution for intimidation and harassment arising out of telephone calls to an Indiana phone number which were placed in Michigan, where the messages were recorded and received in Indiana and the calls produced a result, intimidation and harassment, in Indiana. Brehm v. State, 558 N.E.2d 906, 588 N.E.2d 906, 1990 Ind. App. LEXIS 1119 (1990).

Lesser Included Offenses.

The element of intimidation which distinguishes that crime from both robbery and confinement is the verbal communication of a threat to induce compliance with the communicator's will. Wethington v. State, 560 N.E.2d 496, 1990 Ind. LEXIS 185 (1990).

Where defendant was charged with robbery and carjacking for forcing victim to sign over title to victim's car and then beating victim, intimidation and battery were not inherent lesser included offenses of robbery and carjacking. Waibel v. State, 808 N.E.2d 750, 2004 Ind. App. LEXIS 937 (2004).

Racketeering.

—Civil Liability.

To establish that a defendant's racketeering activities damaged or injured a civil plaintiff, the plaintiff must demonstrate that the defendant's actions "proximately caused" the injury. Raybestos Prods. Co. v. Younger, 54 F.3d 1234, 1995 U.S. App. LEXIS 7689 (7th Cir. Ind. 1995).

Right to Bear Arms.

The right to carry a properly licensed handgun is protected by Ind. Const., Art. 1, § 32, and the due process clause of U.S. Const., Amend. 14, and the display of a properly licensed firearm does not, in itself, constitute a threat under this section. Gaddis v. State, 680 N.E.2d 860, 1997 Ind. App. LEXIS 529 (1997).

Sentence.

Determination of the appropriate habitual offender enhancement was within the range set forth in IC 35-50-2-8 and was left to the trial court's discretion and the relevant statutes did not impose a requirement that habitual offender enhancement had to be accompanied by a statement providing explanation for the length of the enhancement; thus, the trial court did not abuse its discretion by imposing a four-and-one-half-year habitual offender enhancement on one of defendant's intimidation convictions based on prior felonies. Montgomery v. State, 878 N.E.2d 262, 2007 Ind. App. LEXIS 2742 (2007).

When defendant pleaded guilty to felony child molesting, felony neglect of a dependent, felony child exploitation, felony criminal confinement, felony battery, and three counts of felony intimidation, he properly received consecutive sentences, and his aggregate term of 71 years in prison was not inappropriate under AP. 7(B) when the heinous nature of his actions was balanced against his lack of a significant criminal history and his guilty plea; defendant meticulously planned out the hour and a half of terror he inflicted on the victim, his five-year-old grandson, by creating costumes and characters and setting up cameras; a letter written by defendant supported the assessment that defendant was minimizing his culpability; defendant had benefited from his guilty plea in that no additional charges were filed; and in light of the overwhelming evidence against him, his decision to plead guilty was a pragmatic one. Lavoie v. State, — N.E.2d —, 2009 Ind. App. LEXIS 513 (2009).

Where defendant's threat to commit a forcible felony upon defendant's wife and child was based upon the wife's miscarriage, the length of the intimidation accompanied by the wife's frantic attempts to escape for the safety of both her and her child was sufficient to merit the imposition of the advisory sentence under IC 35-45-2-1. Clara v. State, 899 N.E.2d 733, 2009 Ind. App. LEXIS 68 (2009).

Threats.

Where defendant told the owner of a coin collection that had been stolen that he would withhold information concerning such collection unless his money demands were met, such an offer constituted a threat as much as an offer to inflict physical harm. Blackwood v. State, 157 Ind. App. 286, 299 N.E.2d 622, 1973 Ind. App. LEXIS 1008 (1973).

The defendant's telephone communication to a judge that a prisoner would dismiss his civil action against the judge in exchange for being released from prison was not a "threat" within the meaning of this section. Jackson v. State, 570 N.E.2d 1344, 1991 Ind. App. LEXIS 780 (1991).

Where defendant's alleged threats were neither serious nor taken seriously, whether defendant intended that those threatened engage in conduct against their will and whether his communications to them, objectively viewed, were threats were questions of fact for the jury to decide. Owens v. State, 659 N.E.2d 466, 1995 Ind. LEXIS 181 (1995).

Use of Deadly Weapon.

Evidence showing that the defendant "reached for" or "unsnapped" his knife was sufficient for the jury to find that he used a deadly weapon to accomplish his purpose. Kuchel v. State, 570 N.E.2d 910, 1991 Ind. LEXIS 79 (1991).

Since the statute does not make it an offense to be "armed" with a deadly weapon, to the extent that the title of the information, the jury verdict forms, and the abstract of judgment all incorrectly labeled the crime as "Intimidation While Armed With A Deadly Weapon," they were in error. Funk v. State, 714 N.E.2d 746, 1999 Ind. App. LEXIS 1286 (1999).

Cited:

Evansville Book Mart, Inc. v. Indianapolis, 477 F. Supp. 128, 1979 U.S. Dist. LEXIS 9640 (S.D. Ind. 1979); Moss v. State, 433 N.E.2d 852, 1982 Ind. App. LEXIS 1155 (1982); Nation v. State, 445 N.E.2d 565, 1983 Ind. LEXIS 762 (1983); Clark v. State, 447 N.E.2d 1076, 1983 Ind. LEXIS 807 (1983); Potter v. State, 666 N.E.2d 93, 1996 Ind. App. LEXIS 753 (1996); Wright v. State, 688 N.E.2d 224, 1997 Ind. App. LEXIS 1742 (1997); Allen v. State, 725 N.E.2d 472, 2000 Ind. App. LEXIS 328 (2000); Scott v. State, 829 N.E.2d 161, 2005 Ind. App. LEXIS 1051 (2005); McMahon v. State, 856 N.E.2d 743, 2006 Ind. App. LEXIS 2333 (2006); Forgey v. State, 886 N.E.2d 16, 2008 Ind. App. LEXIS 1024 (2008).

RESEARCH REFERENCES

Indiana Law Review.
Survey: Criminal Law and Procedure: Recent Developments in Indiana Criminal Law and Procedure, 35 Ind. L. Rev. 1347 (2002).

Res Gestae.
Criminal Justice Notes 7/05: Intimidation - use of deadly weapon; close proximity to weapon insufficient, 49 (No. 3) Res Gestae 30 (2005).
Criminal Justice Notes 7/06: Intimidation--insufficient evidence, 50 (No. 3) Res Gestae 37 (2006).

Collateral References.
Admonitions against perjury or threats to prosecute potential defense witness, inducing refusal to testify, as prejudicial error. 88 A.L.R.4th 388.
Construction and application of § 2A6.1 of United States Sentencing Guidelines (USSG § 2A6.1), pertaining to sentence to be imposed for making threatening communications. 148 A.L.R. Fed. 501.

35-45-2-2. Harassment.

(a) A person who, with intent to harass, annoy, or alarm another person but with no intent of legitimate communication:

(1) makes a telephone call, whether or not a conversation ensues;

(2) communicates with a person by telegraph, mail, or other form of written communication;

(3) transmits an obscene message, or indecent or profane words, on a Citizens Radio Service channel; or

(4) uses a computer network (as defined in IC 35-43-2-3(a)) or other form of electronic communication to:

(A) communicate with a person; or

(B) transmit an obscene message or indecent or profane words to a person;

commits harassment, a Class B misdemeanor.

(b) A message is obscene if:

(1) the average person, applying contemporary community standards, finds that the dominant theme of the message, taken as a whole, appeals to the prurient interest in sex;

(2) the message refers to sexual conduct in a patently offensive way; and

(3) the message, taken as a whole, lacks serious artistic, literary, political, or scientific value.

History.
IC 35-45-2-2, as added by Acts 1976, P.L.148, § 5; 1977, P.L.340, § 72; 1977, P.L.343, § 1; 1978, P.L.82, § 4; P.L.216-1996, § 22.

Cross References.
Penalties for misdemeanors, IC 35-50-1, IC 35-50-3, IC 35-50-5-2.

NOTES TO DECISIONS

ANALYSIS

Constitutionality.
Construction.
Distinguished from Intimidation.
Evidence.
—Circumstantial Evidence.
—Insufficient.
—Intent.
—Intent of Legitimate Communication.
—Prior Acts.
—Testimony of Phone Company Employees.
Freedom of Speech.
Invasion of Privacy.
Jurisdiction.

Constitutionality.
The words "harass, annoy or alarm" and "legiti-

mate" are not unconstitutionally vague although not defined in the statute since the statute requires a specific intent. Kinney v. State, 404 N.E.2d 49, 1980 Ind. App. LEXIS 1454 (1980).

Construction.
Where statute contains the words "obscene, lewd, lascivious, filthy or indecent" in the disjunctive it implies a separate meaning to each of the words. Hott v. State, 400 N.E.2d 206, 1980 Ind. App. LEXIS 1319 (1980), cert. denied, 449 U.S. 1132, 101 S. Ct. 954, 67 L. Ed. 2d 119, 1981 U.S. LEXIS 686 (1981).

Distinguished from Intimidation.
A comparison of IC 35-45-2-1 and this section shows that intimidation requires proof of an additional fact which harassment does not, that is, the

Distinguished from Intimidation. (Cont'd)
perpetrator entertains the intent that the other
person be placed in fear of retaliation for a prior
lawful act. A comparison further shows that harassment requires proof of an additional fact which
intimidation does not, that is, the perpetrator
entertains the intent to harass, annoy, or alarm
the other person. Intimidation and harassment are
two offenses under the same elements test, and the
legislature intended that cumulative punishments
be allowed for convictions under those statutes in a
single trial. Haynes v. State, 656 N.E.2d 505, 1995
Ind. App. LEXIS 1318 (1995).

Evidence.

—Circumstantial Evidence.
Identification of a telephone caller may be based
upon circumstantial evidence. Zinn v. State, 424
N.E.2d 1058, 1981 Ind. App. LEXIS 1605 (1981).

—Insufficient.
Evidence which proved merely that the call or
calls in question originated from a telephone number assigned to defendant without other evidence
showing either that she had sole access to the use
of that line or that she had some reason or moti-
vation for making the telephone calls was insufficient to support her conviction under this section
beyond a reasonable doubt. Zinn v. State, 424
N.E.2d 1058, 1981 Ind. App. LEXIS 1605 (1981).

An imprisoned father who sent sexually explicit
letters to his daughter, with whom he had maintained a continuing incestuous relationship, was
not proven to have intended to harass, annoy, or
alarm his daughter by sending the letters, where
the evidence most favorable to the state did not
indicate that he knew, at the time of writing, that
the letters upset her or that she wished for the
letters to cease. Schnitz v. State, 475 N.E.2d 59,
1985 Ind. App. LEXIS 2236 (1985).

Evidence was insufficient to support defendant's
conviction of harassment, based on one phone call
to his former employer, where his request, made to
the employer's wife, to speak to "diaper rash face
Charlie," although discourteous, was itself a legitimate communication. Leuteritz v. State, 534
N.E.2d 265, 1989 Ind. App. LEXIS 107 (1989).

Evidence was insufficient to support a conviction
under this section, where the defendant student
authored a document which described violent acts
to be inflicted upon another student, and it was
intercepted by school personnel and eventually
delivered to the student named in the document,
since the defendant did not know that the document would be intercepted and transmitted
through various intermediaries to the other student. J.T. v. State, 718 N.E.2d 1119, 1999 Ind. App.
LEXIS 1840 (1999).

State failed to prove that appellant juvenile's
postings on a private page of a popular Internet
site were made with the expectation that the
principal they focused on would actually learn of
them or see them; therefore, adjudicating appellant delinquent on the basis that the postings
constituted harassment was error. A.B. v. State,
885 N.E.2d 1223, 2008 Ind. LEXIS 363 (2008).

As affirmative evidence showed that the postings appellant juvenile made on a public group
page of a popular Internet site were a legitimate
communication of appellant's anger over disciplinary action taken against a friend by a school
principal, state failed to prove that appellant had
violated IC 35-45-2-2(a)(4) with regard to the postings. A.B. v. State, 885 N.E.2d 1223, 2008 Ind.
LEXIS 363 (2008).

—Intent.
Where the evidence revealed that defendant
persisted in undesired communication with victims despite their protests, whether defendant's
eccentricity so impaired his thinking that he did
not intend to harass the victims was a question
reserved for the trier of fact; the jury determined
that the state proved each element of the crime of
harassment, including the intent element, beyond
a reasonable doubt. Crose v. State, 650 N.E.2d
1187, 1995 Ind. App. LEXIS 603 (1995).

Where defendant, ignoring permanent protective order obtained by victim, began making numerous telephone calls to victim, which were sexually explicit and included threats against victim,
the evidence was sufficient to support trial court's
conclusion defendant had the intent to harass,
annoy or alarm victim, and had no intent of legitimate conversation. Burton v. State, 665 N.E.2d
924, 1996 Ind. App. LEXIS 718 (1996).

—Intent of Legitimate Communication.
Where evidence was presented to establish that
defendant made phone calls which annoyed and
harassed the complaining witness and no personal
or business transactions occurred during those
phone calls court could reasonably conclude that
no intent of legitimate communication existed.
Kinney v. State, 404 N.E.2d 49, 1980 Ind. App.
LEXIS 1454 (1980).

A finding that "no intent of legitimate communication existed," is a factual determination which
will be disturbed only upon a showing that no
substantial evidence of probative value exists from
which the trier of fact could reasonably infer the
defendant was guilty beyond a reasonable doubt.
Brehm v. State, 558 N.E.2d 906, 588 N.E.2d 906,
1990 Ind. App. LEXIS 1119 (1990).

—Prior Acts.
Prior misconduct evidence to prove defendant's
intent was properly introduced where defendant
put her intent at issue by stating in her opening
statement the issue was whether or not she made
telephone call with the intent to annoy or harass
witness and whether or not she intended legitimate communication. Christian-Hornaday v.
State, 649 N.E.2d 669, 1995 Ind. App. LEXIS 433
(1995).

Prior phone calls were similar enough to the
calls for which defendant was charged, and occurring within one month of the charged conduct,
were close enough in time to the charged conduct
to be genuinely relevant and admissible under
Rules Evid. R. 403 and Evid. R. 404. Christian-
Hornaday v. State, 649 N.E.2d 669, 1995 Ind. App.
LEXIS 433 (1995).

Probative value of prior misconduct evidence

Evidence. (Cont'd)

—Prior Acts. (Cont'd)
outweighed the danger of unfair prejudice where it lent credence to witness's story because prior phone calls contained many of the details found in calls for which defendant was charged, evidence of the prior telephone calls was highly probative because there were no witnesses to the calls, and any potential prejudice was minimized by the final jury instructions. Christian-Hornaday v. State, 649 N.E.2d 669, 1995 Ind. App. LEXIS 433 (1995).

—Testimony of Phone Company Employees.
The fact that telephone company employee when testifying gave wrong number as the one on which the dial number recorder was installed was not fatal to the state's case where the exhibits of the actual rolls of tape showed the correct number. Kinney v. State, 404 N.E.2d 49, 1980 Ind. App. LEXIS 1454 (1980).

Freedom of Speech.
Juvenile's delinquency adjudication for harassment, which arose out of a posting the juvenile placed on a schoolmate's personal internet web page, was reversed based on Ind. Const. art. 1, § 9 free speech considerations; the adjudication under the harassment statute restricted an expressive activity, and the speech involved -- criticism of principal's body piercing policy -- was political speech protected that was protected under the state constitution. A.B. v. State, 863 N.E.2d 1212, 2007 Ind. App. LEXIS 694 (2007), transfer granted, 878 N.E.2d 212, 2007 Ind. LEXIS 883 (2007).

Invasion of Privacy.
Where chief of police and prosecuting attorney were called at their homes at 11 o'clock at night and indecent language was used there was an invasion of a substantial interest in privacy and such action was not protected by U.S. Const., Amend. 1. Hott v. State, 400 N.E.2d 206, 1980 Ind. App. LEXIS 1319 (1980), cert. denied, 449 U.S. 1132, 101 S. Ct. 954, 67 L. Ed. 2d 119, 1981 U.S. LEXIS 686 (1981).

Jurisdiction.
Indiana court had jurisdiction over a prosecution for intimidation and harassment arising out of telephone calls to an Indiana phone number which were placed in Michigan, where the messages were recorded and received in Indiana and the calls produced a result, intimidation and harassment, in Indiana. Brehm v. State, 558 N.E.2d 906, 588 N.E.2d 906, 1990 Ind. App. LEXIS 1119 (1990).

RESEARCH REFERENCES

Collateral References.
Telephone calls as nuisance. 53 A.L.R.4th 1153.

35-45-2-3. Unlawful use of a party line or citizens radio service channel.

(a) A person who knowingly or intentionally:

(1) Refuses to yield a party line upon request by another person who states that he wishes to make an emergency call from a telephone on that party line;

(2) Refuses to yield a Citizens Radio Service channel upon request by another person who states that he wishes to make an emergency call on that channel; or

(3) Obtains the use of a party line or Citizens Radio Service channel by falsely stating that he wishes to make an emergency call;
commits unlawful use of a communications medium, a Class B misdemeanor.

(b) "Party line" means a common telephone line for two (2) or more subscribers.

(c) "Emergency call" means a telephone call or radio message in which the caller or sender reasonably believes that a human being or property is in jeopardy and that prompt summoning of aid is essential.

History.
IC 35-45-2-3, as added by Acts 1976, P.L.148, § 5; 1977, P.L.340, § 73; 1977, P.L.343, § 2.

Cross References.
Penalties for misdemeanors, IC 35-50-1, IC 35-50-3, IC 35-50-5-2.

35-45-2-4. Unlawful disclosure.

(a) This section does not apply to an employee who discloses information under IC 35-33.5.

(b) An employee of a telegraph company who knowingly or intentionally discloses the contents of a message sent or received, to a person other than a sender or receiver or authorized agent of either, commits unlawful disclosure, a Class A infraction.

(c) An employee of a telephone company who knowingly or intentionally discloses the contents of a conversation over a line of the company commits unlawful disclosure, a Class A infraction.

History.
IC 35-45-2-4, as added by Acts 1977, P.L.26, § 23; P.L.161-1990, § 4.

Cross References.
Infraction and ordinance violation enforcement proceedings, IC 34-28-5.

RESEARCH REFERENCES

Collateral References.
Search and seizure of telephone company records pertaining to subscriber as violation of subscriber's constitutional rights. 76 A.L.R.4th 536.

35-45-2-5. Interference with the reporting of a crime.

A person who, with the intent to commit, conceal, or aid in the commission of a crime, knowingly or intentionally interferes with or prevents an individual from:
(1) using a 911 emergency telephone system;
(2) obtaining medical assistance; or
(3) making a report to a law enforcement officer;
commits interference with the reporting of a crime, a Class A misdemeanor.

History.
P.L.71-2002, § 1.

Cross References.
Penalties for misdemeanors, IC 35-50-1, IC 35-50-3, IC 35-50-5-2.

NOTES TO DECISIONS

ANALYSIS

Evidence.
—Sufficient.

Evidence.

—Sufficient.
Victim's testimony that when she was trying to call 911, defendant pushed her against the back door, yelled at her, and tried to take her phone, and that, when she ran into the living room to call 911, defendant followed her and pushed her over the arm of the sofa, that she was unable to call 911 because defendant was lying on top of her, holding her arm, and pulling her hair, supported the conviction of interference with the reporting of a crime. Mathis v. State, 859 N.E.2d 1275, 2007 Ind. App. LEXIS 32 (2007).

CHAPTER 3

POISONING PUBLIC WATER — LITTERING

35-45-3-1. [Repealed.]

Compiler's Notes.
This section, concerning poisoning public water, was repealed by P.L.137-2007, § 37, effective July 1, 2007.

35-45-3-2. Littering.

(a) A person who recklessly, knowingly, or intentionally places or leaves refuse on property of another person, except in a container provided for refuse, commits littering, a Class B infraction. However, the offense is a Class A infraction if the refuse is placed or left in, on, or within one hundred (100) feet of a body of water that is under the jurisdiction of the:

(1) department of natural resources; or

(2) United States Army Corps of Engineers.

Notwithstanding IC 34-28-5-4(a), a judgment of not more than one thousand dollars ($1,000) shall be imposed for each Class A infraction committed under this section.

(b) "Refuse" includes solid and semisolid wastes, dead animals, and offal.

(c) Evidence that littering was committed from a moving vehicle other than a public conveyance constitutes prima facie evidence that it was committed by the operator of that vehicle.

History.
IC 35-45-3-2, as added by Acts 1976, P.L. 148, § 5; 1977, P.L.340, § 75; P.L.155-1985, § 2; P.L.137-2007, § 36, emergency eff. July 1, 2007; P.L.231-2007, § 4, emergency eff. July 1, 2007.

Cross References.
Infraction and ordinance violation enforcement proceedings, IC 34-28-5.

NOTES TO DECISIONS

In General.
Fact that utility company unloaded poles on shoulder of highway did not violate statute making it a misdemeanor to dump wood or logs upon public highway. Copeland v. Public Service Co., 123 Ind. App. 345, 108 N.E.2d 273, 1952 Ind. App. LEXIS 215 (1952), superseded by statute as stated in, Carter v. Indianapolis Power & Light Co., 837 N.E.2d 509, 2005 Ind. App. LEXIS 2129 (2005).

35-45-3-3. Throwing burning material from moving motor vehicle.

A person who throws from a moving motor vehicle:

(1) a lighted cigarette, cigar, or match; or

(2) other burning material;

commits a Class A infraction.

History.
P.L.35-2002, § 1.

Cross References.
Infraction and ordinance violation enforcement proceedings, IC 34-28-5.

CHAPTER 4

PUBLIC INDECENCY — PROSTITUTION

35-45-4-1. Public indecency — Indecent exposure.

(a) A person who knowingly or intentionally, in a public place:

(1) engages in sexual intercourse;

(2) engages in deviate sexual conduct;

(3) appears in a state of nudity with the intent to arouse the sexual desires of the person or another person; or

(4) fondles the person's genitals or the genitals of another person;

commits public indecency, a Class A misdemeanor.

(b) A person at least eighteen (18) years of age who knowingly or intentionally, in a public place, appears in a state of nudity with the intent to be seen by a child less than sixteen (16) years of age commits public indecency, a Class A misdemeanor.

(c) However, the offense under subsection (a) or subsection (b) is a Class D felony if the person who commits the offense has a prior unrelated conviction:

(1) under subsection (a) or (b); or

(2) in another jurisdiction, including a military court, that is substantially equivalent to an offense described in subsection (a) or (b).

(d) As used in this section, "nudity" means the showing of the human male or female genitals, pubic area, or buttocks with less than a fully opaque covering, the showing of the female breast with less than a fully opaque covering of any part of the nipple, or the showing of covered male genitals in a discernibly turgid state.

(e) A person who, in a place other than a public place, with the intent to be seen by persons other than invitees and occupants of that place:

    (1) engages in sexual intercourse;

    (2) engages in deviate sexual conduct;

    (3) fondles the person's genitals or the genitals of another person; or

    (4) appears in a state of nudity;

where the person can be seen by persons other than invitees and occupants of that place commits indecent exposure, a Class C misdemeanor.

History.
IC 35-45-4-1, as added by Acts 1976, P.L.148, § 5; 1977, P.L. 340, § 76; P.L.189-1984, § 1; P.L.215-1997, § 1; P.L.121-2000, § 1; P.L.123-2003, § 2.

Cross References.
Penalties for misdemeanors, IC 35-50-1, IC 35-50-3, IC 35-50-5-2.

Sex offense victim, child in need of services, IC 31-34-1-3.

Obscenity and pornography, IC 35-49-1-1 — IC 35-49-3-4.

Defenses relating to culpability, IC 35-41-3-1 — IC 35-41-3-10.

NOTES TO DECISIONS

ANALYSIS

Constitutionality.
—Police Powers.
—Vagueness.
Buttock.
Construction.
Conviction Set Aside.
Evidence.
—Depraved Sexual Instinct Rule.
—Insufficient.
—Prior Acts.
Fondles.
Indictment or Information.
Minimum Requirements.
Municipal Ordinances.
Nonobscene Dancing.
Nudist Club.
Public Place.
Purpose.
Substantial Government Interest.

Constitutionality.
The summary dismissal by the United States Supreme Court of three appeals from Indiana courts which had overturned the public nudity statute as against the tenets of freedom of expression constituted a ruling that the Indiana statute was constitutional in the face of an overbreadth attack, and, thus, the Court of Appeals was compelled to reverse a district court's holding that the statute was overbroad and "chilled" the first amendment rights of free speech. Glen Theatre, Inc. v. Pearson, 802 F.2d 287, 1986 U.S. App. LEXIS 31500 (7th Cir. Ind. 1986).

The Indiana statutory requirement that dancers in adult entertainment establishments must wear pasties and a G-string does not violate the First Amendment. Barnes v. Glen Theatre, Inc., 501 U.S. 560, 115 L. Ed. 2d 504, 111 S. Ct. 2456, 1991 U.S. LEXIS 3633 (1991).

—Police Powers.
This section is not overbroad and is constitutional as a valid exercise of the police powers of the state. State v. Baysinger, 272 Ind. 236, 397 N.E.2d 580, 1979 Ind. LEXIS 790 (1979), appeal dismissed, 446 U.S. 931, 100 S. Ct. 2146, 64 L. Ed. 2d 783, 1980 U.S. LEXIS 1531 (1980), appeal dismissed, 449 U.S. 806, 101 S. Ct. 52, 66 L. Ed. 2d 10, 1980 U.S. LEXIS 2564 (1980).

—Vagueness.
This statute is not vague because the words "public place" are not defined. State v. Baysinger, 272 Ind. 236, 397 N.E.2d 580, 1979 Ind. LEXIS 790 (1979), appeal dismissed, 446 U.S. 931, 100 S. Ct. 2146, 64 L. Ed. 2d 783, 1980 U.S. LEXIS 1531 (1980), appeal dismissed, 449 U.S. 806, 101 S. Ct. 52, 66 L. Ed. 2d 10, 1980 U.S. LEXIS 2564 (1980).

Buttock.
The term "buttock" has not been defined statutorily by the legislature. The term apparently lacks a legal meaning, but "buttock" has been defined as "Either of the two rounded prominences on the human torso that are posterior to the hips and formed by the gluteal muscles and underlying structures," and absent any argument to the contrary, the court used this definition. Turner v. State, 650 N.E.2d 705, 1995 Ind. App. LEXIS 519 (1995), cert. denied, 516 U.S. 1162, 116 S. Ct. 1050, 134 L. Ed. 2d 196, 1996 U.S. LEXIS 1650 (1996).

Construction.

IC 35-42-4-5(c), like IC 34-45-4-1(b)(1), does not require that a defendant's conduct be witnessed by a child or that the child be aware of the defendant's conduct; instead, it simply requires that a child under the age of 14 be at the place where the defendant's conduct occurs. Baumgartner v. State, 891 N.E.2d 1131, 2008 Ind. App. LEXIS 1788 (2008).

Conviction Set Aside.

A conviction for public indecency was set aside where the only act which could arguably constitute public indecency was the very act of fellatio which was the basis of a prostitution conviction. Blanton v. State, 533 N.E.2d 190, 1989 Ind. App. LEXIS 52 (1989).

Evidence.

Victim's testimony that defendant exposed his penis to her at approximately noon in the parking lot of a shopping mall was sufficient evidence to support a conviction of public indecency. Orr v. State, 612 N.E.2d 213, 1993 Ind. App. LEXIS 403 (1993).

State need not prove that children under the age of 16 actually witnessed the defendant's act since such a requirement would bring about an absurd result as the statute was intended to protect children under the age of 16 from the mere potential that they might see an individual commit the act of public indecency as defined in IC 35-45-4-1. Glotzbach v. State, 783 N.E.2d 1221, 2003 Ind. App. LEXIS 302 (2003).

Sufficient evidence existed to convict defendant of violating IC 35-45-4-1 where a 17 year-old girl, who had heard a funny noise, looked up, and saw defendant masturbating in the public library, identified defendant's photograph from a photograph array one week after the incident, and defendant's car was identified leaving the library. Glotzbach v. State, 783 N.E.2d 1221, 2003 Ind. App. LEXIS 302 (2003).

—Depraved Sexual Instinct Rule.

In prosecution for public indecency and attempted criminal deviate conduct, admission of evidence pursuant to the depraved sexual instinct rule was error. Orr v. State, 612 N.E.2d 213, 1993 Ind. App. LEXIS 403 (1993).

—Insufficient.

In a prosecution under prior statute, the fact that defendant took out his private parts for the purpose of having sexual intercourse in a private dwelling, not open to view from a public place, did not constitute the offense of public indecency. Wainscott v. State, 89 Ind. App. 452, 166 N.E. 666, 1929 Ind. App. LEXIS 166 (1929).

Defendant's conviction for public indecency was reversed, because although evidence was sufficient to infer that defendant urinated in public, it was not sufficient to establish that he exposed his penis while doing so. Townsend v. State, 750 N.E.2d 416, 2001 Ind. App. LEXIS 1074 (2001).

—Prior Acts.

Testimony concerning alleged acts of indecency and exhibitionism committed by defendant prior to time of alleged crime was not relevant to the issues under the charge of robbery. Baker v. State, 236 Ind. 55, 138 N.E.2d 641, 1956 Ind. LEXIS 242 (1956).

Fondles.

Conduct in tapping an undercover officer's thigh and working his way upward until he was tapping the officer's genital area was "handling" the officer "lingeringly" and thereby constituted an act of fondling within the meaning of subdivision (a)(4), and was fairly covered by the language of the statute to sustain the defendant's conviction. Marshall v. State, 602 N.E.2d 144, 1992 Ind. App. LEXIS 1592 (1992).

Where the charging information alleged not only genital nudity in restroom stall but also the fondling of another person's genitals, and there was testimony that such act occurred while the defendant was reaching across the stall partition, such conduct exceeded the bounds of the private area and thereby constituted criminal conduct in a public place. Chubb v. State, 640 N.E.2d 44, 1994 Ind. LEXIS 119 (1994).

Indictment or Information.

An indictment for the use of obscene language had to set forth the language used, or show an excuse for not doing so. State v. Burrell, 86 Ind. 313, 1882 Ind. LEXIS 685 (1882).

Minimum Requirements.

A G-string violates the minimum requirements of this section. Turner v. State, 650 N.E.2d 705, 1995 Ind. App. LEXIS 519 (1995), cert. denied, 516 U.S. 1162, 116 S. Ct. 1050, 134 L. Ed. 2d 196, 1996 U.S. LEXIS 1650 (1996).

Municipal Ordinances.

Municipal ordinances which attempt to regulate massage parlors by providing for suspension or revocation of the parlor's license as the penalty for violation are not precluded by this section, since the ordinances establish a licensing scheme while the state statutes establish a penal scheme. Indianapolis v. Wright, 267 Ind. 471, 371 N.E.2d 1298, 1978 Ind. LEXIS 584 (1978), appeal dismissed, 439 U.S. 804, 99 S. Ct. 60, 58 L. Ed. 2d 97, 1978 U.S. LEXIS 2481 (1978).

Trial court properly granted a county partial summary judgment and permanently enjoined a landowner from operating a sexually-oriented business on its property as the landowner violated several ordinances by not obtaining a building permit before conducting renovations totally over $5,000 and, therefore, was not entitled to nonconforming use status; further, the portions of the sexually-oriented business ordinances at issue did not unconstitutionally burden protected speech. Plaza Group Props., LLC v. Spencer County Plan Comm'n, 877 N.E.2d 877, 2007 Ind. App. LEXIS 2744 (2007).

Nonobscene Dancing.

Nonobscene nude dancing as entertainment is a form of expression entitled to limited First Amend-

Nonobscene Dancing. (Cont'd)
ment protection. Miller v. Civil City of South Bend, 887 F.2d 826, 1989 U.S. App. LEXIS 15975 (7th Cir. Ind. 1989).

Nonobscene nude dancing performed as entertainment is expression and as such is entitled to limited protection under the first amendment. Miller v. Civil City of South Bend, 904 F.2d 1081, 1990 U.S. App. LEXIS 8532 (7th Cir. Ind. 1990), vacated en banc, — F.2d —, 1991 U.S. App. LEXIS 20033 (7th Cir. 1991), rev'd, 501 U.S. 560, 115 L. Ed. 2d 504, 111 S. Ct. 2456, 1991 U.S. LEXIS 3633 (1991).

Nudist Club.
Operating a nudist club under a charter issued by the state did not so violate the statute on public indecency as to preclude the operator of the club from being granted the right to equitable relief by seeking an injunction. Martinal v. Lake O'Woods Club, Inc., 140 Ind. App. 358, 208 N.E.2d 722, 1965 Ind. App. LEXIS 468 (1965), superseded, 248 Ind. 252, 225 N.E.2d 183, 1967 Ind. LEXIS 426 (1967).

Public Place.
A public highway was prima facie a public place. State v. Waggoner, 52 Ind. 481, 1876 Ind. LEXIS 50 (1876); State v. Moriarty, 74 Ind. 103, 1881 Ind. LEXIS 109 (1881); Rosenstein v. State, 9 Ind. App. 290, 36 N.E. 652, 1894 Ind. App. LEXIS 36 (1894); Woodworth v. State, 185 Ind. 582, 114 N.E. 86, 1916 Ind. LEXIS 70 (1916).

A private locked room in a massage parlor in which two consenting persons engage in promiscuous conduct is not a "public place" within the meaning of this statute. Lasko v. State, 409 N.E.2d 1124, 1980 Ind. App. LEXIS 1655 (1980).

A common dance floor and surrounding booths which existed inside the confines of a book store advertising adult entertainment constituted a "public place" within the meaning of this section. Adims v. State, 461 N.E.2d 740, 1984 Ind. App. LEXIS 2481 (1984).

The defendant's act of exposing his genitals through a "glory hole" between two adult film-viewing booths constituted conduct in a public place so as to subject the defendant to prosecution and conviction for public indecency. Thompson v. State, 482 N.E.2d 1372, 1985 Ind. App. LEXIS 2815 (1985).

Conduct of a woman who danced nude in a room where she could only be seen by a person in a booth, the door of which was closed through the entire performance, did not occur in a "public place." Sweeney v. State, 486 N.E.2d 651, 1985 Ind. App. LEXIS 3014 (1985).

Nudity within the confines of an enclosed bathroom stall falls outside the proscription of the public indecency statute. Chubb v. State, 627 N.E.2d 842, 1994 Ind. App. LEXIS 20 (1994), superseded, 640 N.E.2d 44, 1994 Ind. LEXIS 119 (1994).

A restroom stall, enclosed by partitions of sufficient height so that users' conduct or condition is not visible to the casual public eye, is not a public place. Chubb v. State, 640 N.E.2d 44, 1994 Ind. LEXIS 119 (1994).

Although one's vehicle may be a "home on wheels" in certain circumstances, a person driving a semi-trailer truck on the state's highways is in a place where members of the public are free to go without restraint, and is subject to the prohibition on appearing nude. Whatley v. State, 708 N.E.2d 66, 1999 Ind. App. LEXIS 551, 95 A.L.R.5th 705 (1999).

It is not the observation of nudity that this statute proscribes, but rather the knowing and intentional appearance in public in a state of nudity. Whatley v. State, 708 N.E.2d 66, 1999 Ind. App. LEXIS 551, 95 A.L.R.5th 705 (1999).

Student who was expelled from school for allowing another student to photograph him in shower was entitled to summary judgment on claim that his substantive due process rights were violated; student did not engage in public indecency within meaning of public indecency statute because shower was not public place. Tun v. Fort Wayne Cmty. Sch., 326 F. Supp. 2d 932, 2004 U.S. Dist. LEXIS 13925 (N.D. Ind. 2004), rev'd, 398 F.3d 899, 2005 U.S. App. LEXIS 2647 (7th Cir. Ind. 2005).

Purpose.
This and other public indecency statutes were designed to protect morals and public order. Barnes v. Glen Theatre, Inc., 501 U.S. 560, 115 L. Ed. 2d 504, 111 S. Ct. 2456, 1991 U.S. LEXIS 3633 (1991).

Substantial Government Interest.
The public indecency statute furthers a substantial government interest in protecting order and morality. This interest is unrelated to the suppression of free expression. Barnes v. Glen Theatre, Inc., 501 U.S. 560, 115 L. Ed. 2d 504, 111 S. Ct. 2456, 1991 U.S. LEXIS 3633 (1991).

Cited:
Owens v. State, 424 N.E.2d 169, 1981 Ind. App. LEXIS 1584 (1981); State v. Harris, 433 N.E.2d 399, 1982 Ind. App. LEXIS 1387 (1982); Elliott v. State, 435 N.E.2d 302, 1982 Ind. App. LEXIS 1217 (1982); Erhardt v. State, 468 N.E.2d 224, 1984 Ind. LEXIS 947 (1984).

RESEARCH REFERENCES

Indiana Law Review.
Survey: Criminal Law and Procedure, 37 Ind. L. Rev. 1003 (2004).

Collateral References.
Modern concept of obscenity. 5 A.L.R.3d 1158.
Indecent exposure: what is "person". 63 A.L.R.4th 1040.

Regulation of exposure of female, but not male breasts. 67 A.L.R.5th 431.

What constitutes "public place" within meaning of state statute or local ordinance prohibiting indecency or commission of sexual act in public place. 95 A.L.R.5th 229.

35-45-4-1.5. Public nudity.

(a) As used in this section, "nudity" has the meaning set forth in section 1(d) [IC 35-45-4-1(d)] of this chapter.

(b) A person who knowingly or intentionally appears in a public place in a state of nudity commits public nudity, a Class C misdemeanor.

(c) A person who knowingly or intentionally appears in a public place in a state of nudity with the intent to be seen by another person commits a Class B misdemeanor. However, the offense is a Class D felony if the person has a prior unrelated conviction under this subsection or under subsection (d).

(d) A person who knowingly or intentionally appears in a state of nudity:

(1) in or on school grounds;

(2) in a public park; or

(3) with the intent to arouse the sexual desires of the person or another person,

in a department of natural resources owned or managed property;

commits a Class A misdemeanor. However, the offense is a Class D felony if the person has a prior unrelated conviction under this subsection or under subsection (c).

History.
P.L.123-2003, § 3.

Penalties for misdemeanors, IC 35-50-1, IC 35-50-3, IC 35-50-5-2.

Cross References.
Penalties for felonies, IC 35-50-1, IC 35-50-2, IC 35-50-5-2.

NOTES TO DECISIONS

ANALYSIS

Constitutionality.
Intent.

Constitutionality.
Public nudity statute, IC 35-45-4-1.5(c), was not void for vagueness, as it sufficiently apprised defendant that being visibly nude to persons in a public place, which included defendant's front yard, violated the statute. Weideman v. State, 890 N.E.2d 28, 2008 Ind. App. LEXIS 1509 (2008).

Intent.
Evidence did not support conviction for public nudity as a Class B misdemeanor but did support a conviction for public nudity as a Class C misdemeanor where there was no evidence that defendant intended to be seen. Weideman v. State, 890 N.E.2d 28, 2008 Ind. App. LEXIS 1509 (2008).

RESEARCH REFERENCES

Indiana Law Review.
Survey: Criminal Law and Procedure, 37 Ind. L. Rev. 1003 (2004).

Res Gestae.
Criminal Justice Notes 7/08: Public nudity -

vagueness challenge, 52 (No. 3) Res Gestae 35 (2008).

35-45-4-2. Prostitution.

A person who knowingly or intentionally:

(1) Performs, or offers or agrees to perform, sexual intercourse or deviate sexual conduct; or

(2) Fondles, or offers or agrees to fondle, the genitals of another person; for money or other property commits prostitution, a Class A misdemeanor. However, the offense is a Class D felony if the person has two (2) prior convictions under this section.

History.
IC 35-45-4-2, as added by Acts 1976, P.L. 148,

§ 5; 1977, P.L.340, § 77; 1979, P.L.301, § 1; P.L.310-1983, § 3.

Cross References.
Incest, IC 35-46-1-3.
Penalties for felonies, IC 35-50-1, IC 35-50-2, IC 35-50-5-2.
Penalties for misdemeanors, IC 35-50-1, IC 35-50-3, IC 35-50-5-2.

Sex crimes, IC 35-42-4-1 — IC 35-42-4-3.
Sex offense victim, child in need of services, IC 31-34-1-3.

NOTES TO DECISIONS

ANALYSIS

Constitutionality.
—Equal Protection.
Construction.
Construction with Other Laws.
Distinguished from Promoting Prostitution.
Double Jeopardy.
Evidence.
—Sufficient.
"Fondle" Defined.
Indictment or Information.
Legislative History.
Municipal Ordinances.
Offer.
Penetration.
"Prostitute" Defined.

Constitutionality.
Statute did not violate the Eighth Amendment by punishing a status regardless of whether activity was performed within the state but proscribes only certain conduct or activity carried on within the state. Sumpter v. State, 261 Ind. 471, 306 N.E.2d 95, 1974 Ind. LEXIS 355 (1974), appeal dismissed, 419 U.S. 811, 95 S. Ct. 25, 42 L. Ed. 2d 38, 1974 U.S. LEXIS 2245 (1974).

This section is not unconstitutionally vague. Owens v. State, 424 N.E.2d 169, 1981 Ind. App. LEXIS 1584 (1981).

Indiana's prostitution statute could constitutionally be applied to prohibit the auto-erotic conduct of a female defendant who was convicted of prostitution without a determination that her conduct in performing a "bed dance" and inserting a sexual device in her anus was obscene. Webb v. State, 575 N.E.2d 1066, 1991 Ind. App. LEXIS 1319 (1991).

—Equal Protection.
A defendant in a prostitution prosecution is not denied equal protection of the law because a witness for the state is not prosecuted for patronizing a prostitute for involvement in the incident for which the defendant is prosecuted. Young v. State, 446 N.E.2d 624, 1983 Ind. App. LEXIS 2754 (1983).

A conviction for public indecency was set aside where the only act which could arguably constitute public indecency was the very act of fellatio which was the basis of a prostitution conviction. Blanton v. State, 533 N.E.2d 190, 1989 Ind. App. LEXIS 52 (1989).

Construction.
Prostitution was committed when female involved committed or offered to commit her part in act of sexual intercourse for hire, and did not relate to any attempt to commit such act. Williams v. State, 256 Ind. 228, 267 N.E.2d 840, 1971 Ind. LEXIS 619 (1971).

The term "prostitution" comprehended both the actual commission and the solicitation of sexual intercourse for hire. Senst v. State, 162 Ind. App. 357, 319 N.E.2d 663, 1974 Ind. App. LEXIS 842 (1974).

Property within meaning of prostitution statute included anything of value and included personal property, money, labor and services; accordingly, evidence was sufficient to sustain conviction for prostitution where defendant agreed to perform sex act in exchange for car ride across town. Edwards v. State, 803 N.E.2d 1249, 2004 Ind. App. LEXIS 295 (2004).

Construction with Other Laws.
IC 35-45-4-2 and IC 35-50-2-8 compliment each other, and the prostitution statute is not a discreet, separate, and independent habitual offender statute; read together, they provide for a progressive scheme of punishment, and because they can be harmonized, both enhancement provisions may be simultaneously applied. State v. Dennis, 686 N.E.2d 901, 1997 Ind. App. LEXIS 1541 (1997).

Distinguished from Promoting Prostitution.
The legislature did not intend for prosecuting attorneys to have the discretion to charge an offense as a Class C felony under IC 35-45-4-4 merely because the prostitute invites the customer into his home; the business manager of a prostitution enterprise typically imposes a greater harm on society than the sole practitioner. State v. Hartman, 602 N.E.2d 1011, 1992 Ind. LEXIS 255 (1992).

Since the employee of an escort service arranged a rendezvous with a person who had contacted that escort service and later fondled the person's genitals when the person came to the employee's residence, it was improper to charge the employee with promoting prostitution, a Class C felony. State v. Hartman, 602 N.E.2d 1011, 1992 Ind. LEXIS 255 (1992).

Double Jeopardy.
The prostitution and obscene performance statutes are not in conflict. Both statutes prohibit certain conduct; neither statute explicitly authorizes any conduct proscribed by the other. A conflict between the statutes is not created by the possibility the overlapping proscriptions may give rise to double jeopardy issue or by the inclusion of an obscenity provision in only one of the two statutes. Webb v. State, 575 N.E.2d 1066, 1991 Ind. App. LEXIS 1319 (1991).

Evidence.

—Sufficient.

Testimony of a police officer that he was solicited by a woman other than the defendant for a "two-girl party" which would cost ten dollars for a "half and half" and, upon his consenting, the defendant led the way to a house, where she demanded her money and stated that it was for the same thing the other woman had agreed to do was sufficient to sustain a conviction of the violation of the statute. Williams v. State, 254 Ind. 4, 256 N.E.2d 913, 1970 Ind. LEXIS 509 (1970).

Testimony of police officer that defendant waved at him as he passed her in unmarked car, that when he stopped she asked if he wanted a date, that she told him price would be $15 for "a straight lay or a half and half," and that she got into his car when he indicated he would accept her offer, was sufficient to support conviction on charge of prostitution. Williams v. State, 256 Ind. 228, 267 N.E.2d 840, 1971 Ind. LEXIS 619 (1971).

Evidence sufficient to support conviction. Wright v. State, 456 N.E.2d 733, 1983 Ind. App. LEXIS 3625 (1983).

"Fondle" Defined.

"Fondle" as used in this section clearly and unequivocally refers to consensual physical contact between persons which may or may not be manual. Owens v. State, 424 N.E.2d 169, 1981 Ind. App. LEXIS 1584 (1981).

Indictment or Information.

An indictment charging a person with being a prostitute had to state the facts constituting the offense. Delano v. State, 66 Ind. 348, 1879 Ind. LEXIS 171 (1879).

The same count of an indictment could charge all the offenses defined by the statute without being bad for duplicity. Fahnestock v. State, 102 Ind. 156, 1 N.E. 372, 1885 Ind. LEXIS 26 (1885); State v. Stout, 112 Ind. 245, 13 N.E. 715, 1887 Ind. LEXIS 388 (1887).

Charging a female with committing fornication for hire charged an offense. Stanton v. State, 27 Ind. App. 105, 60 N.E. 999, 1901 Ind. App. LEXIS 22 (1901).

Legislative History.

The trial court did not err in refusing to consider the legislative history of this section. Owens v. State, 424 N.E.2d 169, 1981 Ind. App. LEXIS 1584 (1981).

Where the opinion of the attorney general dealt with the status of this section before its enactment, that opinion, in a manner similar to legislative journal entries, is not persuasive authority for the courts. Owens v. State, 424 N.E.2d 169, 1981 Ind. App. LEXIS 1584 (1981).

Municipal Ordinances.

Municipal ordinances which attempt to regulate massage parlors by providing for suspension or revocation of the parlor's license as the penalty for violation are not precluded by this section, since the ordinances establish a licensing scheme while the state statutes establish a penal scheme. Indianapolis v. Wright, 267 Ind. 471, 371 N.E.2d 1298, 1978 Ind. LEXIS 584 (1978), appeal dismissed, 439 U.S. 804, 99 S. Ct. 60, 58 L. Ed. 2d 97, 1978 U.S. LEXIS 2481 (1978).

Offer.

Contention that the crime charged was an "attempt" to commit a crime and since arrest was made before an actual "attempt" was made was without effect since the statute and the crime charged was of an "offer" to commit the act. Wilson v. State, 258 Ind. 3, 278 N.E.2d 569, 1972 Ind. LEXIS 519 (1972), cert. denied, 408 U.S. 928, 92 S. Ct. 2494, 33 L. Ed. 2d 341, 1972 U.S. LEXIS 2095 (1972).

Penetration.

Neither the statutory definition of deviate sexual conduct nor the statute proscribing prostitution requires the participation of more than one person in the act of penetration. Webb v. State, 575 N.E.2d 1066, 1991 Ind. App. LEXIS 1319 (1991).

"Prostitute" Defined.

A "prostitute," within the meaning of the statute, was a woman who had indiscriminate sexual intercourse with men. Fahnestock v. State, 102 Ind. 156, 1 N.E. 372, 1885 Ind. LEXIS 26 (1885); Nichols v. State, 127 Ind. 406, 26 N.E. 839, 1891 Ind. LEXIS 222 (1891).

Cited:

Lasko v. State, 409 N.E.2d 1124, 1980 Ind. App. LEXIS 1655 (1980); South Bend v. Bowman, 434 N.E.2d 104, 1982 Ind. App. LEXIS 1167 (1982); Loy v. State, 443 N.E.2d 111, 1982 Ind. App. LEXIS 1541 (1982); Pritchett v. Heil, 756 N.E.2d 561, 2001 Ind. App. LEXIS 1754 (2001); Hernandez v. State, 785 N.E.2d 294, 2003 Ind. App. LEXIS 421 (2003).

35-45-4-3. Patronizing a prostitute.

A person who knowingly or intentionally pays, or offers or agrees to pay, money or other property to another person:

(1) For having engaged in, or on the understanding that the other person will engage in, sexual intercourse or deviate sexual conduct with the person or with any other person; or

(2) For having fondled, or on the understanding that the other person will fondle, the genitals of the person or any other person;

commits patronizing a prostitute, a Class A misdemeanor. However, the offense is a Class D felony if the person has two (2) prior convictions under this section.

History.
IC 35-45-4-3, as added by Acts 1976, P.L.148, § 5; 1977, P.L.340, § 78; 1979, P.L.301, § 2; P.L.310-1983, § 4.

Cross References.
Penalties for felonies, IC 35-50-1, IC 35-50-2, IC 35-50-5-2.

Penalties for misdemeanors, IC 35-50-1, IC 35-50-3, IC 35-50-5-2.

NOTES TO DECISIONS

ANALYSIS

Constitutionality.
Associating with Prostitute.
Boarders.
Character of House.
Indictment.

Constitutionality.
Statute punishing any male who frequented or visited a house of ill fame except as a physician, who associated with known prostitutes, who frequented or visited a gambling house, or who was engaged in a house of prostitution, did not violate § 22 of Art. 4 of the Constitution, prohibiting local or special laws, nor § 23 of Art. 4, requiring laws of uniform operation, nor the privilege and immunity clause of the U.S. Constitution. State v. Griffin, 226 Ind. 279, 79 N.E.2d 537, 1948 Ind. LEXIS 161 (1948).

Associating with Prostitute.
Conviction could be had for associating with one female. Jessop v. State, 14 Ind. App. 257, 42 N.E. 950, 1896 Ind. App. LEXIS 243 (1896).

Boarders.
A boarder at a house of ill fame could be con-

victed. Weideman v. State, 4 Ind. App. 397, 30 N.E. 920, 1892 Ind. App. LEXIS 129 (1892).

Character of House.
Evidence of reputation of house and visitors thereat was admissible. Betts v. State, 93 Ind. 375, 1884 Ind. LEXIS 761 (1884); Whitlock v. State, 4 Ind. App. 432, 30 N.E. 934, 1892 Ind. App. LEXIS 135 (1892).
It was a question of fact to be determined from the evidence whether a house was one of ill fame, assignation, or prostitution. Fahnestock v. State, 102 Ind. 156, 1 N.E. 372, 1885 Ind. LEXIS 26 (1885).

Indictment.
The same count of an indictment could charge all the offenses defined by the statute relating to prostitution without being bad for duplicity. Fahnestock v. State, 102 Ind. 156, 1 N.E. 372, 1885 Ind. LEXIS 26 (1885); State v. Stout, 112 Ind. 245, 13 N.E. 715, 1887 Ind. LEXIS 388 (1887).

Cited:
South Bend v. Bowman, 434 N.E.2d 104, 1982 Ind. App. LEXIS 1167 (1982); Young v. State, 446 N.E.2d 624, 1983 Ind. App. LEXIS 2754 (1983).

35-45-4-4. Promoting prostitution.

A person who:
(1) Knowingly or intentionally entices or compels another person to become a prostitute;
(2) Knowingly or intentionally procures, or offers or agrees to procure, a person for another person for the purpose of prostitution;
(3) Having control over the use of a place, knowingly or intentionally permits another person to use the place for prostitution;
(4) Receives money or other property from a prostitute, without lawful consideration, knowing it was earned in whole or in part from prostitution; or
(5) Knowingly or intentionally conducts or directs another person to a place for the purpose of prostitution;
commits promoting prostitution, a Class C felony. However, the offense is a Class B felony under subdivision (1) if the person enticed or compelled is under eighteen (18) years of age.

History.
IC 35-45-4-4, as added by Acts 1976, P.L.148, § 5; 1977, P.L.340, § 79; 1978, P.L.148, § 6.

Cross References.
Contributing to the delinquency of a minor, IC 35-46-1-8.

Penalties for felonies, IC 35-50-1, IC 35-50-2, IC 35-50-5-2.

NOTES TO DECISIONS

Analysis

Constitutionality.
—Sentence.
Character and Reputation.
Continuing Offense.
Distinguished from Prostitution.
Elements of Keeping House of Ill Fame.
Entice or Compel.
Evidence.
—In General.
—Admissibility.
—Insufficient.
—Sufficiency.
—Witnesses.
Husband and Wife Conducting House.
Indictment or Information.
—Enticement.
—Keeping House of Ill Fame.
Injunction.
Lesser Included Offense of Keeping House.
Place for Prostitution.
—Control.
Receiving Money or Other Property.
Remarks by Prosecutor.
Renting House.
Review on Appeal.
Sentence.
—Reasonable.
—Revised.

Constitutionality.

—Sentence.

Even though the range of permitted sentences for a prostitution promoter is longer than the sentencing range for a prostitute, there is nothing incongruous or unfair about the legislature's decision to punish the two crimes differently, and the state constitution's proportionality clause is not violated; in light of the presumption of constitutionality of statutes, a defendant asserting unconstitutionality of a sentencing statute bears a heavy burden. Jones v. State, 766 N.E.2d 1258, 2002 Ind. App. LEXIS 653 (2002).

Character and Reputation.

The female must have possessed actual personal virtue, and previous acts of illicit sexual intercourse on her part could be proved in defense. Lyons v. State, 52 Ind. 426, 1876 Ind. LEXIS 34 (1876).

Reputation of the house could be proved in a prosecution for keeping a house of ill fame. Betts v. State, 93 Ind. 375, 1884 Ind. LEXIS 761 (1884); Whitlock v. State, 4 Ind. App. 432, 30 N.E. 934, 1892 Ind. App. LEXIS 135 (1892).

Reputation of defendant for virtue and chastity could not be proved in a prosecution for renting a house to be kept as a house of ill fame. Graeter v. State, 105 Ind. 271, 4 N.E. 461, 1886 Ind. LEXIS 441 (1886).

It was necessary that it be a house of ill fame or other place of like character. Miller v. State, 121 Ind. 294, 23 N.E. 94, 1889 Ind. LEXIS 61 (1889).

Reputation of a house of ill fame, its keeper and inmates, could be proved in a prosecution for keeping such house. Christison v. State, 177 Ind. 363, 98 N.E. 113, 1912 Ind. LEXIS 32 (1912).

The state could show that defendant's general reputation for chastity and virtue was bad, as a part of the original case. Schultz v. State, 200 Ind. 1, 161 N.E. 5, 1928 Ind. LEXIS 29 (1928).

Continuing Offense.

Keeping a house of ill fame was a continuing offense, and a conviction barred a prosecution for keeping the same house prior to the return of the indictment. Freeman v. State, 119 Ind. 501, 21 N.E. 1101, 1889 Ind. LEXIS 320 (1889).

Distinguished from Prostitution.

The legislature did not intend for prosecuting attorneys to have the discretion to charge an offense as a Class C felony under this section merely because the prostitute invites the customer into his home; the business manager of a prostitution enterprise typically imposes a greater harm on society than the sole practitioner. State v. Hartman, 602 N.E.2d 1011, 1992 Ind. LEXIS 255 (1992).

Since the employee of an escort service arranged a rendezvous with a person who had contacted that escort service and later fondled the person's genitals when the person came to the employee's residence, it was improper to charge the employee with promoting prostitution, a Class C felony. State v. Hartman, 602 N.E.2d 1011, 1992 Ind. LEXIS 255 (1992).

Elements of Keeping House of Ill Fame.

Manifest in the term keeping a house of ill fame, is the requirement that the accused have knowledge, actual or constructive, of the illegal practices and the necessity that the accused is shown to be the tenant or owner and thereby possessing the means to control the conduct of illegal activity. Senst v. State, 162 Ind. App. 357, 319 N.E.2d 663, 1974 Ind. App. LEXIS 842 (1974).

The term prostitution comprehends both the actual commission and the solicitation of sexual intercourse for hire. Senst v. State, 162 Ind. App. 357, 319 N.E.2d 663, 1974 Ind. App. LEXIS 842 (1974).

Entice or Compel.

The word "entice," as used in subdivision (1), means to wrongfully invite, solicit, allure, coax, tempt, attract, or delude another person to engage in prostitution. Mure v. State, 468 N.E.2d 591, 1984 Ind. App. LEXIS 2973 (1984).

A conviction under subdivision (1) does not require that the party solicited actually engage in

Entice or Compel. (Cont'd)

acts of prostitution. Mure v. State, 468 N.E.2d 591, 1984 Ind. App. LEXIS 2973 (1984).

Evidence.

—In General.

Legal evidence tending to support the fact that defendant kept house of ill fame was essential to conviction. Sullivan v. State, 200 Ind. 43, 161 N.E. 265, 1928 Ind. LEXIS 36 (1928).

In a prosecution under subsection (1) of this section the state need only show that the accused enticed or compelled the victim to commit an act of prostitution; it need not prove that defendant induced her to embark upon a career of prostitution. Nation v. State, 445 N.E.2d 565, 1983 Ind. LEXIS 762 (1983).

—Admissibility.

Statements made by inmates of the house, taken in connection with all the circumstances, were held admissible over the objection that the defendant was not present at such conversation. Schultz v. State, 200 Ind. 1, 161 N.E. 5, 1928 Ind. LEXIS 29 (1928).

Admission of testimony of police officers as to reputation to prove that a certain bar was a house of ill fame was a denial of defendant's right of confrontation guaranteed by the Sixth Amendment and Art. 1, § 13 of the Indiana Constitution. Senst v. State, 162 Ind. App. 357, 319 N.E.2d 663, 1974 Ind. App. LEXIS 842 (1974).

In a trial for the offense of keeping a house of ill fame it was not error to permit the introduction of testimony as to prior arrests which occurred at the location. Senst v. State, 162 Ind. App. 357, 319 N.E.2d 663, 1974 Ind. App. LEXIS 842 (1974).

—Insufficient.

Conviction for procuring female as inmate for a house of prostitution was not sustained by evidence. La Mar v. State, 231 Ind. 508, 109 N.E.2d 614, 1953 Ind. LEXIS 147 (1953).

Evidence that a girl was brought to a house of prostitution operated by the defendants by someone other than the defendants without evidence of any action by defendants to induce her to enter or remain in the house was insufficient to convict defendants of procuring her to inhabit a house of prostitution. Graham v. State, 249 Ind. 119, 231 N.E.2d 28, 1967 Ind. LEXIS 358 (1967).

Because defendant, who sought to take photographs of and have sex with a minor, was the same as a customer seeking a prostitute, there was an insufficient evidentiary foundation for promoting prostitution under IC 35-45-4-4; therefore, defendant's conviction could not stand. Hayes v. State, 879 N.E.2d 1179, 2008 Ind. App. LEXIS 123 (2008).

—Sufficiency.

One who took his daughter, under 18 years of age, to a brothel for the purpose of having sexual intercourse with men, and commanded or instructed her to submit thereto, was guilty under former § 2001, R.S. 1881. Stevens v. State, 112 Ind. 433, 14 N.E. 251, 1887 Ind. LEXIS 426 (1887).

Evidence held sufficient to sustain conviction.

Schultz v. State, 200 Ind. 1, 161 N.E. 5, 1928 Ind. LEXIS 29 (1928); Sullivan v. State, 200 Ind. 43, 161 N.E. 265, 1928 Ind. LEXIS 36 (1928); Matthews v. State, 200 Ind. 53, 161 N.E. 271, 1928 Ind. LEXIS 38 (1928).

Evidence amply supported charge of procuring a female for house of prostitution where defendant took the prosecuting witness, a 15-year-old girl, to his home to meet a woman who worked out of it as a prostitute, purchased her clothing, and the girl went with the other woman to "work on" a designated street and performed acts of prostitution for money in defendant's home. Patterson v. State, 251 Ind. 580, 244 N.E.2d 221, 1969 Ind. LEXIS 403 (1969), cert. denied, 396 U.S. 829, 90 S. Ct. 81, 24 L. Ed. 2d 80, 1969 U.S. LEXIS 909 (1969).

Where evidence showed that defendant was unemployed, lived with the prostitute 2½ years, was present when she returned with "clients" and escorted her around so that she could engage in prostitution, it was sufficient to support a finding that defendant had actual knowledge of how she earned the money that he regularly received. Brown v. State, 254 Ind. 504, 260 N.E.2d 876, 1970 Ind. LEXIS 575 (1970).

Testimony of prostitute that she turned a certain amount of money over to defendant on a certain date which money she had obtained by prostitution was substantial evidence of probative value from which the trier of fact could have reasonably inferred that defendant was guilty beyond a reasonable doubt of pandering. Kleinrichert v. State, 260 Ind. 537, 297 N.E.2d 822, 1973 Ind. LEXIS 563 (1973).

Where undercover police officer registered at hotel and when manager took him to his room he asked if a woman was available to which manager replied it was possible and later a woman came to officer's room, asked how much money he had and when officer told her she asked if he had more and left when he said no, and later manager came to his room and asked what the problem was and officer told manager about the money and showed manager how much money he had after which manager said "okay" and left and then woman returned to officer's room and offered herself for prostitution, the evidence was sufficient to convict manager under this section. Whorton v. State, 412 N.E.2d 1219, 1980 Ind. App. LEXIS 1787 (1980).

Evidence supported defendant's conviction where she told an undercover officer that she would be able to get him oral sex for $65 and arranged for another female to meet with him for that purpose. Luginbuhl v. State, 507 N.E.2d 620, 1987 Ind. App. LEXIS 2667 (1987).

Overwhelming evidence that the defendant and everyone else connected with the massage parlor knew the employees would be engaging in prostitution, and evidence that the defendant was exercising a high degree of control over the business and made a profit, was sufficient to sustain convictions for promoting prostitution. Lee v. State, 569 N.E.2d 717, 1991 Ind. App. LEXIS 605 (1991).

The evidence at trial clearly indicated that the owner knew the women were engaging in prostitution at the massage parlor. He was present during a conversation about supplying condoms

Evidence. (Cont'd)

—Sufficiency. (Cont'd)

and contraceptives to the women at work; he was masturbated by one woman and a new employee during a training session; he warned the manager about the business being investigated and watched by the Vice Division; he instructed the manager to take down license plate numbers of the cars driven by customers so he could have them checked. In addition, he received income because of the prostitution at the massage parlor. The evidence was clearly sufficient to convict him of corrupt business influence and promoting prostitution. Lee v. State, 580 N.E.2d 374, 1991 Ind. App. LEXIS 1832 (1991).

Evidence that a sexual favor was performed almost immediately after an undercover officer's second appointment with a masseuse was sufficient to permit retrial of the proprietor on one count of promoting prostitution; since only one alleged offense could be retried, however, the evidence was insufficient as a matter of law to permit retrial on the other charge, corrupt business influence, which required a showing of a pattern of racketeering. Hernandez v. State, 785 N.E.2d 294, 2003 Ind. App. LEXIS 421 (2003).

Where defendant struck up conversation with undercover officer posing as prostitute and offered to enter into escort service business with officer and where defendant used derogatory term to describe "prostitute" to inform officer of capacity in which officer would work with defendant, there was sufficient evidence to convict defendant of promoting prostitution under IC 35-45-4-4; evidence supported inference that derogatory term meant "prostitute" and that defendant was discussing illegal escort service rather than legitimate one. Dorn v. State, 819 N.E.2d 516, 2004 Ind. App. LEXIS 2573 (2004).

—Witnesses.

It was error to permit witness to answer affirmatively questions which were double in form and improperly assumed a fact in issue. Sullivan v. State, 200 Ind. 43, 161 N.E. 265, 1928 Ind. LEXIS 36 (1928).

Husband and Wife Conducting House.

A husband living with his wife who conducted a house of ill fame could be convicted of keeping such house. Hunter v. State, 14 Ind. App. 683, 43 N.E. 452, 1896 Ind. App. LEXIS 308 (1896).

Indictment or Information.

Counts of an affidavit charging the offense in the language of the statute were sufficient. Anderson v. State, 195 Ind. 329, 145 N.E. 311, 1924 Ind. LEXIS 139 (1924).

—Enticement.

An indictment had to allege that the female was enticed or taken for the purpose of indiscriminate intercourse with men. Osborn v. State, 52 Ind. 526, 1876 Ind. LEXIS 63 (1876); Nichols v. State, 127 Ind. 406, 26 N.E. 839, 1891 Ind. LEXIS 222 (1891).

The indictment should have specified the character of the house or place to which the female was

enticed or taken. Miller v. State, 121 Ind. 294, 23 N.E. 94, 1889 Ind. LEXIS 61 (1889).

The indictment should have shown to what particular place or house the female was enticed or taken, but a judgment would not be arrested for this omission. Nichols v. State, 127 Ind. 406, 26 N.E. 839, 1891 Ind. LEXIS 222 (1891).

An affidavit charging the enticing of a female to a house of ill fame for the purpose of prostitution, and describing the location of the house with particularity, was sufficient. Clark v. State, 183 Ind. 159, 108 N.E. 516, 1915 Ind. LEXIS 31 (1915).

—Keeping House of Ill Fame.

An indictment for keeping a house of ill fame was sufficient if it followed the language of the statute. Betts v. State, 93 Ind. 375, 1884 Ind. LEXIS 761 (1884); Graeter v. State, 105 Ind. 271, 4 N.E. 461, 1886 Ind. LEXIS 441 (1886).

If it were alleged that the names of the persons resorting to a house of ill fame were unknown, strict proof of the allegation was not required. Dutton v. State, 2 Ind. App. 448, 28 N.E. 995, 1891 Ind. App. LEXIS 196 (1891).

It was not necessary to describe the real estate on which a house of ill fame was situate. Johnson v. State, 13 Ind. App. 299, 41 N.E. 550, 1895 Ind. App. LEXIS 232 (1895).

An affidavit for keeping a house of ill fame was sufficient if it substantially followed the language of the statute. Woodward v. State, 174 Ind. 743, 93 N.E. 169, 1910 Ind. LEXIS 170 (1910); Winegardner v. State, 181 Ind. 525, 104 N.E. 969, 1914 Ind. LEXIS 65 (1914); Eley v. State, 183 Ind. 161, 108 N.E. 516, 1915 Ind. LEXIS 32 (1915).

An indictment charging defendant with keeping a house of ill fame was sufficient as against the objections that it failed to locate the place or name the persons resorting thereto. Sullivan v. State, 200 Ind. 43, 161 N.E. 265, 1928 Ind. LEXIS 36 (1928).

Injunction.

In a contempt proceeding for violation of an injunction against the operation of a house of prostitution, testimony of witnesses as to the ownership of the premises and open and notorious violations, was sufficient to sustain a finding that defendant was the owner of the premises and had knowledge of the violation of the injunction. Crawford v. State, 227 Ind. 665, 87 N.E.2d 877, 1949 Ind. LEXIS 178 (1949).

Evidence of prostitution at a truck stop without evidence identifying it with the legal description of the premises alleged in plaintiff's complaint was insufficient to sustain a judgment enjoining the defendant from using the premises described in the complaint for purposes of lewdness or prostitution. Moran v. State, 255 Ind. 540, 265 N.E.2d 703, 1971 Ind. LEXIS 700 (1971).

Lesser Included Offense of Keeping House.

Living in a house of ill fame is not a lesser offense included in keeping a house of ill fame. Sumpter v. State, 264 Ind. 117, 340 N.E.2d 764, 1976 Ind. LEXIS 439 (1976), cert. denied, 425 U.S. 952, 96 S. Ct. 1727, 48 L. Ed. 2d 196, 1976 U.S. LEXIS 1469 (1976).

Place for Prostitution.

—Control.

A night manager of a hotel with control over the processes of guest registration and the assignment of rooms had the requisite control over the hotel as provided in clause (3) of this section. Whorton v. State, 412 N.E.2d 1219, 1980 Ind. App. LEXIS 1787 (1980).

Receiving Money or Other Property.

A person may be guilty of receiving money from a prostitute, "knowing it was earned in whole or in part from prostitution," even though the alleged act of prostitution did not occur, since "knowing" in the context of the statute is a mental state, which the trier of fact may reasonably infer from the circumstances. Gibson v. State, 514 N.E.2d 318, 1987 Ind. App. LEXIS 3146 (1987).

Remarks by Prosecutor.

A remark by the prosecutor in his closing argument that defendant might have to serve two to ten years or might have to serve less than two years was not prejudicial to defendant since it was a matter of common knowledge. Patterson v. State, 251 Ind. 580, 244 N.E.2d 221, 1969 Ind. LEXIS 403 (1969), cert. denied, 396 U.S. 829, 90 S. Ct. 81, 24 L. Ed. 2d 80, 1969 U.S. LEXIS 909 (1969).

Renting House.

In prosecutions for renting a house to be kept as a house of ill fame, actual knowledge on the part of the lessor did not need to be proved, but the fact could be proved by circumstantial evidence. Graeter v. State, 105 Ind. 271, 4 N.E. 461, 1886 Ind. LEXIS 441 (1886).

Review on Appeal.

In a prosecution for keeping a house of ill fame, where the evidence overwhelmingly supported a conviction, the Supreme Court would not set the verdict aside for irregular rulings on matters of evidence. Kline v. State, 194 Ind. 334, 142 N.E. 713, 1924 Ind. LEXIS 41 (1924).

A judgment of conviction would not be reversed, although the evidence was weak, where, to do so, would require the Supreme Court to weigh the evidence. Matthews v. State, 200 Ind. 53, 161 N.E. 271, 1928 Ind. LEXIS 38 (1928).

Sentence.

—Reasonable.

There was nothing inappropriate about a 17-year sentence under IC 35-45-4-4 for a woman who accepted cash in exchange for allowing multiple men to molest her 12-year old daughter. Day v. State, 898 N.E.2d 471, 2008 Ind. App. LEXIS 2610 (2008).

—Revised.

Sentence imposed upon defendant for promoting prostitution was revised because the nature of defendant's offense did not warrant an enhanced sentence for a Class B felony under IC 35-45-4-4 and IC 35-50-2-5 as defendant's promotion of prostitution was highly attenuated. In addition, the appellate court found that: (1) defendant only attempted to, and did not actually, perform sex acts on one occasion; (2) defendant did not abuse a position of trust; and (3) although defendant's criminal history was not inconsequential, defendants' convictions were not significant aggravators in relation to the Class B felony offense. Hayes v. State, 906 N.E.2d 819, 2009 Ind. LEXIS 462 (2009).

Cited:

South Bend v. Bowman, 434 N.E.2d 104, 1982 Ind. App. LEXIS 1167 (1982); Young v. State, 446 N.E.2d 624, 1983 Ind. App. LEXIS 2754 (1983).

RESEARCH REFERENCES

Indiana Law Review.

Update — Criminal Law and Procedure, 26 Ind. L. Rev. 891 (1993).

35-45-4-5. Voyeurism.

(a) A person:
  (1) who:
    (A) peeps; or
    (B) goes upon the land of another with the intent to peep;
into an occupied dwelling of another person; or
  (2) who peeps into an area where an occupant of the area reasonably can be expected to disrobe, including:
    (A) restrooms;
    (B) baths;
    (C) showers; and
    (D) dressing rooms;
without the consent of the other person, commits voyeurism, a Class B misdemeanor.

(b) However, the offense under subsection (a) is a Class D felony if:

(1) it is knowingly or intentionally committed by means of a camera, a video camera, or any other type of video recording device; or

(2) the person who commits the offense has a prior unrelated conviction:

(A) under this section; or

(B) in another jurisdiction, including a military court, for an offense that is substantially similar to an offense described in this section.

(c) "Peep" means any looking of a clandestine, surreptitious, prying, or secretive nature.

History.
IC 35-45-4-5, as added by P.L.311-1983, § 31; P.L.301-1995, § 1; P.L.215-1997, § 2; P.L.7-2005, § 1.

Compiler's Notes.
P.L.7-2005, § 2, effective July 1, 2005, provides:

"The enhanced penalty under IC 35-45-4-5(b)(2), as added by this act, applies only if at least one (1) of the offenses is committed after June 30, 2005."

NOTES TO DECISIONS

ANALYSIS

Attorney Misconduct.
Lack of Consent.

Attorney Misconduct.
The strong element of concealment attendant to clandestine surveillance of attorney who pled guilty to six counts of voyeurism implicated his honesty and trustworthiness, and brought into question his fitness as one who could be trusted to keep his client's secrets or give legal advice. In re Haecker, 664 N.E.2d 1176, 1996 Ind. LEXIS 42 (1996).

Lack of Consent.
Trial court reasonably inferred the lack of consent necessary under IC 35-45-4-5(a) to establish defendant was engaged in voyeurism from evidence that defendant was observed standing on an air conditioning unit at 5 a.m. in the morning peering into the victim's bathroom window and that defendant fled when confronted by one of the victim's neighbors. Saxton v. State, 790 N.E.2d 98, 2003 Ind. LEXIS 523 (2003).

Cited:
Lee v. State, 826 N.E.2d 131, 2005 Ind. App. LEXIS 671 (2005).

RESEARCH REFERENCES

Valparaiso University Law Review.
Scowl Because You're on Candid Camera: Privacy and Video Surveillance, 31 Val. U.L. Rev. 1079 (1997).

CHAPTER 5

GAMBLING

35-45-5-1. Definitions.

(a) The definitions in this section apply throughout this chapter.

(b) "Electronic gaming device" means any electromechanical device, electrical device, or machine that satisfies at least one (1) of the following requirements:

(1) It is a contrivance which for consideration affords the player an opportunity to obtain money or other items of value, the award of which is determined by chance even if accomplished by some skill, whether or not the prize is automatically paid by the contrivance.

(2) It is a slot machine or any simulation or variation of a slot machine.

(3) It is a matchup or lineup game machine or device operated for consideration, in which two (2) or more numerals, symbols, letters, or icons align in a winning combination on one (1) or more lines vertically, horizontally, diagonally, or otherwise, without assistance by the player. The use of a skill stop is not considered assistance by the player.

(4) It is a video game machine or device operated for consideration to play poker, blackjack, any other card game, keno, or any simulation or variation of these games, including any game in which numerals, numbers, pictures, representations, or symbols are used as an equivalent or substitute for the cards used in these games.

The term does not include a toy crane machine or any other device played for amusement that rewards a player exclusively with a toy, a novelty, candy, other noncash merchandise, or a ticket or coupon redeemable for a toy, a novelty, or other noncash merchandise that has a wholesale value of not more than the lesser of ten (10) times the amount charged to play the amusement device one (1) time or twenty-five dollars ($25).

(c) "Gain" means the direct realization of winnings.

(d) "Gambling" means risking money or other property for gain, contingent in whole or in part upon lot, chance, or the operation of a gambling device, but it does not include participating in:

(1) bona fide contests of skill, speed, strength, or endurance in which awards are made only to entrants or the owners of entries; or

(2) bona fide business transactions that are valid under the law of contracts.

(e) "Gambling device" means:

(1) a mechanism by the operation of which a right to money or other property may be credited, in return for consideration, as the result of the operation of an element of chance;

(2) a mechanism that, when operated for a consideration, does not return the same value or property for the same consideration upon each operation;

(3) a mechanism, furniture, fixture, construction, or installation designed primarily for use in connection with professional gambling;

(4) a policy ticket or wheel; or

(5) a subassembly or essential part designed or intended for use in connection with such a device, mechanism, furniture, fixture, construction, or installation.

In the application of this definition, an immediate and unrecorded right to replay mechanically conferred on players of pinball machines and similar amusement devices is presumed to be without value.

(f) "Gambling information" means:

(1) a communication with respect to a wager made in the course of professional gambling; or

(2) information intended to be used for professional gambling.

(g) "Interactive computer service" means an Internet service, an information service, a system, or an access software provider that provides or enables computer access to a computer served by multiple users. The term includes the following:

(1) A service or system that provides access or is an intermediary to the Internet.

(2) A system operated or services offered by a library, school, state educational institution, or private postsecondary educational institution.

(h) "Operator" means a person who owns, maintains, or operates an Internet site that is used for interactive gambling.

(i) "Profit" means a realized or unrealized benefit (other than a gain) and includes benefits from proprietorship or management and unequal advantage in a series of transactions.

(j) "Tournament" means a contest in which:

(1) the consideration to enter the contest may take the form of a separate entry fee or the deposit of the required consideration to play in any manner accepted by the:

(A) video golf machine; or

(B) pinball machine or similar amusement device described in subsection (m)(2);

on which the entrant will compete;

(2) each player's score is recorded; and

(3) the contest winner and other prize winners are determined by objectively comparing the recorded scores of the competing players.

(k) "Toy crane machine" means a device that is used to lift prizes from an enclosed space by manipulating a mechanical claw.

(l) For purposes of this chapter:

(1) a card game; or

(2) an electronic version of a card game;

is a game of chance and may not be considered a bona fide contest of skill.

(m) In the application of the definition of gambling set forth in subsection (d), the payment of consideration to participate in a tournament conducted on:

(1) video golf games; or

(2) pinball machines and similar amusement devices that award no prizes other than to mechanically confer an immediate and unrecorded right to replay on players that is presumed to be without value under this section;

is not considered gambling even if the value of a prize awarded in the course of the tournament exceeds the amount of the player's consideration.

History.

IC 35-45-5-1, as added by Acts 1976, P.L.148, § 5; 1977, P.L.340, § 80; P.L.70-2005, § 2; P.L.2-2007, § 377, eff. July 1, 2007; P.L.227-2007, § 64, emergency eff. July 1, 2007; P.L.3-2008, § 252, emergency eff. March 13, 2008.

NOTES TO DECISIONS

Analysis

Business Accounting.
"Gambling Device."
—Federal Indictment.
—Purchase of Out-of-State Lottery Tickets.
Lotteries.
—Purchase of Out-of-State Tickets.
Pinball Machines.
—Exception.
"Profit."
—Wages.
Tip Books.
Value of Amusement.

Business Accounting.

Because both the ownership of and the profits from electronic poker and video slot machines were illegal under IC 35-45-5-4, any accounting of a partnership could not include the value of or the profits from those machines. Monar v. Hurt, 791 N.E.2d 280, 2003 Ind. App. LEXIS 1247 (2003).

"Gambling Device."

There is no blatant ambiguity in this section which clearly defines "gambling" and "gambling devices," and assuming operation of a certain machine did not constitute gambling based upon the skill exception, it did not follow that its lawful use ipso facto insulated that machine from a violation of the gambling device prohibition. State v. Maillard, 695 N.E.2d 637, 1998 Ind. App. LEXIS 907 (1998).

"Free Spin" machine was found to be a gambling device since when a player put a dollar in the machine it ejected a sports card and then allowed the player to play a video game in which, if the player earned prize credits, he could redeem the point score for cash at the rate of five cents per

"Gambling Device." (Cont'd)
prize credit. Jack Eiser Sales Co. v. Wilson, 752
N.E.2d 225, 2001 Ind. App. LEXIS 1241 (2001).

Cardboard cards sold from vending machines by
corporation that had discount coupon on one side
and cash prize game on other side and which gave
purchaser chance to win money or property con-
stitued illegal gambling device. F.A.C.E. Trading,
Inc. v. Carter, 821 N.E.2d 38, 2005 Ind. App.
LEXIS 74 (2005).

—Federal Indictment.
This section did not control the definition of an
"amusement device" for the purpose of the meaning of a federal indictment charging that the
defendants travelled in interstate commerce with
the intent to extort money from a business supplying and servicing "electronic game and amusement
machines," which included electronic poker machines, which might have been classified as "gambling devices" under this section. United States v.
Esposito, 771 F.2d 283, 1985 U.S. App. LEXIS
22603 (7th Cir. Ind. 1985), cert. denied, 475 U.S.
1011, 106 S. Ct. 1187, 89 L. Ed. 2d 302, 1986 U.S.
LEXIS 241 (1986).

—Purchase of Out-of-State Lottery Tickets.
Out-of-state corporation which proposed to purchase lottery tickets from other states for Indiana
residents, for profit, would have engaged in illegal
gambling, and its equipment for the transmission
and receipt of information constituted gambling
devices. L.E. Servs. v. State Lottery Comm'n, 646
N.E.2d 334, 1995 Ind. App. LEXIS 76 (1995).

Lotteries.

—Purchase of Out-of-State Tickets.
By accepting, or offering to accept, money from
Indiana residents for the purchase of out-of-state
lottery tickets, and by profiting from that activity,
an out-of-state corporation violated this section.
L.E. Servs. v. State Lottery Comm'n, 646 N.E.2d
334, 1995 Ind. App. LEXIS 76 (1995).

Pinball Machines.
The statutes pertaining to gambling made the
maintaining of pinball machines which record the
right of replay mala prohibita. Peachey v. Boswell,
240 Ind. 604, 167 N.E.2d 48, 1960 Ind. LEXIS 233,
89 A.L.R.2d 801 (1960).

—Exception.
Although appellee's machines may have had
certain physical resemblances to so-called one-ball
machines and metered free-play pinball machines
which did not produce free-play mechanically, it
could not be said that it was unreasonable or

arbitrary to distinguish between such machines
and appellee's machines which gave only a mechanically conferred immediate right to replay.
Tinder v. Music Operating, Inc., 237 Ind. 33, 142
N.E.2d 610, 1957 Ind. LEXIS 247 (1957).

Where an affidavit that the informant believed
defendant did wrongfully store, keep and possess a
gambling device and slot machine charged violation of Acts 1935, ch. 321, § 2, it was sufficient as
against the contention that it was necessary to
negate the exception regarding right to replay
contained in prior section. Worl v. State, 243 Ind.
116, 183 N.E.2d 594, 1962 Ind. LEXIS 140 (1962).

A pinball machine containing a meter visible to
the player which showed the number of unplayed
games for which the player had prepaid plus any
unused replay rights the player had won was not
within the exception of prior section that immediate and unrecorded right to replay mechanically
conferred on players should be presumed to be
without value and was a gambling device within
the definition of said section. Eads v. J. & J. Sales
Corp., 257 Ind. 485, 275 N.E.2d 802, 1971 Ind.
LEXIS 564 (1971).

"Profit."

—Wages.
Under the statutory definition of profit, a weekly
paycheck in exchange for services would be a
profit. Accordingly, when defendants, as part of
their employment, collected proceeds from gambling operations and received a paycheck for doing
it, they accepted, for profit, money risked in gambling. Auten v. State, 542 N.E.2d 215, 1989 Ind.
App. LEXIS 777 (1989).

Tip Books.
Since legislature defines gambling device as a
"mechanism" this would exclude a tip book from
the operation of the law as a gambling device.
Higdon v. State, 241 Ind. 501, 173 N.E.2d 58, 1961
Ind. LEXIS 158 (1961).

Value of Amusement.
The argument that only those machines were
illegal under prior statute defining "slot machine"
which by the insertion of a coin and by operation of
chance the user becomes entitled to "money, credit
or something of value" was without merit as it
could not be claimed that amusement itself is
valueless. Worl v. State, 243 Ind. 116, 183 N.E.2d
594, 1962 Ind. LEXIS 140 (1962).

Cited:
Kaszuba v. Zientara, 495 N.E.2d 761, 1986 Ind.
App. LEXIS 2815 (1986); Lashbrook v. State, 550
N.E.2d 772, 1990 Ind. App. LEXIS 228 (1990);
United States v. Cross, 113 F. Supp. 2d 1253, 2000
U.S. Dist. LEXIS 13184 (S.D. Ind. 2000).

OPINIONS OF ATTORNEY GENERAL

Scoring machine in which a nickel is placed and
a number of balls shot at holes for the purpose of
determining the score, where the score determines
whether or not the player is to be rewarded and the

amount of the award, is a gambling device and
illegal. 1935, p. 23.

A freegame meter, visible to the player of a
pinball machine, is a "recorder" and does render a

machine equipped with such a meter illegal as a "gambling device" regardless of whether the right to replay is mechanically or electronically conferred. 1968, No. 32, p. 213.

Fund raising functions at which sums of money and other door prizes are awarded to ticket holders, were gambling functions within the definitions of IC 35-45-5-1 and were in violation of former Ind. Const., art. 15, § 8. 1980, No. 80-1, p. 1.

Since Bingo is a game of chance, it constitutes gambling within the meaning of this section and IC 35-45-5-2. 1987, No. 87-21, p. 105 (for regulation of Bingo games, see IC 4-32.2).

When a person physically located in Indiana wagers over the Internet, both the persons making and taking the bet violate Indiana law, because the gambler is knowingly or intentionally risking money for gain based on lot or chance. 1998, No. 98-8.

A "skill slot" machine was a gambling device within the meaning of the statute by virtue of the fact that property or value could be credited as the result of the operation of an "element of chance" and because "phantom pays" did not return the same property for the same consideration upon each operation. 2001, No. 2001-9.

RESEARCH REFERENCES

Collateral References.

Paraphernalia or appliances used for recording gambling transactions or receiving or furnishing gambling information as gaming "devices" within criminal statute or ordinance. 1 A.L.R.3d 726.

Validity, construction, and application of statutes or ordinances involved in prosecutions for possession of bookmaking paraphernalia. 51 A.L.R.4th 796.

Validity, construction, and application of stat-utes or ordinances involved in prosecutions for transmission of wagers or wagering information related to bookmaking. 53 A.L.R.4th 801.

Private contests and lotteries: entrants' rights and remedies. 64 A.L.R.4th 1021.

Validity, construction, and application of statute or ordinance prohibiting or regulating use or occupancy of premises for bookmaking or pool selling. 82 A.L.R.4th 356.

35-45-5-2. Unlawful gambling.

(a) A person who knowingly or intentionally engages in gambling commits unlawful gambling.

(b) Except as provided in subsection (c), unlawful gambling is a Class B misdemeanor.

(c) An operator who knowingly or intentionally uses the Internet to engage in unlawful gambling:

    (1) in Indiana; or

    (2) with a person located in Indiana;

commits a Class D felony.

History.

IC 35-45-5-2, as added by Acts 1976, P.L.148, § 5; 1977, P.L.340, § 81; P.L.70-2005, § 3.

Compiler's Notes.

P.L.70-2005, § 8, effective July 1, 2005, provides: "IC 35-45-5-2 and IC 35-45-5-3, both as amended by this act, apply only to crimes committed after June 30, 2005."

Cross References.

Gambling debts and losses, IC 34-16-1.

Penalties for felonies, IC 35-50-1, IC 35-50-2, IC 35-50-5-2.

State lottery exempt from anti-lottery laws, IC 4-30-18-4.

NOTES TO DECISIONS

ANALYSIS

Constitutionality.
Conviction for Keeping Gambling House.
Enforcement of Gambling Claim.
Evidence.
Horserace Premiums.
Included Offenses.
Indictment.
—Gambler.
—Gaming.
—Visiting Gambling House.

Instructions.
Jurisdiction.
Out-of-State Lottery.
Police Power.
Proof.
Pyramid Scheme.
Visiting Gambling House Generally.
What Constitutes Gaming.
Witnesses.

Constitutionality.

Indiana's anti-gambling statutes do not violate

Constitutionality. (Cont'd)
Ind. Const., art. 1, § 23 and the equal protection clause of the fourteenth amendment to the United States Constitution. American Legion Post # 113 v. State, 656 N.E.2d 1190, 1995 Ind. App. LEXIS 1364 (1995).

Conviction for Keeping Gambling House.
Conviction of a person for keeping a gambling house did not prevent his prosecution for being a common gambler, or of frequenting the house kept by himself. De Haven v. State, 2 Ind. App. 376, 28 N.E. 562, 1891 Ind. App. LEXIS 180 (1891).

Enforcement of Gambling Claim.
The law will not aid either of the parties in enforcing a claim against the other growing out of a gambling transaction. Vaughn v. Glibota, 108 Ind. App. 156, 27 N.E.2d 400, 1940 Ind. App. LEXIS 26 (1940).
Recovery would not be granted plaintiff for money loaned to defendant for a gambling purpose. Vaughn v. Glibota, 108 Ind. App. 156, 27 N.E.2d 400, 1940 Ind. App. LEXIS 26 (1940).

Evidence.
Circumstantial evidence was admissible to show that a house was used for gaming. Roberts v. State, 25 Ind. App. 366, 58 N.E. 203, 1900 Ind. App. LEXIS 100 (1900); Neeld v. State, 25 Ind. App. 603, 58 N.E. 734, 1900 Ind. App. LEXIS 142 (1900).

Horserace Premiums.
The offering of premiums to the owners of horses whose horse would make the best time in trials of speed was not illegal. Alvord v. Smith, 63 Ind. 58, 1878 Ind. LEXIS 308 (1878); Mullen v. Beech Grove Driving Park, 64 Ind. 202, 1878 Ind. LEXIS 464 (1878).

Included Offenses.
Gambling is not a lesser included offense of professional gambling. Auten v. State, 542 N.E.2d 215, 1989 Ind. App. LEXIS 777 (1989).

Indictment.

—Gambler.
An indictment against a person for frequenting a place where gambling was permitted did not need to aver the kind of games permitted, nor that the defendant gambled. Howard v. State, 64 Ind. 516, 1878 Ind. LEXIS 530 (1878).
An indictment that charged a person with being a professional gambler by charging him with frequenting places where gambling was permitted had to allege with what purpose he frequented such places. State v. Allen, 69 Ind. 124, 1879 Ind. LEXIS 34 (1879).
An indictment charging a person with being a common gambler could, in the same count, allege that the defendant was guilty of all the acts specified in the statute defining such offense. Bickell v. State, 32 Ind. App. 656, 70 N.E. 548, 1904 Ind. App. LEXIS 131 (1904).
In charging a person with being a common gambler, the kind or character of gambling in-

dulged in should have been alleged. Bickell v. State, 32 Ind. App. 656, 70 N.E. 548, 1904 Ind. App. LEXIS 131 (1904).

—Gaming.
The particular game played did not need to be stated in the indictment, but some description thereof should be given. State v. Maxwell, 1839 Ind. LEXIS 118 (1839); Webster v. State, 8 Blackf. 400, 1847 Ind. LEXIS 45 (1847).
An indictment for gaming had to name the persons engaged in the game, and with whom the bet was made, if known. Butler v. State, 1840 Ind. LEXIS 17 (1840); State v. Stallings, 3 Ind. 531 (1852).
The indictment should state the amount lost or won. Long v. State, 13 Ind. 480, 13 Ind. 566, 1859 Ind. LEXIS 511 (1859).
An indictment, alleging the winning or losing on the result of an election before the election was held, was bad. State v. Windell, 60 Ind. 300, 1878 Ind. LEXIS 8 (1878).

—Visiting Gambling House.
In charging the frequenting or visiting of a gambling house, it was not necessary to give any particular description of the house or its location more than that the house was situated in a designated county. State v. Bridgewater, 171 Ind. 1, 85 N.E. 715, 1908 Ind. LEXIS 87 (1908); State v. Henson, 171 Ind. 725, 85 N.E. 718, 1908 Ind. LEXIS 153 (1908); Christison v. State, 177 Ind. 363, 98 N.E. 113, 1912 Ind. LEXIS 32 (1912); State v. Anderson, 177 Ind. 437, 98 N.E. 289, 1912 Ind. LEXIS 36 (1912).
In charging a person with visiting a gambling house, it was not necessary to allege that such person did not visit such house as physician to treat a patient, as the clause in prior statute making the exception as to physicians applied only to houses of ill fame. Christison v. State, 177 Ind. 363, 98 N.E. 113, 1912 Ind. LEXIS 32 (1912).
In charging the offenses of visiting a gambling house, it was sufficient to make the charge in the language of the statute defining the offense, and the word "gaming-house" was equivalent to the word "gambling-house." State v. Frederick, 183 Ind. 509, 109 N.E. 747, 1915 Ind. LEXIS 87 (1915).

Instructions.
Refusal of instruction that defendant could not be convicted for violation of gaming laws unless he himself gambled was not error under common gambler statute, where it was established that gambling was permitted. Mitchell v. State, 233 Ind. 16, 115 N.E.2d 595, 1953 Ind. LEXIS 283 (1953), cert. denied, 347 U.S. 975, 74 S. Ct. 786, 98 L. Ed. 1114, 1954 U.S. LEXIS 2064 (1954).

Jurisdiction.
If a professional gambler went into a county on lawful business, and did not gamble therein, he could not be indicted in such county for being a professional gambler. Bowe v. State, 25 Ind. 415, 1865 Ind. LEXIS 254 (1865).

Out-of-State Lottery.
An Indiana agreement to purchase an Illinois

Out-of-State Lottery. (Cont'd)

lotto ticket, in Illinois, is not an illegal and immoral agreement and is not unenforceable by Indiana courts. Kaszuba v. Zientara, 506 N.E.2d 1, 1987 Ind. LEXIS 874 (1987).

Out-of-state corporation which proposed to purchase lottery tickets from other states for Indiana residents, for profit, proposed to accept, or offer to accept, for profit, money to be risked in gambling, and its activities constituted illegal gambling. L.E. Servs. v. State Lottery Comm'n, 646 N.E.2d 334, 1995 Ind. App. LEXIS 76 (1995).

Police Power.

State's regulation of gambling does not constitute an unreasonable exercise of police power. American Legion Post # 113 v. State, 656 N.E.2d 1190, 1995 Ind. App. LEXIS 1364 (1995).

Proof.

The proof had to correspond to the allegations in the indictment as to the persons between whom the bet was made, and as to the losing or winning of money or articles. Tate v. State, 1839 Ind. LEXIS 77 (1839); Iseley v. State, 8 Blackf. 403, 1847 Ind. LEXIS 47 (1847); Jackson v. State, 4 Ind. 560, 1853 Ind. LEXIS 205 (1853); Carr v. State, 50 Ind. 178, 1875 Ind. LEXIS 86 (1875); Middaugh v. State, 103 Ind. 78, 2 N.E. 292, 1885 Ind. LEXIS 478 (1885).

It was not necessary to prove the winning or losing of the exact sum laid in the indictment. Parsons v. State, 2 Ind. 499, 1851 Ind. LEXIS 107 (1851); Alexander v. State, 99 Ind. 450, 1885 Ind. LEXIS 130 (1885).

Proof that the accused was once in a gambling house would not sustain a charge of frequenting such place. Green v. State, 109 Ind. 175, 9 N.E. 781, 1887 Ind. LEXIS 125 (1887); Roberts v. State, 25 Ind. App. 366, 58 N.E. 203, 1900 Ind. App. LEXIS 100 (1900).

Pyramid Scheme.

"Airplane investment program" pyramid scheme was an illegal lottery, and constituted illegal gambling, where participants were required to pay for a "seat" and thereby risk money for gain. Lashbrook v. State, 550 N.E.2d 772, 1990 Ind. App. LEXIS 228 (1990).

Visiting Gambling House Generally.

A single visit to a gambling house constituted an offense. Roberts v. State, 25 Ind. App. 366, 58 N.E. 203, 1900 Ind. App. LEXIS 100 (1900).

The fact that a house was a gambling house could be established by circumstances. Roberts v. State, 25 Ind. App. 366, 58 N.E. 203, 1900 Ind. App. LEXIS 100 (1900).

On the charge of visiting a gambling house, proof could be made of the reputation of the house and of the visitors found therein. Christison v. State, 177 Ind. 363, 98 N.E. 113, 1912 Ind. LEXIS 32 (1912).

What Constitutes Gaming.

Betting on a horse race was gaming. Cheesum v. State, 1847 Ind. LEXIS 14 (1846); Wade v. Deming, 9 Ind. 34, 9 Ind. 35, 1857 Ind. LEXIS 477 (1857).

An indictment would lie upon a conditional contract for the sale of property depending upon the result of an election. Parsons v. State, 2 Ind. 499, 1851 Ind. LEXIS 107 (1851); Hizer v. State, 12 Ind. 289, 12 Ind. 330, 1859 Ind. LEXIS 138 (1859).

When persons played a game under an arrangement that the loser was to pay for the use of any article used in playing the game, it was gaming. Mount v. State, 7 Ind. 521, 7 Ind. 654, 1856 Ind. LEXIS 374 (1856); Crawford v. State, 33 Ind. 304, 1870 Ind. LEXIS 111 (1870); Alexander v. State, 99 Ind. 450, 1885 Ind. LEXIS 130 (1885).

To make a bet or wager criminal, it had to be made upon some of the things included within the statute relating to gaming. Smoot v. State, 18 Ind. 18, 1862 Ind. LEXIS 221 (1862); Alvord v. Smith, 63 Ind. 58, 1878 Ind. LEXIS 308 (1878).

Betting on the result of an election was gaming. Frazee v. State, 58 Ind. 8, 1877 Ind. LEXIS 126 (1877).

Offering premiums or rewards for the exhibition or contests of skill or speed was not gaming. Alvord v. Smith, 63 Ind. 58, 1878 Ind. LEXIS 308 (1878); Mullen v. Beech Grove Driving Park, 64 Ind. 202, 1878 Ind. LEXIS 464 (1878).

Witnesses.

Persons who were parties to a bet could be compelled to testify as to the same, on condition of being exempted from prosecution. Frazee v. State, 58 Ind. 8, 1877 Ind. LEXIS 126 (1877).

Cited:

In re Brown, 86 B.R. 944, 1988 U.S. Dist. LEXIS 4870 (N.D. Ind. 1988); State v. Allen, 525 N.E.2d 1267, 1988 Ind. App. LEXIS 515 (1988); Lashbrook v. State, 550 N.E.2d 772, 1990 Ind. App. LEXIS 228 (1990).

OPINIONS OF ATTORNEY GENERAL

Since Bingo is a game of chance, it constitutes gambling within the meaning of IC 35-45-5-1 and this section. 1987, No. 87-21, p. 105 (for regulation of Bingo games, see IC 4-32.2).

RESEARCH REFERENCES

Collateral References.

Private contests and lotteries: entrants' rights and remedies. 64 A.L.R.4th 1021.

Validity, construction, and application of statute or ordinance prohibiting or regulating use or occupancy of premises for bookmaking or pool selling. 82 A.L.R.4th 356.

35-45-5-3. Professional gambling.

(a) A person who knowingly or intentionally:

(1) engages in pool-selling;

(2) engages in bookmaking;

(3) maintains, in a place accessible to the public, slot machines, one-ball machines or variants thereof, pinball machines that award anything other than an immediate and unrecorded right of replay, roulette wheels, dice tables, or money or merchandise pushcards, punchboards, jars, or spindles;

(4) conducts lotteries or policy or numbers games or sells chances therein;

(5) conducts any banking or percentage games played with cards, dice, or counters, or accepts any fixed share of the stakes therein; or

(6) accepts, or offers to accept, for profit, money, or other property risked in gambling;

commits professional gambling, a Class D felony. However, the offense is a Class C felony if the person has a prior unrelated conviction under this subsection.

(b) An operator who knowingly or intentionally uses the Internet to:

(1) engage in pool-selling:

(A) in Indiana; or

(B) in a transaction directly involving a person located in Indiana;

(2) engage in bookmaking:

(A) in Indiana; or

(B) in a transaction directly involving a person located in Indiana;

(3) maintain, on an Internet site accessible to residents of Indiana, the equivalent of:

(A) slot machines;

(B) one-ball machines or variants of one-ball machines;

(C) pinball machines that award anything other than an immediate and unrecorded right of replay;

(D) roulette wheels;

(E) dice tables; or

(F) money or merchandise pushcards, punchboards, jars, or spindles;

(4) conduct lotteries or policy or numbers games or sell chances in lotteries or policy or numbers games:

(A) in Indiana; or

(B) in a transaction directly involving a person located in Indiana;

(5) conduct any banking or percentage games played with the computer equivalent of cards, dice, or counters, or accept any fixed share of the stakes in those games:

(A) in Indiana; or

(B) in a transaction directly involving a person located in Indiana; or

(6) accept, or offer to accept, for profit, money or other property risked in gambling:

(A) in Indiana; or

(B) in a transaction directly involving a person located in Indiana;

commits professional gambling over the Internet, a Class D felony.

History.

IC 35-45-5-3, as added by Acts 1976, P.L.148, § 5; 1977, P.L.340, § 82; P.L.70-2005, § 4; P.L.227-2007, § 65, emergency eff. July 1, 2007.

Compiler's Notes.

P.L.227-2007, § 71, effective July 1, 2007, provides:

"(a) IC 35-45-5-3 and IC 35-45-5-4, both as amended by this act, apply only to crimes committed after June 30, 2007.

"(b) IC 35-45-5-3.5, as added by this act, applies only to crimes and infractions committed after June 30, 2007."

Cross References.

Penalties for felonies, IC 35-50-1, IC 35-50-2, IC 35-50-5-2.

Pinball machines as gambling devices, see annotations to IC 35-45-5-1.

NOTES TO DECISIONS

Constitutionality.

The legislature was acting within its constitutional powers in designating pinball machines which record the right of replay as gambling devices and providing that anyone maintaining them in any place accessible to the public is guilty of professional gambling. Peachey v. Boswell, 240 Ind. 604, 167 N.E.2d 48, 1960 Ind. LEXIS 233, 89 A.L.R.2d 801 (1960).

The use and maintaining of pinball machines was legally proscribed by the legislature, and the owner cannot complain that he is prevented from conducting a business (of maintaining such machines) which is unlawful and thus deprived of the property right without due process of law. Peachey v. Boswell, 240 Ind. 604, 167 N.E.2d 48, 1960 Ind. LEXIS 233, 89 A.L.R.2d 801 (1960).

Subdivision (6) is not unconstitutionally vague. Auten v. State, 542 N.E.2d 215, 1989 Ind. App. LEXIS 777 (1989).

Indiana's anti-gambling statutes do not violate Ind. Const., art. 1, § 23 and the equal protection clause of the fourteenth amendment to the United States Constitution. American Legion Post # 113 v. State, 656 N.E.2d 1190, 1995 Ind. App. LEXIS 1364 (1995).

—Equal Protection.

In light of the heavy case load facing a prosecutor, failure to prosecute charitable organizations in no way established that defendants were denied equal protection of the law. Lee v. State, 397 N.E.2d 1047, 1979 Ind. App. LEXIS 1484 (1979), cert. denied, 449 U.S. 983, 101 S. Ct. 399, 66 L. Ed. 2d 245, 1980 U.S. LEXIS 3906 (1980).

Applicability.

Mere bettors on the Super Bowl are not committing professional gambling under subdivision (6). Auten v. State, 542 N.E.2d 215, 1989 Ind. App. LEXIS 777 (1989).

Betting on Election Generally.

If property was sold to be paid for or not according to the result of an election, the parties were subject to a criminal prosecution. Parsons v. State, 2 Ind. 499, 1851 Ind. LEXIS 107 (1851); Hizer v. State, 12 Ind. 289, 12 Ind. 330, 1859 Ind. LEXIS 138 (1859); Davis v. Leonard, 69 Ind. 213, 1879 Ind. LEXIS 56 (1879).

The offense under Acts 1857, ch. 26, § 1, p. 35 consisted in betting or wagering money or property on the result of an election without regard to losing or winning such money or property. Frazee v. State, 58 Ind. 8, 1877 Ind. LEXIS 126 (1877).

If property was to be paid for or not, as an election may result, the purchaser could not be charged with losing money on the result of the election. Wagner v. State, 63 Ind. 250, 1878 Ind. LEXIS 345 (1878).

Bingo.

Bingo played for a prize received by chance or lot in exchange for consideration is a lottery and prohibited by this section. Pruitt v. State, 557 N.E.2d 684, 1990 Ind. App. LEXIS 959 (1990) (for regulation of Bingo games, see IC 4-32.2).

Elements of Offense.

The gravamen of the crime of professional gambling is not the harm done to a third party, but rather the acceptance or offer to accept, for profit, money risked in gambling and the offense is complete when there is acceptance or offer to accept; the party who bets the money is really only a collateral element to the offense. Robb v. State, 15 Ind. Dec. 137, 239 N.E.2d 154 (Ind. 1968).

The elements of a violation of subdivision (6) of this section are that a person must (1) knowingly or intentionally, (2) accept, or offer to accept, (3) for profit, (4) money risked in gambling. L.E. Servs. v. State Lottery Comm'n, 646 N.E.2d 334, 1995 Ind. App. LEXIS 76 (1995).

—Knowingly or Intentionally.

The interpretation of "knowing and intentionally" in this section pertains to the operation of a gambling device rather than knowledge or intent to violate a specific statute. United States v. Cross, 113 F. Supp. 2d 1253, 2000 U.S. Dist. LEXIS 13184 (S.D. Ind. 2000).

Evidence.

—Admissibility.

When lottery tickets could be produced, parol evidence of their contents was not admissible. Whitney v. State, 10 Ind. 306, 10 Ind. 404, 1858 Ind. LEXIS 901 (1858).

—Circumstantial.

Professional gambling may be proven by circumstantial evidence. Walker v. State, 155 Ind. App. 404, 293 N.E.2d 35, 1973 Ind. App. LEXIS 1234 (1973), cert. denied, 414 U.S. 1158, 94 S. Ct. 916, 39 L. Ed. 2d 110, 1974 U.S. LEXIS 1616 (1974); State v. Stone, 160 Ind. App. 226, 311 N.E.2d 446, 1974 Ind. App. LEXIS 1036 (1974).

—Insufficient.

In a prosecution for violation of lottery statute, evidence that accused sold certain cards, to be used in the operation of a lottery, but not showing that accused had any part in the lottery by the use of such tickets, was sufficient to authorize a conviction. McDaniels v. State, 185 Ind. 245, 113 N.E. 1004, 1916 Ind. LEXIS 44 (1916).

—Sufficient.

Evidence that defendant owned the premises, was present during the game, that dealers collected chips which were not retained by them, and other evidence was sufficient to establish a prima facie case that defendant had accepted a fixed share of the poker game stakes. State v. Stone, 160 Ind. App. 226, 311 N.E.2d 446, 1974 Ind. App. LEXIS 1036 (1974).

Where patrons relinquished control over their money, and defendant accepted the money risked to play bingo and other games on behalf of the enterprise, defendant exerted "control" over the patrons' money to an extent other than that to which they had consented, and by promising a performance, the payment of a share of the proceeds to certain charitable organizations that defendant and his affiliates knew would not be performed, defendant's acts enabled the operators of the enterprise to accept money risked in gambling for profit, and he could be convicted as a principal whether or not he committed every element of the crime of professional gambling himself. Dix v. State, 639 N.E.2d 363, 1994 Ind. App. LEXIS 1142 (1994).

Indictment or Information.

—Betting on Election.

An indictment was not bad for alleging that the bet was made the day after the election was held. State v. Little, 1842 Ind. LEXIS 98 (1842).

An indictment alleging the winning or losing of an article on the result of an election, alleged to have taken place after the return of the indictment, was bad. State v. Windell, 60 Ind. 300, 1878 Ind. LEXIS 8 (1878).

—Lottery.

An indictment for making a lottery for the division of property should describe the property. Markle v. State, 3 Ind. 535 (1852).

An indictment for selling lottery tickets should describe the tickets, or show an excuse for not doing so. Whitney v. State, 10 Ind. 306, 10 Ind. 404, 1858 Ind. LEXIS 901 (1858).

An indictment for selling a share or chance in a lottery substantially in the language of the statute was sufficient. Trout v. State, 111 Ind. 499, 12 N.E. 1005, 1887 Ind. LEXIS 290 (1887).

In charging a person with acting as the agent of a lottery or gift enterprise, it was sufficient to follow the language of the statute and allege generally that such person acted as the agent of a designated lottery. Nichols v. State, 28 Ind. App. 674, 63 N.E. 783, 1902 Ind. App. LEXIS 87 (1902).

An indictment charging aiding and abetting another in the commission of the crime defined by lottery statute had to charge either the selling of a lottery ticket or tickets or the selling of share or shares in a lottery scheme or gift enterprise, or that accused acted as agent for a lottery scheme or gift enterprise, as well as that he aided or abetted the commission of one of these offenses. McDaniels v. State, 185 Ind. 245, 113 N.E. 1004, 1916 Ind. LEXIS 44 (1916).

Indictment for lottery was sufficient as a general rule, if offense was charged in language of statute defining crime, or in terms substantially equivalent thereto. State v. McNulty, 228 Ind. 497, 92 N.E.2d 839, 1950 Ind. LEXIS 161 (1950).

The words "make" and "draw" were not generic terms, and they embrace many thoughts. Their use in indictment charging lottery was not improper. State v. McNulty, 228 Ind. 497, 92 N.E.2d 839, 1950 Ind. LEXIS 161 (1950).

Fact that indictment under lottery statute used word "lottery scheme" instead of "lottery" was unimportant. State v. McNulty, 228 Ind. 497, 92 N.E.2d 839, 1950 Ind. LEXIS 161 (1950).

Injunction.

Where the maintenance of pinball machines is made legal only on the basis of the statutory presumption that the free games awarded were "without value" and such presumption as to value might well disappear in the light of facts which might be presented in another particular case, an injunction against officers was contrary to law to the extent that it attempted to unconditionally and perpetually enjoin officers from interfering with or intimidating owners, lessees, operators or employees of the locations where such pinball machines were located. Tinder v. Music Operating, Inc., 237 Ind. 33, 142 N.E.2d 610, 1957 Ind. LEXIS 247 (1957).

Judicial Notice.

Courts would take judicial notice as to who was elected to an office at a general election. Hizer v. State, 12 Ind. 289, 12 Ind. 330, 1859 Ind. LEXIS 138 (1859).

Courts would take judicial notice that a "gift enterprise" was a scheme for the division of property by chance, and was a lottery. Lohman v. State, 81 Ind. 15, 1881 Ind. LEXIS 985 (1881).

Justification of Conduct.

—Assurances by Police.

A person operating a gambling device cannot

Justification of Conduct. (Cont'd)

—Assurances by Police. (Cont'd)
justify his conduct on the grounds that certain law enforcement officials assured him that operation of the machine would not result in criminal prosecution where the person was never told the operation of the machine would not violate state gambling laws, but, rather, was assured that use of the machine would be an acceptable level of gambling in the community. It is not the office of any law enforcement official to grant citizens a license to violate the law. In re Property Located at Marriott Inn, 505 Marriott Drive, 456 N.E.2d 444, 1983 Ind. App. LEXIS 3596 (1983), cert. denied, Carson v. Indiana, 470 U.S. 1005, 105 S. Ct. 1359, 84 L. Ed. 2d 380, 1985 U.S. LEXIS 1165 (1985).

Legislative Determination.
Whether or not the possession of pinball machines with the recorded right to replay should be made a crime in Indiana is a matter of policy to be determined by the legislature and not by the courts. Peachey v. Boswell, 240 Ind. 604, 167 N.E.2d 48, 1960 Ind. LEXIS 233, 89 A.L.R.2d 801 (1960).

Legislative Intent.
The legislature intended to distinguish between "professional gambling" as defined in the act, and "social pastimes" not for profit, and which do not affect the public. Peachey v. Boswell, 240 Ind. 604, 167 N.E.2d 48, 1960 Ind. LEXIS 233, 89 A.L.R.2d 801 (1960).

The clear intention of the legislature was to prohibit the use and maintaining of pinball machines which are equipped with recording devices that may be used to compute "payoffs". Peachey v. Boswell, 240 Ind. 604, 167 N.E.2d 48, 1960 Ind. LEXIS 233, 89 A.L.R.2d 801 (1960).

Lesser Included Offenses.
Gambling is not a lesser included offense of professional gambling. Auten v. State, 542 N.E.2d 215, 1989 Ind. App. LEXIS 777 (1989).

Lotteries.
The former constitutional provision against lotteries was in restraint of legislative authority to authorize lottery schemes in this state or the sale of tickets within the state in schemes organized without the state. Riggs v. Adams, 12 Ind. 175, 12 Ind. 199, 1859 Ind. LEXIS 107 (1859).

The lottery privilege conferred on Vincennes University by the territorial legislature of 1807, was abrogated by former Ind. Const., Art. 15, § 8. State v. Woodward, 89 Ind. 110, 1882 Ind. LEXIS 1022 (1882).

Nature of Defendant's Interest.
Under the statutory definition of profit, a weekly paycheck in exchange for services would be a profit. Accordingly, when defendants, as part of their employment, collected proceeds from gambling operations and received a paycheck for doing it, they accepted, for profit, money risked in gam-

bling. Auten v. State, 542 N.E.2d 215, 1989 Ind. App. LEXIS 777 (1989).

The statute does not require the state to prove the defendants had a fixed share of the stakes, or that the defendants had an ownership interest in the enterprise. Auten v. State, 542 N.E.2d 215, 1989 Ind. App. LEXIS 777 (1989).

Place Accessible to Public.
The phrase "in any place accessible to the public" means any place where the public is invited and is free to go upon special or implied invitation, a place available to all or a certain segment of the public. Peachey v. Boswell, 240 Ind. 604, 167 N.E.2d 48, 1960 Ind. LEXIS 233, 89 A.L.R.2d 801 (1960).

The phrase "in any place accessible to the public" does not create any privileged class, or permit the unrestricted use of such pinball machines in private homes, clubs or other nonprofit organizations, or in any other place not accessible to the public. Peachey v. Boswell, 240 Ind. 604, 167 N.E.2d 48, 1960 Ind. LEXIS 233, 89 A.L.R.2d 801 (1960).

The proscription of pinball machines with recorded right to replay in any place accessible to the public rests upon a reasonable basis. It does not violate the provisions of Ind. Const., art. 1, § 23 or the 14th Amendment of the Constitution of the United States. Peachey v. Boswell, 240 Ind. 604, 167 N.E.2d 48, 1960 Ind. LEXIS 233, 89 A.L.R.2d 801 (1960); Murley v. State, 240 Ind. 655, 168 N.E.2d 205, 1960 Ind. LEXIS 240 (1960).

The term "public place" as used in the statutes pertains to gambling, includes any place for the time being that is made public by the assemblage of people who go there with or without invitation and without restraint. Peachey v. Boswell, 240 Ind. 604, 167 N.E.2d 48, 1960 Ind. LEXIS 233, 89 A.L.R.2d 801 (1960).

The presence of the phrase "in any place accessible to the public" as used in this section does not render this antigambling statute unconstitutional as establishing an unreasonable and arbitrary classification. State v. Hi-Jinks, Inc., 242 Ind. 621, 181 N.E.2d 526, 1962 Ind. LEXIS 233 (1962).

Police Power.
This section does not violate or invade any fundamental right of the citizens of Indiana, and pinball machines, as described therein, come clearly within the ambit of the police power, and the legislature, by the exercise of such power, had the right to proscribe them and their use. Peachey v. Boswell, 240 Ind. 604, 167 N.E.2d 48, 1960 Ind. LEXIS 233, 89 A.L.R.2d 801 (1960).

State's regulation of gambling does not constitute an unreasonable exercise of police power. American Legion Post # 113 v. State, 656 N.E.2d 1190, 1995 Ind. App. LEXIS 1364 (1995).

Premiums Offered in Contests.
Premiums or rewards offered in contests or exhibitions of speed or skill did not constitute gaming. Alvord v. Smith, 63 Ind. 58, 1878 Ind. LEXIS 308 (1878); Mullen v. Beech Grove Driving Park, 64 Ind. 202, 1878 Ind. LEXIS 464 (1878).

Principal or Accomplice.

An active participant in the crimes of professional gambling or theft can be charged as a principal yet convicted as an accomplice in the crime; there is no distinction between the responsibility of a principal and an accomplice. Dix v. State, 639 N.E.2d 363, 1994 Ind. App. LEXIS 1142 (1994).

Purpose.

The purpose of prior section was to prohibit "professional gambling" as defined herein. Peachey v. Boswell, 240 Ind. 604, 167 N.E.2d 48, 1960 Ind. LEXIS 233, 89 A.L.R.2d 801 (1960).

Search and Seizure.

Where the operation of appellee's pinball machines was presumed to be legal under this act, the trial court had jurisdiction to enjoin their seizure by the prosecuting attorney. Tinder v. Music Operating, Inc., 237 Ind. 33, 142 N.E.2d 610, 1957 Ind. LEXIS 247 (1957).

An officer who merely saw "policy slips" hanging out of the defendant's pocket did not see a misdemeanor committed within his view and his arrest and search of the defendant was illegal. Brooks v. State, 249 Ind. 291, 231 N.E.2d 816, 1967 Ind. LEXIS 385 (1967).

Single Transaction.

A single transaction can support convictions of professional gambling under subsection (4). The form of professional gambling with which the defendant was charged is an offense which does not need to occur over a period of time but rather occurs with each lottery incident. Pruitt v. State, 557 N.E.2d 684, 1990 Ind. App. LEXIS 959 (1990).

Since a prosecution for professional gambling contemplated prosecution for a single act, and since the offense of bribery requires the conferring of a benefit with intent to control the performance of an act related to the employment of an official, the defendant could not be convicted of bribing a county prosecutor seven times when the intent was to induce the official not to prosecute him a single time. Winn v. State, 722 N.E.2d 345, 1999 Ind. App. LEXIS 2223 (1999).

Time of Offense.

Former statutes did not make time of the essence of professional gambling offenses; it was enough to show that the crime had been committed before the affidavit was filed and within the statute of limitations. Robb v. State, 15 Ind. Dec. 137, 239 N.E.2d 154 (Ind. 1968).

Validity of Contract.

Any contract entered into in violation of lottery statute was null and void and against public policy. Sumner v. Union Trust Co., 116 Ind. App. 684, 66 N.E.2d 621, 1946 Ind. App. LEXIS 162 (1946).

Where the special finding of facts conclusively established that a business enterprise conducted by decedent and claimant pursuant to a written contract was a lottery and gambling enterprise in which the parties were equally interested, and that funds deposited by decedent in a bank and which were wrongfully converted by him to his own use and not included in a final settlement had between the parties were funds which were received under the illegal contract, and that claimant's right to one half of such bank deposit could only be established by reference to the written contract and the unlawful and illegal enterprise and business operated pursuant thereto, claimant was not entitled to recover one half of the deposit. Sumner v. Union Trust Co., 116 Ind. App. 684, 66 N.E.2d 621, 1946 Ind. App. LEXIS 162 (1946).

What Constituted Lottery.

All schemes for the division of property by chance were lotteries. Whitney v. State, 10 Ind. 306, 10 Ind. 404, 1858 Ind. LEXIS 901 (1858); Swain v. Bussell, 10 Ind. 331, 1858 Ind. LEXIS 925 (1858); Crews v. State, 38 Ind. 28, 1871 Ind. LEXIS 206 (1871); Hudelson v. State, 94 Ind. 426, 1884 Ind. LEXIS 85 (1884); Lynch v. Rosenthal, 144 Ind. 86, 42 N.E. 1103, 31 L.R.A. 835, 1896 Ind. LEXIS 153 (1896); Emshwiler v. Tyner, 21 Ind. App. 347, 52 N.E. 459, 1899 Ind. App. LEXIS 101 (1899); Utz v. Wolf, 72 Ind. App. 572, 126 N.E. 327, 1920 Ind. App. LEXIS 50 (1920).

Plans which were not unlawful could be adopted by the owners of property for a distribution thereof by chance. McCleary v. Chipman, 32 Ind. App. 489, 68 N.E. 320, 1903 Ind. App. LEXIS 241 (1903).

A "suit club" was not necessarily a lottery or gift enterprise. State v. Bailey, 183 Ind. 215, 108 N.E. 753, 1915 Ind. LEXIS 43 (1915).

A contract for distribution of stamps to exchange for lottery tickets for interest in automobile was held void as a "gift enterprise" in violation of lottery statute. Utz v. Wolf, 72 Ind. App. 572, 126 N.E. 327, 1920 Ind. App. LEXIS 50 (1920).

Witnesses.

The parties could be compelled to testify, but they could not afterwards be prosecuted for the offense. Frazee v. State, 58 Ind. 8, 1877 Ind. LEXIS 126 (1877).

Cited:

State v. Foreman, 662 N.E.2d 929, 1996 Ind. LEXIS 20, 61 A.L.R.5th 757 (1996).

RESEARCH REFERENCES

Collateral References.

Entrapment to commit offense with respect to gambling or lotteries. 31 A.L.R.2d 1212.

Right to enjoin rival or competitor from illegal acts or practices amounting to crime. 90 A.L.R.2d 7.

Validity, construction, and application of statute or ordinance prohibiting or regulating use of messenger services to place wagers in pari-mutuel pool. 78 A.L.R.4th 483.

Validity, construction, and application of statute or ordinance prohibiting or regulating use or occupancy of premises for bookmaking or pool selling. 82 A.L.R.4th 356.

Validity of state or local gross receipts tax on gambling. 21 A.L.R.5th 812.

35-45-5-3.5. Possession of electronic gaming device or maintaining professional gambling site — Penalties.

(a) Except as provided in subsection (c), a person who possesses an electronic gaming device commits a Class A infraction.

(b) A person who knowingly or intentionally accepts or offers to accept for profit, money, or other property risked in gambling on an electronic gaming device possessed by the person commits maintaining a professional gambling site, a Class D felony. However, the offense is a Class C felony if the person has a prior unrelated conviction under this subsection.

(c) Subsection (a) does not apply to a person who:
   (1) possesses an antique slot machine;
   (2) restricts display and use of the antique slot machine to the person's private residence; and
   (3) does not use the antique slot machine for profit.

(d) As used in this section, "antique slot machine" refers to a slot machine that is:
   (1) at least forty (40) years old; and
   (2) possessed and used for decorative, historic, or nostalgic purposes.

History.
P.L.227-2007, § 66, emergency eff. July 1, 2007.

Cross References.
Infraction and ordinance violation enforcement proceedings, IC 34-28-5.
Penalties for felonies, IC 35-50-1, IC 35-50-2, IC 35-50-5-2.

Compiler's Notes.
P.L.227-2007, § 71, effective July 1, 2007, provides:

"(a) IC 35-45-5-3 and IC 35-45-5-4, both as amended by this act, apply only to crimes committed after June 30, 2007.

"(b) IC 35-45-5-3.5, as added by this act, applies only to crimes and infractions committed after June 30, 2007."

35-45-5-4. Promoting professional gambling.

(a) Except as provided in subsections (b) and (d), a person who:
   (1) knowingly or intentionally owns, manufactures, possesses, buys, sells, rents, leases, repairs, or transports a gambling device, or offers or solicits an interest in a gambling device;
   (2) before a race, game, contest, or event on which gambling may be conducted, knowingly or intentionally transmits or receives gambling information by any means, or knowingly or intentionally installs or maintains equipment for the transmission or receipt of gambling information; or
   (3) having control over the use of a place, knowingly or intentionally permits another person to use the place for professional gambling;
commits promoting professional gambling, a Class D felony. However, the offense is a Class C felony if the person has a prior unrelated conviction under this section.

(b) Subsection (a)(1) does not apply to a boat manufacturer who:
   (1) transports or possesses a gambling device solely for the purpose of installing that device in a boat that is to be sold and transported to a buyer; and
   (2) does not display the gambling device to the general public or make the device available for use in Indiana.

(c) When a public utility is notified by a law enforcement agency acting within its jurisdiction that any service, facility, or equipment furnished by it is being used or will be used to violate this section, it shall discontinue or refuse to furnish that service, facility, or equipment, and no damages, penalty, or forfeiture, civil or criminal, may be found against a public utility for an act done in compliance with such a notice. This subsection does not prejudice the right of a person affected by it to secure an appropriate determination, as otherwise provided by law, that the service, facility, or equipment should not be discontinued or refused, or should be restored.

(d) Subsection (a)(1) does not apply to a person who:

(1) possesses an antique slot machine;

(2) restricts display and use of the antique slot machine to the person's private residence; and

(3) does not use the antique slot machine for profit.

(e) As used in this section, "antique slot machine" refers to a slot machine that is:

(1) at least forty (40) years old; and

(2) possessed and used for decorative, historic, or nostalgic purposes.

History.

IC 35-45-5-4, as added by Acts 1976, P.L.148, § 5; 1977, P.L.340, § 83; P.L.164-1990, § 1; P.L.20-1995, § 19; P.L.227-2007, § 67, emergency eff. July 1, 2007.

Compiler's Notes.

P.L.227-2007, § 71, effective July 1, 2007, provides:

"(a) IC 35-45-5-3 and IC 35-45-5-4, both as amended by this act, apply only to crimes committed after June 30, 2007.

"(b) IC 35-45-5-3.5, as added by this act, applies only to crimes and infractions committed after June 30, 2007."

Cross References.

Penalties for felonies, IC 35-50-1, IC 35-50-2, IC 35-50-5-2.

NOTES TO DECISIONS

ANALYSIS

In General.
Constitutionality.
Affidavit.
Continuous Offense.
Destruction of Devices.
Evidence.
—Circumstantial.
—Sufficient.
"Gaming" and "Gambling."
Indictment.
—Advertising Lottery.
—Keeping Gaming House.
— —Knowledge of Defendant.
—Keeping or Exhibiting Gaming Device.
Instructions to Jury.
Larceny.
Out-of-State Lottery.
Persons Subject to Penalty.
Police Power.
Purpose.
Renting House for Gaming Purposes.
—Constitutionality.
—Former Rule.
Variance.
What Constitutes Gaming Devices.
What Constitutes Keeping Gaming House.

In General.

The keeper of any device or apparatus who permitted games to be played thereon, the loser to pay for the use of such device or apparatus, was liable. Blanton v. State, 1841 Ind. LEXIS 43 (1841); Mount v. State, 7 Ind. 521, 7 Ind. 654, 1856 Ind. LEXIS 374 (1856); Crawford v. State, 33 Ind. 304, 1870 Ind. LEXIS 111 (1870); Hamilton v. State, 75 Ind. 586, 1881 Ind. LEXIS 325 (1881); Alexander v. State, 99 Ind. 450, 1885 Ind. LEXIS 130 (1885); White v. State, 37 Ind. App. 95, 76 N.E. 554, 1906 Ind. App. LEXIS 15 (1906).

Sheriff was properly charged with misdemeanor where it was alleged that sheriff, on behalf of another, made offer to citizen to install slot machine to be operated on shares. State v. Sutherlin, 228 Ind. 587, 92 N.E.2d 923, 1950 Ind. LEXIS 173 (1950).

Accusation for removal of sheriff from office charging that sheriff declared intention to refuse to do duty in case of certain persons installing gambling devices failed to charge crime. State v. Sutherlin, 228 Ind. 587, 92 N.E.2d 923, 1950 Ind. LEXIS 173 (1950).

Because both the ownership of and the profits from electronic poker and video slot machines were illegal under IC 35-45-5-4, any accounting of a partnership could not include the value of or the profits from those machines. Monar v. Hurt, 791 N.E.2d 280, 2003 Ind. App. LEXIS 1247 (2003).

Constitutionality.

Indiana's anti-gambling statutes do not violate Ind. Const., art. 1, § 23 and the equal protection clause of the fourteenth amendment to the United States Constitution. American Legion Post # 113 v. State, 656 N.E.2d 1190, 1995 Ind. App. LEXIS 1364 (1995).

Affidavit.

An affidavit which charged among other things that the defendants "... did then and there unlawfully ... knowingly ... possess and exhibit to the general public ... a certain gaming device known as a pinball machine," was sufficient to withstand a motion in arrest of judgment. Murley v. State, 240 Ind. 655, 168 N.E.2d 205, 1960 Ind. LEXIS 240 (1960).

An affidavit that the informant believes defendant did wrongfully store, keep and possess a gambling device and slot machine must be deemed sufficient as against the contention that it was

Affidavit. (Cont'd)
necessary to negate the exception relating to right to replay contained in former statute, since the latter law repealed this law only so far as in conflict and no conflict had ever been shown as to slot machines which did not award only free games mechanically. Worl v. State, 243 Ind. 116, 183 N.E.2d 594, 1962 Ind. LEXIS 140 (1962).

The fact that the affidavit used the expression "gambling device" in addition to the words "slot machine" did not ipso facto render the affidavit insufficient. Worl v. State, 243 Ind. 116, 183 N.E.2d 594, 1962 Ind. LEXIS 140 (1962).

Continuous Offense.
The keeping of a gaming house was a continuous offense, and a conviction barred a prosecution for all acts prior to the date in the indictment. State v. Lindley, 14 Ind. 353, 14 Ind. 430, 1860 Ind. LEXIS 177 (1860).

Destruction of Devices.
Articles or devices which could be used only for gaming, or some other unlawful purpose, could be seized and destroyed without notice. State v. Derry, 171 Ind. 18, 85 N.E. 765, 1908 Ind. LEXIS 89 (1908).

Evidence.
When the charge was for permitting gaming, and it was alleged that certain articles were bet and wagered, the proof had to correspond to the allegation. Carr v. State, 50 Ind. 178, 1875 Ind. LEXIS 86 (1875).

The statute providing what evidence was sufficient to prove that a place was rented for gaming was constitutional. Morgan v. State, 117 Ind. 569, 19 N.E. 154, 1888 Ind. LEXIS 178 (1888); Voght v. State, 124 Ind. 358, 24 N.E. 680, 1890 Ind. LEXIS 331 (1890).

Persons familiar with gaming apparatus could express an opinion as to the use of certain devices or articles used for gaming. Douglas v. State, 18 Ind. App. 289, 48 N.E. 9, 1897 Ind. App. LEXIS 207 (1897).

—Circumstantial.
On a charge for renting property to be used for gaming, it had to be proved that the renting was for such purpose, but the fact could have been proved by circumstantial evidence. Rodifer v. State, 74 Ind. 21, 1881 Ind. LEXIS 88 (1881); Morgan v. State, 117 Ind. 569, 19 N.E. 154, 1888 Ind. LEXIS 178 (1888); Voght v. State, 124 Ind. 358, 24 N.E. 680, 1890 Ind. LEXIS 331 (1890).

Permitting a house to be used for gaming could be proved by circumstantial evidence. Roberts v. State, 25 Ind. App. 366, 58 N.E. 203, 1900 Ind. App. LEXIS 100 (1900); Neeld v. State, 25 Ind. App. 603, 58 N.E. 734, 1900 Ind. App. LEXIS 142 (1900).

—Sufficient.
Where defendant maintained an office and was in charge of the premises and there were facts adduced from which it could be inferred that defendant had full awareness of the presence of gambling and gambling equipment on the premises the evidence was sufficient to support a conviction for keeping a gaming house. Andrews v. State, 162 Ind. App. 698, 321 N.E.2d 235, 1975 Ind. App. LEXIS 982 (1975).

Evidence was sufficient that slot machines were operational or readily convertible into machines adapted for gambling where photographs showed that the machines were located in the immediate proximity of other devices which were obviously used for gambling purposes and the machines contained money. B. P. O. E. # 576, Elks Club v. State, 413 N.E.2d 660, 1980 Ind. App. LEXIS 1825 (1980).

"Gaming" and "Gambling."
The words "gaming" and "gambling" are used interchangeably by the legislature. State v. Frederick, 183 Ind. 509, 109 N.E. 747, 1915 Ind. LEXIS 87 (1915).

Indictment.

—Advertising Lottery.
The gravamen of the offense defined in the statute prohibiting the writing, advertising, or publishing an account of a lottery, gift enterprise, or scheme of chance, was the advertising of, and giving publicity to, a contemplated lottery, gift enterprise, or scheme of chance. The charge had to show that the lottery, gift enterprise, or scheme of chance referred to in the advertisement was such in fact. State v. Bailey, 183 Ind. 215, 108 N.E. 753, 1915 Ind. LEXIS 43 (1915).

—Keeping Gaming House.
An indictment for keeping a house to be used for gaming did not need to aver that gaming had actually taken place. State v. Miller, 1841 Ind. LEXIS 19 (1841); McAlpin v. State, 3 Ind. 567 (1852); Sowle v. State, 11 Ind. 398, 11 Ind. 492, 1859 Ind. LEXIS 557 (1859); State v. Pancake, 74 Ind. 15, 1881 Ind. LEXIS 86 (1881).

An indictment for keeping a gaming house could charge that the house was kept for, and was used for, gaming. Dormer v. State, 2 Ind. 308, 1850 Ind. LEXIS 136 (1850); Crawford v. State, 33 Ind. 304, 1870 Ind. LEXIS 111 (1870); Davis v. State, 100 Ind. 154, 1885 Ind. LEXIS 180 (1885).

An indictment for suffering a house to be used for gaming had to aver that gambling had taken place, and state the names of the persons engaged therein. Sowle v. State, 11 Ind. 398, 11 Ind. 492, 1859 Ind. LEXIS 557 (1859); State v. Noland, 29 Ind. 212, 1867 Ind. LEXIS 405 (1867).

An indictment charging that at the time and place named, defendant, "being then and there the keeper of a building and room in said county and state, did then and there permit said building and room to be used and occupied for gaming by certain persons, to wit … and did permit such persons in and about such building to play faro, poker, and other games of chance for money," was sufficient. Christ v. State, 33 Ind. App. 488, 69 N.E. 269, 1903 Ind. App. LEXIS 266 (1903).

An indictment for keeping a gaming house did not need to allege the name of any person who

Indictment. (Cont'd)

—Keeping Gaming House. (Cont'd)
played there. James v. State, 190 Ind. 629, 130 N.E. 115, 1921 Ind. LEXIS 138 (1921); Lee v. State, 191 Ind. 515, 132 N.E. 582, 1921 Ind. LEXIS 60 (1921).

If an indictment for keeping a building for gaming unnecessarily alleged the playing by certain named persons therein, the state did not need to prove that all the persons thus described actually engaged in gaming therein. James v. State, 190 Ind. 629, 130 N.E. 115, 1921 Ind. LEXIS 138 (1921); Howard v. State, 191 Ind. 232, 131 N.E. 403, 1921 Ind. LEXIS 29 (1921); Lee v. State, 191 Ind. 515, 132 N.E. 582, 1921 Ind. LEXIS 60 (1921).

Where an indictment charged both the offense of keeping a building for gaming, and of knowingly permitting certain individuals to engage in gaming therein, and the evidence showed defendant's guilt of the former but not the latter offense, a general verdict of guilty was deemed a verdict of guilty of the offense sufficiently proved. James v. State, 190 Ind. 629, 130 N.E. 115, 1921 Ind. LEXIS 138 (1921); Howard v. State, 191 Ind. 232, 131 N.E. 403, 1921 Ind. LEXIS 29 (1921); Lee v. State, 191 Ind. 515, 132 N.E. 582, 1921 Ind. LEXIS 60 (1921).

— —Knowledge of Defendant.
When the charge was for permitting gaming to be carried on, the proof had to show that the defendant knew of the gaming. Padgett v. State, 68 Ind. 46, 1879 Ind. LEXIS 541 (1879); Hamilton v. State, 75 Ind. 586, 1881 Ind. LEXIS 325 (1881); Barnaby v. State, 106 Ind. 539, 7 N.E. 231, 1886 Ind. LEXIS 156 (1886).

An indictment for renting property to be used for gaming did not need to state to whom the property was rented. Kleespies v. State, 106 Ind. 383, 7 N.E. 186, 1886 Ind. LEXIS 131 (1886); Fisher v. State, 2 Ind. App. 365, 28 N.E. 565, 1891 Ind. App. LEXIS 178 (1891).

On a charge of keeping or renting a house for gaming, the owner did not need to have notice of gaming. Fisher v. State, 2 Ind. App. 365, 28 N.E. 565, 1891 Ind. App. LEXIS 178 (1891).

An indictment for permitting gaming had to allege that the owner of the property knew of the gaming. Emperly v. State, 13 Ind. App. 393, 41 N.E. 840, 1895 Ind. App. LEXIS 256 (1895).

—Keeping or Exhibiting Gaming Device.
An indictment for keeping a gaming apparatus had to allege that it was kept for the purpose of wagering articles of value thereon. Carr v. State, 50 Ind. 178, 1875 Ind. LEXIS 86 (1875).

An indictment for keeping gaming apparatus did not need to allege that any game was played thereon nor state the names of any persons playing on such apparatus. State v. Thomas, 50 Ind. 292, 1875 Ind. LEXIS 118 (1875).

An indictment for exhibiting a gambling device for gain and to win money did not need to give the particular name of the device. Pemberton v. State, 85 Ind. 507, 1882 Ind. LEXIS 592 (1882).

Indictments for keeping and exhibiting gaming devices did not need to describe the particular place or building where the same were kept, naming the county and state being sufficient. App v. State, 90 Ind. 73, 1883 Ind. LEXIS 182 (1883); Keith v. State, 90 Ind. 89, 1883 Ind. LEXIS 188 (1883), overruled, Bledsoe v. State, 223 Ind. 675, 64 N.E.2d 160, 1945 Ind. LEXIS 160 (1945).

Instructions to Jury.
In a prosecution for unlawfully keeping a room to be used and occupied for gaming, where the uncontradicted evidence showed that defendant for five months before the indictment was in charge of a room in which he managed, conducted, and carried on a business of gaming, there was no issue as to ownership or proprietorship of the room or building, and any instruction on such subject would have been improper. Flatters v. State, 189 Ind. 287, 127 N.E. 5, 1920 Ind. LEXIS 23 (1920).

In prosecution for violation of gaming laws, refusal of instruction that appellant could not be convicted if evidence showed that defendant did not keep device involved for gaming with another person for purpose of gaining money and did not use device to play games himself for purpose of obtaining money from other persons was correct because this section provides that conviction may be based on the allowance of the use of the device for gaming purposes. Mitchell v. State, 233 Ind. 16, 115 N.E.2d 595, 1953 Ind. LEXIS 283 (1953), cert. denied, 347 U.S. 975, 74 S. Ct. 786, 98 L. Ed. 1114, 1954 U.S. LEXIS 2064 (1954).

Larceny.
Property illegally held and used for gambling purposes was subject of larceny. Smith v. State, 187 Ind. 253, 118 N.E. 954, 1918 Ind. LEXIS 24, L.R.A. (n.s.) 1918D688 (1918).

Out-of-State Lottery.
Out-of-state corporation which proposed to purchase lottery tickets from other states for Indiana residents, for profit, would have engaged in illegal gambling, and its equipment for the transmission and receipt of information constituted gambling devices. L.E. Servs. v. State Lottery Comm'n, 646 N.E.2d 334, 1995 Ind. App. LEXIS 76 (1995).

Persons Subject to Penalty.
Persons who knowingly owned, rented, leased or possessed any gambling device, as defined by the statute relating to gambling, whether they were placed or stored in places accessible to the public, or in private homes, religious, patriotic, charitable, or fraternal clubs were subject to the penalty provided. Peachey v. Boswell, 240 Ind. 604, 167 N.E.2d 48, 1960 Ind. LEXIS 233, 89 A.L.R.2d 801 (1960).

Police Power.
State's regulation of gambling does not constitute an unreasonable exercise of police power. American Legion Post # 113 v. State, 656 N.E.2d 1190, 1995 Ind. App. LEXIS 1364 (1995).

Purpose.
The purpose of the act pertaining to gambling is to prohibit all persons from seeking profit from gambling as defined by the act. The most effective

Purpose. (Cont'd)

way to prevent the making of a profit from professional gambling would be to prohibit the manufacture, possession, renting, leasing and transporting of devices used in such gambling. Peachey v. Boswell, 240 Ind. 604, 167 N.E.2d 48, 1960 Ind. LEXIS 233, 89 A.L.R.2d 801 (1960).

Renting House for Gaming Purposes.

—Constitutionality.

Section 242 of Acts 1881 (Spec. Sess.), ch. 36, relating to evidence that a place was rented for the purpose of gaming, was held not unconstitutional on the ground that it prohibited the jury from determining the fact. Morgan v. State, 117 Ind. 569, 19 N.E. 154, 1888 Ind. LEXIS 178 (1888); Voght v. State, 124 Ind. 358, 24 N.E. 680, 1890 Ind. LEXIS 331 (1890).

—Former Rule.

To sustain a prosecution under a former law of this nature it was necessary to prove that the defendant had rented the house to someone for gaming purposes. Rodifer v. State, 74 Ind. 21, 1881 Ind. LEXIS 88 (1881).

Variance.

On a charge of keeping or exhibiting a certain kind of device or gaming apparatus, the proof had to correspond to the allegation as to the character of the device or apparatus. Bartender v. State, 51 Ind. 73, 1875 Ind. LEXIS 228 (1875); Squier v. State, 66 Ind. 317, 1879 Ind. LEXIS 165 (1879); Sumner v. State, 74 Ind. 52, 1881 Ind. LEXIS 96 (1881).

Proof that a witness before a grand jury, in a prosecution for permitting persons to remain in defendant's building for the purpose of gaming, knew the names of the persons engaged in gambling, was not a fatal variance from an indictment alleging that such persons were unknown to the grand jurors, where the evidence showed a continuing offense and the names of the persons engaged in the gambling were only an incidental matter. Jessup v. State, 14 Ind. App. 230, 42 N.E. 948, 1896 Ind. App. LEXIS 239 (1896).

What Constitutes Gaming Devices.

Keeping and exhibiting dice for gain, and to be used for gaming, was a violation of the statute. White v. State, 37 Ind. App. 95, 76 N.E. 554, 1906 Ind. App. LEXIS 15 (1906).

Slot machines by which players may by chance obtain articles of an uncertain character or value are gaming devices. Ferguson v. State, 178 Ind. 568, 99 N.E. 806, 1912 Ind. LEXIS 120, 42 L.R.A. (n.s.) 720 (1912).

"Checkerboards," which were in fact "punch boards," the only practical use for which was the carrying on of a game of chance for prizes, were gaming devices. Hatton v. Casey, 93 Ind. App. 336, 178 N.E. 303, 1931 Ind. App. LEXIS 126 (1931).

"Policy slips" were not gambling devices within the meaning of this section. Brooks v. State, 249 Ind. 291, 231 N.E.2d 816, 1967 Ind. LEXIS 385 (1967).

What Constitutes Keeping Gaming House.

The keeping of a room where games were played, and the players were permitted to wager the price of playing the game upon the result thereof, was keeping a gaming house. Crawford v. State, 33 Ind. 304, 1870 Ind. LEXIS 111 (1870); Hamilton v. State, 75 Ind. 586, 1881 Ind. LEXIS 325 (1881).

Cited:

State v. Allen, 525 N.E.2d 1267, 1988 Ind. App. LEXIS 515 (1988); United States v. Cross, 113 F. Supp. 2d 1253, 2000 U.S. Dist. LEXIS 13184 (S.D. Ind. 2000).

RESEARCH REFERENCES

Collateral References.

Paraphernalia or appliances used for recording gambling transactions or receiving or furnishing gambling information as gaming devices within criminal statute or ordinance. 1 A.L.R.3d 726.

Validity, construction, and application of statutes or ordinances involved in prosecutions for possession of bookmaking paraphernalia. 51 A.L.R.4th 796.

35-45-5-4.5. Notice to operator of illegal activity — Manner of service.

(a) A prosecuting attorney may send written notice to an operator described in section 2(c) or 3(b) [IC 35-45-5-2(c) or IC 35-45-5-3(b)] of this chapter. The notice must:

(1) specify the illegal gambling activity;

(2) state that the operator has not more than thirty (30) days after the date the notice is received to remove the illegal gambling activity; and

(3) state that failure to remove the illegal gambling activity not more than thirty (30) days after receiving the notice may result in the filing of criminal charges against the operator.

A prosecuting attorney who sends a notice under this section shall forward a copy of the notice to the attorney general. The attorney general shall maintain a depository to collect, maintain, and retain each notice sent under this section.

(b) The manner of service of a notice under subsection (a) must be:

(1) in compliance with Rule 4.1, 4.4, 4.6, or 4.7 of the Indiana Rules of Trial Procedure; or

(2) by publication in compliance with Rule 4.13 of the Indiana Rules of Trial Procedure if service cannot be made under subdivision (1) after a diligent search for the operator.

(c) A notice served under subsection (a):

(1) is admissible in a criminal proceeding under this chapter; and

(2) constitutes prima facie evidence that the operator had knowledge that illegal gambling was occurring on the operator's Internet site.

(d) A person outside Indiana who transmits information on a computer network (as defined in IC 35-43-2-3) and who knows or should know that the information is broadcast in Indiana submits to the jurisdiction of Indiana courts for prosecution under this section.

History.
P.L.70-2005, § 5.

35-45-5-4.6. Computer service may block transmissions that violate chapter.

(a) An interactive computer service may, on its own initiative, block the receipt or transmission through its service of any commercial electronic mail message that it reasonably believes is or will be sent in violation of this chapter.

(b) An interactive computer service is not liable for such action.

History.
P.L.70-2005, § 6.

35-45-5-4.7. Computer service has right of action against person who transmits electronic messages that violate chapter — Defense — Damages — Jurisdiction.

(a) An interactive computer service that handles or retransmits a commercial electronic mail message has a right of action against a person who initiates or assists the transmission of the commercial electronic mail message that violates this chapter.

(b) This chapter does not provide a right of action against:

(1) an interactive computer service;

(2) a telephone company;

(3) a CMRS provider (as defined in IC 36-8-16.5-6);

(4) a cable operator (as defined in 47 U.S.C. 522(5)); or

(5) any other entity that primarily provides connectivity to an operator;

if the entity's equipment is used only to transport, handle, or retransmit information that violates this chapter and is not capable of blocking the retransmission of information that violates this chapter.

(c) It is a defense to an action under this section if the defendant shows by a preponderance of the evidence that the violation of this chapter resulted from a good faith error and occurred notwithstanding the maintenance of procedures reasonably adopted to avoid violating this chapter.

(d) If the plaintiff prevails in an action filed under this section, the plaintiff is entitled to the following:

(1) An injunction to enjoin future violations of this chapter.

(2) Compensatory damages equal to any actual damage proven by the plaintiff to have resulted from the initiation of the commercial electronic mail message. If the plaintiff does not prove actual damage, the plaintiff is entitled to presumptive

damages of five hundred dollars ($500) for each commercial electronic mail message that violates this chapter and that is sent by the defendant:
  (A) to the plaintiff; or
  (B) through the plaintiff's interactive computer service.
  (3) The plaintiff's reasonable attorney's fees and other litigation costs reasonably incurred in connection with the action.
(e) A person outside Indiana who:
  (1) initiates or assists the transmission of a commercial electronic mail message that violates this chapter; and
  (2) knows or should know that the commercial electronic mail message will be received in Indiana;
submits to the jurisdiction of Indiana courts for purposes of this chapter.

History.
  P.L.70-2005, § 7; P.L.27-2006, § 60.

35-45-5-5. Pari-mutuel wagering excluded.

The provisions of this chapter do not apply to pari-mutuel wagering conducted at racetrack locations or satellite facilities licensed for pari-mutuel wagering under IC 4-31.

History.
  IC 35-45-5-5, as added by Acts 1977, P.L. 47, § 3;
P.L.341-1989(ss), § 13; P.L.24-1992, § 61.

NOTES TO DECISIONS

Constitutional Prohibition of Lotteries.
  The pari-mutuel wagering law (Acts 1977, P.L. 47) is unconstitutional since it violates the constitutional provision prohibiting lotteries. State v. Nixon, 270 Ind. 192, 384 N.E.2d 152, 1979 Ind. LEXIS 629 (1979) But see Indiana Gaming Comm'n v. Moseley, 643 N.E.2d 296, 1994 Ind. LEXIS 152 (1994).

35-45-5-6. Lottery ticket sales excluded.

This chapter does not apply to the sale of lottery tickets authorized by IC 4-30.

History.
  P.L.341-1989(ss), § 14.

35-45-5-7. Information concerning pari-mutuel wagering or certain games of chance excluded.

This chapter does not apply to the publication or broadcast of an advertisement, a list of prizes, or other information concerning:
  (1) pari-mutuel wagering on horse races or a lottery authorized by the law of any state;
  (2) a game of chance operated in accordance with IC 4-32.2; or
  (3) a gambling game operated in accordance with IC 4-35.

History.
  P.L.217-1991, § 1; P.L.91-2006, § 13; P.L.233-2007, § 33, emergency eff. May 11, 2007.

35-45-5-8. Gambling devices authorized under IC 4-32.2 excluded.

This chapter does not apply to the sale or use of gambling devices authorized under IC 4-32.2.

History.
P.L.24-1992, § 62; P.L.91-2006, § 14.

35-45-5-10. Applicability of chapter.

This chapter does not apply to riverboat gambling authorized by IC 4-33.

History.
P.L.277-1993(ss), § 132.

Compiler's Notes.
This chapter does not contain a section 9 (IC 35-45-5-9).

35-45-5-11. Chapter not applicable to gambling game authorized by IC 4-35.

This chapter does not apply to a gambling game authorized by IC 4-35.

History.
P.L.233-2007, § 34, emergency eff. May 11, 2007.

35-45-5-12. Chapter not applicable to certain gambling games licensed under IC 4-36.

This chapter does not apply to the following gambling games licensed or authorized under IC 4-36:

(1) Raffles and winner take all drawings conducted under IC 4-36-5-1.

(2) Type II gambling games.

History.
P.L.95-2008, § 16, eff. July 1, 2008; P.L.108-2009, § 23, emergency eff. July 1, 2009.

Amendments.
The 2009 amendment deleted the (2) designa-

tion following ""Raffles""; added ""conducted under IC 4-36-5-1"" in (1); redesignated former (3) as (2); and made a stylistic change.

CHAPTER 6

RACKETEER INFLUENCED AND CORRUPT ORGANIZATIONS

35-45-6-1. Definitions.

(a) The definitions in this section apply throughout this chapter.

(b) "Documentary material" means any document, drawing, photograph, recording, or other tangible item containing compiled data from which information can be either obtained or translated into a usable form.

(c) "Enterprise" means:

(1) a sole proprietorship, corporation, limited liability company, partnership, business trust, or governmental entity; or

(2) a union, an association, or a group, whether a legal entity or merely associated in fact.

(d) "Pattern of racketeering activity" means engaging in at least two (2) incidents of racketeering activity that have the same or similar intent, result, accomplice, victim, or method of commission, or that are otherwise interrelated by distinguishing characteristics that are not isolated incidents. However, the incidents are a pattern of racketeering activity only if at least one (1) of the incidents occurred after

August 31, 1980, and if the last of the incidents occurred within five (5) years after a prior incident of racketeering activity.

(e) "Racketeering activity" means to commit, to attempt to commit, to conspire to commit a violation of, or aiding and abetting in a violation of any of the following:

(1) A provision of IC 23-19, or of a rule or order issued under IC 23-19.
(2) A violation of IC 35-45-9.
(3) A violation of IC 35-47.
(4) A violation of IC 35-49-3.
(5) Murder (IC 35-42-1-1).
(6) Battery as a Class C felony (IC 35-42-2-1).
(7) Kidnapping (IC 35-42-3-2).
(8) Human and sexual trafficking crimes (IC 35-42-3.5).
(9) Child exploitation (IC 35-42-4-4).
(10) Robbery (IC 35-42-5-1).
(11) Carjacking (IC 35-42-5-2).
(12) Arson (IC 35-43-1-1).
(13) Burglary (IC 35-43-2-1).
(14) Theft (IC 35-43-4-2).
(15) Receiving stolen property (IC 35-43-4-2).
(16) Forgery (IC 35-43-5-2).
(17) Fraud (IC 35-43-5-4(1) through IC 35-43-5-4(10)).
(18) Bribery (IC 35-44-1-1).
(19) Official misconduct (IC 35-44-1-2).
(20) Conflict of interest (IC 35-44-1-3).
(21) Perjury (IC 35-44-2-1).
(22) Obstruction of justice (IC 35-44-3-4).
(23) Intimidation (IC 35-45-2-1).
(24) Promoting prostitution (IC 35-45-4-4).
(25) Professional gambling (IC 35-45-5-3).
(26) Maintaining a professional gambling site (IC 35-45-5-3.5(b)).
(27) Promoting professional gambling (IC 35-45-5-4).
(28) Dealing in or manufacturing cocaine or a narcotic drug (IC 35-48-4-1).
(29) Dealing in or manufacturing methamphetamine (IC 35-48-4-1.1).
(30) Dealing in a schedule I, II, or III controlled substance (IC 35-48-4-2).
(31) Dealing in a schedule IV controlled substance (IC 35-48-4-3).
(32) Dealing in a schedule V controlled substance (IC 35-48-4-4).
(33) Dealing in marijuana, hash oil, or hashish (IC 35-48-4-10).
(34) Money laundering (IC 35-45-15-5).
(35) A violation of IC 35-47.5-5.
(36) A violation of any of the following:
　(A) IC 23-14-48-9.
　(B) IC 30-2-9-7(b).
　(C) IC 30-2-10-9(b).
　(D) IC 30-2-13-38(f).

History.
IC 35-45-6-1, as added by Acts 1980, P.L.199, § 2; P.L.190-1984, § 1; P.L.180-1991, § 10; P.L.8-1993, § 511; P.L.230-1993, § 4; P.L.112-1998, § 1; P.L.17-2001, § 16; P.L.123-2002, § 41; P.L.151-2006, § 17; P.L.173-2006, § 53; P.L.1-2007, § 234, emergency eff. March 30, 2007; P.L.27-2007, § 31, eff. July 1, 2008; P.L.227-2007, § 68, emergency eff. July 1, 2007; P.L.3-2008, § 253, emergency eff. July 1, 2008; P.L.143-2009, § 48, emergency eff. July 1, 2009.

Compiler's Notes.
P.L.227-2007, § 72, effective July 1, 2007, provides:
"(a) IC 35-45-6-1, as amended by this act, applies only to crimes committed after June 30, 2007."
P.L.112-1998, § 3, effective July 1, 1998, provides:
"IC 35-45-6-1, as amended by this act, and IC 35-45-15, as added by this act, apply only to offenses committed after June 30, 1998."

P.L.143-2009, § 49, effective July 1, 2009, provides:
"IC 30-2-13-38 and IC 35-45-6-1, both as amended by this act, apply only to crimes committed after June 30, 2009."

Amendments.
The 2009 amendment added (e)(36).

Cross References.
Criminal gang, IC 34-6-2-32, IC 35-45-9-1.

NOTES TO DECISIONS

ANALYSIS

Applicability.
"Enterprise" Construed.
Evidence.
—Intimidation.
—Sufficient.
Pattern of Racketeering.
Preemption.
Promoting Professional Gambling.
Proximate Cause Requirement.
Securities Act Violations.
Separate Convictions.
Sufficiency of RICO Violation Claim.

Applicability.
Indiana's Racketeer Influenced and Corrupt Organization Act (RICO) statute sweeps more broadly than the federal statute in that it speaks in IC 35-45-6-2(3) of "conducting or otherwise participating in the activities of an enterprise." Clearly, "activities" encompasses a wider range of exploits than "conduct" and does not require "an element of direction"; as such, Indiana's RICO statute applies to all those employed by or associated with an enterprise who knowingly or intentionally conduct or otherwise participate in the activities of an enterprise through a pattern of racketeering activity, whether as generals or foot soldiers. Keesling v. Beegle, 858 N.E.2d 980, 2006 Ind. App. LEXIS 2630 (2006), transfer granted and vacated, 869 N.E.2d 455, 2007 Ind. LEXIS 249.

"Enterprise" Construed.
This section included a corporation within its definition of an "enterprise" even before the 1984 amendment adding the term "corporation." Alvers v. State, 489 N.E.2d 83, 1986 Ind. App. LEXIS 2339 (1986).

Evidence.

—Intimidation.
Only the defendant's intent that the plaintiff change his course of conduct is necessary to establish "intimidation;" because the plaintiff need not rely on the defendant's threats in order to establish a violation, the injury and damages resulting from such violations cannot logically be limited to "reliance damages." Evidence that defendant's "intimidation" or "pattern" of "intimidation" in some other way damaged plaintiff would suffice to establish a submissible case under the Indiana Racketeer Influenced and Corrupt Organization statute. Raybestos Prods. Co. v. Younger, 54 F.3d 1234, 1995 U.S. App. LEXIS 7689 (7th Cir. Ind. 1995).

—Sufficient.
A relationship was established between alleged incidents of racketeering activity where the defendant accepted payment for precious metals, promised delivery of the metals within a short period of time or on demand, and failed to deliver all or parts of the purchases. The threat of continued activity was shown by the lengthy duration of the scheme prior to the time the defendant closed the coin shop, and the defendant's stated intention to continue in the coin business. Kollar v. State, 556 N.E.2d 936, 1990 Ind. App. LEXIS 773 (1990).

Insured's claim under IC 34-24-2-6 against insurer and agent was sufficient to defeat motion for summary judgment where insured presented evidence that insurer engaged in pattern of racketeering activity in violation of IC 35-45-6-1 by inter alia: (1) attaching written instrument to insurance policy which arguably constituted making or uttering of false written instrument, as defined by IC 35-43-5-1(r), in violation of IC 35-43-5-2; and (2) by being both perpetrator and beneficiary of alleged crime pursuant to IC 35-45-6-2(1). Zinman v. Cont'l Cas. Co., — F. Supp. 2d —, 2003 U.S. Dist. LEXIS 18957 (S.D. Ind. 2003).

Under actual evidence test, defendant's conviction of conspiracy to commit burglary in addition to burglary did not violate double jeopardy since there was no need to consider any evidence of actual burglaries in order to find guilt on conspiracy charge. Waldon v. State, 829 N.E.2d 168, 2005 Ind. App. LEXIS 1053 (2005).

Pattern of Racketeering.
Proof of a "pattern of racketeering" requires a showing that the incidents of racketeering activity are related and they amount to or pose a threat of continued criminal activity. Kollar v. State, 556 N.E.2d 936, 1990 Ind. App. LEXIS 773 (1990).

Plaintiffs failed to allege the requisite continuity, where they alleged only one general scheme, two victims, four acts, and a time period of three months, thus alleging only a short-term, closed-end fraud which did not constitute a pattern of activity. Yoder Grain, Inc. v. Antalis, 722 N.E.2d 840, 2000 Ind. App. LEXIS 61 (2000), overruled in part, Keesling v. Beegle, 880 N.E.2d 1202, 2008 Ind. LEXIS 171 (2008).

Summary judgment was granted because run-of-the-mill sales puffery did not give rise to a claim of mail fraud and extension of credit was not against the law in IC 4-33-9-15; therefore these claims were not predicate offenses for gambler's federal Racketeer Influenced and Corrupt Organizations Act (RICO), 18 U.S.C.S. §§ 1961 et seq., or his Indiana RICO claim under IC 35-45-6-1. Williams v. Aztar Ind. Gaming Corp., — F. Supp. 2d —, 2003 U.S. Dist. LEXIS 6450 (S.D. Ind. 2003), vacated, 351 F.3d 294, 2003 U.S. App. LEXIS 24454 (7th Cir. Ind. 2003).

Preemption.

Indiana's anti-racketeering statute, IC 35-45-6-1 and IC 35-45-6-2, is not preempted by the federal statute prohibiting racketeer influenced and corrupt organizations (18 U.S.C.S. §§ 1961-1968). Alvers v. State, 489 N.E.2d 83, 1986 Ind. App. LEXIS 2339 (1986).

Promoting Professional Gambling.

Out-of-state corporation which proposed to purchase lottery tickets from other states for Indiana residents, for profit, violated the Indiana Civil Remedies for Racketeering Activity Statute, and its president and vice president committed the crime of corrupt business influence. L.E. Servs. v. State Lottery Comm'n, 646 N.E.2d 334, 1995 Ind. App. LEXIS 76 (1995).

Proximate Cause Requirement.

To establish that a defendant's racketeering activities damaged or injured a civil plaintiff, the plaintiff must demonstrate that the defendant's actions "proximately caused" the injury. Raybestos Prods. Co. v. Younger, 54 F.3d 1234, 1995 U.S. App. LEXIS 7689 (7th Cir. Ind. 1995).

Securities Act Violations.

Allegations defendant engaged in unlawful conduct in violation of the Indiana Securities Act could also support allegations of a pattern of racketeering entitling plaintiff to relief under the Indiana Racketeer and Corrupt Organizations Act. Wesleyan Pension Fund v. First Albany Corp., 964 F. Supp. 1255, 1997 U.S. Dist. LEXIS 5934 (S.D. Ind. 1997).

Separate Convictions.

The Indiana legislature intended separate convictions for a Racketeer Influenced and Corrupt Organizations Act (RICO) violation and its predicate offenses. State v. Allen, 646 N.E.2d 965, 1995 Ind. App. LEXIS 15 (1995).

Sufficiency of RICO Violation Claim.

Where consumer filed counterclaim in federal district court claiming that satellite TV company violated Indiana Racketeer-Influenced Corrupt Organization (RICO) statute, IC 35-45-6, and the Indiana Crime Victim Relief Act, IC 34-24-3-1, counterclaim was dismissed because court did not have diversity jurisdiction pursuant to 28 U.S.C.S. § 1332, since consumer did not meet amount in controversy requirement, and because court declined supplemental jurisdiction under 28 U.S.C.S. § 1367, since consumer did not plead RICO claims with particularity as required by Fed. R. Civ. P. 9(b). Directv v. Edwards, 293 F. Supp. 2d 873, 2003 U.S. Dist. LEXIS 21818 (N.D. Ind. 2003).

Because Indiana's "baby RICO" statute is modeled after federal RICO statute and federal law is relied upon when interpreting and applying it, plaintiffs' baby RICO claims were dismissed for failure to state cause of action after their federal claims were dismissed for failing to demonstrate necessary continuity for pattern of racketeering and for pleading only one predicate act of racketeering with required particularity. Decatur Ventures, LLC v. Stapleton Ventures, Inc., 373 F. Supp. 2d 829, 2005 U.S. Dist. LEXIS 17222 (S.D. Ind. 2005), dismissed in part, — F. Supp. 2d —, 2006 U.S. Dist. LEXIS 30507 (S.D. Ind. 2006).

In a case involving alleged fraudulent mortgage applications and violations of the Racketeer Influenced and Corrupt Organizations Act (RICO), 18 U.S.C.S. §§ 1961 et seq., defendants were not entitled to dismissal of the alleged violations of Indiana's RICO statute, IC 35-45-6-1 et seq., because that statute was modeled after the federal RICO statute, and federal law is relied upon when interpreting and applying the Indiana act. Since it had been determined that the complaint adequately pled violations of the federal RICO statute, it also adequately pled violations of Indiana's RICO statute. Decatur Ventures, LLC v. Stapleton Ventures, Inc., — F. Supp. 2d —, 2006 U.S. Dist. LEXIS 55512 (S.D. Ind. 2006).

Cited:

Kahn v. State, 493 N.E.2d 790, 1986 Ind. App. LEXIS 2616 (1986); Lee v. State, 569 N.E.2d 717, 1991 Ind. App. LEXIS 605 (1991); Mendenhall v. Goldsmith, 59 F.3d 685, 1995 U.S. App. LEXIS 16604 (7th Cir. Ind. 1995); AGS Capital Corp. v. Prod. Action Int'l, LLC, 884 N.E.2d 294, 2008 Ind. App. LEXIS 725 (2008).

RESEARCH REFERENCES

Indiana Law Journal.

The Applicability of Civil RICO to Toxic Waste Polluters, 62 Ind. L.J. 451 (1987).

Indiana Law Review.

The RICO/CRRA Trap: Troubling Implications for Adult Expression, 23 Ind. L. Rev. 109 (1990).

Notre Dame Law Review.

Civil RICO: Prior Criminal Conviction and Burden of Proof, 60 Notre Dame L. Rev. 566.

A Uniform Limitation Period for Civil RICO, 61 Notre Dame L. 495 (1986).

Treble Damages Under RICO: Characterization and Computation, 61 Notre Dame L. 526 (1986).

Equitable Relief Under Civil RICO: Reflections on *Religious Technology Center v. Wollersheim*:

Will Civil RICO Be Effective Only Against White-Collar Crime? 62 Notre Dame L. Rev. 526 (1987).

Note, Functions of the RICO Enterprise Concept, 64 Notre Dame L. Rev. 646 (1989).

Oscar v. University Students Cooperative Ass'n: Can Citizens Use RICO to Rid Neighborhoods of Drug Houses?, 67 Notre Dame L. Rev. 799 (1992).

Collateral References.

Criminal prosecutions under state RICO statutes for engaging in organized criminal activity. 89 A.L.R.5th 629.

Validity, construction, and application of Racketeer Influenced and Corrupt Organization Act, 18 U.S.C.A. § 1961 et seq. — Supreme Court cases. 171 A.L.R. Fed. 1.

35-45-6-2. Corrupt business influence.

A person:

(1) Who has knowingly or intentionally received any proceeds directly or indirectly derived from a pattern of racketeering activity, and who uses or invests those proceeds or the proceeds derived from them to acquire an interest in property or to establish or to operate an enterprise;

(2) Who through a pattern of racketeering activity, knowingly or intentionally acquires or maintains, either directly or indirectly, an interest in or control of property or an enterprise; or

(3) Who is employed by or associated with an enterprise, and who knowingly or intentionally conducts or otherwise participates in the activities of that enterprise through a pattern of racketeering activity;

commits corrupt business influence, a Class C felony.

History.
IC 35-45-6-2, as added by Acts 1980, P.L.199, § 2; P.L.211-1991, § 9.

Penalties for felonies, IC 35-50-1, IC 35-50-2, IC 35-50-5-2.

Cross References.
Civil remedies for racketeering activity, IC 34-24-2.

NOTES TO DECISIONS

ANALYSIS

Constitutionality.
Applicability.
Attorneys.
Conspiracy.
Distinctiveness.
Double Jeopardy.
Evidence.
—Sufficient.
False Representations.
Limitations Period.
Out-of-State Crime.
Pattern of Racketeering Activity.
Preemption.
Prostitution.
Securities Act Violations.

Constitutionality.
This chapter and former IC 34-4-30.5 (Civil Remedies for Racketeering Activity Statute; now see IC 34-24-2), insofar as they pertained to the predicate offense of obscenity, did not violate the First and Fourteenth Amendments of the United States Constitution. 4447 Corp. v. Goldsmith, 504 N.E.2d 559, 1987 Ind. LEXIS 844 (1987), rev'd, 489 U.S. 46, 103 L. Ed. 2d 34, 109 S. Ct. 916, 1989 U.S. LEXIS 648 (1989); State v. Sappenfield, 505 N.E.2d 504, 1987 Ind. App. LEXIS 2529 (Ind. App. 1987), aff'd, 489 U.S. 46, 103 L. Ed. 2d 34, 109 S. Ct. 916, 1989 U.S. LEXIS 648 (1989).

There is no constitutional bar to Indiana's inclusion of substantive obscenity violations among the predicate offenses under its RICO (Racketeer Influenced and Corrupt Organizations) statute. Ft. Wayne Books v. Indiana, 489 U.S. 46, 103 L. Ed. 2d 34, 109 S. Ct. 916, 1989 U.S. LEXIS 648 (1989).

The alleged predicate acts used in a RICO (Racketeer Influenced and Corrupt Organizations)/obscenity prosecution need not be "affirmed convictions." As long as the standard of proof is the proper one with respect to all of the elements of the RICO allegation — including proof, beyond a reasonable doubt, of the requisite number of constitutionally-proscribable predicate acts — all of the relevant constitutional requirements have been met. Ft. Wayne Books v. Indiana, 489 U.S. 46, 103 L. Ed. 2d 34, 109 S. Ct. 916, 1989 U.S. LEXIS 648 (1989).

Pretrial seizure of a bookstore owner's books and films was unconstitutional where there had been no judicial determination that the seized items were "obscene" or that a RICO (Racketeer Influenced and Corrupt Organizations) violation had occurred. Ft. Wayne Books v. Indiana, 489 U.S. 46, 103 L. Ed. 2d 34, 109 S. Ct. 916, 1989 U.S. LEXIS 648 (1989).

This chapter is not unconstitutionally vague and overbroad and does not fail to provide notice of precisely what conduct is prohibited. Flinn v. State, 563 N.E.2d 536, 1990 Ind. LEXIS 240 (1990).

Collateral estoppel applied to civil action to declare underlying obscenity statute unconstitutional, where the record indicated that the state court found the obscenity statute constitutional in criminal prosecution of civil plaintiffs. A necessary implicit finding by the state court, coupled with language that indicates awareness of the issues, was sufficient to preclude relitigation. Studio Art Theatre v. City of Evansville, 76 F.3d 128, 1996 U.S. App. LEXIS 1294 (7th Cir. Ind. 1996), cert. denied, 519 U.S. 866, 117 S. Ct. 177, 136 L. Ed. 2d 117, 1996 U.S. LEXIS 5457 (1996).

Applicability.
Indiana's Racketeer Influenced and Corrupt Or-

Applicability. (Cont'd)

ganization Act (RICO) statute sweeps more broadly than the federal statute in that it speaks in IC 35-45-6-2(3) of "conducting or otherwise participating in the activities of an enterprise." Clearly, "activities" encompasses a wider range of exploits than "conduct" and does not require "an element of direction"; as such, Indiana's RICO statute applies to all those employed by or associated with an enterprise who knowingly or intentionally conduct or otherwise participate in the activities of an enterprise through a pattern of racketeering activity, whether as generals or foot soldiers. Keesling v. Beegle, 858 N.E.2d 980, 2006 Ind. App. LEXIS 2630 (2006), transfer granted and vacated, 869 N.E.2d 455, 2007 Ind. LEXIS 249.

Because IC 35-45-6-2(3) uses language significantly broader than that of 18 U.S.C.S. § 1962(c), it imposes racketeer influenced and corrupt organizations (RICO) liability both on persons at and below a racketeering enterprise's managerial or supervisory level. Keesling v. Beegle, 880 N.E.2d 1202, 2008 Ind. LEXIS 171 (2008).

Attorneys.

While an attorney may be liable under the state racketeering statute for his involvement in his clients' activities, an attorney was not so liable where he merely provided legal services to aid his clients in carrying out business transactions and where there was no allegation that he was directing his clients to engage in particular transactions. Yoder Grain, Inc. v. Antalis, 722 N.E.2d 840, 2000 Ind. App. LEXIS 61 (2000), overruled in part, Keesling v. Beegle, 880 N.E.2d 1202, 2008 Ind. LEXIS 171 (2008).

Conspiracy.

When the definition of "racketeering activity" is correlated with the definition of "pattern of racketeering activity," it is clear that a conspiracy can be used as only one of the two predicate offenses required for a Racketeer Influenced and Corrupt Organization violation. Koger v. State, 513 N.E.2d 1250, 1987 Ind. App. LEXIS 3122 (1987).

Distinctiveness.

Complaint stated a cause of action under the Indiana Racketeer and Corrupt Organizations Act (RICO) by sufficiently alleging a structure, continuity, or common course of conduct by the alleged RICO enterprises distinct and separate from the alleged RICO persons. Wesleyan Pension Fund v. First Albany Corp., 964 F. Supp. 1255, 1997 U.S. Dist. LEXIS 5934 (S.D. Ind. 1997).

Double Jeopardy.

Defendant's conviction for corrupt business influence, as well as for the predicate offenses of attempted theft and theft, did not violate double jeopardy. Dellenbach v. State, 508 N.E.2d 1309, 1987 Ind. App. LEXIS 2746 (1987).

The trial court's sentencing of the defendant for the predicate offenses of theft as well as for the offense of corrupt business influence does not violate the prohibition against double jeopardy. Swedarsky v. State, 569 N.E.2d 740, 1991 Ind. App. LEXIS 607 (1991).

The Indiana legislature intended separate convictions for a Racketeer Influenced and Corrupt Organizations Act (RICO) violation and its predicate offenses. State v. Allen, 646 N.E.2d 965, 1995 Ind. App. LEXIS 15 (1995).

A prosecution for a Racketeer Influenced and Corrupt Organizations Act (RICO) violation based upon a predicate offense of conspiracy to possess with intent to deliver and to deliver cocaine in violation of 21 U.S.C.S. § 846 did not violate Indiana's double jeopardy statute. State v. Allen, 646 N.E.2d 965, 1995 Ind. App. LEXIS 15 (1995).

A defendant may be convicted of both a racketeer influenced and corrupt organizations (RICO) statute violation and of its predicate offenses, since to constrain law enforcement to choose either to convict on the predicate offenses or to idly wait until a drug dealer has committed enough crimes to constitute a RICO violation would frustrate the very purpose for which the statute was enacted. Chavez v. State, 722 N.E.2d 885, 2000 Ind. App. LEXIS 67 (2000).

Evidence.

—Sufficient.

Even though business burglary enterprise coordinated by defendant did not last long, threat of its continuity was sufficient to support defendant's conviction of corrupt business influence. Waldon v. State, 829 N.E.2d 168, 2005 Ind. App. LEXIS 1053 (2005).

Evidence that defendant, through a corporation at which defendant served as president and chief executive officer, failed to refund clients for early-billed and previously received payments for training that was not completed was sufficient to support a conviction for corrupt business influence. Hightower v. State, 866 N.E.2d 356, 2007 Ind. App. LEXIS 1015 (2007).

Evidence that defendant offered to sell products that defendant did not possess, that defendant informed buyers that defendant had the products, that defendant received payment for the agreed upon purchase prices, and that defendant never shipped products supported defendant's conviction for corrupt business influence. Long v. State, 867 N.E.2d 606, 2007 Ind. App. LEXIS 1202 (2007).

False Representations.

Even if defendant did represent that either he or his corporation actually owned real estate that was to be the collateral for certain transactions, as compared to his merely controlling or having access to real estate, the documentary information he provided plaintiffs clearly conflicted with his verbal representation, and thus the plaintiffs were not entitled to reasonably rely on the characterization. Puller Mortgage Assocs. v. Keegan, 829 F. Supp. 1507, 1993 U.S. Dist. LEXIS 11516 (S.D. Ind. 1993).

Limitations Period.

Racketeering charge under IC 35-45-6-2 was time-barred under IC 35-41-4-2, as defendant's allegedly false statements in 2003 and 2004 about homicides he had investigated until 1990 as an

Limitations Period. (Cont'd)
Indiana police officer did not relate to the official duties he was performing as a federal police officer at the time he made the statements and thus were not the predicate offenses required to establish a continuation of a pattern of racketeering activity. Furthermore, the fact that defendant had moved to Florida did not mean that he had concealed himself so as to toll the limitations period, and his alleged coercive influence over witnesses he was alleged to have threatened and intimidated with regard to the homicide investigation had ceased, at the latest, when he moved from Indiana to Florida in 1996. State v. Lindsay, 862 N.E.2d 314, 2007 Ind. App. LEXIS 434 (2007).

Out-of-State Crime.
Prior convictions for the underlying offenses are not required to prove a pattern of racketeering activity. 4447 Corp. v. Goldsmith, 504 N.E.2d 559, 1987 Ind. LEXIS 844 (1987), rev'd, 489 U.S. 46, 103 L. Ed. 2d 34, 109 S. Ct. 916, 1989 U.S. LEXIS 648 (1989).

A burglary in Ohio could not be construed as an incident of "racketeering activity" within the statutory framework of Indiana's Racketeer Influenced and Corrupt Organization (RICO) prohibitions, since IC 35-45-6-1 defines "racketeering activity" as violations of specifically enumerated Indiana penal provisions, one of which is "burglary (IC 35-43-2-1)." The specific reference to IC 35-43-2-1 renders it impossible to consider the Ohio burglary as one of two incidents of racketeering activity necessary for an Indiana RICO conviction; however, the defendant's possession of the stolen items in Indiana, after transporting them from Ohio, violated IC 35-43-4-2(a), regardless of whether he also committed theft in Ohio by stealing the same subject matter. Koger v. State, 513 N.E.2d 1250, 1987 Ind. App. LEXIS 3122 (1987).

Evidence was sufficient to establish a pattern of racketeering activity where purchases of stolen cars were apparently made for the purpose of "retagging" the cars with salvage cars' public identification numbers. Wojtowicz v. State, 545 N.E.2d 562, 1989 Ind. LEXIS 309 (1989).

Evidence that the defendant exercised a high degree of control over the operation of a massage parlor, including handling the books, collecting and distributing money, providing condoms and other supplies to employees free of charge, handling credit card transactions, and that defendant knew employees would be engaging in prostitution, was sufficient to sustain convictions for corrupt business influence. Lee v. State, 569 N.E.2d 717, 1991 Ind. App. LEXIS 605 (1991).

Well-established sexual activity of the defendants during their employment at a massage parlor amounted to aiding and abetting promoting prostitution and such evidence supported convictions for corrupt business influence. Lee v. State, 569 N.E.2d 717, 1991 Ind. App. LEXIS 605 (1991).

Pattern of Racketeering Activity.
Where the defendant had legally abandoned its trash bags, and therefore could not show the plaintiffs, by removing the bags from a dumpster,

had committed criminal trespass, burglary or theft, or received stolen property, there could be no "pattern of racketeering activity" giving rise to liability for corrupt business influence. Long v. Dilling Mech. Contrs., Inc., 705 N.E.2d 1022, 1999 Ind. App. LEXIS 159 (1999).

Plaintiffs failed to allege the requisite continuity, where they alleged only one general scheme, two victims, four acts, and a time period of three months, thus alleging only a short-term, closed-end fraud which did not constitute a pattern of activity. Yoder Grain, Inc. v. Antalis, 722 N.E.2d 840, 2000 Ind. App. LEXIS 61 (2000), overruled in part, Keesling v. Beegle, 880 N.E.2d 1202, 2008 Ind. LEXIS 171 (2008).

Evidence that a sexual favor was performed almost immediately after an undercover officer's second appointment with a masseuse was sufficient to permit retrial of the proprietor on one count of promoting prostitution; since only one alleged offense could be retried, however, the evidence was insufficient as a matter of law to permit retrial on the other charge, corrupt business influence, which required a showing of a pattern of racketeering. Hernandez v. State, 785 N.E.2d 294, 2003 Ind. App. LEXIS 421 (2003).

Insured's claim under IC 34-24-2-6 against insurer and agent was sufficient to defeat motion for summary judgment where insured presented evidence that insurer engaged in pattern of racketeering activity in violation of IC 35-45-6-1 by inter alia: (1) attaching written instrument to insurance policy which arguably constituted making or uttering of false written instrument, as defined by IC 35-43-5-1(r), in violation of IC 35-43-5-2; and (2) by being both perpetrator and beneficiary of alleged crime pursuant to IC 35-45-6-2(1). Zinman v. Cont'l Cas. Co., — F. Supp. 2d —, 2003 U.S. Dist. LEXIS 18957 (S.D. Ind. 2003).

Attorney's motion to dismiss claims under 18 U.S.C.S. § 1962(c) and (d) and IC 35-45-6-2 on the ground that the board members failed to allege a pattern of racketeering activity sufficient to support either claim was denied because the vast amount of participants and beneficiaries of the pension plan at issue and the distinct injuries inflicted by the alleged activities satisfied the continuity prong. Brugos v. Nannenga, — F. Supp. 2d —, 2005 U.S. Dist. LEXIS 31148 (N.D. Ind. 2005).

In an action in which plaintiff appealed from a judgment of the district court dismissing his claims against defendants under the Racketeer Influenced and Corrupt Organizations Act (RICO), 18 U.S.C.S. § 1962(a)-(d), as well as its Indiana counterpart, IC 35-45-6-2, the judgment was affirmed where: (1) even if defendants may have used misleading tactics in their various efforts to obtain the rights to the product, the case lacked any of the hallmarks of a RICO violation because there was no pattern of fraudulent or racketeering behavior; (2) the state courts and the U.S. Patent and Trademark Office itself had ample tools to correct any individual instances of fraud or other misconduct; and (3) plaintiff's allegations, even construed generously in his favor, could not support a time period longer than ten months. That time period, during which only a few allegedly

Pattern of Racketeering Activity. (Cont'd) fraudulent acts took place, was too short to show the necessary continuity for a "pattern" of racketeering. Jennings v. Auto Meter Prods., 495 F.3d 466, 2007 U.S. App. LEXIS 17618 (7th Cir. Ind. 2007).

Preemption.
Indiana's anti-racketeering statute, IC 35-45-6-1 and IC 35-45-6-2, is not preempted by the federal statute prohibiting racketeer influenced and corrupt organizations (18 U.S.C.S. §§ 1961-1968). Alvers v. State, 489 N.E.2d 83, 1986 Ind. App. LEXIS 2339 (1986).

Prostitution.
The evidence at trial clearly indicated that the owner knew the women were engaging in prostitution at the massage parlor. He was present during a conversation about supplying condoms and contraceptives to the women at work; he was masturbated by one woman and a new employee during a training session; he warned the manager about the business being investigated and watched by the Vice Division; he instructed the manager to take down license plate numbers of the cars driven by customers so he could have them checked. In addition, he received income because of the prostitution at the massage parlor. The evidence was clearly sufficient to convict him of corrupt business

influence and promoting prostitution. Lee v. State, 580 N.E.2d 374, 1991 Ind. App. LEXIS 1832 (1991).

Securities Act Violations.
Allegations defendant engaged in unlawful conduct in violation of the Indiana Securities Act could also support allegations of a pattern of racketeering entitling plaintiff to relief under the Indiana Racketeer and Corrupt Organizations Act. Wesleyan Pension Fund v. First Albany Corp., 964 F. Supp. 1255, 1997 U.S. Dist. LEXIS 5934 (S.D. Ind. 1997).

Cited:
Hewell v. State, 471 N.E.2d 1235, 1984 Ind. App. LEXIS 3161 (1984); Kahn v. State, 493 N.E.2d 790, 1986 Ind. App. LEXIS 2616 (1986); Design Time, Inc. v. Synthetic Diamond Technology, Inc., 674 F. Supp. 1564, 1987 U.S. Dist. LEXIS 11531 (N.D. Ind. 1987); Hewell v. State, 507 N.E.2d 241, 1987 Ind. App. LEXIS 2629 (1987); Studio Art Theatre, Inc. v. State, 530 N.E.2d 750, 1988 Ind. App. LEXIS 925 (1988); Doe v. Indiana Black Expo, 923 F. Supp. 137, 1996 U.S. Dist. LEXIS 5526 (S.D. Ind. 1996); AGS Capital Corp. v. Prod. Action Int'l, LLC, 884 N.E.2d 294, 2008 Ind. App. LEXIS 725 (2008); Kemp v. State, 887 N.E.2d 102, 2008 Ind. App. LEXIS 1159 (2008).

RESEARCH REFERENCES

Indiana Law Review.
Evidentiary Use of Other Crime Evidence: A Survey of Recent Trends in Criminal Procedure, 20 Ind. L. Rev. 183 (1987).

Res Gestae.
Recent Decisions 2/08: Indiana Corrupt Business Influence Act imposes liability on persons at

and below enterprise's managerial or supervisory level, 51 (No. 10) Res Gestae 22 (2008).

Collateral References.
Commencement of limitation period for criminal prosecution under Racketeer Influenced and Corrupt Organizations Act (RICO) (18 U.S.C.S. §§ 1961-1968). 89 A.L.R. Fed. 887.

CHAPTER 7

LOANSHARKING

35-45-7-1. Definitions.

As used in this chapter:

"Loan" means any transaction described in section 3 [IC 35-45-7-3] of this chapter, whether or not the transaction is in the form of a loan as defined in IC 24-4.5-3-106, and without regard to whether the person making the loan is regularly engaged in making consumer loans, consumer credit sales, or consumer leases.

"Principal" includes the monetary value of property which has been loaned from one (1) person to another person.

"Rate" means the monetary value of the consideration received per annum or due per annum, calculated according to the actuarial method on the unpaid balance of the principal.

History.
IC 35-45-7-1, as added by Acts 1980, P.L.207,
§ 1; P.L.247-1983, § 24.

35-45-7-2. Loansharking a felony.

A person who, in exchange for the loan of any property, knowingly or intentionally receives or contracts to receive from another person any consideration, at a rate greater than two (2) times the rate specified in IC 24-4.5-3-508(2)(a)(i), commits loansharking, a Class D felony. However, loansharking is a Class C felony if force or the threat of force is used to collect or to attempt to collect any of the property loaned or any of the consideration for the loan.

History.
IC 35-45-7-2, as added by Acts 1980, P.L. 207,
§ 1.

Cross References.
Penalties for felonies, IC 35-50-1, IC 35-50-2, IC 35-50-5-2.

NOTES TO DECISIONS

Contracts.
Fact that consumer alleged that the loan agreement contracts that the consumer entered into with the cash advance company were illegal under Indiana's loansharking statute, IC 35-45-7-2, et seq., and the Indiana Consumer Credit Code, IC 24-4.5-3-508, did not render an arbitration agreement, which was signed contemporaneously with the loan agreement, invalid. Conner v. Instant Cash Advance, — F. Supp. 2d —, 2003 U.S. Dist. LEXIS 2584 (S.D. Ind. 2003).

Cited:
Edmonds v. Nat'l Check Bureau, Inc., — F. Supp. 2d —, 2003 U.S. Dist. LEXIS 17476 (S.D. Ind. 2003).

OPINIONS OF ATTORNEY GENERAL

Indiana's consumer credit and loansharking statutes are not inconsistent and can be interpreted harmoniously; that is, lenders may contract for and receive one or more $33 loan finance charges, so long as the resulting annual percentage rate does not exceed the interest limit established in the loansharking statute. 2000, No. 2000-1.

RESEARCH REFERENCES

Indiana Law Review.
Consumer Law: Consumer Transactions: Movement Toward a More Progressive Approach, 34 Ind. L. Rev. 599 (2001).
Survey: Commercial and Consumer Law: Indiana's Revised Article 9 and Other Developments in Commercial and Consumer Law, 35 Ind. L. Rev. 1239 (2002).

Res Gestae.
Appellate civil case law update, 45 (No. 3) Res Gestae 15 (2001).

35-45-7-3. Applicability of chapter.

(a) This chapter applies only:
(1) To consumer loans, consumer related loans, consumer credit sales, consumer related sales, and consumer leases, as those terms are defined in IC 24-4.5, subject to adjustment, where applicable, of the dollar amounts set forth in those definitions under IC 24-4.5-1-106;
(2) To any loan primarily secured by an interest in land or sale of an interest in land that is a mortgage transaction (as defined in IC 24-4.5-1-301) if the transaction is otherwise a consumer loan or consumer credit sale; and
(3) To any other loan transaction or extension of credit, regardless of the amount of the principal of the loan or extension of credit, if unlawful force or the threat of force is used to collect or to attempt to collect any of the property loaned or any of the consideration for the loan or extension of credit in question.

(b) This chapter applies regardless of whether the contract is made directly or indirectly, and whether the receipt of the consideration is received or is due to be received before or after the maturity date of the loan.

History.
IC 35-45-7-3, as added by Acts 1980, P.L.207, § 1; P.L.247-1983, § 25; P.L.14-1992, § 164; P.L.122-1994, § 121.

35-45-7-4. Loan involving loansharking void.

A loan or a contract for a loan which is made through loansharking is void.

History.
IC 35-45-7-4, as added by Acts 1980, P.L.207, § 1.

CHAPTER 8

CONSUMER PRODUCT TAMPERING

Section
35-45-8-1. "Consumer product" defined.
35-45-8-2. "Labeling" defined.

Section
35-45-8-3. Consumer product tampering.

35-45-8-1. "Consumer product" defined.

As used in this chapter, "consumer product" means:
(1) A food, drug, device, or cosmetic (as defined under IC 16-18-2-82, IC 16-18-2-94, IC 16-18-2-101(a), or IC 16-18-2-135(a)); or
(2) An item designed to be consumed for personal care or for performing household services.

History.
P.L.326-1987, § 4; P.L.2-1993, § 186.

35-45-8-2. "Labeling" defined.

As used in this chapter, "labeling" has the meaning set forth in IC 16-18-2-198(a)[repealed].

History.
P.L.326-1987, § 4; P.L.2-1993, § 187.

Compiler's Notes.
Subsection (a), referred to in this section, was repealed by P.L.137-1996, § 62.

35-45-8-3. Consumer product tampering.

A person who:
(1) Recklessly, knowingly, or intentionally introduces a poison, a harmful substance, or a harmful foreign object into a consumer product; or
(2) With intent to mislead a consumer of a consumer product, tampers with the labeling of a consumer product;
that has been introduced into commerce commits consumer product tampering, a Class D felony. However, the offense is a Class C felony if it results in harm to a person, and it is a Class B felony if it results in serious bodily injury to another person.

History.
P.L.326-1987, § 4.

Cross References.
False reporting, IC 35-44-2-2.

Penalties for felonies, IC 35-50-1, IC 35-50-2, IC 35-50-5-2.

RESEARCH REFERENCES

Collateral References.
Liability for injury or death allegedly caused by spoilage, contamination, or other deleterious condition of food or food product. 2 A.L.R.5th 1.

CHAPTER 9

CRIMINAL GANG CONTROL

35-45-9-1. "Criminal gang" defined.

As used in this chapter, "criminal gang" means a group with at least three (3) members that specifically:
    (1) either:
        (A) promotes, sponsors, or assists in; or
        (B) participates in; or
    (2) requires as a condition of membership or continued membership;
the commission of a felony or an act that would be a felony if committed by an adult or the offense of battery (IC 35-42-2-1).

History.
P.L.180-1991, § 11; P.L.140-1994, § 5; P.L.192-2007, § 9, eff. July 1, 2007.

NOTES TO DECISIONS

ANALYSIS

Constitutionality.
Evidence.
—In General.
—Insufficient.
—Sufficient.

Constitutionality.
The gang statute, IC 35-45-9-1 et seq., gives persons of ordinary intelligence fair warning of the proscribed unprotected conduct, and is thus not unconstitutionally vague. Helton v. State, 624 N.E.2d 499, 1993 Ind. App. LEXIS 1447 (1993), cert. denied, 520 U.S. 1119, 117 S. Ct. 1252, 137 L. Ed. 2d 333, 1997 U.S. LEXIS 1699 (1997).

Indiana and federal constitutional protections of free speech and free association do not provide protection for associations made in furtherance of crimes or criminal conspiracy, and the act of associating with compatriots in crime is not a protected associations right. Helton v. State, 624 N.E.2d 499, 1993 Ind. App. LEXIS 1447 (1993), cert. denied, 520 U.S. 1119, 117 S. Ct. 1252, 137 L. Ed. 2d 333, 1997 U.S. LEXIS 1699 (1997).

The Gang Statute gives persons of ordinary intelligence fair warning of the prohibited conduct and does not encourage arbitrary or discriminatory enforcement, and thus is not unconstitution-

ally vague. Jackson v. State, 634 N.E.2d 532, 1994 Ind. App. LEXIS 581 (1994).

The Indiana Gang Statute is not unconstitutionally overbroad because it does not substantially prohibit activities protected by the First Amendment. Jackson v. State, 634 N.E.2d 532, 1994 Ind. App. LEXIS 581 (1994).

This chapter is not unconstitutionally vague, since it puts individuals on notice of what the legislature considers to be a criminal gang and that participation in these groups is prohibited. Klein v. State, 698 N.E.2d 296, 1998 Ind. LEXIS 233 (1998).

This chapter does not unconstitutionally punish for status alone, because membership in a gang, by itself, does not provide the basis for prosecution; the state must prove that the individual was aware of the gang's criminal purpose. Klein v. State, 698 N.E.2d 296, 1998 Ind. LEXIS 233 (1998).

Evidence.

—In General.
To demonstrate membership in criminal gang within meaning of IC 35-45-9-1, there must be proof that person: (1) is active member of group with five or more members that promotes, sponsors, assists in, or participates in or requires as

Evidence. (Cont'd)

—In General. (Cont'd)
condition of membership or continued membership commission of felony or act that would be felony if committed by adult or a battery; (2) has knowledge of group's criminal advocacy; and (3) has specific intent to further group's criminal goals. Kelly v. State, 813 N.E.2d 1179, 2004 Ind. App. LEXIS 1709 (2004).

—Insufficient.
Where the state's only evidence that battery was gang related was that defendant was a gang member, but there was no nexus between his alleged gang membership and the crime, there was insufficient evidence of probative value to sustain conviction for criminal gang activity. Trice v. State, 693 N.E.2d 649, 1998 Ind. App. LEXIS 585 (1998).

—Sufficient.
Where the jury could infer that the commission of the offense of battery was a condition of continued membership in the defendant's group, and the evidence showed that the group committed burglary, a felony, the evidence supported a finding that the group was a criminal gang, and there was evidence of more than mere membership in the group sufficient to support a finding that defendant actively participated, and to support his conviction of criminal gang activity. Jackson v. State, 634 N.E.2d 532, 1994 Ind. App. LEXIS 581 (1994).

Evidence that defendant participated with group of five people in executing plan to confront, beat, rob, and humiliate victim was sufficient to support conviction for criminal gang activity. Kelly v. State, 813 N.E.2d 1179, 2004 Ind. App. LEXIS 1709 (2004).

Cited:
A.B. v. State, 733 N.E.2d 29, 2000 Ind. App. LEXIS 1154 (2000); Inlow v. Inlow, 797 N.E.2d 810, 2003 Ind. App. LEXIS 1979 (2003).

RESEARCH REFERENCES

Indiana Law Review.
Update — Criminal Law & Procedure, 25 Ind. L. Rev. 1157 (1992).
Recent Developments in Indiana Criminal Law and Procedure, 28 Ind. L. Rev. 819 (1995).

Res Gestae.
Criminal justice notes, 37 Res Gestae 384 (1994).

Collateral References.
Validity, construction, and application of "hazing" statutes. 30 A.L.R.5th 683.

35-45-9-2. "Threatens" defined.

As used in this chapter, "threatens" includes a communication made with the intent to harm a person or the person's property or any other person or the property of another person.

History.
P.L.180-1991, § 11.

35-45-9-3. Criminal gang activity.

A person who knowingly or intentionally actively participates in a criminal gang commits criminal gang activity, a Class D felony.

History.
P.L.180-1991, § 11.

Cross References.
Penalties for felonies, IC 35-50-1, IC 35-50-2, IC 35-50-5-2.

NOTES TO DECISIONS

Analysis

Constitutionality.
Evidence.
—Insufficient.
—Sufficient.

Constitutionality.
This chapter is not unconstitutionally vague, since it puts individuals on notice of what the legislature considers to be a criminal gang and that participation in these groups is prohibited.

Klein v. State, 698 N.E.2d 296, 1998 Ind. LEXIS 233 (1998).
This chapter does not unconstitutionally punish for status alone, because membership in a gang, by itself, does not provide the basis for prosecution; the state must prove that the individual was aware of the gang's criminal purpose. Klein v. State, 698 N.E.2d 296, 1998 Ind. LEXIS 233 (1998).

Evidence.

—Insufficient.
Where the state's only evidence that battery was

Evidence. (Cont'd)

—Insufficient. (Cont'd)
gang related was that defendant was a gang member, but there was no nexus between his alleged gang membership and the crime, there was insufficient evidence of probative value to sustain conviction for criminal gang activity. Trice v. State, 693 N.E.2d 649, 1998 Ind. App. LEXIS 585 (1998).

Conviction for criminal gang activity was reversed where, aside from a police officer's testimony about the size and illegal activities of a specific gang and his belief that defendant was a member, the state presented no substantive evidence of a nexus between defendant's alleged gang membership and the crimes for which he was charged and convicted. Robinson v. State, 730 N.E.2d 185, 2000 Ind. App. LEXIS 864 (2000).

There was insufficient evidence to convict defendant for criminal gang activity where the state presented no evidence that defendant was an "active" gang member, nor any evidence that defendant had the specific intent to further the gang's criminal goals when he stabbed and attempted to rob the victim. The state's case consisted only of evidence that defendant, at some point, was a member of a gang that commits criminal offenses, and this was not enough. Ferrell v. State, 746 N.E.2d 48, 2001 Ind. LEXIS 294 (2001).

The evidence was not sufficient to support a conviction for criminal gang activity where the state presented no evidence that defendant had the specific intent to further the gang's criminal goals when he stabbed and attempted to rob the victim. The state's case consisted only of evidence that defendant was a member of a gang that commits criminal offenses, and that was not enough. Kilpatrick v. State, 746 N.E.2d 52, 2001 Ind. LEXIS 295 (2001).

Defendant's conviction of criminal gang activity under IC 35-45-9-3 was not supported by sufficient evidence, because the State failed to establish a nexus between defendant's gang membership and the crimes with which defendant was charged. Robles v. State, 758 N.E.2d 581, 2001 Ind. App. LEXIS 1986 (2001).

Because the state only proved that defendant belonged to a gang of four members, the evidence was insufficient to establish that defendant was an active member of a gang with five or more members as required by former version of IC 35-45-9-3; therefore, defendant's delinquency adjudication for criminal gang activity was reversed. G.R. v. State, 893 N.E.2d 774, 2008 Ind. App. LEXIS 2097 (2008).

—Sufficient.
Where the jury could infer that the commission of the offense of battery was a condition of continued membership in the defendant's group, and the evidence showed that the group committed burglary, a felony, the evidence supported a finding that the group was a criminal gang, and there was evidence of more than mere membership in the group sufficient to support a finding that defendant actively participated, and to support his conviction of criminal gang activity. Jackson v. State, 634 N.E.2d 532, 1994 Ind. App. LEXIS 581 (1994).

Evidence that defendant participated with group of five people in executing plan to confront, beat, rob, and humiliate victim was sufficient to support conviction for criminal gang activity. Kelly v. State, 813 N.E.2d 1179, 2004 Ind. App. LEXIS 1709 (2004).

RESEARCH REFERENCES

Res Gestae.
Criminal justice notes, 37 Res Gestae 384 (1994).

Collateral References.
Criminal prosecutions under state RICO stat-

utes for engaging in organized criminal activity. 89 A.L.R.5th 629.

35-45-9-4. Criminal gang intimidation.

A person who threatens another person because the other person:
    (1) Refuses to join a criminal gang; or
    (2) Has withdrawn from a criminal gang;
commits criminal gang intimidation, a Class C felony.

History.
    P.L.180-1991, § 11.

Cross References.
    Penalties for felonies, IC 35-50-1, IC 35-50-2, IC 35-50-5-2.

NOTES TO DECISIONS

Evidence.

—Sufficient.
    Where there was evidence that, because juvenile refused to join the a particular gang, members of

Evidence. (Cont'd)

—Sufficient. (Cont'd)
the gang regularly chased, cursed, and threatened the juvenile and his family, and that a member of the gang shot the juvenile's dog, the evidence was sufficient to prove that the gang was a criminal gang. A.B. v. State, 733 N.E.2d 29, 2000 Ind. App. LEXIS 1154 (2000).

Intra-gang Activity.
The legislature did not exempt all intra-gang activity from the gang statute, IC 35-45-9-1 et seq., even where gang members consent to being abused. Helton v. State, 624 N.E.2d 499, 1993 Ind. App. LEXIS 1447 (1993), cert. denied, 520 U.S. 1119, 117 S. Ct. 1252, 137 L. Ed. 2d 333, 1997 U.S. LEXIS 1699 (1997).

35-45-9-5. Criminal gang recruitment.

(a) Except as provided in subsection (b), an individual who knowingly or intentionally solicits, recruits, entices, or intimidates another individual to join a criminal gang commits criminal gang recruitment, a Class D felony.

(b) The offense under subsection (a) is a Class C felony if:

(1) the solicitation, recruitment, enticement, or intimidation occurs within one thousand (1,000) feet of school property; or

(2) the individual who is solicited, recruited, enticed, or intimidated is less than eighteen (18) years of age.

History.
P.L.192-2007, § 10, eff. July 1, 2007.

Cross References.
Penalties for felonies, IC 35-50-1, IC 35-50-2, IC 35-50-5-2.

35-45-9-6. Restitution to victim.

In addition to any sentence or fine imposed on a criminal gang member for committing a felony or misdemeanor, the court shall order a criminal gang member convicted of a felony or misdemeanor to make restitution to the victim of the crime under IC 35-50-5-3.

History.
P.L.192-2007, § 11, eff. July 1, 2007.

CHAPTER 10

STALKING

35-45-10-1. "Stalk" defined.

As used in this chapter, "stalk" means a knowing or an intentional course of conduct involving repeated or continuing harassment of another person that would cause a reasonable person to feel terrorized, frightened, intimidated, or threatened and that actually causes the victim to feel terrorized, frightened, intimidated, or threatened. The term does not include statutorily or constitutionally protected activity.

History.
P.L.242-1993, § 4.

NOTES TO DECISIONS

ANALYSIS

Constitutionality.
Attempting to Locate Victim.
Double Jeopardy.
—Invasion of Privacy.
"Repeated."
Sufficiency of Evidence.

Constitutionality.

Stalking statutes are not void for vagueness because stalking is an offense which involves a knowing or intentional course of conduct, and the reasonableness standards contained in the statutes provide a constraining and intelligible enforcement standard for those charged with enforcing the statutes. Johnson v. State, 648 N.E.2d 666, 1995 Ind. App. LEXIS 304 (1995).

Attempting to Locate Victim.

Evidence was sufficient to show that defendant directed his conduct toward the victim and that his actions actually caused her to suffer emotional distress where he repeatedly and continuingly pursued the victim in an attempt to locate her, he hid his identity and disturbed operation of the shelter where she lived, and a reasonable person could suffer emotional distress under the circumstances. Johnson v. State, 648 N.E.2d 666, 1995 Ind. App. LEXIS 304 (1995).

Double Jeopardy.

Defendant's conviction for stalking and his 180-day sentence which he served for violating a protective order did not constitute double jeopardy as they were not the "same offense" under Ind. Const. art. 1, § 14. Simms v. State, 791 N.E.2d 225, 2003 Ind. App. LEXIS 1213 (2003).

—Invasion of Privacy.

The offenses of stalking and invasion of privacy require proof of different facts and are not the same for double jeopardy purposes; stalking requires proof that the perpetrator entertain the intent to cause another to feel terrorized, frightened, intimidated or threatened, and invasion of privacy requires proof the defendant violated a protective order issued under former IC 34-4-5.1. Burton v. State, 665 N.E.2d 924, 1996 Ind. App. LEXIS 718 (1996).

The manner in which the offenses of stalking and invasion of privacy were charged relieved the state of proving additional facts to gain defendant's conviction for invasion of privacy beyond those required to prove stalking conviction, and therefore convictions for both offenses were barred by double jeopardy principles. Burton v. State, 665 N.E.2d 924, 1996 Ind. App. LEXIS 718 (1996).

"Repeated."

The term "repeated" in the anti-stalking law means "more than once." Johnson v. State, 721 N.E.2d 327, 1999 Ind. App. LEXIS 2209 (1999).

Sufficiency of Evidence.

Where defendant had threatened to kill the victim, assaulted the victim, continually left threatening messages on the victim's phone, and finally shot at the victim, it was reasonable for the jury to infer the victim felt terrorized, frightened, intimidated, and threatened in convicting defendant of stalking. Simms v. State, 791 N.E.2d 225, 2003 Ind. App. LEXIS 1213 (2003).

Defendant's eight year sentence for stalking was appropriate where the victim received 69 calls from defendant within a three month period and there was witness testimony that defendant followed the victim, showed up at her workplace, and called her friends. Smith v. State, 839 N.E.2d 780, 2005 Ind. App. LEXIS 2442 (2005).

As the freedom to be on a public street is one of the personal liberties guaranteed by the federal constitution and nothing occurred that would remotely indicate to defendant that his conduct of parking across the street from the alleged victim's home on multiple occasions with binoculars was impermissible, such as a protective order, evidence was insufficient to support his conviction for stalking under IC 35-45-10-5(a). VanHorn v. State, 889 N.E.2d 908, 2008 Ind. App. LEXIS 1507 (2008).

Cited:

Landis v. State, 726 N.E.2d 801, 2000 Ind. App. LEXIS 441 (2000); Garza v. State, 736 N.E.2d 323, 2000 Ind. App. LEXIS 1584 (2000); Garmene v. LeMasters, 743 N.E.2d 782, 2001 Ind. App. LEXIS 302 (2001); Essany v. Bower, 790 N.E.2d 148, 2003 Ind. App. LEXIS 1056 (2003).

RESEARCH REFERENCES

Indiana Law Review.

Anti-Stalker Legislation: A Legislative Attempt to Surmount the Inadequacies of Protective Orders, 27 Ind. L. Rev. 449 (1993).

Notre Dame Law Review.

From Imprudence to Crime: Anti-Stalking Laws, 68 Notre Dame L. Rev. 819 (1993).

Res Gestae.

Criminal Justice Notes 7/08: Repeated presence on public street insufficient to support stalking conviction, 52 (No. 3) Res Gestae 35 (2008).

Collateral References.

Validity, construction, and application of stalking statutes. 29 A.L.R.5th 487.

35-45-10-2. "Harassment" defined.

As used in this chapter, "harassment" means conduct directed toward a victim that includes but is not limited to repeated or continuing impermissible contact that would cause a reasonable person to suffer emotional distress and that actually causes the victim to suffer emotional distress. Harassment does not include statutorily or constitutionally protected activity, such as lawful picketing pursuant to labor disputes or lawful employer-related activities pursuant to labor disputes.

History.
P.L.242-1993, § 4.

NOTES TO DECISIONS

ANALYSIS

Sufficiency of Evidence.
Workplace Violence Restraining Orders Act.

Sufficiency of Evidence.
Where defendant had threatened to kill the victim, assaulted the victim, continually left threatening messages on the victim's phone, and finally shot at the victim, it was reasonable for the jury to infer the victim felt terrorized, frightened, intimidated, and threatened in convicting defendant of stalking. Simms v. State, 791 N.E.2d 225, 2003 Ind. App. LEXIS 1213 (2003).

As the freedom to be on a public street is one of the personal liberties guaranteed by the federal constitution and nothing occurred that would remotely indicate to defendant that his conduct of parking across the street from the alleged victim's home on multiple occasions with binoculars was impermissible, such as a protective order, evidence was insufficient to support his conviction for stalking under IC 35-45-10-5(a). VanHorn v. State, 889 N.E.2d 908, 2008 Ind. App. LEXIS 1507 (2008).

Workplace Violence Restraining Orders Act.
Restraining order was properly entered in favor of an administration and against an attendee pursuant to the Workplace Violence Restraining Orders Act, IC 34-26-6-1 et seq., because there was sufficient evidence that the attendee's actions at meetings of the Indiana Council on Independent Living (ICOIL) would have caused a reasonable person to suffer emotional distress and actually caused the victim to suffer emotional distress; it was shown that an ICOIL member, who witnessed the attendee's verbal and physical outbursts on at least 15 occasions, left one meeting because she no longer felt safe. It was reasonable for the trial court to find that reasonable persons at ICOIL meetings would have suffered, and, in fact, suffered emotional distress due to these outbursts, and the evidence also established that the administration's employee actually suffered emotional distress as a result of the attendee's conduct. Torres v. Ind. Family & Soc. Servs. Admin., 905 N.E.2d 24, 2009 Ind. App. LEXIS 741 (2009).

Cited:
Garza v. State, 736 N.E.2d 323, 2000 Ind. App. LEXIS 1584 (2000).

RESEARCH REFERENCES

Res Gestae.
Criminal Justice Notes 7/08: Repeated presence on public street insufficient to support stalking conviction, 52 (No. 3) Res Gestae 35 (2008).

Alternative Dispute Resolution: All things ADR considered: Mediator testimony leads to reversal, 52 (No. 3) Res Gestae 39 (2008).

35-45-10-3. "Impermissible contact" defined.

As used in this chapter, "impermissible contact" includes but is not limited to knowingly or intentionally following or pursuing the victim.

History.
P.L.242-1993, § 4.

NOTES TO DECISIONS

Sufficiency of Evidence.
Where defendant had threatened to kill the victim, assaulted the victim, continually left

threatening messages on the victim's phone, and finally shot at the victim, it was reasonable for the jury to infer the victim felt terrorized, frightened,

Sufficiency of Evidence. (Cont'd)
intimidated, and threatened in convicting defendant of stalking. Simms v. State, 791 N.E.2d 225, 2003 Ind. App. LEXIS 1213 (2003).

Telephone messages, without more, may amount to "impermissible contact" sufficient to support stalking conviction. Smith v. State, 802 N.E.2d 948, 2004 Ind. App. LEXIS 160 (2004).

As the freedom to be on a public street is one of the personal liberties guaranteed by the federal constitution and nothing occurred that would remotely indicate to defendant that his conduct of parking across the street from the alleged victim's home on multiple occasions with binoculars was impermissible, such as a protective order, evidence was insufficient to support his conviction for stalking under IC 35-45-10-5(a). VanHorn v. State, 889 N.E.2d 908, 2008 Ind. App. LEXIS 1507 (2008).

35-45-10-4. "Victim" defined.

As used in this chapter, "victim" means a person who is the object of stalking.

History.
P.L.242-1993, § 4.

35-45-10-5. Violation — Penalties.

(a) A person who stalks another person commits stalking, a Class D felony.
(b) The offense is a Class C felony if at least one (1) of the following applies:
   (1) A person:
      (A) stalks a victim; and
      (B) makes an explicit or an implicit threat with the intent to place the victim in reasonable fear of:
         (i) sexual battery (as defined in IC 35-42-4-8);
         (ii) serious bodily injury; or
         (iii) death.
   (2) A protective order to prevent domestic or family violence, a no contact order, or other judicial order under any of the following statutes has been issued by the court to protect the same victim or victims from the person and the person has been given actual notice of the order:
      (A) IC 31-15 and IC 34-26-5 or IC 31-1-11.5 before its repeal (dissolution of marriage and legal separation).
      (B) IC 31-34, IC 31-37, or IC 31-6-4 before its repeal (delinquent children and children in need of services).
      (C) IC 31-32 or IC 31-6-7 before its repeal (procedure in juvenile court).
      (D) IC 34-26-5 or IC 34-26-2 and IC 34-4-5.1 before their repeal (protective order to prevent abuse).
      (E) IC 34-26-6 (workplace violence restraining orders).
   (3) The person's stalking of another person violates an order issued as a condition of pretrial release, including release on bail or personal recognizance, or pretrial diversion if the person has been given actual notice of the order.
   (4) The person's stalking of another person violates a no contact order issued as a condition of probation if the person has been given actual notice of the order.
   (5) The person's stalking of another person violates a protective order issued under IC 31-14-16-1 and IC 34-26-5 in a paternity action if the person has been given actual notice of the order.
   (6) The person's stalking of another person violates an order issued in another state that is substantially similar to an order described in subdivisions (2) through (5) if the person has been given actual notice of the order.
   (7) The person's stalking of another person violates an order that is substantially similar to an order described in subdivisions (2) through (5) and is issued by an Indian:
      (A) tribe;
      (B) band;
      (C) pueblo;

(D) nation; or

(E) organized group or community, including an Alaska Native village or regional or village corporation as defined in or established under the Alaska Native Claims Settlement Act (43 U.S.C. 1601 et seq.);

that is recognized as eligible for the special programs and services provided by the United States to Indians because of their special status as Indians if the person has been given actual notice of the order.

(8) A criminal complaint of stalking that concerns an act by the person against the same victim or victims is pending in a court and the person has been given actual notice of the complaint.

(c) The offense is a Class B felony if:

(1) the act or acts were committed while the person was armed with a deadly weapon; or

(2) the person has an unrelated conviction for an offense under this section against the same victim or victims.

(d) Notwithstanding subsection (a), the court may enter judgment of conviction of a Class A misdemeanor and sentence accordingly if the court finds mitigating circumstances. The court may consider the mitigating circumstances in IC 35-38-1-7.1(c) in making a determination under this subsection. However, the criteria listed in IC 35-38-1-7.1(c) do not limit the matters the court may consider in making its determination.

(e) Notwithstanding subsection (b), the court may enter judgment of conviction of a Class D felony and sentence accordingly if the court finds mitigating circumstances. The court may consider the mitigating circumstances in IC 35-38-1-7.1(c) in making a determination under this subsection. However, the criteria listed in IC 35-38-1-7.1(c) do not limit the matters the court may consider in making its determination.

History.
P.L.242-1993, § 4; P.L.225-1996, § 1; P.L.1-1997, § 150; P.L.1-1998, § 198; P.L.280-2001, § 52; P.L.133-2002, § 66.

Penalties for misdemeanors, IC 35-50-1, IC 35-50-3, IC 35-50-5-2.

Cross References.
Penalties for felonies, IC 35-50-1, IC 35-50-2, IC 35-50-5-2.

NOTES TO DECISIONS

ANALYSIS

Constitutionality.
Double Jeopardy.
Evidence.
—Insufficient.
—Prior Acts.
—Second Charge.
—Sufficient.
Multiple Convictions.
Predicate Offenses.
Sentencing.
Victim's Fear.

Constitutionality.
Since, at the time the defendant committed the acts comprising a second charge of stalking, he was on notice that his behavior would be punished more severely based upon the prior criminal complaint involving the same victim, the requirement that the state need prove beyond a reasonable

doubt only the fact of a pending charge, and not that the defendant actually stalked the victim the first time, did not contravene the due process clause. Johnson v. State, 721 N.E.2d 327, 1999 Ind. App. LEXIS 2209 (1999).

The elevation of the potential penalty for a second charge of stalking, by which the legislature sought to deter defendants from continuing the criminal behavior while the first charge moved toward trial, was reasonably related to the characteristics of stalkers, and did not contravene the equal privileges and immunities clause of the state constitution. Johnson v. State, 721 N.E.2d 327, 1999 Ind. App. LEXIS 2209 (1999).

Double Jeopardy.
There was no double jeopardy violation where the evidence presented at trial and the state's comments during opening and closing argument showed that there was no reasonable possibility that the two stalking convictions were based upon

Double Jeopardy. (Cont'd)
the same factual evidence. Peckinpaugh v. State, 743 N.E.2d 1238, 2001 Ind. App. LEXIS 460 (2001).

Defendant's conviction for stalking and his 180-day sentence which he served for violating a protective order did not constitute double jeopardy as they were not the "same offense" under Ind. Const., art. 1, § 14. Simms v. State, 791 N.E.2d 225, 2003 Ind. App. LEXIS 1213 (2003).

Evidence.

—Insufficient.

As the freedom to be on a public street is one of the personal liberties guaranteed by the federal constitution and nothing occurred that would remotely indicate to defendant that his conduct of parking across the street from the alleged victim's home on multiple occasions with binoculars was impermissible, such as a protective order, evidence was insufficient to support his conviction for stalking under IC 35-45-10-5(a). VanHorn v. State, 889 N.E.2d 908, 2008 Ind. App. LEXIS 1507 (2008).

—Prior Acts.

Introduction of prior acts requires reversal of denial of motion to bifurcate, where evidence of the prior acts is of no probative value on the issue of guilt, in that those acts do not tend to prove any disputed fact in issue but only to contaminate the jury's thinking. Landis v. State, 693 N.E.2d 570, 1998 Ind. App. LEXIS 355 (1998), transfer granted, 706 N.E.2d 180, 1998 Ind. LEXIS 720 (1998), aff'd, 704 N.E.2d 113, 1998 Ind. LEXIS 681 (1998).

The fact that the defendant was acquitted of a first stalking charge did not preclude the court from considering evidence supporting that charge where the same evidence was also probative of a second stalking charge, since it bore on other elements of the second charge such as his intent and the victim's fear and emotional distress, even though it could not be used to establish the repeated or continuing nature of the defendant's actions. Johnson v. State, 721 N.E.2d 327, 1999 Ind. App. LEXIS 2209 (1999).

Defendant's prior bad acts were not presented to prove his character, in contravention of Rule Evid. R. 404(b), but were admitted to prove the specific elements of the crime of stalking. Landis v. State, 726 N.E.2d 801, 2000 Ind. App. LEXIS 441 (2000), transfer granted, 741 N.E.2d 1256, 2000 Ind. LEXIS 1033 (2000), superseded, 749 N.E.2d 1130, 2001 Ind. LEXIS 534 (Ind. 2001).

—Second Charge.

A second stalking charge which carried an enhanced penalty because of a pending charge at the time defendant committed the acts comprising the second charge, could only be supported by actions subsequent to the filing of the initial charge. Johnson v. State, 721 N.E.2d 327, 1999 Ind. App. LEXIS 2209 (1999).

—Sufficient.

Evidence was sufficient to support conviction for stalking where victim saw defendant near her dance studio a number of times, watching her, and each of the encounters caused her to feel terrorized, frightened, intimidated, or threatened. Waldon v. State, 684 N.E.2d 206, 1997 Ind. App. LEXIS 1124 (1997).

Evidence supported the conclusion that the defendant engaged in a course of conduct involving repeated harassment of the victim, where he, on three different occasions during the same night, banged on the victim's window and door, requested to be let in, and berated the victim; it made no difference that the behavior occurred over a short period of time. Johnson v. State, 721 N.E.2d 327, 1999 Ind. App. LEXIS 2209 (1999).

Where the stalker's repeated flowers, notes, and phone calls to the victim were continuous over a two-year period, despite the fact that defendant knew the victim did not appreciate or welcome his advances and comments to her, the jury could have properly inferred that the victim was reasonable to feel terrorized, frightened, intimidated or threatened, and the evidence was sufficient to convict. Garza v. State, 736 N.E.2d 323, 2000 Ind. App. LEXIS 1584 (2000).

Where defendant had threatened to kill the victim, assaulted the victim, continually left threatening messages on the victim's phone, and finally shot at the victim, it was reasonable for the jury to infer the victim felt terrorized, frightened, intimidated, and threatened in convicting defendant of stalking. Simms v. State, 791 N.E.2d 225, 2003 Ind. App. LEXIS 1213 (2003).

Evidence was sufficient to convict defendant of offenses of intimidation and stalking based on messages sent by defendant where jury could have reasonably concluded that more than one of messages was threatening and that messages amounted to impermissible contact that would cause a reasonable person emotional distress. Smith v. State, 802 N.E.2d 948, 2004 Ind. App. LEXIS 160 (2004).

Multiple Convictions.

A defendant may be convicted of separate counts of stalking the same victim if the respective series of incidents upon which the charges are based can be divided into distinct and separate series. Peckinpaugh v. State, 743 N.E.2d 1238, 2001 Ind. App. LEXIS 460 (2001).

Predicate Offenses.

Intent of legislative revision was not to bar use of prior stalking charge as predicate offense for purpose of elevating class of felony charge. Landis v. State, 693 N.E.2d 570, 1998 Ind. App. LEXIS 355 (1998), transfer granted, 706 N.E.2d 180, 1998 Ind. LEXIS 720 (1998), aff'd, 704 N.E.2d 113, 1998 Ind. LEXIS 681 (1998).

Sentencing.

Trial court did not abuse its discretion in considering defendant's misdemeanor convictions as an aggravating factor or that the aggravating factors substantially outweighed the mitigating factors. Additionally, the sentence imposed was not inappropriate in light of the nature of the offense and the character of the offender where defendant

Sentencing. (Cont'd)
threatened to kill the victim, assaulted the victim, continued to leave threatening messages on the victim's phone, and finally shot at the victim as she was getting into her truck. Simms v. State, 791 N.E.2d 225, 2003 Ind. App. LEXIS 1213 (2003).

Victim's Fear.
Evidence of the defendant's long course of bad behavior toward the victim and its direct impact on the feelings she might have had at the time the defendant committed the acts comprising the charge of stalking was probative of the victim's actual fear. Johnson v. State, 721 N.E.2d 327, 1999 Ind. App. LEXIS 2209 (1999).

Cited:
Hendricks v. State, 649 N.E.2d 1050, 1995 Ind. App. LEXIS 437 (1995).

CHAPTER 11

ABUSE OF A CORPSE

Section
35-45-11-1. When chapter does not apply.
35-45-11-2. Abuse of a corpse defined — Penalties.

35-45-11-1. When chapter does not apply.

(a) This chapter does not apply to the use of a corpse for:
(1) Scientific;
(2) Medical;
(3) Organ transplantation;
(4) Historical;
(5) Forensic; or
(6) Investigative;
purposes.
(b) This chapter does not apply to:
(1) A funeral director;
(2) An embalmer; or
(3) An employee of an individual described in subdivision (1) or (2);
engaged in the individual's normal scope of practice and employment.

History.
P.L.249-1993, § 1.

35-45-11-2. Abuse of a corpse defined — Penalties.

A person who knowingly or intentionally:
(1) mutilates a corpse;
(2) has sexual intercourse or sexual deviate conduct with the corpse; or
(3) opens a casket with the intent to commit an act described in subdivision (1) or (2);
commits abuse of a corpse, a Class D felony.

History.
P.L.249-1993, § 1; P.L.52-1997, § 56.

Cross References.
Penalties for felonies, IC 35-50-1, IC 35-50-2, IC 35-50-5-2.

NOTES TO DECISIONS

Admission of Photographs.
In trial of defendant for numerous crimes, including murder and abuse of corpse, photographs of victim's burnt corpse and pictures of car in which she was burned were properly admitted to support elements necessary to establish abuse of corpse. Collins v. State, 826 N.E.2d 671, 2005 Ind. App. LEXIS 734 (2005), cert. denied, 546 U.S.

Admission of Photographs. (Cont'd)
1108, 163 L. Ed. 2d 885, 126 S. Ct. 1058, 2006 U.S.
LEXIS 639 (2006).

CHAPTER 12

CODE GRABBING DEVICES

Section
35-45-12-1. "Code grabbing device" defined.
35-45-12-2. Possession or use of code grabbing
          device.

35-45-12-1. "Code grabbing device" defined.

As used in this chapter, "code grabbing device" means a device that is capable of:
  (1) Receiving and recording the code signal sent by the transmitter of:
    (A) A motor vehicle security alarm system;
    (B) A motor vehicle automatic door locking system; or
    (C) A residential or commercial automatic garage door opening system; and
  (2) Disarming:
    (A) A motor vehicle security alarm system;
    (B) A motor vehicle automatic door locking system; or
    (C) A residential or commercial automatic garage door opening system.

History.
  P.L.302-1995, § 1.

35-45-12-2. Possession or use of code grabbing device.

A person who, while committing a crime or to further the commission of a crime, knowingly or intentionally:
  (1) Possesses a code grabbing device; or
  (2) Uses a code grabbing device to disarm the security alarm system of a motor vehicle;
commits a Class C misdemeanor.

History.
  P.L.302-1995, § 1.

Cross References.
  Penalties for misdemeanors, IC 35-50-1, IC 35-50-3, IC 35-50-5-2.

CHAPTER 13

UNAUTHORIZED USE OF TELECOMMUNICATIONS SERVICES

35-45-13-1. "Manufacture of an unlawful telecommunications device" defined.

As used in this chapter, "manufacture of an unlawful telecommunications device" means:

(1) the production or assembly of an unlawful telecommunications device; or

(2) the modification, alteration, programming, or reprogramming of a telecommunications device to render it capable of acquiring or facilitating the acquisition of telecommunications service without the consent of the telecommunications service provider.

History.
P.L.216-1996, § 23.

35-45-13-2. "Publish" defined.

As used in this chapter, "publish" means the communication or dissemination of information to at least one (1) person by any of the following methods:

(1) Orally.

(2) In person.

(3) By telephone, radio, or television.

(4) In a writing of any kind, including a letter, memorandum, circular handbill, newspaper, magazine article, or book.

History.
P.L.216-1996, § 23.

35-45-13-3. "Telecommunications device" defined.

As used in this chapter, "telecommunications device" means:

(1) a type of instrument, device, machine, or piece of equipment that is capable of transmitting or receiving telephonic, electronic, or radio communications;

(2) a part of an instrument, a device, a machine, or a piece of equipment that is capable of transmitting or receiving telephonic, electronic, or radio communications; or

(3) a computer circuit, a computer chip, an electronic mechanism, or any other component that is capable of facilitating the transmission or reception of telephonic, electronic, or radio communications.

History.
P.L.216-1996, § 23.

35-45-13-4. "Telecommunications services" defined.

As used in this chapter, "telecommunications service" means a service provided for a charge or compensation to facilitate the origination, transmission, emission, or reception of signs, signals, data, writings, images, sounds, or intelligence of any nature by:

(1) telephone, including cellular or other wireless telephones;

(2) wire;

(3) radio; or

(4) an electromagnetic, a photoelectronic, or a photo-optical system.

History.
P.L.216-1996, § 23.

35-45-13-5. "Telecommunications service provider" defined.

As used in this chapter, "telecommunications service provider" means a person or an entity:

(1) providing telecommunications service, including a cellular, paging, or other wireless communications company; or

(2) that, for a fee, supplies the facility, cell site, mobile telephone switching office, or other equipment for a telecommunications service.

History.
P.L.216-1996, § 23.

35-45-13-6. "Unlawful telecommunications device" defined.

(a) As used in this chapter, "unlawful telecommunications device" means a telecommunications device that:

(1) is capable of; or

(2) has been altered, modified, programmed, or reprogrammed, alone or in conjunction with another access device or other equipment, to render the telecommunications device capable of;

acquiring or facilitating the acquisition of an electronic serial number, a mobile identification number, or a personal identification number of any telecommunications service without the consent of a telecommunications service provider.

(b) The term does not include a device operated by a law enforcement agency in the course of its activities.

History.
P.L.216-1996, § 23.

35-45-13-7. Unauthorized use of telecommunication services.

A person who knowingly or intentionally:

(1) makes, distributes, possesses, uses, or assembles an unlawful telecommunications device that is designed, adapted, or used to:

(A) commit a theft of telecommunications service;

(B) acquire or facilitate the acquisition of telecommunications service without the consent of the telecommunications service provider; or

(C) conceal, or assist another in concealing, from a telecommunication services provider or authority, or from another person with enforcement authority, the existence or place of origin or destination of telecommunications;

(2) sells, possesses, distributes, gives, transports, or otherwise transfers to another or offers or advertises for sale:

(A) an unlawful telecommunications device, with the intent to use the unlawful telecommunications device or allow the device to be used for a purpose described in subdivision (1), or while knowing or having reason to believe that the device is intended to be so used;

(B) plans or instructions for making or assembling an unlawful telecommunications device, knowing or having reason to believe that the plans or instructions are intended to be used for making or assembling an unlawful telecommunications device; or

(C) material, including hardware, cables, tools, data, computer software, or other information or equipment, knowing that the purchaser or a third person intends to use the material in the manufacture of an unlawful telecommunications device; or

(3) publishes:

(A) the number or code of an existing, a canceled, a revoked, or a nonexistent telephone number, credit number, or other credit device; or

(B) the method of numbering or coding that is employed in the issuance of telephone numbers, credit numbers, or other credit devices;
with knowledge or reason to believe that the information may be used to avoid the payment of a lawful telephone or telegraph toll charge;
commits unauthorized use of telecommunication services, a Class A misdemeanor. However, if the commission of the offense involves at least five (5) unlawful telecommunications devices the offense is a Class D felony.

History.
P.L.216-1996, § 23.

Cross References.
Penalties for felonies, IC 35-50-1, IC 35-50-2, IC 35-50-5-2.

Penalties for misdemeanors, IC 35-50-1, IC 35-50-3, IC 35-50-5-2.

35-45-13-8. Restitution — Civil actions.

(a) The court may, in addition to any other sentence imposed for a conviction under this chapter, order a person convicted under this chapter to make restitution for the offense.

(b) A person or an entity that is the victim of an offense under this chapter may, in a civil action brought in the circuit or superior court in the county in which the person who committed the offense under this chapter was convicted, obtain appropriate relief, including preliminary and other equitable or declaratory relief, compensatory and punitive damages, reasonable investigation expense, court costs, and attorney's fees.

History.
P.L.216-1996, § 23.

CHAPTER 14

UNLAWFUL SOLICITATION

35-45-14-1. "Attorney" defined.

As used in this chapter, "attorney" means an individual in good standing admitted to the practice of law in Indiana or another state.

History.
P.L.216-1997, § 1.

35-45-14-2. Solicitation by non-attorneys — Receipt of compensation from attorney.

A person who is not an attorney and who:
(1) knowingly or intentionally solicits, advises, requests, or induces another person to bring an action in a court; and
(2) in making a solicitation under subdivision (1), directly or indirectly receives any compensation, fee, or commission from the attorney for the solicitation;
commits unlawful solicitation, a Class A misdemeanor.

History.
P.L.216-1997, § 1; P.L.64-2001, § 2.

Cross References.
Penalties for misdemeanors, IC 35-50-1, IC 35-50-3, IC 35-50-5-2.

CHAPTER 15

MONEY LAUNDERING

35-45-15-1. "Criminal activity" defined.

As used in this chapter, "criminal activity" means any offense that:
(1) is classified as a felony under Indiana or United States law; or
(2) occurs in another state and is punishable by confinement for more than one
(1) year under the laws of that state.

History.
P.L.112-1998, § 2.

35-45-15-2. "Funds" defined.

As used in this chapter, "funds" includes the following:
(1) Coin or paper money of the United States or any other country that is designated as legal tender and that circulates and is customarily used and accepted as a medium of exchange in the country of issue.
(2) United States silver certificates, United States Treasury notes, and Federal Reserve System notes.
(3) Official foreign bank notes that are customarily used and accepted as a medium of exchange in a foreign country.
(4) Foreign bank drafts.

History.
P.L.112-1998, § 2.

35-45-15-3. "Law enforcement officer" defined.

As used in this chapter, "law enforcement officer" includes a federal enforcement officer.

History.
P.L.112-1998, § 2.

35-45-15-4. "Proceeds" defined.

As used in this chapter, "proceeds" means funds acquired or derived directly or indirectly from, produced through, or realized through an act.

History.
P.L.112-1998, § 2.

35-45-15-5. Money laundering — Defenses.

(a) A person that knowingly or intentionally:
(1) acquires or maintains an interest in, receives, conceals, possesses, transfers, or transports the proceeds of criminal activity;

(2) conducts, supervises, or facilitates a transaction involving the proceeds of criminal activity; or

(3) invests, expends, receives, or offers to invest, expend, or receive, the proceeds of criminal activity or funds that are the proceeds of criminal activity, and the person knows that the proceeds or funds are the result of criminal activity;

commits money laundering, a Class D felony. However, the offense is:

(A) a Class C felony if the value of the proceeds or funds is at least fifty thousand dollars ($50,000);

(B) a Class C felony if a person commits the crime with the intent to:

(i) commit or promote an act of terrorism; or

(ii) obtain or transport a weapon of mass destruction; and

(C) a Class B felony if the value of the proceeds or funds is at least fifty thousand dollars ($50,000) and a person commits the crime with the intent to:

(i) commit or promote an act of terrorism; or

(ii) obtain or transport a weapon of mass destruction.

(b) It is a defense to prosecution under this section that the person acted with intent to facilitate the lawful seizure, forfeiture, or disposition of funds or other legitimate law enforcement purpose under Indiana or United States law.

(c) It is a defense to prosecution under this section that:

(1) the transaction was necessary to preserve a person's right to representation as guaranteed by the Sixth Amendment of the United States Constitution or Article 1, Section 13, of the Constitution of the State of Indiana; or

(2) the funds were received as bona fide legal fees by a licensed attorney and, at the time of the receipt of the funds, the attorney did not have actual knowledge that the funds were derived from criminal activity.

History.
P.L.112-1998, § 2; P.L.123-2002, § 42.

NOTES TO DECISIONS

ANALYSIS

Double Jeopardy.
Evidence.

Double Jeopardy.

Convictions for money laundering and forgery did not violate Indiana's double jeopardy clause; the unique fact supporting the forgery conviction was that defendant uttered or presented a forged check to the bank for deposit into defendant's account, and the unique fact supporting the money laundering conviction was that defendant agreed to receive and deposit the altered checks. Scott v. State, 867 N.E.2d 690, 2007 Ind. App. LEXIS 1211 (2007).

Evidence.

Conviction for money laundering was supported by evidence that defendant lied to a detective when defendant stated that it was the first time defendant had ever tried to cash a check in this sort of business and that defendant had corresponded by email with individuals involved in similar schemes, supporting a reasonable inference that defendant knew that agreeing to accept and deposit the checks sent to defendant was facilitating illegal activity. Scott v. State, 867 N.E.2d 690, 2007 Ind. App. LEXIS 1211 (2007).

Cited:

State v. Jackson, 864 N.E.2d 431, 2007 Ind. App. LEXIS 771 (2007).

RESEARCH REFERENCES

Indiana Law Review.
Survey: Criminal Law and Procedure: Recent

Developments in Indiana, 32 Ind. L. Rev. 789 (1999).

CHAPTER 16

MALICIOUS MISCHIEF

35-45-16-1. "HIV" defined.

(a) As used in this chapter, "HIV" refers to the human immunodeficiency virus.

(b) The term includes acquired immune deficiency syndrome (AIDS) and AIDS related complex.

History.
  P.L.88-2002, § 2.

35-45-16-2. Malicious mischief — Malicious mischief with food.

(a) A person who recklessly, knowingly, or intentionally places human:
  (1) blood;
  (2) semen;
  (3) urine; or
  (4) fecal waste;
in a location with the intent that another person will involuntarily touch the blood, semen, urine, or fecal waste commits malicious mischief, a Class B misdemeanor.

(b) An offense described in subsection (a) is a:
  (1) Class D felony if the person knew or recklessly failed to know that the blood, urine, or waste was infected with:
    (A) hepatitis B;
    (B) HIV; or
    (C) tuberculosis;
  (2) Class C felony if:
    (A) the person knew or recklessly failed to know that the blood, urine, or waste was infected with hepatitis B and the offense results in the transmission of hepatitis B to the other person; or
    (B) the person knew or recklessly failed to know that the waste was infected with tuberculosis and the offense results in the transmission of tuberculosis to the other person; and
  (3) Class B felony if:
    (A) the person knew or recklessly failed to know that the waste was infected with HIV; and
    (B) the offense results in the transmission of HIV to the other person.

(c) A person who recklessly, knowingly, or intentionally places human:
  (1) blood;
  (2) body fluid; or
  (3) fecal waste;
in a location with the intent that another person will ingest the blood, body fluid, or fecal waste, commits malicious mischief with food, a Class A misdemeanor.

(d) An offense described in subsection (c) is:
  (1) a Class D felony if the person knew or recklessly failed to know that the blood, body fluid, or fecal waste was infected with:
    (A) hepatitis B;
    (B) HIV; or
    (C) tuberculosis;
  (2) a Class C felony if:

(A) the person knew or recklessly failed to know that the blood, body fluid, or fecal waste was infected with hepatitis B and the offense results in the transmission of hepatitis B to the other person; or

(B) the person knew or recklessly failed to know that the blood, body fluid, or fecal waste was infected with tuberculosis and the offense results in the transmission of tuberculosis to the other person; and

(3) a Class B felony if:

(A) the person knew or recklessly failed to know that the blood, body fluid, or fecal waste was infected with HIV; and

(B) the offense results in the transmission of HIV to the other person.

History.
P.L.88-2002, § 2.

Penalties for misdemeanors, IC 35-50-1, IC 35-50-3, IC 35-50-5-2.

Cross References.
Penalties for felonies, IC 35-50-1, IC 35-50-2, IC 35-50-5-2.

CHAPTER 17

PANHANDLING

35-45-17-1. "Panhandling" defined.

(a) As used in this chapter, "panhandling" means to solicit an individual:
(1) on a street or in another public place; and
(2) by requesting an immediate donation of money or something else of value.
(b) The term includes soliciting an individual:
(1) by making an oral request;
(2) in exchange for:
(A) performing music;
(B) singing; or
(C) engaging in another type of performance; or
(3) by offering the individual an item of little or no monetary value in exchange for money or another gratuity under circumstances that would cause a reasonable individual to understand that the transaction is only a donation.
(c) The term does not include an act of passively standing, sitting, performing music, singing, or engaging in another type of performance:
(1) while displaying a sign or other indication that a donation is being sought; and
(2) without making an oral request other than in response to an inquiry by another person.

History.
P.L.140-2005, § 8.

35-45-17-2. Panhandling — Misdemeanor.

A person who knowingly or intentionally does any of the following commits panhandling, a Class C misdemeanor:
(1) Panhandling after sunset and before sunrise.
(2) Panhandling when the individual being solicited is:
(A) at a bus stop;
(B) in a:
(i) vehicle; or

(ii) facility;
used for public transportation;
    (C) in a motor vehicle that is parked or stopped on a public street or alley, unless the person soliciting the individual has the approval to do so by a unit of local government that has jurisdiction over the public street or alley;
    (D) in the sidewalk dining area of a restaurant; or
    (E) within twenty (20) feet of:
        (i) an automated teller machine; or
        (ii) the entrance to a bank.
  (3) Panhandling while touching the individual being solicited without the solicited individual's consent.
  (4) Panhandling while the individual being solicited is standing in line and waiting to be admitted to a commercial establishment.
  (5) Panhandling while blocking:
    (A) the path of the individual being solicited; or
    (B) the entrance to a building or motor vehicle.
  (6) Panhandling while using profane or abusive language:
    (A) during a solicitation; or
    (B) after the individual being solicited has declined to donate money or something else of value.
  (7) Panhandling while making a statement, a gesture, or another communication to the individual being solicited that would cause a reasonable individual to:
    (A) fear for the individual's safety; or
    (B) feel compelled to donate.
  (8) Panhandling with at least one (1) other individual.
  (9) Panhandling and then following or accompanying the solicited individual without the solicited individual's consent after the solicited individual has declined to donate money or something else of value.

History.
  P.L.140-2005, § 8.

Compiler's Notes.
  P.L.140-2005, § 10, effective July 1, 2005, provides:
  "IC 35-44-2-2, as amended by this act, and IC 35-45-17-2, as added by this act, apply only to crimes committed after June 30, 2005."

Cross References.
  Penalties for felonies, IC 35-50-1, IC 35-50-2, IC 35-50-5-2.
  Penalties for misdemeanors, IC 35-50-1, IC 35-50-3, IC 35-50-5-2.

NOTES TO DECISIONS

ANALYSIS

Evidence.
—Sufficient.

Evidence.

—Sufficient.
  Conviction for panhandling, as a Class C misde-

meanor under IC 35-45-17-2 was supported by sufficient evidence where the evidence showed that defendant solicited money from an officer and then stepped in front of the officer several times to repeatedly ask for money after the officer told defendant that he did not carry money. Alvies v. State, 895 N.E.2d 1237, 2008 Ind. App. LEXIS 2497 (2008).

CHAPTER 18

COMBATIVE FIGHTING

35-45-18-1. "Combative fighting" defined.

(a) As used in this chapter, "combative fighting" (also known as "toughman fighting", "badman fighting", and "extreme fighting") means a match, contest, or exhibition that involves at least (2) contestants, with or without gloves or protective headgear, in which the contestants:

(1) use their:

(A) hands;

(B) feet; or

(C) both hands and feet;

to strike each other; and

(2) compete for a financial prize or any item of pecuniary value.

(b) The term does not include:

(1) a boxing, sparring, or unarmed combat match regulated under IC 25-9;

(2) mixed martial arts (as defined by IC 25-9-1-0.3).

(3) martial arts, as regulated by the state athletic commission in rules adopted under IC 25-9-1-4.5;

(4) professional wrestling, as regulated by the state athletic commission in rules adopted under IC 25-9-1-4.5; or

(5) a match, contest, or game in which a fight breaks out among the participants as an unplanned, spontaneous event and not as an intended part of the match, contest, or game.

History.

P.L.112-2007, § 2, eff. July 1, 2007; P.L.160-2009, § 49, eff. July 1, 2009.

Amendments.

The 2009 amendment added ""or unarmed combat"" in (b)(1); deleted former (b)(2) and (b)(3), which read: ""(2) ultimate fighting, as defined by the state boxing commission in rules adopted under IC 25-9-1-4.5; (3) Ultimate Fighting Champi-onships, as defined by the state boxing commission in rules adopted under IC 25-9-1-4.5""; redesignated former (b)(4) through (b)(7) as (b)(2) through (b)(5); substituted ""(as defined by IC 25-9-1-0.3)"" for ""as defined by the state boxing commission in rules adopted under IC 25-9-1-4.5"" in (b)(2); substituted ""regulated by the state athletic"" for ""defined by the state boxing"" in (b)(3) and (b)(4); and made a related change.

35-45-18-2. Participation in combative fighting unlawful — Penalty.

A person who knowingly or intentionally participates in combative fighting commits unlawful combative fighting, a Class C misdemeanor.

History.

P.L.112-2007, § 2, eff. July 1, 2007.

Compiler's Notes.

P.L.112-2007, § 3, effective July 1, 2007, provides:

"IC 35-45-18-2 and IC 35-45-18-3, both as added by this act, apply only to crimes committed after June 30, 2007."

Cross References.

Penalties for misdemeanors, IC 35-50-1, IC 35-50-3, IC 35-50-5-2.

35-45-18-3. Promoting or organizing combative fighting unlawful — Penalty.

A person who knowingly or intentionally promotes or organizes combative fighting commits unlawful promotion or organization of combative fighting, a Class A misdemeanor. However, the offense is a Class D felony if, within the five (5) years preceding the commission of the offense, the person had a prior unrelated conviction under this section.

History.

P.L.112-2007, § 2, eff. July 1, 2007.

Compiler's Notes.

P.L.112, § 3, effective July 1, 2007, provides:

"IC 35-45-18-2 and IC 35-45-18-3, both as added by this act, apply only to crimes committed after June 30, 2007."

Cross References.
Penalties for felonies, IC 35-50-1, IC 35-50-2, IC 35-50-5-2.

CHAPTER 19

FAILURE TO REPORT A DEAD BODY

35-45-19-1. Applicability.

This chapter does not:
    (1) apply to the driver of a vehicle involved in an accident that:
        (A) results in the death of a person; and
        (B) must be reported under IC 9-26-1-1; or
    (2) supersede any law governing the reporting of a death by a hospital, health care facility, or provider.

History.
P.L.68-2008, § 1, eff. July 1, 2008.

35-45-19-2. "Public safety officer" defined.

As used in this chapter, "public safety officer" means:
    (1) a law enforcement officer;
    (2) a correctional officer;
    (3) a state university police officer;
    (4) a firefighter;
    (5) an emergency medical technician; or
    (6) a paramedic.

History.
P.L.68-2008, § 1, eff. July 1, 2008.

35-45-19-3. Knowingly or intentionally failing to report dead body — Misdemeanor.

A person who:
    (1) discovers or has custody of the body of a deceased person when it appears the deceased person died:
        (A) by violence, suicide, or accident;
        (B) suddenly, while in apparent good health;
        (C) while unattended;
        (D) from poisoning or an overdose of drugs;
        (E) as the result of a disease that may constitute a threat to public health;
        (F) as the result of:
            (i) a disease;
            (ii) an injury;
            (iii) a toxic effect; or
            (iv) unusual exertion;
    incurred within the scope of the deceased person's employment;
        (G) due to sudden infant death syndrome;
        (H) as the result of a diagnostic or therapeutic procedure; or
        (I) under any other suspicious or unusual circumstances; and

(2) knowingly or intentionally fails to report the body of the deceased person to a:

    (A) public safety officer;

    (B) coroner;

    (C) physician; or

    (D) 911 telephone call center;

within three (3) hours after finding the body;

commits failure to report a dead body, a Class A misdemeanor.

History.
  P.L.68-2008, § 1, eff. July 1, 2008.

"IC 35-45-19-3, as added by this act, applies only to offenses committed after June 30, 2008."

Compiler's Notes.
  P.L.68-2008, § 2, effective July 1, 2008, provides:

CHAPTER 20

DISPENSING CONTACT LENSES WITHOUT A PRESCRIPTION

35-45-20-1. "Prescription" defined.

As used in this chapter, "prescription" means a written or electronically transmitted contact lens prescription or order that:

  (1) is issued by an optometrist licensed under IC 25-24 or a physician licensed under IC 25-22.5; and

  (2) was issued within the previous year.

History.
  P.L.49-2009, § 1, eff. July 1, 2009.

35-45-20-2. Dispensing contact lens to individual who does not have prescription constitutes infraction.

A person who dispenses a contact lens, including a contact lens without corrective power, to an individual who does not have a prescription for the contact lens being dispensed commits a Class A infraction.

History.
  P.L.49-2009, § 1, eff. July 1, 2009.

Cross References.
  Infraction and ordinance violation enforcement proceedings, IC 34-28-5.

ARTICLE 46

MISCELLANEOUS OFFENSES

CHAPTER 1

OFFENSES AGAINST THE FAMILY

35-46-1-1. Definitions.

As used in this chapter:

"Dependent" means:

(1) an unemancipated person who is under eighteen (18) years of age; or

(2) a person of any age who has a mental or physical disability.

"Endangered adult" has the meaning set forth in IC 12-10-3-2.

"Support" means food, clothing, shelter, or medical care.

"Tobacco business" means a sole proprietorship, corporation, partnership, or other enterprise in which:

(1) the primary activity is the sale of tobacco, tobacco products, and tobacco accessories; and

(2) the sale of other products is incidental.

History.
IC 35-46-1-1, as added by Acts 1976, P.L.148, § 6; 1977, P.L.340, § 84; P.L.185-1984, § 2;

P.L.208-1986, § 1; P.L.41-1987, § 19; P.L.2-1992, § 881; P.L.256-1996, § 10; P.L.99-2007, § 210, emergency eff. May 2, 2007.

NOTES TO DECISIONS

Dependent.

IC 35-46-1-4 does not criminalize conduct that occurs prior to a child's birth because an unborn child is not a "dependent" pursuant to this section and IC 35-46-1-4. The plain language of IC 35-46-1-4 contemplates only acts that place one who is a dependent at the time of the conduct at issue in a dangerous situation, not acts that place a future dependent in a dangerous situation. Herron v. State, 729 N.E.2d 1008, 2000 Ind. App. LEXIS 859 (2000).

Use of victim's status as dependent as aggravating factor in sentencing defendant for crime of neglect of dependent under IC 35-46-1-4 was improper. Nybo v. State, 799 N.E.2d 1146, 2003 Ind. App. LEXIS 2286 (2003).

Where defendant pled guilty to neglect of a dependent under IC 35-46-1-4, a sentencing court erred by finding an aggravating factor based on defendant's alleged need for corrective or rehabilitative services because insufficient findings were made; a specific and individualized statement explaining why extended incarceration was appropriate was needed. However, the trial court properly considered the victim's age (under 15 months old) in relation to the nature of the case and the circumstances of the crime. Edwards v. State, 842 N.E.2d 849, 2006 Ind. App. LEXIS 257 (2006).

Cited:

Bean v. State, 460 N.E.2d 936, 1984 Ind. LEXIS 769 (1984); Lomax v. State, 510 N.E.2d 215, 1987 Ind. App. LEXIS 2857 (1987); Mallory v. State, 563 N.E.2d 640, 1990 Ind. App. LEXIS 1610 (1990); State v. Springer, 585 N.E.2d 27, 1992 Ind. App. LEXIS 54 (1992); Kile v. State, 729 N.E.2d 211, 2000 Ind. App. LEXIS 811 (2000); Edwards v. State, 730 N.E.2d 1286, 2000 Ind. App. LEXIS 1056 (2000); Sanders v. State, 734 N.E.2d 646, 2000 Ind. App. LEXIS 1338 (2000); Lush v. State, 783 N.E.2d 1191, 2003 Ind. App. LEXIS 265 (2003).

RESEARCH REFERENCES

Collateral References.

Criminal liability under statutes penalizing abuse or neglect or the institutionalized infirm. 60 A.L.R.4th 1153.

35-46-1-1.7. "Tobacco" defined.

As used in this chapter, "tobacco" includes:
(1) Chewing tobacco;
(2) Cigars, cigarettes, and snuff that contain tobacco; and
(3) Pipe tobacco.

History.
P.L.318-1987, § 2.

35-46-1-2. Bigamy.

(a) A person who, being married and knowing that his spouse is alive, marries again commits bigamy, a Class D felony.

(b) It is a defense that the accused person reasonably believed that he was eligible to remarry.

History.
IC 35-46-1-2, as added by Acts 1976, P.L.148, § 6; 1977, P.L.340, § 85.

Cross References.
Penalties for felonies, IC 35-50-1, IC 35-50-2, IC 35-50-5-2.

NOTES TO DECISIONS

ANALYSIS

Burden of Proof.
Cohabitation.
Indictment or Information.
Knowledge of Other Spouse's Marriage.
Presumption of Validity.
Prima Facie Case.
Proof of Marriage.
Reasonable Belief.
Religious Belief.

Burden of Proof.

Proof had to be made beyond a reasonable doubt that a former husband or wife was living at the time of the alleged bigamous marriage. Squire v. State, 46 Ind. 459, 1874 Ind. LEXIS 118 (1874).

The defendant had the burden of proving that a former marriage had been legally dissolved. Fletcher v. State, 169 Ind. 77, 81 N.E. 1083, 1907 Ind. LEXIS 32 (1907); Long v. State, 192 Ind. 524, 137 N.E. 49, 1922 Ind. LEXIS 93, 24 A.L.R. 1234 (1922).

Cohabitation.

The former IC 35-1-81-1 concerning bigamy did not make bigamous cohabitation a crime, but a crime was committed when a bigamous ceremonial marriage was consummated. Green v. State, 232 Ind. 596, 115 N.E.2d 211, 1953 Ind. LEXIS 250 (1953).

Indictment or Information.

An indictment for bigamy did not need to aver the time and place of the first marriage, the person solemnizing the same, nor the maiden name of the first wife. Hutchins v. State, 28 Ind. 34, 1867 Ind. LEXIS 181 (1867).

Knowledge of Other Spouse's Marriage.

Where defendant had no knowledge at the time of his marriage that his wife's husband was alive, had been told that the husband was dead, and believed the husband to be dead, the defendant was not guilty of aiding in the commission of bigamy. In re Evrard, 263 Ind. 435, 333 N.E.2d 765, 1975 Ind. LEXIS 324 (1975).

Presumption of Validity.

Marriages were presumed to be legal. Boulden v. McIntire, 119 Ind. 574, 21 N.E. 445, 1889 Ind. LEXIS 335 (1889).

The presumption in favor of the validity of a marriage consummated according to the forms of law is one of the strongest known. Bruns v. Cope, 182 Ind. 289, 105 N.E. 471, 1914 Ind. LEXIS 132 (1914), overruled, National City Bank v. Bledsoe, 237 Ind. 130, 144 N.E.2d 710, 1957 Ind. LEXIS 256 (1957).

Prima Facie Case.

If the first husband or wife was proved to have been living at the time the second marriage was contracted, that fact, with due proof of the two marriages, made a prima facie case against a defendant charged with bigamy. Fletcher v. State, 169 Ind. 77, 81 N.E. 1083, 1907 Ind. LEXIS 32 (1907); Lesueur v. State, 176 Ind. 448, 95 N.E. 239, 1911 Ind. LEXIS 147 (1911).

Proof of Marriage.

In prosecutions for bigamy, the former marriage could be proved by the admissions of the defendant. State v. Seals, 16 Ind. 352, 1861 Ind. LEXIS 178 (1861); Squire v. State, 46 Ind. 459, 1874 Ind. LEXIS 118 (1874).

The marriage license and certificate of marriage indorsed thereon were competent evidence of marriage. Squire v. State, 46 Ind. 459, 1874 Ind. LEXIS 118 (1874).

Reasonable Belief.

If the accused had good reason to believe, and did actually believe, that at the time of the second marriage, the former marriage had been set aside, he was not guilty of bigamy. Squire v. State, 46 Ind. 459, 1874 Ind. LEXIS 118 (1874).

Religious Belief.

The fact that defendant's religious belief was such that he did not feel bound to observe the law against bigamy did not constitute a defense to the crime, and should not mitigate the punishment of one found guilty of the offense. Long v. State, 192 Ind. 524, 137 N.E. 49, 1922 Ind. LEXIS 93, 24 A.L.R. 1234 (1922).

RESEARCH REFERENCES

Collateral References.

Mistaken belief in existence, validity, or effect of divorce or separation as defense to prosecution for bigamy or allied offense. 56 A.L.R.2d 915.

35-46-1-3. Incest.

(a) A person eighteen (18) years of age or older who engages in sexual intercourse or deviate sexual conduct with another person, when the person knows that the other person is related to the person biologically as a parent, child, grandparent, grandchild, sibling, aunt, uncle, niece, or nephew, commits incest, a Class C felony. However, the offense is a Class B felony if the other person is less than sixteen (16) years of age.

(b) It is a defense that the accused person's otherwise incestuous relation with the other person was based on their marriage, if it was valid where entered into.

History.

IC 35-46-1-3, as added by Acts 1976, P.L.148, § 6; 1977, P.L.340, § 86; P.L.158-1987, § 5; P.L.79-1994, § 16.

Cross References.

Penalties for felonies, IC 35-50-1, IC 35-50-2, IC 35-50-5-2.

Sex offense victim, child in need of services, IC 31-34-1-3.

NOTES TO DECISIONS

In General.

If a stepfather had intercourse with his stepdaughter, knowing her to be such, whether by force or otherwise, he was guilty of incest. Norton v. State, 106 Ind. 163, 6 N.E. 126, 1886 Ind. LEXIS 84 (1886).

Acquittal of One Party.

When the parties to the incestuous intercourse were both guilty under the law, the acquittal of one would be a discharge of the other. Baumer v. State, 49 Ind. 544, 1875 Ind. LEXIS 40 (1875).

Child.

Natural parents whose children have been adopted are not excluded from the prohibitions of the incest statute. Bohall v. State, 546 N.E.2d 1214, 1989 Ind. LEXIS 347 (1989).

Construction.

—Sexual Intercourse.

"Sexual intercourse" is defined as carnal copulation of male and female implying actual penetration of the organs of the latter. Salsman v. State, 244 Ind. 180, 191 N.E.2d 502, 1963 Ind. LEXIS 174 (1963).

The testimony of defendant's daughter that he engaged in sexual intercourse with her, when her definition of sexual intercourse was "when the male penis touches the vagina," was sufficient to prove penetration, because Indiana incest law does not require that the vagina be penetrated, only that the female sex organ be penetrated. Winters v. State, 727 N.E.2d 758, 2000 Ind. App. LEXIS 603 (2000).

Contact with Sex Organ or Anus.

In the absence of any evidence from which it could be inferred beyond a reasonable doubt that defendant engaged in conduct involving his mouth and the child's genitalia, his penis and the child's mouth or anus, or the child's mouth and his penis, the convictions for child molesting and incest involving the child could not stand. Shackelford v. State, 622 N.E.2d 1340, 1993 Ind. App. LEXIS 1412 (1993).

Double Jeopardy.

The prohibition against double jeopardy would not permit the defendant's incest conviction to stand where a single act of sexual intercourse underlay his convictions for both incest and child molesting/sexual intercourse. Acuna v. State, 581 N.E.2d 961, 1991 Ind. App. LEXIS 1986 (1991).

Based on the actual evidence adduced at trial, defendant's convictions for both child molesting and incest violated the state constitutional prohibition against double jeopardy. Schaefer v. State, 750 N.E.2d 787, 2001 Ind. App. LEXIS 871 (2001).

Evidence.

In an incest prosecution against a defendant involving sexual intercourse with his stepdaughter, it is not necessary to produce the marriage certificate to prove a valid marriage of the defendant to the victim's mother; the fact of marriage can be proven by the use of deeds reciting the grantors to be husband and wife. Pearman v. State, 499 N.E.2d 277, 1986 Ind. App. LEXIS 3118 (1986) (decided prior to the 1987 amendment, which deleted "stepparent" and "stepchild" from the list of prohibited relationships).

—Biological Relationship.

State sufficiently established defendant was victim's biological father, by showing victim's mother and defendant were divorced, victim had defendant's family name, defendant paid child support for victim, and victim referred to defendant throughout trial as her "father." Jackson v. State, 682 N.E.2d 564, 1997 Ind. App. LEXIS 887 (1997).

—Character of Victim.

On a charge against a father for incest with his daughter, her character for chastity was not in issue. Kidwell v. State, 63 Ind. 384, 1878 Ind. LEXIS 375 (1878).

—Confession.

Defendant's incest conviction under IC 35-46-1-3 was improper because defendant's confession was inadmissible as a violation of his right against self-incrimination where confession was made after detective impliedly promised defendant that defendant would not be prosecuted if sex with

Evidence. (Cont'd)

—Confession. (Cont'd)
defendant's adult niece was consensual. McGhee v. State, 899 N.E.2d 35, 2008 Ind. App. LEXIS 2612 (2008).

—Insufficient.
Where the only reasonable inference which could be drawn was that prosecuting witness experienced a feeling, such evidence was not of sufficient probative value to satisfy the burden of proving the corpus delicti with respect to the alleged unlawful act of sexual intercourse. Salsman v. State, 244 Ind. 180, 191 N.E.2d 502, 1963 Ind. LEXIS 174 (1963).

Father's one-time letter to 18-year-old daughter, containing money and solicitation of sexual favors "some night", did not constitute urging or the seeking of immediate action, and therefore was insufficient evidence to sustain a conviction for attempted incest. Mettler v. State, 697 N.E.2d 502, 1998 Ind. App. LEXIS 1258 (1998).

—Photograph.
It was not error to permit admission of photograph of victim taken three years before trial where the appearance of victim changed greatly between the time of the offense and trial. Mahoney v. State, 180 Ind. App. 358, 388 N.E.2d 591, 1979 Ind. App. LEXIS 1145 (1979).

—Prior Similar Acts.
After proof of incestuous intercourse, proof of prior acts of indecent familiarity between the parties was admissible. State v. Markins, 95 Ind. 464, 1884 Ind. LEXIS 223 (1884); Lefforge v. State, 129 Ind. 551, 29 N.E. 34, 1891 Ind. LEXIS 96 (1891), overruled, Burk v. State, 185 Ind. 47, 113 N.E. 294, 1916 Ind. LEXIS 12 (1916).

Evidence regarding other sex offenses similar to that charged was admissible. Ward v. State, 246 Ind. 374, 205 N.E.2d 148, 1965 Ind. LEXIS 363 (1965).

Evidence of prior similar acts was admissible in prosecutions for incest under the general rule as to admissibility of prior criminal acts in cases involving a "depraved sexual instinct." Woods v. State, 250 Ind. 132, 235 N.E.2d 479, 1968 Ind. LEXIS 624 (1968).

Admission of evidence of prior similar acts in a prosecution for incest is permitted. Mahoney v. State, 180 Ind. App. 358, 388 N.E.2d 591, 1979 Ind. App. LEXIS 1145 (1979).

Evidence of uncharged sex crimes which defendant perpetrated on the victims was relevant to establish his depraved sexual instinct in a trial for child molesting and incest. Baxter v. State, 522 N.E.2d 362, 1988 Ind. LEXIS 108 (1988).

—Sufficient.
Evidence held sufficient to sustain conviction. Newton v. State, 456 N.E.2d 736, 1983 Ind. App. LEXIS 3623 (1983).

Evidence was sufficient to support defendant's convictions for child molesting and incest. Baxter v. State, 522 N.E.2d 362, 1988 Ind. LEXIS 108 (1988).

Evidence was sufficient to sustain defendant's convictions for incest, criminal deviate conduct, and child molesting. Dinger v. State, 540 N.E.2d 39, 1989 Ind. LEXIS 187 (1989).

Evidence was sufficient to support defendant's conviction for incest. Bohall v. State, 546 N.E.2d 1214, 1989 Ind. LEXIS 347 (1989); Acuna v. State, 581 N.E.2d 961, 1991 Ind. App. LEXIS 1986 (1991).

—Victim as Witness.
Convictions for incest and child molesting may rest upon the uncorroborated testimony of the victim. Baxter v. State, 522 N.E.2d 362, 1988 Ind. LEXIS 108 (1988).

The uncorroborated testimony of the victim was sufficient to support the conviction of the defendant, notwithstanding the defendant's assertion that the testimony was insufficient where his ex-wife testified that she did not recall the victim staying with the family at the time of the first incident and that she was asleep in an adjacent room at the time of the second incident, as the victim's testimony was not inherently contradictory or coerced. Spurlock v. State, 718 N.E.2d 773, 1999 Ind. App. LEXIS 1879 (1999).

Because the trial judge found the victim, defendant's daughter, was a credible witness, and the victim testified that she had to watch a pornographic movie with defendant while naked and then have sex with him, there was sufficient evidence to convict defendant of incest. Sargent v. State, 875 N.E.2d 762, 2007 Ind. App. LEXIS 2400 (2007).

—Victim's Out-of-Court Statements.
Where the victims testified and were cross-examined at trial, their out-of-court statements, related by other witnesses, were admissible. Baxter v. State, 522 N.E.2d 362, 1988 Ind. LEXIS 108 (1988).

Indictment or Information.

—Knowledge of Relationship.
The indictment had to charge that the accused knew of the relationship between the parties. Williams v. State, 2 Ind. 439, 1850 Ind. LEXIS 187 (1850).

An indictment for incest between a stepmother and stepson had to allege that each knew of the relationship existing between them. Baumer v. State, 49 Ind. 544, 1875 Ind. LEXIS 40 (1875).

Intoxication.
Voluntary drunkenness would neither excuse nor palliate the crime of incest. Colee v. State, 75 Ind. 511, 1881 Ind. LEXIS 310 (1881).

Knowledge of Relationship.
It was not necessary to allege that the child knew the defendant to be her parent, but it was sufficient to allege that the parent had knowledge of the relationship. Woods v. State, 250 Ind. 132, 235 N.E.2d 479, 1968 Ind. LEXIS 624 (1968).

Marital Privilege.
Answer of wife of defendant regarding defendant's emotional state was not subject to exclusion

Marital Privilege. (Cont'd)
under the marital privilege. Mahoney v. State, 180 Ind. App. 358, 388 N.E.2d 591, 1979 Ind. App. LEXIS 1145 (1979).

Morality of Victim.
The morality of the victim in a prosecution for incest is not at issue. Mahoney v. State, 180 Ind. App. 358, 388 N.E.2d 591, 1979 Ind. App. LEXIS 1145 (1979).

Rape.
In a prosecution under an affidavit charging incest and rape in separate counts, there was no fatal inconsistency in the finding of guilty on the charge of incest and acquittal on the charge of rape, even though the evidence was sufficient to sustain a conviction of rape. Flowers v. State, 221 Ind. 448, 48 N.E.2d 56, 1943 Ind. LEXIS 208 (1943).

A person may be found guilty of rape under circumstances which also constituted the offense of incest. Haddock v. State, 246 Ind. 669, 207 N.E.2d 813, 1965 Ind. LEXIS 412 (1965).

Sentence.
Where defendant was convicted of making his 16-year-old daughter watch a pornographic movie with him while naked and then have sex with him, defendant had a prior battering conviction as to his six-year-old son, and defendant was on probation, defendant's aggregate six year sentence for incest was appropriate. Sargent v. State, 875 N.E.2d 762, 2007 Ind. App. LEXIS 2400 (2007).

Stepchild.
This section proscribes sexual intercourse with any stepchild, and this includes a situation when the stepparent and stepchild are related by affinity. State v. Buckles, 508 N.E.2d 54, 1987 Ind. App. LEXIS 2683 (1987) (decided under section as it existed prior to the 1987 amendment, which deleted "stepparent" and "stepchild" from the list of prohibited relationships).

Testimony.

—Regarding Pregnancy.
It was not error for trial court to permit testimony regarding pregnancy which clearly did not result from the act with which defendant was charged. Mahoney v. State, 180 Ind. App. 358, 388 N.E.2d 591, 1979 Ind. App. LEXIS 1145 (1979).

—Uncorroborated.
A conviction for incest may be based upon the uncorroborated testimony of the prosecuting witness. Mahoney v. State, 180 Ind. App. 358, 388 N.E.2d 591, 1979 Ind. App. LEXIS 1145 (1979).

Uncle-Niece.

—Consanguinity Required.
The incest statute requires a relationship by consanguinity between an uncle and a niece. State v. Anderson, 484 N.E.2d 640, 1985 Ind. App. LEXIS 2928 (1985).

Cited:
Kelly v. State, 452 N.E.2d 907, 1983 Ind. LEXIS 926 (1983); Doe v. O'Connor, 790 N.E.2d 985, 2003 Ind. LEXIS 574 (2003).

RESEARCH REFERENCES

Indiana Law Review.
Recent Developments in Indiana Criminal Law and Procedure, 28 Ind. L. Rev. 819 (1995).

Survey: Criminal Law and Procedure, 37 Ind. L. Rev. 1003 (2004).

Valparaiso University Law Review.
Indiana's Criminal Treatment of Abusive Parents: Problems in Need of Solutions, 24 Val. U.L. Rev. 553 (1990).

Collateral References.
Consent as element of incest. 36 A.L.R.2d 1299.

Sexual abuse of child by parent as ground for termination of parent's right to child. 58 A.L.R.3d 1074.

Admissibility, in incest prosecution, of evidence of alleged victim's prior sexual acts with persons other than accused. 97 A.L.R.3d 967.

Sexual intercourse between persons related by half blood as incest. 34 A.L.R.5th 723.

35-46-1-4. Neglect of a dependent — Child selling.

(a) A person having the care of a dependent, whether assumed voluntarily or because of a legal obligation, who knowingly or intentionally:

(1) places the dependent in a situation that endangers the dependent's life or health;

(2) abandons or cruelly confines the dependent;

(3) deprives the dependent of necessary support; or

(4) deprives the dependent of education as required by law;
commits neglect of a dependent, a Class D felony.

(b) However, the offense is:

(1) a Class C felony if it is committed under subsection (a)(1), (a)(2), or (a)(3) and:

(A) results in bodily injury; or

(B) is:

(i) committed in a location where a person is violating IC 35-48-4-1 (delivery, financing, or manufacture of cocaine, methamphetamine, or a narcotic drug); or

(ii) the result of a violation of IC 35-48-4-1 (delivery, financing, or manufacture of cocaine, methamphetamine, or a narcotic drug);

(2) a Class B felony if it is committed under subsection (a)(1), (a)(2), or (a)(3) and results in serious bodily injury;

(3) a Class A felony if it is committed under subsection (a)(1), (a)(2), or (a)(3) by a person at least eighteen (18) years of age and results in the death of a dependent who is less than fourteen (14) years of age; and

(4) a Class C felony if it is committed under subsection (a)(2) and consists of cruel confinement or abandonment that:

(A) deprives a dependent of necessary food, water, or sanitary facilities;

(B) consists of confinement in an area not intended for human habitation; or

(C) involves the unlawful use of handcuffs, a rope, a cord, tape, or a similar device to physically restrain a dependent.

(c) It is a defense to a prosecution based on an alleged act under this section that:

(1) the accused person left a dependent child who was, at the time the alleged act occurred, not more than thirty (30) days of age with an emergency medical provider who took custody of the child under IC 31-34-2.5 when:

(A) the prosecution is based solely on the alleged act of leaving the child with the emergency medical services provider; and

(B) the alleged act did not result in bodily injury or serious bodily injury to the child; or

(2) the accused person, in the legitimate practice of the accused person's religious belief, provided treatment by spiritual means through prayer, in lieu of medical care, to the accused person's dependent.

(d) Except for property transferred or received:

(1) under a court order made in connection with a proceeding under IC 31-15, IC 31-16, IC 31-17, or IC 31-35 (or IC 31-1-11.5 or IC 31-6-5 before their repeal); or

(2) under IC 35-46-1-9(b);

a person who transfers or receives any property in consideration for the termination of the care, custody, or control of a person's dependent child commits child selling, a Class D felony.

History.
IC 35-46-1-4, as added by Acts 1976, P.L.148, § 6; 1977, P.L.340, § 87; 1978, P.L.144, § 8; 1980, P.L.208, § 1; 1981, P.L.299, § 2; 1981, P.L.301, § 3; P.L.1-1997, § 151; P.L.197-1999, § 6; P.L.133-2000, § 10; P.L.46-2004, § 1; P.L.26-2006, § 2; P.L.15-2007, § 1, eff. July 1, 2007; P.L.109-2007, § 1, eff. July 1, 2007.

Compiler's Notes.
P.L.15-2007, § 2, effective July 1, 2007, and P.L.109-2007, § 2, effective July 1, 2007, provides: "IC 35-46-1-4, as amended by this act, applies only to crimes committed after June 30, 2007."

Cross References.
Child molestation and exploitation, IC 35-42-4-3, IC 35-42-4-4.
Civil action for support, IC 31-16-2.
Delinquent children and children in need of services, IC 31-37, IC 31-34.
Enforcement of support orders, Uniform Interstate Family Support Act, IC 31-18.
Parent-child relationship, termination, IC 31-35.
Penalties for felonies, IC 35-50-1, IC 35-50-2, IC 35-50-5-2.

NOTES TO DECISIONS

ANALYSIS

In General.
Constitutionality.
Abandonment.
Appeal.
Applicability.
Circuit Court as Juvenile Court.

Competency of Dependent.
Conditions of Probation.
Contempt Proceedings.
Cruel Confinement.
Divorce.
Double Jeopardy.
—Manslaughter.

—Murder and Felony Neglect.
—Separate Acts.
Education.
Elements.
—Care of a Dependent.
—Compulsory Attendance Law.
Evidence.
—Admissibility.
—Circumstantial.
—Danger.
—Defendant's Personality.
—Expert.
—Insufficient.
—Knowledge.
—Photographs.
—Physician-Patient Privilege.
—Prior Mistreatment.
—Sufficient.
Health or Life at Risk.
Included Offenses.
Indictment or Information.
—Amendment.
—Sufficiency.
Injury Resulting in Death.
Instructions.
—Civil Remedy.
Intent.
Jurisdiction.
Knowledge.
Necessary Support.
Parental Responsibility.
Prosecutorial Vindictiveness.
Protection of Child by Parent.
Psychological, Mental, or Emotional Injury.
Religious Belief.
—Burden of Proof.
Sentence.
—Aggravating Circumstances.
—Double Jeopardy.
—Separate Victims.
Severance of Offenses.
Support Furnished by Others.
Suspension of Judgment.
Testimony.
—Admissible.
Token Amounts of Support.
Unborn Child.

In General.

Parents may be convicted of cruelty to their children. Hinkle v. State, 127 Ind. 490, 26 N.E. 777, 1891 Ind. LEXIS 245 (1891); Hornbeck v. State, 16 Ind. App. 484, 45 N.E. 620, 1896 Ind. App. LEXIS 402 (1896).

The father of a child could not be convicted of neglecting it because of his refusal to furnish support while it lived with others when he had a home and desired that the child live with and be supported by him. Wheeler v. State, 51 Ind. App. 622, 100 N.E. 25, 1912 Ind. App. LEXIS 147 (1912).

There is no requirement that the person charged with the crime be the legal guardian or natural parent of the child or incompetent adult. Bean v. State, 460 N.E.2d 936, 1984 Ind. LEXIS 769 (1984).

This section encompasses not only those persons

having legal responsibility of a child, but also those persons who have voluntarily assumed responsibility. Shoup v. State, 570 N.E.2d 1298, 1991 Ind. App. LEXIS 716 (1991).

Even though other statutes are specifically directed to the protection of adults in residential health care facilities, such fact does not make this section inapplicable to the administrator of a health care provider. State v. Springer, 585 N.E.2d 27, 1992 Ind. App. LEXIS 54 (1992).

Defendant's knowing exposure of his infant son to a drug deal constituted child neglect under IC 35-46-1-4. Cleasant v. State, 779 N.E.2d 1260, 2002 Ind. App. LEXIS 2145 (2002).

Constitutionality.

A former statute on this subject [IC 35-14-1-4] was not void for vagueness. Worthington v. State, 409 N.E.2d 1261, 1980 Ind. App. LEXIS 1680 (1980).

This section is not unconstitutionally vague. Klagiss v. State, 585 N.E.2d 674, 1992 Ind. App. LEXIS 77 (1992), cert. denied, 506 U.S. 819, 113 S. Ct. 66, 121 L. Ed. 2d 33, 1992 U.S. LEXIS 5623 (1992); State v. Springer, 585 N.E.2d 27, 1992 Ind. App. LEXIS 54 (1992).

IC 35-46-1-4 violated the Proportionality Clause, Ind. Const. art. 1, § 16, because if a jury found a defendant guilty of cruel confinement of a dependent, it could characterize the crime as either a Class C felony or a Class D felony; thus, a defendant could receive a harsher sentence than another defendant for the same crime. Poling v. State, 853 N.E.2d 1270, 2006 Ind. App. LEXIS 1938 (2006).

Abandonment.

A father cannot be convicted for desertion of his children and leaving them without a reasonable means of support, in the absence of proof of desertion. Manners v. State, 210 Ind. 648, 5 N.E.2d 300, 1936 Ind. LEXIS 283 (1936).

The fact that defendant's children arrived at a truckstop tired, dirty, and hungry for some unexplained reason and remained there for approximately seven and a half hours before defendant appeared searching for them is not alone sufficient to sustain a conviction under this section. Reynolds v. State, 254 Ind. 478, 260 N.E.2d 793, 1970 Ind. LEXIS 571 (1970).

Appeal.

Only evidence favorable to the state would have been considered on appeal in determining whether the evidence was sufficient to support conviction for contributing to neglect of defendant's children. Woolbright v. State, 90 Ind. App. 704, 169 N.E. 883, 1930 Ind. App. LEXIS 25 (1930).

A prosecution for neglect of minor children and encouraging their delinquency, although referred to in the record on appeal and in the briefs as occurring in the Miami Circuit Court, must have been considered as having been in such court sitting as a juvenile court, and hence the court of appeals and not the Supreme Court had jurisdiction of the appeal from a judgment of conviction by

Appeal. (Cont'd)

a jury of the offense. Tyler v. State, 223 Ind. 519, 62 N.E.2d 626, 1945 Ind. LEXIS 136 (1945).

Applicability.

The phrase "person having the care of a dependent" does not have a technical meaning; the term "person" has its plain and ordinary meaning and "dependent" refers to an adult as well as a child. Thus, this section was applicable to the administrator of a health care facility providing service to adults. State v. Springer, 585 N.E.2d 27, 1992 Ind. App. LEXIS 54 (1992).

Circuit Court as Juvenile Court.

The former section contemplated that prosecution could have been in the circuit court exercising its juvenile jurisdiction in a county not having sufficient population to have a special juvenile court. Tyler v. State, 223 Ind. 519, 62 N.E.2d 626, 1945 Ind. LEXIS 136 (1945).

Competency of Dependent.

This section does not require that the competence of the dependent be legally adjudicated. State v. Springer, 585 N.E.2d 27, 1992 Ind. App. LEXIS 54 (1992).

Conditions of Probation.

Where mother was convicted of the neglect of a dependent, and although the trial court was attempting to prevent a similar tragedy from occurring in the future in light of the mother's criminal history, demonstrably poor parenting skills, and apparently unsuccessful involvement with social service agencies, the court's order that defendant mother not become pregnant while on probation excessively impinged upon her privacy right of procreation and served no discernible rehabilitative purpose. Trammell v. State, 751 N.E.2d 283, 2001 Ind. App. LEXIS 1047 (2001).

Contempt Proceedings.

Where a father was found guilty in 1943 of child neglect under the former section, and the court placed him on probation, he was entitled to discharge after two years and could not be punished for contempt in 1948, and any remedy against him would have been by a new proceeding for child neglect. Schultz v. State, 227 Ind. 33, 83 N.E.2d 784, 1949 Ind. LEXIS 108 (1949).

Cruel Confinement.

The element of "confines" requires (1) substantial interference with liberty (2) which rises to the level of being cruel. Hartbarger v. State, 555 N.E.2d 485, 1990 Ind. App. LEXIS 638 (1990).

Confining a child to his bedroom at night, and not permitting him to associate with his siblings when his parents were not present, for a period of two weeks, did not constitute cruel confinement as a matter of law. Hartbarger v. State, 555 N.E.2d 485, 1990 Ind. App. LEXIS 638 (1990).

The cruel nature of a confinement is to be determined by an objective standard. Demontigney v. State, 593 N.E.2d 1270, 1992 Ind. App. LEXIS 1011 (1992).

"Cruelly confines" as used in this section means confinement which is likely to result in a harm such as disfigurement, mental distress, extreme pain or hurt, or gross degradation, but does not necessarily endanger the dependent's life or health. People of ordinary intelligence can determine, within a given situation, whether a confinement of a dependent is cruel or not. Demontigney v. State, 593 N.E.2d 1270, 1992 Ind. App. LEXIS 1011 (1992).

Divorce.

A father cannot be convicted for failure to make stated payments for the use of the mother in support of their children where the court granted a divorce and gave the mother custody of the children, since the father could not desert children whose care and custody were awarded to the mother. Manners v. State, 210 Ind. 648, 5 N.E.2d 300, 1936 Ind. LEXIS 283 (1936).

Double Jeopardy.

Prior proceeding under former IC 31-5-7-1 et seq. to remove child from custody of parents did not render prosecution for cruelty and neglect of child double jeopardy. Hunter v. State, 172 Ind. App. 397, 360 N.E.2d 588, 1977 Ind. App. LEXIS 769 (1977), cert. denied, Hunter v. Indiana, 434 U.S. 906, 98 S. Ct. 306, 54 L. Ed. 2d 193, 1977 U.S. LEXIS 3679 (1977).

There was no double jeopardy bar to convictions for both neglect of a dependent and involuntary manslaughter where there was substantial evidence to support a conviction under each individually. Bean v. State, 460 N.E.2d 936, 1984 Ind. LEXIS 769 (1984).

Defendant parents were placed in double jeopardy where the neglect and reckless homicide charges upon which they were convicted were both based upon the parents' failure to provide medical treatment to their child during his illness and the pattern of neglect was the means by which the reckless homicide was committed. Hall v. State, 493 N.E.2d 433, 1986 Ind. LEXIS 1159 (1986).

Defendant was not subjected to double jeopardy on charges for battery and neglect of dependent child where the acts constituting neglect were separate from the battery, even if the acts of neglect may have overlapped with some of the acts contained in the battery charge. Hughes v. State, 508 N.E.2d 1289, 1987 Ind. App. LEXIS 2742 (1987).

Convictions and sentences for neglect and battery did not constitute double jeopardy where defendant pleaded guilty to informations which on their face described different criminal actions, the neglect information referring to cigarette burnings which were separate, independent and distinct from beatings described in the battery indictment. Christie v. State, 536 N.E.2d 531, 1989 Ind. App. LEXIS 252 (1989).

Where the state relied on the same conduct or a single act by defendant, namely his operation of a motor vehicle while intoxicated, to support the charges for both Operating a Vehicle While Intoxicated (IC 9-30-5-2) and Neglect of a Dependent (IC 35-46-1-4), when the state proved that defendant

Double Jeopardy. (Cont'd)
committed neglect of a dependent, it necessarily proved his guilt for operating a vehicle while intoxicated; thus, defendant's Neglect of a Dependent and Operating While Intoxicated convictions and sentences violated the prohibition against double jeopardy. Kellogg v. State, 636 N.E.2d 1262, 1994 Ind. App. LEXIS 813 (1994).

Two convictions, one for neglect of dependent in violation of IC 35-46-1-4(a)(1) and the other for battery in violation of IC 35-42-2-1(a)(1), did not violate common law rule prohibiting dual convictions for same act where there was no reasonable possibility that jury used same evidence to support both neglect and battery charges; specifically, while same evidence may have established infant was dependant and under 14, additional evidentiary facts were clearly required to prove defendant had care, custody and control of infant and that defendant was at least 18 years of age. Vandergriff v. State, 812 N.E.2d 1084, 2004 Ind. App. LEXIS 1580 (2004).

Defendant's conviction of two counts of neglect as to each of three victims under IC 35-46-1-4 did not violate double jeopardy under Ind. Const. art. 1, § 14 under the "essential elements" test. There was evidence that defendant hog-tied three victims with duct tape on at least one occasion, thus confining them pursuant to the first three counts, and that he locked each of them in a closet for an extended time on another, thus knowingly endangering their life or health pursuant to the last three counts. Poling v. State, 853 N.E.2d 1270, 2006 Ind. App. LEXIS 1938 (2006).

—Manslaughter.
Although the state presented sufficient evidence to prove that the mother committed both involuntary manslaughter and neglect of a dependent resulting in death, the double jeopardy clause of the Indiana Constitution prohibits a conviction for both crimes because she cannot be convicted twice for one death. Sanders v. State, 734 N.E.2d 646, 2000 Ind. App. LEXIS 1338 (2000).

—Murder and Felony Neglect.
Conviction on both murder and felony neglect constituted double jeopardy where the state used the same evidence of the child's freshly-inflicted injuries to establish both the serious bodily injury required for Class B felony neglect and the knowing killing required for murder. Roby v. State, 742 N.E.2d 505, 2001 Ind. LEXIS 188 (2001).

Convictions of murder and of neglect of dependent, as a class A felony, violated double jeopardy because both charged offenses were still based on the same bodily injury to the child victim; only when deemed a class D offense, which did not include a bodily injury element, did the neglect conviction avoid a double jeopardy violation. For defendant's revised conviction of class D felony neglect, the appropriate sentence was three years, to be served consecutively with the sentence for murder. Strong v. State, 870 N.E.2d 442, 2007 Ind. LEXIS 575 (2007).

—Separate Acts.
Where neither of the acts underlying defendant's convictions, i.e., placing infant's face in scalding water and subsequently failing to seek medical treatment, was the means by which the other act was accomplished, the two acts were separate and distinct, not continuous, and each comprised a violation of subsection (a)(1) of this section; because defendant's convictions were based upon two separate acts, conviction of two counts of neglect of a dependent did not violate the Fifth Amendment double jeopardy prohibition. Taylor v. State, 644 N.E.2d 612, 1994 Ind. App. LEXIS 1778 (1994).

Education.
Education required by law for a child was the education selected by the custodial parent; there was ample evidence to convict defendant of educational neglect where the child did not attend the public school he had been enrolled in by his custodial parent while at non-custodial parent's home. Hampton v. State, 754 N.E.2d 1037, 2001 Ind. App. LEXIS 1601 (2001).

Elements.
It is not significant that there was little evidence that defendant's dependent son was restrained or confined, since under this section confinement is not a necessary element, and the offense does not require that the state show that the victim was subject to the health-threatening conditions for a certain length of time. Lomax v. State, 510 N.E.2d 215, 1987 Ind. App. LEXIS 2857 (1987).

While the statutory phrase "places the dependent in a situation" perhaps implies more than an instantaneous isolated occurrence, the statute does not require proof that the dependent was subjected to the situation for a certain length of time. Wilson v. State, 525 N.E.2d 619, 1988 Ind. App. LEXIS 583 (1988).

In order to convict a person under this section, the state must prove that he subjected the dependent to danger which is actual and appreciable. Wilson v. State, 525 N.E.2d 619, 1988 Ind. App. LEXIS 583 (1988).

In order to convict a person under this section, the state must prove that the actor subjected the dependent to a danger which was actual and appreciable. This does not mean that the injury must be actual. Johnson v. State, 555 N.E.2d 1362, 1990 Ind. App. LEXIS 806 (1990).

—Care of a Dependent.
Assuming care of a dependent voluntarily, even if that dependent is not the defendant's child, is sufficient to prove care of a dependent. Kellogg v. State, 636 N.E.2d 1262, 1994 Ind. App. LEXIS 813 (1994).

—Compulsory Attendance Law.
The state is required to prove more than a person's violation of the compulsory attendance law in order to convict that person of felony neglect; the state must also prove that, as a result of the child's failure to attend school, the child failed to acquire the knowledge and training taught at the school. Hamilton v. State, 694 N.E.2d 1171, 1998 Ind. App. LEXIS 737 (1998).

Evidence.

—Admissibility.

Where defendant was charged with neglect of her 40-year-old son, the testimony of a doctor regarding his observation of the son about nine months after the events leading to the neglect charge, which testimony tended to buttress his opinion regarding the child's mental disability at the time of the events, was relevant, the disability and resulting dependency being material issues of fact. Lomax v. State, 510 N.E.2d 215, 1987 Ind. App. LEXIS 2857 (1987).

Battered Women's Syndrome evidence is relevant and admissible in a neglect of a dependent case to negate a defendant's intent to commit the crime charged. Barrett v. State, 675 N.E.2d 1112, 1996 Ind. App. LEXIS 1734 (1996), superseded by statute as stated in, Marley v. State, 747 N.E.2d 1123, 2001 Ind. LEXIS 473 (2001).

—Circumstantial.

The unexplained severe condition of the child and the defendant's conflicting explanations of the child's injuries was not sufficient circumstantial evidence to support a conviction of cruelty and neglect of the child. Howard v. State, 162 Ind. App. 487, 319 N.E.2d 849, 1974 Ind. App. LEXIS 864 (1974).

Where defendant stepparent was the sole person in charge of the toddler victim when life-threatening injuries occurred, and delayed taking the child to seek medical care, it was reasonable to infer that defendant had committed the offense of neglect of a defendant. Lush v. State, 783 N.E.2d 1191, 2003 Ind. App. LEXIS 265 (2003).

—Danger.

Actual or appreciable danger was shown since both of the child's physicians testified that an injury to the skull of this injury's seriousness posed a strong possibility of injury to the baby's brain underneath the fracture. Sample v. State, 601 N.E.2d 457, 1992 Ind. App. LEXIS 1595 (1992).

Although the so-called "hostage" game, which consisted of taping the children's wrists and ankles, was somewhat bizarre and not something many child development experts would condone, there was insufficient evidence that playing the game exposed the children to a substantial, actual, and appreciable risk of mental or physical harm; furthermore, there was insufficient evidence that defendants were subjectively aware of a high probability that the children were endangered by the taping. Gross v. State, 817 N.E.2d 306, 2004 Ind. App. LEXIS 2233 (2004).

—Defendant's Personality.

Where mother left her child in custody of person whom she knew was mistreating her child, it was not error to exclude evidence as to the passive or dependent personality of the mother since the qualities of meekness, timidity or dependence could not negate the mother's awareness of the dangerousness of the situation. Smith v. State, 408 N.E.2d 614, 1980 Ind. App. LEXIS 1610 (1980).

There was sufficient evidence to find that defendant knew of nursing home patient's propensities to engage in deviate sexual behavior when she took two girls, ages 11 and 12, to visit him and allegedly showed them how to perform oral sex on him, and a sentence of three years was not unreasonable considering that there was also a baby in the room at the time of the incident. Harrison v. State, 644 N.E.2d 888, 1994 Ind. App. LEXIS 1779 (1994).

—Expert.

The trial court did not abuse its discretion in refusing to permit the defendant's expert witnesses to answer hypothetical questions concerning the dependent's fatal injury since they were based on facts not in evidence. Klagiss v. State, 585 N.E.2d 674, 1992 Ind. App. LEXIS 77 (1992), cert. denied, 506 U.S. 819, 113 S. Ct. 66, 121 L. Ed. 2d 33, 1992 U.S. LEXIS 5623 (1992).

—Insufficient.

Defendant's conviction for neglect of a dependent was reversed where the state failed to carry its burden of proving the child's health was placed in actual, appreciable danger by defendant's failure to obtain medical treatment for her. Dayton v. State, 501 N.E.2d 482, 1986 Ind. App. LEXIS 3272 (1986).

State failed to show that due to children's absences from school their educations were harmed to such an extent that they were deprived of the acquisition of knowledge required of children their age; therefore, mother's conviction for neglect of a dependent was reversed. Hamilton v. State, 694 N.E.2d 1171, 1998 Ind. App. LEXIS 737 (1998).

Defendant's Class A misdemeanor conviction for neglect of a dependent under IC 35-46-1-4 was reversed because the state failed to provide evidence that when defendant left her seven-year-old son home alone for approximately three hours, she had a subjective awareness of a high probability that he was placed in a dangerous situation, and thus did not prove the mens rea element of the crime. Scruggs v. State, 883 N.E.2d 189, 2008 Ind. App. LEXIS 615 (2008).

—Knowledge.

The defendant knowingly endangered the health or life of his dependent son by not seeking medical treatment for his son for at least two weeks, despite his admitted knowledge that his son exhibited symptoms of infantile starvation, including vomiting and tantrums. Such evidence met the required level of culpability; i.e., the actor was subjectively aware of a high probability that he placed the dependent in a dangerous situation. Armour v. State, 479 N.E.2d 1294, 1985 Ind. LEXIS 881 (1985).

Testimony regarding the defendant's knowledge of her mother's propensity for violence to young children was sufficient to prove that the defendant knowingly placed her child in a dangerous situation when she left the child in the care of her mother, who beat the child. Caldwell v. State, 497 N.E.2d 610, 1986 Ind. App. LEXIS 2955 (1986).

Defendant's subjective knowledge could be inferred, where he and his wife had been advised to seek medical treatment for the benefit of both his wife and of her baby prior to its birth, and they

Evidence. (Cont'd)

—Knowledge. (Cont'd)
were informed that a strep infection was discovered in the amniotic fluid, prompting the doctor to again recommend immediate hospitalization. Fout v. State, 575 N.E.2d 340, 1991 Ind. App. LEXIS 1225 (1991).

—Photographs.
Where state contended that child was cruelly mistreated and neglected by defendants after having been returned to their custody from foster parent, photograph was properly admitted in evidence depicting condition of such child prior to return to defendants, in order to assist jury in visualizing that which foster parent was describing orally on rebuttal. Loftis v. State, 256 Ind. 417, 269 N.E.2d 746, 1971 Ind. LEXIS 648 (1971).

Where child was beaten and not taken to the hospital until the next morning, it was proper to admit photographs of the child showing the location of the bruises taken shortly before death. Perkins v. State, 181 Ind. App. 461, 392 N.E.2d 490, 1979 Ind. App. LEXIS 1245 (1979).

It was not error to show photographs of deceased child showing bruises. Worthington v. State, 409 N.E.2d 1261, 1980 Ind. App. LEXIS 1680 (1980).

—Physician-Patient Privilege.
There is no physician-patient privilege with respect to cases involving cruelty to a child. Hunter v. State, 172 Ind. App. 397, 360 N.E.2d 588, 1977 Ind. App. LEXIS 769 (1977), cert. denied, Hunter v. Indiana, 434 U.S. 906, 98 S. Ct. 306, 54 L. Ed. 2d 193, 1977 U.S. LEXIS 3679 (1977).

—Prior Mistreatment.
Where defendant was charged with neglect of child whose death was caused by mistreatment of the child by his wife, evidence of prior instances of mistreatment of the child was admissible to show that defendant could have become aware of such abuse. Worthington v. State, 409 N.E.2d 1261, 1980 Ind. App. LEXIS 1680 (1980).

—Sufficient.
Where defendant had left his children in an automobile parked on a city street for several hours while the temperature was below freezing while he was in a tavern drinking beer, evidence was sufficient to sustain conviction. Helwig v. State, 238 Ind. 559, 153 N.E.2d 437, 1958 Ind. LEXIS 263 (1958).

Where defendant knew of the situation in which she placed her child and allowed him to remain resulting in his death it was sufficient to establish the corpus delicti of the crime of neglect of a dependent. Smith v. State, 408 N.E.2d 614, 1980 Ind. App. LEXIS 1610 (1980).

Evidence that defendant knew that her boyfriend had raped her seven-year-old daughter and that her daughter had contracted venereal disease from him, and that she continued to permit him to spend nights in the apartment she shared with her daughter, thereby exposing the child to prolonged emotional distress and to the danger of a renewed attack, supported conviction for knowingly neglecting a dependent under paragraph (a)(1) of this section. Ware v. State, 441 N.E.2d 20, 1982 Ind. App. LEXIS 1447 (1982).

Evidence was sufficient to support conviction. Bean v. State, 460 N.E.2d 936, 1984 Ind. LEXIS 769 (1984); Smith v. State, 718 N.E.2d 794, 1999 Ind. App. LEXIS 1918 (1999); Germaine v. State, 718 N.E.2d 1125, 1999 Ind. App. LEXIS 1876 (1999).

There was sufficient evidence presented to the trial court to justify the finding of guilty of neglect beyond a reasonable doubt where the evidence showing neglect was the placing of children in a tub and leaving them there while knowing that very hot water was supplied to the tub and that the children were able to, and many times did, turn the water faucets themselves. Howard v. State, 481 N.E.2d 1315, 1985 Ind. LEXIS 941 (1985); Johnson v. State, 555 N.E.2d 1362, 1990 Ind. App. LEXIS 806 (1990).

In a prosecution for abandonment of a child, evidence which consisted of a doctor's testimony that the defendant's condition was consistent with the recent delivery of a close-to-full-term baby one to three weeks earlier, witnesses who testified that the defendant appeared to be pregnant, and a human leucocyte antigen blood test that indicated a 99.98867% probability that defendant was the mother, was sufficient to support the finding that the defendant was the child's mother. Davis v. State, 476 N.E.2d 127, 1985 Ind. App. LEXIS 2266 (1985).

Evidence was sufficient to support defendant's conviction of neglect of a dependent, where her baby was found in a very filthy condition that caused severe diaper rash and sores about its body and there was evidence of bruises on the baby's body, apparently sustained at different times, and witnesses testified to the fact that defendant not only neglected the child's personal care but that she failed to seek medical attention when the need was apparent. McClaskey v. State, 540 N.E.2d 41, 1989 Ind. LEXIS 191 (1989).

The culpability requirement of knowing or intentional conduct is provided by evidence that defendant continually neglected to provide adequate nutrition and reasonably clean living conditions despite having had extensive prior counseling, instruction and hands-on guidance with respect to the care and feeding of babies and as to general homemaking skills. Rinker v. State, 565 N.E.2d 344, 1991 Ind. App. LEXIS 17 (1991).

The evidence, and the inferences which it reasonably supported, was sufficient to sustain the conviction for neglect of a dependent. Klagiss v. State, 585 N.E.2d 674, 1992 Ind. App. LEXIS 77 (1992), cert. denied, 506 U.S. 819, 113 S. Ct. 66, 121 L. Ed. 2d 33, 1992 U.S. LEXIS 5623 (1992).

Since, in addition to the circumstantial evidence of knowledge offered from the child's physicians that the child would have been exhibiting symptoms of a serious injury and from the defendant's sister that the child was behaving as if she was in pain at the time she took the child into her care, the defendant admitted that she had observed changes in the bump after the fall and that she knew that the injury needed medical attention; thus, there was sufficient evidence to permit the

Evidence. (Cont'd)

—Sufficient. (Cont'd)
jury to infer that the defendant was aware of a high probability that by failing to obtain prompt medical treatment for her daughter after she had fallen on the floor, she was placing her child in a situation which endangered her life and health. Sample v. State, 601 N.E.2d 457, 1992 Ind. App. LEXIS 1595 (1992).

The state presented ample evidence from which the jury could infer the existence beyond a reasonable doubt of each requisite element of the crime of neglect of a dependent, where the jury could reasonably conclude that defendant abused child in a manner which caused the child to die of a severed bowel. Lloyd v. State, 669 N.E.2d 980, 1996 Ind. LEXIS 115 (1996).

Where mother herself inflicted the injuries to her toddler's abdomen that required medical treatment, and the mother failed to seek necessary medical attention for the toddler until it was too late, there was ample evidence to support the mother's conviction of neglect of a dependent resulting in death. Sanders v. State, 734 N.E.2d 646, 2000 Ind. App. LEXIS 1338 (2000).

Evidence which showed that stepmother watched her husband hit his daughter on the back of the head with a large wooden paddle and then failed to seek medical treatment for the daughter even though the daughter's health deteriorated markedly over the course of one week was sufficient to sustain the stepmother's conviction for neglect of a dependent causing serious bodily injury. Brown v. State, 770 N.E.2d 275, 2002 Ind. LEXIS 505 (2002).

Sufficient evidence existed to support defendant's conviction for neglect of his dependent children, who incurred multiple and numerous bone fractures, where defendant was children's primary caregiver and admitted that no one else inflicted injury upon them, where defendant's contention that children suffered from bone deficiency disease was proven false, and where defendant did not provide medical aid to them; lack of medical insurance as claimed by defendant was not defense to crime of neglect of dependent and, in fact, defendant could have obtained medical insurance for children through wife's employer. Wright v. State, 818 N.E.2d 540, 2004 Ind. App. LEXIS 2414 (2004), transfer granted, — N.E.2d —, 2005 Ind. LEXIS 567 (2005), superseded, 829 N.E.2d 928, 2005 Ind. LEXIS 556 (2005).

Evidence as to the condition of defendant's children and the testimony of medical experts that the injuries to the children were the product of intentional acts rather than falls or accidents was sufficient to support the convictions. Wright v. State, 829 N.E.2d 928, 2005 Ind. LEXIS 556 (2005).

Lack of physical injury did not preclude felony neglect of dependent conviction where defendant's extreme conduct, which included requiring child to kneel on broom handle with his arms extended holding weighted objects for up to two hours, amounted to infliction of unreasonable and prolonged pain capable of causing "actual and appreciable" psychological harm. Williams v. State, 829 N.E.2d 198, 2005 Ind. App. LEXIS 1098 (2005).

Because there was sufficient evidence to support the jury's finding that the baby was alive when born, as an expert testified that the baby likely lived for six hours after being born, the evidence that defendant mother did not seek any medical attention for the baby, but rather wrapped it in a towel and stuffed it in a box and denied its existence, was sufficient evidence to support her conviction for neglect of a dependent. Robinson v. State, 894 N.E.2d 1038, 2008 Ind. App. LEXIS 2232 (2008).

Health or Life at Risk.
Subsection (a)(1) will be construed as though the word "may" were excluded, so that this section is to be regarded as applying to situations that endanger the life or health of a dependent. The placement itself must expose the dependent to a danger which is actual and appreciable. State v. Downey, 476 N.E.2d 121, 1985 Ind. LEXIS 795 (1985); White v. State, 547 N.E.2d 831, 1989 Ind. LEXIS 368 (Ind. 1989); McCullough v. State, 608 N.E.2d 1009, 1993 Ind. App. LEXIS 113 (1993).

Subsection (a)(1), which includes the phrase "may endanger" was not unconstitutionally vague in the defendant's case, where the evidence showed that they left a newborn baby by the side of a deserted road, in a wooded area, outside the view of passersby, despite the assertion that the phrase "may endanger" was so vague that even reasonable conduct could be construed to be dangerous. Davis v. State, 476 N.E.2d 127, 1985 Ind. App. LEXIS 2266 (1985).

Evidence of malnutrition, in and of itself, does not support the conclusion that the person's health or life is at risk or in danger; consequently, without evidence which did not exist in this record, the fact finder had no basis to reasonably infer that the malnutrition suffered by the two children was such that their health was at risk or lives were endangered. Ricketts v. State, 598 N.E.2d 597, 1992 Ind. App. LEXIS 1344 (1992).

Included Offenses.
Assault and battery was not a lesser included offense in cruelty and neglect of children. Hunter v. State, 172 Ind. App. 397, 360 N.E.2d 588, 1977 Ind. App. LEXIS 769 (1977), cert. denied, Hunter v. Indiana, 434 U.S. 906, 98 S. Ct. 306, 54 L. Ed. 2d 193, 1977 U.S. LEXIS 3679 (1977).

Indictment or Information.
An affidavit (predecessor of information) attempting to charge wife desertion without alleging that the wife was not guilty of immoral conduct, and child desertion without alleging that the children were living within the state, or that the accused was able to support the children was bad. Crumley v. State, 204 Ind. 396, 184 N.E. 533, 1933 Ind. LEXIS 22 (1933).

A charge of cruelty and neglect of children could not be joined with a charge of contributing to the delinquency of a minor in the same count of an indictment. Ault v. State, 249 Ind. 545, 233 N.E.2d 480, 1968 Ind. LEXIS 741 (1968).

Indictment or Information. (Cont'd)

The information need not specifically recite the precise words of the statute so long as it adequately conveys to the defendant the conduct which allegedly violated the statute. Carson v. State, 271 Ind. 203, 391 N.E.2d 600, 1979 Ind. LEXIS 660 (1979).

The charge of endangerment "and/or" abandonment in the indictment effectively charged the defendants with both acts. The inclusion of "and/or" did not hamper their ability to understand the nature of the charge or to prepare a defense. Davis v. State, 476 N.E.2d 127, 1985 Ind. App. LEXIS 2266 (1985).

An indictment which closely tracked the language of this section was sufficient to inform the administrator of a health care provider of the charges against him. State v. Springer, 585 N.E.2d 27, 1992 Ind. App. LEXIS 54 (1992).

—Amendment.

Amendment of information by substituting the words "be cruel to" for "abuse" was one of form and not of substance. Carson v. State, 271 Ind. 203, 391 N.E.2d 600, 1979 Ind. LEXIS 660 (1979).

—Sufficiency.

Indictments charging the defendant physician with neglect of elderly patients, and specifying the date and place of the alleged offenses and identifying the defendant and the victims by name in language paralleling the statute, were sufficient to inform the defendant of the charges against him. Kerlin v. State, 573 N.E.2d 445, 1991 Ind. App. LEXIS 943 (1991).

Injury Resulting in Death.

Neglect of a dependent resulting in serious bodily injury, a Class B felony, can be charged when the injury results in death. Hill v. State, 535 N.E.2d 153, 1989 Ind. App. LEXIS 168 (1989).

Evidence sufficiently supported the element of serious bodily injury in a prosecution for neglect of a dependent as a Class B felony, based upon the death of the accused's six-year-old daughter, because the defendant's act of deprivation of medical support resulted in a substantial risk of death, so substantial that death, in fact, occurred. Mallory v. State, 563 N.E.2d 640, 1990 Ind. App. LEXIS 1610 (1990).

Petitioner failed to satisfy petitioner's burden of proof in a post-conviction petition pursuant to Ind. Post-Conviction Rule 1(5), as defense counsel was not ineffective for failing to sufficiently examine the State's theory as to how the child died, where petitioner was convicted of neglect of a dependent resulting in serious bodily injury in violation of IC 35-46-1-4; to prove the crime, the State did not have to show how the child died, but merely that petitioner knowingly placed the child in danger. Reynolds v. State, 783 N.E.2d 357, 2003 Ind. App. LEXIS 210 (2003).

Instructions.

An instruction that "Person having the care, custody or control of any child need not have specific intent to commit the crime of neglect of a child, but merely allowing an act inconsistent with the child's well-being to be committed will support a conviction for neglect of a child" was proper. Worthington v. State, 409 N.E.2d 1261, 1980 Ind. App. LEXIS 1680 (1980).

—Civil Remedy.

It was proper for court to refuse to instruct jury that a civil remedy may be available. Hunter v. State, 172 Ind. App. 397, 360 N.E.2d 588, 1977 Ind. App. LEXIS 769 (1977), cert. denied, Hunter v. Indiana, 434 U.S. 906, 98 S. Ct. 306, 54 L. Ed. 2d 193, 1977 U.S. LEXIS 3679 (1977).

Intent.

It was no defense to a charge of involuntary manslaughter through child neglect that a parent was unaware of the sickly condition of the child when the parent might readily have discovered the condition had he accorded the child reasonable care and attention. Eaglen v. State, 249 Ind. 144, 231 N.E.2d 147, 1967 Ind. LEXIS 362 (1967).

A parent need not have specific intent to commit cruelty and neglect to children. Hunter v. State, 172 Ind. App. 397, 360 N.E.2d 588, 1977 Ind. App. LEXIS 769 (1977), cert. denied, Hunter v. Indiana, 434 U.S. 906, 98 S. Ct. 306, 54 L. Ed. 2d 193, 1977 U.S. LEXIS 3679 (1977).

Where evidence was presented that the defendant confessed to leaving her four-year-old son in her apartment for several days after beating him, returning to find him dead, the jury could reasonably infer that she knowingly abandoned the victim. Jones v. State, 701 N.E.2d 863, 1998 Ind. App. LEXIS 1964 (1998).

Jurisdiction.

The offense under this section being a Class D felony a charge under this section could not be tried by a court having jurisdiction of misdemeanors only. Childers v. State, 411 N.E.2d 157, 1980 Ind. App. LEXIS 1717 (1980).

Knowledge.

Because knowledge, like intent, is a mental state of the actor, the trier of fact must resort to reasonable inferences based on an examination of the surrounding circumstances to reasonably infer the existence of knowledge. Perkins v. State, 181 Ind. App. 461, 392 N.E.2d 490, 1979 Ind. App. LEXIS 1245 (1979).

The insertion in the statute of the words "knowingly" or "intentionally" only requires that the state prove that the defendant's parent was aware of the facts that would alert a reasonable parent under the circumstances to take affirmative action to protect the child and it is within the legitimate province of the trier of fact to infer from the totality of the circumstances whether or not the requisite awareness was present or whether or not the action of the parent was reasonable. Smith v. State, 408 N.E.2d 614, 1980 Ind. App. LEXIS 1610 (1980).

In order to be convicted of knowingly neglecting a dependent under paragraph (a)(1) of this section, accused must have been subjectively aware of high probability that he placed dependent in a danger-

Knowledge. (Cont'd)
ous situation. Ware v. State, 441 N.E.2d 20, 1982 Ind. App. LEXIS 1447 (1982).

To convict a caretaker under the theory of neglect of a dependent the state must show the caretaker was subjectively aware of a high probability that he or she placed the defendant in a dangerous situation. Caldwell v. State, 497 N.E.2d 610, 1986 Ind. App. LEXIS 2955 (1986).

The failure of one who is not the full-time custodian of the child to report child abuse by the child's custodial natural parent is insufficient by itself to establish knowingly placing dependent in a dangerous situation. Fisher v. State, 548 N.E.2d 1177, 1990 Ind. App. LEXIS 26 (1990).

Where defendant was not shown to have subjective knowledge of the danger to which she was exposing her child, her conviction could not stand. Fout v. State, 619 N.E.2d 311, 1993 Ind. App. LEXIS 984 (1993).

A person knowingly commits neglect of a child when he is subjectively aware of a high probability that he placed the child in a dangerous situation. Thames v. State, 653 N.E.2d 517, 1995 Ind. App. LEXIS 919 (1995).

Necessary Support.
When a wife and children had a means of support, whether in their own right, or furnished by the husband, he was not criminally liable for deserting them. State v. Rice, 106 Ind. 139, 5 N.E. 906, 1886 Ind. LEXIS 77 (1886).

Parental Responsibility.
The criminal neglect of one parent is no excuse for the criminal neglect of the other, but, if anything, one parent's duty to look after his children increases when the other is guilty of neglect. Eaglen v. State, 249 Ind. 144, 231 N.E.2d 147, 1967 Ind. LEXIS 362 (1967).

Prosecutorial Vindictiveness.
Fact that defendant was not charged with child neglect until he refused to testify at the trial of his wife for causing the death of the child did not indicate prosecutorial vindictiveness. Worthington v. State, 409 N.E.2d 1261, 1980 Ind. App. LEXIS 1680 (1980).

Protection of Child by Parent.
Where mother was aware that father had been previously convicted of fondling their daughter, and he testified at the trial, independent of his written statement to police, that he discussed his sexual feelings for their daughter with mother, she was aware that the family was no longer involved in professional counseling, the family of four lived in a very small house and thus the proximity of the events to mother should have placed her on notice of father's behavior, and the record was replete with suggestions that the daughter had developed behavioral problems to the point of running away from home, the evidence was sufficient to convict mother of neglect of a dependent when she did not take any action to protect the child. Muehe v. State, 646 N.E.2d 980, 1995 Ind. App. LEXIS 144 (1995).

A parent's failure to take appropriate steps to protect his or her child from the abuse of the other parent is tantamount to neglect of that child, not to mention moral complicity with the base crime being perpetrated upon the child by the other parent. In a situation where it is the other parent perpetuating the abuse upon the child, the non-abusing parent is under an even greater duty to takes steps necessary to prevent the abuse. Muehe v. State, 646 N.E.2d 980, 1995 Ind. App. LEXIS 144 (1995).

Psychological, Mental, or Emotional Injury.
The neglect statute applies to the psychological, mental, and emotional injuries which are inflicted upon children by deviate conduct. Harrison v. State, 644 N.E.2d 888, 1994 Ind. App. LEXIS 1779 (1994).

Religious Belief.
Prayer is not permitted as a defense when a caretaker engages in omissive conduct which results in the child's death. Hall v. State, 493 N.E.2d 433, 1986 Ind. LEXIS 1159 (1986).

—Burden of Proof.
When a defendant raises the religious treatment defense, he bears the burden of proving it, as an issue of fact, and the burden is not on the state to negate the defense. Bergmann v. State, 486 N.E.2d 653, 1985 Ind. App. LEXIS 3026 (1985).

Sentence.
Where defendant was convicted of neglect of a dependent and also for involuntary manslaughter under IC 35-42-1-4 arising out of the same circumstances it was improper to impose a sentence for neglect of a dependent when sentence had been imposed for the greater offense of involuntary manslaughter. Smith v. State, 408 N.E.2d 614, 1980 Ind. App. LEXIS 1610 (1980).

—Aggravating Circumstances.
Although the trial court improperly relied on a reduced sentence depricating the seriousness of the offense as an aggravating circumstance, the trial court did not abuse its discretion by imposing the maximum sentence for defendant's two convictions under (a)(1), where the victim's age, which is not an element of the offense, was properly considered as an aggravating circumstance. Kile v. State, 729 N.E.2d 211, 2000 Ind. App. LEXIS 811 (2000).

Use of victim's status as dependent as aggravating factor in sentencing defendant for crime of neglect of dependent under IC 35-46-1-4 was improper. Nybo v. State, 799 N.E.2d 1146, 2003 Ind. App. LEXIS 2286 (2003).

Where defendant pled guilty to neglect of a dependent under IC 35-46-1-4, a sentencing court erred by finding an aggravating factor based on defendant's alleged need for corrective or rehabilitative services because insufficient findings were made; a specific and individualized statement explaining why extended incarceration was appropriate was needed. However, the trial court properly considered the victim's age (under 15 months old) in relation to the nature of the case and the

Sentence. (Cont'd)

—Aggravating Circumstances. (Cont'd)
circumstances of the crime. Edwards v. State, 842 N.E.2d 849, 2006 Ind. App. LEXIS 257 (2006).

Defendant's 12-year concurrent sentences for battery and neglect of a dependent were not inappropriate given the aggravating circumstance of his criminal history, which the trial court found outweighed the mitigating factor of defendant's guilty plea, and the potentially life-threatening injuries to the victim, his son. Defendant could have received 20 years for each offense, and the trial court was not required to find his abusive childhood to be a mitigating factor. Niemeyer v. State, 865 N.E.2d 674, 2007 Ind. App. LEXIS 862 (2007).

Sentence of 50 years for neglect of a dependent as a Class A felony was appropriate where defendant admitted to tying up the victim, defendant's daughter, smacking her across the face, and putting tape over her mouth; defendant also permitted the victim to become malnourished and dehydrated and aided his wife in forcing the victim to sleep on the floor in a plastic pan in a room built off of the garage with the door tied shut and with no heating. Gauvin v. State, 878 N.E.2d 515, 2007 Ind. App. LEXIS 2999 (2007).

Defendant's 34-year sentence for two counts of neglect under IC 35-46-1-4 was revised under AP. 7 to consecutive sentences of nine years, for placing the hands of child victim under hot water, causing severe burns and pain, and eight years for delay in seeking medical treatment. Cardwell v. State, 895 N.E.2d 1219, 2008 Ind. LEXIS 1049 (2008).

Trial court did not abuse its discretion in sentencing defendant mother to 30-years' imprisonment based upon her conviction for neglect of a dependent where the court found an aggravating factor based on her position of care where she left her child in a box in the basement after it was born where the child, who one expert stated died after birth, was not found until two days later. Robinson v. State, 894 N.E.2d 1038, 2008 Ind. App. LEXIS 2232 (2008).

When defendant pleaded guilty to felony child molesting, felony neglect of a dependent, felony child exploitation, felony criminal confinement, felony battery, and three counts of felony intimidation, he properly received consecutive sentences, and his aggregate term of 71 years in prison was not inappropriate under AP. 7(B) when the heinous nature of his actions was balanced against his lack of a significant criminal history and his guilty plea; defendant meticulously planned out the hour and a half of terror he inflicted on the victim, his five-year-old grandson, by creating costumes and characters and setting up cameras; a letter written by defendant supported the assessment that defendant was minimizing his culpability; defendant had benefited from his guilty plea in that no additional charges were filed; and in light of the overwhelming evidence against him, his decision to plead guilty was a pragmatic one. Lavoie v. State, — N.E.2d —, 2009 Ind. App. LEXIS 513 (2009).

—Double Jeopardy.
Sentences for both neglect of a dependent and reckless homicide violated double jeopardy since the parents' failure to provide medical treatment to their son during his illness was the basis for both convictions, and therefore, the Supreme Court vacated the convictions and sentences for neglect of a dependent. Hall v. State, 493 N.E.2d 433, 1986 Ind. LEXIS 1159 (1986).

—Separate Victims.
Where there were three separate victims, defendant's three children, each of whom was entitled to support, three separate crimes were committed, and it was not error for the trial court to impose separate sentences for each offense. Geans v. State, 623 N.E.2d 435, 1993 Ind. App. LEXIS 1320 (1993).

Severance of Offenses.
Defendants waived the right to sever the offenses of confinement and neglect by failure to make a timely motion. Parrish v. State, 459 N.E.2d 391, 1984 Ind. App. LEXIS 2289 (1984).

Support Furnished by Others.
Where a wife, deserted by her husband, was sheltered and protected by her parents, but she could not rely on them for more than temporary partial support, it afforded no defense to a prosecution for desertion. Kistler v. State, 190 Ind. 149, 129 N.E. 625, 1921 Ind. LEXIS 86 (1921).

Although others may as a matter of fact be furnishing support, the father's duty still exists. Denning v. Star Pub. Co., 94 Ind. App. 300, 180 N.E. 685, 1932 Ind. App. LEXIS 176 (1932).

Suspension of Judgment.
Judgments rendered by juvenile courts under the former provisions could have been suspended on conditions. Spade v. State, 44 Ind. App. 529, 89 N.E. 604, 1909 Ind. App. LEXIS 207 (1908).

Testimony.

—Admissible.
Testimony of daughter that her father attacked her with a knife, in a proceeding in the juvenile division of the superior court brought by welfare department to obtain wardship of children, was admissible in subsequent criminal proceeding against father for assault and battery and neglect of children, such daughter then being deceased. Spence v. State, 182 Ind. App. 62, 393 N.E.2d 277, 1979 Ind. App. LEXIS 1310 (1979).

Token Amounts of Support.
Where defendant provided some support in the form of clothing to each of his dependent children, but total amount of support provided was minimal at best, although substantial amounts of food, clothing and shelter may preclude criminal liability, the token amounts provided were simply not enough to avoid prosecution, and the state presented sufficient evidence to show that he failed to support his dependent children. Geans v. State, 623 N.E.2d 435, 1993 Ind. App. LEXIS 1320 (1993).

Unborn Child.

This section does not criminalize conduct that occurs prior to a child's birth because an unborn child is not a "dependent" pursuant to this section and IC 35-46-1-1. The plain language of this section contemplates only acts that place one who is a dependent at the time of the conduct at issue in a dangerous situation, not acts that place a future dependent in a dangerous situation. Herron v. State, 729 N.E.2d 1008, 2000 Ind. App. LEXIS 859 (2000).

Mother could not be charged with neglect of a dependent for using cocaine during her pregnancy because an unborn child was not a "dependent." Herron v. State, 729 N.E.2d 1008, 2000 Ind. App. LEXIS 859 (2000).

Cited:

Mayes v. State, 440 N.E.2d 678, 1982 Ind.

LEXIS 991 (1982); McMichael v. State, 471 N.E.2d 726, 1984 Ind. App. LEXIS 3105 (1984); Dowler v. State, 547 N.E.2d 1069, 1989 Ind. LEXIS 380 (1989); Millspaugh v. County Dep't of Public Welfare, 937 F.2d 1172, 1991 U.S. App. LEXIS 15200 (7th Cir. Ind. 1991); Eastman v. State, 611 N.E.2d 139, 1993 Ind. App. LEXIS 295 (1993); Mitchell v. State, 726 N.E.2d 1228, 2000 Ind. LEXIS 299 (2000); Cline v. State, 726 N.E.2d 1249, 2000 Ind. LEXIS 298 (2000); Healthscript, Inc. v. State, 740 N.E.2d 562, 2000 Ind. App. LEXIS 2027 (2000); Burdine v. State, 751 N.E.2d 260, 2001 Ind. App. LEXIS 956 (2001); Planned Parenthood v. Carter, 854 N.E.2d 853, 2006 Ind. App. LEXIS 1947 (2006); State v. Campos, 845 N.E.2d 1074, 2006 Ind. App. LEXIS 658 (2006).

RESEARCH REFERENCES

Indiana Law Review.

Surrogate Motherhood Legislation: A Sensible Starting Point, 20 Ind. L. Rev. 879 (1987).

Indiana's Neglect of a Dependent Statute: Uses and Abuses, 28 Ind. L. Rev. 447 (1995).

Choosing Life: Proposing Immunity for Mothers Who Abandon Their Newborns, 35 Ind. L. Rev. 569 (2002).

Res Gestae.

Criminal Justice Notes # 2: Ineffective assistance of counsel, 46 (No. 9) Res Gestae 22 (2003).

Criminal Justice Notes 9/06: Proportionality - unconstitutional where same act can constitute two different levels of felonies, 50 (No. 5) Res Gestae 40 (2006).

Valparaiso University Law Review.

Note, Testimony of Children Via Closed Circuit Television in Indiana: Face (to Television) to Face

Confrontation, 23 Val. U.L. Rev. 455 (1989).

Indiana's Criminal Treatment of Abusive Parents: Problems in Need of Solutions, 24 Val. U.L. Rev. 553 (1990).

Collateral References.

Criminal responsibility of father as affected by decree of divorce or separation requiring support by him. 73 A.L.R.2d 960.

Sufficiency of evidence to establish parent's knowledge or allowance of child's sexual abuse by another under statute permitting termination of parental rights for "allowing" or "knowingly allowing" such abuse to occur. 53 A.L.R.5th 499.

Parents' criminal liability for failure to provide medical attention to their children. 118 A.L.R.5th 253.

35-46-1-5. Nonsupport of a child.

(a) A person who knowingly or intentionally fails to provide support to the person's dependent child commits nonsupport of a child, a Class D felony. However, the offense is a Class C felony if the total amount of unpaid support that is due and owing for one (1) or more children is at least fifteen thousand dollars ($15,000).

(b) It is a defense that the child had abandoned the home of his family without the consent of his parent or on the order of a court, but it is not a defense that the child had abandoned the home of his family if the cause of the child's leaving was the fault of his parent.

(c) It is a defense that the accused person, in the legitimate practice of his religious belief, provided treatment by spiritual means through prayer, in lieu of medical care, to his dependent child.

(d) It is a defense that the accused person was unable to provide support.

History.

IC 35-46-1-5, as added by Acts 1976, P.L.148,

§ 6; 1977, P.L.340, § 88; 1978, P.L.144, § 9; P.L.213-1996, § 4; P.L.123-2001, § 4.

Cross References.

Civil action for support, IC 31-16-2.

Delinquent children and children in need of services, IC 31-37, IC 31-34.

Enforcement of support orders, Uniform Inter-

state Family Support Act, IC 31-18.

Parent-child relationship, termination, IC 31-35.

Penalties for felonies, IC 35-50-1, IC 35-50-2, IC 35-50-5-2.

NOTES TO DECISIONS

Constitutionality.

The support obligations of the defendant, charged with nonsupport of his child, did not constitute a "debt," and therefore the constitutional proscription against imprisonment for debt was inapplicable to his case. Davis v. State, 481 N.E.2d 434, 1985 Ind. App. LEXIS 2695 (1985).

It is not constitutionally impermissible to require the defendant, charged with nonsupport of his child under this section, to bear the burden of proving his defense of inability to pay. Davis v. State, 481 N.E.2d 434, 1985 Ind. App. LEXIS 2695 (1985); Davis v. Barber, 853 F.2d 1418, 1988 U.S. App. LEXIS 11105 (7th Cir. Ind. 1988), cert. denied, 489 U.S. 1021, 109 S. Ct. 1143, 103 L. Ed. 2d 203, 1989 U.S. LEXIS 708 (1989).

Because the offense of nonsupport of a dependent child under this section does not include ability to pay as an element of the offense, the state of Indiana does not violate a father's due process rights by requiring him to bear the burden of proving his inability to pay as an affirmative defense, nor does such a statutory scheme violate the substantive protections of the due process clause. Davis v. Barber, 657 F. Supp. 469, 1987 U.S. Dist. LEXIS 4020 (N.D. Ind. 1987), aff'd, 853 F.2d 1418, 1988 U.S. App. LEXIS 11105 (7th Cir. Ind. 1988).

The support statute clearly informs parents that criminal penalties can attach to failure to support children, and therefore is not unconstitutionally vague. Boss v. State, 702 N.E.2d 782, 1998 Ind. App. LEXIS 2187 (1998).

—Ex Post Facto Application.

The state charged the defendants with failure to provide support after the date the statute was enacted; therefore, the court erred in dismissing the charge as a Class C felony based upon debt incurred before the enactment of the statute as an ex post facto law violation. State v. Land, 688 N.E.2d 1307, 1997 Ind. App. LEXIS 1750 (1997).

Conviction of a Class C felony under IC 35-46-1-5(a) does not violate either the state or federal constitutional ex post facto prohibition in cases where: (1) at least $10,000 in arrearage accrued before the enactment of the 1996 amendment; or (2) the amount accruing after the amendment is less than $10,000, so long as the total arrearage is at least $10,000. Wiggins v. State, 727 N.E.2d 1, 2000 Ind. App. LEXIS 502 (2000).

Burden of Proof.

In a prosecution for nonsupport of a dependent child, in view of the definitions in IC 35-41-2-2, the prosecution has the burden of proving beyond a reasonable doubt: (1) that the accused either had the conscious objective or was aware of a high probability that he was failing to provide support; and (2) that he actually failed to provide support. Davis v. Barber, 657 F. Supp. 469, 1987 U.S. Dist. LEXIS 4020 (N.D. Ind. 1987), aff'd, 853 F.2d 1418, 1988 U.S. App. LEXIS 11105 (7th Cir. Ind. 1988).

—Inability to Pay.

The defense of inability to pay does not negate the element of knowingly or intentionally failing to pay support, but is a defense to the crime charged which the defendant has the burden of proving. Blatchford v. State, 673 N.E.2d 781, 1996 Ind. App. LEXIS 1600 (1996).

Civil Liability.

Statutes making a father liable criminally for failure to support his minor children do not take away or lessen his legal obligation to support them. Miami Coal Co. v. Peskir, 80 Ind. App. 115, 139 N.E. 684, 1923 Ind. App. LEXIS 100 (1923).

Collateral Estoppel.

Trial court properly held that a felony nonsupport defendant was collaterally estopped from arguing the validity of the underlying child support order. The state was invoking offensive collateral estoppel rather than defendant invoking defensive collateral estoppel, and to hold that strict mutuality and identity of parties were required would

Collateral Estoppel. (Cont'd)
allow all nonsupport defendants to challenge the underlying support orders; furthermore, defendant had had a full and fair opportunity to litigate the validity of the support calculation. Stephens v. State, 874 N.E.2d 1027, 2007 Ind. App. LEXIS 2323 (2007).

Construction.
Since the legislature declined to mention the term "children" with regard to Class C felony, it is not appropriate to incorporate the word. State v. Moore, 688 N.E.2d 917, 1997 Ind. App. LEXIS 1744 (1997).

Defenses.

—Incarceration.
Incarceration is not an absolute bar to parent's conviction for nonsupport of a dependant child as a Class C felony. Cooper v. State, 760 N.E.2d 660, 2001 Ind. App. LEXIS 2228 (2001).
Where defendant had previously been held in civil contempt for failure to pay child support and had been committed to work release until arrearage was paid off, subsequent criminal conviction for nonsupport of dependent child did not violate double jeopardy prohibition. Jones v. State, 812 N.E.2d 820, 2004 Ind. App. LEXIS 1459 (2004).

Evidence.

—Circumstantial.
In a prosecution for wilful failure to provide for minor children, the element of wilfulness, like any other fact, may be proved by circumstantial evidence. Francis v. State, 223 Ind. 186, 59 N.E.2d 565, 1945 Ind. LEXIS 94 (1945).

—Dependent Relationship.
Where, in a prosecution for failure to provide necessities of life to a minor child, there was evidence that defendant admitted in a paternity proceeding, which was subsequently dismissed, that he was the father of the child, that defendant and the child's mother were thereafter married and defendant acknowledged the child as his, and a finding and judgment of divorce to the mother declared the child to be a child of the marriage, a judgment of conviction was supported by sufficient evidence. Small v. State, 226 Ind. 38, 77 N.E.2d 578, 1948 Ind. LEXIS 132 (1948).

—Intent.
In a prosecution for wilful failure to provide for minor children, evidence that accused would voluntarily leave his employment and then loaf about town and go to shows, and that twice during the year preceding the filing of the charge he had passed a physical examination in applying for work, was sufficient to authorize an inference of wilfulness and perversity of design, notwithstanding other evidence as to illness of accused and his ability to work at hard labor. Francis v. State, 223 Ind. 186, 59 N.E.2d 565, 1945 Ind. LEXIS 94 (1945).
Under the former law which required proof that a parent "wilfully neglects to furnish" support for

his child, it was not necessary to prove the element of wilfulness by direct or positive evidence, but the evidence had to indicate more than mere carelessness and neglect. Hudson v. State, 175 Ind. App. 237, 370 N.E.2d 983, 1977 Ind. App. LEXIS 1064 (1977).
Where defendant was neither physically nor mentally incapacitated but had voluntarily quit his job in favor of a life of petty crime, and where the children's mother repeatedly admonished defendant to get a job and contribute to the children's support, to which reprimands defendant's response was invariably noncommittal, there was sufficient evidence to support a finding that defendant was deliberately pursuing an irresponsible lifestyle and wilfully neglecting to provide support for his children. Hudson v. State, 175 Ind. App. 237, 370 N.E.2d 983, 1977 Ind. App. LEXIS 1064 (1977).
Evidence that defendant was aware of his child support order and that he was in arrears for over $15,000 was sufficient to show intent in a Class C felony nonsupport case. The jury was not required to accept testimony that defendant thought that his father was making his payments. Stephens v. State, 874 N.E.2d 1027, 2007 Ind. App. LEXIS 2323 (2007).

—Sufficient.
Defendant never asserted that he provided his child with food, clothing, shelter, or medical care so as to relieve him of criminal liability for nonsupport, and although defendant had made some child support payments, he had come no where close to meeting his obligation; the amounts he paid were mere token amounts of support, and where he did not visit significantly with the child, the record did not support any inference that he provided the child with any meaningful amount of food, clothing, shelter, or medical care. Gustman v. State, 660 N.E.2d 353, 1996 Ind. App. LEXIS 16 (1996).
Prosecutor established a prima facie case of non-payment against obligor spouse, who admitted that he failed to make his child support payments, that he did not attempt to obtain relief from asset freeze to provide for his child's support or obtain other employment, but custodial spouse petitioned for and obtained from federal court release of sufficient assets to cover obligor's child support obligations. Wilcox v. State, 664 N.E.2d 379, 1996 Ind. App. LEXIS 569 (1996).
Although defendant provided support in the areas of food, clothing and medical bills, this support was minimal or token, and defendant's support arrearages were sufficient to support conviction under this section. Grimes v. State, 693 N.E.2d 1361, 1998 Ind. App. LEXIS 601 (1998).
Evidence was sufficient to convict defendant of nonsupport of a child where defendant accrued an arrearage of $12,030 and paid only $120 of his court-ordered obligation during an 11-year period; any support defendant directly provided to his child during one summer was minimal or token in light of the large arrearage. Cooper v. State, 760 N.E.2d 660, 2001 Ind. App. LEXIS 2228 (2001).
It was not error to find that a felony nonsupport defendant had not proven an inability to pay.

Evidence. (Cont'd)

—Sufficient. (Cont'd)
Although an accountant testified that defendant had no income in 2005, cross-examination showed that his conclusions were based only upon defendant's representations, and although defendant claimed that he had been unsuccessful in his business, he had never sought to modify his support obligation. Stephens v. State, 874 N.E.2d 1027, 2007 Ind. App. LEXIS 2323 (2007).

—Tax Interception Payments.
The defendant's conviction for nonsupport was upheld where he knowingly or intentionally failed to provide child support in a sum greater than $10,000 during a given period. Payments made under a tax interception order, which reduced the arrearages below $10,000, could not be credited until such time as the funds were received by the county. Long v. State, 716 N.E.2d 51, 1999 Ind. App. LEXIS 1475 (1999).

—Wilfulness.
Circumstantial evidence that defendant had contributed nothing towards child support for six years, and that in that time he had traveled and married twice, was insufficient to support a conviction where there was no proof relating to defendant's employment or capacity for employment during that period and therefore no proof of wilfulness. Burris v. State, 178 Ind. App. 327, 382 N.E.2d 963, 1978 Ind. App. LEXIS 1151 (1978).

Instructions.

—Venue.
In a prosecution for failing to provide a minor child with the necessities of life, venue need not be mentioned in an instruction as one of the elements of the crime. Small v. State, 226 Ind. 38, 77 N.E.2d 578, 1948 Ind. LEXIS 132 (1948).

Intent.
Where the facts show a deliberate and perverse design not to furnish shelter for children, a father could not say that he was always willing to provide for his children, and that therefore his failure to do so was not wilful. Hummel v. State, 73 Ind. App. 12, 126 N.E. 444, 1920 Ind. App. LEXIS 64 (1920).

Multiple Prosecutions.
A parent who has not made child support payments can be prosecuted again under this section, where the previous prosecution was for a specific period of time in the past which did not overlap the periods of time at issue in the subsequent prosecution. Boss v. State, 702 N.E.2d 782, 1998 Ind. App. LEXIS 2187 (1998).

Where a father was convicted of three offenses for non-support of his three children, but the continuing offenses were arbitrarily divided into separate time periods in order to multiply the penalties, remand for vacation of two of the convictions and for resentencing was required. Boss v. State, 702 N.E.2d 782, 1998 Ind. App. LEXIS 2187 (1998).

Parental Responsibility.
No demand or request need be made upon a father to supply the needs of his children, where his wife left home, taking his children, under conditions justifying her leaving because of immoral conditions in the home. Hummel v. State, 73 Ind. App. 12, 126 N.E. 444, 1920 Ind. App. LEXIS 64 (1920).

Parent's obligation to support his child continues during his life unless removed or shifted in some way recognized by the law. Vigo American Clay Co. v. Kelley, 82 Ind. App. 675, 147 N.E. 301, 1925 Ind. App. LEXIS 269 (1925).

Indiana has long recognized the obligation of both parents to support their children. Straub v. B.M.T. by Todd, 626 N.E.2d 848, 1993 Ind. App. LEXIS 1710 (1993), superseded, 645 N.E.2d 597, 1994 Ind. LEXIS 219 (1994).

—Parent Deprived of Custody.
The father of infant children is not released from his duty to provide for their support because he is deprived of the custody. State v. Yocum, 182 Ind. 478, 106 N.E. 705, 1914 Ind. LEXIS 154 (1914).

The granting of a divorce to the wife, with custody of the children to her and an order against the husband for support of the children, does not cancel a bond for their support, given in a previous criminal prosecution, and the sureties on such bond continue liable thereon. Bohler v. State, 95 Ind. App. 107, 181 N.E. 535, 1932 Ind. App. LEXIS 83 (1932).

Sentence.
Trial court properly found that the nature of defendant's crime was particularly egregious, where his criminal nonsupport had taken place over many years and had resulted in a large arrearage, and defendant had failed to visit with the child; the maximum sentence was appropriate, with one year suspended based upon the mitigating factor that defendant had no prior criminal record. Gustman v. State, 660 N.E.2d 353, 1996 Ind. App. LEXIS 16 (1996).

Although the trial court imposed the presumptive four-year sentence and then suspended two years, the case would be remanded to the trial court because it failed to identify all significant aggravating and mitigating circumstances, explain why it found each circumstance, and indicate how it balanced those factors to arrive at a sentencing decision imposing less than the presumptive sentence. Wiggins v. State, 727 N.E.2d 1, 2000 Ind. App. LEXIS 502 (2000).

Trial court's entry of judgment of conviction for Class D felony following guilty plea by defendant for crime of nonsupport of dependent was facially invalid since trial court failed to provide detailed reasons on record required for reducing felony from Class C to Class D; accordingly, trial court's later correction of conviction to Class C felony was analogous to correction of a facially invalid sentence and was valid despite defendant's argument that trial court had no jurisdiction to modify judgment after accepting plea agreement. Ennis v. State, 806 N.E.2d 804, 2004 Ind. App. LEXIS 674 (2004).

Sentence. (Cont'd)

Under the doctrine of amelioration, defendant, who was convicted of nonsupport of a dependent child and owed $13,296.44 in back child support, should have been sentenced to a class D felony, rather than a class C felony, because defendant was sentenced after IC 35-46-1-5(a) was amended to require an arrearage of more than $15,000 for class C felony, and the new statute contained no saving clause, the new statute did have an ameliorative effect in defendant's case, the full intent of the legislature could not be determined, and defendant would have been convicted under the new statute's effective date even if defendant's trial had not been continued for more than five years. Turner v. State, 870 N.E.2d 1083, 2007 Ind. App. LEXIS 1732 (2007).

—Enhancement.

The statute criminalizes the present act of failing to provide child support and enhances it if the amount due and owing at the time of the underlying act is in excess of $10,000; the statute does not criminalize the failure to pay past due support. State v. Land, 688 N.E.2d 1307, 1997 Ind. App. LEXIS 1750 (1997).

Defendant's non-support of his eight children, born to three different mothers, was not a single episode of criminal conduct, as three separate households (with different sets of victims) were deprived of support for dependent children; therefore, consecutive sentences were properly imposed for three counts of violating IC 35-46-1-5. Gilliam v. State, — N.E.2d —, 2009 Ind. App. LEXIS 284 (2009).

Where defendant was convicted of three counts of non-support, involving eight dependent children born to three different women, his 24-year sentence, with nine years to serve and 15 years suspended to probation, was appropriate pursuant to AP. 7(B) in view of the large arrearage he accumulated (over $121,000), the number of victims, and his lengthy criminal history. Gilliam v. State, — N.E.2d —, 2009 Ind. App. LEXIS 284 (2009).

—Restitution.

Civil statute of limitations of IC 34-11-2-10 did not apply to a criminal restitution case under IC 35-46-1-5, because criminal restitution was a portion of a sentence, and because the criminal restitution statute did not incorporate the civil statute of limitations, it did not apply. McKenney v. State, 848 N.E.2d 1127, 2006 Ind. App. LEXIS 1113 (2006).

Support Arrearages.

The fact that a parent owes a substantial amount of support arrearage is not necessarily dispositive in determining criminal liability; provision of food, clothing, shelter or medical care may be considered support when assessing criminal liability. Grimes v. State, 693 N.E.2d 1361, 1998 Ind. App. LEXIS 601 (1998).

Although defendant could introduce his prior imprisonment as an affirmative defense to nonpayment of child support, his incarceration was not an absolute bar to conviction; the verdict was supported by sufficient evidence. Dishmon v. State, 770 N.E.2d 855, 2002 Ind. App. LEXIS 962 (2002).

Support Furnished by Others.

A husband has no right to rely on wife's statement that her father would support her and their children, upon her leaving husband's home on account of immoral conditions therein. Hummel v. State, 73 Ind. App. 12, 126 N.E. 444, 1920 Ind. App. LEXIS 64 (1920).

Although others may as a matter of fact be furnishing support, the father's duty under this section still exists. Denning v. Star Pub. Co., 94 Ind. App. 300, 180 N.E. 685, 1932 Ind. App. LEXIS 176 (1932).

Venue.

If, on the divorce of the parents of children, the mother is given the custody of the children, and an order is made that the father contribute to their support, and the mother removes to another county and takes the children with her, a prosecution against the father for failure to provide for such children should be brought in the county where the mother resides. State v. Yocum, 182 Ind. 478, 106 N.E. 705, 1914 Ind. LEXIS 154 (1914).

Voluntariness.

The general voluntariness statute, IC 35-41-2-1, does not apply to this section. Here the legislature has specifically provided that involuntariness, in the form of inability to pay, is an affirmative defense, and this specific legislative mandate must prevail over the more general voluntariness statute. Davis v. Barber, 853 F.2d 1418, 1988 U.S. App. LEXIS 11105 (7th Cir. Ind. 1988), cert. denied, 489 U.S. 1021, 109 S. Ct. 1143, 103 L. Ed. 2d 203, 1989 U.S. LEXIS 708 (1989).

Cited:

Miller v. Morris, 270 Ind. 505, 386 N.E.2d 1203, 1979 Ind. LEXIS 784 (1979); In re H., 437 N.E.2d 119, 1982 Ind. App. LEXIS 1298 (1982); Haas v. Chater, 79 F.3d 559, 1996 U.S. App. LEXIS 3909 (7th Cir. Ind. 1996).

RESEARCH REFERENCES

Res Gestae.

Criminal Justice Notes 8/07: Doctrine of amelioration, 51 (No. 4) Res Gestae 40 (2007).

Collateral References.

Parent's child support liability as affected by other parent's fraudulent misrepresentation regarding sterility or use of birth control, or refusal to abort pregnancy. 2 A.L.R.5th 337.

35-46-1-6. Nonsupport of a spouse.

(a) A person who knowingly or intentionally fails to provide support to his spouse, when the spouse needs support, commits nonsupport of a spouse, a Class D felony.

(b) It is a defense that the accused person was unable to provide support.

History.
IC 35-46-1-6, as added by Acts 1976, P.L.148, § 6; 1977, P.L.340, § 89; 1978, P.L.144, § 10.

Cross References.
Civil action for support, IC 31-16-2.

Enforcement of support orders, Uniform Interstate Family Support Act, IC 31-18.
Penalties for felonies, IC 35-50-1, IC 35-50-2, IC 35-50-5-2.

NOTES TO DECISIONS

Cited:
Parrish v. State, 459 N.E.2d 391, 1984 Ind. App. LEXIS 2289 (1984).

RESEARCH REFERENCES

Collateral References.
Abandonment, desertion, or refusal to support on part of surviving spouse as affecting marital rights in deceased spouse's estate. 13 A.L.R.3d 446.

35-46-1-7. Nonsupport of a parent.

(a) A person who knowingly or intentionally fails to provide support to his parent, when the parent is unable to support himself, commits nonsupport of a parent, a Class A misdemeanor.

(b) It is a defense that the accused person had not been supported by the parent during the time he was a dependent child under eighteen (18) years of age, unless the parent was unable to provide support.

(c) It is a defense that the accused person was unable to provide support.

History.
IC 35-46-1-7, as added by Acts 1976, P.L.148, § 6; 1977, P.L.340, § 90; 1978, P.L.144, § 11.

Cross References.
Civil action for support, IC 31-16-2.

Duty to support parent, IC 31-16-17.
Enforcement of support orders, Uniform Interstate Family Support Act, IC 31-18.
Penalties for misdemeanors, IC 35-50-1, IC 35-50-3, IC 35-50-5-2.

NOTES TO DECISIONS

ANALYSIS

Ability to Provide Support.
Conduct of Parent.
Indictment or Information.
—Proportionate Liability.
—Support of Child by Parent.
Intent.
Support of Child by Parent.

Ability to Provide Support.
The former IC 35-14-6-1 required that the defendant be financially able to support his parents, not merely gainfully employed, and there had to be evidence with reference to the living expenses and obligations of the defendant which came prior to any legal requirement that he support his parents. Davis v. State, 251 Ind. 201, 240 N.E.2d 54, 1968 Ind. LEXIS 558 (1968).

Conduct of Parent.
The neglect of child to maintain or support parents is not excused by reason of personal conduct of parents during or subsequent to minority of child. Lanham v. State, 208 Ind. 79, 194 N.E. 625, 1935 Ind. LEXIS 199 (1935).

Indictment or Information.

—Proportionate Liability.
In a prosecution against children for failure to support their parent, where there are several children, the indictment, in order to be good, is not required to allege, and the state is not required to prove, that the defendant's proportionate liability has been determined and fixed, and that he has failed and refused to obey the order and to contribute the amount thus fixed by the court. State v.

Indictment or Information. (Cont'd)

—Proportionate Liability. (Cont'd)
Hoffman, 213 Ind. 125, 11 N.E.2d 698, 1937 Ind. LEXIS 389 (1937).

—Support of Child by Parent.
An indictment or affidavit was not required to allege that the parent supported and maintained the defendant child during its minority, as that was a matter of defense. Lundy v. State, 195 Ind. 368, 145 N.E. 485, 1924 Ind. LEXIS 146 (1924).

Intent.
The neglect of the child to maintain or support parents must be wilful in order to constitute an offense within this section. Lanham v. State, 208 Ind. 79, 194 N.E. 625, 1935 Ind. LEXIS 199 (1935).

Support of Child by Parent.
It cannot be said that the children have been supported by the father "when such children were minors" where the father has abandoned his family and left the mother and four minor children to shift for themselves, and where his forced contribution to their support was obviously inadequate to furnish the necessaries of life including at least a common school and high school education, and where the minor children themselves contributed a substantial portion of the support of the family. Lanham v. State, 208 Ind. 79, 194 N.E. 625, 1935 Ind. LEXIS 199 (1935).

The former IC 35-14-6-1 applied only to children whose parents either maintained a home for them throughout their minority or, in lieu thereof, supported them in other surroundings. Hindman v. State, 221 Ind. 611, 50 N.E.2d 913, 1943 Ind. LEXIS 233 (1943).

35-46-1-8. Contributing to the delinquency of a minor.

(a) A person at least eighteen (18) years of age who knowingly or intentionally encourages, aids, induces, or causes a person less than eighteen (18) years of age to commit an act of delinquency (as defined by IC 31-37-1 or IC 31-37-2) commits contributing to delinquency, a Class A misdemeanor.

(b) However, the offense described in subsection (a) is a Class C felony:
  (1) if:
    (A) the person committing the offense is at least twenty-one (21) years of age and knowingly or intentionally furnishes:
      (i) an alcoholic beverage to a person less than eighteen (18) years of age in violation of IC 7.1-5-7-8 when the person committing the offense knew or reasonably should have known that the person furnished the alcoholic beverage was less than eighteen (18) years of age; or
      (ii) a controlled substance (as defined in IC 35-48-1-9) or a drug (as defined in IC 9-13-2-49.1) in violation of Indiana law; and
    (B) the consumption, ingestion, or use of the alcoholic beverage, controlled substance, or drug is the proximate cause of the death of any person; or
  (2) if the person committing the offense knowingly or intentionally encourages, aids, induces, or causes a person less than eighteen (18) years of age to commit an act that would be a felony if committed by an adult under any of the following:
    (A) IC 35-48-4-1.
    (B) IC 35-48-4-1.1.
    (C) IC 35-48-4-2.
    (D) IC 35-48-4-3.
    (E) IC 35-48-4-4.
    (F) IC 35-48-4-4.5.
    (G) IC 35-48-4-4.6.
    (H) IC 35-48-4-5.

History.
IC 35-46-1-8, as added by Acts 1976, P.L.148, § 6; 1977, P.L.340, § 91; 1978, P.L.144, § 12; 1979, P.L.276, § 58; P.L.216-1996, § 24; P.L.1-1997, § 152; P.L.46-2004, § 2; P.L.2-2005, § 126; P.L.1-2006, § 533; P.L.151-2006, § 18.

Compiler's Notes.
This section was amended by P.L.1-2006 and P.L.151-2006, neither act referring to the other. However, because P.L.1-2006 appears to have made no change to the text of the section, the section is set out as amended by P.L.151-2006.

Cross References.
Child molestation, exploitation, IC 35-42-4-3, IC 35-42-4-4.
Delinquent children, children in need of services, IC 31-37, IC 31-34.

Penalties for felonies, IC 35-50-1, IC 35-50-2, IC 35-50-5-2.
Penalties for misdemeanors, IC 35-50-1, IC 35-50-3, IC 35-50-5-2.

NOTES TO DECISIONS

ANALYSIS

In General.
Acts of Delinquency.
—Alcoholic Beverages.
—Immoral Conduct.
Age.
—Burden of Proof.
—Knowledge.
Appeal.
—Jurisdiction.
Change of Venue.
Double Jeopardy.
Encouragement.
Evidence.
—Insufficient.
—Sufficient.
Indictment or Information.
—Knowledge.
Jurisdiction.
Trial and Finding.

In General.
Parents could have been convicted of contributing to the delinquency of a child because of neglect and failure to support such child. Spade v. State, 44 Ind. App. 529, 89 N.E. 604, 1909 Ind. App. LEXIS 207 (1908).
Conviction for encouraging delinquency of a female child under 18 years of age could not have been had under an indictment for rape, as a necessarily included offense. Gouchenour v. State, 202 Ind. 231, 173 N.E. 191, 1930 Ind. LEXIS 36 (1930).

Acts of Delinquency.
Where the act of remaining away from home was not an act of delinquency, a person could not be convicted of contributing to the delinquency of a minor by encouraging the minor not to return to his home. Shorter v. State, 166 Ind. App. 171, 334 N.E.2d 710, 1975 Ind. App. LEXIS 1335 (1975).

—Alcoholic Beverages.
One who invited a boy under 16 years of age into his saloon, and gave him beer to drink and permitted him to remain therein for half an hour, and drink beer given him by another, was guilty under the former section. Murphy v. State, 61 Ind. App. 226, 111 N.E. 806, 1916 Ind. App. LEXIS 50 (1916).

—Immoral Conduct.
If a man had illicit sexual intercourse with a girl under 17 years of age, he could have been convicted of encouraging the delinquency of such girl. Tullis v. Shaw, 169 Ind. 662, 83 N.E. 376, 1908 Ind. LEXIS 80 (1908).
The gist of the offense of encouraging a boy to commit sodomy was not the actual doing of the immoral act by the boy, but was the act of the adult

in encouraging him to do it. Montgomery v. State, 115 Ind. App. 189, 57 N.E.2d 943, 1944 Ind. App. LEXIS 149 (1944).

Age.
The physical condition, size, and physical appearance of the juvenile as a witness on the stand was sufficient to establish that the defendant, who admitted making no inquiries as to her age, knew her to be under 18 years of age when committing the acts alleged to have contributed to her delinquency. Davidson v. State, 249 Ind. 419, 233 N.E.2d 173, 1968 Ind. LEXIS 726 (1968).

—Burden of Proof.
When the defendant claimed that the minor was, or had the appearance of having been, of full age, the burden was on him to show the fact. Mulread v. State, 107 Ind. 62, 7 N.E. 884, 1886 Ind. LEXIS 298 (1886); Taylor v. State, 107 Ind. 483, 8 N.E. 450, 1886 Ind. LEXIS 376 (1886); Fehn v. State, 3 Ind. App. 568, 29 N.E. 1137, 1892 Ind. App. LEXIS 53 (1892).
The state must prove the defendant's age by substantial evidence of probative value. Bowens v. State, 578 N.E.2d 377, 1991 Ind. App. LEXIS 1575 (1991).

—Knowledge.
It was not an essential element of the offense defined in the former section that the person charged with the crime had knowledge that the child was under the age of 18. Marsh v. State, 104 Ind. App. 377, 8 N.E.2d 121, 1937 Ind. App. LEXIS 61 (1937).

Appeal.
In a prosecution under the former section for contributing to the delinquency of a girl under 18 years of age, no question was presented for review on appeal, where the trial judge failed to make a finding of fact on which to base judgment. Femeyer v. State, 85 Ind. App. 596, 152 N.E. 853, 1926 Ind. App. LEXIS 179 (1926).

—Jurisdiction.
An appeal from a judgment of the juvenile court, in an action for contributing to the delinquency of a minor, had to be taken to the appellate court (now court of appeals), and not the Supreme Court. Taughinbaugh v. State, 200 Ind. 334, 163 N.E. 598, 1928 Ind. LEXIS 74 (1928).

Change of Venue.
Where defendant in juvenile court was charged with contributing to delinquency of child and trial judge believed defendant was entitled to change of judge, but that defendant was in error in requesting change to criminal court, juvenile court erred in not following law he thought proper and in not

Change of Venue. (Cont'd)
taking steps to secure change of judge. State ex rel. Harper v. Hoffman, 228 Ind. 641, 94 N.E.2d 756, 1950 Ind. LEXIS 178 (1950).

Double Jeopardy.
Trial court committed fundamental error by sentencing defendant under this section and for theft under IC 35-43-4-2 as these offenses were essentially the same for purposes of double jeopardy. Cornes v. State, 467 N.E.2d 425, 1984 Ind. App. LEXIS 2886 (1984).

Under actual evidence test, defendant's convictions of burglary, theft, criminal mischief, and contributing to delinquency of minors did not violate double jeopardy because each of first three offenses could be established without introducing evidence of contributing to delinquency charge, even though defendant's child and other minors were instruments through which defendant carried out all of crimes charged. Waldon v. State, 829 N.E.2d 168, 2005 Ind. App. LEXIS 1053 (2005).

Encouragement.
Encouragement of minors to use intoxicating liquors is not limited to the direct, positive acts of giving, inviting or urging the minors to drink but may be any purposeful acts or combination of acts by adults which embolden, incite or induce minors to become delinquent by drinking. Wedmore v. State, 235 Ind. 341, 133 N.E.2d 842, 1956 Ind. LEXIS 160 (1956).

Evidence.

—Insufficient.
Mere presence of defendant at an all night beer party of teenagers in his apartment, without evidence that he had invited them or influenced them to drink beer, was insufficient for conviction. Gray v. State, 249 Ind. 523, 233 N.E.2d 468, 1968 Ind. LEXIS 736 (1968); Sayers v. State, 249 Ind. 532, 12 Ind. Dec. 698, 233 N.E.2d 470, 1968 Ind. LEXIS 738 (1968).

Probation officer's negative answer to the question, "Were there any other adults in the house at the time?" amounted to only a scintilla of defendant's adult status and was insufficient to prove his age. Bowens v. State, 578 N.E.2d 377, 1991 Ind. App. LEXIS 1575 (1991).

—Sufficient.
A conviction of contributing to the delinquency of a minor could be sustained where defendant made false representations to the minor's parents as to his whereabouts, allowed the minor to remain at a party where alcohol had been brought with the aid of the minor and where defendant was aware of the minor's consumption of alcohol, although the defendant took no affirmative action to encourage the minor to drink and was absent from the premises for some period of time. Reeves v. State, 161 Ind. App. 240, 315 N.E.2d 397, 1974 Ind. App. LEXIS 928 (1974).

Evidence was sufficient to support defendant's conviction of contributing to the delinquency of a minor, a Class A misdemeanor, when an underage drinking party was held at defendant's home; although the evidence might not have established that defendant actually supplied the juveniles with alcohol, the trial court could have reasonably inferred that defendant knew that minors were drinking in her basement when considering the amount of alcohol that was in the house and the number of individuals who were coming and going from the residence. Rush v. State, 881 N.E.2d 46, 2008 Ind. App. LEXIS 254 (2008).

Indictment or Information.
Adults prosecuted under the former section were entitled to have the accusation conform to the provisions of the Code of Criminal Procedure. Oliver v. State, 195 Ind. 65, 144 N.E. 612, 1924 Ind. LEXIS 108 (1924); Pease v. State, 74 Ind. App. 572, 129 N.E. 337, 1921 Ind. App. LEXIS 138 (1921).

—Knowledge.
Indictment did not charge knowledge on part of defendant in "knowingly" encouraging violation, and was therefore defective. Embry v. State, 229 Ind. 179, 96 N.E.2d 274, 1951 Ind. LEXIS 131 (1951).

Jurisdiction.
Juvenile courts had jurisdiction to hear and assess punishment for encouraging children to commit delinquencies as defined by the former section. Tullis v. Shaw, 169 Ind. 662, 83 N.E. 376, 1908 Ind. LEXIS 80 (1908).

If the juvenile court had jurisdiction, its judgments could not have been collaterally attacked on the hearing of habeas corpus proceedings. Tullis v. Shaw, 169 Ind. 662, 83 N.E. 376, 1908 Ind. LEXIS 80 (1908).

Trial and Finding.
Where the affidavit was defective for omission of the allegation that defendant knew said house of prostitution to be such, it was not error for the court to set aside its finding and judgment of guilty on such affidavit, and put defendant on trial on an amended affidavit containing such omitted allegation, where the first affidavit would not support a judgment of guilty. Marsh v. State, 104 Ind. App. 377, 8 N.E.2d 121, 1937 Ind. App. LEXIS 61 (1937).

Cited:
Nation v. State, 445 N.E.2d 565, 1983 Ind. LEXIS 762 (1983); Harder v. State, 501 N.E.2d 1117, 1986 Ind. App. LEXIS 3270 (1986); Allen v. State, 596 N.E.2d 280, 1992 Ind. App. LEXIS 1134 (1992); Stevens v. State, 689 N.E.2d 487, 1997 Ind. App. LEXIS 1794 (1997); State v. Jackson, 864 N.E.2d 431, 2007 Ind. App. LEXIS 771 (2007).

RESEARCH REFERENCES

Collateral References.

Criminal liability for contributing to delinquency of minor as affected by the fact that minor has not become a delinquent. 18 A.L.R.3d 824.

Mens rea or guilty intent as necessary element

of offense of contributing to delinquency or dependency of minor. 31 A.L.R.3d 848.

Giving, selling, or prescribing dangerous drugs as contributing to the delinquency of a minor. 36 A.L.R.3d 1292.

35-46-1-9. Profiting from an adoption.

(a) Except as provided in subsection (b), a person who, with respect to an adoption, transfers or receives any property in connection with the waiver of parental rights, the termination of parental rights, the consent to adoption, or the petition for adoption commits profiting from an adoption, a Class D felony.

(b) This section does not apply to the transfer or receipt of:

(1) reasonable attorney's fees;

(2) hospital and medical expenses concerning childbirth and pregnancy incurred by the adopted person's birth mother;

(3) reasonable charges and fees levied by a child placing agency licensed under IC 31-27 or the department of child services;

(4) reasonable expenses for psychological counseling relating to adoption incurred by the adopted person's birth parents;

(5) reasonable costs of housing, utilities, and phone service for the adopted person's birth mother during the second or third trimester of pregnancy and not more than six (6) weeks after childbirth;

(6) reasonable costs of maternity clothing for the adopted person's birth mother;

(7) reasonable travel expenses incurred by the adopted person's birth mother that relate to the pregnancy or adoption;

(8) any additional itemized necessary living expenses for the adopted person's birth mother during the second or third trimester of pregnancy and not more than six (6) weeks after childbirth, not listed in subdivisions (5) through (7) in an amount not to exceed one thousand dollars ($1,000); or

(9) other charges and fees approved by the court supervising the adoption, including reimbursement of not more than actual wages lost as a result of the inability of the adopted person's birth mother to work at her regular, existing employment due to a medical condition, excluding a psychological condition, if:

(A) the attending physician of the adopted person's birth mother has ordered or recommended that the adopted person's birth mother discontinue her employment; and

(B) the medical condition and its direct relationship to the pregnancy of the adopted person's birth mother are documented by her attending physician.

In determining the amount of reimbursable lost wages, if any, that are reasonably payable to the adopted person's birth mother under subdivision (9), the court shall offset against the reimbursable lost wages any amounts paid to the adopted person's birth mother under subdivisions (5) and (8) and any unemployment compensation received by or owed to the adopted person's birth mother.

(c) Except as provided in this subsection, payments made under subsection (b)(5) through (b)(9) may not exceed three thousand dollars ($3,000) and must be disclosed to the court supervising the adoption. The amounts paid under subsection (b)(5) through (b)(9) may exceed three thousand dollars ($3,000) to the extent that a court in Indiana with jurisdiction over the child who is the subject of the adoption approves the expenses after determining that:

(1) the expenses are not being offered as an inducement to proceed with an adoption; and

(2) failure to make the payments may seriously jeopardize the health of either the child or the mother of the child and the direct relationship is documented by a licensed social worker or the attending physician.

(d) The payment limitation under subsection (c) applies to the total amount paid under subsection (b)(5) through (b)(9) in connection with an adoption from all prospective adoptive parents, attorneys, and licensed child placing agencies.

(e) An attorney or licensed child placing agency shall inform a birth mother of the penalties for committing adoption deception under section 9.5 [IC 35-46-1-9.5] of this chapter before the attorney or agency transfers a payment for adoption related expenses under subsection (b) in relation to the birth mother.

(f) The limitations in this section apply regardless of the state or country in which the adoption is finalized.

History.
IC 35-46-1-9, as added by Acts 1980, P.L.208, § 2; P.L.117-1990, § 6; P.L.2-1992, § 882; P.L.81-1992, § 39; P.L.1-1993, § 241; P.L.4-1993, § 326; P.L.5-1993, § 333; P.L.226-1996, § 1; P.L.200-1999, § 32; P.L.130-2005, § 14; P.L.145-2006, § 371; P.L.146-2007, § 18, eff. July 1, 2007; P.L.146-2008, § 683, emergency eff. March 19, 2008.

Compiler's Notes.
P.L.130-2005, § 15, effective July 1, 2005, provides:
"IC 35-46-1-9, as amended by this act, applies only to crimes committed after June 30, 2005."

Cross References.
Penalties for felonies, IC 35-50-1, IC 35-50-2, IC 35-50-5-2.

RESEARCH REFERENCES

Indiana Law Review.
Surrogate Motherhood Legislation: A Sensible Starting Point, 20 Ind. L. Rev. 879 (1987).

35-46-1-9.5. Adoption deception.

A person who is a birth mother, or a woman who holds herself out to be a birth mother, and who knowingly or intentionally benefits from adoption related expenses paid:
(1) when the person knows or should have known that the person is not pregnant;
(2) by or on behalf of a prospective adoptive parent who is unaware that at the same time another prospective adoptive parent is also paying adoption related expenses described under section 9(b) [IC 35-46-1-9(b)] of this chapter in an effort to adopt the same child; or
(3) when the person does not intend to make an adoptive placement;
commits adoption deception, a Class A misdemeanor. In addition to any other penalty imposed under this section, a court may order the person who commits adoption deception to make restitution to a prospective adoptive parent, attorney, or licensed child placing agency that incurs an expense as a result of the offense.

History.
P.L.200-1999, § 33; P.L.61-2003, § 21; P.L.146-2007, § 19, eff. July 1, 2007.

Cross References.
Penalties for misdemeanors, IC 35-50-1, IC 35-50-3, IC 35-50-5-2.

NOTES TO DECISIONS

Cited:
State v. Jackson, 864 N.E.2d 431, 2007 Ind. App. LEXIS 771 (2007).

35-46-1-10. Sale of tobacco by an individual to persons under 18 years of age.

(a) A person who knowingly:

(1) sells or distributes tobacco to a person less than eighteen (18) years of age; or

(2) purchases tobacco for delivery to another person who is less than eighteen (18) years of age;

commits a Class C infraction. For a sale to take place under this section, the buyer must pay the seller for the tobacco product.

(b) It is not a defense that the person to whom the tobacco was sold or distributed did not smoke, chew, or otherwise consume the tobacco.

(c) The following defenses are available to a person accused of selling or distributing tobacco to a person who is less than eighteen (18) years of age:

(1) The buyer or recipient produced a driver's license bearing the purchaser's or recipient's photograph, showing that the purchaser or recipient was of legal age to make the purchase.

(2) The buyer or recipient produced a photographic identification card issued under IC 9-24-16-1, or a similar card issued under the laws of another state or the federal government, showing that the purchaser or recipient was of legal age to make the purchase.

(3) The appearance of the purchaser or recipient was such that an ordinary prudent person would believe that the purchaser or recipient was not less than the age that complies with regulations promulgated by the federal Food and Drug Administration.

(d) It is a defense that the accused person sold or delivered the tobacco to a person who acted in the ordinary course of employment or a business concerning tobacco:

(1) agriculture;

(2) processing;

(3) transporting;

(4) wholesaling; or

(5) retailing.

(e) As used in this section, "distribute" means to give tobacco to another person as a means of promoting, advertising, or marketing the tobacco to the general public.

(f) Unless a person buys or receives tobacco under the direction of a law enforcement officer as part of an enforcement action, a person who sells or distributes tobacco is not liable for a violation of this section unless the person less than eighteen (18) years of age who bought or received the tobacco is issued a citation or summons under section 10.5 [IC 35-46-1-10.5] of this chapter.

(g) Notwithstanding IC 34-28-5-4(c), civil penalties collected under this section must be deposited in the Richard D. Doyle youth tobacco education and enforcement fund (IC 7.1-6-2-6).

History.
IC 35-46-1-10, as added by Acts 1980, P.L.209, § 1; P.L.330-1983, § 1; P.L.318-1987, § 3; P.L.125-1988, § 4; P.L.177-1999, § 10; P.L.1-2001, § 37; P.L.204-2001, § 65; P.L.252-2003, § 17.

however, the amendment by P.L.204-2001 did not incorporate the substitution of "IC 34-28-5-5(c)" for "IC 34-28-5-4(c)" in subsection (g) as amended by P.L.1-2001. The compiler has set out subsection (g) as amended by P.L.1-2001, § 37.

Compiler's Notes.
The amendment by P.L.204-2001 purported to amend this section as amended by P.L.1-2001;

Cross References.
Infraction and ordinance violation enforcement proceedings, IC 34-28-5.

NOTES TO DECISIONS

Cited:
State v. Shelton, 692 N.E.2d 947, 1998 Ind. App.
LEXIS 348 (1998).

RESEARCH REFERENCES

Collateral References.
Civil liability for tobacco sales to minors. 55
A.L.R.4th 1238.

35-46-1-10.1. Violations of IC 7.1-5-7-8 regarding recklessly furnishing alcoholic beverage to minors — Penalties imposed.

(a) If a permit holder or an agent or employee of a permit holder violates IC 7.1-5-7-8 on the licensed premises, in addition to any other penalty, a civil judgment may be imposed against the permit holder as follows:

(1) If the licensed premises at that specific business location has not been issued a citation or summons for a violation of IC 7.1-5-7-8 in the previous one hundred eighty (180) days, a civil penalty of up to two hundred dollars ($200).

(2) If the licensed premises at that specific business location has had one (1) citation or summons for a violation of IC 7.1-5-7-8 in the previous one hundred eighty (180) days, a civil penalty of up to four hundred dollars ($400).

(3) If the licensed premises at that specific business location has had two (2) citations or summonses for a violation of IC 7.1-5-7-8 in the previous one hundred eighty (180) days, a civil penalty of up to seven hundred dollars ($700).

(4) If the licensed premises at that specific business location has had three (3) or more citations or summonses for a violation of IC 7.1-5-7-8 in the previous one hundred eighty (180) days, a civil penalty of up to one thousand dollars ($1,000).

(b) The defenses set forth in IC 7.1-5-7-5.1 are available to a permit holder in an action under this section.

(c) Unless a person less than twenty-one (21) years of age buys or receives an alcoholic beverage under the direction of a law enforcement officer as part of an enforcement action, a permit holder that sells alcoholic beverages is not liable under this section unless the person less than twenty-one (21) years of age who bought or received the alcoholic beverage is charged for violating IC 7.1-5-7-7.

(d) All civil penalties collected under this section shall be deposited in the alcohol and tobacco commission's enforcement and administration fund under IC 7.1-4-10.

History.
P.L.94-2008, § 61, emergency eff. July 1, 2008.

35-46-1-10.2. Sale of tobacco by a retail establishment to persons under 18 years of age.

(a) A retail establishment that sells or distributes tobacco to a person less than eighteen (18) years of age commits a Class C infraction. For a sale to take place under this section, the buyer must pay the retail establishment for the tobacco product. Notwithstanding IC 34-28-5-4(c), a civil judgment for an infraction committed under this section must be imposed as follows:

(1) If the retail establishment at that specific business location has not been issued a citation or summons for a violation of this section in the previous one hundred eighty (180) days, a civil penalty of up to two hundred dollars ($200).

(2) If the retail establishment at that specific business location has had one (1) citation or summons issued for a violation of this section in the previous one hundred eighty (180) days, a civil penalty of up to four hundred dollars ($400).

(3) If the retail establishment at that specific business location has had two (2) citations or summonses issued for a violation of this section in the previous one hundred eighty (180) days, a civil penalty of up to seven hundred dollars ($700).

(4) If the retail establishment at that specific business location has had three (3) or more citations or summonses issued for a violation of this section in the previous one hundred eighty (180) days, a civil penalty of up to one thousand dollars ($1,000).

A retail establishment may not be issued a citation or summons for a violation of this section more than once every twenty-four (24) hours for each specific business location.

(b) It is not a defense that the person to whom the tobacco was sold or distributed did not smoke, chew, or otherwise consume the tobacco.

(c) The following defenses are available to a retail establishment accused of selling or distributing tobacco to a person who is less than eighteen (18) years of age:

(1) The buyer or recipient produced a driver's license bearing the purchaser's or recipient's photograph showing that the purchaser or recipient was of legal age to make the purchase.

(2) The buyer or recipient produced a photographic identification card issued under IC 9-24-16-1 or a similar card issued under the laws of another state or the federal government showing that the purchaser or recipient was of legal age to make the purchase.

(3) The appearance of the purchaser or recipient was such that an ordinary prudent person would believe that the purchaser or recipient was not less than the age that complies with regulations promulgated by the federal Food and Drug Administration.

(d) It is a defense that the accused retail establishment sold or delivered the tobacco to a person who acted in the ordinary course of employment or a business concerning tobacco:

(1) agriculture;

(2) processing;

(3) transporting;

(4) wholesaling; or

(5) retailing.

(e) As used in this section, "distribute" means to give tobacco to another person as a means of promoting, advertising, or marketing the tobacco to the general public.

(f) Unless a person buys or receives tobacco under the direction of a law enforcement officer as part of an enforcement action, a retail establishment that sells or distributes tobacco is not liable for a violation of this section unless the person less than eighteen (18) years of age who bought or received the tobacco is issued a citation or summons under section 10.5 [IC 35-46-1-10.5] of this chapter.

(g) Notwithstanding IC 34-28-5-5(c), civil penalties collected under this section must be deposited in the Richard D. Doyle youth tobacco education and enforcement fund (IC 7.1-6-2-6).

(h) A person who violates subsection (a) at least six (6) times in any one hundred eighty (180) day period commits habitual illegal sale of tobacco, a Class B infraction.

History.
P.L.177-1999, § 11; P.L.14-2000, § 72; P.L.1-2001, § 38; P.L.250-2003, § 17; P.L.252-2003, § 18; P.L.94-2008, § 62, emergency eff. July 1, 2008.

Cross References.
Infraction and ordinance violation enforcement proceedings, IC 34-28-5.

35-46-1-10.5. Purchase, acceptance, or possession of tabacco by person under 18 years of age — Defense.

(a) A person less than eighteen (18) years of age who:

(1) purchases tobacco;

(2) accepts tobacco for personal use; or

(3) possesses tobacco on his person;

commits a Class C infraction.

(b) It is a defense under subsection (a) that the accused person acted in the ordinary course of employment in a business concerning tobacco:

(1) agriculture;

(2) processing;

(3) transporting;

(4) wholesaling; or

(5) retailing.

History.
P.L.125-1988, § 5; P.L.256-1996, § 13.

Cross References.
Infraction and ordinance violation enforcement proceedings, IC 34-28-5.

35-46-1-11. Notice concerning prohibition on sale of tobacco to persons under 18 years — Penalty for failure to post.

(a) A tobacco vending machine that is located in a public place must bear the following conspicuous notices:

(1) A notice:

(A) that reads as follows, with the capitalization indicated: "If you are under 18 years of age, YOU ARE FORBIDDEN by Indiana law to buy tobacco from this machine."; or

(B) that:

(i) conveys a message substantially similar to the message described in clause (A); and

(ii) is formatted with words and in a form authorized under the rules adopted by the alcohol and tobacco commission.

(2) A notice that reads as follows, "Smoking by Pregnant Women May Result in Fetal Injury, Premature Birth, and Low Birth Weight."

(3) A notice printed in letters and numbers at least one-half (½) inch high that displays a toll free phone number for assistance to callers in quitting smoking, as determined by the state department of health.

(b) A person who owns or has control over a tobacco vending machine in a public place and who:

(1) fails to post a notice required by subsection (a) on the vending machine; or

(2) fails to replace a notice within one (1) month after it is removed or defaced;

commits a Class C infraction.

(c) An establishment selling tobacco at retail shall post and maintain in a conspicuous place, at the point of sale, the following:

(1) Signs printed in letters at least one-half (½) inch high, reading as follows:

(A) "The sale of tobacco to persons under 18 years of age is forbidden by Indiana law."

(B) "Smoking by Pregnant Women May Result in Fetal Injury, Premature Birth, and Low Birth Weight."

(2) A sign printed in letters and numbers at least one-half (½) inch high that displays a toll free phone number for assistance to callers in quitting smoking, as determined by the state department of health.

(d) A person who:

(1) owns or has control over an establishment selling tobacco at retail; and

(2) fails to post and maintain the sign required by subsection (c);

commits a Class C infraction.

History.
IC 35-46-1-11, as added by P.L.330-1983, § 2; P.L.318-1987, § 4; P.L.204-2001, § 66; P.L.94-2008, § 63, emergency eff. July 1, 2008.

Cross References.
Infraction and ordinance violation enforcement proceedings, IC 34-28-5.

35-46-1-11.2. Operation of tobacco business within two hundred feet of school — Penalty.

(a) This section does not apply to a tobacco business:
(1) operating as a tobacco business before April 1, 1996; or
(2) that begins operating as a tobacco business after April 1, 1996, if at the time the tobacco business begins operation the tobacco business is not located in an area prohibited under this section.

(b) A person may not operate a tobacco business within two hundred (200) feet of a public or private elementary or secondary school, as measured between the nearest point of the premises occupied by the tobacco business and the nearest point of a building used by the school for instructional purposes.

(c) A person who violates this section commits a Class C misdemeanor.

History.
P.L.256-1996, § 11.

Cross References.
Penalties for misdemeanors, IC 35-50-1, IC 35-50-3, IC 35-50-5-2.

35-46-1-11.3. [Repealed.]

Compiler's Notes.
This section, concerning advertisement of tobacco products and penalty, was repealed by P.L.250-2003, § 19, effective July 1, 2003. Prior to its repeal, this section had been amended by P.L.252-2003, § 19.

35-46-1-11.5. Sale or distribution of tobacco by use of coin machine.

(a) Except for a coin machine that is placed in or directly adjacent to an entranceway or an exit, or placed in a hallway, a restroom, or another common area that is accessible to persons who are less than eighteen (18) years of age, this section does not apply to a coin machine that is located in the following:
(1) That part of a licensed premises (as defined in IC 7.1-1-3-20) where entry is limited to persons who are at least eighteen (18) years of age.
(2) Private industrial or office locations that are customarily accessible only to persons who are at least eighteen (18) years of age.
(3) Private clubs if the membership is limited to persons who are at least eighteen (18) years of age.
(4) Riverboats where entry is limited to persons who are at least twenty-one (21) years of age and on which lawful gambling is authorized.

(b) As used in this section, "coin machine" has the meaning set forth in IC 35-43-5-1.

(c) Except as provided in subsection (a), an owner of a retail establishment may not:
(1) distribute or sell tobacco by use of a coin machine; or
(2) install or maintain a coin machine that is intended to be used for the sale or distribution of tobacco.

(d) An owner of a retail establishment who violates this section commits a Class C infraction. A citation or summons issued under this section must provide notice that the coin machine must be moved within two (2) business days. Notwithstanding IC 34-28-5-4(c), a civil judgment for an infraction committed under this section must be imposed as follows:
(1) If the owner of the retail establishment has not been issued a citation or summons for a violation of this section in the previous ninety (90) days, a civil penalty of fifty dollars ($50).

(2) If the owner of the retail establishment has had one (1) citation or summons issued for a violation of this section in the previous ninety (90) days, a civil penalty of two hundred fifty dollars ($250).

(3) If the owner of the retail establishment has had two (2) citations or summonses issued for a violation of this section in the previous ninety (90) days for the same machine, the coin machine shall be removed or impounded by a law enforcement officer having jurisdiction where the violation occurs.

An owner of a retail establishment may not be issued a citation or summons for a violation of this section more than once every two (2) business days for each business location.

(e) Notwithstanding IC 34-28-5-5(c), civil penalties collected under this section must be deposited in the Richard D. Doyle youth tobacco education and enforcement fund established under IC 7.1-6-2-6.

History.
P.L.49-1990, § 20; P.L.177-1999, § 13; P.L.14-2000, § 73; P.L.1-2001, § 40; P.L.252-2003, § 20.

Cross References.
Infraction and ordinance violation enforcement proceedings, IC 34-28-5.

35-46-1-11.7. Persons under 18 years of age prohibited from entering retail stores that have as primary purpose sale of tobacco products.

(a) A retail establishment that has as its primary purpose the sale of tobacco products may not allow an individual who is less than eighteen (18) years of age to enter the retail establishment.

(b) An individual who is less than eighteen (18) years of age may not enter a retail establishment described in subsection (a).

(c) A retail establishment described in subsection (a) must conspicuously post on all entrances to the retail establishment the following:

(1) A sign in boldface type that states "NOTICE: It is unlawful for a person less than 18 years old to enter this store.".

(2) A sign printed in letters and numbers at least one-half (½) inch high that displays a toll free phone number for assistance to callers in quitting smoking, as determined by the state department of health.

(d) A person who violates this section commits a Class C infraction. Notwithstanding IC 34-28-5-4(c), a civil judgment for an infraction committed under this section must be imposed as follows:

(1) If the person has not been cited for a violation of this section in the previous one hundred eighty (180) days, a civil penalty of up to two hundred dollars ($200).

(2) If the person has had one (1) violation in the previous one hundred eighty (180) days, a civil penalty of up to four hundred dollars ($400).

(3) If the person has had two (2) violations in the previous one hundred eighty (180) days, a civil penalty of up to seven hundred dollars ($700).

(4) If the person has had three (3) or more violations in the previous one hundred eighty (180) days, a civil penalty of up to one thousand dollars ($1,000).

A person may not be cited more than once every twenty-four (24) hours.

(e) Notwithstanding IC 34-28-5-5(c), civil penalties collected under this section must be deposited in the Richard D. Doyle youth tobacco education and enforcement fund established under IC 7.1-6-2-6.

(f) A person who violates subsection (a) at least six (6) times in any one hundred eighty (180) day period commits habitual illegal entrance by a minor, a Class B infraction.

History.
P.L.177-1999, § 14; P.L.14-2000, § 74; P.L.1-

2001, § 41; P.L.252-2003, § 21; P.L.94-2008, § 64, emergency eff. July 1, 2008.

Cross References.
Infraction and ordinance violation enforcement
proceedings, IC 34-28-5.

35-46-1-11.8. Sale by retail establishment of cigarettes through self-service display other than coin operated machine — Infraction — Disposition of civil penalties.

(a) As used in this section, "self-service display" means a display that contains cigarettes in an area where a customer:

(1) is permitted; and

(2) has access to the cigarettes without assistance from a sales person.

(b) This section does not apply to a self-service display located in a retail establishment that:

(1) has a primary purpose to sell cigarettes; and

(2) prohibits entry by persons who are less than eighteen (18) years of age.

(c) The owner of a retail establishment that sells or distributes cigarettes through a self-service display, other than a coin operated machine operated under IC 35-46-1-11 or IC 35-46-1-11.5, commits a Class C infraction.

(d) Notwithstanding IC 34-28-5-5(c), civil penalties collected under this section must be deposited in the Richard D. Doyle youth tobacco education and enforcement fund (IC 7.1-6-2-6).

History.
P.L.37-2007, § 1, eff. July 1, 2007.

Cross References.
Infraction and ordinance violation enforcement
proceedings, IC 34-28-5.

35-46-1-12. Exploitation of dependent or endangered adult.

(a) Except as provided in subsection (b), a person who recklessly, knowingly, or intentionally exerts unauthorized use of the personal services or the property of:

(1) an endangered adult; or

(2) a dependent eighteen (18) years of age or older;

for the person's own profit or advantage or for the profit or advantage of another person commits exploitation of a dependent or an endangered adult, a Class A misdemeanor.

(b) The offense described in subsection (a) is a Class D felony if:

(1) the fair market value of the personal services or property is more than ten thousand dollars ($10,000); or

(2) the endangered adult or dependent is at least sixty (60) years of age.

(c) Except as provided in subsection (d), a person who recklessly, knowingly, or intentionally deprives an endangered adult or a dependent of the proceeds of the endangered adult's or the dependent's benefits under the Social Security Act or other retirement program that the division of family resources has budgeted for the endangered adult's or dependent's health care commits financial exploitation of an endangered adult or a dependent, a Class A misdemeanor.

(d) The offense described in subsection (c) is a Class D felony if:

(1) the amount of the proceeds is more than ten thousand dollars ($10,000); or

(2) the endangered adult or dependent is at least sixty (60) years of age.

(e) It is not a defense to an offense committed under subsection (b)(2) or (d)(2) that the accused person reasonably believed that the endangered adult or dependent was less than sixty (60) years of age at the time of the offense.

(f) It is a defense to an offense committed under subsection (a), (b), or (c) if the accused person:

(1) has been granted a durable power of attorney or has been appointed a legal guardian to manage the affairs of an endangered adult or a dependent; and

(2) was acting within the scope of the accused person's fiduciary responsibility.

History.

IC 35-46-1-12, as added by Acts 1981, P.L.299, § 3; P.L.185-1984, § 3; P.L.37-1990, § 26; P.L.2-1992, § 883; P.L.4-1993, § 327; P.L.5-1993, § 334; P.L.145-2001, § 1; P.L.145-2006, § 372; P.L.146-2008, § 684, emergency eff. March 19, 2008.

Cross References.

Penalties for felonies, IC 35-50-1, IC 35-50-2, IC 35-50-5-2.

Penalties for misdemeanors, IC 35-50-1, IC 35-50-3, IC 35-50-5-2.

NOTES TO DECISIONS

ANALYSIS

Evidence.
Theft Distinguished.

Evidence.

The evidence supported defendant's conviction for exploiting an endangered adult where defendant recklessly, knowingly, or intentionally deprived the victim of her property for defendant's own advantage. Edwards v. State, 730 N.E.2d 1286, 2000 Ind. App. LEXIS 1056 (2000).

Theft Distinguished.

The theft statute and the exploitation statute differ in their culpability requirements, theft requiring knowing or intentional conduct, but this section may be violated by knowing, intentional, or reckless conduct. Edwards v. State, 730 N.E.2d 1286, 2000 Ind. App. LEXIS 1056 (2000).

Verdicts were not inconsistent where the jury found that defendant did not intend to deprive the victim of any value or use of the victim's property, but that defendant did exercise control for her own profit or advantage or the profit or advantage of another, and therefore, found defendant guilty of exploitation of an endangered adult, but not guilty of theft. Edwards v. State, 724 N.E.2d 616, 2000 Ind. App. LEXIS 207 (2000).

35-46-1-13. Endangered adult — Failure to report battery, neglect or exploitation — Unlawful disclosure of information — Communication of report to adult protective services unit.

(a) A person who:

(1) believes or has reason to believe that an endangered adult is the victim of battery, neglect, or exploitation as prohibited by this chapter, IC 35-42-2-1(a)(2)(C), or IC 35-42-2-1(a)(2)(E); and

(2) knowingly fails to report the facts supporting that belief to the division of disability and rehabilitative services, the division of aging, the adult protective services unit designated under IC 12-10-3, or a law enforcement agency having jurisdiction over battery, neglect, or exploitation of an endangered adult; commits a Class B misdemeanor.

(b) An officer or employee of the division or adult protective services unit who unlawfully discloses information contained in the records of the division of aging under IC 12-10-3-12 through IC 12-10-3-16 commits a Class C infraction.

(c) A law enforcement agency that receives a report that an endangered adult is or may be a victim of battery, neglect, or exploitation as prohibited by this chapter, IC 35-42-2-1(a)(2)(C), or IC 35-42-2-1(a)(2)(E) shall immediately communicate the report to the adult protective services unit designated under IC 12-10-3.

(d) An individual who discharges, demotes, transfers, prepares a negative work performance evaluation, reduces benefits, pay, or work privileges, or takes other action to retaliate against an individual who in good faith makes a report under IC 12-10-3-9 concerning an endangered individual commits a Class A infraction.

History.

IC 35-46-1-13, as added by Acts 1981, P.L.299, § 4; P.L.185-1984, § 4; P.L.39-1985, § 3; P.L.41-1987, § 20; P.L.42-1987, § 14; P.L.2-1992, § 884; P.L.4-1993, § 328; P.L.5-1993, § 335; P.L.2-1997, § 75; P.L.281-2003, § 4; P.L.141-2006, § 112.

Cross References.

Infraction and ordinance violation enforcement proceedings, IC 34-28-5.

Penalties for misdemeanors, IC 35-50-1, IC 35-50-3, IC 35-50-5-2.

NOTES TO DECISIONS

ANALYSIS

Discharge of Patient to Care of Suspected Abuser.
Standard of Conduct.

Discharge of Patient to Care of Suspected Abuser.

Duty not to discharge a patient to the care of a suspected abuser may sometimes be included in a hospital's general duty of care toward a patient, or in the alternative may arise by virtue of requirements to report abuse of certain endangered adults under IC 35-46-1-13. McSwane v. Bloomington Hosp. & Healthcare Sys., 882 N.E.2d 244, 2008 Ind. App. LEXIS 495 (2008).

Where a decedent was killed by her ex-husband after being released into his care by a hospital, it was error to grant summary judgment to the hospital; under its statutory reporting duty under IC 35-46-1-13, a hospital might have a duty not to release a patient to the care of a suspected abuser, and because the decedent had been given opiates

and other medications and was advised not to make any important decisions, this gave rise to an issue of fact as to whether she was an endangered adult under IC 12-10-3-2(b). McSwane v. Bloomington Hosp. & Healthcare Sys., 882 N.E.2d 244, 2008 Ind. App. LEXIS 495 (2008).

Standard of Conduct.

Courts may adopt as the standard of conduct of a reasonable man the requirements of a legislative enactment or an administrative regulation whose purpose is found to be exclusively or in part (a) to protect a class of persons that includes the one whose interest is invaded, (b) to protect the particular interest which is invaded, (c) to protect that interest against the kind of harm which has resulted and (d) to protect that interest against the particular hazard from which the harm results; IC 35-46-1-13 meets that standard. McSwane v. Bloomington Hosp. & Healthcare Sys., 882 N.E.2d 244, 2008 Ind. App. LEXIS 495 (2008).

35-46-1-14. Immunity from civil or criminal liability — Exceptions.

Any person acting in good faith who:

(1) makes or causes to be made a report of neglect, battery, or exploitation under this chapter, IC 35-42-2-1(a)(2)(C), or IC 35-42-2-1(a)(2)(E);

(2) makes or causes to be made photographs or x-rays of a victim of suspected neglect or battery of an endangered adult or a dependent eighteen (18) years of age or older; or

(3) participates in any official proceeding or a proceeding resulting from a report of neglect, battery, or exploitation of an endangered adult or a dependent eighteen (18) years of age or older relating to the subject matter of that report; is immune from any civil or criminal liability that might otherwise be imposed because of these actions. However, this section does not apply to a person accused of neglect, battery, or exploitation of an endangered adult or a dependent eighteen (18) years of age or older.

History.
IC 35-46-1-14, as added by Acts 1981, P.L.299, § 5; P.L.185-1984, § 5; P.L.2-1997, § 76; P.L.2-1998, § 81; P.L.2-2005, § 127.

35-46-1-15. [Repealed.]

Compiler's Notes.
This section, concerning invasion of privacy, was repealed by P.L.1-1991, § 200, effective April 23, 1991. For present similar provisions, see IC 35-46-1-15.1.

35-46-1-15.1. Invasion of privacy.

A person who knowingly or intentionally violates:

(1) a protective order to prevent domestic or family violence issued under IC 34-26-5 (or, if the order involved a family or household member, under IC 34-26-2 or IC 34-4-5.1-5 before their repeal);

(2) an ex parte protective order issued under IC 34-26-5 (or, if the order involved a family or household member, an emergency order issued under IC 34-26-2 or IC 34-4-5.1 before their repeal);

(3) a workplace violence restraining order issued under IC 34-26-6;

(4) a no contact order in a dispositional decree issued under IC 31-34-20-1, IC 31-37-19-1, or IC 31-37-5-6 (or IC 31-6-4-15.4 or IC 31-6-4-15.9 before their repeal) or an order issued under IC 31-32-13 (or IC 31-6-7-14 before its repeal) that orders the person to refrain from direct or indirect contact with a child in need of services or a delinquent child;

(5) a no contact order issued as a condition of pretrial release, including release on bail or personal recognizance, or pretrial diversion;

(6) a no contact order issued as a condition of probation;

(7) a protective order to prevent domestic or family violence issued under IC 31-15-5 (or IC 31-16-5 or IC 31-1-11.5-8.2 before their repeal);

(8) a protective order to prevent domestic or family violence issued under IC 31-14-16-1 in a paternity action;

(9) a no contact order issued under IC 31-34-25 in a child in need of services proceeding or under IC 31-37-25 in a juvenile delinquency proceeding;

(10) an order issued in another state that is substantially similar to an order described in subdivisions (1) through (9);

(11) an order that is substantially similar to an order described in subdivisions (1) through (9) and is issued by an Indian:

(A) tribe;

(B) band;

(C) pueblo;

(D) nation; or

(E) organized group or community, including an Alaska Native village or regional or village corporation as defined in or established under the Alaska Native Claims Settlement Act (43 U.S.C. 1601 et seq.);

that is recognized as eligible for the special programs and services provided by the United States to Indians because of their special status as Indians;

(12) an order issued under IC 35-33-8-3.2; or

(13) an order issued under IC 35-38-1-30;

commits invasion of privacy, a Class A misdemeanor. However, the offense is a Class D felony if the person has a prior unrelated conviction for an offense under this section.

History.
P.L.1-1991, § 201; P.L.49-1993, § 14, P.L.242-1993, § 5; P.L.1-1994, § 170; P.L.23-1994, § 17; P.L.303-1995, § 1; P.L.1-1997, § 153; P.L.37-1997, § 3; P.L.1-1998, § 199; P.L.280-2001, § 53; P.L.1-2002, § 150; P.L.133-2002, § 67; P.L.104-2008, § 22, emergency eff. July 1, 2008.

NOTES TO DECISIONS

ANALYSIS

Double Jeopardy.
—Battery.
—Civil Contempt.
—Stalking.
Evidence.
—Sufficient.
—Insufficient.
Probable Cause.

Double Jeopardy.

—Battery.
For double jeopardy purposes, battery is not the same offense as invasion of privacy, and there was no constitutional barrier to imposing consecutive sentences for each of these offenses. Fulk v. State, 686 N.E.2d 165, 1997 Ind. App. LEXIS 1498 (1997).

—Civil Contempt.
Because contempt court stayed sentence of defendant to jail time pending defendant's compliance with the terms of restraining order and court imposed conditions, the contempt court's sentence was a civil contempt sanction, and, therefore, not punitive in nature but coercive, and did not constitute a jeopardy for double jeopardy analysis, so that subsequent invasion of privacy charge did not constitute double jeopardy. Webster v. State, 673 N.E.2d 509, 1996 Ind. App. LEXIS 1591 (1996).

—Stalking.
The offenses of stalking and invasion of privacy required proof of different facts and were not the same for double jeopardy purposes; stalking required proof that the perpetrator entertained the intent to cause another to feel terrorized, frightened, intimidated or threatened, and invasion of privacy required proof the defendant violated a

Double Jeopardy. (Cont'd)

—Stalking. (Cont'd)
protective order issued under former IC 34-4-5.1. Burton v. State, 665 N.E.2d 924, 1996 Ind. App. LEXIS 718 (1996).

The manner in which the offenses of stalking and invasion of privacy were charged relieved the state of proving additional facts to gain defendant's conviction for invasion of privacy beyond those required to prove stalking conviction, and therefore convictions for both offenses was barred by double jeopardy principles. Burton v. State, 665 N.E.2d 924, 1996 Ind. App. LEXIS 718 (1996).

Evidence.

—Sufficient.
Where defendant had knowledge of emergency protective order from family of victim and from police officer who told defendant of the emergency protective order and the parameters of the order, and the next day came within 1,000 feet of victim in violation of the order, the evidence was sufficient that defendant knowingly violated the order. Hendricks v. State, 649 N.E.2d 1050, 1995 Ind. App. LEXIS 437 (1995).

The evidence was sufficient that defendant contacted the victim's family in violation of the permanent protective order even though the telephone calls were made collect and the charges were refused. Hendricks v. State, 649 N.E.2d 1050, 1995 Ind. App. LEXIS 437 (1995).

There was sufficient evidence to support defendant's conviction of invasion of privacy under IC 35-46-1-15.1(1) when an officer had explicitly given defendant oral notice of a protective order that ordered defendant to stay away from the wife's residence. Even if the wife had consented to defendant's presence, this did not negate any element of the offense; moreover, IC 34-26-5-11 stated that an invitation by a petitioner who obtained a protec-tive order did not waive or nullify the order. Dixon v. State, 869 N.E.2d 516, 2007 Ind. App. LEXIS 1496 (2007).

—Insufficient.
Where defendant's wife had obtained protective order against him, defendant's request to domestic violence advocate to contact wife for him was insufficient to support conviction for invasion of privacy where there was no evidence that advocate actually contacted wife on defendant's behalf. Huber v. State, 805 N.E.2d 887, 2004 Ind. App. LEXIS 573 (2004).

Probable Cause.
Denial of defendant's motion to suppress evidence was proper where the officer had knowledge of facts and circumstances that would have warranted a person of reasonable caution to believe that defendant had committed an invasion of privacy; a protective order had been issued barring defendant from abusing, harassing, or disturbing the peace of a 16-year-old female, and she was in the back seat of a vehicle in which he was a passenger. Winebrenner v. State, 790 N.E.2d 1037, 2003 Ind. App. LEXIS 1195 (2003).

Police officers were entitled to summary judgment based on doctrine of qualified immunity in plaintiff's 42 U.S.C.S. § 1983 action alleging false arrest; officers' knowledge that emergency protective order had been issued against plaintiff and that plaintiff continued to violate protective order by driving by victim's house in violation of IC 35-46-1-15.1 constituted probable cause for arrest. Howell v. Clapp, — F. Supp. 2d —, 2004 U.S. Dist. LEXIS 2441 (S.D. Ind. 2004).

Cited:
Carter v. Johnson, 745 N.E.2d 237, 2001 Ind. App. LEXIS 301 (2001).

35-46-1-16. Maintenance of confidential information relating to persons convicted under IC 35-46-1-15.1.

The law enforcement agency with custody of a person who is sentenced to a term of imprisonment of more than ten (10) days following conviction of a crime under section 15.1 [IC 35-46-1-15.1] of this chapter shall maintain a confidential record of the:

(1) Name;

(2) Address; and

(3) Telephone number;

of each person that the person convicted under section 15.1 of this chapter is required to refrain from direct or indirect contact with under an order described by section 15.1 of this chapter.

History.
P.L.53-1989, § 10; P.L.1-1991, § 202.

35-46-1-17. Restrictions on access to confidential information maintained under IC 35-46-1-16.

A person convicted of a crime under section 15.1 [IC 35-46-1-15.1] of this chapter may not have access to the information maintained under section 16 [IC 35-46-1-16] of this chapter.

History.
  P.L.53-1989, § 11; P.L.1-1991, § 203.

35-46-1-18. Notice of release of or hearing for persons convicted under IC 35-46-1-15.1.

The law enforcement agency having custody of a person who is sentenced to a term of imprisonment of more than ten (10) days following conviction of a crime under section 15.1 [IC 35-46-1-15.1] of this chapter shall:
  (1) Provide each person described in section 16 [IC 35-46-1-16] of this chapter with written notification of:
    (A) The release of a person convicted of a crime under section 15.1 of this chapter; and
    (B) The date, time, and place of any substantive hearing concerning a violation of section 15.1 of this chapter by a person who is sentenced to a term of imprisonment of more than ten (10) days following conviction of a crime under section 15.1 of this chapter; and
  (2) Attempt to notify each person described in section 16 of this chapter by telephone to provide the information described in subdivision (1).

History.
  P.L.53-1989, § 12; P.L.1-1991, § 204.

35-46-1-19. Time limit for providing notice under IC 35-46-1-18.

The law enforcement agency shall:
  (1) Provide written notice; and
  (2) Attempt notification by telephone;
under section 18 [IC 35-46-1-18] of this chapter at least twenty-four (24) hours before the release or hearing.

History.
  P.L.53-1989, § 13.

35-46-1-20. Enforcement of foreign protection order.

A law enforcement officer shall enforce a foreign protection order (as defined in IC 34-6-2-48.5) in conformity with the procedures in IC 34-26-5-17.

History.
  P.L.280-2001, § 54; P.L.133-2002, § 68.

35-46-1-21. Unauthorized adoption advertising.

(a) Only a person that is an attorney licensed to practice law or a child placing agency licensed under the laws of any state or the District of Columbia may place a paid advertisement or paid listing of the person's telephone number, on the person's own behalf, in a telephone directory that:
  (1) a child is offered or wanted for adoption; or
  (2) the person is able to place, locate, or receive a child for adoption.
(b) A person that publishes a telephone directory that is distributed in Indiana:
  (1) shall include, at the beginning of any classified heading for adoption and adoption services, a statement that informs directory users that only attorneys licensed to practice law and licensed child placing agencies may legally provide adoption services under Indiana law; and

(2) may publish an advertisement described in subsection (a) in the telephone directory only if the advertisement contains the following:

(A) For an attorney licensed to practice law, the person's attorney number.

(B) For a child placing agency licensed under the laws of any state or the District of Columbia, the number on the person's child placing agency license.

(c) A person who knowingly or intentionally violates subsection (a) commits unauthorized adoption advertising, a Class A misdemeanor.

History.
P.L.146-2007, § 20, eff. July 1, 2007.

by this act, apply only to crimes committed after June 30, 2007."

Compiler's Notes.
P.L.146-2007, § 22, effective July 1, 2007, provides:
"IC 35-46-1-21 and IC 35-46-1-22, both as added

Cross References.
Penalties for misdemeanors, IC 35-50-1, IC 35-50-3, IC 35-50-5-2.

35-46-1-22. Unauthorized adoption facilitation.

(a) As used in this section, "adoption services" means at least one (1) of the following services that is provided for compensation, an item of value, or reimbursement, either directly or indirectly, and provided either before or after the services are rendered:

(1) Arranging for the placement of a child.

(2) Identifying a child for adoption.

(3) Matching adoptive parents with biological parents.

(4) Arranging or facilitating an adoption.

(5) Taking or acknowledging consents or surrenders for termination of parental rights for adoption purposes.

(6) Performing background studies on:

(A) a child who is going to be adopted; or

(B) adoptive parents.

(7) Making determinations concerning the best interests of a child and the appropriateness in placing the child for adoption.

(8) Postplacement monitoring of a child before the child is adopted.

(b) As used in this section, the term "adoption services" does not include the following:

(1) Legal services provided by an attorney licensed in Indiana.

(2) Adoption related services provided by a governmental entity or a person appointed to perform an investigation by the court.

(3) General education and training on adoption issues.

(4) Postadoption services, including supportive services to families to promote the well-being of members of adoptive families or birth families.

(c) This section does not apply to the following persons:

(1) The department of child services, an agency or person authorized to act on behalf of the department of child services, or a similar agency or county office with similar responsibilities in another state.

(2) The division of family resources, an agency or person authorized to act on behalf of the division of family resources, or a similar agency or county office with similar responsibilities in another state.

(3) A child placing agency licensed under the laws of Indiana or another state.

(4) An attorney licensed to practice law in Indiana or another state.

(5) A prospective biological parent or adoptive parent acting on the individual's own behalf.

(d) A person who knowingly or intentionally provides, engages in, or facilitates adoption services to a birth parent or prospective adoptive parent who resides in Indiana commits unauthorized adoption facilitation, a Class A misdemeanor.

History.
P.L.146-2007, § 21, eff. July 1, 2007; P.L.146-2008, § 685, emergency eff. March 19, 2008.

Compiler's Notes.
P.L.146-2007, § 22, effective July 1, 2007, provides:

"IC 35-46-1-21 and IC 35-46-1-22, both as added by this act, apply only to crimes committed after June 30, 2007."

CHAPTER 2

OFFENSES RELATING TO CIVIL RIGHTS

35-46-2-1. Civil rights violation.

A person who knowingly or intentionally denies to another person, because of color, creed, disability, national origin, race, religion, or sex, the full and equal use of the services, facilities, or goods in:

(1) An establishment that caters or offers its services, facilities, or goods to the general public; or

(2) A housing project owned or subsidized by a governmental entity;

commits a civil rights violation, a Class B misdemeanor.

History.
IC 35-46-2-1, as added by Acts 1976, P.L.148, § 6; 1977, P.L.340, § 92; P.L.23-1993, § 162.

Cross References.
Blind and disabled persons' rights, IC 16-32-3.
Discrimination because of race, color, religion or national origin, IC 22-9-1-1, IC 22-9-1-2.

Penalties for misdemeanors, IC 35-50-1, IC 35-50-3, IC 35-50-5-2.

Public improvement contracts, race discrimination in employment of labor prohibited, IC 5-16-6-1.

NOTES TO DECISIONS

ANALYSIS

In General.
Evidence.
No Private Cause of Action.

In General.
Denial, on account of race or color, of entertainment at a hotel by the clerk thereof renders the proprietor liable. Fruchey v. Eagleson, 15 Ind. App. 88, 43 N.E. 146, 1896 Ind. App. LEXIS 19 (1896).

Evidence.
In an action by a black woman based upon the contention that she was denied admission to the ground floor of the theater because of her race, evidence that defendant refused plaintiff because he did not like her and because he did not know if she had authority to use the ticket presented by her since it had been purchased by a white person earlier in the day was insufficient as a defense, since it was of such a character that to believe it would involve an absurd and unreasonable conclusion. Bailey v. Washington Theatre Co., 112 Ind. App. 336, 41 N.E.2d 819, 1942 Ind. App. LEXIS 53 (1942).

No Private Cause of Action.
Legislature, by imposing criminal penalty for violation of this section, did not intend it to be enforced through a private cause of action. Right Reason Publs. v. Silva, 691 N.E.2d 1347, 1998 Ind. App. LEXIS 139 (1998).

RESEARCH REFERENCES

Collateral References.
What constitutes private club or association not otherwise open to public that is exempt from state civil rights statute. 83 A.L.R.5th 467.

35-46-2-2. Discrimination in jury selection.

A public servant having the duty to select or summon persons for grand jury or trial jury service who knowingly or intentionally fails to select or summon a person because of color, creed, disability, national origin, race, religion, or sex commits discrimination in jury selection, a Class A misdemeanor.

History.
IC 35-46-2-2, as added by Acts 1976, P.L.148, § 6; 1977, P.L.340, § 93; P.L.23-1993, § 163.

Cross References.
Penalties for misdemeanors, IC 35-50-1, IC 35-50-3, IC 35-50-5-2.

RESEARCH REFERENCES

Collateral References.
Age group underrepresentation in grand jury or petit jury venire. 62 A.L.R.4th 859.

CHAPTER 3

OFFENSES RELATING TO ANIMALS

35-46-3-0.5. Definitions.

The following definitions apply throughout this chapter:

(1) "Abandon" means to desert an animal or to leave the animal permanently in a place without making provision for adequate long term care of the animal. The term does not include leaving an animal in a place that is temporarily vacated for the protection of human life during a disaster.

(2) "Beat" means to unnecessarily or cruelly strike an animal, or to throw the animal against an object causing the animal to suffer severe pain or injury. The term does not include reasonable training or disciplinary techniques.

(3) "Mutilate" means to wound, injure, maim, or disfigure an animal by irreparably damaging the animal's body parts or to render any part of the animal's body useless. The term includes bodily injury involving:

(A) serious permanent disfigurement;

(B) serious temporary disfigurement;

(C) permanent or protracted loss or impairment of the function of a bodily part or organ; or

(D) a fracture.

(4) "Neglect" means:

(A) endangering an animal's health by failing to provide or arrange to provide the animal with food or drink, if the animal is dependent upon the person for the provision of food or drink;

(B) restraining an animal for more than a brief period in a manner that endangers the animal's life or health by the use of a rope, chain, or tether that:

(i) is less than three (3) times the length of the animal;

(ii) is too heavy to permit the animal to move freely; or

(iii) causes the animal to choke;

(C) restraining an animal in a manner that seriously endangers the animal's life or health;

(D) failing to:

(i) provide reasonable care for; or

(ii) seek veterinary care for;

an injury or illness to a dog or cat that seriously endangers the life or health of the dog or cat; or

(E) leaving a dog or cat outside and exposed to:

(i) excessive heat without providing the animal with a means of shade from the heat; or

(ii) excessive cold if the animal is not provided with straw or another means of protection from the cold;

regardless of whether the animal is restrained or kept in a kennel.

(5) "Torture" means:

(A) to inflict extreme physical pain or injury on an animal with the intent of increasing or prolonging the animal's pain; or

(B) to administer poison to a domestic animal (as defined in section 12(d) [IC 35-46-3-12(d)] of this chapter) or expose a domestic animal to a poisonous substance with the intent that the domestic animal ingest the substance and suffer harm, pain, or physical injury.

History.

P.L.171-2007, § 5, eff. July 1, 2007; P.L.111-2009, § 10, eff. July 1, 2009.

Compiler's Notes.

P.L.111-2009, § 15, effective July 1, 2009, provides:

"IC 15-21-2-3, IC 15-21-3-1, and IC 15-21-3-2, all as added by this act, and IC 35-46-3-0.5, IC 35-46-3-7, IC 35-46-3-10, and IC 35-46-3-12, all as amended by this act, apply only to crimes committed after June 30, 2009."

Amendments.

The 2009 amendment added ""or arrange to provide"" in (4)(A); added ""in a manner that endangers the animal's life or health"" in (4)(B); added (4)(C) through (4)(E); deleted ""sole"" following ""animal with the"" in (5)(A); in (5)(B), substituted ""domestic animal"" for ""cat or dog"" wherever it appears and added ""(as defined in section 12(d) of this chapter)""; and made related and stylistic changes.

35-46-3-1. Harboring a non-immunized dog.

A person who knowingly or intentionally harbors a dog that is over the age of six (6) months and not immunized against rabies commits harboring a non-immunized dog, a Class C infraction. However, the offense is a Class B misdemeanor if the dog causes bodily injury by biting a person.

History.

IC 35-46-3-1, as added by Acts 1976, P.L.148, § 6; 1977, P.L.340, § 94.

Cross References.

Infraction and ordinance violation enforcement proceedings, IC 34-28-5.

Penalties for misdemeanors, IC 35-50-1, IC 35-50-3, IC 35-50-5-2.

RESEARCH REFERENCES

Collateral References.
Who "harbors" or "keeps" dog under animal liability statute. 64 A.L.R.4th 963.
Liability of owner or operator of business pre-

mises for injury to patron by dog or cat. 67 A.L.R.4th 976.
Liability for injuries caused by cat. 68 A.L.R.4th 823.

35-46-3-2. [Repealed.]

Compiler's Notes.
This section, relating to cruelty to animals and to animal fighting contests, was repealed by

P.L.193-1987, § 17. For present similar provisions, see IC 35-46-3-3 et seq.

35-46-3-3. "Animal" defined.

As used in this chapter, "animal" does not include a human being.

History.
P.L.193-1987, § 6.

35-46-3-4. "Animal fighting contest" defined.

As used in this chapter, "animal fighting contest" means a conflict between two (2) or more animals. The term does not include a conflict that is unorganized or accidental.

History.
P.L.193-1987, § 7.

35-46-3-4.3. "Animal fighting paraphernalia" defined.

As used in this chapter, "animal fighting paraphernalia" means equipment used to train or condition animals for participation in an animal fighting contest.

History.
P.L.76-2002, § 2.

35-46-3-4.5. Law enforcement animal.

(a) As used in this chapter, "law enforcement animal" means an animal that is owned or used by a law enforcement agency for the principal purposes of:
　(1) aiding in:
　　(A) the detection of criminal activity;
　　(B) the enforcement of laws; and
　　(C) the apprehension of offenders; and
　(2) ensuring the public welfare.
(b) The term includes, but is not limited to, the following:
　(1) A horse.
　(2) An arson investigation dog.
　(3) A bomb detection dog.
　(4) A narcotic detection dog.
　(5) A patrol dog.

History.
P.L.213-1997, § 2; P.L.9-2003, § 1.

35-46-3-5. Applicability of chapter — Exempt activities — Authorization for destruction of animal by electrocution.

(a) Except as provided in subsections (b) through (c), this chapter does not apply to the following:

(1) Fishing, hunting, trapping, or other conduct authorized under IC 14-22.

(2) Conduct authorized under IC 15-20-2.

(3) Veterinary practices authorized by standards adopted under IC 25-38.1-2-14.

(4) Conduct authorized by a local ordinance.

(5) Acceptable farm management practices.

(6) Conduct authorized by IC 15-17, and rules adopted under IC 15-17 for state or federally inspected livestock slaughtering facilities and state or federal animal disease control programs.

(7) A research facility registered with the United States Department of Agriculture under the federal Animal Welfare Act (7 U.S.C. 2131 et seq.).

(8) Destruction of a vertebrate defined as a pest under IC 15-16-5-24.

(9) Destruction of or injury to a fish.

(10) Destruction of a vertebrate animal that is:

(A) endangering, harassing, or threatening livestock or a domestic animal; or

(B) destroying or damaging a person's property.

(11) Destruction of an animal by an animal control program, including an animal control facility, an animal shelter, or a humane society.

(12) Destruction of an injured or ill animal by an individual to prevent the animal from prolonged suffering.

(13) Conduct not resulting in serious injury or illness to the animal that is incidental to exhibiting an animal for show, competition, or display, or that is incidental to transporting the animal for show, competition, or display.

(14) Parking an animal.

(15) Humane destruction of an animal that the person owns.

(b) Section 1 [IC 35-46-3-1] of this chapter applies to conduct described in subsection (a).

(c) Destruction of an animal by electrocution is authorized under this section only if it is conducted by a person who is engaged in an acceptable farm management practice, by a research facility registered with the United States Department of Agriculture under the Animal Welfare Act, or for the animal disease diagnostic laboratory established under IC 21-46-3-1, a research facility licensed by the United States Department of Agriculture, a college, or a university.

History.

P.L.193-1987, § 8; P.L.2-1993, § 188; P.L.1-1995, § 76; P.L.137-1996, § 74; P.L.41-1998, § 1; P.L.2-2007, § 378, eff. July 1, 2007; P.L.171-2007, § 6, eff. July 1, 2007; P.L.2-2008, § 79, eff. July 1, 2008; P.L.111-2009, § 11, eff. July 1, 2009.

Amendments.

The 2009 amendment, in (a)(6), substituted ""IC 15-17"" for ""IC 15-17-5"" twice and added ""and state or federal animal disease control programs"" and added (a)(11) through (a)(15).

NOTES TO DECISIONS

ANALYSIS

Indictment or Information.
Injury.
Intent.
Name of Owner.

Indictment or Information.

In a charge of cruelty to animals, the method of torture and effect produced should have been stated. State v. Bruner, 111 Ind. 98, 12 N.E. 103, 1887 Ind. LEXIS 219 (1887).

Where each count of an indictment charging cruelty to animals averred in detail the specific acts complained of as constituting such cruelty, and the acts were of such character as to leave it a matter of common knowledge that their effect was necessarily harmful to the animal, the indictment was sufficient without alleging that the acts produced an ill effect. Moore v. State, 183 Ind. 114, 107 N.E. 1, 1914 Ind. LEXIS 186 (1914).

An affidavit (predecessor of information) charging that accused unlawfully inflicted needless cruelty upon dogs by unlawfully and cruelly confining

Indictment or Information. (Cont'd) them in a vehicle which was of insufficient size to accommodate them "without" overcrowding them was not subject to a motion to quash on the ground that the use of the word "without" made the charge uncertain, for the only reasonable interpretation of that part of the affidavit was that defendant inflicted needless cruelty on the dogs by confining them in a vehicle where they were overcrowded. McCloskey v. State, 222 Ind. 514, 53 N.E.2d 1012, 1944 Ind. LEXIS 155 (1944).

Injury.

No particular description of the injury needed to be given; if the charge followed the language of the statute, it was sufficient. State v. Giles, 125 Ind. 124, 25 N.E. 159, 1890 Ind. LEXIS 403 (1890).

Intent.

The killing of an animal in good faith to protect the person or property was not criminal. Hunt v. State, 3 Ind. App. 383, 29 N.E. 933, 1892 Ind. App. LEXIS 26 (1892).

Name of Owner.

In a prosecution for cruelty to animals, the name of the owner did not need to be stated, but, if stated, it should have been proved as alleged. State v. Bruner, 111 Ind. 98, 12 N.E. 103, 1887 Ind. LEXIS 219 (1887).

35-46-3-6. Applicability — Impoundment of animal — Posting bond to recover animal — Investigation by state veterinarian — Additional penalties — Termination of right to possession.

(a) This section does not apply to a violation of section 1 [IC 35-46-3-1] of this chapter.

(b) Any law enforcement officer or any other person having authority to impound animals who has probable cause to believe there has been a violation of this chapter or IC 15-20-1-4 may take custody of the animal involved.

(c) The owner of an animal that has been impounded under this section may prevent disposition of the animal by an animal shelter that is caring for the animal by posting, not later than ten (10) days after the animal has been impounded, a bond with the court in an amount sufficient to provide for the animal's care and keeping for at least thirty (30) days, beginning from the date the animal was impounded. The owner may renew a bond by posting a new bond, in an amount sufficient to provide for the animal's care and keeping for at least an additional thirty (30) days, not later than ten (10) days after the expiration of the period for which a previous bond was posted. If a bond expires and is not renewed, the animal shelter may determine disposition of the animal, subject to court order. If the owner of an animal impounded under this section is convicted of an offense under this chapter or IC 15-20-1-4, the owner shall reimburse the animal shelter for the expense of the animal's care and keeping. If the owner has paid a bond under this subsection, the animal shelter may euthanize an animal if a veterinarian determines that an animal is suffering extreme pain.

(d) If the owner requests, the court having jurisdiction of criminal charges filed under this chapter or IC 15-20-1 shall hold a hearing to determine whether probable cause exists to believe that a violation of this chapter or IC 15-20-1 has occurred. If the court determines that probable cause does not exist, the court shall order the animal returned to its owner, and the return of any bond posted by its owner.

(e) Whenever charges are filed under this chapter, the court shall appoint the state veterinarian under IC 15-17-4-1 or the state veterinarian's designee to:

(1) investigate the condition of the animal and the circumstances relating to the animal's condition; and

(2) make a recommendation to the court under subsection (f) regarding the confiscation of the animal.

(f) The state veterinarian or the state veterinarian's designee who is appointed under subsection (e) shall do the following:

(1) Make a recommendation to the court concerning whether confiscation is necessary to protect the safety and well-being of the animal.

(2) If confiscation is recommended under subdivision (1), recommend a manner for handling the confiscation and disposition of the animal that is in the best interests of the animal.

The state veterinarian or the state veterinarian's designee who submits a recommendation under this subsection shall articulate to the court the reasons supporting the recommendation.

(g) The court:

(1) shall give substantial weight to; and

(2) may enter an order based upon;

a recommendation submitted under subsection (f).

(h) If a person is convicted of an offense under this chapter or IC 15-20-1, the court may impose the following additional penalties against the person:

(1) A requirement that the person pay the costs of caring for an animal involved in the offenses that are incurred during a period of impoundment authorized under subsection (b).

(2) An order terminating or imposing conditions on the person's right to possession, title, custody, or care of:

(A) an animal that was involved in the offense; or

(B) any other animal in the custody or care of the person.

(i) If a person's right to possession, title, custody, or care of an animal is terminated under subsection (h), the court may:

(1) award the animal to a humane society or other organization that has as its principal purpose the humane treatment of animals; or

(2) order the disposition of the animal as recommended under subsection (f).

History.
P.L.193-1987, § 9; P.L.166-1993, § 5; P.L.176-1993, § 6; P.L.14-2000, § 75; P.L.76-2002, § 3;

P.L.171-2007, § 7, eff. July 1, 2007; P.L.2-2008, § 80, eff. July 1, 2008.

NOTES TO DECISIONS

ANALYSIS

Costs of Caring for Animals.
Sale of Seized Animals.
Seizure of neglected animals.

Costs of Caring for Animals.
The trial court did not err in ordering the owner to pay for labor and materials to construct structures for the maintenance of horses and for veterinary bills while they were in the custody and care of the county. Lykins v. State, 726 N.E.2d 1265, 2000 Ind. App. LEXIS 564 (2000).

Sale of Seized Animals.
Owner of cattle had no cause of action against

police officer who seized allegedly neglected cattle pursuant to a warrant, where the police had no facilities to care for the cattle, which were sold by the individual caretakers to satisfy liens against the owner for caretaking costs. Campbell v. Chappelow, 95 F.3d 576, 1996 U.S. App. LEXIS 23467 (7th Cir. Ind. 1996).

Seizure of neglected animals.
In an action charging defendant with animal neglect, it was wholly appropriate for animal control to intervene for the limited purpose of opposing defendant's request to sell the animals in clear contravention of IC 35-46-3-6. Baxter v. State, 891 N.E.2d 110, 2008 Ind. App. LEXIS 1671 (2008).

35-46-3-7. Abandonment or neglect of vertebrate animal — Defense.

(a) A person who:

(1) has a vertebrate animal in the person's custody; and

(2) recklessly, knowingly, or intentionally abandons or neglects the animal;

commits cruelty to an animal, a Class A misdemeanor. However, except for a conviction under section 1 [IC 35-46-3-1] of this chapter, the offense is a Class D felony if the person has a prior unrelated conviction under this chapter.

(b) It is a defense to a prosecution for abandoning a vertebrate animal under this section that the person who had the animal in the person's custody reasonably believed that the vertebrate animal was capable of surviving on its own.

(c) For purposes of this section, an animal that is feral is not in a person's custody.

History.
P.L.193-1987, § 10; P.L.171-2007, § 8, eff. July 1, 2007; P.L.111-2009, § 12, eff. July 1, 2009.

Compiler's Notes.
P.L.111-2009, § 15, effective July 1, 2009, provides:
"IC 15-21-2-3, IC 15-21-3-1, and IC 15-21-3-2, all as added by this act, and IC 35-46-3-0.5, IC 35-46-3-7, IC 35-46-3-10, and IC 35-46-3-12, all as amended by this act, apply only to crimes committed after June 30, 2009."

Amendments.
The 2009 amendment added the (a)(1) and (a)(2)

designations; added ""in the person's custody"" in (a)(1); in the concluding language of (a), substituted ""Class A misdemeanor"" for ""Class B misdemeanor"" in the first sentence and added the second sentence; in (b), added ""for abandoning a vertebrate animal"" and substituted ""person who had the animal in the person's custody"" for ""owner""; added (c); and made stylistic changes.

Cross References.
Penalties for felonies, IC 35-50-1, IC 35-50-2, IC 35-50-5-2.
Penalties for misdemeanors, IC 35-50-1, IC 35-50-3, IC 35-50-5-2.

NOTES TO DECISIONS

ANALYSIS

Evidence.
Sale of Seized Animals.

Evidence.
Evidence was sufficient to support a conviction of cruelty to an animal where it was shown that the defendant kept animals in an inhumanely hot environment, that the animals were not properly inoculated and were confined without adequate food or water. Reynolds v. State, 569 N.E.2d 680, 1991 Ind. App. LEXIS 559 (1991).

The jury could have inferred beyond a reasonable doubt from the facts set forth at trial that the owner knowingly, recklessly, or intentionally, neglected three horses. Lykins v. State, 726 N.E.2d 1265, 2000 Ind. App. LEXIS 564 (2000).

Evidence of a dog's starved appearance, injured leg, and frost bitten extremities was sufficient to allow the trial judge to infer that defendant failed

to feed and care for the dog. Trimble v. State, 848 N.E.2d 278, 2006 Ind. LEXIS 423 (2006).

Evidence was not sufficient to support convictions for four counts of Class B misdemeanor neglect of an animal with regard to four dead horses because the state failed to present evidence as to the cause of death of the four dead horses. Baxter v. State, 891 N.E.2d 110, 2008 Ind. App. LEXIS 1671 (2008).

Sale of Seized Animals.
Owner of cattle had no cause of action against police officer who seized allegedly neglected cattle pursuant to a warrant, where the police had no facilities to care for the cattle, which were sold by the individual caretakers to satisfy liens against the owner for caretaking costs. Campbell v. Chappelow, 95 F.3d 576, 1996 U.S. App. LEXIS 23467 (7th Cir. Ind. 1996).

RESEARCH REFERENCES

Collateral References.
What constitutes offense of cruelty to animals — modern cases. 6 A.L.R.5th 733.

35-46-3-8. Possession of animal for purposes of animal fighting contest.

A person who knowingly or intentionally purchases or possesses an animal for the purpose of using the animal in an animal fighting contest commits a Class D felony.

History.
P.L.193-1987, § 11; P.L.171-2007, § 9, eff. July 1, 2007.

Compiler's Notes.
P.L.171-2007, § 13, effective July 1, 2007, provides:
"(a) Except as provided in subsection (b), IC 35-46-3-8 and IC 35-46-3-12, both as amended by this act, and IC 35-46-3-12.5 and IC 35-46-3-14, both as added by this act, apply only to crimes committed after June 30, 2007.

"(b) IC 35-46-3-12(d), as amended by this act, applies only to:
"(1) crimes; and
"(2) delinquent acts that would be crimes if committed by an adult;
"that are committed after June 30, 2007."

Cross References.
Penalties for felonies, IC 35-50-1, IC 35-50-2, IC 35-50-5-2.

35-46-3-8.5. Possession of animal fighting paraphernalia.

A person who knowingly or intentionally possesses animal fighting paraphernalia with the intent to commit a violation of IC 35-46-3-9 commits possession of animal fighting paraphernalia, a Class B misdemeanor. However, the offense is a Class A misdemeanor if the person has a prior unrelated conviction under this section.

History.
P.L.76-2002, § 4.

Cross References.
Penalties for misdemeanors, IC 35-50-1, IC 35-50-3, IC 35-50-5-2.

35-46-3-9. Animal fighting contests prohibited.

A person who knowingly or intentionally:
    (1) Promotes or stages an animal fighting contest;
    (2) Uses an animal in a fighting contest; or
    (3) Attends an animal fighting contest having an animal in the person's possession;
commits a Class D felony.

History.
P.L.193-1987, § 12.

Cross References.
Penalties for felonies, IC 35-50-1, IC 35-50-2, IC 35-50-5-2.

NOTES TO DECISIONS

ANALYSIS

Evidence.
—Knowledge.
—Sufficient.

Evidence.

—Knowledge.
Where defendant was charged with promoting or staging an animal fighting contest and using an animal in a fighting contest, and defendant stated he had no knowledge of dogs fighting on his property or how dogs became injured, explaining dogs must have been wounded by accident, the court properly admitted evidence of an injured dog and several dead dogs found on defendant's property to prove knowledge or lack of accident. Fuller v. State, 674 N.E.2d 576, 1996 Ind. App. LEXIS 1858 (1996).

—Sufficient.
Evidence of dog fighting was sufficient, where blood stains, dead animals, and two men holding dogs in an apparent ready position for a fight where found on defendant's property, a witness testified defendant owned one of the wounded dogs, and there was expert testimony injuries to dog were from a fighting contest. Fuller v. State, 674 N.E.2d 576, 1996 Ind. App. LEXIS 1858 (1996).

35-46-3-9.5. Promoting an animal fighting contest.

A person who knowingly or intentionally:
    (1) possesses animal fighting paraphernalia with the intent to commit a violation of IC 35-46-3-9; and
    (2) possesses, harbors, or trains a dog, cock, fowl, or bird bearing:
        (A) a scar;
        (B) a wound; or
        (C) an injury;
consistent with participation in or training for an animal fighting contest;
commits promoting an animal fighting contest, a Class D felony.

History.
P.L.76-2002, § 5.

Cross References.
Penalties for felonies, IC 35-50-1, IC 35-50-2, IC 35-50-5-2.

35-46-3-10. Attending animal fighting contest prohibited.

A person who knowingly or intentionally attends a fighting contest involving animals commits cruelty to an animal, a Class A misdemeanor. However, except for a conviction under section 1 [IC 35-46-3-1] of this chapter, the offense is a Class D felony if the person has a prior unrelated conviction under this chapter.

History.
P.L.193-1987, § 13; P.L.111-2009, § 13, eff. July 1, 2009.

Compiler's Notes.
P.L.111-2009, § 15, effective July 1, 2009, provides:
"IC 15-21-2-3, IC 15-21-3-1, and IC 15-21-3-2, all as added by this act, and IC 35-46-3-0.5, IC 35-46-3-7, IC 35-46-3-10, and IC 35-46-3-12, all as amended by this act, apply only to crimes committed after June 30, 2009."

Amendments.
The 2009 amendment added the second sentence.

Cross References.
Penalties for felonies, IC 35-50-1, IC 35-50-2, IC 35-50-5-2.
Penalties for misdemeanors, IC 35-50-1, IC 35-50-3, IC 35-50-5-2.

35-46-3-11. Law enforcement animal — Mistreatment — Interference with official duties — Restitution.

(a) A person who knowingly or intentionally:
(1) strikes, torments, injures, or otherwise mistreats a law enforcement animal; or
(2) interferes with the actions of a law enforcement animal while the animal is engaged in assisting a law enforcement officer in the performance of the officer's duties;
commits a Class A misdemeanor.
(b) An offense under subsection (a)(1) is a Class D felony if the act results in:
(1) serious permanent disfigurement;
(2) unconsciousness;
(3) permanent or protracted loss or impairment of the function of a bodily member or organ; or
(4) death;
of the law enforcement animal.
(c) It is a defense that the accused person:
(1) engaged in a reasonable act of training, handling, or discipline; and
(2) acted as an employee or agent of a law enforcement agency.
(d) In addition to any sentence or fine imposed for a conviction of an offense under this section, the court may order the person convicted to make restitution to the person or law enforcement agency owning the animal for reimbursement of:
(1) veterinary bills; and
(2) replacement costs of the animal if the animal is disabled or killed.

History.
P.L.193-1987, § 14; P.L.213-1997, § 3; P.L.9-2003, § 2.

Penalties for misdemeanors, IC 35-50-1, IC 35-50-3, IC 35-50-5-2.

Cross References.
Penalties for felonies, IC 35-50-1, IC 35-50-2, IC 35-50-5-2.

35-46-3-11.3. Search and rescue dog — Interference with or mistreatment — Defenses — Restitution.

(a) As used in this section, "search and rescue dog" means a dog that receives special training to locate or attempt to locate by air scent or ground or water tracking a person who is an offender or is lost, trapped, injured, or incapacitated.

(b) A person who knowingly or intentionally:

(1) interferes with the actions of a search and rescue dog while the dog is performing or is attempting to perform a search and rescue task; or

(2) strikes, torments, injures, or otherwise mistreats a search and rescue dog;

commits a Class A misdemeanor.

(c) An offense under subsection (b)(2) is a Class D felony if the act results in:

(1) serious permanent disfigurement;

(2) unconsciousness;

(3) permanent or protracted loss or impairment of the function of a bodily member or organ; or

(4) death;

of the search and rescue dog.

(d) It is a defense that the accused person:

(1) engaged in a reasonable act of training, handling, or disciplining the search and rescue dog; or

(2) reasonably believed the conduct was necessary to prevent injury to the accused person or another person.

(e) In addition to any sentence or fine imposed for a conviction of an offense under this section, the court may order the person to make restitution to the person who owns the search and rescue dog for reimbursement of:

(1) veterinary bills; and

(2) replacement costs of the dog if the dog is disabled or killed.

History.
P.L.9-2003, § 3.

Penalties for misdemeanors, IC 35-50-1, IC 35-50-3, IC 35-50-5-2.

Cross References.
Penalties for felonies, IC 35-50-1, IC 35-50-2, IC 35-50-5-2.

35-46-3-11.5. Service animal — Interference with assistance to impaired persons — Penalty — Defenses.

(a) As used in this section, "service animal" means an animal that a person who is impaired by:

(1) blindness or any other visual impairment;

(2) deafness or any other aural impairment;

(3) a physical disability; or

(4) a medical condition;

relies on for navigation, assistance in performing daily activities, or alert signals regarding the onset of the person's medical condition.

(b) A person who knowingly or intentionally:

(1) interferes with the actions of a service animal; or

(2) strikes, torments, injures, or otherwise mistreats a service animal;

while the service animal is engaged in assisting an impaired person described in subsection (a) commits a Class A misdemeanor.

(c) An offense under subsection (b)(2) is a Class D felony if the act results in the:

(1) serious permanent disfigurement;

(2) unconsciousness;

(3) permanent or protracted loss or impairment of the function of a bodily member or organ; or

(4) death;

of the service animal.

(d) It is a defense that the accused person:

(1) engaged in a reasonable act of training, handling, or disciplining the service animal; or

(2) reasonably believed the conduct was necessary to prevent injury to the accused person or another person.

History.
P.L.143-1996, § 2; P.L.9-2003, § 4.

Cross References.
Penalties for felonies, IC 35-50-1, IC 35-50-2, IC 35-50-5-2.

Penalties for misdemeanors, IC 35-50-1, IC 35-50-3, IC 35-50-5-2.

35-46-3-12. Cruelty to an animal — Intentionally beating an animal.

(a) This section does not apply to a person who euthanizes an injured, a sick, a homeless, or an unwanted domestic animal if:

(1) the person is employed by a humane society, an animal control agency, or a governmental entity operating an animal shelter or other animal impounding facility; and

(2) the person euthanizes the domestic animal in accordance with guidelines adopted by the humane society, animal control agency, or governmental entity operating the animal shelter or other animal impounding facility.

(b) A person who knowingly or intentionally beats a vertebrate animal commits cruelty to an animal, a Class A misdemeanor. However, the offense is a Class D felony if:

(1) the person has a previous, unrelated conviction under this section; or

(2) the person committed the offense with the intent to threaten, intimidate, coerce, harass, or terrorize a family or household member.

(c) A person who knowingly or intentionally tortures or mutilates a vertebrate animal commits torturing or mutilating a vertebrate animal, a Class D felony.

(d) As used in this subsection, "domestic animal" means an animal that is not wild. The term is limited to:

(1) cattle, calves, horses, mules, swine, sheep, goats, dogs, cats, poultry, ostriches, rhea, and emus; and

(2) an animal of the bovine, equine, ovine, caprine, porcine, canine, feline, camelid, cervidae, or bison species.

A person who knowingly or intentionally kills a domestic animal without the consent of the owner of the domestic animal commits killing a domestic animal, a Class D felony.

(e) It is a defense to a prosecution under this section that the accused person:

(1) reasonably believes the conduct was necessary to:

(A) prevent injury to the accused person or another person;

(B) protect the property of the accused person from destruction or substantial damage; or

(C) prevent a seriously injured vertebrate animal from prolonged suffering; or

(2) engaged in a reasonable and recognized act of training, handling, or disciplining the vertebrate animal.

(f) When a court imposes a sentence or enters a dispositional decree under this section, the court:

(1) shall consider requiring:

(A) a person convicted of an offense under this section; or

(B) a child adjudicated a delinquent child for committing an act that would be a crime under this section if committed by an adult;

to receive psychological, behavioral, or other counseling as a part of the sentence or dispositional decree; and

(2) may order an individual described in subdivision (1) to receive psychological, behavioral, or other counseling as a part of the sentence or dispositional decree.

History.
P.L.193-1987, § 15; P.L.41-1998, § 2; P.L.132-2002, § 1; P.L.7-2007, § 1 eff. July 1, 2007; P.L.171-2007, § 10, eff. July 1, 2007; P.L.111-2009, § 14, eff. July 1, 2009.

Compiler's Notes.
P.L.111-2009, § 15, effective July 1, 2009, provides:
"IC 15-21-2-3, IC 15-21-3-1, and IC 15-21-3-2, all as added by this act, and IC 35-46-3-0.5, IC 35-46-3-7, IC 35-46-3-10, and IC 35-46-3-12, all as amended by this act, apply only to crimes committed after June 30, 2009."

Amendments.
The 2009 amendment deleted former (b)(2), which read: ""the person knowingly or intentionally tortures or mutilates a vertebrate animal""; redesignated former (b)(3), (c), and (d) as (b)(2), (e), and (f); added (c) and (d); deleted ""concerning a person described in subdivision (1)"" following ""this section"" in the introductory language of (f); and made a related change.

Cross References.
Penalties for felonies, IC 35-50-1, IC 35-50-2, IC 35-50-5-2.
Penalties for misdemeanors, IC 35-50-1, IC 35-50-3, IC 35-50-5-2.

NOTES TO DECISIONS

ANALYSIS

Defenses.
—Preventing Suffering.
Sentence.
Shooting.

Defenses.
Defendant's cropping of the ears of two dogs without anesthetic was not a reasonable and recognized act of handling the dogs, and his convictions of cruelty to an animal and practicing veterinary medicine without a license were affirmed. Elisea v. State, 777 N.E.2d 46, 2002 Ind. App. LEXIS 1712 (2002).

—Preventing Suffering.
Where defendant slit throat of injured goose, after gunshot resulted in injury to the goose's wing, this act constituted mutilation in its plain, or ordinary and usual, sense; it was for the trier of fact to determine the weight and credibility to be afforded his claim that he killed the goose to prevent it from suffering. Boushehry v. State, 648 N.E.2d 1174, 1995 Ind. App. LEXIS 227 (1995).

Sentence.
Maximum sentence for cruelty to animal in violation of IC 35-46-3-12(b) was not inappropriate given nature of defendant's character and nature of offense; trial court balanced factors under IC 35-38-1-7.1(a) including defendant's lengthy criminal history and fact that defendant, after pleading guilty, told presentence investigator that he did not commit crime. Hedger v. State, 824 N.E.2d 417, 2005 Ind. App. LEXIS 432 (2005).
Fact that aggravating factors used to impose maximum sentence for offense of cruelty to an animal were not determined by jury did not violate Sixth Amendment where one aggravating factor, criminal history, did not require jury determination, and other aggravating factor, risk of recidivism, was also based upon criminal history. Hedger v. State, 824 N.E.2d 417, 2005 Ind. App. LEXIS 432 (2005).
Maximum sentence for conviction of torturing a vertebrate animal was proper under circumstances in which defendant held his girlfriend's dog, who was trying to protect the girlfriend during an argument she had with defendant, by the collar and repeatedly stabbed it to death, and then tossed the dog's carcass into the yard toward approaching officers; defendant's criminal history included two aggravated assault convictions, two aggravated assault with a deadly weapon convictions, and burglary of an occupied dwelling. Williams v. State, 861 N.E.2d 714, 2007 Ind. App. LEXIS 264 (2007).

Shooting.
The act of shooting goose was not enough alone to establish cruelty to an animal by either torture or mutilation. Boushehry v. State, 648 N.E.2d 1174, 1995 Ind. App. LEXIS 227 (1995).
Evidence was sufficient to support defendants' convictions on charges of cruelty to an animal, where evidence showed that a cat that defendants shot did not die instantly and that the 30 projectiles that struck the cat repeatedly caused its body to be altered radically so as to be imperfect or mutilated. Hall v. State, 791 N.E.2d 257, 2003 Ind. App. LEXIS 1231 (2003).

Cited:
Roose v. State, 610 N.E.2d 256, 1993 Ind. App. LEXIS 80 (1993).

RESEARCH REFERENCES

Indiana Law Review.
Survey: Criminal Law and Procedure: Recent Developments in Indiana, 32 Ind. L. Rev. 789 (1999).

Collateral References.
Damages for killing or injuring dog. 61 A.L.R.5th 635.

35-46-3-12.5. Domestic violence animal cruelty — Penalty.

A person who knowingly or intentionally kills a vertebrate animal with the intent to threaten, intimidate, coerce, harass, or terrorize a family or household member commits domestic violence animal cruelty, a Class D felony.

History.
P.L.171-2007, § 11, eff. July 1, 2007.

Compiler's Notes.
P.L.171-2007, § 13, effective July 1, 2007, provides:
"(a) Except as provided in subsection (b), IC 35-46-3-8 and IC 35-46-3-12, both as amended by this act, and IC 35-46-3-12.5 and IC 35-46-3-14, both as added by this act, apply only to crimes committed after June 30, 2007.

"(b) IC 35-46-3-12(d), as amended by this act, applies only to:
"(1) crimes; and
"(2) delinquent acts that would be crimes if committed by an adult;
"that are committed after June 30, 2007."

Cross References.
Penalties for felonies, IC 35-50-1, IC 35-50-2, IC 35-50-5-2.

35-46-3-13. Cruelty to an animal — Removal of trained attack dog's vocal chords.

(a) A person who knowingly or intentionally removes the vocal cords of a trained attack dog commits cruelty to an animal, a Class A misdemeanor.

(b) It is a defense to a prosecution under this section that the accused person reasonably believes that the conduct was necessary to prevent a seriously injured dog from prolonged injury.

History.
P.L.76-2002, § 7.

Cross References.
Penalties for misdemeanors, IC 35-50-1, IC 35-50-3, IC 35-50-5-2.

35-46-3-14. Bestiality — Penalty.

A person who knowingly or intentionally performs an act involving:
(1) a sex organ of a person and the mouth or anus of an animal;
(2) a sex organ of an animal and the mouth or anus of a person;
(3) any penetration of the human female sex organ by an animal's sex organ; or
(4) any penetration of an animal's sex organ by the human male sex organ;
commits bestiality, a Class D felony.

History.
P.L.171-2007, § 12, eff. July 1, 2007.

Compiler's Notes.
P.L.171-2007, § 13, effective July 1, 2007, provides:
"(a) Except as provided in subsection (b), IC 35-46-3-8 and IC 35-46-3-12, both as amended by this act, and IC 35-46-3-12.5 and IC 35-46-3-14, both as added by this act, apply only to crimes committed after June 30, 2007.

"(b) IC 35-46-3-12(d), as amended by this act, applies only to:
"(1) crimes; and
"(2) delinquent acts that would be crimes if committed by an adult;
"that are committed after June 30, 2007."

Cross References.
Penalties for felonies, IC 35-50-1, IC 35-50-2, IC 35-50-5-2.

35-46-3-15. Applicability of section — Exemptions — Destruction of animal — Penalty.

(a) This section does not apply to the following:

(1) A state or federally inspected livestock slaughtering facility (for conduct authorized by IC 15-17-5 and rules adopted under that chapter).

(2) An animal disease diagnostic laboratory established under IC 21-46-3-1.

(3) A postsecondary educational institution.

(4) A research facility licensed by the United States Department of Agriculture.

(b) As used in this section, "animal" has the meaning set forth in IC 35-46-3-3.

(c) A person who knowingly or intentionally destroys or authorizes the destruction of an animal by:

(1) placing the animal in a decompression chamber and lowering the pressure of or the oxygen content in the air surrounding the animal; or

(2) electrocution;

commits a Class B misdemeanor.

History.
P.L.2-2008, § 13, eff. July 1, 2008.

Penalties for misdemeanors, IC 35-50-1, IC 35-50-3, IC 35-50-5-2.

Cross References.
Penalties for felonies, IC 35-50-1, IC 35-50-2, IC 35-50-5-2.

CHAPTER 4

FAILURE TO DISCLOSE RECRUITMENT

35-46-4-1. "Agent contract" defined.

As used in this chapter, "agent contract" means a contract or agreement in which a student athlete authorizes a person to negotiate or solicit on behalf of the student athlete:

(1) an agreement with a professional sports team for:

(A) the employment of the student athlete by a professional sports team or organization; or

(B) the employment of the student athlete as a professional athlete; or

(2) an endorsement contract.

History.
P.L.184-1988, § 1; P.L.54-2001, § 7.

NOTES TO DECISIONS

ANALYSIS

Evidence.
—Sufficient.

Evidence.

—Sufficient.
Where the state offered overwhelming testimony

that defendant was the perpetrator of the crime, the exclusion of his alibi evidence was, at most, harmless error. Palmer v. State, 654 N.E.2d 844, 1995 Ind. App. LEXIS 1011 (1995).

Valparaiso University Law Review.
Sports Agents Representing Athletes: The Need

for Comprehensive State Legislation, 24 Val. U.L.
Rev. 481 (1990).

35-46-4-1.5. "Endorsement contract" defined.

As used in this chapter, "endorsement contract" means an agreement under which a student athlete is employed or receives consideration to use, on behalf of the other party, any value that the student athlete may have because of publicity, reputation, following, or fame obtained because of athletic ability or performance. The term includes the value of any part of the student athlete's right of publicity (as defined in IC 32-36-1-7).

History.
P.L.54-2001, § 8; P.L.1-2003, § 96.

35-46-4-2. "Professional sports service contract" defined.

As used in this chapter, "professional sports services contract" means a contract or agreement in which a person is employed or agrees to render services:
(1) as a player on a professional sports team;
(2) as a professional athlete; or
(3) with a professional sports organization.

History.
P.L.184-1988, § 1; P.L.54-2001, § 9.

35-46-4-3. "Student athlete" defined.

As used in this chapter, "student athlete" means a person who is:
(1) enrolled or intends to enroll in a course of study in a public or private college or university; and
(2) eligible to engage in, or may be eligible in the future to engage in, an intercollegiate sporting event, contest, exhibition, or program for the college or university in which the person is enrolled or intends to enroll.

History.
P.L.184-1988, § 1; P.L.54-2001, § 10.

35-46-4-4. Failure to disclose recruitment — Penalty.

A person who knowingly or intentionally:
(1) enters into an agent contract, an endorsement contract, or a professional sports services contract with a student athlete; and
(2) no later than ten (10) days before the contract is executed, fails to give written notice to the head of the athletic department for the college or university in which the student athlete is enrolled as a student or intends to enroll as a student that identifies:
(A) the name and business address of each party to the contract;
(B) whether the contract is an agent contract, an endorsement contract, or a professional sports services contract; and
(C) the date that the contract will be executed;
commits failure to disclose recruitment, a Class D felony.

History.
P.L.184-1988, § 1; P.L.54-2001, § 11.

Cross References.
Penalties for felonies, IC 35-50-1, IC 35-50-2, IC 35-50-5-2.

CHAPTER 5

OFFENSES AGAINST PUBLIC SENSIBILITY

35-46-5-1. Unlawful transfer of human organ.

(a) As used in this section, "fetal tissue" means tissue from an infant or a fetus who is stillborn or aborted.

(b) As used in this section, "human organ" means the kidney, liver, heart, lung, cornea, eye, bone marrow, bone, pancreas, or skin of a human body.

(c) As used in this section, "item of value" means money, real estate, funeral related services, and personal property. "Item of value" does not include:

(1) the reasonable payments associated with the removal, transportation, implantation, processing, preservation, quality control, and storage of a human organ; or

(2) the reimbursement of travel, housing, lost wages, and other expenses incurred by the donor of a human organ related to the donation of the human organ.

(d) A person who intentionally acquires, receives, sells, or transfers in exchange for an item of value:

(1) a human organ for use in human organ transplantation; or

(2) fetal tissue;

commits unlawful transfer of human tissue, a Class C felony.

History.
P.L.131-1992, § 2; P.L.217-1997, § 1.

Cross References.
Penalties for felonies, IC 35-50-1, IC 35-50-2, IC 35-50-5-2.

NOTES TO DECISIONS

Cited:
Bolin v. Wingert, 764 N.E.2d 201, 2002 Ind. LEXIS 198 (2002).

RESEARCH REFERENCES

Valparaiso University Law Review.
"Brother, Can You Spare a Liver?" Five Ways to Increase Organ Donation, 31 Val. U.L. Rev. 1 (1996).

35-46-5-2. Cloning activities prohibited — Felony.

(a) This section does not apply to in vitro fertilization.

(b) As used in this section, "cloning" has the meaning set forth in IC 16-18-2-56.5.

(c) A person who knowingly or intentionally:

(1) participates in cloning;

(2) implants or attempts to implant a cloned human embryo into a uterine environment to initiate a pregnancy; or

(3) ships or receives a cloned human embryo;

commits unlawful participation in human cloning, a Class D felony.

3

History.
P.L.126-2005, § 9.

Cross References.
Penalties for felonies, IC 35-50-1, IC 35-50-2, IC 35-50-5-2.

35-46-5-3. Unlawful transfer of human organism — Felony — Applicability of section.

(a) A person who knowingly or intentionally purchases or sells a human ovum, zygote, embryo, or fetus commits unlawful transfer of a human organism, a Class C felony.

(b) This section does not apply to the following:

(1) The transfer to or receipt by a woman donor of an ovum of an amount for:

(A) earnings lost due to absence from employment;

(B) travel expenses;

(C) hospital expenses;

(D) medical expenses; and

(E) recovery time in an amount not to exceed three thousand dollars ($3,000);

concerning a treatment or procedure to enhance human reproductive capability through in vitro fertilization, gamete intrafallopian transfer, or zygote intrafallopian transfer.

(2) The following types of stem cell research:

(A) Adult stem cell.

(B) Fetal stem cell, as long as the biological parent has given written consent for the use of the fetal stem cells.

History.
P.L.126-2005, § 10.

Cross References.
Penalties for felonies, IC 35-50-1, IC 35-50-2, IC 35-50-5-2.

35-46-5-4. Falsifying, forging, concealing, defacing, or obliterating document making gift of body part — Misdemeanor.

An individual who, in order to obtain a financial gain, intentionally falsifies, forges, conceals, defaces, or obliterates a document that:

(1) expresses;

(2) makes an amendment or revocation of; or

(3) refuses;

a gift of organs, tissues, eyes, or other body parts intended to be used in research or in transplants, commits a Class A misdemeanor.

History.
P.L.147-2007, § 18, eff. July 1, 2007.

Cross References.
Penalties for misdemeanors, IC 35-50-1, IC 35-50-3, IC 35-50-5-2.

CHAPTER 6

GLUE SNIFFING

35-46-6-1. "Model glue" defined.

As used in this chapter, "model glue" means a glue or cement containing toluene or acetone, or both.

History.
  P.L.2-1993, § 189; P.L.151-2006, § 19.

35-46-6-2. Penalty.

A person who, with intent to cause a condition of intoxication, euphoria, excitement, exhilaration, stupefaction, or dulling of the senses, ingests or inhales the fumes of:
  (1) model glue; or
  (2) a substance that contains:
    (A) toluene;
    (B) acetone;
    (C) benzene;
    (D) N-butyl nitrite;
    (E) any aliphatic nitrite, unless prescribed by a physician;
    (F) butane;
    (G) amyl butrate;
    (H) isobutyl nitrate;
    (I) freon;
    (J) chlorinated hydrocarbons;
    (K) methylene chloride;
    (L) hexane;
    (M) ether;
    (N) chloroform; or
    (O) halothane; or
  (3) any other chemical having the property of releasing toxic vapors;
commits inhaling toxic vapors, a Class B misdemeanor.

History.
  P.L.2-1993, § 189; P.L.151-2006, § 20.

Cross References.
  Penalties for misdemeanors, IC 35-50-1, IC 35-50-3, IC 35-50-5-2.

NOTES TO DECISIONS

ANALYSIS

Identification of Substance.
Sufficiency of Evidence.

Identification of Substance.
  Testimony as to the nature of a compound may be based on a witness' experience with it if the circumstances support the conclusion that the witness' identification is reliable. Vasquez v. State, 741 N.E.2d 1214, 2001 Ind. LEXIS 74 (2001).

Sufficiency of Evidence.
  Police officer's testimony that he saw defendant breathing into bag, found half-empty tube of glue on defendant that tested positive for Toluene, and noticed that defendant had dazed expression and appeared disoriented was sufficient to sustain defendant's conviction for glue sniffing. Upp v. State, 808 N.E.2d 706, 2004 Ind. App. LEXIS 900 (2004).

35-46-6-3. Use or distribution of nitrous oxide.

A person who knowingly or intentionally uses or distributes nitrous oxide with intent to cause a condition of intoxication, euphoria, excitement, exhilaration, stupefaction, or dulling of the senses of another person, unless the nitrous oxide is to be used for medical purposes, commits a Class B misdemeanor. However, the offense is a Class A misdemeanor if the person has a prior unrelated conviction under this section.

History.
  P.L.163-1994, § 1; P.L.218-1997, § 1.

Cross References.
  Penalties for misdemeanors, IC 35-50-1, IC 35-50-3, IC 35-50-5-2.

CHAPTER 7

OFFENSES AGAINST PERSONS RECEIVING CARE

35-46-7-1. "Health care provider" defined.

As used in this chapter, "health care provider" means:
(1) a hospital licensed under IC 16-21;
(2) a health facility licensed under IC 16-28;
(3) a housing services establishment that is required to file a disclosure statement under IC 12-15;
(4) a continuing care retirement community that is required to file a disclosure statement under IC 23-2-4;
(5) a home health agency licensed under IC 16-27;
(6) a hospice licensed under IC 16-25;
(7) an entity that provides licensed or certified health care professionals to:
    (A) a health care provider; or
    (B) a person who is in need of, or receives, professional health care services;
(8) a community mental health center (as defined in IC 12-7-2-38);
(9) a private psychiatric hospital licensed under IC 12-25;
(10) a state institution (as defined in IC 12-7-2-184); or
(11) a community residential facility for the developmentally disabled that is licensed under IC 12-28-5.

History.
    P.L.139-2002, § 1.

35-46-7-2. Applicability of chapter.

This chapter does not apply to the following:
(1) A gift or donation of money or other asset given to:
    (A) a health care provider in the corporate name of the health care provider; or
    (B) a health care provider that is organized under Section 501(c)(3) of the Internal Revenue Code.
(2) A gift or loan of money or other asset given by a person who receives services from a health care provider to a member of the person's family who:
    (A) is employed by a health care provider; or
    (B) owns, wholly or jointly, a health care provider.
(3) A bequest of personal property or devise of real property made in an executable will as described in IC 29-1-5-5 to a health care provider or an owner, employee, or agent of a health care provider.
(4) The purchase of a security (as defined in IC 23-19-1-2(28)) that is traded on a national or regional exchange.
(5) A gift or gratuity, not exceeding five hundred dollars ($500) in the aggregate per year per person receiving services from the health care provider, to an employee of a health care provider.
(6) A gift or donation of money or other asset given to purchase or otherwise acquire a product, service, or amenity for the use, entertainment, or enjoyment of persons receiving services from a health care provider.

History.
  P.L.139-2002, § 1; P.L.27-2007, § 32, eff. July 1,
2008.

35-46-7-3. Execution of transaction — Writing requirement — Return of assets.

(a) The following transactions are subject to the requirements of subsection (b):

(1) A gift, a donation, a loan, or an investment from a person who receives services from a health care provider to:

(A) the health care provider; or

(B) an owner, employee, or agent of the health care provider.

(2) A loan or an investment from a person who receives services from a health care provider to the health care provider in the corporate name of the health care provider.

(b) A transaction under subsection (a) must be executed by a competent person (including a person other than the health care provider exercising a durable power of attorney on behalf of the donor) in writing and witnessed by two (2) disinterested parties. Each witness shall sign a document that describes the transaction in the presence of:

(1) the person who makes the transaction; and

(2) the other witness.

(c) A health care provider, or an owner, an employee, or an agent of a health care provider, who:

(1) receives a gift, a donation, a loan, or an investment from a person who receives services from a health care provider; and

(2) fails to comply with the requirements of subsection (b);

commits a Class A infraction. Without regard to the amount of the transaction, the court that imposes the penalty for the infraction violation may, upon the request of the prosecuting attorney, order the person to return assets or repay money received in violation of this section, plus interest from the date of the transaction, to the person who made the gift, donation, loan, or investment. In addition, if the court finds that the person knowingly violated the requirements of subsection (b), the court may order the person to pay treble damages and reasonable attorney's fees.

History.
  P.L.139-2002, § 1.

Cross References.
  Infraction and ordinance violation enforcement proceedings, IC 34-28-5.

CHAPTER 8

UNLAWFUL RECORDING

35-46-8-1. Applicability of chapter.

This chapter does not apply to a law enforcement officer acting within the scope of the officer's employment.

History.
  P.L.94-2005, § 6.

"IC 35-46-8, as added by this act, applies only to crimes committed after June 30, 2005."

Compiler's Notes.
  P.L.94-2005, § 7, effective July 1, 2005, provides:

35-46-8-2. "Audiovisual recording device" defined.

As used in this chapter, "audiovisual recording device" means:
(1) a digital or an analog photographic or video camera; or
(2) any other technology capable of enabling the recording or transmission of a motion picture or other audiovisual work;
regardless of whether audiovisual recording is the sole or primary purpose of the device.

History.
P.L.94-2005, § 6.

35-46-8-3. "Motion picture exhibition facility" defined.

(a) As used in this chapter, "motion picture exhibition facility" means:
(1) an indoor or outdoor screening venue; or
(2) any other premises;
where motion pictures or other audiovisual works are shown to the public for a charge, regardless of whether an admission fee is charged.
(b) The term does not include a dwelling.

History.
P.L.94-2005, § 6.

35-46-8-4. Unlawful recording — Class B misdemeanor — Defense.

(a) A person who knowingly or intentionally uses an audiovisual recording device in a motion picture exhibition facility with the intent to transmit or record a motion picture commits unlawful recording, a Class B misdemeanor.
(b) It is a defense to a prosecution under this section that the accused person had the written permission of the motion picture exhibition facility owner to transmit or record the motion picture.

History.
P.L.94-2005, § 6.

Cross References.
Penalties for misdemeanors, IC 35-50-1, IC 35-50-3, IC 35-50-5-2.

35-46-8-5. Forfeiture or destruction of unlawful recordings and recording devices.

In addition to a criminal penalty imposed for an offense under this chapter, a court may order the forfeiture, destruction, or other disposition of:
(1) all unauthorized copies of motion pictures or other audiovisual works; and
(2) any audiovisual recording devices or other equipment used in connection with the offense.

History.
P.L.94-2005, § 6.

ARTICLE 47

REGULATION OF WEAPONS AND INSTRUMENTS OF VIOLENCE

CHAPTER 1

DEFINITIONS

35-47-1-1. Applicability of definitions in chapter.

The definitions in this chapter apply throughout this article.

History.
   IC 35-47-1-1, as added by P.L.311-1983, § 32.

NOTES TO DECISIONS

Right to Carry Handguns.
   There is a state-created right to bear arms which includes the right to carry a handgun with a license, provided that all of the requirements of the Indiana Firearms Act are met. This right is pro-tected by the Due Process Clause of the Fourteenth Amendment and is both a property and liberty interest for purposes of 42 U.S.C.S. § 1983. Kellogg v. Gary, 562 N.E.2d 685, 1990 Ind. LEXIS 226 (1990).

RESEARCH REFERENCES

Collateral References.
   Validity of state gun control legislation under state constitutional provisions securing the right to bear arms. 86 A.L.R.4th 931.

35-47-1-2. Alcohol abuser.

   "Alcohol abuser" means an individual who has had two (2) or more alcohol related offenses, any one (1) of which resulted in conviction by a court or treatment in an alcohol abuse facility within three (3) years prior to the date of the application.

History.
   IC 35-47-1-2, as added by P.L.311-1983, § 32.

NOTES TO DECISIONS

Cited:
Johnson v. Patterson, 570 N.E.2d 93, 1991 Ind. App. LEXIS 662 (1991).

35-47-1-3. Dealer.

"Dealer" means any person who holds himself out as a buyer and seller of handguns on a regular and continuing basis.

History.
IC 35-47-1-3, as added by P.L.311-1983, § 32.

35-47-1-4. Drug abuser.

"Drug abuser" means an individual who has had two (2) or more violations of IC 35-48-1, IC 35-48-2, IC 35-48-3, or IC 35-48-4, any one (1) of which resulted in conviction by a court or treatment in a drug abuse facility within five (5) years prior to the date of application.

History.
IC 35-47-1-4, as added by P.L.311-1983, § 32.

NOTES TO DECISIONS

Cited:
Johnson v. Patterson, 570 N.E.2d 93, 1991 Ind.

App. LEXIS 662 (1991); Seel v. State, 739 N.E.2d 170, 2000 Ind. App. LEXIS 1922 (2000).

35-47-1-5. Firearm.

"Firearm" means any weapon:
   (1) that is:
     (A) capable of expelling; or
     (B) designed to expel; or
   (2) that may readily be converted to expel;
a projectile by means of an explosion.

History.
IC 35-47-1-5, as added by P.L.311-1983, § 32; P.L.3-2008, § 254, emergency eff. March 13, 2008.

NOTES TO DECISIONS

ANALYSIS

Pellet Gun.
Proof.
—Operable Gun.

Pellet Gun.
Where defendant was charged with the illegal use of a handgun, a firearm, and the state clearly established, through the uncontroverted testimony of a deputy, that his pellet gun was not a handgun, there was a variance between the information, the instructions, and the proof produced at trial. Thus, the evidence was insufficient to convict defendant of the crimes with which he was charged: (1) criminal confinement while armed with a deadly weapon as a Class B felony; or (2) criminal recklessness as a Class D felony because he was not armed with a deadly weapon. Miller v. State, 616 N.E.2d 750, 1993 Ind. App. LEXIS 785 (1993).

Proof.

—Operable Gun.
Indiana law does not require that the state prove a handgun is operable to obtain a conviction of carrying a handgun without a license; the fact that the handgun was designed to expel a projectile by means of an explosion is sufficient. Manley v. State, 656 N.E.2d 277, 1995 Ind. App. LEXIS 1272 (1995).

Evidence was sufficient to support defendant's conviction for carrying a handgun without a license as a Class C felony in violation of IC 35-47-2-1; even though the handgun found in her purse

Proof. (Cont'd)

—Operable Gun. (Cont'd)
was disassembled, it met the definition of a "firearm" because it could be readily converted to expel a projectile by means of an explosion, IC 35-47-1-5, and could be fired with one hand, IC 35-47-1-6, and the state produced sufficient evidence that she did

not possess a license to carry it. Staten v. State, 844 N.E.2d 186, 2006 Ind. App. LEXIS 477 (2006).

Cited:
 Hatchett v. State, 740 N.E.2d 920, 2000 Ind. App. LEXIS 2054 (2000); Alexander v. State, 768 N.E.2d 971, 2002 Ind. App. LEXIS 804 (2002).

35-47-1-5.5. Gun show.

"Gun show" has the meaning set forth in 27 CFR 478.100.

History.
 P.L.148-1987, § 2; P.L.1-2006, § 534.

35-47-1-6. Handgun.

"Handgun" means any firearm:
   (1) Designed or adapted so as to be aimed and fired from one (1) hand, regardless of barrel length; or
   (2) Any firearm with:
      (A) A barrel less than sixteen (16) inches in length; or
      (B) An overall length of less than twenty-six (26) inches.

History.
 IC 35-47-1-6, as added by P.L.311-1983, § 32.

NOTES TO DECISIONS

ANALYSIS

Handgun.
Pellet Gun.
Sawed-Off Shotgun.

Handgun.
 Evidence was sufficient to support defendant's conviction for carrying a handgun without a license as a Class C felony in violation of IC 35-47-2-1; even though the handgun found in her purse was disassembled, it met the definition of a "firearm" because it could be readily converted to expel a projectile by means of an explosion, IC 35-47-1-5, and could be fired with one hand, IC 35-47-1-6, and the state produced sufficient evidence that she did not possess a license to carry it. Staten v. State, 844 N.E.2d 186, 2006 Ind. App. LEXIS 477 (2006).

Pellet Gun.
 Where defendant was charged with the illegal use of a handgun, a firearm, and the state clearly established, through the uncontroverted testimony of a deputy, that his pellet gun was not a handgun, there was a variance between the information, the instructions, and the proof produced at trial. Thus,

the evidence was insufficient to convict defendant of the crimes with which he was charged: (1) criminal confinement while armed with a deadly weapon as a Class B felony; or (2) criminal recklessness as a Class D felony because he was not armed with a deadly weapon. Miller v. State, 616 N.E.2d 750, 1993 Ind. App. LEXIS 785 (1993).

Sawed-Off Shotgun.
 Since a firearm is considered a handgun under this section regardless of length if such firearm is designed or adapted to be fired from one hand, a shotgun with the stock removed and a pistol grip added required a license, and the evidence was sufficient to support the defendant's conviction of carrying a handgun without a license. Estep v. State, 716 N.E.2d 986, 1999 Ind. App. LEXIS 1705 (1999).

Cited:
 Johnson v. Patterson, 570 N.E.2d 93, 1991 Ind. App. LEXIS 662 (1991); Hatchett v. State, 740 N.E.2d 920, 2000 Ind. App. LEXIS 2054 (2000); Alexander v. State, 768 N.E.2d 971, 2002 Ind. App. LEXIS 804 (2002).

35-47-1-7. Proper person.

"Proper person" means a person who:
   (1) does not have a conviction for resisting law enforcement under IC 35-44-3-3 within five (5) years before the person applies for a license or permit under this chapter;

(2) does not have a conviction for a crime for which the person could have been sentenced for more than one (1) year;

(3) does not have a conviction for a crime of domestic violence (as defined in IC 35-41-1-6.3), unless a court has restored the person's right to possess a firearm under IC 35-47-4-7;

(4) is not prohibited by a court order from possessing a handgun;

(5) does not have a record of being an alcohol or drug abuser as defined in this chapter;

(6) does not have documented evidence which would give rise to a reasonable belief that the person has a propensity for violent or emotionally unstable conduct;

(7) does not make a false statement of material fact on the person's application;

(8) does not have a conviction for any crime involving an inability to safely handle a handgun;

(9) does not have a conviction for violation of the provisions of this article within five (5) years of the person's application; or

(10) does not have an adjudication as a delinquent child for an act that would be a felony if committed by an adult, if the person applying for a license or permit under this chapter is less than twenty-three (23) years of age.

History.
IC 35-47-1-7, as added by P.L.311-1983, § 32; P.L.191-1984, § 1; P.L.148-1987, § 3; P.L.269- 1995, § 5; P.L.49-2005, § 1; P.L.118-2007, § 34, eff. July 1, 2007.

NOTES TO DECISIONS

Cited:
Johnson v. Patterson, 570 N.E.2d 93, 1991 Ind. App. LEXIS 662 (1991); United States v. Wagner, 976 F.2d 354, 1992 U.S. App. LEXIS 24334 (7th Cir. Ind. 1992); State v. Bailey, 716 N.E.2d 67, 1999 Ind. App. LEXIS 1486 (1999).

RESEARCH REFERENCES

Collateral References.
What amounts to "control" under state statute making it illegal for felon to have possession or control of firearm or other dangerous weapon. 66 A.L.R.4th 1240.

35-47-1-8. Proper reason.

"Proper reason" means for the defense of oneself or the state of Indiana.

History.
IC 35-47-1-8, as added by P.L.311-1983, § 32.

35-47-1-9. Retail.

"Retail" means the sale of handguns singly or in small quantities to one who intends to be the ultimate user thereof.

History.
IC 35-47-1-9, as added by P.L.311-1983, § 32.

35-47-1-10. Sawed-off shotgun.

"Sawed-off shotgun" means:

(1) A shotgun having one (1) or more barrels less than eighteen (18) inches in length; and

(2) Any weapon made from a shotgun (whether by alteration, modification, or otherwise) if the weapon as modified has an overall length of less than twenty-six (26) inches.

History.
IC 35-47-1-10, as added by P.L.311-1983, § 32.

NOTES TO DECISIONS

Dual Definitions.
This section provides two definitions of "sawed-off shotgun": (1) a shotgun having one or more barrels less than 18 inches; and (2) any weapon made from a shotgun if its overall length is less than 26 inches. A shotgun with a barrel length of less than 18 inches comes within one of the statutory definitions of sawed-off shotgun, the overall length of his shotgun being irrelevant. Brook v. State, 448 N.E.2d 1249, 1983 Ind. App. LEXIS 2943 (1983).

Evidence was sufficient to convict defendant of dealing in a sawed-off shotgun, where the shotgun he was in possession of at the time of his arrest violated both definitions of a sawed-off shotgun, in that it was one-half inch shorter than the legally permissible overall length for shotguns under IC 35-47-1-10(2) and had a barrel four and one-half inches shorter than the length permissible under IC 35-47-1-10(1). Hall v. State, 791 N.E.2d 257, 2003 Ind. App. LEXIS 1231 (2003).

Legislative Intent.
A careful reading of the definitions of "sawed-off shotgun" reveals two legislative intentions. The overall rationale for the legislative ban of sawed-off shotguns centers on their concealability and therefore likely use for criminal purposes rather than for sport or hunting. Secondly, the legislature, while condemning sawed-off shotguns when used as weapons, recognized the legitimate use of shotguns for hunting and sporting purposes. Thus, a shotgun having one or more barrels less than 18 inches in length is forbidden because with such a barrel length a shotgun has a decreased range and therefore minimal utility as a hunting and sporting tool. Brook v. State, 448 N.E.2d 1249, 1983 Ind. App. LEXIS 2943 (1983).

Cited:
Brim v. State, 471 N.E.2d 672, 1984 Ind. LEXIS 1055 (1984); Murphy v. State, 499 N.E.2d 1077, 1986 Ind. LEXIS 1373 (1986); Ben-Yisrayl v. State, 729 N.E.2d 102, 2000 Ind. LEXIS 483 (2000).

35-47-1-11. Shotgun.

"Shotgun" means a weapon designed or redesigned, made or remade, and intended to be fired from the shoulder and designed or redesigned and made or remade to use the energy of the explosive in a fixed shotgun shell to fire through a smooth bore either a number of ball shot or a single projectile for each single pull of the trigger.

History.
IC 35-47-1-11, as added by P.L.311-1983, § 32.

NOTES TO DECISIONS

Handgun.
Since a firearm is considered a handgun under IC 35-47-1-6 regardless of length if such firearm is designed or adapted to be fired from one hand, a shotgun with the stock removed and a pistol grip added required a license, and the evidence was sufficient to support the defendant's conviction of carrying a handgun without a license. Estep v.

State, 716 N.E.2d 986, 1999 Ind. App. LEXIS 1705 (1999).

Cited:
Johnson v. Patterson, 570 N.E.2d 93, 1991 Ind. App. LEXIS 662 (1991); Hall v. State, 791 N.E.2d 257, 2003 Ind. App. LEXIS 1231 (2003).

35-47-1-12. Superintendent.

"Superintendent" refers to the superintendent of the Indiana state police department.

History.
IC 35-47-1-12, as added by P.L.311-1983, § 32.

35-47-1-13. Wholesale.

"Wholesale" means the sale of handguns singly or in bulk lots to one lawfully licensed to deal in handguns, or the sale of a handgun to a governmental law enforcement agency for issue to its employees.

History.
IC 35-47-1-13, as added by P.L.311-1983, § 32.

CHAPTER 2

HANDGUNS

35-47-2-1. License required to carry handgun.

(a) Except as provided in subsection (b) and section 2 [IC 35-47-2-2] of this chapter, a person shall not carry a handgun in any vehicle or on or about the person's body, except in the person's dwelling, on the person's property or fixed place of business, without a license issued under this chapter being in the person's possession.

(b) Unless the person's right to possess a firearm has been restored under IC 35-47-4-7, a person who has been convicted of domestic battery under IC 35-42-2-1.3 may not possess or carry a handgun in any vehicle or on or about the person's body in the person's dwelling or on the person's property or fixed place of business.

History.
IC 35-47-2-1, as added by P.L.311-1983, § 32; P.L.326-1987, § 1; P.L.195-2003, § 6; P.L.98-2004, § 155; P.L.118-2007, § 35, eff. July 1, 2007.

Cross References.
Applicability of chapter to electronic stun weapon or taser, IC 35-47-8-4.

NOTES TO DECISIONS

Analysis

Constitutionality.
—Equal Protection.
Burden of Proof.
—Constitutionality.
"Carry" Construed.
Constructive Possession.

Convicted Felon.
Double Jeopardy.
Dwelling.
Evidence.
—Admissibility.
—Insufficient.
—Sufficient.
Exceptions.

Indictment or Information.
Intent.
Jury Trial.
—Number of Jurors.
Knowing and Voluntary Possession.
Lesser Included Offense.
License.
Manifest Necessity.
Nonresidents.
Place of Abode.
Plea.
—Voluntary and Intelligent.
Proof.
—Operable Gun.
Right to Carry Handgun.
Robbery.
Search and Seizure.
—Juveniles.
—Officer's Reasonable Fear.
Self-Defense.
Sentence.
—Errors.

Constitutionality.

—Equal Protection.
There is no disparate treatment among those similarly situated under the child handgun statute, IC 35-47-10-5, and this section, the adult handgun statute. Person v. State, 661 N.E.2d 587, 1996 Ind. App. LEXIS 144 (1996).

Burden of Proof.
It is the burden of the defendant to prove he comes within one of the exceptions to this section. Morgan v. State, 427 N.E.2d 1131, 1981 Ind. App. LEXIS 1728 (1981) (decided under former IC 35-23-4.1-3).

Trial court erred in granting defendant's motion to dismiss charges for carrying a gun without a license on school property because the State was not required to prove that the gun was in operable condition to support the charges; accordingly, the fact that the gun was an antique handgun in inoperable condition was of no significance as the gun met the statutory definition of a firearm in that it was designed to expel projectiles by means of an explosion. State v. Gibbs, 769 N.E.2d 594, 2002 Ind. App. LEXIS 819 (2002).

—Constitutionality.
The burden placed on a defendant by IC 35-47-2-24 to prove he has a license or is otherwise exempt from prosecution under this section does not unconstitutionally infringe on a person's right to keep and bear arms as granted by Ind. Const., Art. 1, § 32. Lewis v. State, 484 N.E.2d 77, 1985 Ind. App. LEXIS 2887 (1985).

"Carry" Construed.
When referring to the carrying of a handgun on or about one's person, as distinguished from carrying a handgun in a vehicle, this section proscribes having on one's person an unlicensed handgun. Conviction of the offense does not require proof that the weapon was conveyed or transported from one place to another. McAnalley v. State, 514 N.E.2d 831, 1987 Ind. LEXIS 1105 (1987).

While mere presence in a vehicle with multiple riders and multiple weapons is not sufficient to establish a violation under this section, a driver, or passenger who has a gun at his feet in plain view, and without a license for carrying the gun, may be convicted of carrying a gun. Henderson v. State, 715 N.E.2d 833, 1999 Ind. LEXIS 686, 88 A.L.R.5th 727 (1999).

The language of this section encompasses more than moving about with a firearm attached to one's body. Henderson v. State, 715 N.E.2d 833, 1999 Ind. LEXIS 686, 88 A.L.R.5th 727 (1999).

This section does not speak in terms of possessing a handgun but rather in terms of carrying a handgun, and the undisputed fact that the weapons were found in a vehicle in defendant's rented storage facility was, as a matter of law, insufficient to support the inference that defendant at one time carried or will carry the weapons on his person or in a vehicle; therefore, the handguns were not subject to forfeiture under IC 35-33-5-5. Seel v. State, 739 N.E.2d 170, 2000 Ind. App. LEXIS 1922 (2000).

Evidence that defendant took the handgun out of the car, moved it toward the officer, and then continued to hold the handgun in his hand during the time that he was struggling with the officer was sufficient to prove beyond a reasonable doubt that defendant did carry the handgun on his person in a place that was not his dwelling, property, or fixed place of business as required for a conviction for carrying a handgun without a license. Sowell v. State, 784 N.E.2d 980, 2003 Ind. App. LEXIS 367 (2003).

Constructive Possession.
A passenger in a motor vehicle had primary control over an automatic pistol lying between his feet and was in the best position to gain actual control of the weapon, as he easily could have reached it, while it would have been difficult, if not impossible, for the driver to reach. It could be inferred, therefore, that he had the requisite knowledge and control, i.e., that he had "constructive possession" of the pistol. Taylor v. State, 482 N.E.2d 259, 1985 Ind. LEXIS 943 (1985).

Constructive possession of a handgun is not sufficient to sustain a conviction for carrying a handgun without a license. Walker v. State, 631 N.E.2d 1, 1994 Ind. App. LEXIS 174 (1994).

Where defendant was a passenger in a car stopped for leaving parking lot without lights on, gun was under defendant's seat where it could not be seen, and there was no evidence that defendant had been seen carrying gun shortly before being stopped, constructive possession of gun could not be inferred. D.C.C. v. State, 695 N.E.2d 1015, 1998 Ind. App. LEXIS 943 (1998).

A passenger in the front seat of an automobile, without more, is not deemed to possess a gun located on the floor behind the driver, nor is passenger deemed to "carry" a gun located in the trunk. Henderson v. State, 715 N.E.2d 833, 1999 Ind. LEXIS 686, 88 A.L.R.5th 727 (1999).

When a car has multiple passengers, and a gun is near a back seat passenger without a permit, a

Constructive Possession. (Cont'd)
jury can infer possession by that passenger, especially when the testimony indicates that the passenger tried to hide the weapon. Henderson v. State, 715 N.E.2d 833, 1999 Ind. LEXIS 686, 88 A.L.R.5th 727 (1999).

Evidence was sufficient to support a conviction based on constructive possession, where, while outside a motel room, state troopers heard yelling and heard a bullet being chambered in a semi-automatic weapon, upon entry into the room, the troopers found four people and identified the defendant as the person yelling, a gun was found under a mattress, and the defendant admitted that the gun was his. Winters v. State, 719 N.E.2d 1279, 1999 Ind. App. LEXIS 2043 (1999).

Evidence was sufficient to support defendant's conviction for possession of a handgun without a license after defendant was found sitting on the gun in a vehicle; state proved that defendant was in the best position in the vehicle to exercise control over the gun, no evidence showed it belonged to somebody else, and the circumstances supported a finding that defendant constructively possessed the gun. Deshazier v. State, 877 N.E.2d 200, 2007 Ind. App. LEXIS 2724 (2007).

Other than defendant juvenile's proximity to a gun, there was no other evidence to suggest that defendant had the capability to maintain control and dominion of the gun; accordingly, since the evidence was insufficient to prove that defendant constructively possessed the handgun, defendant was improperly adjudicated a delinquent child for violating IC 35-47-2-1. E.D. v. State, 905 N.E.2d 505, 2009 Ind. App. LEXIS 812 (2009).

Convicted Felon.
Assuming Indiana restores to convicted felons the limited right to possess handguns in their dwellings, the exception did not aid a defendant charged with possession of a firearm while a convicted felon in violation of federal law who was not in his dwelling when he possessed the handgun. United States v. Wagner, 976 F.2d 354, 1992 U.S. App. LEXIS 24334 (7th Cir. Ind. 1992).

Double Jeopardy.
Where defendant argued that documents pertaining to his felony conviction for carrying a handgun without a permit were erroneously admitted into evidence, claiming they did not pertain to a prior "unrelated" felony because the handgun conviction would have been a misdemeanor were it not for an earlier burglary conviction and that made the handgun and burglary convictions related, which amounted to using the burglary conviction twice for a sentence enhancement, it was held that, in this section on the handgun violation and IC 35-50-2-8 on habitual offenders, the defendant's prior conduct placed him in a different status. That status is not an additional crime, but merely permits trial courts to enhance a given penalty by reason of the status of the offender, and such enhanced penalty does not constitute double jeopardy. Hampton v. State, 526 N.E.2d 1154, 1988 Ind. LEXIS 233 (1988).

For double jeopardy purposes, the offense of possession of a handgun without a license has an element that criminal recklessness as a Class D felony does not, and possession of a handgun is not an inherently included offense of criminal recklessness. Fields v. State, 676 N.E.2d 27, 1997 Ind. App. LEXIS 11 (1997).

Punishment for both a class A misdemeanor under IC 35-47-2-1 and a class C felony under IC 35-47-2-23 violated the double jeopardy prohibition. Henderson v. State, 686 N.E.2d 911, 1997 Ind. App. LEXIS 1560 (1997), transfer granted, 698 N.E.2d 1182 (Ind. 1998), aff'd, 690 N.E.2d 706, 1998 Ind. LEXIS 2 (1998).

Since criminal recklessness as a Class D felony requires the possession of a deadly weapon, and violation of the statutory provision proscribing possession of a handgun without a license requires only possession of a deadly weapon, the element necessary for a conviction for the latter offense does not require proof different from the elements necessary to prove the former, and convictions for both offenses violate double jeopardy. Collier v. State, 715 N.E.2d 940, 1999 Ind. App. LEXIS 1466 (1999).

Defendant's conviction and sentence for carrying a handgun without a license was vacated where there was a reasonable possibility that the trial court used the same evidentiary facts to establish the essential elements of both unlawful possession of a firearm as a serious violent felon, and carrying a handgun without a license. Hatchett v. State, 740 N.E.2d 920, 2000 Ind. App. LEXIS 2054 (2000).

There was no double jeopardy violation under the statutory evidence test or the actual evidence test for defendant's convictions for pointing a firearm under IC 35-47-4-3, and for carrying a handgun without a license under this section, because the two convictions do not constitute multiple punishments for the same offense in violation of the Indiana double jeopardy clause. Armstrong v. State, 742 N.E.2d 972, 2001 Ind. App. LEXIS 23 (2001).

There was no double jeopardy violation where distinct evidentiary facts were used to prove that defendant committed robbery while armed with a handgun, and a lack of evidentiary facts was used to prove that the defendant did not have a license to carry that handgun. Defendant failed to demonstrate a reasonable possibility that the same evidentiary facts may have been used to establish the essential elements of each challenged offense. Newman v. State, 751 N.E.2d 265, 2001 Ind. App. LEXIS 965 (2001).

Appeals court affirmed defendant's convictions of IC 35-42-2-2 criminal recklessness, a class D felony, and IC 35-47-2-1 carrying a handgun without a license, a class C felony, since proof that the defendant carried the handgun somewhere other than his dwelling, property, or fixed place of business, was not required to obtain a conviction for criminal recklessness as a class D felony, and proof that he created a substantial risk of bodily injury to another was not required to obtain a conviction for carrying a handgun without a license; since each offense required proof of an additional fact that the other did not, defendant's convictions did

Double Jeopardy. (Cont'd)
not violate the Double Jeopardy Clause. Woods v. State, 768 N.E.2d 1024, 2002 Ind. App. LEXIS 803 (2002).

Defendant's conviction of IC 35-47-2-1, carrying a handgun without a license, and IC 35-47-4-5, unlawful possession of a firearm by a serious violent felon, violated Indiana's Double Jeopardy Clause, Ind. Const. art. 1, § 14 since the essential elements of one challenged offense also established all of the essential elements of the other challenged offense. Alexander v. State, 768 N.E.2d 971, 2002 Ind. App. LEXIS 804 (2002), clarified, 772 N.E.2d 476, 2002 Ind. App. LEXIS 1195 (2002).

Dwelling.

A motel room was not the defendant's dwelling where there was no evidence that he intended to eat or sleep in the room or that he registered or paid for the room. Winters v. State, 719 N.E.2d 1279, 1999 Ind. App. LEXIS 2043 (1999).

For purposes of IC 35-47-2-1, a dwelling does not include the common areas serving a person's apartment; defendant's possession of a loaded handgun in the hallway outside his apartment was a violation of this section. Robertson v. State, 765 N.E.2d 138, 2002 Ind. LEXIS 244 (2002).

Evidence.

—Admissibility.

A defendant's admission, made to police officers investigating a disturbance, that he had no permit to carry a pistol was admissible in evidence as was testimony by police officers in charge of records that they had no record of an application for a permit from the defendant. Johnson v. State, 256 Ind. 497, 269 N.E.2d 879, 1971 Ind. LEXIS 665 (1971), cert. denied, 405 U.S. 921, 92 S. Ct. 958, 30 L. Ed. 2d 792, 1972 U.S. LEXIS 3653 (1972).

Photograph of dead accomplice and a narration of a shooting incident occurring immediately after the crime charged were properly admissible at trial for the crimes of armed robbery and possession of an unlicensed handgun, as part of the res gestae and as evidence of flight and as reason for possession of the gun. Frasier v. State, 262 Ind. 59, 312 N.E.2d 77, 1974 Ind. LEXIS 268 (1974), cert. denied, 419 U.S. 1092, 95 S. Ct. 686, 42 L. Ed. 2d 686, 1974 U.S. LEXIS 3842 (1974).

While officer who was waiting to search house in which heroin buys had been made saw defendant leave premises and drive away and radioed to another officer to stop him, and after being stopped he stepped from the car and officer saw a gun, the seizure of the gun was proper and properly admitted in evidence. Walker v. State, 173 Ind. App. 263, 363 N.E.2d 1026, 1977 Ind. App. LEXIS 857 (1977).

Defendant's conviction of carrying a handgun without a license was reversed where the trial court abused its discretion by permitting admission of irrelevant and prejudicial evidence of a shotgun barrel, duct tape, and ski mask found in the car in which defendant was a passenger; the shotgun, the duct tape, and the ski mask had no

relevancy to the issue of defendant's guilt or innocence on the charge of possessing an unlicensed handgun, nor did they prove or disprove any material fact in the case. Brown v. State, 747 N.E.2d 66, 2001 Ind. App. LEXIS 749 (2001).

—Insufficient.

Where pistol was found in tackle box in trunk of defendant's car parked in front of his residence but there was no evidence that pistol had been or was about to be transported, trial court properly directed verdict in favor of defendant because of insufficient evidence on the element "carry." State v. Cox, 156 Ind. App. 548, 297 N.E.2d 920, 1973 Ind. App. LEXIS 1163 (1973).

The fact a gun was found under the passenger seat of a car in which defendant had ridden was insufficient to establish possession. Frasier v. State, 262 Ind. 59, 312 N.E.2d 77, 1974 Ind. LEXIS 268 (1974), cert. denied, 419 U.S. 1092, 95 S. Ct. 686, 42 L. Ed. 2d 686, 1974 U.S. LEXIS 3842 (1974).

The defendant's conviction for carrying a handgun without a license was reversed since the mere evidence that the defendant was a passenger in the front seat of a vehicle in which a revolver was found on the driver's side floor of the back seat was, as a matter of law, insufficient to support beyond a reasonable doubt the inference that he once possessed the gun on his person. Cole v. State, 588 N.E.2d 1316, 1992 Ind. App. LEXIS 447 (1992).

Where information charged defendant with carrying a handgun on or about his person or in a vehicle, but there was no evidence that defendant had control over the vehicle in which the handgun was found, and he was neither driving the car nor was he the car's owner, the state failed to prove an essential element necessary for conviction based on carrying an unlicensed handgun in a vehicle. Walker v. State, 631 N.E.2d 1, 1994 Ind. App. LEXIS 174 (1994).

Where a passenger in a car knew a gun owned and licensed by the driver was at his feet, the evidence was insufficient to sustain a conviction for carrying a handgun where there was no evidence of any movement or action to suggest that the passenger exercised dominion. Henderson v. State, 715 N.E.2d 833, 1999 Ind. LEXIS 686, 88 A.L.R.5th 727 (1999).

There was insufficient evidence to support defendant's IC 35-47-2-1 conviction where: (1) defendant did not have direct physical control over a handgun found in a car, which was owned and had been driven that evening by defendant's cousin; (2) there was no evidence that the clothes upon which the gun was found were defendant's; (3) the mere fact defendant was alone in the car when police found the gun did not establish that defendant possessed it; (4) although the gun was in the middle of the back seat, and defendant had reclined defendant's seat, possession of a gun found in the rear of a vehicle is not imputed to a person in the front passenger seat; and (5) defendant evidenced no awareness of the gun when approached by police, made no furtive gestures, and made no incriminating statements. Jones v. State,

Evidence. (Cont'd)

—Insufficient. (Cont'd)
881 N.E.2d 1095, 2008 Ind. App. LEXIS 2223 (2008).

—Sufficient.
Evidence that defendant used handgun on night of alleged crime, and that at trial state introduced pistol identified as strongly resembling one defendant had on such night, was sufficient to support conviction of carrying pistol in violation of statute, especially in view of photograph of such pistol as it was found. Thomas v. State, 256 Ind. 309, 268 N.E.2d 609, 1971 Ind. LEXIS 631 (1971).

Evidence that search of gun license records failed to reveal any license issued to defendant was sufficient to support conviction of carrying pistol without license, notwithstanding such search was made by police licensing supervisor rather than police superintendent. Thomas v. State, 256 Ind. 309, 268 N.E.2d 609, 1971 Ind. LEXIS 631 (1971).

Evidence that defendant went to residence of others with pistol and caused general disturbance in presence of five witnesses by displaying pistol, that two of such five witnesses testified unequivocally as to defendant's actions at trial, and that defendant was not licensed to carry firearms on date of offense, was sufficient to support conviction of violation of statute. Anness v. State, 256 Ind. 368, 269 N.E.2d 8, 1971 Ind. LEXIS 640 (1971).

Even when the pistol was not introduced as evidence, the testimony that the defendant was carrying the pistol in a place not his abode or business and that defendant did not have a license was sufficient evidence to sustain a conviction of carrying a pistol without a license. Wilson v. State, 164 Ind. App. 665, 330 N.E.2d 356, 1975 Ind. App. LEXIS 1199 (1975).

Defendant need not be found to have been carrying pistol on or about his person in order to be found in violation of former IC 35-23-4.1-3, where he was driver of vehicle in which pistol was found underneath driver's seat. Klopfenstein v. State, 439 N.E.2d 1181, 1982 Ind. App. LEXIS 1408 (1982).

Even when a gun is not introduced as evidence, the testimony of an eyewitness that the defendant was carrying a pistol in a place other than his dwelling or business and testimony that the defendant did not have a license to carry a handgun on that date is sufficient to sustain a conviction for carrying a handgun without a license. Youngblood v. State, 515 N.E.2d 522, 1987 Ind. LEXIS 1134 (1987).

Where victim observed defendant carrying a pistol approximately 20 minutes after the shooting incident, police officer responded to a call which reported that a red Cadillac had been involved, police officer then stopped an automobile matching the description only blocks away from victim's residence, and police officer seized a pistol from beneath the seat; this evidence permitted the factfinder to conclude that defendant was armed and that he discarded the handgun under the seat prior to officer's stop of the automobile. Ferrell v. State, 656 N.E.2d 839, 1995 Ind. App. LEXIS 1331 (1995).

Evidence was sufficient to support conviction where defendant was sitting in the back seat of a car when police officers approached him, officers saw him remove something from his pants and place the object next to him in the car, and then officers saw that the object was a gun. Henderson v. State, 686 N.E.2d 911, 1997 Ind. App. LEXIS 1560 (1997), transfer granted, 698 N.E.2d 1182 (Ind. 1998), aff'd, 690 N.E.2d 706, 1998 Ind. LEXIS 2 (1998).

Evidence was sufficient to support convictions for carrying a handgun without a license and being a habitual offender; fingerprint expert properly identified plaintiff in court and arrest reports and orders of convictions sufficiently linked defendant to offenses to show plaintiff was the person convicted of each crime. Sides v. State, 693 N.E.2d 1310, 1998 Ind. LEXIS 37 (1998), overruled, Jones v. State, 863 N.E.2d 333, 2007 Ind. App. LEXIS 573 (2007).

Where the defendant presented no evidence that he possessed a valid gun license, and evidence was introduced that he shot the victim from a car, thus showing possession of a handgun outside his dwelling or business, there was sufficient evidence to sustain a conviction for carrying a handgun without a license. Williams v. State, 700 N.E.2d 784, 1998 Ind. LEXIS 484 (1998).

Evidence sufficient to support the defendant's conviction was presented where two witnesses observed the defendant chase and shoot the victim, and another witness observed the victim laying on the ground while the defendant, carrying a handgun, walked away. Dobbins v. State, 721 N.E.2d 867, 1999 Ind. LEXIS 1191 (1999).

There was sufficient evidence from which a jury could have reasonably concluded that the defendant killed the victim where there was both an eyewitness and a corroborating witness identifying the defendant as the shooter. Newson v. State, 721 N.E.2d 237, 1999 Ind. LEXIS 1251 (1999).

There was sufficient evidence to support the defendant's conviction for carrying a handgun without a license where he was in the back seat of a car from which shots were fired, where the officer who stopped the car noticed the defendant handing something to another passenger who then threw objects out of the car, and where four firearms were later found near the car. Wallace v. State, 722 N.E.2d 910, 2000 Ind. App. LEXIS 78 (2000).

Where a witness at trial testified he saw defendant carrying a handgun and defendant failed to present evidence that he possessed a valid license to carry a weapon, this was sufficient evidence to establish the elements of carrying a handgun without a license. Skaggs v. State, 751 N.E.2d 318, 2001 Ind. App. LEXIS 1102 (2001).

Evidence was sufficient to sustain defendant's conviction for carrying a handgun without a license where: a man, armed with a gun and dressed as the defendant, shot the victim in the stomach; the man ordered the other victim to open the register and lie on the floor; the man stole money from the register; and defendant had over $300 in small bills on his person when he was arrested. Hill v. State, 773 N.E.2d 336, 2002 Ind. App.

Evidence. (Cont'd)

—Sufficient. (Cont'd)

LEXIS 1331 (2002), clarified, 777 N.E.2d 795, 2002 Ind. App. LEXIS 1816 (Ind. Ct. App. 2002), cert. denied, 540 U.S. 832, 124 S. Ct. 79, 157 L. Ed. 2d 59, 2003 U.S. LEXIS 6188 (2003).

Evidence that defendant was driving car and knew there was handgun in car was sufficient to convict defendant of carrying handgun without license. Thurman v. State, 793 N.E.2d 318, 2003 Ind. App. LEXIS 1511 (2003).

Evidence was sufficient to affirm defendant's conviction for possessing handgun with no license in violation of IC 35-47-2-1 and IC 35-47-2-23(c) where handgun was in plain view in close proximity to defendant in vehicle in which defendant was passenger. Grim v. State, 797 N.E.2d 825, 2003 Ind. App. LEXIS 1978 (2003).

Defendant's conviction for carrying handgun without license was sufficiently supported by police officer's testimony that he observed handgun drop from defendant's waistband; furthermore, trial court did not err in admitting statement "Did they find the gun" made by defendant to his sister at scene of crime. Stokes v. State, 828 N.E.2d 937, 2005 Ind. App. LEXIS 1056 (2005), cert. denied, 547 U.S. 1043, 164 L. Ed. 2d 339, 126 S. Ct. 1623, 2006 U.S. LEXIS 2563 (2006).

State presented sufficient evidence to support defendant's conviction for carrying a handgun without a license as a Class C felony where state showed that defendant did not have a license for the handgun that he threw away when police came by searching for somebody involved in drug activity and shined a spotlight on him standing behind a car just before he tossed gun under car; defendant could not show that he had a recognized, justifiable reason for carrying the gun without a permit, as the evidence showed that defendant did not live at the residence where police confronted him and the residence was not defendant's fixed place of business. Campbell v. State, 841 N.E.2d 624, 2006 Ind. App. LEXIS 131 (2006).

Evidence was sufficient to support defendant's conviction for carrying a handgun without a license as a Class C felony in violation of IC 35-47-2-1; even though the handgun found in her purse was disassembled, it met the definition of a "firearm" because it could be readily converted to expel a projectile by means of an explosion, IC 35-47-1-5, and could be fired with one hand, IC 35-47-1-6, and the state produced sufficient evidence that she did not possess a license to carry it. Staten v. State, 844 N.E.2d 186, 2006 Ind. App. LEXIS 477 (2006).

Officer found a handgun within easy reach in an unlocked glove compartment of defendant's car and the magazine for the handgun was in the trunk. As neither defendant nor the officer could say definitively that the gun required the magazine to be in place in order to be fired, the jury could have found that defendant failed to prove under IC 35-47-2-2(11) that the gun was unloaded or was in a secure wrapper; therefore, defendant was properly convicted of violating IC 35-47-2-1. Tormoehlen v. State, 848 N.E.2d 326, 2006 Ind. App. LEXIS 998 (2006).

There was sufficient evidence to convict defendant of voluntary manslaughter under IC 35-42-1-3, attempted aggravated battery under IC 35-42-2-1.5, and carrying a handgun without a license under IC 35-47-2-1 because a victim-eyewitness testified that defendant was the shooter of her boyfriend and that he also shot at her, and any inconsistencies in her testimony were not so significant that they rendered her testimony incredibly dubious. It was for the jury to decide the weight and credibility to assign to her testimony, and her testimony was sufficient to support the jury's determination that defendant was the shooter. Gleaves v. State, 859 N.E.2d 766, 2007 Ind. App. LEXIS 15 (2007).

Evidence was sufficient to support defendant's convictions for murder and carrying a handgun without a license, as the evidence presented in defendant's case showed that defendant went to an apartment building with a gun looking for a man who allegedly owed money to defendant, that defendant shot and fatally wounded the man once defendant found him, and that defendant did not have a license for the gun that defendant possessed. Dixson v. State, 865 N.E.2d 704, 2007 Ind. App. LEXIS 913 (2007).

Testimony of two witnesses, one of whom knew defendant, was sufficient to prove defendant possessed and used a firearm at the time in question, as both, one after being reminded of a prior identification, identified defendant as the shooter in a photo lineup, and defendant did not contend that the lineup was unduly suggestive. Stewart v. State, 866 N.E.2d 858, 2007 Ind. App. LEXIS 1085 (2007).

Exceptions.

In establishing the elements of the offense of carrying a pistol away from home or place of business without a license, the prosecution did not have to negate the exception of transporting from place of purchase while unloaded and in secure wrapper. Gray v. State, 159 Ind. App. 200, 305 N.E.2d 886, 1974 Ind. App. LEXIS 1109 (1974).

Indictment or Information.

Where the affidavit substantially followed the words of the statute, it was sufficient as against a motion to quash on the ground that the facts stated therein did not constitute a public offense. State v. Stephens, 241 Ind. 586, 174 N.E.2d 51, 1961 Ind. LEXIS 167 (1961).

Intent.

Voluntary intoxication was no defense in a prosecution for carrying a pistol without a license where statute did not require proof of specific criminal intent. Day v. State, 251 Ind. 399, 241 N.E.2d 357, 1968 Ind. LEXIS 586 (1968).

Where statute did not require defendant to know of the licensing requirements contained in it, it was only necessary that the defendant intended to do the act which was a violation of the statute. Johnson v. State, 256 Ind. 497, 269 N.E.2d 879, 1971 Ind. LEXIS 665 (1971), cert. denied, 405 U.S. 921, 92 S. Ct. 958, 30 L. Ed. 2d 792, 1972 U.S. LEXIS 3653 (1972).

Intent. (Cont'd)

Trial court did not err in entering judgment of conviction following bench trial on charge of disturbing cemetery without permit in violation of IC 14-21-1-26.5; state was only required to prove that defendant committed criminal act under that statute, which it did, and state was not also required to prove that defendant knew he did not have development plan to make cemetery alterations Scalpelli v. State, 827 N.E.2d 1193, 2005 Ind. App. LEXIS 929 (2005).

Jury Trial.

—Number of Jurors.

Where defendant was charged with a class A misdemeanor in violation of IC 35-47-2-1, and charged with a class C felony under IC 35-47-2-23(c)(2)(B), he should only have been charged with the class C felony, and he was entitled to a twelve-member jury. Henderson v. State, 686 N.E.2d 911, 1997 Ind. App. LEXIS 1560 (1997), transfer granted, 698 N.E.2d 1182 (Ind. 1998), aff'd, 690 N.E.2d 706, 1998 Ind. LEXIS 2 (1998).

A defendant who was charged with one count of carrying a handgun without a license, a Class A misdemeanor, and with another count of carrying a handgun without a license with a prior felony conviction, a Class C felony, was charged with a Class C felony, even though it would have been a less serious offense without a prior conviction, and defendant was entitled to be tried by a twelve-person jury. Henderson v. State, 690 N.E.2d 706, 1998 Ind. LEXIS 2 (1998).

Because the right to a 12-member jury is a purely statutory matter of trial procedure, and thus not a fundamental right, a defendant's failure to make an express objection to the trial court either personally or through his counsel constitutes a valid waiver of the right. Croney v. State, 710 N.E.2d 212, 1999 Ind. App. LEXIS 735 (1999).

Knowing and Voluntary Possession.

Where defendant was handed a gun by person in whose car she was riding, and she accepted the gun because she was afraid of that person, she knowingly accepted possession of the gun and had voluntary possession thereof, and her conviction was proper. Nichols v. State, 683 N.E.2d 1358, 1997 Ind. App. LEXIS 1159 (1997).

Lesser Included Offense.

Carrying a handgun without a license is not a lesser-included offense of felony murder during the commission of a robbery. Griffith v. State, 791 N.E.2d 235, 2003 Ind. App. LEXIS 1230 (2003), overruled in part, Phares v. State, 796 N.E.2d 305, 2003 Ind. App. LEXIS 1750 (Ind. Ct. App. 2003).

License.

Proof that a defendant does not possess a license to carry a handgun is not an element of the statute. Proof that the defendant had a license is an exception to the offense, and the burden is on him to prove he possessed a valid license. Washington v. State, 517 N.E.2d 77, 1987 Ind. LEXIS 1199 (1987).

License acquired after being cited for carrying a handgun without a license is not a "valid license" sufficient to require that the charge be dismissed pursuant to IC 35-47-2-24(b). A "valid license" is one that is valid at the time the handgun is carried. Tormoehlen v. State, 848 N.E.2d 326, 2006 Ind. App. LEXIS 998 (2006).

Defendant, after being charged with carrying a handgun without a valid license, in violation of IC 35-47-2-1, obtained a handgun license. He was properly convicted of the crime because under IC 35-47-2-24(b) only presentation of a license that was valid at the time the handgun was carried would negate the crime. Tormoehlen v. State, 848 N.E.2d 326, 2006 Ind. App. LEXIS 998 (2006).

Manifest Necessity.

In order to negate a claim of necessity, the state must disprove at least one element of the defense beyond a reasonable doubt. Dozier v. State, 709 N.E.2d 27, 1999 Ind. App. LEXIS 601 (1999).

Where a high school student had adequate alternatives to taking a loaded gun to school to protect himself against possible gang retaliation, namely telling his parents about threats, reporting those threats to the police, and contacting school authorities, his defense of manifest necessity could not stand. Dozier v. State, 709 N.E.2d 27, 1999 Ind. App. LEXIS 601 (1999).

Nonresidents.

There was nothing in the statute that exempted residents of another state from the requirement of obtaining a license to carry pistols. Garcia v. State, 260 Ind. 131, 292 N.E.2d 810, 1973 Ind. LEXIS 502 (1973).

Place of Abode.

Under prior law the phrase "the place of abode" did not include public streets or alleys regardless of who owned the lands on which the streets or alleys were situated. Dunbar v. State, 162 Ind. App. 375, 319 N.E.2d 630, 1974 Ind. App. LEXIS 844 (1974).

Plea.

—Voluntary and Intelligent.

Where defendant was charged with carrying a handgun without a permit and dealing in sawed-off shotguns and it was apparent that the court recognized from his initial answers the potential for an insufficient factual basis but his counsel interjected and questioned him in such a fashion as to establish constructive possession of the weapons and pointed out the potential problems of proving the elements of the offenses, but nevertheless requested the court to accept the plea due to the beneficial nature of the state's sentencing recommendation, defendant could not successfully claim his plea was involuntary or unintelligent since he was aware of the possible deficiencies in the factual basis and urged the court to accept his plea. Harvey v. State, 498 N.E.2d 1231, 1986 Ind. LEXIS 1320 (1986).

Proof.

—Operable Gun.

Indiana law does not require that the state prove a handgun is operable to obtain a conviction of carrying a handgun without a license; the fact that the handgun was designed to expel a projectile by means of an explosion is sufficient. Manley v. State, 656 N.E.2d 277, 1995 Ind. App. LEXIS 1272 (1995).

Right to Carry Handgun.

There is a state-created right to bear arms which includes the right to carry a handgun with a license, provided that all of the requirements of the Indiana Firearms Act are met. This right is protected by the Due Process Clause of the Fourteenth Amendment and is both a property and liberty interest for purposes of 42 U.S.C.S. § 1983. Kellogg v. Gary, 562 N.E.2d 685, 1990 Ind. LEXIS 226 (1990).

Where there was no evidence on record showing whether marijuana was found on defendant prior to police learning house which was subject of search warrant was not his, search of defendant was not incident to valid arrest for carrying handgun without a license, since it is not a violation to carry an unlicensed gun on one's own property. Perkins v. State, 695 N.E.2d 612, 1998 Ind. App. LEXIS 791 (1998).

Where officer responding to domestic disturbance complaint encountered defendant outside house and informed defendant that he was going to perform pat-down search, at which time defendant informed officer that he had handgun in his belt, and officer then arrested defendant, insufficient facts existed to support officer's investigatory stop of defendant on defendant's property; accordingly, defendant's motion to suppress gun, which was basis of charge against defendant of unlawful possession of firearm by serious violent felon, was properly granted, since officer did not know that defendant was serious violent felon when he performed investigatory stop. State v. Atkins, 834 N.E.2d 1028, 2005 Ind. App. LEXIS 1797 (2005).

Robbery.

The trial court did not erroneously make inconsistent findings when it determined that the defendant was not guilty of carrying a handgun without a license, but guilty of using a handgun to commit robbery and confinement where defendant was charged with carrying a handgun without a license as a Class D felony by alleging that the defendant had a prior conviction for the same type of offense, since conviction of the unlicensed handgun count as charged would have required not only proof that defendant was carrying a handgun, but also proof that defendant had previously been convicted of a similar offense and the acquittal does not necessarily and exclusively compel the conclusion that defendant was unarmed. Townsend v. State, 498 N.E.2d 1198, 1986 Ind. LEXIS 1305 (1986).

Search and Seizure.

Defendant and the vehicle in which he was a passenger were unlawfully detained beyond the parameters of a routine traffic stop and the ensuing search and seizure was unconstitutional; therefore, defendant's conviction, based on evidence obtained through an unlawful search, was reversed. Tumblin v. State, 736 N.E.2d 317, 2000 Ind. App. LEXIS 1581 (2000).

—Juveniles.

The protective search of a juvenile just outside classroom was permissible where the school safety officer received information from a student about the juvenile that caused her to remove the juvenile from the classroom, and her concern for her safety caused her to conduct a patdown search. In re C.S., 735 N.E.2d 273, 2000 Ind. App. LEXIS 1468 (2000).

—Officer's Reasonable Fear.

Defendant's furtive movements to the right of his body and hesitation at following the officer's commands, coupled with the fact that he wore an empty shoulder holster, provided a basis for a reasonable belief that the officer or others were in danger, and it was during this initial investigatory stop that the officer's right to conduct a limited weapons search of the passenger compartment of the vehicle to protect himself and others arose, even though he conducted the search after the defendant was in handcuffs and he no longer felt threatened. State v. Dodson, 733 N.E.2d 968, 2000 Ind. App. LEXIS 1206 (2000).

The patdown search was illegal where the record did not disclose specific facts that would have caused the officer, while making a routine traffic stop, to entertain a reasonable fear for his safety in issuing a citation or making an arrest. Tumblin v. State, 736 N.E.2d 317, 2000 Ind. App. LEXIS 1581 (2000).

Self-Defense.

Where the court denied the jury consideration of defendant's claim of self-defense, the instruction was in error because it ignored any nexus between the crime and the shooting; the error was reversible because on the undisputed evidence that defendant did not possess a firearms license, it denied him consideration of his claim of self-defense. Harvey v. State, 652 N.E.2d 876, 1995 Ind. App. LEXIS 738 (1995).

Sentence.

—Errors.

Where there was an inconsistency between the judge's in-court pronouncement of sentence and the subsequent abstract of judgment, and the Chronological Case Summary entry lengthened the sentence, the original in-court sentence was reinstated and the subsequent contradictory language vacated. Whatley v. State, 685 N.E.2d 48, 1997 Ind. LEXIS 130 (1997).

Cited:

Woods v. State, 471 N.E.2d 691, 1984 Ind. LEXIS 1058 (1984); Lucas v. State, 501 N.E.2d 480, 1986 Ind. App. LEXIS 3257 (1986); Fletcher v. State, 505 N.E.2d 491, 1987 Ind. App. LEXIS 2510 (1987);

Hall v. State, 524 N.E.2d 1279, 1988 Ind. LEXIS 205 (1988); Hazzard v. State, 642 N.E.2d 1368, 1994 Ind. LEXIS 151 (1994); Meriweather v. State, 659 N.E.2d 133, 1995 Ind. App. LEXIS 1572 (1995); Sears v. State, 668 N.E.2d 662, 1996 Ind. LEXIS 82 (1996); Valance v. Wisel, 110 F.3d 1269, 1997 U.S. App. LEXIS 6538 (7th Cir. Ind. 1997); Jenkins v. State, 677 N.E.2d 624, 1997 Ind. App. LEXIS 288 (1997); Hazzard v. State, 694 N.E.2d 283, 1998 Ind. LEXIS 56 (1998); Ramsey v. State, 723 N.E.2d 869, 2000 Ind. LEXIS 113 (2000); Emerson v. State, 724 N.E.2d 605, 2000 Ind. LEXIS 184 (2000); Perez v. State, 728 N.E.2d 234, 2000 Ind. App. LEXIS 743 (2000); VanZandt v. State, 731 N.E.2d 450, 2000 Ind. App. LEXIS 894 (2000); Bush v. State, 732 N.E.2d 250, 2000 Ind. App. LEXIS 1146 (2000); Scruggs v. State, 737 N.E.2d 385, 2000 Ind. LEXIS 981 (2000); Mickens v. State, 742 N.E.2d 927, 2001 Ind. LEXIS 189 (2001); Mayes v. State, 744 N.E.2d 390, 2001 Ind. LEXIS 217 (2001); Hopkins v. State, 747 N.E.2d 598, 2001 Ind. App. LEXIS 706 (2001); Burgett v. State, 758 N.E.2d 571, 2001 Ind. App. LEXIS 1978 (2001); Patton v. State, 760 N.E.2d 672, 2002 Ind. App. LEXIS 7 (2002); B.K.C. v. State, 781 N.E.2d 1157, 2003 Ind. App. LEXIS 1 (2003); Jackson v. State, 785 N.E.2d 615, 2003 Ind. App. LEXIS 456 (2003); State v. Gladney, 793 N.E.2d 264, 2003 Ind. App. LEXIS 1502 (2003); Harris v. State, 884 N.E.2d 399, 2008 Ind. App. LEXIS 729 (2008).

RESEARCH REFERENCES

Res Gestae.
Criminal justice notes, 37 Res Gestae 478 (1994).
Criminal Justice Notes 10/03: Constructive possession — handgun, drugs and paraphernalia in vehicle. 47 (No. 6) Res Gestae 43 (2004).

Collateral References.
Fact that gun was broken, dismantled, or inoperable as affecting criminal responsibility under weapons statute. 81 A.L.R.4th 745.
Validity of state gun control legislation under state constitutional provisions securing the right to bear arms. 86 A.L.R.4th 931.
What constitutes "constructive possession" of unregistered or otherwise prohibited weapon under state law. 88 A.L.R.5th 121.

35-47-2-2. Persons excepted.

Section 1 [IC 35-47-2-1] of this chapter does not apply to:
(1) Marshals;
(2) Sheriffs;
(3) The commissioner of the department of correction or persons authorized by him in writing to carry firearms;
(4) Judicial officers;
(5) Law enforcement officers;
(6) Members of the armed forces of the United States or of the national guard or organized reserves while they are on duty;
(7) Regularly enrolled members of any organization duly authorized to purchase or receive such weapons from the United States or from this state who are at or are going to or from their place of assembly or target practice;
(8) Employees of the United States duly authorized to carry handguns;
(9) Employees of express companies when engaged in company business;
(10) Any person engaged in the business of manufacturing, repairing, or dealing in firearms or the agent or representative of any such person having in his possession, using, or carrying a handgun in the usual or ordinary course of that business; or
(11) Any person while carrying a handgun unloaded and in a secure wrapper from the place of purchase to his dwelling or fixed place of business, or to a place of repair or back to his dwelling or fixed place of business, or in moving from one dwelling or business to another.

History.
IC 35-47-2-2, as added by P.L.311-1983, § 32.

NOTES TO DECISIONS

ANALYSIS

Burden of Proof.
Express Companies.
Gun Unloaded and in Secure Wrapper.
Law-Enforcement Officers.
Nonresidents.
Secure Wrapper.

Burden of Proof.

It was not necessary to negate in the indictment the exceptions mentioned in law and it was not incumbent upon the state to prove the defendant did not fall within these exceptions. Day v. State, 251 Ind. 399, 241 N.E.2d 357, 1968 Ind. LEXIS 586 (1968).

The burden was on the defendant to prove that he came within one of the exceptions. Moore v. State, 267 Ind. 270, 369 N.E.2d 628, 1977 Ind. LEXIS 496 (1977).

Express Companies.

Any ambiguity regarding the term "express companies" in subdivision (9) has been resolved by the legislature's definition of "express company" in former IC 8-2.1-21-1, enacted effective July 1, 1989. State v. Turner, 567 N.E.2d 783, 1991 Ind. LEXIS 28 (1991).

Gun Unloaded and in Secure Wrapper.

Where defendant, who had no license to carry gun, admitted that gun was under front seat of automobile but that cylinder was removed and was in grocery bag on back seat, and there was evidence that gun could have been reassembled easily, evidence was sufficient for jury to find that defendant did not come within the exception that the gun was unloaded and in a secure wrapper. Beck v. State, 414 N.E.2d 970, 1981 Ind. App. LEXIS 1214 (1981) (decided under former IC 35-23-4.1-4).

Officer found a handgun within easy reach in an unlocked glove compartment of defendant's car and the magazine for the handgun was in the trunk. As neither defendant nor the officer could say definitively that the gun required the magazine to be in place in order to be fired, the jury could have found that defendant failed to prove under IC 35-47-2-2(11) that the gun was unloaded or was in a secure wrapper; therefore, defendant was properly convicted of violating IC 35-47-2-1. Tormoehlen v. State, 848 N.E.2d 326, 2006 Ind. App. LEXIS 998 (2006).

Law-Enforcement Officers.

Where affidavit on which accused was arrested charged him with carrying "concealed upon his person a revolver," and the agreed statement of facts upon which the case was submitted to court alleged that accused was "at the time of his arrest a duly appointed deputy constable" in a certain township in the state, such statement of facts did not show that accused was a deputy constable at time and place the alleged offense was committed. McIntire v. State, 170 Ind. 163, 83 N.E. 1005, 1908 Ind. LEXIS 15 (1908).

Nonresidents.

There was nothing in the statute that exempted residents of another state from the requirements of obtaining a license to carry pistols. Garcia v. State, 260 Ind. 131, 292 N.E.2d 810, 1973 Ind. LEXIS 502 (1973).

Secure Wrapper.

Carrying a pistol by one's side in one's belt was not carrying it in a "secure wrapper" as required to meet the exception. Gray v. State, 159 Ind. App. 200, 305 N.E.2d 886, 1974 Ind. App. LEXIS 1109 (1974).

Cited:

Lewis v. State, 484 N.E.2d 77, 1985 Ind. App. LEXIS 2887 (1985).

35-47-2-3. Issuance of licenses.

(a) A person desiring a license to carry a handgun shall apply:

(1) to the chief of police or corresponding law enforcement officer of the municipality in which the applicant resides;

(2) if that municipality has no such officer, or if the applicant does not reside in a municipality, to the sheriff of the county in which the applicant resides after the applicant has obtained an application form prescribed by the superintendent; or

(3) if the applicant is a resident of another state and has a regular place of business or employment in Indiana, to the sheriff of the county in which the applicant has a regular place of business or employment.

The superintendent and local law enforcement agencies shall allow an applicant desiring to obtain or renew a license to carry a handgun to submit an application electronically under this chapter if funds are available to establish and maintain an electronic application system.

(b) The law enforcement agency which accepts an application for a handgun license shall collect the following application fees:

(1) From a person applying for a four (4) year handgun license, a ten dollar ($10) application fee, five dollars ($5) of which shall be refunded if the license is not issued.

(2) From a person applying for a lifetime handgun license who does not currently possess a valid Indiana handgun license, a fifty dollar ($50) application fee, thirty dollars ($30) of which shall be refunded if the license is not issued.

(3) From a person applying for a lifetime handgun license who currently possesses a valid Indiana handgun license, a forty dollar ($40) application fee, thirty dollars ($30) of which shall be refunded if the license is not issued.

Except as provided in subsection (h), the fee shall be deposited into the law enforcement agency's firearms training fund or other appropriate training activities fund and used by the agency to train law enforcement officers in the proper use of firearms or in other law enforcement duties, or to purchase firearms or firearm related equipment, or both for the law enforcement officers employed by the law enforcement agency. The state board of accounts shall establish rules for the proper accounting and expenditure of funds collected under this subsection.

(c) The officer to whom the application is made shall ascertain the applicant's name, full address, length of residence in the community, whether the applicant's residence is located within the limits of any city or town, the applicant's occupation, place of business or employment, criminal record, if any, and convictions (minor traffic offenses excepted), age, race, sex, nationality, date of birth, citizenship, height, weight, build, color of hair, color of eyes, scars and marks, whether the applicant has previously held an Indiana license to carry a handgun and, if so, the serial number of the license and year issued, whether the applicant's license has ever been suspended or revoked, and if so, the year and reason for the suspension or revocation, and the applicant's reason for desiring a license. The officer to whom the application is made shall conduct an investigation into the applicant's official records and verify thereby the applicant's character and reputation, and shall in addition verify for accuracy the information contained in the application, and shall forward this information together with the officer's recommendation for approval or disapproval and one (1) set of legible and classifiable fingerprints of the applicant to the superintendent.

(d) The superintendent may make whatever further investigation the superintendent deems necessary. Whenever disapproval is recommended, the officer to whom the application is made shall provide the superintendent and the applicant with the officer's complete and specific reasons, in writing, for the recommendation of disapproval.

(e) If it appears to the superintendent that the applicant:

(1) has a proper reason for carrying a handgun;

(2) is of good character and reputation;

(3) is a proper person to be licensed; and

(4) is:

(A) a citizen of the United States; or

(B) not a citizen of the United States but is allowed to carry a firearm in the United States under federal law;

the superintendent shall issue to the applicant a qualified or an unlimited license to carry any handgun lawfully possessed by the applicant. The original license shall be delivered to the licensee. A copy shall be delivered to the officer to whom the application for license was made. A copy shall be retained by the superintendent for at least four (4) years in the case of a four (4) year license. The superintendent may adopt guidelines to establish a records retention policy for a lifetime license. A four (4) year license shall be valid for a period of four (4) years from the date of issue. A lifetime license is valid for the life of the individual receiving the license. The license of police officers, sheriffs or their deputies, and law enforcement officers of the United States government who have been honorably retired by a lawfully created pension board or its equivalent after twenty (20) or more years of service, shall be valid for the life of these individuals. However, a lifetime license is automatically revoked if the license holder does not remain a proper person.

(f) At the time a license is issued and delivered to a licensee under subsection (e), the superintendent shall include with the license information concerning handgun safety rules that:

(1) neither opposes nor supports an individual's right to bear arms; and

(2) is:

(A) recommended by a nonprofit educational organization that is dedicated to providing education on safe handling and use of firearms;

(B) prepared by the state police department; and

(C) approved by the superintendent.

The superintendent may not deny a license under this section because the information required under this subsection is unavailable at the time the superintendent would otherwise issue a license. The state police department may accept private donations or grants to defray the cost of printing and mailing the information required under this subsection.

(g) A license to carry a handgun shall not be issued to any person who:

(1) has been convicted of a felony;

(2) has had a license to carry a handgun suspended, unless the person's license has been reinstated;

(3) is under eighteen (18) years of age;

(4) is under twenty-three (23) years of age if the person has been adjudicated a delinquent child for an act that would be a felony if committed by an adult; or

(5) has been arrested for a Class A or Class B felony, or any other felony that was committed while armed with a deadly weapon or that involved the use of violence, if a court has found probable cause to believe that the person committed the offense charged.

In the case of an arrest under subdivision (5), a license to carry a handgun may be issued to a person who has been acquitted of the specific offense charged or if the charges for the specific offense are dismissed. The superintendent shall prescribe all forms to be used in connection with the administration of this chapter.

(h) If the law enforcement agency that charges a fee under subsection (b) is a city or town law enforcement agency, the fee shall be deposited in the law enforcement continuing education fund established under IC 5-2-8-2.

(i) If a person who holds a valid license to carry a handgun issued under this chapter:

(1) changes the person's name;

(2) changes the person's address; or

(3) experiences a change, including an arrest or a conviction, that may affect the person's status as a proper person (as defined in IC 35-47-1-7) or otherwise disqualify the person from holding a license;

the person shall, not later than thirty (30) days after the date of a change described under subdivision (3), and not later than sixty (60) days after the date of the change described under subdivision (1) or (2), notify the superintendent, in writing, of the event described under subdivision (3) or, in the case of a change under subdivision (1) or (2), the person's new name or new address.

(j) The state police shall indicate on the form for a license to carry a handgun the notification requirements of subsection (i).

(k) The state police department shall adopt rules under IC 4-22-2 to implement an electronic application system under subsection (a). Rules adopted under this section must require the superintendent to keep on file one (1) set of classifiable and legible fingerprints from every person who has received a license to carry a handgun so that a person who applies to renew a license will not be required to submit an additional set of fingerprints.

History.

IC 35-47-2-3, as added by P.L.311-1983, § 32; P.L.26-1990, § 15; P.L.48-1993, § 5; P.L.140-1994, § 6; P.L.269-1995, § 6; P.L.2-1996, § 284; P.L.27-

2001, § 1; P.L.120-2001, § 1; P.L.49-2005, § 2; P.L.187-2005, § 3; P.L.190-2006, § 2; P.L.155-2007, § 1, eff. July 1, 2007.

NOTES TO DECISIONS

ANALYSIS

Application for Permit to Carry Handgun.
Refusal to Make Applications Available.

Application for Permit to Carry Handgun.
Where application for permit to carry handgun was because of need for self-protection, superintendent of state police had no power to deny application on ground that applicant did not have a proper reason to be so licensed but where there was conflicting evidence as to applicant's suitability to be licensed the matter was remanded for the determination of such issue. Schubert v. De Bard, 398 N.E.2d 1339, 1980 Ind. App. LEXIS 1260 (1980) (decided under former IC 35-23-4.1-5).

Refusal to Make Applications Available.
Where chief of police refused to make applications for gun permits available at his office, it was within the discretion of the court to grant a preliminary injunction enjoining such chief of police from interfering with the distribution of applications for handgun permits. Motley v. Kellogg, 409 N.E.2d 1207, 1980 Ind. App. LEXIS 1699 (1980) (decided under former IC 35-23-4.1-5).

Cited:
Valance v. Wisel, 110 F.3d 1269, 1997 U.S. App. LEXIS 6538 (7th Cir. Ind. 1997); Murray v. State, 742 N.E.2d 932, 2001 Ind. LEXIS 192 (2001).

35-47-2-4. Qualified licenses — Unlimited licenses.

(a) Licenses to carry handguns shall be either qualified or unlimited, and are valid for:
   (1) four (4) years from the date of issue in the case of a four (4) year license; or
   (2) the life of the individual receiving the license in the case of a lifetime license.
A qualified license shall be issued for hunting and target practice. The superintendent may adopt rules imposing limitations on the use and carrying of handguns under a license when handguns are carried by a licensee as a condition of employment. Unlimited licenses shall be issued for the purpose of the protection of life and property.

(b) In addition to the application fee, the fee for:
   (1) a qualified license shall be:
      (A) five dollars ($5) for a four (4) year qualified license;
      (B) twenty-five dollars ($25) for a lifetime qualified license from a person who does not currently possess a valid Indiana handgun license; or
      (C) twenty dollars ($20) for a lifetime qualified license from a person who currently possesses a valid Indiana handgun license; and
   (2) an unlimited license shall be:
      (A) thirty dollars ($30) for a four (4) year unlimited license;
      (B) seventy-five dollars ($75) for a lifetime unlimited license from a person who does not currently possess a valid Indiana handgun license; or
      (C) sixty dollars ($60) for a lifetime unlimited license from a person who currently possesses a valid Indiana handgun license.
The superintendent shall charge a twenty dollar ($20) fee for the issuance of a duplicate license to replace a lost or damaged license. These fees shall be deposited in accordance with subsection (e).

(c) Licensed dealers are exempt from the payment of fees specified in subsection (b) for a qualified license or an unlimited license.

(d) The following officers of this state or the United States who have been honorably retired by a lawfully created pension board or its equivalent after at least twenty (20) years of service or because of a disability are exempt from the payment of fees specified in subsection (b):

(1) Police officers.

(2) Sheriffs or their deputies.

(3) Law enforcement officers.

(4) Correctional officers.

(e) Fees collected under this section shall be deposited in the state general fund.

(f) The superintendent may not issue a lifetime qualified license or a lifetime unlimited license to a person who is a resident of another state. The superintendent may issue a four (4) year qualified license or a four (4) year unlimited license to a person who is a resident of another state and who has a regular place of business or employment in Indiana as described in section 3(a)(3) [IC 35-47-2-3(a)(3)] of this chapter.

History.
IC 35-47-2-4, as added by P.L.311-1983, § 22; P.L.209-1986, § 1; P.L.148-1987, § 4; P.L.75-1989, § 9; P.L.190-2006, § 3; P.L.1-2007, § 235, emergency eff. March 30, 2007; P.L.155-2007, § 2, eff. July 1, 2007.

NOTES TO DECISIONS

Double Jeopardy.
Defendant's convictions for robbery and carrying a handgun without a license are not the same offense under Indiana's double jeopardy clause. Ho v. State, 725 N.E.2d 988, 2000 Ind. App. LEXIS 435 (2000).

35-47-2-5. Suspension or revocation of licenses.

(a) The superintendent may suspend or revoke any license issued under this chapter if he has reasonable grounds to believe that the person's license should be suspended or revoked.

(b) Documented evidence that a person is not a "proper person" to be licensed as defined by IC 35-47-1-7, or is prohibited under section 3(g)(5) [IC 35-47-2-3(g)(5)] of this chapter from being issued a license, shall be grounds for immediate suspension or revocation of a license previously issued under this chapter. However, if a license is suspended or revoked based solely on an arrest under section 3(g)(5) of this chapter, the license shall be reinstated upon the acquittal of the defendant in that case or upon the dismissal of the charges for the specific offense.

(c) A person who fails to promptly return his license after written notice of suspension or revocation commits a Class A misdemeanor. The observation of a handgun license in the possession of a person whose license has been suspended or revoked constitutes a sufficient basis for the arrest of that person for violation of this subsection.

(d) The superintendent shall establish rules under IC 4-22-2 concerning the procedure for suspending or revoking a person's license.

History.
IC 35-47-2-5, as added by P.L.311-1983, § 32; P.L.140-1994, § 7; P.L.2-1996, § 285; P.L.120-2001, § 2; P.L.1-2006, § 535.

Cross References.
Penalties for misdemeanors, IC 35-50-1, IC 35-50-3, IC 35-50-5-2.

35-47-2-6. Time for review of applications.

(a) Every initial application for any license under this chapter shall be granted or rejected within sixty (60) days after the application is filed.

(b) The period during which an application for the renewal of an existing license may be filed begins one hundred eighty (180) days before the expiration of the existing license. If the application for renewal of an existing license is filed within thirty (30) days of its expiration, the existing license is automatically extended until the application for renewal is passed upon.

History.
IC 35-47-2-6, as added by P.L.311-1983, § 32; P.L.190-2006, § 4.

35-47-2-7. Prohibited sales or transfers.

(a) Except an individual acting within a parent-minor child or guardian-minor protected person relationship or any other individual who is also acting in compliance with IC 35-47-10, a person may not sell, give, or in any other manner transfer the ownership or possession of a handgun or assault weapon [firearm] (as defined in IC 35-50-2-11) to any person under eighteen (18) years of age.

(b) It is unlawful for a person to sell, give, or in any manner transfer the ownership or possession of a handgun to another person who the person has reasonable cause to believe:

(1) Has been:
(A) Convicted of a felony; or
(B) Adjudicated a delinquent child for an act that would be a felony if committed by an adult, if the person seeking to obtain ownership or possession of the handgun is less than twenty-three (23) years of age;
(2) Is a drug abuser;
(3) Is an alcohol abuser; or
(4) Is mentally incompetent.

History.
IC 35-47-2-7, as added by P.L.311-1983, § 32; P.L.33-1989, § 126; P.L.140-1994, § 8; P.L.269-1995, § 7.

Compiler's Notes.
The bracketed reference to firearm was inserted by the compiler to reflect the 1996 amendment to IC 35-50-2-11.

NOTES TO DECISIONS

ANALYSIS

Civil Liability.
Negligence.
Strict Liability.

Civil Liability.
Persons who sold dangerous weapons to minors were liable for the damages resulting from the use thereof. Binford v. Johnston, 82 Ind. 426, 1882 Ind. LEXIS 154 (1882); Gartin v. Meredith, 153 Ind. 16, 53 N.E. 936, 1899 Ind. LEXIS 5 (1899).

Negligence.
A genuine issue of fact, precluding summary judgment, existed concerning whether a pawn shop owner committed negligence per se in selling a firearm to a mentally ill customer, and whether the customer's subsequent use of the weapon to commit murder was a foreseeable result. Rubin v. Johnson, 550 N.E.2d 324, 1990 Ind. App. LEXIS 157 (1990).

Homeowners were required to use reasonable care in storing a handgun in the homeowners' home, as public policy favored the safe storage of firearms, and the constitutional right to bear arms, under Ind. Const., art. 1, § 32, did not shield the homeowners from negligence claims tangentially related to the exercise of the right to bear arms;

the Indiana Legislature deemed the safety risk associated with the possession of handguns by certain individuals too high, as set forth in IC 35-47-2-7, and implicit within that statute was a recognition that a degree of responsibility was associated with handgun ownership. Estate of Heck v. Stoffer, 786 N.E.2d 265, 2003 Ind. LEXIS 293 (2003).

Strict Liability.
Presumption that legislature intends to include culpable mental state in criminal statute may be overcome where factors decisively indicate otherwise. The conclusion the legislature intended to make a violation of this section an offense not requiring a culpable mental state was supported by the facts that transfer of a gun to a minor presents a danger to the public and the age of a minor can be easily ascertained; the factors of severity of punishment and expected number of prosecutions which militate against strict liability are insufficient to overcome this conclusion. State v. Shelton, 692 N.E.2d 947, 1998 Ind. App. LEXIS 348 (1998).

Cited:
Johnson v. Patterson, 570 N.E.2d 93, 1991 Ind. App. LEXIS 662 (1991); Howard v. United States, 962 F.2d 651, 1992 U.S. App. LEXIS 8892 (7th Cir.

Ind. 1992); United States v. Wagner, 976 F.2d 354,
1992 U.S. App. LEXIS 24334 (7th Cir. Ind. 1992).

RESEARCH REFERENCES

Indiana Law Review.
Recent Developments in Indiana Criminal Law
and Procedure, 28 Ind. L. Rev. 819 (1995).
Survey: Criminal Law and Procedure: Recent
Developments in Indiana, 32 Ind. L. Rev. 789
(1999).

Res Gestae.
Recent Decisions 4/03: Appellate civil law case
update: Parents whose son took their gun owed
duty to police officer killed by said gun, 47 (No. 1)
Res Gestae 15 (2003).

Collateral References.
What amounts to "control" under state statute
making it illegal for felon to have possession or
control of firearm or other dangerous weapon. 66
A.L.R.4th 1240.
Fact that gun was broken, dismantled, or inoperable as affecting criminal responsibility under
weapons statute. 81 A.L.R.4th 745.
Firearm or ammunition manufacturer or seller's
liability for injuries caused to another by use of
gun in committing crime. 88 A.L.R.5th 1.

35-47-2-8. Persons to whom sale regulations apply.

The regulation of the sale of handguns imposed by this chapter shall apply equally
to an occasional sale, trade, or transfer between individual persons and to retail
transactions between dealers and individual persons.

History.
IC 35-47-2-8, as added by P.L.311-1983, § 32;
P.L.17-1997, § 6.

35-47-2-9 — 35-47-2-13. [Repealed.]

Compiler's Notes.
IC 35-47-2-9 — IC 35-47-2-12, concerning the
manner of the sale or transfer of handguns, application forms, searches of law enforcement records,
and unlawful delivery of handguns, were repealed
by P.L.17-1997, § 9, effective November 30, 1998.

IC 35-47-2-13, concerning records of lawful
transfers of handguns and application forms as
proof of ownership, was repealed by P.L.17-1997,
§ 10, effective May 13, 1997.
For present similar provisions, see IC 35-47-2.5.

35-47-2-14. License requirements for retail dealer — Failure to display license.

A retail dealer who:
(1) Sells;
(2) Trades;
(3) Transfers;
(4) Exposes for sale, trade, or transfer; or
(5) Possesses with intent to sell, trade, or transfer;
any handgun without being licensed under sections 15 and 16 [IC 35-47-2-15 and IC
35-47-2-16] of this chapter and without displaying his license at all times commits
a Class B misdemeanor.

History.
IC 35-47-2-14, as added by P.L.311-1983, § 32.

Cross References.
Penalties for misdemeanors, IC 35-50-1, IC 35-
50-3, IC 35-50-5-2.

35-47-2-15. Issuance of retail handgun dealer's license — Investigation and fingerprinting.

(a) A person desiring a retail handgun dealer's license shall apply to the sheriff of
the county in which he resides, or if he is a resident of another state and has a
regular place of business in Indiana, then to the sheriff of the county in which he has
a regular place of business. The applicant shall state his name, full address,

occupation, sex, race, age, place of birth, date of birth, nationality, height, weight, build, color of eyes, color of hair, complexion, scars and marks, and any criminal record (minor traffic offenses excepted). The officer to whom the application is made shall verify the application and search his records concerning the applicant's character and reputation.

(b) The officer to whom the application is made shall send to the superintendent:

(1) The verified application;

(2) The results of the officer's investigation; and

(3) The officer's recommendation for approval or disapproval of the application; in as many copies as the superintendent shall designate, and one (1) set of legible and classifiable fingerprints of the applicant. The superintendent may make whatever further investigation he deems necessary. Whenever disapproval is recommended by the officer to whom the application was made, he shall provide the superintendent and the applicant with his complete reasons for the disapproval in writing. If the officer to whom the application is made recommends approval, he shall instruct the applicant in the proper method of taking legible and classifiable fingerprints. If it appears to the superintendent that the applicant is of good character and reputation and a proper person to be licensed, he shall issue to the applicant a retail handgun dealer's license which shall be valid for a period of two (2) years from the date of issue. The fee for the license shall be twenty dollars ($20), which shall be deposited with the officer to whom the application is made, who shall in turn forward it to the superintendent for deposit with the treasurer of state when the application is approved by the superintendent. In the event that the application is disapproved by the superintendent, the fee shall be returned to the applicant along with the complete reasons, in writing, for the disapproval.

(c) No retail dealer's license shall be issued to any person who has been:

(1) Convicted of a felony; or

(2) Adjudicated a delinquent child for an act that would be a felony if committed by an adult, if the person applying for the retail dealer's license is less than twenty-three (23) years of age;

in Indiana or any other state or country.

(d) A retail dealer's license shall permit the licensee to sell handguns at retail within this state subject to the conditions specified in this chapter. The license may be suspended or revoked in accordance with applicable law, and the licensee may be subject to punishment as provided in this chapter.

History.
IC 35-47-2-15, as added by P.L.311-1983, § 32; P.L.191-1984, § 4; P.L.269-1995, § 9.

35-47-2-16. License-designated business site — Display of license — Restrictions on sale of handguns — Display, sale or transfer at gun shows.

(a) A retail dealer's business shall be carried on only in the site designated in the license. A separate license shall be required for each separate retail outlet. Whenever a licensed dealer moves his place of business, he shall promptly notify the superintendent, who shall at once issue an amended license certificate valid for the balance of the license period. This subsection does not apply to sales at wholesale.

(b) The license, certified by the issuing authority, shall be displayed on the business premises in a prominent place where it can be seen easily by prospective customers.

(c) No handgun shall be sold:

(1) In violation of any provision of this chapter; or

(2) Under any circumstances unless the purchaser is personally known to the seller or presents clear evidence of his identity.

(d) Notwithstanding subsection (a), a retail dealer may display, sell, or transfer handguns at a gun show in accordance with this chapter and federal law.

History.
IC 35-47-2-16, as added by P.L.311-1983, § 32;
P.L.191-1984, § 5; P.L.148-1987, § 5.

35-47-2-17. False information — Confiscation and disposal of handgun.

No person, in purchasing or otherwise securing delivery of a handgun or in applying for a license to carry a handgun, shall give false information or offer false evidence of identity. In addition to any penalty provided by this chapter, any handgun obtained through false information shall be subject to confiscation and disposition as provided in this chapter. Upon notice of a violation of this section by the superintendent, it shall be the duty of the sheriff or chief of police or corresponding officer of the jurisdiction in which the purchaser resides to confiscate the firearm and retain it as evidence pending trial for the offense.

History.
IC 35-47-2-17, as added by P.L.311-1983, § 32.

35-47-2-18. Alteration, removal or obliteration of identifying marks prohibited — Possession of such handguns prohibited.

No person shall:
(1) Change, alter, remove, or obliterate the name of the maker, model, manufacturer's serial number, or other mark of identification on any handgun; or
(2) Possess any handgun on which the name of the maker, model, manufacturer's serial number, or other mark of identification has been changed, altered, removed, or obliterated;
except as provided by applicable United States statute.

History.
IC 35-47-2-18, as added by P.L.311-1983, § 32.

NOTES TO DECISIONS

ANALYSIS

Elements.
—Knowing Alteration.
Evidence.
—Sufficient.
Proof of Exemption.

Elements.

—Knowing Alteration.
In a prosecution under this section for possession of a handgun with an altered serial number, the state must prove that a defendant had knowledge of the serial number's alteration. Wagerman v. State, 597 N.E.2d 13, 1992 Ind. App. LEXIS 1227 (1992).

Evidence.

—Sufficient.
Testimony by apprehending police officers that a handgun was found with the defendant's belongings and that the serial number had been scratched off was sufficient to convict defendant for possession of a handgun with an obliterated serial number. Hanson v. State, 704 N.E.2d 152, 1999 Ind. App. LEXIS 6 (1999).

Where the state's expert testified that the gun's serial number had been "ground, filed," and had "some kind of abrasion device" applied to it, with the result that the serial number was materially transformed or obscured, this evidence was sufficient for a jury to find that the serial number on defendant's gun was changed, altered, removed, or obliterated, as prohibited by IC 35-47-2-18. Chambliss v. State, 746 N.E.2d 73, 2001 Ind. LEXIS 346 (2001).

Defendant's conviction of possession of an altered handgun under IC 35-47-2-18 and IC 35-47-2-23(b) was supported by sufficient evidence, based on testimony by an officer that the area where the serial number had been was "very shiny," and the fact that defendant had been in possession of the gun for over a week. Robles v. State, 758 N.E.2d 581, 2001 Ind. App. LEXIS 1986 (2001).

Proof of Exemption.
IC 35-47-2-19 is an exemption under the chapter on handguns which the state is not required to

Proof of Exemption. (Cont'd)
negate, and prosecution of the offense of possession of a handgun with an obliterated serial number does not require proof of when the handgun was manufactured as an element of the offense. McKeller v. State, 620 N.E.2d 744, 1993 Ind. App. LEXIS 1139 (1993).

Cited:
Robinson v. State, 730 N.E.2d 185, 2000 Ind. App. LEXIS 864 (2000).

RESEARCH REFERENCES

Indiana Law Review.
Update — Criminal Law and Procedure, 26 Ind. L. Rev. 891 (1993).

35-47-2-19. Firearms exempted.

This chapter does not apply to any firearm not designed to use fixed cartridges or fixed ammunition, or any firearm made before January 1, 1899.

History.
IC 35-47-2-19, as added by P.L.311-1983, § 32.

NOTES TO DECISIONS

Applicability.
This section is an exemption under the chapter on handguns which the state is not required to negate, and prosecution of the offense of possession of a handgun with an obliterated serial number does not require proof of when the handgun was manufactured as an element of the offense. McKeller v. State, 620 N.E.2d 744, 1993 Ind. App. LEXIS 1139 (1993).

35-47-2-20. Effect of full or conditional pardon.

(a) A full pardon from the governor of Indiana for:
(1) A felony other than a felony that is included in IC 35-42; or
(2) A violation of this chapter;
removes any disability under this chapter imposed because of that offense, if fifteen (15) years have elapsed between the time of the offense and the application for a license under this chapter.

(b) A conditional pardon described in IC 11-9-2-4 for:
(1) A felony; or
(2) A violation of this chapter;
removes a disability under this chapter if the superintendent determines after an investigation that circumstances have changed since the pardoned conviction was entered to such an extent that the pardoned person is likely to handle handguns in compliance with the law.

History.
IC 35-47-2-20, as added by P.L.311-1983, § 32;
P.L.191-1984, § 6; P.L.148-1987, § 6.

NOTES TO DECISIONS

Cited:
United States v. Wagner, 976 F.2d 354, 1992 U.S. App. LEXIS 24334 (7th Cir. Ind. 1992).

35-47-2-21. Foreign licenses.

(a) Retail dealers' licenses issued by other states or foreign countries will not be recognized in Indiana except for sales at wholesale.

(b) Licenses to carry handguns, issued by other states or foreign countries, will be recognized according to the terms thereof but only while the holders are not residents of Indiana.

History.
IC 35-47-2-21, as added by P.L.311-1983, § 32.

35-47-2-22. Use of false or altered handgun license unlawful.

It is unlawful for any person to use, or to attempt to use, a false, counterfeit, spurious, or altered handgun-carrying license to obtain a handgun contrary to the provisions of this chapter.

History.
IC 35-47-2-22, as added by P.L.311-1983, § 32.

35-47-2-23. Violation of chapter.

(a) A person who violates section 3, 4, 5, 14, 15, or 16 [IC 35-47-2-3, IC 35-47-2-4, IC 35-47-2-5, IC 35-47-2-14, IC 35-47-2-15, or IC 35-47-2-16] of this chapter commits a Class B misdemeanor.

(b) A person who violates section 7, 17, or 18 [IC 35-47-2-7, IC 35-47-2-17, or IC 35-47-2-18] of this chapter commits a Class C felony.

(c) A person who violates section 1 [IC 35-47-2-1] of this chapter commits a Class A misdemeanor. However, the offense is a Class C felony:
  (1) if the offense is committed:
    (A) on or in school property;
    (B) within one thousand (1,000) feet of school property; or
    (C) on a school bus; or
  (2) if the person:
    (A) has a prior conviction of any offense under:
      (i) this subsection; or
      (ii) subsection (d); or
    (B) has been convicted of a felony within fifteen (15) years before the date of the offense.

(d) A person who violates section 22 [IC 35-47-2-22] of this chapter commits a Class A misdemeanor. However, the offense is a Class D felony if the person has a prior conviction of any offense under this subsection or subsection (c), or if the person has been convicted of a felony within fifteen (15) years before the date of the offense.

History.
IC 35-47-2-23, as added by P.L.311-1983, § 32; P.L.16-1984, § 20; P.L.140-1994, § 9; P.L.17-1997, § 7.

Penalties for misdemeanors, IC 35-50-1, IC 35-50-3, IC 35-50-5-2.

Cross References.
Penalties for felonies, IC 35-50-1, IC 35-50-2, IC 35-50-5-2.

NOTES TO DECISIONS

Analysis

Constitutionality.
—Cruel and Unusual Punishment.
—Double Jeopardy.
—Proportionality.
Evidence.
—Sufficient.
Guilty Pleas.
Jury Trial.
—Number of Jurors.
Necessity Defense.
Proof Required.
Robbery.

Self-Defense.
Search and Seizure.
Sentence.
—Enhancement.
— —Time Limits.
—Errors.

Constitutionality.

—Cruel and Unusual Punishment.

Sentence of four years imprisonment enhanced by 30 years based on defendant's status as an habitual offender for conviction of illegal possession of a handgun, a Class D felony, did not constitute cruel and unusual punishment. Woods v. State, 471 N.E.2d 691, 1984 Ind. LEXIS 1058 (1984).

—Double Jeopardy.

Use of the same prior felony conviction to raise possession of a handgun from a Class A misdemeanor to a Class D felony under subsection (c) and then to enhance the penalty under IC 35-50-2-8 does not doubly punish defendant for the same past crime and thus does not constitute double jeopardy. Woods v. State, 471 N.E.2d 691, 1984 Ind. LEXIS 1058 (1984).

Punishment for both a class A misdemeanor under IC 35-47-2-1 and a class C felony under IC 35-47-2-23 violated the double jeopardy prohibition. Henderson v. State, 686 N.E.2d 911, 1997 Ind. App. LEXIS 1560 (1997), transfer granted, 698 N.E.2d 1182 (Ind. 1998), aff'd, 690 N.E.2d 706, 1998 Ind. LEXIS 2 (1998).

Defendant's conviction of IC 35-47-2-1, carrying a handgun without a license, and IC 35-47-4-5, unlawful possession of a firearm by a serious violent felon, violated Indiana's Double Jeopardy Clause, Ind. Const. art. 1, § 14 since the essential elements of one challenged offense also established all of the essential elements of the other challenged offense. Alexander v. State, 768 N.E.2d 971, 2002 Ind. App. LEXIS 804 (2002), clarified, 772 N.E.2d 476, 2002 Ind. App. LEXIS 1195 (2002).

—Proportionality.

This section does not violate the proportionality requirement of Ind. Const., Art. 1, § 16. State v. Moss-Dwyer, 686 N.E.2d 109, 1997 Ind. LEXIS 171 (1997).

Evidence.

—Sufficient.

Evidence was sufficient to support conviction where defendant was sitting in the back seat of a car when police officers approached him, officers saw him remove something from his pants and place the object next to him in the car, and then officers saw that the object was a gun. Henderson v. State, 686 N.E.2d 911, 1997 Ind. App. LEXIS 1560 (1997), transfer granted, 698 N.E.2d 1182 (Ind. 1998), aff'd, 690 N.E.2d 706, 1998 Ind. LEXIS 2 (1998).

The state presented evidence which supported an inference that the defendants either constructively possessed, actually possessed, or knew of the presence and nature of the handgun, therefore the trial judge should not have granted the motion for judgment on the evidence. State v. Hill, 688 N.E.2d 1280, 1997 Ind. App. LEXIS 1745 (1997).

There was sufficient evidence from which a jury could have reasonably concluded that the defendant killed the victim where there was both an eyewitness and a corroborating witness identifying the defendant as the shooter. Newson v. State, 721 N.E.2d 237, 1999 Ind. LEXIS 1251 (1999).

Defendant's conviction of possession of an altered handgun under IC 35-47-2-18 and IC 35-47-2-23(b) was supported by sufficient evidence, based on testimony by an officer that the area where the serial number had been was "very shiny," and the fact that defendant had been in possession of the gun for over a week. Robles v. State, 758 N.E.2d 581, 2001 Ind. App. LEXIS 1986 (2001).

Evidence that defendant was driving car and knew there was handgun in car was sufficient to convict defendant of carrying handgun without license. Thurman v. State, 793 N.E.2d 318, 2003 Ind. App. LEXIS 1511 (2003).

Evidence was sufficient to affirm defendant's conviction for possessing handgun with no license in violation of IC 35-47-2-1 and IC 35-47-2-23(c) where handgun was in plain view in close proximity to defendant in vehicle in which defendant was passenger. Grim v. State, 797 N.E.2d 825, 2003 Ind. App. LEXIS 1978 (2003).

Defendant's conviction for carrying handgun without license was sufficiently supported by police officer's testimony that he observed handgun drop from defendant's waistband; furthermore, trial court did not err in admitting statement "Did they find the gun" made by defendant to his sister at scene of crime. Stokes v. State, 828 N.E.2d 937, 2005 Ind. App. LEXIS 1056 (2005), cert. denied, 547 U.S. 1043, 164 L. Ed. 2d 339, 126 S. Ct. 1623, 2006 U.S. LEXIS 2563 (2006).

State presented sufficient evidence to support defendant's conviction for carrying a handgun without a license as a Class C felony where state showed that defendant did not have a license for the handgun that he threw away when police came by searching for somebody involved in drug activity and shined a spotlight on him standing behind a car just before he tossed gun under car; defendant could not show that he had a recognized, justifiable reason for carrying the gun without a permit, as the evidence showed that defendant did not live at the residence where police confronted him and the residence was not defendant's fixed place of business. Campbell v. State, 841 N.E.2d 624, 2006 Ind. App. LEXIS 131 (2006).

Evidence was sufficient to support defendant's convictions for murder and carrying a handgun without a license, as the evidence presented in defendant's case showed that defendant went to an apartment building with a gun looking for a man who allegedly owed money to defendant, that defendant shot and fatally wounded the man once defendant found him, and that defendant did not have a license for the gun that defendant possessed. Dixson v. State, 865 N.E.2d 704, 2007 Ind. App. LEXIS 913 (2007).

Evidence was sufficient to sustain defendant's

Evidence. (Cont'd)

—Sufficient. (Cont'd)
convictions for murder, attempted murder, possession of a firearm by a serious violent felon, and carrying a handgun without a license. A witness's testimony was not incredibly dubious, as there was not a complete lack of circumstantial evidence, and the inconsistencies in the testimony were brought to the jury's attention by defense counsel and were to be considered by the jury. Gray v. State, 871 N.E.2d 408, 2007 Ind. App. LEXIS 1810 (2007).

Guilty Pleas.
Stipulation as to defendant's prior conviction for carrying a handgun without a license did not constitute a guilty plea, and the trial court did not err by failing to read defendant any advisement of rights which would be waived by pleading guilty. Whatley v. State, 685 N.E.2d 48, 1997 Ind. LEXIS 130 (1997).

Jury Trial.

—Number of Jurors.
Where defendant was charged with a class A misdemeanor in violation of IC 35-47-2-1, and charged with a class C felony under IC 35-47-2-23(c)(2)(B), he should only have been charged with the class C felony, and he was entitled to a twelve-member jury. Henderson v. State, 686 N.E.2d 911, 1997 Ind. App. LEXIS 1560 (1997), transfer granted, 698 N.E.2d 1182 (Ind. 1998), aff'd, 690 N.E.2d 706, 1998 Ind. LEXIS 2 (1998).
A defendant who was charged with one count of carrying a handgun without a license, a Class A misdemeanor, and with another count of carrying a handgun without a license with a prior felony conviction, a Class C felony, was charged with a Class C felony, even though it would have been a less serious offense without a prior conviction, and defendant was entitled to be tried by a twelve-person jury. Henderson v. State, 690 N.E.2d 706, 1998 Ind. LEXIS 2 (1998).

Necessity Defense.
In order to negate a claim of necessity, the state must disprove at least one element of the defense beyond a reasonable doubt. Dozier v. State, 709 N.E.2d 27, 1999 Ind. App. LEXIS 601 (1999).
Where a high school student had adequate alternatives to taking a loaded gun to school to protect himself against possible gang retaliation, namely telling his parents about threats, reporting those threats to the police, and contacting school authorities, his defense of manifest necessity could not stand. Dozier v. State, 709 N.E.2d 27, 1999 Ind. App. LEXIS 601 (1999).

Proof Required.
Where defendant was charged with the illegal use of a handgun, a firearm, and the state clearly established, through the uncontroverted testimony of a deputy, that his pellet gun was not a handgun, there was a variance between the information, the instructions, and the proof produced at trial. Thus, the evidence was insufficient to convict defendant

of the crimes with which he was charged: (1) criminal confinement while armed with a deadly weapon as a Class B felony; or (2) criminal recklessness as a Class D felony because he was not armed with a deadly weapon. Miller v. State, 616 N.E.2d 750, 1993 Ind. App. LEXIS 785 (1993).

Robbery.
The trial court did not erroneously make inconsistent findings when it determined that the defendant was not guilty of carrying a handgun without a license, but guilty of using a handgun to commit robbery and confinement where defendant was charged with carrying a handgun without a license as a Class D felony by alleging that the defendant had a prior conviction for the same type of offense, since conviction of the unlicensed handgun count as charged would have required not only proof that defendant was carrying a handgun, but also proof that defendant had previously been convicted of a similar offense and the acquittal does not necessarily and exclusively compel the conclusion that defendant was unarmed. Townsend v. State, 498 N.E.2d 1198, 1986 Ind. LEXIS 1305 (1986).

Self-Defense.
Where the court denied the jury consideration of defendant's claim of self-defense, the instruction was in error because it ignored any nexus between the crime and the shooting; the error was reversible because on the undisputed evidence that defendant did not possess a firearms license, it denied him consideration of his claim of self-defense. Harvey v. State, 652 N.E.2d 876, 1995 Ind. App. LEXIS 738 (1995).

Search and Seizure.
The protective search of a juvenile just outside classroom was permissible where the school safety officer received information from a student about the juvenile that caused her to remove the juvenile from the classroom, and her concern for her safety caused her to conduct the pat down search that revealed the gun. In re C.S., 735 N.E.2d 273, 2000 Ind. App. LEXIS 1468 (2000).

Sentence.

—Enhancement.
Jury's finding of two prior unrelated felony convictions met the habitual offender requirement, and the same finding supported the enhancement of his handgun conviction to a class C felony. McCants v. State, 686 N.E.2d 1281, 1997 Ind. LEXIS 183 (1997).
In light of the statutory construction favoring more specific statutes as opposed to more general ones and because of the rule of lenity, a misdemeanor conviction under the handgun statute, once elevated to a felony due to a prior felony conviction, should not be enhanced again under the general habitual offender statute. Ross v. State, 729 N.E.2d 113, 2000 Ind. LEXIS 484 (2000), superseded by statute as stated in, Mills v. State, 855 N.E.2d 296, 2006 Ind. App. LEXIS 2126 (2006).

Sentence. (Cont'd)

—Enhancement. (Cont'd)
— —Time Limits.
Subsection (c)(2)(B) unambiguously states an offense is elevated if defendant has been convicted of a felony within 15 years, and the 15 years begins to run upon defendant's conviction and not when the offense was committed. Jenkins v. State, 677 N.E.2d 624, 1997 Ind. App. LEXIS 288 (1997).

—Errors.
Where there was an inconsistency between the judge's in-court pronouncement of sentence and the subsequent abstract of judgment, and the Chronological Case Summary entry lengthened the sentence, the original in-court sentence was reinstated and the subsequent contradictory language vacated. Whatley v. State, 685 N.E.2d 48, 1997 Ind. LEXIS 130 (1997).

Cited:
Fletcher v. State, 505 N.E.2d 491, 1987 Ind. App.

LEXIS 2510 (1987); Sears v. State, 668 N.E.2d 662, 1996 Ind. LEXIS 82 (1996); Valance v. Wisel, 110 F.3d 1269, 1997 U.S. App. LEXIS 6538 (7th Cir. Ind. 1997); Ramsey v. State, 723 N.E.2d 869, 2000 Ind. LEXIS 113 (2000); Perez v. State, 728 N.E.2d 234, 2000 Ind. App. LEXIS 743 (2000); Bush v. State, 732 N.E.2d 250, 2000 Ind. App. LEXIS 1146 (2000); State v. Dodson, 733 N.E.2d 968, 2000 Ind. App. LEXIS 1206 (2000); Campbell v. State, 734 N.E.2d 248, 2000 Ind. App. LEXIS 1297 (2000); Hatchett v. State, 740 N.E.2d 920, 2000 Ind. App. LEXIS 2054 (2000); Murray v. State, 742 N.E.2d 932, 2001 Ind. LEXIS 192 (2001); Mitchell v. State, 745 N.E.2d 775, 2001 Ind. LEXIS 300 (2001); Lockett v. State, 747 N.E.2d 539, 2001 Ind. LEXIS 458 (2001); Conrad v. State, 747 N.E.2d 575, 2001 Ind. App. LEXIS 703 (2001); State v. Downey, 770 N.E.2d 794, 2002 Ind. LEXIS 542 (2002); Jackson v. State, 785 N.E.2d 615, 2003 Ind. App. LEXIS 456 (2003); Scott v. State, 855 N.E.2d 1068, 2006 Ind. App. LEXIS 2262 (2006); Harris v. State, 884 N.E.2d 399, 2008 Ind. App. LEXIS 729 (2008).

RESEARCH REFERENCES

Indiana Law Review.
Recent Developments in Indiana Criminal Law and Procedure, 28 Ind. L. Rev. 819 (1995).

Res Gestae.
Criminal Justice Notes 10/03: Constructive pos-

session — handgun, drugs and paraphernalia in vehicle. 47 (No. 6) Res Gestae 43 (2004).

35-47-2-24. Burden of proof — When prosecutions dismissed.

(a) In an information or indictment brought for the enforcement of any provision of this chapter, it is not necessary to negate any exemption specified under this chapter, or to allege the absence of a license required under this chapter. The burden of proof is on the defendant to prove that he is exempt under section 2 [IC 35-47-2-2] of this chapter, or that he has a license as required under this chapter.

(b) Whenever a person who has been arrested or charged with a violation of section 1 [IC 35-47-2-1] of this chapter presents a valid license to the prosecuting attorney or establishes that he is exempt under section 2 of this chapter, any prosecution for a violation of section 1 of this chapter shall be dismissed immediately, and all records of an arrest or proceedings following arrest shall be destroyed immediately.

History.
IC 35-47-2-24, as added by P.L.311-1983, § 32.

NOTES TO DECISIONS

ANALYSIS

Constitutionality.
—Double Jeopardy.
Applicability.

Constitutionality.
The burden placed on a defendant by this section to prove he has a license or is otherwise exempt from prosecution under IC 35-47-2-1 does not unconstitutionally infringe on a person's right to keep and bear arms as granted by Ind. Const., art. 1,

§ 32. Lewis v. State, 484 N.E.2d 77, 1985 Ind. App. LEXIS 2887 (1985).

—Double Jeopardy.
For double jeopardy purposes, the offense of possession of a handgun without a license has an element that criminal recklessness as a Class D felony does not, and possession of a handgun is not an inherently included offense of criminal recklessness. Fields v. State, 676 N.E.2d 27, 1997 Ind. App. LEXIS 11 (1997).
There was no double jeopardy violation where

Constitutionality. (Cont'd)

—Double Jeopardy. (Cont'd)
distinct evidentiary facts were used to prove that defendant committed robbery while armed with a handgun, and a lack of evidentiary facts was used to prove that the defendant did not have a license to carry that handgun. Defendant failed to demonstrate a reasonable possibility that the same evidentiary facts may have been used to establish the essential elements of each challenged offense. Newman v. State, 751 N.E.2d 265, 2001 Ind. App. LEXIS 965 (2001).

Applicability.
IC 35-47-2-19 is an exemption under the chapter on handguns which the state is not required to negate, and prosecution of the offense of possession of a handgun with an obliterated serial number does not require proof of when the handgun was manufactured as an element of the offense. McKeller v. State, 620 N.E.2d 744, 1993 Ind. App. LEXIS 1139 (1993).

Once the state has established that the defendant carried a handgun on or about his person, away from his residence or place of business, the burden shifts to the defendant to demonstrate that he possessed a valid license. Harris v. State, 716 N.E.2d 406, 1999 Ind. LEXIS 807 (1999).

License acquired after being cited for carrying a handgun without a license is not a "valid license" sufficient to require that the charge be dismissed pursuant to IC 35-47-2-24(b). A "valid license" is one that is valid at the time the handgun is carried. Tormoehlen v. State, 848 N.E.2d 326, 2006 Ind. App. LEXIS 998 (2006).

Defendant, after being charged with carrying a handgun without a valid license, in violation of IC 35-47-2-1, obtained a handgun license. He was properly convicted of that crime because under IC 35-47-2-24(b) only presentation of a license that was valid at the time the handgun was carried would negate the crime. Tormoehlen v. State, 848 N.E.2d 326, 2006 Ind. App. LEXIS 998 (2006).

CHAPTER 2.5

SALE OF HANDGUNS

35-47-2.5-1. Applicability.

(a) This chapter does not apply to the following:

(1) Transactions between persons who are licensed as firearms importers or collectors or firearms manufacturers or dealers under 18 U.S.C. 923.

(2) Purchases by or sales to a law enforcement officer or agent of the United States, the state, or a county or local government.

(3) Indiana residents licensed to carry handguns under IC 35-47-2-3.

(b) Notwithstanding any other provision of this chapter, the state shall participate in the NICS if federal funds are available to assist the state in participating in the NICS. If:

(1) the state participates in the NICS; and

(2) there is a conflict between:

(A) a provision of this chapter; and

(B) a procedure required under the NICS;

the procedure required under the NICS prevails over the conflicting provision of this chapter.

History.
P.L.17-1997, § 8; P.L.190-2006, § 5.

35-47-2.5-2. "Dealer" defined.

As used in this chapter, "dealer" includes any person licensed under 18 U.S.C. 923.

History.
P.L.17-1997, § 8.

35-47-2.5-2.5. "NICS" defined.

As used in this chapter, "NICS" refers to the National Instant Criminal Background Check System maintained by the Federal Bureau of Investigation in accordance with the federal Brady Handgun Violence Prevention Act (18 U.S.C. 921 et seq.).

History.
P.L.190-2006, § 6.

35-47-2.5-3. Completion of Form 4473.

A person purchasing a handgun from a dealer shall complete and sign Bureau of Alcohol, Tobacco, Firearms and Explosives Form 4473.

History.
P.L.17-1997, § 8; P.L.190-2006, § 7; P.L.155-2007, § 3, eff. July 1, 2007.

35-47-2.5-4. Dealer's responsibilities.

(a) A dealer may not sell, rent, trade, or transfer from the dealer's inventory a handgun to a person until the dealer has done all of the following:
(1) Obtained from the prospective purchaser a completed and signed Form 4473 as specified in section 3 [IC 35-47-2.5-3] of this chapter.
(2) Contacted NICS:
(A) by telephone; or
(B) electronically;
to request a background check on the prospective purchaser.
(3) Received authorization from NICS to transfer the handgun to the prospective purchaser.
(b) The dealer shall record the NICS transaction number on Form 4473 and retain Form 4473 for auditing purposes.

History.
P.L.17-1997, § 8; P.L.190-2006, § 8.

35-47-2.5-5. Photographic identification required — Other documentation of residence.

(a) To establish personal identification and residence in Indiana for purposes of this chapter, a dealer must require a prospective purchaser to present one (1) photographic identification form issued by a governmental agency of the state or by the United States Department of Defense, or other documentation of residence.
(b) Except when photographic identification was issued by the United States Department of Defense, other documentation of residence must show an address identical to that shown on the photographic identification form or as amended by proper notice of change of address filed with the issuing authority. Suitable other documentation of residence includes:

(1) evidence of currently paid personal property tax or real estate tax, a current lease, utility, or telephone bill, a voter registration card, a bank check, a passport, an automobile registration, or a hunting or fishing license;

(2) other current identification allowed as evidence of residency by 27 CFR 178.124 and United States Alcohol, Tobacco, and Firearms Ruling 79-7; or

(3) other documentation of residence, determined to be acceptable by the state police department, that corroborates that the prospective purchaser currently resides in Indiana.

(c) If the photographic identification was issued by the United States Department of Defense, permanent orders may be used as documentation of residence.

History.
    P.L.17-1997, § 8.

35-47-2.5-6 — 35-47-2.5-11. [Repealed.]

Compiler's Notes.
    These sections, concerning duties of state police, were repealed by P.L. 190-2006, § 10, effective July 1, 2006.

35-47-2.5-12. False statement a felony.

A person who knowingly or intentionally makes a materially false statement on Form 4473 completed under section 3 [IC 35-47-2.5-3] of this chapter commits a Class D felony.

History.
    P.L.17-1997, § 8; P.L.190-2006, § 9; P.L.155-2007, § 4, eff. July 1, 2007.

Cross References.
    Penalties for felonies, IC 35-50-1, IC 35-50-2, IC 35-50-5-2.

35-47-2.5-13. Violation by dealer a misdemeanor.

Except as otherwise provided in this chapter, a dealer who knowingly or intentionally sells, rents, trades, or transfers a handgun in violation of this chapter commits a Class A misdemeanor.

History.
    P.L.17-1997, § 8.

Cross References.
    Penalties for misdemeanors, IC 35-50-1, IC 35-50-3, IC 35-50-5-2.

35-47-2.5-14. Exemptions for children and resale of guns.

(a) This section does not apply to a person who provides a handgun to the following:

(1) A child who is attending a hunters safety course or a firearms safety course or an adult who is supervising the child during the course.

(2) A child engaging in practice in using a firearm for target shooting at an established range or in an area where the discharge of a firearm is not prohibited or is supervised by:

(A) a qualified firearms instructor; or

(B) an adult who is supervising the child while the child is at the range.

(3) A child engaging in an organized competition involving the use of a firearm or participating in or practicing for a performance by an organized group under Section 501(c)(3) of the Internal Revenue Code that uses firearms as a part of a performance or an adult who is involved in the competition or performance.

(4) A child who is hunting or trapping under a valid license issued to the child under IC 14-22.

(5) A child who is traveling with an unloaded firearm to or from an activity described in this section.

(6) A child who:

(A) is on real property that is under the control of the child's parent, an adult family member of the child, or the child's legal guardian; and

(B) has permission from the child's parent or legal guardian to possess a firearm.

(b) A person who purchases a handgun with the intent to:

(1) resell or otherwise provide the handgun to another person who the person knows or has reason to believe is ineligible for any reason to purchase or otherwise receive from a dealer a handgun; or

(2) transport the handgun out of the state to be resold or otherwise provided to another person who the transferor knows is ineligible to purchase or otherwise receive a firearm;

commits a Class D felony.

(c) If the violation of this section involves a transfer of more than one (1) handgun, the offense is a Class C felony.

History.
P.L.17-1997, § 8.

Cross References.
Penalties for felonies, IC 35-50-1, IC 35-50-2, IC 35-50-5-2.

35-47-2.5-15. Violation of exemptions a felony.

(a) A person who is ineligible to purchase or otherwise receive or possess a handgun in Indiana who knowingly or intentionally solicits, employs, or assists any person in violating section 14 [IC 35-47-2.5-14] of this chapter commits a Class D felony.

(b) If the violation involves a transfer of more than one (1) handgun, the offense is a Class C felony.

History.
P.L.17-1997, § 8.

Cross References.
Penalties for felonies, IC 35-50-1, IC 35-50-2, IC 35-50-5-2.

CHAPTER 3

DISPOSAL OF CONFISCATED WEAPONS

35-47-3-1. Disposal of confiscated weapons.

All firearms confiscated pursuant to statute shall, upon conviction of the person for the offense for which the confiscation was made, be disposed of in accordance with this chapter.

History.
IC 35-47-3-1, as added by P.L.311-1983, § 32.

NOTES TO DECISIONS

In General.
All firearms confiscated by the state, for what-

ever reason and irrespective of the state statute the forfeiting defendant had violated, were to be

In General. (Cont'd)
disposed of in the manner provided by former IC 35-23-4.1-16. State v. Souder, 444 N.E.2d 891, 1983 Ind. App. LEXIS 2591 (1983).

35-47-3-2. Firearms not required to be registered — Return to rightful owner — Disposal by law enforcement agency.

(a) This section applies only to firearms which are not required to be registered in the National Firearms Registration and Transfer Record.

(b) Firearms shall be returned to the rightful owner at once following final disposition of the cause if a return has not already occurred under the terms of IC 35-33-5. If the rightful ownership is not known the law enforcement agency holding the firearm shall make a reasonable attempt to ascertain the rightful ownership and cause the return of the firearm. However, nothing in this chapter shall be construed as requiring the return of firearms to rightful owners who have been convicted for the misuse of firearms. In such cases, the court may provide for the return of the firearm in question or order that the firearm be at once delivered:

(1) Except as provided in subdivision (2), to the sheriff's department of the county in which the offense occurred; or

(2) To the city or town police force that confiscated the firearm, if:

(A) A member of the city or town police force confiscated the firearm; and

(B) The city or town has a population of more than two thousand five hundred (2,500) and less than two hundred fifty thousand (250,000).

(c) The receiving law enforcement agency shall dispose of firearms under subsection (b), at the discretion of the law enforcement agency, not more than one hundred twenty (120) days following receipt by use of any of the following procedures:

(1) Public sale of the firearms to the general public as follows:

(A) Notice of the sale shall be:

(i) Posted for ten (10) days in the county courthouse in a place readily accessible to the general public; and

(ii) Advertised in the principal newspaper of the county for two (2) days in an advertisement that appears in the newspaper at least five (5) days prior to the sale.

(B) Disposition of the firearm shall be by public auction in a place convenient to the general public, with disposition going to the highest bidder. However, no firearm shall be transferred to any bidder if that bidder is not lawfully eligible to receive and possess firearms according to the laws of the United States and Indiana.

(C) All handguns transferred under this subdivision shall also be transferred according to the transfer procedures set forth in this article.

(D) Money collected pursuant to the sales shall first be used to defray the necessary costs of administering this subdivision with any surplus to be:

(i) Deposited into the receiving law enforcement agency's firearms training fund, if the law enforcement agency is a county law enforcement agency, or into a continuing education fund established under IC 5-2-8-2, if the law enforcement agency is a city or town law enforcement agency; and

(ii) Used by the agency exclusively for the purpose of training law enforcement officers in the proper use of firearms or other law enforcement duties, if the law enforcement agency is a county law enforcement agency, or for law enforcement purposes, if the law enforcement agency is a city or town law enforcement agency.

(2) Sale of the firearms to a licensed firearms dealer as follows:

(A) Notice of the sale must be:

(i) Posted for ten (10) days in the county courthouse in a place readily accessible to the general public; and

(ii) Advertised in the principal newspaper of the county for two (2) days in an advertisement that appears in the newspaper at least five (5) days before the sale.

(B) Disposition of the firearm shall be by auction with disposition going to the highest bidder who is a licensed firearms dealer.

(C) Money collected from the sales shall first be used to defray the necessary costs of administering this subdivision and any surplus shall be:

(i) Deposited into the receiving law enforcement agency's firearms training fund or other appropriate training activities fund; and

(ii) Used by the agency exclusively for the purpose of training law enforcement officers in the proper use of firearms or other law enforcement duties.

(3) Sale or transfer of the firearms to another law enforcement agency.

(4) Release to the state police department laboratory or other forensic laboratory administered by the state or a political subdivision (as defined in IC 36-1-2-13) for the purposes of research, training, and comparison in conjunction with the forensic examination of firearms evidence.

(5) Destruction of the firearms.

(d) Notwithstanding the requirement of this section mandating disposal of firearms not more than one hundred twenty (120) days following receipt, the receiving law enforcement agency may at its discretion hold firearms it may receive until a sufficient number has accumulated to defray the costs of administering this section if a delay does not exceed one hundred eighty (180) days from the date of receipt of the first firearm in the sale lot. In any event, all confiscated firearms shall be disposed of as promptly as possible.

(e) When a firearm is delivered to the state police department laboratory or other forensic laboratory under subsection (c)(4) and the state police department laboratory or other forensic laboratory determines the laboratory has no further need for the firearm in question, the laboratory shall return the firearm to the law enforcement agency for disposal under subsection (c).

History.
IC 35-47-3-2, as added by P.L.311-1983, § 32;
P.L.209-1986, § 2; P.L.57-1992, § 7; P.L.48-1993, § 7.

NOTES TO DECISIONS

Cited:
Indiana State Police v. Don's Guns & Galleries,
674 N.E.2d 565, 1996 Ind. App. LEXIS 1607 (1996).

OPINIONS OF ATTORNEY GENERAL

In cases where the rightful owner of the confiscated firearm cannot be found, a city police department must deliver all confiscated and unclaimed firearms held by it to the sheriff of the county wherein the offense involving the firearm occurred; the sheriff shall then sell the firearms to the highest lawfully eligible bidder at public auction, hold the firearms for the purpose of instruction, research and law enforcement, or destroy the firearms as provided by law on court order. 1978, No. 29, p. 82; 2 IR 179, issued under former IC 35-23-4.1-16.

35-47-3-3. Firearms required to be registered — Return to rightful owner — Delivery to law enforcement agency.

(a) This section applies to firearms that are required to be registered in the National Firearms Registration and Transfer Record.

(b) Firearms shall be returned to the rightful owner at once following final disposition of the cause, if such return has not already occurred under the terms of IC 35-33-5, and if such owner remains lawfully entitled to possess such firearms according to applicable United States and Indiana statutes. If rightful ownership is not known, the law enforcement agency holding the firearm shall make a reasonable and diligent effort to ascertain the rightful ownership and cause the return of the firearm being held, providing the owner remains lawfully entitled to possess such firearms.

(c) Firearms that are not returnable under this section shall be at once delivered to:

(1) The sheriff's department of the county in which the offense occurred, unless subdivision (2) applies; or

(2) The city or town police force that confiscated the firearm if:

(A) A member of the city or town police force confiscated the firearm; and

(B) The city or town has a population of more than two thousand five hundred (2,500) and less than two hundred fifty thousand (250,000);

following final disposition of the cause.

(d) When firearms are sent to a law enforcement agency under subsection (c), the law enforcement agency may upon request release the firearms to the state police department laboratory or other forensic laboratory administered by the state or a political subdivision (as defined in IC 36-1-2-13) for the purposes of research, training, and comparison in conjunction with the forensic examination of firearms evidence.

(e) The receiving law enforcement agency or laboratory shall cause the registry of such firearms in the United States National Firearms Registration and Transfer Record within thirty (30) days following receipt from the court.

(f) The court may order such firearms as are not returnable destroyed, specifying the exact manner of destruction and requiring the receiving law enforcement agency or laboratory to make due return to the ordering court the time, date, method of destruction, and disposition of the remains of the destroyed firearm.

(g) No portion of this section shall be construed as requiring the receiving law enforcement agency or laboratory to retain firearms which are inoperable or unserviceable, or which the receiving law enforcement agency or laboratory may choose to transfer as public property in the ordinary course of lawful commerce and exchange.

History.
IC 35-47-3-3, as added by P.L.311-1983, § 32; P.L.209-1986, § 3; P.L.57-1992, § 8.

35-47-3-4. Unlawful disposal of confiscated firearms.

A person who knowingly or intentionally:

(1) Delivers a confiscated firearm to a person convicted of a felony:

(A) Involving use of a firearm; and

(B) Which is the basis of the confiscation;

(2) Delivers a confiscated firearm to another with knowledge that there is a rightful owner to whom the firearm must be returned; or

(3) Fails to deliver a confiscated firearm to the sheriff's department, a city or town police force, the state police department laboratory or a forensic laboratory under this chapter, the state under IC 14-22-39-6, or for disposition after a determination that the rightful owner of the firearm cannot be ascertained or is no longer entitled to possess the confiscated firearm;

commits a Class D felony.

History.
IC 35-47-3-4, as added by P.L.311-1983, § 32; P.L.209-1986, § 4; P.L.57-1992, § 9; P.L.1-1995, § 77.

Cross References.
Penalties for felonies, IC 35-50-1, IC 35-50-2, IC 35-50-5-2.

CHAPTER 4
MISCELLANEOUS PROVISIONS

Section
35-47-4-1. Sale or delivery of deadly weapon to intoxicated person unlawful.
35-47-4-2. Making loan secured by mortgage, deposit or pledge of handgun unlawful.
35-47-4-3. Pointing a firearm.
35-47-4-4. [Repealed.]

Section
35-47-4-5. Possession of firearm by serious violent felon.
35-47-4-6. Possession of firearm by domestic batterer.
35-47-4-7. Restoration of right to possess firearm by person who has been convicted of domestic violence — Procedure.

35-47-4-1. Sale or delivery of deadly weapon to intoxicated person unlawful.

A person who sells, barters, gives, or delivers any deadly weapon to any person at the time in a state of intoxication, knowing him to be in a state of intoxication, or to any person who is in the habit of becoming intoxicated, and knowing him to be a person who is in the habit of becoming intoxicated, commits a Class B misdemeanor.

History.
IC 35-47-4-1, as added by P.L.311-1983, § 32.

Cross References.
Penalties for misdemeanors, IC 35-50-1, IC 35-50-3, IC 35-50-5-2.

RESEARCH REFERENCES

Collateral References.
Fact that gun was unloaded as affecting criminal responsibility. 68 A.L.R.4th 507.

Fact that gun was broken, dismantled, or inoperable as affecting criminal responsibility under weapons statute. 81 A.L.R.4th 745.

35-47-4-2. Making loan secured by mortgage, deposit or pledge of handgun unlawful.

A person who makes a loan secured by a:
(1) Mortgage;
(2) Deposit; or
(3) Pledge;
of a handgun commits a Class B misdemeanor.

History.
IC 35-47-4-2, as added by P.L.311-1983, § 32.

Cross References.
Penalties for misdemeanors, IC 35-50-1, IC 35-50-3, IC 35-50-5-2.

35-47-4-3. Pointing a firearm.

(a) This section does not apply to a law enforcement officer who is acting within the scope of the law enforcement officer's official duties or to a person who is justified in using reasonable force against another person under:
(1) IC 35-41-3-2; or
(2) IC 35-41-3-3.
(b) A person who knowingly or intentionally points a firearm at another person commits a Class D felony. However, the offense is a Class A misdemeanor if the firearm was not loaded.

History.
P.L.296-1995, § 2.

Penalties for misdemeanors, IC 35-50-1, IC 35-50-3, IC 35-50-5-2.

Cross References.
Penalties for felonies, IC 35-50-1, IC 35-50-2, IC 35-50-5-2.

NOTES TO DECISIONS

ANALYSIS

Construction.
Double Jeopardy.
Evidence.
—Exculpatory.
Jury Instructions.
Multiple Convictions.
Sentence.
Status of Offense.
Sufficiency of Evidence.

Construction.

Fact that gun is unloaded is mitigating factor that reduces defendant's culpability from felony to misdemeanor, but is not an affirmative defense. Adkins v. State, 887 N.E.2d 934, 2008 Ind. LEXIS 453 (2008).

Double Jeopardy.

Pointing a firearm and criminal recklessness, both of which required knowingly or intentionally pointing a firearm at another person, were the same offense for double jeopardy purposes and convictions for both offenses violated the state and federal constitutions. Bracksieck v. State, 691 N.E.2d 1273, 1998 Ind. App. LEXIS 109 (1998), amended, 1998 Ind. App. LEXIS 599 (Ind. Ct. App. Apr. 23, 1998).

There was no double jeopardy violation under the statutory evidence test or the actual evidence test for defendant's convictions for pointing a firearm under this section and for carrying a handgun without a license under IC 35-47-2-1, because the two convictions do not constitute multiple punishments for the same offense in violation of the Indiana double jeopardy clause. Armstrong v. State, 742 N.E.2d 972, 2001 Ind. App. LEXIS 23 (2001).

Evidence.

—Exculpatory.

Conviction was reversed where the state wrongly withheld evidence in the form of testimony of an independent eyewitness who did not see a gun, and this testimony could have created a reasonable doubt that did not otherwise exist. Penley v. State, 734 N.E.2d 287, 2000 Ind. App. LEXIS 1335 (2000).

Jury Instructions.

Jury instruction did not improperly shift the burden of proving that the gun was unloaded to defendant; the instruction given was proper and, even if erroneous, any error was harmless because the evidence demonstrated that the gun was loaded and thus, defendant's only defense was that he was in a different city at the time of the incident. Adkins v. State, 870 N.E.2d 465, 2007 Ind. App. LEXIS 1585 (2007), transfer granted and vacated, 878 N.E.2d 212, 2007 Ind. LEXIS 881 (2007).

Because defendant offered no evidence to suggest that a firearm was unloaded when he pointed

it at the victim and there was ample evidence from which to conclude that the gun was loaded since witnesses heard gunshots when defendant went outside, defendant did not place the question of whether his gun was unloaded at issue and so the state had no obligation to prove that it was loaded; thus, while the trial court's jury instruction, which placed the burden on defendant to show the gun was not loaded, was in error, the error was harmless. Adkins v. State, 887 N.E.2d 934, 2008 Ind. LEXIS 453 (2008).

Multiple Convictions.

Although all three of defendant's convictions for pointing a firearm stem from a single incident, the evidence shows that he pointed a handgun at three different individuals, and the record further supports an inference that these were three separate and distinct pointings of a firearm rather than one continuous action. Armstrong v. State, 742 N.E.2d 972, 2001 Ind. App. LEXIS 23 (2001).

Evidence that defendant waved a firearm at the three individuals in the confined space of an automobile and thus put each occupant at risk of injury from the discharge of the firearm was sufficient to support multiple convictions under IC 35-47-4-3(b). Brown v. State, 790 N.E.2d 1061, 2003 Ind. App. LEXIS 1203 (2003).

Sentence.

Because defendant's felony offenses, which included possession of cocaine, resisting law enforcement, and pointing firearm, constituted single episode of criminal conduct, IC 35-50-1-2(b) permitted trial court to impose consecutive sentences totaling 30 years for felonies; accordingly, trial court's imposition of consecutive sentences totaling 26 years did not violate IC 35-50-1-2. Johnican v. State, 804 N.E.2d 211, 2004 Ind. App. LEXIS 324 (2004).

Trial court's imposition of maximum sentence for crime of pointing firearm, a Class D felony under IC 35-47-4-3, was appropriate pursuant to AP. 7(B) in light of nature of offense and character of offender; defendant had extensive history of offenses against individuals and circumstance of his crime, pointing gun at friend in whose home he was guest, and doing so over argument whether or not to babysit friend's child, made defendant one of worst offenders charged with that crime. Spears v. State, 811 N.E.2d 485, 2004 Ind. App. LEXIS 1331 (2004).

Pursuant to IC 35-50-2-7, trial court properly enhanced defendant's sentence for conviction of pointing firearm, a Class D felony under IC 35-47-4-3, to maximum sentence of three years. Spears v. State, 811 N.E.2d 485, 2004 Ind. App. LEXIS 1331 (2004).

Status of Offense.

Under IC 35-47-4-3(b), a defendant is entitled to a Class A misdemeanor rather than a Class D felony only if the evidence affirmatively demonstrates that the firearm was not loaded. Brown v. State, 790 N.E.2d 1061, 2003 Ind. App. LEXIS 1203 (2003).

Status of Offense. (Cont'd)

If a defendant charged with Class D felony pointing a firearm seeks instead to be convicted of Class A misdemeanor pointing a firearm, the defendant must place the fact of the gun having been unloaded at issue if the state's evidence has not done so; once at issue, the state must then prove beyond a reasonable doubt that the firearm was loaded. Adkins v. State, 887 N.E.2d 934, 2008 Ind. LEXIS 453 (2008).

Sufficiency of Evidence.

It was within the jury's province to believe the victim's testimony rather than defendant's testimony, and the testimony of the victim alone is sufficient to support a conviction; therefore, the state presented sufficient evidence to establish beyond a reasonable doubt that defendant pointed a loaded firearm at the victim. Nantz v. State, 740 N.E.2d 1276, 2001 Ind. App. LEXIS 10 (2001).

Cited:

Brown v. State, 790 N.E.2d 1061, 2003 Ind. App. LEXIS 1203 (2003); Collins v. State, 826 N.E.2d 671, 2005 Ind. App. LEXIS 734 (2005); Baber v. State, 834 N.E.2d 146, 2005 Ind. App. LEXIS 1683 (2005); Ransley v. State, 850 N.E.2d 443, 2006 Ind. App. LEXIS 1341 (2006); Forgey v. State, 886 N.E.2d 16, 2008 Ind. App. LEXIS 1024 (2008).

RESEARCH REFERENCES

Res Gestae.

Criminal Justice Notes 6/08: Burden of proving firearm was loaded, 52 (No. 2) Res Gestae 37 (2008).

35-47-4-4. [Repealed.]

Compiler's Notes.

This section, concerning possession of certain firearms by convicted felons, was repealed by P.L.247-1999, § 2, effective July 1, 1999.

35-47-4-5. Possession of firearm by serious violent felon.

(a) As used in this section, "serious violent felon" means a person who has been convicted of:

(1) committing a serious violent felony in:

(A) Indiana; or

(B) any other jurisdiction in which the elements of the crime for which the conviction was entered are substantially similar to the elements of a serious violent felony; or

(2) attempting to commit or conspiring to commit a serious violent felony in:

(A) Indiana as provided under IC 35-41-5-1 or IC 35-41-5-2; or

(B) any other jurisdiction in which the elements of the crime for which the conviction was entered are substantially similar to the elements of attempting to commit or conspiring to commit a serious violent felony.

(b) As used in this section, "serious violent felony" means:

(1) murder (IC 35-42-1-1);

(2) voluntary manslaughter (IC 35-42-1-3);

(3) reckless homicide not committed by means of a vehicle (IC 35-42-1-5);

(4) battery as a:

(A) Class A felony (IC 35-42-2-1(a)(5));

(B) Class B felony (IC 35-42-2-1(a)(4)); or

(C) Class C felony (IC 35-42-2-1(a)(3));

(5) aggravated battery (IC 35-42-2-1.5);

(6) kidnapping (IC 35-42-3-2);

(7) criminal confinement (IC 35-42-3-3);

(8) rape (IC 35-42-4-1);

(9) criminal deviate conduct (IC 35-42-4-2);

(10) child molesting (IC 35-42-4-3);

(11) sexual battery as a Class C felony (IC 35-42-4-8);

(12) robbery (IC 35-42-5-1);

(13) carjacking (IC 35-42-5-2);

(14) arson as a Class A felony or Class B felony (IC 35-43-1-1(a));

(15) burglary as a Class A felony or Class B felony (IC 35-43-2-1);

(16) assisting a criminal as a Class C felony (IC 35-44-3-2);

(17) resisting law enforcement as a Class B felony or Class C felony (IC 35-44-3-3);

(18) escape as a Class B felony or Class C felony (IC 35-44-3-5);

(19) trafficking with an inmate as a Class C felony (IC 35-44-3-9);

(20) criminal gang intimidation (IC 35-45-9-4);

(21) stalking as a Class B felony or Class C felony (IC 35-45-10-5);

(22) incest (IC 35-46-1-3);

(23) dealing in or manufacturing cocaine or a narcotic drug (IC 35-48-4-1);

(24) dealing in methamphetamine (IC 35-48-4-1.1);

(25) dealing in a schedule I, II, or III controlled substance (IC 35-48-4-2);

(26) dealing in a schedule IV controlled substance (IC 35-48-4-3); or

(27) dealing in a schedule V controlled substance (IC 35-48-4-4).

(c) A serious violent felon who knowingly or intentionally possesses a firearm commits unlawful possession of a firearm by a serious violent felon, a Class B felony.

History.
P.L.247-1999, § 1; P.L.14-2000, § 76; P.L.17-2001, § 17; P.L.222-2001, § 5; P.L.151-2006, § 21.

Cross References.
Penalties for felonies, IC 35-50-1, IC 35-50-2, IC 35-50-5-2.

NOTES TO DECISIONS

In General.
Court properly used defendant's prior conviction of Class C felony battery to support both possession of firearm by serious violent felon conviction and habitual offender finding. Townsend v. State, 793 N.E.2d 1092, 2003 Ind. App. LEXIS 1526 (2003).

Since defendant's status as serious violent felon was element of crime charged, namely, unlawful possession of firearm by serious violent felon, IC 35-47-4-5, state's references at trial to defendant as "violent felon," "serious violent felon," or "felon" were not unduly prejudicial to extent that appellate counsel should have raised issue. Imel v. State, 830 N.E.2d 913, 2005 Ind. App. LEXIS 1185 (2005).

Since defendant's status as a serious violent felon was an element of the crime charged, unlawful possession of a firearm by a serious violent felon, IC 35-47-4-5, the State's references at trial to defendant as a "violent felon," "serious violent felon," or "felon" were not unduly prejudicial to the extent that appellate counsel should have raised this issue. Imel v. State, 830 N.E.2d 913, 2005 Ind. App. LEXIS 1185 (2005).

Constitutionality.
Because the 1999 amended and recodified version of this section merely prohibits the possession of a firearm by a serious violent felon, and neither re-punished defendant for a crime he committed in 1996, nor enhanced the penalty for the crime, defendant's ex post facto challenge failed. Teer v. State, 738 N.E.2d 283, 2000 Ind. App. LEXIS 1832 (2000).

Although handgun ownership is a liberty and property interest protectible under substantive due process, the legislative decision to prevent serious violent felons from possessing potentially deadly weapons cannot be said to be without rational basis. Teer v. State, 738 N.E.2d 283, 2000 Ind. App. LEXIS 1832 (2000).

The legislature's method of defining the class of serious violent felons does not violate the first element of the test for constitutionality under Ind. Const., art. 1, § 23, and the serious violent felon statute's apparent lack of "mathematical nicety," that is, its omission of a few other arguably violent crimes, does not render it unconstitutional. Hatchett v. State, 740 N.E.2d 920, 2000 Ind. App. LEXIS 2054 (2000).

Defendant's right to due process was not violated where the trial court refused to conduct bifurcated proceedings so that the jury would not be told of defendant's criminal confinement conviction before it determined whether he was in possession of a firearm. The court properly tried him under circumstances that allowed his prior felony conviction for criminal confinement to be introduced during the trial to prove the unlawful possession of a firearm by a serious violent felon. Spearman v. State, 744 N.E.2d 545, 2001 Ind. App. LEXIS 368 (2001).

IC 35-47-4-5, which prohibits serious violent felons from knowingly or intentionally possessing weapons, does not violate the privileges or immunities clause under Ind. Const., art. 1, § 23, or a public policy favoring reformation of felons, or the

Constitutionality. (Cont'd)

right to bear arms guarantee of Ind. Const., art. 1, § 32, or the equal protection guarantee of U.S. Const., Amend. 14, because defendant was not a member of a protected class and the law has a rational relationship to preventing violence. Baker v. State, 747 N.E.2d 633, 2001 Ind. App. LEXIS 755 (2001).

Double Jeopardy.

Defendant's conviction and sentence for carrying a handgun without a license was vacated where there was a reasonable possibility that the trial court used the same evidentiary facts to establish the essential elements of both unlawful possession of a firearm as a serious violent felon, and carrying a handgun without a license. Hatchett v. State, 740 N.E.2d 920, 2000 Ind. App. LEXIS 2054 (2000).

Defendant's conviction of IC 35-47-2-1, carrying a handgun without a license, and IC 35-47-4-5, unlawful possession of a firearm by a serious violent felon, violated Indiana's Double Jeopardy Clause, Ind. Const. art 1, § 14 since the essential elements of one challenged offense also established all of the essential elements of the other challenged offense. Alexander v. State, 768 N.E.2d 971, 2002 Ind. App. LEXIS 804 (2002), clarified, 772 N.E.2d 476, 2002 Ind. App. LEXIS 1195 (2002).

Where defendant's conviction for possession of firearm by serious violent felon was reversed on grounds that only evidence that prior offense was a serious violent felony was inadmissible hearsay, defendant could be retried without violating double jeopardy prohibition because evidence, including hearsay, had not been insufficient to convict, and, in new trial, state could establish that prior offense was serious violent felony by other means. Rhone v. State, 825 N.E.2d 1277, 2005 Ind. App. LEXIS 724 (2005).

Because defendant did not waive a double jeopardy argument by pleading guilty without a bargained-for benefit, and because the same underlying felony could not be used to support defendant's conviction under IC 35-47-4-5 for unlawful possession of a firearm by a serious violent felon and a habitual offender enhancement under IC 35-50-2-8, the sentencing defect could be remedied on remand. Graham v. State, 903 N.E.2d 538, 2009 Ind. App. LEXIS 643 (2009).

Elements.

Under IC 35-47-4-5, the legal status of the offender is an essential element of the crime, and the act (the possession) is illegal only if performed by one occupying that status. Bayes v. State, 779 N.E.2d 77, 2002 Ind. App. LEXIS 1966 (2002).

IC 35-47-4-5(c) does not require proof that defendant knew he was a serious violent felon; statute merely requires that defendant knowingly or intentionally possessed firearm after having been convicted of serious violent felony. Rhone v. State, 825 N.E.2d 1277, 2005 Ind. App. LEXIS 724 (2005).

Evidence.

—Insufficient.

Defendant's conviction of unlawful possession of a firearm by serious violent felon under IC 35-47-4-5 was improper where only evidence that the homicide underlying his previous conviction for reckless homicide was committed by means other than a vehicle was affidavit for probable cause, which was inadmissible hearsay. Rhone v. State, 825 N.E.2d 1277, 2005 Ind. App. LEXIS 724 (2005).

In prosecution for possession of firearm by serious violent felon, affidavit for probable cause was hearsay and should not have been admitted to prove that the homicide underlying defendant's prior conviction for reckless homicide was committed by means other than a vehicle; affidavit did not fall under public record exception, Evid. R. 803(8), since it contained factual findings and was prepared for advocacy purposes. Rhone v. State, 825 N.E.2d 1277, 2005 Ind. App. LEXIS 724 (2005).

Although a prior conviction can be proven by other means besides an entry of judgment that complies with TR. 58, an unsigned abstract fails to represent the trial court's final judgment and therefore standing alone is insufficient to prove a prior conviction for purposes of proving a defendant's status as a serious violent felon and a habitual offender. Accordingly, when an unsigned abstract was the only evidence of defendant's prior conviction, defendant's conviction under IC 35-47-4-5(c) and his enhancement under IC 35-38-1-3 could not stand. Abdullah v. State, 847 N.E.2d 1031, 2006 Ind. App. LEXIS 986 (2006).

—Sufficient.

In prosecution of defendant for unlawful possession of firearm by serious violent felon, sufficient evidence supported jury's finding that defendant had constructive possession of gun found under seat in vehicle in which he was passenger where gun was under his seat and he made furtive movements when police stopped vehicle; furthermore, defendant's argument that it was improper to try him on severed charges of robbery and unlawful possession of a firearm by serious violent felon on same day to same jury was rejected since defendant agreed to severance and agreed to incorporate evidence from robbery trial into trial on gun possession charge. Causey v. State, 808 N.E.2d 139, 2004 Ind. App. LEXIS 881 (2004).

Evidence that defendant told police that they would find guns in a duffle bag in defendant's bedroom closet and under the mattress, that defendant had possession of the key to a Pepsi machine containing cocaine, that cocaine was found in defendant's possession, and that defendant ran from police was sufficient to support defendant's convictions for dealing in cocaine, a Class A felony, possession of cocaine and a firearm, a Class C felony, and possession of a handgun by a serious violent felon, a Class B felony. Massey v. State, 816 N.E.2d 979, 2004 Ind. App. LEXIS 2119 (2004).

Where eyewitness identified defendant from array of six photographs depicting different African-American males of roughly the same age with similar expressions, similar haircuts, and similar mustaches and goatees, photographic array was

Evidence. (Cont'd)

—Sufficient. (Cont'd)

not impermissibly suggestive. Dillard v. State, 827 N.E.2d 570, 2005 Ind. App. LEXIS 826 (2005).

Sufficient evidence supported defendant's conviction for possession of firearm by serious violent felon where: (1) defendant's prior burglary conviction showed he was serious violent felon; and (2) he constructively possessed firearm by occupying, with others, motel room in which firearm was in plain view within proximity of defendant. Tate v. State, 835 N.E.2d 499, 2005 Ind. App. LEXIS 1904 (2005).

Evidence was sufficient to sustain defendant's convictions for murder, attempted murder, possession of a firearm by a serious violent felon, and carrying a handgun without a license. A witness's testimony was not incredibly dubious, as there was not a complete lack of circumstantial evidence, and the inconsistencies in the testimony were brought to the jury's attention by defense counsel and were to be considered by the jury. Gray v. State, 871 N.E.2d 408, 2007 Ind. App. LEXIS 1810 (2007).

Based on defendant's statement to the police that he intended to sell the gun which was found in a jacket in his home, it was clear that, at one point, defendant had direct physical control over the handgun; that was sufficient to establish that he possessed the firearm. Craig v. State, 883 N.E.2d 218, 2008 Ind. App. LEXIS 622 (2008).

Jury Instructions.

In prosecution under IC 35-47-4-5, jury should have been instructed that only non-vehicular reckless homicide qualified as serious violent felony. Rhone v. State, 825 N.E.2d 1277, 2005 Ind. App. LEXIS 724 (2005).

Although the trial court erred in instructing the jury in defendant's case where he was on trial for Class B felony unlawful possession of a firearm by a serious violent felon that defendant had a prior robbery conviction, because such evidence did not bear upon the accused's guilt in the current proceeding and could taint the proceeding, the appellate court concluded that the trial court's instruction in that regard was harmless since defendant's conviction on the current charge was clearly sustained by the evidence and the instruction likely did not impact the jury's verdict. Ray v. State, 846 N.E.2d 1064, 2006 Ind. App. LEXIS 827 (2006).

Sentence.

The legislature has prohibited those who have committed serious violent felonies from possessing firearms, presumably to make it harder for them to continue committing other violent crimes; therefore, a sentencing range of six to twenty years is not unconstitutionally disproportionate for possession of a firearm by a serious violent felon. Hatchett v. State, 740 N.E.2d 920, 2000 Ind. App. LEXIS 2054 (2000).

Defendant convicted of unlawful possession of a firearm by a serious violent felon may not have his sentence enhanced under the general habitual offender statute by proof of the same felony used to establish that defendant was a serious violent felon. Conrad v. State, 747 N.E.2d 575, 2001 Ind. App. LEXIS 703 (2001).

The unusually lethal capabilities of the weapons in question were properly taken into account as aggravating factors in convicting defendant as a principal in aiding and abetting a convicted felon in obtaining weapons that the felon used to kill and maim others; however, since the trial court improperly considered depreciation of the seriousness of the offense as an aggravator, even though it was not considering imposition of a minimal sentence, and since the trial court failed to indicate how it had weighed the various factors, remand for further sentencing proceedings was ordered. Meadows v. State, 785 N.E.2d 1112, 2003 Ind. App. LEXIS 520 (2003).

Because defendant chose to remain silent when offered chance to dispute accuracy of presentence investigation report that detailed prior felony convictions, defendant waived any challenge to use of that prior criminal history to enhance his sentences for robbery and possession of firearm. Dillard v. State, 827 N.E.2d 570, 2005 Ind. App. LEXIS 826 (2005).

Trial court did not err in sentencing defendant on his convictions on two counts of being a serious violent felon in possession of a firearm and a count of false informing to 20 years on each possession count, to be served consecutively, and 180 days suspended on the false informing count to be served concurrently to the sentences on the possession counts in a case where he purchased assault weapons that he gave to a known felon who could not possess them, the known felon was involved in a police chase in which the weapons were used to shoot a police officer to death and wound a bystander permanently, and defendant falsely reported that the weapons had been stolen; the sentence was justified in light of the nature of the crime and defendant's character. Meadows v. State, 853 N.E.2d 1032, 2006 Ind. App. LEXIS 1888 (2006).

Though the trial court erred in using the felony supporting an inmate's serious violent felon (SVF) conviction as part of the criminal history justifying an enhanced sentence for the same SVF offense, defense counsel's failure to object did not prejudice him, as the remainder of his extensive criminal and delinquent history supported the enhanced sentence. Reed v. State, 857 N.E.2d 19, 2006 Ind. App. LEXIS 2375 (2006), transfer granted and vacated, — N.E.2d —, 2007 Ind. LEXIS 756 (2007), superseded, 866 N.E.2d 767, 2007 Ind. LEXIS 361 (2007).

Trial court did not err in ordering an inmate's sentence for one serious violent felon (SVF) conviction to run consecutive to a sentence imposed for another such conviction, as IC 35-50-1-2 permits consecutive sentences for separate SVF convictions. Thus, the failure of trial counsel to object and appellate counsel to present the issue on appeal did not prejudice the inmate. Reed v. State, 857 N.E.2d 19, 2006 Ind. App. LEXIS 2375 (2006), transfer granted and vacated, — N.E.2d —, 2007 Ind. LEXIS 756 (2007), superseded, 866 N.E.2d 767, 2007 Ind. LEXIS 361 (2007).

Sentence. (Cont'd)

IC 35-50-1-2 permits the imposition of consecutive sentences for separate convictions where appropriate, including multiple serious violent felon convictions. Reed v. State, 857 N.E.2d 19, 2006 Ind. App. LEXIS 2375 (2006), transfer granted and vacated, — N.E.2d —, 2007 Ind. LEXIS 756 (2007), superseded, 866 N.E.2d 767, 2007 Ind. LEXIS 361 (2007).

No error occurred in denying defendant's motion for post-conviction relief in which defendant argued that the trial court should not have been able to use defendant's prior voluntary manslaughter conviction to both prove defendant's conviction for possession of a firearm by a serious violent felon and to enhance defendant's sentence for being a habitual offender; while defendant's contention was true, defendant waived that claim by not raising it at defendant's sentencing or on direct appeal, and, instead, pleading guilty and waiting to raise it in a motion for postconviction relief. Mills v. State, 868 N.E.2d 446, 2007 Ind. LEXIS 473 (2007).

Defendant's 20-year sentence for possession of a firearm by a serious violent felon was appropriate in light of the nature of the offense and the character of the offender where he eluded police for 10 days, admitted to using cocaine, had prior convictions for entering to commit a felony, second degree burglary, and Class A felony murder, for which he was on probation when he committed the offense at issue. Craig v. State, 883 N.E.2d 218, 2008 Ind. App. LEXIS 622 (2008).

When Bifurcated Trial Necessary.

Prejudice from evidence necessary to sustain conviction for unlawful possession of firearm by serious violent felon outweighed its probative value for robbery charge, requiring reversal of convictions, since defendant's status as serious violent felon was not essential element of robbery; defendant's request for bifurcated trial should have been granted. Hines v. State, 801 N.E.2d 634, 2004 Ind. LEXIS 77 (2004).

In a murder case, defendant was entitled to post-conviction relief on the ground of ineffective assistance of appellate counsel because counsel should have argued that the trial court abused its discretion under IC 35-34-1-11(a) in denying severance of a charge of unlawful possession of a firearm by a serious violent felon, as defined in IC 35-47-4-5(a); the case law in this area was unclear. Gray v. State, 841 N.E.2d 1210, 2006 Ind. App. LEXIS 174 (2006).

When Bifurcated Trial Not Necessary.

Prosecution's reference to defendant as a serious violent felon during trial of defendant for crime of unlawful possession of a firearm by serious violent felon, which was only crime with which defendant was charged, did not require bifurcation of trial as, inter alia, the trial court ordered that the state limit its use of the "serious violent felon" language, even during voir dire, in order to offset any prejudice to defendant. Dugan v. State, 860 N.E.2d 1288, 2007 Ind. App. LEXIS 237 (2007).

Cited:

Person v. State, 764 N.E.2d 743, 2002 Ind. App. LEXIS 380 (2002); Rotz v. State, 894 N.E.2d 989, 2008 Ind. App. LEXIS 2161 (2008).

RESEARCH REFERENCES

Indiana Law Review.

Survey: Constitutional Law: Indiana Constitutional Developments: Laches, Sentences, and Privacy, 39 Ind. L. Rev. 847 (2006).

Res Gestae.

Criminal Justice Notes 10/03: Bifurcated trial — Defendant charged with robbery and possession of firearm by serious violent felon. 47 (No. 5) Res Gestae 36 (2003).

Collateral References.

What constitutes "constructive possession" of unregistered or otherwise prohibited weapon under state law. 88 A.L.R.5th 121.

35-47-4-6. Possession of firearm by domestic batterer.

(a) A person who has been convicted of domestic battery under IC 35-42-2-1.3 and who knowingly or intentionally possesses a firearm commits unlawful possession of a firearm by a domestic batterer, a Class A misdemeanor.

(b) It is a defense to a prosecution under this section that the person's right to possess a firearm has been restored under IC 35-47-4-7.

History.

P.L.195-2003, § 7; P.L.98-2004, § 156; P.L.118-2007, § 36, eff. July 1, 2007.

Cross References.

Penalties for misdemeanors, IC 35-50-1, IC 35-50-3, IC 35-50-5-2.

NOTES TO DECISIONS

ANALYSIS

Evidence.
—Sufficient.

Evidence.

—Sufficient.

There was sufficient evidence to support defen-

Evidence. (Cont'd)

—Sufficient. (Cont'd)
dant's convictions of possession of a firearm by a convicted domestic batterer as a class A misdemeanor and criminal mischief as a class B misdemeanor when defendant had allegedly fired a gun into the air during an argument in his yard, then used the butt of the gun to break a windshield of a car driven by his former girlfriend's roommate. In addition to impeachment testimony by an officer, the evidence included the roommate's identification of defendant on a 911 recording, the recovery of shell casings and a live round from defendant's yard, officers' discovery of a gun consistent with the one used in the crime in a detached garage behind defendant's house, and defendant's threatening statement to the roommate and the former girlfriend as he was taken into custody. Gayden v. State, 863 N.E.2d 1193, 2007 Ind. App. LEXIS 652 (2007).

RESEARCH REFERENCES

Res Gestae.
    Criminal Justice Notes 8/05: Confrontation clause under Crawford, 49 (No. 4) Res Gestae 43 (2005).

35-47-4-7. Restoration of right to possess firearm by person who has been convicted of domestic violence — Procedure.

(a) Notwithstanding IC 35-47-2, IC 35-47-2.5, the restoration of the right to serve on a jury under IC 33-28-5-18, or the restoration of the right to vote under IC 3-7-13-5, and except as provided in subsections (b), (c), and (f), a person who has been convicted of a crime of domestic violence may not possess a firearm after the person's release from imprisonment or lawful detention.

(b) Not earlier than five (5) years after the date of conviction, a person who has been convicted of a crime of domestic violence may petition the court for restoration of the person's right to possess a firearm. In determining whether to restore the person's right to possess a firearm, the court shall consider the following factors:

(1) Whether the person has been subject to:
(A) a protective order;
(B) a no contact order;
(C) a workplace violence restraining order; or
(D) any other court order that prohibits the person from possessing a firearm.

(2) Whether the person has successfully completed a substance abuse program, if applicable.

(3) Whether the person has successfully completed a parenting class, if applicable.

(4) Whether the person still presents a threat to the victim of the crime.

(5) Whether there is any other reason why the person should not possess a firearm, including whether the person failed to satisfy a specified condition under subsection (c) or whether the person has committed a subsequent offense.

(c) The court may condition the restoration of a person's right to possess a firearm upon the person's satisfaction of specified conditions.

(d) If the court denies a petition for restoration of the right to possess a firearm, the person may not file a second or subsequent petition until one (1) year has elapsed after the filing of the most recent petition.

(e) A person has not been convicted of a crime of domestic violence for purposes of subsection (a) if the conviction has been expunged or if the person has been pardoned.

(f) The right to possess a firearm shall be restored to a person whose conviction is reversed on appeal or on postconviction review at the earlier of the following:

(1) At the time the prosecuting attorney states on the record that the charges that gave rise to the conviction will not be refiled.

(2) Ninety (90) days after the final disposition of the appeal or the postconviction proceeding.

History.
P.L.118-2007, § 37, eff. July 1, 2007.

CHAPTER 4.5

REGULATION OF LASER POINTERS

35-47-4.5-1. Exemptions.

This chapter does not apply to the use of a laser pointer:
(1) for educational purposes by individuals engaged in an organized meeting or training class; or
(2) during the normal course of work or trade activities.

History.
P.L.70-2000, § 1.

35-47-4.5-2. "Laser pointer" defined.

As used in this chapter, "laser pointer" means a device that emits light amplified by the stimulated emission of radiation that is visible to the human eye.

History.
P.L.70-2000, § 1.

35-47-4.5-3. "Public safety officer" defined.

As used in this chapter, "public safety officer" means:
(1) a state police officer;
(2) a county sheriff;
(3) a county police officer;
(4) a correctional officer;
(5) an excise police officer;
(6) a county police reserve officer;
(7) a city police officer;
(8) a city police reserve officer;
(9) a conservation enforcement officer;
(10) a gaming agent;
(11) a town marshal;
(12) a deputy town marshal;
(13) a state educational institution police officer appointed under IC 21-39-4;
(14) a probation officer;
(15) a firefighter (as defined in IC 9-18-34-1);
(16) an emergency medical technician;
(17) a paramedic;
(18) a member of a consolidated law enforcement department established under IC 36-3-1-5.1; or
(19) a gaming control officer.

History.
P.L.70-2000, § 1; P.L.170-2005, § 18; P.L.227-2005, § 11; P.L.1-2006, § 536; P.L.2-2007, § 379, emergency eff. July 1, 2007; P.L.227-2007, § 69, emergency eff. July 1, 2007; P.L.3-2008, § 255, emergency eff. March 13, 2008.

35-47-4.5-4. Directing light at a public safety officer.

A person who knowingly or intentionally directs light amplified by the stimulated emission of radiation that is visible to the human eye or any other electromagnetic radiation from a laser pointer at a public safety officer or a state police motor carrier inspector without the consent of the public safety officer or state police motor carrier inspector commits a Class B misdemeanor.

History.
P.L.70-2000, § 1; P.L.232-2003, § 2.

RESEARCH REFERENCES

Indiana Law Review.
Criminal Law and Procedure: Recent Develop-
ments in Indiana Criminal Law and Procedure, 34 Ind. L. Rev. 645 (2001).

CHAPTER 5

PROHIBITED WEAPONS AND OTHER INSTRUMENTS OF VIOLENCE

35-47-5-1. [Repealed.]

Compiler's Notes.
This section, concerning the sale or possession of explosive or inflammable substances, was repealed by P.L.123-2002, § 51, effective July 1, 2002. For present similar provisions, see IC 35-47.5-5.

35-47-5-2. Knife with automatically opening blade prohibited.

It is a Class B misdemeanor for a person to manufacture, possess, display, offer, sell, lend, give away, or purchase any knife with a blade that:
(1) opens automatically; or
(2) may be propelled;
by hand pressure applied to a button, device containing gas, spring, or other device in the handle of the knife.

History.
IC 35-47-5-2, as added by P.L.311-1983, § 32; P.L.70-2000, § 2.

Cross References.
Penalties for misdemeanors, IC 35-50-1, IC 35-50-3, IC 35-50-5-2.

NOTES TO DECISIONS

Constitutionality.
IC 35-47-5-2 is rationally calculated to advance the public good; thus, it is a valid exercise of the state's police power. Lacy v. State, — N.E.2d —, 2009 Ind. App. LEXIS 526 (2009).

IC 35-47-5-2 was not unconstitutional under Ind. Const., art. 1, § 32 as applied to defendant, who was convicted of possession of a switchblade; switchblades were not typically possessed by law-abiding citizens for self-defense and since statute

Constitutionality. (Cont'd)
did not ban all knives, it did not materially burden

defendant's right to defend herself. Lacy v. State,
— N.E.2d —, 2009 Ind. App. LEXIS 526 (2009).

35-47-5-2.5. Possession of knife on school property or on a school bus.

(a) As used in this section, "knife" means an instrument that:
(1) consists of a sharp edged or sharp pointed blade capable of inflicting cutting, stabbing, or tearing wounds; and
(2) is intended to be used as a weapon.

(b) The term includes a dagger, dirk, poniard, stiletto, switchblade knife, or gravity knife.

(c) A person who recklessly, knowingly, or intentionally possesses a knife on:
(1) school property (as defined in IC 35-41-1-24.7);
(2) a school bus (as defined in IC 20-27-2-8); or
(3) a special purpose bus (as defined in IC 20-27-2-10);

commits a Class B misdemeanor. However, the offense is a Class A misdemeanor if the person has a previous unrelated conviction under this section and a Class D felony if the offense results in bodily injury or serious bodily injury to another person.

(d) This section does not apply to a person who possesses a knife:
(1) if:
(A) the knife is provided to the person by the school corporation or possession of the knife is authorized by the school corporation; and
(B) the person uses the knife for a purpose authorized by the school corporation; or
(2) if the knife is secured in a motor vehicle.

History.
P.L.72-2006, § 9.

Compiler's Notes.
P.L.72-2006, § 10, effective July 1, 2006, provides:
"IC 35-47-5-2.5, as added by this act, applies only to crimes committed after June 30, 2006."

Cross References.
Penalties for felonies, IC 35-50-1, IC 35-50-2, IC 35-50-5-2.
Penalties for misdemeanors, IC 35-50-1, IC 35-50-3, IC 35-50-5-2.

35-47-5-3, 35-47-5-4. [Repealed.]

Compiler's Notes.
IC 35-47-5-3, concerning the prohibition of exposing or offering knucks, a sling-shot or a billy for sale, was repealed by P.L.269-1995, § 10, effective July 1, 1995.

IC 35-47-5-4, concerning dealing in sawed-off shotguns, was repealed by P.L.1-1990, § 350. For present similar provisions, see IC 35-47-5-4.1.

35-47-5-4.1. Dealing in sawed-off shotguns prohibited — Exceptions.

(a) A person who:
(1) Manufactures;
(2) Causes to be manufactured;
(3) Imports into Indiana;
(4) Keeps for sale;
(5) Offers or exposes for sale; or
(6) Gives, lends, or possesses;
any sawed-off shotgun commits dealing in a sawed-off shotgun, a Class D felony.

(b) The presence of a weapon referred to in subsection (a) in a motor vehicle (as defined under IC 9-13-2-105(a)) except for school buses and a vehicle operated in the transportation of passengers by a common carrier (as defined in IC 8-2.1-17-4) creates an inference that the weapon is in the possession of the persons occupying the motor vehicle. However, the inference does not apply to all the persons occupying the motor vehicle if the weapon is found upon, or under the control of, one (1) of the occupants. In addition, the inference does not apply to a duly licensed driver of a motor vehicle for hire who finds the weapon in the licensed driver's motor vehicle in the proper pursuit of the licensed driver's trade.

(c) This section does not apply to a law enforcement officer who is acting in the course of the officer's official duties or to a person who manufactures or imports for sale or sells a sawed-off shotgun to a law enforcement agency.

History.
P.L.1-1990, § 351; P.L.2-1991, § 107.

Cross References.
Penalties for felonies, IC 35-50-1, IC 35-50-2, IC 35-50-5-2.

NOTES TO DECISIONS

ANALYSIS

"Crime of Violence."
"Dealing."
Defenses.
Evidence.
—Seizure.
—Sufficient.
Intent.
Plea.
—Voluntary and Intelligent.
"Possession."
Proof.

"Crime of Violence."
Dealing in a sawed-off shotgun in violation of IC 35-47-5-4.1 was a "crime of violence" because possession of a sawed-off shotgun is an offense which involves conduct that presents a serious potential risk of physical injury to another, thereby rendering it a crime of violence under federal sentencing guidelines. United States v. Best, 250 F.3d 1084, 2001 U.S. App. LEXIS 8729 (7th Cir. Ind. 2001), cert. denied, 534 U.S. 924, 122 S. Ct. 279, 151 L. Ed. 2d 205, 2001 U.S. LEXIS 7052 (2001).

"Dealing."
The term "dealing" as it appears in this section is obviously used in the broad sense of a course of conduct as opposed to the limited sense in which it is used in other statutes, such as those which define the offense of dealing in controlled substances. Brook v. State, 448 N.E.2d 1249, 1983 Ind. App. LEXIS 2943 (1983).

Defenses.
Reliance on IC 35-47-5-5 is in the nature of a defense, and thus the defendant has the burden of showing that he falls within its purview. Had the legislature intended to place the burden on the state, the date of manufacture would have been included as an element within former IC 35-47-5-4. Rafiq v. State, 495 N.E.2d 749, 1986 Ind. App. LEXIS 2812 (1986).

Evidence.

—Seizure.
Shotgun in closet at defendant's mother's apart-

ment was in plain view and officer had probable cause to seize it, where he believed it was sawed-off and that it was contraband. Peterson v. State, 674 N.E.2d 528, 1996 Ind. LEXIS 167 (1996), cert. denied, 522 U.S. 1078, 118 S. Ct. 858, 139 L. Ed. 2d 757, 1998 U.S. LEXIS 520 (1998).

—Sufficient.
There was sufficient evidence to support the jury's verdicts of guilty of attempted murder, battery, and possession of a sawed-off gun. Tunstall v. State, 451 N.E.2d 1077, 1983 Ind. LEXIS 917 (1983).
Evidence held to be sufficient to support conviction of possession of a sawed-off shotgun under former IC 35-47-5-4. Miller v. State, 498 N.E.2d 53, 1986 Ind. App. LEXIS 3020 (1986).
Evidence was sufficient to convict defendant of dealing in a sawed-off shotgun where the shotgun he was in possession of at the time of his arrest was one-half inch shorter than the legally permissible overall length for shotguns under IC 35-47-1-10(2) and had a barrel four and one-half inches shorter than the length permissible under IC 35-47-1-10(1). Hall v. State, 791 N.E.2d 257, 2003 Ind. App. LEXIS 1231 (2003).
Evidence against defendant, who was convicted of counterfeiting as a Class D felony and possession of a sawed-off shotgun as a Class D felony, was sufficient. A printer and counterfeit money were found in a locked closet in defendant's house, and defendant provided the police with the key to the closet; the sawed-off shotgun was found in defendant's bedroom. Duso v. State, 866 N.E.2d 321, 2007 Ind. App. LEXIS 1009 (2007).

Intent.
There is nothing within the provisions concerning sawed-off shotguns indicating possession of a sawed-off shotgun was intended as a crime of specific rather than general intent. Brook v. State, 448 N.E.2d 1249, 1983 Ind. App. LEXIS 2943 (1983).

Plea.

—Voluntary and Intelligent.
Where defendant was charged with carrying a handgun without a permit and dealing in sawed-off shotguns and it is apparent that the court

Plea. (Cont'd)

—Voluntary and Intelligent. (Cont'd)
recognized from his initial answers the potential for an insufficient factual basis but his counsel interjected and questioned him in such a fashion as to establish constructive possession of the weapons and pointed out the potential problems of proving the elements of the offenses, but nevertheless requested the court to accept the plea due to the beneficial nature of the state's sentencing recommendation, defendant could not successfully claim his plea was involuntary or unintelligent under former IC 35-47-5-4 since he was aware of the possible deficiencies in the factual basis and urged the court to accept his plea. Harvey v. State, 498 N.E.2d 1231, 1986 Ind. LEXIS 1320 (1986).

"Possession."
The term "possession" as used in former IC

35-47-5-4 meant knowing control or custody. Doss v. State, 470 N.E.2d 732, 1984 Ind. App. LEXIS 3041 (1984).

Proof.
Violation of former IC 35-47-5-4 could be proved by mere possession of a sawed-off shotgun. Rafiq v. State, 495 N.E.2d 749, 1986 Ind. App. LEXIS 2812 (1986).

Cited:
United States v. Dudley, 854 F. Supp. 570, 1994 U.S. Dist. LEXIS 7520 (S.D. Ind. 1994); Ben-Yisrayl v. State, 729 N.E.2d 102, 2000 Ind. LEXIS 483 (2000); Hall v. State, 791 N.E.2d 257, 2003 Ind. App. LEXIS 1231 (2003).

RESEARCH REFERENCES

Collateral References.
Fact that gun was broken, dismantled, or inop-

erable as affecting criminal responsibility under weapons statute. 81 A.L.R.4th 745.

35-47-5-5. Firearms exempted.

This chapter does not apply to any firearm not designed to use fixed cartridges or fixed ammunition, or any firearm made before January 1, 1899.

History.
IC 35-47-5-5, as added by P.L.311-1983, § 32.

NOTES TO DECISIONS

ANALYSIS

Burden of Proof.
Instructions.

Burden of Proof.
Reliance on this section is in the nature of a defense, and thus the defendant has the burden of showing that he falls within its purview. Had the legislature intended to place the burden on the state, the date of manufacture would have been included as an element within former IC 35-47-5-4.

Rafiq v. State, 495 N.E.2d 749, 1986 Ind. App. LEXIS 2812 (1986).

Instructions.
Where the defendant tendered an instruction which informed the jury of the existence of this section, but presented no evidence of the gun's date of manufacture, there was no evidentiary basis for the instruction and it was properly refused. Rafiq v. State, 495 N.E.2d 749, 1986 Ind. App. LEXIS 2812 (1986).

35-47-5-6. Interstate firearms sales.

(a) Any resident of Indiana:
(1) Who is eighteen (18) years of age or older; and
(2) Who is not prohibited by law from obtaining, possessing, or using a firearm;
may purchase or obtain a rifle or shotgun in Ohio, Kentucky, Michigan, or Illinois.
(b) Any resident of Ohio, Kentucky, Michigan, or Illinois:
(1) Who is eighteen (18) years of age or older; and
(2) Who is not prohibited by the laws of Indiana, his domicile, or the United States from obtaining, possessing, or using a firearm;
may purchase or obtain a rifle, shotgun, or ammunition for a rifle or a shotgun in Indiana.
(c) Any transaction under this section is subject to the provisions of the Gun Control Act of 1968 (82 Stat. 1213, 18 U.S.C. 0.922(B)(3)).

History.
IC 35-47-5-6, as added by P.L.311-1983, § 32.

35-47-5-7. [Repealed.]

Compiler's Notes.
This section, concerning manufacture, operation or possession of a bulletproof motor vehicle, was repealed by P.L.175-1984, § 5.

35-47-5-8. Ownership or possession of machine gun prohibited.

A person who owns or possesses a machine gun commits a Class C felony.

History.
IC 35-47-5-8, as added by P.L.311-1983, § 32; P.L.104-2000, § 3; P.L.123-2002, § 43.

Cross References.
Penalties for felonies, IC 35-50-1, IC 35-50-2, IC 35-50-5-2.

NOTES TO DECISIONS

ANALYSIS

Evidence.
—Sufficient.
Fireworks.
"Possess."
—Constructive Possession.

Evidence.

—Sufficient.
Evidence supported the defendant's conviction of possession of a bomb loaded with explosives where it was shown that he had retrieved a bomb from his car, activated the bomb, placed it under the victim's car, and told his son he would detonate it later by remote control when the victim was in the car. Sutton v. State, 571 N.E.2d 1299, 1991 Ind. App. LEXIS 900 (1991).

The evidence was sufficient to find defendant guilty of possessing a bomb where officers discovered firearms, ammunition, two electric blasting caps, wire, and a battery operated detonation switch, and defendant admitted that the items belonged to him. Austill v. State, 745 N.E.2d 859, 2001 Ind. App. LEXIS 502 (2001).

Fireworks.
The element of purpose or design distinguishes bombs from fireworks, so that possession of a firework is not a lesser included offense of possession of a bomb. A "bomb" is an explosive device designed to release destructive material or force, whereas a "firework" is a composition or device designed for the purpose of producing a visible or audible effect. Smithhart v. State, 591 N.E.2d 149, 1992 Ind. App. LEXIS 652 (1992).

"Possess."
The word "possess" encompasses within its meaning the elements of volition, intent and conscious knowledge, and these words are elements of the offense. Satterfield v. State, 468 N.E.2d 571, 1984 Ind. App. LEXIS 2944 (1984) (decided under former IC 35-23-3-1).

—Constructive Possession.
Where the prosecution made no showing that defendant personally possessed the bombs, that he made efforts to hide them, or that the room, or desk, in which the bombs were found was habitually used by defendant, there was no evidence to show constructive possession by the defendant. Satterfield v. State, 468 N.E.2d 571, 1984 Ind. App. LEXIS 2944 (1984) (decided under former IC 35-23-3-1).

RESEARCH REFERENCES

Collateral References.
Fact that gun was broken, dismantled, or inoperable as affecting criminal responsibility under weapons statute. 81 A.L.R.4th 745.

35-47-5-9. Operation of loaded machine gun prohibited.

A person who operates a loaded machine gun commits a Class B felony.

History.
IC 35-47-5-9, as added by P.L.311-1983, § 32; P.L.104-2000, § 4; P.L.123-2002, § 44.

Cross References.
Penalties for felonies, IC 35-50-1, IC 35-50-2, IC 35-50-5-2.

Indiana Law Journal.
The New First Amendment and Its Impact on
the Second, 68 Ind. L.J. 679 (1993).

35-47-5-10. Exemptions to machine gun prohibitions.

The provisions of section 8 or 9 [IC 35-47-5-8 or IC 35-47-5-9] of this chapter shall not be construed to apply to any of the following:

(1) Members of the military or naval forces of the United States, National Guard of Indiana, or Indiana State Guard, when on duty or practicing.

(2) Machine guns kept for display as relics and which are rendered harmless and not usable.

(3) Any of the law enforcement officers of this state or the United States while acting in the furtherance of their duties.

(4) Persons lawfully engaged in the display, testing, or use of fireworks.

(5) Agencies of state government.

(6) Persons permitted by law to engage in the business of manufacturing, assembling, conducting research on, or testing machine guns, airplanes, tanks, armored vehicles, or ordnance equipment or supplies while acting within the scope of such business.

(7) Persons possessing, or having applied to possess, machine guns under applicable United States statutes. Such machine guns must be transferred as provided in this article.

(8) Persons lawfully engaged in the manufacture, transportation, distribution, use or possession of any material, substance, or device for the sole purpose of industrial, agricultural, mining, construction, educational, or any other lawful use.

History.
IC 35-47-5-10, as added by P.L.311-1983, § 32;
P.L.104-2000, § 5; P.L.123-2002, § 45.

35-47-5-11. Use of armor-piercing handgun ammunition prohibited — Exception.

(a) As used in this section, "armor-piercing handgun ammunition" means a cartridge that:

(1) Can be fired in a handgun; and

(2) Will, upon firing, expel a projectile that has a metal core and an outer coating of plastic.

(b) A person who knowingly or intentionally:

(1) Manufactures;

(2) Possesses;

(3) Transfers possession of; or

(4) Offers to transfer possession of;

armor-piercing handgun ammunition commits a Class C felony.

(c) This section does not apply to nylon coated ammunition, plastic shot capsules, or ammunition designed to be used in rifles or shotguns.

(d) This section does not apply to a law enforcement officer who is acting in the course of the officer's official duties or to a person who manufactures or imports for sale or sells armor-piercing handgun ammunition to a law enforcement agency.

History.
IC 35-47-5-11, as added by P.L.332-1983, § 1;
P.L.327-1987, § 2.

Cross References.
Penalties for felonies, IC 35-50-1, IC 35-50-2, IC 35-50-5-2.

35-47-5-12. Manufacture, sale or possession of Chinese throwing star.

(a) A person who:
(1) Manufactures;
(2) Causes to be manufactured;
(3) Imports into Indiana;
(4) Keeps for sale;
(5) Offers or exposes for sale; or
(6) Gives, lends, or possesses;
a Chinese throwing star commits a Class C misdemeanor.

(b) As used in this section, "Chinese throwing star" means a throwing-knife, throwing-iron, or other knife-like weapon with blades set at different angles.

History.
P.L.318-1985, § 2.

Cross References.
Penalties for misdemeanors, IC 35-50-1, IC 35-50-3, IC 35-50-5-2.

35-47-5-13. Unlawful use of body armor.

(a) As used in this section, "body armor" means bullet resistant metal or other material worn by a person to provide protection from weapons or bodily injury.

(b) A person who knowingly or intentionally uses body armor while committing a felony commits unlawful use of body armor, a Class D felony.

History.
P.L.227-1996, § 1.

Cross References.
Penalties for felonies, IC 35-50-1, IC 35-50-2, IC 35-50-5-2.

NOTES TO DECISIONS

ANALYSIS

Constitutionality.
Sentencing.

Constitutionality.
The bodily armor statute, IC 35-47-5-13, was not unconstitutionally vague under the actual facts of the case; defendant's specific conduct controlled his vagueness claim. Haggard v. State, 771 N.E.2d 668, 2002 Ind. App. LEXIS 1098 (2002).

Sentencing.
Defendant's criminal acts resulting in convictions for possession of cocaine, battery by body waste, resisting law enforcement, battery resulting in bodily injury, and unlawful use of body armor were all causally related; accordingly, no grounds existed for trial court to order sentence for unlawful use of body armor to run consecutively to concurrent sentences for other crimes. Haggard v. State, 810 N.E.2d 751, 2004 Ind. App. LEXIS 1154 (2004).

CHAPTER 6

WEAPONS ON AIRCRAFT

35-47-6-0.5. Exceptions.

(a) Except as provided in subsection (b), this chapter does not apply to an official or employee:

(1) of:
    (A) the United States;
    (B) a state or political subdivision of a state;
    (C) an operator (as defined in IC 5-23-2-8); or
    (D) any other entity that has been granted statutory authority to enforce the penal laws of Indiana;
(2) who has been granted the power to effect arrests under Indiana law; and
(3) who has been authorized by the official's or employee's agency or employer to carry firearms.

(b) An individual described in subsection (a) is subject to the applicable regulations of the United States concerning the possession and carriage of firearms on aircraft or in areas of an airport to which access is controlled by the inspection of persons and property.

History.
  P.L.84-1996, § 2; P.L.49-1997, § 67.

35-47-6-1. Possession of deadly weapon when boarding aircraft prohibited.

A person who boards a commercial or charter aircraft having in his possession:
    (1) A firearm;
    (2) An explosive; or
    (3) Any other deadly weapon;
commits a Class C felony.

History.
  IC 35-47-6-1, as added by P.L.311-1983, § 32.

Cross References.
  Penalties for felonies, IC 35-50-1, IC 35-50-2, IC 35-50-5-2.

RESEARCH REFERENCES

Collateral References.
  Fact that gun was unloaded as affecting criminal responsibility. 68 A.L.R.4th 507.
  Fact that gun was broken, dismantled, or inoperable as affecting criminal responsibility under weapons statute. 81 A.L.R.4th 745.

Validity, construction, and application of provisions of Federal Aviation Act (49 U.S.C.S. Appx. § 1472(i)-(l), (n)) punishing air piracy and certain acts aboard aircraft in flight, or boarding aircraft. 109 A.L.R. Fed. 488.

35-47-6-1.1. Undisclosed transport of dangerous device.

(a) As used in this section, "dangerous device" means:
    (1) a firearm;
    (2) a destructive device (as defined in IC 35-47.5-2-4); or
    (3) a weapon of mass destruction (IC 35-41-1-29.4).

(b) A person who checks an item to be transported on a commercial passenger airline and who:
    (1) knows the item contains a dangerous device; and
    (2) knowingly or intentionally fails to disclose orally or in writing to the person to whom possession of the item is delivered for carriage that the item contains a dangerous device;
commits undisclosed transport of a dangerous device, a Class A misdemeanor.

History.
  P.L.50-2005, § 2.

Compiler's Notes.
  P.L.50-2005, § 3, effective July 1, 2005, provides:

"IC 35-47-6-1.1, as added by this act, applies only to offenses committed after June 30, 2005."

Cross References.
  Penalties for misdemeanors, IC 35-50-1, IC 35-50-3, IC 35-50-5-2.

35-47-6-1.3. Possession of firearm, explosive, or deadly weapon in airport.

A person who knowingly or intentionally enters an area of an airport to which access is controlled by the inspection of persons and property while the person:
(1) possesses:
(A) a firearm;
(B) an explosive; or
(C) any other deadly weapon; or
(2) has access to property that contains:
(A) a firearm;
(B) an explosive; or
(C) any other deadly weapon;
commits a Class A misdemeanor.

History.
P.L.84-1996, § 3.

Cross References.
Penalties for misdemeanors, IC 35-50-1, IC 35-50-3, IC 35-50-5-2.

35-47-6-1.4. Unauthorized entry into inspection-controlled areas of airports.

(a) This section does not apply to a person who is:
(1) employed by:
(A) an airport;
(B) an airline; or
(C) a law enforcement agency; and
(2) acting lawfully within the scope of the person's employment.
(b) A person who knowingly or intentionally enters an area of an airport to which access is controlled by the inspection of persons or property without submitting to the inspection commits a Class A misdemeanor.

History.
P.L.59-2002, § 3.

Cross References.
Penalties for misdemeanors, IC 35-50-1, IC 35-50-3, IC 35-50-5-2.

35-47-6-1.6. Use or threat of force to disrupt operation of aircraft — Hijacking an aircraft.

(a) A person who knowingly or intentionally uses force or violence or the threat of force or violence to disrupt the operation of an aircraft commits a Class B felony.
(b) A person who knowingly or intentionally uses force or violence or the threat of force or violence to hijack an aircraft in flight commits a Class A felony.
(c) For purposes of this section, an aircraft is considered to be in flight while the aircraft is:
(1) on the ground in Indiana:
(A) after the doors of the aircraft are closed for takeoff; and
(B) until the aircraft takes off;
(2) in the airspace above Indiana; or
(3) on the ground in Indiana:
(A) after the aircraft lands; and
(B) before the doors of the aircraft are opened after landing.

History.
P.L.59-2002, § 4.

Cross References.
Penalties for felonies, IC 35-50-1, IC 35-50-2, IC 35-50-5-2.

35-47-6-2. [Repealed.]

Compiler's Notes.
This section, concerning exemptions, was repealed by P.L.84-1996, § 4, effective March 7, 1996. For present similar provisions, see IC 35-47-6-0.5.

35-47-6-3. Consent of purchaser of airline ticket to search of person or personal belongings.

Any person purchasing a ticket to board any commercial or charter aircraft shall by such purchase consent to a search of his person or personal belongings by the company selling said ticket to him. In case said person shall refuse to submit to a search of his person or personal belongings by said aircraft company, the person refusing may be denied the right to board said commercial or charter aircraft.

History.
IC 35-47-6-3, as added by P.L.311-1983, § 32.

35-47-6-4. Immunity of airline company from liability.

No action, either at law or equity, shall be brought against any commercial or charter airline company operating in Indiana for the refusal of said company to permit a person to board said aircraft where said person has refused to be searched as set out in section 3 [IC 35-47-6-3] of this chapter.

History.
IC 35-47-6-4, as added by P.L.311-1983, § 32.

CHAPTER 7

REPORTS OF WOUNDS AND BURN INJURIES

35-47-7-1. Report of injuries from gun, firearm, knife, ice pick or other sharp or pointed instrument.

Every case of a bullet wound, gunshot wound, powder burn, or any other injury arising from or caused by the discharge of a firearm, and every case of a wound which is likely to or may result in death and is actually or apparently inflicted by a knife, ice pick, or other sharp or pointed instrument, shall be reported at once to the law enforcement authorities of the county, city, or town in which the person reporting is located by either the physician attending or treating the case, or by the manager, superintendent, or other person in charge if the case is treated in a hospital, clinic, sanitarium, or other facility or institution. A person who violates this section commits a Class A misdemeanor.

History.
IC 35-47-7-1, as added by P.L.311-1983, § 32.

Cross References.
Penalties for misdemeanors, IC 35-50-1, IC 35-50-3, IC 35-50-5-2.

35-47-7-2. Exceptions.

The provisions of this chapter shall not apply to a wound or other injury received by a member of the armed forces of the United States or the state while engaged in the actual performance of duty.

History.
  IC 35-47-7-2, as added by P.L.311-1983, § 32.

35-47-7-3. Burn injury reports.

(a) As used in this section, "burn" includes chemical burns, flash burns, and thermal burns.

(b) If a person is treated for:

  (1) A second or third degree burn to ten percent (10%) or more of the body;

  (2) Any burn to the upper respiratory tract or laryngeal edema due to the inhalation of superheated air; or

  (3) A burn that results in serious bodily injury;

the physician treating the person, or the hospital administrator or the hospital administrator's designee of the hospital or ambulatory outpatient surgical center (if the person is treated in a hospital or outpatient surgical center), shall report the case to the state fire marshal within seventy-two (72) hours. This report may be made orally or in writing and shall be considered confidential information.

(c) If a person is treated for a second or third degree burn to less than ten percent (10%) of the body, the attending physician may report the case to the state fire marshal under subsection (b).

(d) The state fire marshal shall ascertain the following when a report is made under this chapter:

  (1) Victim's name, address, and date of birth.

  (2) Address where burn injury occurred.

  (3) Date and time of injury.

  (4) Degree of burns and percent of body burned.

  (5) Area of body burned.

  (6) Injury severity.

  (7) Apparent cause of burn injury.

  (8) Name and address of reporting facility.

  (9) Attending physician.

History.
  P.L.328-1987, § 1.

35-47-7-4. Reporting of dog bite cases.

The:

  (1) Physician who treats a person for a dog bite or an apparent dog bite; or

  (2) Administrator or the administrator's designee of the hospital or outpatient surgical center if a person is treated in a hospital or an outpatient surgical center for a dog bite or an apparent dog bite;

shall report the case to the Indiana state department of health not more than seventy-two (72) hours after the time the person is treated. The report may be made orally or in writing.

History.
  P.L.176-1993, § 7.

35-47-7-5. Reporting of injuries caused by manufacture or use of destructive devices.

The:

(1) physician who treats a person; or

(2) administrator or the administrator's designee of the hospital or outpatient surgical center where a person was treated;

who has reason to believe that the physician or hospital is treating a person for an injury that was inflicted while the person was making or using a destructive device shall report the case to a local law enforcement agency not more than seventy-two (72) hours after the person is treated. The report may be made orally or in writing.

History.
P.L.123-2002, § 46.

35-47-7-6. [Repealed.]

Compiler's Notes.
This section, concerning firework or pyrotechnic injury reports, was repealed by P.L.187-2006, § 18, effective March 27, 2006.

35-47-7-7. Reports to state by practitioners, hospitals and outpatient surgical centers of injuries resulting from fireworks or pyrotechnics.

(a) If:

(1) a practitioner (as defined in IC 25-1-9-2) initially treats a person for an injury and identifies the person's injury as resulting from fireworks or pyrotechnics, the practitioner; or

(2) a hospital or an outpatient surgical center initially treats a person for an injury and the administrator of the hospital or outpatient surgical center identifies the person's injury as resulting from fireworks or pyrotechnics, the administrator or the administrator's designee;

shall report the case to the state health data center of the state department of health not more than five (5) business days after the time the person is treated. The report may be made in writing on a form prescribed by the state department of health.

(b) A person submitting a report under subsection (a) shall make a reasonable attempt to include the following information:

(1) The name, address, and age of the injured person.

(2) The date and time of the injury and the location where the injury occurred.

(3) If the injured person was less than eighteen (18) years of age at the time of the injury, whether an adult was present when the injury occurred.

(4) Whether the injured person consumed an alcoholic beverage within three (3) hours before the occurrence of the injury.

(5) A description of the firework or pyrotechnic that caused the injury.

(6) The nature and extent of the injury.

(c) A report made under this section is confidential for purposes of IC 5-14-3-4(a)(1).

(d) The state department of health shall compile the data collected under this section and submit a report of the compiled data to the legislative council in an electronic format under IC 5-14-6 not later than December 31 of each year.

History.
P.L.187-2006, § 17.

CHAPTER 8

ELECTRONIC STUN WEAPONS, TASERS, AND STUN GUNS

35-47-8-1. "Electronic stun weapon" defined.

As used in this chapter, "electronic stun weapon" means any mechanism that is:
  (1) Designed to emit an electronic, magnetic, or other type of charge that exceeds the equivalency of a five (5) milliamp sixty (60) hertz shock; and
  (2) Used for the purpose of temporarily incapacitating a person.

History.
  P.L.318-1985, § 3.

35-47-8-2. "Stun gun" defined.

As used in this chapter, "stun gun" means any mechanism that is:
  (1) Designed to emit an electronic, magnetic, or other type of charge that equals or does not exceed the equivalency of a five (5) milliamp sixty (60) hertz shock; and
  (2) Used for the purpose of temporarily incapacitating a person.

History.
  P.L.318-1985, § 3.

35-47-8-3. "Taser" defined.

As used in this chapter, "taser" means any mechanism that is:
  (1) Designed to emit an electronic, magnetic, or other type of charge or shock through the use of a projectile; and
  (2) Used for the purpose of temporarily incapacitating a person.

History.
  P.L.318-1985, § 3.

35-47-8-4. Applicability of IC 35-47-2.

IC 35-47-2 applies to an electronic stun weapon or taser.

History.
  P.L.318-1985, § 3.

35-47-8-5. Purchase, possession, sale or use of stun gun.

  (a) A person eighteen (18) years of age or over may purchase or possess a stun gun.
  (b) A person who sells or furnishes a stun gun to a person who is less than eighteen (18) years of age commits a Class B misdemeanor.
  (c) A person who uses a stun gun in the commission of a crime commits a Class A misdemeanor.
  (d) A person who uses a stun gun on a law enforcement officer while the officer is performing the officer's duties commits a Class D felony.

History.
P.L.318-1985, § 3.

Penalties for misdemeanors, IC 35-50-1, IC 35-50-3, IC 35-50-5-2.

Cross References.
Penalties for felonies, IC 35-50-1, IC 35-50-2, IC 35-50-5-2.

CHAPTER 9

POSSESSION OF FIREARMS ON SCHOOL PROPERTY AND SCHOOL BUSES

35-47-9-1. Security guards — School functions.

This chapter does not apply to the following:
(1) A:
(A) Federal;
(B) State; or
(C) Local;
law enforcement officer.
(2) A person who has been employed or authorized by:
(A) A school; or
(B) Another person who owns or operates property being used by a school for a school function;
to act as a security guard, perform or participate in a school function, or participate in any other activity authorized by a school.
(3) A person who:
(A) May legally possess a firearm; and
(B) Possesses the firearm in a motor vehicle that is being operated by the person to transport another person to or from a school or a school function.

History.
P.L.140-1994, § 11.

NOTES TO DECISIONS

No Affirmative Defense.
Defendant was properly convicted of possession of firearms on school property, a Class D felony, IC 35-47-9-2; three witnesses testified without objection that defendant admitted owning both the car and the handgun, and as such, any error in the admission of the handgun taken from defendant's vehicle could only be considered harmless pursuant to TR. 61, and defendant failed to prove an affirmative defense pursuant to IC 35-47-9-1(3), because defendant was not operating his car when a student initially saw the handgun in the car. Newson v. State, 785 N.E.2d 1155, 2003 Ind. App. LEXIS 528 (2003).

35-47-9-2. Possession of firearm on school property or school bus.

A person who possesses a firearm:
(1) In or on school property;
(2) In or on property that is being used by a school for a school function; or
(3) On a school bus;
commits a Class D felony.

History.

P.L.140-1994, § 11.

Cross References.

Penalties for felonies, IC 35-50-1, IC 35-50-2, IC 35-50-5-2.

NOTES TO DECISIONS

Conviction Proper.

Defendant was properly convicted of possession of firearms on school property, a Class D felony, IC 35-47-9-2; three witnesses testified without objection that defendant admitted owning both the car and the handgun, and as such, any error in the admission of the handgun taken from defendant's vehicle could only be considered harmless pursuant to TR. 61, and defendant failed to prove an affirmative defense pursuant to IC 35-47-9-1(3), because defendant was not operating his car when a student initially saw the handgun in the car. Newson v. State, 785 N.E.2d 1155, 2003 Ind. App. LEXIS 528 (2003).

Search and Seizure.

The protective search of a juvenile just outside classroom was permissible where the school safety officer received information from a student about the juvenile that caused her to remove the juvenile from the classroom, and her concern for her safety caused her to conduct a pat down search. In re C.S., 735 N.E.2d 273, 2000 Ind. App. LEXIS 1468 (2000).

Detection by trained dogs of scent of narcotics coming from high school defendant's vehicle, which was parked in high school parking lot, provided probable cause to search vehicle; therefore, defendant, who was charged with possession of firearm on school property in violation of IC 35-47-9-2, was not entitled to suppression of evidence discovered in search. Myers v. State, 806 N.E.2d 350, 2004 Ind. App. LEXIS 678 (2004), transfer granted, 812 N.E.2d 806, 2004 Ind. LEXIS 512 (2004), aff'd, 839 N.E.2d 1154, 2005 Ind. LEXIS 1136 (2005).

CHAPTER 10

CHILDREN AND HANDGUNS

35-47-10-1. Applicability.

This chapter does not apply to the following:

(1) A child who is attending a hunters safety course or a firearms safety course or an adult who is supervising the child during the course.

(2) A child engaging in practice in using a firearm for target shooting at an established range or in an area where the discharge of a firearm is not prohibited or supervised by:

(A) a qualified firearms instructor; or

(B) an adult who is supervising the child while the child is at the range.

(3) A child engaging in an organized competition involving the use of a firearm or participating in or practicing for a performance by an organized group under Section 501(c) (3) of the Internal Revenue Code that uses firearms as a part of a performance or an adult who is involved in the competition or performance.

(4) A child who is hunting or trapping under a valid license issued to the child under IC 14-22.

(5) A child who is traveling with an unloaded firearm to or from an activity described in this section.

(6) A child who:

(A) is on real property that is under the control of the child's parent, an adult family member of the child, or the child's legal guardian; and

(B) has permission from the child's parent or legal guardian to possess a firearm.

(7) A child who:

(A) is at the child's residence; and

(B) has the permission of the child's parent, an adult family member of the child, or the child's legal guardian to possess a firearm.

History.
P.L.140-1994, § 12; P.L.1-1995, § 78; P.L.203-1996, § 2.

ferred to in subdivision (3) above, may be found at 26 U.S.C.S. § 501.

Compiler's Notes.
Section 501 of the Internal Revenue Code, re-

NOTES TO DECISIONS

Criminal Court Jurisdiction.
Former IC 31-6-2-1.1 was made applicable to crimes committed after July 1, 1994, and provided that criminal courts rather than juvenile courts had jurisdiction over a child for alleged violations of this chapter if the child was 16 or over at the time of the violation. Person v. State, 661 N.E.2d 587, 1996 Ind. App. LEXIS 144 (1996).

RESEARCH REFERENCES

Indiana Law Review.
Recent Developments in Indiana Criminal Law and Procedure, 28 Ind. L. Rev. 819 (1995).

35-47-10-2. "Adult" defined.

As used in this chapter, "adult" means a person who is at least eighteen (18) years of age.

History.
P.L.140-1994, § 12.

35-47-10-3. "Child" defined.

As used in this chapter, "child" means a person who is less than eighteen (18) years of age.

History.
P.L.140-1994, § 12.

NOTES TO DECISIONS

In General.
Sufficient evidence supported juvenile defendant's conviction for dangerous possession of firearm where defendant kicked in door to father's locked bedroom to retrieve semi-automatic rifle and father testified that defendant did not have permission to possess rifle. Gall v. State, 811 N.E.2d 969, 2004 Ind. App. LEXIS 1384 (2004).

35-47-10-4. "Loaded" defined.

As used in this chapter, "loaded" means having any of the following:

(1) A cartridge in the chamber or cylinder of a firearm.

(2) Ammunition in close proximity to a firearm so that a person can readily place the ammunition in the firearm.

History.
P.L.140-1994, § 12; P.L.203-1996, § 3.

35-47-10-5. Dangerous possession of firearm.

A child who knowingly, intentionally, or recklessly:

(1) possesses a firearm for any purpose other than a purpose described in section 1 [IC 35-47-10-1] of this chapter; or

(2) provides a firearm to another child with or without remuneration for any purpose other than a purpose described in section 1 of this chapter;

commits dangerous possession of a firearm, a Class A misdemeanor. However, the offense is a Class C felony if the child has a prior conviction under this section.

History.
P.L.140-1994, § 12; P.L.203-1996, § 4.

Penalties for misdemeanors, IC 35-50-1, IC 35-50-3, IC 35-50-5-2.

Cross References.
Penalties for felonies, IC 35-50-1, IC 35-50-2, IC 35-50-5-2.

NOTES TO DECISIONS

ANALYSIS

Constitutionality.
Evidence.
Possession.
Trial As Adult.

Constitutionality.
There is no disparate treatment among those similarly situated under this section, the child handgun statute, and the adult handgun statute, IC 35-47-2-1. Person v. State, 661 N.E.2d 587, 1996 Ind. App. LEXIS 144 (1996).

IC 35-47-10-5 does not violate privileges and immunities clause of Ind. Const., art. 1, § 23, and 16-year-old defendant, who was convicted of dangerous possession of firearm, criminal recklessness, and attempted murder, failed to show that statute was unconstitutional as applied to him based on disparate treatment since he did not show that his treatment was different from treatment of any other juvenile charged with multiple offenses including offense listed in IC 31-30-1-4. Gall v. State, 811 N.E.2d 969, 2004 Ind. App. LEXIS 1384 (2004).

Evidence.
Evidence was insufficient to prove that defendant was under the age of 18, as required for the dangerous possession of a firearm by a child conviction; the testimony presented only indicated that a witness knew defendant in high school but did not indicate what grade defendant had been in or how old he was. Stewart v. State, 866 N.E.2d 858, 2007 Ind. App. LEXIS 1085 (2007).

Because defendant stole a car knowing that there were children in it, and then took a purse from the car and shot at the children's father, the evidence was sufficient to support convictions under IC 35-42-3-2(a)(2), IC 35-43-4-2(a), IC 35-41-5-1, IC 35-42-1-1, IC 35-47-10-5 for kidnapping, theft, attempted murder, and dangerous possession of a firearm; however, defendant's conviction under IC 5-42-3-3(a)(2), (b)(2)(A) for confinement merged with the kidnapping conviction. Taylor v. State, 879 N.E.2d 1198, 2008 Ind. App. LEXIS 131 (2008).

Possession.
The evidence sufficiently supported the trial court's judgment that defendant had the capability and intent to exercise dominion and control over the handgun, and thus "possess" it within the meaning of this section. Person v. State, 661 N.E.2d 587, 1996 Ind. App. LEXIS 144 (1996).

Sufficient evidence supported 16-year-old defendant's conviction for dangerous possession of firearm where defendant kicked in door to father's locked bedroom to retrieve semi-automatic rifle and father testified that defendant did not have permission to possess rifle. Gall v. State, 811 N.E.2d 969, 2004 Ind. App. LEXIS 1384 (2004).

Trial As Adult.
Defendant, who was 16-years-old at time of offense, was properly charged and tried in adult criminal court with dangerous possession of firearm; furthermore, joinder of that offense with attempted murder charge also supported adult criminal court jurisdiction pursuant to IC 35-34-1-9(a)(2). Gall v. State, 811 N.E.2d 969, 2004 Ind. App. LEXIS 1384 (2004).

35-47-10-6. Provision of firearm by adult to child.

An adult who knowingly, intentionally, or recklessly provides a firearm to a child for any purpose other than those described in section 1 [IC 35-47-10-1] of this chapter, with or without remuneration, commits dangerous control of a firearm, a Class C felony. However, the offense is a Class B felony if the adult has a prior conviction under this section.

History.
  P.L.140-1994, § 12; P.L.203-1996, § 5.

Cross References.
  Penalties for felonies, IC 35-50-1, IC 35-50-2, IC 35-50-5-2.

NOTES TO DECISIONS

Constructive Possession.
  Constructive possession is established by showing defendant has the intent and capability to maintain control over contraband. Where defendant has exclusive possession of the premises, an inference is permitted that defendant knew of its presence and was capable of controlling it; where possession is non-exclusive, the inference is not permitted absent additional circumstances. Person v. State, 661 N.E.2d 587, 1996 Ind. App. LEXIS 144 (1996).

35-47-10-7. Dangerous control of a child.

A child's parent or legal guardian who knowingly, intentionally, or recklessly permits the child to possess a firearm:
  (1) while:
    (A) aware of a substantial risk that the child will use the firearm to commit a felony; and
    (B) failing to make reasonable efforts to prevent the use of a firearm by the child to commit a felony; or
  (2) when the child has been convicted of a crime of violence or has been adjudicated as a juvenile for an offense that would constitute a crime of violence if the child were an adult;
commits dangerous control of a child, a Class C felony. However, the offense is a Class B felony if the child's parent or legal guardian has a prior conviction under this section.

History.
  P.L.140-1994, § 12; P.L.203-1996, § 6.

Cross References.
  Penalties for felonies, IC 35-50-1, IC 35-50-2, IC 35-50-5-2.

35-47-10-8. Additional incarceration.

(a) In addition to any criminal penalty imposed for an offense under this chapter, the court shall order the following:
  (1) That a person who has committed an offense be incarcerated for five (5) consecutive days in an appropriate facility.
  (2) That the additional five (5) day term must be served within two (2) weeks after the date of sentencing.
(b) Notwithstanding IC 35-50-6, a person does not earn credit time while serving an additional five (5) day term of imprisonment imposed by a court under this section.

History.
  P.L.140-1994, § 12.

NOTES TO DECISIONS

ANALYSIS

Constitutionality.
—Equal Protection.
—Excessive Penalties.

Constitutionality.
—Equal Protection.
  Article 1, § 23 of the Indiana Constitution is not violated by the mandatory executed sentence im-

Constitutionality. (Cont'd)

—Equal Protection. (Cont'd)
posed upon children under this section. Person v. State, 661 N.E.2d 587, 1996 Ind. App. LEXIS 144 (1996).

—Excessive Penalties.
The nature and extent of penal sanctions are primarily legislative considerations and there is no constitutional violation of either section 16 or section 18 of the Indiana Constitution when the legislature determines that children who dangerously possess handguns should serve a mandatory five day jail term. Person v. State, 661 N.E.2d 587, 1996 Ind. App. LEXIS 144 (1996).

35-47-10-9. Consecutive sentencing of offense under IC 35-47-2-7.

A court shall impose consecutive sentences upon a person who has a conviction under this chapter and a conviction under IC 35-47-2-7.

History.
P.L.140-1994, § 12.

35-47-10-10. Placement of child in quasi-military program.

When sentencing a child who has committed an offense under this chapter, a court may elect to place the child in a facility that uses a quasi-military program for rehabilitative purposes.

History.
P.L.140-1994, § 12.

CHAPTER 11

LOCAL REGULATION OF FIREARMS

35-47-11-1. Applicability.

(a) Section 2 [IC 35-47-11-2] of this chapter applies to all units (as defined in IC 36-1-2-23). All other sections of this chapter apply to all units other than townships.

(b) This chapter applies only if a statute expressly grants a legislative body the authority to adopt an emergency ordinance under this chapter.

(c) This chapter does not affect the validity of an ordinance adopted before, and in effect on, January 1, 1994.

History.
P.L.140-1994, § 13.

35-47-11-2. Regulation of ownership, sale, transfer, etc. of firearms or ammunition.

Notwithstanding IC 36-1-3, a unit may not regulate in any manner the ownership, possession, sale, transfer, or transportation of firearms (as defined in IC 35-47-1-5) or ammunition except as follows:

(1) This chapter does not apply to land, buildings, or other real property owned or administered by a unit, except highways (as defined in IC 8-23-1-23) or public highways (as defined in IC 8-2.1-17-14).

(2) Notwithstanding the limitation in this section, a unit may use the unit's

planning and zoning powers under IC 36-7-4 to prohibit the sale of firearms within two hundred (200) feet of a school by a person having a business that did not sell firearms within two hundred (200) feet of a school before April 1, 1994.

(3) Notwithstanding the limitation in this section, a legislative body of a unit other than a township may adopt an emergency ordinance or a unit other than a township may take other action allowed under section 6 [IC 35-47-11-6] of this chapter to regulate the sale of firearms anywhere within the unit for a period of not more than seventy-two (72) hours after the regulatory action takes effect.

History.
P.L.140-1994, § 13.

35-47-11-3. Emergency ordinance — Adoption for disaster.

The legislative body of a unit may adopt an emergency ordinance under this chapter if:

(1) a disaster (as defined in IC 10-14-3-1) has occurred or is likely to occur in the unit; and

(2) a local disaster emergency has been declared in the unit under IC 10-14-3-29.

History.
P.L.140-1994, § 13; P.L.2-2003, § 98.

35-47-11-4. Emergency ordinance — Adoption procedure.

Notwithstanding any other law, if the conditions described under section 3 [IC 35-47-11-3] of this chapter are present within a unit, the legislative body of the unit may adopt an emergency ordinance under this chapter:

(1) Without complying with the public notice and public meeting provisions of:
  (A) IC 5-14-1.5; or
  (B) Any other statute;
(2) On the same day that the ordinance is presented to the legislative body; and
(3) By a majority vote of the members of the legislative body.

History.
P.L.140-1994, § 13.

35-47-11-5. Time of taking effect — Expiration.

An emergency ordinance adopted under section 4 [IC 35-47-11-4] of this chapter:
(1) Takes effect on the date and at the time of the adoption of the ordinance; and
(2) Expires the earlier of:
  (A) Seventy-two (72) hours after the time of the adoption of the ordinance; or
  (B) A time specified in the emergency ordinance.

History.
P.L.140-1994, § 13.

35-47-11-6. Restriction on firearms for 72 hours.

If:
(1) The conditions described under section 3 [IC 35-47-11-3] of this chapter are present within a unit;
(2) An unsuccessful attempt is made to convene the legislative body for the purpose of adopting an emergency ordinance under this chapter; and

(3) In the case of a municipality, an unsuccessful attempt is made to convene the works board to act under this chapter as if the works board were the legislative body;

the executive of a municipality or the presiding officer of a county executive may declare a restriction on the sale of firearms anywhere within the unit for a period of not more than seventy-two (72) hours after the restriction is declared. A declaration under this section has the same effect as an ordinance adopted under section 4 [IC 35-47-11-4] of this chapter and becomes effective and expires as provided in section 5 [IC 35-47-11-5] of this chapter.

History.
P.L.140-1994, § 13.

CHAPTER 12

WEAPONS OF MASS DESTRUCTION

35-47-12-1. Use with intent to carry out terrorism.

A person who knowingly or intentionally:
(1) possesses;
(2) manufactures;
(3) places;
(4) disseminates; or
(5) detonates;
a weapon of mass destruction with the intent to carry out terrorism commits a Class B felony. However, the offense is a Class A felony if the conduct results in serious bodily injury or death of any person.

History.
P.L.156-2001, § 13; P.L.123-2002, § 47.

Cross References.
Penalties for felonies, IC 35-50-1, IC 35-50-2, IC 35-50-5-2.

35-47-12-2. Agricultural terrorism.

A person who knowingly or intentionally:
(1) possesses;
(2) manufactures;
(3) places;
(4) disseminates; or
(5) detonates;
a weapon of mass destruction with the intent to damage, destroy, sicken, or kill crops or livestock of another person without the consent of the other person commits agricultural terrorism, a Class C felony.

History.
P.L.156-2001, § 13; P.L.123-2002, § 48.

Cross References.
Penalties for felonies, IC 35-50-1, IC 35-50-2, IC 35-50-5-2.

35-47-12-3. Terroristic mischief.

A person who knowingly or intentionally places or disseminates a device or substance with the intent to cause a reasonable person to believe that the device or substance is a weapon of mass destruction (as defined in IC 35-41-1-29.4), commits terroristic mischief, a Class C felony. However, the offense is a Class B felony if, as a result of the terroristic mischief:

(1) a physician prescribes diagnostic testing or medical treatment for any person other than the person who committed the terroristic mischief; or

(2) a person suffers serious bodily injury.

History.
   P.L.123-2002, § 49.

Cross References.
   Penalties for felonies, IC 35-50-1, IC 35-50-2, IC 35-50-5-2.

CHAPTER 13

RETIRED LAW ENFORCEMENT OFFICERS IDENTIFICATION FOR CARRYING FIREARMS

35-47-13-1 — 35-47-13-6. [Repealed.]

Compiler's Notes.
   This chapter, as enacted by P.L.140-2005, concerning retired law enforcement officers identifica-tion for carrying firearms, was repealed by P.L.1-2006, § 588, effective March 24, 2006.

CHAPTER 13

PROCEEDINGS FOR THE SEIZURE AND RETENTION OF A FIREARM

35-47-13-1 — 35-47-13-9. [Repealed.]

Compiler's Notes.
   This chapter, as enacted by P.L.187-2005, concerning proceedings for the seizure and retention of a firearm, was repealed by P.L.1-2006, § 588, effective March 24, 2006.

CHAPTER 14

PROCEEDINGS FOR THE SEIZURE AND RETENTION OF A FIREARM

35-47-14-1. "Dangerous individual" defined.

(a) For the purposes of this chapter, an individual is "dangerous" if:

(1) the individual presents an imminent risk of personal injury to the individual or to another individual; or

(2) the individual may present a risk of personal injury to the individual or to another individual in the future and the individual:

(A) has a mental illness (as defined in IC 12-7-2-130) that may be controlled by medication, and has not demonstrated a pattern of voluntarily and consistently taking the individual's medication while not under supervision; or

(B) is the subject of documented evidence that would give rise to a reasonable belief that the individual has a propensity for violent or emotionally unstable conduct.

(b) The fact that an individual has been released from a mental health facility or has a mental illness that is currently controlled by medication does not establish that the individual is dangerous for the purposes of this chapter.

History.
P.L.1-2006, § 537.

35-47-14-2. Warrant for search and seizure of firearm.

A circuit or superior court may issue a warrant to search for and seize a firearm in the possession of an individual who is dangerous if:

(1) a law enforcement officer provides the court a sworn affidavit that:

(A) states why the law enforcement officer believes that the individual is dangerous and in possession of a firearm; and

(B) describes the law enforcement officer's interactions and conversations with:

(i) the individual who is alleged to be dangerous; or

(ii) another individual, if the law enforcement officer believes that information obtained from this individual is credible and reliable;

that have led the law enforcement officer to believe that the individual is dangerous and in possession of a firearm;

(2) the affidavit specifically describes the location of the firearm; and

(3) the circuit or superior court determines that probable cause exists to believe that the individual is:

(A) dangerous; and

(B) in possession of a firearm.

History.
P.L.1-2006, § 537.

35-47-14-3. Seizure without warrant — Submission of written statement by law enforcement officer.

(a) If a law enforcement officer seizes a firearm from an individual whom the law enforcement officer believes to be dangerous without obtaining a warrant, the law enforcement officer shall submit to the circuit or superior court having jurisdiction over the individual believed to be dangerous a written statement under oath or affirmation describing the basis for the law enforcement officer's belief that the individual is dangerous.

(b) The court shall review the written statement submitted under subsection (a). If the court finds that probable cause exists to believe that the individual is dangerous, the court shall order the law enforcement agency having custody of the firearm to retain the firearm. If the court finds that there is no probable cause to believe that the individual is dangerous, the court shall order the law enforcement agency having custody of the firearm to return the firearm to the individual.

(c) This section does not authorize a law enforcement officer to perform a warrantless search or seizure if a warrant would otherwise be required.

History.
P.L.1-2006, § 537.

35-47-14-4. Filing of return of warrant.

If a court issued a warrant to seize a firearm under this chapter, the law enforcement officer who served the warrant shall, not later than forty-eight (48) hours after the warrant was served, file a return with the court that:
(1) states that the warrant was served; and
(2) sets forth:
(A) the time and date on which the warrant was served;
(B) the name and address of the individual named in the warrant; and
(C) the quantity and identity of any firearms seized by the law enforcement officer.

History.
P.L.1-2006, § 537.

35-47-14-5. Hearing.

(a) Not later than fourteen (14) days after a return is filed under section 4 [IC 35-47-14-4] of this chapter or a written statement is submitted under section 3 [IC 35-47-14-3] of this chapter, the court shall conduct a hearing to determine whether the seized firearm should be:
(1) returned to the individual from whom the firearm was seized; or
(2) retained by the law enforcement agency having custody of the firearm.
(b) The court shall set the hearing date as soon as possible after the return is filed under section 4 of this chapter. The court shall inform:
(1) the prosecuting attorney; and
(2) the individual from whom the firearm was seized;
of the date, time, and location of the hearing. The court may conduct the hearing at a facility or other suitable place not likely to have a harmful effect upon the individual's health or well-being.

History.
P.L.1-2006, § 537.

35-47-14-6. Burden of proof in hearing — Retention of firearm by law enforcement agency — Return of firearm.

(a) In a hearing conducted under section 5 [IC 35-47-14-5] of this chapter, the state has the burden of proving all material facts by clear and convincing evidence.
(b) If the court, in a hearing under section 5 of this chapter, determines that the state has proved by clear and convincing evidence that the individual is dangerous, the court may order that the law enforcement agency having custody of the seized firearm retain the firearm. In addition, if the individual has received a license to carry a handgun, the court shall suspend the individual's license to carry a handgun. If the court determines that the state has failed to prove that the individual is dangerous, the court shall order the law enforcement agency having custody of the firearm to return the firearm to the individual from whom it was seized.
(c) If the court, in a hearing under section 5 of this chapter, orders a law enforcement agency to retain a firearm, the law enforcement agency shall retain the firearm until the court orders the firearm returned or otherwise disposed of.

History.
P.L.1-2006, § 537.

35-47-14-7. Return of firearm to owner.

If the court, in a hearing conducted under section 5 [IC 35-47-14-5] of this chapter, determines that:
(1) the individual from whom a firearm was seized is dangerous; and
(2) the firearm seized from the individual is owned by another individual;
the court may order the law enforcement agency having custody of the firearm to return the firearm to the owner of the firearm.

History.
P.L.1-2006, § 537.

35-47-14-8. Petition for return of firearm after hearing.

(a) At least one hundred eighty (180) days after the date on which a court orders a law enforcement agency to retain an individual's firearm under section 6(b) [IC 35-47-14-6(b)] of this chapter, the individual may petition the court for return of the firearm.
(b) Upon receipt of a petition described in subsection (a), the court shall:
(1) enter an order setting a date for a hearing on the petition; and
(2) inform the prosecuting attorney of the date, time, and location of the hearing.
(c) The prosecuting attorney shall represent the state at the hearing on a petition under this section.
(d) In a hearing on a petition under this section, the individual:
(1) may be represented by an attorney; and
(2) must prove by a preponderance of the evidence that the individual is not dangerous.
(e) If, upon the completion of the hearing and consideration of the record, the court finds that the individual is not dangerous, the court shall order the law enforcement agency having custody of the firearm to return the firearm to the individual.
(f) If the court denies an individual's petition under this section, the individual may not file a subsequent petition until at least one hundred eighty (180) days after the date on which the court denied the petition.

History.
P.L.1-2006, § 537.

35-47-14-9. Destruction or permanent disposal of firearm.

If at least five (5) years have passed since a court conducted the first hearing to retain a firearm under this chapter, the court, after giving notice to the parties and conducting a hearing, may order the law enforcement agency having custody of the firearm to destroy or otherwise permanently dispose of the firearm.

History.
P.L.1-2006, § 537.

CHAPTER 15

RETIRED LAW ENFORCEMENT OFFICERS IDENTIFICATION FOR CARRYING FIREARMS

35-47-15-1. "Firearm" defined.

As used in this chapter, "firearm" has the meaning set forth in 18 U.S.C. 926C(e).

History.
P.L.1-2006, § 538.

35-47-15-2. "Law enforcement agency" defined.

As used in this chapter, "law enforcement agency" means an agency or department of:
(1) the state; or
(2) a political subdivision of the state;
whose principal function is the apprehension of criminal offenders.

History.
P.L.1-2006, § 538.

35-47-15-3. "Law enforcement officer" defined.

As used in this chapter, "law enforcement officer" has the meaning set forth in IC 35-41-1-17(a). The term includes an arson investigator employed by the office of the state fire marshal.

History.
P.L.1-2006, § 538.

35-47-15-4. Annual photographic identification.

After June 30, 2005, all law enforcement agencies shall issue annually to each person who has retired from that agency as a law enforcement officer a photographic identification.

History.
P.L.1-2006, § 538.

35-47-15-5. Evidence of training and qualification standards.

(a) In addition to the photographic identification issued under section 4 [IC 35-47-15-4] of this chapter, after June 30, 2005, a retired law enforcement officer who carries a concealed firearm under 18 U.S.C. 926C must obtain annually, for each type of firearm that the retired officer intends to carry as a concealed firearm, evidence that the retired officer meets the training and qualification standards for carrying that type of firearm that are established:
(1) by the retired officer's law enforcement agency, for active officers of the agency; or
(2) by the state, for active law enforcement officers in the state.
A retired law enforcement officer bears any expense associated with obtaining the evidence required under this subsection.
(b) The evidence required under subsection (a) is one (1) of the following:
(1) For compliance with the standards described in subsection (a)(1), an endorsement issued by the retired officer's law enforcement agency with or as part of the photographic identification issued under section 4 of this chapter.

(2) For compliance with the standards described in subsection (a)(2), a certification issued by the state.

History.
P.L.1-2006, § 538.

35-47-15-6. Immunity from liability of agency providing evidence required by IC 35-47-15-5.

An entity that provides evidence required under section 5 [IC 35-47-15-5] of this chapter is immune from civil or criminal liability for providing the evidence.

History.
P.L.1-2006, § 538.

ARTICLE 47.5

CONTROLLED EXPLOSIVES

CHAPTER 1

APPLICABILITY

35-47.5-1-1. Applicability.

This article does not apply to the following:
(1) Fertilizers, propellant actuated devices, or propellant activated industrial tools:
   (A) manufactured;
   (B) imported;
   (C) distributed; or
   (D) used;
for their designed purposes.
(2) A pesticide that is:
   (A) manufactured;
   (B) stored;
   (C) transported;
   (D) distributed;
   (E) possessed; or
   (F) used;
for its designed purposes or in accordance with Chapter 7 of Title 2, the federal Insecticide, Fungicide, and Rodenticide Act, 61 Stat. 163, as amended, and the federal Environmental Pesticide Control Act of 1972, P.L.92-516, as amended.

History.
P.L.123-2002, § 50.

Compiler's Notes.
The Federal Insecticide, Fungicide, and Roden-

ticide Act can be found generally at 7 U.S.C. § 136 et seq.

CHAPTER 2
DEFINITIONS

35-47.5-2-1. Applicability.

The definitions in this chapter apply throughout this article.

History.
P.L.123-2002, § 50.

35-47.5-2-2. Booby trap.

"Booby trap" means a device meant to cause death or bodily injury by:
(1) hiding the device; or
(2) activating the device by trip wires, switches, antidisturbance, or other remote means.

History.
P.L.123-2002, § 50.

35-47.5-2-3. Commission.

"Commission" refers to the fire prevention and building safety commission established by IC 22-12-2-1.

History.
P.L.123-2002, § 50.

35-47.5-2-4. Destructive device.

(a) "Destructive device" means:
(1) an explosive, incendiary, or overpressure device that is configured as a:
(A) bomb;
(B) grenade;
(C) rocket with a propellant charge of more than four (4) ounces;
(D) missile having an explosive or incendiary charge of more than one-quarter (¼) ounce;
(E) mine;
(F) Molotov cocktail; or
(G) device that is substantially similar to an item described in clauses (A) through (F);
(2) a type of weapon that may be readily converted to expel a projectile by the action of an explosive or other propellant through a barrel that has a bore diameter of more than one-half (½) inch; or
(3) a combination of parts designed or intended for use in the conversion of a device into a destructive device.
(b) The term does not include the following:
(1) A pistol, rifle, shotgun, or weapon suitable for sporting or personal safety purposes or ammunition.

(2) A device that is neither designed nor redesigned for use as a weapon.

(3) A device that, although originally designed for use as a weapon, is redesigned for use as a signaling, pyrotechnic, line throwing, safety, or similar device.

(4) A surplus military ordnance sold, loaned, or given by authority of the appropriate official of the United States Department of Defense.

History.
P.L.123-2002, § 50.

35-47.5-2-5. Detonator.

"Detonator" means a device containing a detonating charge that is used to initiate detonation in an explosive, including the following:
(1) Electric blasting caps.
(2) Blasting caps for use with safety fuses.
(3) Detonating cord delay connectors.
(4) Blasting caps for use with a shock tube.
(5) Improvised devices designed to function as a detonator.

History.
P.L.123-2002, § 50.

35-47.5-2-6. Distribute.

"Distribute" means the actual, constructive, or attempted transfer from one (1) person to another.

History.
P.L.123-2002, § 50.

35-47.5-2-7. Explosives.

"Explosives" means a chemical compound or other substance or mechanical system intended to produce an explosion capable of causing injury to persons or damage to property or containing oxidizing and combustible units or other ingredients in such proportions or quantities that ignition, fire, friction, concussion, percussion, or detonation may produce an explosion capable of causing injury to persons or damage to property, including the substances designated in IC 35-47.5-3. The term does not include the following:
(1) A model rocket and model rocket engine designed, sold, and used to propel recoverable aero models.
(2) A paper cap in which the explosive content does not average more than twenty-five hundredths (0.25) grains of explosive mixture per paper cap for toy pistols, toy cannons, toy canes, toy guns, or other devices using paper caps unless the paper cap is used as a component of a destructive device.

History.
P.L.123-2002, § 50.

35-47.5-2-8. Hoax device.

"Hoax device" or "replica" means a device or article that has the appearance of a destructive device or detonator.

History.
P.L.123-2002, § 50.

35-47.5-2-9. Incendiary.

"Incendiary" means a flammable liquid or compound with a flash point not greater than one hundred fifty (150) degrees Fahrenheit, as determined by a Tagliabue or an equivalent closed cup device, including gasoline, kerosene, fuel oil, or a derivative of these substances.

History.
P.L.123-2002, § 50.

NOTES TO DECISIONS

Applicability.
In an arson case, judicial requirement that proof of the corpus delicti of arson show that fire was "incendiary" does not refer to the definition of "incendiary" in IC 35-47.5-2-9 because (1) that definition only applies to "controlled explosives" under IC 35-47 and (2) judicial requirement was adopted before IC 35-47.5-2-9 was enacted. Williams v. State, 837 N.E.2d 615, 2005 Ind. App. LEXIS 2186 (2005).

35-47.5-2-10. Division.

"Division" refers to the division of fire and building safety.

History.
P.L.123-2002, § 50; P.L.1-2006, § 539.

35-47.5-2-11. Overpressure device.

"Overpressure device" means:
  (1) a frangible container filled with an explosive gas or expanding gas that is designed or constructed to cause the container to break or fracture in a manner that is capable of causing death, bodily harm, or property damage; or
  (2) a container filled with an explosive gas or expanding gas or chemicals that generate an expanding gas.

History.
P.L.123-2002, § 50.

NOTES TO DECISIONS

In General.
Device not designed for use as weapon is not "destructive device" within meaning of IC 35-47.5-5-2; accordingly, where juvenile exploded homemade bomb in backyard but demonstrated no intent to use device as weapon, juvenile could not be charged with possession of destructive device in violation of IC 35-47.5-5-2 but could be charged with lesser offense of use of overpressure device in violation of IC 35-47.5-5-9. A.H. v. State, 794 N.E.2d 1147, 2003 Ind. App. LEXIS 1643 (2003).

35-47.5-2-12. Property.

"Property" means real or personal property of any kind, including money, choses in action, and other similar interests in property.

History.
P.L.123-2002, § 50.

35-47.5-2-13. Regulated explosive.

(a) "Regulated explosive" includes:
    (1) a destructive device; and
    (2) an explosive.
(b) The term does not include the following:

(1) An explosive in a manufactured article that is designed and packaged in a manner that is likely to prevent an explosion resulting in property damage or personal injury. A manufactured article to which this subdivision applies includes fixed ammunition for small arms, a firework, and a safety fuse match.

(2) Gasoline, kerosene, naphtha, turpentine, or benzine.

(3) An explosive that is being transported on or in a vessel, railroad car, or highway vehicle in conformity with the regulations adopted by the United States Department of Transportation.

(4) A blasting explosive that is transported or used for agricultural purposes and that is in a quantity that does not exceed two hundred (200) pounds.

(5) Ammonium nitrate or other explosive compounds kept for mining purposes at coal mines regulated under IC 14-34.

History.
P.L.123-2002, § 50.

CHAPTER 3

CLASSIFICATION OF REGULATED EXPLOSIVES

Section
35-47.5-3-1. Regulated explosives.

35-47.5-3-1. Regulated explosives.

The following materials are regulated explosives within the meaning of this article:

(1) Acetylides of heavy metals.

(2) Aluminum containing polymeric propellant.

(3) Aluminum ophorite explosive.

(4) Amatex.

(5) Amatol.

(6) Ammonal.

(7) Ammonium nitrate explosive mixtures, cap sensitive.

(8) Ammonium nitrate explosive mixtures, noncap sensitive.

(9) Aromatic nitro-compound explosive mixtures.

(10) Ammonium perchlorate explosive mixtures.

(11) Ammonium perchlorate composite propellant.

(12) Ammonium picrate (picrate of ammonia, explosive D).

(13) Ammonium salt lattice with isomorphously substituted inorganic salts.

(14) Ammonium tri-iodide.

(15) ANFO (ammonium nitrate-fuel oil).

(16) Baratol.

(17) Baronol.

(18) BEAF (1,2-bis (2,2-difluoro-2-nitroacetoxyethane)).

(19) Black powder.

(20) Black powder based explosive mixtures.

(21) Blasting agents, nitro-carbo-nitrates, including noncap sensitive slurry and water-gel explosives.

(22) Blasting caps.

(23) Blasting gelatin.

(24) Blasting powder.

(25) BTNEC (bis (trinitroethyl) carbonate).

(26) Bulk salutes.

(27) BTNEN (bis (trinitroethyl) nitramine).

(28) BTTN (1,2,4 butanetriol trinitrate).

(29) Butyl tetryl.

(30) Calcium nitrate explosive mixture.

(31) Cellulose hexanitrate explosive mixture.

(32) Chlorate explosive mixtures.

(33) Composition A and variations.

(34) Composition B and variations.

(35) Composition C and variations.

(36) Copper acetylide.

(37) Cyanuric triazide.

(38) Cyclotrimethylenetrinitramine (RDX).

(39) Cyclotetramethylenetetranitramine (HMX).

(40) Cyclonite (RDX).

(41) Cyclotol.

(42) DATB (diaminotrinitrobenzene).

(43) DDNP (diazodinitrophenol).

(44) DEGDN (diethyleneglycol dinitrate).

(45) Detonating cord.

(46) Detonators.

(47) Dimethylol dimethyl methane dinitrate composition.

(48) Dinitroethyleneurea.

(49) Dinitroglycerine (glycerol dinitrate).

(50) Dinitrophenol.

(51) Dinitrophenolates.

(52) Dinitrophenyl hydrazine.

(53) Dinitroresorcinol.

(54) Dinitrotoluene-sodium nitrate explosive mixtures.

(55) DIPAM.

(56) Dipicryl sulfone.

(57) Dipicrylamine.

(58) DNDP (dinitropentano nitrile).

(59) DNPA (2,2-dinitropropyl acrylate).

(60) Dynamite.

(61) EDDN (ethylene diamine dinitrate).

(62) EDNA.

(63) Ednatol.

(64) EDNP (ethyl 4,4-dinitropentanoate).

(65) Erythritol tetranitrate explosives.

(66) Esters of nitro substituted alcohols.

(67) EGDN (ethylene glycol dinitrate).

(68) Ethyl-tetryl.

(69) Explosive conitrates.

(70) Explosive gelatins.

(71) Explosive mixtures containing oxygen releasing inorganic salts and hydrocarbons.

(72) Explosive mixtures containing oxygen releasing inorganic salts and nitro bodies.

(73) Explosive mixtures containing oxygen releasing inorganic salts and water insoluble fuels.

(74) Explosive mixtures containing oxygen releasing inorganic salts and water soluble fuels.

(75) Explosive mixtures containing sensitized nitromethane.

(76) Explosive mixtures containing tetranitromethane (nitroform).

(77) Explosive nitro compounds of aromatic hydrocarbons.

(78) Explosive organic nitrate mixtures.

(79) Explosive liquids.
(80) Explosive powders.
(81) Flash powder.
(82) Fulminate of mercury.
(83) Fulminate of silver.
(84) Fulminating gold.
(85) Fulminating mercury.
(86) Fulminating platinum.
(87) Fulminating silver.
(88) Gelatinized nitrocellulose.
(89) Gem-dinitro aliphatic explosive mixtures.
(90) Guanyl nitrosamino guanyl tetrazene.
(91) Guanyl nitrosamino guanylidene hydrazine.
(92) Hexogene or octogene and a nitrated N-methylaniline.
(93) Hexolites.
(94) HMX(cyclo-l,3,5,7-tetramethylene-2,4,6,8-tetranitramine; octogen).
(95) Hydrazinium nitrate/hydrazine/aluminum explosive system.
(96) Hydrazoic acid.
(97) Igniter cord.
(98) Igniters.
(99) Initiating tube systems.
(100) KDNBF (potassium dinitrobenzo-furoxane).
(101) Lead azide.
(102) Lead mannite.
(103) Lead mononitroresorcinate.
(104) Lead picrate.
(105) Lead salts, explosive.
(106) Lead styphnate (styphnate of lead, lead trinitroresorcinate).
(107) Liquid nitrated polyol and trimethylolethane.
(108) Liquid oxygen explosives.
(109) Magnesium ophorite explosives.
(110) Mannitol hexanitrate.
(111) MDNP (methyl 4,4-dinitropentanoate).
(112) MEAN (monoethanolamine nitrate).
(113) Mercuric fulminate.
(114) Mercury oxalate.
(115) Mercury tartrate.
(116) Metriol trinitrate.
(117) Minol-2 (40% TNT, 40% ammonium nitrate, 20% aluminum).
(118) MMAN (monomethylamine nitrate); methylamine nitrate.
(119) Mononitrotoluene-nitroglycerin mixture.
(120) Monopropellants.
(121) NIBTN (nitroisobutametriol trinitrate).
(122) Nitrate sensitized with gelled nitroparaffin.
(123) Nitrated carbohydrate explosive.
(124) Nitrated glucoside explosive.
(125) Nitrated polyhydric alcohol explosives.
(126) Nitrates of soda explosive mixtures.
(127) Nitric acid and a nitro aromatic compound explosive.
(128) Nitric acid and carboxylic fuel explosive.
(129) Nitric acid explosive mixtures.
(130) Nitro aromatic explosive mixtures.
(131) Nitro compounds of furane explosive mixtures.
(132) Nitrocellulose explosive.

(133) Nitroderivative of urea explosive mixture.

(134) Nitrogelatin explosive.

(135) Nitrogen trichloride.

(136) Nitrogen tri-iodide.

(137) Nitroglycerine (NG, RNG, nitro, glyceryl trinitrate, trinitroglycerine).

(138) Nitroglycide.

(139) Nitroglycol (ethylene glycol dinitrate, EGDN).

(140) Nitroguanidine explosives.

(141) Nitroparaffins explosive grade and ammonium nitrate mixtures.

(142) Nitronium perchlorate propellant mixtures.

(143) Nitrostarch.

(144) Nitro substituted carboxylic acids.

(145) Nitrourea.

(146) Octogen (HMX).

(147) Octol (75% HMX, 25% TNT).

(148) Organic amine nitrates.

(149) Organic nitramines.

(150) PBX (RDX and plasticizer).

(151) Pellet powder.

(152) Penthrinite composition.

(153) Pentolit.

(154) Perchlorate explosive mixtures.

(155) Peroxide based explosive mixtures.

(156) PETN (nitropentaerythrite, pentaerythrite tetranitrate, pentaerythritol tetranitrate).

(157) Picramic acid and its salts.

(158) Picramide.

(159) Picrate of potassium explosive mixtures.

(160) Picratol.

(161) Picric acid (manufactured as an explosive).

(162) Picryl chloride.

(163) Picryl fluoride.

(164) PLX (95% nitromethane, 5% ethylenediamine).

(165) Polynitro aliphatic compounds.

(166) Polyolpolynitrate-nitrocellulose explosive gels.

(167) Potassium chlorate and lead sulfocyanate explosive.

(168) Potassium nitrate explosive mixtures.

(169) Potassium nitroaminotetrazole.

(170) Pyrotechnic compositions.

(171) PYX (2,6-bis(picrylamino)-3,5-dinitropyridine).

(172) RDX (cyclonite, hexogen, T4,cyclo-1,3, 5,-trimethylene-2,4,6,-rinitramine; hexahydro-1,3,5-trinitro-S-triazine).

(173) Safety fuse.

(174) Salutes (bulk).

(175) Salts of organic amino sulfonic acid explosive mixture.

(176) Silver acetylide.

(177) Silver azide.

(178) Silver fulminate.

(179) Silver oxalate explosive mixtures.

(180) Silver styphnate.

(181) Silver tartrate explosive mixtures.

(182) Silver tetrazene.

(183) Slurried explosive mixtures of water, inorganic oxidizing salt, gelling agent, fuel, and sensitizer, cap sensitive.

(184) Smokeless powder.

(185) Sodatol.

(186) Sodium amatol.

(187) Sodium azide explosive mixture.

(188) Sodium dinitro-ortho-cresolate.

(189) Sodium nitrate-potassium nitrate explosive mixture.

(190) Sodium picramate.

(191) Special fireworks (as defined in IC 22-11-14-1).

(192) Squibs.

(193) Styphnic acid explosives.

(194) Tacot (tetranitro-2,3,5,6-dibenzo-l,3a,4,6a tetrazapentalene).

(195) TATB (triaminotrinitrobenzene).

(196) TATP (triacetone triperoxide).

(197) TEGDN (triethylene glycol dinitrate).

(198) Tetrazene (tetracene, tetrazine, l(5-tetrazolyl)-4-guanyl tetrazene hydrate).

(199) Tetranitrocarbazole.

(200) Tetryl (2,4,6 tetranitro-N-methylaniline).

(201) Tetrytol.

(202) Thickened inorganic oxidizer salt slurried explosive mixture.

(203) TMETN (trimethylolethane trinitrate).

(204) TNEF (trinitroethyl formal).

(205) TNEOC (trinitroethylorthocarbonate).

(206) TNEOF (trinitroethylorthoformate).

(207) TNT (trinitrotoluene, trotyl, trilite, triton).

(208) Torpex.

(209) Tridite.

(210) Trimethylol ethyl methane trinitrate composition.

(211) Trimethylolthane trinitrate-nitrocellulose.

(212) Trimonite.

(213) Trinitroanisole.

(214) Trinitrobenzene.

(215) Trinitrobenzoic acid.

(216) Trinitrocresol.

(217) Trinitro-meta-cresol.

(218) Trinitronaphthalene.

(219) Trinitrophenetol.

(220) Trinitrophloroglucinol.

(221) Trinitroresorcinol.

(222) Tritonal.

(223) Urea nitrate.

(224) Water bearing explosives having salts of oxidizing acids and nitrogen bases, sulfates, or sulfamates, cap sensitive.

(225) Water in oil emulsion explosive compositions.

(226) Xanthamonas hydrophilic colloid explosive mixture.

History.
P.L.123-2002, § 50.

RESEARCH REFERENCES

Collateral References.
31A Am. Jur. 2d Explosions and Explosives, §§ 7
— 16.

CHAPTER 4

REGISTRATION AND CONTROL

35-47.5-4-1. Manufacturing inspection.

The division shall carry out a program to periodically inspect places where regulated explosives are manufactured.

History.
P.L.123-2002, § 50; P.L.1-2006, § 540.

35-47.5-4-2. Insurance requirements.

(a) The division may order any person engaged in the manufacture or handling of a regulated explosive and any person with control over a place where regulated explosives are manufactured or handled to maintain insurance covering fire and explosion losses. The order is not effective until sixty (60) days after the date that notice of the order is received.

(b) The state fire marshal shall specify the insurance required under subsection (a) in an amount not less than ten thousand dollars ($10,000) nor more than two hundred fifty thousand dollars ($250,000).

(c) Proof of the insurance required under this section must be maintained with the department of insurance.

(d) The insurance commissioner may exempt a person from the insurance requirements under this section if an applicant for the exemption submits proof that the applicant has the financial ability to discharge all judgments in the amount specified by the state fire marshal. The insurance commissioner may revoke an exemption under this subsection if the commissioner requires additional proof of financial ability and:

(1) the exempted person fails to comply with the order; or

(2) the insurance commissioner determines that the exempted person has failed to provide adequate proof of financial ability.

History.
P.L.123-2002, § 50; P.L.1-2006, § 541.

35-47.5-4-3. Storage inspection.

The division shall carry out a program to periodically inspect places where regulated explosives are stored.

History.
P.L.123-2002, § 50; P.L.1-2006, § 542.

35-47.5-4-4. Regulated explosives magazine permit.

(a) The division shall issue a regulated explosives magazine permit to maintain an explosives magazine to an applicant who qualifies under section 5 [IC 35-47.5-4-5] of this chapter.

(b) A permit issued under subsection (a) expires one (1) year after it is issued. The permit is limited to storage of the types and maximum quantities of explosives specified in the permit in the place covered by the permit and under the construction and location requirements specified in the rules of the commission.

History.
P.L.123-2002, § 50; P.L.1-2006, § 543.

35-47.5-4-4.5. "Regulated amusement device".

(a) This section does not apply to:

(1) a person who is regulated under IC 14-34; or

(2) near surface or subsurface use of regulated explosives associated with oil and natural gas:

(A) exploration;

(B) development;

(C) production; or

(D) abandonment activities or procedures.

(b) The commission shall adopt rules under IC 4-22-2 to:

(1) govern the use of a regulated explosive; and

(2) establish requirements for the issuance of a license for the use of a regulated explosive.

(c) The commission shall include the following requirements in the rules adopted under subsection (b):

(1) Relicensure every three (3) years after the initial issuance of a license.

(2) Continuing education as a condition of relicensure.

(3) An application for licensure or relicensure must be submitted to the division on forms approved by the commission.

(4) A fee for licensure and relicensure.

(5) Reciprocal recognition of a license for the use of a regulated explosive issued by another state if the licensure requirements of the other state are substantially similar to the licensure requirements established by the commission.

(d) A person may not use a regulated explosive unless the person has a license issued under this section for the use of a regulated explosive.

(e) The division shall carry out the licensing and relicensing program under the rules adopted by the commission.

(f) As used in this section, "regulated explosive" does not include either of the following:

(1) Consumer fireworks (as defined in 27 CFR 555.11).

(2) Commercially manufactured black powder in quantities not to exceed fifty (50) pounds, if the black powder is intended to be used solely for sporting, recreational, or cultural purposes in antique firearms or antique devices.

History.
P.L.35-2004, § 2; P.L.25-2004, § 6; P.L.2-2005, § 128; P.L.80-2005, § 7; P.L.1-2006, § 544.

35-47.5-4-5. Qualifications for permit.

(a) To qualify for a regulated explosives permit, an applicant must:

(1) submit information on the form provided by the state fire marshal describing:

(A) the location of the affected magazine;

(B) the types and maximum quantities of explosives that will be kept in the place covered by the application; and

(C) the distance that the affected magazine will be located from the nearest highway, railway, and structure that is also used as a place of habitation or assembly other than for the manufacture of explosives;

(2) except as provided in subdivision (3), demonstrate through an inspection that the magazine is constructed and located in accordance with the rules adopted by the commission;

(3) demonstrate through an inspection that smoking, matches, open flames, and spark producing devices are not allowed within a room containing an indoor magazine; and

(4) pay the fee under IC 22-12-6-6.

(b) To qualify for the renewal of a regulated explosives permit, the applicant must pay the fee under IC 22-12-6-6.

History.
P.L.123-2002, § 50.

35-47.5-4-6. Violations — Exemptions.

(a) This section does not apply to storage that is exempted from the requirements of this section in the rules adopted by the commission under IC 22-13-3.

(b) A person who:

(1) stores a regulated explosive;

(2) has control over a regulated explosive that is stored; or

(3) has control over a place where a regulated explosive is stored;

without a regulated explosives magazine permit issued under this chapter that covers the storage commits a Class C infraction.

History.
P.L.123-2002, § 50.

Cross References.
Infraction and ordinance violation enforcement proceedings, IC 34-28-5.

35-47.5-4-7. Reporting of injuries related to manufacture of destructive devices.

A physician or hospital that has reason to believe that the physician or hospital is treating a person for an injury inflicted while the person was making or using a destructive device shall report the injury to a local law enforcement agency under IC 35-47-7-5.

History.
P.L.123-2002, § 50.

CHAPTER 5

OFFENSES RELATING TO REGULATED EXPLOSIVES

35-47.5-5-1. Applicability.

Sections 2, 3, 4, 5, and 6 [IC 35-47.5-5-2, IC 35-47.5-5-3, IC 35-47.5-5-4, IC 35-47.5-5-5, and IC 35-47.5-5-6] of this chapter do not apply to the following:

(1) A person authorized to manufacture, possess, transport, distribute, or use a destructive device or detonator under the laws of the United States, as amended, or under Indiana law when the person is acting in accordance with the laws, regulations, and rules issued under federal or Indiana law.

(2) A person who is issued a permit for blasting or surface coal mining by the director of the department of natural resources under IC 14-34 when the person is acting under the laws and rules of Indiana and any ordinances and regulations of the political subdivision or authority of the state where blasting or mining operations are being performed.

(3) Fireworks (as defined in IC 22-11-14-1) and a person authorized by the laws of Indiana and of the United States to manufacture, possess, distribute, transport, store, exhibit, display, or use fireworks.

(4) A law enforcement agency, a fire service agency, the department of homeland security, or an emergency management agency of Indiana, an agency or an authority of a political subdivision of the state or the United States, and an employee or authorized agent of the United States while in performance of official duties.

(5) A law enforcement officer, a fire official, or an emergency management official of the United States or any other state if that person is attending training in Indiana.

(6) The armed forces of the United States or of Indiana.

(7) Research or educational programs conducted by or on behalf of a college, university, or secondary school that are:

(A) authorized by the chief executive officer of the educational institution or the officer's designee; or

(B) conducted under the policy of the educational institution;

and conducted in accordance with the laws of the United States and Indiana.

(8) The use of explosive materials in medicines and medicinal agents in forms prescribed by the most recent published edition of the official United States Pharmacopoeia or the National Formulary.

(9) Small arms ammunition and reloading components of small arms ammunition.

(10) Commercially manufactured black powder in quantities not to exceed fifty (50) pounds, percussion caps, safety and pyrotechnic fuses, quills, quick and slow matches, and friction primers intended to be used solely for sporting, recreational, or cultural purposes in antique firearms or antique devices.

(11) An explosive that is lawfully possessed for use in legitimate agricultural or business activities.

History.
P.L.123-2002, § 50; P.L.1-2006, § 545.

35-47.5-5-2. Unauthorized possession, manufacture, transportation or distribution of destructive devices.

A person who knowingly or intentionally:

(1) possesses;

(2) manufactures;

(3) transports;

(4) distributes;

(5) possesses with the intent to distribute; or

(6) offers to distribute;

a destructive device, unless authorized by law, commits a Class C felony.

History.
P.L.123-2002, § 50.

Cross References.
Conviction of felony or misdemeanor, effect on

license or certificate holder, IC 25-1-1.1-1.
Penalties for felonies, IC 35-50-1, IC 35-50-2, IC 35-50-5-2.

NOTES TO DECISIONS

ANALYSIS

Evidence.
—Not Sufficient.
—Sufficient.
Lesser-Included Offense.
Ultra-Hazardous Activity.

Evidence.

—Not Sufficient.
Device not designed for use as weapon is not "destructive device" within meaning of IC 35-47.5-5-2; accordingly, where juvenile exploded home-made bomb in backyard but demonstrated no intent to use device as weapon, juvenile could not be charged with possession of destructive device in violation of IC 35-47.5-5-2 but could be charged with lesser offense of use of overpressure device in violation of IC 35-47.5-5-9. A.H. v. State, 794 N.E.2d 1147, 2003 Ind. App. LEXIS 1643 (2003).

—Sufficient.
Evidence held sufficient to sustain conviction. Crowe v. State, 456 N.E.2d 439, 1983 Ind. App. LEXIS 3604 (1983).

Lesser-Included Offense.
Use of overpressure device does not qualify as inherently included offense of possession of destructive device nor does possession of destructive device necessarily constitute use of overpressure device. A.H. v. State, 794 N.E.2d 1147, 2003 Ind. App. LEXIS 1643 (2003).

Ultra-Hazardous Activity.
Whether the storage of dynamite in any particular circumstance is an ultra-hazardous activity must be determined on a case-by-case basis. Bridges v. Kentucky Stone Co., 425 N.E.2d 125, 1981 Ind. LEXIS 825 (1981).

RESEARCH REFERENCES

Collateral References.
Liability in connection with fire or explosion of

explosives while being stored or transported. 35 A.L.R.3d 1177.

35-47.5-5-3. Possession, manufacture, transportation or distribution by convicted felon.

A person who has been convicted of a felony by an Indiana court or a court of any other state, the United States, or another country and knowingly or intentionally:
(1) possesses;
(2) manufactures;
(3) transports;
(4) distributes;
(5) possesses with the intent to distribute; or
(6) offers to distribute;
a regulated explosive commits a Class C felony. However, the offense is a Class B felony if the person has a prior unrelated conviction for an offense under this section.

History.
P.L.123-2002, § 50.

Cross References.
Penalties for felonies, IC 35-50-1, IC 35-50-2, IC 35-50-5-2.

35-47.5-5-4. Distribution to convicted felon.

A person who knowingly or intentionally distributes a regulated explosive to a person who has been convicted of a felony by an Indiana court or a court of another state, the United States, or another country commits a Class C felony.

History.
P.L.123-2002, § 50.

Cross References.
Penalties for felonies, IC 35-50-1, IC 35-50-2, IC 35-50-5-2.

35-47.5-5-5. Distribution to minor.

A person who knowingly or intentionally distributes or offers to distribute:
(1) a destructive device;
(2) an explosive; or
(3) a detonator;
to a person who is less than eighteen (18) years of age commits a Class B felony.

History.
P.L.123-2002, § 50.

Cross References.
Penalties for felonies, IC 35-50-1, IC 35-50-2, IC 35-50-5-2.

35-47.5-5-6. Possession, manufacture, transportation or distribution of hoax device.

A person who:
(1) manufactures;
(2) possesses;
(3) transports;
(4) distributes; or
(5) uses;
a hoax device or replica with the intent to cause another to believe that the hoax device or replica is a destructive device or detonator commits a Class D felony.

History.
P.L.123-2002, § 50.

Cross References.
Penalties for felonies, IC 35-50-1, IC 35-50-2, IC 35-50-5-2.

35-47.5-5-7. Obstruction of law enforcement.

A person who knowingly or intentionally hinders or obstructs:
(1) a law enforcement officer;
(2) a fire official;
(3) an emergency management official;
(4) an animal trained to detect destructive devices; or
(5) a robot or mechanical device designed or used by a law enforcement officer, fire official, or emergency management official;
of Indiana or of the United States in the detection, disarming, or destruction of a destructive device commits a Class B felony.

History.
P.L.123-2002, § 50.

Cross References.
Penalties for felonies, IC 35-50-1, IC 35-50-2, IC 35-50-5-2.

35-47.5-5-8. Possession, transportation, receipt, placing or detonation of destructive device or explosive to kill, injure or intimidate.

A person who:
(1) possesses;
(2) transports;
(3) receives;
(4) places; or
(5) detonates;

a destructive device or explosive with the knowledge or intent that it will be used to kill, injure, or intimidate an individual or to destroy property commits a Class A felony.

History.
P.L.123-2002, § 50.

Cross References.
Penalties for felonies, IC 35-50-1, IC 35-50-2, IC 35-50-5-2.

35-47.5-5-9. Use of overpressure device.

A person who knowingly or intentionally uses an overpressure device commits a Class A misdemeanor. However, the offense is a Class D felony if the person has a prior unrelated conviction for an offense under this section.

History.
P.L.123-2002, § 50.

Penalties for misdemeanors, IC 35-50-1, IC 35-50-3, IC 35-50-5-2.

Cross References.
Penalties for felonies, IC 35-50-1, IC 35-50-2, IC 35-50-5-2.

NOTES TO DECISIONS

ANALYSIS

Sufficient Evidence.
Lesser-Included Offense.

Sufficient Evidence.
Device not designed for use as weapon is not "destructive device" within meaning of IC 35-47.5-5-2; accordingly, where juvenile exploded homemade bomb in backyard but demonstrated no intent to use device as weapon, juvenile could not be charged with possession of destructive device in violation of IC 35-47.5-5-2 but could be charged with lesser offense of use of overpressure device in violation of IC 35-47.5-5-9. A.H. v. State, 794 N.E.2d 1147, 2003 Ind. App. LEXIS 1643 (2003).

Lesser-Included Offense.
Use of overpressure device does not qualify as inherently included offense of possession of destructive device nor does possession of destructive device necessarily constitute use of overpressure device. A.H. v. State, 794 N.E.2d 1147, 2003 Ind. App. LEXIS 1643 (2003).

35-47.5-5-10. Deployment of booby trap.

A person who knowingly or intentionally deploys a booby trap commits a Class D felony.

History.
P.L.123-2002, § 50.

Cross References.
Penalties for felonies, IC 35-50-1, IC 35-50-2, IC 35-50-5-2.

35-47.5-5-11. Violation of rules regarding use of regulated explosives.

A person who recklessly violates a rule regarding the use of a regulated explosive adopted by the commission under IC 35-47.5-4-4.5 commits a Class A misdemeanor. However, the offense is a Class D felony if the violation of the rule proximately causes bodily injury or death.

History.
P.L.35-2004, § 3.

Penalties for misdemeanors, IC 35-50-1, IC 35-50-3, IC 35-50-5-2.

Cross References.
Penalties for felonies, IC 35-50-1, IC 35-50-2, IC 35-50-5-2.

ARTICLE 48

CONTROLLED SUBSTANCES

CHAPTER 1

DEFINITIONS

35-48-1-1. [Repealed.]

Compiler's Notes.

This section, containing definitions for this article, was repealed by P.L.5-1988, § 208. For present similar provisions, see IC 35-48-1-2 through IC 35-48-1-27.

35-48-1-2. Applicability of definitions.

The definitions in this chapter apply throughout this article.

History.

P.L.5-1988, § 182.

RESEARCH REFERENCES

Collateral References.

State law criminal liability of licensed physician for prescribing or dispensing drug or similar controlled substance. 13 A.L.R.5th 1.

35-48-1-3. Administer.

"Administer" means the direct application of a controlled substance, whether by injection, inhalation, ingestion, or any other means, to the body of a patient or research subject by:

(1) A practitioner or by his authorized agent; or

(2) The patient or research subject at the direction and in the presence of the practitioner.

History.
P.L.5-1988, § 183.

35-48-1-4. Advisory committee.

"Advisory committee" refers to the controlled substances advisory committee established under IC 35-48-2-1.

History.
P.L.5-1988, § 184.

35-48-1-5. Agent.

"Agent" means an authorized person who acts on behalf of, or at the direction of, a manufacturer, distributor, or dispenser, but it does not include a common or contract carrier, public warehouseman, or employee of the carrier or warehouseman.

History.
P.L.5-1988, § 185.

35-48-1-6. Board.

"Board" refers to the Indiana state board of pharmacy.

History.
P.L.5-1988, § 186.

35-48-1-7. Cocaine.

"Cocaine" includes coca leaves and any salt, compound, or derivative of coca leaves, and any salt, compound, isomer, derivative, or preparation which is chemically equivalent or identical to any of these substances. However, decocainized coca leaves or extraction of coca leaves that do not contain cocaine or ecgonine are not included.

History.
P.L.5-1988, § 187.

35-48-1-8. [Repealed.]

Compiler's Notes.
This section, concerning the definition of "committee," was repealed by P.L.3-1989, § 224.

35-48-1-9. Controlled substance.

"Controlled substance" means a drug, substance, or immediate precursor in schedule I, II, III, IV, or V under:
(1) IC 35-48-2-4, IC 35-48-2-6, IC 35-48-2-8, IC 35-48-2-10, or IC 35-48-2-12, if IC 35-48-2-14 does not apply; or
(2) A rule adopted by the board, if IC 35-48-2-14 applies.

History.
P.L.5-1988, § 189.

NOTES TO DECISIONS

In General.
As defined by IC 35-48-1-9, "controlled substance" does not include precursors listed in IC 35-48-4-14.5, but rather includes only those drugs,

In General. (Cont'd)
substances, or immediate precursors identified in statutes defining schedules of controlled substances; accordingly, under strict reading of IC 35-48-1-9, precursors listed in IC 35-48-4-14.5(a) are not "controlled substances" and thus not "drugs" for purpose of establishing predicate substance offense under IC 35-50-2-10, unless they are included in Schedules I, II, III, IV, or V. Murray v. State, 798 N.E.2d 895, 2003 Ind. App. LEXIS 2149 (2003).

Defendant's conviction for public intoxication under prior version of IC 7.1-5-1-3, which required that intoxication be caused by use of alcohol or "controlled substance" as that term was defined by IC 35-48-1-9, required reversal, since defendant's intoxication due to glue sniffing was not crime under former version of statute. Upp v. State, 808 N.E.2d 706, 2004 Ind. App. LEXIS 900 (2004).

35-48-1-9.3. Controlled substance analog.

(a) "Controlled substance analog" means a substance:

(1) the chemical structure of which is substantially similar to that of a controlled substance included in schedule I or II and that has; or

(2) that a person represents or intends to have;

a narcotic, stimulant, depressant, or hallucinogenic effect on the central nervous system substantially similar to or greater than the narcotic, stimulant, depressant, or hallucinogenic effect on the central nervous system of a controlled substance included in schedule I or II.

(b) The definition set forth in subsection (a) does not include:

(1) a controlled substance;

(2) a substance for which there is an approved new drug application;

(3) a substance for which an exemption is in effect for investigational use by a person under Section 505 of the federal Food, Drug and Cosmetic Act (chapter 675, 52 Stat. 1052 (21 U.S.C. 355)), to the extent that conduct with respect to the substance is permitted under the exemption; or

(4) a substance to the extent not intended for human consumption before an exemption takes effect regarding the substance.

History.
P.L.225-2003, § 1.

NOTES TO DECISIONS

In General.
Defendant's conviction of possession of a controlled substance analog, IC 35-48-1-9.3(a), was reversed, because the active ingredient in a plant called khat which defendant possessed was not a listed controlled substance under IC 35-48-2-4, and the state failed to show that it was a controlled substance analog, as it failed to show that the effect of the active ingredient, cathinone, was comparable to the effect of methcathinone, which was a controlled substance. Mohamed v. State, 843 N.E.2d 553, 2006 Ind. App. LEXIS 367 (2006).

35-48-1-10. Counterfeit substance.

"Counterfeit substance" means a controlled substance which, or the container or labeling of which, without authorization, bears the trademark, trade name, or other identifying mark, imprint, number, or device, or any likeness thereof, of a manufacturer, distributor, or dispenser other than the person who in fact manufactured, distributed, or dispensed the substance.

History.
P.L.5-1988, § 190.

35-48-1-11. Delivery.

"Delivery" means:

(1) An actual or constructive transfer from one (1) person to another of a controlled substance, whether or not there is an agency relationship; or

(2) The organizing or supervising of an activity described in subdivision (1).

History.
  P.L.5-1988, § 191; P.L.165-1990, § 1.

NOTES TO DECISIONS

ANALYSIS

Delivery.
"Delivery" defined.
Evidence Insufficient.
Evidence Sufficient.

Delivery.
  The defendant's action of giving controlled substance to his girlfriend with instructions to deliver it to a third person constituted "constructive transfer" which was the equivalent of "delivery" under this section. Laird v. State, 483 N.E.2d 68, 1985 Ind. LEXIS 975 (1985).
  Because, in anticipation of a purchase, the defendant agreed to sell the drugs and had them in his possession for that purpose, but before he handed the drugs to the buyer the transaction was interrupted by the police and the defendant instead placed the controlled substance in his mouth and attempted to flee, there was no transfer and thus no delivery. Simmons v. State, 585 N.E.2d 1341, 1992 Ind. App. LEXIS 174 (1992).
  Confidential informant (CI) was not searched for drugs prior to controlled drug purchase after which the defendant ended up with the money that the police provided and the CI ended up with drugs. Since the CI did not testify that he bought the drugs from the defendant, there was no direct evidence, only speculation, that the defendant delivered the drugs under IC 35-48-1-11, so there was insufficient evidence that defendant violated IC 35-48-4-1(b). Watson v. State, 839 N.E.2d 1291, 2005 Ind. App. LEXIS 2452 (2005).
  Under the definition of "delivery" in IC 35-48-1-11, delivery under IC 35-48-4-1 does not have to be directly from the hand of a defendant; therefore, when defendant delivered cocaine to a second person, who in turn delivered it to a confidential informant, it was of no moment that defendant did not know the identity of the person to whom the second person intended to deliver and did deliver the cocaine. Reinhardt v. State, 881 N.E.2d 15, 2008 Ind. App. LEXIS 248 (2008).

"Delivery" defined.
  Definition of "delivery" in IC 35-48-1-11 does not require intent to relinquish control or possession of the controlled substance to another individual. It merely requires the actual or constructive transfer of the controlled substance. Cline v. State, 860 N.E.2d 647, 2007 Ind. App. LEXIS 108 (2007).

Evidence Insufficient.
  Where a controlled buyer is not searched prior to the controlled buy and the controlled buyer does not testify at trial, a defendant's possession of the buy money is insufficient to sustain a conviction under IC 35-48-4-1(b). Watson v. State, 839 N.E.2d 1291, 2005 Ind. App. LEXIS 2452 (2005).

Evidence Sufficient.
  Sufficient evidence supported defendant's conviction for dealing in cocaine where defendant bought cocaine for undercover officer from third party, and whether defendant or third party handed drugs to the officer was irrelevant. Smalley v. State, 732 N.E.2d 1231, 2000 Ind. App. LEXIS 1204 (2000).
  When defendant, who had been stopped by an officer for speeding, handed a bag of marijuana to his passenger and told the passenger to hide it, he had "delivered" the marijuana to the passenger under IC 35-48-1-11. Thus, the evidence was sufficient to support his conviction of felony dealing in marijuana in violation of IC 35-48-4-10, although the small amount of marijuana, its packaging in a single bag, and defendant's possession of drug paraphernalia did not support the inference that defendant possessed the marijuana with intent to deliver it to another in a sale, barter, or gift transaction. Cline v. State, 860 N.E.2d 647, 2007 Ind. App. LEXIS 108 (2007).

Cited:
  Lay v. State, 659 N.E.2d 1005, 1995 Ind. LEXIS 174 (1995); Hurst v. Dep't of State Revenue, 721 N.E.2d 370, 1999 Ind. Tax LEXIS 53 (1999); Cockrell v. State, 743 N.E.2d 799, 2001 Ind. App. LEXIS 414 (2001); Smith v. State, 835 N.E.2d 1072, 2005 Ind. App. LEXIS 1983 (2005).

35-48-1-12. Dispense.

  "Dispense" means to deliver a controlled substance to an ultimate user or research subject by or pursuant to the lawful order of a practitioner and includes the prescribing, administering, packaging, labeling, or compounding necessary to prepare the substance for that delivery.

History.
  P.L.5-1988, § 192.

RESEARCH REFERENCES

Collateral References.
  State law criminal liability of licensed physician for prescribing or dispensing drug or similar controlled substance. 13 A.L.R.5th 1.

35-48-1-13. Dispenser.

"Dispenser" means a practitioner who dispenses.

History.
P.L.5-1988, § 193.

RESEARCH REFERENCES

Res Gestae.
Criminal Justice Notes: Maintaining a common
nuisance, 46 (No. 5) Res Gestae 26 (2002).

35-48-1-14. Distribute.

"Distribute" means to deliver other than by administering or dispensing a controlled substance.

History.
P.L.5-1988, § 194.

35-48-1-15. Distributor.

"Distributor" means a person who distributes.

History.
P.L.5-1988, § 195.

35-48-1-16. Drug.

"Drug" has the meaning set forth in IC 16-42-19-2. It does not include devices or their components, parts, or accessories, nor does it include food.

History.
P.L.5-1988, § 196; P.L.2-1993, § 190.

35-48-1-17. Immediate precursor.

"Immediate precursor" means a substance which the board has found to be and by rule designates as being the principal compound commonly used or produced primarily for use, and which is an immediate chemical intermediate used or likely to be used in the manufacture of a controlled substance, the control of which is necessary to prevent, curtail, or limit manufacture.

History.
P.L.5-1988, § 197.

35-48-1-18. Manufacture.

"Manufacture" means:
(1) the production, preparation, propagation, compounding, conversion, or processing of a controlled substance, either directly or indirectly by extraction from substances of natural origin, independently by means of chemical synthesis, or by a combination of extraction and chemical synthesis, and includes any packaging or repackaging of the substance or labeling or relabeling of its container. It does not include the preparation, compounding, packaging, or labeling of a controlled substance:
(A) by a practitioner as an incident to his administering or dispensing of a controlled substance in the course of his professional practice; or

(B) by a practitioner, or by his authorized agent under his supervision, for the purpose of, or as an incident to, research, teaching, or chemical analysis and not for sale; or

(2) the organizing or supervising of an activity described in subdivision (1).

History.
P.L.5-1988, § 198; P.L.165-1990, § 2; P.L.17-2001, § 18.

NOTES TO DECISIONS

ANALYSIS

Controlled Substance Excise Tax.
Evidence of Manufacturing.
Finished Product.
Former Personal Use Exception.
Start of Manufacturing Process.

Controlled Substance Excise Tax.
Possession of marijuana, whether the possessor manufactured it or not, is taxable. Horrall v. Indiana Dep't of State Revenue, 687 N.E.2d 1219, 1997 Ind. Tax LEXIS 33 (1997).

Evidence of Manufacturing.
Baggies and scales as well as crack cocaine itself found on premises where defendant lived and among his personal possessions established existence of drug manufacturing process and was sufficient to prove constructive possession of illegal drugs. Jones v. State, 807 N.E.2d 58, 2004 Ind. App. LEXIS 752 (2004).

There was sufficient evidence to support defendant's dealing in methamphetamine conviction. For methamphetamine to have been manufactured, defendant would have had to extract the methamphetamine from a substance found in a pitcher and then allowed it to dry; although the evidence showed that defendant had not yet produced pure methamphetamine, testimony reflected that methamphetamine was extracted from the substance in the pitcher. Moore v. State, 869 N.E.2d 489, 2007 Ind. App. LEXIS 1488 (2007).

Finished Product.
Defendant's trial counsel was not ineffective in failing to pursue line of questioning regarding whether methcathinone, which defendant was accused of dealing, was finished product because no element of offense required that schedule I controlled substance be "finished product." Johnson v. State, 832 N.E.2d 985, 2005 Ind. App. LEXIS 1448 (2005).

Evidence that police found in defendant's truck and house was sufficient to support defendant's conviction for dealing in methamphetamine where the state presented additional evidence explaining how those ingredients and items found were commonly used to make methamphetamine; reasonable trier of fact could have concluded that defendant was in the process of manufacturing methamphetamine when defendant was arrested even if defendant had not created a finished product. Robertson v. State, 877 N.E.2d 507, 2007 Ind. App. LEXIS 2734 (2007).

Former Personal Use Exception.
Where the trial court erred in giving a jury instruction which failed to include the personal use exception under former IC 35-48-1-18, the defendant's conviction under IC 35-48-4-2 and IC 35-48-4-14.5 would be reversed. Poe v. State, 775 N.E.2d 681, 2002 Ind. App. LEXIS 1530 (2002).

Evidence that law enforcement officers found enough material on defendant's property to manufacturer only nine grams of methamphetamine was not sufficient to sustain defendant's conviction for dealing in a schedule II controlled substance by manufacturing methamphetamine, in violation of IC 35-48-4-2, because the state was required to prove that defendant manufactured the drug for use by others, under former IC 35-48-1-18, to obtain a conviction, and the evidence was not sufficient to prove that defendant manufactured the drug for the use of others. Culbertson v. State, 792 N.E.2d 573, 2003 Ind. App. LEXIS 1364 (2003).

Start of Manufacturing Process.
Since a bag containing ephedrine powder was found in the possession of defendant, the process of extraction, and thus, the process to manufacture methamphetamine, had begun, and there was sufficient evidence to support defendant's conviction for manufacturing methamphetamine. Dawson v. State, 786 N.E.2d 742, 2003 Ind. App. LEXIS 630 (2003).

Cited:
Bradley v. State, 765 N.E.2d 204, 2002 Ind. App. LEXIS 458 (2002); Bush v. State, 772 N.E.2d 1020, 2002 Ind. App. LEXIS 1262 (2002); Traylor v. State, 817 N.E.2d 611, 2004 Ind. App. LEXIS 2229 (2004).

35-48-1-19. Marijuana.

"Marijuana" means any part of the plant genus Cannabis whether growing or not; the seeds thereof; the resin extracted from any part of the plant, including hashish and hash oil; any compound, manufacture, salt, derivative, mixture, or preparation of the plant, its seeds or resin. It does not include the mature stalks of the plant; fiber produced from the stalks; oil or cake made from the seeds of the plant; any other compound, manufacture, salt, derivative, mixture, or preparation of the mature stalks (except the resin extracted therefrom); or the sterilized seed of the plant which is incapable of germination.

History.
P.L.5-1988, § 199.

NOTES TO DECISIONS

Cited:
Lycan v. State, 671 N.E.2d 447, 1996 Ind. App. LEXIS 1262 (1996).

35-48-1-20. Narcotic drug.

"Narcotic drug" means any of the following, whether produced directly or indirectly by extraction from substances of vegetable origin, independently by means of chemical synthesis, or by a combination of extraction and chemical synthesis:

(1) Opium and opiate, and any salt, compound, derivative, or preparation of opium or opiate.

(2) Any salt, compound, isomer, derivative, or preparation thereof which is chemically equivalent or identical to any of the substances referred to in subdivision (1) of this definition, but not including the isoquinoline alkaloids of opium.

(3) Opium poppy and poppy straw.

History.
P.L.5-1988, § 200.

NOTES TO DECISIONS

ANALYSIS

Addiction-Forming Quality.
Determination by State Board.
Marijuana.
Paregoric.

Addiction-Forming Quality.
Any drug which the Indiana board of pharmacy defined as a "narcotic drug" within the provisions of the Narcotic Drug Act had to have an addiction-forming or an addiction-sustaining quality similiar to any narcotic drug expressly defined in the act itself. Burk v. State, 257 Ind. 407, 275 N.E.2d 1, 1971 Ind. LEXIS 553, 50 A.L.R.3d 1279 (1971).

Determination by State Board.
The former statute did not delegate the power to define a narcotic drug to the Indiana board of pharmacy, but limited the board to determining, after reasonable notice and opportunity for hearing, whether a certain drug fell within the definition of a "narcotic drug" as that term was used in

the Narcotic Drug Act. Burk v. State, 257 Ind. 407, 275 N.E.2d 1, 1971 Ind. LEXIS 553, 50 A.L.R.3d 1279 (1971).

Marijuana.
A person could not be convicted under the Narcotic Drug Law for possession of marijuana where he was charged with possession of a dangerous drug and at the time of such possession marijuana was not included within the provisions of the Dangerous Drug Act. Healey v. State, 154 Ind. App. 55, 288 N.E.2d 781, 1972 Ind. App. LEXIS 877 (1972).

Paregoric.
Under the former statute defining a "narcotic drug," paregoric containing two grains or less of opium was not excluded as a narcotic drug within the definition. Merritt v. State, 245 Ind. 362, 198 N.E.2d 867, 1964 Ind. LEXIS 217 (1964).

35-48-1-21. Opiate.

"Opiate" means a substance having an addiction-forming or addiction-sustaining liability similar to morphine or being capable of conversion into a drug having addiction-forming or addiction-sustaining liability. It does not include, unless specifically designated as controlled under IC 35-48-2, the dextrorotatory isomer of 3-methoxy-n-methylmorphinan and its salts (dextromethorphan). It does include its racemic and levorotatory forms.

History.
P.L.5-1988, § 201.

35-48-1-22. Opium poppy.

"Opium poppy" means the plant of the species Papaver somniferum L., except its seeds.

History.
P.L.5-1988, § 202.

35-48-1-23. Poppy straw.

"Poppy straw" means any part, except the seeds, of the opium poppy, after mowing.

History.
P.L.5-1988, § 203.

35-48-1-24. Practitioner.

"Practitioner" means a physician, dentist, veterinarian, scientific investigator, pharmacy, hospital, or other institution or individual licensed, registered, or otherwise permitted to distribute, dispense, conduct research with respect to, or administer a controlled substance in the course of professional practice or research in Indiana.

History.
P.L.5-1988, § 204.

35-48-1-25. Prescription drug.

"Prescription drug" means a controlled substance or a legend drug (as defined in IC 16-18-2-199).

History.
P.L.5-1988, § 205; P.L.2-1993, § 191.

35-48-1-26. Production.

"Production" includes the manufacture, planting, cultivation, growing, or harvesting of a controlled substance.

History.
P.L.5-1988, § 206.

35-48-1-27. Ultimate user.

"Ultimate user" means a person who lawfully possesses a controlled substance for the person's own use, for the use of a member of the person's household, or for administering to an animal owned by the person or by a member of the person's household.

History.
    P.L.5-1988, § 207.

NOTES TO DECISIONS

Marijuana.
    Defendant could not be an ultimate user under this section of marijuana because he intended to construct a "hemp hut," because there is no "hemp hut" exemption to the general rule that possession of marijuana is illegal. Horrall v. Indiana Dep't of State Revenue, 687 N.E.2d 1219, 1997 Ind. Tax LEXIS 33 (1997).

CHAPTER 2

CLASSIFICATION OF DRUGS

35-48-2-1. Authority to control — Appointment of advisory committee.

(a) The board shall administer this article and may recommend to the general assembly the addition, deletion, or rescheduling of all substances listed in the schedules in sections 4, 6, 8, 10, and 12 [IC 35-48-2-4, IC 35-48-2-6, IC 35-48-2-8, IC 35-48-2-10, and IC 35-48-2-12] of this chapter by submitting in an electronic format under IC 5-14-6 a report of such recommendations to the legislative council. In making a determination regarding a substance, the board shall consider the following:

(1) The actual or relative potential for abuse.

(2) The scientific evidence of its pharmacological effect, if known.

(3) The state of current scientific knowledge regarding the substance.

(4) The history and current pattern of abuse.

(5) The scope, duration, and significance of abuse.

(6) The risk to public health.

(7) The potential of the substance to produce psychic or physiological dependence liability.

(8) Whether the substance is an immediate precursor of a substance already controlled under this article.

(b) After considering the factors enumerated in subsection (a), the board shall make findings and recommendations concerning the control of the substance if it finds the substance has a potential for abuse.

(c) If the board finds that a substance is an immediate precursor, substances which are precursors of the controlled precursor shall not be subject to control solely because they are precursors of the controlled precursor.

(d) If any substance is designated or rescheduled to a more restrictive schedule as a controlled substance under federal law and notice is given to the board, the board shall recommend similar control of the substance under this article in the board's report to the general assembly, unless the board objects to inclusion or rescheduling.

In that case, the board shall publish the reasons for objection and afford all interested parties an opportunity to be heard. At the conclusion of the hearing, the board shall publish its findings.

(e) If a substance is rescheduled to a less restrictive schedule or deleted as a controlled substance under federal law, the substance is rescheduled or deleted under this article. If the board objects to inclusion, rescheduling, or deletion of the substance, the board shall notify the chairman of the legislative council not more than thirty (30) days after the federal law is changed and the substance may not be rescheduled or deleted until the conclusion of the next complete session of the general assembly. The notice from the board to the chairman of the legislative council must be published.

(f) There is established a sixteen (16) member controlled substances advisory committee to serve as a consultative and advising body to the board in all matters relating to the classification, reclassification, addition to, or deletion from of all substances classified as controlled substances in schedules I to IV or substances not controlled or yet to come into being. In addition, the advisory committee shall conduct hearings and make recommendations to the board regarding revocations, suspensions, and restrictions of registrations as provided in IC 35-48-3-4. All hearings shall be conducted in accordance with IC 4-21.5-3. The advisory committee shall be made up of:

(1) two (2) physicians licensed under IC 25-22.5, one (1) to be elected by the medical licensing board of Indiana from among its members and one (1) to be appointed by the governor;

(2) two (2) pharmacists, one (1) to be elected by the state board of pharmacy from among its members and one (1) to be appointed by the governor;

(3) two (2) dentists, one (1) to be elected by the state board of dentistry from among its members and one (1) to be appointed by the governor;

(4) the state toxicologist or the designee of the state toxicologist;

(5) two (2) veterinarians, one (1) to be elected by the state board of veterinary medical examiners from among its members and one (1) to be appointed by the governor;

(6) one (1) podiatrist to be elected by the board of podiatric medicine from among its members;

(7) one (1) advanced practice nurse with authority to prescribe legend drugs as provided by IC 25-23-1-19.5 who is:

(A) elected by the state board of nursing from among the board's members; or

(B) if a board member does not meet the requirements under IC 25-23-1-19.5 at the time of the vacancy on the advisory committee, appointed by the governor;

(8) the superintendent of the state police department or the superintendent's designee;

(9) three (3) members appointed by the governor who have demonstrated expertise concerning controlled substances; and

(10) one (1) member appointed by the governor who is a psychiatrist with expertise in child and adolescent psychiatry.

(g) All members of the advisory committee elected by a board shall serve a term of one (1) year and all members of the advisory committee appointed by the governor shall serve a term of four (4) years. Any elected or appointed member of the advisory committee, may be removed for cause by the authority electing or appointing the member. If a vacancy occurs on the advisory committee, the authority electing or appointing the vacating member shall elect or appoint a successor to serve the unexpired term of the vacating member. The board shall acquire the recommendations of the advisory committee pursuant to administration over the controlled substances to be or not to be included in schedules I to V, especially in the implementation of scheduled substances changes as provided in subsection (d).

(h) Authority to control under this section does not extend to distilled spirits, wine, or malt beverages, as those terms are defined or used in IC 7.1, or to tobacco.

(i) The board shall exclude any nonnarcotic substance from a schedule if that substance may, under the Federal Food, Drug, and Cosmetic Act or state law, be sold over the counter without a prescription.

History.
IC 35-48-2-1, as added by Acts 1976, P.L.148, § 7; 1977, P.L.344, § 1; P.L.137-1985, § 17; P.L.200-1987, § 4; P.L.188-1989, § 4; P.L.33-1993, § 73; P.L.163-1994, § 2; P.L.177-1997, § 8; P.L.14-2000, § 77; P.L.107-2002, § 31; P.L.28-2004, § 178.

Compiler's Notes.
The reference in the second sentence of subsection (f) to IC 35-48-3-4 probably should be to IC

35-48-3-5, as the latter section is the one which provides for the duties of the advisory committee relative to registrations.

The Federal Food, Drug, and Cosmetic Act, referred to in subsection (i), may be found at 21 U.S.C.S. §§ 301 et seq.

Cross References.
Employment of inspector-investigators to enforce controlled substances law, IC 25-26-13-5.

NOTES TO DECISIONS

ANALYSIS

Evidence.
Thioridazine.

Evidence.
Whether the substance in question is within the statutory prohibition is an issue for the jury to resolve, and evidence on the issue may come in the form of lay testimony and circumstantial evidence. Grayson v. State, 593 N.E.2d 1200, 1992 Ind. App. LEXIS 920 (1992).

Thioridazine.
Since neither Mellaril, its generic name Thioridazine, nor an immediate precursor is listed in any of the schedules I through V in this chapter, the tranquilizer is not a controlled substance and its possession is not a criminal act. Gee v. State, 454 N.E.2d 1265, 1983 Ind. App. LEXIS 3477 (1983).

RESEARCH REFERENCES

Indiana Law Journal.
Constitutional Analysis of Indiana's Controlled Substance Excise Tax, 70 Ind. L.J. 1301 (1995).

Valparaiso University Law Review.
Problems in Defending a Drug Case, 8 Val. U.L. Rev. 615.

35-48-2-1.1. [Repealed.]

Compiler's Notes.
This section, concerning the annual report on the advisory committee, expired by its own terms on June 30, 1993, and was repealed by P.L.2-1995, § 140, effective May 5, 1995.

35-48-2-1.5. Advisory committee — Election of chairperson and officers — Meetings — Quorum — Adoption of rules — Staff and facilities — Per diem and expenses.

(a) The advisory committee shall annually elect a chairperson and any other officers that the advisory committee determines necessary from among its members.

(b) Meetings of the advisory committee may be called by:
(1) the advisory committee chairperson; or
(2) a majority of the members of the advisory committee.

(c) Seven (7) members of the committee constitute a quorum.

(d) Notwithstanding IC 1-1-4-1, if at least a quorum of its members are present at a meeting, the committee may take an action by an affirmative vote of at least a majority of the members present and voting.

(e) The advisory committee shall adopt rules under IC 4-22-2 to:

(1) set standards related to the registration and control of the manufacture, distribution, and dispensing of controlled substances, including record keeping requirements;

(2) set fees described in IC 25-1-8; and

(3) carry out its responsibilities under IC 35-48-2 through IC 35-48-3.

(f) The Indiana professional licensing agency shall provide staff and facilities to the advisory committee under IC 25-1-5.

(g) Each member of the committee who is not a state employee is entitled to the minimum salary per diem provided by IC 4-10-11-2.1(b). Such a member is also entitled to reimbursement for traveling expenses and other expenses actually incurred in connection with the member's duties, as provided in the state travel policies and procedures established by the department of administration and approved by the budget agency.

(h) Each member of the committee who is a state employee is entitled to reimbursement for traveling expenses and other expenses actually incurred in connection with the member's duties, as provided in the state travel policies and procedures established by the department of administration and approved by the budget agency.

History.
P.L.200-1987, § 5; P.L.1-2006, § 546.

35-48-2-2. Nomenclature.

The controlled substances listed in the schedules in sections 4, 6, 8, 10 and 12 [IC 35-48-2-4, IC 35-48-2-6, IC 35-48-2-8, IC 35-48-2-10, and IC 35-48-2-12] of this chapter are included by whatever official, common, usual, chemical, or trade name designated. The number placed in brackets after each substance is its federal Drug Enforcement Administration Controlled Substances Code Number which is to be used for identification purposes on certain certificates of registration.

History.
IC 35-48-2-2, as added by Acts 1976, P.L.148, § 7; 1979, P.L.303, § 2.

NOTES TO DECISIONS

Cited:
Sherelis v. State, 498 N.E.2d 973, 1986 Ind. LEXIS 1306 (1986); McKean v. State, 500 N.E.2d 1184, 1986 Ind. LEXIS 1402 (1986).

RESEARCH REFERENCES

Valparaiso University Law Review.
Problems in Defending a Drug Case, 8 Val. U.L. Rev. 615.

35-48-2-3. Schedule I tests.

(a) The board shall recommend placement of a substance in schedule I under this chapter if it finds that the substance:

(1) Has high potential for abuse; and

(2) Has no accepted medical use in treatment in the United States or lacks accepted safety for use in treatment under medical supervision.

(b) The board may recommend placement of a substance in schedule I under this chapter if it finds that the substance is classified as a controlled substance in schedule I under federal law.

History.
  IC 35-48-2-3, as added by Acts 1976, P.L.148,
§ 7; P.L.200-1987, § 6.

RESEARCH REFERENCES

Valparaiso University Law Review.
  Problems in Defending a Drug Case, 8 Val. U.L.
Rev. 615.

35-48-2-4. Schedule I.

  (a) The controlled substances listed in this section are included in schedule I.
  (b) Opiates. Any of the following opiates, including their isomers, esters, ethers, salts, and salts of isomers, esters, and ethers, unless specifically excepted by rule of the board or unless listed in another schedule, whenever the existence of these isomers, esters, ethers, and salts is possible within the specific chemical designation:
  Acetyl-alpha-methylfentanyl (N-[1-(1-methyl-2-phenethyl)-4-piperidinyl]-N-phenylacetamide) (9815)
  Acetylmethadol (9601)
  Allylprodine (9602)
  Alpha-methylthiofentanyl (N-[1-methyl-2-(2- thienyl)ethyl-4-piperidinyl]-N-phenylpropanamide) (9832)
  Alphacetylmethadol (9603)
  Alphameprodine (9604)
  Alphamethadol (9605)
  Alphamethylfentanyl (9814)
  Benzethidine (9606)
  Beta-hydroxy-3-methylfentanyl (9831).Other name: N-[1-(2-hydroxy-2-phenethyl)-3-methyl-4-piperidinyl]-N-phenylpropanamide.
  Beta-hydroxyfentanyl (N-[1-(2-hydroxy-2- phenethyl)-4-piperidinyl]-N-phenylpropanamide) (9830)
  Betacetylmethadol (9607)
  Betameprodine (9608)
  Betamethadol (9609)
  Betaprodine (9611)
  Clonitazene (9612)
  Dextromoramide (9613)
  Diampromide (9615)
  Diethylthiambutene (9616)
  Difenoxin (9168)
  Dimenoxadol (9617)
  Dimepheptanol (9618)
  Dimethylthiambutene (9619)
  Dioxaphetyl butyrate (9621)
  Dipipanone (9622)
  Ethylmethylthiambutene (9623)
  Etonitazene (9624)
  Etoxeridine (9625)
  Furethidine (9626)
  Hydroxypethidine (9627)
  Ketobemidone (9628)
  Levomoramide (9629)
  Levophenacylmorphan (9631)
  3-Methylfentanyl [N-[3-methyl-1-(2-phenylethyl)-4-piperidyl]-N-phenyl-propanimide](9813)

3-Methylthiofentanyl (N-[(3-methyl-1-(2-thienyl)ethyl-4- piperidinyl]-N-phenyl-propanamide) (9833)

MPPP (1-methyl-4-phenyl-4-propionoxypiperidine) (9961)

Morpheridine (9632)

N-[1-benzyl-4-piperidyl]-N-phenylpropanamide (benzylfentanyl), including any isomers, salts, or salts of isomers (9818)

N-[1-(2-thienyl)methyl-4-piperidyl]-N-phenylpropanamide (thenylfentanyl), including any isomers, salts, or salts of isomers (9834)

Noracymethadol (9633)

Norlevorphanol (9634)

Normethadone (9635)

Norpipanone (9636)

Para-fluorofentanyl (N-(4-fluorophenyl)-N- [1-(2-phenethyl)-4-piperidinyl] pro-panamide (9812)

Phenadoxone (9637)

Phenampromide (9638)

Phenomorphan (9647)

Phenoperidine (9641)

PEPAP [1-(2-phenethyl)-4-phenyl-4-acetoxypiperidine] (9663)

Piritramide (9642)

Proheptazine (9643)

Properidine (9644)

Propiram (9649)

Racemoramide (9645)

Thiofentanyl (N-phenyl-N-[1-(2-thienyl)ethyl-4- piperidinyl]-propanamide) (9835)

Tilidine (9750)

Trimeperidine (9646)

(c) Opium derivatives. Any of the following opium derivatives, their salts, isomers, and salts of isomers, unless specifically excepted by rule of the board or unless listed in another schedule, whenever the existence of these salts, isomers, and salts of isomers is possible within the specific chemical designation:

Acetorphine (9319)

Acetyldihydrocodeine (9051)

Benzylmorphine (9052)

Codeine methylbromide (9070)

Codeine-N-Oxide (9053)

Cyprenorphine (9054)

Desomorphine (9055)

Dihydromorphine (9145)

Drotebanol (9335)

Etorphine (except hydrochloride salt) (9056)

Heroin (9200)

Hydromorphinol (9301)

Methyldesorphine (9302)

Methyldihydromorphine (9304)

Morphine methylbromide (9305)

Morphine methylsulfonate (9306)

Morphine-N-Oxide (9307)

Myrophine (9308)

Nicocodeine (9309)

Nicomorphine (9312)

Normorphine (9313)

Pholcodine (9314)

Thebacon (9315)

(d) Hallucinogenic substances. Any material, compound, mixture, or preparation which contains any quantity of the following hallucinogenic, psychedelic, or psychogenic substances, their salts, isomers, and salts of isomers, unless specifically excepted by rule of the board or unless listed in another schedule, whenever the existence of these salts, isomers, and salts of isomers is possible within the specific chemical designation:

(1) 1-[1-(2-thienyl)cyclohexyl]pyrrolidine (7473). Other name: TCPy.

(2) 4-Bromo-2, 5-Dimethoxyamphetamine (7391). Some trade or other names: 4-Bromo-2, 5-Dimethoxy-a-methylphenethylamine; 4-Bromo-2, 5-DMA.

(3) 4-Bromo-2, 5-dimethoxphenethylamine (7392). Some trade or other names: 2-[4-bromo-2,5-dimethoxyphenyl]-1-aminoethane; alpha-desmethyl DOB; 2C-B, Nexus.

(4) 2, 5-Dimethoxy-4-ethylamphet-amine (7399). Other name: DOET.

(5) 2, 5-Dimethoxy-4-(n)-propylthiophenethylamine (7348). Other name: 2C-T-7.

(6) 2, 5-Dimethoxyamphetamine (7396). Some trade or other names: 2, 5-Dimethoxy-a-methylphenethylamine; 2, 5-DMA.

(7) 4-Methoxyamphetamine (7411). Some trade or other names: 4-Methoxy-a-methylphenethylamine; Paramethoxyamphetamine; PMA.

(8) 5-Methoxy-3, 4-methylenedioxy amphetamine (7401). Other Name: MMDA.

(9) 5-Methoxy-N, N-diisopropyltryptamine, including any isomers, salts, or salts of isomers (7439). Other name: 5-MeO-DIPT.

(10) 4-methyl-2, 5-dimethoxyamphetamine (7395). Some trade and other names: 4-methyl-2, 5-dimethoxy-a-methylphenethylamine; DOM; and STP.

(11) 3, 4-methylenedioxy amphetamine (7400). Other name: MDA.

(12) 3,4-methylenedioxy-N-ethylamphetamine (7404). Other names: N-ethyl-alpha-methyl-3,4(methylenedioxy) phenethylamine; N-ethyl MDA; MDE; and MDEA.

(13) 3, 4-methylenedioxymethamphetamine (MDMA) (7405).

(14) 3, 4, 5-trimethoxy amphetamine (7390). Other name: TMA.

(15) Alpha-ethyltryptamine (7249). Some trade and other names: Etryptamine; Monase; [alpha]-ethyl-1H-indole-3-ethanamine; 3-(2-aminobutyl) indole; [alpha]-ET; and AET.

(16) Alpha-methyltryptamine (7432). Other name: AMT.

(17) Bufotenine (7433). Some trade and other names: 3-(B-Dimethylaminoethyl)-5-hydroxyindole; 3-(2-dimethylaminonethyl)-5-indolol; N, N-dimethylserotonin; 5-hydroxy-N, N-dimethyltryptamine; mappine.

(18) Diethyltryptamine (7434). Some trade or other names: N, N-Diethyltryptamine; DET.

(19) Dimethyltrytamine (7435). Some trade or other names: DMT.

(20) Ibogaine (7260). Some trade and other names: 7-Ethyl-6, 6b, 7, 8, 9, 10, 12, 13-octahydro-2-methoxy-6, 9-methano-5H-pyrido (1', 2': 1, 2, azepino 4, 5-b) indole; tabernanthe iboga.

(21) Lysergic acid diethylamide (7315). Other name: LSD.

(22) Marijuana (7360).

(23) Mescaline (7381).

(24) Parahexyl (7374). Some trade or other names: 3-Hexyl-1-hydroxy-7, 8, 9, 10-Tetrahydro-6, 6, 9-trimethyl-6H-dibenzo (b,d) pyran; Snyhexyl.

(25) Peyote (7415), including:

(A) all parts of the plant that are classified botanically as lophophora williamsii lemaire, whether growing or not;

(B) the seeds thereof;

(C) any extract from any part of the plant; and

(D) every compound, manufacture, salt, derivative, mixture, or preparation of the plant, its seeds, or extracts.

(26) N-ethyl-3-piperidyl benzilate (7482). Other name: DMZ.

(27) N-hydroxy-3,4-methylenedioxyamphetamine (7402). Other names: N-hydroxy-alpha-methyl-3,4 (methylenedioxy)phenethylamine; and N-hydroxy MDA.

(28) N-methyl-3-piperidyl benzilate (7484). Other name: LBJ.

(29) Psilocybin (7437).

(30) Psilocyn (7438).

(31) Tetrahydrocannabinols (7370), including synthetic equivalents of the substances contained in the plant, or in the resinous extractives of Cannabis, sp. and synthetic substances, derivatives, and their isomers with similar chemical structure and pharmacological activity such as:

(A) π^1cis or trans tetrahydrocannabinol, and their optical isomers;

(B) π^6cis or trans tetrahydrocannabinol, and their optical isomers; and

(C) $\pi^3{}_4$ cis or trans tetrahydrocannabinol, and their optical isomers.

Since nomenclature of these substances is not internationally standardized, compounds of these structures, regardless of numerical designation of atomic positions are covered. Other name: THC.

(32) Ethylamine analog of phencyclidine (7455). Some trade or other names: N-Ethyl-1-phenylcyclohexylamine; (1-phenylcyclohexyl) ethylamine; N-(1-phenylcyclohexyl) ethylamine; cyclohexamine; PCE.

(33) Pyrrolidine analog of phencyclidine (7458). Some trade or other names: 1-(1-phenylcyclohexyl)-pyrrolidine; PCP$_y$; PHP.

(34) Thiophene analog of phencyclidine (7470). Some trade or other names: 1-(1-(2-thienyl) cyclohexyl) piperidine; 2-Thienyl Analog of Phencyclidine; TPCP.

(e) Depressants. Unless specifically excepted in a rule adopted by the board or unless listed in another schedule, any material, compound, mixture, or preparation which contains any quantity of the following substances having a depressant effect on the central nervous system, including its salts, isomers, and salts of isomers whenever the existence of such salts, isomers, and salts of isomers is possible within the specific chemical designation:

Gamma-hydroxybutyric acid (other names include GHB; gamma-hydroxybutyrate; 4-hydroxybutanoic acid; sodium oxybate; sodium oxybutyrate) (2010)

Mecloqualone (2572)

Methaqualone (2565)

(f) Stimulants. Unless specifically excepted or unless listed in another schedule, any material, compound, mixture, or preparation that contains any quantity of the following substances having a stimulant effect on the central nervous system, including its salts, isomers, and salts of isomers:

([+/-]) cis-4-methylaminorex (([+/-])cis-4,5- dihydro-4-methyl-5-phenyl-2-oxazolamine) (1590)

Aminorex (1585). Other names: aminoxaphen; 2-amino-5-phenyl-2-oxazoline; or 4,5-dihydro-5-phenyl-2-oxazolamine or 4,5-dihydro-5-phenyl-2-oxazolamine.

Cathinone (1235). Some trade or other names: 2-amino-1-phenyl-1-propanone; alpha-aminopropiophenone; 2-aminopropiophenone; and norephedrone.

Fenethylline (1503)

N-Benzylpiperazine (7493). Other names: BZP; and 1-benzylpiperazine.

N-ethylamphetamine (1475)

Methcathinone (1237) Some other trade names: 2-Methylamino-1-Phenylpropan-I-one; Ephedrone; Monomethylpropion; UR 1431.

N, N-dimethylamphetamine (1480). Other names: N, N-alpha-trimethyl-benzeneethanamine; and N, N-alpha-trimethylphenethylamine.

History.
IC 35-48-2-4, as added by Acts 1976, P.L.148,
§ 7; 1979, P.L.303, § 3; 1981, P.L.170, § 2; P.L.333-1983, § 1; P.L.327-1985, § 1; P.L.156-

1986, § 4; P.L.156-1986, § 5; P.L.200-1987, § 7; P.L.163-1994, § 3; P.L.2-1996, § 286; P.L.288-2001, § 15; P.L.22-2008, § 1, eff. July 1, 2008.

Cross References.
Significance of numbers in brackets following names of substances, IC 35-48-2-2.

NOTES TO DECISIONS

ANALYSIS

Constitutionality.
—Vagueness.
Evidence.
—Controlled Substance.
Heroin.
Instructions.
Marijuana.
Unlisted Substance.

Constitutionality.

—Vagueness.
The Indiana Controlled Substance Act as it relates to Psilocybin and Psilocyn is not unconstitutionally vague; Indiana's statutory scheme gives persons of ordinary intelligence fair warning of the prohibited conduct and does not encourage arbitrary or discriminatory enforcement; thus the statutes are not unconstitutionally vague, either on their face or as applied to defendant. Bemis v. State, 652 N.E.2d 89, 1995 Ind. App. LEXIS 719 (1995).

Evidence.

—Controlled Substance.
Where the statute provided that marijuana was a controlled substance, it was not necessary for the state to introduce evidence to show that marijuana was a controlled substance. Russell v. State, 182 Ind. App. 386, 395 N.E.2d 791, 1979 Ind. App. LEXIS 1359 (1979).

Heroin.
Under former IC 35-24.1-2-4, which designated heroin a controlled substance, and former IC 35-24.1-4.1-6, which imposed an additional penalty for possession of a "controlled narcotic substance" in an "aggregate weight of ten grams or more," possession of more than 10 grams of a substance containing heroin did not subject the defendant to the additional penalty absent proof that the substance was pure heroin, since there was no indication in either of the statutes that the substance intended to be controlled was one which merely contained some quantity of heroin. Hutcherson v. State, 178 Ind. App. 8, 381 N.E.2d 877, 1978 Ind. App. LEXIS 1053 (1978).

Instructions.
It was proper for the court to instruct the jury that the statute defined marijuana as a controlled substance. Russell v. State, 182 Ind. App. 386, 395 N.E.2d 791, 1979 Ind. App. LEXIS 1359 (1979).

Marijuana.
The classification of marijuana with hard narcotic drugs was not violative of the equal protection clause of the U.S. Constitution. Ross v. State, 172 Ind. App. 484, 360 N.E.2d 1015, 1977 Ind. App. LEXIS 782 (1977).

Unlisted Substance.
Defendant's conviction of possession of a controlled substance analog, IC 35-48-1-9.3(a), was reversed, because the active ingredient in a plant called khat which defendant possessed was not a listed controlled substance under IC 35-48-2-4, and the state failed to show that it was a controlled substance analog, as it failed to show that the effect of the active ingredient, cathinone, was comparable to the effect of methcathinone, which was a controlled substance. Mohamed v. State, 843 N.E.2d 553, 2006 Ind. App. LEXIS 367 (2006).

Cited:
Whalen v. State, 442 N.E.2d 14, 1982 Ind. App. LEXIS 1487 (1982); Hunt v. State, 459 N.E.2d 730, 1984 Ind. LEXIS 751 (1984); Hall v. State, 497 N.E.2d 916, 1986 Ind. LEXIS 1277 (1986); Lay v. State, 659 N.E.2d 1005, 1995 Ind. LEXIS 174 (1995); Quick v. State, 660 N.E.2d 598, 1996 Ind. App. LEXIS 24 (1996); Brown v. State, 744 N.E.2d 989, 2001 Ind. App. LEXIS 456 (2001).

RESEARCH REFERENCES

Res Gestae.
The Legal Aspects of Mushrooms Addendum (Samuel R. Rosen), 23 Res Gestae 528.

35-48-2-5. Schedule II tests.

(a) The board shall recommend placement of a substance in schedule II under this chapter if it finds that:

(1) The substance has high potential for abuse;

(2) The substance has currently accepted medical use in treatment in the United States, or currently accepted medical use with severe restrictions; and

(3) The abuse of the substance may lead to severe psychological or physical dependence.

(b) The board may recommend placement of a substance in schedule II under this chapter if it finds that the substance is classified as a controlled substance in schedule II under federal law.

History.
IC 35-48-2-5, as added by Acts 1976, P.L.148,
§ 7; P.L.200-1987, § 8.

35-48-2-6. Schedule II.

(a) The controlled substances listed in this section are included in schedule II.

(b) Any of the following substances, except those narcotic drugs listed in other schedules, whether produced directly or indirectly by extraction from substances of vegetable origin, or independently by means of chemical synthesis, or by combination of extraction and chemical synthesis:

(1) Opium and opiate, and any salt, compound, derivative, or preparation of opium or opiate, excluding apomorphine, dextrorphan, nalbuphine, naloxone, naltrexone, and their respective salts but including:

(A) raw opium (9600);
(B) opium extracts (9610);
(C) opium fluid extracts (9620);
(D) powdered opium (9639);
(E) granulated opium (9640);
(F) tincture of opium (9630);
(G) codeine (9050);
(H) dihydroetorphine (9334);
(I) ethylmorphine (9190);
(J) etorphine hydrochloride (9059);
(K) hydrocodone (9193);
(L) hydromorphone (9150);
(M) metopon (9260);
(N) morphine (9300);
(O) oxycodone (9143);
(P) oxymorphone (9652); and
(Q) thebaine (9333).

(2) Any salt, compound, isomer, derivative, or preparation thereof which is chemically equivalent or identical with any of the substances referred to in subdivision (b)(1) of this section, but not including the isoquinoline alkaloids of opium.

(3) Opium poppy and poppy straw.

(4) Cocaine (9041).

(5) Concentrate of poppy straw (the crude extract of poppy straw in either liquid, solid, or powder form which contains the phenanthrene alkaloids of the opium poppy) (9670).

(c) Opiates. Any of the following opiates, including their isomers, esters, ethers, salts, and salts of isomers, esters, and ethers whenever the existence of these isomers, esters, ethers, and salts is possible within the specific chemical designation:

Alfentanil (9737)
Alphaprodine (9010)
Anileridine (9020)
Bezitramide (9800)
Bulk dextropropoxyphene (nondosage forms) (9273)

Carfentanil (9743)
Dihydrocodeine (9120)
Diphenoxylate (9170)
Fentanyl (9801)
Isomethadone (9226)
Levo-alphacetylmethadol (9648). Other names: Levo-alpha-acetylmethadol; levomethadyl acetate; and LAAM.
Levomethorphan (9210)
Levorphanol (9220)
Metazocine (9240)
Methadone (9250)
Methadone-Intermediate, 4-cyano-2-dimethyl-amino-4, 4-diphenyl butane (9254)
Moramide-Intermediate, 2-methyl-3-morpholino-1, 1-diphenylpropane- carboxylic acid (9802)
Pethidine (Meperidine) (9230)
Pethidine-Intermediate- A, 4-cyano-1-methyl-4-phenylpiperidine (9232)
Pethidine-Intermediate-B, ethyl-4-phenylpiperidine-4-carboxylate (9233)
Pethidine-Intermediate-C,1-methyl-4-phenylpiperidine-4-carbo xylic acid (9234)
Phenazodine (9715)
Piminodine (9730)
Racemethorphan (9732)
Racemorphan (9733)
Remifentanil (9739)
Sufentanil (9740)

(d) Stimulants. Any material compound, mixture, or preparation which contains any quantity of the following substances having a potential for abuse associated with a stimulant effect on the central nervous system:

(1) Amphetamine, its salts, optical isomers, and salts of its optical isomers (1100).

(2) Methamphetamine, including its salts, isomers, and salts of its isomers (1105).

(3) Phenmetrazine and its salts (1631).

(4) Methylphenidate (1724).

(e) Depressants. Unless specifically excepted by rule of the board or unless listed in another schedule, any material, compound, mixture, or preparation which contains any quantity of the following substances having a depressant effect on the central nervous system, including its salts, isomers, and salts of isomers whenever the existence of such salts, isomers, and salts of isomers is possible within the specific chemical designation:

Amobarbital (2125)
Glutethimide (2550)
Pentobarbital (2270)
Phencyclidine (7471)
Secobarbital (2315)

(f) Immediate precursors. Unless specifically excepted by rule of the board or unless listed in another schedule, any material, compound, mixture, or preparation which contains any quantity of the following substances:

(1) Immediate precursor to amphetamine and methamphetamine: Phenylacetone (8501). Some trade or other names: phenyl-2-propanone; P2P; benzyl methyl ketone; methyl benzyl ketone.

(2) Immediate precursors to phencyclidine (PCP):

(A) 1-phenylcyclohexylamine (7460); or

(B) 1-piperidinocyclohexanecarbonitrile (PCC) (8603).

(g) Hallucinogenic substances:

Nabilone (7379). Other name: (+/-)-trans-3- (1,1-dimethylheptyl)-6, 6a, 7, 8, 10, 10a-hexahydro-1-hydroxy -6, 6-dimethyl-9H-dibenzo [b,d] pyran-9-one.

History.
IC 35-48-2-6, as added by Acts 1976, P.L.148, § 7; 1979, P.L.303, § 4; 1981, P.L.170, § 3; P.L.333-1983, § 2; P.L.77-1984, § 13; P.L.327-1985, § 2; P.L.156-1986, § 5; P.L.329-1987, § 1; P.L.31-1998, § 9; P.L.22-2008, § 2, eff. July 1, 2008.

Cross References.
Significance of numbers in brackets following names of substances, IC 35-48-2-2.

NOTES TO DECISIONS

ANALYSIS

Cocaine.
Drugs Not Enumerated by Act.
Evidence.
—Testimony of Pharmacists.
Judicial Notice.

Cocaine.
The listing of cocaine in Schedule II clearly includes cocaine hydrochloride. Sherelis v. State, 498 N.E.2d 973, 1986 Ind. LEXIS 1306 (1986).

Drugs Not Enumerated by Act.
The prosecution must prove an essential element, that the substance involved (methadone) was indeed a prohibited drug within the statutory definition. White v. State, 161 Ind. App. 568, 316 N.E.2d 699, 1974 Ind. App. LEXIS 976 (1974).

Where a prohibited substance (methadone) as identified was not specifically enumerated by the act, the state could nevertheless establish it as a legally defined narcotic drug by submitting some additional extrinsic evidence describing its chemical identity, characteristics, ingredients, or derivation so as to bring it within the definition; the gap may not be closed by resorting to the doctrine of judicial notice since as a general rule that doctrine is restricted to matters of common knowledge, a description that does not apply to the chemistry of drugs such as methadone hydrochloride. White v. State, 161 Ind. App. 568, 316 N.E.2d 699, 1974 Ind. App. LEXIS 976 (1974).

Evidence.

—Testimony of Pharmacists.
It was proper to permit an experienced pharmacist to testify that preludin was a tablet containing phenmetrazine which was a class II controlled substance although the witness had never analyzed such tablets. Ralston v. State, 412 N.E.2d 239, 1980 Ind. App. LEXIS 1736 (1980).

Judicial Notice.
The fact that phenmetrazine is a controlled substance is a matter of which the trial court would take judicial notice. Ralston v. State, 412 N.E.2d 239, 1980 Ind. App. LEXIS 1736 (1980).

Cited:
Thorne v. State, 429 N.E.2d 644, 1981 Ind. LEXIS 959 (1981); Forehand v. State, 479 N.E.2d 552, 1985 Ind. LEXIS 865 (1985); Clayton v. State, 491 N.E.2d 534, 1986 Ind. LEXIS 1109 (1986); McKean v. State, 500 N.E.2d 1184, 1986 Ind. LEXIS 1402 (1986); Sherelis v. Duckworth, 675 F. Supp. 1144, 1987 U.S. Dist. LEXIS 11690 (N.D. Ind. 1987); Conn v. State, 535 N.E.2d 1176, 1989 Ind. LEXIS 88 (1989); Secor v. Department of State Revenue, — N.E.2d —, 2000 Ind. Tax LEXIS 24 (2000); Teer v. State, 738 N.E.2d 283, 2000 Ind. App. LEXIS 1832 (2000); Krise v. State, 746 N.E.2d 957, 2001 Ind. LEXIS 394 (2001); Dawson v. State, 786 N.E.2d 742, 2003 Ind. App. LEXIS 630 (2003); Tapely v. State, 886 N.E.2d 61, 2008 Ind. App. LEXIS 1015 (2008).

35-48-2-7. Schedule III tests.

(a) The board shall recommend placement of a substance in schedule III under this chapter if it finds that:

(1) The substance has a potential for abuse less than the substances listed in schedule [schedules] I and II under this chapter;

(2) The substance has currently accepted medical use in treatment in the United States; and

(3) Abuse of the substance may lead to moderate or low physical dependence or high psychological dependence.

(b) The board may recommend placement of a substance in schedule III under this chapter if it finds that the substance is classified as a controlled substance in schedule III under federal law.

History.
IC 35-48-2-7, as added by Acts 1976, P.L.148, § 7; P.L.200-1987, § 9.

Compiler's Notes.
The bracketed word "schedules" was inserted by the compiler for clarity.

35-48-2-8. Schedule III.

(a) The controlled substances listed in this section are included in schedule III.

(b) Stimulants. Unless specifically excepted or unless listed in another schedule, any material, compound, mixture, or preparation which contains any quantity of the following substances having a stimulant effect on the central nervous system, including its salts, isomers (whether optical, position, or geometric), and salts of such isomers whenever the existence of such salts, isomers, and salts of isomers is possible within the specific chemical designation:

(1) Those compounds, mixtures, or preparations in dosage unit form containing any stimulant substances listed in schedule II which compounds, mixtures, or preparations were listed on April 1, 1986, as excepted compounds under 21 CFR 1308.32, and any other drug of the quantitative composition shown in that list for those drugs or that is the same except that it contains a lesser quantity of controlled substances (1405).

(2) Benzphetamine (1228).

(3) Chlorphentermine (1645).

(4) Clortermine (1647).

(5) Phendimetrazine (1615).

(c) Depressants. Unless specifically excepted or unless listed in another schedule, any material, compound, mixture, or preparation which contains any quantity of the following substances having a depressant effect on the central nervous system:

(1) Any compound, mixture, or preparation containing:

    (A) amobarbital (2126);

    (B) secobarbital (2316);

    (C) pentobarbital (2271); or

    (D) any of their salts;

and one (1) or more other active medicinal ingredients which are not listed in any schedule.

(2) Any suppository dosage form containing:

    (A) amobarbital (2126);

    (B) secobarbital (2316);

    (C) pentobarbital (2271); or

    (D) any of their salts;

and approved by the Food and Drug Administration for marketing only as a suppository.

(3) Any substance which contains any quantity of a derivative of barbituric acid, or any salt thereof (2100).

(4) Chlorhexadol (2510).

(5) Embutramide (2020).

(6) Lysergic acid (7300).

(7) Lysergic acid amide (7310).

(8) Methyprylon (2575).

(9) Sulfondiethylmethane (2600).

(10) Sulfonethylmethane (2605).

(11) Sulfonmethane (2610).

(12) A combination product containing Tiletamine and Zolazepam or any salt thereof (Telazol) (7295).

(13) Any drug product containing gamma-hydroxybutyric acid, including its salts, isomers, and salts of isomers, for which an application is approved under section 505 of the federal Food, Drug and Cosmetic Act, 21 U.S.C. 301 et seq. (2012).

(d) Nalorphine (a narcotic drug) (9400).

(e) Narcotic Drugs. Unless specifically excepted or unless listed in another schedule, any material, compound, mixture, or preparation containing any of the following narcotic drugs, or their salts calculated as the free anhydrous base or alkaloid, in the following limited quantities:

(1) Not more than 1.8 grams of codeine, per 100 milliliters or not more than 90 milligrams per dosage unit, with an equal or greater quantity of an isoquinoline alkaloid of opium (9803).

(2) Not more than 1.8 grams of codeine, per 100 milliliters or not more than 90 milligrams per dosage unit, with one (1) or more active, nonnarcotic ingredients in recognized therapeutic amounts (9804).

(3) Not more than 300 milligrams of dihydrocodeinone, per 100 milliliters or not more than 15 milligrams per dosage unit, with a fourfold or greater quantity of an isoquinoline alkaloid of opium (9805).

(4) Not more than 300 milligrams of dihydrocodeinone, per 100 milliliters or not more than 15 milligrams per dosage unit, with one (1) or more active nonnarcotic ingredients in recognized therapeutic amounts (9806).

(5) Not more than 1.8 grams of dihydrocodeine, per 100 milliliters or not more than 90 milligrams per dosage unit, with one (1) or more active, nonnarcotic ingredients in recognized therapeutic amounts (9807).

(6) Not more than 300 milligrams of ethylmorphine, per 100 milliliters or not more than 15 milligrams per dosage unit, with one (1) or more active, nonnarcotic ingredients in recognized therapeutic amounts (9808).

(7) Not more than 500 milligrams of opium per 100 milliliters or per 100 grams or not more than 25 milligrams per dosage unit, with one (1) or more active, nonnarcotic ingredients in recognized therapeutic amounts (9809).

(8) Not more than 50 milligrams of morphine, per 100 milliliters or per 100 grams with one (1) or more active nonnarcotic ingredients in recognized therapeutic amounts (9810).

(9) Buprenorphine (9064).

(f) Anabolic steroid (as defined in 21 U.S.C. 802(41)(A) and 21 U.S.C. 802(41)(B)).

(g) The board shall except by rule any compound, mixture, or preparation containing any stimulant or depressant substance listed in subsections (b) through (e) from the application of any part of this article if the compound, mixture, or preparation contains one (1) or more active medicinal ingredients not having a stimulant or depressant effect on the central nervous system, and if the admixtures are included therein in combinations, quantity, proportion, or concentration that vitiate the potential for abuse of the substances which have a stimulant or depressant effect on the central nervous system.

(h) Any material, compound, mixture, or preparation which contains any quantity of Ketamine (7285).

(i) Hallucinogenic substances:

Dronabinol (synthetic) in sesame oil and encapsulated in a soft gelatin capsule in a United States Food and Drug Administration approved drug product (7369).

History.

IC 35-48-2-8, as added by Acts 1976, P.L.148, § 7; 1977, P.L.2, § 86; 1979, P.L.303, § 5; 1981, P.L.170, § 4; P.L.333-1983, § 3; P.L.200-1987, § 10; P.L.48-1991, § 76; P.L.1-1994, § 171; P.L.31-1998, § 10; P.L.288-2001, § 16; P.L.22-2008, § 3, eff. July 1, 2008.

Cross References.

Significance of numbers in brackets following names of substances, IC 35-48-2-2.

NOTES TO DECISIONS

Codeine.

Codeine is not specifically designated a schedule III controlled substance in the Indiana Code in all cases. Barnett v. State, 579 N.E.2d 84, 1991 Ind. App. LEXIS 1574 (1991).

Evidentiary Burden of State.

Even if acetaminophen with codeine is recognized by chemists as a schedule III controlled substance, the state may not rely on the doctrine of judicial notice to meet its evidentiary burden regarding the drug's chemical composition and characteristics. Barnett v. State, 579 N.E.2d 84, 1991 Ind. App. LEXIS 1574 (1991).

35-48-2-9. Schedule IV tests.

(a) The board shall recommend placement of a substance in schedule IV under this chapter if it finds that:

(1) The substance has a low potential for abuse relative to substances in schedule III under this chapter;

(2) The substance has currently accepted medical use in treatment in the United States; and

(3) Abuse of the substance may lead to limited physical dependence or psychological dependence relative to the substances in schedule III under this chapter.

(b) The board may recommend placement of a substance in schedule IV under this chapter if it finds that the substance is classified as a controlled substance in schedule IV under federal law.

History.
IC 35-48-2-9, as added by Acts 1976, P.L.148, § 7; P.L.200-1987, § 11.

35-48-2-10. Schedule IV.

(a) The controlled substances listed in this section are included in schedule IV.

(b) Narcotic drugs. Unless specifically excepted in a rule adopted by the board or unless listed in another schedule, any material, compound, mixture, or preparation containing any of the following narcotic drugs, or their salts calculated as the free anhydrous base or alkaloid, in the following limited quantities:

(1) Not more than 1 milligram of difenoxin (9618) and not less than 25 micrograms of atropine sulfate per dosage unit.

(2) Dextropropoxyphene (alpha- (+)-4-dimethylamino-1,2- diphenyl-3-methyl-2-propionoxybutane (9278).

(c) Depressants. Unless specifically excepted in a rule adopted by the board or unless listed in another schedule, any material, compound, mixture, or preparation which contains any quantity of the following substances, including its salts, isomers, and salts of isomers whenever the existence of such salts, isomers, and salts of isomers is possible within the specific chemical designation:

Alprazolam (2882).
Barbital (2145).
Bromazepam (2748).
Camazepam (2749).
Carisoprodol.
Chloral betaine (2460).
Chloral hydrate (2465).
Chlordiazepoxide (2744).
Clobazam (2751).
Clonazepam (2737).
Clorazepate (2768).

Clotiazepam (2752).
Cloxazolam (2753).
Delorazepam (2754).
Diazepam (2765).
Dichloralphenazone (2467).
Estazolam (2756).
Ethchlorvynol (2540).
Ethinamate (2545).
Ethyl loflazepate (2758).
Fludiazepam (2759).
Flunitrazepam (2763).
Flurazepam (2767).
Halazepam (2762).
Haloxazolam (2771).
Ketazolam (2772).
Loprazolam (2773).
Lorazepam (2885).
Lormetazepam (2774).
Mebutamate (2800).
Medazepam (2836).
Meprobamate (2820).
Methohexital (2264).
Methylphenobarbital (mephobarbital) (2250).
Midazolam (2884).
Nimetazepam (2837).
Nitrazepam (2834).
Nordiazepam (2838).
Oxazepam (2835).
Oxazolam (2839).
Paraldehyde (2585).
Petrichloral (2591).
Phenobarbital (2285).
Pinazepam (2883).
Prazepam (2764).
Quazepam (2881).
Temazepam (2925).
Tetrazepam (2886).
Triazolam (2887).
Zaleplon (2781).
Zolpidem (Ambien) (2783).
Zopiclone (2784).

(d) Fenfluramine. Any material, compound, mixture, or preparation which contains any quantity of the following substances, including its salts, isomers (whether optical, position, or geometric), and salts of such isomers, whenever the existence of such salts, isomers, and salts of isomers is possible.

Fenfluramine (1670).

(e) Stimulants. Unless specifically excepted in a rule adopted by the board or unless listed in another schedule, any material, compound, mixture, or preparation which contains any quantity of the following substances having a stimulant effect on the central nervous system, including its salts, isomers (whether optical, position, or geometric), and salts of such isomers whenever the existence of such salts, isomers, and salts of isomers is possible within the specific chemical designation:

Cathine ((+)-norpseudoephedrine) (1230).
Diethylpropion (1610).

Fencamfamin (1760).

Fenproporex (1575).

Mazindol (1605).

Mefenorex (1580).

Modafinil (1680).

Phentermine (1640).

Pemoline (including organometallic complexes and chelates thereof) (1530).

Pipradrol (1750).

Sibutramine (1675).

SPA ((-)-1-dimethylamino-1,2-diphenylethane (1635).

(f) Other substances. Unless specifically excepted or unless listed in another schedule, any material, compound, mixture, or preparation which contains any quantity of the following substances including its salts:

Butorphanol (including its optical isomers) (9720).

Pentazocine (9709).

(g) The board may except by rule any compound, mixture, or preparation containing any depressant substance listed in subsection (b), (c), (d), (e), or (f) from the application of any part of this article if the compound, mixture, or preparation contains one (1) or more active medicinal ingredients not having a depressant effect on the central nervous system, and if the admixtures are included therein in combinations, quantity, proportion, or concentration that vitiate the potential for abuse of the substances which have a depressant effect on the central nervous system.

History.

IC 35-48-2-10, as added by Acts 1976, P.L.148, § 7; 1977, P.L.344, § 2; 1979, P.L.303, § 6; 1981, P.L.170, § 5; P.L.333-1983, § 4; P.L.77-1984, § 14; P.L.200-1987, § 12; P.L.288-2001, § 17; P.L.8-2004, § 3; P.L.22-2008, § 4, eff. July 1, 2008.

Cross References.

Significance of numbers in brackets following names of substances, IC 35-48-2-2.

NOTES TO DECISIONS

Cited:

State v. Isaacs, 794 N.E.2d 1120, 2003 Ind. App. LEXIS 1634 (2003).

35-48-2-11. Schedule V tests.

(a) The board shall recommend placement of a substance in schedule V under this chapter if it finds that:

(1) The substance has low potential for abuse relative to the controlled substances listed in schedule IV under this chapter;

(2) The substance has currently accepted medical use in treatment in the United States; and

(3) The substance has limited physical dependence or psychological dependence liability relative to the controlled substances listed in schedule IV under this chapter.

(b) The board may recommend placement of a substance in schedule V under this chapter if it finds that the substance is classified as a controlled substance in schedule V under federal law.

History.

IC 35-48-2-11, as added by Acts 1976, P.L.148, § 7; P.L.200-1987, § 13.

35-48-2-12. Schedule V.

(a) The controlled substances listed in this section are included in schedule V.

(b) Narcotic drugs containing nonnarcotic active medicinal ingredients. Any compound, mixture, or preparation containing any of the following narcotic drugs, or their salts calculated as the free anhydrous base or alkaloid, in the following quantities, which shall include one (1) or more nonnarcotic active medicinal ingredients in sufficient proportion to confer upon the compound, mixture, or preparation, valuable medicinal qualities other than those possessed by the narcotic drug alone:

(1) Not more than 200 milligrams of codeine per 100 milliliters or per 100 grams.

(2) Not more than 100 milligrams of dihydrocodeine per 100 milliliters or per 100 grams.

(3) Not more than 100 milligrams of ethylmorphine per 100 milliliters or per 100 grams.

(4) Not more than 2.5 milligrams of diphenoxylate and not less than 25 micrograms of atropine sulfate per dosage unit.

(5) Not more than 100 milligrams of opium per 100 milliliters or per 100 grams.

(6) Not more than 0.5 milligrams of difenoxin (9168), and not less than 25 micrograms of atropine sulfate per dosage unit.

(c) Pregabalin (2782).

(d) Pyrovalerone (1485).

History.
IC 35-48-2-12, as added by Acts 1976, P.L.148, § 7; 1979, P.L.303, § 7; 1981, P.L.170, § 6; P.L.327-1985, § 3; P.L.22-2008, § 5, eff. July 1, 2008.

Cross References.
Significance of numbers in brackets following names of substances, IC 35-48-2-2.

35-48-2-13. [Repealed.]

Compiler's Notes.
This section, concerning republishing of schedules of controlled substances, was repealed by Acts 1979, P.L. 303, § 13. For authority of state board of pharmacy as to controlled substances, see IC 35-48-2-1.

35-48-2-14. Reclassification of controlled substances — Rules of board.

(a) The board may adopt rules under IC 4-22-2 to reclassify a controlled substance:

(1) From a more restrictive schedule to a less restrictive schedule; or

(2) As a substance that is not a controlled substance;
if the board finds that the substance qualifies for reclassification under this chapter and that the same reclassification has been made in a controlled substance schedule under federal law.

(b) If the board reclassifies a controlled substance under subsection (a), the board shall recommend the same reclassification to the general assembly under section 1 [IC 35-48-2-1] of this chapter.

(c) Notwithstanding a provision in this chapter that classifies a controlled substance in a more restrictive schedule than a rule adopted under subsection (a), a person who manufactures, distributes, dispenses, possesses, or uses a controlled substance in compliance with the requirements applicable to the less restrictive schedule to which a controlled substance is reclassified under subsection (a) does not commit an offense under this article.

(d) Notwithstanding a provision in this chapter that classifies a substance as a controlled substance, a person does not commit an offense under this article if the board has reclassified the controlled substance as a substance that is not a controlled substance.

History.
P.L.200-1987, § 14.

CHAPTER 3

REGISTRATION AND CONTROL

35-48-3-1. Rules and regulations — Fees.

The board may promulgate rules and charge reasonable fees relating to the registration and control of the manufacture, distribution, and dispensing of controlled substances within this state.

History.
IC 35-48-3-1, as added by Acts 1976, P.L.148, § 7.

Cross References.
Employment of inspector-investigators to enforce controlled substances law, IC 25-26-13-5.

NOTES TO DECISIONS

Cited:
Hall v. Dep't of State Revenue, 720 N.E.2d 1287, 1999 Ind. Tax LEXIS 54 (1999).

35-48-3-2. Humane societies and animal control agencies.

(a) Any humane society, animal control agency, or governmental entity operating an animal shelter or other animal impounding facility is entitled to receive a limited permit only for the purpose of buying, possessing, and using:

(1) sodium pentobarbital to euthanize injured, sick, homeless, or unwanted domestic pets and animals;

(2) ketamine and ketamine products to anesthetize or immobilize fractious domestic pets and animals; and

(3) a combination product containing tiletamine and zolazepam as an agent for the remote chemical capture of domestic pets or animals that otherwise cannot be restrained or captured.

(b) A humane society, animal control agency, or governmental entity entitled to receive a permit under this chapter must:

(1) apply to the board according to the rules established by the board;

(2) pay annually to the board a fee set by the board for the limited permit; and

(3) submit proof, as determined by the board, that the employees of an applicant who will handle a controlled substance are sufficiently trained to use and administer the controlled substance.

(c) All fees collected by the board under this section shall be credited to the state board of pharmacy account.

(d) Storage, handling, and use of controlled substances obtained according to this section are subject to the rules adopted by the board.

History.
   IC 35-48-3-2, as added by Acts 1976, P.L.148,
§ 7; P.L.193-1987, § 16; P.L.136-2001, § 1.

35-48-3-3. Registration of manufacturers, distributors, etc., generally.

(a) Every person who manufactures or distributes any controlled substance within this state or who proposes to engage in the manufacture or distribution of any controlled substance within this state, must obtain biennially a registration issued by the board in accordance with its rules.

(b) Every person who dispenses or proposes to dispense any controlled substance within Indiana must have a registration issued by the board in accordance with its rules. A registration issued to a dispenser under this subsection expires whenever the dispenser's license as a practitioner expires. The board shall renew a dispenser's registration under this subsection concurrently with any state license authorizing the dispenser to act as a practitioner.

(c) Persons registered by the board under this article to manufacture, distribute, dispense, or conduct research with controlled substances may possess, manufacture, distribute, dispense, or conduct research with those substances to the extent authorized by their registration and in conformity with the other provisions of this chapter.

(d) The following persons need not register and may lawfully possess controlled substances under this article:

   (1) An agent or employee of any registered manufacturer, distributor, or dispenser of any controlled substance if he is acting in the usual course of his business or employment.

   (2) A common or contract carrier or warehouseman, or an employee thereof, whose possession of any controlled substance is in the usual course of business or employment.

   (3) An ultimate user or a person in possession of any controlled substance under a lawful order of a practitioner or in lawful possession of a schedule V substance.

(e) The board may waive by rule the requirement for registration of certain manufacturers, distributors, or dispensers if it finds it consistent with the public health and safety.

(f) A separate registration is required at each principal place of business or professional practice where the applicant manufactures, distributes, dispenses, or possesses controlled substances.

(g) The board may inspect the establishment of a registrant or applicant for registration in accordance with the board's rules.

History.
   IC 35-48-3-3, as added by Acts 1976, P.L.148,
§ 7; P.L.156-1986, § 6.

NOTES TO DECISIONS

Physicians.
   A physician who issues prescriptions without a legitimate purpose or outside the usual course of his professional practice may be prosecuted for dealing in a controlled substance. Alarcon v. State, 573 N.E.2d 477, 1991 Ind. App. LEXIS 980 (1991).

RESEARCH REFERENCES

Collateral References.
State law criminal liability of licensed physician

for prescribing or dispensing drug or similar controlled substance. 13 A.L.R.5th 1.

35-48-3-4. Criteria for registration of manufacturers and distributors — Registration of practitioners — Registration to conduct research or instructional activities.

(a) The board shall register an applicant to manufacture or distribute controlled substances unless it determines that the issuance of that registration would be inconsistent with the public interest. In determining the public interest, the board shall consider:

(1) Maintenance of effective controls against diversion of controlled substances into other than legitimate medical, scientific, or industrial channels;

(2) Compliance with applicable state and local law;

(3) Any convictions of the applicant under any federal and state laws relating to any controlled substance;

(4) Past experience in the manufacture or distribution of controlled substances, and the existence in the applicant's establishment of effective controls against diversion;

(5) Furnishing by the applicant of false or fraudulent material in any application filed under this article;

(6) Suspension or revocation of the applicant's federal registration to manufacture, distribute, or dispense controlled substances as authorized by federal law; and

(7) Any other factors relevant to and consistent with the public health and safety.

(b) Registration under subsection (a) of this section does not entitle a registrant to manufacture and distribute controlled substances in schedules I or II other than those specified in the registration.

(c) Practitioners must be registered to dispense any controlled substances or to conduct research with controlled substances in schedules II through V if they are authorized to dispense or conduct research under the law of this state. The board need not require separate registration under this chapter for practitioners engaging in research with nonnarcotic controlled substances in schedules II through V where the registrant is already registered under this chapter in another capacity, to the extent authorized by his registration in that other capacity.

(d) Registration to conduct research or instructional activities with controlled substances in schedules I through V does not entitle a registrant to conduct research or instructional activities with controlled substances other than those approved by the controlled substances advisory committee in accordance with the registration.

Compliance by manufacturers and distributors with the provisions of the federal law respecting registration (excluding fees) entitles them to be registered under this article.

History.
IC 35-48-3-4, as added by Acts 1976, P.L.148, § 7; 1981, P.L.170, § 7.

35-48-3-5. Denial, revocation, and suspension of registration.

(a) An application for registration or re-registration submitted pursuant to and a registration issued under section 3 [IC 35-48-3-3] of this chapter to manufacture, distribute, or dispense a controlled substance may be denied, suspended, or revoked by the board upon a finding by the advisory committee that the applicant or registrant:

(1) has furnished false or fraudulent material information in any application filed under this article;

(2) has violated any state or federal law relating to any controlled substance;

(3) has had his federal registration suspended or revoked to manufacture, distribute, or dispense controlled substances; or

(4) has failed to maintain reasonable controls against diversion of controlled substances into other than legitimate medical, scientific, or industrial channels.

(b) The board may limit revocation or suspension of a registration or the denial of an application for registration or re-registration to the particular controlled substance with respect to which grounds for revocation, suspension, or denial exist.

(c) If the board suspends or revokes a registration or denies an application for re-registration, all controlled substances owned or possessed by the registrant at the time of suspension or the effective date of the revocation or denial order may be placed under seal. The board may require the removal of such substances from the premises. No disposition may be made of substances under seal until the time for taking an appeal has elapsed or until all appeals have been concluded unless a court, upon application therefor, orders the sale of perishable substances and the deposit of the proceeds of the sale with the court. Upon a revocation or denial order becoming final, all controlled substances may be forfeited to the state.

(d) The board shall promptly notify the drug enforcement administration of all orders suspending or revoking registration, all orders denying any application for registration or re-registration, and all forfeitures of controlled substances.

(e) If the Drug Enforcement Administration terminates, denies, suspends, or revokes a federal registration for the manufacture, distribution, or dispensing of controlled substances, a registration issued by the board under this chapter is automatically suspended.

(f) The board may reinstate a registration that has been suspended under subsection (e), after a hearing, if the board is satisfied that the applicant is able to manufacture, distribute, or dispense controlled substances with reasonable skill and safety to the public. As a condition of reinstatement, the board may impose disciplinary or corrective measures authorized under IC 25-1-9-9 or this article.

History.
IC 35-48-3-5, as added by Acts 1976, P.L.148, § 7; 1981, P.L.170, § 8; P.L.197-2007, § 93, eff. July 1, 2007.

35-48-3-6. Order to show cause.

(a) Before recommending a denial, suspension, or revocation of a registration, or before refusing a renewal of registration, the advisory committee shall serve upon the applicant or registrant an order to show cause why registration should not be denied, revoked, or suspended, or why the renewal should not be denied. The order to show cause shall contain a statement of the basis therefor and shall call upon the applicant or registrant to appear before the advisory committee at a time and place not less than thirty (30) days after the date of service of the order, but in the case of a denial or renewal of registration the show cause order shall be served not later than thirty (30) days before the expiration of the registration. These proceedings shall be conducted in accordance with IC 4-21.5 without regard to any criminal prosecution or other proceeding. Proceedings to refuse renewal of registration shall not abate the existing registration which shall remain in effect pending the outcome of the administrative hearing.

(b) The advisory committee may recommend suspension, and the board may suspend, without an order to show cause, any registration simultaneously with the institution of proceedings under section 4 [IC 35-48-3-4] of this chapter, or where renewal of registration is refused, if it finds that there is an imminent danger to the public health or safety which warrants this action. The suspension shall continue in effect until the conclusion of the proceedings, including judicial review thereof, unless sooner withdrawn by the board or dissolved by a court of competent jurisdiction.

(c) If an applicant for re-registration (who is doing business under a registration previously granted and not revoked nor suspended) has applied for re-registration at least forty-five (45) days before the date on which the existing registration is due to expire, the existing registration of the applicant shall automatically be extended and continue in effect until the date on which the board so issues its order. The board may extend any other existing registration under the circumstances contemplated in this section even though the registrant failed to apply for re-registration at least forty-five (45) days before expiration of the existing registration, with or without request by the registrant, if the board finds that such extension is not inconsistent with the public health and safety.

History.
IC 35-48-3-6, as added by Acts 1976, P.L.148, § 7; P.L.7-1987, § 166.

35-48-3-7. Records of registrants.

Persons registered to manufacture, distribute, or dispense controlled substances under this article shall keep records and maintain inventories in conformance with the record-keeping and inventory requirements of federal law and with any additional rules the board issues.

History.
IC 35-48-3-7, as added by Acts 1976, P.L.148, § 7.

NOTES TO DECISIONS

ANALYSIS

Paregoric.
Records Required.

Paregoric.
The statute exempted paregoric containing two grains or less of opium from the provisions with reference to a physician's prescription, but did not exempt the seller from the requirement of keeping a record of the sales nor the buyer from the penal provision when obtaining the same by use of deceit, fraud or the use of a false name. Merritt v. State, 245 Ind. 362, 198 N.E.2d 867, 1964 Ind. LEXIS 217 (1964).

Records Required.
Notwithstanding that purchases of certain narcotic drugs with a minimum opium content were exempt from the requirement that a prescription be obtained, it was necessary that a record be kept of those to whom the sales were made. Merritt v. State, 245 Ind. 362, 198 N.E.2d 867, 1964 Ind. LEXIS 217 (1964).

35-48-3-8. Order forms.

Controlled substances in schedules I and II shall be distributed by a registrant to another registrant only pursuant to an order form. Compliance with the provisions of federal law respecting order forms is deemed compliance with this section.

History.
IC 35-48-3-8, as added by Acts 1976, P.L.148, § 7.

35-48-3-9. Prescriptions.

(a) Except for dosages medically required for a period of not more than forty-eight (48) hours that are dispensed by or on the direction of a practitioner or medication dispensed directly by a practitioner, other than a pharmacy, to an ultimate user, no controlled substance in schedule II may be dispensed without the written prescription of a practitioner.

(b) In emergency situations, as defined by rule of the board, schedule II drugs may be dispensed upon oral prescription of a practitioner, reduced promptly to writing and filed by the pharmacy. Prescriptions shall be retained in conformity with the requirements of section 7 [IC 35-48-3-7] of this chapter. No prescription for a schedule II substance may be refilled.

(c) Except for dosages medically required for a period of not more than forty-eight (48) hours that are dispensed by or on the direction of a practitioner, or medication dispensed directly by a practitioner, other than a pharmacy, to an ultimate user, a controlled substance included in schedule III or IV, which is a prescription drug as determined under IC 16-42-19, shall not be dispensed without a written or oral prescription of a practitioner. The prescription shall not be filled or refilled more than six (6) months after the date thereof or be refilled more than five (5) times, unless renewed by the practitioner. Prescriptions for schedule III, IV, and V controlled substances may be transmitted by facsimile from the practitioner or the agent of the practitioner to a pharmacy. The facsimile prescription is equivalent to an original prescription to the extent permitted under federal law.

(d) A controlled substance included in schedule V shall not be distributed or dispensed other than for a medical purpose.

History.
  IC 35-48-3-9, as added by Acts 1976, P.L.148, § 7; P.L.2-1993, § 192; P.L.163-1994, § 4; P.L.204-2005, § 21.

NOTES TO DECISIONS

ANALYSIS

Good Faith.
Instructions.

Good Faith.
  Where a physician was prosecuted for unlawfully selling and administering morphine, his lack of good faith was sufficiently established, where the evidence showed among other things that the party to whom the sale was made told the accused that she might sell a portion of the morphine and thereby get money to buy more morphine. Smith v. State, 214 Ind. 169, 13 N.E.2d 562, 1938 Ind. LEXIS 159 (1938).
  In the prosecution of a physician for unlawfully selling and furnishing morphine, the words "good faith" pertaining to sales of narcotics, did not need any definition other than that implied by the words themselves. Smith v. State, 214 Ind. 169, 13 N.E.2d 562, 1938 Ind. LEXIS 159 (1938).
  Instructions in the prosecution of a physician for unlawfully selling and administering morphine,

that when a physician attended a patient it was presumed that whatever treatment he gave was given in good faith, that good faith meant good intention and the honest exercise of his best judgment as to the needs of his patient, and that error of judgment was not sufficient evidence of lack of good faith, were not erroneous, but sufficiently informed the jury that good faith sale or administration of morphine meant without unlawful intention. Smith v. State, 214 Ind. 169, 13 N.E.2d 562, 1938 Ind. LEXIS 159 (1938).

Instructions.
  In prosecution for possession of controlled substance, an instruction that "Except when dispensed directly by a practitioner no controlled substance in schedule II may be dispensed without the written prescription of a practitioner" was proper even though the pharmacist to whom forged prescription was taken testified that he had accepted telephone orders for prescriptions from doctors. Ralston v. State, 412 N.E.2d 239, 1980 Ind. App. LEXIS 1736 (1980).

35-48-3-10. [Repealed.]

Compiler's Notes.
  This section, prescribing controlled substances to treat weight reduction or control obesity, was

repealed by P.L.157-1999, § 2, effective May 5, 1999. For present similar provisions, see IC 35-48-3-11.

35-48-3-11. Prescribing controlled substances to treat weight reduction or control obesity.

(a) Only a physician licensed under IC 25-22.5 may treat a patient with a

Schedule III or Schedule IV controlled substance for the purpose of weight reduction or to control obesity.

(b) A physician licensed under IC 25-22.5 may not prescribe, dispense, administer, supply, sell, or give any amphetamine, sympathomimetic amine drug, or compound designated as a Schedule III or Schedule IV controlled substance under IC 35-48-2-8 and IC 35-48-2-10 for a patient for purposes of weight reduction or to control obesity, unless the physician does the following:

    (1) Determines:

        (A) through review of:

            (i) the physician's records of prior treatment of the patient; or

            (ii) the records of prior treatment of the patient provided by a previous treating physician or weight loss program;

        that the physician's patient has made a reasonable effort to lose weight in a treatment program using a regimen of weight reduction based on caloric restriction, nutritional counseling, behavior modification, and exercise without using controlled substances; and

        (B) that the treatment described in clause (A) has been ineffective for the physician's patient.

    (2) Obtains a thorough history and performs a thorough physical examination of the physician's patient before initiating a treatment plan using a Schedule III or Schedule IV controlled substance for purposes of weight reduction or to control obesity.

(c) A physician licensed under IC 25-22.5 may not begin and shall discontinue using a Schedule III or Schedule IV controlled substance for purposes of weight reduction or to control obesity after the physician determines in the physician's professional judgment that:

    (1) the physician's patient has failed to lose weight using a treatment plan involving the controlled substance;

    (2) the controlled substance has provided a decreasing contribution toward further weight loss for the patient unless continuing to take the controlled substance is medically necessary or appropriate for maintenance therapy;

    (3) the physician's patient:

        (A) has a history of; or

        (B) shows a propensity for;

    alcohol or drug abuse; or

    (4) the physician's patient has consumed or disposed of a controlled substance in a manner that does not strictly comply with a treating physician's direction.

History.
P.L.157-1999, § 1; P.L.37-2001, § 1.

CHAPTER 4

OFFENSES RELATING TO CONTROLLED SUBSTANCES

35-48-4-0.5. "Controlled substance analog" defined.

For purposes of this chapter, a "controlled substance analog" is considered to be a controlled substance in schedule I if the analog is in whole or in part intended for human consumption.

History.
    P.L.225-2003, § 2.

35-48-4-1. Dealing in cocaine or a narcotic drug.

(a) A person who:
    (1) knowingly or intentionally:
        (A) manufactures;
        (B) finances the manufacture of;
        (C) delivers; or
        (D) finances the delivery of;
cocaine or a narcotic drug, pure or adulterated, classified in schedule I or II; or
    (2) possesses, with intent to:
        (A) manufacture;
        (B) finance the manufacture of;
        (C) deliver; or
        (D) finance the delivery of;
cocaine or a narcotic drug, pure or adulterated, classified in schedule I or II;
commits dealing in cocaine or a narcotic drug, a Class B felony, except as provided in subsection (b).
    (b) The offense is a Class A felony if:
        (1) the amount of the drug involved weighs three (3) grams or more;
        (2) the person:
            (A) delivered; or
            (B) financed the delivery of;
the drug to a person under eighteen (18) years of age at least three (3) years junior to the person; or
        (3) the person manufactured, delivered, or financed the delivery of the drug:
            (A) on a school bus; or
            (B) in, on, or within one thousand (1,000) feet of:
                (i) school property;
                (ii) a public park;
                (iii) a family housing complex; or
                (iv) a youth program center.

History.

IC 35-48-4-1, as added by Acts 1976, P.L.148, § 7; 1977, P.L.340, § 96; 1979, P.L.303, § 8; P.L.296-1987, § 5; P.L.165-1990, § 3; P.L.296-1995, § 3; P.L.65-1996, § 11; P.L.17-2001, § 19; P.L.151-2006, § 22.

Compiler's Notes.

P.L.151-2006, § 29, effective July 1, 2006, provides:

"IC 35-48-4-1.1 and IC 35-48-4-6.1, both as added by this act, and IC 35-48-4-1, IC 35-48-4-6, IC 35-48-4-14.5, and IC 35-48-4-14.7, all as amended by this act, apply only to crimes committed after June 30, 2006."

Cross References.

Defenses relating to culpability, IC 35-41-3-1 — IC 35-41-3-10.

Employment of inspector-investigators to enforce controlled substances law, IC 25-26-13-5.

Failure to pay excise tax required by IC 6-7-3 as factor in sentencing, IC 6-7-3-18.

Penalties for felonies, IC 35-50-1, IC 35-50-2, IC 35-50-5-2.

NOTES TO DECISIONS

Constitutionality.

Where defendant was charged with possession of heroin and not any other drugs, he could not object that the former statute was unconstitutional because of power given to board of pharmacy to determine additional drugs to be "narcotic drugs." Lander v. State, 238 Ind. 680, 154 N.E.2d 507, 1958 Ind. LEXIS 277 (1958).

Interpreting section to mean that offense can be classified as a Class A felony based on the weight of the drug and the substance with which it is mixed is not unconstitutional on the ground that it would unequally penalize persons who sell identical amounts of pure cocaine — the inequality based on whether the cocaine was mixed with enough other substance to make an aggregate weight in excess

Constitutionality. (Cont'd)
of three grams. Lawhorn v. State, 452 N.E.2d 915, 1983 Ind. LEXIS 927 (1983).

This section is not unconstitutionally vague. Sherelis v. Duckworth, 675 F. Supp. 1144, 1987 U.S. Dist. LEXIS 11690 (N.D. Ind. 1987), aff'd without op., 866 F.2d 432, 1988 U.S. App. LEXIS 18155 (7th Cir. Ind. 1988).

Motion challenging constitutionality of this section on claim of cruel and unusual punishment was properly denied on authority of prior cases. Lopez v. State, 527 N.E.2d 1119, 1988 Ind. LEXIS 248 (1988).

Increased penalties for drug offenders who commit their offenses near school property is constitutional. Reynolds/Herr v. State, 582 N.E.2d 833, 1991 Ind. App. LEXIS 2116 (1991).

Subsection (b), which enhances the offense of delivery of cocaine to a Class A felony if the amount of the drug involved weighs three grams or more, is not unconstitutionally vague and does not offend the rights of due process and equal protection nor does it violate the proportionality requirement of Ind. Const. Art. 1, § 16. Coleman v. State, 588 N.E.2d 1335, 1992 Ind. App. LEXIS 468 (1992).

—Due Process.
The classification of cocaine as a narcotic did not violate procedural due process. Hall v. State, 273 Ind. 425, 403 N.E.2d 1382, 1980 Ind. LEXIS 686 (1980).

—Overbreadth.
This section was not overbroad because nothing distinguished defendant's drug transaction from thousands of other drug transactions other than proximity to a school; courts engage in overbreadth analysis in determining when an otherwise valid criminal statute impermissibly encompasses constitutionally protected activity. Defendant did not show how the enhancement of dealing in cocaine from a Class B to a Class A felony could result in such an over-reaching application that constitutionally protected activities were improperly punished. Schnitz v. State, 650 N.E.2d 717, 1995 Ind. App. LEXIS 569 (1995), aff'd, 666 N.E.2d 919, 1996 Ind. LEXIS 64 (1996).

Burden of Proof.

—Proximity to Park.
State failed to meet its burden of proving beyond a reasonable doubt either that defendant was within 1000 feet of a park for more than a brief time or that persons under the age of 18 were within 1000 feet of the park to prove a violation of IC 35-48-4-1(b)(3)(B). Harrison v. State, — N.E.2d —, 2009 Ind. App. LEXIS 346 (2009).

—Proximity to School Property.
The state was not required to show that defendant knew he was within 1,000 feet of the school when the drug transaction occurred. Schnitz v. State, 650 N.E.2d 717, 1995 Ind. App. LEXIS 569 (1995), aff'd, 666 N.E.2d 919, 1996 Ind. LEXIS 64 (1996).

This section creates a strict liability enhance-ment and it is unnecessary for the state to prove a defendant had actual knowledge that sale of cocaine was occurring within 1,000 feet of a school. Walker v. State, 668 N.E.2d 243, 1996 Ind. LEXIS 65 (1996).

Where the state, in proving that the defendant's drug transaction took place within 1,000 feet of a school, elicited testimony from an associate superintendent of schools regarding the ownership of the property, and from a county surveyor regarding the distance involved, this testimony, coupled with the defendant's admission that he was "right down the street from a school" was sufficient to support a conviction for dealing in cocaine within 1,000 feet of school property. Dixon v. State, 712 N.E.2d 1086, 1999 Ind. App. LEXIS 1195 (1999).

Chain of Custody.
Where informant was strip searched before he entered his home, delivery of drug to informant was made in his home and informant then went outside where he was picked up by police officer and drug was surrendered to police officer and its custody from that time until trial was accounted for there was a sufficient chain of custody for its introduction into evidence. Coker v. State, 399 N.E.2d 857, 1980 Ind. App. LEXIS 1302 (1980).

To establish a proper chain of custody, the prosecution need only present evidence that strongly suggests the exact whereabouts of the evidence at all times. Gardner v. State, 514 N.E.2d 1261, 1987 Ind. LEXIS 1117 (1987).

The state need not establish a perfect chain of custody, and any gaps impact solely on the weight, not the admissibility, of the evidence. Johnson v. State, 594 N.E.2d 817, 1992 Ind. App. LEXIS 1003 (1992).

The trial court did not commit error when it allowed the state to introduce into evidence cocaine allegedly delivered from defendant to a paid police informant, when the informant did not testify at trial so as to identify the cocaine exhibit, where police officer performed a complete search of confidential informant's person and clothing, the officer had an unobstructed view of the confidential informant handing defendant money and defendant dropping something into the confidential informant's hand, and from the time he left the car until he returned, the confidential informant had had no contact with anyone but defendant and had not left the officer's sight. Collins v. State, 645 N.E.2d 1089, 1995 Ind. App. LEXIS 8 (1995), aff'd, 659 N.E.2d 509, 1995 Ind. LEXIS 202 (1995).

Cocaine.
Cocaine hydrochloride is a controlled substance within the meaning of this section. Sherelis v. State, 498 N.E.2d 973, 1986 Ind. LEXIS 1306 (1986); Sherelis v. Duckworth, 675 F. Supp. 1144, 1987 U.S. Dist. LEXIS 11690 (N.D. Ind. 1987), aff'd without op., 866 F.2d 432, 1988 U.S. App. LEXIS 18155 (7th Cir. Ind. 1988).

Conspiracy.
Evidence held sufficient to support a conviction for conspiracy to commit dealing in a narcotic

Conspiracy. (Cont'd)
drug. Altman v. State, 466 N.E.2d 716, 1984 Ind. LEXIS 922 (1984).

Mere knowledge of, or presence at, a drug transaction and association with co-conspirators is insufficient evidence of conspiracy. Kats v. State, 559 N.E.2d 348, 1990 Ind. App. LEXIS 1189 (1990).

Circumstantial evidence supported defendant's conviction for conspiracy to commit dealing in cocaine, where there was testimony showing that defendant had been a runner for her co-conspirator and that the two had packaged cocaine for sale. Snow v. State, 560 N.E.2d 69, 1990 Ind. App. LEXIS 1272 (1990).

Intent to deliver cocaine to police officers could be inferred from the evidence of the defendant's accepting money from the officers for the ostensible purpose of obtaining cocaine, and returning to negotiate a higher price. The failure of delivery merely demonstrated that the underlying offense was not committed. Because there is no requirement that the underlying felony actually be committed or even attempted, the evidence was sufficient to sustain conviction for conspiracy to deal in cocaine. Hammond v. State, 594 N.E.2d 509, 1992 Ind. App. LEXIS 1068 (1992).

Evidence was sufficient to show that defendant and deceased coconspirator had entered into an agreement to deal in cocaine and had committed an act in furtherance of the agreement, where a witness testified that coconspirator acknowledged on several occasions that he and defendant were involved in the sale of cocaine, and the witness provided eyewitness testimony describing defendant's direct participation in at least one drug transaction. Leslie v. State, 670 N.E.2d 898, 1996 Ind. App. LEXIS 1194 (1996).

Evidence that car in which defendant was backseat passenger contained chemical reagents or precursors to manufacture of methamphetamine while in Indiana was sufficient to prove venue in Indiana and therefore to support defendant's conviction for conspiracy to commit dealing in methamphetamine; defendant's argument that evidence was insufficient to support conspiracy conviction because he dealt with his co-conspirators in Illinois and committed no act in furtherance of conspiracy in Indiana was rejected. Smith v. State, 809 N.E.2d 938, 2004 Ind. App. LEXIS 1100 (2004).

Convictions for conspiracy to sell more than three grams of cocaine was proper based on aggregate weight of two cocaine sales to informant and agreement as to location of sales and preparation and transportation of cocaine. Simmons v. State, 828 N.E.2d 449, 2005 Ind. App. LEXIS 948 (2005).

Construction.

—"Drug."
The antecedent of "drug" in the second sentence of this section is the drug discussed in the first sentence, which is "narcotic drug, pure or adulterated." Lawhorn v. State, 452 N.E.2d 915, 1983 Ind. LEXIS 927 (1983).

—"School."
Trial court did not err in taking judicial notice that a head start school was a school within the meaning of this section. Woods v. State, 654 N.E.2d 1153, 1995 Ind. LEXIS 114 (1995).

Parochial kindergarten was a school within the meaning of IC 35-41-1-24.7 and IC 35-48-4-1. French v. State, 778 N.E.2d 816, 2002 Ind. LEXIS 891 (2002).

—"School Property."
The term "school property" in the statutes need not refer to an entire building. Bailey v. State, 603 N.E.2d 1376, 1992 Ind. App. LEXIS 1822 (1992).

Construction With Other Law.
Neither the text nor the history of the Vienna Convention on Consular Relations clearly provides a private right of action in United States courts to set aside a criminal conviction and sentence for violation of consular notification provisions; therefore, the state's failure to inform defendant of his rights under Article 36 of the Convention, and the state's failure to notify the Mexican Consulate of defendant's arrest, did not prejudice defendant's fundamental rights of due process and his convictions and sentence should not be vacated. Zavala v. State, 739 N.E.2d 135, 2000 Ind. App. LEXIS 1768 (2000).

Constructive Possession.
One's possession of a substance may be constructive only and need not be actual and exclusive to create criminal liability. Jeffers v. State, 485 N.E.2d 81, 1985 Ind. LEXIS 1026 (1985).

Constructive possession is defined as "the intent and capability to maintain dominion and control over the illegal drugs." The defendant's exclusive control of the premises where drugs are found will support an inference of intent to maintain dominion and control over the drugs. However, when the premises are not within the exclusive control of the defendant, the inference of intent must be supported by additional circumstances showing the defendant had knowledge of the presence of the drugs. Kelley v. State, 555 N.E.2d 1341, 1990 Ind. App. LEXIS 809 (1990).

—Evidence.
Where defendant obtained drug from hiding place, sold half of it to police agent and placed the remainder in his pocket, he could be convicted and sentenced for the crime of possession of a controlled substance in addition to the crime of delivery of a controlled substance. Kruckeberg v. State, 268 Ind. 643, 377 N.E.2d 1351, 1978 Ind. LEXIS 722 (1978), cert. denied, 439 U.S. 990, 99 S. Ct. 590, 58 L. Ed. 2d 665, 1978 U.S. LEXIS 4050 (1978).

Constructive possession may be proved by circumstantial evidence from which the care, management and control over the item in question may be inferred. Jeffers v. State, 485 N.E.2d 81, 1985 Ind. LEXIS 1026 (1985).

Where the state showed neither that the defendant stayed in the area where cocaine was found, nor could they place any other identifying marks or possessions of the defendant with the drugs seized, and where the drugs were not found in the defendant's immediate control, it was insufficient for a

Constructive Possession. (Cont'd)

—Evidence. (Cont'd)
showing of constructive possession that the defendant was in possession of drugs in the past, and the conviction was reversed. Caruthers v. State, 698 N.E.2d 765, 1998 Ind. LEXIS 232 (1998).

Constructive possession of cocaine was sufficiently shown where the defendant possessed the key to the trunk where the drug was found, where he had been living out of the vehicle, and where his clothes were found in the trunk near the cocaine. Goliday v. State, 708 N.E.2d 4, 1999 Ind. LEXIS 163 (1999).

Conviction for possession of cocaine was supported by sufficient evidence where defendant, driving his girlfriend's car, was the only person in the car, admitted to hiding the drugs in the car, and drugs were found in 29 separate plastic bags. White v. State, 772 N.E.2d 408, 2002 Ind. LEXIS 631 (2002).

Doctrine of Completeness.
Both witnesses' statement to the police and his deposition were admissible under the doctrine of completeness, which allows a party to place the remainder of a statement or document before the jury after the opposing party has introduced a portion of that statement or document into evidence; however, the remainder of the statement or document is subject to the general rules of admissibility, and any portions found immaterial, irrelevant, or prejudicial must be redacted. Evans v. State, 643 N.E.2d 877, 1994 Ind. LEXIS 183 (1994).

Double Jeopardy.
Because delivery charge was based upon the sale of a single rock of cocaine to undercover officer, while possession charge was based upon the possession of additional rocks of cocaine, double jeopardy was not offended. Morgan v. State, 648 N.E.2d 1164, 1995 Ind. App. LEXIS 212 (1995), aff'd in part, vacated in part, 675 N.E.2d 1067, 1996 Ind. LEXIS 198 (1996).

Separate convictions for dealing and possession based upon a single sale of narcotics may be sustained, but to do so the state must make clear that only the quantity sold forms the basis of the dealing charge, while only the quantity retained after the sale forms the basis of the possession charge. If this is not made clear, proof that the defendant dealt narcotics could also form the basis for proving that the defendant first possessed narcotics, allowing a defendant to be convicted twice for possessing and dealing the same drug, which is forbidden. Johnson v. State, 659 N.E.2d 242, 1995 Ind. App. LEXIS 1657 (1995).

The defendant was not sentenced for the lesser included offense of possession of cocaine; that conviction could not stand where he was also convicted of possession with intent to deliver, since double jeopardy considerations bar separate conviction and sentencing where conviction of a greater crime cannot be had without commission of the lesser offense. O'Neal v. State, 716 N.E.2d 82, 1999 Ind. App. LEXIS 1491 (1999).

—Collateral Estoppel.
Defendant, who contended his prosecution in one county was barred by the doctrine of collateral estoppel due to his acquittal in another county on charges relating to the same drug sting operation, failed to present sufficient evidence to demonstrate that the jury in the first county had found that the police entrapped him during the entire series of drug transactions and not just those transactions which occurred in county where he was first prosecuted. Smith v. State, 670 N.E.2d 360, 1996 Ind. App. LEXIS 1090 (1996).

—Excise Taxes.
The offense of failure to pay the substance excise tax on cocaine differs from the offense of dealing in cocaine only in the respect that a less serious harm or risk of harm to the same public interest in deterrence is required to establish the commission of the excise tax offense. Therefore, the offense of failure to pay the substance excise tax on cocaine was an included offense of the dealing in cocaine under IC 35-41-1-16(3), and convictions for both offenses were precluded by IC 35-38-1-6. Collins v. State, 645 N.E.2d 1089, 1995 Ind. App. LEXIS 8 (1995), aff'd, 659 N.E.2d 509, 1995 Ind. LEXIS 202 (1995).

Because each element of the offense of delivering cocaine is encompassed by the elements of the Controlled Substance Excise Tax's (CSET's) criminal penalty, the two statutes cannot be said to punish different offenses. Rather, the delivery offense is a lesser-included offense of the CSET's criminal sanction. Collins v. State, 659 N.E.2d 509, 1995 Ind. LEXIS 202 (1995).

—Possession and Dealing.
Convictions for both dealing in cocaine and possession of cocaine did not violate double jeopardy standards where evidence was presented at trial that defendant sold and delivered cocaine to a confidential informant, and evidence was also presented that later that same day, as a result of a search warrant, there was evidence to establish that defendant possessed cocaine, evidence sufficient for the jury to conclude defendant had committed two separate crimes. Castillo v. State, 734 N.E.2d 299, 2000 Ind. App. LEXIS 1356 (2000), transfer granted, 753 N.E.2d 2, 2001 Ind. LEXIS 67 (2001), aff'd, 741 N.E.2d 1196, 2001 Ind. LEXIS 14 (Ind. 2001).

Under the double jeopardy clause of the United States Constitution, the jury's determination of guilt on the possession of cocaine charge but deadlock on the dealing charge did not preclude the state from retrying defendant for the dealing offense. Davenport v. State, 734 N.E.2d 622, 2000 Ind. App. LEXIS 1313 (2000).

Where same evidence, seized in same episode, was used to convict defendant of both cocaine possession and possession with intent to deliver, double jeopardy principles were violated, requiring reversal of cocaine possession convictions. Donnegan v. State, 809 N.E.2d 966, 2004 Ind. App. LEXIS 1101 (2004).

Convictions of possession of methamphetamine

Double Jeopardy. (Cont'd)

—Possession and Dealing. (Cont'd)
in excess of three grams with intent to deliver and manufacture of methamphetamine in excess of three grams did not violate the Ind. Const., art. 1, § 14 double jeopardy clause because the state carefully parsed the evidence at trial, relying primarily on the finished product found at the time of defendant's arrest to support the possession offense and the unfinished product found at the time of arrest to support the manufacturing offense; additionally, the state presented two separate theories of conduct in support of the possession and manufacturing offenses, and sufficiently distinguished the two offenses and provided independent evidence to support both. Storey v. State, 875 N.E.2d 243, 2007 Ind. App. LEXIS 2365 (2007).

Double jeopardy considerations barred defendant's convictions for both IC 35-48-4-1(a) cocaine dealing and IC 35-48-4-6(a) cocaine possession since conviction on the dealing charge necessarily included possession; only cocaine introduced into evidence was that found in the baggies defendant delivered to an officer and none was found on his person or in the baggie he threw while attempting to resist arrest. Harrison v. State, — N.E.2d —, 2009 Ind. App. LEXIS 346 (2009).

—Violated.
Where the state chose to allege the commission of the underlying felony, dealing in cocaine, as the requisite overt act in furtherance of the conspiracy to deal in cocaine, and the jury was instructed that in order to sustain its burden of proof on the conspiracy charge, the state must prove the agreement along with the delivery of cocaine on the five dates alleged, and with respect to the dealing charge, the state had only to prove the same five deliveries, the state was required to prove no facts to obtain the conviction for dealing in cocaine in addition to those facts it was required to prove to obtain the conviction for conspiracy. Thus, dealing in cocaine was not merely an offense that occurred in the same criminal episode as the conspiracy, it was a necessary element of the conspiracy as charged. The acts of delivery to substantiate the delivery charges were "precisely coextensive" with the overt acts alleged in support of the conspiracy charge, and the language of the instruction made it evident that the factual basis underlying the conspiracy charge was the same conduct alleged by the state to establish the delivery charges. As a result, defendant was placed in double jeopardy. Derado v. State, 622 N.E.2d 181, 1993 Ind. LEXIS 179 (1993).

Since the same cocaine supported both the dealing and possession charges, defendant's conviction of possession of cocaine was vacated. Mack v. State, 736 N.E.2d 801, 2000 Ind. App. LEXIS 1659 (2000).

The dealing in cocaine Class B felony count was vacated on double jeopardy grounds where defendant was also charged with possession of cocaine, since the imposition of concurrent sentences did not cure the double jeopardy violation. Carroll v. State, 740 N.E.2d 1225, 2000 Ind. App. LEXIS 2032 (2000).

Where same evidence used to convict defendant of manufacturing methamphetamine in excess of three grams was sole evidence used to convict defendant of possession of methamphetamine in excess of three grams, defendant's conviction and sentence on possession offense was vacated on double jeopardy grounds. Caron v. State, 824 N.E.2d 745, 2005 Ind. App. LEXIS 519 (2005).

Elements.
The state was not required to show independently that cocaine is a Schedule II substance in order to present a case for dealing in cocaine. Hall v. State, 557 N.E.2d 3, 1990 Ind. App. LEXIS 936 (1990).

Since the defendant dropped a bag containing cocaine as he fled from a police officer, the defendant at most committed only one act of possession of cocaine and could not be convicted and sentenced for both dealing in cocaine and possession of cocaine. Stephens v. State, 588 N.E.2d 564, 1992 Ind. App. LEXIS 335 (1992).

Possession constitutes a material element of the crime of dealing in cocaine and supports that conviction. Therefore, because the admissible evidence presented does not support a finding that the defendant possessed cocaine, the separate conviction for dealing cocaine cannot stand. In re J.L., 599 N.E.2d 208, 1992 Ind. App. LEXIS 1350 (1992).

In order to convict the defendant for possession of cocaine with intent to deliver, the state had to prove the defendant had knowledge of the nature of the substance and its presence. Jernigan v. State, 612 N.E.2d 609, 1993 Ind. App. LEXIS 432 (1993).

State's failure to prove that the defendant exercised any control over the premises where drugs were found warranted reversal of his conviction under this section for lack of sufficient evidence indicating personal possession over the actual drugs. Moore v. State, 613 N.E.2d 849, 1993 Ind. App. LEXIS 544 (1993).

Defendant was not denied his fundamental right to require the State to prove each element of cocaine dealing offense within 1000 feet of a school or park under IC 35-48-4-1 where: (1) a parochial kindergarten was within 1000 feet of the crime; (2) a park was within 1000 feet of the crime; (3) a city employee testified that a computer-generated calculation of the distance between the school and the park had been made; and (4) a police officer testified to physically measuring the distances. French v. State, 778 N.E.2d 816, 2002 Ind. LEXIS 891 (2002).

Entrapment.
The mere fact that in a prosecution for the unlawful sale of morphine, the purchaser was cooperating with the state and federal officials in making the purchase, did not entitle the defendant to an acquittal under the "entrapment rule." Smith v. State, 214 Ind. 169, 13 N.E.2d 562, 1938 Ind. LEXIS 159 (1938).

It was not entrapment for a state's witness by prearrangement with police to purchase codeine

Entrapment. (Cont'd)

sulphate from defendant upon offer by defendant for the purpose of obtaining evidence against defendant. Neusbaum v. State, 249 Ind. 297, 230 N.E.2d 772, 1967 Ind. LEXIS 386 (1967).

Where police gave an informer money to make a purchase of heroin and, after the purchase, a search of the defendant's apartment disclosed no other heroin, there was no evidence that the defendant had previously offered to sell heroin to the informer, and there was no evidence that he had made previous sales, such evidence was indicative of entrapment and insufficient to convict the defendant of the illegal sale. Gray v. State, 249 Ind. 629, 231 N.E.2d 793, 1967 Ind. LEXIS 400 (1967).

Where a police officer had witnessed, if not partaken in, an illegal sale of drugs made by defendant to a third person, the fact the police officer first suggested a subsequent sale to him was not entrapment as he had acquired the information which supplied probable cause during his investigation and before the transaction. Telfare v. State, 163 Ind. App. 413, 324 N.E.2d 270, 1975 Ind. App. LEXIS 1051 (1975).

There was sufficient evidence of probable cause for the state to set into operation a scheme to trap (make a controlled purchase) the defendant. Riding v. State, 265 Ind. 106, 350 N.E.2d 629, 1976 Ind. LEXIS 355 (1976).

Where informer who made the purchase of heroin testified that when he went to defendant's residence defendant asked how much he wanted and then measured the required quantity with measuring scoops and kept that which remained, there was evidence from which a reasonable person could infer that the transaction was not an isolated sale which would not have occurred without inducement and there was no entrapment. Mendez v. State, 267 Ind. 67, 367 N.E.2d 1081, 1977 Ind. LEXIS 465 (1977).

There was sufficient evidence for jury to find that there had been no entrapment where there was testimony that he was attempting to engage another person as a seller of heroin for him. Davila v. State, 172 Ind. App. 425, 360 N.E.2d 283, 1977 Ind. App. LEXIS 772 (1977).

There was no entrapment where police officer learned from informant, whom police officer had reasonable ground to believe was a reliable source, that defendant was a dealer in heroin. Henry v. State, 269 Ind. 1, 379 N.E.2d 132, 1978 Ind. LEXIS 730 (1978).

In a trial for dealing in cocaine, where defendant did not deny that the transaction took place, but raised the defense of entrapment which he contended the state failed to disprove, it was held that there was evidence that defendant was willing to take part in the transaction although he insisted he was an unwilling participant merely doing a favor for a friend; it was for the jury to decide whose version of the events to believe, and there was sufficient evidence from which the jury could have found that defendant was predisposed, i.e., had the necessary intent, to deliver cocaine. Koke v. State, 498 N.E.2d 1326, 1986 Ind. App. LEXIS 3086 (1986).

Evidence.

—Admissibility.

Where police officer was observing area from a vacant building and upon seeing what appeared to him a drug transaction, he reported the occurrence to another officer by radio who stopped the car in which defendant was riding and after asking defendant to get out of the car, defendant began fighting with the officer and after being subdued and arrested on charge of resisting arrest defendant was asked to open his left hand from which a bundle of heroin dropped to the ground, the heroin was properly admitted in evidence as against contention that heroin was obtained as result of illegal detention. Burhannon v. State, 172 Ind. App. 680, 361 N.E.2d 928, 1977 Ind. App. LEXIS 814 (1977).

Where officer who was waiting to search house in which heroin buys had been made saw defendant leave house and drive away and radioed to another officer to stop him, heroin found on him when he was stopped was properly admissible in evidence. Walker v. State, 173 Ind. App. 263, 363 N.E.2d 1026, 1977 Ind. App. LEXIS 857 (1977).

The defendant's identification as a supplier of cocaine was at issue, and the paraphernalia seized tended to show that the defendant possessed the equipment necessary to process cocaine. The paraphernalia was therefore relevant to the crime charged and was admissible even though it also tended to suggest the additional crime of possession or use. Kelley v. State, 555 N.E.2d 1341, 1990 Ind. App. LEXIS 809 (1990).

An evidentiary harpoon occurs when the prosecution places inadmissible evidence before the jury for the deliberate purpose of prejudicing the jurors against the defendant. To prevail on such a claim of error, the defendant must show that: (1) the prosecution acted deliberately to prejudice the jury; and (2) the evidence was inadmissible. Evans v. State, 643 N.E.2d 877, 1994 Ind. LEXIS 183 (1994).

A syringe was not likely to lead the jury to decide the case on improper grounds, and the state rightly introduced the evidence to support witness' claim that he was the user, not the dealer, in the transaction. Evans v. State, 643 N.E.2d 877, 1994 Ind. LEXIS 183 (1994).

Videotaped evidence of surveillance of defendant and a confederate as they consummated drug sales from porch of house provided ample circumstantial evidence that defendant possessed cocaine later found in house with intent to distribute and had conspired with other person to do so. Stokes v. State, 801 N.E.2d 1263, 2004 Ind. App. LEXIS 63 (2004).

Adequate probable cause existed for search warrant of defendant's residence that led to defendant's arrest for possession of methamphetamine; driver and passenger of van independently identified defendant as source of methamphetamine after van was stopped and found to contain methamphetamine. Soliz v. State, 832 N.E.2d 1022, 2005 Ind. App. LEXIS 1466 (2005).

Items of evidence in trial for dealing in cocaine which defendant challenged, namely, baggies, razor blade, residue, marijuana, a marijuana tray,

Evidence. (Cont'd)

—Admissibility. (Cont'd)

handguns, a "tin" holding ammunition, and a scooter, were directly relevant to the issue of intent to deliver and were therefore admissible and did not violate defendant's right to a fair trial. Eaton v. State, 889 N.E.2d 297, 2008 Ind. LEXIS 497 (2008), cert. denied, Eaton v. Indiana, 129 S. Ct. 1986, 173 L. Ed. 2d 1090, 2009 U.S. LEXIS 2987 (U.S. 2009).

—Aggregate Weight.

Where there was evidence to show that there was 10.98 grams of the powder, it was sufficient to show violation of delivering ten grams or more without showing that a quantitative test had been made. Hall v. State, 273 Ind. 425, 403 N.E.2d 1382, 1980 Ind. LEXIS 686 (1980).

This section and all those involving controlled substance dealing utilize the weight of the entire substance delivered by the dealer. This is the statutory meaning as well as the usage and meaning common in drug trafficking. Lawhorn v. State, 452 N.E.2d 915, 1983 Ind. LEXIS 927 (1983).

Evidence that the substance delivered weighed 6.617 grams and contained 35.2 percent pure cocaine, so that the pure cocaine portion of the delivered substance thus weighed approximately 2.3 grams, could support a Class A felony, 30-year sentence. Lawhorn v. State, 452 N.E.2d 915, 1983 Ind. LEXIS 927 (1983).

The Indiana Supreme Court's construction of this section that the entire weight of the substance delivered and not just of the actual drug amount, should be considered in determining the class of the crime, was guided by rational principles and did not rise to the level of discrimination or arbitrariness reviewable by a federal court in a habeas petition. Cox v. Duckworth, 620 F. Supp. 98, 1984 U.S. Dist. LEXIS 21719 (N.D. Ind. 1984).

The total weight of the delivered drug and not its pure component is to be considered in prosecutions under this section. Tobias v. State, 479 N.E.2d 508, 1985 Ind. LEXIS 863 (1985).

In light of the confidential informant's testimony, the officer's testimony was not so prejudicial as to deny defendant a fair trial, because the complained of evidence was at most cumulative, and therefore insufficient to establish prejudice. Meagher v. State, 726 N.E.2d 260, 2000 Ind. LEXIS 245 (2000).

Defendant's conviction of possession of cocaine in excess of three grams with intent to deliver under IC 35-48-4-1(b)(1) was supported by sufficient evidence, because for such a conviction the total weight of the delivered drug and not its pure component was to be considered, the total weight of the nine rocks of crack cocaine exceeded three grams, and the testing of a representative sample consisting of two rocks of cocaine was sufficient. Woodford v. State, 752 N.E.2d 1278, 2001 Ind. LEXIS 686 (2001), cert. denied, 535 U.S. 999, 122 S. Ct. 1564, 152 L. Ed. 2d 486, 2002 U.S. LEXIS 2538 (2002).

IC 35-48-4-1 does not prohibit state from charging and proving conspiracy to deal in cocaine in excess of three grams even though no single buy

involves more than three grams. Simmons v. State, 828 N.E.2d 449, 2005 Ind. App. LEXIS 948 (2005).

Evidence was sufficient to establish that defendant possessed at least three grams of cocaine during controlled buy where state laid proper foundation for testimony establishing cocaine's weight and witness established that scale used was calibrated annually and checked immediately before its use. Smith v. State, 829 N.E.2d 64, 2005 Ind. App. LEXIS 1037 (2005).

Where defendant argued that defendant's conviction of possession of cocaine weighing three grams or more with intent to deliver in violation of IC 35-48-4-1 was not supported by sufficient evidence because the state allegedly failed to meet its burden of establishing the weight of the cocaine and failed to prove that the weighing scales were calibrated before and after use, the argument failed; defendant did not object to the testimony of the drug chemist who testified as to the weight of the cocaine, defendant failed to object to the state's foundation regarding the accuracy of the scales, and the evidence showed that the weight of the cocaine was over 26 grams. Samaniego-Hernandez v. State, 839 N.E.2d 798, 2005 Ind. App. LEXIS 2450 (2005).

—Chain of Custody.

In a prosecution for the delivery of heroin, where only the most remote possibility existed that an exhibit had been tampered with, and evidence introduced by the state strongly suggested the whereabouts of the exhibit at all times, the chain of custody was sufficient to permit the introduction of the exhibit. Mendez v. State, 267 Ind. 309, 370 N.E.2d 323, 1977 Ind. LEXIS 502 (1977).

—Controlled Substances.

Heroin is a controlled substance as a matter of law and it was not necessary for the state to introduce the statute or evidence to show that heroin is a controlled substance. Mendez v. State, 267 Ind. 67, 367 N.E.2d 1081, 1977 Ind. LEXIS 465 (1977).

—Corroboration of Testimony.

The uncorroborated testimony of a narcotics agent was sufficient to support a verdict. Winfield v. State, 248 Ind. 95, 223 N.E.2d 576, 1967 Ind. LEXIS 404 (1967).

—Defendant's Use As Informant.

In a trial for dealing in cocaine and dealing in a Schedule II controlled substance, the trial court did not commit reversible error in denying defendant's motion for a mistrial based on a police officer's testimony that defendant had worked undercover for him in the past, where the prosecuting attorney asked the officer if he was able to recognize defendant's voice on a tape and among the questions asked him to substantiate his ability to recognize her voice was the question: "And has she worked as a confidential informant for the Evansville Police Narcotics Department?," to which he answered "Yes." The question and answer were simply a foundational basis to establish the officer's familiarity with defendant and the trial court

Evidence. (Cont'd)

—Defendant's Use As Informant. (Cont'd)
did not abuse its discretion. Hampton v. State, 526 N.E.2d 1154, 1988 Ind. LEXIS 233 (1988).

—Delivery.
Sufficient evidence supported defendant's conviction for dealing in cocaine where defendant bought cocaine for undercover officer from third party, and whether defendant or third party handed drugs to the officer was irrelevant. Smalley v. State, 732 N.E.2d 1231, 2000 Ind. App. LEXIS 1204 (2000).

Under the definition of "delivery" in IC 35-48-1-11, delivery under IC 35-48-4-1 does not have to be directly from the hand of a defendant; therefore, when defendant delivered cocaine to a second person, who in turn delivered it to a confidential informant, it was of no moment that defendant did not know the identity of the person to whom the second person intended to deliver and did deliver the cocaine. Reinhardt v. State, 881 N.E.2d 15, 2008 Ind. App. LEXIS 248 (2008).

Under IC 35-48-4-1, the act which is criminalized is the act of delivering cocaine; prohibition applies to the deliverer or transferor and not to the recipient and therefore the latter's identity is not an essential element of the offense; accordingly, state must prove that a delivery took place to someone but not to any particular person. Reinhardt v. State, 881 N.E.2d 15, 2008 Ind. App. LEXIS 248 (2008).

—Hearsay.
Where officer observing area from vacant building informed another officer of what appeared to be a drug transaction and such other officer made the arrest, testimony of the arresting officer as to what the officer making the observation told him was hearsay and not properly admitted, however, such admission was harmless error where the facts were proved by other legitimate evidence. Burhannon v. State, 172 Ind. App. 680, 361 N.E.2d 928, 1977 Ind. App. LEXIS 814 (1977).

Where hearsay testimony of police officer that defendant had a reputation for selling drugs to high school students and dealing in stolen property was admitted without identification as to time, place or persons involved and other evidence as to predisposition was meager, the admission of such hearsay was reversible error. Price v. State, 397 N.E.2d 1043, 1979 Ind. App. LEXIS 1483 (1979).

—Identity of Substance.
Where an officer's identification of a substance as heroin was based upon three tests, there was sufficient evidence to support a finding that the substance was heroin, although there was testimony that the result of one of the tests could have been produced by other substances, as well as heroin. Patterson v. State, 255 Ind. 22, 262 N.E.2d 520, 1970 Ind. LEXIS 446 (1970).

Circumstantial evidence was sufficient to find that substance defendant was dealing in was crack cocaine where informant, who participated in controlled buy, testified to long history of addiction to crack cocaine and positively identified substance purchased from defendant, which informant ingested following sale, as crack cocaine. Jones v. State, 807 N.E.2d 58, 2004 Ind. App. LEXIS 752 (2004).

—Inadmissible.
Search warrant was invalid, and cocaine seized in the search was inadmissible. Bryant v. State, 655 N.E.2d 103, 1995 Ind. App. LEXIS 1093 (1995).

Police violated defendant's Fifth Amendment right to counsel, requiring reversal of his convictions for possession of and manufacturing methamphetamine, when they interrogated defendant at police station after defendant asserted right to counsel during drive to station; while being driven to station, police officer mentioned that all persons involved, including defendant's wife, were going to be prosecuted, which constituted threat that led to subsequent written confession made by defendant. Storey v. State, 830 N.E.2d 1011, 2005 Ind. App. LEXIS 1270 (2005).

—Incredible Dubiosity Rule.
Items found in defendant's purse and defendant's flight provided independent evidence supporting her convictions for dealing in methamphetamine, conspiracy to deal in methamphetamine and resisting law enforcement, and existence of such evidence made incredible dubiosity rule inapplicable to defendant. Jacobs v. State, 802 N.E.2d 995, 2004 Ind. App. LEXIS 203 (2004).

—Insufficient.
Conviction for dealing in a narcotic which was based merely on the visual identification of the substance involved was reversed as being based on insufficient evidence. Copeland v. State, 430 N.E.2d 393, 1982 Ind. App. LEXIS 1048 (1982).

Where the state did not produce any evidence as to whether the scale used to weigh cocaine had been tested either before or after the drugs were weighed, and where the evidence of the weight of cocaine contained in a police lab report, which was admitted for the limited purpose of showing that the substance was cocaine, was not considered by the court, the state failed to produce sufficient evidence to support a conviction for a Class A felony. Wattley v. State, 721 N.E.2d 353, 1999 Ind. App. LEXIS 2211 (1999).

The evidence was insufficient to establish, by a preponderance, that defendant agreed with the dealer to sell cocaine, and because the crime was charged without evidence that defendant agreed with the dealer, no conspiracy was established, and the trial court abused its discretion when it allowed the dealer's hearsay statements into evidence under Evid. R. 801(d)(2)(E). Cockrell v. State, 743 N.E.2d 799, 2001 Ind. App. LEXIS 414 (2001).

Since there was no evidence indicating that defendant, who was involved in one cocaine transaction, was party to agreement concerning four other cocaine transactions, other than fact that he associated with persons involved in those transactions, defendant could not be convicted of conspiracy for dealing cocaine as Class A felony; court

Evidence. (Cont'd)

—Insufficient. (Cont'd)
rejected state's argument that because defendant agreed to deal cocaine on one occasion, inevitable and reasonable inference is that he was party to agreement to do so on four other occasions. Washington v. State, 807 N.E.2d 793, 2004 Ind. App. LEXIS 844 (2004).

Confidential informant (CI) was not searched for drugs prior to controlled drug purchase after which the defendant ended up with the money that the police provided and the CI ended up with drugs. Since the CI did not testify that he bought the drugs from the defendant, there was no direct evidence, only speculation, that the defendant delivered the drugs under IC 35-48-1-11, so there was insufficient evidence that defendant violated IC 35-48-4-1(b). Watson v. State, 839 N.E.2d 1291, 2005 Ind. App. LEXIS 2452 (2005).

Where a controlled buyer is not searched prior to the controlled buy and the controlled buyer does not testify at trial, a defendant's possession of the buy money is insufficient to sustain a conviction under IC 35-48-4-1(b). Watson v. State, 839 N.E.2d 1291, 2005 Ind. App. LEXIS 2452 (2005).

—Intermediate Stage.
Even though a batch of methamphetamine was still in process of being produced, as opposed to having been completely manufactured, the evidence was sufficient to convict defendant of manufacturing a controlled substance where the process of manufacture was well under way and the amount of methamphetamine being produced was far in excess of the statutory minimum weight. Traylor v. State, 817 N.E.2d 611, 2004 Ind. App. LEXIS 2229 (2004).

—Other Offenses.
Where defense on charge of sale of heroin was entrapment, it was not error to admit packets of heroin taken from car after defendant's arrest as against objection that such evidence imputed an additional crime, since the presence of additional heroin in the car supported the inference that defendant was willing and able to engage in the sale of heroin when the opportunity presented itself. Henry v. State, 269 Ind. 1, 379 N.E.2d 132, 1978 Ind. LEXIS 730 (1978).

In trial of defendants on charge of delivering a controlled substance it was not error to introduce evidence that they previously had attempted to obtain a prescription at a doctor's office for the same drug they were charged with delivering. Perry v. State, 181 Ind. App. 553, 393 N.E.2d 204, 1979 Ind. App. LEXIS 1279 (1979).

—Predisposition.
Where court permitted informant to testify that he had previously sold heroin for defendant to show that defendant was predisposed to commit the crime and admonished jury that any evidence of prior dealings was not proof of the crime for which defendant was charged, the admission of such testimony was not error. Hicks v. State, 272 Ind. 350, 397 N.E.2d 973, 1979 Ind. LEXIS 809 (1979).

—Prior Statements.
Where a party impeaches a witness using portions of a prior statement that is in certain respects inconsistent with the witness' testimony at trial and implies that the witness has an improper motive in testifying, the opposing party may put the inconsistencies in context for the jury by introducing the remainder of the statement under the doctrine of completeness and may introduce the same prior statement as generally consistent with the witness' testimony in order to rebut the charge of recent fabrication or improper motive or influence. Evans v. State, 643 N.E.2d 877, 1994 Ind. LEXIS 183 (1994).

—Proximity to School or Public Park.
There was no evidence in the record that the site of the cocaine delivery, which took place inside defendant's house, was contained within officer's measurement, and the state failed to present sufficient evidence from which the jury could find beyond a reasonable doubt that defendant dealt cocaine within 1,000 feet of school property. Doty v. State, 730 N.E.2d 175, 2000 Ind. App. LEXIS 900 (2000).

—Search and Seizure.
Where informant had told police officer that defendant usually carried heroin in a cigarette package and when defendant was arrested after making sale police did not find a cigarette package containing extra heroin on defendant's person, it was proper to search car in which defendant arrived and cigarette package containing heroin found therein was properly introduced in evidence. Henry v. State, 269 Ind. 1, 379 N.E.2d 132, 1978 Ind. LEXIS 730 (1978).

Where officer's determination that the item was contraband was contemporaneous with his weapons search, the warrantless seizure of the marijuana was justified. Walker v. State, 661 N.E.2d 869, 1996 Ind. App. LEXIS 170 (1996).

A closed Tylenol bottle containing crack, located beneath a vehicle's passenger seat where defendant was sitting, did not constitute contraband in plain view. Lampkins v. State, 685 N.E.2d 698, 1997 Ind. LEXIS 155 (1997).

An investigatory stop was not warranted where defendant committed no crime in the officer's presence, and the initial traffic stop was based solely on an anonymous tip. Washington v. State, 740 N.E.2d 1241, 2000 Ind. App. LEXIS 2045 (2000).

Police officers did not violate defendant's right against unreasonable search and seizure by walking drug detection dog around defendant's car while police officer wrote warning ticket for traffic offense committed by defendant, notwithstanding that defendant had parked car at his house before K-9 unit arrived; drug evidence obtained from search of car following dog's drug alert was admissible. Myers v. State, 812 N.E.2d 146, 2004 Ind. App. LEXIS 1385 (2004), transfer granted, — N.E.2d —, 2004 Ind. LEXIS 1004 (2004), superseded, 839 N.E.2d 1146, 2005 Ind. LEXIS 1135 (2005).

—State of Mind.
Where all of an informant's statements were

Evidence. (Cont'd)

—State of Mind. (Cont'd)
offered, not to prove the truth of any of the assertions contained in them, but as evidence of the effect they had upon defendant and upon his decision to participate in the drug transaction, they should have been admitted as an utterance offered to evidence the state of mind which ensued in another person as a consequence of the utterance, since such an utterance does not run afoul of the hearsay rule. Koke v. State, 498 N.E.2d 1326, 1986 Ind. App. LEXIS 3086 (1986).

—Sufficient.
In the prosecution of a physician for unlawful sale or furnishing of morphine to a person, the verdict of guilty was not unlawful because there was no proof that the sale was not authorized by a federal law, where no federal law was pointed out as authorizing the sale. Smith v. State, 214 Ind. 169, 13 N.E.2d 562, 1938 Ind. LEXIS 159 (1938).

The testimony of officers that they observed an informer go to the automobile, driven to the scene by the defendant and containing a passenger, and then gave the officers a morphine tablet he had purchased from the defendant, in addition to their finding morphine tablets in the car, was sufficient to warrant the court finding the defendant was in possession of narcotics. Pinkston v. State, 251 Ind. 306, 241 N.E.2d 138, 1968 Ind. LEXIS 574 (1968).

Where there was an insufficient quantity of the substance seized on which to conduct a chemical analysis, the identification of the substance as heroin could be established by the opinion testimony of a drug addict with a demonstrated familiarity with heroin. Locklayer v. State, 162 Ind. App. 64, 317 N.E.2d 868, 1974 Ind. App. LEXIS 799 (1974).

The testimony of a one-time addict turned police informer is sufficient evidence to sustain a conviction. Jones v. State, 166 Ind. App. 160, 334 N.E.2d 716, 1975 Ind. App. LEXIS 1336 (1975).

Evidence was sufficient to convict defendant of unlawfully dealing in heroin where the drugs were transported in a car driven by defendant, a packet of heroin was taken from the car by codefendant after conferring with defendant, and police officer after purchasing from codefendant complained to defendant that the packet might not be full and defendant stated that it was, and additional packets were found on the floor of the car in front of the driver's seat. Henry v. State, 269 Ind. 1, 379 N.E.2d 132, 1978 Ind. LEXIS 730 (1978).

Where there were sufficient facts from which trier of fact could infer that transaction was not merely an isolated sale and that the necessary predisposition to commit the offense existed evidence was sufficient to overcome defense of entrapment although only one sale was shown to have been made. Stewart v. State, 271 Ind. 169, 390 N.E.2d 1018, 1979 Ind. LEXIS 782 (1979).

Where evidence showed that one of the defendants delivered a narcotic drug to undercover police officer for which the undercover police officer paid an amount of money and other defendant agreed to sale and there was further evidence that such other defendant had been involved in passing forged prescriptions for the same drug, evidence was sufficient for conviction of delivery of a controlled substance. Perry v. State, 181 Ind. App. 553, 393 N.E.2d 204, 1979 Ind. App. LEXIS 1279 (1979).

Evidence was sufficient to convict defendant of dealing in a narcotic drug where he drove person carrying narcotic drug to informant's home, introduced person carrying drug to informant, remained there while sale was made by person carrying drug and then drove such person away from informant's home. Coker v. State, 399 N.E.2d 857, 1980 Ind. App. LEXIS 1302 (1980); Jernigan v. State, 612 N.E.2d 609, 1993 Ind. App. LEXIS 432 (1993).

Where evidence showed that police officer, after receiving information from informant, went to car in which defendant was sitting, that defendant then threw heroin on the ground and another officer testified that the amount of heroin recovered indicated it was for sale rather than personal use and there was no evidence indicating defendant used heroin, evidence was sufficient to show possession with intent to deliver. Thompson v. State, 400 N.E.2d 1151, 1980 Ind. App. LEXIS 1330 (1980).

Evidence was sufficient to rebut defendant's entrapment defense. Henrichs v. State, 455 N.E.2d 599, 1983 Ind. LEXIS 1016 (1983).

Evidence was sufficient to support a conviction for dealing in cocaine where two police officers testified to a meeting between defendant and one of the officers to sell the officer a packet later determined to be cocaine, even though defense witnesses testified that defendant was with them in another city on that date. Berkman v. State, 459 N.E.2d 44, 1984 Ind. App. LEXIS 2284 (1984).

Evidence was sufficient to support conviction. Hunt v. State, 459 N.E.2d 730, 1984 Ind. LEXIS 751 (1984); Mullins v. State, 504 N.E.2d 570, 1987 Ind. LEXIS 846 (1987).

When chemical analysis of the substance allegedly sold in violation of this section is impossible because of unavailability of the substance (for example, where it has been swallowed by the purchaser), visual identification by an officer who witnessed the transaction, together with other corroborative evidence, may be sufficient circumstantial evidence to support a conviction. Clifton v. State, 499 N.E.2d 256, 1986 Ind. LEXIS 1358 (1986); Jernigan v. State, 612 N.E.2d 609, 1993 Ind. App. LEXIS 432 (1993).

Evidence was sufficient to support conviction of dealing in cocaine. Burgos v. State, 512 N.E.2d 1101, 1987 Ind. LEXIS 1073 (1987); Elmore v. State, 657 N.E.2d 1216, 1995 Ind. LEXIS 167 (Ind. 1995).

Evidence was sufficient to support dealing convictions, where the jury could infer defendants' intent to deliver, based on circumstantial evidence of defendants' possession of 272 grams of cocaine. Enamorado v. State, 534 N.E.2d 740, 1989 Ind. LEXIS 43 (1989).

State proved every element of the offenses of dealing in cocaine, notwithstanding the facts that the state relied on the testimony of a confidential

Evidence. (Cont'd)

—Sufficient. (Cont'd)

informant, and that no cocaine was found on the person of the defendant, where there was substantial and probative evidence that defendant actively participated in both the arrangement and execution of the transaction. Johnson v. State, 659 N.E.2d 242, 1995 Ind. App. LEXIS 1657 (1995).

Because the legislature intended to use the weight of the entire substance as delivered to be considered in prosecutions, the state was not required to prove purity of the product, and evidence of delivery of packaged material weighing more than three grams was sufficient to sustain a conviction for dealing in cocaine. Riley v. State, 711 N.E.2d 489, 1999 Ind. LEXIS 306 (1999).

Evidence of identification of the defendant by an informant both at the scene of the crime and at trial was sufficient to sustain the defendant's drug convictions. Toney v. State, 715 N.E.2d 367, 1999 Ind. LEXIS 577 (1999).

There was ample evidence to support defendant's conviction where a witness clearly saw him in daylight hours, recognized him from previous contacts and gave the police an accurate description, and where a police officer confirmed that the defendant's voice was that of the individual he overheard making a drug transaction with the witness. In re Pressler, 721 N.E.2d 1245, 1999 Ind. LEXIS 1254 (1999).

Evidence including an officer's testimony clearly describing the details of a drug purchase operation and identifying defendant as the individual who sold him cocaine, and a recording of the transaction, was sufficient to support defendant's conviction for dealing in cocaine. Stroud v. State, 787 N.E.2d 430, 2003 Ind. App. LEXIS 743 (2003).

Evidence that defendant received mail at the address where drugs and a firearm were located, and defendant's testimony that he lived at the house, that the drugs were his, and that he was watching the firearm for a friend, was sufficient to establish that defendant knowingly possessed cocaine, marijuana, and the firearm found in his house. Allen v. State, 787 N.E.2d 473, 2003 Ind. App. LEXIS 753 (2003).

Evidence was sufficient to convict defendant of dealing in methamphetamine when a search of the trailer occupied by defendant revealed evidence, partially in plain view, of numerous reagents and equipment used for the manufacture of methamphetamine, there was a small amount of methamphetamine found in a "snort tube," and constructive possession of the items by defendant could be inferred when defendant was found hiding under the bed during the search, witnesses had identified the trailer as a methamphetamine lab, defendant had a recipe for making methamphetamine in his wallet, and defendant's relative had asked defendant to live in the trailer while he was gone. Floyd v. State, 791 N.E.2d 206, 2003 Ind. App. LEXIS 1208 (2003).

In prosecution for dealing in cocaine and possession of cocaine, evidence, which included defendant's continual presence in residence where cocaine was found and cocaine found on woman who had just left residence, was sufficient to prove possession and intent to deliver. Stokes v. State, 800 N.E.2d 647, 2003 Ind. App. LEXIS 2354 (2003), vacated, Strokes v. State, 2004 Ind. App. LEXIS 2 (Ind. Ct. App. Jan. 7, 2004).

Evidence was sufficient to establish defendant's constructive possession of marijuana and cocaine with intent to deliver where defendant and codefendant were shown to be only residents of premises where drugs were found and where codefendant testified at length about their joint drug business and where they kept their stash. Donnegan v. State, 809 N.E.2d 966, 2004 Ind. App. LEXIS 1101 (2004).

Evidence that defendant told police that they would find guns in a duffle bag in defendant's bedroom closet and under the mattress, that defendant had possession of the key to a Pepsi machine containing cocaine, that cocaine was found in defendant's possession, and that defendant ran from police was sufficient to support defendant's convictions for dealing in cocaine, a Class A felony, possession of cocaine and a firearm, a Class C felony, and possession of a handgun by a serious violent felon, a Class B felony. Massey v. State, 816 N.E.2d 979, 2004 Ind. App. LEXIS 2119 (2004).

Evidence that defendant's residence smelled of ether, contained red air tank which smelled of anhydrous ammonia, contained two starting fluid ether cans, contained lithium source, and that white powder residue was present on various items, when combined with evidence explaining how these ingredients and objects are used in manufacture of methamphetamine, was sufficient to support defendant's conviction for dealing in methamphetamine as class B felony. Lovell v. State, 813 N.E.2d 393, 2004 Ind. App. LEXIS 1626 (2004).

In an action charging defendant with dealing in methamphetamine as class B felony, evidence presented by state was sufficient to support inference that defendant's behavior was not consistent with that of "practitioner" within meaning of IC 35-48-18(1)(A)-(B); accordingly, it was reasonable for jury to conclude that defendant was not acting as "practitioner" and trial court properly denied defendant's motion for judgment on evidence. Lovell v. State, 813 N.E.2d 393, 2004 Ind. App. LEXIS 1626 (2004).

Where police officers found in defendant's trailer a mirror with small pipe on it, handgun, several jars, starting fluid cans with holes in them, empty salt container, coffee grinder, aspirin bottle with pseudophedrine tablets, and bottle of acetone, and defendant stated that he and his wife had been paid to "cook" methamphetamine, evidence was sufficient to convict defendant of dealing in narcotics regardless of fact that no finished methamphetamine was found in trailer. Hill v. State, 825 N.E.2d 432, 2005 Ind. App. LEXIS 601 (2005).

Where detective searched confidential informant, gave him $150, and placed electronic wire on him, and defendant twice paid another individual $50 to deliver cocaine to informant and then return

Evidence. (Cont'd)

—Sufficient. (Cont'd)
to defendant with money, there was sufficient evidence to convict defendant of two counts of aiding, inducing, or causing dealing in cocaine. Johnson v. State, 831 N.E.2d 163, 2005 Ind. App. LEXIS 1269 (2005).

Despite the slight indication of powder cocaine in the sample, the state gave reasonable assurances that the cocaine passed through the parties' hands in an undisturbed condition because: (1) before the controlled drug purchase, a deputy searched the informant who was acting as the buyer; (2) the informant was in the deputy's sight until he entered defendant's vehicle; (3) the informant entered the backseat of defendant's car and purchased the drugs; and (4) when the informant returned to the deputy, he showed the deputy the baggie of drugs; defendant simply requested that the appellate court reweigh evidence and judge the credibility of the witnesses, which it could not do. There was evidence in the record to support the assertion that defendant sold the informant over three grams of cocaine; thus, the state presented evidence of probative value from which the trial court could have found defendant guilty beyond a reasonable doubt of dealing in cocaine as a class A felony. Whaley v. State, 843 N.E.2d 1, 2006 Ind. App. LEXIS 164 (2006).

Evidence that 9.56 grams of methamphetamine was found in defendant's garage, separated into 11 packages, gave rise to a reasonable inference that defendant intended to deliver the drugs and therefore supported defendant's conviction for dealing in methamphetamine. Hirshey v. State, 852 N.E.2d 1008, 2006 Ind. App. LEXIS 1676 (2006).

Evidence was sufficient to sustain the defendant's dealing in methamphetamine conviction where there were three grams of methamphetamine and a scale present in a mobile home and the defendant and a co-conspirator had asked another person to come back later so they could "get rid of their stuff." Richardson v. State, 856 N.E.2d 1222, 2006 Ind. App. LEXIS 2376 (2006).

Conviction for possession of cocaine with intent to deliver was supported by evidence that defendant was the only person who stood between the car and the house during the incident, that grocery bag was in plain view and appeared to have been placed against the house recently, defendant was very defensive and kept insisting that he was innocent of any wrongdoing even before asked about his presence, and defendant possessed almost 100 times the amount courts have previously found sufficient to prove intent to deliver. Gault v. State, 861 N.E.2d 728, 2007 Ind. App. LEXIS 301 (2007), transfer granted, 869 N.E.2d 457, 2007 Ind. LEXIS 310 (2007), aff'd in part, superseded in part, 878 N.E.2d 1260, 2008 Ind. LEXIS 43 (2008).

Evidence was sufficient to support defendant's conviction for dealing in cocaine as a class B felony in violation of IC 35-48-4-1; defendant was found leaning over the inside of a wishing well after police officers approached a drug buy at which defendant was present, both of defendant's hands were found inside of the wishing well, a baggie containing cocaine with an amount consistent with distribution had been freshly placed there, and money was found nearby on the ground. Davis v. State, 863 N.E.2d 1218, 2007 Ind. App. LEXIS 693 (2007).

Evidence presented at trial that during a controlled buy supervised by a drug task force, a confidential informant, who had been searched by the officers and given buy money, gave defendant $240 and defendant gave the informant over four grams of cocaine in return, along with evidence that defendant called the informant from jail and discouraged informant from testifying against defendant at trial, was sufficient to support defendant's conviction. Hale v. State, 875 N.E.2d 438, 2007 Ind. App. LEXIS 2382 (2007).

Evidence that police found in defendant's truck and house was sufficient to support defendant's conviction for dealing in methamphetamine where the state presented additional evidence explaining how those ingredients and items found were commonly used to make methamphetamine; reasonable trier of fact could have concluded that defendant was in the process of manufacturing methamphetamine when defendant was arrested even if defendant had not created a finished product. Robertson v. State, 877 N.E.2d 507, 2007 Ind. App. LEXIS 2734 (2007).

Evidence was sufficient to sustain defendant's cocaine dealing conviction where it showed that he lived at a residence where a substantial amount of foot and vehicular traffic occurred and items connected to drug activity and to defendant were found inside the residence. Turner v. State, 878 N.E.2d 286, 2007 Ind. App. LEXIS 2764 (2007).

Sufficient evidence supported defendant's conviction for possession of cocaine with intent to deliver, a violation of former IC 35-48-4-1, even though defendant's possession was non-exclusive; court considered the following additional circumstances: (1) defendant made incriminating statements and mingled the cocaine with other items defendant owned; (2) defendant possessed a jacket, and the drugs were found in the jacket pocket; (3) upon defendant's arrival at a middle school, defendant indicated that he was there to recover his jacket, which his nephew had worn to school that morning; (4) defendant was very anxious and became concerned when he believed that it was taking too long to have his jacket sent to the office; (5) an officer testified that defendant behaved in an evasive and deceptive manner after being informed that cocaine had been found in the jacket pocket and he avoided eye contact with the officer, attempted to shift the blame for the cocaine possession to his 12-year-old nephew, and he lied to the officer regarding whether his nephew's mother was able to pick up the nephew from school; (6) the nephew told another officer that the cocaine was not his and admitted that the jacket belonged to defendant; (7) the bag of drugs recovered from the jacket pocket contained nine rocks of crack cocaine that were individually packaged in "baggie corners, which were a typical packaging agent for drug dealers and were a common way to transport, store, and distribute narcotics; and (8) a detective testified that he believed the packaging of the nine

Evidence. (Cont'd)

—Sufficient. (Cont'd)
rocks of crack cocaine found in the jacket was indicative of an individual who was dealing in narcotics. Washington v. State, — N.E.2d —, 2009 Ind. App. LEXIS 358 (2009).

Forfeiture.
State failed to establish its burden under IC 34-24-1-4 to show that the subject property in the forfeiture case was subject to seizure under IC 34-24-1-1(a)(2); there was a complete lack of evidence that the owner's money was connected to a drug offense pursuant to IC 35-48-4-1 et seq., as the owner's drug charge was unrelated to the events that led to the seizure of the owner's money, and there was no evidence that the owner possessed the box containing scales that was found in the car with the owner and others. Ivy v. State, 847 N.E.2d 963, 2006 Ind. App. LEXIS 866 (2006).

Identification of Defendant.
The trial court erred when it denied defendant's motion for mistrial where the detective was the only identification witness and he testified that he identified defendant after he was shown photographs of people known to deal in cocaine in the area. Mack v. State, 736 N.E.2d 801, 2000 Ind. App. LEXIS 1659 (2000).

Identification of Drug.
Where there was an insufficient quantity of the substance seized on which to conduct a chemical analysis, the identification of the substance as heroin could be established by the opinion testimony of a drug addict with a demonstrated familiarity with heroin. State v. Cooley, 162 Ind. App. 482, 319 N.E.2d 868, 1974 Ind. App. LEXIS 863 (1974).

Indictment and Information.
Where heroin was purchased on March 23 but information was not filed until November 8, there was no lack of due process in the absence of a showing of prejudice by the delay. Burress v. State, 173 Ind. App. 286, 363 N.E.2d 1036, 1977 Ind. App. LEXIS 864 (1977).

Where original information charged defendant with selling "0.315g." of heroin it was not error to permit the information to be amended to show "3.15g." of heroin since it did not change the crime or affect the penalty. Henry v. State, 269 Ind. 1, 379 N.E.2d 132, 1978 Ind. LEXIS 730 (1978).

Addition of the term "narcotic drug" or "controlled substance" to indictment for delivery of cocaine was mere surplusage, which was not detrimental to the defense. Marts v. State, 432 N.E.2d 18, 1982 Ind. LEXIS 771 (1982).

Fact that defendant did not personally deliver cocaine to a confidential informant, but to a second person who delivered the cocaine to the informant, did not create a fatal variance between the charge of dealing cocaine under IC 35-48-4-1 and the evidence; identity of the recipient was surplusage and did not mislead defendant. Reinhardt v. State, 881 N.E.2d 15, 2008 Ind. App. LEXIS 248 (2008).

—Sufficient.
The state's information, amended subsequent to defendant's motion for a more definite statement, adequately set forth the required elements where it alleged that defendant knowingly or intentionally intended to deal cocaine or a narcotic drug and that defendant agreed with an undercover officer to commit dealing, and the amended information set forth acts in furtherance of the conspiracy which included: (1) that defendant traveled to Kokomo and told the undercover officer he wanted to purchase cocaine in excess of three grams; (2) that defendant agreed to pay undercover officer a $5,000 down payment for a kilo of cocaine; (3) that defendant telephoned the undercover officer and agreed to conduct the purchase of the cocaine on June 2, 1990; and (4) that defendant and the undercover officer completed an exchange of U.S. currency for the purchase of one kilo of a substance purported to be cocaine on June 12, 1990. Grant v. State, 623 N.E.2d 1090, 1993 Ind. App. LEXIS 1388 (1993).

Intent.
A conviction for possession with intent to deliver may be sustained upon circumstantial evidence. Knowles v. State, 571 N.E.2d 1308, 1991 Ind. App. LEXIS 895 (1991).

Possession of a large quantity of cocaine is circumstantial evidence of intent to deal. Knowles v. State, 571 N.E.2d 1308, 1991 Ind. App. LEXIS 895 (1991).

—Inferences.
A quantity permitting an inference of predisposition to sell is one which could not be personally consumed or utilized and therefore of necessity available for delivery. Montego v. State, 517 N.E.2d 74, 1987 Ind. LEXIS 1202 (1987).

From evidence showing that the defendant possessed 140 grams of 98 percent pure cocaine, the jury could properly infer that he had the requisite intent to deliver. Knowles v. State, 571 N.E.2d 1308, 1991 Ind. App. LEXIS 895 (1991).

The defendant's exclusive possession of a vehicle was sufficient to raise a reasonable inference of intent, even where he was not the owner of the vehicle. Goliday v. State, 708 N.E.2d 4, 1999 Ind. LEXIS 163 (1999).

—To Deliver.
Possession of a large amount of narcotics is circumstantial evidence of intent to deliver. The probative value of quantity in proving intent increases as the quantity itself becomes greater. Montego v. State, 517 N.E.2d 74, 1987 Ind. LEXIS 1202 (1987).

Evidence was sufficient to support a reasonable inference of guilt on the element of intent to deliver, where heroin in defendant's possession was valued at $555, was in excess of three grams, and was in 37 balloons, each containing one-tenth to two-tenths of a gram. Adamov v. State, 536 N.E.2d 281, 1989 Ind. LEXIS 103 (1989).

The state must prove that defendant had the intent to deliver in order to gain a conviction of possession of cocaine with intent to deliver. Be-

Intent. (Cont'd)

—To Deliver. (Cont'd)

cause intent is a mental state, and because it is often the case that an actor does not verbally express intent, the trier of fact must usually resort to reasonable inferences based on examination of the surrounding circumstances to determine the existence of the requisite intent. Chandler v. State, 581 N.E.2d 1233, 1991 Ind. LEXIS 218 (1991).

The amount of cocaine found in the defendant's vehicle (.88 grams) was insufficient to support a reasonable inference of intent to deliver, and the defendant's conviction for dealing in cocaine should therefore be reversed. Isom v. State, 589 N.E.2d 245, 1992 Ind. App. LEXIS 795 (1992).

A total weight of 1.76 grams of cocaine was not a quantity consistent with business use, and the record was devoid of any other evidence supporting the inference that the defendant intended to deal the drugs, the evidence, as a matter of law, could not support the inference that the defendant intended to deliver the cocaine, and his conviction was reversed. Johnson v. State, 594 N.E.2d 817, 1992 Ind. App. LEXIS 1003 (1992).

Where the jury learned that appellant possessed approximately 25 grams of cocaine in various forms, and the evidence also showed that he had a handgun and nearly $6,000 in cash, a reasonable trier of fact could have concluded beyond a reasonable doubt that an individual possessing a significant amount of cocaine subdivided into small bags, a substantial sum of cash, and a gun, intended to deliver the cocaine. Hazzard v. State, 642 N.E.2d 1368, 1994 Ind. LEXIS 151 (1994).

There was sufficient evidence to support jury's conclusion defendant possessed cocaine with intent to deliver where companion testified he manufactured the cocaine and put it in baggies, had a ledger book with names of customers and their purchases and had a pager and defendant also told officer he did not make much money and never sold to kids. Stewart v. State, 688 N.E.2d 1254, 1997 Ind. LEXIS 219 (1997).

Given that the defendant was arrested during the course of a traffic stop in the middle of the night, the fact that he did not have with him the equipment to enable him to weigh crack cocaine with scientific precision was not enough to shed reasonable doubt on his intent to deal. O'Neal v. State, 716 N.E.2d 82, 1999 Ind. App. LEXIS 1491 (1999).

Evidence that defendant possessed 5.6225 grams of cocaine packed in 45 bundles, coupled with the testimony of an officer, a "skilled" witness, that said evidence indicated an intent to deliver rather than consume the substance for personal use, was sufficient to show defendant's intent to distribute and thus, to support his conviction for possession of cocaine with intent to deliver. Davis v. State, 791 N.E.2d 266, 2003 Ind. App. LEXIS 1233 (2003).

There was sufficient evidence of intent to deliver to convict defendant of dealing in cocaine under IC 35-48-4-1; defendant made multiple incriminating statements and expert testimony established that

amount of cocaine possessed by defendant, 10.07 grams, its packaging, and $351 possessed by defendant were consistent with dealing in cocaine. Dandridge v. State, 810 N.E.2d 746, 2004 Ind. App. LEXIS 1152 (2004).

Jury Instructions.

Where the state charged defendant with "knowingly" delivering cocaine, and the jury instruction used the phrase "knowingly or intentionally", if the jury acted under the "intentionally" part of the instruction, then they necessarily concluded that defendant also acted "knowingly," and the instruction did not constitute reversible error. Palmer v. State, 654 N.E.2d 844, 1995 Ind. App. LEXIS 1011 (1995).

Where there was no serious evidentiary dispute regarding the weight of the cocaine, the trial court did not err in refusing to instruct the jury on the lesser included offense of possession with intent to deliver an amount less than three grams. Norwood v. State, 670 N.E.2d 32, 1996 Ind. App. LEXIS 1017 (1996).

The second sentence of the instruction, which added the phrase, "you may infer that the defendant possessed the cocaine with the intent to deliver" was not improper because it called on the jury to perform its traditional role as the trier of fact, and sufficiently recognized the authority of the jury to make its own determination of whether defendant possessed a large amount of cocaine and had the requisite intent to deliver it. Whitney v. State, 750 N.E.2d 342, 2001 Ind. LEXIS 538 (2001).

—Unanimous Verdict.

The trial court did not instruct the jurors that they were required to render a unanimous verdict regarding which dealing crime defendant committed, and given the facts, some jurors could have believed that defendant committed the earlier dealing crime, while other jurors believed that defendant committed the dealing violation later that same day, denying defendant a unanimous verdict. Castillo v. State, 734 N.E.2d 299, 2000 Ind. App. LEXIS 1356 (2000), transfer granted, 753 N.E.2d 2, 2001 Ind. LEXIS 67 (2001), aff'd, 741 N.E.2d 1196, 2001 Ind. LEXIS 14 (Ind. 2001).

Lesser Included Offenses.

Where information charged defendant with possession of heroin "with intent to deliver" and defendant made motion for finding of not guilty after state's evidence, it was not error for court to find defendant not guilty of possession with intent to deliver but guilty of lesser included offense of possession. Clark v. State, 173 Ind. App. 295, 363 N.E.2d 1045, 1977 Ind. App. LEXIS 863 (1977).

The sale of a legend drug is not a lesser included offense of dealing in narcotics. Copeland v. State, 430 N.E.2d 393, 1982 Ind. App. LEXIS 1048 (1982).

It is factually not possible to include IC 35-48-4-5 as a lesser included offense of this section. This section requires proof that the substance delivered contains cocaine or another specified controlled

Lesser Included Offenses. (Cont'd)
substance. On the other hand, IC 35-48-4-5 requires proof that a counterfeit substance, a substance which by definition eliminates cocaine or other controlled substances, be delivered. Tomlinson v. State, 540 N.E.2d 78, 1989 Ind. App. LEXIS 486 (1989).

Where the charge of possessing a drug is a lesser-included offense of dealing in that drug, the offender cannot be convicted and sentenced on both the greater and lesser offenses. Ratcliff v. State, 578 N.E.2d 359, 1991 Ind. LEXIS 168 (1991).

Possession of cocaine is an inherently included lesser offense of dealing in cocaine. Frierson v. State, 572 N.E.2d 536, 1991 Ind. App. LEXIS 933 (1991); Reynolds/Herr v. State, 582 N.E.2d 833, 1991 Ind. App. LEXIS 2116 (1991); Abron v. State, 591 N.E.2d 634, 1992 Ind. App. LEXIS 793 (1992); Johnson v. State, 594 N.E.2d 817, 1992 Ind. App. LEXIS 1003 (1992).

Trial court did not err by refusing to give a lesser included offense instruction on possession of cocaine, where evidence adduced at trial did not create a serious evidentiary dispute regarding delivery of cocaine, since defendant's argument was directed not to the distinguishing element between dealing and possession, but rather to his participation in any crime. Sledge v. State, 677 N.E.2d 82, 1997 Ind. App. LEXIS 85 (1997).

Where the elements of visiting or maintaining a building, structure, vehicle or other place were absent from information charging dealing cocaine, neither visiting nor maintaining a common nuisance was a factually included lesser offense, and trial court properly refused tendered instructions on those offenses. Sledge v. State, 677 N.E.2d 82, 1997 Ind. App. LEXIS 85 (1997).

Possession of cocaine is not an inherently lesser-included offense of dealing in cocaine, because the possession with intent to deliver offense requires possession of an amount greater than three grams, which is not an element of the offense of dealing cocaine, and the dealing offense also requires actual delivery whereas the possession offense merely requires the intent to deliver. Carroll v. State, 740 N.E.2d 1225, 2000 Ind. App. LEXIS 2032 (2000).

Defendant was not entitled to have a conviction for possession of chemical reagents or precursors with intent to manufacture vacated as a lesser included offense to a conviction for dealing in methamphetamine, because it would not have been impossible to commit the dealing offense without first committing the possession offense. Floyd v. State, 791 N.E.2d 206, 2003 Ind. App. LEXIS 1208 (2003).

Conviction and sentences for both attempting to manufacture methamphetamine and manufacturing methamphetamine did not constitute error despite defendants contention that attempt offense was included within manufacturing offense; evidence showed that defendant had already created at least three grams of methamphetamine and was in process of creating at least three grams more. Wilhelmus v. State, 824 N.E.2d 405, 2005 Ind. App. LEXIS 433 (2005).

Where defendant was convicted of dealing in cocaine as class A felony, trial court correctly refused to enter judgment of conviction on jury's additional guilty verdict for possession of cocaine and a firearm, since latter offense, which involved same cocaine, was necessarily included in dealing offense. Kendall v. State, 825 N.E.2d 439, 2005 Ind. App. LEXIS 607 (2005), transfer granted, — N.E.2d —, 2006 Ind. LEXIS 563 (2006), aff'd in part, superseded in part, 849 N.E.2d 1109, 2006 Ind. LEXIS 551 (2006).

Defendant's felony conviction for dealing cocaine was affirmed, but his conviction for Class C felony possession of cocaine and a firearm could not stand because the Class A conviction was a greater offense, the Class C conviction was for a lesser offense, and a judgment and sentence could not be entered on the lesser offense in a case where defendant had been found guilty of the greater offense. Hardister v. State, 849 N.E.2d 563, 2006 Ind. LEXIS 552 (2006).

Counsel on direct appeal was not ineffective where the plain reading of IC 35-48-4-6(b)(1)(B) (2002) and IC 35-48-4-1 did not demonstrate that an inmate would have been entitled to immediate relief had his counsel raised the issue that possession of cocaine and a firearm was a lesser-included offense of dealing in cocaine. Brown v. State, 880 N.E.2d 1226, 2008 Ind. App. LEXIS 308 (2008).

Multiple Transactions.

Where defendant sold the same drug to the same informant on several occasions over a short period of time, presumably, the police could have set up any number of additional transactions, each time adding an additional count against defendant; while the police may find it necessary to conduct a series of buys, the trial court should be leery of sentencing a defendant to consecutive terms for each count. A sentence of 120 years was inappropriate. Gregory v. State, 644 N.E.2d 543, 1994 Ind. LEXIS 197 (1994).

Necessary Intent.

Where offense consists of a violation of statute the only intent necessary is the intent to commit the actions proscribed by the statute and where there was evidence of delivery of the narcotics would not matter that defendant may have intended to return the money to the informant. Hicks v. State, 272 Ind. 350, 397 N.E.2d 973, 1979 Ind. LEXIS 809 (1979).

Pharmacists.

There is no language in this section that prohibits the charging of a pharmacist with this offense. Tobias v. State, 479 N.E.2d 508, 1985 Ind. LEXIS 863 (1985).

Possession.

—Dominion and Control.

Defendant's intent to maintain dominion and control over cocaine was shown where cocaine was in a bottle under defendant's seat in the car, easily within his reach, and there was testimony that defendant and codefendant had gone to Atlanta to

Possession. (Cont'd)

—Dominion and Control. (Cont'd)
get some drugs a few days earlier, and the car in which defendant was riding did not stop when a police officer tried to pull it over, even though defendant was not driving. Lampkins v. State, 682 N.E.2d 1268, 1997 Ind. LEXIS 91 (1997), modified, 685 N.E.2d 698, 1997 Ind. LEXIS 155 (1997).

Possessory Interest.

—Shown.
Based upon utility bills found in a residence, which were properly admitted, a reasonable fact finder could have determined that defendant had a possessory interest in the premises, and this possessory interest, coupled with the evidence that 15 grams of cocaine, packaged in two-to-three gram packets, paraphernalia, including a triple beam scale and a cutting agent, and $1200 in cash, $450 of which was marked, were seized in common areas of the residence, was sufficient to sustain his conviction of dealing in cocaine a Class A felony. Wilson v. State, 606 N.E.2d 1314, 1993 Ind. App. LEXIS 60 (1993).

Prior Conviction.
Prior conviction for possession of less than ten grams of heroin met requirements of recidivist provision in former IC 35-24.1-4.1-1. Hutcherson v. State, 441 N.E.2d 962, 1982 Ind. LEXIS 1017 (1982).

Review on Appeal.
Inasmuch as defendant failed to adequately raise and preserve the issue of entrapment, the alleged error was waived. Thurston v. State, 169 Ind. App. 543, 349 N.E.2d 722, 1976 Ind. App. LEXIS 951 (1976).

Sale.
Even if the sale of cocaine was not a commercial transaction but merely a friendly gesture between users, it was a violation of the law which did not distinguish between "commercial" and "friendly" sales. Telfare v. State, 163 Ind. App. 413, 324 N.E.2d 270, 1975 Ind. App. LEXIS 1051 (1975).

School Property.
Since a community center building was used as a classroom site for a remedial program for students who failed to succeed in a regular education setting, a school corporation paid $1,500 rent per academic year for use of the classroom, classes were conducted for grades seven through 12, student access to other parts of the building was unrestricted and a certified teacher taught the curriculum which was consistent with the regularly scheduled classes, the building constituted school property to support an enhancement of the defendant's sentence. Bailey v. State, 603 N.E.2d 1376, 1992 Ind. App. LEXIS 1822 (1992).

—Knowledge.
State need not prove that cocaine dealer knew he dealt cocaine within 1000 feet of a school in order to convict dealer of dealing in cocaine as a

class A felony. Schnitz v. State, 666 N.E.2d 919, 1996 Ind. LEXIS 64 (1996).

Search and Seizure.
Defendant's consent to search was not constitutionally defective, and because the expressed objects of the officer's search were drugs and weapons, when defendant gave the officer permission to search his person for drugs and weapons, a reasonable person would have understood defendant's consent to include permission to search defendant's outer clothing, including his back pants pocket, which might reasonably contain those specified items. Pinkney v. State, 742 N.E.2d 956, 2001 Ind. App. LEXIS 8 (2001).
Where officers responded to residential alarm that defendant accidentally set off and officers were then given consent to look around house for officer safety and to make sure no one else was in house, officer's search of small tin, which contained cocaine, exceeded scope of defendant's consent to search, requiring suppression of evidence obtained in search. Buckley v. State, 797 N.E.2d 845, 2003 Ind. App. LEXIS 1981 (2003).

Sentence.
The sentences provided for in former IC 35-24.1-4.1-1 were not grossly out of proportion to the severity of the crimes. Hall v. State, 273 Ind. 425, 403 N.E.2d 1382, 1980 Ind. LEXIS 686 (1980).
Sentence of 30 years' imprisonment for dealing in cocaine did not constitute cruel and unusual punishment. Marts v. State, 432 N.E.2d 18, 1982 Ind. LEXIS 771 (1982).
Twenty-year term for dealing in cocaine in an amount of three grams or more is not unreasonable. Stroud v. State, 517 N.E.2d 780, 1988 Ind. LEXIS 3 (1988).
A 110-year sentence imposed on a habitual offender convicted of dealing in cocaine was not disproportionate, excessive, and cruel and unusual in violation of the Eighth Amendment and the Indiana Bill of Rights. McCollum v. State, 582 N.E.2d 804, 1991 Ind. LEXIS 246 (1991).
Even though the defendants' convictions all stemmed from possession of several controlled substances at the same place and time, since they were found guilty of violating only three statutory provisions, the trial court erred when it sentenced the defendants on all five counts charged. Everroad v. State, 570 N.E.2d 38, 1991 Ind. App. LEXIS 618 (1991), superseded, 590 N.E.2d 567, 1992 Ind. LEXIS 132 (1992).
By classifying dealing in cocaine as a Class B felony, the legislature has made the determination that dealing in cocaine is a serious offense, and by increasing the crime from a Class B felony to a Class A felony for committing the offense within 1,000 feet of a school, the legislature has determined that schoolchildren need extra protection from the adverse effects of drug trafficking; there was no constitutional infirmity in defendant's conviction, and the legislative enhancement which is entirely reasonable. Defendant's 30-year sentence was not disproportionate to either the nature or the gravity of the offense he committed. Schnitz v. State, 650 N.E.2d 717, 1995 Ind. App. LEXIS 569

Sentence. (Cont'd)

(1995), aff'd, 666 N.E.2d 919, 1996 Ind. LEXIS 64 (1996).

The court could not suspend 15 years under the possession of cocaine charge because the minimum sentence for a Class A felony is 20 years, and the court may only suspend that part of the sentence which is in excess of the minimum. Morgan v. State, 675 N.E.2d 1067, 1996 Ind. LEXIS 198 (1996), superseded by statute as stated in, Allen v. State, 722 N.E.2d 1246, 2000 Ind. App. LEXIS 12 (2000).

Trial court violated defendant's Sixth Amendment rights by imposing an enhanced sentence upon defendant's conviction of dealing methamphetamine, IC 35-48-4-1, as only two of the mitigating factors considered by the trial court were proper under the Blakely doctrine, and those aggravators were outweighed by mitigating factors. Morgan v. State, 829 N.E.2d 12, 2005 Ind. LEXIS 533 (2005).

Where defendant was sentenced to 35 years in prison after defendant was convicted of possession of cocaine weighing three grams or more with intent to deliver, a Class A felony, in violation of IC 35-48-4-1, the trial court did not err under IC 35-50-2-4 in enhancing defendant's sentence, and the sentence did not violate AP. 7(B); defendant failed to bring to the trial court's attention defendant's lack of education, defendant failed to raise at sentencing the argument that defendant's status as an illegal alien was a mitigating circumstance, and there was no basis in the record to find that the sentence was inappropriate under AP. 7(B) based on defendant's character or the nature of the offense. Samaniego-Hernandez v. State, 839 N.E.2d 798, 2005 Ind. App. LEXIS 2450 (2005).

Defendant sold an undercover police officer 970.8 grams methamphetamine; for context, pursuant to IC 35-48-4-1, delivery of only three or more grams of methamphetamine elevates dealing in methamphetamine to an A felony. That fact, taken with defendant's guilty plea and lack of felony criminal history, made the presumptive sentence for a Class B felony an appropriate sentence; thus, defendant's 10-year sentence was appropriate. Rivera v. State, 841 N.E.2d 1169, 2006 Ind. App. LEXIS 170 (2006), transfer granted and vacated, — N.E.2d —, 2006 Ind. LEXIS 670 (2006), aff'd in part, superseded in part, 851 N.E.2d 299, 2006 Ind. LEXIS 667 (2006).

Because defendant was in possession of 74.74 grams of cocaine when he was arrested, he was facing a minimum of 20 years if he did not plead guilty, and his criminal history involved offenses against persons and property; accordingly, his sentence of 15 years was not inappropriate for his convictions under IC 35-48-4-1(a)(1) and 35-48-4-7(a). Swain v. State, 870 N.E.2d 1058, 2007 Ind. App. LEXIS 1721 (2007).

While the trial court erred in finding the amount of cocaine an aggravating circumstance since defendant pled guilty to a lesser charge, it did properly find defendant's criminal history an aggravating circumstance. Swain v. State, 870 N.E.2d 1058, 2007 Ind. App. LEXIS 1721 (2007).

Given defendant's lengthy and unrelenting criminal history and the trial court's previous decision to impose the maximum sentence for his Class A felony convictions, defendant should likewise face the 20-year maximum sentence for his Class B felony convictions for dealing in cocaine and possession of cocaine. Bell v. State, 881 N.E.2d 1080, 2008 Ind. App. LEXIS 437 (2008).

Trial court did not err in sentencing defendant to 40 years imprisonment after he pleaded guilty to Class A felony dealing in cocaine, which was 10 years more than the advisory sentence, because the trial court properly declined to accord significant weight to defendant's plea; the trial court found that defendant's willingness to accept responsibility was not significant because he received a substantial benefit from the plea agreement. Sanchez v. State, 891 N.E.2d 174, 2008 Ind. App. LEXIS 1673 (2008).

Although the trial court erred in treating defendant's Level of Service Inventory-Revised score as an aggravator, it was not error to impose the advisory sentence of 30 years for dealing in cocaine as a Class A felony when the other aggravators were defendant's criminal history, his consumption of alcohol as a child, and his use of an alias in past encounters with law enforcement, and the mitigators were acceptance of responsibility, remorse, hardship on his four children, and his cooperation with police. Rhodes v. State, 896 N.E.2d 1193, 2008 Ind. App. LEXIS 2545 (2008).

Imposing the advisory sentence of 30 years for dealing in cocaine as a Class A felony was not inappropriate when defendant admitted to possessing almost 60 grams of cocaine with the intent to sell it; defendant had a criminal history that included possession of cocaine; defendant had used an alias in past encounters with police; defendant was cooperative with police and admitted that the drugs were his; defendant pleaded guilty in exchange for the dismissal of two other charges; and defendant had children. Rhodes v. State, 896 N.E.2d 1193, 2008 Ind. App. LEXIS 2545 (2008).

—Aggravating Circumstances.

Where the sentencing court identified five aggravating circumstances that were improper and no valid aggravators, the imposition of the enhanced sentence was not justified. Stone v. State, 727 N.E.2d 33, 2000 Ind. App. LEXIS 565 (2000).

Trial court did not abuse its discretion in considering and balancing aggravating and mitigating circumstances in sentencing defendant to 15 years imprisonment with five years suspended for dealing methamphetamine where defendant helped his drug supplier and an accomplice assemble methamphetamine lab in his girlfriend's trailer, which included placing tank of anhydrous ammonia directly underneath children's bedroom. Glass v. State, 801 N.E.2d 204, 2004 Ind. App. LEXIS 9 (2004).

—Aggravating Factors.

Whether the imposition of a reduced or suspended sentence would depreciate the seriousness of the crime is a factor which may be used as an aggravator only when the trial court is considering imposing a sentence of shorter duration than the

Sentence. (Cont'd)

—Aggravating Factors. (Cont'd)

presumptive sentence. Lee v. State, 689 N.E.2d 435, 1997 Ind. LEXIS 224 (1997).

Aggravating factors considered by the trial judge supported enhancement of the presumptive sentence where defendant had a history of criminal and delinquent acts, crime occurred after defendant was arrested and had agreed to plead guilty to another Class A felony and the chances of defendant committing another crime were great. Lee v. State, 689 N.E.2d 435, 1997 Ind. LEXIS 224 (1997).

Because dealing in three grams or more of cocaine is an element of the offense of Class A dealing in cocaine, the trial court could not approve a plea agreement and then circumvent it by sentencing the defendant using the amount of cocaine in defendant's possession as an aggravator. Carlson v. State, 716 N.E.2d 469, 1999 Ind. App. LEXIS 1468 (1999).

Since the trial court was not obligated to accept a plea agreement by which the defendant pled guilty to an included offense in the Class A offense of dealing in cocaine, it could not circumvent the agreement by sentencing the defendant using the distinguishing element of that offense as an aggravator. Carlson v. State, 716 N.E.2d 469, 1999 Ind. App. LEXIS 1468 (1999).

Sentence of 45 years for possession of methamphetamine in excess of three grams with intent to deliver was proper despite possible error in considering amount of methamphetamine seized as sentence aggravator since other aggravators justified enhanced sentence. Soliz v. State, 832 N.E.2d 1022, 2005 Ind. App. LEXIS 1466 (2005).

Although the trial court improperly found one aggravator, since there were four remaining aggravators, defendant's sentence of 50 years with five years suspended for conspiracy to deal in cocaine was proper. The sentence was not inappropriate in light of the nature of his crime and his character. Vazquez v. State, 839 N.E.2d 1229, 2005 Ind. App. LEXIS 2454 (2005).

As the risks methamphetamine and its manufacture pose to the general public have been factored into the crime of dealing in methamphetamine, in violation of IC 35-48-4-1, and there was no evidence that defendant's crime posed a greater risk to the public than any other manufacturing operation would, the court could not use the "lessor sentence would depreciate the seriousness of the crime" aggravator when it imposed the presumptive sentence. However, that defendant's three-year-old son lived in the house where the drug was being manufactured did support the trial court's consideration of that aggravator in refusing to reduce or suspend the presumptive sentence under former IC 35-50-2-4. Burgess v. State, 854 N.E.2d 35, 2006 Ind. App. LEXIS 1890 (2006).

Defendant was convicted of dealing in methamphetamine, in violation of IC 35-48-4-1(a)(1), (b)(3). Despite defendant's lack of prior convictions, the trial court, in imposing the presumptive 30-year sentence, properly found as an aggravator that he was at risk to reoffend, because it found he was an addict who would do anything to obtain the drug.

Burgess v. State, 854 N.E.2d 35, 2006 Ind. App. LEXIS 1890 (2006).

Under defendant's plea bargain, the state had agreed to cap his sentence for dealing in methamphetamine, in violation of IC 35-48-4-1, at the presumptive range. Therefore, the trial court, pursuant to former IC 35-50-2-4, properly considered as an aggravator the fact that a lesser sentence would depreciate the seriousness of the crime, since it was deciding whether to reduce, not enhance, the presumptive sentence. Burgess v. State, 854 N.E.2d 35, 2006 Ind. App. LEXIS 1890 (2006).

Defendant's 50-year sentence for Class A felony under IC 35-48-4-1 was appropriate given defendant's extensive criminal history, which included 26 misdemeanors and four felonies, and fact that defendant was on parole from earlier cocaine conviction when arrested. Hale v. State, 875 N.E.2d 438, 2007 Ind. App. LEXIS 2382 (2007).

Trial court properly sentenced defendant to 40 years imprisonment after he pleaded guilty to Class A felony dealing in cocaine, which was 10 years more than the advisory sentence, because defendant's illegal alien status was a valid aggravator; the trial court found that defendant's status as an illegal alien reflected disregard for the law. Sanchez v. State, 891 N.E.2d 174, 2008 Ind. App. LEXIS 1673 (2008).

Defendant's 18-year sentence for violating IC 35-48-4-1 was not inappropriate, under AP. 7(B), given defendant's character: (1) defendant's criminal history included prior convictions of dealing in cocaine, furnishing alcohol to a minor, and operating while suspended; (2) defendant had a Class C felony battery charge pending against him at the time of sentencing for the instant matter; and (3) defendant admitted his previous association with a criminal organization; although defendant's love for and interaction with his daughters was to be admired, his character also indicated a disregard for the health and safety of the children around him, which was exhibited by his leaving drugs in a location accessible to children. Washington v. State, — N.E.2d —, 2009 Ind. App. LEXIS 358 (2009).

—Consecutive Sentences.

Imposition of consecutive sentences for three counts of dealing cocaine was not manifestly unreasonable, where the sales spanned a period of almost two months, defendant was sentenced according to a plea agreement, and he was not sentenced to the maximum term under the agreement. Pritscher v. State, 675 N.E.2d 727, 1996 Ind. App. LEXIS 1739 (1996).

—Excessive.

In light of the nature of the offense and the character of the offender, the maximum sentence allowed by law for dealing in cocaine as a Class A felony was clearly unreasonable; the 50-year sentence was vacated and the presumptive sentence of 30 years was imposed. Evans v. State, 725 N.E.2d 850, 2000 Ind. LEXIS 233 (2000).

—Legislative Intent.

Purveyors of cocaine and illegal narcotic drugs are a menace to society, and the legislature has

Sentence. (Cont'd)

—Legislative Intent. (Cont'd)
determined that the crime of knowingly or intentionally delivering cocaine weighing three grams or more is so reprehensible that it warrants sentencing as a Class A felony. Evans v. State, 725 N.E.2d 850, 2000 Ind. LEXIS 233 (2000).

—Presumptive Sentence.
Because the trial court found no significant aggravating or mitigating circumstances, the imposition of presumptive sentences for each guilty offense was appropriate. Meagher v. State, 726 N.E.2d 260, 2000 Ind. LEXIS 245 (2000).

—Reasonable.
Defendant's 18-year sentence for violating IC 35-48-4-1 was not inappropriate, under AP. 7(B), given the nature of the offense, where defendant (1) placed 2.10 grams of crack cocaine divided into nine separate rocks, packaged for sale, in the pocket of a jacket that he left accessible to his emotionally disabled 12-year-old nephew; (2) the nephew, seemingly unaware of the drugs in the jacket pocket, wore the jacket to school; (3) defendant went to the school to retrieve the jacket, at which time the drugs were discovered; (4) when questioned about the crack cocaine, defendant exhibited evasive and deceptive behavior; and (5) he lied to police and tried to shift the blame for the drugs to his nephew. Washington v. State, — N.E.2d —, 2009 Ind. App. LEXIS 358 (2009).

Defendant's 12-year sentence for conspiracy to deal in cocaine under IC 35-48-4-1 and IC 35-41-5-2 was proper as defendant was the ringleader in an operation, using couriers to lessen the time in which the illicit drugs were in defendant's possession, and defendant was on probation at the time of the offense due to a prior possession of marijuana conviction. Vaughen v. State, — N.E.2d —, 2009 Ind. App. LEXIS 875 (2009).

—Unreasonable.
The jury could have reasonably inferred defendant's intent to deal crack cocaine from his possession of several hundred dollars and 11.3 grams of the drug with no means to ingest it. Love v. State, 741 N.E.2d 789, 2001 Ind. App. LEXIS 6 (2001).

Trial court erred in enhancing by 15 years defendant's sentence for possession of methamphetamine in excess of three grams with intent to deliver; mitigating factors, namely defendant's age of 20 and lack of criminal record, outweighed aggravating factors, namely that defendant had other drugs on his person, gave false testimony about his involvement, and failed to appear at trial. Merlington v. State, 814 N.E.2d 269, 2004 Ind. LEXIS 782 (2004).

Intent to possess cocaine does not make a conspiracy conviction a substance offense; thus, defendant's conviction for conspiracy to commit possession of cocaine was not a substance offense, and the evidence was insufficient to sustain defendant's status as an habitual substance offender. Therefore, the trial court was directed to vacate the habitual substance offender enhancement that was attached to Count I, dealing in cocaine as a class A felony. Whaley v. State, 843 N.E.2d 1, 2006 Ind. App. LEXIS 164 (2006).

Use of Military Personnel.
The federal Posse Comitatus Act does not prohibit the use of military personnel acting as undercover agents to assist local police. Hall v. State, 557 N.E.2d 3, 1990 Ind. App. LEXIS 936 (1990).

Venue.
Sufficient evidence established that Hamilton county was proper venue for prosecution of defendant dealing in narcotic drugs; although defendant actually delivered drugs in Marion county, defendant offered his services in Hamilton county, procured help of another drug dealer in Hamilton county, and collected money to buy drugs while in Hamilton county. Smith v. State, 835 N.E.2d 1072, 2005 Ind. App. LEXIS 1983 (2005).

Voluntary Statements of Witness.
The trial court did not err in denying two motions of defendant for mistrial based upon voluntary statements made by a police officer on cross-examination by defendant where, in each instance the court sustained defendant's motion to strike the statement and admonished the jury to disregard it. Duke v. State, 249 Ind. 466, 233 N.E.2d 159, 1968 Ind. LEXIS 731 (1968).

Cited:
Thomas v. State, 428 N.E.2d 231, 1981 Ind. LEXIS 917 (1981); Downer v. State, 429 N.E.2d 953, 1982 Ind. LEXIS 718 (1982); Ryan v. State, 431 N.E.2d 115, 1982 Ind. LEXIS 747 (1982); Crowdus v. State, 431 N.E.2d 796, 1982 Ind. LEXIS 760 (1982); Collins v. State, 431 N.E.2d 802, 1982 Ind. LEXIS 758 (1982); Watkins v. State, 436 N.E.2d 83, 1982 Ind. LEXIS 839 (1982); Powers v. State, 440 N.E.2d 1096, 1982 Ind. LEXIS 988 (1982); Pineiro v. State, 434 N.E.2d 135, 1982 Ind. App. LEXIS 1169 (1982); Huff v. State, 443 N.E.2d 1234, 1983 Ind. App. LEXIS 2507 (1983); Martinez v. State, 451 N.E.2d 39, 1983 Ind. LEXIS 888 (1983); Moore v. State, 471 N.E.2d 684, 1984 Ind. LEXIS 1062 (1984); Murray v. State, 479 N.E.2d 1283, 1985 Ind. LEXIS 869 (1985); Riley v. State, 489 N.E.2d 58, 1986 Ind. LEXIS 1023 (1986); Morales v. State, 492 N.E.2d 334, 1986 Ind. App. LEXIS 2574 (1986); Clark v. Munster, — F. Supp. —, 115 F.R.D. 609, 1987 U.S. Dist. LEXIS 12885 (N.D. Ind. 1987); Williams v. State, 529 N.E.2d 323, 1988 Ind. LEXIS 299 (1988); Majors v. State, 568 N.E.2d 1065, 1991 Ind. App. LEXIS 435 (1991); McDandal v. State, 615 N.E.2d 430, 1993 Ind. LEXIS 83 (1993); Esquerdo v. State, 640 N.E.2d 1023, 1994 Ind. LEXIS 126 (1994); Lycan v. State, 671 N.E.2d 447, 1996 Ind. App. LEXIS 1262 (1996); McGowan v. State, 671 N.E.2d 872, 1996 Ind. App. LEXIS 1271 (1996); Hazzard v. State, 694 N.E.2d 283, 1998 Ind. LEXIS 56 (1998); Lee v. State, 694 N.E.2d 719, 1998 Ind. LEXIS 53 (1998); Price v. State, 725 N.E.2d 82, 2000 Ind. LEXIS 208 (2000); Crouse v. Indiana Dep't of State Revenue, — N.E.2d —, 2000 Ind. Tax LEXIS 50 (2000); Graham v. State, 738 N.E.2d 1096, 2000 Ind. App. LEXIS 1982 (2000); Huffines v. State, 739 N.E.2d

1093, 2000 Ind. App. LEXIS 2057 (2000); Mitchell v. State, 745 N.E.2d 775, 2001 Ind. LEXIS 300 (2001); Martin v. State, 748 N.E.2d 428, 2001 Ind. App. LEXIS 891 (2001); Caudle v. State, 749 N.E.2d 616, 2001 Ind. App. LEXIS 898 (2001); Fuller v. State, 752 N.E.2d 235, 2001 Ind. App. LEXIS 1290 (2001); Ashley v. State, 757 N.E.2d 1037, 2001 Ind. App. LEXIS 1864 (2001); Bunch v. State, 760 N.E.2d 1163, 2002 Ind. App. LEXIS 22 (2002); Wertz v. State, 771 N.E.2d 677, 2002 Ind. App. LEXIS 1129 (2002); Smith v. State, 780 N.E.2d 1214, 2003 Ind. App. LEXIS 13 (2003); O'Connor v. State, 789 N.E.2d 504, 2003 Ind. App. LEXIS 908 (2003); Kelley v. State, 825 N.E.2d 420, 2005 Ind. App. LEXIS 599 (2005); Seals v. State, 846 N.E.2d 1070, 2006 Ind. App. LEXIS 826 (2006); Baird v. State, 854 N.E.2d 398, 2006 Ind. App. LEXIS 1951 (2006); Tyson v. State, 868 N.E.2d 855, 2007 Ind. App. LEXIS 1322 (2007).

RESEARCH REFERENCES

Indiana Law Review.

Recent Developments In Indiana Criminal Law and Procedure: Case Developments in 1995, 29 Ind. L. Rev. 860 (1996).

Taxation: Developments in Indiana Taxation, 34 Ind. L. Rev. 1003 (2001).

Collateral References.

Admissibility, in criminal prosecution, of expert opinion allegedly stating whether drugs were possessed with intent to distribute — state cases. 83 A.L.R.4th 629.

Defense of necessity, duress, or coercion in prosecution for violation of state narcotics laws. 1 A.L.R.5th 938.

Sufficiency of evidence that possessor of cocaine had intent to distribute it, so as to violate 21 U.S.C.S. § 841(a)(1). 80 A.L.R. Fed. 397.

When may offender found guilty of multiple crimes under Comprehensive Drug Abuse Prevention and Control Act of 1970 (21 U.S.C.S. §§ 841-851) be punished for only one offense. 80 A.L.R. Fed. 794.

Admissibility of expert evidence concerning meaning of narcotics code language in federal prosecution for narcotics dealing — modern cases. 104 A.L.R. Fed. 230.

Validity, construction, and application of state statutes prohibiting sale or possession of controlled substances within specified distance of schools. 27 A.L.R.5th 593.

35-48-4-1.1. Dealing in methamphetamine.

(a) A person who:
  (1) knowingly or intentionally:
    (A) manufactures;
    (B) finances the manufacture of;
    (C) delivers; or
    (D) finances the delivery of;
methamphetamine, pure or adulterated; or
  (2) possesses, with intent to:
    (A) manufacture;
    (B) finance the manufacture of;
    (C) deliver; or
    (D) finance the delivery of;
methamphetamine, pure or adulterated;
commits dealing in methamphetamine, a Class B felony, except as provided in subsection (b).

(b) The offense is a Class A felony if:
  (1) the amount of the drug involved weighs three (3) grams or more;
  (2) the person:
    (A) delivered; or
    (B) financed the delivery of;
the drug to a person under eighteen (18) years of age at least three (3) years junior to the person; or
  (3) the person manufactured, delivered, or financed the delivery of the drug:
    (A) on a school bus; or
    (B) in, on, or within one thousand (1,000) feet of:
      (i) school property;
      (ii) a public park;
      (iii) a family housing complex; or
      (iv) a youth program center.

History.
P.L.151-2006, § 23.

Cross References.
Penalties for felonies, IC 35-50-1, IC 35-50-2, IC 35-50-5-2.

NOTES TO DECISIONS

ANALYSIS

Constitutionality.
Double Jeopardy.
Jury Instructions.
Lesser Included Offense.
Sentence.
Sufficiency of Evidence.

Constitutionality.
IC 35-48-4-1.1 adequately advises the public of the proscribed conduct, namely, possessing methamphetamine with the intent to manufacture methamphetamine; IC 35-48-4-1.1 is therefore not unconstitutionally vague. Micheau v. State, 893 N.E.2d 1053, 2008 Ind. App. LEXIS 2029 (2008).

Double Jeopardy.
Defendant's convictions for Count I (IC 35-48-4-1.1) and Count IV (IC 35-48-4-11) did not violate Ind. Const., art. 1, § 14, Indiana's Double Jeopardy Clause because the state distinguished and set forth independent evidence of dealing in methamphetamine as a Class B felony (Count I) and possession of marijuana as a Class A misdemeanor (Count VI); therefore, there was no error in imposing a sentence on each count under IC 35-38-1-6. Micheau v. State, 893 N.E.2d 1053, 2008 Ind. App. LEXIS 2029 (2008).

Jury Instructions.
In defendant's prosecution on a charge of dealing in methamphetamine based on a theory that defendant assisted another individual in the manufacture of methamphetamine, the trial court did not err in giving an accomplice liability instruction as the instruction did not highlight particular evidentiary facts offered to establish the elements of dealing in methamphetamine; instead, it merely informed the jury that factors such as presence and acquiescence were proper matters for consideration in determining accomplice liability; and instruction did not mislead the jury as to the applicable law nor did it invade the province of the jury to determine whether the elements of the charged crimes had been established. Fowler v. State, — N.E.2d —, 2009 Ind. App. LEXIS 121 (2009).

Lesser Included Offense.
Sentence on Count II for possession of methamphetamine as a Class D felony (IC 35-48-4-6.1) had to be vacated because Count II was a lesser included offense of Count I for dealing in methamphetamine (IC 35-48-4-1.1). Micheau v. State, 893 N.E.2d 1053, 2008 Ind. App. LEXIS 2029 (2008).

Sentence.
Twenty-year sentence for violating IC 35-48-4-1.1 was not inappropriate given the nature of the offense; defendant agreed to create methamphetamine with others, he offered his knowledge of producing methamphetamine by agreeing to serve as the "cook," he used his truck to bring the necessary ingredients to the residence, proceeded to process the methamphetamine in the barn, and directed others as to how to help him make the drug. Gregory v. State, 885 N.E.2d 697, 2008 Ind. App. LEXIS 1149 (2008).

Twenty-year sentence for violating IC 35-48-4-1.1 was not inappropriate given defendant's character; defendant had a criminal history, including convictions for driving while under the influence, possession of drug paraphernalia, theft, and illegal possession of chemical for manufacture. Gregory v. State, 885 N.E.2d 697, 2008 Ind. App. LEXIS 1149 (2008).

Convictions for Count I, dealing in methamphetamine as a Class B felony (IC 35-48-4-1.1), and Count VI, attempted dealing in methamphetamine as a Class A felony (IC 35-48-4-1.1 and IC 35-41-5-1), did not violate the Proportionality Clause of the Indiana Constitution. Micheau v. State, 893 N.E.2d 1053, 2008 Ind. App. LEXIS 2029 (2008).

Sufficiency of Evidence.
There was sufficient other circumstantial and direct evidence to support a conviction for violating IC 35-48-4-1.1, so there was no reason to apply the incredible dubiosity rule to an accomplice's testimony; discrepancies between his trial testimony and earlier statements made to the police and in depositions did not render his testimony incredibly dubious since there was no showing that his testimony was inherently improbable, equivocal, or wholly uncorroborated. Gregory v. State, 885 N.E.2d 697, 2008 Ind. App. LEXIS 1149 (2008).

There was sufficient evidence to support a conviction for violating IC 35-48-4-1.1, which evidence included store surveillance video and store receipts showing that defendant bought paper towels and batteries used in methamphetamine lab. Gregory v. State, 885 N.E.2d 697, 2008 Ind. App. LEXIS 1149 (2008).

Although the charging information cited IC 35-48-4-1.1(a)(2) instead of IC 35-48-4-1.1(a)(1), the allegation in the charging information related to the latter, and It was the allegation in the body of the information that defined the crime and not the cited statute. Micheau v. State, 893 N.E.2d 1053, 2008 Ind. App. LEXIS 2029 (2008).

Because the evidence permitted a reasonable conclusion that two independent offenses were committed for which defendant could have been separately punished, an attempt charge was not a lesser included offense of a dealing in methamphetamine charge; evidence of numerous items commonly used in the production of methamphetamine and .48 grams of methamphetamine were found in defendant's residence supported a convic-

Sufficiency of Evidence. (Cont'd)

tion under IC 35-48-4-1.1 for dealing in methamphetamine as a Class B felony and evidence that the police found 12.96 grams of ephedrine and pseudoephedrine that could yield at least three grams of methamphetamine supported the conviction under IC 35-48-4-11 for attempted dealing in methamphetamine as a Class A felony. Micheau v. State, 893 N.E.2d 1053, 2008 Ind. App. LEXIS 2029 (2008).

Defendant's conviction for dealing in methamphetamine was supported by evidence showing that methamphetamine precursors and paraphernalia were found in virtually every room of defendant's house, that defendant had carried at least some of the items into the house, and that methamphetamine residue was found on a plate in the kitchen. Fowler v. State, — N.E.2d —, 2009 Ind. App. LEXIS 121 (2009).

Sufficient evidence supported a conviction for violating IC 35-48-4-1.1(a)(2)(C), (b)(1): (1) admission of defendant's cell phone text messages was harmless error; (2) the conviction was supported by substantial independent evidence of guilt such that there was no substantial likelihood that the questioned evidence contributed to the conviction; (3) the trooper testified that defendant possessed approximately 33 doses of methamphetamine at the time of his arrest; (4) the methamphetamine was packaged in nine plastic bags; and (5) defendant had a large amount of cash in his possession and two cellular telephones. Hape v. State, 903 N.E.2d 977, 2009 Ind. App. LEXIS 637 (2009).

While a trial court improperly permitted a trooper, as an Evid. R. 701 skilled witness, to testify about the physiological effect of a particular amount of the drug upon an individual, it was perfectly acceptable for the trooper to testify about a typical dose amount of methamphetamine and how much methamphetamine is typically packaged in a baggie; defendant's conviction for possession of methamphetamine with the intent to deal (a violation of IC 35-48-4-1.1(a)(2)(C), (b)(1)) was supported by substantial independent evidence of guilt, and this error was therefore harmless. Hape v. State, 903 N.E.2d 977, 2009 Ind. App. LEXIS 637 (2009).

35-48-4-2. Dealing in a schedule I, II, or III controlled substance.

(a) A person who:
  (1) knowingly or intentionally:
    (A) manufactures;
    (B) finances the manufacture of;
    (C) delivers; or
    (D) finances the delivery of;
a controlled substance, pure or adulterated, classified in schedule I, II, or III, except marijuana, hash oil, or hashish; or
  (2) possesses, with intent to:
    (A) manufacture;
    (B) finance the manufacture of;
    (C) deliver; or
    (D) finance the delivery of;
a controlled substance, pure or adulterated, classified in schedule I, II, or III, except marijuana, hash oil, or hashish;
commits dealing in a schedule I, II, or III controlled substance, a Class B felony, except as provided in subsection (b).

(b) The offense is a Class A felony if:
  (1) the person:
    (A) delivered; or
    (B) financed the delivery of;
the substance to a person under eighteen (18) years of age at least three (3) years junior to the person; or
  (2) the person delivered or financed the delivery of the substance:
    (A) on a school bus; or
    (B) in, on, or within one thousand (1,000) feet of:
      (i) school property;
      (ii) a public park;
      (iii) a family housing complex; or
      (iv) a youth program center.

History.
IC 35-48-4-2, as added by Acts 1976, P.L.148, § 7; 1977, P.L.340, § 97; 1979, P.L.303, § 9; P.L.296-1987, § 6; P.L.165-1990, § 4; P.L.296-1995, § 4; P.L.65-1996, § 12; P.L.17-2001, § 20.

Cross References.
Penalties for felonies, IC 35-50-1, IC 35-50-2, IC 35-50-5-2.

NOTES TO DECISIONS

ANALYSIS

Constitutionality.
Accessories.
Amount.
Corpus Delicti.
Dealing.
Double Jeopardy.
Elements.
Evidence.
—Chain of Custody.
—Defendant's Use as Informant.
—Entrapment.
—Insufficient.
—Other Offenses.
—Probable Cause.
—Sufficient.
Former Personal Use Exception.
Informants.
—Perjury.
Intent.
—Inferred from Possession.
Manufacturing and Dealing Distinguished.
Manufacturing Process.
Multiple Offenses.
Possession of Precursors with Intent to Manufacture.
Review on Appeal.
Sale of Controlled Substance.
School Premises.
Search and Seizure.
Sentence.

Constitutionality.
The Indiana Controlled Substance Act as it relates to Psilocybin and Psilocyn is not unconstitutionally vague; Indiana's statutory scheme gives persons of ordinary intelligence fair warning of the prohibited conduct and does not encourage arbitrary or discriminatory enforcement; thus, the statutes are not unconstitutionally vague, either on their face or as applied to defendant. Bemis v. State, 652 N.E.2d 89, 1995 Ind. App. LEXIS 719 (1995).

Accessories.
Although defendant did not participate in the sale negotiations and was not seen to receive any of the money for the purchase, where he was present during the negotiations, drove the person actually making the sale to the place where the heroin was obtained, and was present in the house when the heroin was delivered to the police officer, evidence was sufficient for a conviction. Gilliam v. State, 270 Ind. 71, 383 N.E.2d 297, 1978 Ind. LEXIS 841 (1978).

Amount.
The presence of any identifiable amount of a controlled substance is sufficient to sustain a con-

viction. Schwartz v. State, 177 Ind. App. 258, 379 N.E.2d 480, 1978 Ind. App. LEXIS 988 (1978).

Corpus Delicti.
For the preliminary purpose of determining whether a confession is admissible, the state must present evidence independent of the confession establishing that the specific crime charged was committed by someone, which may be shown by circumstantial evidence. On the other hand, in order to sustain a conviction, the corpus delicti must be proved beyond a reasonable doubt. In determining the sufficiency of the evidence for conviction, the confession may be considered along with the independent evidence. Harkrader v. State, 553 N.E.2d 1231, 1990 Ind. App. LEXIS 577 (1990).

Dealing.
The term "dealing" as it appeared in former IC 35-47-5-4 (see now IC 35-47-5-4.1, dealing in sawed-off shotguns) was obviously used in the broad sense of a course of conduct as opposed to the limited sense in which it is used in other statutes, such as those which define the offense of dealing in controlled substances. Brook v. State, 448 N.E.2d 1249, 1983 Ind. App. LEXIS 2943 (1983).

Double Jeopardy.
Where possession and delivery counts stemmed from the same factual basis, and only one delivery took place, the possession charge was only a lesser included offense of the sale charge. Cyrus v. State, 269 Ind. 461, 381 N.E.2d 472, 1978 Ind. LEXIS 800 (1978), cert. denied, 441 U.S. 935, 99 S. Ct. 2058, 60 L. Ed. 2d 664, 1979 U.S. LEXIS 1758 (1979).

Where defendant retained a residue of a substance after a delivery transaction, possession of the controlled substance was not a lesser included offense of the delivery offense. Bates v. State, 178 Ind. App. 153, 381 N.E.2d 552, 1978 Ind. App. LEXIS 1074 (1978).

Where the trial court "merged" the sentence imposed for possession with the sentence imposed for dealing, the procedure was inappropriate, as conviction and sentencing on both the greater and lesser included offenses violated double jeopardy principles. Mason v. State, 532 N.E.2d 1169, 1989 Ind. LEXIS 15 (1989), cert. denied, 490 U.S. 1049, 109 S. Ct. 1960, 104 L. Ed. 2d 428, 1989 U.S. LEXIS 2202 (1989).

Circumstantial evidence of possession with intent to deliver is sufficient to support a conviction. Mason v. State, 532 N.E.2d 1169, 1989 Ind. LEXIS 15 (1989), cert. denied, 490 U.S. 1049, 109 S. Ct. 1960, 104 L. Ed. 2d 428, 1989 U.S. LEXIS 2202 (1989).

The offenses of dealing by manufacturing and

Double Jeopardy. (Cont'd)
dealing by possession with the intent to deliver were intended by the legislature to be distinct crimes for which cumulative punishment may be imposed. The imposition of consecutive sentences on the two counts therefore did not violate the double jeopardy clause of the federal Constitution. Bigler v. State, 602 N.E.2d 509, 1992 Ind. App. LEXIS 1575 (1992).

While the crime of possession of a controlled substance may always be committed once the crime of manufacturing by processing or production is complete and the chemicals are synthesized into a controlled substance, it is not true that the offense of possession with the intent to deliver is necessarily established by the same proof. In this case, the defendant harbored two distinct criminal intents: to knowingly or purposefully manufacture, and then to deliver the substance he had manufactured. The state's proof established that the defendant was both a manufacturer and a retailer. The Indiana legislature has criminalized both forms of dealing. Bigler v. State, 602 N.E.2d 509, 1992 Ind. App. LEXIS 1575 (1992).

Because no distinction whatsoever as to which LSD defendant was accused of dealing and which he was accused of possessing was indicated by the charging document, the state did not separate the dealing and possession charges adequately to sustain the separate convictions, and defendant could not be convicted and sentenced for both dealing and possession with intent to deliver. Quick v. State, 660 N.E.2d 598, 1996 Ind. App. LEXIS 24 (1996).

There was no reasonable possibility that the jury relied on the same evidentiary facts to establish the essential elements of both manufacturing methamphetamine under IC 35-48-4-2(a)(1)(A) and possession of precursors under IC 35-48-4-14.5(c)(2) where the state presented ample evidence that defendant manufactured methamphetamine, but that evidence could not support a conviction for possession of precursors without the additional evidence that defendant possessed at least two precursors. Goffinet v. State, 775 N.E.2d 1227, 2002 Ind. App. LEXIS 1647 (2002).

Defendant's convictions of possession of anhydrous ammonia and of possession of chemical reagents or precursors violated double jeopardy under the Fifth Amendment and Ind. Const., art. 1, § 14 because they were necessarily included in defendant's conviction for dealing in methamphetamine. Defendant could not have been in the process of manufacturing methamphetamine without possessing anhydrous ammonia and reagents or precursors. Moore v. State, 869 N.E.2d 489, 2007 Ind. App. LEXIS 1488 (2007).

Elements.
Defendant's trial counsel was not ineffective in failing to pursue line of questioning regarding whether methcathinone, which defendant was accused of dealing, was finished product because no element of offense required that schedule I controlled substance be "finished product." Johnson v. State, 832 N.E.2d 985, 2005 Ind. App. LEXIS 1448 (2005).

Court rejected defendant's claim that jury's unsupervised use of a sound recording and equipment during deliberations violated his substantial rights; defendant had admitted that he gave drugs to a confidential informant, but claimed that he did not accept money for the drugs, but the recording did not address that point and acceptance of money for drugs was not an element of the offense of dealing in a Schedule III controlled substance, IC 35-48-4-2(a). Hall v. State, 897 N.E.2d 979, 2008 Ind. App. LEXIS 2561 (2008).

Evidence.

—Chain of Custody.
Where, after police officer received packet of heroin, he placed it in plastic envelope, sealed it with evidence tape and wrapped it in an envelope for mailing to the state police laboratory and chemist who analyzed it testified that he received the package still wrapped and bearing the registered mail receipt stub, evidence was sufficient to show chain of custody although persons who received package from mail carrier and took it to chemist did not testify. Gilliam v. State, 270 Ind. 71, 383 N.E.2d 297, 1978 Ind. LEXIS 841 (1978).

Where chain of possession was completely established by the evidence, the fact that arresting officer described the capsule as white with a white powder, and the chemist that tested it described it as a clear capsule with a tan powder, did not make the evidence of chain of custody insufficient. Williams v. State, 270 Ind. 573, 387 N.E.2d 1317, 1979 Ind. LEXIS 603 (1979).

Where officer described the chain of custody of substance from the time of purchase by informant, taking it to his office, to the property room which was protected by burglary prevention device and its transfer to the state police laboratory it was proper to admit such substance as an exhibit even though it was admitted that for brief periods of time it would have been possible for others to have had access to the substance. Holt v. State, 272 Ind. 544, 400 N.E.2d 130, 1980 Ind. LEXIS 597 (1980).

—Defendant's Use as Informant.
In a trial for dealing in cocaine and dealing in a Schedule II controlled substance, the trial court did not commit reversible error in denying defendant's motion for a mistrial based on a police officer's testimony that defendant had worked undercover for him in the past, where the prosecuting attorney asked the officer if he was able to recognize defendant's voice on a tape and among the questions asked him to substantiate his ability to recognize her voice was the question: "And has she worked as a confidential informant for the Evansville Police Narcotics Department?," to which he answered "Yes." The question and answer were simply a foundational basis to establish the officer's familiarity with defendant and the trial court did not abuse its discretion. Hampton v. State, 526 N.E.2d 1154, 1988 Ind. LEXIS 233 (1988).

—Entrapment.
Where undercover police officer saw defendant counting pills and asked him if he wanted to sell them and how much he wanted for them and

Evidence. (Cont'd)

—Entrapment. (Cont'd)
defendant immediately said he would sell them and stated his price, evidence was sufficient for the finder of fact to find that defendant was predisposed to commit the crime and therefore was not entrapped. Moore v. State, 181 Ind. App. 362, 391 N.E.2d 1168, 1979 Ind. App. LEXIS 1256 (1979).

Where police informant arranged for a meeting between the defendant and two police officers at which time defendant sold officers a controlled substance and offered to sell them more than they wanted, and defendant also told officers to come by anytime they wanted something, the evidence was sufficient for the jury to have found that defendant was predisposed to dealing in the controlled substance and that there was no entrapment. Johnson v. State, 413 N.E.2d 686, 1980 Ind. App. LEXIS 1869 (1980).

Where purchaser, after being introduced to defendant, indicated he wanted to purchase a certain drug and after defendant purchased the drugs, arrangements were made for subsequent purchases and when subsequent purchases were made if defendant did not have the drug desired encouraged purchaser to take a different drug, there was sufficient evidence to show that defendant was predisposed to commit the offense and therefore sufficient to overcome the defense of entrapment. Sowers v. State, 416 N.E.2d 466, 1981 Ind. App. LEXIS 1257 (1981).

Where after meeting, defendant made an immediate agreement to sell and made available to undercover officer the desired quantity of marijuana and cocaine and stated that he would be receiving more cocaine over the weekend which represented an amount larger than the casual user would have in his possession, the jury could logically infer that defendant was in the business of selling and that the police merely afforded defendant an opportunity to commit the crime. Grogg v. State, 417 N.E.2d 1175, 1981 Ind. App. LEXIS 1303 (1981).

There was sufficient evidence to rebut the defense of entrapment and show a predisposition to deal in controlled substances where defendant was familiar with prices and sources for marijuana and cocaine, possessed at least ten one-ounce bags of marijuana, and demonstrated a willingness to engage in future transactions. Gitary v. State, 503 N.E.2d 1241, 1987 Ind. App. LEXIS 2380 (1987).

—Insufficient.
The following evidence was insufficient to support a conviction for dealing, particularly as to the element of requisite intent: The defendant possessed $260 worth of heroin, an amount which a heavy user may need in a single day; he threw the heroin, contained in a package of 26 bundles, out of his car window; and his outward physical appearance, after a cursory inspection, seemed to indicate he himself was not a user. Further, since the information by which the defendant was charged tracked almost exactly the statutory language of this section, with no indication that the prosecutor intended to also charge the defendant with posses-

sion, the prosecution was limited to the offense of dealing, and the appellate court could not reduce the offense. O'Grady v. State, 481 N.E.2d 115, 1985 Ind. App. LEXIS 2644 (1985), overruled, Wright v. State, 658 N.E.2d 563, 1995 Ind. LEXIS 162 (1995).

Evidence that law enforcement officers found enough material on defendant's property to manufacturer only nine grams of methamphetamine was not sufficient to sustain defendant's conviction for dealing in a schedule II controlled substance by manufacturing methamphetamine, in violation of IC 35-48-4-2, because the state was required to prove that defendant manufactured the drug for use by others, under former IC 35-48-1-18, to obtain a conviction, and the evidence was not sufficient to prove that defendant manufactured the drug for the use of others. Culbertson v. State, 792 N.E.2d 573, 2003 Ind. App. LEXIS 1364 (2003).

Conviction for dealing in a schedule II substance, as a Class A felony under IC 35-48-4-2, was reduced to a class B felony, because the State failed to rebut defendant's justification defense under IC 34-48-4-16; the transaction which lasted, at most, for 20 minutes, at 3:00 a.m., was, as a matter of law, brief, and the transaction took place in a location where no children were present. While under different circumstances, a 20-minute transaction could fall under the category of a Class A felony because of the proximity to children or the potential for contact with youth, such was not the case. Gallagher v. State, — N.E.2d —, 2009 Ind. App. LEXIS 892 (2009).

—Other Offenses.
Where defendant, charged with sale of drugs, testified that she had previously been addicted to the use of drugs and at the time of the alleged sale took some drugs but did not deliver any, it was proper to bring out on rebuttal that police officer had previously made drug purchases from defendant. Gilliam v. State, 270 Ind. 71, 383 N.E.2d 297, 1978 Ind. LEXIS 841 (1978).

—Probable Cause.
Probable cause affidavit for search warrant based on two-day-old information was not per se "stale" and trial court did not err in refusing to quash search warrant or in admitting in evidence the drugs seized thereunder. Sowers v. State, 416 N.E.2d 466, 1981 Ind. App. LEXIS 1257 (1981).

—Sufficient.
Where witness had been strip searched by police prior to his entering tavern, where he communicated with defendant, and emerged shortly thereafter with three bags of heroin, evidence was sufficient to support finding that defendant delivered narcotics to witness. Shipp v. State, 265 Ind. 108, 350 N.E.2d 619, 1976 Ind. LEXIS 356 (1976).

Where evidence showed that two police agents purchased narcotics from defendant, evidence was sufficient to support conviction, despite testimony of state's witness under grant of immunity that he rather than the defendant had delivered the narcotics. Rosell v. State, 265 Ind. 173, 352 N.E.2d 750, 1976 Ind. LEXIS 366 (1976).

Evidence. (Cont'd)

—Sufficient. (Cont'd)

The testimony of the informer established all of the essential elements of the crime of sale of a narcotic drug, for in addition to his testimony concerning the actual exchange, the informer also gave testimony to show that the drug sale was not authorized by law and this testimony alone was sufficient to sustain a conviction for the sale of heroin. Stewart v. State, 170 Ind. App. 696, 354 N.E.2d 749, 1976 Ind. App. LEXIS 1049 (1976).

Where person soliciting police officer to sell drug was asked if she could supply more and she said she would have "to see her man" and she went and talked to defendant and then came back after which the sale was made, and after being in police custody she said that defendant supplied her with the drug, evidence was sufficient to convict defendant although at trial she denied defendant supplied her with the drug but said it was another person. Foor v. State, 172 Ind. App. 618, 360 N.E.2d 1273, 1977 Ind. App. LEXIS 804 (1977).

Despite the defendant's contention that the drugs in question were owned by a third party, his transfer of the drugs to an undercover policeman in exchange for cash is sufficient to support his conviction for delivering a controlled substance. Wilhelm v. State, 446 N.E.2d 621, 1983 Ind. App. LEXIS 2753 (1983).

Evidence was sufficient to support a conviction. Schlabach v. State, 459 N.E.2d 740, 1984 Ind. App. LEXIS 2341 (1984).

The evidence was held to be sufficient to sustain the defendant's conviction for attempting to receive stolen property, food stamp coupons, dealing in controlled substances, secobarbital, methamphetamine, and amphetamine. Cavendish v. State, 496 N.E.2d 46, 1986 Ind. LEXIS 1227 (1986).

Evidence that defendant agreed to trade anhydrous ammonia for methamphetamine, but asked a friend to give an informant some of her methamphetamine because he could not locate the drug among his belongings, was sufficient to sustain defendant's conviction for dealing in a schedule II controlled substance by delivering methamphetamine, in violation of IC 34-48-4-2. Culbertson v. State, 792 N.E.2d 573, 2003 Ind. App. LEXIS 1364 (2003).

Where defendant was convicted of dealing in a controlled substance in violation of IC 35-48-4-2, there was sufficient evidence that defendant manufactured methamphetamine to convict defendant; an experienced crime scene investigator testified as to the many items used in manufacturing methamphetamine that were found at the house where defendant was found, there was testimony of defendant's actions attempting to dispose of or hide incriminating evidence, and there was testimony as to the odor inside the house. Ikemire v. State, 852 N.E.2d 640, 2006 Ind. App. LEXIS 1601 (2006).

There was sufficient evidence to support defendant's dealing in methamphetamine conviction. For methamphetamine to have been manufactured, defendant would have had to extract the methamphetamine from a substance found in a pitcher and then allowed it to dry; although the evidence showed that defendant had not yet produced pure methamphetamine, testimony reflected that methamphetamine was extracted from the substance in the pitcher. Moore v. State, 869 N.E.2d 489, 2007 Ind. App. LEXIS 1488 (2007).

Former Personal Use Exception.

Where the trial court erred in giving a jury instruction which failed to include the personal use exception under former IC 35-48-1-18, the defendant's conviction under IC 35-48-4-2 and IC 35-48-4-14.5 would be reversed. Poe v. State, 775 N.E.2d 681, 2002 Ind. App. LEXIS 1530 (2002).

Informants.

Refusal of court to order identification of informant who accompanied undercover police officer to defendant's residence where police officer purchased drug from defendant was not error especially where there had been threats against informant's life. Craig v. State, 403 N.E.2d 925, 1980 Ind. App. LEXIS 1431 (1980).

Fact that information that witness for the state was previously involved in drug sales to federal agents and for that reason he became an informant was not made known to defense prior to trial did not require new trial where such information was made known to jury during trial. Carey v. State, 275 Ind. 321, 416 N.E.2d 1252, 1981 Ind. LEXIS 683 (1981).

—Perjury.

Perjury by informant, testifying for state concerning his prior involvement in making deliveries to law enforcement officer, that he had someone else make the deliveries, and perjury as to number of law enforcement officers in room when he telephoned defendant to make arrangements for delivery to defendant did not require new trial. Carey v. State, 275 Ind. 321, 416 N.E.2d 1252, 1981 Ind. LEXIS 683 (1981).

Intent.

—Inferred from Possession.

The illegal possession of large quantities of narcotics does not create a presumption of intent to deliver, but may support an inference of intent. Romack v. State, 446 N.E.2d 1346, 1983 Ind. App. LEXIS 2780 (1983).

Manufacturing and Dealing Distinguished.

Proof of manufacture is not an element of dealing by possession with the intent to deliver; proof of the intent to deliver is not necessary to establish that a defendant knowingly manufactured in all cases. It would be possible to engage in manufacturing as that term has been defined by statute without ever having the intent to deliver what one produces because even manufacturing by production, propagation, conversion, or processing for one's own use is manufacturing. Neither offense is statutorily included in the other. Bigler v. State, 602 N.E.2d 509, 1992 Ind. App. LEXIS 1575 (1992).

Manufacturing Process.

IC 35-48-4-2 does not require that the manufac-

Manufacturing Process. (Cont'd)
turing process be completed or that there be actual product before someone could be found to have manufactured a controlled substance; since a bag containing ephedrine powder was found in the possession of defendant, the process of extraction, and thus, the process to manufacture methamphetamine, had begun, and there was sufficient evidence to support defendant's conviction for manufacturing methamphetamine. Dawson v. State, 786 N.E.2d 742, 2003 Ind. App. LEXIS 630 (2003).

Multiple Offenses.
The involvement of two buyers creates more than one sales transaction and thereby creates multiple offenses. Hurst v. State, 464 N.E.2d 19, 1984 Ind. App. LEXIS 2672 (1984).

Possession of Precursors with Intent to Manufacture.
Sole distinguishing factor between conviction for manufacturing methamphetamine under IC 35-48-4-2 and conviction for possession of precursors with intent to manufacture methamphetamine is that one may be guilty of possessing chemical precursors with intent to manufacture without actually beginning manufacturing process, whereas manufacturing process must at least have been started in order to be deemed guilty of manufacturing methamphetamine. Murray v. State, 798 N.E.2d 895, 2003 Ind. App. LEXIS 2149 (2003).

Review on Appeal.
Since defendant did not challenge the sufficiency of the evidence to support the judge's determination that the police had probable cause to instigate the entrapment, although the evidence was circumstantial, it was sufficient to withstand defendant's challenge of entrapment on appeal. Shipp v. State, 265 Ind. 108, 350 N.E.2d 619, 1976 Ind. LEXIS 356 (1976).

Sale of Controlled Substance.
Although it is only necessary to prove delivery of a controlled substance and not a sale, where police officer saw the money change hands and found the money on defendant after the arrest, it was not error to permit testimony with respect to such money. Williams v. State, 270 Ind. 573, 387 N.E.2d 1317, 1979 Ind. LEXIS 603 (1979).

School Premises.
Not requiring the difficult proof as to whether children were actually present at school at the time a drug transaction occurred does not make this section unconstitutional. Morse v. State, 593 N.E.2d 194, 1992 Ind. LEXIS 162 (1992).
The trial court committed no error when it instructed the jury that it had taken judicial notice that Howe Military Institution is a school within the meaning of the law, but the jury was not required to accept the fact as conclusive. Haley v. State, 736 N.E.2d 1250, 2000 Ind. App. LEXIS 1646 (2000).

Search and Seizure.
Where defendant attacks the adequacy of police search procedures, the challenge is directed to the weight and credibility of the evidence presented not to the burden of proof. Hudson v. State, 462 N.E.2d 1077, 1984 Ind. App. LEXIS 2534 (1984).

Sentence.
Consecutive sentences were inappropriate for defendant who was enticed by the police to make additional drug buys as part of a sting operation, resulting in defendant's conviction of five counts of drug related offenses and sentence to both maximum and consecutive sentences. Hendrickson v. State, 690 N.E.2d 765, 1998 Ind. App. LEXIS 32 (1998).

Cited:
Thorne v. State, 429 N.E.2d 644, 1981 Ind. LEXIS 959 (1981); Madaras v. State, 425 N.E.2d 670, 1981 Ind. App. LEXIS 1650 (1981); Huff v. State, 440 N.E.2d 465, 1982 Ind. LEXIS 965 (1982); Warthan v. State, 440 N.E.2d 657, 1982 Ind. LEXIS 977 (1982); Powers v. State, 440 N.E.2d 1096, 1982 Ind. LEXIS 988 (1982); Everroad v. State, 442 N.E.2d 994, 1982 Ind. LEXIS 1038 (1982); Indiana Bd. of Pharmacy v. Crick, 433 N.E.2d 32, 1982 Ind. App. LEXIS 1129 (1982); Bubb v. State, 434 N.E.2d 120, 1982 Ind. App. LEXIS 1176 (1982); Hudson v. State, 443 N.E.2d 834, 1983 Ind. LEXIS 725 (1983); Huff v. State, 443 N.E.2d 1234, 1983 Ind. App. LEXIS 2507 (1983); McCann v. State, 446 N.E.2d 1293, 1983 Ind. LEXIS 801 (1983); Hudak v. State, 446 N.E.2d 615, 1983 Ind. App. LEXIS 2727 (1983); Vanyo v. State, 450 N.E.2d 524, 1983 Ind. LEXIS 875 (1983); Priestley v. State, 451 N.E.2d 88, 1983 Ind. App. LEXIS 3130 (1983); Smith v. State, 452 N.E.2d 160, 1983 Ind. App. LEXIS 3224 (1983); McKrill v. State, 452 N.E.2d 946, 1983 Ind. LEXIS 939 (1983); Forehand v. State, 479 N.E.2d 552, 1985 Ind. LEXIS 865 (1985); Tevis v. State, 480 N.E.2d 214, 1985 Ind. LEXIS 902 (1985); Herrod v. State, 491 N.E.2d 538, 1986 Ind. LEXIS 1110 (1986); Hall v. State, 497 N.E.2d 916, 1986 Ind. LEXIS 1277 (1986); Lay v. State, 659 N.E.2d 1005, 1995 Ind. LEXIS 174 (1995); Hopkins v. State, 668 N.E.2d 686, 1996 Ind. App. LEXIS 814 (1996); Jennings v. State, 714 N.E.2d 730, 1999 Ind. App. LEXIS 1283 (1999); Huffines v. State, 739 N.E.2d 1093, 2000 Ind. App. LEXIS 2057 (2000); Leitch v. State, 736 N.E.2d 1284, 2000 Ind. App. LEXIS 1766 (2000); Griffin v. State, 756 N.E.2d 572, 2001 Ind. App. LEXIS 1762 (2001); Creekmore v. State, 800 N.E.2d 230, 2003 Ind. App. LEXIS 2341 (2003); Duncan v. State, 857 N.E.2d 955, 2006 Ind. LEXIS 1028 (2006).

Collateral References.
Admissibility, in criminal prosecution, of expert opinion allegedly stating whether drugs were possessed with intent to distribute — state cases. 83 A.L.R.4th 629.

35-48-4-3. Dealing in a schedule IV controlled substance.

(a) A person who:
(1) knowingly or intentionally:
(A) manufactures;
(B) finances the manufacture of;
(C) delivers; or
(D) finances the delivery of;
a controlled substance, pure or adulterated, classified in schedule IV; or
(2) possesses, with intent to manufacture or deliver, a controlled substance, pure or adulterated, classified in schedule IV;
commits dealing in a schedule IV controlled substance, a Class C felony, except as provided in subsection (b).
(b) The offense is a Class B felony if:
(1) the person:
(A) delivered; or
(B) financed the delivery of;
the substance to a person under eighteen (18) years of age at least three (3) years junior to the person; or
(2) the person delivered or financed the delivery of the substance:
(A) on a school bus; or
(B) in, on, or within one thousand (1,000) feet of:
(i) school property;
(ii) a public park;
(iii) a family housing complex; or
(iv) a youth program center.

History.
IC 35-48-4-3, as added by Acts 1976, P.L.148, § 7; 1977, P.L.340, § 98; P.L.296-1987, § 7; P.L.165-1990, § 5; P.L.296-1995, § 5; P.L.65-1996, § 13; P.L.17-2001, § 21.

Cross References.
Penalties for felonies, IC 35-50-1, IC 35-50-2, IC 35-50-5-2.

NOTES TO DECISIONS

"Dealing."
The term "dealing" as it appeared in former IC 35-47-5-4 (dealing in sawed-off shotguns) was obviously used in the broad sense of a course of conduct as opposed to the limited sense in which it was used in other statutes, such as those which define the offense of dealing in controlled substances. Brook v. State, 448 N.E.2d 1249, 1983 Ind. App. LEXIS 2943 (1983).

Evidence.

—Admissibility.
Where defendant's truck was impounded after defendant crashed the truck in a parking lot while attempting to flee from an arrest, and the truck's contents were inventoried pursuant to the community care taking function and established police procedures, the inventory search exception to the warrant requirement of U.S. Const. amend. IV applied to money that was found in a suitcase inside the truck, and, accordingly, the money was not subject to suppression. Ratliff v. State, 770 N.E.2d 807, 2002 Ind. LEXIS 544 (2002).

—Chain of Custody.
Where evidence showed that state police officer, after receiving drug from defendant, placed it in an evidence bag which he initialed, placed it in his briefcase which he placed in the trunk of his

Evidence. (Cont'd)

—Chain of Custody. (Cont'd)

automobile which was kept locked until he delivered it to the state police chemist who tested it and returned it to the officer there was a sufficient chain of custody. Drollinger v. State, 274 Ind. 99, 409 N.E.2d 1084, 1980 Ind. LEXIS 740 (1980).

—Sufficient.

The uncorroborated testimony of an informant-buyer is sufficient to sustain a conviction under this section. Simmons v. State, 585 N.E.2d 1341, 1992 Ind. App. LEXIS 174 (1992).

—Vials.

Admission of unopened vials and identification of Valium as diazepam by a chemist was proper in the context of the trial since the defendant was taped during the transaction identifying what she had obtained as Valium; the defendant admitted in court that she had delivered Valium obtained from the medical stores of the nursing home where she was employed; and the vials delivered by her were labelled by the manufacturer as containing Valium and were intact as to labeling and seal. Morris v. State, 604 N.E.2d 665, 1992 Ind. App. LEXIS 1852 (1992).

Physicians.

A physician who issues prescriptions without a legitimate purpose or outside the usual course of his professional practice may be prosecuted for violation of this section. Alarcon v. State, 573 N.E.2d 477, 1991 Ind. App. LEXIS 980 (1991).

Proof.

The proof required under subsection (a)(2) of this section is not sufficient to prove a violation under subsection (a)(1). Simmons v. State, 585 N.E.2d 1341, 1992 Ind. App. LEXIS 174 (1992).

This section defines at least two separate offenses for dealing in a controlled substance rather than a single offense provable by alternative means, as argued by the State. Simmons v. State, 585 N.E.2d 1341, 1992 Ind. App. LEXIS 174 (1992).

Cited:

Powers v. State, 440 N.E.2d 1096, 1982 Ind. LEXIS 988 (1982); Ramirez v. State, 455 N.E.2d 609, 1983 Ind. App. LEXIS 3503 (1983).

RESEARCH REFERENCES

Collateral References.

Admissibility, in criminal prosecution, of expert opinion allegedly stating whether drugs were possessed with intent to distribute — state cases. 83 A.L.R.4th 629.

Sufficiency of evidence that possessor of controlled substance other than cocaine, heroin, or marijuana had intent to distribute it, so as to violate 21 U.S.C.S. § 841(a)(1). 80 A.L.R. Fed. 507.

State law criminal liability of licensed physician for prescribing or dispensing drug or similar controlled substance. 13 A.L.R.5th 1.

35-48-4-4. Dealing in a schedule V controlled substance.

(a) A person who:

    (1) knowingly or intentionally:

        (A) manufactures;

        (B) finances the manufacture of;

        (C) delivers; or

        (D) finances the delivery of;

a controlled substance, pure or adulterated, classified in schedule V; or

    (2) possesses, with intent to:

        (A) manufacture;

        (B) finance the manufacture of;

        (C) deliver; or

        (D) finance the delivery of;

a controlled substance, pure or adulterated, classified in schedule V;

commits dealing in a schedule V controlled substance, a Class D felony, except as provided in subsection (b).

(b) The offense is a Class B felony if:

    (1) the person:

        (A) delivered; or

        (B) financed the delivery of;

the substance to a person under eighteen (18) years of age at least three (3) years junior to the person; or

    (2) the person delivered or financed the delivery of the substance:

        (A) on a school bus; or

(B) in, on, or within one thousand (1,000) feet of:
(i) school property;
(ii) a public park;
(iii) a family housing complex; or
(iv) a youth program center.

History.
IC 35-48-4-4, as added by Acts 1976, P.L.148, § 7; P.L.340, § 99; P.L.296-1987, § 8; P.L.165- 1990, § 6; P.L.296-1995, § 6; P.L.65-1996, § 14; P.L.17-2001, § 22.

NOTES TO DECISIONS

"Dealing."
The term "dealing" as it appeared in former IC 35-47-5-4 (dealing in sawed-off shotguns) was obviously used in the broad sense of a course of conduct as opposed to the limited sense in which it was used in other statutes, such as those which define the offense of dealing in controlled substances. Brook v. State, 448 N.E.2d 1249, 1983 Ind. App. LEXIS 2943 (1983).

RESEARCH REFERENCES

Collateral References.
Admissibility, in criminal prosecution, of expert opinion allegedly stating whether drugs were possessed with intent to distribute — state cases. 83 A.L.R.4th 629.

35-48-4-4.1. Dumping controlled substance waste.

(a) A person who dumps, discharges, discards, transports, or otherwise disposes of:
(1) chemicals, knowing the chemicals were used in the illegal manufacture of a controlled substance or an immediate precursor; or
(2) waste, knowing that the waste was produced from the illegal manufacture of a controlled substance or an immediate precursor;
commits dumping controlled substance waste, a Class D felony.

(b) It is not a defense in a prosecution under subsection (a) that the person did not manufacture the controlled substance or immediate precursor.

History.
P.L.17-2001, § 23.

Cross References.
Penalties for felonies, IC 35-50-1, IC 35-50-2, IC 35-50-5-2.

NOTES TO DECISIONS

ANALYSIS

Evidence.
—Sufficient.

Evidence.

—Sufficient.
State provided evidence that, outside of defendant's residence, police found a backhoe next to a hole that contained empty containers of denatured alcohol, camp fuel, xylene, and naptha, and that each of the cans were labeled as chemicals used in the manufacture of methamphetamine, and, thus, the state presented sufficient evidence to support defendant's conviction for dumping controlled substance waste as a Class D felony. Redden v. State, 850 N.E.2d 451, 2006 Ind. App. LEXIS 1340 (2006).

35-48-4-4.5. Dealing in substance represented to be controlled substance.

(a) A person who knowingly or intentionally delivers or finances the delivery of any substance, other than a controlled substance or a drug for which a prescription is required under federal or state law, that:
(1) Is expressly or impliedly represented to be a controlled substance;

(2) Is distributed under circumstances that would lead a reasonable person to believe that the substance is a controlled substance; or

(3) By overall dosage unit appearance, including shape, color, size, markings, or lack of markings, taste, consistency, or any other identifying physical characteristic of the substance, would lead a reasonable person to believe the substance is a controlled substance;

commits dealing in a substance represented to be a controlled substance, a Class D felony.

(b) In determining whether representations have been made, subject to subsection (a)(1), or whether circumstances of distribution exist, subject to subsection (a)(2), the trier of fact may consider, in addition to other relevant factors, the following:

(1) Statements made by the owner or other person in control of the substance, concerning the substance's nature, use, or effect.

(2) Statements made by any person, to the buyer or recipient of the substance, that the substance may be resold for profit.

(3) Whether the substance is packaged in a manner uniquely used for the illegal distribution of controlled substances.

(4) Whether:

(A) The distribution included an exchange of, or demand for, money or other property as consideration; and

(B) The amount of the consideration was substantially greater than the reasonable retail market value of the substance.

History.
IC 35-48-4-4.5, as added by Acts 1981, P.L.305, § 1; P.L.210-1986, § 1; P.L.165-1990, § 7.

Cross References.
Penalties for felonies, IC 35-50-1, IC 35-50-2, IC 35-50-5-2.

NOTES TO DECISIONS

Analysis

"Dealing."
Double Jeopardy.
Equal Protection.
Information.
Jury Instructions.
Proof.

"Dealing."
The term "dealing" as it appeared in former IC 35-47-5-4 (dealing in sawed-off shotguns) was obviously used in the broad sense of a course of conduct as opposed to the limited sense in which it was used in other statutes, such as those which define the offense of dealing in controlled substances. Brook v. State, 448 N.E.2d 1249, 1983 Ind. App. LEXIS 2943 (1983).

Double Jeopardy.
Defendant could not be convicted and sentenced separately for distributing a substance represented to be a controlled substance and possession of a substance represented to be a controlled substance, where the state made no distinction in the charging information and did not provide a clear distinction by introducing some evidence of a possible possession aside from the quantity sold. Townsend v. State, 673 N.E.2d 503, 1996 Ind. App. LEXIS 1588 (1996).

Equal Protection.
Defendant's right to equal protection under law was not violated where the prosecutor was afforded the discretion to choose whether to charge his conduct as a Class C or a Class D felony, since overlapping statutes which carry differing penalties do not violate equal protection absent a showing that the two statutes are utilized to treat different recognizable classes of defendants differently, and where defendant had not asserted that he was a member of a recognizable or suspect class, nor had he asserted that the state charged him with the more serious felony to treat him differently than anyone else, there was no equal protection violation. Conner v. State, 613 N.E.2d 484, 1993 Ind. App. LEXIS 529 (1993), superseded, 626 N.E.2d 803, 1993 Ind. LEXIS 213 (1993).

Information.
Charging information did not deny defendant due process because it sufficiently informed him of the charge against him, where charging information in both title and in body of count indicated that the state was charging defendant with "distributing" a look-a-like substance and not "delivery," and the information specifically indicated that defendant was being charged with a Class C felony. Townsend v. State, 673 N.E.2d 503, 1996 Ind. App. LEXIS 1588 (1996).

Jury Instructions.

There was no error resulting from the trial court's deletion of the word "controlled" before the word "substance" in challenged jury instructions. It was inconceivable that the legislature intended proof of the distribution of a controlled substance in a prosecution for the distribution of a noncontrolled substance represented to be a controlled substance, and therefore, the trial court's instructions could not have prejudiced defendant and there was no reversible error. Conner v. State, 613 N.E.2d 484, 1993 Ind. App. LEXIS 529 (1993), superseded, 626 N.E.2d 803, 1993 Ind. LEXIS 213 (1993).

Proof.

The present statutory scheme, which was clearly intended to prohibit the distribution of noncontrolled substances represented to be controlled substances, does not require proof of a distribution of a controlled substance. Conner v. State, 613 N.E.2d 484, 1993 Ind. App. LEXIS 529 (1993), superseded, 626 N.E.2d 803, 1993 Ind. LEXIS 213 (1993).

Where defendant delivered 16 bags of noncontrolled plant material he represented to be marijuana in exchange for $1,600, his case was fairly covered by this section and IC 35-48-4-4.6. Conner v. State, 613 N.E.2d 484, 1993 Ind. App. LEXIS 529 (1993), superseded, 626 N.E.2d 803, 1993 Ind. LEXIS 213 (1993).

Where the defendant was engaged in selling a substance that he expressly represented could be sold as cocaine for a profit, where he packaged the substance in a manner "uniquely used for the illegal distribution of controlled substances," and where the distribution of this substance included an exchange of money in an amount "substantially greater than the reasonable market value of the substance," the evidence was sufficient to support a conviction for dealing in a substance represented to be a controlled substance. Riley v. State, 711 N.E.2d 489, 1999 Ind. LEXIS 306 (1999).

Cited:

Smith v. State, 586 N.E.2d 890, 1992 Ind. App. LEXIS 152 (1992).

35-48-4-4.6. Manufacture or distribution of substance represented to be controlled substance.

(a) A person who knowingly or intentionally:

(1) manufactures;

(2) finances the manufacture of;

(3) advertises;

(4) distributes; or

(5) possesses with intent to manufacture, finance the manufacture of, advertise, or distribute;

a substance described in section 4.5 [IC 35-48-4-4.5] of this chapter commits a Class C felony.

(b) A person who knowingly or intentionally possesses a substance described in section 4.5 of this chapter commits a Class C misdemeanor. However, the offense is a Class A misdemeanor if the person has a previous conviction under this section.

(c) In any prosecution brought under this section it is not a defense that the person believed the substance actually was a controlled substance.

(d) This section does not apply to the following:

(1) The manufacture, financing the manufacture of, processing, packaging, distribution, or sale of noncontrolled substances to licensed medical practitioners for use as placebos in professional practice or research.

(2) Persons acting in the course and legitimate scope of their employment as law enforcement officers.

(3) The retention of production samples of noncontrolled substances produced before September 1, 1986, where such samples are required by federal law.

History.

P.L.210-1986, § 2; P.L.165-1990, § 8; P.L.150-1999, § 1; P.L.225-2003, § 3.

Penalties for misdemeanors, IC 35-50-1, IC 35-50-3, IC 35-50-5-2.

Cross References.

Penalties for felonies, IC 35-50-1, IC 35-50-2, IC 35-50-5-2.

NOTES TO DECISIONS

ANALYSIS

Constitutionality.
—Vagueness.
Burden of Proof.
Double Jeopardy.
Equal Protection.
Information.
Jury Instructions.
Proof.
—Intent.
Sentence.
—Not Proportional.

Constitutionality.

—Vagueness.

The defect in the statutory scheme, that this section requires proof that a defendant distributed any substance other than a controlled substance, while the statutory definition of the term "distribute" in IC 35-48-1-14 relates only to the delivery of controlled substances, is hypertechnical in nature and does not mislead a person of ordinary intelligence regarding the illegality of the distribution of a noncontrolled substance represented to be a controlled substance; therefore, the statute is not unconstitutionally vague. Conner v. State, 613 N.E.2d 484, 1993 Ind. App. LEXIS 529 (1993), superseded, 626 N.E.2d 803, 1993 Ind. LEXIS 213 (1993).

Burden of Proof.

Under this section, the state is required to prove a negative, and where a police detective involved in defendant's arrest testified that the subject plant material "sure didn't look like marijuana," this testimony, in combination with the test results from the state laboratory indicating that the two samples taken from the batch did not contain marijuana, sufficiently supported defendant's conviction. Conner v. State, 613 N.E.2d 484, 1993 Ind. App. LEXIS 529 (1993), superseded, 626 N.E.2d 803, 1993 Ind. LEXIS 213 (1993).

Double Jeopardy.

Defendant could not be convicted and sentenced separately for distributing a substance represented to be a controlled substance and possession of a substance represented to be a controlled substance, where the state made no distinction in the charging information and did not provide a clear distinction by introducing some evidence of a possible possession aside from the quantity sold. Townsend v. State, 673 N.E.2d 503, 1996 Ind. App. LEXIS 1588 (1996).

Equal Protection.

Defendant's right to equal protection under law was not violated where the prosecutor was afforded the discretion to choose whether to charge his conduct as a Class C or a Class D felony, since overlapping statutes which carry differing penalties do not violate equal protection absent a showing that the two statutes are utilized to treat different recognizable classes of defendants differently, and where defendant had not asserted that he was a member of a recognizable or suspect class, nor had he asserted that the state charged him with the more serious felony to treat him differently than anyone else, there was no equal protection violation. Conner v. State, 613 N.E.2d 484, 1993 Ind. App. LEXIS 529 (1993), superseded, 626 N.E.2d 803, 1993 Ind. LEXIS 213 (1993).

Defendant's conviction under this section did not violate equal protection because this section requires a disproportionate penalty and a different evidentiary burden than the statutes prohibiting the delivery of real marijuana; the statutory scheme is not necessarily unreasonable, nor does it provide for a level of proof disproportionate to that required in the prosecution of "real" drug offenses, and therefore, there was no equal protection violation. Conner v. State, 613 N.E.2d 484, 1993 Ind. App. LEXIS 529 (1993), superseded, 626 N.E.2d 803, 1993 Ind. LEXIS 213 (1993).

Information.

Charging information did not deny defendant due process because it sufficiently informed him of the charge against him, where charging information in both title and in body of count indicated that the state was charging defendant with "distributing" a look-a-like substance and not "delivery," and the information specifically indicated that defendant was being charged with a Class C felony. Townsend v. State, 673 N.E.2d 503, 1996 Ind. App. LEXIS 1588 (1996).

Jury Instructions.

There was no error resulting from the trial court's deletion of the word "controlled" before the word "substance" in challenged jury instructions. It was inconceivable that the legislature intended proof of the distribution of a controlled substance in a prosecution for the distribution of a noncontrolled substance represented to be a controlled substance, and therefore, the trial court's instructions could not have prejudiced defendant and there was no reversible error. Conner v. State, 613 N.E.2d 484, 1993 Ind. App. LEXIS 529 (1993), superseded, 626 N.E.2d 803, 1993 Ind. LEXIS 213 (1993).

Proof.

The present statutory scheme, which was clearly intended to prohibit the distribution of noncontrolled substances represented to be controlled substances, does not require proof of a distribution of a controlled substance. Conner v. State, 613 N.E.2d 484, 1993 Ind. App. LEXIS 529 (1993), superseded, 626 N.E.2d 803, 1993 Ind. LEXIS 213 (1993).

Where defendant delivered 16 bags of noncontrolled plant material he represented to be marijuana in exchange for $1,600, his case was fairly covered by IC 35-48-4-4.5 and this section. Conner v. State, 613 N.E.2d 484, 1993 Ind. App. LEXIS 529 (1993), superseded, 626 N.E.2d 803, 1993 Ind. LEXIS 213 (1993).

Proof. (Cont'd)

The requisite intent in the prosecution of a case involving distribution of a noncontrolled substance represented to be a controlled substance may be proven by circumstantial evidence. Conner v. State, 613 N.E.2d 484, 1993 Ind. App. LEXIS 529 (1993), superseded, 626 N.E.2d 803, 1993 Ind. LEXIS 213 (1993).

—Intent.

Where defendant sold a batch of plant material that he represented to be marijuana, and the plant material was not marijuana nor did it even look like marijuana, from this evidence, the jury could reasonably have infered that he knew the substance he sold was not marijuana. Conner v. State, 613 N.E.2d 484, 1993 Ind. App. LEXIS 529 (1993),

superseded, 626 N.E.2d 803, 1993 Ind. LEXIS 213 (1993).

Sentence.

—Not Proportional.

Application of this section to defendant who sold fake marijuana to informant violated the constitutional requirement that all penalties be in proportion to the nature of the offense where defendant's six year prison term was twice the maximum penalty available had he actually sold marijuana to the police informant. Such a doubling of the penalty was out of proportion to the nature of his offense. Conner v. State, 626 N.E.2d 803, 1993 Ind. LEXIS 213 (1993).

RESEARCH REFERENCES

Collateral References.

Admissibility, in criminal prosecution, of expert opinion allegedly stating whether drugs were possessed with intent to distribute — state cases. 83 A.L.R.4th 629.

35-48-4-5. Dealing in a counterfeit substance.

A person who:

    (1) Knowingly or intentionally:

        (A) Creates;

        (B) Delivers; or

        (C) Finances the delivery of;

a counterfeit substance; or

    (2) Possesses, with intent to:

        (A) Deliver; or

        (B) Finance the delivery of;

a counterfeit substance;

commits dealing in a counterfeit substance, a Class D felony.

History.

IC 35-48-4-5, as added by Acts 1976, P.L.148, § 7; 1977, P.L.340, § 100; P.L.165-1990, § 9.

Cross References.

Penalties for felonies, IC 35-50-1, IC 35-50-2, IC 35-50-5-2.

NOTES TO DECISIONS

Lesser Included Offenses.

It is factually not possible to include this section as a lesser included offense of IC 35-48-4-1. IC 35-48-4-1 requires proof that the substance delivered contains cocaine or another specified controlled substance. On the other hand, this section

requires proof that a counterfeit substance, a substance which by definition eliminates cocaine or other controlled substances, be delivered. Tomlinson v. State, 540 N.E.2d 78, 1989 Ind. App. LEXIS 486 (1989).

RESEARCH REFERENCES

Collateral References.

Admissibility, in criminal prosecution, of expert opinion allegedly stating whether drugs were possessed with intent to distribute — state cases. 83 A.L.R.4th 629.

Validity, construction, and effect of state statute regulating sale of counterfeit or imitation controlled substances. 84 A.L.R.4th 936.

35-48-4-6. Possession of a narcotic drug.

(a) A person who, without a valid prescription or order of a practitioner acting in the course of the practitioner's professional practice, knowingly or intentionally possesses cocaine (pure or adulterated) or a narcotic drug (pure or adulterated) classified in schedule I or II, commits possession of cocaine or a narcotic drug, a Class D felony, except as provided in subsection (b).

(b) The offense is:

(1) a Class C felony if:

(A) the amount of the drug involved (pure or adulterated) weighs three (3) grams or more; or

(B) the person was also in possession of a firearm (as defined in IC 35-47-1-5);

(2) a Class B felony if the person in possession of the cocaine or narcotic drug possesses less than three (3) grams of pure or adulterated cocaine or a narcotic drug:

(A) on a school bus; or

(B) in, on, or within one thousand (1,000) feet of:

(i) school property;

(ii) a public park;

(iii) a family housing complex; or

(iv) a youth program center; and

(3) a Class A felony if the person possesses the cocaine or narcotic drug in an amount (pure or adulterated) weighing at least three (3) grams:

(A) on a school bus; or

(B) in, on, or within one thousand (1,000) feet of:

(i) school property;

(ii) a public park;

(iii) a family housing complex; or

(iv) a youth program center.

History.
IC 35-48-4-6, as added by Acts 1976, P.L.148, § 7; 1977, P.L.340, § 101; 1979, P.L.303, § 10; P.L.138-1983, § 3; P.L.296-1987, § 9; P.L.296-1995, § 7; P.L.65-1996, § 15; P.L.188-1999, § 7; P.L.17-2001, § 24; P.L.151-2006, § 24.

Compiler's Notes.
P.L.151-2006, § 29, effective July 1, 2006, provides:

"IC 35-48-4-1.1 and IC 35-48-4-6.1, both as added by this act, and IC 35-48-4-1, IC 35-48-4-6, IC 35-48-4-14.5, and IC 35-48-4-14.7, all as amended by this act, apply only to crimes committed after June 30, 2006."

Cross References.
Penalties for felonies, IC 35-50-1, IC 35-50-2, IC 35-50-5-2.

NOTES TO DECISIONS

Analysis

In General.
Constitutionality.
Aggregate Weight.
Constructive Possession.
—Nonexclusive Control over Premises.
—Vehicles.
Control.
Defenses.
Determination of Amount of Substance.
Double Jeopardy.
—Dealing and Possession.
"Drug Involved."
Elements.
—Proximity to School Property.
— —Persons in Moving Vehicles.
—Youth Program Center.

—Youth Program Shelter.
Entrapment.
Evidence.
—Admissibility.
—Chain of Possession.
—Circumstantial.
—Harmless Error.
—Not Sufficient.
—Prior Convictions.
—Proximity to School or Park.
—Street Value.
—Sufficient.
Inconsistent Verdicts.
Indictment or Information.
—Failure to Cite Statutory Provisions.
—Lysergic Acid Diethylamide.
Intent.

—To Deliver.
—To Possess.
Jury Instructions.
Knowledge.
—Of Possession and Character.
—Of Possession of Narcotic Drug.
—Of Presence.
Lesser Included Offenses.
Premises.
Search and Seizure.
—Investigatory Stop.
Search Warrant.
Sentence.
—Fines.
— —Indigency Hearing Required.
"Without Valid Prescription or Order."

In General.

There was nothing indefinite or uncertain in the statute, as every person was put on notice that the possession of a narcotic drug was unlawful except as authorized by the laws of the United States or the state of Indiana. Stanley v. State, 252 Ind. 37, 245 N.E.2d 149, 1969 Ind. LEXIS 321 (1969).

Constitutionality.

Increased penalties for drug offenders who commit their offenses near school property is constitutional. Reynolds/Herr v. State, 582 N.E.2d 833, 1991 Ind. App. LEXIS 2116 (1991).

The portion of IC 35-48-4-6 pertaining to a 1,000 foot enhancement is not void for vagueness, notwithstanding the failure of the statute to explicitly provide for the use of a line-of-sight technique for measuring distance. Reed v. State, 720 N.E.2d 431, 1999 Ind. App. LEXIS 2106 (1999).

The language of IC 35-48-4-6 is neither indefinite nor uncertain; rather, the language clearly and unambiguously puts any person of ordinary intelligence on notice that possessing cocaine within 1,000 feet of any school property, public park, family housing complex or youth program is a Class B felony. Manigault v. State, 881 N.E.2d 679, 2008 Ind. App. LEXIS 307 (2008).

The language of IC 35-48-4-6 was not unconstitutionally vague or overbroad as applied to the facts of a case in which defendant possessed cocaine while on the property of a motel, which was a family housing complex pursuant to IC 35-41-1-10.5. Manigault v. State, 881 N.E.2d 679, 2008 Ind. App. LEXIS 307 (2008).

Because IC 35-48-4-6(b)(2)(B) had already been determined to be constitutional in another case involving a motel which qualified as a "family housing complex" under IC 35-41-1-10.5(2), namely, Manigault v. State, 881 N.E.2d 679, 2008 Ind. App. LEXIS 307 (2008), defendant's constitutional argument was rejected. Robinson v. State, 888 N.E.2d 1267, 2008 Ind. App. LEXIS 1338 (2008).

Aggregate Weight.

The term "aggregate weight" was not meant to include noncontrolled substances; rather, it referred to all the controlled substance found in an accused's possession. Hutcherson v. State, 178 Ind. App. 8, 381 N.E.2d 877, 1978 Ind. App. LEXIS 1053 (1978).

Constructive Possession.

A conviction of illegal possession could be based upon evidence that the regulated substance, while not found on the person of the defendant, was in a place under his dominion and control; if possession was established, knowledge of the character of the drug and the fact that it was possessed could be inferred therefrom, and such possession need not have been exclusive and the substance could be possessed jointly by a person and another without a showing that the person had actual physical control thereof. Thomas v. State, 260 Ind. 1, 291 N.E.2d 557, 1973 Ind. LEXIS 480 (1973).

Evidence was sufficient to support conviction of defendant for possession of narcotic drugs where, when police entered house, defendant was found seated at a table with another person with two packages of heroin upon the table, such a factual situation being sufficient for the trial court to determine that the defendant had the intent and capability to maintain control over the heroin and thus was in "constructive possession" of the heroin. Thomas v. State, 260 Ind. 1, 291 N.E.2d 557, 1973 Ind. LEXIS 480 (1973).

Where a packet of heroin was found in the rear of the police car in which defendant had been placed, constructive possession sufficient to base a conviction could be inferred. Phillips v. State, 160 Ind. App. 647, 313 N.E.2d 101, 1974 Ind. App. LEXIS 1092 (1974).

A conviction under prior law could be based on actual or constructive possession of heroin. Phillips v. State, 160 Ind. App. 647, 313 N.E.2d 101, 1974 Ind. App. LEXIS 1092 (1974).

Where heroin was found in the bedroom of an apartment rented by defendant, dominion and control and knowledge of the presence of the drug sufficient to establish constructive possession could be inferred. Jones v. State, 163 Ind. App. 454, 324 N.E.2d 828, 1975 Ind. App. LEXIS 1057 (1975).

Where police officer observed defendant in the presence of his girlfriend while she was injecting herself with heroin and cocaine near a wastebasket wherein drugs were found, the evidence was sufficient to allow a reasonable inference that defendant had constructive possession of the drugs. Pettigrew v. State, 164 Ind. App. 297, 328 N.E.2d 236, 1975 Ind. App. LEXIS 1149 (1975).

In a prosecution for constructive possession, the element of intent is proved by evidence of the accused's knowledge of the nature of the substance and its presence, and may be inferred where possession and access to the premises is exclusive; otherwise there must be additional circumstances in evidence supporting the inference. Hutcherson v. State, 178 Ind. App. 8, 381 N.E.2d 877, 1978 Ind. App. LEXIS 1053 (1978).

Where a conviction is based on constructive possession, there must be evidence showing the accused's intent and capability to maintain control and dominion over the substance and proof of a possessory interest in the premises where a controlled substance is found is adequate to show capability to control. Hutcherson v. State, 178 Ind. App. 8, 381 N.E.2d 877, 1978 Ind. App. LEXIS 1053 (1978).

Constructive Possession. (Cont'd)

Where defendant stipulated that he was the owner of the house where the substances were found and was the only person present when the search warrant was executed and provided keys to various cabinets, evidence was sufficient to show possession since constructive possession may be proven from evidence that substance was in a place where defendant exercised dominion and control. Craig v. State, 403 N.E.2d 925, 1980 Ind. App. LEXIS 1431 (1980).

Evidence was sufficient to show that defendant had constructive possession of heroin found in residence where he had keys to residence and let the officers with search warrant in, had told an officer that he lived there, and pointed out a shoebox in a closet which contained heroin, although the apartment in question was leased to defendant's girlfriend. Tinnin v. State, 275 Ind. 203, 416 N.E.2d 116, 1981 Ind. LEXIS 674 (1981).

Constructive possession is shown where there is an intent and a capability to maintain dominion and control over the narcotics. Fyock v. State, 436 N.E.2d 1089, 1982 Ind. LEXIS 862 (1982).

The evidence was sufficient to support the conclusion that defendant was in constructive possession of heroin. Ferguson v. State, 485 N.E.2d 888, 1985 Ind. LEXIS 1047 (1985).

A finding of constructive possession must be supported by a determination that defendant had both the intent and the capability to maintain control and dominion over the illegal drugs (cocaine and marijuana) found in the bedroom. Brooks v. State, 526 N.E.2d 1027, 1988 Ind. App. LEXIS 573 (1988).

Facts, together with the reasonable inferences drawn therefrom, supported the jury's determination of defendant's constructive possession of cocaine and marijuana. Brooks v. State, 526 N.E.2d 1027, 1988 Ind. App. LEXIS 573 (1988).

Constructive possession requires the intent and the capability to maintain dominion and control over the illegal drugs. Stephens v. State, 588 N.E.2d 564, 1992 Ind. App. LEXIS 335 (1992).

Evidence was sufficient to sustain conviction for possession of cocaine even though defendant did not have cocaine in his possession when he was stopped where police officer saw defendant drop the package containing cocaine which was retrieved by another officer, and defendant later made statement to officers: "I didn't think you saw me." Hicks v. State, 609 N.E.2d 1165, 1993 Ind. App. LEXIS 173 (1993).

Evidence was sufficient to convict defendant of possession of cocaine, as a Class C felony, because the State proved that he had constructive possession of all of the cocaine found in the hotel room. Armour v. State, 762 N.E.2d 208, 2002 Ind. App. LEXIS 141 (2002).

In absence of actual possession of drugs while in possession of firearm, constructive possession may support conviction for offense if state shows that defendant had both capability and intent to maintain dominion and control over contraband; control in this sense concerns defendant's relation to place where substance is found and whether defendant had power, by way of legal authority or in practical sense, to control place where, or item in which, substance was found; proof of possessory interest in premises in which illegal drugs are found is adequate to show capability to maintain control and dominion over them, and possessory interest in premises does not require actual ownership of premises. Allen v. State, 798 N.E.2d 490, 2003 Ind. App. LEXIS 2111 (2003).

Evidence was sufficient to convict defendant of possession of cocaine while in possession of firearm under constructive possession theory where drugs and firearm were found in his apartment. Allen v. State, 798 N.E.2d 490, 2003 Ind. App. LEXIS 2111 (2003).

Where person's control over premises is nonexclusive, intent to maintain dominion and control over contraband found on premises may be inferred from additional circumstances that indicate person knew of presence of contraband; these additional circumstance include: (1) incriminating statements by the defendant; (2) attempted flight or furtive gestures; (3) a drug manufacturing setting; (4) proximity of the defendant to the drugs; (5) drugs in plain view; and (6) location of the drugs in close proximity to items owned by the defendant. Allen v. State, 798 N.E.2d 490, 2003 Ind. App. LEXIS 2111 (2003).

Defendant's intent to maintain dominion and control over cocaine seized in apartment that defendant shared with another person could be inferred where drugs were found in plain view in close proximity to items owned by defendant and defendant pointed handgun at police officers when they entered apartment to execute search warrant. Allen v. State, 798 N.E.2d 490, 2003 Ind. App. LEXIS 2111 (2003).

In trial at which defendant was convicted of possession of cocaine and drug paraphernalia found in her purse, fundamental error requiring reversal of conviction occurred during voir dire when trial court gave jury venire example of constructive possession that was similar to facts of case. Merritt v. State, 822 N.E.2d 642, 2005 Ind. App. LEXIS 223 (2005).

—Nonexclusive Control over Premises.

Although defendant shared premises with another, evidence was sufficient to show constructive possession of heroin in defendant where, during search of premises when police officers found a package, defendant remarked it contained dummy bags and other occupant of the premises testified at trial that she did not know the heroin was there. Mills v. State, 177 Ind. App. 432, 379 N.E.2d 1023, 1978 Ind. App. LEXIS 1012 (1978).

Where defendant enjoyed nonexclusive possession of the premises and fled from police in response to his girlfriend's warning cry, the evidence was sufficient to support a finding of constructive possession. Hutcherson v. State, 178 Ind. App. 8, 381 N.E.2d 877, 1978 Ind. App. LEXIS 1053 (1978).

The following evidence was sufficient to establish that the defendant, who did not have exclusive possession of the premises searched, had "constructive possession" of the heroin found therein, i.e., had the capability and the intent to control the

Constructive Possession. (Cont'd)

—Nonexclusive Control over Premises. (Cont'd)

heroin: (1) He was present in the small bedroom where a heroin-filled syringe was in plain view; and (2) he fled when the police effected their entry. Lewis v. State, 482 N.E.2d 487, 1985 Ind. App. LEXIS 2730 (1985).

If the legal authority or practical ability to control the premises is nonexclusive, the defendant's capability to exercise control over the substance may be inferred but only if there is some independent evidence from which the trier of fact may infer the defendant's intent to exercise such control. In re J.L., 599 N.E.2d 208, 1992 Ind. App. LEXIS 1350 (1992).

Where defendant was found in a barricaded house with two other individuals, none of whom owned the house, and cocaine and marijuana were in plain view in close proximity to defendant, this was sufficient to establish defendant's constructive possession of the drugs and to convict defendant of possession of cocaine in violation of IC 35-48-4-6 and possession of marijuana in violation of IC 35-48-4-11. Matthews v. State, 792 N.E.2d 934, 2003 Ind. App. LEXIS 1413 (2003).

Defendant's constructive possession of drugs found in search of house occupied by defendant and his cousin could not be inferred from police discovery, in search of house while defendant was not present, of contraband in closed containers in basement laundry room cabinet and other incriminating material found primarily in cousin's bedroom; there was no showing that contraband would have been within defendant's plain view. Gee v. State, 810 N.E.2d 338, 2004 Ind. LEXIS 535 (2004).

—Vehicles.

Constructive possession of items found in a vehicle may be imputed to the driver of the vehicle, and evidence showing that not only was the cocaine found in the vehicle which defendant was driving, but that it was found directly under the seat upon which he was sitting, supported a conviction under this section. Woods v. State, 640 N.E.2d 1089, 1994 Ind. App. LEXIS 1355 (1994).

Possession of cocaine found within a car was imputed to the driver of the car, where the bag of cocaine was found in the front ashtray between the driver and passenger seats, an area easily accessible to the driver, and where there was direct testimony that driver knew about and actually handled the cocaine during the transaction. Johnson v. State, 659 N.E.2d 242, 1995 Ind. App. LEXIS 1657 (1995).

Where cocaine was found on the driver's seat of the car the defendant was driving, it was reasonable to infer that the defendant knew of its presence and had the intent and capability of controlling the drug. Macklin v. State, 701 N.E.2d 1247, 1998 Ind. App. LEXIS 2024 (1998).

Defendant's exclusive possession of the car where the cocaine was found, along with the evidence of his marijuana use in the car, established his intent and ability to control the cocaine that was found in a hidden compartment of the car.

Whitney v. State, 726 N.E.2d 823, 2000 Ind. App. LEXIS 507 (2000).

Control.

Where defendant did not have exclusive control of the apartment where the drugs were found, but there was evidence of attempted flight and flushing a toilet upon confrontation with an imminent police search, the trier of fact was entitled to infer that she knew of the presence of the drugs and had control of them. Martin v. State, 175 Ind. App. 503, 372 N.E.2d 1194, 1978 Ind. App. LEXIS 818 (1978).

Defenses.

It is no defense that defendant had possession of cocaine only to hide it from police, and that it was not his cocaine. McClendon v. State, 671 N.E.2d 486, 1996 Ind. App. LEXIS 1365 (1996).

Determination of Amount of Substance.

Purity of a drug, and thus amount possessed, need not be demonstrated only by quantitative chemical analysis. Jones v. State, 435 N.E.2d 616, 1982 Ind. App. LEXIS 1228 (1982).

Double Jeopardy.

Where defendant obtained drug from hiding place, sold half of it to police agent and placed the remainder in his pocket he could be convicted and sentenced for the crime of possession of a controlled substance in addition to the crime of delivery of a controlled substance. Kruckeberg v. State, 268 Ind. 643, 377 N.E.2d 1351, 1978 Ind. LEXIS 722 (1978), cert. denied, 439 U.S. 990, 99 S. Ct. 590, 58 L. Ed. 2d 665, 1978 U.S. LEXIS 4050 (1978).

Trial court erred in convicting and sentencing the defendant on two counts of possession of cocaine, where he was charged and convicted, in effect, of two violations which arose from his single act of simultaneous possession of two packages of cocaine. Young v. State, 564 N.E.2d 968, 1991 Ind. App. LEXIS 14 (1991).

Where the charge of possessing a drug is a lesser-included offense of dealing in that drug, the offender cannot be convicted and sentenced on both the greater and lesser offenses. Ratcliff v. State, 578 N.E.2d 359, 1991 Ind. LEXIS 168 (1991); Abron v. State, 591 N.E.2d 634, 1992 Ind. App. LEXIS 793 (1992).

This section required the state to prove defendant possessed cocaine within 1000 feet of school property. IC 6-7-3-11 contains no such element, and in turn required that the state prove defendant possessed cocaine without having paid the Controlled Substance Excise Tax, which this section does not require. Because each offense contained an element which the other did not, defendant's double jeopardy rights were not violated. Whitt v. State, 659 N.E.2d 512, 1995 Ind. LEXIS 203 (1995).

Defendant's conviction for failure to pay the Controlled Substance Excise Tax was contemporaneous with his underlying conviction for possession of cocaine within 1000 feet of school property, and thus double jeopardy was not implicated.

Double Jeopardy. (Cont'd)

Charley v. State, 651 N.E.2d 300, 1995 Ind. App. LEXIS 600 (1995).

Separate convictions for dealing and possession based upon a single sale of narcotics may be sustained, but to do so the state must make clear that only the quantity sold forms the basis of the dealing charge, while only the quantity retained after the sale forms the basis of the possession charge. If this is not made clear, proof that the defendant dealt narcotics could also form the basis for proving that the defendant first possessed narcotics, allowing a defendant to be convicted twice for possessing and dealing the same drug, which is forbidden. Johnson v. State, 659 N.E.2d 242, 1995 Ind. App. LEXIS 1657 (1995).

The defendant was not sentenced for the lesser included offense of possession of cocaine, which conviction could not stand where he was also convicted of possession with intent to deliver. Since double jeopardy considerations bar separate conviction and sentencing where conviction of a greater crime cannot be had without commission of the lesser offense. O'Neal v. State, 716 N.E.2d 82, 1999 Ind. App. LEXIS 1491 (1999).

Although police found cocaine both on his person and in his house, the trial court erred and the double jeopardy clause was violated when the court convicted defendant of two counts of possession of cocaine, because he possessed cocaine only once. Campbell v. State, 734 N.E.2d 248, 2000 Ind. App. LEXIS 1297 (2000).

Since the same cocaine supported both the dealing and possession charges, defendant's conviction of possession of cocaine was vacated. Mack v. State, 736 N.E.2d 801, 2000 Ind. App. LEXIS 1659 (2000).

Defendant's two convictions for possession of cocaine violated double jeopardy prohibition of Ind. Const. art. 1, § 14 as the convictions were not separate crimes in that defendant was convicted for two counts of possession, using the same cocaine, but each count was enhanced by a separate additional circumstance: proximity to a school and possessing a handgun. The judgment was remanded with instruction to vacate one of the convictions. Scott v. State, 855 N.E.2d 1068, 2006 Ind. App. LEXIS 2262 (2006).

—Dealing and Possession.

Convictions for both dealing in cocaine and possession of cocaine did not violate double jeopardy standards where evidence was presented at trial that defendant sold and delivered cocaine to a confidential informant, and evidence was also presented that later that same day defendant possessed cocaine. The evidence adduced at trial was sufficient for the jury to conclude that defendant had committed two separate crimes at two different times. Castillo v. State, 734 N.E.2d 299, 2000 Ind. App. LEXIS 1356 (2000), transfer granted, 753 N.E.2d 2, 2001 Ind. LEXIS 67 (2001), aff'd, 741 N.E.2d 1196, 2001 Ind. LEXIS 14 (Ind. 2001).

Under the double jeopardy clause of the United States Constitution, the jury's determination of guilt on the possession of cocaine charge but dead-lock on the dealing charge did not preclude the state from retrying defendant for the dealing offense. Davenport v. State, 734 N.E.2d 622, 2000 Ind. App. LEXIS 1313 (2000).

Where same evidence, seized in same episode, was used to convict defendant of both cocaine possession and possession with intent to deliver, double jeopardy principles were violated, requiring reversal of cocaine possession convictions. Donnegan v. State, 809 N.E.2d 966, 2004 Ind. App. LEXIS 1101 (2004).

Double jeopardy considerations barred defendant's convictions for both IC 35-48-4-1(a) cocaine dealing and IC 35-48-4-6(a) cocaine possession since conviction on the dealing charge necessarily included possession; only cocaine introduced into evidence was that found in the baggies defendant delivered to an officer and none was found on his person or in the baggie he threw while attempting to resist arrest. Harrison v. State, — N.E.2d —, 2009 Ind. App. LEXIS 346 (2009).

"Drug Involved."

The phrase "drug involved" in the second sentence (now subsection (b)(1)) includes both cocaine and the narcotic drug previously mentioned in the section. Collins v. State, 549 N.E.2d 89, 1990 Ind. App. LEXIS 92 (1990).

Elements.

Since the defendant dropped a bag containing cocaine as he fled from a police officer, the defendant at most committed only one act of possession of cocaine and could not be convicted and sentenced for both dealing in cocaine and possession of cocaine. Stephens v. State, 588 N.E.2d 564, 1992 Ind. App. LEXIS 335 (1992).

State's failure to prove that the defendant exercised any control over the premises where the drugs were found, warranted reversal of his conviction under this section for lack of sufficient evidence indicating personal possession over the actual drugs. Moore v. State, 613 N.E.2d 849, 1993 Ind. App. LEXIS 544 (1993).

In order to convict a defendant of possession of cocaine while in possession of firearm, state is required to prove beyond reasonable doubt that defendant knowingly or intentionally possessed cocaine while also possessing firearm. Allen v. State, 798 N.E.2d 490, 2003 Ind. App. LEXIS 2111 (2003).

IC 35-48-4-6 did not violate the Privileges and Immunities Clause of Ind. Const., art. 1, § 23 because it did not create two classes of citizens, those charged with simple possession and those charged with the offense elevated by location. The inherent characteristic that distinguishes a person charged with a Class D felony from the person charged with a Class B felony is the proximity to places where children congregate. Manigault v. State, 881 N.E.2d 679, 2008 Ind. App. LEXIS 307 (2008).

Even though drug-free zones had been expanded, IC 35-48-4-6 did not violate defendant's right to equal protection under the Fourteenth Amendment. Enhanced penalties for controlled substance violations within 1,000 feet of parks,

Elements. (Cont'd)

family housing complexes and youth program centers were rationally related to the legitimate governmental interest of protecting children from the perils and dangers associated with drug trafficking. Manigault v. State, 881 N.E.2d 679, 2008 Ind. App. LEXIS 307 (2008).

—Proximity to School Property.

There is no requirement that police apprehend defendant within one thousand feet of school property; it is sufficient that the jury heard evidence from which they could reasonably infer that defendant possessed the drug within one thousand feet of school. Anderson v. State, 649 N.E.2d 1060, 1995 Ind. App. LEXIS 469 (1995).

Testimony that school was 496 feet from house and that officer observed defendant from time he left house until he was arrested while in possession of cocaine was sufficient to support conviction for possession of cocaine within 1000 feet of school. Chandler v. State, 816 N.E.2d 464, 2004 Ind. App. LEXIS 2054 (2004).

— —Persons in Moving Vehicles.

The enhancement for possession within 1000 feet of school property applies to an occupant of a moving vehicle in that zone, and enhancement of defendant's convictions for possession of cocaine and possession of a controlled substance where he was pulled over in a school zone and the substances were found on him and in his car did not violate his right to equal protection. Polk v. State, 683 N.E.2d 567, 1997 Ind. LEXIS 117 (1997).

—Youth Program Center.

Conviction for Class A felony violation of IC 35-48-4-6(b)(3)(B)(iv) could not stand; a community church was and remained a church and was not converted into a youth program center by reason of its faith-based activities for young people. Bi-weekly Girl Scout troop meetings and mentoring of children by adult members of the congregation were accessory or incidental to the existence and identity as a church; and, the church was not a youth program center--it remained a church notwithstanding the incidental activities not solely religious in nature. Whatley v. State, 906 N.E.2d 259, 2009 Ind. App. LEXIS 837 (2009).

—Youth Program Shelter.

Defendant's constitutional challenge to IC 35-41-1-29' s definition of a "youth program center" under IC 35-41-1-10.5 gained no support from the bright line rule mentioned in Manigault or Polk. Manigault involved a family housing complex, i.e., a motel; Polk stated that knowledge or notice of a "youth program center" was not required for constitutionality; and, in defendant's case, if a community church was a "youth program center," defendant's conviction for possession of cocaine as a Class A felony, under IC 35-48-4-6(b)(3)(B)(iv), had to stand. Whatley v. State, 906 N.E.2d 259, 2009 Ind. App. LEXIS 837 (2009).

Entrapment.

The quantum of evidence necessary to support the probable cause to set in motion an entrapment scheme is minimal, for example, it is less than that required to support a search warrant. Williams v. State, 408 N.E.2d 123, 1980 Ind. App. LEXIS 1579 (1980).

Where the offer of the police to help out probation violator on this violation in exchange for assistance was pressure upon the violator to supply truthful information, a statement to the police that the defendant possessed heroin provided the necessary "entrapment probable cause." Williams v. State, 408 N.E.2d 123, 1980 Ind. App. LEXIS 1579 (1980).

Evidence.

It is not necessary in a prosecution for possession for the prosecution to prove that the defendant did not have a prescription or order from a professional practitioner to have possession of the drugs. Gilbert v. State, 426 N.E.2d 1333, 1981 Ind. App. LEXIS 1701 (1981).

—Admissibility.

Where police officers found narcotics in defendant's car when he was arrested for running a stop sign, the evidence was properly admitted by the trial court. Neely v. State, 240 Ind. 362, 164 N.E.2d 110, 1960 Ind. LEXIS 193 (1960).

Where officers had reason to believe that defendant was in house and went into house to serve a bench warrant for defendant's arrest on another matter, and when in house found narcotic drugs on dining room table where defendant had been sitting, such drugs were subject to seizure and admissible in evidence. Cannon v. State, 414 N.E.2d 578, 1980 Ind. App. LEXIS 1858 (1980).

Marijuana in the form of a "blunt" and plastic baggies containing marijuana and cocaine were inadmissible because the evidence was seized in violation of defendant's Fourth Amendment rights where the police officer did not have reasonable suspicion that defendant was about to commit a crime or had committed a crime. Dowdell v. State, 747 N.E.2d 564, 2001 Ind. App. LEXIS 618 (2001).

State trooper was allowed to pat-down defendant before placing him in police cruiser for transport to the next exit on an interstate highway and the trial court properly denied defendant's motion to suppress marijuana found during pat-down and cocaine found during an inventory search that was conducted after the defendant's car was impounded; however, the trial court erred by imposing consecutive sentences without stating its reason for doing so on the record. Lewis v. State, 755 N.E.2d 1116, 2001 Ind. App. LEXIS 1642 (2001).

Police, who had reasonable suspicion that defendant was involved in illegal activity that was occurring inside a house, were justified in following the defendant when he fled inside the house and in strip searching the defendant, after they saw items of drug paraphernalia and drugs in plain view, and arrested the defendant and everyone else who was present. Frye v. State, 757 N.E.2d 684, 2001 Ind. App. LEXIS 1763 (2001), cert. denied, 535 U.S. 1103, 122 S. Ct. 2308, 152 L. Ed. 2d 1063, 2002 U.S. LEXIS 3956 (2002).

Since the police had probable cause to arrest

Evidence. (Cont'd)

—Admissibility. (Cont'd)
defendant for disorderly conduct resulting from defendant's involvement in a multi-person altercation, the search of defendant's person, as well as a rag that had been in defendant's immediate control, was lawful as a search incident to an arrest; thus, the motion to suppress was properly denied. Moffitt v. State, 817 N.E.2d 239, 2004 Ind. App. LEXIS 2194 (2004).

In prosecution for possession of methamphetamine, trial court did not err in admitting into evidence statements defendant made at police station that he was involved in drug dealing and that he had disposed of a safe from cousin's house or in admitting into evidence methamphetamine found in safe; defendant's claim that his *Miranda* rights were violated was rejected since court concluded that defendant voluntarily went to police station and could have left station without making statements in response to questions by police officers. Kelley v. State, 825 N.E.2d 420, 2005 Ind. App. LEXIS 599 (2005).

—Chain of Possession.
Where, in the case of seized or purchased narcotics, the object offered in evidence had passed out of the possession of the original receiver and into the possession of others, a chain of possession must have been established to avoid any claim of substitution, tampering or mistake, and a failure to submit such proof could have resulted in the exclusion of the evidence or testimony as to its characteristics. Graham v. State, 253 Ind. 525, 255 N.E.2d 652, 1970 Ind. LEXIS 626 (1970).

Despite discrepancy over whether glass tube containing cocaine was contained in a plastic container or bottle or baggie, the evidence was sufficient to provide reasonable assurance that the evidence remained undisturbed in the transfer of the heat-sealed evidence envelope from police officer to drug chemist for analysis of the contents of that envelope. Katner v. State, 640 N.E.2d 388, 1994 Ind. App. LEXIS 1209 (1994), aff'd, 655 N.E.2d 345, 1995 Ind. LEXIS 138 (1995).

—Circumstantial.
Evidence showing that a person had heroin within his system was circumstantial evidence tending to show he was in possession of the drug prior to the injection. Smith v. State, 161 Ind. App. 636, 316 N.E.2d 841, 1974 Ind. App. LEXIS 987 (1974).

Possession may be constructive as well as actual and may be inferred from circumstantial evidence. Smith v. State, 165 Ind. App. 60, 330 N.E.2d 771, 1975 Ind. App. LEXIS 1221 (1975).

Defendant was properly convicted of possession of methamphetamine because a jury was able to compare the amount of the drug found in a dresser at a home where defendant lived with that of the homeowner's testimony regarding how much of the drug had been observed. Halsema v. State, 783 N.E.2d 1199, 2003 Ind. App. LEXIS 299 (2003), transfer granted, 804 N.E.2d 746, 2003 Ind. LEXIS 657 (2003), superseded, 823 N.E.2d 668, 2005 Ind. LEXIS 197 (2005).

—Harmless Error.
Although it was error for detective to volunteer testimony that another officer had told him that defendant was a convicted felon, the surrounding circumstances of defendant's uncontested possession of marijuana and a firearm without a permit supported the jury's conclusion that defendant also possessed the cocaine, and any possible impact of the detective's testimony about defendant's felony record was negated by the surrounding circumstances. Perez v. State, 728 N.E.2d 234, 2000 Ind. App. LEXIS 743 (2000).

—Not Sufficient.
In trial of defendant for possession of methamphetamine within 1000 feet of a school, state failed to prove essential element of crime by not producing evidence that methamphetamine possessed by defendant weighed at least three grams; state's argument that jurors were able to examine bag containing the methamphetamine and use their common sense and experience to determine whether it weighed at least three grams was rejected. Halsema v. State, 823 N.E.2d 668, 2005 Ind. LEXIS 197 (2005).

—Prior Convictions.
Defendant's prior convictions for drug offenses occurring at his place of business, one conviction being seven years old and the other 13, were inadmissible, because the transactions were too remote and dissimilar to be relevant as part of a common scheme or plan. Clark v. State, 536 N.E.2d 493, 1989 Ind. LEXIS 105 (1989).

—Proximity to School or Park.
There was sufficient evidence that elementary school was "school property," and testimony of detective provided a rational inference that defendant possessed cocaine within one thousand feet of school property, where he stated he went to the location of the arrest and measured the distance from that location to the location of the elementary school. Whitt v. State, 659 N.E.2d 512, 1995 Ind. LEXIS 203 (1995).

Because there are no statutory requirements regarding the method of measurement, and because there is no complex scientific process necessary to obtain a measurement of distance, the state was not required to offer expert testimony regarding the operation or accuracy of the measuring device used, and officer's testimony was sufficient to lay an adequate foundation prior to admission of distance of defendant's possession of cocaine from school. Charley v. State, 651 N.E.2d 300, 1995 Ind. App. LEXIS 600 (1995).

The evidence was sufficient for a reasonable jury to find defendant guilty of possession of cocaine within 1,000 feet of a public park. Tardy v. State, 728 N.E.2d 904, 2000 Ind. App. LEXIS 808 (2000).

—Street Value.
It was not error to admit evidence of the street value of the heroin seized. Gooden v. State, 401 N.E.2d 93, 1980 Ind. App. LEXIS 1341 (1980).

—Sufficient.
Where the evidence showed that defendant was

Evidence. (Cont'd)

—Sufficient. (Cont'd)
arrested in the city of Indianapolis while in a car parked in the middle of a street for improper parking, and at the time of arrest he was searched, and the search disclosed among other things, 20 capsules containing a white powder, and an analysis of one of the capsules showed that the powder contained heroin, it was sufficient to sustain a conviction. Wilson v. State, 240 Ind. 66, 161 N.E.2d 484, 1959 Ind. LEXIS 251 (1959).

Evidence that police officer observed known narcotics user inject himself with hypodermic contraption, that user's arm was bleeding slightly in area of injection, and that user appeared to be under influence of narcotics, was sufficient for arrest of user on charge of violation of statute. Sanchez v. State, 256 Ind. 140, 267 N.E.2d 374, 1971 Ind. LEXIS 601 (1971).

Evidence was sufficient to support conviction for possession of heroin where police officers testified that they had received information that a large amount of drug traffic was being conducted at a certain address and that defendant would be present at the address with a large quantity of heroin, that they subsequently placed the house under surveillance and followed defendant as he left the house whereupon they observed him remove two envelopes from his pocket which he threw to the ground, and that after detaining defendant they analyzed the contents of the packets and determined that they contained heroin. Glenn v. State, 154 Ind. App. 474, 290 N.E.2d 103, 1972 Ind. App. LEXIS 925 (1972).

Where state's evidence indicated that tests showed an opium derivative was present in substance found on defendant and no contradictory evidence was offered, evidence was sufficient to sustain conviction. Jones v. State, 260 Ind. 463, 296 N.E.2d 407, 1973 Ind. LEXIS 550 (1973).

Where one of two police officers who searched defendant testified that he was wearing pants in which they found heroin and defendant testified he was wearing pants at the time, but one of the officers, at a previous trial of another, testified the defendant was wearing only underclothes, it was reasonable to conclude that the previous testimony was in error and that the evidence sustained the conviction. Wright v. State, 164 Ind. App. 266, 328 N.E.2d 253, 1975 Ind. App. LEXIS 1143 (1975).

Where police officers observed defendant acting suspiciously and followed him when he drove away recklessly and later when they accosted him observed him attempt to dispose of a cigarette package found to contain two bundles of heroin, the evidence was sufficient to sustain the conviction for possession. Wadlington v. State, 164 Ind. App. 255, 328 N.E.2d 458, 1975 Ind. App. LEXIS 1140 (1975).

Where evidence is introduced as to each element of the crime with which the defendant is charged, a verdict of conviction is supported by sufficient evidence. Taylor v. State, 265 Ind. 433, 355 N.E.2d 247, 1976 Ind. LEXIS 404 (1976).

Evidence showing heroin was found in the defendant's pocket is sufficient by itself to sustain a conviction for possession of a narcotic drug. Robinson v. State, 454 N.E.2d 873, 1983 Ind. App. LEXIS 3455 (1983).

Evidence held sufficient to convict for possession of heroin. Ferguson v. State, 485 N.E.2d 888, 1985 Ind. LEXIS 1047 (1985).

Evidence held sufficient to sustain conviction for possession of cocaine. Hammond v. State, 594 N.E.2d 509, 1992 Ind. App. LEXIS 1068 (1992).

Evidence was sufficient to support conviction for possession of cocaine where handcuffed defendant was placed in back seat of police car, police officer testified that he had checked the car earlier and there was no cocaine in his car, defendant was the only person to occupy the back seat, and cocaine was found in back seat after defendant had occupied the back seat. Polk v. State, 683 N.E.2d 567, 1997 Ind. LEXIS 117 (1997).

Evidence of identification of the defendant by an informant both at the scene of the crime and at trial was sufficient to sustain the defendant's drug convictions. Toney v. State, 715 N.E.2d 367, 1999 Ind. LEXIS 577 (1999).

Evidence that defendant received mail at the address the drugs and a firearm were located, and defendant's testimony that he lived at the house, that the drugs were his, and that he was watching the firearm for a friend, was sufficient to establish that defendant knowingly possessed cocaine, marijuana, and the firearm found in his house. Allen v. State, 787 N.E.2d 473, 2003 Ind. App. LEXIS 753 (2003).

Evidence was sufficient to convict defendant of possessing methamphetamine when a search of the trailer occupied by defendant revealed evidence, partially in plain view, of numerous reagents and equipment used for the manufacture of methamphetamine, there was a small amount of methamphetamine found in a "snort tube," and constructive possession of the items by defendant could be inferred when defendant was found hiding under the bed during the search, witnesses had identified the trailer as a methamphetamine lab, defendant had a recipe for making methamphetamine in his wallet, and defendant's relative had asked defendant to live in the trailer while he was gone. Floyd v. State, 791 N.E.2d 206, 2003 Ind. App. LEXIS 1208 (2003).

Baggies and scales as well as crack cocaine itself found on premises where defendant lived and among his personal possessions established existence of drug manufacturing process and was sufficient to prove constructive possession of illegal drugs. Jones v. State, 807 N.E.2d 58, 2004 Ind. App. LEXIS 752 (2004).

Although chemist who analyzed scale taken from defendant after traffic stop could not determine amount of cocaine residue on scale, he did detect cocaine, and that evidence, along with other evidence, sustained defendant's conviction for possession of cocaine. Beeler v. State, 807 N.E.2d 789, 2004 Ind. App. LEXIS 845 (2004).

Evidence that defendant told police that they would find guns in a duffle bag in defendant's bedroom closet and under the mattress, that defendant had possession of the key to a Pepsi machine containing cocaine, that cocaine was

Evidence. (Cont'd)

—Sufficient. (Cont'd)
found in defendant's possession, and that defendant ran from police was sufficient to support defendant's convictions for dealing in cocaine, a Class A felony, possession of cocaine and a firearm, a Class C felony, and possession of a handgun by a serious violent felon, a Class B felony. Massey v. State, 816 N.E.2d 979, 2004 Ind. App. LEXIS 2119 (2004).

Sufficient evidence linked defendant to cocaine found in cigarette package at traffic intersection; officer saw defendant throw cigarette package out of car window, another officer found package, and defendant admitted to throwing package. Williams v. State, 818 N.E.2d 970, 2004 Ind. App. LEXIS 2417 (2004), aff'd, 838 N.E.2d 1019, 2005 Ind. LEXIS 1110 (2005).

In trial of defendant for possession of methamphetamine within 1000 feet of a school, state failed to prove essential element of crime by not producing evidence that methamphetamine possessed by defendant weighed at least three grams; state's argument that jurors were able to examine bag containing the methamphetamine and use their common sense and experience to determine whether it weighed at least three grams was rejected. Halsema v. State, 823 N.E.2d 668, 2005 Ind. LEXIS 197 (2005).

Defendant was not entitled to reversal of his conviction for possession of cocaine because sufficient evidence supported the conviction; an officer testified that he saw defendant place his closed fist into a blue bin and then remove his empty hand, that defendant ran from the officer, and that the officer subsequently recovered cocaine from the bin. Hayes v. State, 876 N.E.2d 373, 2007 Ind. App. LEXIS 3056 (2007).

Inconsistent Verdicts.
Defendant's conviction for possession of cocaine in a family housing complex was reversed because the jury's verdicts were inconsistent when the jury acquitted defendant of the lesser included offense of possession of cocaine since acquittal on possession of cocaine logically negated a necessary element of possession of cocaine in a family housing complex; the only evidence of possession of cocaine was the cocaine allegedly found under the mattress in defendant's apartment, and there was no evidence that defendant possessed cocaine at any other time or at any other place. Beattie v. State, — N.E.2d —, 2009 Ind. App. LEXIS 660 (2009).

Indictment or Information.
Affidavit charging that defendant did "unlawfully and feloniously possess certain narcotic drugs, to wit: heroin" was sufficient, since statute did not require any specific quantity to be possessed. Lander v. State, 238 Ind. 680, 154 N.E.2d 507, 1958 Ind. LEXIS 277 (1958).

Information charging that defendant "did unlawfully, knowingly, intentionally and feloniously possess a controlled substance" was valid although not including the words "without a valid prescription or order of a practitioner acting in the course

of his professional practice." Craig v. State, 403 N.E.2d 925, 1980 Ind. App. LEXIS 1431 (1980).

In a case in which defendant was convicted for Class D felony possession of a narcotic drug, the trial court did not err by allowing the state to amend the information one week before trial; defendant's substantial rights were not prejudiced by the amendment because defendant had a reasonable opportunity to prepare for and defend against the charge against him. Jones v. State, 863 N.E.2d 333, 2007 Ind. App. LEXIS 573 (2007).

—Failure to Cite Statutory Provisions.
Where defendant was charged with attempting to commit the crime of possession of a controlled substance by knowingly presenting a forged prescription to be filled for preludin the failure of the state to cite the statutory provision did not place defendant in a position of uncertainty as to whether the state intended to present evidence of attempted possession of a narcotic drug. Ralston v. State, 412 N.E.2d 239, 1980 Ind. App. LEXIS 1736 (1980).

—Lysergic Acid Diethylamide.
The chemical lysergic acid diethylamide (commonly known as LSD) was never defined by the Narcotic Drug Act as a narcotic drug so that a motion to quash an indictment for the use of LSD should have been sustained. Burk v. State, 257 Ind. 407, 275 N.E.2d 1, 1971 Ind. LEXIS 553, 50 A.L.R.3d 1279 (1971). (LSD is now listed in IC 35-48-2-4).

Intent.

—To Deliver.
Possessing a large amount of a narcotic substance is circumstantial evidence of intent to deliver. The more narcotics a person possesses, the stronger the inference that he intended to deliver it and not consume it personally. Berry v. State, 574 N.E.2d 960, 1991 Ind. App. LEXIS 1180 (1991).

—To Possess.
Intent to possess is proved by evidence of accused's knowledge of the nature of the substance and its presence. Fyock v. State, 436 N.E.2d 1089, 1982 Ind. LEXIS 862 (1982).

Jury Instructions.
Where defendant's conviction for violating IC 35-48-4-6 was subject to enhancement because he was arrested in a park, he was not entitled to an instruction under IC 35-48-4-16, which provided a defense if no one under 18 was in the park at the time, as the testimony showed only that it was unknown whether anyone under 18 was in the park at the time defendant was arrested. Stringer v. State, 853 N.E.2d 543, 2006 Ind. App. LEXIS 1804 (2006).

Knowledge.

—Of Possession and Character.
While actual knowledge of the heroin possessed and its character is required, this knowledge may be inferred from the fact the item was found in a place under the accused's dominion and control.

Knowledge. (Cont'd)

—Of Possession and Character. (Cont'd)
Phillips v. State, 160 Ind. App. 647, 313 N.E.2d 101, 1974 Ind. App. LEXIS 1092 (1974).

—Of Possession of Narcotic Drug.
Evidence was sufficient to show possession of narcotic drugs where the drugs were spread on table where defendant had been sitting and there was evidence that defendant knew the illegal nature of such drugs. Cannon v. State, 414 N.E.2d 578, 1980 Ind. App. LEXIS 1858 (1980).

Although the presence of metabolites in urine may be circumstantial evidence of possession of cocaine, the mere presence of metabolites is not prima facie evidence of prior possession and presence of metabolites in a person's bodily systems does not amount to a knowledgeable possession of the substance. State v. Vorm, 570 N.E.2d 109, 1991 Ind. App. LEXIS 666 (1991).

—Of Presence.
Where defendant, with his wife, was joint occupant of the apartment where the drugs were found, but the only persons present at the time of the search were his wife and a houseguest who was not a casual visitor and who had access to the room where the drugs were found, there was insufficient evidence that defendant had knowledge of the presence of the drugs. Martin v. State, 175 Ind. App. 503, 372 N.E.2d 1194, 1978 Ind. App. LEXIS 818 (1978).

Where the accused did not have exclusive control of the premises, it may not be inferred that he knew of the presence of the drugs and had control of them, unless there are other incriminating statements or circumstances tending to buttress such an inference. Martin v. State, 175 Ind. App. 503, 372 N.E.2d 1194, 1978 Ind. App. LEXIS 818 (1978).

Where access to and control of premises where drugs were found was not exclusive there must be additional evidence of incriminating statements or circumstances to raise an inference of knowledge. Gooden v. State, 401 N.E.2d 93, 1980 Ind. App. LEXIS 1341 (1980).

Where there was abundant evidence that heroin was found in defendant's apartment, and there was evidence from which the jury could infer that defendant knew of the presence of the drug, the evidence was sufficient. Williams v. State, 408 N.E.2d 123, 1980 Ind. App. LEXIS 1579 (1980).

Evidence was insufficient to affirm defendant's conviction for possessing narcotic drug since, although carrying case containing methamphetamine was found under passenger seat of car in which he was sitting, there was no evidence that defendant knew case contained methamphetamine. Grim v. State, 797 N.E.2d 825, 2003 Ind. App. LEXIS 1978 (2003).

Sufficient evidence supported an inference that defendant knew about the cocaine and paraphernalia in a car and had the ability to control it: he apologized to an officer for reaching his hands between the seat, confessed that he had just purchased two rocks of cocaine and had just smoked one, and explained that crack and crack pipes were

in the car in violation of IC 35-48-4-8.3(b) and IC 35-48-4-6(b)(2)(B)(i). Atwood v. State, 905 N.E.2d 479, 2009 Ind. App. LEXIS 738 (2009).

Lesser Included Offenses.
An accused was not entitled to an instruction with reference to an offense which was not a lesser included offense and keeping a common nuisance was not a lesser included offense of illegal possession of narcotics. Certain v. State, 261 Ind. 101, 300 N.E.2d 345, 1973 Ind. App. LEXIS 426 (1973).

Where information charged defendant with possession of heroin "with intent to deliver" and defendant made motion for finding of not guilty after state's evidence, it was not error for court to find defendant not guilty of possession with intent to deliver but guilty of lesser included offense of possession. Clark v. State, 173 Ind. App. 295, 363 N.E.2d 1045, 1977 Ind. App. LEXIS 863 (1977).

Trial court did not err by refusing to give a lesser included offense instruction on possession of cocaine, where evidence adduced at trial did not create a serious evidentiary dispute regarding delivery of cocaine, since defendant's argument was directed not to the distinguishing element between dealing and possession, but rather to his participation in any crime. Sledge v. State, 677 N.E.2d 82, 1997 Ind. App. LEXIS 85 (1997).

Where defendant was convicted of dealing in cocaine as class A felony, trial court correctly refused to enter judgment of conviction on jury's additional guilty verdict for possession of cocaine and a firearm, since latter offense, which involved same cocaine, was necessarily included in dealing offense. Kendall v. State, 825 N.E.2d 439, 2005 Ind. App. LEXIS 607 (2005), transfer granted, — N.E.2d —, 2006 Ind. LEXIS 563 (2006), aff'd in part, superseded in part, 849 N.E.2d 1109, 2006 Ind. LEXIS 551 (2006).

Counsel on direct appeal was not ineffective where the plain reading of IC 35-48-4-6(b)(1)(B) (2002) and IC 35-48-4-1 did not demonstrate that an inmate would have been entitled to immediate relief had his counsel raised the issue that possession of cocaine and a firearm was a lesser-included offense of dealing in cocaine. Brown v. State, 880 N.E.2d 1226, 2008 Ind. App. LEXIS 308 (2008).

There was no error in refusing defendant's tendered instruction of Class C possession of cocaine as a lesser included offense of Class A felony for possessing more than three grams of cocaine within 1,000 feet of school property, IC 35-48-4-6(b)(3); defendant had more than 24 grams of cocaine within 20 to 50 feet of a day care center and there was no serious evidentiary dispute about whether the day care at issue was licensed. Danner v. State, 900 N.E.2d 9, 2008 Ind. App. LEXIS 2631 (2008).

Premises.
Although premises in which heroin was found were rented under a different name than that of defendant there was sufficient evidence of possession by defendant where it was shown that the person using the name under which the premises were rented was the same person as defendant.

Premises. (Cont'd)
Hoskins v. State, 174 Ind. App. 475, 174 Ind. App. 480, 367 N.E.2d 1388, 1977 Ind. App. LEXIS 998 (1977).

Search and Seizure.

Where an officer had, two days before the arrest, been informed by two men with criminal records that the defendant was selling heroin and, a few minutes before the arrest, was informed by one of the men whom he had several times previously used as an informer and found to be reliable in his information that he had just purchased heroin from defendant and that defendant was in a certain barbershop with heroin in his possession and the officer thereupon went to the barbershop, arrested defendant, searched him, and found heroin, the arrest and search were lawful and the heroin was admissible in evidence. Wagner v. State, 249 Ind. 457, 233 N.E.2d 236, 1968 Ind. LEXIS 730 (1968), overruled, Johnson v. State, 254 Ind. 465, 260 N.E.2d 782, 1970 Ind. LEXIS 569 (1970), overruled, Weigel v. State, 252 Ind. 464, 250 N.E.2d 368, 1969 Ind. LEXIS 371 (1969).

Where the defendant threw away a container of narcotics in the presence of police, who recovered it, such narcotics were not admissible in evidence where their discard was induced by the defendant's illegal arrest and threatened illegal search. Bowles v. State, 256 Ind. 27, 267 N.E.2d 56, 1971 Ind. LEXIS 578 (1971).

Where there was no contention that the arrest of passenger of car which defendant was driving was unlawful, officers were entitled to search the area of the vehicle within passenger's immediate control, including under the front seat, and upon discovering that the license plate did not belong to the car, that the car might be stolen, and that the passenger had an outstanding warrant for his arrest on felony charges, the officers' belief that they might be in danger was reasonable, justifying a search of the car for weapons; the evidence obtained as a result of the search of the car was properly admitted in defendant's conviction under this section. Woods v. State, 640 N.E.2d 1089, 1994 Ind. App. LEXIS 1355 (1994).

Where decision to impound vehicle was a proper exercise of the community caretaking function because vehicle otherwise would have been left unattended on a public street, and inventory search of vehicle was conducted in a routine manner pursuant to standard department procedures, the fact that officer reflected on passenger's furtive movements prior to his arrest did not render defendant's counsel ineffective for failing to object to search and resulting seizure of cocaine. Peete v. State, 678 N.E.2d 415, 1997 Ind. App. LEXIS 384 (1997).

Where there was no indication that a police officer instantaneously ascertained that the substance in the defendant's watch pocket was either a weapon or contraband in the form of cocaine, but only that he "believed" it could "possibly" have been a narcotic, based largely on the location of the contraband and the neighborhood in which the search took place, the search exceeded the permis-sible bounds of a legitimate patdown, and remand for vacation of the conviction for possession of cocaine was required. Johnson v. State, 710 N.E.2d 925, 1999 Ind. App. LEXIS 734 (1999).

The crack cocaine was inadmissible where the pat down was not lawful because the only facts upon which the officers relied to conduct a pat down were defendant's presence in an area known for drugs and defendant having his hands in his pockets. Swanson v. State, 730 N.E.2d 205, 2000 Ind. App. LEXIS 875 (2000).

Where the evidence found in defendant's house was not derivative evidence, but was itself the product of an illegal search, the taint may not be removed even though this same evidence would have been discovered through lawful means, and the trial court should have granted the order to suppress. LaMunion v. State, 740 N.E.2d 576, 2000 Ind. App. LEXIS 2044 (2000).

Officers lacked probable cause to search children's backpack they saw in open trunk of car because there was no information that backpack had been involved in nearby robbery; argument that exigent circumstances existed to justify search, namely, possibility owner of car would return and drive car away, was rejected, since one officer could have gone to obtain warrant while other remained with car. Jones v. State, 814 N.E.2d 298, 2004 Ind. App. LEXIS 1763 (2004).

Where the purpose of a traffic stop was satisfied when a police officer determined that defendant had a valid temporary license plate, cocaine seized thereafter was obtained in violation of the Fourth Amendment, and defendant's motion to suppress the cocaine should have been granted. Young v. State, 886 N.E.2d 636, 2008 Ind. App. LEXIS 1155 (2008).

—Investigatory Stop.

Evidence of an exchange of something between defendant and a third party, and defendant's act of walking away when he saw police was not a sufficient basis for an investigatory stop where there was no evidence that defendant was in a high crime area or that the officer knew that either party was involved in criminal activity. The officer's suspicion was based merely on a hunch that the two were involved in criminal activity and was not a sufficient basis for an investigatory stop. Williams v. State, 745 N.E.2d 241, 2001 Ind. App. LEXIS 308 (2001).

Search Warrant.

A search warrant issued within three days after the drugs were seen in a residence was not based on information that was too old and was valid. Tinnin v. State, 275 Ind. 203, 416 N.E.2d 116, 1981 Ind. LEXIS 674 (1981).

In an interlocutory appeal, pursuant to IC 35-33-5-1 and IC 35-33-5-2, the trial court did not err in finding that a substantial basis existed to conclude that probable cause was present because the trash that the officers legally retrieved from defendant's household contained both drug paraphernalia and evidence of cocaine. Given the presence of cocaine, and the fact that the possession of cocaine

Search Warrant. (Cont'd)
itself was a crime under IC 35-48-4-6, the search warrant was based upon probable cause, and the evidence discovered during the execution of the warrant was admissible; thus, defendant's motion to suppress was properly denied. Love v. State, 842 N.E.2d 420, 2006 Ind. App. LEXIS 223 (2006).

Sentence.
Where the trial judge suspended a two to ten year sentence and ordered the defendant to serve out his fine at the State Farm, and sentence at State Farm was improper, court had power to correct such sentence, where he wanted some time served; by removing the suspended sentence and ordering the defendant to serve the two to ten year sentence. State v. Irvin, 259 Ind. 610, 291 N.E.2d 70, 1973 Ind. LEXIS 589 (1973).

Consecutive sentences were not improper for multiple sales of a single drug to one informant, where defendant was sentenced after pleading guilty pursuant to an agreement which provided that the court had discretion to order concurrent or consecutive sentences, the trial court questioned defendant to be sure he understood the sentence and terms of the plea agreement, and the length of the sentence was not inappropriate to the offense or the offender. Ragland v. State, 670 N.E.2d 51, 1996 Ind. App. LEXIS 1092 (1996).

Where the defendant was given the presumptive 30 year sentence after pleading guilty to possessing cocaine within 1,000 feet of a school zone, a strict liability offense, the sentence was in proportion to the crime. Miller v. State, 709 N.E.2d 48, 1999 Ind. App. LEXIS 619 (1999).

Trial court erred by attaching defendant's habitual offender enhancement to conviction under IC 35-48-4-6 for possession of cocaine since that conviction was ineligible for enhancement under IC 35-50-2-8(b). Johnican v. State, 804 N.E.2d 211, 2004 Ind. App. LEXIS 324 (2004).

Because defendant's felony offenses, which included possession of cocaine, resisting law enforcement, and pointing firearm, constituted single episode of criminal conduct, IC 35-50-1-2(b) permitted trial court to impose consecutive sentences totaling 30 years for felonies; accordingly, trial court's imposition of consecutive sentences totaling 26 years did not violate IC 35-50-1-2. Johnican v. State, 804 N.E.2d 211, 2004 Ind. App. LEXIS 324 (2004).

Intent to possess cocaine does not make a conspiracy conviction a substance offense; thus, defendant's conviction for conspiracy to commit possession of cocaine was not a substance offense, and the evidence was insufficient to sustain defendant's status as an habitual substance offender. Therefore, the trial court was directed to vacate the habitual substance offender enhancement that was attached to Count I, dealing in cocaine as a class A felony. Whaley v. State, 843 N.E.2d 1, 2006 Ind. App. LEXIS 164 (2006).

Enhancement of defendant's cocaine possession offense from a Class D felony to a Class B felony did not violate the proportionality clause of Ind. Const., art. 1, § 16 where IC 35-48-4-6 clearly required an additional element before possession of cocaine could be charged as a Class B felony; even if there were few, if any, locations within a county that weren't either within or accessed by passing within one of the forbidden areas, prosecutors nonetheless had to prove proximity to a site listed in IC 35-48-4-6(b) to obtain a conviction for a Class B felony. Manigault v. State, 881 N.E.2d 679, 2008 Ind. App. LEXIS 307 (2008).

There was no error in sentencing defendant to the maximum sentence of 50 years for his conviction of, inter alia, felony possession of cocaine as a Class A felony for possessing more than three grams of cocaine within 1,000 feet of school property, IC 35-48-4-6(b)(3), where the record disclosed that defendant had more than 24 grams of cocaine when he was stopped within 20 to 50 feet of a licensed day care center and had convictions for Class A felony dealing in cocaine, Class B felony dealing in cocaine, Class D felony possession of cocaine, and two convictions for Class B felony robbery. Danner v. State, 900 N.E.2d 9, 2008 Ind. App. LEXIS 2631 (2008).

—Fines.
Where the trial court imposed, inter alia, a fine upon defendant for a possession of cocaine conviction, the fine was vacated, as the plea agreement did not provide for a fine; the imposition of the fine was not contemplated by the parties in reaching their agreement, and the trial court erred in varying the terms of the sentence as set out in the plea agreement. Briscoe v. State, 783 N.E.2d 790, 2003 Ind. App. LEXIS 266 (2003).

Trial court was not required to examine defendant's ability to pay before imposing a $200 fee, following defendant's conviction for methamphetamine possession, a Class D felony, under IC 35-48-4-6, as the minimum $200 fee was required by IC 33-19-6-9, regardless of ability to pay. Taylor v. State, 786 N.E.2d 285, 2003 Ind. App. LEXIS 561 (2003).

— —Indigency Hearing Required.
With regard to defendant's conviction for possession of cocaine, while the appointment of trial counsel and appellate counsel implied that the trial court knew of defendant's indigency, and the presentence investigation report provided the trial court with some information regarding defendant's financial position, such facts were not conclusive as to defendant's ability to pay fees; thus, the trial court erred when it failed to conduct a hearing on the issue, and remand was required to hold a hearing on defendant's indigency because defendant's sentence included the imposition of a fee. Briscoe v. State, 783 N.E.2d 790, 2003 Ind. App. LEXIS 266 (2003).

"Without Valid Prescription or Order."
The phrase "without a valid prescription or order of a practitioner" states an exception to and not an element of the crime of possession. Gilbert v. State, 426 N.E.2d 1333, 1981 Ind. App. LEXIS 1701 (1981).

Cited:
Morgan v. State, 427 N.E.2d 14, 1981 Ind. App.

LEXIS 1691 (1981); Everroad v. State, 442 N.E.2d 994, 1982 Ind. LEXIS 1038 (1982); Hudson v. State, 443 N.E.2d 834, 1983 Ind. LEXIS 725 (1983); O'Grady v. State, 481 N.E.2d 115, 1985 Ind. App. LEXIS 2644 (1985); In re Payne, 494 N.E.2d 1283, 1986 Ind. LEXIS 1188 (1986); Evans v. State, 566 N.E.2d 1037, 1991 Ind. App. LEXIS 178 (1991); Esquerdo v. State, 640 N.E.2d 1023, 1994 Ind. LEXIS 126 (1994); Mitchell v. State, 659 N.E.2d 112, 1995 Ind. LEXIS 188 (1995); Stone v. State, 671 N.E.2d 499, 1996 Ind. App. LEXIS 1485 (1996); Price v. State, 725 N.E.2d 82, 2000 Ind. LEXIS 208 (2000); Navaretta v. State, 726 N.E.2d 787, 2000 Ind. LEXIS 246 (2000); Stone v. State, 727 N.E.2d 33, 2000 Ind. App. LEXIS 565 (2000); Robinson v. State, 730 N.E.2d 185, 2000 Ind. App. LEXIS 864 (2000); Graham v. State, 738 N.E.2d 1096, 2000 Ind. App. LEXIS 1982 (2000); Huffines v. State, 739 N.E.2d 1093, 2000 Ind. App. LEXIS 2057 (2000); Kirby v. State, 746 N.E.2d 440, 2001 Ind. App. LEXIS 711 (2001); Caudle v. State, 749 N.E.2d 616, 2001 Ind. App. LEXIS 898 (2001); Fuller v. State, 752 N.E.2d 235, 2001 Ind. App. LEXIS 1290 (2001); Prewitt v. State, 761 N.E.2d 862, 2002 Ind. App. LEXIS 18 (2002); Jones v. State, 790 N.E.2d 536, 2003 Ind. App. LEXIS 1102 (2003); Winebrenner v. State, 790 N.E.2d 1037, 2003 Ind. App. LEXIS 1195 (2003); Stokes v. State, 801 N.E.2d 1263, 2004 Ind. App. LEXIS 63 (2004); Fermaglich v. Indiana, — F. Supp. 2d —, 2004 U.S. Dist. LEXIS 24539 (S.D. Ind. 2004); Cotto v. State, 829 N.E.2d 520, 2005 Ind. LEXIS 562 (2005); Baird v. State, 854 N.E.2d 398, 2006 Ind. App. LEXIS 1951 (2006); Fentress v. State, 863 N.E.2d 420, 2007 Ind. App. LEXIS 579 (2007); Cade v. State, 872 N.E.2d 186, 2007 Ind. App. LEXIS 1919 (2007); Bell v. State, 881 N.E.2d 1080, 2008 Ind. App. LEXIS 437 (2008).

RESEARCH REFERENCES

Res Gestae.

Criminal Justice Notes 10/03: Constructive possession — handgun, drugs and paraphernalia in vehicle. 47 (No. 6) Res Gestae 43 (2004).

Criminal Justice Notes 6/04: Constructive possession not shown, 48 (No. 2) Res Gestae 32 (2004).

Collateral References.

Minimum quantity of drug required to support claim that defendant is guilty of criminal "possession" of drug under state law. 4 A.L.R.5th 1.

Validity, construction, and application of state statutes prohibiting sale or possession of controlled substances within specified distance of schools. 27 A.L.R.5th 593.

35-48-4-6.1. Possession of methamphetamine.

(a) A person who, without a valid prescription or order of a practitioner acting in the course of the practitioner's professional practice, knowingly or intentionally possesses methamphetamine (pure or adulterated) commits possession of methamphetamine, a Class D felony, except as provided in subsection (b).

(b) The offense is:

(1) a Class C felony if:

(A) the amount of the drug involved (pure or adulterated) weighs three (3) grams or more; or

(B) the person was also in possession of a firearm (as defined in IC 35-47-1-5);

(2) a Class B felony if the person in possession of the methamphetamine possesses less than three (3) grams of pure or adulterated methamphetamine:

(A) on a school bus; or

(B) in, on, or within one thousand (1,000) feet of:

(i) school property;

(ii) a public park;

(iii) a family housing complex; or

(iv) a youth program center; and

(3) a Class A felony if the person possesses the methamphetamine in an amount (pure or adulterated) weighing at least three (3) grams:

(A) on a school bus; or

(B) in, on, or within one thousand (1,000) feet of:

(i) school property;

(ii) a public park;

(iii) a family housing complex; or

(iv) a youth program center.

History.
P.L.151-2006, § 25.

Compiler's Notes.
P.L.151-2006, § 29, effective July 1, 2006, provides: "IC 35-48-4-1.1 and IC 35-48-4-6.1, both as added by this act, and IC 35-48-4-1, IC 35-48-4-6,

IC 35-48-4-14.5, and IC 35-48-4-14.7, all as amended by this act, apply only to crimes committed after June 30, 2006."

Cross References.
Penalties for felonies, IC 35-50-1, IC 35-50-2, IC 35-50-5-2.

NOTES TO DECISIONS

Lesser Included Offenses.
Sentence on Count II for possession of methamphetamine as a Class D felony (IC 35-48-4-6.1) had to be vacated because Count II was a lesser included offense of Count I for dealing in methamphetamine (IC 35-48-4-1.1). Micheau v. State, 893 N.E.2d 1053, 2008 Ind. App. LEXIS 2029 (2008).

Sufficiency of Evidence.
Defendant's conviction for dealing in methamphetamine was supported by evidence showing that methamphetamine precursors and paraphernalia were found in virtually every room of defendant's house, that defendant had carried at least some of the items into the house, and that methamphetamine residue was found on a plate in the kitchen. Fowler v. State, — N.E.2d —, 2009 Ind. App. LEXIS 121 (2009).

35-48-4-7. Possession of a controlled substance.

(a) A person who, without a valid prescription or order of a practitioner acting in the course of his professional practice, knowingly or intentionally possesses a controlled substance (pure or adulterated) classified in schedule I, II, III, or IV, except marijuana or hashish, commits possession of a controlled substance, a Class D felony. However, the offense is a Class C felony if the person in possession of the controlled substance possesses the controlled substance:
  (1) on a school bus; or
  (2) in, on, or within one thousand (1,000) feet of:
    (A) school property;
    (B) a public park;
    (C) a family housing complex; or
    (D) a youth program center.
(b) A person who, without a valid prescription or order of a practitioner acting in the course of his professional practice, knowingly or intentionally obtains:
  (1) more than four (4) ounces of schedule V controlled substances containing codeine in any given forty-eight (48) hour period unless pursuant to a prescription;
  (2) a schedule V controlled substance pursuant to written or verbal misrepresentation; or
  (3) possession of a schedule V controlled substance other than by means of a prescription or by means of signing an exempt narcotic register maintained by a pharmacy licensed by the Indiana state board of pharmacy;
commits a Class D felony.

History.
IC 35-48-4-7, as added by Acts 1976, P.L.148, § 7; 1977, P.L.340, § 102; P.L.138-1983, § 4; P.L.327-1985, § 4; P.L.296-1987, § 10; P.L.296-1995, § 8; P.L.65-1996, § 16; P.L.17-2001, § 25.

Cross References.
Penalties for felonies, IC 35-50-1, IC 35-50-2, IC 35-50-5-2.

NOTES TO DECISIONS

—Invalid Prescription.
—Other Offenses.
—Prior Convictions.
—Prosecutorial Statements.
—Search and Seizure.
—Sufficient.
—Testimony of Pharmacists.
Exemptions or Exceptions.
Indictment or Information.
—Failure to Cite Statutory Provisions.
—Sufficiency.
Jury Instructions.
Knowledge and Intent.
Lesser Included Offenses.
Merger of Verdicts.
School Property.
—Persons in Moving Vehicles.
Search Warrants.
Sentence.

Amount.

Any identifiable amount of an illegal drug is sufficient to convict. Brown v. State, 177 Ind. App. 607, 380 N.E.2d 609, 1978 Ind. App. LEXIS 1038 (1978).

Constructive Possession.

Where aside from defendant's wife's possessory interest in the apartment where marijuana was found, the evidence was undisputed that the landlord entered the apartment, took control, and leased it to someone else and that workmen had entered the apartment to renovate it, defendant did not have exclusive control of the apartment so as to put him in constructive possession of the marijuana. Solano v. State, 426 N.E.2d 705, 1981 Ind. App. LEXIS 1674 (1981).

To establish constructive possession of a controlled substance, the state must prove the defendant was capable of controlling the contraband and intended to do so. Proof of a possessory interest in the premises where contraband was found is adequate to show capability to control. Evidence that contraband was found hidden in a person's dresser is sufficient to prove the person intended to control it. Robinson v. State, 454 N.E.2d 873, 1983 Ind. App. LEXIS 3455 (1983).

Evidence was sufficient to support a conviction for unlawful "constructive possession" of contraband found within the defendants' joint residency, within the kitchen refrigerator and upon a tray sitting upon a bench or table in the bedroom. Carnes v. State, 480 N.E.2d 581, 1985 Ind. App. LEXIS 2634 (1985).

Because, at the time of the arrest, the defendant's acquaintance was pouring heroin through a funnel into a balloon, on the dresser near where the defendant was sitting was a Dormin bottle containing 24 balloons filled with heroin, in an open drawer of the dresser were two bottles of Dormin, a cooker cap containing heroin residue, a bottle of diphenhydramine, and a billfold containing paraphernalia for packaging heroin, the evidence is sufficient to support the inference that the defendant was aware of the presence and character of the heroin to support a finding of construc-

tive possession. Young v. State, 562 N.E.2d 424, 1990 Ind. App. LEXIS 1448 (1990).

Police officer had probable cause to charge defendant with unlawful possession of controlled substance where officer found two Lortab pills in owner's abandoned truck during inventory search, where Lortab was controlled substance under IC 35-48-4-7, where officer found no evidence of prescription for Lortab, and where officer was not required to seek more information about defendant's possession of Lortab before filing charge. Welty v. McLanahan, — F. Supp. 2d —, 2004 U.S. Dist. LEXIS 9144 (S.D. Ind. 2004).

"Dealing."

The term "dealing" as it appeared in former IC 35-47-5-4 (dealing in sawed-off shotguns) was obviously used in the broad sense of a course of conduct as opposed to the limited sense in which it was used in other statutes, such as those which define the offense of dealing in controlled substances. Brook v. State, 448 N.E.2d 1249, 1983 Ind. App. LEXIS 2943 (1983).

Defenses.

—Prescription.

Under this section, where the state must prove that the defendant knowingly or intentionally possessed a controlled substance, the existence of a valid prescription for that substance is a defense to the offense of possession. Schuller v. State, 625 N.E.2d 1243, 1993 Ind. App. LEXIS 1502 (1993).

Double Jeopardy.

Where possession and delivery counts stemmed from the same factual basis, and only one delivery took place, the possession charge was only a lesser included offense of the sale charge. Cyrus v. State, 269 Ind. 461, 381 N.E.2d 472, 1978 Ind. LEXIS 800 (1978), cert. denied, 441 U.S. 935, 99 S. Ct. 2058, 60 L. Ed. 2d 664, 1979 U.S. LEXIS 1758 (1979).

Where defendant was convicted on all three counts of a three-count indictment charging possession of controlled substances in schedules I, III and IV, the trial court erred in imposing sentences on all three counts and the judgments and sentences on two of the judgments should be vacated. Martin v. State, 176 Ind. App. 99, 374 N.E.2d 543, 1978 Ind. App. LEXIS 864 (1978).

Where defendant forged a prescription and by use of the prescription attempted to obtain controlled substances at four different drug stores there could be only one conviction for attempted possession of a controlled substance and not four. Perry v. State, 177 Ind. App. 334, 379 N.E.2d 531, 1978 Ind. App. LEXIS 996 (1978).

The offenses of forgery and uttering a forged instrument were not necessarily lesser included offenses of the crime of attempting to obtain a controlled substance. Dolan v. State, 178 Ind. App. 127, 381 N.E.2d 543, 1978 Ind. App. LEXIS 1069 (1978).

Where defendant retained a residue of a substance after a delivery transaction, possession of the controlled substance was not a lesser included

Double Jeopardy. (Cont'd)
offense of the delivery offense. Bates v. State, 178 Ind. App. 153, 381 N.E.2d 552, 1978 Ind. App. LEXIS 1074 (1978).

Convictions for possession of a controlled substance and obtaining a controlled substance violated the statutory prohibition against multiple punishments for the same offense. Loman v. State, 640 N.E.2d 745, 1994 Ind. App. LEXIS 1345 (1994).

Assessment of controlled substance excise tax (CSET) in amount of $871,437.50 against person who pled guilty to maintaining common nuisance did not violate double jeopardy because element of possession, which was required for assessment of CSET, was not required to establish essential elements of maintaining common nuisance; furthermore, CSET was legislatively intended as an addition to any criminal penalties or forfeitures. Newby v. Ind. Dep't of State Revenue, 826 N.E.2d 173, 2005 Ind. Tax LEXIS 24 (2005).

Evidence.

—Chain of Custody.
Chain of custody was adequate despite mailing of small envelope containing drug sample to police laboratory since it was probable that the sample had not been tampered with during mailing, and despite fact that seven or eight persons had access to the sample while it was at the laboratory, there being no evidence that any unauthorized person had tampered with the sample. Downing v. State, 178 Ind. App. 144, 381 N.E.2d 554, 1978 Ind. App. LEXIS 1075 (1978).

—Inferences.
In that defendant assisted his companion in obtaining drugs by forgery and deception, and by uttering forged prescriptions, it was reasonable to infer that he knew of the presence of those drugs in the glove compartment of his leased automobile, and that therefore, he had sufficient control over those drugs to support his conviction for possession. Dolan v. State, 178 Ind. App. 127, 381 N.E.2d 543, 1978 Ind. App. LEXIS 1069 (1978).

—Insufficient.
Where there was no evidence supporting an allegation that defendant accompanied codefendant and a third party as they went from town to town passing forged prescriptions, evidence that defendant was with codefendant when codefendant was apprehended was by itself insufficient to support defendant's convictions for forgery, uttering a forged instrument, deception, and possession of a controlled substance. Dolan v. State, 178 Ind. App. 127, 381 N.E.2d 543, 1978 Ind. App. LEXIS 1069 (1978).

—Invalid Prescription.
Where the evidence established that the defendant obtained a prescription by fraud, the factfinder properly concluded that the prescription was not valid. Schuller v. State, 625 N.E.2d 1243, 1993 Ind. App. LEXIS 1502 (1993).

—Other Offenses.
Even though defendant was charged with the attempted possession of a controlled substance, it was proper to admit evidence that defendant aided, induced or caused another to commit the offense charged. Ralston v. State, 412 N.E.2d 239, 1980 Ind. App. LEXIS 1736 (1980).

—Prior Convictions.
Where defendant testified, it was proper to question defendant about prior conviction for possession of controlled substance, which conviction was on appeal, as a means of impeaching defendant's testimony where jury was given a cautionary instruction regarding their consideration of prior crimes for impeachment purposes only. Craig v. State, 403 N.E.2d 925, 1980 Ind. App. LEXIS 1431 (1980).

—Prosecutorial Statements.
Statement by prosecutor that defendant "is a drug dealer" in final argument in prosecution for possession of a controlled substance when there was no evidence to support such statement constituted reversible error. Flynn v. State, 177 Ind. App. 360, 379 N.E.2d 548, 1978 Ind. App. LEXIS 1003 (1978).

—Search and Seizure.
Where defendant invited undercover police officers to enter his residence, where quantities of a controlled substance were clearly visible, and where defendant offered to obtain some of the substance for the officers, there was probable cause for defendant's arrest, and his subsequent search fell within the exception to the search warrant requirement made for a search subsequent to lawful arrest. McBride v. State, 178 Ind. App. 160, 381 N.E.2d 562, 1978 Ind. App. LEXIS 1077 (1978).

Where officer testified at suppression hearing that, before entering the apartment, he did not believe or suspect that the occupants of the apartment were committing any type of criminal activity besides violating the noise ordinance of the town, the officer did not have facts upon which he could reasonably have concluded that the occupants were engaging in or were the victims of criminal activity, and the search was illegal. Hanna v. State, 726 N.E.2d 384, 2000 Ind. App. LEXIS 511 (2000).

Where defendant's truck was impounded after defendant crashed the truck in a parking lot while attempting to flee from an arrest, and the truck's contents were inventoried pursuant to the community care taking function and established police procedures, the inventory search exception to the warrant requirement of U.S. Const. amend. IV applied to money that was found in a suitcase inside the truck, and, accordingly, the money was not subject to suppression. Ratliff v. State, 770 N.E.2d 807, 2002 Ind. LEXIS 544 (2002).

Since identity of pills was not immediately apparent to police officer, removal of pill bottle from defendant's pants pocket during Terry search for weapons and subsequent testing of pills exceeded permissible bounds of legitimate pat-down; accordingly, trial court abused its discretion in denying defendant's motion to suppress evidence obtained

Evidence. (Cont'd)

—Search and Seizure. (Cont'd)
from testing of pills. Burkett v. State, 785 N.E.2d 276, 2003 Ind. App. LEXIS 409 (2003).

—Sufficient.
Where substance was found in defendant's clothing evidence was sufficient to show that he knowingly possessed the substance. Clark v. State, 400 N.E.2d 172, 1980 Ind. App. LEXIS 1307 (1980).

Where police found PCP and drug paraphernalia in defendant's apartment and defendant was a regular user, evidence of possession was sufficient. Norris v. State, 275 Ind. 608, 419 N.E.2d 129, 1981 Ind. LEXIS 724 (1981).

A possessory interest in the premises where the contraband is found is sufficient to establish the capability to maintain control. Solano v. State, 426 N.E.2d 705, 1981 Ind. App. LEXIS 1674 (1981); Burgin v. State, 431 N.E.2d 864, 1982 Ind. App. LEXIS 1090 (1982).

Evidence abandoned by defendant as the result of a lawful investigatory stop was admissible at trial, and with the admission of those items, the evidence was sufficient to sustain the convictions of possession of a controlled substance and carrying a handgun without a license. Gipson v. State, 459 N.E.2d 366, 1984 Ind. LEXIS 743 (1984).

Where defendant was arrested for disorderly conduct and public intoxication, and an inventory search revealed a used and worn aspirin tin being carried in his pocket, in which were nine pills including one containing phenobarbital, it was reasonable for the jury to infer that he knew what kind of pills he was carrying in a well-used tin in his own pocket, and the evidence of possession of a schedule IV controlled substance was not insufficient. Bastin v. State, 510 N.E.2d 229, 1987 Ind. App. LEXIS 2883 (1987).

Evidence was sufficient to sustain defendant's conviction, where he did not dispute his possession of mushrooms containing psilocyn, a controlled substance naturally occurring in the mushrooms, which do not grow naturally in Indiana. Kail v. State, 528 N.E.2d 799, 1988 Ind. App. LEXIS 659 (1988).

Fact that dollar bill containing drugs was found next to passenger seat of car in which defendant was riding and that items recovered from vehicle were used in manufacturing methamphetamine were sufficient to sustain conviction for possession of controlled substance. Boner v. State, 796 N.E.2d 1249, 2003 Ind. App. LEXIS 1919 (2003).

Evidence that defendant possessed unmarked bottle of pills, that he produced no prescription for pills, and that he did not claim until after his arrest that he was taking the pills to his mother was sufficient for appellate court to uphold defendant's conviction for possession of controlled substance, since to conclude otherwise would have been invasion of jury's responsibility to judge credibility of witnesses and weigh evidence. Shirley v. State, 803 N.E.2d 251, 2004 Ind. App. LEXIS 209 (2004).

—Testimony of Pharmacists.
It was proper to permit an experienced pharmacist to testify that preludin was a tablet containing phenmetrazine which was a class II controlled substance although the witness had never analyzed such tablets. Ralston v. State, 412 N.E.2d 239, 1980 Ind. App. LEXIS 1736 (1980).

Exemptions or Exceptions.
Because of the provisions of former IC 16-6-8.5-6 which made it unnecessary for the state to negate exceptions and which placed the burden of proof of any exemption or exception on the person claiming it, it was not necessary for the state to either plead or prove that phenmetrazine, a class II controlled substance, was not marijuana or hashish. Ralston v. State, 412 N.E.2d 239, 1980 Ind. App. LEXIS 1736 (1980).

Possession of a valid prescription was an exception to the crime of possession in this section; therefore former IC 16-6-8.5-6(a) placed the burden of proving a valid prescription on the defendant. Burgin v. State, 431 N.E.2d 864, 1982 Ind. App. LEXIS 1090 (1982).

Indictment or Information.

—Failure to Cite Statutory Provisions.
Where defendant was charged with attempting to commit the crime of possession of a controlled substance by knowingly presenting a forged prescription to be filled for preludin, the failure of the state to cite the statutory provision did not place defendant in a position of uncertainty as to whether the state intended to present evidence of attempted possession of a narcotic drug under IC 35-48-4-6. Ralston v. State, 412 N.E.2d 239, 1980 Ind. App. LEXIS 1736 (1980).

—Sufficiency.
An information which charged defendant with attempting to commit the crime of possession of a controlled substance by knowingly presenting a forged prescription to be filled for preludin was sufficient to appraise defendant of the charge notwithstanding the statutory section was not stated and preludin was not described in the words of this section. Ralston v. State, 412 N.E.2d 239, 1980 Ind. App. LEXIS 1736 (1980).

Jury Instructions.
Where defendant's conviction for violating IC 35-48-4-7 was subject to enhancement because he was arrested in a park, he was not entitled to an instruction under IC 35-48-4-16, which provided a defense if no one under 18 was in the park at the time, as the testimony showed only that it was unknown whether anyone under 18 was in the park at the time defendant was arrested. Stringer v. State, 853 N.E.2d 543, 2006 Ind. App. LEXIS 1804 (2006).

Knowledge and Intent.
Evidence that the accused had exclusive control over the premises permits a reasonable inference that he had knowledge of or intent possession of the contraband. Solano v. State, 426 N.E.2d 705, 1981 Ind. App. LEXIS 1674 (1981).

Exclusive possession of the premises where contraband is found is sufficient to show intent to

Knowledge and Intent. (Cont'd)
control the contraband. Burgin v. State, 431 N.E.2d 864, 1982 Ind. App. LEXIS 1090 (1982).

When a person does not have exclusive possession of the premises where contraband is found, some additional evidence is necessary to show intent to control. Burgin v. State, 431 N.E.2d 864, 1982 Ind. App. LEXIS 1090 (1982).

Lesser Included Offenses.
Attempted possession of a controlled substance was not a lesser included offense of forgery within the double jeopardy provision of the fifth amendment and therefore defendant could be sentenced for both the attempted possession and the uttering of a forged prescription to obtain possession of a controlled substance. Ralston v. State, 412 N.E.2d 239, 1980 Ind. App. LEXIS 1736 (1980).

Merger of Verdicts.
Where jury found defendant guilty of both possession and dealing in a controlled substance and judge in entering judgment stated that verdict of guilty of possession merged in the finding of guilty on the greater offense of dealing in a controlled substance, and defendant was declared guilty of only the crime of dealing in a controlled substance for which he was sentenced, errors involving the possession count were not subject to review on appeal. Johnson v. State, 413 N.E.2d 686, 1980 Ind. App. LEXIS 1869 (1980).

School Property.

—Persons in Moving Vehicles.
The enhancement for possession within 1000 feet of school property applies to an occupant of a moving vehicle in that zone, and enhancement of defendant's convictions of possession of cocaine and possession of a controlled substance did not violate his right to equal protection. Polk v. State, 683 N.E.2d 567, 1997 Ind. LEXIS 117 (1997).

Search Warrants.
Where police officer who swore out affidavit for search warrant to search premises lost visual contact of informant who was making a controlled buy for police officer for about 20 seconds it was not so substantial as to affect probable cause and evidence obtained by search was properly intro-duced. Whirley v. State, 408 N.E.2d 629, 1980 Ind. App. LEXIS 1607 (1980).

Sentence.
Because defendant had failed to respond positively to more lenient punishments in the past, and the trial court properly weighed aggravating and mitigating circumstances, her ten-year sentence, consisting of concurrent advisory sentences for burglary, a class B felony, and possession within 1000 feet of a school, a class C felony, was appropriate. Thomas-Collins v. State, 868 N.E.2d 557, 2007 Ind. App. LEXIS 1315 (2007).

Because defendant was in possession of 74.74 grams of cocaine when he was arrested, he was facing a minimum of 20 years if he did not plead guilty, and his criminal history involved offenses against persons and property; accordingly, his sentence of 15 years was not inappropriate for his convictions under IC 35-48-4-1(a)(1) and IC 35-48-4-7(a). Swain v. State, 870 N.E.2d 1058, 2007 Ind. App. LEXIS 1721 (2007).

While the trial court erred in finding the amount of cocaine an aggravating circumstance since defendant pled guilty to a lesser charge, it did properly find defendant's criminal history an aggravating circumstance. Swain v. State, 870 N.E.2d 1058, 2007 Ind. App. LEXIS 1721 (2007).

Cited:
Fyock v. State, 428 N.E.2d 58, 1981 Ind. App. LEXIS 1741 (1981); Elliott v. State, 435 N.E.2d 302, 1982 Ind. App. LEXIS 1217 (1982); Flaherty v. State, 443 N.E.2d 340, 1982 Ind. App. LEXIS 1539 (1982); Priestley v. State, 451 N.E.2d 88, 1983 Ind. App. LEXIS 3130 (1983); Borst v. State, 459 N.E.2d 751, 1984 Ind. App. LEXIS 2337 (1984); Crabtree v. State, 479 N.E.2d 70, 1985 Ind. App. LEXIS 2496 (1985); O'Grady v. State, 481 N.E.2d 115, 1985 Ind. App. LEXIS 2644 (1985); Davis v. State, 642 N.E.2d 987, 1994 Ind. App. LEXIS 1602 (1994); Huffines v. State, 739 N.E.2d 1093, 2000 Ind. App. LEXIS 2057 (2000); Kirby v. State, 746 N.E.2d 440, 2001 Ind. App. LEXIS 711 (2001); Bradley v. State, 765 N.E.2d 204, 2002 Ind. App. LEXIS 458 (2002); Creekmore v. State, 800 N.E.2d 230, 2003 Ind. App. LEXIS 2341 (2003); Stanley v. State, 849 N.E.2d 626, 2006 Ind. App. LEXIS 1103 (2006).

RESEARCH REFERENCES

Collateral References.
Minimum quantity of drug required to support claim that defendant is guilty of criminal "possession" of drug under state law. 4 A.L.R.5th 1.

Drug abuse: what constitutes illegal construc-tive possession under 21 U.S.C. § 841(a)(1), prohibiting possession of a controlled substance with intent to manufacture, distribute, or dispense the same. 87 A.L.R. Fed. 309.

35-48-4-8. [Repealed.]

Compiler's Notes.
This section, concerning possession of and dealing in paraphernalia, was repealed by Acts 1980, P.L.115, § 5. For present similar provisions, see IC 35-48-4-8.3.

35-48-4-8.1. Manufacture of paraphernalia.

(a) A person who manufactures, finances the manufacture of, or designs an instrument, a device, or other object that is intended to be used primarily for:

(1) Introducing into the human body a controlled substance;

(2) Testing the strength, effectiveness, or purity of a controlled substance; or

(3) Enhancing the effect of a controlled substance;

in violation of this chapter commits a Class A infraction for manufacturing paraphernalia.

(b) A person who:

(1) Knowingly or intentionally violates this section; and

(2) Has a previous judgment for violation of this section;

commits manufacture of paraphernalia, a Class D felony.

History.
IC 35-48-4-8.1, as added by Acts 1980, P.L.115, § 2; P.L.202-1989, § 3; P.L.165-1990, § 10.

Penalties for felonies, IC 35-50-1, IC 35-50-2, IC 35-50-5-2.

Cross References.
Infraction and ordinance violation enforcement proceedings, IC 34-28-5.

NOTES TO DECISIONS

ANALYSIS

Constitutionality.
—Cruel and Unusual Punishment.
—Free Speech.
—Interstate Commerce.
—Not Overbroad.
—Statutory Classifications.
—Vagueness.
Elements.
—"Manufactures or Designs."
Intent of Violator.

Constitutionality.
The Indiana drug paraphernalia provisions are not violative of either the First Amendment or the due process clause. Nova Records, Inc. v. Sendak, 706 F.2d 782, 1983 U.S. App. LEXIS 28783 (7th Cir. Ind. 1983).

—Cruel and Unusual Punishment.
Drug paraphernalia statutes do not permit cruel and unusual punishment of innocent activity in violation of the Eighth Amendment, for the statutes insure that those lacking the requisite intent or knowledge will not be subjected to any punishment whatsoever. Nova Records, Inc. v. Sendak, 504 F. Supp. 938, 1980 U.S. Dist. LEXIS 15832 (S.D. Ind. 1980), aff'd, 706 F.2d 782, 1983 U.S. App. LEXIS 28783 (7th Cir. Ind. 1983).

—Free Speech.
The intent requirements of the Indiana drug paraphernalia statutes prevent a wholesale assault on unpopular, but legal, commercial or symbolic speech, and the statutes do not impermissibly restrict protected commercial or symbolic speech. Nova Records, Inc. v. Sendak, 504 F. Supp. 938, 1980 U.S. Dist. LEXIS 15832 (S.D. Ind. 1980), aff'd, 706 F.2d 782, 1983 U.S. App. LEXIS 28783 (7th Cir. Ind. 1983).

—Interstate Commerce.
The effect of the drug paraphernalia provisions, if any, on interstate commerce will be both incidental and fully justified. Nova Records, Inc. v. Sendak, 504 F. Supp. 938, 1980 U.S. Dist. LEXIS 15832 (S.D. Ind. 1980), aff'd, 706 F.2d 782, 1983 U.S. App. LEXIS 28783 (7th Cir. Ind. 1983).

—Not Overbroad.
Drug paraphernalia statutes are not facially overbroad because reasonable people can readily tell whether their conduct will be violative of the law since it is their own state of mind which is ultimately determinative. Nova Records, Inc. v. Sendak, 504 F. Supp. 938, 1980 U.S. Dist. LEXIS 15832 (S.D. Ind. 1980), aff'd, 706 F.2d 782, 1983 U.S. App. LEXIS 28783 (7th Cir. Ind. 1983).

—Statutory Classifications.
Drug paraphernalia statutes on their face create no statutory classifications not reasonably related to a legitimate state purpose, and to the extent that subsequent events show a disproportionate impact of enforcement on enterprises in the nature of those operated by plaintiffs, such result may be justified on the basis of the recognized likelihood that such shops will contain objects constituting paraphernalia under the statutes. Nova Records, Inc. v. Sendak, 504 F. Supp. 938, 1980 U.S. Dist. LEXIS 15832 (S.D. Ind. 1980), aff'd, 706 F.2d 782, 1983 U.S. App. LEXIS 28783 (7th Cir. Ind. 1983).

—Vagueness.
Drug paraphernalia statutes are not unconstitutionally vague where persons of ordinary intelligence are put on notice that items intended for ingesting, testing, or enhancing the effect of a controlled substance will be deemed to fall within the category of drug paraphernalia to the detriment of one who manufactures, designs, delivers,

Constitutionality. (Cont'd)

—Vagueness. (Cont'd)
or possesses such items with the intent that they be so used, and law enforcement officials are, in addition to the stated uses, made keenly aware via the statutory language that objects alone, without specific unlawful intent, will not serve as a basis for conviction under the statutes. Nova Records, Inc. v. Sendak, 504 F. Supp. 938, 1980 U.S. Dist. LEXIS 15832 (S.D. Ind. 1980), aff'd, 706 F.2d 782, 1983 U.S. App. LEXIS 28783 (7th Cir. Ind. 1983).

In this section and former IC 35-48-4-8.2 (see now IC 35-48-4-8.5), an object was made subject to the statute if the alleged violator "intends it to be used primarily for" introducing a controlled substance into the body, testing the strength, effectiveness, or purity of a controlled substance, or enhancing the effect of such a substance. The "primarily" requirement ensured that the defendant who anticipated both legal and illegal uses of an item could be convicted only if his intent that it be used illegally predominated. Therefore the inclusion of the word "primarily" in this context did not render the statute unconstitutionally vague.

Nova Records, Inc. v. Sendak, 706 F.2d 782, 1983 U.S. App. LEXIS 28783 (7th Cir. Ind. 1983).

Elements.

—"Manufactures or Designs."
The section which prohibited dealing in paraphernalia, former IC 35-48-4-8.2 (see now IC 35-48-4-8.5), differed from this section only in that the operative word was "delivers" rather than "manufactures or designs." Nova Records, Inc. v. Sendak, 706 F.2d 782, 1983 U.S. App. LEXIS 28783 (7th Cir. Ind. 1983).

Intent of Violator.
The scienter requirement in the drug paraphernalia provisions is not merely an intent to design, manufacture, distribute, or possess items that could be deemed drug paraphernalia. The Indiana statute "defines" the scope of its prohibition by reference to the intent of the violator. Nova Records, Inc. v. Sendak, 706 F.2d 782, 1983 U.S. App. LEXIS 28783 (7th Cir. Ind. 1983).

RESEARCH REFERENCES

Notre Dame Law Review.
The Constitutionality of Anti-Drug Paraphernalia Laws — The Smoke Clears, 58 Notre Dame L. Rev. 833.

35-48-4-8.2. [Repealed.]

Compiler's Notes.
This section, concerning dealing in paraphernalia, was repealed by P.L.1-1991, § 205, effective April 23, 1991. For present similar provisions, see IC 35-48-4-8.5.

35-48-4-8.3. Possession of paraphernalia.

(a) A person who possesses a raw material, an instrument, a device, or other object that the person intends to use for:
(1) introducing into the person's body a controlled substance;
(2) testing the strength, effectiveness, or purity of a controlled substance; or
(3) enhancing the effect of a controlled substance;
in violation of this chapter commits a Class A infraction for possessing paraphernalia.

(b) A person who knowingly or intentionally violates subsection (a) commits a Class A misdemeanor. However, the offense is a Class D felony if the person has a prior unrelated judgment or conviction under this section.

(c) A person who recklessly possesses a raw material, an instrument, a device, or other object that is to be used primarily for:
(1) introducing into the person's body a controlled substance;
(2) testing the strength, effectiveness, or purity of a controlled substance; or
(3) enhancing the effect of a controlled substance;
in violation of this chapter commits reckless possession of paraphernalia, a Class B misdemeanor. However, the offense is a Class D felony if the person has a previous judgment or conviction under this section.

History.
IC 35-48-4-8.3, as added by Acts 1980, P.L.115, § 4; P.L.202-1989, § 5; P.L.166-1990, § 2; P.L.58-2003, § 1.

Cross References.

Infraction and ordinance violation enforcement proceedings, IC 34-28-5.

Penalties for felonies, IC 35-50-1, IC 35-50-2, IC 35-50-5-2.

Penalties for misdemeanors, IC 35-50-1, IC 35-50-3, IC 35-50-5-2.

NOTES TO DECISIONS

Constitutionality.

The Indiana drug paraphernalia provisions are not violative of either the First Amendment or the due process clause. Nova Records, Inc. v. Sendak, 706 F.2d 782, 1983 U.S. App. LEXIS 28783 (7th Cir. Ind. 1983).

—Cruel and Unusual Punishment.

Drug paraphernalia statutes do not permit cruel and unusual punishment of innocent activity in violation of the Eighth Amendment, for the statutes insure that those lacking the requisite intent or knowledge will not be subjected to any punishment whatsoever. Nova Records, Inc. v. Sendak, 504 F. Supp. 938, 1980 U.S. Dist. LEXIS 15832 (S.D. Ind. 1980), aff'd, 706 F.2d 782, 1983 U.S. App. LEXIS 28783 (7th Cir. Ind. 1983).

—Disproportionate Penalties.

Penalties for drug paraphernalia offenses set out in IC 35-48-4-8.3(a) and (c), the former an infraction for possession and the latter a felony for reckless possession, were not unconstitutionally disproportionate; reckless possession was deemed more culpable than intentional possession. Avant v. State, 779 N.E.2d 538, 2002 Ind. App. LEXIS 1928 (2002).

—Free Speech.

The intent requirements of the Indiana drug paraphernalia statutes prevent a wholesale assault on unpopular, but legal, commercial or symbolic speech, and the statutes do not impermissibly restrict protected commercial or symbolic speech.

Nova Records, Inc. v. Sendak, 504 F. Supp. 938, 1980 U.S. Dist. LEXIS 15832 (S.D. Ind. 1980), aff'd, 706 F.2d 782, 1983 U.S. App. LEXIS 28783 (7th Cir. Ind. 1983).

—Interstate Commerce.

The effect of the drug paraphernalia provisions, if any, on interstate commerce will be both incidental and fully justified. Nova Records, Inc. v. Sendak, 504 F. Supp. 938, 1980 U.S. Dist. LEXIS 15832 (S.D. Ind. 1980), aff'd, 706 F.2d 782, 1983 U.S. App. LEXIS 28783 (7th Cir. Ind. 1983).

—Not Overbroad.

Drug paraphernalia statutes are not facially overbroad because reasonable people can readily tell whether their conduct will be violative of the law since it is their own state of mind which is ultimately determinative. Nova Records, Inc. v. Sendak, 504 F. Supp. 938, 1980 U.S. Dist. LEXIS 15832 (S.D. Ind. 1980), aff'd, 706 F.2d 782, 1983 U.S. App. LEXIS 28783 (7th Cir. Ind. 1983).

—Statutory Classifications.

Drug paraphernalia statutes on their face create no statutory classifications not reasonably related to a legitimate state purpose, and to the extent that subsequent events show a disproportionate impact of enforcement on enterprises in the nature of those operated by plaintiffs, such result may be justified on the basis of the recognized likelihood that such shops will contain objects constituting paraphernalia under the statutes. Nova Records, Inc. v. Sendak, 504 F. Supp. 938, 1980 U.S. Dist. LEXIS 15832 (S.D. Ind. 1980), aff'd, 706 F.2d 782, 1983 U.S. App. LEXIS 28783 (7th Cir. Ind. 1983).

—Vagueness.

Drug paraphernalia statutes are not unconstitutionally vague where persons of ordinary intelligence are put on notice that items intended for ingesting, testing, or enhancing the effect of a controlled substance will be deemed to fall within the category of drug paraphernalia to the detriment of one who manufactures, designs, delivers, or possesses such items with the intent that they be so used, and law enforcement officials are, in addition to the stated uses, made keenly aware via the statutory language that objects alone, without specific unlawful intent, will not serve as a basis for conviction under the statutes. Nova Records, Inc. v. Sendak, 504 F. Supp. 938, 1980 U.S. Dist. LEXIS 15832 (S.D. Ind. 1980), aff'd, 706 F.2d 782, 1983 U.S. App. LEXIS 28783 (7th Cir. Ind. 1983).

Elements.

—Possession.

Evidence was sufficient to show constructive

Elements. (Cont'd)

—Possession. (Cont'd)

possession of paraphernalia, and intent to control and exercise dominion over the paraphernalia, where the defendant was in close personal proximity to contraband which was in plain view and engaged both in furtive conduct and attempted flight. Testimony by the defendant's spouse that the paraphernalia was hers alone was merely conflicting evidence, resolution of which rested solely with the trier of fact. Crabtree v. State, 479 N.E.2d 70, 1985 Ind. App. LEXIS 2496 (1985).

Evidence.

—Intent.

Evidence that defendant was in possession of certain instruments often used by narcotics users to unlawfully administer narcotic drugs was insufficient, standing alone, to prove requisite intent to unlawfully administer and use narcotic drugs. Taylor v. State, 256 Ind. 170, 267 N.E.2d 383, 1971 Ind. LEXIS 608 (1971).

Intent to unlawfully use the possessed instruments was an element of the crime which had to be proven beyond a reasonable doubt. Eskridge v. State, 258 Ind. 363, 281 N.E.2d 490, 1972 Ind. LEXIS 572 (1972).

Mere evidence of possession coupled with flight and attempted concealment did not establish the necessary intent to sustain a conviction. Bradley v. State, 153 Ind. App. 421, 287 N.E.2d 759, 1972 Ind. App. LEXIS 762 (1972).

Intent to use an instrument for illegal drug use may be inferred from circumstantial evidence, such as from evidence of previous convictions for drug use, and from former drug use and the presence of needle marks on defendant's arms. McConnell v. State, 540 N.E.2d 100, 1989 Ind. App. LEXIS 501 (1989).

Police officer's testimony that the substance found in the bowl of a smoking pipe appeared to be marijuana was sufficient evidence from which the jury could infer that the substance was marijuana and that defendant intended to use the pipe in connection with marijuana. McConnell v. State, 540 N.E.2d 100, 1989 Ind. App. LEXIS 501 (1989).

—Seizure.

Object police officer identified during pat down search as pipe used to smoke marijuana would be contraband under the plain feel doctrine and therefore subject to seizure. Burkett v. State, 691 N.E.2d 1241, 1998 Ind. App. LEXIS 97 (1998).

Since there was probable cause to arrest defendant, based on the smell of marijuana emanating from his vehicle, the pat-down search and search of his vehicle were proper, and his motion to suppress was properly denied. Sebastian v. State, 726 N.E.2d 827, 2000 Ind. App. LEXIS 501 (2000).

—Sufficiency.

Testimony of officer, qualified as an expert in the area of narcotics violations, that the accused had puncture marks, the type of marks found on narcotic users, coupled with accused's admission of past use was sufficient to show that the accused was a user of narcotics and that he intended to use "outfit," found in his possession, to unlawfully administer the narcotic drugs. Stevens v. State, 257 Ind. 386, 275 N.E.2d 12, 1971 Ind. LEXIS 549 (1971).

Possession of the contraband and blood-stained toilet tissue, coupled with discovery of puncture marks on defendant's swollen forearm, when taken together, were sufficient evidence that defendant's possession of the contraband was with "intent to unlawfully administer and use narcotic drugs." Dabner v. State, 258 Ind. 179, 279 N.E.2d 797, 1972 Ind. LEXIS 543 (1972).

Testimony by officer that appellant had just injected himself with narcotics which was borne out by the physical condition of appellant as well as by the presence of a cooker, matches, eyedropper, needle and a fresh puncture mark on appellant's arm supplied sufficient evidence of probative value from which the trier of facts could reasonably infer the appellant was guilty beyond a reasonable doubt. Irvin v. State, 258 Ind. 528, 282 N.E.2d 825, 1972 Ind. LEXIS 598 (1972).

Where defendant under arrest attempted to conceal narcotics "outfit," had fresh needle marks on arms, later exhibited narcotics withdrawal symptoms and admitted he was an addict with a $25.00 a day habit, there was sufficient evidence of intent to sustain a conviction. Sargent v. State, 153 Ind. App. 430, 287 N.E.2d 795, 1972 Ind. App. LEXIS 763 (1972).

Where defendant fidgeted in the seat as though trying to hide or retrieve something as the officer approached the vehicle, and residue encrusted crack pipe was lying on the car seat where defendant had been sitting immediately prior to exiting the car, the evidence was sufficient to support an inference that defendant possessed the pipe with the intent to use it to smoke crack. Trigg v. State, 725 N.E.2d 446, 2000 Ind. App. LEXIS 311 (2000).

Possession of a straw was not reckless for purposes of reckless possession of drug paraphernalia where: (1) there was no evidence the straw was ever out of defendant's pocket until the police removed it; (2) there was no evidence of the harm that might result from possession of the straw in defendant's pocket; (3) there was no evidence that possession of the straw showed a disregard of the harm that might result from defendant's conduct or that it involved a substantial deviation from acceptable standards of conduct; and (4) the evidence demonstrated only that defendant possessed the straw. Bocko v. State, 769 N.E.2d 658, 2002 Ind. App. LEXIS 903 (2002).

Evidence was insufficient to affirm defendant's conviction for possession of paraphernalia because, while evidence was sufficient to show he knew of presence of paraphernalia and could easily have asserted dominion and control over it, state did not prove possession was "reckless," since no evidence was presented of harm which might result from defendant's constructive possession of paraphernalia or that defendant acted in total disregard of any such harm. Grim v. State, 797 N.E.2d 825, 2003 Ind. App. LEXIS 1978 (2003).

Defendant's conviction of possession of para-

Evidence. (Cont'd)

—Sufficiency. (Cont'd)
phernalia under IC 35-48-4-8.3(c)(2) was reversed for lack of evidence that cigarette papers in defendant's possession could have been used to "test" strength, effectiveness or purity of marijuana. Atkinson v. State, 810 N.E.2d 1190, 2004 Ind. App. LEXIS 1269 (2004).

Trial court erred in convicting defendant of reckless possession of paraphernalia; the police officer's investigatory stop of defendant based on an anonymous tip was impermissible because the officer's conduct was not based on reasonable suspicion that defendant was involved in criminal activity, especially since the officer did not corroborate the information he received regarding defendant, and, in any event, the evidence was not sufficient to show recklessness since the state did not show defendant's conduct involved "possible harm." Castner v. State, 840 N.E.2d 362, 2006 Ind. App. LEXIS 14 (2006).

Although the trial court erroneously admitted a laboratory report into evidence, because the evidence, including the erroneously-admitted laboratory report, was sufficient to support defendant's conviction for possession of paraphernalia under IC 35-48-4-8.3, a retrial would not offend double jeopardy principles. McMurrar v. State, 905 N.E.2d 527, 2009 Ind. App. LEXIS 815 (2009).

Hypodermic Syringe.
It was not necessary for the state to show that a hypodermic syringe or needle had been adapted for the use of narcotic drugs by injection, the words "adapted for the use of narcotic drugs by injection" having been limited to the words "any instrument." Moore v. State, 248 Ind. 109, 223 N.E.2d 899, 1967 Ind. LEXIS 406 (1967).

A medicine dropper with a compressible rubber bulb attached is a hypodermic syringe. Dorsey v. State, 254 Ind. 409, 260 N.E.2d 800, 1970 Ind. LEXIS 562 (1970).

Intent of Violator.
The scienter requirement in the drug paraphernalia provisions is not merely an intent to design, manufacture, distribute, or possess items that could be deemed drug paraphernalia. The Indiana statute "defines" the scope of its prohibition by reference to the intent of the violator. Nova Records, Inc. v. Sendak, 706 F.2d 782, 1983 U.S. App. LEXIS 28783 (7th Cir. Ind. 1983).

Jury Instructions.
Although the trial court's instructions were incomplete in not specifying the manner in which it was charged that rolling papers and a roach clip might be used to constitute paraphernalia, the trial court did not commit fundamental error in failing to specify such usage. Spindler v. State, 555 N.E.2d 1319, 1990 Ind. App. LEXIS 761 (1990).

Possession.

—Constructive Possession.
Constructive possession of items found in a car might have been imputed to the driver and was established where the defendant had the intent and capability to maintain dominion and control over the contraband, because exclusive possession of a vehicle properly raised a reasonable inference of intent. State v. Emry, 753 N.E.2d 19, 2001 Ind. App. LEXIS 1180 (2001).

Defendant was properly convicted of possession of paraphernalia where the State proved constructive possession given defendant's proximity to the paraphernalia in a car and evidence of defendant's ability and intent to maintain dominion and control. Halsema v. State, 783 N.E.2d 1199, 2003 Ind. App. LEXIS 299 (2003), transfer granted, 804 N.E.2d 746, 2003 Ind. LEXIS 657 (2003), superseded, 823 N.E.2d 668, 2005 Ind. LEXIS 197 (2005).

In trial at which defendant was convicted of possession of cocaine and drug paraphernalia found in her purse, fundamental error requiring reversal of conviction occurred during voir dire when trial court gave jury venire example of constructive possession that was similar to facts of case. Merritt v. State, 822 N.E.2d 642, 2005 Ind. App. LEXIS 223 (2005).

—Evidence Insufficient.
Where state prosecuted defendant for possession of drug paraphernalia, which included a pipe, cigarette papers and two scales, there was not enough evidence to uphold conviction because no evidence was introduced to show that the paraphernalia was intended to be used for "enhancing the effect of a controlled substance" outside of their mere presence. Harrison v. State, 469 N.E.2d 22, 1984 Ind. App. LEXIS 2978 (1984).

—Evidence Sufficient.
Sufficient evidence supported an inference that defendant knew about the cocaine and paraphernalia in a car and had the ability to control it: he apologized to an officer for reaching his hands between the seat, confessed that he had just purchased two rocks of cocaine and had just smoked one, and explained that crack and crack pipes were in the car in violation of IC 35-48-4-8.3(b) and 35-48-4-6(b)(2)(B)(i). Atwood v. State, 905 N.E.2d 479, 2009 Ind. App. LEXIS 738 (2009).

—Reckless Possession.
Possession of paraphernalia was not made reckless by presence of children; accordingly, defendant's conviction for reckless possession of paraphernalia was reversed. Bean v. State, 818 N.E.2d 148, 2004 Ind. App. LEXIS 2325 (2004).

Search and Seizure.
Trial court properly convicted defendant of reckless possession of paraphernalia, IC 35-48-4-8.3(c), given that an investigatory stop and a patdown search of defendant which discovered a crack pipe did not violate defendant's rights under the Fourth Amendment to the United States Constitution and Ind. Const. Art. 1, § 11, as the arresting officer had reasonable suspicion that criminal activity was about to occur based on defendant's behavior inside a drugstore, the officer had reasonable suspi-

Search and Seizure. (Cont'd)
cion that defendant might be armed, and because defendant consented to allowing the officer to remove a crack pipe from defendant's pocket. Clenna v. State, 782 N.E.2d 1029, 2003 Ind. App. LEXIS 132 (2003).

Officer's observation of a crack pipe on the driver's seat of defendant's vehicle shortly after defendant exited the vehicle provided the officer with probable cause to arrest defendant for possession of paraphernalia as a Class A misdemeanor. Kyles v. State, 888 N.E.2d 809, 2008 Ind. App. LEXIS 1326 (2008).

Title of Act.
The title of former Acts 1935, ch. 280, which read, "An act defining and relating to narcotic

drugs and to make uniform the law with reference thereto" and the title of the amendment thereto were not too narrow and restrictive for the enactment of criminal penalties connected with the possession of hypodermic needles and syringes used for the purpose of administering drugs. Von Hauger v. State, 255 Ind. 666, 266 N.E.2d 197, 1971 Ind. LEXIS 714 (1971).

Cited:
Navaretta v. State, 726 N.E.2d 787, 2000 Ind. LEXIS 246 (2000); Roberts v. State, 725 N.E.2d 441, 2000 Ind. App. LEXIS 310 (2000); Hanna v. State, 726 N.E.2d 384, 2000 Ind. App. LEXIS 511 (2000); State v. Glass, 769 N.E.2d 639, 2002 Ind. App. LEXIS 901 (2002); State v. Downey, 770 N.E.2d 794, 2002 Ind. LEXIS 542 (2002).

RESEARCH REFERENCES

Notre Dame Law Review.
The Constitutionality of Anti-Drug Paraphernalia Laws — The Smoke Clears, 58 Notre Dame L. Rev. 833.

Res Gestae.
Criminal Justice Notes: Evidence sufficient to support conviction of reckless possession of paraphernalia. 47 (No. 5) Res Gestae 36 (2003).
Criminal Justice Notes 10/03: Constructive possession — handgun, drugs and paraphernalia in vehicle. 47 (No. 6) Res Gestae 43 (2004).

Valparaiso University Law Review.
Paraphernalia for Marijuana and Hashish Use: Possession Statutes and Indiana's Pipe Dream, 10 Val. U.L. Rev. 353.

Collateral References.
Propriety of instruction of jury on "conscious avoidance" of knowledge of nature of substance or transaction in prosecution for possession or distribution of drugs. 109 A.L.R. Fed. 710.

35-48-4-8.5. Dealing in paraphernalia.

(a) A person who keeps for sale, offers for sale, delivers, or finances the delivery of a raw material, an instrument, a device, or other object that is intended to be or that is designed or marketed to be used primarily for:

(1) ingesting, inhaling, or otherwise introducing into the human body marijuana, hash oil, hashish, or a controlled substance;

(2) testing the strength, effectiveness, or purity of marijuana, hash oil, hashish, or a controlled substance;

(3) enhancing the effect of a controlled substance;

(4) manufacturing, compounding, converting, producing, processing, or preparing marijuana, hash oil, hashish, or a controlled substance;

(5) diluting or adulterating marijuana, hash oil, hashish, or a controlled substance by individuals; or

(6) any purpose announced or described by the seller that is in violation of this chapter;
commits a Class A infraction for dealing in paraphernalia.

(b) A person who knowingly or intentionally violates subsection (a) commits a Class A misdemeanor. However, the offense is a Class D felony if the person has a prior unrelated judgment or conviction under this section.

(c) A person who recklessly keeps for sale, offers for sale, or delivers an instrument, a device, or other object that is to be used primarily for:

(1) ingesting, inhaling, or otherwise introducing into the human body marijuana, hash oil, hashish, or a controlled substance;

(2) testing the strength, effectiveness, or purity of marijuana, hash oil, hashish, or a controlled substance;

(3) enhancing the effect of a controlled substance;

(4) manufacturing, compounding, converting, producing, processing, or preparing marijuana, hash oil, hashish, or a controlled substance;

(5) diluting or adulterating marijuana, hash oil, hashish, or a controlled substance by individuals; or

(6) any purpose announced or described by the seller that is in violation of this chapter;

commits reckless dealing in paraphernalia, a Class B misdemeanor. However, the offense is a Class D felony if the person has a previous judgment or conviction under this section.

(d) This section does not apply to the following:

(1) Items marketed for use in the preparation, compounding, packaging, labeling, or other use of marijuana, hash oil, hashish, or a controlled substance as an incident to lawful research, teaching, or chemical analysis and not for sale.

(2) Items marketed for or historically and customarily used in connection with the planting, propagating, cultivating, growing, harvesting, manufacturing, compounding, converting, producing, processing, preparing, testing, analyzing, packaging, repackaging, storing, containing, concealing, injecting, ingesting, or inhaling of tobacco or any other lawful substance.

History.
P.L.1-1991, § 206; P.L.58-2003, § 2.

Cross References.
Infraction and ordinance violation enforcement proceedings, IC 34-28-5.

Penalties for felonies, IC 35-50-1, IC 35-50-2, IC 35-50-5-2.

Penalties for misdemeanors, IC 35-50-1, IC 35-50-3, IC 35-50-5-2.

NOTES TO DECISIONS

ANALYSIS

Constitutionality.
—Cruel and Unusual Punishment.
—Free Speech.
—Interstate Commerce.
—Not Overbroad.
—Statutory Classifications.
—Vagueness.
Elements.
—"Delivers."
Intent of Violator.

Constitutionality.
The Indiana drug paraphernalia provisions were not violative of either the First Amendment or the due process clause. Nova Records, Inc. v. Sendak, 706 F.2d 782, 1983 U.S. App. LEXIS 28783 (7th Cir. Ind. 1983).

—Cruel and Unusual Punishment.
Drug paraphernalia statutes do not permit cruel and unusual punishment of innocent activity in violation of the Eighth Amendment, for the statutes insure that those lacking the requisite intent or knowledge will not be subjected to any punishment whatsoever. Nova Records, Inc. v. Sendak, 504 F. Supp. 938, 1980 U.S. Dist. LEXIS 15832 (S.D. Ind. 1980), aff'd, 706 F.2d 782, 1983 U.S. App. LEXIS 28783 (7th Cir. Ind. 1983).

Because IC 35-48-4-8.5(a) was a strict-liability offense and did not require proof of a culpable mental state, whereas a misdemeanor conviction under the statute required proof of at least reckless culpability, there was no support for the asser-

tion that the punishment under IC 35-48-4-8.5 rose as the culpability required for the offense declined, so the penalties under IC 35-48-4-8.5 were constitutional because they were proportional to the nature of the offense. Hevenor v. State, 784 N.E.2d 937, 2003 Ind. App. LEXIS 169 (2003).

Faithful reading of IC 35-48-4-8.5(c) does not create a proportionality problem when it is read in conjunction with IC 35-48-4-8.5(a) as IC 35-48-4-8.5(a) does not require a mens rea of "knowingly" or "intentionally" for an infraction violation; rather, subsection (a) is a strict-liability offense and thus does not require proof of a culpable mental state, so its lesser penalty is not disproportionate to the penalty for the misdemeanor offense in IC 35-48-4-8.5(c), requiring a reckless mental state. Hevenor v. State, 784 N.E.2d 937, 2003 Ind. App. LEXIS 169 (2003).

—Free Speech.
The intent requirements of the Indiana drug paraphernalia statutes prevent a wholesale assault on unpopular, but legal, commercial or symbolic speech, and the statutes do not impermissibly restrict protected commercial or symbolic speech. Nova Records, Inc. v. Sendak, 504 F. Supp. 938, 1980 U.S. Dist. LEXIS 15832 (S.D. Ind. 1980), aff'd, 706 F.2d 782, 1983 U.S. App. LEXIS 28783 (7th Cir. Ind. 1983).

—Interstate Commerce.
The effect of the drug paraphernalia provisions, if any, on interstate commerce will be both inciden-

Constitutionality. (Cont'd)

—Interstate Commerce. (Cont'd)
tal and fully justified. Nova Records, Inc. v. Sendak, 504 F. Supp. 938, 1980 U.S. Dist. LEXIS 15832 (S.D. Ind. 1980), aff'd, 706 F.2d 782, 1983 U.S. App. LEXIS 28783 (7th Cir. Ind. 1983).

—Not Overbroad.
Drug paraphernalia statutes are not facially overbroad because reasonable people can readily tell whether their conduct will be violative of the law since it is their own state of mind which is ultimately determinative. Nova Records, Inc. v. Sendak, 504 F. Supp. 938, 1980 U.S. Dist. LEXIS 15832 (S.D. Ind. 1980), aff'd, 706 F.2d 782, 1983 U.S. App. LEXIS 28783 (7th Cir. Ind. 1983).

Reading IC 35-48-4-8.5(a) as written (without a culpability requirement) did not expose dealers of purely innocent items to Class A infractions, as IC 35-48-4-8.5(d)(2) provided that items marketed for or customarily used in connection with tobacco or any other lawful substances did not fall under the governance of the statute; even without a culpability requirement, dealers were not subject to a Class A infraction if their wares were customarily used for legal purposes. Hevenor v. State, 784 N.E.2d 937, 2003 Ind. App. LEXIS 169 (2003).

—Statutory Classifications.
Drug paraphernalia statutes on their face create no statutory classifications not reasonably related to a legitimate state purpose, and to the extent that subsequent events show a disproportionate impact of enforcement on enterprises in the nature of those operated by plaintiffs, such result may be justified on the basis of the recognized likelihood that such shops will contain objects constituting paraphernalia under the statutes. Nova Records, Inc. v. Sendak, 504 F. Supp. 938, 1980 U.S. Dist. LEXIS 15832 (S.D. Ind. 1980), aff'd, 706 F.2d 782, 1983 U.S. App. LEXIS 28783 (7th Cir. Ind. 1983).

—Vagueness.
Drug paraphernalia statutes are not unconstitutionally vague where persons of ordinary intelligence are put on notice that items intended for ingesting, testing, or enhancing the effect of a controlled substance will be deemed to fall within the category of drug paraphernalia to the detriment of one who manufactures, designs, delivers, or possesses such items with the intent that they be so used, and law enforcement officials are, in addition to the stated uses, made keenly aware via the statutory language that objects alone, without specific unlawful intent, will not serve as a basis for conviction under the statutes. Nova Records, Inc. v. Sendak, 504 F. Supp. 938, 1980 U.S. Dist.

LEXIS 15832 (S.D. Ind. 1980), aff'd, 706 F.2d 782, 1983 U.S. App. LEXIS 28783 (7th Cir. Ind. 1983).

In IC 35-48-4-8.1 and former IC 35-48-4-8.2, an object was made subject to the statute if the alleged violator intended it to be used primarily for introducing a controlled substance into the body, testing the strength, effectiveness, or purity of a controlled substance, or enhancing the effect of such a substance. The "primarily" requirement ensured that the defendant who anticipated both legal and illegal uses of an item could be convicted only if his intent that it be used illegally predominated. Therefore the inclusion of the word "primarily" in this context did not render the statute unconstitutionally vague. Nova Records, Inc. v. Sendak, 706 F.2d 782, 1983 U.S. App. LEXIS 28783 (7th Cir. Ind. 1983).

Elements.

—"Delivers."
Former IC 35-48-4-8.2 differed from the manufacturing section, IC 35-48-4-8.1, only in that the operative word was "delivers" rather than "manufactures or designs." Nova Records, Inc. v. Sendak, 706 F.2d 782, 1983 U.S. App. LEXIS 28783 (7th Cir. Ind. 1983).

Intent of Violator.
The scienter requirement in the drug paraphernalia provisions is not merely an intent to design, manufacture, distribute, or possess items that could be deemed drug paraphernalia. The Indiana statute "defines" the scope of its prohibition by reference to the intent of the violator. Nova Records, Inc. v. Sendak, 706 F.2d 782, 1983 U.S. App. LEXIS 28783 (7th Cir. Ind. 1983).

While IC 35-48-4-8.5(a) contains the word "intended," the word "intended" does not define the culpable mental state required for the subsection, but rather "intended" is part of the relative clause modifying the antecedents "raw material, an instrument, a device, or other object"; there is no language in subsection (a) indicating the level of culpability required for the infraction offense. Hevenor v. State, 784 N.E.2d 937, 2003 Ind. App. LEXIS 169 (2003).

Because a violation of IC 35-48-4-8.5(a) was a Class A infraction, the element of criminal intent was not required for that subsection. Hevenor v. State, 784 N.E.2d 937, 2003 Ind. App. LEXIS 169 (2003).

Cited:
Bryant v. State, 660 N.E.2d 290, 1995 Ind. LEXIS 205, 64 A.L.R.5th 867 (1995).

35-48-4-9. [Repealed.]

Compiler's Notes.
This section, concerning possession of and dealing in paraphernalia, was repealed by Acts 1980,

P.L.115, § 5. For present similar provisions, see IC 35-48-4-8.5.

35-48-4-10. Dealing in marijuana, hash oil, or hashish.

(a) A person who:
  (1) knowingly or intentionally:
    (A) manufactures;
    (B) finances the manufacture of;
    (C) delivers; or
    (D) finances the delivery of;
marijuana, hash oil, or hashish, pure or adulterated; or
  (2) possesses, with intent to:
    (A) manufacture;
    (B) finance the manufacture of;
    (C) deliver; or
    (D) finance the delivery of;
marijuana, hash oil, or hashish, pure or adulterated;
commits dealing in marijuana, hash oil, or hashish, a Class A misdemeanor, except as provided in subsection (b).

(b) The offense is:
  (1) a Class D felony if:
    (A) the recipient or intended recipient is under eighteen (18) years of age;
    (B) the amount involved is more than thirty (30) grams but less than ten (10) pounds of marijuana or two (2) grams but less than three hundred (300) grams of hash oil or hashish; or
    (C) the person has a prior conviction of an offense involving marijuana, hash oil, or hashish; and
  (2) a Class C felony if the amount involved is ten (10) pounds or more of marijuana or three hundred (300) or more grams of hash oil or hashish or the person delivered or financed the delivery of marijuana, hash oil, or hashish:
    (A) on a school bus; or
    (B) in, on, or within one thousand (1,000) feet of:
      (i) school property;
      (ii) a public park;
      (iii) a family housing complex; or
      (iv) a youth program center.

History.
IC 35-48-4-10, as added by Acts 1976, P.L. 148, § 7; 1977, P.L. 340, § 105; 1979, P.L. 303, § 11; 1982, P.L. 204, § 38; P.L.296-1987, § 11; P.L.165-1990, § 12; P.L.296-1995, § 9; P.L.65-1996, § 17; P.L.17-2001, § 26.

Cross References.
Penalties for felonies, IC 35-50-1, IC 35-50-2, IC 35-50-5-2.

NOTES TO DECISIONS

—Consecutive Sentences.
—Enhanced.

Attempts.
This section applies to inchoate crimes, including attempts. Berry v. State, 561 N.E.2d 832, 1990 Ind. App. LEXIS 1394 (1990).

Double Jeopardy.
Where the charge of possessing a drug is a lesser included offense of dealing in that drug, the offender cannot be convicted and sentenced on both the greater and lesser offenses. Ratcliff v. State, 578 N.E.2d 359, 1991 Ind. LEXIS 168 (1991).

Defendant, who contended his prosecution in one county was barred by the doctrine of collateral estoppel due to his acquittal in another county on charges relating to the same drug sting operation, failed to present sufficient evidence to demonstrate that the jury in the first county had found that the police entrapped him during the entire series of drug transactions and not just those transactions which occurred in county where he was first prosecuted. Smith v. State, 670 N.E.2d 360, 1996 Ind. App. LEXIS 1090 (1996).

Where defendant was arrested in December 1992 for dealing in and possession of marijuana, and the Controlled Substance Excise Tax (CSET) was assessed and proceedings initiated to collect the tax in January 1993, jeopardy attached when he received notice of the assessment, and a subsequent trial in January 1994 for the underlying drug offenses which were the basis of the CSET assessment violated the double jeopardy clause. Garcia v. State, 686 N.E.2d 883, 1997 Ind. App. LEXIS 1502 (1997).

The state constitution's proscription of multiple punishments for the same offense was violated where the state was relieved of the requirement to present evidence to prove dealing in marijuana charges independent of the evidence required to prove conspiracy charges, because the manner in which the defendant was charged and the jury was instructed rendered the occurrence of the substantive crime an overt act in furtherance of the conspiracy. Chavez v. State, 722 N.E.2d 885, 2000 Ind. App. LEXIS 67 (2000).

Entrapment.
There was no entrapment where defendant had a reputation as a source for obtaining drugs, had informed a police informant three days before the purchase of drugs that he had narcotics for sale, and had sold the informant drugs on prior occasions. McCarty v. State, 167 Ind. App. 396, 338 N.E.2d 738, 1975 Ind. App. LEXIS 1449 (1975).

Proof of probable cause is not required before police officer makes a purchase of marijuana to avoid defense of entrapment. Maynard v. State, 174 Ind. App. 202, 367 N.E.2d 5, 1977 Ind. App. LEXIS 952 (1977).

Where evidence showed that police officer had made purchase prior to date when purchase was made, that police officer knew the price and obtained marijuana within 45 minutes after request was made and also knew prices for larger amounts,

there was no evidence of entrapment. Maynard v. State, 174 Ind. App. 202, 367 N.E.2d 5, 1977 Ind. App. LEXIS 952 (1977).

Where police officer, along with informant whom police officer had not previously known, went to defendant's home and informant initiated a discussion concerning "tea" but defendant indicated he was out of "tea" at the moment, and then informant inquired about marijuana and defendant indicated he had some, offered some to the informant and police officer to try and then sold some to the police officer, evidence was sufficient to show a predisposition on part of defendant to commit the offense so as to overcome defense of entrapment. Horn v. State, 178 Ind. App. 415, 382 N.E.2d 1012, 1978 Ind. App. LEXIS 1095 (1978).

Where defense was entrapment by a certain police officer it was not error to refuse testimony of witness that such officer had encouraged persons to engage in drug traffic where such witness knew nothing of the case that was being tried. Drollinger v. State, 274 Ind. 99, 409 N.E.2d 1084, 1980 Ind. LEXIS 740 (1980).

Where there was evidence of defendant's ability to obtain a supply of drugs within a few minutes, several different schemes to accomplish the sale, multiple sales to officers and a large supply of drugs in the possession of defendant there was sufficient evidence to show a predisposition to commit the crime and the question of whether there was entrapment was for the trier of fact. Silva v. State, 410 N.E.2d 1342, 1980 Ind. App. LEXIS 1664 (1980).

Where after meeting, defendant made an immediate agreement to sell marijuana to undercover officer and also made statements concerning a forthcoming shipment which represented an amount larger than a casual user would have in his possession, the jury could logically infer that defendant was in the business of selling and that the police merely afforded defendant an opportunity to commit the crime. Grogg v. State, 417 N.E.2d 1175, 1981 Ind. App. LEXIS 1303 (1981).

There was sufficient evidence to rebut the defense of entrapment and show a predisposition to deal in controlled substances where defendant was familiar with prices and sources for marijuana and cocaine, possessed at least 10 one-ounce bags of marijuana, and demonstrated a willingness to engage in future transactions. Gitary v. State, 503 N.E.2d 1241, 1987 Ind. App. LEXIS 2380 (1987).

In a prosecution for dealing in marijuana as a Class C felony, IC 35-48-4-10(b)(2), as police did not induce defendant to receive a package containing over 10 pounds of marijuana, but merely afforded him an opportunity to commit the crime, there was no entrapment under IC 35-41-3-9(b). Espinoza v. State, 859 N.E.2d 375, 2006 Ind. App. LEXIS 2636 (2006).

Evidence.

—Admissibility.
Evidence of other drug transactions tending to prove defendant's common scheme and plan of marijuana peddling was admissible. Manuel v. State, 267 Ind. 436, 370 N.E.2d 904, 1977 Ind. LEXIS 525 (1977).

—Amount.

The fact that marijuana recovered contained portions of the marijuana plant not included within the statutory definition of marijuana does not prevent the entire amount recovered from being considered with respect to the enhancement under this section based upon the amount involved; however, external water weight, not included for the purposes of trafficking the marijuana, is not to be included in the aggregate weight of the drug delivered. Lycan v. State, 671 N.E.2d 447, 1996 Ind. App. LEXIS 1262 (1996).

Defendant was convicted of dealing in marijuana as a Class C felony. As he failed to object to the admission of evidence that the drugs weighed over 10 pounds, he could not argue on appeal that no foundation had been laid as to the accuracy of the scale used to weigh the drugs. Espinoza v. State, 859 N.E.2d 375, 2006 Ind. App. LEXIS 2636 (2006).

—Chain of Custody.

Where officer described the chain of custody of substance from the time of purchase by informant, taking it to his office, to the property room which was protected by burglary prevention device and its transfer to the state police laboratory, it was proper to admit such substance as an exhibit even though it was admitted that for brief periods of time it would have been possible for others to have had access to the substance. Holt v. State, 272 Ind. 544, 400 N.E.2d 130, 1980 Ind. LEXIS 597 (1980).

Where evidence showed that state police officer, after receiving drug from defendant, placed it in an evidence bag which he initialed, placed it in his briefcase which he placed in the trunk of his automobile which was kept locked until he delivered it to the state police chemist who tested it and returned it to the officer, there was a sufficient chain of custody. Drollinger v. State, 274 Ind. 99, 409 N.E.2d 1084, 1980 Ind. LEXIS 740 (1980).

Evidence showing sufficient chain of custody. Burst v. State, 499 N.E.2d 1140, 1986 Ind. App. LEXIS 3217 (1986).

Where defendant received over 10 pounds of marijuana shipped from another state and was convicted of dealing in marijuana as a Class C felony, a gap in the chain of custody went to the weight, not the admissibility, of the evidence. Espinoza v. State, 859 N.E.2d 375, 2006 Ind. App. LEXIS 2636 (2006).

—Cross-Examination.

Where defendant, in attempting to show police harassment of defendant, questioned witness concerning the stopping of defendant's car by police for faulty brake lights, a question by prosecutor on cross-examination as to whether marijuana was found in car, was proper to show that police may have other reasons for stopping car. Haynes v. State, 411 N.E.2d 659, 1980 Ind. App. LEXIS 1745 (1980).

—Intent.

Circumstantial evidence of intent to deliver such as scales, plastic bags, and other paraphernalia is

sufficient to support a conviction. Kail v. State, 528 N.E.2d 799, 1988 Ind. App. LEXIS 659 (1988).

A quantity permitting an inference of predisposition to sell is an amount that could not be personally consumed or used and therefore of necessity is available for delivery or sale. Kail v. State, 528 N.E.2d 799, 1988 Ind. App. LEXIS 659 (1988).

Marijuana found in plain view in the defendant's bedroom and the testimony provided by police officers as to the conduct of their search created a reasonable inference for the jury to find the defendant intended to package and sell marijuana. Ladd v. State, 710 N.E.2d 188, 1999 Ind. App. LEXIS 425 (1999).

—Other Offenses.

Where defense was entrapment by a certain police officer and defendant testified that such officer had signed every probable cause affidavit that had been filed against him, it was not error to question defendant about other charges brought against him that were not signed by such officer. Drollinger v. State, 274 Ind. 99, 409 N.E.2d 1084, 1980 Ind. LEXIS 740 (1980).

Evidence of uncharged crimes near the time and place of the charged crime may be admitted on the theory of res gestae. Haynes v. State, 411 N.E.2d 659, 1980 Ind. App. LEXIS 1745 (1980).

—Over 30 Grams of Marijuana Involved.

The phrase in subsection (b), "the offense specified in subsection (a)," causes the added penalty to affix even where the drug is "adulterated," and evidence that the police chemist tested the contents of the bags and found the bags contained marijuana, and he also found them to contain some other vegetable material, and that the total weight of the substance in the two bags was 52.2 grams, is therefore sufficient to support the jury's finding that defendant delivered more than 30 grams of "pure or adulterated" marijuana. Burst v. State, 499 N.E.2d 1140, 1986 Ind. App. LEXIS 3217 (1986).

—Search and Seizure.

Where police officers, by posing as other than police officers, were invited into house and they saw marijuana in plain view, warrantless arrests were justified and officers were also justified in walking through house in search of other marijuana. Ingle v. State, 176 Ind. App. 695, 63 Ind. Dec. 129, 377 N.E.2d 885, 1978 Ind. App. LEXIS 1073, 1978 Ind. App. LEXIS 950 (1978), rehearing denied, 176 Ind. App. 695, 65 Ind. Dec. 217, 381 N.E.2d 887, 1978 Ind. App. LEXIS 1073 (1978).

Where informant set up a buy of a controlled substance to take place at a certain location and police followed the informant to such location, and after defendant got in informant's car the police stopped the car after it went a short distance and then searched the defendant, such search was made with probable cause and controlled substance found on defendant was properly admissible in evidence. Rihl v. State, 413 N.E.2d 1046, 1980 Ind. App. LEXIS 1847 (1980).

—Sufficient.

Testimony of one witness to purchasing mari-

Evidence. (Cont'd)

—Sufficient. (Cont'd)

juana from defendant and of the arresting officer, although contradicted by testimony of defendant, was sufficient to support a conviction. Turner v. State, 248 Ind. 401, 229 N.E.2d 469, 1967 Ind. LEXIS 456 (1967).

There was sufficient evidence to support defendant's two convictions of dealing in marijuana. Mack v. State, 457 N.E.2d 200, 1983 Ind. LEXIS 1069 (1983).

Evidence was sufficient to prove defendant delivered marijuana within 1,000 feet of a school. Crocker v. State, 563 N.E.2d 617, 1990 Ind. App. LEXIS 1570 (1990).

Evidence that defendant received mail at the address where drugs and a firearm were located, and defendant's testimony that he lived at the house, that the drugs were his, and that he was watching the firearm for a friend, was sufficient to establish that defendant knowingly possessed cocaine, marijuana, and the firearm found in his house. Allen v. State, 787 N.E.2d 473, 2003 Ind. App. LEXIS 753 (2003).

When defendant, who had been stopped by an officer for speeding, handed a bag of marijuana to his passenger and told the passenger to hide it, he had "delivered" the marijuana to the passenger under IC 35-48-1-11. Thus, the evidence was sufficient to support his conviction of felony dealing in marijuana in violation of IC 35-48-4-10, although the small amount of marijuana, its packaging in a single bag, and defendant's possession of drug paraphernalia did not support the inference that defendant possessed the marijuana with intent to deliver it to another in a sale, barter, or gift transaction. Cline v. State, 860 N.E.2d 647, 2007 Ind. App. LEXIS 108 (2007).

— —Possession.

Where there was evidence that defendant rented house where marijuana was found, that he took package from mailbox, that he was one of two persons in house when police arrived, that marijuana was found in house, that defendant pointed out location of package in house and that inner liner of package was broken open, evidence was sufficient to show possession. Russell v. State, 182 Ind. App. 386, 395 N.E.2d 791, 1979 Ind. App. LEXIS 1359 (1979).

Where the material seized constituted 50 pounds, and three random samples taken from the material confirmed that marijuana was present and police officer testified that based on his experience the entire 50 pounds was marijuana, evidence was sufficient for jury to find that defendant possessed marijuana in excess of 30 grams. Stayton v. State, 400 N.E.2d 784, 1980 Ind. App. LEXIS 1309 (1980).

Evidence held sufficient to support conviction for possession of marijuana but held insufficient to support a conviction for dealing in marijuana. Wilburn v. State, 442 N.E.2d 1098, 1982 Ind. LEXIS 1065 (1982).

There was sufficient evidence that defendant possessed marijuana where witnesses testified that defendant had possessed suitcase and that the suitcase contained marijuana; it was not necessary to demonstrate defendant was in possession of the marijuana when it was recovered. Lycan v. State, 671 N.E.2d 447, 1996 Ind. App. LEXIS 1262 (1996).

Where police officers searched only that portion of the defendant's residence in which other people did not reside, and found bags of marijuana in a bedroom which contained many of the defendant's personal items, many of these items being in plain view, the evidence established drugs were found in plain view and in close proximity to items owned by the defendant, leading to the conclusion that the defendant had the capability to maintain dominion and control over the marijuana. Ladd v. State, 710 N.E.2d 188, 1999 Ind. App. LEXIS 425 (1999).

Included Offenses.

Manufacturing marijuana includes the offense of possession with intent to manufacture. The proof required to establish manufacture of marijuana necessarily establishes possession as well; one cannot knowingly or intentionally manufacture the drug without also possessing it to that end. Mudd v. State, 483 N.E.2d 782, 1985 Ind. App. LEXIS 2838 (1985).

—Conspiracy.

The offenses of dealing in marijuana and conspiracy to commit dealing in marijuana are not the same under the statutory elements test, in that the latter offense requires an agreement to deal in the drug and an overt act in furtherance of the agreement, but not that any marijuana be possessed with the intent to deliver, while a conviction for dealing in marijuana requires an actual possession of marijuana with the intent to deliver. Chavez v. State, 722 N.E.2d 885, 2000 Ind. App. LEXIS 67 (2000).

Indictment or Information.

—Prior Convictions.

Under this section, the charging information must be drafted so that any allegations of any prior convictions appear on a page separate from that containing allegations of foundation charge, and a determination of whether a drug-dealing charge should be aggravated must be made only if and after a conviction is rendered on the foundation charge. Sweet v. State, 439 N.E.2d 1144, 1982 Ind. LEXIS 954 (1982).

—Conviction of Uncharged Included Offense.

Where defendants were charged in the information with dealing in marijuana and maintaining a common nuisance, the trial court erred in convicting them of possession of marijuana, a charge against which the defendants were not prepared to defend. Crawford v. State, 502 N.E.2d 1361, 1987 Ind. App. LEXIS 2319 (1987), overruled, Wright v. State, 658 N.E.2d 563, 1995 Ind. LEXIS 162 (1995).

Informants.

It is the general policy to prevent the disclosure

Informants. (Cont'd)

of an informant's identity unless such disclosure is relevant to the defense or necessary for a fair trial and since the state has the privilege of withholding the identity of the informant, the burden is upon the defendant to demonstrate an exception and where defendant only showed the mere presence of the informant during the sale, it was not error for the trial court to refuse to allow the defendant to depose the informant. Silva v. State, 410 N.E.2d 1342, 1980 Ind. App. LEXIS 1664 (1980).

Defendant's conviction was reversed because an anonymous telephone tip, absent any independent indicia of reliability or any officer-observed confirmation of the caller's prediction of the defendant's future behavior, is not enough to permit police to detain a citizen and subject him or her to a *Terry* stop and the attendant interruption of liberty required to accomplish it. Washington v. State, 740 N.E.2d 1241, 2000 Ind. App. LEXIS 2045 (2000).

Instructions.

The giving of an instruction that the burden of proof to establish the defense of entrapment by a preponderance of the evidence was on the defendant was reversible error. Silva v. State, 410 N.E.2d 1342, 1980 Ind. App. LEXIS 1664 (1980).

"Marijuana."

—Nonnarcotic Substances.

As used in paragraph (b)(1)(B), "marijuana" does not include nonnarcotic substances present with marijuana. Romack v. State, 446 N.E.2d 1346, 1983 Ind. App. LEXIS 2780 (1983).

Merger.

Where dealing and possession charges arise from the same act, it cannot be said that each charge requires proof of an element that the other does not. Hence, dealing and possession convictions for that act would be merged. Howard v. State, 422 N.E.2d 440, 1981 Ind. App. LEXIS 1502 (1981).

Nonnarcotic Adulterants.

Since the statute uses the words "pure or adulterated" defendant could be convicted of dealing in marijuana in excess of 30 grams notwithstanding that a portion of the total weight may have been attributed to nonnarcotic adulterants or dilutents. Grogg v. State, 417 N.E.2d 1175, 1981 Ind. App. LEXIS 1303 (1981).

School Property.

A state university student was improperly convicted of two Class C felonies for selling marijuana from his dormitory room because that was not "school property" within the meaning of subsection (b)(2). Pridgeon v. State, 569 N.E.2d 722, 1991 Ind. App. LEXIS 614 (1991).

A surveyor's line-of-sight technique to determine the 1,000-foot perimeter around school property conforms to the legislative intent, although the defendant argued the line-of-sight measurement was irrational because neither the defendants nor the school children walk through obstacles such as buildings, homes, fences, concrete barriers, creeks, or the like. Steelman v. State, 602 N.E.2d 152, 1992 Ind. App. LEXIS 1593 (1992).

—Intent.

Although it is incumbent upon the state to prove that a defendant knowingly or intentionally delivered marijuana in order to secure a conviction for dealing, the state is not required to prove that a defendant knowingly or intentionally was within 1,000 feet of school property to support an enhanced sentence for dealing marijuana. Williford v. State, 571 N.E.2d 310, 1991 Ind. App. LEXIS 775 (1991).

Although it was not obvious to the defendant that his apartment was within 1,000 feet of school property, since the school was two streets away from his apartment and the school property could not have been seen from the street on which his apartment building was located, and it took an expert surveyor to determine his apartment building was within 959 feet of the southern and westernmost corner of the school property, the state did not have to prove the defendant knew he was within 1,000 feet of the school when he delivered marijuana. Steelman v. State, 602 N.E.2d 152, 1992 Ind. App. LEXIS 1593 (1992).

Sentence.

Where defendant was convicted of selling more than 29 times the minimum prohibited quantity of marijuana a sentence which was only 60 percent of the maximum was not excessive. Manuel v. State, 267 Ind. 436, 370 N.E.2d 904, 1977 Ind. LEXIS 525 (1977).

The penalty of five to 20 years for the delivery of marijuana does not constitute cruel and unusual punishment. Ross v. State, 172 Ind. App. 484, 360 N.E.2d 1015, 1977 Ind. App. LEXIS 782 (1977).

Although crime was committed under former law prior to the effective date of a new law which provided for a reduced sentence, sentence should have been under new law. Maynard v. State, 174 Ind. App. 202, 367 N.E.2d 5, 1977 Ind. App. LEXIS 952 (1977).

Where defendant did not seek application of new law's penalty provisions, it was not error to grant state's motion in limine preventing defendant from mentioning the fact that the penalty for the sale of marijuana had been reduced since the crime was committed which fact defendant sought to introduce as a mitigating factor, where the penalty set by the jury was the minimum permitted under the law under which defendant was convicted. Lewandowski v. State, 271 Ind. 4, 389 N.E.2d 706, 1979 Ind. LEXIS 620 (1979).

Where defendant was sentenced to 12 years imprisonment for unlawful dealing in a controlled substance more than a year prior to the effective date of this section, he could not claim that his sentence was excessive because it was greater than that provided for in the new law. Watford v. State, 270 Ind. 262, 384 N.E.2d 1030, 1979 Ind. LEXIS 631 (1979).

Where law in effect at time crime was committed was repealed and new law enacted by P.L.338 -

Sentence. (Cont'd)

1975 effective prior to trial, the effect of which was to reduce the penalty for dealing in marijuana when the amount was less than 30 grams and the amount involved in the instant case was less than 30 grams the sentence should have been that which was provided in the new law. Lewandowski v. State, 271 Ind. 4, 389 N.E.2d 706, 1979 Ind. LEXIS 620 (1979).

Defendant received over 10 pounds of marijuana shipped from another state, was babysitting children when the drugs arrived, and was an illegal immigrant who carried an invalid driver's license under a false name. The fact that he had no criminal record did not make his four-year presumptive sentence for dealing in marijuana as a Class C felony inappropriate. Espinoza v. State, 859 N.E.2d 375, 2006 Ind. App. LEXIS 2636 (2006).

Defendant received over 10 pounds of marijuana shipped from another state. The trial court properly imposed the four-year presumptive sentence for dealing in marijuana as a Class C felony, as it was not obliged to give significant weight to defendant's proposed mitigating factors -- his lack of a criminal history, his support of his children, and his employment at the time of his arrest. Espinoza v. State, 859 N.E.2d 375, 2006 Ind. App. LEXIS 2636 (2006).

—Consecutive Sentences.

The trial court did not err in imposing consecutive sentences where defendant pled guilty to three counts of dealing in marijuana, a Class D felony. Howard v. State, 626 N.E.2d 574, 1993 Ind. App. LEXIS 1636 (1993).

Consecutive sentences totaling 15 years for convictions resulting from two controlled buys of marijuana from defendant by the same informant four months apart were not manifestly unreasonable, where defendant agreed to plead guilty to two counts of dealing marijuana, and was informed of the presumptive term of imprisonment and maximum penalty which could be imposed and that the sentences could run consecutively. Weaver v. State, 676 N.E.2d 22, 1997 Ind. App. LEXIS 5 (1997).

Consecutive sentences were inappropriate for defendant who was enticed by the police to make additional drug buys as part of a sting operation, resulting in defendant's conviction of five counts of drug related offenses and sentence to both maximum and consecutive sentences. Hendrickson v. State, 690 N.E.2d 765, 1998 Ind. App. LEXIS 32 (1998).

—Enhanced.

Trial court properly enhanced sentence of defendant who pled guilty to two counts of dealing marijuana, where defendant was informed that his Class A misdemeanors would be enhanced to Class D felonies because he committed a prior, unrelated Class D felony which had been reduced to a Class A misdemeanor. Weaver v. State, 676 N.E.2d 22, 1997 Ind. App. LEXIS 5 (1997).

Cited:

Haynes v. State, 431 N.E.2d 83, 1982 Ind. LEXIS 737 (1982); Jones v. State, 435 N.E.2d 616, 1982 Ind. App. LEXIS 1228 (1982); Smith v. State, 451 N.E.2d 57, 1983 Ind. App. LEXIS 3075 (1983); Barnett v. State, 493 N.E.2d 1286, 1986 Ind. App. LEXIS 2655 (1986); Lather v. Berg, 519 N.E.2d 755, 1988 Ind. App. LEXIS 240 (1988); Street v. State, 567 N.E.2d 1180, 1991 Ind. App. LEXIS 400 (1991); Esquerdo v. State, 640 N.E.2d 1023, 1994 Ind. LEXIS 126 (1994); Davis v. State, 642 N.E.2d 987, 1994 Ind. App. LEXIS 1602 (1994); Johnson v. State, 659 N.E.2d 116, 1995 Ind. LEXIS 190 (1995); Fassinger v. State, 666 N.E.2d 58, 1996 Ind. LEXIS 48 (1996); State v. Mohler, 694 N.E.2d 1129, 1998 Ind. LEXIS 52 (1998); Price v. State, 725 N.E.2d 82, 2000 Ind. LEXIS 208 (2000); Everroad v. State, 730 N.E.2d 222, 2000 Ind. App. LEXIS 899 (2000); Mendoza v. State, 737 N.E.2d 784, 2000 Ind. App. LEXIS 1647 (2000); Vanzo v. State, 738 N.E.2d 1061, 2000 Ind. App. LEXIS 1901 (2000); Antrim v. State, 745 N.E.2d 246, 2001 Ind. App. LEXIS 309 (2001); O'Connor v. State, 789 N.E.2d 504, 2003 Ind. App. LEXIS 908 (2003); Creekmore v. State, 800 N.E.2d 230, 2003 Ind. App. LEXIS 2341 (2003); $ 100 v. State, 822 N.E.2d 1001, 2005 Ind. App. LEXIS 224 (2005); Rotz v. State, 894 N.E.2d 989, 2008 Ind. App. LEXIS 2161 (2008).

RESEARCH REFERENCES

Indiana Law Review.

Taxation: Developments in Indiana Taxation, 34 Ind. L. Rev. 1003 (2001).

Valparaiso University Law Review.

Paraphernalia for Marijuana and Hashish Use: Possession Statutes and Indiana's Pipe Dream, 10 Val. U.L. Rev. 353.

Collateral References.

Admissibility, in criminal prosecution, of expert opinion allegedly stating whether drugs were possessed with intent to distribute — state cases. 83 A.L.R.4th 629.

Validity, construction, and application of state statutes prohibiting sale or possession of controlled substances within specified distance of schools. 27 A.L.R.5th 593.

35-48-4-11. Possession of marijuana, hash oil, or hashish.

A person who:

(1) Knowingly or intentionally possesses (pure or adulterated) marijuana, hash oil, or hashish;

(2) Knowingly or intentionally grows or cultivates marijuana; or

(3) Knowing that marijuana is growing on his premises, fails to destroy the marijuana plants;

commits possession of marijuana, hash oil, or hashish, a Class A misdemeanor. However, the offense is a Class D felony (i) if the amount involved is more than thirty (30) grams of marijuana or two (2) grams of hash oil or hashish, or (ii) if the person has a prior conviction of an offense involving marijuana, hash oil, or hashish.

History.

IC 35-48-4-11, as added by Acts 1976, P.L. 148, § 7; 1977, P.L. 340, § 106; 1979, P.L. 303, § 12; P.L.138-1983, § 5.

NOTES TO DECISIONS

ANALYSIS

Amount.
Arrest.
Constructive Possession.
Control.
Controlled Substance Excise Tax.
Conviction of Uncharged Included Offense.
Double Jeopardy.
—Controlled Substance Excise Tax.
Evidence.
—Admissibility.
—Amount.
—Chain of Possession.
—Insufficient.
—Possession.
—Sufficient.
Instructions.
Knowledge or Intent.
Merger.
—Conspiracy.
—Dealing.
Premises.
Search and Seizure.
Search Warrants.
Sentence.
Sufficiency of Evidence.
Ultimate User.
Verdict.
Verdict Form.
Violation by Attorney.

Amount.

Under prior law, the state was not required to prove the amount of marijuana in the possession of the accused nor that he was not authorized to possess marijuana. Heldman v. State, 163 Ind. App. 395, 324 N.E.2d 281, 1975 Ind. App. LEXIS 1048 (1975).

Only the portion of the confiscated substance consisting of pure marijuana, that is, marijuana as defined by former IC 35-48-1-1 (see now IC 35-48-1-19), could be taken into account in determining whether to convict defendant of the basic offense of possession or aggravated offense; however, purity of drug need not have been demonstrated only by quantitative chemical analysis. Jones v. State, 435 N.E.2d 616, 1982 Ind. App. LEXIS 1228 (1982).

Arrest.

Where an experienced narcotics officer was admitted to a room which smelled of marijuana and viewed an ashtray containing what he believed were marijuana cigarettes, there were sufficient facts to establish probable cause for a warrantless arrest. Heldman v. State, 163 Ind. App. 395, 324 N.E.2d 281, 1975 Ind. App. LEXIS 1048 (1975).

Constructive Possession.

In prosecution for possession of marijuana, persons who were merely passengers in car did not have constructive possession of marijuana found in the trunk, although constructive possession would have been imputed to the owner and driver of the car, since there was evidence from which control over the automobile by these two persons could have been inferred. Corrao v. State, 154 Ind. App. 525, 290 N.E.2d 484, 1972 Ind. App. LEXIS 930 (1972).

Where defendant stipulated that he was the owner of the house where the substances were found and was the only person present when the search warrant was executed and provided keys to various cabinets, evidence was sufficient to show possession since constructive possession may be proven from evidence that substance was in a place where defendant exercised dominion and control. Craig v. State, 403 N.E.2d 925, 1980 Ind. App. LEXIS 1431 (1980).

Evidence was sufficient to support a conviction for unlawful "constructive possession" of contraband found within the defendants' joint residency, within the kitchen refrigerator and upon a tray sitting upon a bench or table in the bedroom. Carnes v. State, 480 N.E.2d 581, 1985 Ind. App. LEXIS 2634 (1985).

Evidence was sufficient to support defendant's conviction for constructive possession of marijuana which was seized on a bed, where defendant unlocked the front door of a residence and directed police officers to his bedroom, where the marijuana was in plain view. Smith v. State, 505 N.E.2d 81, 1987 Ind. App. LEXIS 2462 (1987).

A finding of constructive possession must be supported by a determination that defendant had both the intent and the capability to maintain control and dominion over the illegal drugs (cocaine and marijuana) found in the bedroom.

Constructive Possession. (Cont'd)
Brooks v. State, 526 N.E.2d 1027, 1988 Ind. App. LEXIS 573 (1988).

Facts, together with the reasonable inferences drawn therefrom, supported the jury's determination of defendant's constructive possession of cocaine and marijuana. Brooks v. State, 526 N.E.2d 1027, 1988 Ind. App. LEXIS 573 (1988).

Constructive possession is defined as the intent and capability to maintain control and dominion over the drugs. The capability to exert control is the defendant's ability to reduce the substance to his personal possession or to direct its disposition or use. Rumple v. State, 529 N.E.2d 861, 1988 Ind. App. LEXIS 803 (1988).

State failed to produce additional evidence inferring defendant's knowledge of the presence of marijuana and its illegal character where, although defendant had originally been the front seat passenger, which would place him in closest proximity to the marijuana, it was not in plain view to infer his knowledge of its presence; mere presence where drugs are located or association with persons who possess drugs is not alone sufficient to support a finding of constructive possession. Godar v. State, 643 N.E.2d 12, 1994 Ind. App. LEXIS 1685 (1994).

Constructive possession of items found in a car might have been imputed to the driver and was established where the defendant had the intent and capability to maintain dominion and control over the contraband, because exclusive possession of a vehicle properly raised a reasonable inference of intent. State v. Emry, 753 N.E.2d 19, 2001 Ind. App. LEXIS 1180 (2001).

Defendant was properly convicted of possession of marijuana where the State proved constructive possession given defendant's proximity to the marijuana in a car and evidence of defendant's ability and intent to maintain dominion and control. Halsema v. State, 783 N.E.2d 1199, 2003 Ind. App. LEXIS 299 (2003), transfer granted, 804 N.E.2d 746, 2003 Ind. LEXIS 657 (2003), superseded, 823 N.E.2d 668, 2005 Ind. LEXIS 197 (2005).

Where defendant was found in a barricaded house with two other individuals, none of whom owned the house, and cocaine and marijuana were in plain view in close proximity to defendant, this was sufficient to establish defendant's constructive possession of the drugs and to convict defendant of possession of cocaine in violation of IC 35-48-4-6 and possession of marijuana in violation of IC 35-48-4-11. Matthews v. State, 792 N.E.2d 934, 2003 Ind. App. LEXIS 1413 (2003).

Evidence was sufficient to establish defendant's constructive possession of marijuana and cocaine with intent to deliver where defendant and codefendant were shown to be only residents of premises where drugs were found and where codefendant testified at length about their joint drug business and where they kept their stash. Donnegan v. State, 809 N.E.2d 966, 2004 Ind. App. LEXIS 1101 (2004).

Defendant's constructive possession of drugs found in search of house occupied by defendant and his cousin could not be inferred from police discovery, in search of house while defendant was not present, of contraband in closed containers in basement laundry room cabinet and other incriminating material found primarily in cousin's bedroom; there was no showing that contraband would have been within defendant's plain view. Gee v. State, 810 N.E.2d 338, 2004 Ind. LEXIS 535 (2004).

Control.
Where defendant did not have exclusive control of the apartment where the marijuana was found, but there was evidence of attempted flight and flushing a toilet upon confrontation with an imminent police search, the trier of fact was entitled to infer that she knew of the presence of the drugs and had control of them. Martin v. State, 175 Ind. App. 503, 372 N.E.2d 1194, 1978 Ind. App. LEXIS 818 (1978).

Controlled Substance Excise Tax.
Possession of marijuana, whether the possessor manufactured it or not, is taxable. Horrall v. Indiana Dep't of State Revenue, 687 N.E.2d 1219, 1997 Ind. Tax LEXIS 33 (1997).

Conviction of Uncharged Included Offense.
Where defendants were charged in the information with dealing in marijuana and maintaining a common nuisance, the trial court erred in convicting them of possession of marijuana, a charge against which the defendants were not prepared to defend. Crawford v. State, 502 N.E.2d 1361, 1987 Ind. App. LEXIS 2319 (1987), overruled, Wright v. State, 658 N.E.2d 563, 1995 Ind. LEXIS 162 (1995).

Double Jeopardy.
Where the charge of possessing a drug is a lesser included offense of dealing in that drug, the offender cannot be convicted and sentenced on both the greater and lesser offenses. Ratcliff v. State, 578 N.E.2d 359, 1991 Ind. LEXIS 168 (1991).

Where defendant was arrested in December 1992 for dealing in and possession of marijuana, and the Controlled Substance Excise Tax (CSET) was assessed and proceedings initiated to collect the tax in January 1993, jeopardy attached when he received notice of the assessment, and a subsequent trial in January 1994 for the underlying drug offenses which were the basis of the CSET assessment violated the double jeopardy clause. Garcia v. State, 686 N.E.2d 883, 1997 Ind. App. LEXIS 1502 (1997).

Delinquency petition based on marijuana possession did not subject juvenile to double jeopardy when, based on same possession charge, juvenile had already been subjected to forfeiture proceeding under IC 34-24-1-1, since civil forfeiture was not punishment for Fifth Amendment purposes. C.R.M. v. State, 799 N.E.2d 555, 2003 Ind. App. LEXIS 2236 (2003).

Once state established possession of marijuana by cultivation under IC 35-48-4-11(2), it also established possession of marijuana under IC 35-48-4-11(1), since it is not possible to cultivate marijuana

Double Jeopardy. (Cont'd)
without having either actual or constructive possession of marijuana; accordingly, two offenses were not distinct under same elements test, and double jeopardy clause was violated by defendant's conviction of both offenses. Britt v. State, 810 N.E.2d 1077, 2004 Ind. App. LEXIS 1206 (2004).

Defendant's convictions for Count I (IC 35-48-4-1.1) and Count IV (IC 35-48-4-11) did not violate Ind. Const., art. 1, § 14, Indiana's Double Jeopardy Clause because the state distinguished and set forth independent evidence of dealing in methamphetamine as a Class B felony (Count I) and possession of marijuana as a Class A misdemeanor (Count VI); therefore, there was no error in imposing a sentence on each count under IC 35-38-1-6. Micheau v. State, 893 N.E.2d 1053, 2008 Ind. App. LEXIS 2029 (2008).

—Controlled Substance Excise Tax.
Department of revenue's assessment of the controlled substance excise tax (CSET) against defendant was a jeopardy; therefore, his criminal prosecution for failure to pay the CSET constituted a second jeopardy in violation of his double jeopardy rights under the United States and Indiana Constitutions, as did his criminal prosecutions for growing and possessing marijuana. Bryant v. State, 660 N.E.2d 290, 1995 Ind. LEXIS 205, 64 A.L.R.5th 867 (1995), cert. denied, 519 U.S. 926, 117 S. Ct. 293, 136 L. Ed. 2d 213, 64 A.L.R.5th 867, 1996 U.S. LEXIS 6135 (1996).

Assessment of controlled substance excise tax (CSET) in amount of $871,437.50 against person who pled guilty to maintaining common nuisance did not violate double jeopardy because element of possession, which was required for assessment of CSET, was not required to establish essential elements of maintaining common nuisance; furthermore, CSET was legislatively intended as an addition to any criminal penalties or forfeitures. Newby v. Ind. Dep't of State Revenue, 826 N.E.2d 173, 2005 Ind. Tax LEXIS 24 (2005).

Evidence.

—Admissibility.
Where testimony of an officer, that marijuana cigarette butts were clearly visible to him when he was first within the dwelling in an attempt to make a purchase, was accepted by the trial court, the court on appeal must accept it and hold that the evidence was not the product of a search. Heldman v. State, 163 Ind. App. 395, 324 N.E.2d 281, 1975 Ind. App. LEXIS 1048 (1975).

Where officers saw defendant in a parked car near picnic grounds with his head lying against the window, it was proper for officers to investigate to see if he was all right, but after defendant said he was all right officers had no further right, because of the fact he appeared groggy and one of the officers had heard "a lot of things about him," to make him get out of the car to check his identification, and marijuana discovered at that time was not admissible in evidence. Madison v. State, 171 Ind. App. 492, 357 N.E.2d 911, 1976 Ind. App. LEXIS 1118 (1976).

Testimony that defendant offered to trade two bags of marijuana for another's stereo was relevant to show that the defendant knowingly possessed the marijuana and therefore, was correctly admitted into evidence by the trial court. Howard v. State, 422 N.E.2d 440, 1981 Ind. App. LEXIS 1502 (1981).

Where police officer testified that he had been on the police force for 14 years, that he had conducted numerous field tests on substances suspected of being marijuana, and that he was well acquainted with marijuana due to his police service, the fact that officer was unable to testify concerning the chemicals used or the reason for the chemical reaction to demonstrate the presence of marijuana did not render his use of the "field test" inadmissible. There was no error in the introduction of the result of the field test or officer's opinion as to the fact that the tested substance was marijuana. Eckstein v. State, 526 N.E.2d 693, 1988 Ind. LEXIS 218 (1988).

Marijuana in the form of a "blunt" and plastic baggies containing marijuana and cocaine was inadmissible because the evidence was seized in violation of defendant's Fourth Amendment rights where the police officer did not have reasonable suspicion that defendant was about to commit a crime or had committed a crime. Dowdell v. State, 747 N.E.2d 564, 2001 Ind. App. LEXIS 618 (2001).

State trooper was allowed to pat-down defendant before placing him in police cruiser for transport to the next exit on an interstate highway and the trial court properly denied defendant's motion to suppress marijuana found during pat-down and cocaine found during an inventory search that was conducted after the defendant's car was impounded. Lewis v. State, 755 N.E.2d 1116, 2001 Ind. App. LEXIS 1642 (2001).

Since the police had probable cause to arrest defendant for disorderly conduct resulting from defendant's involvement in a multi-person altercation, the search of defendant's person, as well as a rag that had been in his immediate control, was lawful as a search incident to an arrest; thus, the motion to suppress was properly denied. Moffitt v. State, 817 N.E.2d 239, 2004 Ind. App. LEXIS 2194 (2004).

Defendant was properly convicted of possession of marijuana because a police officer's testimony about discovering a warrant for defendant's arrest was not inadmissible hearsay when the officer testified about the warrant to explain her course of action; to the extent that the officer's testimony was offered to establish the existence of a warrant, that information pertained to whether the marijuana was admissible, and the existence of a warrant was not an element of the state's case but pertained only to the admissibility of evidence obtained under the warrant. Lewis v. State, — N.E.2d —, 2009 Ind. App. LEXIS 652 (2009).

—Amount.
Where test sample was taken from a pile of marijuana stalks two and one-half feet tall and eight feet in diameter weighing 130 pounds, there was sufficient evidence from which jury could find the possession of more than 30 grams of mari-

Evidence. (Cont'd)

—Amount. (Cont'd)
juana. Scott v. State, 404 N.E.2d 1190, 1980 Ind. App. LEXIS 1478 (1980).

—Chain of Possession.
Where evidence was introduced showing the exact location of marijuana from the time it was obtained by the arresting officers until it was introduced at the trial, the mere possibility of tampering was not sufficient to overcome the state's proof of chain of authority. Heldman v. State, 163 Ind. App. 395, 324 N.E.2d 281, 1975 Ind. App. LEXIS 1048 (1975).

—Insufficient.
Where defendant was arrested on assault and battery charge in front of place which he gave as his address and police allowed him to carry bag of groceries into house, and two days later, while defendant was incarcerated, police searched such house, which was occupied by a woman and two children, for objects used in connection with assault, and during such search found marijuana in upstairs bedroom closet, such evidence was insufficient to show possession of marijuana by defendant. Pier v. State, 400 N.E.2d 209, 1980 Ind. App. LEXIS 1321 (1980).

Mere presence in the vicinity or association with one having possession of drugs is not sufficient to sustain a conviction. Haynes v. State, 431 N.E.2d 83, 1982 Ind. LEXIS 737 (1982).

There was insufficient evidence to convict defendant of possession of marijuana in violation of IC 35-48-4-11 and of maintaining a common nuisance in violation of IC 35-48-4-13, as the state failed to prove that defendant had exclusive control over the premises where the marijuana was found, for there was no evidence that indicated whether defendant was the only resident of the house or that defendant's control was otherwise exclusive, and the state failed to prove that defendant constructively possessed the drugs, as there was no evidence of incriminating statements or behavior by defendant, nor was there evidence that the marijuana was close to defendant or defendant's possessions, or was in defendant's plain view. Smith v. State, 787 N.E.2d 458, 2003 Ind. App. LEXIS 740 (2003).

State failed to prove that defendant had actual or constructive possession of marijuana found at house frequented by defendant; there was no testimony as to presence of defendant's clothes or personal belongings, and presence of some of defendant's papers in house was insufficient to prove exclusive possession. Chandler v. State, 816 N.E.2d 464, 2004 Ind. App. LEXIS 2054 (2004).

—Possession.
Fact that passenger in car had bag of marijuana did not constitute evidence of actual or constructive possession of marijuana by driver of car. Crowder v. State, 398 N.E.2d 1352, 1980 Ind. App. LEXIS 1263 (1980).

Evidence indicating that defendant carried marijuana from a house and placed it on an automobile console was enough to show that he had actual possession of the marijuana. Smith v. State, 505 N.E.2d 81, 1987 Ind. App. LEXIS 2462 (1987).

Evidence was insufficient to support defendant's conviction for possession of marijuana, where, at most, the state proved that he held a plastic bag containing marijuana for a brief period of seven seconds before passing it to another individual. Loudermilk v. State, 523 N.E.2d 769, 1988 Ind. App. LEXIS 371 (1988).

The state was not required to show that defendant possessed the bag of marijuana at the time of his apprehension, or at the time the officers discovered the bag, only that defendant was knowingly or intentionally capable of maintaining dominion and control over the marijuana on the date identified in defendant's charging information. Womack v. State, 738 N.E.2d 320, 2000 Ind. App. LEXIS 1892 (2000).

—Sufficient.
Evidence that defendant was found with quantities of marijuana in his pockets and offered no evidence or legal authority for such possession was sufficient to sustain conviction. Sanchez v. State, 256 Ind. 140, 267 N.E.2d 374, 1971 Ind. LEXIS 601 (1971).

Where defendant dropped packet of marijuana, there was sufficient evidence to infer that he had possession or control. McGowan v. State, 156 Ind. App. 344, 296 N.E.2d 667, 1973 Ind. App. LEXIS 1128 (1973).

Where marijuana was found in defendant's residence which he shared with his wife and children, and defendant had previously told informant that he had marijuana growing in his yard and pictures of the growing marijuana were found, including one in which defendant was in the picture, and one bag of marijuana was found in defendant's dresser drawer, there was sufficient evidence to show constructive possession of the marijuana. Perry v. State, 418 N.E.2d 1214, 1981 Ind. App. LEXIS 1343 (1981).

Exclusive possession of the premises where contraband is found is sufficient to show intent to control the contraband. Burgin v. State, 431 N.E.2d 864, 1982 Ind. App. LEXIS 1090 (1982).

Proof of a possessory interest in the place where the contraband is found is sufficient to establish the capability to maintain control over the substance. Burgin v. State, 431 N.E.2d 864, 1982 Ind. App. LEXIS 1090 (1982).

Evidence was sufficient to support conviction. Snyder v. State, 460 N.E.2d 522, 1984 Ind. App. LEXIS 2878 (1984).

Evidence was sufficient to sustain defendant's conviction for possession of marijuana under IC 35-48-4-11(1) where marijuana was found in the freezer and there was no indication that defendant's housemates exclusively used the freezer. Goffinet v. State, 775 N.E.2d 1227, 2002 Ind. App. LEXIS 1647 (2002).

Evidence that marijuana was within defendant's reach was sufficient to show that he was able to reduce the marijuana to his personal possession, and defendant's flight from vehicle was sufficient to support the reasonable inference that defendant was aware of the marijuana's presence; thus conviction for possession of marijuana was affirmed.

Evidence. (Cont'd)

—Sufficient. (Cont'd)
Holmes v. State, 785 N.E.2d 658, 2003 Ind. App. LEXIS 515 (2003).

Instructions.
Where the jury was instructed that it should find defendant guilty of Class D felony possession if it concluded that defendant had a prior marijuana conviction, such an instruction, standing alone, would violate the dictates of Ind. Const., art. 1, § 19; however, the final paragraph of the court's instruction specifically stated that the jury could decline to convict defendant of Class D felony possession even if the jury found that he had a prior marijuana conviction. Since the jury was instructed as to this option, the court's instruction did not invade the province of the jury or improperly lead the jury to believe that it did not have the discretion to decide the law and the facts afforded under Ind. Const., art. 1, § 19. Womack v. State, 738 N.E.2d 320, 2000 Ind. App. LEXIS 1892 (2000).

Knowledge or Intent.
Where defendant, with his wife, was joint occupant of the apartment where the marijuana was found, but the only persons present at the time of the search were his wife and a houseguest who was not a casual visitor and who had access to the room where the drugs were found, there was insufficient evidence that defendant had knowledge of the presence of the drugs. Martin v. State, 175 Ind. App. 503, 372 N.E.2d 1194, 1978 Ind. App. LEXIS 818 (1978).
Guilty knowledge must be shown in order to convict an accused of marijuana possession. Howard v. State, 422 N.E.2d 440, 1981 Ind. App. LEXIS 1502 (1981).
Evidence held sufficient to show that defendant knowingly or intentionally grew or cultivated marijuana where his wife reported marijuana growing behind her home to the sheriff's department, defendant had resided at a separate residence since early May, 1991, the officer testified that the wife told him the marijuana had been cultivated by her husband, and a neighbor testified that the defendant phoned her on the evening of June 10, 1991 and requested that she pull his marijuana plants before the police arrived, even though defendant denied contacting his neighbor and also denied any connection with the marijuana plants. McClurg v. State, 616 N.E.2d 788, 1993 Ind. App. LEXIS 826 (1993).

Merger.

—Conspiracy.
Conviction for possession of marijuana and conspiracy cannot be merged. Howard v. State, 422 N.E.2d 440, 1981 Ind. App. LEXIS 1502 (1981).

—Dealing.
Where dealing and possession charges arise from the same act, it cannot be said that each charge requires proof of an element that the other does not. Hence, dealing and possession convic-

tions for that act would be merged. Howard v. State, 422 N.E.2d 440, 1981 Ind. App. LEXIS 1502 (1981).

Premises.
Where the accused did not have exclusive control of the premises, it may not be inferred that he knew of the presence of the marijuana and had control of it, unless there are other incriminating statements or circumstances tending to buttress such an inference. Martin v. State, 175 Ind. App. 503, 372 N.E.2d 1194, 1978 Ind. App. LEXIS 818 (1978).

Search and Seizure.
Evidence obtained under a search warrant the affidavit for which was based upon unsupported hearsay without adequate allegations of the reliability of the informant was obtained illegally and defendant's motion to suppress the same should have been sustained. McCurry v. State, 249 Ind. 191, 231 N.E.2d 227, 1967 Ind. LEXIS 368 (1967).
The facts known to the officer at the time he stopped defendant's vehicle were sufficient to warrant the belief of a man of reasonable caution that an investigation was appropriate. Bratcher v. State, 661 N.E.2d 828, 1996 Ind. App. LEXIS 123 (1996).
Where the officer discovered the bag of marijuana during a search for weapons and the incriminating character was immediately apparent to the officer, the search was authorized and the seizure of the marijuana was valid under the United States Constitution. Bratcher v. State, 661 N.E.2d 828, 1996 Ind. App. LEXIS 123 (1996).
Since there was probable cause to arrest defendant, based on the smell of marijuana emanating from his vehicle, the pat-down search and search of his vehicle were proper, and his motion to suppress was properly denied. Sebastian v. State, 726 N.E.2d 827, 2000 Ind. App. LEXIS 501 (2000).
The trial court committed reversible error in denying defendant's motion to suppress marijuana seized from the warrantless search of his van because the scope of the search incident to defendant's arrest should have been limited to his person where he was stopped and arrested, but the marijuana was found in the interior of his van. Gibson v. State, 733 N.E.2d 945, 2000 Ind. App. LEXIS 1150 (2000).
Where the officer received a radio report of possible narcotics dealing by three or four African-American men in the vicinity of a particular city block, the required specificity of information was lacking to give reasonable suspicion to conduct an investigatory stop. Burkett v. State, 736 N.E.2d 304, 2000 Ind. App. LEXIS 1580 (2000).
Defendant's consent to search was not constitutionally defective, and because the expressed objects of the officer's search were drugs and weapons, when defendant gave the officer permission to search his person for drugs and weapons, a reasonable person would have understood defendant's consent to include permission to search defendant's outer clothing, including his back pants pocket, which might reasonably contain those

Search and Seizure. (Cont'd)
specified items. Pinkney v. State, 742 N.E.2d 956, 2001 Ind. App. LEXIS 8 (2001).

Officer lawfully seized plastic bag containing vegetable material after he saw bag in pouch of defendant's sweatshirt while defendant was exiting car prior to lawful search and suspected that vegetable material was marijuana. Crabtree v. State, 762 N.E.2d 217, 2002 Ind. App. LEXIS 148 (2002).

Defendant's Ind. Const., art. 1, § 11 rights were violated where police searched his trash based solely on anonymous tip of drug activity, which, standing alone, did not create reasonable suspicion of illegal activity necessary for search; accordingly, evidence found after search warrant was issued based on evidence found in trash should have been suppressed. Crook v. State, 827 N.E.2d 643, 2005 Ind. App. LEXIS 892 (2005).

Public school safety officer's clear need to determine the identity of a juvenile who was in a high school hallway without a pass and claimed he had no identification justified her pat-down search of him for identification; accordingly, juvenile's Fourth Amendment rights were not violated, and marijuana found in the course of the search was admissible. D.L. v. State, 877 N.E.2d 500, 2007 Ind. App. LEXIS 2729 (2007).

Where the evidence collected as a result of an impermissible Terry stop, including marijuana seized during a search and defendant's subsequent admission that he owned the marijuana, was inadmissible under the Fourth Amendment, and the trial court abused its discretion in admitting it, the conviction for possession of marijuana had to be reversed. Holly v. State, 888 N.E.2d 338, 2008 Ind. App. LEXIS 1258 (2008).

Defendant was properly convicted of possession of marijuana because he was not deprived of his right to challenge the validity of an outstanding warrant for his arrest when defendant made no effort to obtain the warrant, and there was no discovery violation by the state; a police officer's testimony was not inadmissible hearsay when the officer testified about the warrant to explain her course of action, and to the extent that the officer's testimony was offered to establish the existence of a warrant, that information pertained to whether the marijuana was admissible. Lewis v. State, — N.E.2d —, 2009 Ind. App. LEXIS 652 (2009).

Defendant was properly convicted of possession of marijuana because evidence seized from her apartment was admissible when a reasonable person could conclude that defendant had given a police officer consent to search the apartment, and a scrivener's error on the consent to search form did not make the search unreasonable; the officer was clearly interested in searching defendant's apartment, not some other apartment unrelated to the complaint he was investigating, and defendant's actions were consistent with giving consent. Beattie v. State, — N.E.2d —, 2009 Ind. App. LEXIS 660 (2009).

Search Warrants.
Where police officer who swore out affidavit for search warrant for search of premises lost visual contact of informant who was making a controlled buy for police officer for about 20 seconds it was not so substantial as to affect probable cause and evidence obtained by search was properly introduced. Whirley v. State, 408 N.E.2d 629, 1980 Ind. App. LEXIS 1607 (1980).

Sentence.
Where conviction was under counts which charged possession of marijuana and a previous conviction for the same offense, and law provided for lesser sentence in the case of first offenders, sentence was not to have been for first offenders but was a proper sentence for a second offender. Heldman v. State, 163 Ind. App. 395, 324 N.E.2d 281, 1975 Ind. App. LEXIS 1048 (1975).

Where three bags of marijuana were found during one search of defendant's residence he could be charged with only one offense of possession and when convicted and sentenced on three counts the sentences on the other two counts were required to be vacated. Perry v. State, 418 N.E.2d 1214, 1981 Ind. App. LEXIS 1343 (1981).

Although defendant's misdemeanor charge for possession of marijuana was elevated to a felony, he could also be charged as a habitual offender under IC 35-50-2-10 since drug possession misdemeanors and felonies were specifically included in the category of offenses that were subject to habitual substance offender enhancement. State v. Downey, 770 N.E.2d 794, 2002 Ind. LEXIS 542 (2002).

When defendant's sentence for possession of marijuana, which was suspended pursuant to IC 35-50-2-2(c), was ordered to be executed, defendant had a right of allocution to the same extent defendant would have had at a probation revocation hearing. The trial court was not required to ask if defendant wanted to speak as provided by IC 35-38-1-5 and Ind. Const. art. 1, § 13, and defendant waived the right of allocution by not asking to speak or objecting to the lack of opportunity to speak. Hull v. State, 868 N.E.2d 901, 2007 Ind. App. LEXIS 1400 (2007).

Although defendant's eight-year and one-year sentences for child exploitation and possession of marijuana, IC 35-42-4-4(b) and IC 35-48-4-11, respectively, were not inappropriate, they were to be served concurrently. Hayes v. State, 879 N.E.2d 1179, 2008 Ind. App. LEXIS 123 (2008).

Sufficiency of Evidence.
Because the evidence permitted a reasonable conclusion that two independent offenses were committed for which defendant could have been separately punished, an attempt charge was not a lesser included offense of a dealing in methamphetamine charge; evidence of numerous items commonly used in the production of methamphetamine and .48 grams of methamphetamine were found in defendant's residence supported a conviction under IC 35-48-4-1.1 for dealing in methamphetamine as a Class B felony and evidence that the police found 12.96 grams of ephedrine and pseudoephedrine that could yield at least three grams of methamphetamine supported the conviction under IC 35-48-4-11 for attempted dealing in

Sufficiency of Evidence. (Cont'd)
methamphetamine as a Class A felony. Micheau v. State, 893 N.E.2d 1053, 2008 Ind. App. LEXIS 2029 (2008).

Ultimate User.
Defendant could not be an ultimate user under IC 35-48-1-27 of marijuana because he intended to construct a "hemp hut," because there is no "hemp hut" exemption to the general rule that possession of marijuana is illegal. Horrall v. Indiana Dep't of State Revenue, 687 N.E.2d 1219, 1997 Ind. Tax LEXIS 33 (1997).

Verdict.
Where evidence showed police informant had nothing in his possession except $10.00 prior to his meeting with defendant, and that under police observation he met defendant giving him the $10.00 and receiving a package in return which later was identified as marijuana, a verdict which found defendant guilty of possession but not guilty of sale was not inconsistent. Buckner v. State, 252 Ind. 379, 248 N.E.2d 348, 1969 Ind. LEXIS 361 (1969).

Verdict Form.
Where the jury instructions adequately explained the difference between Class A misdemeanor possession and Class D felony possession, and advised the jury of its responsibility to decide the law and facts, the verdict form needed to give the jury the option of convicting defendant of possession as a Class A misdemeanor or as a Class D felony, without specific reference to whether defendant had a prior marijuana conviction. Womack v. State, 738 N.E.2d 320, 2000 Ind. App. LEXIS 1892 (2000).

Violation by Attorney.
Knowing that marijuana is growing on one's premises and failing to destroy the plants is contrary to this section and, accordingly, is violative of DR. 1-102, Code of Prof. Resp. for Attorneys at Law, for which the strongest disciplinary sanction available, disbarment, must be imposed. In re Moore, 453 N.E.2d 971, 1983 Ind. LEXIS 975 (1983).

Cited:
O'Brien v. State, 422 N.E.2d 1266, 1981 Ind. App. LEXIS 1535 (1981); Smith v. State, 427 N.E.2d 11, 1981 Ind. App. LEXIS 1685 (1981);

Everroad v. State, 442 N.E.2d 994, 1982 Ind. LEXIS 1038 (1982); Vanderberg v. State, 434 N.E.2d 936, 1982 Ind. App. LEXIS 1188 (1982); Klopfenstein v. State, 439 N.E.2d 1181, 1982 Ind. App. LEXIS 1408 (1982); Vitaniemi v. State, 440 N.E.2d 5, 1982 Ind. App. LEXIS 1401 (1982); Flaherty v. State, 443 N.E.2d 340, 1982 Ind. App. LEXIS 1539 (1982); Hurley v. State, 446 N.E.2d 1326, 1983 Ind. LEXIS 794 (1983); Borst v. State, 459 N.E.2d 751, 1984 Ind. App. LEXIS 2337 (1984); Castle v. State, 476 N.E.2d 522, 1985 Ind. App. LEXIS 2329 (1985); Marshall v. State, 493 N.E.2d 1317, 1986 Ind. App. LEXIS 2654 (1986); Wood v. State, 592 N.E.2d 740, 1992 Ind. App. LEXIS 856 (1992); Esquerdo v. State, 640 N.E.2d 1023, 1994 Ind. LEXIS 126 (1994); Davis v. State, 642 N.E.2d 987, 1994 Ind. App. LEXIS 1602 (1994); Lycan v. State, 671 N.E.2d 447, 1996 Ind. App. LEXIS 1262 (1996); Stone v. State, 671 N.E.2d 499, 1996 Ind. App. LEXIS 1485 (1996); Rook v. State, 679 N.E.2d 997, 1997 Ind. App. LEXIS 520 (1997); Dunn v. State, 694 N.E.2d 722, 1998 Ind. LEXIS 55 (1998); State v. Mohler, 694 N.E.2d 1129, 1998 Ind. LEXIS 52 (1998); Jennings v. State, 714 N.E.2d 730, 1999 Ind. App. LEXIS 1283 (1999); Price v. State, 725 N.E.2d 82, 2000 Ind. LEXIS 208 (2000); Hanna v. State, 726 N.E.2d 384, 2000 Ind. App. LEXIS 511 (2000); Whitney v. State, 726 N.E.2d 823, 2000 Ind. App. LEXIS 507 (2000); Perez v. State, 728 N.E.2d 234, 2000 Ind. App. LEXIS 743 (2000); Campbell v. State, 734 N.E.2d 248, 2000 Ind. App. LEXIS 1297 (2000); Seel v. State, 739 N.E.2d 170, 2000 Ind. App. LEXIS 1922 (2000); LaMunion v. State, 740 N.E.2d 576, 2000 Ind. App. LEXIS 2044 (2000); Love v. State, 741 N.E.2d 789, 2001 Ind. App. LEXIS 6 (2001); Vanzo v. State, 738 N.E.2d 1061, 2000 Ind. App. LEXIS 1901 (2000); Antrim v. State, 745 N.E.2d 246, 2001 Ind. App. LEXIS 309 (2001); Allen v. State, 743 N.E.2d 1222, 2001 Ind. App. LEXIS 367 (2001); Lineberry v. State, 747 N.E.2d 1151, 2001 Ind. App. LEXIS 800 (2001); Clifft v. Ind. Dep't of Revenue, 748 N.E.2d 449, 2001 Ind. Tax LEXIS 29 (2001); Lark v. State, 755 N.E.2d 1153, 2001 Ind. App. LEXIS 1703 (2001); Bradshaw v. State, 759 N.E.2d 271, 2001 Ind. App. LEXIS 2066 (2001); State v. Glass, 769 N.E.2d 639, 2002 Ind. App. LEXIS 901 (2002); Rybolt v. State, 770 N.E.2d 935, 2002 Ind. App. LEXIS 1005 (2002); Jefferson v. State, 780 N.E.2d 398, 2002 Ind. App. LEXIS 2147 (2002); Winebrenner v. State, 790 N.E.2d 1037, 2003 Ind. App. LEXIS 1195 (2003).

RESEARCH REFERENCES

Indiana Law Journal.
Constitutional Analysis of Indiana's Controlled Substance Excise Tax, 70 Ind. L.J. 1301 (1995).

Indiana Law Review.
Taxation: Developments in Indiana Taxation, 34 Ind. L. Rev. 1003 (2001).

Res Gestae.
Criminal Justice Notes 6/04: Constructive possession not shown, 48 (No. 2) Res Gestae 32 (2004).

Collateral References.
Minimum quantity of drug required to support claim that defendant is guilty of criminal "possession" of drug under state law. 4 A.L.R.5th 1.

35-48-4-12. Conditional discharge for possession as first offense.

If a person who has no prior conviction of an offense under this article or under a law of another jurisdiction relating to controlled substances pleads guilty to possession of marijuana or hashish as a Class A misdemeanor, the court, without entering a judgment of conviction and with the consent of the person, may defer further proceedings and place him in the custody of the court under such conditions as the court determines. Upon violation of a condition of the custody, the court may enter a judgment of conviction. However, if the person fulfills the conditions of the custody, the court shall dismiss the charges against him. There may be only one (1) dismissal under this section with respect to a person.

History.
IC 35-48-4-12, as added by Acts 1976, P.L.148, § 7; 1977, P.L.340, § 107.

NOTES TO DECISIONS

ANALYSIS

In General.
Judicial Discretion.
Violation of Terms.

In General.
This section does not provide that the defendant punished under it is not "convicted," as if it were possible to impose criminal punishment (such as probation and a fine) on a person who had not been convicted of a crime; this section merely provides that no "judgement of conviction" shall be entered. Hill v. Norfolk & W. R. Co., 814 F.2d 1192, 1987 U.S. App. LEXIS 3552 (7th Cir. Ind. 1987).

Judicial Discretion.
A defendant has no right to a conditional discharge since it is a conditional liberty and an alternative to commitment that may be granted at the sole discretion of the trial court. Perkins v. State, 715 N.E.2d 1016, 1999 Ind. App. LEXIS 1481 (1999).

Violation of Terms.
Where the defendant agreed to the terms and conditions of a conditional discharge agreement, and where he was clearly informed that if he violated the conditions he could be convicted and sentenced for the offense, there was no error in entering a judgment of conviction and in sentencing him accordingly when he violated the terms of his release. Perkins v. State, 715 N.E.2d 1016, 1999 Ind. App. LEXIS 1481 (1999).

Cited:
In re Thomas, 472 N.E.2d 609, 1985 Ind. LEXIS 726 (1985); Miller v. State, 783 N.E.2d 772, 2003 Ind. App. LEXIS 268 (2003).

35-48-4-13. Visiting or maintaining a common nuisance.

(a) A person who knowingly or intentionally visits a building, structure, vehicle, or other place that is used by any person to unlawfully use a controlled substance commits visiting a common nuisance, a Class B misdemeanor.

(b) A person who knowingly or intentionally maintains a building, structure, vehicle, or other place that is used one (1) or more times:
  (1) by persons to unlawfully use controlled substances; or
  (2) for unlawfully:
    (A) manufacturing;
    (B) keeping;
    (C) offering for sale;
    (D) selling;
    (E) delivering; or
    (F) financing the delivery of;
  controlled substances, or items of drug paraphernalia as described in IC 35-48-4-8.5;
commits maintaining a common nuisance, a Class D felony.

History.
IC 35-48-4-13, as added by Acts 1976, P.L.148, § 7; 1977, P.L.340, § 108; P.L.210-1986, § 4;

P.L.165-1990, § 13; P.L.1-1991, § 207; P.L.31-1998, § 11; P.L.17-2001, § 27.

NOTES TO DECISIONS

ANALYSIS

In General.
Constitutionality.
Common Nuisance.
—Maintaining Nuisance.
—Visiting a Nuisance.
Continuing Violations.
Double Jeopardy.
Evidence.
—Sufficiency.
Included Offenses.
"Knowingly or Intentionally."
Merger.
Paraphernalia.
Use for Illegal Purposes.
"Visits" Defined.

In General.
It is consistent that a person who does not possess controlled substances may concurrently maintain a building that is used for unlawfully keeping controlled substances. Sayre v. State, 471 N.E.2d 708, 1984 Ind. App. LEXIS 3103 (1984), cert. denied, 475 U.S. 1027, 106 S. Ct. 1226, 89 L. Ed. 2d 336, 1986 U.S. LEXIS 454 (1986).

One must know that a controlled substance is unlawfully used before he can be convicted of visiting a common nuisance. Bass v. State, 512 N.E.2d 460, 1987 Ind. App. LEXIS 3060 (1987), corrected, 517 N.E.2d 1238, 1988 Ind. App. LEXIS 148 (1988).

Constitutionality.
The defendant lacked standing to challenge the constitutionality of the statute, as a contravention of the due process provisions of the Fourteenth Amendment in not requiring those convicted of visiting a common nuisance to have "knowledge" that illicit drugs were kept or used on the premises, because she was not barred by the alleged defect there being sufficient evidence to show defendant actually knew marijuana was kept and used in the apartment. Terrel v. State, 170 Ind. App. 422, 353 N.E.2d 553, 1976 Ind. App. LEXIS 1012 (1976).

Common Nuisance.

—Maintaining Nuisance.
The use of the defendant's wife's car for a drug sale was insufficient to sustain a conviction for maintaining a common nuisance. Plowman v. State, 604 N.E.2d 1219, 1992 Ind. App. LEXIS 1845 (1992).

The "maintains" or "maintaining" language in this section implicitly requires proof of a continuing or recurring violation, and the state must have proof of a defendant's recurring or continuous violation. Bryant v. State, 660 N.E.2d 290, 1995 Ind. LEXIS 205, 64 A.L.R.5th 867 (1995), cert.

denied, 519 U.S. 926, 117 S. Ct. 293, 136 L. Ed. 2d 213, 64 A.L.R.5th 867, 1996 U.S. LEXIS 6135 (1996).

Until it was changed on July 1, 2001, IC 34-48-4-13(b) did not specify that it was a crime to maintain property for the purpose of manufacturing drugs, and the appellate court reversed defendant's conviction for maintaining a common nuisance in February 2001, in violation of former IC 34-48-4-13(b), because the trial court charged the jury that it could find defendant guilty of violating former IC 35-48-4-13 if he used his property to manufacture a controlled substance. Culbertson v. State, 792 N.E.2d 573, 2003 Ind. App. LEXIS 1364 (2003).

Evidence that defendant constructively possessed controlled substance in duplex where he lived was sufficient to convict defendant of maintaining common nuisance on property; defendant's claim that he could not be convicted under IC 35-48-4-13 of maintaining common nuisance on property because he did not sign lease and was not legal tenant of duplex was rejected. Jones v. State, 807 N.E.2d 58, 2004 Ind. App. LEXIS 752 (2004).

—Visiting a Nuisance.
Term "common nuisance" as used within IC 35-48-4-13(a) necessarily requires proof of a continuous or recurrent violation, and the 1998 amendment to IC 35-48-4-13(b) did not change this requirement; where the State offered no evidence with respect to the element of continuous or recurrent violation, a conviction for visiting a common nuisance was reversed. Hale v. State, 785 N.E.2d 641, 2003 Ind. App. LEXIS 462 (2003).

Continuing Violations.
The fact that the defendant sold drugs at the tavern on more than one occasion was merely probative of the continuing violations necessary to establish a single offense. Such evidence was insufficient to support a conviction for separate counts of maintaining a common nuisance. Plowman v. State, 604 N.E.2d 1219, 1992 Ind. App. LEXIS 1845 (1992).

Double Jeopardy.
Department of revenue's assessment of the controlled substance excise tax (CSET) against defendant was a jeopardy; therefore, his subsequent criminal prosecutions for failure to pay the CSET, and for growing and possessing marijuana, violated his double jeopardy rights under the United States and Indiana Constitutions. Bryant v. State, 660 N.E.2d 290, 1995 Ind. LEXIS 205, 64 A.L.R.5th 867 (1995), cert. denied, 519 U.S. 926, 117 S. Ct. 293, 136 L. Ed. 2d 213, 64 A.L.R.5th 867, 1996 U.S. LEXIS 6135 (1996).

Assessment of controlled substance excise tax (CSET) in amount of $871,437.50 against person

Double Jeopardy. (Cont'd)
who pled guilty to maintaining common nuisance did not violate double jeopardy because element of possession, which was required for assessment of CSET, was not required to establish essential elements of maintaining common nuisance; furthermore, CSET was legislatively intended as an addition to any criminal penalties or forfeitures. Newby v. Ind. Dep't of State Revenue, 826 N.E.2d 173, 2005 Ind. Tax LEXIS 24 (2005).

Evidence.

—Sufficiency.
Although nothing was found in the accused's room, evidence that he had slept at the residence where significant amounts of contraband were found and had paid most of the rent for three months and had smoked marijuana there, was sufficient. Mayotte v. State, 172 Ind. App. 252, 360 N.E.2d 34, 1977 Ind. App. LEXIS 752 (1977).

Testimony of the accused that he had previously smoked marijuana on the premises was sufficient to show knowledge of the unlawful use of the house. Mayotte v. State, 172 Ind. App. 252, 360 N.E.2d 34, 1977 Ind. App. LEXIS 752 (1977).

Evidence that defendants resided in the house and were fully aware of drug related activity occurring there was sufficient to support conviction for maintaining a common nuisance. Ewing v. State, 613 N.E.2d 53, 1993 Ind. App. LEXIS 470 (1993), superseded, 629 N.E.2d 1238, 1994 Ind. LEXIS 22 (Ind. 1994).

The large quantity of illegal drugs and drug paraphernalia found in plain view in a house, coupled with the facts that the defendant voluntarily sought refuge in the house and was found in possession of cocaine, was sufficient to support a reasonable inference that the defendant knew the house was used by a person for illegal drug activities, in violation of IC 35-48-4-13(a). Frye v. State, 757 N.E.2d 684, 2001 Ind. App. LEXIS 1763 (2001), cert. denied, 535 U.S. 1103, 122 S. Ct. 2308, 152 L. Ed. 2d 1063, 2002 U.S. LEXIS 3956 (2002).

Evidence was insufficient to support defendant's conviction for maintaining a common nuisance, because the criminal statute making it a violation of the law required that the evidence show that "persons" unlawfully used controlled substances at a home and the evidence in defendant's case only showed that one person was doing so. Hook v. State, 775 N.E.2d 1125, 2002 Ind. App. LEXIS 1590 (2002).

There was insufficient evidence to convict defendant of possession of marijuana in violation of IC 35-48-4-11 and of maintaining a common nuisance in violation of IC 35-48-4-13, as the state failed to prove that defendant had exclusive control over the premises where the marijuana was found, for there was no evidence that indicated whether defendant was the only resident of the house or that defendant's control was otherwise exclusive, and the state failed to prove that defendant constructively possessed the drugs, as there was no evidence of incriminating statements or behavior by defendant, nor was there evidence that the

marijuana was close to defendant or defendant's possessions, or that it was in defendant's plain view. Smith v. State, 787 N.E.2d 458, 2003 Ind. App. LEXIS 740 (2003).

There was insufficient evidence to convict defendant of visiting common nuisance in violation of IC 35-48-4-13 since, although defendant became aware of drug use when she visited property in question, state did not present evidence that drug use occurred on property more than once. Zuniga v. State, 815 N.E.2d 197, 2004 Ind. App. LEXIS 1862 (2004).

Where state failed to prove defendant's constructive possession of marijuana found in house by his exclusive possession of house and failed to prove that defendant knew it was present in house, evidence was insufficient to convict defendant of maintaining common nuisance. Chandler v. State, 816 N.E.2d 464, 2004 Ind. App. LEXIS 2054 (2004).

Evidence was sufficient to show that premises where defendant was arrested had been used many times for methamphetamine production, so as to amount to a common nuisance, where search of a storage area yielded evidence indicating past production of controlled substances. Traylor v. State, 817 N.E.2d 611, 2004 Ind. App. LEXIS 2229 (2004).

Included Offenses.
Where the elements of visiting or maintaining a building, structure, vehicle or other place were absent from information charging dealing cocaine, neither visiting nor maintaining a common nuisance was a factually included lesser offense, and trial court properly refused tendered instructions on those offenses. Sledge v. State, 677 N.E.2d 82, 1997 Ind. App. LEXIS 85 (1997).

"Knowingly or Intentionally."
Knowledge of selling is a necessary element of proving the crime of maintaining a common nuisance. Holmes v. State, 583 N.E.2d 180, 1991 Ind. App. LEXIS 2214 (1991).

Defendant's conviction of maintaining a common nuisance was reversed where, although the state proved that she was present somewhere within the residence during a drug transaction, there was insufficient evidence to establish that she knew her residence was used for the unlawful sale of cocaine. Holmes v. State, 583 N.E.2d 180, 1991 Ind. App. LEXIS 2214 (1991).

Plaintiff was arrested without probable cause in violation of the Fourth Amendment on a charge under IC 35-48-4-13 of maintaining a common nuisance where the circumstances did not corroborate that plaintiff had knowledge of alleged methamphetamine manufacturing activities that occurred in plaintiff's garage; however, the officer was entitled to qualified immunity from plaintiff's 42 U.S.C.S. § 1983 claim because the officer reasonably could have believed that probable cause existed even though that belief was ultimately mistaken. Wheeler v. Lawson, 539 F.3d 629, 2008 U.S. App. LEXIS 17792 (2008).

Merger.
Visiting a common nuisance under this section

Merger. (Cont'd)

and possession of marijuana under IC 35-48-4-11 each require the showing of a fact that the other does not. In the same way, visiting a common nuisance and conspiracy under IC 35-41-5-2 each require proof of an element that the other does not. Consequently, visiting a common nuisance cannot be merged with either possession of marijuana or conspiracy. Howard v. State, 422 N.E.2d 440, 1981 Ind. App. LEXIS 1502 (1981).

Paraphernalia.

Introduction of drug paraphernalia which did not contain controlled substances was error because the evidence was not probative to the issue of whether defendant maintained a common nuisance by keeping controlled substances, but where sufficient other evidence was properly admitted and the defendant did not show how the irrelevant evidence prejudiced her, the error was harmless. Sayre v. State, 471 N.E.2d 708, 1984 Ind. App. LEXIS 3103 (1984), cert. denied, 475 U.S. 1027, 106 S. Ct. 1226, 89 L. Ed. 2d 336, 1986 U.S. LEXIS 454 (1986).

Testimony that paraphernalia associated with the use of controlled substances was found in the lower level of the home and that the defendant was found in the kitchen in the lower level of the home, was insufficient to show that the defendant knew that a controlled substance was being used at the residence. Braster v. State, 596 N.E.2d 278, 1992 Ind. App. LEXIS 1138 (1992).

Use for Illegal Purposes.

Where samples of narcotics were found in refrigerator on premises, and the seller discussed other substances he "would be getting in" in the future, evidence was sufficient to designate house a common nuisance. Wells v. State, 170 Ind. App. 29, 351 N.E.2d 43, 1976 Ind. App. LEXIS 969 (1976).

A suspect fleeing arrest does not convert a public restaurant into a common nuisance by entering it with narcotics in his possession. Bezell v. State, 170 Ind. App. 356, 352 N.E.2d 809, 1976 Ind. App. LEXIS 1007 (1976).

"Visits" Defined.

"Visits" means to come or go to a place generally and is not confined to a concept of staying as a guest. Mayotte v. State, 172 Ind. App. 252, 360 N.E.2d 34, 1977 Ind. App. LEXIS 752 (1977).

Cited:

Hurley v. State, 446 N.E.2d 1326, 1983 Ind. LEXIS 794 (1983); Barnett v. State, 493 N.E.2d 1286, 1986 Ind. App. LEXIS 2655 (1986); Meagher v. State, 726 N.E.2d 260, 2000 Ind. LEXIS 245 (2000); Perez v. State, 728 N.E.2d 234, 2000 Ind. App. LEXIS 743 (2000); Everroad v. State, 730 N.E.2d 222, 2000 Ind. App. LEXIS 899 (2000); Castillo v. State, 734 N.E.2d 299, 2000 Ind. App. LEXIS 1356 (2000); Mendoza v. State, 737 N.E.2d 784, 2000 Ind. App. LEXIS 1647 (2000); Antrim v. State, 745 N.E.2d 246, 2001 Ind. App. LEXIS 309 (2001); Baird v. State, 854 N.E.2d 398, 2006 Ind. App. LEXIS 1951 (2006); Rotz v. State, 894 N.E.2d 989, 2008 Ind. App. LEXIS 2161 (2008).

RESEARCH REFERENCES

Indiana Law Review.

Update — Criminal Law and Procedure, 26 Ind. L. Rev. 891 (1993).

Collateral References.

Validity and construction of state statutes criminalizing the act of permitting real property to be used in connection with illegal drug activities. 24 A.L.R.5th 428.

Validity, construction, and application of state or local law prohibiting maintenance of vehicle for purpose of keeping or selling controlled substances. 31 A.L.R.5th 760.

35-48-4-13.3. Taking a minor or endangered adult into place where controlled substances are unlawfully present, manufactured, offered for sale or financed for delivery.

A person who recklessly, knowingly, or intentionally takes a person less than eighteen (18) years of age or an endangered adult (as defined in IC 12-10-3-2) into a building, structure, vehicle, or other place that is being used by any person to:

(1) unlawfully possess drugs or controlled substances; or

(2) unlawfully:

  (A) manufacture;

  (B) keep;

  (C) offer for sale;

  (D) sell;

  (E) deliver; or

  (F) finance the delivery of;

drugs or controlled substances;

commits a Class A misdemeanor. However, the offense is a Class D felony if the person has a prior unrelated conviction under this section.

History.
P.L.225-2003, § 4.

Penalties for misdemeanors, IC 35-50-1, IC 35-50-3, IC 35-50-5-2.

Cross References.
Penalties for felonies, IC 35-50-1, IC 35-50-2, IC 35-50-5-2.

35-48-4-14. Offenses relating to registration.

(a) A person who:
(1) Is subject to IC 35-48-3 and who recklessly, knowingly, or intentionally distributes or dispenses a controlled substance in violation of IC 35-48-3;
(2) Is a registrant and who recklessly, knowingly, or intentionally:
(A) Manufactures; or
(B) Finances the manufacture of;
a controlled substance not authorized by his registration or distributes or dispenses a controlled substance not authorized by his registration to another registrant or other authorized person;
(3) Recklessly, knowingly, or intentionally fails to make, keep, or furnish a record, a notification, an order form, a statement, an invoice, or information required under this article; or
(4) Recklessly, knowingly, or intentionally refuses entry into any premises for an inspection authorized by this article;
commits a Class D felony.
(b) A person who knowingly or intentionally:
(1) Distributes as a registrant a controlled substance classified in schedule I or II, except under an order form as required by IC 35-48-3;
(2) Uses in the course of the:
(A) Manufacture of;
(B) The financing of the manufacture of; or
(C) Distribution of;
a controlled substance a federal or state registration number that is fictitious, revoked, suspended, or issued to another person;
(3) Furnishes false or fraudulent material information in, or omits any material information from, an application, report, or other document required to be kept or filed under this article; or
(4) Makes, distributes, or possesses a punch, die, plate, stone, or other thing designed to print, imprint, or reproduce the trademark, trade name, or other identifying mark, imprint, or device of another or a likeness of any of the foregoing on a drug or container or labeling thereof so as to render the drug a counterfeit substance;
commits a Class D felony.
(c) A person who knowingly or intentionally acquires possession of a controlled substance by misrepresentation, fraud, forgery, deception, subterfuge, alteration of a prescription order, concealment of a material fact, or use of a false name or false address commits a Class D felony. However, the offense is a Class C felony if the person has a prior conviction of an offense under this subsection.
(d) A person who knowingly or intentionally affixes any false or forged label to a package or receptacle containing a controlled substance commits a Class D felony. However, the offense is a Class C felony if the person has a prior conviction of an offense under this subsection. This subsection does not apply to law enforcement agencies or their representatives while engaged in enforcing IC 16-42-19 or this chapter (or IC 16-6-8 before its repeal).

(e) A person who duplicates, reproduces, or prints any prescription pads or forms without the prior written consent of a practitioner commits a Class D felony. However, the offense is a Class C felony if the person has a prior conviction of an offense under this subsection. This subsection does not apply to the printing of prescription pads or forms upon a written, signed order placed by a practitioner or pharmacist, by legitimate printing companies.

History.
IC 35-48-4-14, as added by Acts 1976, P.L.148, § 7; 1977, P.L.340, § 109; P.L.131-1986, § 3; P.L.165-1990, § 14; P.L.2-1993, § 193.

Cross References.
Penalties for felonies, IC 35-50-1, IC 35-50-2, IC 35-50-5-2.

NOTES TO DECISIONS

ANALYSIS

Fraud or Deceit to Obtain Drug.
Manufacture of Methamphetamine.
Multiple Punishments.
Nature of Controlled Substance.
Prior Conviction.

Fraud or Deceit to Obtain Drug.
That the seller of drugs did not rely on the false name and address given by the purchaser because he knew the purchaser, did not keep the transaction from being a criminal violation; the statute did not require that there be reliance except in the case of use of fraud or deceit. Merritt v. State, 245 Ind. 362, 198 N.E.2d 867, 1964 Ind. LEXIS 217 (1964).

Manufacture of Methamphetamine.
The legislature did not intend that IC 35-48-4-14.5 allow one to be subjected to criminal liability for possession of the ingredients of methamphetamine, but to be excluded from liability if the ingredients were used to manufacture the finished product. Hatcher v. State, 762 N.E.2d 170, 2002 Ind. App. LEXIS 132 (2002).

Multiple Punishments.
Convictions for possession of a controlled substance and obtaining a controlled substance violated the statutory prohibition against multiple punishments for the same offense. Loman v. State, 640 N.E.2d 745, 1994 Ind. App. LEXIS 1345 (1994).

Nature of Controlled Substance.
There was sufficient connection between propoxyphene napsylate and Darvocet to support a conviction for obtaining a controlled substance where defendant, by fraud or deceit, had doctor phone in a prescription for Darvocet, a schedule IV controlled substance, and the pharmacist who received the doctor's call filled the prescription with proposyphene napsylate, the generic equivalent of Darvocet and a schedule IV controlled substance. Loman v. State, 640 N.E.2d 745, 1994 Ind. App. LEXIS 1345 (1994).

Prior Conviction.
A prior conviction of attempt may not be used to increase the penalty for a later conviction of attempt or possession from a Class A misdemeanor to a Class D felony under subsection (c) of this section. Smith v. State, 427 N.E.2d 11, 1981 Ind. App. LEXIS 1685 (1981).

Cited:
Tobias v. State, 479 N.E.2d 508, 1985 Ind. LEXIS 863 (1985); McDonald v. State, 775 N.E.2d 1195, 2002 Ind. App. LEXIS 1635 (2002).

RESEARCH REFERENCES

Collateral References.
Criminality of act of directing to, or recommending, source from which illicit drugs may be purchased. 34 A.L.R.5th 125.

35-48-4-14.5. Possession of two or more chemical reagents or precursors with intent to manufacture — Possession of a firearm.

(a) As used in this section, "chemical reagents or precursors" refers to one (1) or more of the following:
(1) Ephedrine.
(2) Pseudoephedrine.
(3) Phenylpropanolamine.
(4) The salts, isomers, and salts of isomers of a substance identified in subdivisions (1) through (3).
(5) Anhydrous ammonia or ammonia solution (as defined in IC 22-11-20-1).

(6) Organic solvents.
(7) Hydrochloric acid.
(8) Lithium metal.
(9) Sodium metal.
(10) Ether.
(11) Sulfuric acid.
(12) Red phosphorous.
(13) Iodine.
(14) Sodium hydroxide (lye).
(15) Potassium dichromate.
(16) Sodium dichromate.
(17) Potassium permanganate.
(18) Chromium trioxide.
(19) Benzyl cyanide.
(20) Phenylacetic acid and its esters or salts.
(21) Piperidine and its salts.
(22) Methylamine and its salts.
(23) Isosafrole.
(24) Safrole.
(25) Piperonal.
(26) Hydriodic acid.
(27) Benzaldehyde.
(28) Nitroethane.
(29) Gamma-butyrolactone.
(30) White phosphorus.
(31) Hypophosphorous acid and its salts.
(32) Acetic anhydride.
(33) Benzyl chloride.
(34) Ammonium nitrate.
(35) Ammonium sulfate.
(36) Hydrogen peroxide.
(37) Thionyl chloride.
(38) Ethyl acetate.
(39) Pseudoephedrine hydrochloride.

(b) A person who possesses more than ten (10) grams of ephedrine, pseudoephedrine, or phenylpropanolamine, pure or adulterated, commits a Class D felony. However, the offense is a Class C felony if the person possessed:

(1) a firearm while possessing more than ten (10) grams of ephedrine, pseudoephedrine, or phenylpropanolamine, pure or adulterated; or

(2) more than ten (10) grams of ephedrine, pseudoephedrine, or phenylpropanolamine, pure or adulterated, in, on, or within one thousand (1,000) feet of:

    (A) school property;
    (B) a public park;
    (C) a family housing complex; or
    (D) a youth program center.

(c) A person who possesses anhydrous ammonia or ammonia solution (as defined in IC 22-11-20-1) with the intent to manufacture methamphetamine or amphetamine, schedule II controlled substances under IC 35-48-2-6, commits a Class D felony. However, the offense is a Class C felony if the person possessed:

(1) a firearm while possessing anhydrous ammonia or ammonia solution (as defined in IC 22-11-20-1) with intent to manufacture methamphetamine or amphetamine, schedule II controlled substances under IC 35-48-2-6; or

(2) anhydrous ammonia or ammonia solution (as defined in IC 22-11-20-1) with intent to manufacture methamphetamine or amphetamine, schedule II controlled substances under IC 35-48-2-6, in, on, or within one thousand (1,000) feet of:

(A) school property;

(B) a public park;

(C) a family housing complex; or

(D) a youth program center.

(d) Subsection (b) does not apply to a:

(1) licensed health care provider, pharmacist, retail distributor, wholesaler, manufacturer, warehouseman, or common carrier or an agent of any of these persons if the possession is in the regular course of lawful business activities; or

(2) person who possesses more than ten (10) grams of a substance described in subsection (b) if the substance is possessed under circumstances consistent with typical medicinal or household use, including:

(A) the location in which the substance is stored;

(B) the possession of the substance in a variety of:

(i) strengths;

(ii) brands; or

(iii) types; or

(C) the possession of the substance:

(i) with different expiration dates; or

(ii) in forms used for different purposes.

(e) A person who possesses two (2) or more chemical reagents or precursors with the intent to manufacture a controlled substance commits a Class D felony.

(f) An offense under subsection (e) is a Class C felony if the person possessed:

(1) a firearm while possessing two (2) or more chemical reagents or precursors with intent to manufacture a controlled substance; or

(2) two (2) or more chemical reagents or precursors with intent to manufacture a controlled substance in, on, or within one thousand (1,000) feet of:

(A) school property;

(B) a public park;

(C) a family housing complex; or

(D) a youth program center.

(g) A person who sells, transfers, distributes, or furnishes a chemical reagent or precursor to another person with knowledge or the intent that the recipient will use the chemical reagent or precursors to manufacture a controlled substance commits unlawful sale of a precursor, a Class D felony.

History.
P.L.150-1999, § 2; P.L.17-2001, § 28; P.L.225-2003, § 5; P.L.192-2005, § 8; P.L.151-2006, § 26.

Compiler's Notes.
P.L.151-2006, § 29, effective July 1, 2006, provides:
"IC 35-48-4-1.1 and IC 35-48-4-6.1, both as

added by this act, and IC 35-48-4-1, IC 35-48-4-6, IC 35-48-4-14.5, and IC 35-48-4-14.7, all as amended by this act, apply only to crimes committed after June 30, 2006."

Cross References.
Penalties for felonies, IC 35-50-1, IC 35-50-2, IC 35-50-5-2.

NOTES TO DECISIONS

ANALYSIS

"Chemical Reagents or Precursors."
Double Jeopardy.
Evidence.
—Insufficient.
—Sufficient.
Intent.
Manufacture of Methamphetamine.
Personal Use Exception.
Possession and Dealing.
Sentence.

"Chemical Reagents or Precursors."
Defendant's conviction for possession of two or more chemical reagents or precursors with the intent to manufacture methamphetamine was reversed where rubbing alcohol and boxes of pseudoephedrine were found in defendant's car but the state failed to establish rubbing alcohol was an organic solvent, and thus did not prove he possessed two or more of the enumerated chemical reagents or precursors. Dolkey v. State, 750 N.E.2d 460, 2001 Ind. App. LEXIS 1174 (2001).

Overwhelming evidence supported manufactur-

"Chemical Reagents or Precursors." (Cont'd)
ing methamphetamine charge under IC 35-48-4-
2(a)(1)(A) and possession of precursors charge under IC 35-48-4-14.5(c)(2) where the police officer
found pseudoephedrine tablets dissolving in denatured alcohol, two propane tanks modified to dispense anhydrous ammonia, several cans of starting fluid, and an HCl generator in plain view at
defendant's house. Goffinet v. State, 775 N.E.2d
1227, 2002 Ind. App. LEXIS 1647 (2002).

As defined by IC 35-48-1-9, "controlled substance" does not include precursors listed in IC
35-48-4-14.5, but rather includes only those drugs,
substances, or immediate precursors identified in
statutes defining schedules of controlled substances; accordingly, under strict reading of IC
35-48-1-9, precursors listed in IC 35-48-4-14.5(a)
are not "controlled substances" and thus not
"drugs" for purpose of establishing predicate substance offense under IC 35-50-2-10, unless they
are included in Schedules I, II, III, IV, or V. Murray
v. State, 798 N.E.2d 895, 2003 Ind. App. LEXIS
2149 (2003).

Pseudoephedrine hydrochloride is not specifically designated as drug precursor by IC 35-48-4-
14.5; accordingly, where state offered no evidence
that pseudoephedrine hydrochloride possessed by
defendant was pseudoephedrine or a salt of pseudoephedrine, defendant's conviction of possession
of drug precursor was improper; fact that pseudoephedrine hydrochloride was deemed a salt of
pseudoephedrine in a different case was irrelevant
since state is required to prove all elements of
offense charged in every case. Reemer v. State, 817
N.E.2d 626, 2004 Ind. App. LEXIS 2235 (2004),
transfer granted, 831 N.E.2d 736, 2005 Ind. LEXIS
144 (2005), superseded, 835 N.E.2d 1005, 2005
Ind. LEXIS 955 (2005).

Double Jeopardy.

There is no reasonable possibility that the jury
relied on the same evidentiary facts to establish
the essential elements of both manufacturing
methamphetamine under IC 35-48-4-2(a)(1)(A)
and possession of precursors under IC 35-48-4-
14.5(c)(2) where the state presented ample evidence that defendant manufactured methamphetamine, but that evidence could not support a
conviction for possession of precursors without the
additional evidence that defendant possessed at
least two precursors. Goffinet v. State, 775 N.E.2d
1227, 2002 Ind. App. LEXIS 1647 (2002).

Defendant's convictions of possession of anhydrous ammonia and of possession of chemical reagents or precursors violated double jeopardy under the Fifth Amendment and Ind. Const., art. 1,
§ 14 because they were necessarily included in
defendant's conviction for dealing in methamphetamine. Defendant could not have been in the
process of manufacturing methamphetamine without possessing anhydrous ammonia and reagents
or precursors. Moore v. State, 869 N.E.2d 489,
2007 Ind. App. LEXIS 1488 (2007).

Evidence.

—Insufficient.

Evidence was insufficient to affirm defendant's

conviction for possessing two or more chemical
reagents or precursors with intent to manufacture
controlled substances since, although defendant
had dominion and control over both lithium metal
and pseudoephedrine in vehicle in which he was
passenger, lithium metal was in lithium batteries
which were inside box and there was no evidence
from which jury could infer that defendant knew
box contained lithium batteries; furthermore, it
was not shown that defendant had possessory
interest in vehicle or box or that defendant engaged in furtive acts. Grim v. State, 797 N.E.2d
825, 2003 Ind. App. LEXIS 1978 (2003).

Conviction for possession of chemical reagents or
precursors with intent to manufacture as class D
felony was reversed where state failed to present
probative evidence from which jury could have
found that defendant possessed two chemical reagents or precursors as required by statute. Lovell
v. State, 813 N.E.2d 393, 2004 Ind. App. LEXIS
1626 (2004).

—Sufficient.

Evidence consisting of labels on commercial
products was of sufficient probative value to permit fact finder to conclude that defendant possessed sulfuric acid, pseudoephedrine, and
lithium, chemical precursors necessary to convict
defendant for possession of chemical precursors
with intent to manufacture methamphetamine.
Scott v. State, 803 N.E.2d 1231, 2004 Ind. App.
LEXIS 298 (2004).

In trial of defendant for illegal possession of
anhydrous ammonia, admission of Draeger test
results performed by police officer to detect presence of anhydrous ammonia was error because
prosecution did not establish scientific reliability
of test; however, error was harmless, due to existence of other sufficient admissible evidence of
defendant's possession of anhydrous ammonia.
West v. State, 805 N.E.2d 909, 2004 Ind. App.
LEXIS 589 (2004).

In a prosecution under former IC 35-48-4-
14.5(b), drug labels were admissible under Evid. R.
803(17) to prove composition of drug at issue
where drugs were found in unaltered state and
weight and contents of drugs were described in
discarded labels. Reemer v. State, 835 N.E.2d
1005, 2005 Ind. LEXIS 955 (2005).

In prosecution under former IC 35-48-4-14.5(b),
state did not have to prove that pseudoephedrine
hydrochloride possessed by defendant was isomer
of ephedrine. Reemer v. State, 835 N.E.2d 1005,
2005 Ind. LEXIS 955 (2005).

In a prosecution for possession of two or more
methamphetamine chemical reagents or precursors with intent to manufacture (IC 35-48-4-
14.5(e)), even if the trial court erred by admitting a
half-empty bottle's label to prove the bottle contained sulfuric acid, the error was harmless in
view of overwhelming admissible evidence that
she possessed two other methamphetamine precursors or chemical reagents. Forler v. State, 846
N.E.2d 266, 2006 Ind. App. LEXIS 667 (2006).

In a prosecution for possession of two or more
methamphetamine chemical reagents or precur-

Evidence. (Cont'd)

—Sufficient. (Cont'd)

sors with intent to manufacture (IC 35-48-4-14.5(e)), a label from an aerosol can of starting fluid was properly admitted under Evid. R. 803(17) to prove the can contained ether because: (1) the manufacturer would be unlikely to falsely state its product contained a hazardous substance; and (2) common knowledge and experience taught that consumers could not readily replace the contents of aerosol-type cans. Forler v. State, 846 N.E.2d 266, 2006 Ind. App. LEXIS 667 (2006).

Evidence was sufficient to sustain a defendant's conviction under IC 35-48-4-14.5(c) even though the defendant did not have exclusive possession of a mobile home where evidence showed that she had the intent and capability to maintain dominion and control over the mobile home and that ammonia was a component of a gray sludge found in a shed next to the mobile home. Richardson v. State, 856 N.E.2d 1222, 2006 Ind. App. LEXIS 2376 (2006).

Evidence that defendant: (1) knew that all the ingredients for manufacturing methamphetamine were being prepared at a house; (2) helped light incense to cover the smell of ether; (3) remained at the house while other people at the house left to go out into the country to finish the manufacturing process; (4) presumably flickered the lights of the house off and on in response to the honks from a passing car because he was the only person in the house when the police arrived; (5) took 30 seconds to open the door after the police knocked; and (6) claimed to not notice a smell of ether permitted a reasonable person to infer that defendant had intended to be part of the manufacturing process, even if the process had been moved elsewhere. Tapely v. State, 886 N.E.2d 61, 2008 Ind. App. LEXIS 1015 (2008).

Intent.

State proved that driver of truck constructively possessed quantity of chemicals found under his seat these chemicals were not solely for his personal use. Bradley v. State, 765 N.E.2d 204, 2002 Ind. App. LEXIS 458 (2002).

Officer did not have probable cause to arrest suspect under IC 35-48-4-14.5(c) for possession of chemical precursors to methamphetamine based on the presence in the suspect's garage of materials used to manufacture methamphetamine; there was no evidence from which the officer could have inferred that suspect possessed items found in the garage with the intent to manufacture methamphetamine. Wheeler v. Lawson, 539 F.3d 629, 2008 U.S. App. LEXIS 17792 (2008).

Manufacture of Methamphetamine.

The legislature did not intend that IC 35-48-4-14.5 allow one to be subjected to criminal liability for possession of the ingredients of methamphetamine, but to be excluded from liability if the ingredients were used to manufacture the finished product. Hatcher v. State, 762 N.E.2d 170, 2002 Ind. App. LEXIS 132 (2002).

Sole difference in IC 35-48-4-2 and IC 35-48-4-14.5(b) is that one may be guilty of possessing chemical precursors with intent to manufacture without actually beginning the manufacturing process, whereas the manufacturing process must, at the very least, have been started by a defendant in order to be found guilty of manufacturing methamphetamine; since a bag containing ephedrine powder was found in the possession of defendant, the process of extraction, and thus, the process to manufacture methamphetamine, had begun, and there was sufficient evidence to support defendant's conviction for manufacturing methamphetamine. Dawson v. State, 786 N.E.2d 742, 2003 Ind. App. LEXIS 630 (2003).

Evidence was sufficient to convict defendant of possession of chemical reagents or precursors with the intent to manufacture methamphetamine when a search of the trailer occupied by defendant revealed evidence, partially in plain view, of numerous reagents and equipment used for the manufacture of methamphetamine and there was sufficient evidence to infer constructive possession of the items by defendant when defendant was found hiding under the bed during the search, witnesses had identified the trailer as a methamphetamine lab, defendant had a recipe for making methamphetamine in his wallet, and defendant's relative had asked defendant to live in the trailer while he was gone. Floyd v. State, 791 N.E.2d 206, 2003 Ind. App. LEXIS 1208 (2003).

Sole distinguishing factor between conviction for manufacturing methamphetamine under IC 35-48-4-2 and conviction for possession of precursors with intent to manufacture methamphetamine is that one may be guilty of possessing chemical precursors with intent to manufacture without actually beginning manufacturing process, whereas manufacturing process must at least have been started in order to be deemed guilty of manufacturing methamphetamine. Murray v. State, 798 N.E.2d 895, 2003 Ind. App. LEXIS 2149 (2003).

Personal Use Exception.

Where the trial court erred in giving a jury instruction which failed to include the personal use exception under former IC 35-48-1-18, the defendant's conviction under IC 35-48-4-2 and IC 35-48-4-14.5 would be reversed. (Decided prior to the 2001 amendment, deleting the personal use exemption.) Poe v. State, 775 N.E.2d 681, 2002 Ind. App. LEXIS 1530 (2002).

Possession and Dealing.

Defendant was not entitled to have a conviction for possession of chemical reagents or precursors with intent to manufacture vacated as a lesser included offense to a conviction for dealing in methamphetamine, because it would not have been impossible to commit the dealing offense without first committing the precursors offense. Floyd v. State, 791 N.E.2d 206, 2003 Ind. App. LEXIS 1208 (2003).

Sentence.

Because IC 35-48-4-14.5 was not intended to reduce the penalty for attempt to deal in metham-

Sentence. (Cont'd)

phetamine, there was not an amendment, much less an ameliorative amendment, under which defendant should have been sentenced. Hellums v. State, 758 N.E.2d 1027, 2001 Ind. App. LEXIS 2061 (2001).

Cited:

Baird v. State, 854 N.E.2d 398, 2006 Ind. App. LEXIS 1951 (2006).

RESEARCH REFERENCES

Indiana Law Review.

Survey: Criminal Law and Procedure, 37 Ind. L. Rev. 1003 (2004).

Res Gestae.

Criminal Justice Notes 10/03: Constructive pos-

session — handgun, drugs and paraphernalia in vehicle. 47 (No 6) Res Gestae 43 (2004).

35-48-4-14.7. Sales of products containing ephedrine or pseudoephedrine — Storage and reporting requirements.

(a) This section does not apply to the following:

(1) Ephedrine or pseudoephedrine dispensed pursuant to a prescription.

(2) The sale of a drug containing ephedrine or pseudoephedrine to a licensed health care provider, pharmacist, retail distributor, wholesaler, manufacturer, or an agent of any of these persons if the sale occurs in the regular course of lawful business activities. However, a retail distributor, wholesaler, or manufacturer is required to report a suspicious order to the state police department in accordance with subsection (f).

(3) The sale of a drug containing ephedrine or pseudoephedrine by a person who does not sell exclusively to walk-in customers for the personal use of the walk-in customers. However, if the person described in this subdivision is a retail distributor, wholesaler, or manufacturer, the person is required to report a suspicious order to the state police department in accordance with subsection (f).

(b) The following definitions apply throughout this section:

(1) "Constant video monitoring" means the surveillance by an automated camera that:

(A) records at least one (1) photograph or digital image every ten (10) seconds;

(B) retains a photograph or digital image for at least seventy-two (72) hours;

(C) has sufficient resolution and magnification to permit the identification of a person in the area under surveillance; and

(D) stores a recorded photograph or digital image at a location that is immediately accessible to a law enforcement officer.

(2) "Convenience package" means a package that contains a drug having as an active ingredient not more than one hundred twenty (120) milligrams of ephedrine or pseudoephedrine, or both.

(3) "Ephedrine" means pure or adulterated ephedrine.

(4) "Pseudoephedrine" means pure or adulterated pseudoephedrine.

(5) "Suspicious order" means a sale or transfer of a drug containing ephedrine or pseudoephedrine if the sale or transfer:

(A) is a sale or transfer that the retail distributor, wholesaler, or manufacturer is required to report to the United States Drug Enforcement Administration;

(B) appears suspicious to the retail distributor, wholesaler, or manufacturer in light of the recommendations contained in Appendix A of the report to the United States attorney general by the suspicious orders task force under the federal Comprehensive Methamphetamine Control Act of 1996; or

(C) is for cash or a money order in a total amount of at least two hundred dollars ($200).

(6) "Unusual theft" means the theft or unexplained disappearance from a particular retail store of drugs containing ten (10) grams or more of ephedrine, pseudoephedrine, or both in a twenty-four (24) hour period.

(c) This subsection does not apply to a convenience package. A person may sell a drug that contains the active ingredient of ephedrine, pseudoephedrine, or both only if the person complies with the following conditions:

(1) The person does not sell the drug to a person less than eighteen (18) years of age.

(2) The person does not sell drugs containing more than three (3) grams of ephedrine or pseudoephedrine, or both in one (1) transaction.

(3) The person requires:

(A) the purchaser to produce a state or federal identification card;

(B) the purchaser to complete a paper or an electronic log in a format approved by the state police department with the purchaser's name, address, and driver's license or other identification number; and

(C) the clerk who is conducting the transaction to initial or electronically record the clerk's identification on the log.

Records from the completion of a log must be retained for at least two (2) years. A law enforcement officer has the right to inspect and copy a log or the records from the completion of a log in accordance with state and federal law. A person may not sell or release a log or the records from the completion of a log for a commercial purpose. The Indiana criminal justice institute may obtain information concerning a log or the records from the completion of a log from a law enforcement officer if the information may not be used to identify a specific individual and is used only for statistical purposes. A retailer who in good faith releases information maintained under this subsection is immune from civil liability unless the release constitutes gross negligence or intentional, wanton, or willful misconduct. This subdivision expires June 30, 2012.

(4) The person stores the drug:

(A) behind a counter in an area inaccessible to a customer or in a locked display case that makes the drug unavailable to a customer without the assistance of an employee; or

(B) directly in front of the pharmacy counter in the direct line of sight of an employee at the pharmacy counter, in an area under constant video monitoring, if the drug is sold in a retail establishment that:

(i) is a pharmacy; or

(ii) contains a pharmacy that is open for business.

(d) A person may not purchase drugs containing more than three (3) grams of ephedrine, pseudoephedrine, or both in one (1) week.

(e) This subsection only applies to convenience packages. A person may not sell drugs containing more than one hundred twenty (120) milligrams of ephedrine or pseudoephedrine, or both in any one (1) transaction if the drugs are sold in convenience packages. A person who sells convenience packages must secure the convenience packages in at least one (1) of the following ways:

(1) The convenience package must be stored not more than thirty (30) feet away from a checkout station or counter and must be in the direct line of sight of an employee at the checkout station or counter.

(2) The convenience package must be protected by a reliable anti-theft device that uses package tags and detection alarms designed to prevent theft.

(3) The convenience package must be stored in restricted access shelving that permits a purchaser to remove not more than one (1) package every fifteen (15) seconds.

(4) The convenience package must be stored in an area that is under constant video monitoring, and a sign placed near the convenience package must warn that the area is under constant video monitoring.

(f) A retail distributor, wholesaler, or manufacturer shall report a suspicious order to the state police department in writing.

(g) Not later than three (3) days after the discovery of an unusual theft at a particular retail store, the retailer shall report the unusual theft to the state police department in writing. If three (3) unusual thefts occur in a thirty (30) day period at a particular retail store, the retailer shall, for at least one hundred eighty (180) days after the date of the last unusual theft, locate all drugs containing ephedrine or pseudoephedrine at that particular retail store behind a counter in an area inaccessible to a customer or in a locked display case that makes the drug unavailable to customers without the assistance of an employee.

(h) A unit (as defined in IC 36-1-2-23) may not adopt an ordinance after February 1, 2005, that is more stringent than this section.

(i) A person who knowingly or intentionally violates this section commits a Class C misdemeanor. However, the offense is a Class A misdemeanor if the person has a prior unrelated conviction under this section.

(j) Before June 30, 2007, the state police department shall submit a report to the legislative council detailing the effectiveness of this section in reducing the illicit production of methamphetamine. The report must describe the number of arrests or convictions that are attributable to the identification and logging requirements contained in this section, and must include recommendations for future action. The report must be in an electronic format under IC 5-14-6.

History.
P.L.192-2005, § 9; P.L.151-2006, § 27; P.L.186-2007, § 9, eff. July 1, 2007.

"IC 35-48-4-14.5, as amended by this act, and IC 35-48-4-14.7, as added by this act, apply only to offenses committed after June 30, 2005."

Compiler's Notes.
P.L.192-2005, § 11, effective July 1, 2005, provides:

Cross References.
Penalties for misdemeanors, IC 35-50-1, IC 35-50-3, IC 35-50-5-2.

35-48-4-15. Suspension of operator's license and motor vehicle registrations.

(a) If a person is convicted of an offense under section 1, 2, 3, 4, 5, 6, 7, 10, or 11 [IC 35-48-4-1, IC 35-48-4-2, IC 35-48-4-3, IC 35-48-4-4, IC 35-48-4-5, IC 35-48-4-6, IC 35-48-4-7, IC 35-48-4-10, or IC 35-48-4-11] of this chapter, or conspiracy to commit an offense under section 1, 2, 3, 4, 5, 6, 7, 10, or 11 of this chapter, and the court finds that a motor vehicle was used in the commission of the offense, the court shall, in addition to any other order the court enters, order that the person's:

(1) operator's license be suspended;

(2) existing motor vehicle registrations be suspended; and

(3) ability to register motor vehicles be suspended;

by the bureau of motor vehicles for a period specified by the court of at least six (6) months but not more than two (2) years.

(b) If a person is convicted of an offense described in subsection (a) and the person does not hold an operator's license or a learner's permit, the court shall order that the person may not receive an operator's license or a learner's permit from the bureau of motor vehicles for a period of not less than six (6) months.

History.
P.L.67-1990, § 13; P.L.107-1991, § 3; P.L.129-1993, § 2; P.L.64-1994, § 6; P.L.76-2004, § 23.

NOTES TO DECISIONS

Analysis

Constitutionality.
—Due Process.
Suspension Mandatory.

Constitutionality.

Driving is not a fundamental right under the Constitution, and the statute mandating that an individual's operator's license and ability to register motor vehicles be suspended upon conviction for possession of cocaine was not violative of equal protection, substantive due process or the privileges and immunities clause. Maher v. State, 612 N.E.2d 1063, 1993 Ind. App. LEXIS 405 (1993).

—Due Process.

When the private interest, risk of erroneous deprivation, and the governmental interest are balanced there is no violation of a defendant's procedural due process rights, when the defendant's driver's license, license plates, and ability to register a motor vehicle are suspended pursuant to this section; his interest in retaining his operator's license is considerable, but so is the state's interest in imposing criminal punishment, and this section provides significant procedural safeguards, as one can only have one's driver's license suspended under this statute after a lawful conviction and a full sentencing hearing. Mitchell v. State, 659 N.E.2d 112, 1995 Ind. LEXIS 188 (1995).

Since the law recognizes no fundamental right to drive, the state need only show that the law bears a rational relationship to a legitimate state interest, and since this statute only applies to those that have been convicted of one of the enumerated offenses, it bears a rational relationship to the legitimate state interest in punishing lawbreakers and deterring lawbreaking. Mitchell v. State, 659 N.E.2d 112, 1995 Ind. LEXIS 188 (1995).

License suspension under this section does not violate either procedural due process or substantive due process. Walker v. State, 661 N.E.2d 869, 1996 Ind. App. LEXIS 170 (1996).

Suspension Mandatory.

A judge is not prevented from ordering a license suspended if the state does not move for suspension or does not show that the penalty is appropriate; a judge must impose a sentence that conforms to the mandate of the applicable statute. Mitchell v. State, 659 N.E.2d 112, 1995 Ind. LEXIS 188 (1995).

RESEARCH REFERENCES

Res Gestae.

Criminal justice notes, 38 (No. 6) Res Gestae 40 (1994).

35-48-4-16. Defenses to charge of delivery within one thousand feet of school.

(a) For an offense under this chapter that requires proof of:

(1) delivery of cocaine, a narcotic drug, methamphetamine, or a controlled substance;

(2) financing the delivery of cocaine, a narcotic drug, methamphetamine, or a controlled substance; or

(3) possession of cocaine, narcotic drug, methamphetamine, or controlled substance;

within one thousand (1,000) feet of school property, a public park, a family housing complex, or a youth program center, the person charged may assert the defense in subsection (b) or (c).

(b) It is a defense for a person charged under this chapter with an offense that contains an element listed in subsection (a) that:

(1) a person was briefly in, on, or within one thousand (1,000) feet of school property, a public park, a family housing complex, or a youth program center; and

(2) no person under eighteen (18) years of age at least three (3) years junior to the person was in, on, or within one thousand (1,000) feet of the school property, public park, family housing complex, or youth program center at the time of the offense.

(c) It is a defense for a person charged under this chapter with an offense that contains an element listed in subsection (a) that a person was in, on, or within one thousand (1,000) feet of school property, a public park, a family housing complex, or a youth program center at the request or suggestion of a law enforcement officer or an agent of a law enforcement officer.

(d) The defense under this section applies only to the element of the offense that requires proof that the delivery, financing of the delivery, or possession of cocaine, a narcotic drug, methamphetamine, or a controlled substance occurred in, on, or within one thousand (1,000) feet of school property, a public park, a family housing complex, or a youth program center.

History.
P.L.17-2001, § 29.

NOTES TO DECISIONS

ANALYSIS

Constitutionality.
Burden of Proof.
Defense Sufficient.
Jury Instructions.
Mitigating Factors.
Rebuttal of Defense.

Constitutionality.

Sixth Amendment and Ind. Const. art. 1, § 13 claims, that defenses listed under IC 35-48-4-16 were unavailable to defendants in Marion County due to the presence of expanded drug-free zones in the county and thus had affected defendant's right to present a defense and challenge the charge against him, failed where nothing in the record indicated that defendant was prevented from asserting a defense. Manigault v. State, 881 N.E.2d 679, 2008 Ind. App. LEXIS 307 (2008).

Burden of Proof.

Class A felony dealing in cocaine conviction was reduced to a Class B felony because, once defendant put in issue the fact that no person under 18 years of age at least three years junior to defendant was in, on, or within one thousand feet of the park, state failed to rebut IC 35-48-4-16(b)'s statutory mitigating factors beyond a reasonable doubt. Harrison v. State, — N.E.2d —, 2009 Ind. App. LEXIS 346 (2009).

Defense Sufficient.

Because there was no evidence contradicting that defendant was summoned to the confidential informant's apartment by the informant at the behest of the police, defendant established that he was within 1,000 feet of a public park only at the request or suggestion of an agent of a law enforcement officer; thus, defendant established his defense under IC 35-48-4-16(c). Bell v. State, 881 N.E.2d 1080, 2008 Ind. App. LEXIS 437 (2008).

Conviction for dealing in a schedule II substance, as a Class A felony under IC 35-48-4-2, was reduced to a class B felony, because the State failed to rebut defendant's justification defense under IC 34-48-4-16; the transaction which lasted, at most, for 20 minutes, at 3:00 a.m., was, as a matter of

law, brief, and the transaction took place in a location where no children were present. While under different circumstances, a 20-minute transaction could fall under the category of a class A felony because of the proximity to children or the potential for contact with youth, such was not the case. Gallagher v. State, — N.E.2d —, 2009 Ind. App. LEXIS 892 (2009).

Jury Instructions.

Where defendant's conviction for violating IC 35-48-4-6 was subject to enhancement because he was arrested in a park, he was not entitled to an instruction under IC 35-48-4-16, which provided a defense if no one under 18 was in the park at the time, as the testimony showed only that it was unknown whether anyone under 18 was in the park at the time defendant was arrested. Stringer v. State, 853 N.E.2d 543, 2006 Ind. App. LEXIS 1804 (2006).

Mitigating Factors.

IC 35-48-4-16(b) constitutes a mitigating factor that reduces culpability, and therefore a defendant does not have the burden of proof but only the burden of placing the issue in question where the state's evidence has not done so; once at issue, the state must rebut the defense by proving beyond a reasonable doubt either that defendant was within 1000 feet of a public park more than "briefly" or persons under the age of 18 at least three years junior to defendant were within 1000 feet of the public park, because both factors are required to effectuate the mitigation. Harrison v. State, — N.E.2d —, 2009 Ind. App. LEXIS 346 (2009).

Rebuttal of Defense.

Because there was no ironclad rule as to what constituted a "brief" presence within 1000 feet of school property, the State's evidence that defendant was observed for approximately five minutes on a street abutting a school while in possession of contraband was sufficient to rebut defendant's statutory defense under IC 35-48-4-16(b). Griffin v. State, 905 N.E.2d 521, 2009 Ind. App. LEXIS 810 (2009).

35-48-4-17. Environmental cleanup costs of methamphetamine manufacture — Restitution — Reimbursement of law enforcement agencies.

(a) In addition to any other penalty imposed for conviction of an offense under this chapter involving the manufacture or intent to manufacture methamphetamine, a court shall order restitution under IC 35-50-5-3 to cover the costs, if necessary, of an environmental cleanup incurred by a law enforcement agency or other person as a result of the offense.

(b) The amount collected under subsection (a) shall be used to reimburse the law enforcement agency that assumed the costs associated with the environmental cleanup described in subsection (a).

History.
P.L.225-2003, § 6.

CHAPTER 5

REPORTING REQUIREMENTS; SCHOOL PERSONNEL

35-48-5-1 — 35-48-5-6. [Repealed.]

Compiler's Notes.
This chapter, concerning reporting requirements for school personnel, was repealed by P.L.202-1989, § 6.

CHAPTER 6

COMPUTERIZED PRESCRIPTION DATA PROGRAM

35-48-6-1 — 35-48-6-15. [Repealed.]

Compiler's Notes.
This chapter, concerning the computerized prescription data program, expired pursuant to its own terms on June 30, 1993, and was repealed by P.L. 2-1995, § 140, effective May 5, 1995.

IC 35-48-6-1 through IC 35-48-6-5, concerning the prescription abuse study committee, were previously repealed by P.L.3-1989, § 224.

CHAPTER 7

CENTRAL REPOSITORY FOR CONTROLLED SUBSTANCES DATA

35-48-7-1. "Advisory committee" defined.

As used in this chapter, "advisory committee" refers to the controlled substances advisory committee established by IC 35-48-2-1.

History.
P.L.163-1994, § 5.

35-48-7-2. [Repealed.]

Compiler's Notes.
This section, concerning the definition of "central repository", was repealed by P.L.65-2006 § 18, effective July 1, 2007.

35-48-7-2.9. "Dispense" defined.

(a) As used in this chapter, "dispense" has the meaning set forth in IC 35-48-1-12.
(b) The term does not apply to the following:
    (1) A drug administered directly to a patient.
    (2) A drug dispensed by a practitioner, if the quantity dispensed is not more than a seventy-two (72) hour supply of a controlled substance listed in schedule II, III, IV, or V as set forth in IC 35-48-3-9.

History.
P.L.105-2008, § 65, eff. January 1, 2009.

35-48-7-3. [Repealed.]

Compiler's Notes.
This section, concerning definition of "dispenser", was repealed by P.L.105-2008, § 66, effective January 1, 2009.

35-48-7-4. "Exception report" defined.

As used in this chapter, "exception report" means a record of data concerning:
    (1) A practitioner practicing a particular specialty or field of health care;
    (2) A dispenser doing business in a particular location; or
    (3) A recipient;
that indicates dispensing or receiving of controlled substances outside norms for dispensing or receiving controlled substances established by the advisory committee under this chapter.

History.
P.L.163-1994, § 5.

35-48-7-5. "Identification number" defined.

As used in this chapter, "identification number" refers to the following:
    (1) The unique number contained on any of the following:
        (A) A valid driver's license of a recipient or a recipient's representative issued under Indiana law or the law of any other state.
        (B) A recipient's or a recipient representative's valid military identification card.

(C) A valid identification card of a recipient or a recipient's representative issued by:

(i) the bureau of motor vehicles as described in IC 9-24-16-3; or

(ii) any other state and that is similar to the identification card issued by the bureau of motor vehicles.

(D) If the recipient is an animal:

(i) the valid driver's license issued under Indiana law or the law of any other state;

(ii) the valid military identification card; or

(iii) the valid identification card issued by the bureau of motor vehicles and described in IC 9-24-16-3 or a valid identification card of similar description that is issued by any other state;

of the animal's owner.

(2) The identification number or phrase designated by the central repository.

History.
P.L.163-1994, § 5; P.L.204-2005, § 22.

35-48-7-5.2. "INSPECT" defined.

As used in this chapter, "INSPECT" means the Indiana scheduled prescription electronic collection and tracking program established by IC 25-1-13-4.

History.
P.L.65-2006, § 3.

35-48-7-5.4. "Interoperability" defined.

As used in this chapter, "interoperability" refers to the INSPECT program electronically sharing reported information with another state concerning the dispensing of a controlled substance:

(1) to a recipient who resides in the other state; or

(2) prescribed by a practitioner whose principal place of business is located in another state.

History.
P.L.65-2006, § 4.

35-48-7-5.6. "Patient" defined.

As used in this chapter, "patient" means an individual who has requested or received health care services from a provider for the examination, treatment, diagnosis, or prevention of a physical or mental condition.

History.
P.L.65-2006, § 5.

35-48-7-5.8. "Practitioner" defined.

As used in this chapter, "practitioner" means a physician, dentist, veterinarian, podiatrist, nurse practitioner, scientific investigator, pharmacist, hospital, or other institution or individual licensed, registered, or otherwise permitted to distribute, dispense, conduct research with respect to, or administer a controlled substance in the course of professional practice or research in the United States.

History.
P.L.65-2006, § 6.

35-48-7-6. "Recipient" defined.

As used in this chapter, "recipient" means an individual for whom a controlled substance is dispensed.

History.
  P.L.163-1994, § 5.

35-48-7-7. "Recipient representative" defined.

As used in this chapter, "recipient representative" means the individual to whom a controlled substance is dispensed if the recipient is either less than eighteen (18) years of age or unavailable to receive the controlled substance.

History.
  P.L.163-1994, § 5.

35-48-7-7.5. "State" defined.

As used in this chapter, "state" means any state of the United States or the District of Columbia.

History.
  P.L.65-2006, § 7.

35-48-7-8. [Repealed.]

Compiler's Notes.
  This section, concerning controlled substance prescription monitoring program, was repealed by P.L.3-2008, § 269, effective March 13, 2008.

35-48-7-8.1. Advisory committee to provide for controlled substance prescription monitoring program — Components of program.

(a) This section applies after June 30, 2007.

(b) The advisory committee shall provide for a controlled substance prescription monitoring program that includes the following components:

(1) Each time a controlled substance designated by the advisory committee under IC 35-48-2-5 through IC 35-48-2-10 is dispensed, the dispenser shall transmit to the INSPECT program the following information:

(A) The controlled substance recipient's name.

(B) The controlled substance recipient's or the recipient representative's identification number or the identification number or phrase designated by the INSPECT program.

(C) The controlled substance recipient's date of birth.

(D) The national drug code number of the controlled substance dispensed.

(E) The date the controlled substance is dispensed.

(F) The quantity of the controlled substance dispensed.

(G) The number of days of supply dispensed.

(H) The dispenser's United States Drug Enforcement Agency registration number.

(I) The prescriber's United States Drug Enforcement Agency registration number.

(J) An indication as to whether the prescription was transmitted to the pharmacist orally or in writing.

(K) Other data required by the advisory committee.

(2) The information required to be transmitted under this section must be transmitted not more than seven (7) days after the date on which a controlled substance is dispensed.

(3) A dispenser shall transmit the information required under this section by:
  (A) uploading to the INSPECT web site;
  (B) a computer diskette; or
  (C) a CD-ROM disk;
that meets specifications prescribed by the advisory committee.

(4) The advisory committee may require that prescriptions for controlled substances be written on a one (1) part form that cannot be duplicated. However, the advisory committee may not apply such a requirement to prescriptions filled at a pharmacy with a Type II permit (as described in IC 25-26-13-17) and operated by a hospital licensed under IC 16-21, or prescriptions ordered for and dispensed to bona fide enrolled patients in facilities licensed under IC 16-28. The committee may not require multiple copy prescription forms for any prescriptions written. The advisory committee may not require different prescription forms for any individual drug or group of drugs. Prescription forms required under this subdivision must be jointly approved by the committee and by the Indiana board of pharmacy established by IC 25-26-13-3.

(5) The costs of the program.

History.
P.L.65-2006, § 9; P.L.182-2009(ss), § 399, emergency eff. July 1, 2009.

35-48-7-9. [Repealed.]

Compiler's Notes.
This section, concerning the costs of the program, was repealed by P.L.65-2006 § 18, effective July 1, 2007.

35-48-7-10. [Repealed.]

Compiler's Notes.
This section, concerning central repository for collection of information, was repealed by P.L.3-2008, § 269, effective March 13, 2008.

35-48-7-10.1. Required actions of INSPECT program.

(a) This section applies after June 30, 2007.

(b) The INSPECT program must do the following:

(1) Create a data base for information required to be transmitted under section 8.1 [IC 35-48-7-8.1] of this chapter in the form required under rules adopted by the advisory committee, including search capability for the following:
  (A) A controlled substance recipient's name.
  (B) A controlled substance recipient's or recipient representative's identification number.
  (C) A controlled substance recipient's date of birth.
  (D) The national drug code number of a controlled substance dispensed.
  (E) The dates a controlled substance is dispensed.
  (F) The quantities of a controlled substance dispensed.
  (G) The number of days of supply dispensed.
  (H) A dispenser's United States Drug Enforcement Agency registration number.
  (I) A prescriber's United States Drug Enforcement Agency registration number.
  (J) Whether a prescription was transmitted to the pharmacist orally or in writing.

(2) Provide the advisory committee with continuing twenty-four (24) hour a day online access to the data base.

(3) Secure the information collected and the data base maintained against access by unauthorized persons.

(c) The advisory committee may execute a contract with a vendor designated by the advisory committee to perform any function associated with the administration of the INSPECT program.

(d) The INSPECT program may gather prescription data from the Medicaid retrospective drug utilization review (DUR) program established under IC 12-15-35.

(e) The advisory committee may accept and designate grants, public and private financial assistance, and licensure fees to provide funding for the INSPECT program.

History.
P.L.65-2006, § 11.

35-48-7-11. [Repealed.]

Compiler's Notes.
This section, concerning confidentiality of infor- mation, was repealed by P.L.3-2008, § 269, effective March 13, 2008.

35-48-7-11.1. Information received by INSPECT program confidential — Release of confidential information — Procedures for release of confidential information — Use of information as evidence — Civil immunity.

(a) This section applies after June 30, 2007.

(b) Information received by the INSPECT program under section 8.1 [IC 35-48-7-8.1] of this chapter is confidential.

(c) The advisory committee shall carry out a program to protect the confidentiality of the information described in subsection (b). The advisory committee may disclose the information to another person only under subsection (d), (e), or (h).

(d) The advisory committee may disclose confidential information described in subsection (b) to any person who is authorized to engage in receiving, processing, or storing the information.

(e) Except as provided in subsections (f) and (g), the advisory committee may release confidential information described in subsection (b) to the following persons:

(1) A member of the board, the advisory committee, or another governing body that licenses practitioners and is engaged in an investigation, an adjudication, or a prosecution of a violation under any state or federal law that involves a controlled substance.

(2) An investigator for the consumer protection division of the office of the attorney general, a prosecuting attorney, the attorney general, a deputy attorney general, or an investigator from the office of the attorney general, who is engaged in:

(A) an investigation;
(B) an adjudication; or
(C) a prosecution;
of a violation under any state or federal law that involves a controlled substance.

(3) A law enforcement officer who is an employee of:

(A) a local, state, or federal law enforcement agency; or
(B) an entity that regulates controlled substances or enforces controlled substances rules or laws in another state;
that is certified to receive information from the INSPECT program.

(4) A practitioner or practitioner's agent certified to receive information from the INSPECT program.

(5) A controlled substance monitoring program in another state with which Indiana has established an interoperability agreement.

(f) Information provided to an individual under:

(1) subsection (e)(3) is limited to information:

(A) concerning an individual or proceeding involving the unlawful diversion or misuse of a schedule II, III, IV, or V controlled substance; and

(B) that will assist in an investigation or proceeding; and

(2) subsection (e)(4) may be released only for the purpose of:

(A) providing medical or pharmaceutical treatment; or

(B) evaluating the need for providing medical or pharmaceutical treatment to a patient.

(g) Before the advisory committee releases confidential information under subsection (e), the applicant must be approved by the INSPECT program in a manner prescribed by the advisory committee.

(h) The advisory committee may release to:

(1) a member of the board, the advisory committee, or another governing body that licenses practitioners;

(2) an investigator for the consumer protection division of the office of the attorney general, a prosecuting attorney, the attorney general, a deputy attorney general, or an investigator from the office of the attorney general; or

(3) a law enforcement officer who is:

(A) authorized by the state police department to receive the type of information released; and

(B) approved by the advisory committee to receive the type of information released;

confidential information generated from computer records that identifies practitioners who are prescribing or dispensing large quantities of a controlled substance.

(i) The information described in subsection (h) may not be released until it has been reviewed by:

(1) a member of the advisory committee who is licensed in the same profession as the prescribing or dispensing practitioner identified by the data; or

(2) the advisory committee's designee;

and until that member or the designee has certified that further investigation is warranted. However, failure to comply with this subsection does not invalidate the use of any evidence that is otherwise admissible in a proceeding described in subsection (j).

(j) An investigator or a law enforcement officer receiving confidential information under subsection (d), (e), or (h) may disclose the information to a law enforcement officer or an attorney for the office of the attorney general for use as evidence in the following:

(1) A proceeding under IC 16-42-20.

(2) A proceeding under any state or federal law that involves a controlled substance.

(3) A criminal proceeding or a proceeding in juvenile court that involves a controlled substance.

(k) The advisory committee may compile statistical reports from the information described in subsection (b). The reports must not include information that identifies any practitioner, ultimate user, or other person administering a controlled substance. Statistical reports compiled under this subsection are public records.

(l) This section may not be construed to require a practitioner to obtain information about a patient from the data base.

(m) A practitioner is immune from civil liability for an injury, death, or loss to a person solely due to a practitioner seeking or not seeking information from the INSPECT program. The civil immunity described in this subsection does not extend to a practitioner if the practitioner receives information directly from the INSPECT program and then negligently misuses this information. This subsection does not apply to an act or omission that is a result of gross negligence or intentional misconduct.

(n) The advisory committee may review the records of the INSPECT program. If the advisory committee determines that a violation of the law may have occurred, the advisory committee shall notify the appropriate law enforcement agency or the relevant government body responsible for the licensure, regulation, or discipline of practitioners authorized by law to prescribe controlled substances.

History.
P.L.65-2006, § 13.

35-48-7-12. [Repealed.]

Compiler's Notes.
This section, concerning adoption of rules, was repealed by P.L.3-2008, § 269, effective March 13, 2008.

35-48-7-12.1. Advisory committee to adopt rules to implement chapter.

(a) This section applies after June 30, 2007.

(b) The advisory committee shall adopt rules under IC 4-22-2 to implement this chapter, including the following:

(1) Information collection and retrieval procedures for the INSPECT program, including the controlled substances to be included in the program required under section 8.1 [IC 35-48-7-8.1] of this chapter.

(2) Design for the creation of the data base required under section 10.1 [IC 35-48-7-10.1] of this chapter.

(3) Requirements for the development and installation of online electronic access by the advisory committee to information collected by the INSPECT program.

(4) Identification of emergency situations or other circumstances in which a practitioner may prescribe, dispense, and administer a prescription drug specified in section 8.1 of this chapter without a written prescription or on a form other than a form specified in section 8.1(b)(4) [IC 35-48-7-8.1(b)(4)] of this chapter.

(c) The advisory committee may:

(1) Set standards for education courses for individuals authorized to use the INSPECT program.

(2) Identify treatment programs for individuals addicted to controlled substances monitored by the INSPECT program.

(3) Work with impaired practitioner associations to provide intervention and treatment.

History.
P.L.65-2006, § 15.

35-48-7-13. [Repealed.]

Compiler's Notes.
This section, concerning controlled substances data fund established, was repealed by P.L.3-2008, § 269, effective March 13, 2008.

35-48-7-13.1. Controlled substances data fund established — Administration of fund — Source of money — Investment of money in fund.

(a) This section applies after June 30, 2007.

(b) The controlled substances data fund is established to fund the operation of the INSPECT program. The fund shall be administered by the Indiana professional licensing agency.

(c) Expenses of administering the fund shall be paid from money in the fund. The fund consists of grants, public and private financial assistance, and sixteen percent (16%) of the controlled substances registration fees imposed under rules adopted under IC 35-48-3-1.

(d) The treasurer of state shall invest the money in the fund not currently needed to meet the obligations of the fund in the same manner as other public money may be invested.

(e) Money in the fund at the end of a state fiscal year does not revert to the state general fund.

History.
  P.L.65-2006, § 17.

35-48-7-14. Violations of chapter — Penalty.

A person who knowingly or intentionally violates this chapter commits a Class A misdemeanor.

History.
  P.L.163-1994, § 5.

Cross References.
  Penalties for misdemeanors, IC 35-50-1, IC 35-50-3, IC 35-50-5-2.

35-48-7-15. [Repealed.]

Compiler's Notes.
  This section, providing for the expiration of this

chapter on July 1, 2001, was repealed by P.L.214-2001, § 1, effective May 10, 2001.

ARTICLE 49
OBSCENITY AND PORNOGRAPHY

CHAPTER 1
DEFINITIONS

35-49-1-1. Applicability of definitions.

The definitions in this chapter apply throughout this article.

History.
  IC 35-49-1-1, as added by P.L.311-1983, § 33.

Cross References.
  Child participating in obscene performance a child in need of services, IC 31-34-1-4.

NOTES TO DECISIONS

ANALYSIS

Constitutionality.
—Overbroadness.
—Right of Privacy.
—Speech or Press.
—Vagueness.
Construction With Other Law.

Magazines and Films.
Photographs.
Ruling That Law Was Unconstitutional.

Constitutionality.

—Overbroadness.
  The definition of "sexual conduct," as contained

Constitutionality. (Cont'd)

—Overbroadness. (Cont'd)
in former IC 35-30-10.1-1, was not unconstitutional for overbroadness. Porter v. State, 440 N.E.2d 690, 1982 Ind. App. LEXIS 1423 (1982).

—Right of Privacy.
Former IC 35-30-10.1-1 did not constitute an unconstitutional invasion into the right of privacy. Ford v. State, 182 Ind. App. 224, 394 N.E.2d 250, 1979 Ind. App. LEXIS 1343 (1979).

—Speech or Press.
Obscenity is not within the area of constitutionally protected speech or press. Ford v. State, 182 Ind. App. 224, 394 N.E.2d 250, 1979 Ind. App. LEXIS 1343 (1979).

—Vagueness.
Former IC 35-50-10.1-1 was sufficiently clear to give notice of the conduct proscribed and therefore was not unconstitutional for vagueness. Riley v. State, 180 Ind. App. 540, 389 N.E.2d 367, 1979 Ind. App. LEXIS 1158 (1979).
Former IC 35-30-10.1-1 was not unconstitutionally vague or overly broad. Ford v. State, 182 Ind. App. 224, 394 N.E.2d 250, 1979 Ind. App. LEXIS 1343 (1979).

Construction With Other Law.
Evidence that defendant broke into home and

masturbated in front of eight-year-old girl supported conviction for burglary. Sloan v. State, 794 N.E.2d 1128, 2003 Ind. App. LEXIS 1644 (2003).

Magazines and Films.
Magazines and films which explicitly portray in a patently offensive manner sexual intercourse and deviate sexual conduct and which lack serious literary, artistic, political, or scientific value despite the inclusion in the magazines of some insignificant text are obscene. Hagood v. State, 182 Ind. App. 317, 395 N.E.2d 315, 1979 Ind. App. LEXIS 1358 (1979).

Photographs.
Photograph involving nothing more than nudity is not obscene. Smith v. State, 413 N.E.2d 652, 1980 Ind. App. LEXIS 1838 (1980).

Ruling That Law Was Unconstitutional.
Ruling of superior court judge that former IC 35-30-10.1-1 was unconstitutional was binding only on the parties and pending appeal legislature could amend the law removing the alleged unconstitutional provisions as against contention that there was nothing to amend after such ruling. Hagood v. State, 182 Ind. App. 317, 395 N.E.2d 315, 1979 Ind. App. LEXIS 1358 (1979).

OPINIONS OF ATTORNEY GENERAL

The state of Indiana has not preempted the adoption of an ordinance by a city which defines "obscenity" within the First and Fourteenth Amendment guarantees of the United States Constitution as set forth in the generally accepted test under Miller v. California, 413 U.S. 15, 93 S. Ct. 2607, 37 L. Ed. 2d 419, 1973 U.S. LEXIS 149

(1973) and which provides that transmission of "obscenity" will be considered a material breach of a cable television franchise and grounds for suspension or revocation but which does not prescribe any crime, criminal penalty, criminal regulation or fine. Criminal penalties have already been established by 35-49. (1984), No. 84-4, p. 82.

RESEARCH REFERENCES

Indiana Law Review.
Pornography as Group Libel: The Indianapolis Sex Discrimination Ordinance, 18 Ind. L. Rev. 479 (1985).

Valparaiso University Law Review.
Children and Pornography: An Interest Analysis in System Perspective, 19 Val. U.L. Rev. 441 (1985).

35-49-1-2. Distribute.

"Distribute" means to transfer possession for a consideration.

History.
IC 35-49-1-2, as added by P.L.311-1983, § 33.

35-49-1-3. Matter.

"Matter" means:
   (1) any book, magazine, newspaper, or other printed or written material;
   (2) any picture, drawing, photograph, motion picture, digitized image, or other pictorial representation;
   (3) any statue or other figure;

(4) any recording, transcription, or mechanical, chemical, or electrical reproduction; or

(5) any other articles, equipment, machines, or materials.

History.
IC 35-49-1-3, as added by P.L.311-1983, § 33;
P.L.3-2002, § 3.

NOTES TO DECISIONS

Digitized Images.
Although defendant possessed "matter" pursuant to IC 35-49-1-3 for purposes of a conviction for the offense of dissemination of matter harmful to minors, as defendant sent a girl who was 16-year-old but not 18-years-old digitized pictures of defendant's genitals, defendant could not be convicted of that offense. Despite a minor being defined in Indiana as someone under the age of 18, IC 35-49-1-4, the dissemination statute was vague as applied to defendant because the evidence did not show that defendant had fair notice that the pictures of defendant's genitals were patently offensive to prevailing standards in the adult community as a whole, especially since the age for consenting to sexual activity in Indiana was 16-years-old. Salter v. State, 906 N.E.2d 212, 2009 Ind. App. LEXIS 831 (2009).

35-49-1-4. Minor.

"Minor" means any individual under the age of eighteen (18) years.

History.
IC 35-49-1-4, as added by P.L.311-1983, § 33.

35-49-1-5. Nudity.

"Nudity" means:

(1) The showing of the human male or female genitals, pubic area, or buttocks with less than a full opaque covering;

(2) The showing of the female breast with less than a fully opaque covering of any part of the nipple; or

(3) The depiction of covered male genitals in a discernibly turgid state.

History.
IC 35-49-1-5, as added by P.L.311-1983, § 33.

35-49-1-6. Owner.

"Owner" means any person who owns or has legal right to possession of any matter.

History.
IC 35-49-1-6, as added by P.L.311-1983, § 33.

35-49-1-7. Performance.

"Performance" means any play, motion picture, dance, or other exhibition or presentation, whether pictured, animated, or live, performed before an audience of one (1) or more persons.

History.
IC 35-49-1-7, as added by P.L.311-1983, § 33.

NOTES TO DECISIONS

Cited:
Walters v. State, 495 N.E.2d 734, 1986 Ind. LEXIS 1217 (1986); Low v. State, 580 N.E.2d 737, 1991 Ind. App. LEXIS 1881 (1991).

35-49-1-8. Sado-masochistic abuse.

"Sado-masochistic abuse" means flagellation or torture by or upon a person as an act of sexual stimulation or gratification.

History.
IC 35-49-1-8, as added by P.L.311-1983, § 33.

35-49-1-9. Sexual conduct.

"Sexual conduct" means:
(1) Sexual intercourse or deviate sexual conduct;
(2) Exhibition of the uncovered genitals in the context of masturbation or other sexual activity;
(3) Exhibition of the uncovered genitals of a person under sixteen (16) years of age;
(4) Sado-masochistic abuse; or
(5) Sexual intercourse or deviate sexual conduct with an animal.

History.
IC 35-49-1-9, as added by P.L.311-1983, § 33.

NOTES TO DECISIONS

Constitutionality.
Definitions of "sexual conduct" and "deviate sexual conduct" clearly limit the scope of materials that can be found to be obscene and are not constitutionally infirm. Van Sant v. State, 523 N.E.2d 229, 1988 Ind. App. LEXIS 388 (1988).

35-49-1-10. Sexual excitement.

"Sexual excitement" means the condition of human male or female genitals when in a state of sexual stimulation or arousal.

History.
IC 35-49-1-10, as added by P.L.311-1983, § 33.

CHAPTER 2

GENERAL PROVISIONS

35-49-2-1. Obscene matter or performance.

A matter or performance is obscene for purposes of this article if:
(1) The average person, applying contemporary community standards, finds that the dominant theme of the matter or performance, taken as a whole, appeals to the prurient interest in sex;
(2) The matter or performance depicts or describes, in a patently offensive way, sexual conduct; and
(3) The matter or performance, taken as a whole, lacks serious literary, artistic, political, or scientific value.

History.
IC 35-49-2-1, as added by P.L.311-1983, § 33.

Cross References.
Child participating in obscene performance a

child in need of services, IC 31-34-1-4.

Public indecency and indecent exposure, IC 35-45-4-1.

NOTES TO DECISIONS

Constitutionality.

Material which is obscene has been carefully defined by this section. This test is specific enough to put persons on notice of what material is and is not obscene. This section thus satisfies due process requirements and does not operate ex post facto in violation of U.S. Const., art. I, § 10. Sedelbauer v. State, 455 N.E.2d 1159, 1983 Ind. App. LEXIS 3564 (1983).

The Indiana obscenity statute (IC 35-49-2-1) does not violate the First Amendment. Albright v. State, 501 N.E.2d 488, 1986 Ind. App. LEXIS 3274 (1986).

Indiana's obscenity statute tracks the United States Supreme Court's definition of obscenity and is not unconstitutionally overbroad. Van Sant v. State, 523 N.E.2d 229, 1988 Ind. App. LEXIS 388 (1988).

Indiana's obscenity statute does not violate the free speech clause of the Indiana Constitution. Fordyce v. State, 569 N.E.2d 357, 1991 Ind. App. LEXIS 450 (1991).

Indiana's statutory definition of obscenity does not violate the First and Ninth Amendments to the United States Constitution. Fordyce v. State, 569 N.E.2d 357, 1991 Ind. App. LEXIS 450 (1991).

Access to Materials.

Mere fact that some effort is required to access materials does not change the point of distribution or the character of the material, and does not place the material's distribution outside of the obscenity statute. State v. Virtue, 658 N.E.2d 605, 1995 Ind. App. LEXIS 1420 (1995).

Books.

The book "Tropic of Cancer" is not obscene.

Cuffel v. State, 247 Ind. 357, 215 N.E.2d 36, 1966 Ind. LEXIS 362 (1966).

Contemporary Community Standards.

The purpose of the contemporary community standards test of this statute is to ensure the application of a general community standard and, as the statute does not specify whether a statewide or local standard shall be employed in reference to community standards, either standard is permissible as long as the jury is instructed that they are to take a generalized view of the community as a whole rather than expressing personal or aberrant views. Richards v. State, 461 N.E.2d 744, 1984 Ind. App. LEXIS 2479 (1984).

Determination of obscenity depends upon the prevailing community standards. Saliba v. State, 475 N.E.2d 1181, 1985 Ind. App. LEXIS 2267 (1985).

—Comparison Evidence.

To establish a foundation for the admission of comparison evidence on the issue of community standards, there must be a showing that the proffered evidence: (1) is similar to the material in issue; and (2) enjoys a reasonable degree of community acceptance. Fordyce v. State, 569 N.E.2d 357, 1991 Ind. App. LEXIS 450 (1991).

—Determination of Standard.

The majority of the community need not desire to view sexually explicit materials in order to establish community acceptance or tolerance of such materials; rather, the issue concerns the population's perception of what is generally acceptable in the community, considering the intended and probable recipients of the materials. Saliba v. State, 475 N.E.2d 1181, 1985 Ind. App. LEXIS 2267 (1985).

—Expert Testimony.

Due process rights are not violated by the trial court's failure to allow expert testimony on contemporary standards. While expert opinion may be used to define contemporary community standards, it is not required in obscenity cases. Whether materials are obscene can be determined by viewing them. Sedelbauer v. State, 455 N.E.2d 1159, 1983 Ind. App. LEXIS 3564 (1983).

Trial court properly refused to permit a certified sex therapist to testify as to contemporary community standards where, although she was familiar with persons experiencing sexual dysfunction and with sexually explicit material used in treatment of such persons, her testimony did not show knowledge of the general community's sexual functioning or with their use or tolerance of sexually explicit material in or outside the home. Albright v. State, 501 N.E.2d 488, 1986 Ind. App. LEXIS 3274 (1986).

—Instructions.

An instruction to apply local standards presents reversible error only where the record indicates that the instruction materially affected the deliberations of the jury in a manner prejudicial to the defendant. Richards v. State, 461 N.E.2d 744, 1984 Ind. App. LEXIS 2479 (1984).

When an instruction has been given in terms of a local or county-wide standard, the essence of the question of prejudice to the defendant is whether the instruction may have led the jury to apply some specialized test that might differ to the defendant's disadvantage from a generalized "average person, applying contemporary community standards" test. Richards v. State, 461 N.E.2d 744, 1984 Ind. App. LEXIS 2479 (1984).

—Public Opinion Polls.

In a prosecution for distribution of obscene matter which includes as evidence a public opinion poll which attempts to determine the community standards of obscenity, and where foundation testimony detailing methodology employed by the poll comported with generally accepted survey techniques, the trial court cannot exclude such evidence on the basis of choosing between opinions proffered by qualified experts as to the validity of the polling techniques. Saliba v. State, 475 N.E.2d 1181, 1985 Ind. App. LEXIS 2267 (1985).

The testimony of a defense expert who conducted a public opinion poll to determine the community standards regarding the depiction of sexual activities in movies and publications, including a statement that the definitions, standards and methodologies used in the poll were used by "practically all" national polling organizations, provided a complete foundation for admission of the poll in a trial involving distribution of obscene matter. Saliba v. State, 475 N.E.2d 1181, 1985 Ind. App. LEXIS 2267 (1985).

Evidence.

—Sufficient.

Where testimony of police officers gave descriptions of the films which revealed plots or nonexistent plots or story lines connecting a series of sexual acts and films were also shown to jury as exhibits, evidence was sufficient for conviction. American Films, Ltd. v. State, 413 N.E.2d 1091, 1981 Ind. App. LEXIS 1205 (1981).

—Supporting Conviction on Multiple Counts.

Evidence that after defendant began showing an obscene film to one minor boy the boy left and returned with another minor boy, and that defendant then showed both boys obscene photographs and a pornographic magazine before showing them the obscene film, was sufficient to support conclusion that two separate exhibitions of obscene material occurred and thus supported defendant's convictions on two counts of exhibiting an obscene performance. Isaac v. State, 439 N.E.2d 1193, 1982 Ind. App. LEXIS 1405 (1982).

—View.

It was not error to have jury view pictures in a movie theater. American Films, Ltd. v. State, 413 N.E.2d 1091, 1981 Ind. App. LEXIS 1205 (1981).

Motion Pictures.

Both former IC 35-30-10.1-2 and former IC 35-30-10.1-3 prohibited the exhibition of obscene motion pictures. Isaac v. State, 439 N.E.2d 1193, 1982 Ind. App. LEXIS 1405 (1982).

Municipal Ordinances.

Municipal ordinances which attempt to regulate massage parlors by providing for suspension or revocation of the parlor's license as the penalty for violation are not precluded by this section, since the ordinances establish a licensing scheme while the state statutes establish a penal scheme. Indianapolis v. Wright, 267 Ind. 471, 371 N.E.2d 1298, 1978 Ind. LEXIS 584 (1978), appeal dismissed, 439 U.S. 804, 99 S. Ct. 60, 58 L. Ed. 2d 97, 1978 U.S. LEXIS 2481 (1978).

—Discrimination Against Women.

In a federal suit challenging the constitutionality of a city ordinance defining "pornography" as a practice that discriminates against women, abstention was not appropriate. A state court could not have clarified the ordinance's meaning, which was all too clear. The ordinance was not an "ordinary" obscenity law, as this article is, but was designed to be distinctively different, to prohibit explicitly sexual speech that "subordinated" women in specified ways. American Booksellers Asso. v. Hudnut, 771 F.2d 323, 1985 U.S. App. LEXIS 22623 (7th Cir. Ind. 1985), aff'd, 475 U.S. 1001, 106 S. Ct. 1172, 89 L. Ed. 2d 291, 1986 U.S. LEXIS 166 (1986).

Prurient Appeal.

—Deviant Group.

The prurient appeal of material intended for a clearly defined deviant sexual group may be measured by its prurient appeal to that particular group. Sedelbauer v. State, 455 N.E.2d 1159, 1983 Ind. App. LEXIS 3564 (1983).

— —Expert Testimony.

Expert testimony may be allowed in order to guide a jury in determining the prurient appeal of material on a specific deviant group. Sedelbauer v. State, 455 N.E.2d 1159, 1983 Ind. App. LEXIS 3564 (1983).

Single Offense.

Exhibition of an obscene film to more than one person constituted a single offense under former IC 35-30-10.1-3. Isaac v. State, 439 N.E.2d 1193, 1982 Ind. App. LEXIS 1405 (1982).

Cited:

Lewis v. State, 726 N.E.2d 836, 2000 Ind. App. LEXIS 508 (2000).

RESEARCH REFERENCES

Collateral References.

Obscenity prosecutions: Statutory exemption based on dissemination to persons or entities having scientific, educational, or similar justification for possession of such materials. 13 A.L.R.5th 567.

Admissiblility of evidence of public-opinion polls or surveys in obscenity prosecutions on issue whether materials in question are obscene. 58 A.L.R.5th 749.

35-49-2-2. Matter or performance harmful to minors.

A matter or performance is harmful to minors for purposes of this article if:

(1) It describes or represents, in any form, nudity, sexual conduct, sexual excitement, or sado-masochistic abuse;

(2) Considered as a whole, it appeals to the prurient interest in sex of minors;

(3) It is patently offensive to prevailing standards in the adult community as a whole with respect to what is suitable matter for or performance before minors; and

(4) Considered as a whole, it lacks serious literary, artistic, political, or scientific value for minors.

History.

IC 35-49-2-2, as added by P.L.311-1983, § 33.

NOTES TO DECISIONS

ANALYSIS

Constitutionality.
Construction.
Evidence Sufficient.

Constitutionality.

IC 35-49-3-3 and 35-49-2-2 are not unconstitutionally vague since individuals of ordinary intelligence can comprehend the statutes adequately enough to inform them of the proscribed conduct. Zitlaw v. State, 880 N.E.2d 724, 2008 Ind. App. LEXIS 249 (2008).

Defendant's convictions for dissemination of matter harmful to minors in violation of IC 35-49-3-3 had to be reversed, as that statute was impermissibly vague as applied to defendant based on defendant's conduct in sending pictures of defendant's genitals to a girl in Delaware who was between the ages of 16 and 18. The evidence did not show that defendant had fair notice that the pictures of defendant's genitals would be patently offensive to prevailing standards in the adult community as a whole, as required by IC 35-49-3-3, especially since minors in Indiana could consent to sexual activity at the age of 16. Salter v. State, 906 N.E.2d 212, 2009 Ind. App. LEXIS 831 (2009).

Construction.

IC 35-49-2-2(2) and (3) do not require the actual presence of a minor. Zitlaw v. State, 880 N.E.2d 724, 2008 Ind. App. LEXIS 249 (2008).

Evidence Sufficient.

Although nudity alone is not enough to make material legally obscene, where a tape showed defendant naked and engaging in intimate activity with a woman near a bed, the evidence was sufficient to support the conclusion that defendant disseminated matter to a minor that was harmful to minors. Lewis v. State, 726 N.E.2d 836, 2000 Ind. App. LEXIS 508 (2000).

Defendant knew for purposes of IC 35-41-2-2 and IC 35-49-2-2 that a DVD containing nudity and sexual content was playing on a screen mounted in defendant's rearview window for purposes of IC 35-49-3-3 as a duplicate screen was in the center console between defendant and a passenger, and the DVD that was playing on the video screen in the rearview window was housed in the unit on the center console. M.S. v. State, 889 N.E.2d 900, 2008 Ind. App. LEXIS 1504 (2008).

The trial court properly refused to dismiss a charge of engaging in a performance harmful to minors under IC 35-49-3-3(a)(5) where defendant was accused of exposing himself to an officer in a public park in order to get the officer to engage in oral sex because subsection did not require the actual presence of a minor, it was unnecessary for the state to name specific minor victims or to include the phrase "unless each minor is accompanied by the minor's parent or guardian" in the information, IC 35-49-3-3 and IC 35-49-2-2 were not unconstitutionally vague, and defendant's alleged conduct of exposing himself in a public park for the purpose of engaging in oral sex clearly fell within the conduct proscribed by the statutes. Zitlaw v. State, 880 N.E.2d 724, 2008 Ind. App. LEXIS 249 (2008).

35-49-2-3. Warrant required for search or arrest.

(a) Whenever a person:

(1) Offers matter for distribution to the public as stock-in-trade of a lawful business or activity; or

(2) Exhibits matter at a commercial theater showing regularly scheduled performances to the general public;

the person may be arrested under this article only if the arresting officer has first obtained an arrest warrant, and matter may be seized as evidence only if a search warrant has first been obtained.

(b) The quantity of matter seized may encompass no more than is reasonable and necessary for the purpose of obtaining evidence.

(c) If:

(1) The subject of a seizure under this chapter is a motion picture that is allegedly harmful to minors; and

(2) The defendant or owner of the motion picture proves that other copies of the motion picture are not available for exhibition;

the court shall order that the defendant or owner may, at his own expense, copy the motion picture and continue showing the motion picture to adults pending a preliminary determination under section 4(b) [IC 35-49-2-4(b)] of this chapter.

History.
IC 35-49-2-3, as added by P.L.311-1983, § 33.

NOTES TO DECISIONS

ANALYSIS

Constitutionality.
Advance Censorship.
Affidavit or Information.
Evidence.
Warrants for Search and Arrest Obtained Simultaneously.

Constitutionality.
It was a violation of the First Amendment to the United States Constitution to seize a film as obscene prior to an adversary proceeding on the issue of obscenity. Metzger v. Pearcy, 393 F.2d 202, 1968 U.S. App. LEXIS 7163 (7th Cir. Ind. 1968). (A hearing is now provided for in IC 35-49-2-4).

Advance Censorship.
A deputy prosecuting attorney's action in furnishing a list of magazines which he considered in violation of the statute was not authorized by the pernicious literature statute or by any other law of Indiana as it constituted an informal method of law enforcement which was clearly beyond the scope of any authority given the prosecuting attorney. HMH Publishing Co. v. Garrett, 151 F. Supp. 903, 1957 U.S. Dist. LEXIS 3648 (D. Ind. 1957).

Affidavit or Information.
An affidavit (procedural forerunner of an infor-

mation) which charged the selling of obscene literature in the language of the statute, and alleging the literature to be in pamphlet form, and too lewd, lascivious and licentious to set out in the affidavit and to encumber the court record, was sufficient against a motion to quash. Sunderman v. State, 197 Ind. 705, 151 N.E. 829, 1926 Ind. LEXIS 81 (1926).

Evidence.
The testimony of former employee of the defendant that the newspaper in question was brought to the store by the defendant from another state was sufficient to sustain finding that the obscene material was sent into Indiana. Mohney v. State, 257 Ind. 394, 276 N.E.2d 517, 1971 Ind. LEXIS 551 (1971), vacated, 413 U.S. 911, 93 S. Ct. 3040, 37 L. Ed. 2d 1026 (1973).

Warrants for Search and Arrest Obtained Simultaneously.
Where prosecutor obtained an arrest warrant for an adult bookstore employee at the same time he obtained a search warrant for the store, this was in derogation of former IC 35-30-10.1-6 concerning the issuing of a legal arrest warrant. Butts v. Monk, 516 F. Supp. 1, 1980 U.S. Dist. LEXIS 16820 (S.D. Ind. 1980).

RESEARCH REFERENCES

Collateral References.
When is consent voluntarily given so as to justify

search conducted on basis of that consent — Supreme Court cases. 148 A.L.R. Fed 271.

35-49-2-4. Preliminary determination of obscenity at adversary hearing.

(a) Within ten (10) days after:

(1) Matter is obtained by seizure or by purchase under this article; or

(2) The defendant is arrested under this article;

whichever is later, and before trial, the state, the defendant, an owner, or any other party in interest of any matter seized or purchased may apply for and obtain a prompt adversary hearing for the purpose described in subsection (b).

(b) At the adversary hearing, the court shall make a preliminary determination of whether the matter is:

(1) Probably obscene; or

(2) Probably harmful to minors.

History.
IC 35-49-2-4, as added by P.L.311-1983, § 33.

NOTES TO DECISIONS

ANALYSIS

Constitutionality.
—No Denial of Rights Found.
—Vagueness.
Adversary Hearing.
—Notice.
—Preliminary Step.

Constitutionality.

—No Denial of Rights Found.

Where allegedly obscene materials, films and photographs were seized pursuant to a search warrant and owner petitioned for prompt adversary proceedings pursuant to former IC 35-30-10.1-6 to obtain a determination of probable obscenity and the matter was continued once on the petition of the owner and other subsequent hearing dates were scheduled over a period of several months because of conflicts with other court proceedings, there was no denial of First Amendment rights and Supreme Court denied application for writ of mandate to require trial court to advance the matter on the calendar ahead of all other matters except criminal cases. State ex rel. Drost v.

Newton Superior Court, 275 Ind. 297, 416 N.E.2d 1247, 1981 Ind. LEXIS 722 (1981).

—Vagueness.

Former IC 35-30-10.1-6 was clear in its import and therefore not unconstitutional. Hagood v. State, 182 Ind. App. 317, 395 N.E.2d 315, 1979 Ind. App. LEXIS 1358 (1979).

Adversary Hearing.

—Notice.

Where state requests an adversary hearing under the provisions of this section, it is not necessary to send a notice to the defendant of his right to an adversary hearing. Hagood v. State, 182 Ind. App. 317, 395 N.E.2d 315, 1979 Ind. App. LEXIS 1358 (1979).

—Preliminary Step.

The adversary hearing provided by former IC 35-30-10.1-6 to determine if there were probable cause to believe the matter was obscene was merely a preliminary step in the bringing of a criminal action and therefore a change of judge was not required. State ex rel. J. N. S., Inc. v. Marion County Municipal Court, 272 Ind. 86, 396 N.E.2d 361, 1979 Ind. LEXIS 750 (1979).

35-49-2-5. Adoption or enforcement of zoning ordinances not limited.

This article does not limit the power of political subdivisions to adopt or enforce zoning ordinances regulating the use of real property.

History.
IC 35-49-2-5, as added by P.L.311-1983, § 33.

CHAPTER 3

CRIMES

35-49-3-1. Importation or distribution of obscene matter.

A person who knowingly or intentionally:

(1) Sends or brings into Indiana obscene matter for sale or distribution; or

(2) Offers to distribute, distributes, or exhibits to another person obscene matter;

commits a Class A misdemeanor. However, the offense is a Class D felony if the obscene matter depicts or describes sexual conduct involving any person who is or appears to be under sixteen (16) years of age.

History.
IC 35-49-3-1, as added by P.L.311-1983, § 33.

Penalties for misdemeanors, IC 35-50-1, IC 35-50-3, IC 35-50-5-2.

Cross References.
Penalties for felonies, IC 35-50-1, IC 35-50-2, IC 35-50-5-2.

NOTES TO DECISIONS

ANALYSIS

Constitutionality.
Access to Materials.
Community Standards of Obscenity.
—Public Opinion Polls.
Elements.
Entrapment.
—Predisposition.
Evidence.
—Admissibility.
—Circumstantial.
—Sufficiency.
Fictional Depictions.
Instructions.
—Not Justified.
Knowledge Inferred.
Managerial Position.
—Knowledge of Distribution.
—Liability.
Motion Pictures.
Number of Counts Chargeable.
Right to Privacy.
State Regulation.
Statute of Limitations.

Constitutionality.
Fine of $10,000 (under penal provision which has since been repealed) imposed on person who was not an employee of store when he sold magazine but was merely helping out the owner who was absent at the time did not constitute excessive punishment within the meaning of Ind. Const., Art. 1, § 16. Ford v. State, 182 Ind. App. 224, 394 N.E.2d 250, 1979 Ind. App. LEXIS 1343 (1979).

Access to Materials.
Mere fact that some effort is required to access the materials does not change the point of distribution or the character of the material, and does not place the material's distribution outside of the obscenity statute. State v. Virtue, 658 N.E.2d 605, 1995 Ind. App. LEXIS 1420 (1995).

Community Standards of Obscenity.

—Public Opinion Polls.
In a prosecution for distribution of obscene matter, which includes as evidence a public opinion poll which attempts to determine the community standards of obscenity, and where foundation testimony detailing methodology employed by poll taken comported with generally accepted survey techniques, the trial court cannot exclude such evidence on the basis of choosing between opinions proffered by qualified experts as to the validity of the polling techniques. Saliba v. State, 475 N.E.2d 1181, 1985 Ind. App. LEXIS 2267 (1985).

The testimony of a defense expert who conducted a public opinion poll to determine the community standards regarding the depiction of sexual activities in movies and publications, including a statement that the definitions, standards and methodologies used in the poll were used by "practically all" national polling organizations, provided a complete foundation for admission of the poll in a trial involving distribution of obscene matter. Saliba v. State, 475 N.E.2d 1181, 1985 Ind. App. LEXIS 2267 (1985).

Defendant's introduction of public opinion poll may have established the public's acceptance of some types of sexually explicit materials in general, but did not establish community acceptance of the specific type of sexual materials defendant sought to introduce. Van Sant v. State, 523 N.E.2d 229, 1988 Ind. App. LEXIS 388 (1988).

Elements.
Scienter is an element under Indiana's obscenity statute. Van Sant v. State, 523 N.E.2d 229, 1988 Ind. App. LEXIS 388 (1988).

Entrapment.
Where police wrote to defendant and expressed an interest in pornographic pictures and defendant sent him a picture and expressed delight at the prospect of meeting him and showing him his

Entrapment. (Cont'd)
collection, there was no entrapment. Beach v. State, 411 N.E.2d 363, 1980 Ind. App. LEXIS 1582 (1980).

—Predisposition.
The defendant's admitted personal and/or business relationship with a suspected distributor of child pornography, his admitted pedophilic affections, his familiarity with insider terminology, his willingness to forward, by mail, personal photographs to a stranger, his apparent readiness to exhibit his collection, and his admission of having previously traded obscene matter, are sufficient evidence of predisposition to avoid the defense of entrapment and sustain the conviction by the trial court, regardless of the detective's having feigned an interest in obscene matter and presented the defendant with an opportunity to commit the crime. Beach v. State, 411 N.E.2d 363, 1980 Ind. App. LEXIS 1582 (1980).

Evidence.
Evidence that defendant showed the undercover officer materials displaying a woman having sexual intercourse with a dog and a woman having oral sex with a horse and that he displayed these images to the officer for the purpose of making a sale was sufficient to support defendant's convictions under Indiana's obscenity statute. Adams v. State, 804 N.E.2d 1169, 2004 Ind. App. LEXIS 430 (2004).

—Admissibility.
Evidence of events occurring at the time of, or after, the initial contact by the officer with the defendant, or occurring at the time of the commission of the offense, is admissible to show predisposition to commit a crime, in order to defeat a claim of entrapment. Beach v. State, 411 N.E.2d 363, 1980 Ind. App. LEXIS 1582 (1980).

—Circumstantial.
Knowledge of the seller is an essential element of a conviction for distributing obscenity but scienter, like any other legally material fact may be proved by circumstantial evidence. Hagood v. State, 182 Ind. App. 317, 395 N.E.2d 315, 1979 Ind. App. LEXIS 1358 (1979).

—Sufficiency.
Where the magazine involved was itself introduced into evidence, that alone was sufficient evidence for the jury to determine the magazine's obscenity. Ford v. State, 182 Ind. App. 224, 394 N.E.2d 250, 1979 Ind. App. LEXIS 1343 (1979).
Defendant could be convicted of violating former IC 35-30-10.1-2 where he showed his collection of obscene pictures to policeman in the policeman's hotel room. Beach v. State, 411 N.E.2d 363, 1980 Ind. App. LEXIS 1582 (1980).
Material was correctly categorized as obscene. Sedelbauer v. State, 428 N.E.2d 206, 1981 Ind. LEXIS 921 (1981), cert. denied, 455 U.S. 1035, 102 S. Ct. 1739, 72 L. Ed. 2d 153, 1982 U.S. LEXIS 1487 (1982).
Where the magazine itself is introduced into evidence, it alone is sufficient evidence for a deter-

mination of obscenity. The state is not required to present expert testimony; the jury can make its determination based on the material. Peters v. State, 449 N.E.2d 311, 1983 Ind. App. LEXIS 2944 (1983).
Evidence that defendant was the only person in the store when obscene matter was purchased, the only person in control of the store at the time, the store was identified as an adult book store, store racks were filled with magazines similar to the materials in issue, sexual devices were also on the racks, magazines were viewable from the counter, defendant viewed the covers of the magazines before registering the purchase price and the covers were descriptive of the contents, was sufficient to establish defendant's knowledge of the nature of the materials and to support her conviction for the exhibiting, offering to distribute, and distributing of the materials. Van Sant v. State, 523 N.E.2d 229, 1988 Ind. App. LEXIS 388 (1988).

Fictional Depictions.
The enhancement provision in the last sentence of this section applies to depictions of fictional as well as real people under the age of 16. Fordyce v. State, 569 N.E.2d 357, 1991 Ind. App. LEXIS 450 (1991).

Instructions.
Instruction which used the word "pandered" without defining such word was in error. Sedelbauer v. State, 402 N.E.2d 1006, 1980 Ind. App. LEXIS 1398 (1980).
Evidence was sufficient to justify an instruction on pandering. Sedelbauer v. State, 428 N.E.2d 206, 1981 Ind. LEXIS 921 (1981), cert. denied, 455 U.S. 1035, 102 S. Ct. 1739, 72 L. Ed. 2d 153, 1982 U.S. LEXIS 1487 (1982).

—Not Justified.
Fact that store in which film was sold contained signs in window which read "Swingers World Book Store" and "Adult News and Book Store" did not justify an instruction on pandering. Sedelbauer v. State, 405 N.E.2d 566, 1980 Ind. App. LEXIS 1497 (1980), vacated, 428 N.E.2d 206, 1981 Ind. LEXIS 921 (1981).

Knowledge Inferred.
Where magazines contained objectionable material on their covers and defendant who sold magazines placed plastic coverings on them and placed them on the shelves, jury could have inferred knowledge on defendant's part of the nature and content of the magazines. Hagood v. State, 182 Ind. App. 317, 395 N.E.2d 315, 1979 Ind. App. LEXIS 1358 (1979).
Knowledge of contents of allegedly obscene material can be proved by circumstantial evidence; whether defendant charged with distributing obscene material had knowledge of contents of material was for jury where defendant entered into lease under pretense of selling camera and video equipment and where, although defendant did not tend premises himself, he was seen in the store and money was seen to change hands from sales

Knowledge Inferred. (Cont'd)
clerk to defendant and nature of material sold was readily apparent from covers of magazines and videotapes. Porter v. State, 440 N.E.2d 690, 1982 Ind. App. LEXIS 1423 (1982).

Before a person can be convicted of distributing obscene material, he must have knowledge of the nature and contents of the material. However, knowledge may be proved by circumstantial evidence. Peters v. State, 449 N.E.2d 311, 1983 Ind. App. LEXIS 2944 (1983).

The picture on the package of an obscene film may be sufficient to prove that the seller of the film had the knowledge required for conviction under this section. Sedelbauer v. State, 462 N.E.2d 244, 1984 Ind. App. LEXIS 2502 (1984).

Managerial Position.

—Knowledge of Distribution.
Knowledge of distribution of books may be inferred where defendant held a managerial or proprietary position in the book store, the store contained a warning sign with respect to minors and those that may be offended, and he ordered the inventory. Riley v. State, 180 Ind. App. 540, 389 N.E.2d 367, 1979 Ind. App. LEXIS 1158 (1979).

—Liability.
Personal distribution is not a material element of the offense and a person in a managerial or proprietary position in the distribution process may be liable. Riley v. State, 180 Ind. App. 540, 389 N.E.2d 367, 1979 Ind. App. LEXIS 1158 (1979).

Motion Pictures.
Both former IC 35-30-10.1-2 and former IC 35-30-10.1-3 prohibited the exhibition of obscene motion pictures. Isaac v. State, 439 N.E.2d 1193, 1982 Ind. App. LEXIS 1405 (1982).

Number of Counts Chargeable.
Defendant could not be convicted of two counts of exhibiting obscene materials even though he exhibited obscene materials to two minor boys, since exhibition was pursuant to single intent and design. Isaac v. State, 439 N.E.2d 1193, 1982 Ind. App. LEXIS 1405 (1982).

Where one detective purchased two magazines and another detective purchased two films, defendant could be charged with two, but not four, counts of distributing obscene material. Porter v. State, 440 N.E.2d 690, 1982 Ind. App. LEXIS 1423 (1982).

Right to Privacy.
The argument that the defendant had a right to possess and exhibit pornography in the privacy of a hotel room was lacking in cogency where the hotel room was the detective's. Beach v. State, 411 N.E.2d 363, 1980 Ind. App. LEXIS 1582 (1980).

State Regulation.
States have the right to regulate the distribution of obscene matter regardless of whether that matter is distributed to consenting adults. State v. Virtue, 658 N.E.2d 605, 1995 Ind. App. LEXIS 1420 (1995).

In order for the state's regulation of the distribution of obscene videotapes to be constitutional, the state only has to show that the distributor abused his right to freedom of expression in distributing the videotapes. State v. Virtue, 658 N.E.2d 605, 1995 Ind. App. LEXIS 1420 (1995).

Commercial exposure and sale of obscene materials to anyone, including consenting adults, is subject to state regulation. State v. Virtue, 658 N.E.2d 605, 1995 Ind. App. LEXIS 1420 (1995).

Statute of Limitations.
Where time is not of the essence of the offense, the state is not confined to proving the commission on the date alleged in the affidavit or indictment, but may prove the commission at any time within the statutory period of limitations. Thus, in a trial for exhibiting obscene material and disseminating matter harmful to minors, the question is whether the film viewed by the jury was exhibited and displayed to the minor victim at any time within the statutory period of limitations. Walters v. State, 495 N.E.2d 734, 1986 Ind. LEXIS 1217 (1986).

Cited:
Lewis v. State, 726 N.E.2d 836, 2000 Ind. App. LEXIS 508 (2000).

RESEARCH REFERENCES

Valparaiso University Law Review.
Children and Pornography: An Interest Analysis in System Perspective, 19 Val. U.L. Rev. 441 (1985).

Collateral References.
Admissiblility of evidence of public-opinion polls or surveys in obscenity prosecutions on issue whether materials in question are obscene. 58 A.L.R.5th 749.

Construction and application of United States Sentencing Guideline § 2G2.1 et seq., pertaining to child pornography. 145 A.L.R. Fed. 481.

35-49-3-2. Activities related to obscene performance.

A person who knowingly or intentionally engages in, participates in, manages, produces, sponsors, presents, exhibits, photographs, films, or videotapes any obscene performance commits a Class A misdemeanor. However, the offense is a Class

D felony if the obscene performance depicts or describes sexual conduct involving any person who is or appears to be under sixteen (16) years of age.

History.
IC 35-49-3-2, as added by P.L.311-1983, § 33.

Cross References.
Penalties for felonies, IC 35-50-1, IC 35-50-2, IC 35-50-5-2.

Penalties for misdemeanors, IC 35-50-1, IC 35-50-3, IC 35-50-5-2.
Public indecency and indecent exposure, IC 35-45-4-1.

NOTES TO DECISIONS

ANALYSIS

Activity Held Not Violation.
Evidence Sufficient.
Private Setting.
Prostitution.
Purpose.
Single Offense.

Activity Held Not Violation.
Defendant's performance of a semi-nude "bed dance" and a "finger fantasy" involving masturbation of her vagina, in a hotel room while in the company of an undercover police officer, did not violate the obscene performance statute. Low v. State, 580 N.E.2d 737, 1991 Ind. App. LEXIS 1881 (1991).

Evidence Sufficient.
Where defendant who lived in a large apartment complex committed an obscene act at night inside his lighted bedroom with the curtains open, thereby being observed by two occupants of another apartment, evidence was sufficient to support finding that defendant "knowingly or intentionally" engaged in an "obscene performance." Fultz v. State, 473 N.E.2d 624, 1985 Ind. App. LEXIS 2123 (1985).

Private Setting.
The purpose of this section and the legislative intent revealed by the language used, is to prohibit obscene performances of a theatrical, show, or entertainment nature, performed live, or on film or video, before an audience, and not to ban an act in a private setting, no matter how disgusting. Riffel v. State, 549 N.E.2d 1084, 1990 Ind. App. LEXIS 120 (1990).
Obscene act does not have to be done in "private" to violate IC 35-49-1-7, Riffel v. State and Low v.

State to the contrary notwithstanding. Sloan v. State, 794 N.E.2d 1128, 2003 Ind. App. LEXIS 1644 (2003).

Prostitution.
The prostitution and obscene performance statutes are not in conflict. Both statutes prohibit certain conduct; neither statute explicitly authorizes any conduct proscribed by the other. A conflict between the statutes is not created by the possibility the overlapping proscriptions may give rise to double jeopardy issues or by the inclusion of an obscenity provision in only one of the two statutes. Webb v. State, 575 N.E.2d 1066, 1991 Ind. App. LEXIS 1319 (1991).

Purpose.
The obscene performance statute does not seek to prevent the performance of sexual acts for money. That purpose is served elsewhere in the criminal code. The purpose of the statute is to prosecute "obscene performances" as those acts are defined by the statute, whether or not the acts are performed in return for money. Low v. State, 580 N.E.2d 737, 1991 Ind. App. LEXIS 1881 (1991).

Single Offense.
A single, continuous, uninterrupted exhibition of four obscene films for one admission price constituted only one count of exhibiting an obscene performance since the offenses were committed at the same time, in the same place, constituted parts of a continuous criminal design, and were inspired by the same criminal intent. American Film Distributors, Inc. v. State, 471 N.E.2d 3, 1984 Ind. App. LEXIS 3037 (1984).

Cited:
Tinsley v. State, 496 N.E.2d 1306, 1986 Ind. App. LEXIS 2887 (1986).

RESEARCH REFERENCES

Valparaiso University Law Review.
Children and Pornography: An Interest Analysis

in System Perspective, 19 Val. U.L. Rev. 441 (1985).

35-49-3-3. Providing obscene matter and performances before minors.

(a) Except as provided in subsection (b), a person who knowingly or intentionally:
   (1) disseminates matter to minors that is harmful to minors;

(2) displays matter that is harmful to minors in an area to which minors have visual, auditory, or physical access, unless each minor is accompanied by the minor's parent or guardian;

(3) sells, rents, or displays for sale or rent to any person matter that is harmful to minors within five hundred (500) feet of the nearest property line of a school or church;

(4) engages in or conducts a performance before minors that is harmful to minors;

(5) engages in or conducts a performance that is harmful to minors in an area to which minors have visual, auditory, or physical access, unless each minor is accompanied by the minor's parent or guardian;

(6) misrepresents the minor's age for the purpose of obtaining admission to an area from which minors are restricted because of the display of matter or a performance that is harmful to minors; or

(7) misrepresents that the person is a parent or guardian of a minor for the purpose of obtaining admission of the minor to an area where minors are being restricted because of display of matter or performance that is harmful to minors; commits a Class D felony.

(b) This section does not apply if a person disseminates, displays, or makes available the matter described in subsection (a) through the Internet, computer electronic transfer, or a computer network unless:

(1) the matter is obscene under IC 35-49-2-1;

(2) the matter is child pornography under IC 35-42-4-4; or

(3) the person distributes the matter to a child less than eighteen (18) years of age believing or intending that the recipient is a child less than eighteen (18) years of age.

History.

IC 35-49-3-3, as added by P.L.311-1983, § 33; P.L.59-1995, § 4; P.L.3-2002, § 4; P.L.140-2006, § 35.

Compiler's Notes.

P.L.140-2006, § 42, effective July 1, 2006, provides:

"IC 11-8-8-15, IC 11-8-8-17, IC 11-8-8-18, IC 35-42-4-10, and IC 35-44-3-13, all as added by this act, and IC 35-43-1-2, IC 35-42-4-11, and IC 35-49-3-3, all as amended by this act, apply only to crimes committed after June 30, 2006."

Cross References.

Penalties for felonies, IC 35-50-1, IC 35-50-2, IC 35-50-5-2.

Public indecency and indecent exposure, IC 35-45-4-1.

NOTES TO DECISIONS

ANALYSIS

Constitutionality.
Access Element.
Collateral Estoppel.
Construction.
Distance to School or Church.
Evidence Insufficient.
Evidence Sufficient.
Statute of Limitations.

Constitutionality.

IC 35-49-3-3 and IC 35-49-2-2 are not unconstitutionally vague since individuals of ordinary intelligence can comprehend the statutes adequately enough to inform them of the proscribed conduct. Zitlaw v. State, 880 N.E.2d 724, 2008 Ind. App. LEXIS 249 (2008).

Defendant's convictions for dissemination of matter harmful to minors in violation of IC 35-49-3-3 had to be reversed, as that statute was impermissibly vague as applied to defendant based on defendant's conduct in sending pictures of defendant's genitals to a girl in Delaware who was between the ages of 16 and 18. The evidence did not show that defendant had fair notice that the pictures of defendant's genitals would be patently offensive to prevailing standards in the adult community as a whole, as required by IC 35-49-3-3, especially since minors in Indiana could consent to sexual activity at the age of 16. Salter v. State, 906 N.E.2d 212, 2009 Ind. App. LEXIS 831 (2009).

Access Element.

Access element for an IC 35-49-3-3(a)(2) violation may be satisfied even though a minor is not present; minors only have to have the ability to see or hear the conduct or the ability to be present. M.S. v. State, 889 N.E.2d 900, 2008 Ind. App. LEXIS 1504 (2008).

Collateral Estoppel.

Collateral estoppel applied to civil action, by defendant in prior criminal proceeding under this section, seeking to have this section declared unconstitutional, where the record indicated that the state court found the obscenity statute constitutional in the criminal proceeding. A necessary implicit finding by the state court, coupled with language that indicates awareness of the issues, is sufficient to preclude relitigation. Studio Art Theatre v. City of Evansville, 76 F.3d 128, 1996 U.S. App. LEXIS 1294 (7th Cir. Ind. 1996), cert. denied, 519 U.S. 866, 117 S. Ct. 177, 136 L. Ed. 2d 117, 1996 U.S. LEXIS 5457 (1996).

Construction.

Defendant could not be convicted of more than one count of dissemination of matter harmful to minors based on one occurrence, even if there was more than one victim. Scuro v. State, 849 N.E.2d 682, 2006 Ind. App. LEXIS 1206 (2006).

"Access" is defined as "permission, liberty, or ability to enter, approach, or pass to and from a place or to approach or communicate with a person or thing"; accordingly, under the clear and unambiguous definition of "access," a minor need not be present for there to be a violation of IC 35-49-3-3(a)(5); rather, minor only needs to see or hear the conduct. Zitlaw v. State, 880 N.E.2d 724, 2008 Ind. App. LEXIS 249 (2008).

Phrase "unless each minor is accompanied by the minor's parent or guardian" in IC 35-49-3-3(a)(5) is like an affirmative defense and allows a defendant to show that unaccompanied minors did not have access to the place in question, such as strip bar or X-rated movie house, where unaccompanied minors are not usually allowed; in other words, where an unaccompanied minor has no access, there is no crime. Zitlaw v. State, 880 N.E.2d 724, 2008 Ind. App. LEXIS 249 (2008).

Distance to School or Church.

Straight-line measurement is the appropriate method of determining the distance between a place selling matter harmful to minors and a "school or church." Studio Art Theatre, Inc. v. State, 530 N.E.2d 750, 1988 Ind. App. LEXIS 925 (1988), cert. denied, 494 U.S. 1056, 110 S. Ct. 1523, 108 L. Ed. 2d 763, 1990 U.S. LEXIS 1632 (1990).

Evidence Insufficient.

Because the court had before it no evidence that a store which sold and rented adult videos generated the types of secondary effects that could justify the "within 500 feet of a church or school" restriction contained in IC 35-49-3-3(a)(3), the store was granted an injunction which enjoined enforcement of the statute. Video-Home-One, Inc. v. Brizzi, — F. Supp. 2d —, 2005 U.S. Dist. LEXIS 31151 (S.D. Ind. 2005).

Evidence was insufficient to support defendant's convictions for attempted sexual misconduct with a minor and attempted dissemination of matter harmful to minors as the detectives who were conducting the online sting operation were not less than 18 years old. Gibbs v. State, 898 N.E.2d 1240, 2008 Ind. App. LEXIS 2623 (2008).

Evidence Sufficient.

Although nudity alone is not enough to make material legally obscene, where a tape showed defendant naked and engaging in intimate activity with a woman near a bed, the evidence was sufficient to support the conclusion that defendant disseminated matter to a minor that was harmful to minors. Lewis v. State, 726 N.E.2d 836, 2000 Ind. App. LEXIS 508 (2000).

Evidence that defendant broke into home and masturbated in front of eight-year-old girl supported conviction for burglary. Sloan v. State, 794 N.E.2d 1128, 2003 Ind. App. LEXIS 1644 (2003).

The trial court properly refused to dismiss a charge of engaging in a performance harmful to minors under IC 35-49-3-3(a)(5) where defendant was accused of exposing himself to an officer in a public park in order to get the officer to engage in oral sex because subsection did not require the actual presence of a minor, it was unnecessary for the state to name specific minor victims or to include the phrase "unless each minor is accompanied by the minor's parent or guardian" in the information, IC 35-49-3-3 and IC 35-49-2-2 were not unconstitutionally vague, and defendant's alleged conduct of exposing himself in a public park for the purpose of engaging in oral sex clearly fell within the conduct proscribed by the statutes. Zitlaw v. State, 880 N.E.2d 724, 2008 Ind. App. LEXIS 249 (2008).

Defendant knew for purposes of IC 35-41-2-2 and IC 35-49-2-2 that a DVD containing nudity and sexual content was playing on a screen mounted in defendant's rearview window for purposes of IC 35-49-3-3 as a duplicate screen was in the center console between defendant and a passenger, and the DVD that was playing on the video screen in the rearview window was housed in the unit on the center console. M.S. v. State, 889 N.E.2d 900, 2008 Ind. App. LEXIS 1504 (2008).

Access element for defendant's IC 35-49-3-3(a)(2) adjudication as a delinquent was satisfied as defendant was driving on a busy street near a fairground with a DVD mounted on the rearview window playing material that contained nudity and sexual content; the area was a public area, and minors had both auditory and visual access to what occurred in the rear window of defendant's vehicle. M.S. v. State, 889 N.E.2d 900, 2008 Ind. App. LEXIS 1504 (2008).

Statute of Limitations.

Where time is not of the essence of the offense, the state is not confined to proving the commission on the date alleged in the affidavit or indictment, but may prove the commission at any time within the statutory period of limitations. Thus, in a trial for exhibiting obscene material and disseminating matter harmful to minors, the question is whether the film viewed by the jury was exhibited and displayed to the minor victim at any time within the statutory period of limitations. Walters v. State, 495 N.E.2d 734, 1986 Ind. LEXIS 1217 (1986).

Cited:

State v. Shelton, 692 N.E.2d 947, 1998 Ind. App.

LEXIS 348 (1998); Windhorst v. State, 868 N.E.2d
504, 2007 Ind. LEXIS 489 (2007).

OPINIONS OF ATTORNEY GENERAL

A city-county council may not enact an ordinance restricting the display of "sexually provocative written, photographic, printed, sound or published material" which the ordinance declared "to be harmful to minors" since an Indiana law on displaying matter harmful to minors, this section already exists. 1986, No. 86-8, p. 186.

RESEARCH REFERENCES

Res Gestae.
Criminal Justice Notes 1/08-2/08: Performance harmful to minors (even without minors), 51 (No. 8) Res Gestae 39 (2008).

Valparaiso University Law Review.
Children and Pornography: An Interest Analysis in System Perspective, 19 Val. U.L. Rev. 441 (1985).

Collateral References.
Validity of state statutes and administrative regulations regulating internet communications under commerce clause and First Amendment of federal constitution. 98 A.L.R.5th 167.

35-49-3-4. Defenses.

It is a defense to a prosecution under section 3 [IC 35-49-3-3] of this chapter for the defendant to show:

(1) That the matter was disseminated or that the performance was performed for legitimate scientific or educational purposes;

(2) That the matter was disseminated or displayed to or that the performance was performed before the recipient by a bona fide school, museum, or public library that qualifies for certain property tax exemptions under IC 6-1.1-10, or by an employee of such a school, museum, or public library acting within the scope of his employment;

(3) That he had reasonable cause to believe that the minor involved was eighteen (18) years old or older and that the minor exhibited to the defendant a draft card, driver's license, birth certificate, or other official or apparently official document purporting to establish that the minor was eighteen (18) years old or older; or

(4) That he was a salesclerk, motion picture projectionist, usher, or ticket taker, acting within the scope of his employment and that he had no financial interest in the place where he was so employed.

History.
IC 35-49-3-4, as added by P.L.311-1983, § 33.

ARTICLE 50

SENTENCES

CHAPTER 1

GENERAL PROVISIONS

35-50-1-1. Authority to sentence.

The court shall fix the penalty of and sentence a person convicted of an offense.

History.
IC 35-50-1-1, as added by Acts 1976, P.L.148, § 8; 1977, P.L.340, § 110.

NOTES TO DECISIONS

Analysis

In General.
Applicability to Infractions.
Due Process.
Failure of Jury to Impose Sentence.
Failure to Instruct Jury.
Fixing of Punishment a Judicial Function.
Increase in Sentence.
Jury Instructions.
Jury Sentencing Abolished.
Order in Limine.
Restitution.
Right to Trial by Jury Unaffected.
Sentence Enhancement.
Sentence Not Stated in Verdict.
Sentence Under Former Provisions.

In General.

Where defendant was convicted after jury trial of misdemeanor of driving while under the influence of intoxicating liquor, it was the jury's function to fix the fine and imprisonment and it was error for the judge in the trial court to instruct otherwise. Shewmaker v. State, 236 Ind. 49, 138 N.E.2d 290, 1956 Ind. LEXIS 241 (1956).

The general rule is that the Supreme Court will not invade the province of the legislature or the jury and impose a different sentence from that authorized by law or issued by the jury. Manuel v. State, 267 Ind. 436, 370 N.E.2d 904, 1977 Ind. LEXIS 525 (1977).

Trial court was permitted to fix the penalty of and sentence a person convicted of an offense, and it was entitled to sentence defendant on both theft and burglary convictions arising out of defendant's breaking into the home of defendant's parents and taking property of value from it, as the burglary and theft convictions were allowed to merge and defendant could be sentenced on both convictions as such sentencing did not violate double jeopardy. Payne v. State, 777 N.E.2d 63, 2002 Ind. App. LEXIS 1739 (2002).

Applicability to Infractions.

The mandate of this section, as to trial sentencing upon conviction of an offense, has no applicability to a civil judgment entered on a finding of a violation of an infraction. Horne v. State, 572 N.E.2d 1333, 1991 Ind. App. LEXIS 945 (1991).

Due Process.

Where the term imposed by the trial court was the least the jury could have imposed for the offense of which the jury convicted defendant, defendant was not denied due process even though the trial court did not submit the question of appropriate punishment to the jury. Kelsie v. Trigg, 657 F.2d 155, 1981 U.S. App. LEXIS 18353 (7th Cir. Ind. 1981) (decided under former IC 35-8-2-1).

Failure of Jury to Impose Sentence.

Under the former IC 35-8-2-1 which provided for jury sentencing, failure of the jury to impose sentence was considered fundamental error and resulted in a reduction of the defendant's sentence to the minimum penalty. Bates v. State, 178 Ind. App. 153, 381 N.E.2d 552, 1978 Ind. App. LEXIS 1074 (1978).

Where crime was committed prior to October 1, 1977, although trial was held thereafter, the jury alone had the power to fix the punishment for a determinate sentence and if the jury did not fix the penalty the judge could not fix a penalty for more than the minimum period. Haskett v. State, 271 Ind. 648, 395 N.E.2d 229, 1979 Ind. LEXIS 731 (1979).

Failure to Instruct Jury.

It was reversible error for court to fail to instruct jury that the penalty for kidnapping was life imprisonment. Kocher v. State, 270 Ind. 661, 389 N.E.2d 18, 1979 Ind. LEXIS 618 (1979). See, however, Debose v. State, 270 Ind. 675, 389 N.E.2d 272, 1979 Ind. LEXIS 588 (1979) decided under new Criminal Code holding that it is not necessary to instruct jury as to penalty of offense.

Fixing of Punishment a Judicial Function.

It was not error to instruct the jury that in the event of a guilty verdict the fixing of punishment was a judicial function and not the concern of the jury. Garcia v. State, 271 Ind. 510, 394 N.E.2d 106, 1979 Ind. LEXIS 711 (1979).

Judge who asked administrators of penal institution if they could provide adequate and necessary medical treatment for defendant improperly delegated his duty or function to hear and weigh the evidence and make the determination himself. Naked City, Inc. v. State, 460 N.E.2d 151, 1984 Ind. App. LEXIS 2276 (1984).

Increase in Sentence.

There was no error in the court's increasing the defendant's sentence prior to any entry being made in the court's record book, after the defendant, after hearing the initial sentence, began to use rude and profane language toward the judge, since the amended sentence was not manifestly unreasonable in light of the defendant's character and numerous prior offenses. Coleman v. State, 490 N.E.2d 711, 1986 Ind. LEXIS 1055 (1986).

Jury Instructions.

Inasmuch as juries have no duties or powers as to penalties imposed, it is improper for trial judge to permit discussion of possible penalties at request of either party. Williamson v. State, 436 N.E.2d 90, 1982 Ind. LEXIS 841 (1982).

It is error to instruct jury as to penalty involved upon conviction under habitual offender statute, since under present statutory scheme the jury is to play no role in sentencing defendants. Erickson v. State, 438 N.E.2d 269, 1982 Ind. LEXIS 911 (1982).

Inclusion in instructions that a given offense was a certain class of felony did not violate the prohibition against informing the jury as to penalty. Short v. State, 443 N.E.2d 298, 1982 Ind. LEXIS 1063 (1982).

The court does not err in refusing to instruct the jury that the crime charged is a Class D felony. It is only necessary to instruct the jury on the matters necessary for them to adequately understand the case and arrive at a fair verdict, and the fact that the crime is a felony or, specifically, a Class D felony is not necessary information for the jury. Pursuant to this section, fixing the penalty and sentencing the defendant is the function of the court. Wilder v. State, 498 N.E.2d 1295, 1986 Ind. App. LEXIS 3085 (1986).

Though instructions informing the jury of specific penalties are irrelevant, instructions which relieve the jury of any speculation about the sentencing procedure and allow the jury to concentrate on the guilt or innocence of the defendant are permissible. Hatchett v. State, 503 N.E.2d 398, 1987 Ind. LEXIS 823 (1987).

An instruction that, "A person who is convicted of a crime by a jury is sentenced by a judge. By law the judge must hold a sentencing hearing in which a written pre-sentence report and all matters in mitigation and aggravation are considered. After the hearing the judge may have various sentencing alternatives, including imprisonment within a certain range. That is why these instructions do not contain any information concerning the penalties that could be imposed upon a conviction," is not misleading nor confusing because it implies defendant may not be imprisoned if found guilty and is a correct statement of the law. Only the trial court has authority to determine the proper penalty to be given upon a conviction. Willis v. State, 510 N.E.2d 1354, 1987 Ind. LEXIS 1002 (1987), cert. denied, 484 U.S. 1015, 108 S. Ct. 721, 98 L. Ed. 2d 670, 1988 U.S. LEXIS 144 (1988).

Jury Sentencing Abolished.

This provision abolishes jury sentencing. Debose v. State, 270 Ind. 675, 389 N.E.2d 272, 1979 Ind. LEXIS 588 (1979).

Order in Limine.

It did not violate defendant's constitutional rights for court to issue order in limine prohibiting any references pertaining to penalties. Inman v. State, 271 Ind. 491, 393 N.E.2d 767, 1979 Ind. LEXIS 707 (1979).

Restitution.

Although a judge has broad discretion in sentencing he is required to act within the statutorily prescribed limits, and there being no statute providing for the imposition of restitution the imposition of restitution as part of a sentence was a nullity. Barnett v. State, 414 N.E.2d 965, 1981 Ind. App. LEXIS 1216 (1981), superseded by statute as stated in, Smith v. State, 471 N.E.2d 1245, 1984 Ind. App. LEXIS 3182 (1984).

Right to Trial by Jury Unaffected.

A defendant's right to trial by jury is not offended by a statutory scheme which does not require the jury to fix the punishment of the defendant. Williams v. State, 271 Ind. 656, 395 N.E.2d 239, 1979 Ind. LEXIS 734 (1979); Rogers v. State, 272 Ind. 65, 396 N.E.2d 348, 1979 Ind. LEXIS 748 (1979); Wells v. State, 397 N.E.2d 1250, 1979 Ind. App. LEXIS 1481 (1979); Collins v. State, 275 Ind. 86, 415 N.E.2d 46, 1981 Ind. LEXIS 657 (1981), cert. denied, 451 U.S. 991, 101 S. Ct. 2331, 68 L. Ed. 2d 851, 1981 U.S. LEXIS 2139 (1981).

Provision that court shall fix punishment does not violate the right of a trial by jury. Boyd v. State, 396 N.E.2d 920, 1979 Ind. App. LEXIS 1430 (1979).

Sentence Enhancement.

Use of defendant's juvenile adjudications to enhance defendant's sentence for theft and auto theft beyond statutorily prescribed minimum sentence was improper and violated his Sixth Amendment right to trial by jury; juvenile convictions are not prior convictions under Blakely/Apprendi. Pinkston v. State, 836 N.E.2d 453, 2005 Ind. App. LEXIS 2036 (2005).

Sentence Not Stated in Verdict.

Where only one sentence was prescribed by the statute there was no error in the failure of the jury to state the sentence in its verdict. Davis v. State, 271 Ind. 676, 395 N.E.2d 232, 1979 Ind. LEXIS 735 (1979).

Sentence Under Former Provisions.

Where a defendant was sentenced under the old criminal code prior to the effective date of the new criminal code he was not entitled to be resentenced under the new criminal code. Davidovic v. State, 408 N.E.2d 647, 1980 Ind. App. LEXIS 1638 (1980).

Cited:

Kocher v. State, 270 Ind. 661, 389 N.E.2d 18, 1979 Ind. LEXIS 618 (1979); Lyda v. State, 272 Ind. 15, 395 N.E.2d 776, 1979 Ind. LEXIS 755 (1979); Bumgardner v. State, 422 N.E.2d 1244,

1981 Ind. LEXIS 794 (1981); Cornelius v. State, 425 N.E.2d 616, 1981 Ind. LEXIS 818 (1981); State v. Williams, 430 N.E.2d 756, 1982 Ind. LEXIS 730 (1982); Naked City, Inc. v. State, 434 N.E.2d 576, 1982 Ind. App. LEXIS 1170 (1982); Schiro v. State, 451 N.E.2d 1047, 1983 Ind. LEXIS 904 (1983); Stafford v. State, 455 N.E.2d 402, 1983 Ind. App. LEXIS 3505 (1983); Haskett v. State, 467 N.E.2d 32, 1984 Ind. App. LEXIS 2910 (1984); Stout v. State, 479 N.E.2d 563, 1985 Ind. LEXIS 888 (1985); Komyatti v. State, 490 N.E.2d 279, 1986 Ind. LEXIS 1063 (1986); Boyd v. Broglin, 519 N.E.2d 541, 1988 Ind. LEXIS 81 (1988).

RESEARCH REFERENCES

Indiana Law Review.

Survey: Criminal Law and Procedure: Recent Developments in Indiana Criminal Law and Procedure (October 1, 2003, to September 30, 2004), 38 Ind. L. Rev. 999 (2005).

Collateral References.

Guilty plea as affected by fact that sentence

contemplated by plea bargain is subsequently determined to be illegal or unauthorized. 87 A.L.R.4th 384.

When does delay in imposing sentence violate speedy trial provision. 86 A.L.R.4th 340.

35-50-1-2. Consecutive and concurrent terms — Considerations — Maximum for enhanced penalty.

(a) As used in this section, "crime of violence" means the following:

(1) Murder (IC 35-42-1-1).
(2) Attempted murder (IC 35-41-5-1).
(3) Voluntary manslaughter (IC 35-42-1-3).
(4) Involuntary manslaughter (IC 35-42-1-4).
(5) Reckless homicide (IC 35-42-1-5).
(6) Aggravated battery (IC 35-42-2-1.5).
(7) Kidnapping (IC 35-42-3-2).
(8) Rape (IC 35-42-4-1).
(9) Criminal deviate conduct (IC 35-42-4-2).
(10) Child molesting (IC 35-42-4-3).
(11) Sexual misconduct with a minor as a Class A felony under IC 35-42-4-9(a)(2) or a Class B felony under IC 35-42-4-9(b)(2).
(12) Robbery as a Class A felony or a Class B felony (IC 35-42-5-1).
(13) Burglary as a Class A felony or a Class B felony (IC 35-43-2-1).
(14) Operating a motor vehicle while intoxicated causing death (IC 9-30-5-5).
(15) Operating a motor vehicle while intoxicated causing serious bodily injury to another person (IC 9-30-5-4).
(16) Resisting law enforcement as a felony (IC 35-44-3-3).

(b) As used in this section, "episode of criminal conduct" means offenses or a connected series of offenses that are closely related in time, place, and circumstance.

(c) Except as provided in subsection (d) or (e), the court shall determine whether terms of imprisonment shall be served concurrently or consecutively. The court may consider the:

(1) aggravating circumstances in IC 35-38-1-7.1(a); and
(2) mitigating circumstances in IC 35-38-1-7.1(b);

in making a determination under this subsection. The court may order terms of imprisonment to be served consecutively even if the sentences are not imposed at the same time. However, except for crimes of violence, the total of the consecutive terms of imprisonment, exclusive of terms of imprisonment under IC 35-50-2-8 and IC 35-50-2-10, to which the defendant is sentenced for felony convictions arising out of an episode of criminal conduct shall not exceed the advisory sentence for a felony which is one (1) class of felony higher than the most serious of the felonies for which the person has been convicted.

(d) If, after being arrested for one (1) crime, a person commits another crime:

(1) before the date the person is discharged from probation, parole, or a term of imprisonment imposed for the first crime; or

(2) while the person is released:

(A) upon the person's own recognizance; or

(B) on bond;

the terms of imprisonment for the crimes shall be served consecutively, regardless of the order in which the crimes are tried and sentences are imposed.

(e) If the factfinder determines under IC 35-50-2-11 that a person used a firearm in the commission of the offense for which the person was convicted, the term of imprisonment for the underlying offense and the additional term of imprisonment imposed under IC 35-50-2-11 must be served consecutively.

History.
IC 35-50-1-2, as added by Acts 1976, P.L.148, § 8; 1977, P.L.340, § 111; P.L.330-1987, § 1; P.L.164-1994, § 1; P.L.304-1995, § 1; P.L.203-1996, § 7; P.L.219-1997, § 1; P.L.228-2001, § 6; P.L.266-2003, § 2; P.L.71-2005, § 4; P.L.213-2005, § 4; P.L.1-2006, § 549; P.L.126-2008, § 12, eff. July 1, 2008.

Compiler's Notes.
P.L.126-2008, § 13, effective July 1, 2008, provides:
"IC 9-26-1-1, IC 9-26-1-2, IC 9-26-1-6, IC 9-26-1-8, IC 9-26-1-9, IC 9-30-5-3, IC 9-30-5-10, and IC 35-50-1-2, all as amended by this act, apply only to crimes committed after June 30, 2008."

NOTES TO DECISIONS

ANALYSIS

In General.
Constitutionality.
Aggravating Factors.
—Lack of Remorse.
—Not Shown.
Amelioration.
—In General.
—Inapplicable.
Concurrent Sentences.
Consecutive Sentences.
—In General.
—Attempted Murder.
—Contemporaneous Sentencing.
—Enhancement.
—Excessive.
—Federal Sentences.
—Improper.
— —Correction.
—Misdemeanor Convictions.
—Mistrial.
—Modification.
—Pending Charges.
—Presumptive Sentence for Next Greater Offense.
—Prior Commission of Offense.
—Procedure.
—Probation Revocation.
—Proper.
—Serious Bodily Injury.
—Seriousness and Crime.
—Severance.
—Subsequent Offense.
—Vacation of Prior Conviction.
Construction.
—"On Bond".

—Term of Imprisonment.
Crime Committed Pending Appeal.
Crime Committed While Free on Bail.
Crime Committed While on Probation or Parole.
—Probation Granted Prior to Enactment.
—Sentence Prior to Probation Revocation.
Crimes of Violence.
Cruel and Unusual Punishment.
Discretion of Court.
—Considerations.
—Constitutional Prohibitions.
Effective Date.
—Law in Effect When Crime Committed.
Effect of Amendment.
—1994 Amendment.
—1995 Amendment.
Episode of Criminal Conduct.
—Not Shown.
—Shown.
Ex Post Facto Doctrine.
Felony Conviction.
—Theft.
Incarceration in Another State.
Mandatory Sentencing.
Merger.
Mitigating Circumstances.
Parole.
Plea Agreements.
Record.
—Harmless Error.
Refusal to Instruct Jury on This Section.
Review.
Sentence Enhancement.
Separate Episodes.
Statement of Reasons.

—Insufficient.
—Review.
Violation of Probation.
—Proof.

In General.
There is no constitutional right to have sentences run concurrently. Phillips v. State, 425 N.E.2d 119, 1981 Ind. LEXIS 809 (1981); Burnett v. State, 439 N.E.2d 174, 1982 Ind. App. LEXIS 1361 (Ind. App. 1982), criticized, Emerson v. State, 498 N.E.2d 1301, 1986 Ind. App. LEXIS 3082 (1986).

The mandatory part of this section, formerly subsection (b) as it existed prior to the 1995 amendments, only applies if a defendant is on probation, parole, or serving a term of imprisonment at the time the other offenses were committed. Haggard v. State, 445 N.E.2d 969, 1983 Ind. LEXIS 772 (1983), overruled in part, Woodson v. State, 778 N.E.2d 475, 2002 Ind. App. LEXIS 1898 (2002).

Trial courts are permitted to determine whether the terms of imprisonment they impose shall be served concurrently or consecutively by considering aggravating and mitigating circumstances; however, when the trial court finds those circumstances in balance, there is no basis on which to impose consecutive terms. Wentz v. State, 766 N.E.2d 351, 2002 Ind. LEXIS 315 (2002).

Constitutionality.
This section does not constitute an unlawful delegation of legislative power. Mott v. State, 273 Ind. 216, 402 N.E.2d 986, 1980 Ind. LEXIS 659 (1980).

Fact that a defendant in one part of the state might receive concurrent sentences while a defendant in another part of the state might receive consecutive sentences does not make this section a local law in violation of Ind. Const., art. 4, § 22. Mott v. State, 273 Ind. 216, 402 N.E.2d 986, 1980 Ind. LEXIS 659 (1980).

Consecutive sentences under IC 35-50-1-2(c) for two counts of child solicitation premised on trial judge's discretionary findings on certain factors was constitutional. Smylie v. State, 823 N.E.2d 679, 2005 Ind. LEXIS 199 (2005), cert. denied, 126 S. Ct. 545, 163 L. Ed. 2d 459, 2005 U.S. LEXIS 7865 (U.S. 2005), superseded by statute as stated in, Anglemyer v. State, 868 N.E.2d 482, 2007 Ind. LEXIS 490 (2007), superseded by statute as stated in, McMahon v. State, 856 N.E.2d 743, 2006 Ind. App. LEXIS 2333 (2006).

Aggravating Factors.

—Lack of Remorse.
The court did not err in identifying lack of remorse as an aggravating factor. Salone v. State, 652 N.E.2d 552, 1995 Ind. App. LEXIS 783 (1995).

—Not Shown.
Trial court affirmed defendant's convictions on charges of rape, criminal confinement, sexual battery, battery on a police officer, and public intoxication, but remanded the case for further proceedings because the statement which the trial judge made on the record when he imposed sentence did not show that he found at least one aggravating factor that justified his decision to order that defendant serve his sentences consecutively. Wood v. State, 804 N.E.2d 1182, 2004 Ind. App. LEXIS 436 (2004).

Amelioration.

—In General.
Under the doctrine of amelioration, when the penalty for a crime is decreased by an ameliorative amendment enacted after the commission of the crime but before the defendant's sentencing, the defendant may take advantage of the ameliorative amendment. Tedlock v. State, 656 N.E.2d 273, 1995 Ind. App. LEXIS 1146 (1995).

A trial court erred when it sentenced the defendant to an aggregate sentence of more than 10 years for convictions on two counts of attempted battery with a deadly weapon, because the defendant was sentenced after the legislature had enacted an ameliorative amendment to the sentencing statute without including a savings clause, thus making it applicable to the sentence at issue. Martin v. State, 714 N.E.2d 1140, 1999 Ind. App. LEXIS 1208 (1999).

—Inapplicable.
The law in effect when crime was committed and defendant was originally sentenced controlled defendant's sentence on remand, and he was not entitled to the ameliorative benefits of a subsequent amendment, where only portion of original sentencing order requiring sentences run concurrently was vacated. Riffe v. State, 675 N.E.2d 710, 1996 Ind. App. LEXIS 1725 (1996).

Defendant's sentence properly fell within the parameters of this section in force at the time he was sentenced, and he was not entitled to ameliorative amendment prohibiting the total of consecutive terms of imprisonment to exceed the presumptive sentence for a felony one class higher. Pritscher v. State, 675 N.E.2d 727, 1996 Ind. App. LEXIS 1739 (1996).

IC 35-50-2-1.3 did not limit a defendant's consecutive sentences for vehicular homicide to four-year advisory sentences because he committed his crimes before the statute went into effect, and the amelioration doctrine did not require its retroactive application because it was not ameliorative, as it did not limit, beyond IC 35-50-1-2, a trial court's ability to impose consecutive sentences. Barber v. State, 863 N.E.2d 1199, 2007 Ind. App. LEXIS 695 (2007).

Concurrent Sentences.
If the trial court specifically finds no aggravating circumstances are present, and former subsection (b), as it existed prior to the 1995 amendments, does not apply, terms of imprisonment must be imposed to run concurrently with one another. Taylor v. State, 442 N.E.2d 1087, 1982 Ind. LEXIS 1061 (1982).

Where the trial court wanted to impose concurrent sentences for the present crimes because

Concurrent Sentences. (Cont'd)

defendant was 47 years old and in ill health, but, the court imposed consecutive sentences after concluding that his status as a parolee made doing so mandatory under IC 35-50-1-2, the case was remanded to allow the trial court to do what it wanted in the first place: Impose concurrent sentences for the three present offenses, to be served consecutively to any time to be served for violating his out-of-state parole. Le Master v. State, 498 N.E.2d 1185, 1986 Ind. LEXIS 1297 (1986).

Where plaintiff did not suffer any harm by being sentenced to serve concurrent instead of consecutive time, but rather benefited from being able to serve the time concurrently, denial of post-conviction petition was proper. Moredock v. State, 693 N.E.2d 961, 1998 Ind. App. LEXIS 435 (1998).

Trial court did not err in sentencing defendant to 65 years in prison for defendant's shooting of a man who allegedly owed money to defendant, and one year, to be served concurrently, for defendant's carrying of a handgun without a license, which would be served consecutive to an 18-year sentence imposed upon defendant in another cause; the trial court was not required to impose the advisory sentence upon defendant in the current case because the sentences imposed were concurrent sentences, not consecutive sentences, and the consecutive sentence involved was for a crime imposed in another cause not in the current cause. Dixson v. State, 865 N.E.2d 704, 2007 Ind. App. LEXIS 913 (2007).

Concurrent sentences were proper for three out of six crimes for which defendant was convicted where sentencing judge ruled that the three constituted an episode of criminal conduct, i.e., offenses or a connected series of offenses closely related in time, place, and circumstance. Beer v. State, 885 N.E.2d 33, 2008 Ind. App. LEXIS 952 (2008).

Consecutive Sentences.

Where the defendant had more than an adequate opportunity following the first crimes, to conform his behavior to the dictates of the law and, thereby, avoid a consecutive sentence for the second crimes, no constitutional rights of the defendant were violated by the consecutive sentencing. Garrett v. State, 411 N.E.2d 692, 1980 Ind. App. LEXIS 1733 (1980), disapproved, Sides v. State, 490 N.E.2d 318, 1986 Ind. LEXIS 1053 (1986).

The trial court did not subject the defendant to a manifestly unreasonable punishment nor deny him due process in ordering him to serve four sentences on a consecutive basis, where the offenses arose out of the confinement, robbery and repeated sexual attacks on a young woman by three men over a period of several hours, the degree and extent of participation varied among the three defendants, though not attributable to any of the defendants' unwillingness to become involved or their concern for the mental and physical welfare of the victim, that several different offenses had been committed by each defendant, sometimes in simultaneous fashion, these offenses were "heinous, despicable, atrocious and disgust-

ing," and the record clearly showed that the defendant was an active and willing, if sometimes unable, participant in the night's events. Bish v. State, 421 N.E.2d 608, 1981 Ind. LEXIS 758 (1981).

At the very least the judge had to be able to articulate facts in the case that supported a finding of the presence of at least one of the aggravating circumstances listed in former IC 35-50-1A-7 before consecutive terms of imprisonment may be imposed. Taylor v. State, 442 N.E.2d 1087, 1982 Ind. LEXIS 1061 (1982).

Where a defendant confined, attempted to molest, and battered a minor victim in a vicious way, the trial court's imposition of consecutive sentences was not manifestly unreasonable in light of the nature of the offenses and the character of the offender. Barham v. State, 454 N.E.2d 392, 1983 Ind. LEXIS 987 (1983).

When a court imposes consecutive terms of imprisonment, the record should disclose articulated facts that support a finding of the presence of at least one of the aggravating circumstances delineated in former IC 35-38-1-7(b). Brown v. State, 497 N.E.2d 1049, 1986 Ind. LEXIS 1281 (1986).

A history of criminal activity is specifically contemplated as an aggravating circumstance by former IC 35-38-1-7(b)(2) and is a valid basis for the imposition of consecutive sentences. Brown v. State, 497 N.E.2d 1049, 1986 Ind. LEXIS 1281 (1986).

Where a new conviction may constitute a parole violation for which the defendant could be returned to prison, this section requires that the sentences for the present offenses be served consecutive to any time resulting from the parole violation, but this section does not require that each of the sentences for the present crimes be served consecutively to each other, although the trial court could find aggravating circumstances which outweigh any mitigating circumstances and order consecutive sentences for the present offenses. Le Master v. State, 498 N.E.2d 1185, 1986 Ind. LEXIS 1297 (1986).

When a sentence is imposed, the commencement of that sentence cannot be delayed absent specific statutory authorization, and where there is not indication of whether or not the mandatory provision of this section was applicable, the trial judge must give specific reasons for imposing a consecutive sentence; if the record is silent as to any explanation for the order requiring the sentences to run consecutive to any time to be imposed in an unrelated case the cause will be remanded to the trial court with instructions to conduct a new sentencing hearing to specify the legal authority and justification for the consecutive sentence order, or in the alternative to drop it. Erby v. State, 511 N.E.2d 302, 1987 Ind. LEXIS 1004 (1987).

Where defendant pled guilty to kidnapping, rape, criminal deviate conduct, and robbery and was sentenced to consecutive terms totaling 100 years, it was held that the robbery charge has reduced significance compared to the Class A felonies and should be ordered served concurrently, but, in view of defendant's criminal record and pending serious charges of kidnapping of a mother

Consecutive Sentences. (Cont'd)

and her three-year-old child, rape, and criminal deviate conduct, there was justification to require defendant serve his three 30-year presumptive sentences upon the kidnapping, rape, and criminal deviate conduct convictions consecutively. Kubiak v. State, 508 N.E.2d 559, 1987 Ind. App. LEXIS 2718 (1987).

Formerly, subsection (b) of this section required that defendant's sentence for the offense of battery be served consecutively to the sentences for any offenses for which he had been convicted at the time he committed the instant offense and from which he had not been discharged from probation at the time of sentencing for the instant offense. Scott v. State, 632 N.E.2d 761, 1994 Ind. App. LEXIS 386 (1994).

Trial courts may order consecutive sentences only where there is express statutory authority to do so. Harris v. State, 671 N.E.2d 864, 1996 Ind. App. LEXIS 1109 (1996).

Where the defendant was sentenced after the statute went into effect, the trial court had the authority to impose the sentence consecutive to the sentence in another case even though the two sentences were not contemporaneously imposed. Berry v. State, 689 N.E.2d 444, 1997 Ind. LEXIS 244 (1997).

Trial court improperly considered defendant's convictions on charges of attempted murder, robbery, attempted robbery, and criminal confinement in imposing consecutive sentences totaling 122 years where, at time defendant was sentenced, IC 35-50-1-2(c) did not include attempted murder as "crime of violence," did not include robbery or attempted robbery as Class C felonies, and did not include criminal confinement as Class B felony. Hawkins v. State, 794 N.E.2d 1158, 2003 Ind. App. LEXIS 1697 (2003).

Defendant's enhanced and consecutive sentences, amounting to 150 years, for rape, criminal deviate conduct, and criminal confinement were proper given defendant's long criminal history. Foster v. State, 795 N.E.2d 1078, 2003 Ind. App. LEXIS 1734 (2003), overruled in part, Rutherford v. State, 866 N.E.2d 867, 2007 Ind. App. LEXIS 1086 (2007), overruled in part, Stewart v. State, 866 N.E.2d 858, 2007 Ind. App. LEXIS 1085 (2007).

Where orders of judgment of conviction failed to reflect court's oral statement that defendant's convictions in separate bench trials were to be served consecutively, sentence was not facially erroneous, despite state's claim that defendant was required to serve sentences consecutively because defendant was out on bond when he committed second offense; accordingly, state's motion to correct sentence was improper remedy, and since 30-day deadline for direct appeals or post-conviction proceedings had elapsed, state had no remedy to challenge sentence. Hoggatt v. State, 805 N.E.2d 1281, 2004 Ind. App. LEXIS 606 (2004).

Consecutive sentences under IC 35-50-1-2(c) for two counts of child solicitation premised on trial judge's discretionary findings on certain factors was constitutional. Smylie v. State, 823 N.E.2d

679, 2005 Ind. LEXIS 199 (2005), cert. denied, 126 S. Ct. 545, 163 L. Ed. 2d 459, 2005 U.S. LEXIS 7865 (U.S. 2005), superseded by statute as stated in, Anglemyer v. State, 868 N.E.2d 482, 2007 Ind. LEXIS 490 (2007), superseded by statute as stated in, McMahon v. State, 856 N.E.2d 743, 2006 Ind. App. LEXIS 2333 (2006).

Although the ability to recount each charge without referring to the other can provide additional guidance on the question of whether a defendant's conduct constitutes a single episode of criminal conduct for purposes of consecutive sentencing under former IC 35-52-1-2, it is not a critical ingredient in resolving the question. Rather, IC 35-52-1-2(b) speaks in less absolute terms: a connected series of offenses that are closely connected in time, place, and circumstance. Harris v. State, 861 N.E.2d 1182, 2007 Ind. LEXIS 101 (2007).

IC 35-50-2-1.3 adds no restrictions on the ability of trial courts to impose consecutive sentences beyond the restrictions already in place by virtue of IC 35-50-1-2(c). Barber v. State, 863 N.E.2d 1199, 2007 Ind. App. LEXIS 695 (2007).

—In General.

"Appropriate advisory sentence" in IC 35-50-2-1.3, which references IC 35-50-1-2, refers to the total penalty for an episode of criminal conduct; the advisory sentence for a felony which is one class of felony higher than the most serious of the felonies for which the person has been convicted is the "appropriate advisory sentence" for an episode of non-violent criminal conduct. IC 35-50-1-2 in no other way limits the ability of a trial court to impose consecutive sentences; in turn, IC 35-50-2-1.3 imposes no additional restrictions on the ability of trial courts to impose consecutive sentences, and thus is not ameliorative. White v. State, 849 N.E.2d 735, 2006 Ind. App. LEXIS 1198 (2006).

IC 35-50-2-1.3 was not ameliorative and thus did not apply to a defendant whose crimes were committed before it took effect. Even if the statute had been in effect at the time of the offenses, it would not have aided defendant because it placed no restrictions on the ability of trial courts to impose consecutive sentences beyond the restrictions already in place by virtue of IC 35-50-1-2(c). White v. State, 849 N.E.2d 735, 2006 Ind. App. LEXIS 1198 (2006).

—Attempted Murder.

It was not error for court to order sentence for attempted murder to run consecutively to sentences for criminal confinement and sex related offenses. Merrifield v. State, 272 Ind. 579, 400 N.E.2d 146, 1980 Ind. LEXIS 604 (1980).

Trial court did not err in sentencing defendant to 220 years for murder, burglary, three counts of attempted murder, and criminal deviate conduct where his convictions for attempted murder were exempted from the term of imprisonment limitation imposed by this section because he knowingly and intentionally caused serious bodily injury. Greer v. State, 684 N.E.2d 1140, 1997 Ind. LEXIS 127 (1997).

The statutory limitation on imposing consecu-

Consecutive Sentences. (Cont'd)

—Attempted Murder. (Cont'd)

tive sentences does apply to attempted murder convictions, where there is no evidence of any bodily injury. Payne v. State, 688 N.E.2d 164, 1997 Ind. LEXIS 191 (1997).

Limitations on consecutive sentencing do not apply between crimes of violence and those that are not crimes of violence. Therefore, the trial court made no error by ordering the sentence for attempted murder, not in the list of violent crimes, to run consecutive to the other sentences for the violent crimes of murder and robbery. Williams v. State, 741 N.E.2d 1209, 2001 Ind. LEXIS 73 (2001).

Post-conviction court properly held that trial court did not improperly sentence defendant convicted of murder and attempted murder to serve consecutive terms in prison. Ford v. State, 755 N.E.2d 1138, 2001 Ind. App. LEXIS 1656 (2001).

—Contemporaneous Sentencing.

A trial court erred by ordering a sentence to be served consecutively to a sentence in another criminal case; former subsection (a), as it existed prior to the 1995 amendments, is limited to situations in which the trial court is contemporaneously imposing two sentences. Wright v. State, 590 N.E.2d 650, 1992 Ind. App. LEXIS 558 (1992).

For sentences imposed before 1994 amendment of subsection (a), trial court was limited to imposing consecutive sentences to those occasions when the court was contemporaneously imposing two or more sentences. Weaver v. State, 664 N.E.2d 1169, 1996 Ind. LEXIS 39 (1996).

Under former IC 35-50-1-2(a), a trial court had discretion to impose consecutive sentences when it was sentencing for more than one offense in a single proceeding, and all the offenses did not have to be tried together. Totten v. State, 760 N.E.2d 1074, 2001 Ind. App. LEXIS 2143 (2001).

Where the sentence imposed by the trial court upon the inmate's 1989 guilty plea was consecutive to a sentence imposed upon the inmate in another case, the sentence was improper under former IC 35-50-1-2, as the trial court was not contemporaneously imposing the sentences. Lee v. State, 792 N.E.2d 603, 2003 Ind. App. LEXIS 1362 (2003), transfer granted, 804 N.E.2d 754, 2003 Ind. LEXIS 871 (2003), superseded, 816 N.E.2d 35, 2004 Ind. LEXIS 898 (Ind. 2004).

Under former version of IC 35-50-1-2(a) in effect at time of defendant's conviction for felony murder, discretionary authority of trial court to order consecutive sentences was limited to occasions when court was imposing one or more terms of imprisonment at one time; accordingly, trial court did not have statutory authority to order defendant's sentence to run consecutive to earlier sentence imposed in different county. Stites v. State, 810 N.E.2d 1083, 2004 Ind. App. LEXIS 1207 (2004), transfer granted, 822 N.E.2d 977, 2004 Ind. LEXIS 862 (2004), superseded, 829 N.E.2d 527, 2005 Ind. LEXIS 563 (Ind. 2005).

Under IC 35-50-1-2(c) trial court has discretion to order consecutive sentences even when sen-

tences are not contemporaneously imposed; accordingly, trial court neither violated its statutory authority nor abused its discretion by ordering defendant to serve sentence consecutive to sentence imposed by another county. Dixon v. State, 825 N.E.2d 1269, 2005 Ind. App. LEXIS 719 (2005).

Even though his sentences for robbery and burglary were not imposed at the same time, defendant's sentences were properly made consecutive under IC 35-50-1-2(c) because the burglary sentence was imposed later on the same day as the robbery sentence and defendant had already pleaded guilty to the burglary at the time of the first sentence. Shafer v. State, 856 N.E.2d 752, 2006 Ind. App. LEXIS 2334 (2006).

—Enhancement.

The imposition of aggravated sentences which are to be served consecutively is not vindicative and manifestly unreasonable, where the trial court enhanced the sentences because defendant had at least six prior felonies and approximately 11 misdemeanor convictions, it also found that he had committed a serious and brutal crime in which the victim could have easily died, and it was unable to find any mitigating factors. Anderson v. State, 452 N.E.2d 173, 1983 Ind. App. LEXIS 3217 (1983).

While the existence of more than one aggravator is implied if there is to be both sentence enhancement and consecutive sentences, nevertheless, both the enhancement and the consecutive terms of defendant's sentences were authorized where the post-conviction relief court disposed of defendant's application based upon only one aggravator. Staton v. State, 640 N.E.2d 741, 1994 Ind. App. LEXIS 1336 (1994).

The mandatory application of subdivision (d)(2)(B), requiring that a person who commits a crime while released on bond for another crime serve the resulting sentences consecutively, does not preclude a trial court from imposing an enhanced sentence based upon the same crime for which defendant was released on bond. Thorne v. State, 687 N.E.2d 604, 1997 Ind. App. LEXIS 1658 (1997).

Although the trial court did not expressly state that defendant's sentences for his convictions of attempted murder and burglary were enhanced because the felonies resulted in serious bodily injury, the evidence left no doubt that defendant's sentences were enhanced because of the serious bodily injuries inflicted upon the victim. Hollins v. State, 790 N.E.2d 100, 2003 Ind. App. LEXIS 765 (2003).

Enhanced consecutive sentences were proper because, contrary to defendant's argument, IC 35-50-2-1.3 did not restrict consecutive sentences to advisory sentences; it was within the trial court's discretion to sentence defendant to enhanced consecutive sentences, and defendant did not established an abuse of that discretion. As aggravating circumstances, the trial court considered that there was a substantial risk that defendant would commit future crimes, that the nature and circumstances of the offense were particularly disturbing based on defendant's willingness to

Consecutive Sentences. (Cont'd)

—Enhancement. (Cont'd)
harm himself, and that defendant had a particularly serious criminal history, each of which aggravating circumstances was sufficient to warrant the consecutive sentences. Luhrsen v. State, 864 N.E.2d 452, 2007 Ind. App. LEXIS 773 (2007).

—Excessive.
Where the defendant's crimes were committed within half an hour at the same location, and the offenses thus related closely enough in time, place, and circumstance, to warrant that a full description of either offense could not be related without referring to the details of the other, his offenses consisted of an episode of criminal conduct, and the trial court erred in sentencing him to consecutive sentences in excess of more than the presumptive sentence for the most serious felony. Ballard v. State, 715 N.E.2d 1276, 1999 Ind. App. LEXIS 1494 (1999).

The limitation in this section applied to sentences for attempted murder, and that portion of defendant's sentence for two counts of attempted murder to be served consecutively for a total term of 100 years exceeded the statutory limitation under this section. Ellis v. State, 736 N.E.2d 731, 2000 Ind. LEXIS 973 (2000).

Supreme court revised aggregate sentence of 385 years for 26 counts of child molesting and sexual misconduct involving minor to 90 years because sentence was excessive compared to factually similar cases. Serino v. State, 798 N.E.2d 852, 2003 Ind. LEXIS 982 (2003).

Trial court erred in imposing consecutive sentences that amounted to more than the statutory maximum allowed. Puckett v. State, 843 N.E.2d 959, 2006 Ind. App. LEXIS 469 (2006).

—Federal Sentences.
A trial court may order a defendant's state sentence to be served consecutively to his federal sentence. Sweeney v. State, 704 N.E.2d 86, 1998 Ind. LEXIS 672 (1998), cert. denied, 527 U.S. 1035, 119 S. Ct. 2393, 144 L. Ed. 2d 793, 1999 U.S. LEXIS 4437 (1999).

—Improper.
Where trial court specifically found that there were neither aggravating nor mitigating circumstances, it was error to impose consecutive sentences. Brown v. State, 442 N.E.2d 1109, 1982 Ind. LEXIS 1069 (1982).

Where the record shows that the trial court did consider defendant's prior criminal history, the nature and circumstances of the crimes committed, and defendant's character, but he set out only one reason for imposing a sentence to be served consecutive to the sentence in another county — the mandatory provisions of this section, and the Supreme Court found the mandatory provision was not applicable — the Supreme Court must remand the case for a specific and individualized statement of why the facts in the case support the imposition of consecutive terms. Otherwise, the trial court must impose concurrent sentences. Haggard v. State, 445 N.E.2d 969, 1983 Ind.

LEXIS 772 (1983), overruled in part, Woodson v. State, 778 N.E.2d 475, 2002 Ind. App. LEXIS 1898 (2002).

Where use of a deadly weapon is part of the crimes charged, it will not support imposition of consecutive sentences. Burch v. State, 487 N.E.2d 176, 1985 Ind. App. LEXIS 3091 (1985).

A defendant who has not been sentenced for the first offense at the time he commits the second offense does not fall under the mandatory consecutive sentence provisions. Sides v. State, 490 N.E.2d 318, 1986 Ind. LEXIS 1053 (1986).

Former subsection (b), as it existed prior to the 1995 amendments, did not apply to a defendant who was in jail awaiting trial upon burglary and theft charges. When he participated in an assault upon another prisoner because the defendant was not on parole, probation or serving a term of imprisonment at the time the second offense was committed. Killian v. State, 512 N.E.2d 411, 1987 Ind. LEXIS 1045 (1987).

A court was without authority to impose "consecutive" sentencing when at the time sentence was imposed for an offense the defendant had pleaded guilty to but had not yet been sentenced upon another defense. Frazier v. State, 512 N.E.2d 215, 1987 Ind. App. LEXIS 3014 (1987).

Sentencing court exceeded its legislative authorization when it imposed consecutive felony sentences, both of which were enhanced by 30 years, because of habitual offender status, at a single criminal trial. Starks v. State, 523 N.E.2d 735, 1988 Ind. LEXIS 129 (1988).

The sentence previously received from another court in another cause was not a proper subject for the court's consideration in determining the propriety of consecutive sentences, and the court acted beyond the scope of its authority when it ordered the commencement of the instant sentence to be postponed until the completion of the sentence imposed in the previous cause. (Decided prior to the 1994 amendment to IC 35-50-1-2, affecting the court's discretion to impose consecutive sentences). Seay v. State, 550 N.E.2d 1284, 1990 Ind. LEXIS 30 (1990), superseded by statute as stated in, Davidson v. State, 763 N.E.2d 441, 2002 Ind. LEXIS 144 (2002), superseded by statute as stated in, Wilkerson v. State, 728 N.E.2d 239, 2000 Ind. App. LEXIS 771 (2000).

A sentence previously received from another court is no longer a proper subject of consideration in determining the propriety of consecutive sentences. Saylor v. State, 565 N.E.2d 348, 1991 Ind. App. LEXIS 18 (1991).

Trial court lacked statutory authority to order defendant's eight-year sentence for a battery conviction to run consecutively to an earlier imposed thirty-year sentence. Watkins v. State, 588 N.E.2d 1342, 1992 Ind. App. LEXIS 448 (1992).

Discretionary authority to give consecutive sentences under former subsection (a), as it existed prior to the 1995 amendments, is limited to those occasions when a court is meting out two or more terms of imprisonment at one time; thus, the court's order that the sentence run consecutively to a sentence entered previously in another court was

Consecutive Sentences. (Cont'd)

—Improper. (Cont'd)

illegal and could not be sanctioned even though the second sentence was imposed pursuant to a plea agreement. Sinn v. State, 609 N.E.2d 434, 1993 Ind. App. LEXIS 156 (1993).

Where appellant was not on probation, parole, or serving a term of imprisonment, nor released on his own recognizance or on bond for the first charge when he committed the second and third crimes, the trial court was not statutorily required to impose consecutive sentences. Martin v. State, 638 N.E.2d 1349, 1994 Ind. App. LEXIS 1152 (1994).

Where defendant was tried on escape charge separately from conspiracy charge and when he committed the crime of escape he was not on probation, parole, or serving a term of imprisonment; subsection (b)(1) (now (d)(1)) did not mandate that the sentences be served consecutively. Newsome v. State, 654 N.E.2d 11, 1995 Ind. App. LEXIS 936 (1995).

Trial court's imposition of consecutive sentences for a Class A and Class B felony resulting in an aggregate 65-year sentence violated this section. Trei v. State, 658 N.E.2d 131, 1995 Ind. App. LEXIS 1571 (1995).

Where amendment to consecutive sentence statute was enacted after sentencing, it was fundamental error amounting to ineffective assistance for appellate counsel not to present the issue that the sentence was based on an erroneous interpretation of the statute. Nuckles v. State, 691 N.E.2d 211, 1998 Ind. App. LEXIS 88 (1998).

Where the court ordered that the sentences for the two murders be served consecutively because they were "crimes of violence", this articulation fell short of the requirement that a trial court's sentencing statement identify, explain, and evaluate any aggravating circumstances used to impose consecutive sentences. Sanquenetti v. State, 727 N.E.2d 437, 2000 Ind. LEXIS 295 (2000).

Defendant's sentence under subsection (c) of this section should not have exceeded four years, and where defendant was given consecutive sentences of three years for a Class D felony conviction, and one year each for two Class A misdemeanor convictions, the two separate misdemeanor sentences of one year each caused defendant's sentence to be in violation of this section. Purdy v. State, 727 N.E.2d 1091, 2000 Ind. App. LEXIS 601 (2000).

Where charges were joined because the offenses were of the same or similar character, and defendant received consecutive sentences as a result of the joinder, defendant was entitled to have his offenses severed as a matter of right, and his counsel's failure to request severance amounted to deficient performance. Wilkerson v. State, 728 N.E.2d 239, 2000 Ind. App. LEXIS 771 (2000).

The consecutive sentences defendant received for attempted murder and criminal confinement were improper pursuant to IC 35-50-1-2 because only defendant's two convictions of robbery as Class A felonies were "crimes of violence" which could be ordered to be served consecutively. Hopkins v. State, 747 N.E.2d 598, 2001 Ind. App. LEXIS 706 (2001).

Trial court erred as a matter of law when it determined that IC 35-50-1-2(b) required the imposition of consecutive sentences on defendant's second offense since defendant was not on probation, parole, or serving a term of imprisonment at the time he committed his second offense. The sentencing court lacked the authority under IC 35-50-1-2(a) to impose consecutive sentences since the offenses were in no way connected. Dragon v. State, 774 N.E.2d 103, 2002 Ind. App. LEXIS 1407 (2002), transfer granted, 783 N.E.2d 702, 2002 Ind. LEXIS 861 (2002).

Defendant should not have received a consecutive sentence for possession of marijuana where defendant was not out on bond or released on his own recognizance on an intimidation charge, but was found in possession of marijuana at the time of his arrest for intimidation. Jones v. State, 775 N.E.2d 322, 2002 Ind. App. LEXIS 1494 (2002).

Defendant's criminal acts resulting in convictions for possession of cocaine, battery by body waste, resisting law enforcement, battery resulting in bodily injury, and unlawful use of body armor were all causally related; accordingly, no grounds existed for trial court to order sentence for unlawful use of body armor to run consecutively to concurrent sentences for other crimes. Haggard v. State, 810 N.E.2d 751, 2004 Ind. App. LEXIS 1154 (2004).

Imposition of consecutive sentences for an aggregate sentence of greater than 55 years violated IC 35-50-1-2(c) because defendant's convictions arose from a single episode of criminal conduct. Massey v. State, 816 N.E.2d 979, 2004 Ind. App. LEXIS 2119 (2004).

Trial court erroneously imposed 10-year consecutive sentence on top of three other sentences that had not been contemporaneously imposed; however, since defendant received benefit from plea bargain that included the improper sentence, he waived any right to challenge sentence. Gonzales v. State, 831 N.E.2d 845, 2005 Ind. App. LEXIS 1368 (2005).

Trial court's sentencing order was insufficient to support consecutive sentencing because the trial court did not clearly state that the trial court found that the aggravating circumstances outweighed the mitigating circumstances in a case where defendant pled guilty to drug offenses; as a result, the trial court ordered that defendant's case be remanded to the trial court for entry of a clarified sentencing order. Diaz v. State, 839 N.E.2d 1277, 2005 Ind. App. LEXIS 2455 (2005).

Defendant's consecutive sentences violated IC 35-50-1-2 and had to be revised downward, as consecutive sentences arising out of a single episode of criminal conduct, such as were involved in defendant's case where he was arrested as a result of an anonymous tip that drugs were being cooked at a certain residence, could not exceed the advisory sentence for a felony one class higher than the most serious of felonies for which defendant was convicted; since defendant's sentence would be 53 years with improper convictions removed, defendant's sentence had to be changed to 53 years in prison. Hardister v. State, 849 N.E.2d 563, 2006 Ind. LEXIS 552 (2006).

Consecutive Sentences. (Cont'd)

—Improper. (Cont'd)

It was error to sentence defendant to consecutive terms for resisting law enforcement and for possession of chemical reagents or precursors with intent to manufacture methamphetamine, because the crimes constituted a single episode of conduct under IC 35-50-1-2(c). Defendant possessed the ammonia that he was carrying to use in the manufacture of methamphetamine at the same time he was resisting law enforcement by fleeing from police. Cole v. State, 850 N.E.2d 417, 2006 Ind. App. LEXIS 1060 (2006).

Where an inmate contended his consecutive sentences violated former IC 35-50-1-2(c) because his two Class B felonies (two counts of sexual misconduct with a minor in violation of IC 35-42-4-9(a)(1)) involved a single episode of criminal conduct, as the trial transcript of the minors' testimony indicated a connected series of offenses closely connected in time, place, and circumstance, the inmate's appellate counsel was ineffective for failing to include the transcript in the record on appeal. Harris v. State, 861 N.E.2d 1182, 2007 Ind. LEXIS 101 (2007).

Trial court erred in imposing an enhanced and consecutive sentence of two years in prison upon defendant following defendant's conviction for theft; in imposing a consecutive sentence in accordance with IC 35-50-1-2, the trial court was required to use the appropriate advisory sentence, which was six months less than the two-year sentence the trial court imposed. Robertson v. State, 860 N.E.2d 621, 2007 Ind. App. LEXIS 104 (2007), transfer granted, 869 N.E.2d 455, 2007 Ind. LEXIS 251 (2007), aff'd in part, superseded in part, 871 N.E.2d 280, 2007 Ind. LEXIS 618 (2007), overruled in part, Pedraza v. State, 873 N.E.2d 1083, 2007 Ind. App. LEXIS 2182 (2007), abrogated as stated, Dixson v. State, 865 N.E.2d 704, 2007 Ind. App. LEXIS 913 (2007).

Although the trial court did not err in enhancing defendant's sentence for burglary based on the jury's finding that defendant was a habitual offender, it did err in imposing consecutive sentences on defendant for burglary and possession of a handgun by a serious violent felon; imposing consecutive sentences pursuant to IC 35-50-1-2 constituted a double enhancement of which the state Supreme Court had disapproved of in an earlier case. Sweatt v. State, 887 N.E.2d 81, 2008 Ind. LEXIS 426 (2008).

Consecutive sentences for two child molesting convictions were improper because, although the aggravating circumstances were sufficient to warrant imposing enhanced sentences, they were not sufficient to justify imposing consecutive sentences, and the trial court did not explain why the aggravating circumstances warranted consecutive sentences; defendant was in a position of trust with the child victim, who believed defendant was her biological father, defendant molested the victim on multiple occasions other than the crimes charged, and, although defendant's criminal history was not inconsequential, his convictions were not significant aggravators. Harris v. State, 897 N.E.2d 927, 2008 Ind. LEXIS 1277 (2008).

Imposition of consecutive sentences was inappropriate where defendant's convictions resulted from same state-sponsored criminal sting operation. Williams v. State, 891 N.E.2d 621, 2008 Ind. App. LEXIS 2526 (2008).

— —Correction.

The reviewing court is duty bound to correct sentences that violate the trial court's statutory authority to impose consecutive sentences. Ballard v. State, 715 N.E.2d 1276, 1999 Ind. App. LEXIS 1494 (1999).

—Misdemeanor Convictions.

The court refused to interpret this ameliorative statute so as to increase the length of defendant's sentence by virtue of his convictions of misdemeanors rather than felonies. Purdy v. State, 727 N.E.2d 1091, 2000 Ind. App. LEXIS 601 (2000).

—Mistrial.

Judge could impose consecutive sentences for closely related offenses that were first charged in the same information and all tried in the same court, and but for a hung jury and subsequent mistrial on two of four of the counts, the court would have sentenced defendant on all counts contemporaneously; the court was authorized to impose consecutive sentences on those two counts when defendant was convicted following retrial. Buell v. State, 668 N.E.2d 251, 1996 Ind. LEXIS 68 (1996).

—Modification.

When a court modifies a sentence, it is altering an already existing sentence rather than "imposing" a sentence; a trial court may not avoid the limitation on its discretionary authority to order consecutive sentences merely by modifying a sentence which was imposed previously in a separate cause of action. Lamirand v. State, 640 N.E.2d 79, 1994 Ind. App. LEXIS 1256 (1994).

—Pending Charges.

There was no error in the trial court's order that defendant's sentence on current convictions be consecutive to that imposed on a pending cocaine possession charge. Garner v. State, 646 N.E.2d 349, 1995 Ind. App. LEXIS 90 (1995).

Defendant properly received consecutive sentences for intimidation and false reporting where defendant was out on his own recognizance for false reporting when defendant committed the act of intimidation. Jones v. State, 775 N.E.2d 322, 2002 Ind. App. LEXIS 1494 (2002).

—Presumptive Sentence for Next Greater Offense.

After determining the classification of offenses and identifying the presumptive sentence for the next greater classification of offense, the court still has the discretion to impose consecutive sentences for crimes in the second category, provided that the total term of the consecutive sentences does not exceed the presumptive sentence for the next greater offense. Salone v. State, 652 N.E.2d 552, 1995 Ind. App. LEXIS 783 (1995).

Consecutive Sentences. (Cont'd)

—Presumptive Sentence for Next Greater Offense. (Cont'd)

Where defendant was sentenced to consecutive sentences that did not exceed four years, and the most serious offense was battery, a Class D felony, the sentences were not excessive under IC 35-50-1-2(c); the presumptive sentence for the next highest class of felony was four years under IC 35-50-2-6, and the sentence imposed was just under four years. Monyhan v. State, 780 N.E.2d 1187, 2003 Ind. App. LEXIS 7 (2003).

Because defendant's burglary of two neighboring garages were a single episode of criminal conduct under IC 35-50-1-2(c) and were not crimes of violence, consecutive sentences could not exceed the advisory sentence for a felony which was one class of felony higher than the most serious of the felonies for which defendant had been convicted; as defendant was convicted of two Class C felonies, and the advisory sentence for a Class B felony was 10 years under IC 35-50-2-5, the trial court's imposition of consecutive sentences totaling 12 years violated IC 35-50-1-2(c). Henson v. State, 881 N.E.2d 36, 2008 Ind. App. LEXIS 255 (2008).

—Prior Commission of Offense.

Trial court erred as a matter of law when it determined that the imposition of consecutive sentences was required as to defendant's second offense; because defendant committed the offense of failing to return to lawful detention before being convicted and sentenced on the cocaine dealing offenses, consecutive terms were not mandatory under IC 35-50-1-2(d)(1). Williams v. State, 787 N.E.2d 461, 2003 Ind. App. LEXIS 741 (2003).

—Procedure.

The court first must determine the length of a sentence within the prescribed, statutory range, and then must determine what portion of that sentence, if any, should be suspended. Only then must a court consult this section to determine whether a consecutive sentence may or must be imposed, and in the event that the court decides to impose a sentence consecutive to another sentence, the court also must adhere to requirements set forth in this section with respect to the procedure to be followed in imposing consecutive sentences. Atchely v. State, 730 N.E.2d 758, 2000 Ind. App. LEXIS 891 (2000).

—Probation Revocation.

Defendant, prior to pleading guilty to theft and burglary charges, was not entitled to an advisement as to the possibility of consecutive sentencing as a result of his probation revocation. Arnold v. State, 539 N.E.2d 969, 1989 Ind. App. LEXIS 450 (1989).

Trial court's order that defendant's sentence for resisting law enforcement be served consecutive to any sentence to be imposed in probation revocation proceedings was proper where defendant was on probation when he committed the offense. Garner v. State, 646 N.E.2d 349, 1995 Ind. App. LEXIS 90 (1995).

Although the state referred to the wrong date in its petition and during the revocation hearing, plaintiff testified to the actual date that the incident occurred on, and to the fact that he reported to his home detention supervisor on the same day, so that the court could have reasonably inferred he was on probation at the time of the incident, despite the state's typographical error. Sutton v. State, 689 N.E.2d 452, 1997 Ind. App. LEXIS 1741 (1997).

Because the issue of whether the trial court properly sentenced defendant to consecutive sentences under IC 35-50-1-2 was not before the trial court in the probation revocation proceeding, defendant could not raise the issue in an appeal from defendant's probation revocation. Schlichter v. State, 779 N.E.2d 1155, 2002 Ind. LEXIS 934 (2002).

Where trial court found that defendant's offenses violated probation and ordered defendant to serve remaining six years of previous conviction to run concurrently to sentence for new convictions, trial court violated IC 35-50-1-2(d), which required sentences to run consecutively. Barnett v. State, 834 N.E.2d 169, 2005 Ind. App. LEXIS 1681 (2005).

—Proper.

The defendant was convicted of attempted murder, criminal recklessness, battery, theft, possession of stolen property, and resisting law enforcement, and the trial court ordered the sentences for the felony convictions to be served consecutively. The court found that consecutive sentences were warranted because not imposing them would demean the seriousness of the offense and because the defendant was likely to repeat the offenses if not confined. Both of these factors justified ordering consecutive sentences. Parks v. State, 513 N.E.2d 170, 1987 Ind. LEXIS 1066 (1987).

Trial court did not err in denying defendant credit time for the days spent awaiting trial for jail takeover, where defendant was serving a sentence on an unrelated charge when the jail takeover occurred and he was sentenced to a term consecutive to the prior sentence. Corn v. State, 659 N.E.2d 554, 1995 Ind. LEXIS 219 (1995).

Defendant's four security fraud convictions do not constitute one criminal episode, therefore, the consecutive sentencing of defendant to an aggregate term of 16 years for these four convictions does not violate this section. Tedlock v. State, 656 N.E.2d 273, 1995 Ind. App. LEXIS 1146 (1995).

Where each of three burglaries took place as a distinct episode in itself and each could be described without referring to details of the others, the court did not abuse its discretion in finding the three burglaries not to be a single episode and, therefore, ordering the sentences to be served consecutively. Reynolds v. State, 657 N.E.2d 438, 1995 Ind. App. LEXIS 1414 (1995).

There were sufficient aggravating factors to support the consecutive sentences. Morgan v. State, 675 N.E.2d 1067, 1996 Ind. LEXIS 198 (1996), superseded by statute as stated in, Allen v. State, 722 N.E.2d 1246, 2000 Ind. App. LEXIS 12 (2000).

Imposition of consecutive sentences for three counts of dealing cocaine was not manifestly un-

Consecutive Sentences. (Cont'd)

—Proper. (Cont'd)

reasonable, where the sales spanned a period of almost two months, defendant was sentenced according to a plea agreement, and he was not sentenced to the maximum term under the agreement. Pritscher v. State, 675 N.E.2d 727, 1996 Ind. App. LEXIS 1739 (1996).

Enhanced and consecutive sentences were justified because of the number of times the victims were shot, the fact that the victims were asked to kneel before defendant and face him while he executed them, and the fact that the female victims were repeatedly raped. Mitchem v. State, 685 N.E.2d 671, 1997 Ind. LEXIS 128 (1997).

Where state charged defendant with attempted murder, and where evidence presented demonstrated defendant committed the offense of aggravated battery as a lesser included offense of attempted murder, the restrictions of this section prohibiting sentences for consecutive terms for offenses arising from a single episode of criminal conduct did not apply, because aggravated battery is a crime of violence excepted from the limitations of this section, and the court was not prohibited from ordering the sentences to be served consecutively. Jackson v. State, 698 N.E.2d 809, 1998 Ind. App. LEXIS 1221 (1998).

Where the trial court stated in its sentencing order that it found aggravating circumstances in the defendant's two prior felony convictions and various misdemeanor involvements, and did not find mitigating circumstances, it provided adequate justification for the imposition of consecutive sentences. Taylor v. State, 710 N.E.2d 921, 1999 Ind. LEXIS 355 (1999).

Although the trial court improperly considered the seriousness of the crime in order to impose a consecutive sentence on the defendant, the sentence was upheld where the court found other aggravating factors. Hampton v. State, 719 N.E.2d 803, 1999 Ind. LEXIS 920 (1999).

The judge appropriately found that the advanced age of the victim and the violation of the position of trust occupied by defendant in relation to the victim justified the imposition of consecutive sentences for murder and robbery. Hampton v. State, 719 N.E.2d 803, 1999 Ind. LEXIS 920 (1999).

Where two charges involved the same victim and it appeared that a conspiracy to murder the witness-victim was merely an attempt to finish the prior unsuccessful attempt to kill him, and where the same judge tried both cases, the court was within its discretion to order the sentence for conspiracy to commit murder to run consecutively to the sentence for murder and attempted murder. Elswick v. State, 706 N.E.2d 592, 1999 Ind. App. LEXIS 360 (1999).

There was no error in the imposition of consecutive sentences where the offenses for which the defendant was convicted were committed during two distinct episodes of criminal conduct, and where each episode was unrelated and could be described independently without referring to the specific details of the other. Chavez v. State, 722 N.E.2d 885, 2000 Ind. App. LEXIS 67 (2000).

Defendant was properly sentenced for two theft and two conversion convictions to consecutive terms of imprisonment where the offenses did not constitute a single episode of criminal conduct, because his convictions arose from crimes he committed with four separate checks written on separate dates for different amounts. Hightower v. State, 735 N.E.2d 1209, 2000 Ind. App. LEXIS 1578 (2000).

Subsection (c) places limitations on consecutive sentencing for an episode of criminal conduct except for crimes of violence. Therefore, because murder and robbery are not subject to these limitations, the trial court did not err by ordering the two sentences for murder, the sentence for attempted murder, and the sentence for robbery to run consecutive to each other. Williams v. State, 741 N.E.2d 1209, 2001 Ind. LEXIS 73 (2001).

Where defendant's plan resulted in the attempted murder of several people and the murder of another on different days over a span of two weeks, these events did not constitute a single criminal episode and the trial court did not err in sentencing defendant to consecutive terms for his convictions. O'Connell v. State, 742 N.E.2d 943, 2001 Ind. LEXIS 193 (2001).

Consecutive sentences were proper where defendant's sentence arose from more than one episode of criminal conduct because neither of defendant's acts of sexual misconduct was a necessary prerequisite for the other, and although defendant had sexual intercourse with each of the girls on the same evening and in the same apartment, there was no other connection between the events. Each act was an occurrence that may be viewed as distinct and apart from the other, notwithstanding the fact that the acts were both part of a more comprehensive series. Harris v. State, 749 N.E.2d 57, 2001 Ind. App. LEXIS 759 (2001).

Defendant's sentence was proper where his sentence for involuntary manslaughter, a crime of violence, was ordered to be served consecutive to those for his other convictions of crimes not of violence arising out of a single episode, and these sentences did not exceed ten years, the presumptive sentence for a Class B felony. McCarthy v. State, 751 N.E.2d 753, 2001 Ind. App. LEXIS 1105 (2001).

Trial court was permitted to sentence defendant to consecutive sentences without adhering to the limitations under IC 35-50-1-2(c); defendant's offenses, three counts of battery and one count of attempted battery, were not part of a single episode of criminal conduct as defined under IC 35-50-1-2(b), as each offense occurred in a different time and place. Monyhan v. State, 780 N.E.2d 1187, 2003 Ind. App. LEXIS 7 (2003).

Because defendant's felony offenses, which included possession of cocaine, resisting law enforcement, and pointing firearm, constituted single episode of criminal conduct, IC 35-50-1-2(b) permitted trial court to impose consecutive sentences totaling 30 years for felonies; accordingly, trial court's imposition of consecutive sentences totaling 26

Consecutive Sentences. (Cont'd)

—Proper. (Cont'd)
years did not violate IC 35-50-1-2. Johnican v. State, 804 N.E.2d 211, 2004 Ind. App. LEXIS 324 (2004).

Where state and defendant in trespassing case entered into agreement under which prosecution would be withheld if defendant did not commit another crime for two years, but defendant was shortly thereafter convicted of offense of resisting law enforcement, defendant was properly sentenced to consecutive sentences for the two offenses despite trial court's failure to find any aggravating circumstances; consecutive sentences were mandatory under IC 35-50-1-2(d)(2)(B), since defendant, at time of arrest for second offense, was either released on his own recognizance or on bond within meaning of statute. Christmas v. State, 812 N.E.2d 174, 2004 Ind. App. LEXIS 1397 (2004).

Statutory exemption from consecutive sentences under IC 35-50-1-2(a) did not apply to conviction of felony for knowingly damaging by fire another's property under circumstances that endangered human life, which was neither murder conviction nor felony conviction for which defendant received enhanced sentence due to infliction of serious bodily injury. Mathews v. State, 824 N.E.2d 713, 2005 Ind. App. LEXIS 515 (2005), transfer granted, 841 N.E.2d 183, 2005 Ind. LEXIS 812 (2005), superseded, 849 N.E.2d 578, 2006 Ind. LEXIS 550 (2006).

Trial court did not err in ordering defendant's 20-year sentence for Class B felony arson to be served consecutive to 45-year sentence for Class A felony arson resulting in serious bodily injury. Mathews v. State, 824 N.E.2d 713, 2005 Ind. App. LEXIS 515 (2005), transfer granted, 841 N.E.2d 183, 2005 Ind. LEXIS 812 (2005), superseded, 849 N.E.2d 578, 2006 Ind. LEXIS 550 (2006).

Blakely case was not implicated in situation where trial court ordered consecutive sentences for burglary and robbery convictions pursuant to its discretion under IC 35-50-1-2(c); furthermore, where, at sentencing hearing, defendant admitted to criminal history, trial court could use that history as aggravating factor to support enhanced sentence. Fields v. State, 825 N.E.2d 841, 2005 Ind. App. LEXIS 608 (2005).

Taking digital photographs of child and then disseminating them through the Internet were separate and distinct acts, and each of those acts was separate and distinct from acts of molesting child; imposition of consecutive sentences was therefore appropriate. Hart v. State, 829 N.E.2d 541, 2005 Ind. App. LEXIS 1041 (2005).

Trial court was required to order that the sentence imposed for defendant resisting law enforcement as a Class D felony run consecutively to the sentences imposed on defendant's other two offenses because defendant was on bond for other offenses at the time. Childress v. State, 848 N.E.2d 1073, 2006 Ind. LEXIS 474 (2006).

Though the sentencing court did not use the words, "aggravating circumstances," it properly imposed consecutive sentences under IC 35-50-1-2, as it clearly identified as aggravating factors the fact that there were multiple victims over six months, that defendant knowingly wrote bad checks, and that he failed to pay any restitution. Creekmore v. State, 853 N.E.2d 523, 2006 Ind. App. LEXIS 1803 (2006), clarified, 858 N.E.2d 230, 2006 Ind. App. LEXIS 2529 (2006).

As to two bad checks defendant wrote after the effective date of the amendment to IC 35-38-1-7.1, the trial court was authorized by IC 35-50-1-2(c) to order consecutive terms, and was not required to consider mitigating factors due to the amendment to IC 35-38-1-7.1. Creekmore v. State, 853 N.E.2d 523, 2006 Ind. App. LEXIS 1803 (2006), clarified, 858 N.E.2d 230, 2006 Ind. App. LEXIS 2529 (2006).

IC 35-50-1-2 permits the imposition of consecutive sentences for separate convictions where appropriate, including multiple serious violent felon convictions. Reed v. State, 857 N.E.2d 19, 2006 Ind. App. LEXIS 2375 (2006), transfer granted and vacated, — N.E.2d —, 2007 Ind. LEXIS 756 (2007), superseded, 866 N.E.2d 767, 2007 Ind. LEXIS 361 (2007).

Trial court did not err in ordering an inmate's sentence for one serious violent felon (SVF) conviction to run consecutive to a sentence imposed for another such conviction, as IC 35-50-1-2 permits consecutive sentences for separate SVF convictions. Thus, the failure of trial counsel to object and appellate counsel to present the issue on appeal did not prejudice the inmate. Reed v. State, 857 N.E.2d 19, 2006 Ind. App. LEXIS 2375 (2006), transfer granted and vacated, — N.E.2d —, 2007 Ind. LEXIS 756 (2007), superseded, 866 N.E.2d 767, 2007 Ind. LEXIS 361 (2007).

When defendant was sentenced for the Class C felony of battery, which was committed while defendant was on probation, it was error not to order that sentence be served consecutively to any sentence imposed due to defendant's probation violation because IC 35-50-1-2(d) required that a consecutive sentence be imposed. Mata v. State, 866 N.E.2d 346, 2007 Ind. App. LEXIS 1014 (2007).

Trial court had the authority to impose defendant's 12-year sentence consecutively to his existing sentence because the offenses defendant committed in the counties did not constitute a single episode of criminal conduct since a complete account of each crime could have been given without referring to the other offenses. In light of the independent natures of those offenses, the trial court did not abuse its discretion by ordering defendant's sentence to run consecutively to the trial court's sentence because it was reasonable for the trial court to conclude that defendant should not have benefitted from the time served. Geiger v. State, 866 N.E.2d 830, 2007 Ind. App. LEXIS 1081 (2007), aff'd, transfer granted, — N.E.2d —, 2007 Ind. LEXIS 655 (2007).

When IC 35-50-2-1.3 was read in conjunction with IC 35-50-1-2, it was apparent that the reference to the "appropriate advisory sentence" was meant to apply to situations involving the single episode of criminal conduct limitation on consecutive sentencing. Consequently, the trial court had the authority to impose enhanced, consecutive sentences on defendant, and it did not err by doing

Consecutive Sentences. (Cont'd)

—Proper. (Cont'd)
so. Geiger v. State, 866 N.E.2d 830, 2007 Ind. App. LEXIS 1081 (2007), aff'd, transfer granted, — N.E.2d —, 2007 Ind. LEXIS 655 (2007).

When IC 35-50-2-1.3 is read in conjunction with IC 35-50-1-2, it is apparent that the reference to the "appropriate advisory sentence" was meant to apply to situations involving the single episode of criminal conduct limitation on consecutive sentencing; the statute was not intended to place any other limits on a court's ability to impose consecutive sentences. Accordingly, the trial court had the authority to impose enhanced, consecutive sentences. Mendoza v. State, 869 N.E.2d 546, 2007 Ind. App. LEXIS 1498 (2007).

Trial court did not err in ordering the aggregate sentence for murder, rape, and criminal deviate conduct to run consecutively to the sentence for an unrelated offense. The trial court had found two aggravators, defendant's lengthy criminal record and the brutality of the offenses. Hampton v. State, 873 N.E.2d 1074, 2007 Ind. App. LEXIS 2134 (2007).

Trial court was legally permitted to order defendant's sentences for two counts of operating a vehicle while intoxicated (OWI) causing death, OWI causing serious bodily injury, and having a prior OWI conviction in the last five years, to run consecutively. Pedraza v. State, 873 N.E.2d 1083, 2007 Ind. App. LEXIS 2182 (2007), transfer granted and vacated, 878 N.E.2d 218, 2007 Ind. LEXIS 1005 (2007).

Consecutive sentences were permissibly imposed upon defendant following defendant's convictions for carrying a handgun without a license, resisting law enforcement, and possession of marijuana; although the 12-year aggregate sentence with two years suspended exceeded the advisory sentence, defendant's possession of the handgun and marijuana did not arise out of the same episode of criminal conduct as the acts of resisting arrest and, thus, the possession offenses were not counted in determining whether consecutive sentences were allowed pursuant to IC 35-50-1-2(b). Deshazier v. State, 877 N.E.2d 200, 2007 Ind. App. LEXIS 2724 (2007).

Defendant properly received a total executed sentence of 10 years on three counts of robbery as a Class C felony under IC 35-42-5-1(1) where: (1) defendant benefited significantly from his guilty plea by the state agreeing not to file B felony charges and trial court recognized his limited criminal history, consisting only of a weapons charge and a pending battery charge, as a mitigating factor but discounted its value; (2) victim's injury was a proper aggravator, as the sentences were less than the minimum of the next greater felony; and (3) because of the injury and because there were multiple victims, consecutive sentences were warranted under IC 35-50-1-2(c). Page v. State, 878 N.E.2d 404, 2007 Ind. App. LEXIS 2937 (2007).

Deviation from the presumptive sentence of 30 years under IC 35-50-2-4 for child molesting was not warranted as defendant's extensive criminal history of felony child molesting and sexual battery occurred about 10 years before the current offenses; however, defendant's repeated molestations of the victim, violation of his position of trust as the victim's step-father, and infliction of psychological abuse warranted one sentence being imposed consecutive to one of the other counts under IC 35-50-1-2(c). Smith v. State, 889 N.E.2d 261, 2008 Ind. LEXIS 486 (2008).

Defendant's 34-year sentence for two counts of neglect under IC 35-46-1-4 was revised under AP. 7 to consecutive sentences of nine years, for placing the hands of child victim under hot water, causing severe burns and pain, and eight years for delay in seeking medical treatment. Cardwell v. State, 895 N.E.2d 1219, 2008 Ind. LEXIS 1049 (2008).

Pursuant to IC 35-50-1-2, it was proper for the trial court to consider the aggravating and mitigating factors when determining how to impose the sentences for defendant's crimes; trial court could have relied on defendant's extensive criminal history to enhance the sentences and then relied on the nature and circumstances of the crime to run his criminal confinement sentence consecutively to the other sentences. Smith v. State, 881 N.E.2d 1040, 2008 Ind. App. LEXIS 442 (2008).

Imposition of consecutive sentences was proper because the trial court found defendant's criminal history an aggravating factor under IC 35-50-1-2(c). Beer v. State, 885 N.E.2d 33, 2008 Ind. App. LEXIS 952 (2008).

Defendant committed the instant offense (which included a habitual offender enhancement under IC 35-50-2-8) while placed in a work release program following his prior criminal conviction and had to be returned to probation under IC 35-38-2.6-3(a); therefore, he had not been discharged from his incarceration, pursuant to IC 35-50-1-2(d), and thus trial court was required to order defendant's sentence to be served consecutively to his prior sentence. Breaston v. State, 893 N.E.2d 6, 2008 Ind. App. LEXIS 1940 (2008).

Trial court erred in failing to impose consecutive sentences based on the convictions in two separate causes. Hardley v. State, 893 N.E.2d 1140, 2008 Ind. App. LEXIS 2106 (2008).

Where defendant pled guilty to one count of attempted child molesting as a class A felony and one count of child molesting as a class C felony, consecutive sentences were proper despite defendant's contention that because the offenses involved the same victim and essentially the same conduct the sentences should be concurrent. Powell v. State, 895 N.E.2d 1259, 2008 Ind. App. LEXIS 2502 (2008).

Defendant's non-support of his eight children, born to three different mothers, was not a single episode of criminal conduct, as three separate households (with different sets of victims) were deprived of support for dependent children; therefore, consecutive sentences were properly imposed for three counts of violating IC 35-46-1-5. Gilliam v. State, — N.E.2d —, 2009 Ind. App. LEXIS 284 (2009).

—Serious Bodily Injury.
In determining whether trial court had author-

Consecutive Sentences. (Cont'd)

—Serious Bodily Injury. (Cont'd)
ity to impose consecutive sentences for crimes arising out of a single incident, the reviewing court must determine whether any of the convictions for which the consecutive sentences were imposed constitute convictions for which defendant received the enhanced penalty because the felony resulted in serious bodily injury, and, if so, that defendant knowingly or intentionally caused that injury. Becker v. State, 695 N.E.2d 968, 1998 Ind. App. LEXIS 740 (1998).

—Seriousness and Crime.
The seriousness and heinousness of a crime may not be considered in order to impose consecutive rather than concurrent sentences. Hampton v. State, 719 N.E.2d 803, 1999 Ind. LEXIS 920 (1999).

—Severance.
Where a former version of IC 35-50-1-2 provided at the time of defendant's trial that consecutive sentences could be imposed only in limited circumstances, the court determined that defendant was prejudiced by counsel's failure to seek automatic severance that would have resulted in half the aggregate sentence, so that remand for resentencing was appropriate. Davidson v. State, 735 N.E.2d 325, 2000 Ind. App. LEXIS 1532 (2000), transfer granted, 753 N.E.2d 2, 2001 Ind. LEXIS 26 (2001), aff'd, 763 N.E.2d 441, 2002 Ind. LEXIS 144 (2002).

Petitioner failed to show how he was prejudiced by counsel's failure to move for severance because if the trial court had sentenced petitioner on different days on the cases to which he pleaded guilty, then petitioner would have faced a maximum sentence of 20 years, and when sentenced contemporaneously petitioner was sentenced to an aggregate term of 20 years for the offenses to which he pleaded guilty. Peace v. State, 736 N.E.2d 1261, 2000 Ind. App. LEXIS 1709 (2000).

—Subsequent Offense.
Consecutive sentences were mandatory under subdivision (b)(2) as it existed prior to the 1987 amendment, which rewrote subsection (b), where the subsequent crime was committed after conviction and sentence for the prior crime and while the defendant was free on bond pending appeal. Groff v. State, 488 N.E.2d 711, 1986 Ind. LEXIS 1017 (1986).

Where the defendant commits a crime while on probation from a prior conviction, the trial court is without discretion and errs in not ordering that the sentences for the later convictions be served consecutively to the sentences imposed for the earliest convictions. Bay v. State, 489 N.E.2d 1220, 1986 Ind. App. LEXIS 2428 (1986).

The discretionary authority of the trial court to order consecutive sentences under former subsection (a), as it existed prior to the 1995 amendments, has been limited to those occasions when a court is contemporaneously imposing two or more sentences. Baskin v. State, 586 N.E.2d 938, 1992 Ind. App. LEXIS 196 (1992).

The trial court had no authority to impose a sentence which would run consecutively to sentences for two prior separate offenses. Baskin v. State, 586 N.E.2d 938, 1992 Ind. App. LEXIS 196 (1992).

The legislature intended to require imposition of consecutive sentences where a defendant commits a crime while still on probation or parole from another offense, or where he has been arrested but not yet tried on one offense and commits another offense while released from jail awaiting trial on the pending offense; it would frustrate that intent to determine that former subsection (b)(2) of this section had no application to a defendant who has been arrested and released on bond and then commits an offense after his bond has been revoked but before he has been reapprehended. Douglas v. State, 632 N.E.2d 1150, 1994 Ind. App. LEXIS 383 (1994).

If a court is contemporaneously imposing two or more sentences, it is granted the general statutory authority to order them to be served consecutive to one another under subsection (a) of this section; a sentencing order from one county, requiring that sentences for robbery be served consecutive to the sentence previously imposed in another county, was without statutory authority. Thompson v. State, 634 N.E.2d 775, 1994 Ind. App. LEXIS 615 (1994).

—Vacation of Prior Conviction.
Where defendant committed a 1980 burglary after being convicted and sentenced for a 1978 burglary, and the 1978 conviction was later set aside in October of 1983, the prior conviction, which might have supported the enhanced penalty of consecutive sentences, was vacated. When defendant was resentenced in 1983 there was no basis for the application of former subsection (b), as it existed prior to the 1995 amendments, and the trial court was not required to impose the enhanced penalty of consecutive sentences pursuant thereto. St. John v. State, 529 N.E.2d 371, 1988 Ind. App. LEXIS 792 (1988).

Construction.

—"On Bond".
IC 27-10-2-10 regulates the form of recognizances and affidavits to which bail bondsmen must adhere, but does not otherwise address the vitality of a bond, and does not determine whether a defendant is "on bond" within the meaning of this section in view of an agreement to withhold prosecution. Martin v. State, 645 N.E.2d 1100, 1995 Ind. App. LEXIS 18 (1995).

Defendant was on bond when the state and he executed an agreement to withhold prosecution, whereby if defendant satisfactorily performed the conditions of the agreement, the state agreed to dismiss the charges, but the state would withdraw from the arrangement and proceed with prosecution if he failed to complete his obligations as set out in the agreement. The attachment of conditions rendered the charges against defendant ongoing, and not finally resolved, and until defendant remained subject to the appearance bond, defendant was "on bond" within the meaning of this section until he fully performed the conditions.

Construction. (Cont'd)

—"On Bond". (Cont'd)
Martin v. State, 645 N.E.2d 1100, 1995 Ind. App. LEXIS 18 (1995).

—Term of Imprisonment.
The death penalty is not a "term of imprisonment" within the meaning of subsection (d) of this section, since it features incarceration only while appellate processes persist, does not contemplate a future release into society, and is not a penalty under which a convict is sent to incarceration for some period and then released. State v. Price, 715 N.E.2d 331, 1999 Ind. LEXIS 407 (1999).

Crime Committed Pending Appeal.
Where defendant was free on appeal bond when subsequent offense was committed, the sentence for the subsequent offense must be served consecutively to the first sentence even though the court's order did not specifically state that they were to be consecutive. Hutcherson v. State, 269 Ind. 331, 380 N.E.2d 1219, 1978 Ind. LEXIS 780 (1978).

Crime Committed While Free on Bail.
The provision that sentence for a crime committed while person was free on bail under a previous charge should not be served concurrently with sentence for previous charge was operative even if not mentioned by the trial court when sentencing. Banton v. State, 180 Ind. App. 698, 390 N.E.2d 687, 1979 Ind. App. LEXIS 1207 (1979).

Crime Committed While on Probation or Parole.
Where defendant was convicted of several counts of crime committed while he was on parole the sentences on those counts would run consecutively to the original sentence but as to the several sentences on the new conviction it was within the court's discretion as to whether they should be consecutive or run concurrently with each other. Perry v. State, 177 Ind. App. 334, 379 N.E.2d 531, 1978 Ind. App. LEXIS 996 (1978).

Where, after this law went into effect, defendant committed an offense while on probation for an offense committed before the new law went into effect, a consecutive sentence under the provisions of this section was proper since such sentence was for the new offense and not the prior offense. Dolan v. State, 420 N.E.2d 1364, 1981 Ind. App. LEXIS 1446 (1981).

The trial court was in error where it ordered the defendant to serve his sentence imposed under conviction for attempted murder consecutively with a sentence imposed in a prior case, as the defendant was not on probation, parole, or serving a term of imprisonment at the time for the other crime. Hutchinson v. State, 477 N.E.2d 850, 1985 Ind. LEXIS 821 (1985).

Where the record was devoid of evidence indicating that the defendant committed a crime while on probation, even though he was arrested for the crime while on probation, this section does not apply. Pawloski v. State, 555 N.E.2d 851, 1990 Ind. App. LEXIS 771 (1990).

Former subsection (b), as it existed prior to the 1995 amendments, the mandatory section of the statute, applies only if a defendant is on probation, parole, or serving a term of imprisonment at the time the other offenses are committed. Saylor v. State, 565 N.E.2d 348, 1991 Ind. App. LEXIS 18 (1991).

An order for consecutive sentences for a defendant who, while on probation for the first crime (burglary), committed and was sentenced for the second pair of crimes (theft/criminal mischief) for which the sentences were to be served consecutive to the remainder of the burglary sentence, which was reinstated, was proper. Menifee v. State, 601 N.E.2d 359, 1992 Ind. App. LEXIS 1585 (1992).

If an original order of consecutive sentences is proper, the court is within its power to reinstate that same sentence at a probation violation hearing even though the probation violation is a "different proceeding at a different time." Menifee v. State, 601 N.E.2d 359, 1992 Ind. App. LEXIS 1585 (1992).

—Probation Granted Prior to Enactment.
Where probation was revoked the trial court had no authority to order the previously suspended sentences to run consecutive to a sentence for an offense committed during the probation and prior to revocation on the basis of this section permitting consecutive sentences where crime for which probation was granted occurred prior to the enactment of this section. Young v. State, 413 N.E.2d 1083, 1980 Ind. App. LEXIS 1846 (1980).

—Sentence Prior to Probation Revocation.
Sentences for offenses committed after an arrest for another offense shall be served consecutively, and where a sentence was imposed for illegal possession of a handgun, before the defendant's probation was revoked, defendant could not be granted credit time for his confinement while awaiting trial and sentencing in the handgun case, for the previously suspended sentence. Bischoff v. State, 704 N.E.2d 129, 1998 Ind. App. LEXIS 2020 (1998).

Crimes of Violence.
Burglary, as a Class B felony, is considered a crime of violence, and not subject to the limitation imposed by the sentencing statute. Flynn v. State, 702 N.E.2d 741, 1998 Ind. App. LEXIS 2087 (1998).

Battery is not included in the crimes delineated by the legislature as being a crime of violence. Ballard v. State, 715 N.E.2d 1276, 1999 Ind. App. LEXIS 1494 (1999).

The legislature delineated the exact crimes by name and citation that were to be considered violent crimes, and if battery as a Class C felony had been intended to be included as a crime of violence, it would have appeared in subsection (a) of this section. Maxwell v. State, 731 N.E.2d 459, 2000 Ind. App. LEXIS 1064 (2000).

Because battery as a Class C felony is not a crime of violence, the trial court erred by applying the exception language of the consecutive sentence statute when determining defendant's sentence.

Crimes of Violence. (Cont'd)

Maxwell v. State, 731 N.E.2d 459, 2000 Ind. App. LEXIS 1064 (2000).

Consecutive sentencing among crimes of violence, and consecutive sentencing between a crime of violence and those that are not crimes of violence are exempt from the sentencing limitation. However, the limitation does apply for consecutive sentences between and among those crimes that are not crimes of violence. Ellis v. State, 736 N.E.2d 731, 2000 Ind. LEXIS 973 (2000).

The limitations on the duration of consecutive sentences under IC 35-50-1-2(c) do not apply to crimes of violence, which include murder, burglary, and criminal deviate conduct. Davies v. State, 758 N.E.2d 981, 2001 Ind. App. LEXIS 2030 (2001).

There was no merit to defendant's argument that he could not be given maximum consecutive sentences under IC 35-50-1-2 for murder, rape, and criminal deviate conduct. All three crimes were crimes of violence. Hampton v. State, 873 N.E.2d 1074, 2007 Ind. App. LEXIS 2134 (2007).

Cruel and Unusual Punishment.

So long as the imposition of consecutive sentences is supported by specific and detailed reasons and an indication that the court has considered the goal of rehabilitation, it will not constitute cruel and unusual punishment. Smith v. State, 474 N.E.2d 71, 1985 Ind. LEXIS 752 (1985).

Discretion of Court.

Former subsection (b), as it existed prior to the 1995 amendments, provided for mandatory consecutive sentencing in specific instances but under former subsection (a) the court has discretion to sentence defendant consecutively regardless of whether the provisions of former subsection (b) were met. Ferguson v. State, 273 Ind. 468, 405 N.E.2d 902, 1980 Ind. LEXIS 695 (1980).

Where the burglaries were committed after the defendant was arrested for theft and following his break from jail, and he was not on probation, parole or serving a term of imprisonment, former subsection (b), as it existed prior to the 1995 amendments, was not applicable, and as a result, former subsection (a) applied and the court has wide discretion in determining whether concurrent or consecutive terms shall be served. Garrett v. State, 411 N.E.2d 692, 1980 Ind. App. LEXIS 1733 (1980), disapproved, Sides v. State, 490 N.E.2d 318, 1986 Ind. LEXIS 1053 (1986).

Former subsection (a), as it existed prior to the 1995 amendments, gave the trial court the discretion to determine whether terms of imprisonment shall be served concurrently or consecutively when evidence of the facts of each offense is before the court. Haggard v. State, 445 N.E.2d 969, 1983 Ind. LEXIS 772 (1983), overruled in part, Woodson v. State, 778 N.E.2d 475, 2002 Ind. App. LEXIS 1898 (2002).

It is within the discretion of the trial court to determine whether sentences are to be served concurrently or consecutively. Anderson v. State, 448 N.E.2d 1180, 1983 Ind. LEXIS 849 (1983).

Sentencing is a decision within the trial court's discretion and will be reversed only upon a showing of a manifest abuse of discretion. Allen v. State, 453 N.E.2d 1011, 1983 Ind. LEXIS 968 (1983).

The legislature has granted trial courts the discretion to determine whether sentences are to be served consecutively or concurrently, and a trial court may, upon consideration of relevant facts and information, increase the basic sentences, impose consecutive sentences, or both. Anderson v. State, 452 N.E.2d 173, 1983 Ind. App. LEXIS 3217 (1983).

The trial court is vested with wide discretion to determine whether a presumptive sentence will be enhanced due to aggravating factors involving the particular defendant or crime, and whether terms of multiple convictions will be served concurrently or consecutively. Shippen v. State, 477 N.E.2d 903, 1985 Ind. LEXIS 835 (1985).

Former subsection (a), as it existed prior to the 1995 amendments, gives the trial court wide discretion in determining whether the sentences on multiple convictions are to run concurrently or consecutively. Brown v. State, 497 N.E.2d 1049, 1986 Ind. LEXIS 1281 (1986).

Where the trial court adequately stated the aggravating circumstances relied on to impose consecutive sentences and the court considered the goal of rehabilitation, no abuse of discretion resulted from imposition of consecutive sentences. Kubiak v. State, 508 N.E.2d 559, 1987 Ind. App. LEXIS 2718 (1987).

The general discretionary authority to order one sentence to be served consecutively to another afforded by former subsection (a), as it existed prior to the 1995 amendments, was restricted to those occasions when the sentencing court is contemporaneously meting out two or more terms of imprisonment. Saylor v. State, 565 N.E.2d 348, 1991 Ind. App. LEXIS 18 (1991).

The imposition of consecutive sentences is committed to the trial court's discretion, and a trial court may increase the basic penalties, impose consecutive sentences or both upon consideration of the relevant facts. Steele v. State, 569 N.E.2d 652, 1991 Ind. LEXIS 67 (1991).

—Considerations.

The trial judge may consider the circumstances of the crime committed in determining whether to impose consecutive sentences and this consideration may include the fact that defendant was armed and that he threatened human life. Warfield v. State, 275 Ind. 396, 417 N.E.2d 304, 1981 Ind. LEXIS 699 (1981).

It is within the discretion of the trial court to impose aggravated or consecutive sentences. In deciding such, the trial court may consider the aggravating circumstances listed in former IC 35-38-1-7(b) or any other aggravating circumstances. White v. State, 495 N.E.2d 725, 1986 Ind. LEXIS 1213 (1986).

When a trial court imposes consecutive terms of imprisonment, the record should disclose what factors were considered by the court to be mitigating or aggravating factors. Kahn v. State, 493 N.E.2d 790, 1986 Ind. App. LEXIS 2616 (1986).

The mere absence of collateral brutality is not a mitigating factor and does not mandate sentences

Discretion of Court. (Cont'd)

—Considerations. (Cont'd)
be served concurrently. Kubiak v. State, 508 N.E.2d 559, 1987 Ind. App. LEXIS 2718 (1987).

—Constitutional Prohibitions.
Constitutional prohibitions against cruel and unusual punishment and vindictive justice are a limitation upon the acts of the general assembly and not upon the discretion of a trial court acting within the framework of a statute imposing penalties for the offense. Allen v. State, 453 N.E.2d 1011, 1983 Ind. LEXIS 968 (1983).

Effective Date.
This section has no application when all the crimes involved were committed prior to the time it became effective. Baldock v. State, 177 Ind. App. 355, 379 N.E.2d 539, 1978 Ind. App. LEXIS 998 (1978), disapproved, Frink v. State, 568 N.E.2d 535, 1991 Ind. LEXIS 47 (1991).

—Law in Effect When Crime Committed.
Although this section, in effect when defendant was sentenced, permits either concurrent or consecutive terms, the law in effect when the crimes were committed is controlling and consecutive terms were improper when not authorized by the statute in effect at the time of commission of the crime. Rihl v. State, 413 N.E.2d 1046, 1980 Ind. App. LEXIS 1847 (1980).

Since the penalties imposed for the crimes committed by the defendant were not enhanced, the trial court was restricted by the 1994 version of this section to impose a sentence no greater than the presumptive sentence for a Class A felony in 1994, or 25 years, and eight years for the Class C felony and 1 year for the battery, a Class A misdemeanor, or nine years, for the episode of criminal conduct involving battery and escape, or a maximum sentence of 34 years. Becker v. State, 719 N.E.2d 858, 1999 Ind. App. LEXIS 2036 (1999).

Effect of Amendment.

—1994 Amendment.
The 1994 amendment to this section, which imposed a previously nonexistent limitation upon the trial court's authority to impose consecutive sentences, is ameliorative in nature. Tedlock v. State, 656 N.E.2d 273, 1995 Ind. App. LEXIS 1146 (1995).

—1995 Amendment.
The legislature's 1995 amendment to this section, which added a definition of the term "episode", was intended to clarify, and not change, the 1994 version of the statute. Tedlock v. State, 656 N.E.2d 273, 1995 Ind. App. LEXIS 1146 (1995).

Episode of Criminal Conduct.
Because rape and criminal deviate conduct are crimes of violence as defined by IC 35-50-1-2, the year limitation on consecutive sentences for crimes committed as part of an episode of criminal conduct is not applicable. Sallee v. State, 777 N.E.2d 1204, 2002 Ind. App. LEXIS 1888 (2002).

"Separate victims and separate acts" is not the test of distinct "episodes" for purposes of consecutive sentences under former IC 35-52-1-2. An "episode of criminal conduct" is offenses or a connected series of offenses that are closely connected in time, place, and circumstance; there is no requirement that the victims be the same, and the acts of two crimes are almost always distinct at least in one element. Harris v. State, 861 N.E.2d 1182, 2007 Ind. LEXIS 101 (2007).

—Not Shown.
Where defendant's four acts of molestation involved the same child at different times, each of which could be related without referring to the details of the other, defendant's actions did not constitute an "episode of criminal conduct". Lockhart v. State, 671 N.E.2d 893, 1996 Ind. App. LEXIS 1356 (1996).

Trial court could order sentences for three distinct episodes of defendant's conduct to be served consecutively, because each episode was sufficiently unrelated and could be described independently without referring to the specific details of the other episodes, where burglary and larceny constituted one distinct episode of conduct, defendant committed the crimes of resisting law enforcement and driving while suspended after speeding away in his car when police arrived, a second, distinct episode, and after he was arrested and transported to hospital he committed his final unrelated crime of escape. Newman v. State, 690 N.E.2d 735, 1998 Ind. App. LEXIS 14 (1998).

Where fraudulent checks were cashed over a five day period at two different stores, the offenses did not arise from a single episode. Logan v. State, 693 N.E.2d 1331, 1998 Ind. App. LEXIS 569 (1998).

Where the defendant's three convictions did not constitute a single episode of criminal conduct, in that he entered a home, took a purse and wallet, removed mail from the mailbox, and then entered another home, the limitation on the total sentence imposed by the sentencing statute was not applicable. Flynn v. State, 702 N.E.2d 741, 1998 Ind. App. LEXIS 2087 (1998).

Defendant's convictions did not amount to a single criminal episode where each marijuana sale occurred on different dates and involved different amounts of marijuana, the first sale was initiated by the informant, the second and third sale by defendant, and the third sale was made to an undercover police officer. Mendoza v. State, 737 N.E.2d 784, 2000 Ind. App. LEXIS 1647 (2000).

Defendant's possession of marijuana was a separate and distinct act from his acts of operating while intoxicated and resisting law enforcement, that did not constitute a single episode of criminal conduct; therefore, the trial court was not limited by IC 35-50-1-2(b) in sentencing defendant to consecutive terms of imprisonment. Ratliff v. State, 741 N.E.2d 424, 2000 Ind. App. LEXIS 2185 (2000).

Defendant's six forgeries were not "simultaneous" nor were they "contemporaneous" with one another, and so were not a single episode of criminal conduct. Smith v. State, 770 N.E.2d 290, 2002 Ind. LEXIS 520 (2002).

Episode of Criminal Conduct. (Cont'd)

—Not Shown. (Cont'd)

Single episode considerations did not limit the sentence imposed on defendant for drug dealing and related offenses where the evidence did not indicate that the various offenses, which took place on successive days, were particularly related to each other. Jones v. State, 807 N.E.2d 58, 2004 Ind. App. LEXIS 752 (2004).

Defendant's conduct in stopping his car during police chase and shooting at pursuing officers, then driving on, and then stopping again to shoot at another officer, was not single episode of criminal conduct for sentencing purposes under IC 35-50-1-2(b) but constituted two separate murder attempts for sentencing purposes. Reed v. State, 825 N.E.2d 911, 2005 Ind. App. LEXIS 648 (2005), transfer granted and vacated, 831 N.E.2d 750, 2005 Ind. LEXIS 574 (2005), superseded, 856 N.E.2d 1189, 2006 Ind. LEXIS 1021 (2006).

Defendant's confinement and battery of one victim and the confinement and battery of a second victim were not so closely related in time, place and circumstance as to constitute a single episode of criminal conduct pursuant to IC 35-50-1-2(b). Williams v. State, 889 N.E.2d 1274, 2008 Ind. App. LEXIS 1529 (2008).

—Shown.

Court's imposition of consecutive sentences for robbery, confinement and carrying a handgun without a license violated this section, because all of his convictions stemmed from same episode of criminal conduct, and defendant was entitled to retroactive application of the amendment to this section under the doctrine of amelioration. Timberlake v. State, 679 N.E.2d 1337, 1997 Ind. App. LEXIS 519 (1997).

Where all four offenses were committed by defendant at the same place on the same night, and burglary/arson was committed to conceal burglary/theft, all four counts against defendant related to a single criminal episode as defined by subsection (b). Jennings v. State, 687 N.E.2d 621, 1997 Ind. App. LEXIS 1746 (1997).

Although the record established, and all parties conceded, that the defendant's failure to pay an undivided amount of child support during the same time period for the benefit of four children born of the same marriage constituted one episode of criminal behavior for purposes of sentencing, the court erred when it imposed a five-year sentence on the defendant as a result of a plea agreement knowingly and voluntarily entered into by the defendant when the maximum sentence allowed by law was four years. Smith v. State, 717 N.E.2d 239, 1999 Ind. App. LEXIS 1752 (1999).

Defendant's sentence for his three convictions of pointing a firearm should not have exceeded four years, because a longer sentence would exceed the limits of IC 35-50-1-2(c) which provides that the total sentence that may be imposed for acts arising out of a single episode of criminal conduct cannot exceed the presumptive sentence for the next highest felony. Armstrong v. State, 742 N.E.2d 972, 2001 Ind. App. LEXIS 23 (2001).

Because defendant's felony convictions for three counts of attempted murder and one count of criminal mischief arose out of an episode of criminal conduct, at the time the offenses were committed and tried none were on the list of crimes of violence, and 55 years was the presumptive sentence for the next highest class of felony, the trial court erred in sentencing defendant to a total executed term of 80 years. Fight v. State, 768 N.E.2d 881, 2002 Ind. LEXIS 224 (2002).

Pursuant to the single larceny rule and IC 35-50-1-2(b), (c), defendant's theft by depositing forged checks in the bank in rapid succession was a single criminal episode, and the failure to advise petitioner of this made his guilty pleas and the resulting sentence invalid. Smith v. State, 770 N.E.2d 290, 2002 Ind. LEXIS 520 (2002).

Where defendant pled guilty to burglary, conspiracy to commit burglary, attempted robbery, and conspiracy to commit robbery, conspiracy to commit burglary and attempted robbery constituted one criminal episode; accordingly, under IC 35-50-1-2, longest total allowable sentence was 105 years, 50 years for burglary conviction and 55 years for other convictions. Fields v. State, 825 N.E.2d 841, 2005 Ind. App. LEXIS 608 (2005).

Shots from which attempted murder charges arose were fired within seconds of each other and were thus closely connected in time, place, and circumstance, constituting one episode of conduct within meaning of IC 35-50-1-2(b). Reed v. State, 856 N.E.2d 1189, 2006 Ind. LEXIS 1021 (2006).

Ex Post Facto Doctrine.

The ex post facto doctrine simply forbids a court to retroactively increase the punishment for a crime committed under the old code, and one is not disadvantaged if he receives that penalty to which he was entitled at the time he acted under existing laws. Garrett v. State, 411 N.E.2d 692, 1980 Ind. App. LEXIS 1733 (1980), disapproved, Sides v. State, 490 N.E.2d 318, 1986 Ind. LEXIS 1053 (1986).

Felony Conviction.

—Theft.

Defendant's 1974 theft conviction was not a Class D felony conviction, for purposes of the Habitual Offender Statute. Johnson v. State, 575 N.E.2d 282, 1991 Ind. App. LEXIS 1178 (1991).

Incarceration in Another State.

Indiana defendants are not entitled to credit on an Indiana sentence while incarcerated in another state. Penick v. State, 659 N.E.2d 484, 1995 Ind. LEXIS 191 (1995).

Mandatory Sentencing.

A person must commit another crime after being arrested and before discharge on the other crime for the mandatory sentencing statute to apply. Thompson v. State, 634 N.E.2d 775, 1994 Ind. App. LEXIS 615 (1994).

Merger.

When defendant was convicted of attempted

Merger. (Cont'd)

robbery and conspiracy to commit burglary, the attempted robbery was part of the conspiracy to commit burglary because no "fresh purpose" to commit the attempted robbery arose after the conspiracy to commit the burglary was completed, so defendant could not receive more than the maximum sentence for a burglary, of which he was also convicted, and the maximum sentence for the criminal incident, which consisted of his conspiracy to commit burglary and his attempted robbery. Green v. State, 850 N.E.2d 977, 2006 Ind. App. LEXIS 1386 (2006), transfer granted, — N.E.2d —, 2006 Ind. LEXIS 1037 (2006), aff'd, 856 N.E.2d 703, 2006 Ind. LEXIS 1022 (2006).

Mitigating Circumstances.

The trial court did not err when it failed to find remorse on the part of defendant to be a mitigating circumstance because the trial court is not required to find the presence of mitigating factors, and if the trial court does not find the existence of a mitigating factor after it has been argued by counsel, the trial court is not obligated to explain why it has found that the factor does not exist. Taylor v. State, 735 N.E.2d 308, 2000 Ind. App. LEXIS 1479 (2000).

When the trial court erred as a matter of law in stating that mitigators outweighed aggravators when the mitigators were not clearly delineated and supported by the record, the appellate court conducted its own independent review of consecutive sentences imposed upon defendant. Green v. State, 870 N.E.2d 560, 2007 Ind. App. LEXIS 1664 (2007), transfer granted, 878 N.E.2d 215, 2007 Ind. LEXIS 913 (2007).

Parole.

Former subsection (b), as it existed prior to the 1995 amendments, did not require a defendant to be "on" parole, probation or serving a term of imprisonment; rather, the statutory language speaks of a person who commits a crime during the time period: (1) after he is arrested for another crime; and (2) before he is discharged from probation, parole or imprisonment for that other crime. Ramirez v. State, 455 N.E.2d 609, 1983 Ind. App. LEXIS 3503 (1983), aff'd, 471 U.S. 147, 105 S. Ct. 1860, 85 L. Ed. 2d 113, 1985 U.S. LEXIS 201 (1985).

Nothing in IC 35-50-1-2 indicates an offender may not be on parole for one offense while serving a consecutive sentence. Pallett v. State, — N.E.2d —, 2009 Ind. App. LEXIS 331 (2009).

Plea Agreements.

Because defendant's plea agreement expressly provided that the maximum sentence would be imposed, the trial court was under no duty to explain its reasons for imposing the sentence to which the parties agreed. Bobbitt v. State, 725 N.E.2d 521, 2000 Ind. App. LEXIS 398 (2000).

Record.

When the trial court uses its discretionary power to increase or decrease the basic sentence or impose consecutive terms of imprisonment, the record must disclose what factors were considered by the judge to be mitigating or aggravating circumstances, and the record must further show that the determination of the sentence was based upon a consideration of the facts of the specific crime and the relation of the sentence imposed to the objectives to be served by that sentence. Allen v. State, 453 N.E.2d 1011, 1983 Ind. LEXIS 968 (1983).

Although aggregate sentence on five criminal charges was in accordance with IC 35-50-1-2, aggregate sentence was vacated because record did not reflect sentence imposed for each individual conviction. Murray v. State, 798 N.E.2d 895, 2003 Ind. App. LEXIS 2149 (2003).

—Harmless Error.

Where the record showed that defendant's consecutive sentence was mandatory under the statute, it was unnecessary to go through the formality of remanding the case to the trial court after the trial court erroneously failed to include a statement specifying whether defendant's consecutive sentence was discretionary or mandatory. Miller v. State, 637 N.E.2d 1359, 1994 Ind. App. LEXIS 954 (1994).

Refusal to Instruct Jury on This Section.

Since under the statute the trial court is required to fix the penalty and sentence of the person convicted it was not error to refuse to give this section to the jury as an instruction. Inman v. State, 271 Ind. 491, 393 N.E.2d 767, 1979 Ind. LEXIS 707 (1979).

Review.

If a trial court imposes an enhanced or consecutive sentence upon an invalid aggravator, the appellate court may nonetheless affirm the decision if sufficient aggravating circumstances otherwise exist to support the lower court ruling and it appears that the invalid aggravator had little, if any, impact upon the sentence. Payne v. State, 687 N.E.2d 252, 1997 Ind. App. LEXIS 1659 (1997).

Defendant did not allege that any of the three Robertson exceptions applied that required a trial court to limit itself to imposing the advisory sentence when imposing a consecutive sentence, and, thus, the appellate court could uphold defendant's two-and-one-half year sentence for domestic battery, as a Class D felony, even though the advisory sentence for Class D felonies was one-and-one-half years; exceptions involved: (1) a consecutive sentence for nonviolent felony convictions arising out of a single episode of criminal conduct, according to IC 35-50-1-2; (2) a consecutive sentence imposed as an additional fixed term to a habitual offender, IC 35-50-2-8; or (3) a consecutive sentence imposed as an additional fixed term to a repeat sexual offender under IC 35-50-2-14, and since defendant could not show any of the exceptions applied, a sentence higher than the advisory sentence could be imposed. Freyn v. State, 884 N.E.2d 901, 2008 Ind. App. LEXIS 791 (2008).

Sentence Enhancement.

Although the same aggravating circumstance

Sentence Enhancement. (Cont'd)
may support both decisions, the trial court must separately indicate which factors, if any, support the enhancement and the consecutive sentences. Saucerman v. State, 555 N.E.2d 1351, 1990 Ind. App. LEXIS 807 (1990).

The trial court's failure to find separate aggravating factors to impose both enhanced and consecutive sentences is not fatal to the trial court's sentencing determination, assuming the sentences are otherwise authorized by statute. Ratliff v. State, 741 N.E.2d 424, 2000 Ind. App. LEXIS 2185 (2000).

Separate Episodes.
Crimes of burglary, forgery, and theft committed by defendant on three separate dates over course of more than month and against separate victims did not constitute single episode requiring maximum sentence of 10 years under former IC 35-50-1-2(c) and IC 35-50-2-5; it was possible to give complete account of crimes committed on each date without referring to offenses committed on other dates. Hope v. State, 834 N.E.2d 713, 2005 Ind. App. LEXIS 1791 (2005).

Statement of Reasons.
If the trial court imposes consecutive sentences, IC 35-38-1-3 requires the trial court to include a statement indicating the reasons for selecting the sentence it renders. Pearson v. State, 543 N.E.2d 1141, 1989 Ind. App. LEXIS 921 (1989).

Although a consecutive sentence was mandatory under the provisions of this section, the sentencing court is not exempt from the requirement for a specific statement of the basis for the sentence. Ray v. State, 585 N.E.2d 36, 1992 Ind. App. LEXIS 71 (1992).

Even though the trial court did not state the specific reasons why each factor was aggravating or mitigating, where the trial court engaged in an evaluative balancing process, the court satisfied the requirement of articulating the reasons. Mitchem v. State, 685 N.E.2d 671, 1997 Ind. LEXIS 128 (1997).

When the record indicates court engaged in evaluative and balancing processes in sentencing but did not sufficiently articulate reasons for the sentence imposed, the reasons underlying the sentencing statement requirement have been met. Becker v. State, 695 N.E.2d 968, 1998 Ind. App. LEXIS 740 (1998).

—Insufficient.
Where court's sentencing statement did not specify that victim suffered serious bodily harm, that defendant intended to cause such harm, or that sentences were enhanced because of serious bodily injury, the required factors for imposition of consecutive sentences were not established. Becker v. State, 695 N.E.2d 968, 1998 Ind. App. LEXIS 740 (1998).

—Review.
If the trial court fails to give any statement of reasons for imposing consecutive sentences the cause must be remanded for correction of the

deficiency. However, where a statement of reasons is given but lacks the required specificity, the court of appeals is permitted to review the record to determine if there exists, in fact, an adequate basis for imposing consecutive sentences. Pearson v. State, 543 N.E.2d 1141, 1989 Ind. App. LEXIS 921 (1989).

It is very important for sentencing court to state unequivocally what circumstances justify the sentence imposed in order that a reviewing court can determine the reasonableness or legality of the sentence. Becker v. State, 695 N.E.2d 968, 1998 Ind. App. LEXIS 740 (1998).

Violation of Probation.
This section requires the sentence of a crime committed while on probation to be served consecutively but it does not require that the sentence for the violation of the probation be served consecutively. Dolan v. State, 420 N.E.2d 1364, 1981 Ind. App. LEXIS 1446 (1981).

—Proof.
It was not error for a judge to sentence a defendant and, moments later, in the same consolidated hearing with the same parties, revoke the defendant's probation on a prior conviction without requiring additional proof that the defendant violated his probation by committing the crime for which he was sentenced a few moments earlier. Bane v. State, 579 N.E.2d 1339, 1991 Ind. App. LEXIS 1712 (1991).

Cited:
Duvall v. State, 275 Ind. 188, 415 N.E.2d 718, 1981 Ind. LEXIS 662 (1981); Bumgardner v. State, 422 N.E.2d 1244, 1981 Ind. LEXIS 794 (1981); Pearson v. State, 428 N.E.2d 808, 1981 Ind. App. LEXIS 1769 (1981); Yager v. State, 437 N.E.2d 454, 1982 Ind. LEXIS 874 (1982); Kocher v. State, 439 N.E.2d 1344, 1982 Ind. LEXIS 970 (1982); Hoskins v. State, 441 N.E.2d 419, 1982 Ind. LEXIS 995 (1982); Petruso v. State, 441 N.E.2d 446, 1982 Ind. LEXIS 1013 (1982); Watts v. State, 434 N.E.2d 891, 1982 Ind. App. LEXIS 1183 (1982); Chandler v. State, 451 N.E.2d 319, 1983 Ind. LEXIS 894 (1983); Joy v. State, 460 N.E.2d 551, 1984 Ind. App. LEXIS 2389 (1984); Hennings v. State, 465 N.E.2d 1142, 1984 Ind. App. LEXIS 2793 (1984); Little v. State, 475 N.E.2d 677, 1985 Ind. LEXIS 783 (1985); Chambers v. State, 478 N.E.2d 1234, 1985 Ind. LEXIS 855 (1985); Sides v. State, 480 N.E.2d 572, 1985 Ind. App. LEXIS 2633 (1985); Dunfee v. State, 482 N.E.2d 499, 1985 Ind. App. LEXIS 2765 (1985); Sides v. State, 482 N.E.2d 757 (Ind. App. 1985); Komyatti v. State, 490 N.E.2d 279, 1986 Ind. LEXIS 1063 (1986); Smith v. State, 491 N.E.2d 193, 1986 Ind. LEXIS 1098 (1986); Henderson v. State, 492 N.E.2d 20, 1986 Ind. LEXIS 1130 (1986); Patterson v. State, 500 N.E.2d 1191, 1986 Ind. LEXIS 1408 (1986); Nagy v. State, 505 N.E.2d 434, 1987 Ind. LEXIS 864 (1987); McNeely v. State, 529 N.E.2d 1317, 1988 Ind. App. LEXIS 807 (1988); Jones v. State, 536 N.E.2d 1051, 1989 Ind. App. LEXIS 258 (1989); Bigler v. State, 540 N.E.2d 32, 1989 Ind. LEXIS 189 (1989); Brady v. State, 540 N.E.2d 59, 1989 Ind. App. LEXIS 475

(1989); Parker v. State, 567 N.E.2d 105, 1991 Ind. App. LEXIS 214 (1991); Schick v. State, 570 N.E.2d 918, 1991 Ind. App. LEXIS 669 (1991); Grayson v. State, 593 N.E.2d 1200, 1992 Ind. App. LEXIS 920 (1992); Carrion v. State, 619 N.E.2d 972, 1993 Ind. App. LEXIS 1075 (1993); Liggin v. State, 665 N.E.2d 618, 1996 Ind. App. LEXIS 716 (1996); Dillehay v. State, 672 N.E.2d 956, 1996 Ind. App. LEXIS 1481 (1996); Singer v. State, 674 N.E.2d 11, 1996 Ind. App. LEXIS 1605 (1996); Palmer v. State, 679 N.E.2d 887, 1997 Ind. LEXIS 53 (1997); Richards v. State, 681 N.E.2d 208, 1997 Ind. LEXIS 80 (1997); Spann v. State, 681 N.E.2d 223, 1997 Ind. App. LEXIS 545 (1997); Jennings v. State, 687 N.E.2d 621, 1997 Ind. App. LEXIS 1746 (1997); Ridley v. State, 690 N.E.2d 177, 1997 Ind. LEXIS 213 (1997); Morrow v. State, 690 N.E.2d 183, 1997 Ind. App. LEXIS 210 (1997); Smith v. State, 718 N.E.2d 794, 1999 Ind. App. LEXIS 1918 (1999); McCurry v. State, 718 N.E.2d 1201, 1999 Ind. App. LEXIS 1971 (1999); Allen v. State, 722 N.E.2d 1246, 2000 Ind. App. LEXIS 12 (2000); Lewis v. State, 726 N.E.2d 836, 2000 Ind. App. LEXIS 508 (2000); Collins v. State, 740 N.E.2d 143, 2000 Ind. App. LEXIS 2037 (2000); Stafford v. State, 736 N.E.2d 326, 2000 Ind. App. LEXIS 1585 (2000); Crawford v. State, 755 N.E.2d 565, 2001 Ind. LEXIS 893 (2001); Diedrich v. State, 744 N.E.2d 1004, 2001 Ind. App. LEXIS 413 (2001); Catt v. State, 749 N.E.2d 633, 2001 Ind. ·App. LEXIS 963 (2001); Ingram v. State, 761 N.E.2d 883, 2002 Ind. App. LEXIS 52 (2002); Sallee v. State, 785 N.E.2d 645, 2003 Ind. App. LEXIS 458 (2003); Patton v. State, 837 N.E.2d 576, 2005 Ind. App. LEXIS 2177 (2005); Carneal v. State, 859 N.E.2d 1255, 2007 Ind. App. LEXIS 30 (2007); Brown v. State, — N.E.2d —, 2009 Ind. App. LEXIS 890 (2009).

RESEARCH REFERENCES

Indiana Law Review.
Double Jeopardy Protection — Illusion or Reality?, 13 Ind. L. Rev. 863 (1980).

Update — Criminal Law and Procedure, 26 Ind. L. Rev. 891 (1993).

Recent Developments in Indiana Criminal Law and Procedure, 28 Ind. L. Rev. 819 (1995).

Recent Developments In Indiana Criminal Law and Procedure: Case Developments in 1995, 29 Ind. L. Rev. 860 (1996).

Criminal Law and Procedure: Recent Developments in Indiana Criminal Law and Procedure, 34 Ind. L. Rev. 645 (2001).

Survey: Criminal Law and Procedure: Recent Developments in Indiana Criminal Law and Procedure, 35 Ind. L. Rev. 1347 (2002).

Survey: Criminal Law and Procedure: Recent Developments in Indiana Criminal Law and Procedure (October 1, 2003, to September 30, 2004), 38 Ind. L. Rev. 999 (2005).

Survey: Criminal Law and Procedure: Recent Developments in Indiana Criminal Law and Procedure (October 1, 2004, through September 30, 2005), 39 Ind. L. Rev. 893 (2006).

Res Gestae.
Criminal Justice Notes — Merger, 23 Res Gestae 32.

Criminal Justice Notes, 44 (No. 12) Res Gestae 32 (2000).

Criminal Justice Notes: Appellate sentence review. 47 (No 7) Res Gestae 31 (2004).

Criminal Justice Notes 6/05: Suspended sentences and IC 35-50-1-2(c), 49 (No. 2) Res Gestae 37 (2005).

Criminal Justice Notes 5/08: Double enhancements, 52 (No. 1) Res Gestae 40 (2008).

Collateral References.
Validity, construction, and application of concurrent-sentence doctrine — state cases. 56 A.L.R.5th 385.

35-50-1-3. [Repealed.]

Compiler's Notes.
This section, providing for liability for costs, was repealed by P.L.305-1987, § 38. For present similar provisions, see IC 33-37-2-2.

35-50-1-4. [Repealed.]

Compiler's Notes.
This section, concerning disenfranchising of incarcerated convicts, was repealed by P.L.5-1986, § 61, effective March 4, 1986.

35-50-1-5. Effect of postconviction remedy on subsequent sentencing.

If:

(1) Prosecution is initiated against a petitioner who has successfully sought relief under any proceeding for postconviction remedy and a conviction is subsequently obtained; or

(2) A sentence has been set aside under a postconviction remedy and the successful petitioner is to be resentenced;

the sentencing court may impose a more severe penalty than that originally imposed, and the court shall give credit for time served.

History.
  P.L.179-1984, § 3.

NOTES TO DECISIONS

Retroactivity.
  The amended rule, allowing more severe sentences after post-conviction remedial action, should not apply retroactively, but should apply only to petitions filed after the amendment date because of the potential due process and equal protection issues. Dean v. State, 499 N.E.2d 185, 1986 Ind. LEXIS 1337 (1986).

Cited:
  Linthicum v. State, 511 N.E.2d 1026, 1987 Ind. LEXIS 1019 (1987); Dukes v. State, 661 N.E.2d 1263, 1996 Ind. App. LEXIS 200 (1996); Kincaid v. State, 778 N.E.2d 789, 2002 Ind. LEXIS 856 (2002).

35-50-1-6. Placement in secure private facility.

(a) Before a person who has been convicted of an offense and committed to the department of correction is assigned to a department of correction program or facility under IC 11-10-1, the sentencing court may recommend that the department of correction place the person in a secure private facility (as defined in IC 31-9-2-115) if:

(1) the person was less than sixteen (16) years of age on the date of sentencing; and

(2) the court determines that the person would benefit from the treatment offered by the facility.

(b) A secure private facility may terminate a placement and request the department of correction to reassign a convicted person to another department of correction facility or program.

(c) When a convicted person becomes twenty-one (21) years of age or if a secure private facility terminates a placement under subsection (b) a convicted person shall:

(1) be assigned to a department of correction facility or program under IC 11-10-1-3(b); and

(2) serve the remainder of the sentence in the department of correction facility or program.

(d) A person who is placed in a secure private facility under this section:

(1) is entitled to earn credit time under IC 35-50-6; and

(2) may be deprived of earned credit time as provided under rules adopted by the department of correction under IC 4-22-2.

History.
  P.L.79-1994, § 17; P.L.1-1997, § 154; P.L.1-2002, § 151.

RESEARCH REFERENCES

Indiana Law Review.
  Indiana Constitutional Developments: Incremental Change, 41 Ind. L. Rev. 923 (2008).

35-50-1-7. Notice to victim.

Whenever a court commits a person to the department of correction as a result of a conviction, the court shall notify the department of correction of the last known name and address of any victim of the offense for which the person is convicted.

History.
   P.L.90-2000, § 19.

CHAPTER 1A

ADDITIONAL GENERAL PROVISIONS

35-50-1A-1 — 35-50-1A-18. [Repealed.]

Compiler's Notes.
   This chapter, which was enacted as IC 35-4.1-4 and transferred to this position by the compiler, and concerned the entry of judgment and sentenc-ing, was repealed by Acts 1976, P.L.148, § 29; Acts 1977, P.L.340, § 148; P.L.311-1983, § 49. For present similar provisions, see IC 35-38-1.

CHAPTER 2

SENTENCES FOR FELONIES

35-50-2-1. Definitions.

   (a) As used in this chapter, "Class D felony conviction" means a conviction of a Class D felony in Indiana and a conviction, in any other jurisdiction at any time, with respect to which the convicted person might have been imprisoned for more than one (1) year. However, it does not include a conviction with respect to which the person has been pardoned, or a conviction of a Class A misdemeanor under section 7(b) [IC 35-50-2-7(b)] of this chapter.

   (b) As used in this chapter, "felony conviction" means a conviction, in any jurisdiction at any time, with respect to which the convicted person might have been imprisoned for more than one (1) year. However, it does not include a conviction with respect to which the person has been pardoned, or a conviction of a Class A misdemeanor under section 7(b) of this chapter.

   (c) As used in this chapter, "minimum sentence" means:
       (1) for murder, forty-five (45) years;
       (2) for a Class A felony, twenty (20) years;
       (3) for a Class B felony, six (6) years;
       (4) for a Class C felony, two (2) years; and
       (5) for a Class D felony, one-half (½) year.

History.

IC 35-50-2-1, as added by Acts 1976, P.L.148, § 8; 1977, P.L.340, § 114; P.L.334-1983, § 1; P.L.98-1988, § 8; P.L.243-2001, § 2; P.L.291-2001, § 225.

Compiler's Notes.

This section was separately amended by P.L.243-2001 and by P.L.291-2001, neither act referring to the other. Because the amendments were identical, this section is set out only once.

Cross References.

Compensation for victims of violent crimes, IC 5-2-6.1.

Crimes to be defined by statute, IC 1-1-2-2.

NOTES TO DECISIONS

ANALYSIS

In General.
Amendment of Charge.
Applicability.
Consecutive Sentences.
Convictions in Other Jurisdictions.
—Federal Offenses.
—Indeterminate Sentence.
—Insufficient Evidence.
Felony Conviction.
—Theft.
Instructions.
Minimum Sentence.
Penalties Apportioned.

In General.

Crimes punishable by imprisonment in the state prison were felonies. State v. Smith, 1847 Ind. LEXIS 83 (1847); Hicks v. State, 150 Ind. 293, 50 N.E. 27, 1898 Ind. LEXIS 182 (1898); Mahok v. State, 202 Ind. 473, 174 N.E. 281, 1931 Ind. LEXIS 19 (1931); Knotts v. State, 243 Ind. 501, 187 N.E.2d 571, 1963 Ind. LEXIS 128 (1963); Stevenson v. State, 164 Ind. App. 199, 327 N.E.2d 621, 1975 Ind. App. LEXIS 1129 (1975).

The word "felony" must be interpreted in the light of the definition of the offense. Dougherty v. State, 206 Ind. 678, 191 N.E. 84, 1934 Ind. LEXIS 230 (1934).

Where, in a prosecution for unlawful possession of burglary tools with intent to commit burglary, the affidavit charged that accused had, prior to the attempt set forth in the affidavit, been convicted of a felony, it charged a felony with sufficient certainty and was good as against a motion in arrest of judgment. Dougherty v. State, 206 Ind. 678, 191 N.E. 84, 1934 Ind. LEXIS 230 (1934).

Allegation in affidavit charging receiving stolen goods "feloniously" stolen by two minors was mere surplusage and did not charge minors with the commission of a felony requiring imprisonment in the state prison. McCoy v. State, 241 Ind. 104, 170 N.E.2d 43, 1960 Ind. LEXIS 143 (1960).

A former similar statute (IC 35-1-1-1, repealed) did not require that imprisonment must be in the state prison in order for the offense to be characterized as a felony, but it was sufficient if the offender may be imprisoned in the state prison. Paneitz v. State, 246 Ind. 418, 204 N.E.2d 350, 1965 Ind. LEXIS 368 (1965), cert. denied, 382 U.S. 883, 86 S. Ct. 176, 15 L. Ed. 2d 123, 1965 U.S. LEXIS 500 (1965); In re Sobieski, 246 Ind. 222, 204 N.E.2d 353, 1965 Ind. LEXIS 344 (1965); Bernard v. State, 248 Ind. 688, 230 N.E.2d 536, 1967 Ind. LEXIS 498 (1967).

Amendment of Charge.

Where defendant was convicted in a city court on an affidavit charging assault and battery, and thereafter he appealed to the circuit court, it was error for the circuit court to permit the affidavit to be amended over his objection so as to charge him with assault and battery with intent to kill, since the amendment changed the crime sought to be charged from a misdemeanor to a felony. Drury v. State, 223 Ind. 140, 59 N.E.2d 116, 1945 Ind. LEXIS 86 (1945).

Applicability.

Where no portion of a defendant's sentence was suspended and he did not receive the shortest sentence under either this section or IC 35-50-2-3, any question of whether these statutes conflict was of no legal consequence to him, and he was not entitled to a resentencing hearing. Johnson v. State, 702 N.E.2d 711, 1998 Ind. LEXIS 609 (1998).

Consecutive Sentences.

Where trial court mistakenly believed it was obligated to order defendant's sentences to run consecutively under subsection (b) of this section, and the state conceded that the mandatory provision of subsection (b) was misapplied in this case, but argued the aggravating factors were sufficient to support an order of consecutive sentences under the discretionary provision, IC 35-50-1-2(a) prior to the 1995 amendments (now see IC 35-50-1-2(c)), while the same reasons may have served to justify both enhanced and consecutive sentences, the fact remained that the court appeared to base its order for consecutive sentences on its mistaken interpretation of the statute. Because the mandatory provision was not applicable in this case, the case was remanded for a specific and individualized statement of whether the facts supported the imposition of consecutive terms. Barker v. State, 622 N.E.2d 1336, 1993 Ind. App. LEXIS 1383 (1993).

Convictions in Other Jurisdictions.

Exhibits in prosecution for being a habitual offender which showed that sentences served on prior offenses in California were greater than one year were sufficient to prove that defendant's California convictions were felonies within meaning of this section. Allen v. State, 439 N.E.2d 615, 1982 Ind. LEXIS 936 (1982).

The classification of crimes as felonies or misdemeanors in other states is not relevant for purposes of establishing a prior felony conviction in determining habitual criminal status in Indiana;

Convictions in Other Jurisdictions. (Cont'd)
therefore, because the defendant's prior convictions were both for more than one year imprisonment, the state showed sufficient proof that defendant had two prior felony convictions as required by the habitual offender statute. Galmore v. State, 467 N.E.2d 1173, 1984 Ind. LEXIS 906 (1984).

Evidence that the defendant had been convicted of burglary in another state and that he received a 60-day jail sentence and two years probation was insufficient to establish the defendant's prior conviction for a felony, since the evidence did not indicate that the defendant could have been imprisoned for more than one year for the burglary conviction. Jones v. State, 485 N.E.2d 627, 1985 Ind. LEXIS 1039 (1985).

A foreign state's classification of an offense as a felony or a misdemeanor is not relevant for purposes of establishing a prior felony conviction when determining habitual criminal status in Indiana. Beach v. State, 496 N.E.2d 43, 1986 Ind. LEXIS 1233 (1986).

A decision that the defendant's prior Tennessee conviction was for a felony was erroneous where it was based upon the fact that the Tennessee indictment stated that defendant "feloniously" possessed burglar tools. This is not the test by which Indiana determines whether an earlier judgment was a felony conviction. Cavendish v. State, 496 N.E.2d 46, 1986 Ind. LEXIS 1227 (1986).

Evidence was insuffient to show that the defendant's prior Ohio concealed weapon conviction was for a felony, since the document relating to the conviction was silent as to the potential penalty and a testifying police officer did not know whether the charge had been treated as a misdemeanor or a felony. Straub v. State, 567 N.E.2d 87, 1991 Ind. LEXIS 20 (1991).

The defendant's conviction in Kentucky of Class D felony with a sentence of one to five years met the definition of a felony under the habitual offender statute. Stewart v. State, 688 N.E.2d 1254, 1997 Ind. LEXIS 219 (1997).

—Federal Offenses.
Convictions not within the jurisdiction of the Indiana courts were admissible in a habitual offender determination, and this included convictions to a federal institution when former IC 35-1-1-1 defined "felony" as an offense punishable by imprisonment in the state prison. Denton v. State, 496 N.E.2d 576, 1986 Ind. LEXIS 1252 (1986).

Where person was convicted of a federal offense, for which he received a sentence of two years, he "might have been imprisoned for more than one (1) year" and the offense was a felony under this section. Further, in 1984, he entered a plea of guilty to the charged offense, which the district court ultimately reduced to a conviction. He therefore "had entered a plea of guilty ... to" and "been convicted of a felony (as defined in IC 35-50-2-1)" and "was disqualified from ... being a candidate for an elected office" under IC 3-8-1-5(b)(3)(A) and (B). The election board properly decided that he was disqualified for candidacy and that his name should not be placed on the ballot. Wilson v. Montgomery County Election Bd., 642 N.E.2d 258, 1994 Ind. App. LEXIS 1498 (1994).

—Indeterminate Sentence.
Where statute of another state provided for punishment by imprisonment for not less than one nor more than 15 years, a conviction under such statute as charged in an habitual offender proceeding was a felony conviction as defined in this section. Collins v. State, 275 Ind. 86, 415 N.E.2d 46, 1981 Ind. LEXIS 657 (1981), cert. denied, 451 U.S. 991, 101 S. Ct. 2331, 68 L. Ed. 2d 851, 1981 U.S. LEXIS 2139 (1981).

—Insufficient Evidence.
Where the state relied on the defendant's plea of guilty to an out-of-state offense as one of the requisite prior convictions for an adjudication as an habitual offender, but where, under that state's law, the resulting suspended sentence and placement on probation did not constitute a "conviction," there was insufficient evidence to support his adjudication as an habitual offender. Bochner v. State, 715 N.E.2d 416, 1999 Ind. App. LEXIS 2419 (1999).

Felony Conviction.

—Theft.
Although defendant had bargained for and received a minimal sentence for the crime of theft under former Burns' § 10-3039, notwithstanding the language of "misdemeanor" used in the plea bargain and by the trial court, he had been convicted of a felony. Thus, the trial court did not err in permitting the record of that conviction to be used in the habitual offender phase of a later trial. Wolfe v. State, 512 N.E.2d 185, 1987 Ind. LEXIS 1033 (1987).

Instructions.
There is no prejudice to defendant where trial court's instruction omits the second clause of the definition of "felony conviction" (beginning with "but it does not include") when no evidence is presented to show relevance of clause. Choate v. State, 462 N.E.2d 1037, 1984 Ind. LEXIS 816 (1984).

Minimum Sentence.
This section provides that the minimum sentence for a Class D felony is one year, but IC 35-50-2-7 provides the court may reduce the one and one-half year presumptive sentence for a Class D felony by up to one year, and because IC 35-50-2-7 was most recently amended by the legislature, the minimum sentence for a Class D felony is six months. Antcliff v. State, 688 N.E.2d 166, 1997 Ind. App. LEXIS 759 (1997).

The provisions of IC 35-50-2-3(a) establish the length of murder sentences generally, while those of this section establish, in conjunction with other statutes, what portion of a sentence may be suspended. Johnson v. State, 702 N.E.2d 711, 1998 Ind. LEXIS 609 (1998).

Penalties Apportioned.
Sentencing under the current criminal code appropriately apportions penalties to the nature of the offense as required by Ind. Const., Art. 1, § 16.

Penalties Apportioned. (Cont'd)
Williams v. State, 271 Ind. 656, 395 N.E.2d 239, 1979 Ind. LEXIS 734 (1979); Wells v. State, 397 N.E.2d 1250, 1979 Ind. App. LEXIS 1481 (1979).

Cited:
Griffin v. State, 275 Ind. 107, 415 N.E.2d 60, 1981 Ind. LEXIS 656 (1981); Clay v. State, 440 N.E.2d 466, 1982 Ind. LEXIS 963 (1982); Minneman v. State, 441 N.E.2d 673, 1982 Ind. LEXIS 1011 (1982); Thomas v. State, 443 N.E.2d 1197, 1983 Ind. LEXIS 721 (1983); Mc Brady v. State, 459 N.E.2d 719, 1984 Ind. LEXIS 755 (1984); Washington v. State, 517 N.E.2d 77, 1987 Ind. LEXIS 1199 (1987); Stroud v. State, 517 N.E.2d 780, 1988 Ind. LEXIS 3 (1988); Slocumb v. State, 568 N.E.2d 1068, 1991 Ind. App. LEXIS 448 (1991); Cain v. State, 594 N.E.2d 835, 1992 Ind. App. LEXIS 1062 (1992); Dickson v. State, 624 N.E.2d 472, 1993 Ind. App. LEXIS 1020 (1993); Mayo v. State, 681 N.E.2d 689, 1997 Ind. LEXIS 77 (1997); Smith v. State, 717 N.E.2d 1277, 1999 Ind. App. LEXIS 1922 (1999); Simmons v. State, 773 N.E.2d 823, 2002 Ind. App. LEXIS 1215 (2002); Wolf v. State, 793 N.E.2d 328, 2003 Ind. App. LEXIS 1509 (2003); Holland v. Rizzo, 872 N.E.2d 659, 2007 Ind. App. LEXIS 1932 (2007); Page v. State, 878 N.E.2d 404, 2007 Ind. App. LEXIS 2937 (2007).

RESEARCH REFERENCES

Indiana Law Review.
Survey of Recent Developments in Indiana Evidence Law, 31 Ind. L. Rev. 593 (1998).
Survey: Criminal Law and Procedure: Recent Developments in Indiana Criminal Law and Procedure, 35 Ind. L. Rev. 1347 (2002).

Res Gestae.
Overlooked Consequences of Apprendi: The Unconstitutionality of Indiana's Non-Capital Sentencing, 46 (No. 8) Res Gestae 19 (2003).

35-50-2-1.3. "Advisory sentence" defined — Use of advisory sentences.

(a) For purposes of sections 3 through 7 [IC 35-50-2-3 through IC 35-50-2-7] of this chapter, "advisory sentence" means a guideline sentence that the court may voluntarily consider as the midpoint between the maximum sentence and the minimum sentence.

(b) Except as provided in subsection (c), a court is not required to use an advisory sentence.

(c) In imposing:

(1) consecutive sentences for felony convictions that are not crimes of violence (as defined in IC 35-50-1-2(a)) arising out of an episode of criminal conduct, in accordance with IC 35-50-1-2;

(2) an additional fixed term to an habitual offender under section 8 [IC 35-50-2-8] of this chapter; or

(3) an additional fixed term to a repeat sexual offender under section 14 [IC 35-50-2-14] of this chapter;

a court is required to use the appropriate advisory sentence in imposing a consecutive sentence or an additional fixed term. However, the court is not required to use the advisory sentence in imposing the sentence for the underlying offense.

(d) This section does not require a court to use an advisory sentence in imposing consecutive sentences for felony convictions that do not arise out of an episode of criminal conduct.

History.
P.L.71-2005, § 5; P.L.178-2007, § 4, emergency eff. July 1, 2007.

NOTES TO DECISIONS

ANALYSIS

In General.
Applicability.
Consecutive Sentences.
Underlying Offense.

In General.
Indiana Legislature has amended Indiana's sentencing statutes to provide for advisory sentences rather than presumptive sentences. Childress v. State, 848 N.E.2d 1073, 2006 Ind. LEXIS 474 (2006).

Applicability.

Appellate court was not required to revise defendant's sentence pursuant to Ind. R. App. P. 7(B) because consecutive presumptive sentences were properly imposed for defendant's manslaughter and aggravated battery convictions in that the multiple-victim aggravator tipped the balance so that the aggravators outweighed the mitigators and a 40-year total sentence was not improper in light of the fact that defendant committed separate offenses against two separate victims. A new sentencing scheme codified at IC 35-50-2-1.3 and IC 35-38-1-7.1(d) did not apply in that defendant's offenses were committed before the effective date of the amended scheme. Gleaves v. State, 859 N.E.2d 766, 2007 Ind. App. LEXIS 15 (2007).

IC 35-50-2-1.3 did not limit a defendant's consecutive sentences for vehicular homicide to four-year advisory sentences because he committed his crimes before the statute went into effect, and the amelioration doctrine did not require its retroactive application because it was not ameliorative, as it did not limit, beyond IC 35-50-1-2, a trial court's ability to impose consecutive sentences. Barber v. State, 863 N.E.2d 1199, 2007 Ind. App. LEXIS 695 (2007).

Trial court did not err in sentencing defendant to 65 years in prison for defendant's shooting of a man who allegedly owed money to defendant, and one year, to be served concurrently, for defendant's carrying of a handgun without a license, which would be served consecutive to an 18-year sentence imposed upon defendant in another cause; the trial court was not required to impose the advisory sentence upon defendant in the current case because the sentences imposed were concurrent sentences, not consecutive sentences, and the consecutive sentence involved was for a crime imposed in another cause not in the current cause. Dixson v. State, 865 N.E.2d 704, 2007 Ind. App. LEXIS 913 (2007).

Consecutive Sentences.

"Appropriate advisory sentence" in IC 35-50-2-1.3, which references IC 35-50-1-2, refers to the total penalty for an episode of criminal conduct; the advisory sentence for a felony which is one class of felony higher than the most serious of the felonies for which the person has been convicted is the "appropriate advisory sentence" for an episode of non-violent criminal conduct. IC 35-50-1-2 in no other way limits the ability of a trial court to impose consecutive sentences; in turn, IC 35-50-2-1.3 imposes no additional restrictions on the ability of trial courts to impose consecutive sentences, and thus is not ameliorative. White v. State, 849 N.E.2d 735, 2006 Ind. App. LEXIS 1198 (2006).

IC 35-50-2-1.3 was not ameliorative and thus did not apply to a defendant whose crimes were committed before it took effect. Even if the statute had been in effect at the time of the offenses, it would not have aided defendant because it placed no restrictions on the ability of trial courts to impose consecutive sentences beyond the restrictions already in place by virtue of IC 35-50-1-2(c). White v. State, 849 N.E.2d 735, 2006 Ind. App. LEXIS 1198 (2006).

IC 35-50-2-1.3 adds no restrictions on the ability of trial courts to impose consecutive sentences beyond the restrictions already in place by virtue of IC 35-50-1-2(c). Barber v. State, 863 N.E.2d 1199, 2007 Ind. App. LEXIS 695 (2007).

Enhanced consecutive sentences were proper because, contrary to defendant's argument, IC 35-50-2-1.3 did not restrict consecutive sentences to advisory sentences; it was within the trial court's discretion to sentence defendant to enhanced consecutive sentences, and defendant did not established an abuse of that discretion. As aggravating circumstances, the trial court considered that there was a substantial risk that defendant would commit future crimes, that the nature and circumstances of the offense were particularly disturbing based on defendant's willingness to harm himself, and that defendant had a particularly serious criminal history, each of which aggravating circumstances was sufficient to warrant the consecutive sentences. Luhrsen v. State, 864 N.E.2d 452, 2007 Ind. App. LEXIS 773 (2007).

When IC 35-50-2-1.3 was read in conjunction with IC 35-50-1-2, it was apparent that the reference to the "appropriate advisory sentence" was meant to apply to situations involving the single episode of criminal conduct limitation on consecutive sentencing. Consequently, the trial court had the authority to impose enhanced, consecutive sentences on defendant, and it did not err by doing so. Geiger v. State, 866 N.E.2d 830, 2007 Ind. App. LEXIS 1081 (2007), aff'd, transfer granted, — N.E.2d —, 2007 Ind. LEXIS 655 (2007).

When IC 35-50-2-1.3 is read in conjunction with IC 35-50-1-2, it is apparent that the reference to the "appropriate advisory sentence" was meant to apply to situations involving the single episode of criminal conduct limitation on consecutive sentencing; the statute was not intended to place any other limits on a court's ability to impose consecutive sentences. Accordingly, the trial court had the authority to impose enhanced, consecutive sentences. Mendoza v. State, 869 N.E.2d 546, 2007 Ind. App. LEXIS 1498 (2007).

Trial court erred in imposing an enhanced and consecutive sentence of two years in prison upon defendant following defendant's conviction for theft; in imposing a consecutive sentence in accordance with IC 35-50-1-2, the trial court was required to use the appropriate advisory sentence, which was six months less than the two-year sentence the trial court imposed. Robertson v. State, 860 N.E.2d 621, 2007 Ind. App. LEXIS 104 (2007), transfer granted, 869 N.E.2d 455, 2007 Ind. LEXIS 251 (2007), aff'd in part, superseded in part, 871 N.E.2d 280, 2007 Ind. LEXIS 618 (2007), overruled in part, Pedraza v. State, 873 N.E.2d 1083, 2007 Ind. App. LEXIS 2182 (2007), abrogated as stated, Dixson v. State, 865 N.E.2d 704, 2007 Ind. App. LEXIS 913 (2007).

IC 35-50-2-1.3(c)(1) does not represent a general requirement that a consecutive sentence be for the advisory term, but does no more than retain the fixed maximum sentences permissible under the "episode" and "repeat offender" provisions. Further, the previous version of IC 35-50-2-1.3(c)(1)

Consecutive Sentences. (Cont'd)
was not meant to impose additional restrictions on a trial court's ability to impose consecutive sentences. Robertson v. State, 871 N.E.2d 280, 2007 Ind. LEXIS 618 (2007).

Under former IC 35-50-2-1.3(b), the trial court was not required to use an "advisory" sentence except in the three situations identified in IC 35-50-2-1.3(c), none of which applied to defendant. Therefore, the trial court was not required to impose the 18-month advisory sentence for a class D felony when sentencing defendant to a consecutive term. Robertson v. State, 871 N.E.2d 280, 2007 Ind. LEXIS 618 (2007).

Trial court was legally permitted to order defendant's sentences for two counts of operating a vehicle while intoxicated (OWI) causing death, OWI causing serious bodily injury, and having a prior OWI conviction in the last five years, to run consecutively. Pedraza v. State, 873 N.E.2d 1083, 2007 Ind. App. LEXIS 2182 (2007), transfer granted and vacated, 878 N.E.2d 218, 2007 Ind. LEXIS 1005 (2007).

Trial court did not abuse its discretion in imposing an enhanced sentence of 26 years on two counts of aggravated battery instead of applying the rule of lenity; defendant had not relied on or was harmed by a split in case law concerning imposition of consecutive sentences under a prior version of IC 35-50-2-1.3 and he was repeatedly advised that he faced a possible 40-year prison term. Quiroz v. State, 885 N.E.2d 740, 2008 Ind. App. LEXIS 968 (2008).

Imposition of 13-year consecutive sentences that were imposed for each of two counts of aggravated battery was not an abuse of discretion because the sentences were supported by aggravating factors: defendant had an extensive criminal history, prior leniency had not deterred his behavior, he was on parole when he committed the offenses, and the two victims were significantly injured. Quiroz v. State, 885 N.E.2d 740, 2008 Ind. App. LEXIS 968 (2008).

Underlying Offense.
Last sentence of IC 35-50-2-1.3(c), "the court is not required to use the advisory sentence in imposing the sentence for the underlying offense," applies only to subsections 35-50-2-1.3(c)(2) and (c)(3). "Underlying offense" is a legal term of art that only applies to repeat offender sentencing enhancements, such as IC 35-50-2-1.3(c)(2) and (c)(3); when dealing strictly with consecutive sentences for distinct criminal violations, as under IC 35-50-2-1.3(c)(1), there is no "underlying offense." White v. State, 849 N.E.2d 735, 2006 Ind. App. LEXIS 1198 (2006).

Reference in IC 35-50-2-1.3(c) to "the underlying offense" is meaningful only as to the repeat offender sentencing enhancements found in IC 35-50-2-1.3(c)(2) and (c)(3). It is inapplicable to IC 35-50-2-1.3(c)(1) dealing with the episode limitation because there is no "underlying offense" in the episode calculation. Robertson v. State, 871 N.E.2d 280, 2007 Ind. LEXIS 618 (2007).

Cited:
Weaver v. State, 845 N.E.2d 1066, 2006 Ind. App. LEXIS 660 (2006); Hampton v. State, 873 N.E.2d 1074, 2007 Ind. App. LEXIS 2134 (2007).

RESEARCH REFERENCES

Indiana Law Review.
Survey: Criminal Law and Procedure: Recent Developments in Indiana Criminal Law and Procedure (October 1, 2004, through September 30, 2005), 39 Ind. L. Rev. 893 (2006).
Recent Developments in Indiana Criminal Law and Procedure, 41 Ind. L. Rev. 955 (2008).

Res Gestae.
Criminal Justice Notes 3/07-4/07: Significant legislation: Limitations on consecutive sentences, 50 (No. 10) Res Gestae 37 (2007).
Criminal Justice Notes: Limitations on consecutive sentences, 50 (No. 8) Res Gestae 38 (2007).
Criminal Justice Notes 8/07: Enhanced sentences may be ordered served consecutively, 51 (No. 4) Res Gestae 40 (2007).

35-50-2-1.4. "Criminal gang" defined.

For purposes of section 15 [IC 35-50-2-15] of this chapter, "criminal gang" means a group with at least three (3) members that specifically:
    (1) either:
        (A) promotes, sponsors, or assists in; or
        (B) participates in; or
    (2) requires as a condition of membership or continued membership;
the commission of a felony or an act that would be a felony if committed by an adult or the offense of battery (IC 35-42-2-1).

History.
P.L.109-2006, § 2; P.L.192-2007, § 12, eff. July 1, 2007.

35-50-2-1.5. "Individual with mental retardation" defined.

As used in this chapter, "individual with mental retardation" has the meaning set forth in IC 35-36-9-2.

History.
P.L.158-1994, § 4; P.L.99-2007, § 211, emergency eff. May 2, 2007.

RESEARCH REFERENCES

Collateral References.
Downward departure under state sentencing guidelines permitting downward departure for de-

fendants with significantly reduced mental capacity, including alcohol or drug dependency. 113 A.L.R.5th 597.

35-50-2-1.8. "Sex offense against a child" defined.

As used in this chapter, "sex offense against a child" means an offense under IC 35-42-4 in which the victim is a child less than eighteen (18) years of age.

History.
P.L.53-2005, § 1.

35-50-2-2. Suspension — Probation.

(a) The court may suspend any part of a sentence for a felony, except as provided in this section or in section 2.1 [IC 35-50-2-2.1] of this chapter.

(b) Except as provided in subsection (i), with respect to the following crimes listed in this subsection, the court may suspend only that part of the sentence that is in excess of the minimum sentence, unless the court has approved placement of the offender in a forensic diversion program under IC 11-12-3.7:

(1) The crime committed was a Class A felony or Class B felony and the person has a prior unrelated felony conviction.

(2) The crime committed was a Class C felony and less than seven (7) years have elapsed between the date the person was discharged from probation, imprisonment, or parole, whichever is later, for a prior unrelated felony conviction and the date the person committed the Class C felony for which the person is being sentenced.

(3) The crime committed was a Class D felony and less than three (3) years have elapsed between the date the person was discharged from probation, imprisonment, or parole, whichever is later, for a prior unrelated felony conviction and the date the person committed the Class D felony for which the person is being sentenced. However, the court may suspend the minimum sentence for the crime only if the court orders home detention under IC 35-38-1-21 or IC 35-38-2.5-5 instead of the minimum sentence specified for the crime under this chapter.

(4) The felony committed was:

(A) murder (IC 35-42-1-1);

(B) battery (IC 35-42-2-1) with a deadly weapon or battery causing death;

(C) sexual battery (IC 35-42-4-8) with a deadly weapon;

(D) kidnapping (IC 35-42-3-2);

(E) confinement (IC 35-42-3-3) with a deadly weapon;

(F) rape (IC 35-42-4-1) as a Class A felony;

(G) criminal deviate conduct (IC 35-42-4-2) as a Class A felony;

(H) except as provided in subsection (i), child molesting (IC 35-42-4-3) as a Class A or Class B felony, unless:

(i) the felony committed was child molesting as a Class B felony;

(ii) the victim was not less than twelve (12) years old at the time the offense was committed;

(iii) the person is not more than four (4) years older than the victim, or more than five (5) years older than the victim if the relationship between the person and the victim was a dating relationship or an ongoing personal relationship (not including a family relationship);

(iv) the person did not have a position of authority or substantial influence over the victim; and

(v) the person has not committed another sex offense (as defined in IC 11-8-8-5.2) (including a delinquent act that would be a sex offense if committed by an adult) against any other person;

(I) robbery (IC 35-42-5-1) resulting in serious bodily injury or with a deadly weapon;

(J) arson (IC 35-43-1-1) for hire or resulting in serious bodily injury;

(K) burglary (IC 35-43-2-1) resulting in serious bodily injury or with a deadly weapon;

(L) resisting law enforcement (IC 35-44-3-3) with a deadly weapon;

(M) escape (IC 35-44-3-5) with a deadly weapon;

(N) rioting (IC 35-45-1-2) with a deadly weapon;

(O) dealing in cocaine or a narcotic drug (IC 35-48-4-1) if the court finds the person possessed a firearm (as defined in IC 35-47-1-5) at the time of the offense, or the person delivered or intended to deliver to a person under eighteen (18) years of age at least three (3) years junior to the person and was on a school bus or within one thousand (1,000) feet of:

(i) school property;

(ii) a public park;

(iii) a family housing complex; or

(iv) a youth program center;

(P) dealing in methamphetamine (IC 35-48-4-1.1) if the court finds the person possessed a firearm (as defined in IC 35-47-1-5) at the time of the offense, or the person delivered or intended to deliver the methamphetamine pure or adulterated to a person under eighteen (18) years of age at least three (3) years junior to the person and was on a school bus or within one thousand (1,000) feet of:

(i) school property;

(ii) a public park;

(iii) a family housing complex; or

(iv) a youth program center;

(Q) dealing in a schedule I, II, or III controlled substance (IC 35-48-4-2) if the court finds the person possessed a firearm (as defined in IC 35-47-1-5) at the time of the offense, or the person delivered or intended to deliver to a person under eighteen (18) years of age at least three (3) years junior to the person and was on a school bus or within one thousand (1,000) feet of:

(i) school property;

(ii) a public park;

(iii) a family housing complex; or

(iv) a youth program center;

(R) an offense under IC 9-30-5 (operating a vehicle while intoxicated) and the person who committed the offense has accumulated at least two (2) prior unrelated convictions under IC 9-30-5;

(S) an offense under IC 9-30-5-5(b) (operating a vehicle while intoxicated causing death);

(T) aggravated battery (IC 35-42-2-1.5); or

(U) disarming a law enforcement officer (IC 35-44-3-3.5).

(c) Except as provided in subsection (e), whenever the court suspends a sentence for a felony, it shall place the person on probation under IC 35-38-2 for a fixed period to end not later than the date that the maximum sentence that may be imposed for the felony will expire.

(d) The minimum sentence for a person convicted of voluntary manslaughter may not be suspended unless the court finds at the sentencing hearing that the crime was not committed by means of a deadly weapon.

(e) Whenever the court suspends that part of the sentence of a sex or violent offender (as defined in IC 11-8-8-5) that is suspendible under subsection (b), the court shall place the sex or violent offender on probation under IC 35-38-2 for not more than ten (10) years.

(f) An additional term of imprisonment imposed under IC 35-50-2-11 may not be suspended.

(g) A term of imprisonment imposed under IC 35-47-10-6 or IC 35-47-10-7 may not be suspended if the commission of the offense was knowing or intentional.

(h) A term of imprisonment imposed for an offense under IC 35-48-4-6(b)(1)(B) or IC 35-48-4-6.1(b)(1)(B) may not be suspended.

(i) If a person is:

(1) convicted of child molesting (IC 35-42-4-3) as a Class A felony against a victim less than twelve (12) years of age; and

(2) at least twenty-one (21) years of age;

the court may suspend only that part of the sentence that is in excess of thirty (30) years.

History.

IC 35-50-2-2, as added by Acts 1976, P.L.148, § 8; 1977, P.L.340, § 115; 1979, P.L.305, § 1; 1982, P.L.204, § 39; P.L.334-1983, § 2; P.L.284-1985, § 3; P.L.211-1986, § 1; P.L.98-1988, § 9; P.L.351-1989(ss), § 4; P.L.214-1991, § 2; P.L.240-1991(ss2), § 98; P.L.11-1994, § 17; P.L.96-1996, § 7; P.L.203-1996, § 8; P.L.220-1997, § 1; P.L.188-1999, § 8; P.L.17-2001, § 30; P.L.222-2001, § 6; P.L.238-2001, § 21; P.L.116-2002, § 25; P.L.224-2003, § 126; P.L.85-2004, § 11; P.L.213-2005, § 7; P.L.151-2006, § 28; P.L.140-2006, § 36; P.L.173-2006, § 36; P.L.216-2007, § 50, emergency eff. July 1, 2007; P.L.1-2007, § 236, emergency eff. March 30, 2007; P.L.64-2008, § 2, eff. July 1, 2008.

NOTES TO DECISIONS

Constitutionality.

A statute which prohibits the suspension of sentence does not violate Ind. Const., Art. 1, § 18, prohibiting vindictive justice. State v. Lawson, 272 Ind. 541, 400 N.E.2d 128, 1980 Ind. LEXIS 596 (1980).

This section does not violate the constitution. Davis v. State, 398 N.E.2d 704, 1980 Ind. App. LEXIS 1254 (1980).

Probation is merely a sentencing tool available to trial judges to use when and as they wish; there is no right to a suspended sentence, and therefore, no constitutional issue is presented when a defendant fails to receive consideration of probation regarding a sentence provided by the legislature. Halbig v. State, 525 N.E.2d 288, 1988 Ind. LEXIS 203 (1988).

Motion to declare IC 35-48-4-1 (dealing in narcotic drugs) and this section unconstitutional because defendant's sentence was disproportionate to the offense and therefore constituted cruel and unusual punishment was properly denied since these challenges have already been substantially addressed and rejected as "addressed to the wrong branch of government." Lopez v. State, 527 N.E.2d 1119, 1988 Ind. LEXIS 248 (1988).

Attempted Child Molesting.

Six years of the defendant's ten-year sentence

Attempted Child Molesting. (Cont'd)
for attempted child molesting was nonsuspendable, because this section includes sentences for attempted child molesting. Holt v. State, 561 N.E.2d 830, 1990 Ind. App. LEXIS 1391 (1990).

Attempted Murder.
Sentence imposed upon a defendant for attempted murder was not suspendable, since reference to "murder" in this section also included attempted murder. Haggenjos v. State, 441 N.E.2d 430, 1982 Ind. LEXIS 996 (1982).

Attempted Robbery.
Although not specifically mentioned, IC 35-50-2-2(b)(4)(I) applied to attempted robbery with a deadly weapon; therefore, the trial court properly concluded that it could not suspend defendant's minimum sentence. Strong v. State, — N.E.2d —, 2009 Ind. App. LEXIS 519 (2009).

Conspiracy.
Conspiracy is not one of the offenses that is nonsuspendable under this section. Huff v. State, 443 N.E.2d 1234, 1983 Ind. App. LEXIS 2507 (1983).

Construction With Other Statutes.
Reading the general suspension statute at IC 35-50-2-2 and the juvenile record suspension statute at IC 35-50-2-2.1 in pari materia, and giving effect to the language in the juvenile record suspension statute, "except as provided in" the general suspension statute, indicate that the legislature intended that a trial court's authority to suspend a sentence in excess of the minimum sentence applies to persons with disqualifying juvenile records in the same way as to persons with disqualifying adult records. Saintignon v. State, 749 N.E.2d 1134, 2001 Ind. LEXIS 536 (2001).

IC 9-30-5-15(b) is not irreconcilably in conflict with IC 35-50-2-2(b)(4)(Q) because IC 9-30-5-15(b) operates to require a minimum term of imprisonment in situations where IC 35-50-2-2 is inapplicable. Simmons v. State, 773 N.E.2d 823, 2002 Ind. App. LEXIS 1215 (2002).

Conviction of Prior Felonies.
Court did not err in refusing probation where defendant had been convicted of prior felonies although the sentences he received for such prior crimes were for misdemeanors. Davis v. State, 398 N.E.2d 704, 1980 Ind. App. LEXIS 1254 (1980).

Where the Division of Mental Health, which had discretion as to whether to accept the defendant for treatment, found, during the course of a court-ordered presentence investigation, that the defendant had outstanding warrants pending against her, contrary to what she had averred in her request for treatment in lieu of sentencing, and where the presentence investigation also revealed that the defendant had been convicted of a previous felony, the court was required to sentence her to at least a two-year minimum sentence for the felony to which she had pled, and neither the court nor the prosecutor could have agreed to treatment

in lieu of sentencing. Dyer v. State, 714 N.E.2d 229, 1999 Ind. App. LEXIS 1069 (1999).

Because the uncodified savings clause in Pub. L. No. 2-1991, § 111 (Ind.) permitted prosecutions based on convictions under a repealed statute, the trial court did not err in finding that defendant's 1988 operating while intoxicated (OWI) conviction qualified as one of the two OWI convictions under IC 35-50-2-2(b)(4)(R) and IC 9-30-5-3. Schenk v. State, 895 N.E.2d 1271, 2008 Ind. App. LEXIS 2531 (2008).

Effect of Reduction of Prior Felony Conviction to Misdemeanor.
IC 35-50-2-2(b)(1) non-suspension rule still applied to defendant's sentence for a Class A felony conviction despite the fact that her earlier unrelated Class D felony conviction had been reduced to a misdemeanor after the sentencing on the Class A felony; when defendant was sentenced on the Class A felony, she had a prior unrelated Class D felony conviction, thus reduction of the Class D felony to a misdemeanor had only prospective operation, and trial court therefore had no authority to suspend the sentence on the Class A felony below the minimum at hearing on defendant's later motion to modify sentence. Gardiner v. State, 903 N.E.2d 557, 2009 Ind. App. LEXIS 641 (2009).

Erroneous Suspension.
The court could not suspend fifteen years under the possession of cocaine charge because the minimum sentence for a Class A felony is 20 years, and the court may only suspend that part of the sentence which is in excess of the minimum. Morgan v. State, 675 N.E.2d 1067, 1996 Ind. LEXIS 198 (1996), superseded by statute as stated in, Allen v. State, 722 N.E.2d 1246, 2000 Ind. App. LEXIS 12 (2000).

Where defendant was convicted of robbery as Class B felony and had prior drug possession felony conviction, no part of his sentence could be suspended under IC 35-50-2-2 or IC 35-50-2-2.1, and he therefore fell under IC 35-38-2.6-1(a)(1); accordingly, IC 35-38-2.6 applied to defendant and trial court exceeded its authority under that chapter by placing defendant in community corrections home detention program. State v. Thomas, 827 N.E.2d 577, 2005 Ind. App. LEXIS 827 (2005).

—Correction.
Where a trial court erroneously suspends a sentence in violation of this section, the court has the power to vacate the sentence. Niece v. State, 456 N.E.2d 1081, 1983 Ind. App. LEXIS 3666 (1983).

Habitual Offenders.
When a criminal defendant receives an enhanced sentence under the habitual offender statute, such sentence may not be suspended. State v. Williams, 430 N.E.2d 756, 1982 Ind. LEXIS 730 (1982), superseded by statute as stated in, Bauer v. State, 875 N.E.2d 744, 2007 Ind. App. LEXIS 2391 (2007).

This section pertains only to the suspended sentences for felonies generally. The statute which

Habitual Offenders. (Cont'd)
permits the trial court to reduce the fixed enhancement of 30 years upon a habitual offender determination is IC 35-50-2-8(e). Marsillett v. State, 495 N.E.2d 699, 1986 Ind. LEXIS 1206 (1986).

Although the habitual offender offense is not listed under this section as a sentence that may not be suspended, it is not suspendable. Atkins v. State, 550 N.E.2d 342, 1990 Ind. App. LEXIS 153 (1990).

Since a conviction for dealing or possession of an illegal drug does not count for habitual offender purposes if that crime was not classified a "crime of violence" under IC 35-50-2-2(b)(4) and the defendant has only one or no convictions for illegal drug dealing, the habitual offender enhancement was invalid as it was evident that an earlier conviction could not be used to support an habitual offender enhancement. Williams v. State, 834 N.E.2d 225, 2005 Ind. App. LEXIS 1757 (2005).

Murder.
Although the trial court found the defendant's lack of criminal history to be a mitigating circumstance, there was no error in its failure to find that he was likely to respond affirmatively to probation or short term imprisonment as a mitigating circumstance where those sentences were not options available to the court in a murder case. Angleton v. State, 714 N.E.2d 156, 1999 Ind. LEXIS 555 (1999), cert. denied, 529 U.S. 1132, 120 S. Ct. 2012, 146 L. Ed. 2d 961, 2000 U.S. LEXIS 3480 (2000).

No Ground for Sentence Revision.
Where law at time offense was committed prohibited court from suspending sentence or placing defendant on probation in case of conviction for first-degree burglary fact that this section places no such restriction on the court for the corresponding crime in the present law was no ground for defendant to obtain a revision of his sentence. Holliday v. State, 181 Ind. App. 360, 391 N.E.2d 866, 1979 Ind. App. LEXIS 1252 (1979).

Where the trial court misspoke and stated that defendant was not eligible for less than the presumptive sentence because he was on probation at the time he committed the robbery, the misstatement had no impact upon defendant's sentence, especially in light of defendant's concession that the presumptive sentence would be appropriate. Scott v. State, 840 N.E.2d 376, 2006 Ind. App. LEXIS 26 (2006).

Operating Vehicle While Intoxicated.
Defendant, who pled guilty to operating vehicle while intoxicated (OWI), which was elevated to Class D felony because of two previous OWI offenses, was properly sentenced using general suspension statute, IC 35-50-2(b)(4)(Q). Woodward v. State, 798 N.E.2d 260, 2003 Ind. App. LEXIS 2050 (2003).

Probation.
Probation is a matter addressed to the sound discretion of the trial judge, and may be granted as a substitute for incarceration. It is merely a sentencing tool available to trial judges to use when and as they wish. Campbell v. State, 551 N.E.2d 1164, 1990 Ind. App. LEXIS 370 (1990).

When the trial court suspends the remainder of a sentence pursuant to IC 35-38-1-17(b), the defendant is released to probation by operation of subsection (c). Wilburn v. State, 671 N.E.2d 143, 1996 Ind. App. LEXIS 1237 (1996).

—After Serving Consecutive Sentences.
Subsection (c) does not prohibit the trial court from ordering a person to begin serving a probationary term after serving consecutive sentences. Day v. State, 669 N.E.2d 1072, 1996 Ind. App. LEXIS 1195 (1996).

—Extension.
The trial court was within the statutory guidelines when it ordered defendant to serve an additional one year of probation following his first probation violation, and the fact that the additional year extended the term of defendant's probation beyond that provided for in this section was of no consequence, because this section applies only to the initial suspension of a sentence and placement on probation. If a probationer is found to violate probation, IC 35-38-2-3(g)(2) allows the trial court to order an extension of up to one year. Bailey v. State, 731 N.E.2d 447, 2000 Ind. App. LEXIS 893 (2000).

For parole violation, trial court has authority to extend probationary period for no more than one year beyond original probationary period. Sharp v. State, 817 N.E.2d 644, 2004 Ind. App. LEXIS 2249 (2004).

Role of Court and Jury.
Discretion is vested in the trial court to suspend a sentence unless one of a series of exceptions applies. This decision is not shared with the jury. The same is true of aggravating or mitigating circumstances in the determination of a sentence by the trial judge. Hunt v. State, 455 N.E.2d 307, 1983 Ind. LEXIS 995 (1983).

Suspendable Sentence.
The trial court's conclusion that it was without authority to suspend a defendant's sentence where the defendant was charged with a Class A felony for which the sentence was suspendable was in error, and the court's comments to the effect that it lacked such authority required remand for resentencing. Henning v. State, 477 N.E.2d 547, 1985 Ind. LEXIS 831 (1985).

Probation term in sentence for murder provided for a 30-year prison sentence, and a 30-year probation term was void since probation can be imposed only if a portion of the executed sentence is suspended, and no portion of the 30-year prison sentence could be suspended. Willis v. State, 498 N.E.2d 1029, 1986 Ind. App. LEXIS 3046 (1986).

A trial court may suspend a sentence, place a defendant on probation, and then order a term of imprisonment as a condition of probation. Sutton v. State, 562 N.E.2d 1310, 1990 Ind. App. LEXIS 1526 (1990), cert. denied, 502 U.S. 987, 112 S. Ct. 598, 116 L. Ed. 2d 621, 1991 U.S. LEXIS 6994 (1991).

Suspendable Sentence. (Cont'd)

Trial court erred in finding that the enhancement of defendant's sentence under the habitual substance offender statute could not be suspended, where defendant was being sentenced for his first felony conviction and his sentence for that conviction was properly suspendable. Collins v. State, 583 N.E.2d 761, 1991 Ind. App. LEXIS 2203 (1991).

Because IC 35-50-2-2 was a specific statute for suspended sentences and prevailed over the general sentencing parameters statute, IC 35-50-2-7, the trial court properly applied the specific statute in finding that the minimum non-suspendable part of defendant's sentence for his Class D felony conviction of operating while intoxicated with a prior conviction was one year rather than six months. Snider v. State, 753 N.E.2d 721, 2001 Ind. App. LEXIS 1323 (2001).

Trial court did not abuse its discretion in ordering that defendant serve an executed sentence of 50 years in prison for murder; the trial court was authorized to suspend part of defendant's sentence and, thus, it did not err in concluding that the 52-year imposed sentence could be reduced by two years. Nguyen v. State, 837 N.E.2d 153, 2005 Ind. App. LEXIS 2123 (2005), overruled in part, Childress v. State, 848 N.E.2d 1073, 2006 Ind. LEXIS 474 (2006).

Defendant's plea agreement called for a fixed term of 10 years with the amount of time executed to be determined by the trial court at sentencing; the trial court could have ordered defendant to serve 10 years executed, and, thus, the trial court's decision to suspend four years of defendant's 10-year sentence was clearly within its discretionary power. The appellate court declined defendant's request to review any aggravators and mitigators the trial court might have considered when determining what portion of his sentence should be suspended. Rivera v. State, 841 N.E.2d 1169, 2006 Ind. App. LEXIS 170 (2006), transfer granted and vacated, — N.E.2d —, 2006 Ind. LEXIS 670 (2006), aff'd in part, superseded in part, 851 N.E.2d 299, 2006 Ind. LEXIS 667 (2006).

Trial court properly held that defendant's sentence could not be suspended because she had possessed a firearm when she was dealing in cocaine. Knowledge of the gun was shown by the facts that defendant was in the vehicle in which the gun was found, that she was in close proximity to the gun, that she reached down when she saw officers moving in, and that she admitted that the gun was in the center console with her cell phone; ability to reduce the gun to her personal possession was shown by the close proximity of the gun to defendant and her furtive gesture of reaching downward. Ables v. State, 848 N.E.2d 293, 2006 Ind. App. LEXIS 984 (2006).

Defendant was not entitled to have more than four years of a 10-year sentence for class B felony child molesting suspended under IC 35-50-2-2(b)(4)(H). Laney v. State, 868 N.E.2d 561, 2007 Ind. App. LEXIS 1317 (2007).

When defendant's sentence for possession of marijuana, which was suspended pursuant to IC 35-50-2-2(c), was ordered to be executed, defendant had a right of allocution to the same extent defendant would have had at a probation revocation hearing. The trial court was not required to ask if defendant wanted to speak as provided by IC 35-38-1-5 and Ind. Const. art. 1, § 13, and defendant waived the right of allocution by not asking to speak or objecting to the lack of opportunity to speak. Hull v. State, 868 N.E.2d 901, 2007 Ind. App. LEXIS 1400 (2007).

Because the trial court imposed a six-year sentence, and, pursuant to the terms of IC 35-50-2-2, could have suspended any part of the sentence in excess of three and a half years, once the trial court amended the sentencing order to attach the habitual substance offender finding to an underlying conviction, two years of the resulting enhanced sentence could be suspended. Bauer v. State, 875 N.E.2d 744, 2007 Ind. App. LEXIS 2391 (2007).

Defendant's sentence on several drug and related conviction was affirmed on appeal where IC 35-50-2-2(b)(4)(O) prohibited trial court from suspending any portion of imposed minimum sentence. Turner v. State, 878 N.E.2d 286, 2007 Ind. App. LEXIS 2764 (2007).

Trial court's sentence of three years, with but 240 days suspended, for a conviction of operating a motor vehicle while intoxicated, as a Class D felony, was error; because a Class D felony served as the underlying offense for the habitual substance offender adjudication; pursuant to IC 35-50-2-10(f), the sentencing range for that felony was enhanced such that the new sentencing range was three and a half years to eleven years, and under IC 35-50-2-2(b), the trial court was permitted to only suspend that portion of the sentence in excess of three and a half years where the felony committed was an offense under IC 9-30-5-1 et seq. (operating while intoxicated) and the person who committed the offense had accumulated at least two prior unrelated convictions under IC 9-30-5-1 et seq.; accordingly, because trial court ordered that all but 240 days of defendant's sentence was suspended, that sentence was illegal. Young v. State, 901 N.E.2d 624, 2009 Ind. App. LEXIS 342 (2009).

Cited:

Galloway v. State, 422 N.E.2d 1290, 1981 Ind. App. LEXIS 1533 (1981); Anderson v. State, 426 N.E.2d 674, 1981 Ind. LEXIS 874 (1981); Grassmyer v. State, 426 N.E.2d 1377, 1981 Ind. App. LEXIS 1692 (1981); Vacendak v. State, 431 N.E.2d 100, 1982 Ind. LEXIS 751 (1982); Yager v. State, 437 N.E.2d 454, 1982 Ind. LEXIS 874 (1982); McVey v. State, 438 N.E.2d 770, 1982 Ind. App. LEXIS 1347 (1982); Smith v. State, 439 N.E.2d 634, 1982 Ind. LEXIS 959 (1982); Huff v. State, 440 N.E.2d 465, 1982 Ind. LEXIS 965 (1982); Abercrombie v. State, 441 N.E.2d 442, 1982 Ind. LEXIS 1005 (1982); Carter v. State, 467 N.E.2d 694, 1984 Ind. LEXIS 951 (1984); Lessig v. State, 489 N.E.2d 978, 1986 Ind. App. LEXIS 2399 (1986); Johnson v. State, 490 N.E.2d 333, 1986 Ind. LEXIS 1076 (1986); Willis v. State, 492 N.E.2d 45, 1986 Ind. App. LEXIS 2533 (1986); Stroud v. State, 517 N.E.2d 780, 1988 Ind. LEXIS 3 (1988); Fassoth v. State, 525 N.E.2d 318, 1988 Ind. LEXIS 201

(1988); Jackson v. State, 540 N.E.2d 1232, 1989 Ind. LEXIS 207 (1989); Williams v. State, 541 N.E.2d 921, 1989 Ind. LEXIS 241 (1989); Brock v. State, 558 N.E.2d 872, 1990 Ind. App. LEXIS 1086 (1990); Smith v. State, 621 N.E.2d 325, 1993 Ind. LEXIS 138 (1993); Minor v. State, 641 N.E.2d 85, 1994 Ind. App. LEXIS 1436 (1994); Thorne v. State, 687 N.E.2d 604, 1997 Ind. App. LEXIS 1658 (1997); Wolf v. State, 793 N.E.2d 328, 2003 Ind. App. LEXIS 1509 (2003); Slinkard v. State, 807 N.E.2d 127, 2004 Ind. App. LEXIS 759 (2004); Stanley v. State, 849 N.E.2d 626, 2006 Ind. App. LEXIS 1103 (2006); Ruble v. State, 849 N.E.2d 165, 2006 Ind. App. LEXIS 1114 (2006); Duncan v. State, 857 N.E.2d 955, 2006 Ind. LEXIS 1028 (2006); Howard v. State, 873 N.E.2d 685, 2007 Ind. App. LEXIS 2138 (2007); Ashby v. State, — N.E.2d —, 2009 Ind. App. LEXIS 724 (2009).

RESEARCH REFERENCES

Indiana Law Review.
Recent Developments in Indiana Criminal Law and Procedure, 28 Ind. L. Rev. 819 (1995).
Criminal Law and Procedure: Recent Developments in Indiana Criminal Law and Procedure, 34 Ind. L. Rev. 645 (2001).
Survey: Criminal Law and Procedure: Recent Developments in Indiana Criminal Law and Procedure (October 1, 2004, through September 30, 2005), 39 Ind. L. Rev. 893 (2006).

Res Gestae.
Criminal justice notes, 35 Res Gestae 225 (1993).

Criminal Justice Notes 12/04-1/05: Sentencing after probation revocation, 48 (No. 8) Res Gestae 43 (2005).

Collateral References.
Appealability of order suspending imposition or execution of sentence. 51 A.L.R.4th 939.
Propriety, in criminal case, of Federal District Court order restricting defendant's right to re-enter or stay in United States. 94 A.L.R. Fed. 619.

35-50-2-2.1. Suspension for adult with juvenile record.

(a) Except as provided in subsection (b) or section 2 [IC 35-50-2-2] of this chapter, the court may not suspend a sentence for a felony for a person with a juvenile record when:
(1) The juvenile record includes findings that the juvenile acts, if committed by an adult, would constitute:
(A) One (1) Class A or Class B felony;
(B) Two (2) Class C or Class D felonies; or
(C) One (1) Class C and one (1) Class D felony; and
(2) Less than three (3) years have elapsed between commission of the juvenile acts that would be felonies if committed by an adult and the commission of the felony for which the person is being sentenced.
(b) Notwithstanding subsection (a), the court may suspend any part of the sentence for a felony, except as provided in section 2 of this chapter, if it finds that:
(1) The crime was the result of circumstances unlikely to recur;
(2) The victim of the crime induced or facilitated the offense;
(3) There are substantial grounds tending to excuse or justify the crime, though failing to establish a defense; or
(4) The acts in the juvenile record would not be Class A or Class B felonies if committed by an adult, and the convicted person is to undergo home detention under IC 35-38-1-21 instead of the minimum sentence specified for the crime under this chapter.

History.
P.L.284-1985, § 4; P.L.331-1987, § 1; P.L.98-1988, § 10.

NOTES TO DECISIONS

ANALYSIS

Acts Committed Outside Indiana.

Construction.
Construction With Other Statutes.
Limitations.

Acts Committed Outside Indiana.

The intent of the legislature was for the determination of whether juvenile acts, if committed by an adult, would constitute a Class A or Class B felony to be decided based on Indiana law, regardless of where those juvenile acts were committed. Ashley v. State, 757 N.E.2d 1037, 2001 Ind. App. LEXIS 1864 (2001).

Construction.

A trial court is not required to suspend any portion of a sentence even though it was authorized it to do so. Ashley v. State, 757 N.E.2d 1037, 2001 Ind. App. LEXIS 1864 (2001).

Where defendant was convicted of robbery as Class B felony and had prior drug possession felony conviction, no part of his sentence could be suspended under IC 35-50-2-2 or IC 35-50-2-2.1, and he therefore fell under IC 35-38-2.6-1(a)(1); accordingly, IC 35-38-2.6 applied to defendant and trial court exceeded its authority under that chapter by placing defendant in community corrections

home detention program. State v. Thomas, 827 N.E.2d 577, 2005 Ind. App. LEXIS 827 (2005).

Construction With Other Statutes.

Reading the general suspension statute at IC 35-50-2-2 and the juvenile record suspension statute at IC 35-50-2-2.1 in pari materia, and giving effect to the language in the juvenile record suspension statute, "except as provided in" the general suspension statute, indicate that the legislature intended that a trial court's authority to suspend a sentence in excess of the minimum sentence applies to persons with disqualifying juvenile records in the same way as to persons with disqualifying adult records. Saintignon v. State, 749 N.E.2d 1134, 2001 Ind. LEXIS 536 (2001).

Limitations.

Under the Juvenile Suspension Statute, the trial court could suspend that portion of a person's sentence that was in excess of the minimum sentence. Ashley v. State, 757 N.E.2d 1037, 2001 Ind. App. LEXIS 1864 (2001).

RESEARCH REFERENCES

Indiana Law Review.

Criminal Law and Procedure: Recent Developments in Indiana Criminal Law and Procedure, 34 Ind. L. Rev. 645 (2001).

35-50-2-3. Murder.

(a) A person who commits murder shall be imprisoned for a fixed term of between forty-five (45) and sixty-five (65) years, with the advisory sentence being fifty-five (55) years. In addition, the person may be fined not more than ten thousand dollars ($10,000).

(b) Notwithstanding subsection (a), a person who was:

(1) at least eighteen (18) years of age at the time the murder was committed may be sentenced to:

(A) death; or

(B) life imprisonment without parole; and

(2) at least sixteen (16) years of age but less than eighteen (18) years of age at the time the murder was committed may be sentenced to life imprisonment without parole;

under section 9 [IC 35-50-2-9] of this chapter unless a court determines under IC 35-36-9 that the person is an individual with mental retardation.

History.

IC 35-50-2-3, as added by Acts 1976, P.L.148, § 8; 1977, P.L.340, § 116; P.L.332-1987, § 1; P.L.250-1993, § 1; P.L.164-1994, § 2; P.L.158-1994, § 5; P.L.2-1995, § 128; P.L.148-1995, § 4; P.L.117-2002, § 1; P.L.71-2005, § 6; P.L.99-2007, § 212, emergency eff. May 2, 2007.

Cross References.

Aggravating circumstances, IC 35-38-1-7.1.

Compensation for victims of violent crimes, IC 5-2-6.1.

Mitigating circumstances, IC 35-38-1-7.1.

NOTES TO DECISIONS

Analysis

In General.
Constitutionality.
—Added Years.
—Cruel and Unusual Punishment.
—Due Process/Equal Protection Not Violated.

—Murder and Felony-Murder Convictions.
—Saving Clause.
Applicable Law.
Basic Sentence.
Construction.
Death Sentence.

—Saving Clause.
Fine.
Jury Instructions.
Lesser Included Offenses.
Life Sentence.
Plea Agreement.
Proper to Sentence Under Prior Law.
—Resentencing.
Record Should Disclose Sentencing Factors.
Sentence.
—Age of Defender.
—Age of Offender.
—Aggravating Circumstances.
—Erroneous.
—Improper.
—Murder and Felony Murder.
—Presumptive Sentence Proper.
—Reasonable.
—Suspended Sentence Not Available.
—Unclear Application of Law.
—Unreasonable.
Sentence Enhancement.
—Aggravators.
—Depreciating Seriousness of Crime.
—Mitigators.
Statement of Reasons.

In General.

Under prior law, where one accused of murder in the first degree was found guilty of murder in the second degree, the punishment fixed by the statute at life imprisonment could not be reduced by the judge or jury. O'Neil v. State, 216 Ind. 21, 22 N.E.2d 825, 1939 Ind. LEXIS 234 (1940).

Where there is the killing of but one human being, only one sentence may be imposed for such killing. Birkla v. State, 425 N.E.2d 118, 1981 Ind. LEXIS 810 (1981).

Constitutionality.

Fact that under prior law a person could be sentenced to life imprisonment for either first-degree or second-degree murder did not make such law unconstitutional. Millar v. State, 275 Ind. 465, 417 N.E.2d 1105, 1981 Ind. LEXIS 708 (1981).

A former statute which provided for either life imprisonment or the imposition of a 15- to 25-year prison term for second-degree murder, without setting forth any criteria by which to determine which sentence was to be imposed, was not unconstitutional. Millar v. State, 275 Ind. 465, 417 N.E.2d 1105, 1981 Ind. LEXIS 708 (1981).

—Added Years.

Fact that number of years that may be added for aggravating circumstances exceeds the number of years that may be subtracted for mitigating circumstances, does not violate the constitution. Boyd v. State, 396 N.E.2d 920, 1979 Ind. App. LEXIS 1430 (1979).

A trial court's enhancement of a defendant's presumptive sentence by ten years did not constitute double punishment in violation of the prohibition against double jeopardy, where in sentencing the defendant, who had pled guilty to felony-murder for which the underlying felony was kidnapping, the court not only considered the kidnapping in imposing both the presumptive and enhanced sentences, but also considered the brutal manner in which the murder was committed along with other circumstances of the crime. Rust v. State, 477 N.E.2d 262, 1985 Ind. LEXIS 815 (1985).

—Cruel and Unusual Punishment.

It was not a cruel and unusual punishment to sentence a 19-year-old to a 60-year sentence, although he did not directly commit the murder himself, as this sentence was within the bounds of statutory limits, and not unreasonable based on the facts and circumstances of defendant's conduct. Slone v. State, 496 N.E.2d 401, 1986 Ind. LEXIS 1253 (1986).

—Due Process/Equal Protection Not Violated.

The wide latitude given the court in fixing the sentence does not violate due process or equal protection. Boyd v. State, 396 N.E.2d 920, 1979 Ind. App. LEXIS 1430 (1979).

—Murder and Felony-Murder Convictions.

The defendant was convicted of both murder and felony-murder for the same homicide, an action which was held to be improper double punishment, but the 40-year sentence was not unconstitutional where the trial court sentenced the defendant with regard to only one of the counts of murder. Robinson v. State, 477 N.E.2d 288, 1985 Ind. LEXIS 820 (1985).

—Saving Clause.

In a death penalty case, the interest that appellee has in life is curtailed by the procedures laid out in the death penalty statute, and there is no suspect class affected by the saving clause; accordingly, the appropriate level of scrutiny to apply is the rational basis analysis, which merely requires the classification to bear some rational relationship to a legitimate state interest or goal. State v. Alcorn, 638 N.E.2d 1242, 1994 Ind. LEXIS 96 (1994).

Applicable Law.

P.L.158-1994, which provides a presumptive 40 year sentence for murder subject to a 20 year enhancement, applies to murders during the period between July 1, 1994, and May 5, 1995, rather than P.L.164-1994, which provides a presumptive 50 year sentence for murder subject to a 10 year enhancement. Alvarado v. State, 686 N.E.2d 819, 1997 Ind. LEXIS 160 (1997).

Where defendant was sentenced December 16, 1996 but the crime he committed occurred on June 16, 1995, court incorrectly applied the version of this section as amended by P.L.148-1995, § 4, effective July 1, 1995 when sentencing defendant. Jones v. State, 689 N.E.2d 722, 1997 Ind. LEXIS 218 (1997).

When at the time of killing in July 1994 there were two versions of the sentencing statute for murder, defendant's sentence would be remanded, where there was reason to believe that the court's sentence might have been different had the 40 year presumptive sentence under P.L.158-1994

Applicable Law. (Cont'd)
been applied. Hicks v. State, 690 N.E.2d 215, 1997 Ind. LEXIS 229 (1997).

Where no portion of a defendant's sentence was suspended and he did not receive the shortest sentence under either IC 35-50-2-1 or this section, any question of whether these statutes conflict was of no legal consequence to him, and he was not entitled to a resentencing hearing. Johnson v. State, 702 N.E.2d 711, 1998 Ind. LEXIS 609 (1998).

Basic Sentence.
When a court imposes the basic sentence embodied within a particular criminal statute, the reviewing court will presume that the mandatory considerations were made by the judge, even if the record lacks specificity in enumerating those considerations. Gardner v. State, 270 Ind. 627, 388 N.E.2d 513, 1979 Ind. LEXIS 614 (1979).

Presumptive sentences for murder and Class A felony conspiracy given to an accomplice were not manifestly unreasonable considering the cruel and callous nature of these offenses and the character of the defendant as indicated by the presentence report and by his demeanor before the trial court. Haynes v. State, 479 N.E.2d 572, 1985 Ind. LEXIS 884 (1985).

Where the trial court imposed the presumptive sentence of 40 years for murder but defendant claimed the court failed to consider alleged mitigating circumstances, the court was not bound to attach great weight to such evidence and the record clearly supported the imposition of a basic sentence. Ellis v. State, 508 N.E.2d 790, 1987 Ind. LEXIS 955 (1987).

Sentence was affirmed where judge stated that, in mitigation, he recognized lack of male role model during formative years and age of 18 years at time of crime, but that aggravating factors, including defendant's criminal history at early age, intoxicated state at time of crime, and disregard for hardship his potential incarceration would cause his young child and girlfriend, justified imposition of presumptive sentence. Jones v. State, 698 N.E.2d 289, 1998 Ind. LEXIS 218 (1998).

Construction.
Where different amendments to this section provided presumptive sentences of different terms, which could not be harmonized, the statute had to be strictly construed against the state, and the defendant sentenced according to the lesser term. Smith v. State, 675 N.E.2d 693, 1996 Ind. LEXIS 193 (1996).

The provisions of subsection (a) establish the length of murder sentences generally, while those of section IC 35-50-2-1 establish, in conjunction with other statutes, what portion of a sentence may be suspended. Johnson v. State, 702 N.E.2d 711, 1998 Ind. LEXIS 609 (1998).

Death Sentence.
Death sentence imposed on a 15-year-old murderer, prior to the 1987 amendment of this section, was disproportionate to any other sentence for the same crime, and could therefore not be upheld.

Cooper v. State, 540 N.E.2d 1216, 1989 Ind. LEXIS 216 (1989).

Imposition of the death penalty on a 15-year-old murderer was cruel and unusual punishment even though this section did not contain a minimum age at the time sentence was imposed. Cooper v. State, 540 N.E.2d 1216, 1989 Ind. LEXIS 216 (1989).

Where defendant was sentenced to death in 1992 despite unanimous jury recommendation to the contrary and where Indiana law was changed in 2002 to require unanimous jury recommendation of death before death penalty could be imposed, defendant's death penalty was no longer deemed appropriate, and his sentence was revised to 100 years of imprisonment. Saylor v. State, 808 N.E.2d 646, 2004 Ind. LEXIS 464 (2004).

—Saving Clause.
Where, at the time of the alleged offense of murder of which appellee was charged, the sentence of life imprisonment without parole was not an available option under the statute, appellee's trial was governed by the law that was in effect when the crime was committed; the application of the more recently adopted saving clause did not violate any principle of reformation and neither was it an exercise of vindictive justice. State v. Alcorn, 638 N.E.2d 1242, 1994 Ind. LEXIS 96 (1994).

Fine.
Where defendant was convicted of murder, this section allows the court to impose a fine of up to $10,000. However, where the trial court was aware of defendant's indigency because it appointed pauper appellate counsel, the case was remanded to add language that defendant should not be imprisoned for failure to pay the court-ordered fine of $1,000. Whitehead v. State, 511 N.E.2d 284, 1987 Ind. LEXIS 986, 71 A.L.R.4th 173 (1987), cert. denied, 484 U.S. 1031, 108 S. Ct. 761, 98 L. Ed. 2d 773, 1988 U.S. LEXIS 420 (1988).

Jury Instructions.
Defendant who was charged with a crime that occurred prior to June 30, 1993, was not entitled to a jury instruction that a sentence of life imprisonment was an alternative to the death penalty. Saylor v. State, 686 N.E.2d 80, 1997 Ind. LEXIS 142 (1997), cert. denied, 525 U.S. 831, 119 S. Ct. 84, 142 L. Ed. 2d 66, 1998 U.S. LEXIS 5043 (1998).

Where this section provides that defendant may be sentenced to death or life imprisonment without parole, it was error not to instruct jury on sentence options. Barker v. State, 695 N.E.2d 925, 1998 Ind. LEXIS 76 (1998).

Lesser Included Offenses.
Prior to the 1969 amendment, the return of a verdict of guilty of murder in the first degree and fixing the penalty at life imprisonment where the evidence could have warranted only a verdict of murder in the second degree, were not prejudicial, since the punishment prior to the 1969 amendment could not legally have been less if the verdict of second-degree murder had been returned.

Lesser Included Offenses. (Cont'd)
McPherson v. State, 178 Ind. 583, 99 N.E. 984, 1912 Ind. LEXIS 122 (1912).

The penalty imposed for the lesser included offense of second-degree murder may be the same as that for the greater offense of first-degree murder. Brown v. State, 261 Ind. 619, 308 N.E.2d 699, 1974 Ind. LEXIS 378 (1974).

Life Sentence.

Where statute provided for a sentence for "life," a sentence which provided that defendant should serve a term of his "natural life" was not objectionable. Lock v. State, 273 Ind. 315, 403 N.E.2d 1360, 1980 Ind. LEXIS 678 (1980).

Plea Agreement.

A plea agreement calling for an executed 50-year sentence for murder, which was more than the presumptive sentence for that offense, was properly accepted where both defendant and his counsel were thoroughly questioned by the trial court and defendant received exactly what he agreed to. Payton v. State, 507 N.E.2d 579, 1987 Ind. LEXIS 919 (1987).

Proper to Sentence Under Prior Law.

Where murder was committed and prosecution commenced prior to October 1, 1977, but after post-conviction relief a new trial was had after such date, it was proper to sentence the defendant under the prior law. Lynk v. State, 271 Ind. 445, 393 N.E.2d 751, 1979 Ind. LEXIS 699 (1979).

—Resentencing.

A person who was sentenced to life imprisonment for murder prior to the enactment of this section was not entitled to be resentenced under the provisions of this section. Cooper v. State, 273 Ind. 249, 403 N.E.2d 826, 1980 Ind. LEXIS 663 (1980), cert. denied, 449 U.S. 867, 101 S. Ct. 201, 66 L. Ed. 2d 86, 1980 U.S. LEXIS 3181 (1980).

Record Should Disclose Sentencing Factors.

When a judge increases or decreases the basic sentence or imposes consecutive terms of imprisonment, the record should disclose what factors were considered by the judge to be mitigating or aggravating circumstances. Gardner v. State, 270 Ind. 627, 388 N.E.2d 513, 1979 Ind. LEXIS 614 (1979).

Sentence.

—Age of Defender.

Defendant's 55-year sentence for murder, intimidation, and carrying an unlicensed handgun fell within the range for murder under IC 35-50-2-3 and thus was proper under IC 35-38-1-7.1; the trial court was not required to impose a minimum sentence because of defendant's youth. Moreover, defendant's character and the offenses' nature did not suggest that the appellate court should impose a lesser sentence under Ind. R. App. P. 7, given that defendant had insisted that he could complete a robbery twice attempted in vain, had lain in wait for the victim, had shot him twice, and had laughed and boasted to another prisoner about the murder. Fuller v. State, 852 N.E.2d 22, 2006 Ind. App. LEXIS 1540 (2006).

—Age of Offender.

Statutes addressing the distinctions between the treatment accorded to offenders who are 16 or older and those under 16 evince strong legislative sentiment that a 16 year old should be treated differently from a younger child in at least some respects, although individuals of any age convicted of murder face the same presumptive, minimum, and maximum sentence. Carter v. State, 711 N.E.2d 835, 1999 Ind. LEXIS 356 (1999).

—Aggravating Circumstances.

Any error by the court in using the factor of depreciation of the seriousness of the crime as an aggravating circumstance was overcome because several valid aggravating circumstances were found, including the age of the victim, the heinous nature and circumstances of the crime, and the defendant's lengthy history of criminal and delinquent activity. Mitchell v. State, 726 N.E.2d 1228, 2000 Ind. LEXIS 299 (2000).

Trial court, which imposed 60-year sentence on African-American defendant for felony murder, abused its sentencing discretion by finding that defendant's race was aggravating circumstance on basis that his murder of elderly white woman made people in community afraid of African-Americans; case was therefore remanded for resentencing. Williams v. State, 811 N.E.2d 462, 2004 Ind. App. LEXIS 1276 (2004).

Where defendant was convicted of murdering a girlfriend's 20-month-old daughter, the 60-year sentence was appropriate because: (1) the particularly serious nature of the crime supported the sentence; (2) defendant's nature of the offense argument did not aid the inappropriateness claim; and (3) the notion that the victim's alleged crying or fussiness amounted to a provocation that warranted a reduced sentence was rejected. Book v. State, 880 N.E.2d 1240, 2008 Ind. App. LEXIS 310 (2008).

—Erroneous.

Where the trial court erred in denying defendant's motion to correct an erroneous sentence regarding defendant's conviction for attempted murder, and it was unclear whether defendant was properly credited for both defendant's time served and credit time, remand was required to determine the amount of time defendant actually served prior to sentencing. Robinson v. State, 783 N.E.2d 1206, 2003 Ind. App. LEXIS 297 (2003), op. withdrawn, 2003 Ind. App. LEXIS 963 (Ind. Ct. App. May 9, 2003), op. replaced, 789 N.E.2d 965, 2003 Ind. App. LEXIS 960 (2003).

—Improper.

Where person was convicted of murder in the first degree and felony murder and sentenced to life imprisonment on each count of murder and both were for the same homicide, one sentence would be vacated. Pointon v. State, 274 Ind. 44, 408 N.E.2d 1255, 1980 Ind. LEXIS 779 (1980).

The trial court applied the wrong sentencing statute when it indicated that the sentence was

Sentence. (Cont'd)

—Improper. (Cont'd)

comprised of a presumptive 50-year term plus a 10-year enhancement when the legislature had provided that a 40-year presumptive term, subject to a 20-year enhancement, applied to murders occurring between July 1, 1994 and May 5, 1995. Hicks v. State, 729 N.E.2d 144, 2000 Ind. LEXIS 512 (2000).

Resentencing was required because the court should have applied P.L.158-1994, which provides a presumptive 40-year sentence for murder subject to a 20-year enhancement, rather than P.L.164-1994, which provides a presumptive 50-year sentence for murder subject to a 10-year enhancement. Williams v. State, 733 N.E.2d 919, 2000 Ind. LEXIS 700 (2000).

The trial court has no authority on remand to re-evaluate the aggravating and mitigating factors and modify a presumptive sentence after a final judgment has been entered. Lane v. State, 727 N.E.2d 454, 2000 Ind. App. LEXIS 563 (2000).

—Murder and Felony Murder.

Because only one murder occurred, the trial court cannot sentence a defendant on both murder and felony murder convictions. Martinez Chavez v. State, 534 N.E.2d 731, 1989 Ind. LEXIS 46 (1989); Tapia v. State, 569 N.E.2d 655, 1991 Ind. LEXIS 70 (Ind. App. 1991).

Defendant's 90-year consecutive sentences for felony murder, rape and burglary (violations of IC 35-42-1-1; IC 35-42-4-1(b)(3); and IC 35-43-2-1(1)(B)(i)) were not inappropriate, and the nature of the offenses did not warrant revision under AP. 7(B): (1) defendant raped and murdered a 14-year-old girl, stabbing her 11 times; (2) defendant burglarized another victim's home, taking advantage of his knowledge that she kept the doors to her apartment unlocked; (3) defendant was not remorseful and lacked the ability to empathize with the victims in the case; (4) his youth as a mitigating factor was outweighed by the likelihood of reoffending; (5) in each case, the aggravating circumstances outweighed the mitigating circumstances; (6) the sentences were within the ranges of IC 35-50-2-3 and IC 35-50-2-5; and (7) consecutive sentences were appropriate since the crimes were separate and distinct. Shepherd v. State, — N.E.2d —, 2009 Ind. App. LEXIS 431 (2009).

—Presumptive Sentence Proper.

Concurrent presumptive sentences for the murder and conspiracy to commit robbery charges were appropriate where the aggravating and mitigating circumstances considered were in approximate balance. Sherwood v. State, 749 N.E.2d 36, 2001 Ind. LEXIS 475 (2001).

Trial court did not err in sentencing defendant by applying the aggravator that imposition of a reduced sentence would depreciate the seriousness of the crime to balance three mitigating factors in arriving at the presumptive sentence under IC 35-38-1-7.1(b)(4) because the trial court actually considered a reduced sentenced. Additionally, defendant's Sixth Amendment rights were not violated by the court imposing the presumptive sentence. Davidson v. State, 849 N.E.2d 591, 2006 Ind. LEXIS 548 (2006).

While defendant's mental illness and lack of criminal history merited significant mitigating weight, because she killed both her children by hitting them in the head with a weight and there was longstanding precedent favoring imposition of the presumptive sentence under such circumstances, the imposition of the advisory 55-year sentences, to run consecutively, was not inappropriate. Lopez v. State, 869 N.E.2d 1254, 2007 Ind. App. LEXIS 1577 (2007).

—Reasonable.

Sixty-year sentence for felony murder found not manifestly unreasonable. Randall v. State, 455 N.E.2d 916, 1983 Ind. LEXIS 1017 (1983); Slone v. State, 496 N.E.2d 401, 1986 Ind. LEXIS 1253 (1986).

Forty-five year sentence for felony murder not manifestly unreasonable. Mullens v. State, 456 N.E.2d 411, 1983 Ind. LEXIS 1049 (1983).

Under the facts and circumstances of this case, and further considering a showing of the defendant's history of substantial criminal activity, the appellate court could not conclude that no reasonable person could find the 60-year sentence appropriate. Hitt v. State, 478 N.E.2d 65, 1985 Ind. LEXIS 848 (1985).

Concurrent 45-year sentences for murder were not unreasonable given the defendant's prior conviction for assault with attempt to rob while armed and the circumstances surrounding the murders. Moore v. State, 484 N.E.2d 20, 1985 Ind. LEXIS 1000 (1985); Slone v. State, 496 N.E.2d 401, 1986 Ind. LEXIS 1253 (1986).

Where the court found mitigating factors offset by aggravating circumstances, the imposition of a 40-year sentence for felony murder is reasonable. Stevens v. State, 531 N.E.2d 1175, 1989 Ind. LEXIS 3 (1989).

Sentence of 50 years was affirmed where the trial court found that although defendant was remorseful, the mitigating factor of remorse was outweighed by aggravating circumstances: defendant's criminal record; his fugitive status at the time of the crime; the danger to others occasioned by his carrying and firing a gun in a public place; his inability to compensate or make restitution to the victim's family; and his refusal, though he was not uneducated and was able to discern right from wrong, to explain why he took another life without reason. White v. State, 541 N.E.2d 541, 1989 Ind. App. LEXIS 714 (1989).

A 60-year sentence was not manifestly unreasonable where the trial court found there were no mitigating circumstances, and set forth the following aggravating circumstances: defendant had a past history of criminal and delinquent activity; defendant was in need of correctional or rehabilitative treatment that could best be provided by commitment to a penal facility; imposition of a reduced sentence would depreciate the seriousness of the crime, the defendant showed no or little remorse or regret for his terrible act, no grief over the death of his wife, and the nature of the crime

Sentence. (Cont'd)

—Reasonable. (Cont'd)
and the brutal manner in which it was committed amounted to a cold-blooded execution of the victim wife. Sweany v. State, 607 N.E.2d 387, 1993 Ind. LEXIS 19 (1993).

A 240-year sentence imposed by the trial court was not manifestly unreasonable when the defendant's character, the nature of the offenses, and the imposition of consecutive sentences were taken into account where defendant committed five separate acts of murder, pursued at least three of his victims and shot them several times, shot his 73-year old mother twice in the head and after her murder, moved her body to the bedroom and mopped her blood from the kitchen floor, moved several of the bodies, hiding them in the basement and garden, then fled the scene, disposed of the murder weapon and left the state. Hardebeck v. State, 656 N.E.2d 486, 1995 Ind. App. LEXIS 1312 (1995).

Trial court put considerable thought and deliberation into the length and structure of defendant's sentence, and exhibited compassion for the circumstances under which defendant found himself and the unfortunate struggles throughout his childhood and adolescence, making specific reference to many mitigating circumstances, including his youthful age, that defendant's mother was an alcohol abuser, that defendant had a significant history of psychiatric referrals and diagnoses due to his behavioral problems, that he turned himself in to the authorities and continued to be cooperative with law enforcement authorities and the judiciary; the court considered the many well-founded aggravating circumstances which were supported by the evidence along with the mitigating circumstances, and concluded that the aggravating circumstances outweighed the mitigating circumstances. Brown v. State, 659 N.E.2d 671, 1995 Ind. App. LEXIS 1660 (1995).

Trial court properly considered aggravating and mitigating circumstances where the court considered the brutality of the murder and the fact that defendant continued his attack well after his victims were incapacitated, and also that defendant was provoked, that he lacked a felony record, and that he committed the crimes under the influence of narcotics. Birdsong v. State, 685 N.E.2d 42, 1997 Ind. LEXIS 126 (1997).

Maximum sentence of 60 years imposed by court was proper; no mitigating factors were sufficient to offset the aggravating factors and court adequately explained its reasons for the maximum sentence. Coleman v. State, 694 N.E.2d 269, 1998 Ind. LEXIS 41 (1998).

Where defendant murdered a 14 year old boy while on probation, had a history of criminal activity, but presented substantial evidence demonstrating his lack of intellectual capabilities and his unhappy and often abusive childhood in mitigation, the maximum sentence of 60 years was appropriate. Rhodes v. State, 698 N.E.2d 304, 1998 Ind. LEXIS 240 (1998).

A presumptive 55 year sentence enhanced by

five years, less than the maximum sentence allowed, was not grossly out of proportion for the taking of a human life. Harrison v. State, 699 N.E.2d 645, 1998 Ind. LEXIS 231 (1998).

Sentences totaling 110 years for two murders was reasonable, notwithstanding the defendant's young age and the influence of the defendant's older brother on his actions, where the court identified six aggravating circumstances, properly outlined its reasoning for the defendant's sentences, and adequately balanced the aggravating and mitigating circumstances. Kelly v. State, 719 N.E.2d 391, 1999 Ind. LEXIS 1071 (1999).

The imposition of the presumptive sentence was reasonable where the court considered the defendant's proposed mitigating factors and engaged in a lengthy and thoughtful assessment of aggravating and mitigating circumstances. O'Neill v. State, 719 N.E.2d 1243, 1999 Ind. LEXIS 1081 (1999).

Defendant's sentence was not manifestly unreasonable, where the trial court added only five years to the murder sentence and ten years to attempted murder as enhancements, and ran defendant's sentences concurrently. Johnson v. State, 725 N.E.2d 864, 2000 Ind. LEXIS 239 (2000).

The trial court thoughtfully exercised its discretion in ordering that each presumptive sentence be enhanced by five years and that the sentences be served consecutively. Walter v. State, 727 N.E.2d 443, 2000 Ind. LEXIS 296 (2000).

There was no abuse of the trial court's sentencing discretion in choosing not to assign any significant weight to defendant's claim of remorse, and any weight that might have been assigned to this proffered mitigating circumstance was more than offset by defendant's prior criminal history and the trial court's decision to impose concurrent instead of consecutive sentences for defendant's murder and attempted murder convictions. Evans v. State, 727 N.E.2d 1072, 2000 Ind. LEXIS 411 (2000).

Given the aggravating factors and the fact that the trial court found no mitigating factor, defendant's sentence of 65 years for murder was appropriate under IC 35-50-2-3(a) for the shooting death of the victim who defendant attempted to rob. Williams v. State, 782 N.E.2d 1039, 2003 Ind. App. LEXIS 134 (2003).

Trial court did not err in imposing an executed sentence on defendant of 50 years for murder; the trial court had imposed a 52-year sentence, had suspended two years of that murder sentence, had found an aggravating factor that was supported by the record, and defendant had agreed in pleading guilty that an executed sentence between 40 and 52 years would be appropriate. Nguyen v. State, 837 N.E.2d 153, 2005 Ind. App. LEXIS 2123 (2005), overruled in part, Childress v. State, 848 N.E.2d 1073, 2006 Ind. LEXIS 474 (2006).

Defendant's consecutive, enhanced, IC 35-50-2-3(a) sentences for three murders were based on aggravators that were improper if found without a jury, so the aggravators were removed. The defendant was re-sentenced to 55 years for each of the three murders to be served consecutively. The aggravators that the trial judge found (with no jury findings) were based upon sufficient evidence and supported the consecutive sentences for three

Sentence. (Cont'd)

—Reasonable. (Cont'd)

murders. The four aggravating factors were substantial level of planning and aforethought, failure to accept responsibility, lack of remorse, and certain circumstances of the murders: (1) the shots were fired at close range; (2) the victims were defenseless; (3) one victim was of young age; (4) a level of callousness was demonstrated; and (5) there was a fair amount of time for reflection between the murders. Sowders v. State, 829 N.E.2d 18, 2005 Ind. LEXIS 538 (2005).

Where defendant's sentence was within purview of plea agreement, where number of times victim was shot was proper aggravator, and where sentence was limited to presumptive term, trial court did not abuse its discretion in sentencing defendant to 55 years for murder. Ross v. State, 835 N.E.2d 1090, 2005 Ind. App. LEXIS 1995 (2005).

Trial court did not err in sentencing defendant to 60 years for a murder conviction and 40 years for a conspiracy conviction, with the sentences to run consecutively, under circumstances in which defendant entered into the conspiracy and then facilitated the victim's murder as part of a continuing conspiracy to sell illegal substances; although a co-conspirator pulled the trigger, the murder would not have occurred without defendant's planning of the murder, the conspiracy to commit the murder, the set-up of the victim, and assistance to facilitate the co-conspirator's escape. With reference to defendant's character, his full-time job was breaking the law, and in performing his job, he planned and facilitated the murder. Jack v. State, 870 N.E.2d 444, 2007 Ind. App. LEXIS 1583 (2007).

Defendant's presumptive 55-year sentence for murder was proper. The trial court had not relied upon defendant's mens rea as an aggravating circumstance, but had commented on the execution-style way in which the murder was carried out; defendant had not shown that a 45-year sentence would cause any less hardship on his children than a 55-year sentence; even if the victim, who was "tripping" on drugs, had provoked the situation, defendant had left the scene, then returned with a gun and shot the victim; and even if defendant had not waived steady employment as a mitigating factor, he had presented no information regarding his performance or reasons for termination. McKinney v. State, 873 N.E.2d 630, 2007 Ind. App. LEXIS 2124 (2007).

Defendant's sentence was affirmed because, based on the nature of the offense, defendant's causing the victim to die by punching and kicking him in the head during a fight, and defendant's character and prior criminal history, trial court's imposition of a 60-year sentence for murder, pursuant to IC 35-42-1-1, was not inappropriate under AP. 7(B). Rogers v. State, 878 N.E.2d 269, 2007 Ind. App. LEXIS 2741 (2007).

Sixty-five-year sentence for murder was not inappropriate given the extraordinary brutality of the crime. Newgent v. State, 897 N.E.2d 520, 2008 Ind. App. LEXIS 2585 (2008).

—Suspended Sentence Not Available.

The trial court did not abuse its discretion by failing to find the defendant's status as a father a mitigating circumstance sufficient to show that long-term imprisonment would cause undue hardship, since many persons convicted of serious crimes have one or more children, since counsel did not argue this as a mitigating circumstance at sentencing nor offer any evidence on the point, and since a suspended sentence is not an available option for a murder conviction. Dowdell v. State, 720 N.E.2d 1146, 1999 Ind. LEXIS 1179 (1999).

—Unclear Application of Law.

Where it was unclear whether court applied the version of this section from P.L.158-1994 or the version from P.L.164-1994, case was remanded for new sentencing pursuant to P.L.158-1994. Carter v. State, 686 N.E.2d 1254, 1997 Ind. LEXIS 158 (1997).

—Unreasonable.

Case was remanded for entry of a sentence of 50 years where the maximum sentence of 60 years was manifestly unreasonable and an aggravation of sentence of no more than ten years was required under the circumstances. Christopher v. State, 511 N.E.2d 1019, 1987 Ind. LEXIS 1013 (1987).

Where the court added 20 years for aggravating circumstances and the only relevant and applicable aggravating circumstance identified in the order was the body of trial evidence, and it, standing in opposition to the weight of the mitigating circumstance, was clearly insufficient to warrant a 20-year enhancement to the maximum sentence, a 60-year sentence under the record was manifestly unreasonable. Harrington v. State, 584 N.E.2d 558, 1992 Ind. LEXIS 7 (1992).

In light of appellant's conduct in surrendering himself to the police and providing a full confession to a murder committed 15 years earlier, a sentence of 60 years was unreasonable considering the character of the offender. Brewer v. State, 646 N.E.2d 1382, 1995 Ind. LEXIS 20 (1995).

Where defendant was convicted of murder and burglary for killing his former wife, court order that he have no contact with former in-laws or his children was invalid since no-contact order is not authorized sentence under murder or burglary statutes. Laux v. State, 821 N.E.2d 816, 2005 Ind. LEXIS 93 (2005).

Defendant was prejudiced and deprived of a fair appeal due to his trial counsel's failure to raise his sentence of 60 years' imprisonment for accomplice murder as an issue on direct appeal where the trial court improperly considered aggravators, namely, a psychological evaluation of defendant that was conducted six years prior to the crime and provided no explanation on how it was relevant; defendant's juvenile criminal history since his juvenile crimes were not particularly grave nor related to his murder conviction; heinousness since evidence did not indicate that murder was particularly heinous; furthermore, presentence report recommended 45 years rather than 60. Taylor v. State, 840 N.E.2d 324, 2006 Ind. LEXIS 28 (2006).

Sentence Enhancement.

Although the same aggravating circumstance may support both decisions, the trial court must separately indicate which factors, if any, support the enhancement and the consecutive sentences. Saucerman v. State, 555 N.E.2d 1351, 1990 Ind. App. LEXIS 807 (1990).

Enhancement from the presumptive term of 40 years to a term of 60 years was warranted where defendant was involved in the murder of her husband, and the record was replete with aggravating circumstances, including the fact that she had arranged for the murder of a previous husband. Thacker v. State, 578 N.E.2d 351, 1991 Ind. LEXIS 163 (1991).

Where the presentence report detailed the history of appellant's criminal activity as a juvenile and gave the adjudications that supported the finding of a specific juvenile history, the statement by the trial court that the crime was of a heinous enough nature to constitute an aggravating factor was sufficient to support an enhanced sentence. Harris v. State, 617 N.E.2d 912, 1993 Ind. LEXIS 101 (1993), overruled, Wright v. State, 690 N.E.2d 1098, 1997 Ind. LEXIS 245 (1997).

Trial court did not err in first enhancing the presumptive sentence for murder based upon the habitual offender finding, then enhancing the sentence based upon the aggravating circumstances. James v. State, 643 N.E.2d 321, 1994 Ind. LEXIS 165 (1994).

Given the evidence presented at trial and at sentencing, the Supreme Court held that murder merited an enhanced sentence; however, a 60-year sentence was simply too excessive where appellant pled guilty to the murder charge, thus saving the court time and resources and sparing the victim's family from enduring a full-blown trial. Scheckel v. State, 655 N.E.2d 506, 1995 Ind. LEXIS 141 (1995).

Where sentence for felony murder was 10 years beyond presumptive sentence and was imposed based upon findings that victims were over age of 65 and due to nature and circumstances of crime, sentence violated Sixth Amendment under Blakely because facts supporting findings were not found by jury and were not admitted by defendant. Harris v. State, 824 N.E.2d 432, 2005 Ind. App. LEXIS 478 (2005).

Where murder defendant had her sister turn up volume on stereo while she shot her stepfather twice and then attempted to conceal murder by burning the body, any error in accepting defendant's jury trial waiver without advising defendant that she had right to have jury determine beyond reasonable doubt all facts legally essential to her sentence was deemed harmless. Averitte v. State, 824 N.E.2d 1283, 2005 Ind. App. LEXIS 563 (2005).

—Aggravators.

Although the noncapital sentencing statute, IC 35-38-1-7.1, does not specifically cite the lying in wait element of a crime as a separate aggravator, a court may consider the nature and circumstances of a crime to determine what sentence to impose, and since that factor demonstrates a heightened level of vindictiveness the court's statement reflecting the seriousness of that factor sustained sentence. Taylor v. State, 695 N.E.2d 117, 1998 Ind. LEXIS 71 (1998).

Sentence of 40 years with 20 year enhancement was not manifestly unreasonable where court found aggravating circumstances of elderly victim, defendant's prior misdemeanor conviction for check deception, and nature and circumstances of crime outweighed mitigating factor of defendant's health. Willsey v. State, 698 N.E.2d 784, 1998 Ind. LEXIS 248 (1998).

Where it was apparent from the record that the trial court considered the defendant's mental illness, it was not manifestly unreasonable to add ten years to the presumptive sentence for murder based on aggravating factors found. Garner v. State, 704 N.E.2d 1011, 1998 Ind. LEXIS 674 (1998).

Because the defendant murdered two roommates and the planning of the two murders showed the deliberate nature of the crime, the court did not err when it considered those aggravating factors and imposed a sentence on each count of 65 years with 20 years suspended, to be served consecutively, for a total sentence of 90 years for the two murders. Hull v. State, 839 N.E.2d 1250, 2005 Ind. App. LEXIS 2456 (2005).

Enhancement of defendant's murder sentence for manner in which he handled his relationship with victim, circumstances under which stabbing of victim occurred, and defendant's actions and statements during trial violated defendant's right to trial by jury since facts used to enhance sentence were never determined by jury. Aguilar v. State, 820 N.E.2d 762, 2005 Ind. App. LEXIS 33 (2005), transfer granted, 831 N.E.2d 741, 2005 Ind. LEXIS 257 (2005).

Defendant's consecutive, enhanced, IC 35-50-2-3(a) sentences for three murders were based on aggravators that were improper if found without a jury, so the aggravators were removed. The defendant was re-sentenced to 55 years for each of the three murders to be served consecutively. The aggravators that the trial judge found (with no jury findings) were based upon sufficient evidence and supported the consecutive sentences for three murders. The four aggravating factors were substantial level of planning and aforethought, failure to accept responsibility, lack of remorse, and certain circumstances of the murders: (1) the shots were fired at close range; (2) the victims were defenseless; (3) one victim was of young age; (4) a level of callousness was demonstrated; and (5) there was a fair amount of time for reflection between the murders. Sowders v. State, 829 N.E.2d 18, 2005 Ind. LEXIS 538 (2005).

IC 35-38-1-7.1(a)(2) criminal history that was perhaps significant in terms of the number of burglary, theft, and conversion offenses but relatively insignificant in terms of nature and gravity as related to the instant offense of murder did not support a 60-year statutory maximum sentence under former IC 35-50-2-3; therefore, the trial court abused its discretion when it sentenced defendant to 60 years in prison. Ashworth v. State, — N.E.2d —, 2009 Ind. App. LEXIS 228 (2009).

—**Depreciating Seriousness of Crime.**

Aggravating factor that lesser sentence would depreciate seriousness of crime applies only when considering imposition of a sentence shorter than the presumptive sentence, but where other aggravating circumstances are adequate to support an enhanced sentence, reversal is not required where the court uses an improper aggravating factor. Robinson v. State, 693 N.E.2d 548, 1998 Ind. LEXIS 36 (1998).

—**Mitigators.**

Although the trial court found the defendant's lack of criminal history to be a mitigating circumstance, there was no error in its failure to find that he was likely to respond affirmatively to probation or short term imprisonment as a mitigating circumstance where those sentences were not options available to the court in a murder case. Angleton v. State, 714 N.E.2d 156, 1999 Ind. LEXIS 555 (1999), cert. denied, 529 U.S. 1132, 120 S. Ct. 2012, 146 L. Ed. 2d 961, 2000 U.S. LEXIS 3480 (2000).

Statement of Reasons.

A statement of reasons is generally not required when the presumptive sentence of 40 years is given. Hensley v. State, 497 N.E.2d 1067, 1986 Ind. LEXIS 1286 (1986).

Where trial court identified a particular prior serious crime and the specific manner in which defendant murdered his victim as aggravating circumstances, the sentencing statement was sufficiently specific. Montgomery v. State, 694 N.E.2d 1137, 1998 Ind. LEXIS 57 (1998).

Where aggravating factors in sentence statement were not neatly packaged, but court found in sum that defendant had prior history of violence, unsuccessful history of rehabilitation, and that crime was particularly heinous, enhanced and consecutive sentences were warranted. Brown v. State, 698 N.E.2d 779, 1998 Ind. LEXIS 245 (1998).

Where the trial court found three aggravating circumstances and commented on proffered mitigating circumstances, the fact that the court did not articulate specifically that the aggravating circumstances outweighed the mitigating circum-

stances did not render the sentencing statement unsatisfactory or the sentence of 60 years manifestly unreasonable. Charlton v. State, 702 N.E.2d 1045, 1998 Ind. LEXIS 606 (1998).

Cited:

Jones v. State, 422 N.E.2d 1197, 1981 Ind. LEXIS 778 (1981); Basham v. State, 422 N.E.2d 1206, 1981 Ind. LEXIS 776 (1981); Williams v. State, 430 N.E.2d 759, 1982 Ind. LEXIS 732 (1982); Bryan v. State, 450 N.E.2d 53, 1983 Ind. LEXIS 871 (1983); Smith v. State, 468 N.E.2d 512, 1984 Ind. LEXIS 941 (1984); Butrum v. State, 469 N.E.2d 1174, 1984 Ind. LEXIS 1006 (1984); McHugh v. State, 471 N.E.2d 293, 1984 Ind. LEXIS 1044 (1984); Hicks v. State, 474 N.E.2d 987, 1985 Ind. LEXIS 760 (1985); Eaton v. State, 575 N.E.2d 287, 1991 Ind. App. LEXIS 1229 (1991); Propes v. State, 587 N.E.2d 1291, 1992 Ind. LEXIS 74 (1992); Hampton v. State, 588 N.E.2d 555, 1992 Ind. App. LEXIS 329 (1992); Scheckel v. State, 620 N.E.2d 681, 1993 Ind. LEXIS 117 (1993); Foster v. State, 633 N.E.2d 337, 1994 Ind. App. LEXIS 520 (1994); Burris v. Parke, 948 F. Supp. 1310, 1996 U.S. Dist. LEXIS 19117 (N.D. Ind. 1996); Payne v. State, 688 N.E.2d 164, 1997 Ind. LEXIS 191 (1997); Page v. State, 689 N.E.2d 707, 1997 Ind. LEXIS 208 (1997); Bufkin v. State, 700 N.E.2d 1147, 1998 Ind. LEXIS 505 (1998); Miller v. State, 720 N.E.2d 696, 1999 Ind. LEXIS 1072 (1999); Johnston v. Dobeski, 739 N.E.2d 121, 2000 Ind. LEXIS 1109 (2000); Lambert v. State, 743 N.E.2d 719, 2001 Ind. LEXIS 199 (2001); Fredrick v. State, 755 N.E.2d 1078, 2001 Ind. LEXIS 920 (2001); Monegan v. State, 756 N.E.2d 499, 2001 Ind. LEXIS 925 (2001); McAbee v. State, 770 N.E.2d 802, 2002 Ind. LEXIS 543 (2002); Saylor v. State, 765 N.E.2d 535, 2002 Ind. LEXIS 221 (2002); Brown v. State, 783 N.E.2d 1121, 2003 Ind. LEXIS 201 (2003); Mathews v. State, 824 N.E.2d 713, 2005 Ind. App. LEXIS 515 (2005); Reed v. State, 825 N.E.2d 911, 2005 Ind. App. LEXIS 648 (2005); Moore v. State, 827 N.E.2d 631, 2005 Ind. App. LEXIS 887 (2005); Duncan v. State, 857 N.E.2d 955, 2006 Ind. LEXIS 1028 (2006); McDonald v. State, 868 N.E.2d 1111, 2007 Ind. LEXIS 488 (2007); Anglemyer v. State, 868 N.E.2d 482, 2007 Ind. LEXIS 490 (2007).

RESEARCH REFERENCES

Indiana Law Review.

Survey: Criminal Law and Procedure: Recent Developments in Indiana Criminal Law and Procedure (October 1, 2003, to September 30, 2004), 38 Ind. L. Rev. 999 (2005).

Survey: Criminal Law and Procedure: Recent Developments in Indiana Criminal Law and Procedure (October 1, 2004, through September 30,

2005), 39 Ind. L. Rev. 893 (2006).

Indiana Constitutional Developments: Incremental Change, 41 Ind. L. Rev. 923 (2008).

Res Gestae.

Criminal Justice Notes 7/04: Race as aggravating circumstance in sentencing, 48 (No. 3) Res Gestae 36 (2004).

35-50-2-4. Class A felony.

A person who commits a Class A felony shall be imprisoned for a fixed term of between twenty (20) and fifty (50) years, with the advisory sentence being thirty (30)

years. In addition, the person may be fined not more than ten thousand dollars ($10,000).

History.
IC 35-50-2-4, as added by Acts 1976, P.L.148, § 8; 1977, P.L.340, § 117; P.L.164-1994, § 3; P.L.148-1995, § 5; P.L.71-2005, § 7.

Cross References.
Compensation for victims of violent crimes, IC 5-2-6.1.

NOTES TO DECISIONS

Constitutionality.

—Cruel and Unusual Punishment.
The wide range of penalties which may be imposed for the various classes of felonies in the new criminal code does not invite discrimination and cruel and unusual punishment. Rogers v. State, 272 Ind. 65, 396 N.E.2d 348, 1979 Ind. LEXIS 748 (1979).

Sentence did not constitute cruel and unusual punishment where it was made in accordance with statutory mandate and actually mitigated from the statutorily dictated presumptive terms. Carter v. State, 471 N.E.2d 1111, 1984 Ind. LEXIS 1073 (1984).

The 30-year presumptive sentence for robbery resulting in "bodily injury" does not violate the cruel and unusual punishments clauses of the state and federal constitutions. Payne v. State, 484 N.E.2d 16, 1985 Ind. LEXIS 1001 (1985).

A 50-year sentence for child molestation was not cruel and unusual punishment. Stout v. State, 612 N.E.2d 1076, 1993 Ind. App. LEXIS 409 (1993).

—Double Jeopardy.
The enhanced counts of attempted rape and robbery, each enhanced because of physical injury, violated the defendant's right against double jeopardy because the injuries sustained were part of the same onslaught, and the injuries could not be used to enhance both charges. Wolfe v. State, 549 N.E.2d 1024, 1990 Ind. LEXIS 9 (1990).

Aggravating Factors.
Whether the imposition of a reduced or suspended sentence would depreciate the seriousness of the crime is a factor which may be used as an aggravator only when the trial court is considering imposing a sentence of shorter duration than the presumptive sentence. Lee v. State, 689 N.E.2d 435, 1997 Ind. LEXIS 224 (1997).

Aggravating factors considered by the trial judge supported enhancement of the presumptive sentence where defendant had a history of criminal and delinquent acts, crime occurred after defendant was arrested and had agreed to plead guilty to another Class A felony and the chances of defendant committing another crime were great. Lee v. State, 689 N.E.2d 435, 1997 Ind. LEXIS 224 (1997).

Even though charges based on the defendant's subsequent arrests were dropped due to a plea bargain, the record of arrests was properly considered as an aggravating factor by the trial court in sentencing. Miller v. State, 709 N.E.2d 48, 1999 Ind. App. LEXIS 619 (1999).

AP. 7(B) authorizes revision of sentences when certain broad conditions are satisfied; defendant's criminal history, consisting only of misdemeanors, most of which were alcohol related, was insufficient to justify maximum sentence for class A felony child molesting conviction, since criminal history was manifestly different than molesting charge. Neale v. State, 826 N.E.2d 635, 2005 Ind. LEXIS 398 (2005).

In sentencing defendant for conspiracy to deal in cocaine in excess of three grams, trial court's improper reliance on two aggravators was harmless, since defendant's criminal history alone justified enhanced sentence. Simmons v. State, 828 N.E.2d 449, 2005 Ind. App. LEXIS 948 (2005).

Father's abuse of position of trust was by itself valid aggravator supporting maximum enhancement of sentence for molesting his own child. Hart v. State, 829 N.E.2d 541, 2005 Ind. App. LEXIS 1041 (2005).

Defendant's enhanced sentence of 38 years for each of the two counts of attempted murder, to be served consecutively, was proper where the trial court found defendant's criminal history to be an

Aggravating Factors. (Cont'd)
aggravating factor. Burks v. State, 838 N.E.2d 510, 2005 Ind. App. LEXIS 2268 (2005).

As the risks methamphetamine and its manufacture pose to the general public have been factored into the crime of dealing in methamphetamine, in violation of IC 35-48-4-1, and there was no evidence that defendant's crime posed a greater risk to the public than any other manufacturing operation would, the court could not use the "lessor sentence would depreciate the seriousness of the crime" aggravator when it imposed the presumptive sentence. However, that defendant's three-year-old son lived in the house where the drug was being manufactured did support the trial court's consideration of that aggravator in refusing to reduce or suspend the presumptive sentence under former IC 35-50-2-4. Burgess v. State, 854 N.E.2d 35, 2006 Ind. App. LEXIS 1890 (2006).

Defendant was convicted of dealing in methamphetamine, in violation of IC 35-48-4-1(a)(1), (b)(3). Despite defendant's lack of prior convictions, the trial court, in imposing the presumptive 30-year sentence, properly found as an aggravator that he was at risk to reoffend, because it found he was an addict who would do anything to obtain the drug. Burgess v. State, 854 N.E.2d 35, 2006 Ind. App. LEXIS 1890 (2006).

Under defendant's plea bargain the state had agreed to cap his sentence for dealing in methamphetamine, in violation of IC 35-48-4-1, at the presumptive range. Therefore, pursuant to former IC 35-50-2-4, the trial court properly considered as an aggravator the fact that a lesser sentence would depreciate the seriousness of the crime, since it was deciding whether to reduce, not enhance, the presumptive sentence. Burgess v. State, 854 N.E.2d 35, 2006 Ind. App. LEXIS 1890 (2006).

Defendant's 50-year sentence for two counts of child molesting, one as a Class A felony and one as a Class C felony, was affirmed where the trial court properly assessed significant aggravating weight to the aggravators of abuse of trust and the victim's age because the defendant was the victim's uncle and her babysitter. Garland v. State, 855 N.E.2d 703, 2006 Ind. App. LEXIS 2145 (2006).

Deviation from the presumptive sentence of 30 years under IC 35-50-2-4 for child molesting was not warranted as defendant's extensive criminal history of felony child molesting and sexual battery occurred about 10 years before the current offenses; however, defendant's repeated molestations of the victim, violation of his position of trust as the victim's step-father, and infliction of psychological abuse warranted one sentence being imposed consecutive to one of the other counts under IC 35-50-1-2(c). Smith v. State, 889 N.E.2d 261, 2008 Ind. LEXIS 486 (2008).

Defendant's 50-year sentence for child molestation under IC 35-42-4-3(a)(1), a Class A felony under IC 35-50-2-4, was proper, even though the trial court erred in finding that the offense was committed in the presence of other children and in using the victim's ADHD and bi-polar illness as aggravators, as the trial court assigned great weight to defendant's predatory behavior and likelihood to reoffend, and would probably have imposed the same sentence if the improper aggravators were not considered. Taylor v. State, 891 N.E.2d 155, 2008 Ind. App. LEXIS 1678 (2008).

Trial court did not abuse its discretion in considering defendant mother's position of care as an aggravating factor where defendant was convicted of neglect of a dependent based upon her leaving her child in a box in the basement after it was born where the child was not found until two days later. Robinson v. State, 894 N.E.2d 1038, 2008 Ind. App. LEXIS 2232 (2008).

Basic Sentence.
When the court imposed the basic sentence, the Supreme Court would presume that the mandatory considerations of former IC 35-50-1A-7 were made by the judge. Keys v. State, 271 Ind. 52, 390 N.E.2d 148, 1979 Ind. LEXIS 640 (1979).

—Reasonable.
Imposition of basic presumptive sentence found not to be manifestly unreasonable. Warner v. State, 455 N.E.2d 355, 1983 Ind. LEXIS 998 (1983).

Codefendants.
When one defendant proceeds to trial and his accomplice pleads guilty the sentences need not be identical. Morgan v. State, 275 Ind. 666, 419 N.E.2d 964, 1981 Ind. LEXIS 735 (1981).

Consecutive Sentences.
Where court's imposition of consecutive sentences was based on the fact there were "two separate and distinct incidences of rape," the offered justification did not satisfy the specificity requirement and the cause was remanded for correction of the sentence. Lindsey v. State, 485 N.E.2d 102, 1985 Ind. LEXIS 1031 (1985).

Appropriate aggravating sentencing factors outweighed the mitigating factors, and the 30 year presumptive sentence for each conviction of child molesting was appropriately enhanced by 10 years; however, since the evidence did not establish that the two acts occurred at significantly different times, it was improper to order that the two child molesting by sexual intercourse convictions be served consecutively. Kien v. State, 782 N.E.2d 398, 2003 Ind. App. LEXIS 96 (2003).

Trial court should not have imposed consecutive sentences on defendant's convictions on five counts of deviate sexual conduct, a Class A felony, which under the prior presumptive sentencing scheme pursuant to IC 35-50-2-4 and the trial court's sentencing resulted in a 100-year prison sentence; sentence was excessive because: (1) the trial court did not explain its consecutive-sentence reasoning; (2) the crimes were identical and involved the same child; and (3) defendant's prior criminal history only consisted of six driving-related misdemeanor offenses; accordingly, state Supreme Court revised the total executed sentence to 50 years. Monroe v. State, 886 N.E.2d 578, 2008 Ind. LEXIS 424 (2008).

Consecutive sentences for two child molesting convictions were improper because, although the

Consecutive Sentences. (Cont'd)
aggravating circumstances were sufficient to warrant imposing enhanced sentences, they were not sufficient to justify imposing consecutive sentences, and the trial court did not explain why the aggravating circumstances warranted consecutive sentences; defendant was in a position of trust with the child victim, who believed defendant was her biological father, defendant molested the victim on multiple occasions other than the crimes charged, and, although defendant's criminal history was not inconsequential, his convictions were not significant aggravators. Harris v. State, 897 N.E.2d 927, 2008 Ind. LEXIS 1277 (2008).

Defendant's Criminal Record.
The sole factor of the defendant's criminal record is sufficient to support an enhanced sentence. Schwass v. State, 554 N.E.2d 1127, 1990 Ind. LEXIS 121 (1990).

Single aggravator was sufficient for an enhanced sentence and a criminal history in and of itself was sufficient to support an enhanced sentence; an enhanced sentence of 38 years for dealing in cocaine was affirmed where, although none of the defendant's prior convictions involved the possession or sale of cocaine, the defendant had a number of prior offenses including two involving illegal drug possession. Parker v. State, 773 N.E.2d 867, 2002 Ind. App. LEXIS 1396 (2002).

History of misdemeanors unrelated to defendant's conviction for voluntary manslaughter were not significant aggravators in context of sentencing of defendant; accordingly, trial court abused its discretion in imposing enhanced sentence based on those misdemeanors. Ballard v. State, 808 N.E.2d 729, 2004 Ind. App. LEXIS 935 (2004), transfer granted, 812 N.E.2d 789, 2004 Ind. LEXIS 685 (2004).

Discretion of Trial Court.

—Appellate Review.
Determination of a sentence rests with the discretion of the trial court; an appellate court will not alter a sentence authorized by statute unless the sentence is manifestly unreasonable in light of the offender and offense. Clayton v. State, 658 N.E.2d 82, 1995 Ind. App. LEXIS 1098 (1995), corrected, 658 N.E.2d 82, 1995 Ind. App. LEXIS 1204 (1995).

—Arrests.
Trial court has broad discretion to consider aggravating factors; this discretion includes consideration of arrests not yet reduced to conviction. Clayton v. State, 658 N.E.2d 82, 1995 Ind. App. LEXIS 1098 (1995), corrected, 658 N.E.2d 82, 1995 Ind. App. LEXIS 1204 (1995).

Effect of Amendments to Statute.
Where the changes to the applicable sentencing statute, IC 35-50-2-4, were made prior to defendant's sentencing, the trial court relied upon the amended statute, which provided for advisory rather than presumptive sentences, because the change in the statute was procedural rather than substantive. Samaniego-Hernandez v. State, 839 N.E.2d 798, 2005 Ind. App. LEXIS 2450 (2005).

Illegal Alien.
Placement of juvenile respondent with the department of corrections upon a finding that respondent committed an act that would have constituted class A felony dealing in a schedule I controlled substance within 1,000 feet of a school was proper because, although respondent was a Mexican national in the United States illegally, and argued that he should have been returned to Mexico, the disposition was proper considering the serious nature of respondent's drug-related offense, the likelihood of reoffending, and the trial court's findings regarding respondent's best interests; among other things, respondent had previously been returned to Mexico after committing a crime in Kentucky, but about one month later, illegally reentered the United States with a counterfeit Mexican driver's license, and although respondent's family was in Mexico, he chose to leave them and illegally reenter the United States. J.S. v. State, 881 N.E.2d 26, 2008 Ind. App. LEXIS 256 (2008).

Trial court properly sentenced defendant to 40 years imprisonment after he pleaded guilty to Class A felony dealing in cocaine, which was 10 years more than the advisory sentence, because defendant's illegal alien status was a valid aggravator; the trial court found that defendant's status as an illegal alien reflected disregard for the law. Sanchez v. State, 891 N.E.2d 174, 2008 Ind. App. LEXIS 1673 (2008).

Mitigating Circumstances.
Mitigating circumstances of age, addiction to alcohol and drugs, and belligerent nature, are not mandatory mitigating circumstances. It is the very nature of the criminal to have sociopathic tendencies. Schwass v. State, 554 N.E.2d 1127, 1990 Ind. LEXIS 121 (1990).

Where defendant's eventual capture and arrest were nigh unavoidable, the trial court did not abuse its discretion in failing to find that defendant's voluntary statement to police was a mitigating factor entitled to any significant weight. Battles v. State, 688 N.E.2d 1230, 1997 Ind. LEXIS 196 (1997).

Although there were several aggravating circumstances which the court properly found, and the facts were egregious, defendant's mental illness should have warranted at least some offset to those aggravating circumstances; because defendant's mental illness was well documented and long standing and apparently limited his ability to function, it was entitled to some mitigating weight and warranted a reduction of defendant's total sentence. Archer v. State, 689 N.E.2d 678, 1997 Ind. LEXIS 189 (1997), amended, — N.E.2d —, 1998 Ind. LEXIS 8 (1998).

Sentence of 135 years imposed upon 16-year old defendant who pled guilty to burglary, criminal confinement, criminal deviate conduct, and robbery was not abuse of trial court's discretion where defendant participated in repeated rapes and deviate sexual conduct committed against two women, one of whom was seven months pregnant; trial court properly considered all mitigators pro-

Mitigating Circumstances. (Cont'd)
posed by defendant, including age, troubled childhood, drug and alcohol abuse and his testimony against other defendant. Rose v. State, 810 N.E.2d 361, 2004 Ind. App. LEXIS 1111 (2004).

Trial court did not err in imposing presumptive sentence of 30 years on all four of defendant's attempted murder convictions; trial court was not required to give significant weight to defendant's lack of criminal history. Truax v. State, 856 N.E.2d 116, 2006 Ind. App. LEXIS 2264 (2006).

—Statement of Reasons.
Where defendant received the presumptive sentence for a Class A felony, 30 years, the trial court was under no duty to identify, discuss, or balance mitigating factors. Owensby v. State, 549 N.E.2d 407, 1990 Ind. App. LEXIS 140 (1990).

Punitive Damages.
One consideration in evaluating the excessiveness of a punitive damages award in a civil action is a comparison between the award and criminal penalties for similar conduct. Schimizzi v. Illinois Farmers Ins. Co., 928 F. Supp. 760, 1996 U.S. Dist. LEXIS 7486 (N.D. Ind. 1996).

Retroactivity.
Where defendant's crimes were committed on October 20, 1994, he should have been sentenced pursuant to the 1994 version of this section which became effective July 1, 1994, and was applicable to crimes committed on or after its effective date. Culpepper v. State, 662 N.E.2d 670, 1996 Ind. App. LEXIS 337 (1996).

Robbery Resulting in Serious Bodily Injury.
The offense of robbery resulting in serious bodily injury does not have the seriousness of the crime as a Class A felony legislated into the base sentence so as to prevent the judge from adding to the sentence for aggravated circumstances. McNew v. State, 271 Ind. 214, 391 N.E.2d 607, 1979 Ind. LEXIS 658 (1979).

Sentence Enhancement.
Sentence enhancement is a separate and discrete decision from the imposition of consecutive sentences. Lindsey v. State, 485 N.E.2d 102, 1985 Ind. LEXIS 1031 (1985).

Fifty year enhanced sentence for arson was not excessive due to the defendant's extensive criminal history, which included serious crimes, any attempt to rehabilitate had failed and would probably have continued to fail in the future, and reducing the sentence would have depreciated the seriousness of this type of crime, and since personal injury and property damage resulted from the offense. Faulisi v. State, 602 N.E.2d 1032, 1992 Ind. App. LEXIS 1710 (1992).

Enhancement of presumptive sentences, along with the imposition of consecutive sentences, may be supported by a single aggravating circumstance. Clayton v. State, 658 N.E.2d 82, 1995 Ind. App. LEXIS 1098 (1995), corrected, 658 N.E.2d 82, 1995 Ind. App. LEXIS 1204 (1995).

Where defendant was convicted of a Class A

felony for selling an extraordinary amount of cocaine, and his sentence was enhanced only by five years for two prior felony convictions and several misdemeanors, his enhanced sentence of thirty years was not disproportionate to his offense. McGowan v. State, 671 N.E.2d 872, 1996 Ind. App. LEXIS 1271 (1996), aff'd, 674 N.E.2d 174, 1996 Ind. LEXIS 172 (1996).

A single aggravator may support enhanced sentence for Class A felony. Moore v. State, 691 N.E.2d 1232, 1998 Ind. App. LEXIS 86 (1998).

Where only one of three factors used to enhance defendant's sentence violated Sixth Amendment requirement that enhancement factors either be admitted by defendant or determined by jury, enhanced sentence was valid. Padilla v. State, 822 N.E.2d 288, 2005 Ind. App. LEXIS 216 (2005).

Since jury finding of planning and preparation was not necessary for jury to find defendant guilty of attempted murder, Sixth Amendment prevented trial court from using planning and preparation as aggravating factor justifying enhanced sentence. Edwards v. State, 822 N.E.2d 1106, 2005 Ind. App. LEXIS 278 (2005).

Defendant's 45-year sentence for Class A felony child molesting in violation of IC 35-42-4-3, which was greater than presumptive sentence under IC 35-50-2-4, did not violate defendant's right to jury trial; one of aggravating factors was defendant's criminal record, which factor did not have to be determined by jury, and defendant admitted facts upon which two other aggravating factors were based. Devries v. State, 833 N.E.2d 511, 2005 Ind. App. LEXIS 1585 (2005), overruled in part, Ryle v. State, 842 N.E.2d 320, 2005 Ind. LEXIS 1112 (2005).

While the trial court improperly relied on the victim's age as an aggravator, the error was harmless since the trial court properly relied on the nature of defendant's relationship with the victim and his extensive criminal history as an aggravator in sentencing him to 30 years for child molestation. Johnson v. State, 845 N.E.2d 147, 2006 Ind. App. LEXIS 598 (2006).

Sentence for Attempted Murder.
A sentence of 40 years for attempted murder under the new statute was not too extreme when contrasted with the former 2 to 14 year penalty for assault and battery with intent to kill under the former statute since the new attempt statute (IC 35-41-5-1) specifically states that the attempt to commit murder is a Class A felony. Zickefoose v. State, 270 Ind. 618, 388 N.E.2d 507, 1979 Ind. LEXIS 612 (1979).

The court properly imposed a 30 year sentence for attempted murder and properly added 20 years for aggravating circumstances where the court identified and weighed four aggravating circumstances and three mitigating circumstances. Simmons v. State, 717 N.E.2d 635, 1999 Ind. App. LEXIS 1798 (1999).

Sentence for Child Molesting.
Imposition of the maximum sentence for two counts of child molesting was inappropriate, as the acts committed, while monstrous, did not, stand-

Sentence for Child Molesting. (Cont'd)
ing alone, demonstrate a character of such recalcitrance that it justified a maximum sentence; the court found that the advisory sentence was appropriate. Mishler v. State, 894 N.E.2d 1095, 2008 Ind. App. LEXIS 2386 (2008).

Sentence for Kidnapping.
Where defendant received a 40-year sentence, which was 10 years less than the maximum sentence for kidnapping, the court declined to exercise its constitutional authority under Ind. Const., art. 7, § 4, to revise his sentence. Bassie v. State, 726 N.E.2d 242, 2000 Ind. LEXIS 224 (2000).

Sentence for Voluntary Manslaughter.
In a case in which defendant pleaded guilty to voluntary manslaughter, the trial court appropriately sentenced defendant to 30 years imprisonment. Although defendant was unable to cope with his wife's affair with the victim, there was very little provocation to defendant's violent reaction, and the nature of defendant's crime was extreme under the circumstances. Eversole v. State, 873 N.E.2d 1111, 2007 Ind. App. LEXIS 2186 (2007).

Sentence Not Unreasonable.
A sentence of 40 years for robbery was not unreasonable where a presentence report showed a history of criminal activity and a psychologist felt defendant would be a poor probationary risk. Williams v. State, 271 Ind. 408, 393 N.E.2d 149, 1979 Ind. LEXIS 691 (1979).

A sentence of 40 years for kidnapping, a Class A felony, was not excessive where there were aggravating circumstances. Pine v. State, 274 Ind. 78, 408 N.E.2d 1271, 1980 Ind. LEXIS 737 (1980).

Where the jury found the defendant guilty of conspiracy to commit murder, a Class A felony, for which the presumptive sentence was 30 years, with not more than 10 years subtracted for mitigating circumstances, and where the defendant received the minimum sentence possible, 20 years, with 10 years of that sentence suspended, the sentence was not unreasonable. Sutton v. State, 495 N.E.2d 253, 1986 Ind. App. LEXIS 2763 (1986).

Defendant's sentence was not manifestly unreasonable, where the trial court added only five years to the murder sentence and ten years to attempted murder as enhancements, and ran defendant's sentences concurrently. Johnson v. State, 725 N.E.2d 864, 2000 Ind. LEXIS 239 (2000).

Since defendant's guilty plea to sexual molestation of a six-year-old and other mitigating circumstances, including the fact that he was molested as a child, balanced the aggravating circumstances, defendant's sentence of 50 years was revised to the presumptive sentence of 30 years. Francis v. State, 817 N.E.2d 235, 2004 Ind. LEXIS 988 (2004).

Sentence of juvenile defendant to term of 30 years executed for attempted murder was not inappropriate in light of nature of offense and character of offender; trial court found no mitigating factors and several aggravating factors, including criminal history, marijuana use, and necessity

for correctional rehabilitative treatment. Gall v. State, 811 N.E.2d 969, 2004 Ind. App. LEXIS 1384 (2004).

Where defendant was sentenced to 35 years in prison after defendant was convicted of possession of cocaine weighing three grams or more with intent to deliver, a Class A felony, in violation of IC 35-48-4-1, the trial court did not err under IC 35-50-2-4 in enhancing defendant's sentence, and the sentence did not violate AP. 7(B); defendant failed to bring to the trial court's attention defendant's lack of education, defendant failed to raise at sentencing the argument that defendant's status as an illegal alien was a mitigating circumstance, and there was no basis in the record to find that the sentence was inappropriate under AP. 7(B) based on defendant's character or the nature of the offense. Samaniego-Hernandez v. State, 839 N.E.2d 798, 2005 Ind. App. LEXIS 2450 (2005).

Sentence Reasonable.
Presumptive sentences for murder and Class A felony conspiracy given to an accomplice were not manifestly unreasonable considering the cruel and callous nature of these offenses and the character of the defendant as indicated by the presentence report and by his demeanor before the trial court. Haynes v. State, 479 N.E.2d 572, 1985 Ind. LEXIS 884 (1985).

Where a trial court relied upon two improper aggravating circumstances, but the remaining aggravating circumstances were properly applied, defendant's sentence for Class A felonies was not manifestly unreasonable. Scott v. State, 771 N.E.2d 718, 2002 Ind. App. LEXIS 1135 (2002), overruled, Ludy v. State, 784 N.E.2d 459, 2003 Ind. LEXIS 207 (Ind. 2003), overruled, D'Paffo v. State, 778 N.E.2d 798, 2002 Ind. LEXIS 854 (2002), overruled in part, Louallen v. State, 778 N.E.2d 794, 2002 Ind. LEXIS 853 (2002).

Defendant's fine of $5,000 was appropriate in light of the nature of the offense and the character of the offender where defendant molested a 10-year-old neighbor girl. Johnson v. State, 845 N.E.2d 147, 2006 Ind. App. LEXIS 598 (2006).

Because a 40-year sentence was within the range for a Class A felony under IC 35-50-2-4, and defendant was not entitled to relief as the judgment was final when Blakely was decided and Blakely did not apply retroactively to his case, the trial court did not err in denying his motion to correct an erroneous sentence. Fulkrod v. State, 855 N.E.2d 1064, 2006 Ind. App. LEXIS 2221 (2006).

Trial court did not err in sentencing defendant to 60 years for a murder conviction and 40 years for a conspiracy conviction, with the sentences to run consecutively, under circumstances in which defendant entered into the conspiracy and then facilitated the victim's murder as part of a continuing conspiracy to sell illegal substances; although a co-conspirator pulled the trigger, the murder would not have occurred without defendant's planning of the murder, the conspiracy to commit the murder, the set-up of the victim, and assistance to facilitate the co-conspirator's escape. With refer-

Sentence Reasonable. (Cont'd)

ence to defendant's character, his full-time job was breaking the law, and in performing his job, he planned and facilitated the murder. Jack v. State, 870 N.E.2d 444, 2007 Ind. App. LEXIS 1583 (2007).

Concurrent sentences of 45 years on convictions of possession of methamphetamine in excess of three grams with intent to deliver and manufacture of methamphetamine in excess of three grams were not improper; among other things, given that much of defendant's criminal history related to his lifelong drug and substance abuse, the trial court did not err in finding it a significant aggravating factor in sentencing; because the trial court's statement pertained to the imposition of an enhanced, rather than a reduced, sentence, it did not abuse its discretion in considering "depreciate seriousness" factor to have been an aggravating circumstance. Storey v. State, 875 N.E.2d 243, 2007 Ind. App. LEXIS 2365 (2007).

Defendant's 50-year sentence for child molestation under IC 35-42-4-3(a)(1), a Class A felony under IC 35-50-2-4, was not inappropriate for Ind. Const., art. 7, §§ 4 and 6 and AP. 7(B) purposes as defendant: (1) chose a young victim who did not know defendant; (2) removed the victim to an isolated place; (3) offered the victim money; (4) instructed the victim not to tell anyone about the incident; and (5) lied to two police officers to prevent them from determining that there was a warrant for defendant's arrest. Taylor v. State, 891 N.E.2d 155, 2008 Ind. App. LEXIS 1678 (2008).

Trial court did not abuse its discretion in sentencing defendant mother to 30-years' imprisonment based upon her conviction for neglect of a dependent where she left her child in a box in the basement after it was born where the child, who one expert stated died after birth, was not found until two days later. Robinson v. State, 894 N.E.2d 1038, 2008 Ind. App. LEXIS 2232 (2008).

There was no error in sentencing defendant to the maximum sentence of 50 years for his conviction of, inter alia, felony possession of cocaine as a Class A felony for possessing more than three grams of cocaine within 1,000 feet of school property, IC 35-48-4-6(b)(3), where the record disclosed that defendant had more than 24 grams of cocaine when he was stopped within 20 to 50 feet of a licensed day care center and had convictions for Class A felony dealing in cocaine, Class B felony dealing in cocaine, Class D felony possession of cocaine, and two convictions for Class B felony robbery. Danner v. State, 900 N.E.2d 9, 2008 Ind. App. LEXIS 2631 (2008).

Sentence Under Ameliorative Provision.

Even though ameliorative sentencing provision was promulgated before defendant's sentence, where defendant's trial and sentence was imposed before the effective date of the statute, defendant did not meet the requirements of the doctrine of amelioration, and was not entitled to be sentenced pursuant to the ameliorative statute. Turner v. State, 669 N.E.2d 1024, 1996 Ind. App. LEXIS 1013 (1996).

Sentence Under Former Law.

Where defendant was sentenced under law as it existed at time crime was committed and at time of sentencing, he was not entitled to be resentenced under the provisions of this section after the new criminal code went into effect. Parsley v. State, 273 Ind. 46, 401 N.E.2d 1360, 1980 Ind. LEXIS 636 (1980), cert. denied, 449 U.S. 862, 101 S. Ct. 166, 66 L. Ed. 2d 79, 1980 U.S. LEXIS 3123 (1980).

Sentence Unreasonable.

Where the defendant (a) was 18 years of age, (b) had not as an adult been convicted of a felony, (c) was not armed during the perpetration of the offense, and (d) was convicted of a Class A felony rather than a Class B felony because of injuries received by the victims while defendant and his accomplice were seeking to avoid apprehension rather than as a direct result of force or threat of force in the commission of the burglary, imposing the maximum 50-year sentence upon the defendant under the circumstances was manifestly unreasonable. In view of the trial court's specific finding of aggravating circumstances, the sentence should have been revised from 50 years imprisonment to 35 years imprisonment, consisting of the presumptive sentence of 30 years plus enhancement of five years. Hill v. State, 499 N.E.2d 1103, 1986 Ind. LEXIS 1444 (1986).

Defendant was convicted on two counts of child molestation for performing oral sex on a six-year-old boy, and although crimes against children are particularly contemptible, defendant's was some distance from being the worst offense or defendant the most culpable offender. Therefore, while the aggravating circumstances warranted an enhanced sentence, defendant's aggregate sentence of 80 years was manifestly unreasonable. Walker v. State, 747 N.E.2d 536, 2001 Ind. LEXIS 406 (2001).

Where defendant was nineteen and had never been convicted of a violent crime, the maximum sentence allowed by law for dealing in cocaine as a Class A felony was plainly unreasonable, and his fifty-year sentence was vacated and the case was remanded with instructions to impose the presumptive sentence of thirty years. Love v. State, 741 N.E.2d 789, 2001 Ind. App. LEXIS 6 (2001).

Because a maximum sentence permitted by law should be reserved for the very worst, and defendant's criminal history was not lengthy, did not demonstrate a tendency toward violence or a propensity to commit sexual acts, and was the only proper aggravating factor considered by the trial court, the maximum sentence imposed was manifestly unreasonable. Simmons v. State, 746 N.E.2d 81, 2001 Ind. App. LEXIS 467 (2001).

Defendant's sentence of 80 years for drug offenses and being adjudged a habitual offender was reversed where the trial court's decision to order the two convictions to be served consecutively rendered the aggregate 80-year sentence clearly, plainly, and obviously unreasonable. Perry v. State, 751 N.E.2d 306, 2001 Ind. App. LEXIS 1090 (2001).

Resentencing was ordered where the trial court erred in sentencing defendant to an enhanced term

Sentence Unreasonable. (Cont'd)
of 35 years because it relied on improper aggravating circumstances, and because it failed to consider the significant mitigating factor of mental illness, which defendant presented into evidence. Powell v. State, 751 N.E.2d 311, 2001 Ind. App. LEXIS 1091 (2001).

Trial court properly considered the aggravating and mitigating circumstances surrounding defendant's conviction for sexually molesting a five-year old child; however, because the crime was committed without excessive physical brutality, the use of a weapon, or resulting physical injury, and was a one-time occurrence, the maximum penalty of 50 years was inappropriate. Buchanan v. State, 767 N.E.2d 967, 2002 Ind. LEXIS 371 (2002).

Trial court erred in enhancing by 15 years defendant's sentence for possession of methamphetamine in excess of three grams with intent to deliver; mitigating factors, namely defendant's age of 20 and lack of criminal record, outweighed aggravating factors, namely that defendant had other drugs on his person, gave false testimony about his involvement, and failed to appear at trial. Merlington v. State, 814 N.E.2d 269, 2004 Ind. LEXIS 782 (2004).

While sufficient evidence of a victim's and eyewitnesses' testimony supported defendant's conviction for two counts of child molestation under IC 35-42-4-3(a), (b) for having sex with and touching the breasts of a 13-year-old victim, defendant's enhanced sentence of 40 years was improper when the trial court failed to explain how the enhanced sentence furthered defendant's rehabilitation better than the presumptive sentence of 30 years found in IC 35-50-2-4, and defendant's criminal history, probation status, and use of force did not justify the enhanced sentence when defendant's criminal history was neither sufficiently similar to the child molestation nor weighty enough to warrant consideration as an aggravating factor in enhancing his Class A felony sentence, and the evidence of force did not show a force that was beyond what was necessary to perform sexual intercourse. Prickett v. State, 856 N.E.2d 1203, 2006 Ind. LEXIS 1027 (2006).

Defendant's maximum 50-year sentence for conspiracy to commit murder under IC 35-41-5-2 was reduced under AP. 7(B) and Ind. Const., art. 7, § 4 to the advisory sentence of 30 years under IC 35-50-2-4 given that no one was injured, that both potential victims pleaded for leniency, and that defendant had a history of mental health problems; furthermore, whether defendant had the ability to orchestrate such a scheme absent the encouragement of another inmate, who was awaiting a sentencing hearing and who informed on defendant, was doubtful. Reid v. State, 876 N.E.2d 1114, 2007 Ind. LEXIS 1066 (2007).

Statement of Reasons.
Where defendant received the presumptive sentence for a Class A felony, 30 years, the trial court was under no duty to identify, discuss, or balance mitigating factors. Owensby v. State, 549 N.E.2d 407, 1990 Ind. App. LEXIS 140 (1990).

Where a trial court imposes the presumptive

sentence it has no obligation to explain its reasons for doing so, but where the court listed aggravating and mitigating factors in its sentencing order, it erred by using the facts surrounding a subsequent arrest as an aggravating factor, where the facts were neither proven by the state nor admitted by the defendant. Miller v. State, 709 N.E.2d 48, 1999 Ind. App. LEXIS 619 (1999).

Trial court's failure to identify the proffered mitigating factors in regard to sentencing defendant to 40 years for Class A felony robbery constituted error; however, the error was harmless because the record supported the finding of the two aggravating circumstances identified by the trial court. Further, the mitigating circumstances that the trial court failed to identify would have been accorded little weight; accordingly, the trial court would have imposed the same sentence if it had considered the proper aggravating and mitigating circumstances. Scott v. State, 840 N.E.2d 376, 2006 Ind. App. LEXIS 26 (2006).

Cited:
Vicory v. State, 272 Ind. 683, 400 N.E.2d 1380, 1980 Ind. LEXIS 619 (1980); Pine v. State, 274 Ind. 78, 408 N.E.2d 1271, 1980 Ind. LEXIS 737 (1980); Harris v. State, 425 N.E.2d 112, 1981 Ind. LEXIS 929 (1981); Grassmyer v. State, 426 N.E.2d 1377, 1981 Ind. App. LEXIS 1692 (1981); Gatewood v. State, 430 N.E.2d 781, 1982 Ind. LEXIS 727 (1982); Abercrombie v. State, 441 N.E.2d 442, 1982 Ind. LEXIS 1005 (1982); Petruso v. State, 441 N.E.2d 446, 1982 Ind. LEXIS 1013 (1982); Head v. State, 443 N.E.2d 44, 1982 Ind. LEXIS 1041 (1982); Huff v. State, 443 N.E.2d 1234, 1983 Ind. App. LEXIS 2507 (1983); Allen v. State, 453 N.E.2d 1011, 1983 Ind. LEXIS 968 (1983); Barham v. State, 454 N.E.2d 392, 1983 Ind. LEXIS 987 (1983); Eubank v. State, 456 N.E.2d 1012, 1983 Ind. LEXIS 1062 (1983); Lang v. State, 461 N.E.2d 1110, 1984 Ind. LEXIS 791 (1984); Alvies v. State, 478 N.E.2d 678, 1985 Ind. LEXIS 853 (1985); Shoulders v. State, 480 N.E.2d 211, 1985 Ind. LEXIS 898 (1985); Komyatti v. State, 490 N.E.2d 279, 1986 Ind. LEXIS 1063 (1986); Hansford v. State, 490 N.E.2d 1083, 1986 Ind. LEXIS 1067 (1986); Hestand v. State, 491 N.E.2d 976, 1986 Ind. LEXIS 1104 (1986); Mallery v. State, 499 N.E.2d 1100, 1986 Ind. LEXIS 1370 (1986); Mullins v. State, 504 N.E.2d 570, 1987 Ind. LEXIS 846 (1987); Morris v. State, 508 N.E.2d 11, 1987 Ind. LEXIS 935 (1987); Gee v. State, 508 N.E.2d 787, 1987 Ind. LEXIS 908 (1987); Jackson v. State, 509 N.E.2d 885, 1987 Ind. App. LEXIS 2814 (1987); Lewis v. State, 511 N.E.2d 1054, 1987 Ind. LEXIS 1040 (1987); Greene v. State, 515 N.E.2d 1376, 1987 Ind. LEXIS 1145 (1987); French v. State, 516 N.E.2d 40, 1987 Ind. LEXIS 1182 (1987); Johnson v. State, 518 N.E.2d 1073, 1988 Ind. LEXIS 31 (1988); Smith v. State, 519 N.E.2d 544, 1988 Ind. LEXIS 82 (1988); Douglas v. State, 520 N.E.2d 427, 1988 Ind. LEXIS 43 (1988); Lowrance v. State, 565 N.E.2d 375, 1991 Ind. App. LEXIS 75 (1991); Wright v. State, 665 N.E.2d 2, 1996 Ind. App. LEXIS 669 (1996); Meagher v. State, 726 N.E.2d 260, 2000 Ind. LEXIS 245 (2000); Mann v. State, 742 N.E.2d 1025, 2001 Ind. App. LEXIS 268

(2001); Parker v. State, 754 N.E.2d 614, 2001 Ind. App. LEXIS 1502 (2001); White v. State, 756 N.E.2d 1057, 2001 Ind. App. LEXIS 1818 (2001); Hancock v. State, 758 N.E.2d 995, 2001 Ind. App. LEXIS 2055 (2001); Haycraft v. State, 760 N.E.2d 203, 2001 Ind. App. LEXIS 2225 (2001); Shaw v. State, 771 N.E.2d 85, 2002 Ind. App. LEXIS 1118 (2002); Farmer v. State, 772 N.E.2d 1025, 2002 Ind. App. LEXIS 1261 (2002); Nelson v. State, 792 N.E.2d 588, 2003 Ind. App. LEXIS 1359 (2003); Krumm v. State, 793 N.E.2d 1170, 2003 Ind. App. LEXIS 1529 (2003); Donnegan v. State, 809 N.E.2d 966, 2004 Ind. App. LEXIS 1101 (2004); Jones v. State, 807 N.E.2d 58, 2004 Ind. App. LEXIS 752 (2004); Traylor v. State, 817 N.E.2d 611, 2004 Ind. App. LEXIS 2229 (2004); Dixon v. State, 825 N.E.2d 1269, 2005 Ind. App. LEXIS 719 (2005); Rogers v. State, 868 N.E.2d 414, 2007 Ind. LEXIS 470 (2007); Mendoza v. State, 869 N.E.2d 546, 2007 Ind. App. LEXIS 1498 (2007); Swain v. State, 870 N.E.2d 1058, 2007 Ind. App. LEXIS 1721 (2007); Padgett v. State, 875 N.E.2d 310, 2007 Ind. App. LEXIS 2361 (2007).

RESEARCH REFERENCES

Indiana Law Review.
Recent Developments in Indiana Criminal Law and Procedure, 28 Ind. L. Rev. 819 (1995).

Res Gestae.
Revising Indiana's sentencing scheme: Where do we go now? 48 (No. 1) Res Gestae 14 (2004).

Collateral References.
Downward departure under state sentencing guidelines based on extraordinary family circumstances. 106 A.L.R.5th 377.

35-50-2-5. Class B felony.

A person who commits a Class B felony shall be imprisoned for a fixed term of between six (6) and twenty (20) years, with the advisory sentence being ten (10) years. In addition, the person may be fined not more than ten thousand dollars ($10,000).

History.
IC 35-50-2-5, as added by Acts 1976, P.L.148, § 8; 1977, P.L.340, § 118; P.L.71-2005, § 8.

Cross References.
Compensation for victims of violent crimes, IC 5-2-6.1.

NOTES TO DECISIONS

ANALYSIS

Constitutionality.
—Added Years.
—Cruel and Unusual Punishment.
—Double Jeopardy.
—Sentencing.
Aggravating Circumstances.
—Corrective or Rehabilitative Treatment.
—Past Criminal Record.
—Position of Trust.
—Past Criminal Record.
—Subsequent Offenses.
Alternative to Payment of Fine.
Appeal.
Balancing Aggravating and Mitigating Factors.
Basic Sentence.
Discretion of Court.
—Appellate Review.
—Arrests.
Effective Date.
Penalties Apportioned.
Penalty Fixed by Trial Court.
Plea Agreement.
Sentence Enhancement.
Sentence Imposed Prior to Effective Date.
Sentence Not Unreasonable.
Sentence Unreasonable.
Separate Episodes.

Statement of Aggravating Circumstances.
—Harmless Error.
—Insufficient.
—Sufficient.

Constitutionality.

—Added Years.
Fact that number of years that may be added for aggravating circumstances exceeds the number of years that may be subtracted for mitigating circumstances, does not violate the constitution. Boyd v. State, 396 N.E.2d 920, 1979 Ind. App. LEXIS 1430 (1979).

—Cruel and Unusual Punishment.
Where defendant was convicted of a Class B felony and given the standard sentence under this section, he could not complain that his sentence was cruel and unusual and manifestly unreasonable when compared to the sentence received by a codefendant who was more involved in the burglary. Dorton v. State, 419 N.E.2d 1289, 1981 Ind. LEXIS 738 (1981).

—Double Jeopardy.
The enhanced counts of attempted rape and robbery, each enhanced because of physical injury, violated the defendant's right against double jeop-

Constitutionality. (Cont'd)

—Double Jeopardy. (Cont'd)
ardy because the injuries sustained were part of the same onslaught, and the injuries could not be used to enhance both charges. Wolfe v. State, 549 N.E.2d 1024, 1990 Ind. LEXIS 9 (1990).

Recognizing that defendant's two attempted criminal deviate conduct convictions and defendant's two sexual battery convictions constituted same offense for purposes of double jeopardy, trial court merged two attempted criminal deviate conduct convictions and two sexual battery convictions for sentencing purposes; however, trial court's act of merging without also vacating the convictions was error requiring remand to vacate one attempted criminal deviate conduct conviction and one sexual battery convictions. Morrison v. State, 824 N.E.2d 734, 2005 Ind. App. LEXIS 518 (2005).

—Sentencing.
Trial court should have sentenced defendant under the presumptive sentencing scheme, instead of the advisory sentencing scheme, as the advisory sentencing scheme violated the constitutional prohibition against ex post facto laws under U.S. Const., art. I, § 10 and Ind. Const., art. 1, § 24. Walsman v. State, 855 N.E.2d 645, 2006 Ind. App. LEXIS 2144 (2006).

Aggravating Circumstances.
Where court found aggravating circumstances as set out in former IC 35-50-1A-7 existed, it was proper to impose an additional ten years on the sentence. Harris v. State, 272 Ind. 210, 396 N.E.2d 674, 1979 Ind. LEXIS 765 (1979).

Where court considered prior felony convictions and defendant's admitted involvement in many other home burglaries and also found that defendant fired shots at victim during burglary subjecting victim to grave personal peril, the adding of ten additional years to sentence of burglary for aggravating circumstances was not unreasonable. Holmes v. State, 272 Ind. 435, 398 N.E.2d 1279, 1980 Ind. LEXIS 576 (1980).

It was not error to give the maximum sentence of 20 years where the aggravating circumstances consisted of many prior offenses, the threat of serious harm to the victim, past violations of probation, and others, and lone mitigating circumstance was intoxication which helped to facilitate the commission of the crime. Gibson v. State, 275 Ind. 470, 417 N.E.2d 1111, 1981 Ind. LEXIS 707 (1981).

Any number of years up through, but not more than, 10 may be added at the discretion of the trial court when aggravating circumstances are found. Pilant v. State, 422 N.E.2d 1216, 1981 Ind. LEXIS 786 (1981).

A court may find that the factual details of the manner in which the crimes were committed constitute an aggravating circumstance as long as its finding is a particularized account of the aspect of the crime which illustrated to the court the defendant's deservedness of an enhanced sentence rather than a bare recitation of the elements of the

charges. Wethington v. State, 560 N.E.2d 496, 1990 Ind. LEXIS 185 (1990).

Committing a crime while on parole is a proper aggravating circumstance. Keller v. State, 560 N.E.2d 533, 1990 Ind. LEXIS 196 (1990).

Defendant's sentence following his guilty plea for arson was not excessive, where he received an aggravated sentence of 20 years and the trial judge found his past criminal history and reluctance to admit he suffered from psychological problems as aggravating factors. Collins v. State, 676 N.E.2d 741, 1996 Ind. App. LEXIS 1735 (1996).

Sentence of 20 years imprisonment for Class B felony of child molestation based on aggravating factor of defendant's criminal history of alcohol-related misdemeanors was improper since aggravating factor was too insignificant in relation to Class B felony; accordingly, sentence was reduced to presumptive sentence of 10 years imprisonment. Ruiz v. State, 818 N.E.2d 927, 2004 Ind. LEXIS 1029 (2004).

Where trial court erroneously imposed greater than presumptive terms for offenses of aggravated battery and criminal confinement without jury determination of aggravating factors as required by Sixth Amendment, reviewing court exercised its review and revise power under Ind. Const., art. 7, § 4 and AP. 7(B) to impose legal sentence. Williams v. State, 827 N.E.2d 1127, 2005 Ind. LEXIS 487 (2005).

While the trial judge erred in enhancing each of defendant's two sentences for neglect of a dependent and four sentences for battery based on aggravating circumstances that the judge found, rather than the jury, the judge was permitted to require that three of the sentences were to run consecutively. Wright v. State, 829 N.E.2d 928, 2005 Ind. LEXIS 556 (2005).

Although one aggravating factor used to enhance sentence was erroneously based upon facts not determined by jury or admitted by defendant, remaining three aggravating factors did not violate Sixth Amendment and were sufficient to support enhanced sentence. McNew v. State, 822 N.E.2d 1078, 2005 Ind. App. LEXIS 276 (2005).

Defendant's five prior criminal convictions, which were exempt from Apprendi rule, constituted sufficient aggravator to justify sentence enhancement for sexual misconduct with a minor despite invalidity of other aggravators. Moon v. State, 823 N.E.2d 710, 2005 Ind. App. LEXIS 388 (2005).

Sentencing court erred by enhancing sentence for pleading guilty to Class B felony possession of methamphetamine based on allegations that he possessed 22 grams of methamphetamine and that he was in possession of both firearm and marijuana when he was arrested since those aggravating circumstances were never determined by jury or admitted by defendant. Freeze v. State, 827 N.E.2d 600, 2005 Ind. App. LEXIS 829 (2005).

Failure to rehabilitate should not have been considered separate aggravating circumstance in sentencing defendant for felony burglary conviction but did not warrant modification of 15-year sentence. Gentry v. State, 835 N.E.2d 569, 2005 Ind. App. LEXIS 1930 (2005).

Aggravating Circumstances. (Cont'd)

Where a defendant, a physician, poisoned, bludgeoned, and strangled his 62-year old victim-acquaintance in the victim's home, his 20-year sentence for voluntary manslaughter was not inappropriate nor unreasonable. Reyes v. State, 848 N.E.2d 1081, 2006 Ind. LEXIS 468 (2006).

—Corrective or Rehabilitative Treatment.

Because the trial judge did not articulate how defendant's correctional or rehabilitative treatment could be achieved through the imposition of an enhanced sentence rather than the presumptive sentence, the trial court improperly relied on defendant's need for treatment as an aggravating circumstance. Oberst v. State, 748 N.E.2d 870, 2001 Ind. App. LEXIS 603 (2001).

—Past Criminal Record.

Given defendant's lengthy and unrelenting criminal history and the trial court's previous decision to impose the maximum sentence for his Class A felony convictions, defendant should likewise face the 20-year maximum sentence for his Class B felony convictions for dealing in cocaine and possession of cocaine. Bell v. State, 881 N.E.2d 1080, 2008 Ind. App. LEXIS 437 (2008).

—Position of Trust.

Where the victim and defendant met one another at an auction the month that the events giving rise to the charges occurred, at best defendant could be described as an acquaintance of the victim, and the mere fact that he may have had something in common with the victim did not establish a close and involved relationship characterized as being in a position of trust with that person; therefore, the trial court improperly considered this as an aggravating circumstance. Oberst v. State, 748 N.E.2d 870, 2001 Ind. App. LEXIS 603 (2001).

—Past Criminal Record.

The past criminal record of the defendant may be an aggravating circumstance, justifying the decision to add additional years to the presumptive sentence. Jones v. State, 456 N.E.2d 1025, 1983 Ind. LEXIS 1056 (1983).

The sentencing court properly found the defendant's criminal history was an aggravating circumstance warranting an increase from the presumptive sentence of ten years, specifically, a prior commission of theft. Oglesby v. State, 515 N.E.2d 1082, 1987 Ind. LEXIS 1149 (1987).

Defendant's criminal history, as contained in presentence investigation report and acknowledged by defendant in open court, was sufficient to support enhanced sentence of 18 years for Class B felony; trial court did not abuse its discretion in determining that defendant committed perjury and in not treating his guilty plea and testimony against co-defendant as mitigating factors. McCray v. State, 823 N.E.2d 740, 2005 Ind. App. LEXIS 392 (2005).

—Subsequent Offenses.

In determining whether aggravating circumstances existed court could properly consider subsequent robbery although defendant had not been tried or convicted for the latter offense. Griffin v. State, 273 Ind. 184, 402 N.E.2d 981, 1980 Ind. LEXIS 656 (1980).

Alternative to Payment of Fine.

Where the sentencing court fined the defendant $10,000, but suspended $9,900 on the condition he pay restitution to the victim in the amount of $405 within ten years, and pay the county within nine years for all medical services rendered to the defendant and for court costs, the court had authority to impose the fine and there was no error in the court offering defendant a more attractive penalty as to the medical bills. Mellott v. State, 496 N.E.2d 396, 1986 Ind. LEXIS 1249 (1986), clarified, 500 N.E.2d 173, 1986 Ind. LEXIS 1476 (1986).

Appeal.

Where sentence was for minimum amount allowed by statute court on appeal did not revise sentence. Kyles v. State, 181 Ind. App. 202, 391 N.E.2d 642, 1979 Ind. App. LEXIS 1474 (1979).

Balancing Aggravating and Mitigating Factors.

A sentence of 12 years was proper where mitigating factors found by the court were overcome by aggravating factors. Wolfe v. State, 270 Ind. 81, 383 N.E.2d 317, 1978 Ind. LEXIS 832 (1978).

Where court considered both aggravating and mitigating circumstances, a sentence of 15 years was not error. Hinton v. State, 272 Ind. 297, 397 N.E.2d 282, 1979 Ind. LEXIS 797 (1979).

Sentencing court was not required to find evidence about the state of defendant's mental health was mitigating, and where it considered the evidence and explained its reasons for failing to find the evidence mitigating, it did not abuse its discretion in imposing presumptive sentence. Wilson v. State, 679 N.E.2d 1333, 1997 Ind. App. LEXIS 513 (1997).

Trial court properly enhanced defendant's sentence for rape under IC 35-50-2-5 after concluding that defendant's lack of criminal history was not significant compared to the victim's physical and mental limitations, as well as the fact that defendant was in a position of trust as the victim's caregiver. Matshazi v. State, 804 N.E.2d 1232, 2004 Ind. App. LEXIS 444 (2004).

Trial court has sole discretion to determine weight accorded aggravating or mitigating factors; in arson case, trial court properly considered proffered mitigating factors and decided against accepting them. Julian v. State, 811 N.E.2d 392, 2004 Ind. App. LEXIS 1205 (2004).

Defendant was improperly sentenced to three consecutive 20-year terms after entering an open guilty plea to three counts of robbery while armed with a deadly weapon under IC 35-42-5-1 because the trial court deviated from the presumptive sentence under former IC 35-50-2-5 (1993) but did not consider the mitigating factors, such as defendant's remorse and his open guilty plea, that existed at the time of sentence; while the trial court indicated that it would modify the sentence if defendant underwent, inter alia, drug rehabilitation while in prison, the trial court was unable to

Balancing Aggravating and Mitigating Factors. (Cont'd)

modify sentences under IC 35-38-1-17 after the passage of a year without the prosecutor's consent. Ashby v. State, — N.E.2d —, 2009 Ind. App. LEXIS 724 (2009).

Basic Sentence.

Where defendant was given the basic sentence he could not complain that the provision for additions for aggravating circumstances and subtractions for mitigating circumstances was discriminatory. Boyd v. State, 396 N.E.2d 920, 1979 Ind. App. LEXIS 1430 (1979).

Where defendant was given the basic sentence of ten years, defendant could not complain that provisions for additions to or subtractions from sentence for aggravating or mitigating circumstances violate the constitution since such provisions were not prejudicial to him. Wells v. State, 397 N.E.2d 1250, 1979 Ind. App. LEXIS 1481 (1979).

Sentence of 18 years on conviction of voluntary manslaughter was not unreasonable in light of defendant's prior convictions within a two-year period of drunk and disorderly, mischief and trespass, and drunk, and of a pending burglary charge facing defendant at the time of this offense. Robey v. State, 454 N.E.2d 1221, 1983 Ind. LEXIS 992 (1983).

While the facts that entered into the trial judge's decision to impose the enhanced sentence were perhaps not as detailed as Supreme Court would have liked, there was sufficient evidence in the record to support the imposition of the additional ten years. Blackmon v. State, 455 N.E.2d 586, 1983 Ind. LEXIS 1007 (1983).

Presumptive sentence for Class B felony found not manifestly unreasonable. See Stafford v. State, 455 N.E.2d 402, 1983 Ind. App. LEXIS 3505 (1983).

The trial court does not err in sentencing the defendant to concurrent terms of ten years on child molesting and two years on incest, which are the statutory prescribed sentences. Newton v. State, 456 N.E.2d 736, 1983 Ind. App. LEXIS 3623 (1983).

Discretion of Court.

It is within the trial court's discretion whether the presumptive sentence for a crime will be increased or decreased because of aggravating or mitigating circumstances. Hill v. State, 445 N.E.2d 994, 1983 Ind. LEXIS 764 (1983).

It is discretionary with the trial court whether the presumptive sentence will be enhanced or reduced. Pettiford v. State, 506 N.E.2d 1088, 1987 Ind. LEXIS 901 (1987).

Where the record supported the trial court's findings and the reasons stated were sufficient indications that defendant was in need of an enhanced sentence, the trial court did not abuse its discretion by imposing an enhanced sentence. Barker v. State, 508 N.E.2d 795, 1987 Ind. LEXIS 948 (1987).

Trial court did not abuse its discretion by considering the severity of a victim's injuries and defendant's criminal record as aggravating factors, and refusing to consider testimony about defendant's rehabilitation after he stabbed his victim or the fact that his last conviction was 12 years old as mitigating factors, before trial court sentenced defendant to 20 years' incarceration for aggravated battery, the maximum period of incarceration allowed by law. Settles v. State, 791 N.E.2d 812, 2003 Ind. App. LEXIS 1246 (2003).

Where defendant was convicted of two murders and Class B felony robbery, six-year sentence for robbery was properly ordered to run consecutive to 110-year sentence for murders, despite defendant's argument that robbery sentence should run concurrently. Where defendant's conviction for class A felony robbery was vacated and a trial court was ordered to enter judgment of conviction on a class B felony robbery count, the appellate court ordered the entry of a sentence of six years in prison, to run consecutive to defendant's sentence of 110 years for two counts of murder; in so holding, the court observed that the aggravating factors in defendant's acts outweighed the mitigating factors. Vennard v. State, 803 N.E.2d 678, 2004 Ind. App. LEXIS 234 (2004).

Where defendant committed a carefully planned robbery, lured the victim to an apartment, lay in wait, attacked the victim from behind and choked him, and even though the victim begged his attackers not to kill him in view of his two young children, defendant told his accomplice to stab the victim, defendant's sentences of 13 years for robbery and 6 years for battery, to be served consecutively, for an aggregate sentence of 19 years, was not an abuse of discretion or inappropriate. Moore v. State, — N.E.2d —, 2009 Ind. App. LEXIS 876 (2009).

—Appellate Review.

Determination of a sentence rests with the discretion of the trial court; an appellate court will not alter a sentence authorized by statute unless the sentence is manifestly unreasonable in light of the offender and offense. Clayton v. State, 658 N.E.2d 82, 1995 Ind. App. LEXIS 1098 (1995), corrected, 658 N.E.2d 82, 1995 Ind. App. LEXIS 1204 (1995).

Trial court did not abuse its discretion in imposing defendant's sentence because the sentence imposed was six years less than the maximum sentence for a conviction of child molestation as a class B felony. Bear v. State, 772 N.E.2d 413, 2002 Ind. App. LEXIS 1049 (2002), overruled, Ludy v. State, 784 N.E.2d 459, 2003 Ind. LEXIS 207 (Ind. 2003), overruled, D'Paffo v. State, 778 N.E.2d 798, 2002 Ind. LEXIS 854 (2002), overruled in part, Louallen v. State, 778 N.E.2d 794, 2002 Ind. LEXIS 853 (2002).

—Arrests.

Trial court has broad discretion to consider aggravating factors; this discretion includes consideration of arrests not yet reduced to conviction. Clayton v. State, 658 N.E.2d 82, 1995 Ind. App. LEXIS 1098 (1995), corrected, 658 N.E.2d 82, 1995 Ind. App. LEXIS 1204 (1995).

Effective Date.

Since the maximum sentence for burglary of a

Effective Date. (Cont'd)

dwelling house under the prior law was 20 years and the maximum sentence for burglary of a dwelling house under the new law is also 20 years, the sentence provision under the new law is not amelioratory; it was error for trial court to sentence defendant under provisions of the new law when offense was committed prior to the effective date of the new law. State v. Turner, 178 Ind. App. 562, 383 N.E.2d 428, 1978 Ind. App. LEXIS 1118 (1978).

Penalties Apportioned.

Sentencing under the current criminal code appropriately apportions penalties to the nature of the offense as required by Ind. Const., Art. 1, § 16. Wells v. State, 397 N.E.2d 1250, 1979 Ind. App. LEXIS 1481 (1979).

Penalty Fixed by Trial Court.

Since under the statute the trial court is required to fix the penalty, it was not error to refuse to give this section to the jury as an instruction. Inman v. State, 271 Ind. 491, 393 N.E.2d 767, 1979 Ind. LEXIS 707 (1979).

Plea Agreement.

Fact that court accepted a plea agreement by which defendant was sentenced to the standard sentence for a Class A felony did not prevent the court from imposing the maximum sentence for the Class B felony. Mott v. State, 273 Ind. 216, 402 N.E.2d 986, 1980 Ind. LEXIS 659 (1980).

Defendant's sentence was not disproportionate for three counts of dealing cocaine, where defendant's plea agreement contained a negotiated sentence recommendation. Pritscher v. State, 675 N.E.2d 727, 1996 Ind. App. LEXIS 1739 (1996).

Defendant's sentencing, pursuant to plea agreement in which he agreed to 20-year prison sentence, did not violate Sixth Amendment or Blakely case requiring jury to determine beyond reasonable doubt existence of aggravating factors used to enhance sentence; defendant waived right to jury at sentencing by pleading guilty and his sentence was not enhanced because 20-year sentence he agreed to was imposed pursuant to plea agreement. Smith v. State, 829 N.E.2d 1021, 2005 Ind. App. LEXIS 1153 (2005).

Sentence Enhancement.

Enhancement of presumptive sentences, along with the imposition of consecutive sentences, may be supported by a single aggravating circumstance. Clayton v. State, 658 N.E.2d 82, 1995 Ind. App. LEXIS 1098 (1995), corrected, 658 N.E.2d 82, 1995 Ind. App. LEXIS 1204 (1995).

There was no error in the trial court's sentencing of defendant to the Indiana Department of Correction for a period of 15 years with 10 years executed and 5 years suspended on probation for a conviction of battery resulting in serious bodily injury to a person less than 14 years of age where defendant's 3 year old victim had sustained a series of other injuries, and defendant had been in a position of trust with the victim. Watson v. State, 784 N.E.2d 515, 2003 Ind. App. LEXIS 310 (2003).

Enhanced sentences imposed by trial court following defendant's guilty plea to seven counts of robbery as Class B felony and one count of robbery as Class C felony were vacated; trial court should not have used defendant's admission, made as he was pleading guilty, that he had gone on crime spree in order to enhance his sentences, since doing so was unsupported by case law and unnecessary since trial court could have made some of concurrent sentences consecutive without violating Blakely. Young v. State, 834 N.E.2d 1015, 2005 Ind. LEXIS 877 (2005).

Because defendant chose to remain silent when offered chance to dispute accuracy of presentence investigation report that detailed prior felony convictions, defendant waived any challenge to use of that prior criminal history to enhance his sentences for robbery and possession of firearm. Dillard v. State, 827 N.E.2d 570, 2005 Ind. App. LEXIS 826 (2005).

Trial court abused its discretion when it enhanced defendant's sentence by identifying the seriousness of the crime, which was for armed robbery, as an aggravator when there was no indication that the trial court considered a sentence below the presumptive sentence. Additionally, the trial court erred by using defendant's criminal history as a significant aggravator because defendant's prior offenses, which included juvenile adjudications, were not on a par with the offense for which he was sentenced; furthermore; defendant's CHINS adjudication could not have been considered part of defendant's criminal history on review because the appellate court could not determine from the record whether the CHINS adjudication was based on allegations of delinquency or neglect. Walsman v. State, 855 N.E.2d 645, 2006 Ind. App. LEXIS 2144 (2006).

Two-year sentencing enhancement for possessing material capable of causing bodily injury by an inmate, under IC 35-44-3-9.5, was not inappropriate because: (1) while defendant had been previously attacked, the evidence did not clearly establish that defendant needed a shank to protect himself; (2) defendant had a prior conviction of battery with a deadly weapon; (3) defendant committed several drug and driving offenses prior to his final release date; and (4) the similarity of defendant's previous felony conviction to the present offense and the numerous misdemeanors committed before his first sentence was completed did not reflect favorably on defendant's character. Phillips v. State, 875 N.E.2d 480, 2007 Ind. App. LEXIS 2390 (2007).

Sentence Imposed Prior to Effective Date.

Where crime was committed and sentence imposed prior to the effective date of this section, denial of petition for post-conviction relief to amend sentence to conform to new law was proper, the maximum permissible under either the old or new law being the same. Terrell v. State, 180 Ind. App. 634, 390 N.E.2d 208, 1979 Ind. App. LEXIS 1199 (1979).

Sentence Not Unreasonable.

Where presentence investigation report indi-

Sentence Not Unreasonable. (Cont'd)
cated that defendant had been jailed 26 times, had
been committed to the state farm three times and
previously had been sent to the boy's school, the
maximum sentence was not unreasonable. Hauger
v. State, 273 Ind. 481, 405 N.E.2d 526, 1980 Ind.
LEXIS 692 (1980).

Sentence held not unreasonable. Bray v. State,
430 N.E.2d 1162, 1982 Ind. LEXIS 736 (1982);
Cooper v. State, 461 N.E.2d 1119, 1984 Ind. LEXIS
793 (Ind. 1984).

Sentence of 11 years was not manifestly unreasonable where defendant had sexually molested an
eight-year old victim leaving her with multiple
scars in her rectum and defendant had a history of
criminal activity and was on probation at the time
of the offense, showing that past attempts at
rehabilitation had failed. Tuggle v. State, 457
N.E.2d 1094, 1984 Ind. LEXIS 727 (1984).

A sentence of 20 years for voluntary manslaughter was not unreasonable given the following aggravating factors: the crime was the final occurrence in a series of batterings; the victim was only
five months old, she was infirm, having been blind
from birth, unable to defend herself, and unable to
report these attacks; the victim was the defendant's daughter and he breached his duty to protect and care for her; and he showed little remorse
for his acts. Brown v. State, 512 N.E.2d 173, 1987
Ind. LEXIS 1034 (1987).

In a trial for molesting defendant's two stepsons,
Class B felonies, it was not error to enhance the
presumptive sentence for each crime of which he
was convicted, nor error to order the sentences to
be served consecutively, where these crimes were
committed in private and involved the ability to
deceive others, the crimes involved the building of
trust, and then a continuing pattern of violating
that trust, the court also considered the age of the
victims and defendant's use of threats of force to
get the victims to comply with his demands, and
the record indicated defendant had been involved
in auto theft and alcohol and substance abuse both
as a juvenile and as an adult. Maynard v. State,
513 N.E.2d 641, 1987 Ind. LEXIS 1077 (1987).

The mere fact that an accomplice receives a
lesser sentence does not demonstrate that the trial
court abused its discretion in sentencing a defendant. Keller v. State, 560 N.E.2d 533, 1990 Ind.
LEXIS 196 (1990).

A sentencing range of six to twenty years is not
unconstitutionally disproportionate for possession
of a firearm by a serious violent felon. Teer v. State,
738 N.E.2d 283, 2000 Ind. App. LEXIS 1832
(2000); Hatchett v. State, 740 N.E.2d 920, 2000
Ind. App. LEXIS 2054 (2000).

Trial court did not abuse its discretion in considering defendant's misdemeanor convictions as an
aggravating factor or in finding that the aggravating factors substantially outweighed the mitigating factors. Additionally, the sentence imposed was
not inappropriate in light of the nature of the
offense and the character of the offender where
defendant threatened to kill the victim, assaulted
the victim, continued to leave threatening messages on the victim's phone, and finally shot at the

victim as she was getting into her truck. Simms v.
State, 791 N.E.2d 225, 2003 Ind. App. LEXIS 1213
(2003).

Sentence review under AP. 7(B) was available
after a guilty plea, and sentences totalling 40 years
resulting from two guilty pleas to Class B felonies
and a habitual offender finding were not inappropriate under IC 35-50-2-5 and IC 35-50-2-8(h)
where the nature of the offenses involved ongoing
drug dealing and weapons violations, and the
character of the offender showed that he was a
serial criminal with an interest in financial gain
through the sale of drugs. Weiss v. State, 848
N.E.2d 1070, 2006 Ind. LEXIS 473 (2006).

Trial court did not err in sentencing defendant
on his convictions on two counts of being a serious
violent felon in possession of a firearm and a count
of false informing to 20 years on each possession
count, to be served consecutively, and 180 days
suspended on the false informing count to be
served concurrently to the sentences on the possession counts in a case where he purchased assault weapons that he gave to a known felon who
could not possess them, the known felon was
involved in a police chase in which the weapons
were used to shoot a police officer to death and
wound a bystander permanently, and defendant
falsely reported that the weapons had been stolen;
the sentence was justified in light of the nature of
the crime and defendant's character. Meadows v.
State, 853 N.E.2d 1032, 2006 Ind. App. LEXIS
1888 (2006).

Defendant's aggregate 52-year sentence for convictions of two counts of operating a vehicle while
intoxicated (OWI) causing death, OWI causing
serious bodily injury, and having a prior OWI
conviction in the last five years was 4 years shorter
than the maximum sentence possible, and was not
inappropriate; defendant's BAC was over three
times the legal limit, he had cocaine in his system,
and he was speeding in an area where pedestrians
and traffic were common. Although neither of
defendant's previous convictions involved offenses
nearly as serious as the current offense, they
involved the same illegal and dangerous conduct,
driving while intoxicated. Pedraza v. State, 873
N.E.2d 1083, 2007 Ind. App. LEXIS 2182 (2007),
transfer granted and vacated, 878 N.E.2d 218,
2007 Ind. LEXIS 1005 (2007).

Twenty year sentence imposed under IC 35-50-
2-5 for violating IC 9-30-5-5 was appropriate given
the nature of the offense and defendant's character; defendant had history of substance abuse and
driving under the influence of alcohol. Hale v.
State, 888 N.E.2d 314, 2008 Ind. App. LEXIS 1252
(2008).

Defendant's 90-year consecutive sentences for
felony murder, rape and burglary (violations of IC
35-42-1-1; IC 35-42-4-1(b)(3); and IC 35-43-2-
1(1)(B)(i)) were not inappropriate, and the nature
of the offenses did not warrant revision under AP.
7(B): (1) defendant raped and murdered a 14-year-
old girl, stabbing her 11 times; (2) defendant burglarized another victim's home, taking advantage
of his knowledge that she kept the doors to her
apartment unlocked; (3) defendant was not remorseful and lacked the ability to empathize with

Sentence Not Unreasonable. (Cont'd)
the victims in the case; (4) his youth as a mitigating factor was outweighed by the likelihood of reoffending; (5) in each case, the aggravating circumstances outweighed the mitigating circumstances; (6) the sentences were within the ranges of IC 35-50-2-3 and IC 35-50-2-5; and (7) consecutive sentences were appropriate since the crimes were separate and distinct. Shepherd v. State, — N.E.2d —, 2009 Ind. App. LEXIS 431 (2009).

Pursuant to an AP. 7(B) review, defendant's character justified the imposition of 10-year sentence for arson; although defendant had a personality disorder, his angry and vengeful character was apparent from the record, and his compilation of a hit list for those he claimed had wronged him and the violent fantasies he entertained about them were troublesome given that he acted out one of his revenge fantasies by setting fire to a victim's porch. Schumann v. State, 900 N.E.2d 495, 2009 Ind. App. LEXIS 181 (2009).

Where the trial court focused on defendant's extreme violation of trust as well as the particulars of the crime, defendant did not demonstrate any abuse of discretion in the trial court's sentencing statement or rationale. Considering the revolting nature of his actions in raping his 15-year-old niece and his less than positive character, defendant failed to show the 15-year sentence was inappropriate. Richardson v. State, 906 N.E.2d 241, 2009 Ind. App. LEXIS 828 (2009).

Sentence Unreasonable.

Forty year sentence for burglary with a habitual offender enhancement was inappropriate where there was no violence and marginal pecuniary loss, where defendant committed the burglary and theft while unarmed and while the victim was away from home, where the value of the stolen items was approximately $395, and where defendant's prior burglary conviction occurred more than 20 years before. Frye v. State, 837 N.E.2d 1012, 2005 Ind. LEXIS 1082 (2005).

When defendant received the 20-year maximum under IC 35-50-2-5 for conspiracy to commit burglary under IC 35-43-2-1(1)(B)(i) and IC 35-41-5-2(a) and a 20-year habitual offender enhancement under IC 35-50-2-8, the court revised his sentence to a 20-year aggregate under AP. 7(B) and Ind. Const., art. 7, § 4; since no one was at the burglarized home and neither defendant nor his companion was apparently armed, there was a decreased likelihood of violence, and, furthermore, although defendant, who was 18, had a long criminal history, most of his crimes were juvenile offenses and only one, cruelty to animals, involved violence. Hollin v. State, 877 N.E.2d 462, 2007 Ind. LEXIS 1065 (2007).

Sentence of 20 years for voluntary manslaughter was revised down to 15 years after the appellate court found that defendant had no long history of violence and that the sentence imposed was inappropriate in light of, inter alia, the 23 persons who wrote letters detailing defendant's character attributes, defendant's lack of criminal history, and the fact that defendant accepted responsibility and

pled guilty. Long v. State, 865 N.E.2d 1031, 2007 Ind. App. LEXIS 914 (2007).

Defendant's 34-year sentence for two counts of neglect under IC 35-46-1-4 was revised under AP. 7 to consecutive sentences of nine years, for placing the hands of child victim under hot water, causing severe burns and pain, and eight years for delay in seeking medical treatment. Cardwell v. State, 895 N.E.2d 1219, 2008 Ind. LEXIS 1049 (2008).

Because defendant's burglary of two neighboring garages were a single episode of criminal conduct under IC 35-50-1-2(c) and were not crimes of violence, consecutive sentences could not exceed the advisory sentence for a felony which was one class of felony higher than the most serious of the felonies for which defendant had been convicted; as defendant was convicted of two Class C felonies, and the advisory sentence for a Class B felony was 10 years under IC 35-50-2-5, the trial court's imposition of consecutive sentences totaling 12 years violated IC 35-50-1-2(c). Henson v. State, 881 N.E.2d 36, 2008 Ind. App. LEXIS 255 (2008).

Ten-year sentence was inappropriate in light of the nature of the violations of IC 35-42-4-2 and IC 35-41-5-1 and defendant's character; a revised sentence in the nature of a downward departure from the advisory sentence in IC 35-50-2-5 was appropriate; while the offenses showed a dark side of defendant's personality, his character was particularly mitigating, including his 34 years as a law-abiding citizen and his position as a contributing member of society. Filice v. State, 886 N.E.2d 24, 2008 Ind. App. LEXIS 1152 (2008).

Sentence imposed upon defendant for promoting prostitution was revised because the nature of defendant's offense did not warrant an enhanced sentence for a Class B felony under IC 35-45-4-4 and IC 35-50-2-5 as defendant's promotion of prostitution was highly attenuated. In addition, the appellate court found that: (1) defendant only attempted to, and did not actually, perform sex acts on one occasion; (2) defendant did not abuse a position of trust; and (3) although defendant's criminal history was not inconsequential, defendants' convictions were not significant aggravators in relation to the Class B felony offense. Hayes v. State, 906 N.E.2d 819, 2009 Ind. LEXIS 462 (2009).

Separate Episodes.

Crimes of burglary, forgery, and theft committed by defendant on three separate dates over course of more than month and against separate victims did not constitute single episode requiring maximum sentence of 10 years under former IC 35-50-1-2(c) and IC 35-50-2-5; it was possible to give complete account of crimes committed on each date without referring to offenses committed on other dates. Hope v. State, 834 N.E.2d 713, 2005 Ind. App. LEXIS 1791 (2005).

Consecutive sentences were permissibly imposed upon defendant following defendant's convictions for carrying a handgun without a license, resisting law enforcement, and possession of marijuana; although the 12-year aggregate sentence with two years suspended exceeded the advisory sentence, defendant's possession of the handgun

Separate Episodes. (Cont'd)
and marijuana did not arise out of the same episode of criminal conduct as the acts of resisting arrest and, thus, the possession offenses were not counted in determining whether consecutive sentences were allowed pursuant to IC 35-50-1-2(b). Deshazier v. State, 877 N.E.2d 200, 2007 Ind. App. LEXIS 2724 (2007).

Statement of Aggravating Circumstances.
Where court sentenced defendant to 14 years for a Class B felony but sentencing record contained no statement concerning aggravating circumstances to support the enhanced sentence, the cause was remanded with instructions that the trial court enter his findings, if any, supporting the enhanced sentence, or in the alternative, reduce the sentence to the basic term of ten years. Page v. State, 274 Ind. 264, 410 N.E.2d 1304, 1980 Ind. LEXIS 769 (1980).

—Harmless Error.
Although record of sentencing was inadequate in that it did not inform reviewing court of reasons supporting enhancement of sentence in sufficient detail to allow it to make independent judgment as to reasonableness of sentence, where defendant did not show, by a preponderance of evidence, that sentence was unlawful or manifestly unreasonable, sentence of 15 years for conviction of burglary was upheld. Neville v. State, 439 N.E.2d 1358, 1982 Ind. LEXIS 961 (1982).

Assuming arguendo that the statement of reasons for enhancing sentence was inadequate, but defendant failed to raise this issue in his motion to correct errors, as the alleged error was not fundamental, there was no reversible error. Reese v. State, 452 N.E.2d 936, 1983 Ind. LEXIS 937 (1983).

Any error committed by the trial judge for having failed to recite reasons for imposing an enhanced sentence is not fundamental and is waived by the petitioner's failure to raise the issue in his direct appeal. Barker v. State, 508 N.E.2d 795, 1987 Ind. LEXIS 948 (1987).

Where other, proper aggravating factors support an enhanced sentence, a sentence will not be overturned even if impermissible factors are considered, since a court need list only one aggravating factor to support enhancement. Cheshier v. State, 690 N.E.2d 1226, 1998 Ind. App. LEXIS 35 (1998).

Trial court's imposition of aggravated sentence for conviction of attempted aggravated battery did not violate rule that courts may not impose sentence greater than presumptive sentence based on factor not admitted by defendant or submitted to jury and proven beyond reasonable doubt since there were two other aggravating factors upon which trial court properly based sentence. Berry v. State, 819 N.E.2d 443, 2004 Ind. App. LEXIS 2481 (2004), overruled in part, Waldon v. State, 829 N.E.2d 168, 2005 Ind. App. LEXIS 1053 (2005).

Enhanced sentence for aggravated battery was proper even though trial court improperly considered several aggravating factors that pursuant to Apprendi and Blakely required jury determination

since one of aggravating factors properly considered by trial court was defendant's extensive criminal history, which, standing alone, was sufficient to support enhanced sentence. Rembert v. State, 832 N.E.2d 1130, 2005 Ind. App. LEXIS 1506 (2005).

—Insufficient.
Where defendant was convicted of a Class B felony but there was neither an order book entry nor a sentencing transcript to reflect the trial judge's evaluative process, this record was inadequate for appellate review of the decision to enhance defendant's sentence from the presumptive term. Collier v. State, 498 N.E.2d 1219, 1986 Ind. LEXIS 1319 (1986).

—Sufficient.
Where court stated reasons for finding aggravating circumstances after the filing of a motion to correct errors, such statement was sufficient to show cause for increased sentence. Hardin v. State, 273 Ind. 459, 404 N.E.2d 1354, 1980 Ind. LEXIS 732 (1980).

Where the trial court cited as an aggravating circumstance the defendant's extensive record, dating back to 1964, which encompassed five larceny or theft charges, and, as a mitigating factor, the trial court cited the fact that defendant did not have any prior felony convinction, this was a sufficient statement by the trial court of its reasons for enhancing the sentence. Reese v. State, 452 N.E.2d 936, 1983 Ind. LEXIS 937 (1983).

Where the trial court heard evidence of defendant's previous felony conviction and stated that the aggravating circumstances were: The physical danger involved in holding a knife to the neck of a hostage; defendant's lack of rehabilitation potential; and the lack of remorse shown by him, these findings were sufficient to support an increased sentence. Shields v. State, 523 N.E.2d 411, 1988 Ind. LEXIS 130 (1988).

Where two of the three aggravating factors were inappropriately applied by the trial court, but it did appropriately consider the defendant's criminal history, it was within the court's discretion to rely on the same aggravating circumstance both to enhance the sentence and to order it served consecutively. Adkins v. State, 703 N.E.2d 182, 1998 Ind. App. LEXIS 2249 (1998).

Cited:
Rodriguez v. State, 179 Ind. App. 464, 385 N.E.2d 1208, 1979 Ind. App. LEXIS 1049 (1979); Vicory v. State, 272 Ind. 683, 400 N.E.2d 1380, 1980 Ind. LEXIS 619 (1980); Bish v. State, 421 N.E.2d 608, 1981 Ind. LEXIS 758 (1981); Hightower v. State, 422 N.E.2d 1194, 1981 Ind. LEXIS 777 (1981); Collins v. State, 422 N.E.2d 1250, 1981 Ind. App. LEXIS 1526 (1981); Lewis v. State, 424 N.E.2d 107, 1981 Ind. LEXIS 927 (1981); Alleyn v. State, 427 N.E.2d 1095, 1981 Ind. LEXIS 902 (1981); Boyd v. State, 430 N.E.2d 1146, 1982 Ind. LEXIS 742 (1982); Vacendak v. State, 431 N.E.2d 100, 1982 Ind. LEXIS 751 (1982); Showecker v. State, 432 N.E.2d 1340, 1982 Ind. LEXIS 780 (1982); McManus v. State, 433 N.E.2d 775, 1982

Ind. LEXIS 795 (1982); Darnell v. State, 435 N.E.2d 250, 1982 Ind. LEXIS 821 (1982); Arnold v. State, 436 N.E.2d 288, 1982 Ind. LEXIS 843 (1982); Reed v. State, 438 N.E.2d 704, 1982 Ind. LEXIS 920 (1982); Troxail v. State, 439 N.E.2d 153, 1982 Ind. LEXIS 932 (1982); Hatton v. State, 439 N.E.2d 565, 1982 Ind. LEXIS 948 (1982); Solomon v. State, 439 N.E.2d 570, 1982 Ind. LEXIS 946 (1982); Stanley v. State, 435 N.E.2d 54, 1982 Ind. App. LEXIS 1193 (1982); Disney v. State, 441 N.E.2d 489, 1982 Ind. App. LEXIS 1467 (1982); Tucker v. State, 443 N.E.2d 840, 1983 Ind. LEXIS 723 (1983); Burgess v. State, 444 N.E.2d 1193, 1983 Ind. LEXIS 746 (1983); Cronk v. State, 443 N.E.2d 882, 1983 Ind. App. LEXIS 2509 (1983); Sidener v. State, 446 N.E.2d 965, 1983 Ind. LEXIS 791 (1983); Johnson v. State, 447 N.E.2d 1072, 1983 Ind. LEXIS 811 (1983); Chamness v. State, 447 N.E.2d 1086, 1983 Ind. LEXIS 819 (1983); Robinson v. State, 450 N.E.2d 51, 1983 Ind. LEXIS 853 (1983); Barham v. State, 454 N.E.2d 392, 1983 Ind. LEXIS 987 (1983); Eubank v. State, 456 N.E.2d 1012, 1983 Ind. LEXIS 1062 (1983); Wilson v. State, 458 N.E.2d 654, 1984 Ind. LEXIS 734 (1984); McIntyre v. State, 460 N.E.2d 162, 1984 Ind. App. LEXIS 2360 (1984); Wagner v. State, 471 N.E.2d 669, 1984 Ind. LEXIS 1045 (1984); Carman v. State, 473 N.E.2d 618, 1985 Ind. LEXIS 738 (1985); Steele v. State, 475 N.E.2d 1149, 1985 Ind. LEXIS 786 (1985); Bowen v. State, 478 N.E.2d 44, 1985 Ind. LEXIS 846 (1985); Williams v. State, 481 N.E.2d 1319, 1985 Ind. LEXIS 940 (1985); Inman v. State, 482 N.E.2d 451, 1985 Ind. LEXIS 939 (1985); Markham v. State, 484 N.E.2d 573, 1985 Ind. LEXIS 1010 (1985); Jeffers v. State, 485 N.E.2d 81, 1985 Ind. LEXIS 1026 (1985); Caldwell v. State, 497 N.E.2d 610, 1986 Ind. App. LEXIS 2955 (1986); Brooks v. State, 497 N.E.2d 210, 1986 Ind. LEXIS 1260 (1986); Thomas v. State, 510 N.E.2d 651, 1987 Ind. LEXIS 995 (1987); Criss v. State, 512 N.E.2d 858, 1987 Ind. LEXIS 1061 (1987); Poling v. State, 515 N.E.2d 1074, 1987 Ind. LEXIS 1146 (1987); Creasy v. State, 518 N.E.2d 785, 1988 Ind. LEXIS 32 (1988); Smith v. State, 519 N.E.2d 544, 1988 Ind. LEXIS 82 (1988); Douglas v. State, 520 N.E.2d 427, 1988 Ind. LEXIS 43 (1988); Buza v. State, 529 N.E.2d 334, 1988 Ind. LEXIS 300 (1988); Tiller v. State, 541 N.E.2d 885, 1989 Ind. LEXIS 228 (1989); Dowler v. State, 547 N.E.2d 1069, 1989 Ind. LEXIS 380 (1989); Mallory v. State, 563 N.E.2d 640, 1990 Ind. App. LEXIS 1610 (1990); Okuly v. State, 574 N.E.2d 315, 1991 Ind. App. LEXIS 994 (1991); Allen v. State, 575 N.E.2d 615, 1991 Ind. LEXIS 133 (1991); Meriweather v. State, 659 N.E.2d 133, 1995 Ind. App. LEXIS 1572 (1995); Lockhart v. State, 671 N.E.2d 893, 1996 Ind. App. LEXIS 1356 (1996); Singer v. State, 674 N.E.2d 11, 1996 Ind. App. LEXIS 1605 (1996); Wieland v. State, 736 N.E.2d 1198, 2000 Ind. LEXIS 961 (2000); Boyce v. State, 736 N.E.2d 1206, 2000 Ind. LEXIS 960 (2000); Lewis v. State, 759 N.E.2d 1077, 2001 Ind. App. LEXIS 1987 (2001); Shane v. State, 769 N.E.2d 1195, 2002 Ind. App. LEXIS 955 (2002); McAbee v. State, 770 N.E.2d 802, 2002 Ind. LEXIS 543 (2002); Person v. State, 764 N.E.2d 743, 2002 Ind. App. LEXIS 380 (2002); Schlichter v. State, 766 N.E.2d 801, 2002 Ind. App. LEXIS 652 (2002); Bennett v. State, 787 N.E.2d 938, 2003 Ind. App. LEXIS 762 (2003); Booker v. State, 790 N.E.2d 491, 2003 Ind. App. LEXIS 1042 (2003); Sloan v. State, 794 N.E.2d 1128, 2003 Ind. App. LEXIS 1644 (2003); Saylor v. State, 808 N.E.2d 646, 2004 Ind. LEXIS 464 (2004); Moore v. State, 827 N.E.2d 631, 2005 Ind. App. LEXIS 887 (2005); Johnson v. State, 831 N.E.2d 163, 2005 Ind. App. LEXIS 1269 (2005); Anglemyer v. State, 845 N.E.2d 1087, 2006 Ind. App. LEXIS 662 (2006); White v. State, 847 N.E.2d 1043, 2006 Ind. App. LEXIS 989 (2006); Stanley v. State, 849 N.E.2d 626, 2006 Ind. App. LEXIS 1103 (2006); Stringer v. State, 853 N.E.2d 543, 2006 Ind. App. LEXIS 1804 (2006); Anglemyer v. State, 868 N.E.2d 482, 2007 Ind. LEXIS 490 (2007); Howard v. State, 873 N.E.2d 685, 2007 Ind. App. LEXIS 2138 (2007); Padgett v. State, 875 N.E.2d 310, 2007 Ind. App. LEXIS 2361 (2007); Tubbs v. State, 888 N.E.2d 814, 2008 Ind. App. LEXIS 1325 (2008); Atwood v. State, 905 N.E.2d 479, 2009 Ind. App. LEXIS 738 (2009).

RESEARCH REFERENCES

Indiana Law Review.

Survey: Criminal Law and Procedure: Recent Developments in Indiana Criminal Law and Procedure (October 1, 2004, through September 30, 2005), 39 Ind. L. Rev. 893 (2006).

Collateral References.

Downward departure under state sentencing guidelines based on extraordinary family circumstances. 106 A.L.R.5th 377.

35-50-2-6. Class C felony.

(a) A person who commits a Class C felony shall be imprisoned for a fixed term of between two (2) and eight (8) years, with the advisory sentence being four (4) years. In addition, the person may be fined not more than ten thousand dollars ($10,000).

(b) Notwithstanding subsection (a), if a person has committed nonsupport of a child as a Class C felony under IC 35-46-1-5, upon motion of the prosecuting attorney, the court may enter judgment of conviction of a Class D felony under IC 35-46-1-5 and sentence the person accordingly. The court shall enter in the record detailed reasons for the court's action when the court enters a judgment of conviction of a Class D felony under this subsection.

History.

IC 35-50-2-6, as added by Acts 1976, P.L.148, § 8; 1977, P.L.340, § 119; P.L.167-1990, § 1; P.L.213-1996, § 5; P.L.71-2005, § 9.

Cross References.

Compensation for victims of violent crimes, IC 5-2-6.1.

NOTES TO DECISIONS

Constitutionality.

—Cruel and Unusual Punishment.

A sentence of five years for robbery did not constitute cruel and unusual punishment. Perry v. State, 401 N.E.2d 792, 1980 Ind. App. LEXIS 1383 (1980).

—Double Jeopardy.

The use of prior convictions to find aggravating circumstances and add to penalty and the use of prior convictions to find defendant an habitual offender with the added sentence did not violate the prohibition against double jeopardy. Griffin v. State, 275 Ind. 107, 415 N.E.2d 60, 1981 Ind. LEXIS 656 (1981).

Addition to Basic Term.

—Considerations.

The facts that the defendant was in need of rehabilitative treatment that could best be provided by a penal facility and that the imposition of a lesser sentence would depreciate the seriousness of the crime are considerations which support the addition of three years to the basic term. Parker v. State, 424 N.E.2d 132, 1981 Ind. App. LEXIS 1552 (1981).

Findings regarding the presence of certain aggravating factors, including: (1) history of criminal activity; (2) a need of correctional or rehabilitative treatment for appellant at a penal facility; (3) that a reduced sentence would depreciate the seriousness of the offense; (4) the age of the victim; (5) that the crime might have a serious effect on the victim; (6) that the crime is likely to reoccur; and (7) that the defendant showed no remorse for committing the crime, supported three-year en-

hancement of sentence for child molesting. Caccavallo v. State, 436 N.E.2d 775, 1982 Ind. LEXIS 851 (1982).

In child molestation cases, the age of the child abuse victim (here 23 months) is an appropriate aggravating circumstance to be considered in determining whether to enhance a sentence under this section. Bresson v. State, 498 N.E.2d 91, 1986 Ind. App. LEXIS 3007 (1986).

The defendant's behavior, including theft and aggravated assault and battery involving a knife, and the fact that he picked up a cement block and was threatening to hit one of the persons at the scene immediately after the death of the victim, supported the enhancement of his sentence for involuntary manslaughter. Stanley v. State, 515 N.E.2d 1117, 1987 Ind. LEXIS 1162 (1987).

In imposing sentence for child molesting, a Class C felony, it is proper for the trial court to use defendant's prior uncharged child molesting acts as an aggravating circumstance. Durham v. State, 510 N.E.2d 202, 1987 Ind. App. LEXIS 2880 (1987).

In imposing sentence for child molesting, a Class C felony, it is not improper for the trial court to use as an aggravating circumstance the emotional and psychological effects defendant's acts had on the victim and another child. Durham v. State, 510 N.E.2d 202, 1987 Ind. App. LEXIS 2880 (1987).

Even if the trial court was entitled or required to consider the risk that the defendant would reoffend under former IC 35-38-1-7.1, under Jud. Canon 3(B)(8), trial court should not have considered evidence outside the record in making its determination to sentence the defendant to one year greater than the advisory sentence for a Class C felony under IC 35-50-2-6. Cannon v. State, 839 N.E.2d 185, 2005 Ind. App. LEXIS 2260 (2005), transfer granted and vacated, — N.E.2d —, 2007 Ind. LEXIS 368 (2007), superseded, 866 N.E.2d 770, 2007 Ind. LEXIS 357 (Ind. 2007).

Crime Committed Under Prior Law.

Where crime was committed prior to the effective date of the new criminal code, defendant was properly sentenced under the old law and was not entitled to receive the ameliorative benefits of the new law. Davis v. State, 418 N.E.2d 256, 1981 Ind. App. LEXIS 1324 (1981).

Discretion of Court.

Whether the basic sentence will be increased or decreased due to aggravating or mitigating circumstances is within the trial court's discretion. Wilson v. State, 465 N.E.2d 717, 1984 Ind. LEXIS 871 (1984).

Where defendant committed a carefully planned robbery, lured the victim to an apartment, lay in wait, attacked the victim from behind and choked

Discretion of Court. (Cont'd)
him, and even though the victim begged his attackers not to kill him in view of his two young children, defendant told his accomplice to stab the victim, defendant's sentences of 13 years for robbery and 6 years for battery, to be served consecutively, for an aggregate sentence of 19 years, was not an abuse of discretion or inappropriate. Moore v. State, — N.E.2d —, 2009 Ind. App. LEXIS 876 (2009).

—Appellate Review.
Determination of a sentence rests with the discretion of the trial court; an appellate court will not alter a sentence authorized by statute unless the sentence is manifestly unreasonable in light of the offender and offense. Clayton v. State, 658 N.E.2d 82, 1995 Ind. App. LEXIS 1098 (1995), corrected, 658 N.E.2d 82, 1995 Ind. App. LEXIS 1204 (1995).

— —Presumptions on Appeal.
When the trial court imposes the basic sentence, the Supreme Court will presume that it considered the proper factors in determining that sentence. Wilson v. State, 465 N.E.2d 717, 1984 Ind. LEXIS 871 (1984).

When the trial court imposes the basic sentence, the Court of Appeals will presume that it considered the proper factors in determining that sentence. Hobson v. State, 495 N.E.2d 741, 1986 Ind. App. LEXIS 2756 (1986).

—Arrests.
Trial court has broad discretion to consider aggravating factors; this discretion includes consideration of arrests not yet reduced to conviction. Clayton v. State, 658 N.E.2d 82, 1995 Ind. App. LEXIS 1098 (1995), corrected, 658 N.E.2d 82, 1995 Ind. App. LEXIS 1204 (1995).

Involuntary Manslaughter.
A four-year sentence for involuntary manslaughter is not manifestly unreasonable. Johnson v. State, 480 N.E.2d 600, 1985 Ind. App. LEXIS 2640 (1985), disapproved, Modesitt v. State, 578 N.E.2d 649, 1991 Ind. LEXIS 177 (Ind. 1991).

Defendant's involuntary manslaughter sentence, under IC 35-50-2-6(a), was properly enhanced to the maximum sentence based on: (1) an unusually severe impact on the victim's family, given the loss of the victim's unborn child, which defendant could foresee, as he knew the victim, his wife, was pregnant; (2) defendant's changing version of the facts surrounding the incident; and (3) defendant's extreme recklessness. Sipple v. State, 788 N.E.2d 473, 2003 Ind. App. LEXIS 827 (2003).

Mitigating and Aggravating Factors.
Trial court properly considered aggravating factor that defendant convicted of child molestation was in a position of trust with his victim against mitigating factors that defendant had no prior criminal history and no prior criminal record when the court imposed a 3 year sentence for child molestation, a class C felony, rather than the maximum 4 year sentence. The trial court was not required to consider hardship to defendant's dependents as a mitigating factor. Haun v. State, 792 N.E.2d 69, 2003 Ind. App. LEXIS 1351 (2003).

Trial court has sole discretion to determine weight accorded aggravating or mitigating factors; in arson case, trial court properly considered proffered mitigating factors and decided against accepting them. Julian v. State, 811 N.E.2d 392, 2004 Ind. App. LEXIS 1205 (2004).

Defendant's failure to rehabilitate and his risk of re-offending should not have been considered separate aggravating circumstances under Blakely since those aggravators were not presented to jury; furthermore, while weight given to three mitigating circumstances was less than weight given as aggravator to defendant's criminal history, it was not so much less that maximum sentence was warranted. Neff v. State, 832 N.E.2d 1006, 2005 Ind. App. LEXIS 1454 (2005), transfer granted, — N.E.2d —, 2006 Ind. LEXIS 562 (2006), aff'd in part, superseded in part, 849 N.E.2d 556, 2006 Ind. LEXIS 546 (2006).

Defendant's six-year sentence for operating a motor vehicle while privileges were forfeited for life was not an abuse of discretion, even though the trial court erroneously failed to give mitigating weight to defendant's guilty plea, because it was unlikely that treating plea as mitigator would have changed the sentence, and defendant received a benefit for his plea in the form of the dismissal of a probation revocation petition in another case; accordingly, the trial court's failure to consider plea as mitigator was harmless error. Banks v. State, 841 N.E.2d 654, 2006 Ind. App. LEXIS 160 (2006).

When defendant was sentenced to six years for operating a motor vehicle while privileges were forfeited for life, it was not an abuse of discretion for the trial court not to give mitigating weight to a probation department's level of services inventory (LSI) placing him at a low/moderate risk to reoffend or to nonviolent aspect of his crime because he waived mitigators by not raising them at sentencing; furthermore, mitigators were highly disputable in significance because the LSI was merely a prediction which could be given little weight in light of defendant's subsequent arrests and pending criminal cases and because the nonviolent nature of the crime was apparent at sentencing. Banks v. State, 841 N.E.2d 654, 2006 Ind. App. LEXIS 160 (2006).

When defendant was sentenced to six years for operating a motor vehicle while privileges were forfeited for life, it was not an abuse of discretion for the trial court not to give mitigating weight to his statements of remorse where the statements were somewhat ambivalent and did not indicate that defendant took full responsibility for his actions. Banks v. State, 841 N.E.2d 654, 2006 Ind. App. LEXIS 160 (2006).

When defendant was sentenced to six years for operating a motor vehicle while privileges were forfeited for life, it was not an abuse of discretion for the trial court not to give mitigating weight to his long-term relationship with his girlfriend where he was driving her car when he was arrested and she admitted that she let him drive the car knowing his license had been suspended.

Mitigating and Aggravating Factors. (Cont'd)
Banks v. State, 841 N.E.2d 654, 2006 Ind. App.
LEXIS 160 (2006).

Defendant's 50-year sentence for two counts of
child molesting, one as a Class A felony and one as
a Class C felony, was affirmed where the trial court
properly assessed significant aggravating weight
to the aggravators of abuse of trust and the victim's age because the defendant was the victim's
uncle and was her babysitter. Garland v. State, 855
N.E.2d 703, 2006 Ind. App. LEXIS 2145 (2006).

Findings were sufficient to support the sentence
in a felony battery case pursuant to IC 35-38-1-3
because the trial court adequately described the
factors that supported the eight-year sentence,
namely, defendant's history of criminal behavior
and his violent acts against a pregnant woman
which led to the charges in the case; omission of
the word "aggravating" did not make the trial
court's reasoning any less apparent. Loos v. State,
875 N.E.2d 387, 2007 Ind. App. LEXIS 2376
(2007).

Defendant's challenge to the relative weight of
aggravating and mitigating factors failed on the
merits because, under IC 35-50-2-6, the trial court
was not required to weigh them when imposing
sentence; on appeal, the trial court could not have
been found to have abused its discretion in failing
to weigh those factors. Brattain v. State, 891
N.E.2d 1055, 2008 Ind. App. LEXIS 1681 (2008).

Plea Agreements.
Although the record established, and all parties
conceded, that the defendant's failure to pay an
undivided amount of child support during the
same time period for the benefit of four children
born of the same marriage constituted one episode
of criminal behavior for purposes of sentencing,
the court erred when it imposed a five-year sentence on the defendant as a result of a plea
agreement knowingly and voluntarily entered into
by the defendant when the maximum sentence
allowed by law was four years. Smith v. State, 717
N.E.2d 239, 1999 Ind. App. LEXIS 1752 (1999).

Penalties Apportioned.
Sentencing under the current criminal code ap-
propriately apportions penalties to the nature of
the offense as required by Ind. Const., Art. 1, § 16.
Wells v. State, 397 N.E.2d 1250, 1979 Ind. App.
LEXIS 1481 (1979).

Retroactive Application.
Because the amendment to IC 35-50-2-8 by
P.L.164-1993, § 13, reduced the maximum sentence for Class C felonies, the court should have
sentenced defendant pursuant to the statute in
effect when he was sentenced, and not the statute
in effect when the offense was committed, where
the maximum sentence enhancement for a habitual offender conviction for that defendant would
be reduced under the amended statute from 30
years to 12 years. Elkins v. State, 659 N.E.2d 563,
1995 Ind. App. LEXIS 1633 (1995).

Robbery.

—Sentence Upheld.
A sentence of 48 years for robbing the library at
a children's hospital was upheld where defendant
put three innocent children, two of whom had been
diagnosed as terminally ill, in fear for their own
safety and the safety of the people they loved; he
worked at the hospital and knew the library was
used by the children as a place to relax; and while
he may have been under stress, his stress could not
have been any greater than that of the persons he
chose to rob. Harris v. State, 616 N.E.2d 25, 1993
Ind. App. LEXIS 702 (1993).

Sentence.
A conspiracy count alleged a conspiracy to commit a Class C robbery. It was therefore error to
impose a Class B felony sentence for such a conviction. Jones v. State, 517 N.E.2d 405, 1988 Ind.
LEXIS 16 (1988).

Where defendant was sentenced to consecutive
sentences that did not exceed four years, and the
most serious offense was battery, a Class D felony,
the sentences were not excessive under IC 35-50-
1-2(c); the presumptive sentence for the next highest class of felony was four years under IC 35-50-
2-6, and the sentence imposed was just under four
years. Monyhan v. State, 780 N.E.2d 1187, 2003
Ind. App. LEXIS 7 (2003).

Trial court's entry of judgment of conviction for
Class D felony following guilty plea by defendant
for crime of non-support of dependent was facially
invalid since trial court failed to provide detailed
reasons on record required for reducing felony
from Class C to Class D; accordingly, trial court's
later correction of conviction to Class C felony was
analogous to correction of a facially invalid sentence and was valid despite defendant's argument
that trial court had no jurisdiction to modify judgment after accepting plea agreement. Ennis v.
State, 806 N.E.2d 804, 2004 Ind. App. LEXIS 674
(2004).

While addressing the propriety of defendant's
sentence, the appellate court had to operate under
the earlier "presumptive" sentencing scheme
rather than the "advisory" sentencing scheme enacted by statutory amendment; defendant's offenses were committed when the "presumptive"
sentencing scheme was in force and the advisory
scheme was not to be applied retroactively. Bennett v. State, 862 N.E.2d 1281, 2007 Ind. App.
LEXIS 530 (2007).

Sentence Enhancement.
Enhancement of presumptive sentences, along
with the imposition of consecutive sentences, may
be supported by a single aggravating circumstance. Clayton v. State, 658 N.E.2d 82, 1995 Ind.
App. LEXIS 1098 (1995), corrected, 658 N.E.2d 82,
1995 Ind. App. LEXIS 1204 (1995).

Defendant's four-year sentence for operating a
motor vehicle after driving privileges are forfeited
for life as a Class C felony could not be further
enhanced under the general habitual offender statute. Wood v. State, 734 N.E.2d 296, 2000 Ind. App.
LEXIS 1343 (2000).

Where defendant was convicted of a class C
felony, which carred a statutory maximum sentence of four years and up to four additional years
were permitted if aggravating circumstances were

Sentence Enhancement. (Cont'd)
present, IC 35-50-2-6, defendant's sentence of six years based upon aggravating circumstances that were neither admitted by defendant nor decided by the jury violated U.S. Const. amend. VI; in order to impose greater than the maximum sentence, the aggravating circumstances either had to be admitted by defendant or found by a jury. Milligan v. State, 819 N.E.2d 115, 2004 Ind. App. LEXIS 2473 (2004).

Enhanced sentences imposed by trial court following defendant's guilty plea to seven counts of robbery as Class B felony and one count of robbery as Class C felony were vacated; trial court should not have used defendant's admission, made as he was pleading guilty, that he had gone on crime spree in order to enhance his sentences, since doing so was unsupported by case law and unnecessary since trial court could have made some of concurrent sentences consecutive without violating Blakely. Young v. State, 834 N.E.2d 1015, 2005 Ind. LEXIS 877 (2005).

Defendant's incarceration, which was material element of offense for which he was charged, namely, possession of material capable of causing bodily injury by an inmate, could nevertheless be used as sentence aggravator since defendant committed offense while on probation for different offense; aggravator was derivative of defendant's criminal history and therefore did not violate Blakely case prohibitions. Abney v. State, 822 N.E.2d 260, 2005 Ind. App. LEXIS 214 (2005), overruled in part, Ryle v. State, 842 N.E.2d 320, 2005 Ind. LEXIS 1112 (2005).

Trial court improperly sentenced defendant, who pleaded guilty to battery by means of a deadly weapon, a Class C felony, to an enhanced term, where the particular facts relied upon by the trial court in assessing the nature and circumstances of defendant's crime were not contained within the presentence investigation report. Williams v. State, 840 N.E.2d 433, 2006 Ind. App. LEXIS 33 (2006), clarified, 2006 Ind. App. LEXIS 633 (2006).

Defendant's enhanced sentence under IC 35-50-2-6 for child molesting under IC 35-42-4-3 and sexual misconduct with a minor under IC 35-42-4-9 violated Blakely v. Washington, 542 U.S. 296, 124 S. Ct. 2531, 159 L. Ed. 2d 403, 2004 U.S. LEXIS 4573 (2004) where the sole aggravating factor, that defendant was in a position of trust with his victims, was not proven by the fact that defendant was the victims' aunt; the state did not show that defendant lived in the same neighborhood as the victims; and the testimony of defendant's mother was not an admission by defendant, even though the mother was a defense witness. Williams v. State, 895 N.E.2d 377, 2008 Ind. App. LEXIS 2438 (2008).

Sentence Not Unreasonable.
Imposition of basic presumptive sentence found not to be manifestly unreasonable. Warner v. State, 455 N.E.2d 355, 1983 Ind. LEXIS 998 (1983).

Four-year sentence for robbery found not manifestly unreasonable. Simmons v. State, 455 N.E.2d 1143, 1983 Ind. App. LEXIS 3567 (1983).

A five-year term of imprisonment, with three years suspended, and two years of probation after the sentence, was not "manifestly unreasonable" for violation of former IC 9-11-2-5 (operating a vehicle while intoxicated, resulting in the death of another person). Smith v. State, 496 N.E.2d 778, 1986 Ind. App. LEXIS 2824 (1986).

Imposition of the presumptive five-year sentence for child molesting was not manifestly unreasonable. Phillips v. State, 499 N.E.2d 803, 1986 Ind. App. LEXIS 3130 (1986).

Where sentencing statement indicates a consideration of the facts of the subject crimes and the character of the defendant and adequately provides the reasons and logic supporting the enhanced sentence, it cannot be said no reasonable person could find the sentence appropriate to the particular offenses and offender, and thus, sentence of $10,000 fine and concurrent six and one-half years for burglary and three years for theft is not manifestly unreasonable. Herald v. State, 511 N.E.2d 5, 1987 Ind. App. LEXIS 2911 (1987).

Because defendant did not submit any evidence of the existence of mitigating factors, and because the only mitigating factor listed in the presentence report was defendant's young age and the only aggravating factor listed was defendant's history of criminal activity, defendant's sentence was not manifestly unreasonable where the trial court imposed the presumptive sentence and then suspended three years. Bush v. State, 732 N.E.2d 250, 2000 Ind. App. LEXIS 1146 (2000).

Although the lack of remorse for failure to appear at trial was an improper aggravating factor considered by the court, the two remaining aggravators were sufficient to support the sentence. Angeles v. State, 751 N.E.2d 790, 2001 Ind. App. LEXIS 1193 (2001).

Defendant's maximum sentence was not unreasonable where trial court considered mitigating and aggravating factors and provided reasons without merely restating the elements of the crime; the defendant had strangled her two-year-old son and then when he became unresponsive, she tried to cover up her crime by placing him into a swimming pool. Garrett v. State, 756 N.E.2d 523, 2001 Ind. App. LEXIS 1695 (2001).

Defendant did not receive an inappropriate sentence as his criminal record showed several convictions in the relatively short amount of time of 4 years, at the time of sentencing, defendant was awaiting a jury trial on the charges of resisting law enforcement and possession of marijuana, and, although defendant claimed that he was going to turn himself in, the record revealed that he was residing in a different county and was stopped by police for driving while suspended; thus, contrary to defendant's assertions, that pattern did not show an individual who was changed and would no longer make "mistakes," but someone who had little regard for the law and had not learned from the relative leniency he had been shown previously by several trial courts in sentencing. Anglin v. State, 787 N.E.2d 1012, 2003 Ind. App. LEXIS 800 (2003).

Defendant was properly sentenced to the maximum term of 8 years after pleading guilty to felony

Sentence Not Unreasonable. (Cont'd)
possession of methamphetamine because the trial court did not abuse its discretion in determining that defendant would benefit from an extended incarceration given his repeated criminal acts despite being afforded leniency and past rehabilitation, that the hardship imposed on defendant's children by his incarceration was to be given minimal weight where such hardship would exist for any imprisonment, and that the application of the "depreciating the seriousness of the crime" aggravator was appropriate. Jones v. State, 790 N.E.2d 536, 2003 Ind. App. LEXIS 1102 (2003).

Maximum sentence for Class C felony of child molesting was appropriate for defendant who molested 10-year-old step-daughter; trial court's sentencing statement sufficiently stated reasons for sentencing decision, which included as aggravators violation of bond conditions and violation of position of trust, and which gave little weight to fact that defendant did not have prior serious criminal history because defendant had previously been arrested for possession of drugs. Leffingwell v. State, 810 N.E.2d 369, 2004 Ind. App. LEXIS 1112 (2004).

With respect to deciding whether case is among very worst offenses and defendant among very worst offenders, thus justifying maximum sentence, courts should concentrate less on comparing facts of case to other cases, whether real or hypothetical, and more on focusing on nature, extent, and depravity of offense for which defendant is being sentenced and what it reveals about defendant's character; accordingly, where defendant's actions resulted in death of two persons, as well as injuries to his minor brother, and pre-sentence report listed litany of charges filed against defendant over the years, some of which involved driving while impaired, eight-year sentence for two counts of causing death while operating motor vehicle with Schedule I controlled substance in his body, IC 9-30-5-5, was appropriate. Wilkie v. State, 813 N.E.2d 794, 2004 Ind. App. LEXIS 1640 (2004), overruled, 851 N.E.2d 302, 2006 Ind. LEXIS 666 (2006), overruled in part, 848 N.E.2d 1073, 2006 Ind. LEXIS 474 (2006).

Defendant's eight year sentence for stalking was appropriate where the victim received 69 calls from defendant within a three month period and there was witness testimony that defendant followed the victim, showed up at her workplace, and called her friends. Smith v. State, 839 N.E.2d 780, 2005 Ind. App. LEXIS 2442 (2005).

While defendant did not waive right to challenge propriety of 6-year sentence for burglary and 10-year sentence as habitual offender by pleading guilty to burglary charge, 16-year sentence was nevertheless deemed proper where 6-year sentence was less than maximum sentence for burglary and where eight prior convictions justified enhanced sentence. Mast v. State, 824 N.E.2d 429, 2005 Ind. App. LEXIS 477 (2005), overruled in part, Childress v. State, 848 N.E.2d 1073, 2006 Ind. LEXIS 474 (2006).

Even though defendant's sentence was at the near maximum under the terms of his plea agreement based upon the maximum sentence for a Class C felony of eight years under IC 35-50-2-6, defendant's seven year sentence was not inappropriate under a single standard established by Ind. R. App. P. 7(B) and taking into consideration the relevant circumstances of IC 35-38-1-7.1, as required under IC 35-38-1-3, in that he was a convicted felon on probation and, while intoxicated, pulled a knife on a stranger and then injured an officer trying to apprehend him. McMahon v. State, 856 N.E.2d 743, 2006 Ind. App. LEXIS 2333 (2006).

Sentence of four years, with two executed and two suspended to probation, for defendant's conviction of child solicitation under IC 35-42-4-6(c) was affirmed as the particulars of the offense were not unremarkable and did go beyond the inherent nature of the crime charged; among other things, defendant admitted his intention to bring alcohol to a planned rendezvous with a person he believed to be a 14-year-old girl. Windhorst v. State, 858 N.E.2d 676, 2006 Ind. App. LEXIS 2632 (2006), transfer granted, 869 N.E.2d 447, 2007 Ind. LEXIS 56 (2007), aff'd in part, superseded in part, 868 N.E.2d 504, 2007 Ind. LEXIS 489 (2007).

Six-year sentence for attempted battery with a deadly weapon and possession of a handgun without a license, which was two years more than the advisory sentence, was appropriate where defendant had a prior juvenile delinquency adjudication involving a firearm and multiple victims, including an infant, were involved. Stewart v. State, 866 N.E.2d 858, 2007 Ind. App. LEXIS 1085 (2007).

Six-year sentence for attempted battery with a deadly weapon, which was two years more than the advisory sentence, was appropriate where defendant had a prior criminal history and where multiple victims, including an infant, were involved. Rutherford v. State, 866 N.E.2d 867, 2007 Ind. App. LEXIS 1086 (2007).

Where defendant, who had pled guilty and had no prior criminal record, was 46 at the time of the offense, communicated with the 15-year-old victim by exchanging emails and instant messages, told the victim he was 26, and took her to a mobile home for several days, during which time they engaged in oral sex and fondling, six years was an appropriate sentence for his conviction under IC 35-50-2-6. Blixt v. State, 872 N.E.2d 149, 2007 Ind. App. LEXIS 1910 (Ind. App. 2007).

Defendant's aggregate 52-year sentence for convictions of two counts of operating a vehicle while intoxicated (OWI) causing death, OWI causing serious bodily injury, and having a prior OWI conviction in the last five years was 4 years shorter than the maximum sentence possible, and was not inappropriate; defendant's BAC was over three times the legal limit, he had cocaine in his system, and he was speeding in an area where pedestrians and traffic were common. Although neither of defendant's previous convictions involved offenses nearly as serious as the current offense, they involved the same illegal and dangerous conduct, driving while intoxicated. Pedraza v. State, 873 N.E.2d 1083, 2007 Ind. App. LEXIS 2182 (2007), transfer granted and vacated, 878 N.E.2d 218, 2007 Ind. LEXIS 1005 (2007).

Where defendant was convicted of making his

Sentence Not Unreasonable. (Cont'd)
16-year-old daughter watch a pornographic movie with him while naked and then have sex with him, defendant had a prior battering conviction as to his six-year-old son, and defendant was on probation, defendant's aggregate six year sentence for incest was appropriate. Sargent v. State, 875 N.E.2d 762, 2007 Ind. App. LEXIS 2400 (2007).

There was no error in sentencing defendant to consecutive sentences under IC 35-50-2-6(a) for violating IC 9-30-5-5(a)(1); two passengers were killed due to defendant's inebriated driving and his failure to be honest with families until victims' autopsies demonstrated his guilt showed lack of remorse and diminished acceptance of responsibility. Ricci v. State, 894 N.E.2d 1089, 2008 Ind. App. LEXIS 2384 (2008).

Cited:
Rivera v. State, 179 Ind. App. 295, 385 N.E.2d 455, 1979 Ind. App. LEXIS 1021 (1979); Rodriguez v. State, 179 Ind. App. 464, 385 N.E.2d 1208, 1979 Ind. App. LEXIS 1049 (1979); Woods v. State, 181 Ind. App. 352, 391 N.E.2d 858, 1979 Ind. App. LEXIS 1251 (1979); Davis v. State, 398 N.E.2d 704, 1980 Ind. App. LEXIS 1254 (1980); Vicory v. State, 272 Ind. 683, 400 N.E.2d 1380, 1980 Ind. LEXIS 619 (1980); Gatewood v. State, 430 N.E.2d 781, 1982 Ind. LEXIS 727 (1982); Hernandez v. State, 439 N.E.2d 625, 1982 Ind. LEXIS 958 (1982);

Phillips v. State, 441 N.E.2d 201, 1982 Ind. LEXIS 994 (1982); Cronk v. State, 443 N.E.2d 882, 1983 Ind. App. LEXIS 2509 (1983); Barham v. State, 454 N.E.2d 392, 1983 Ind. LEXIS 987 (1983); Ingram v. State, 463 N.E.2d 483, 1984 Ind. App. LEXIS 2594 (1984); Haskett v. State, 467 N.E.2d 32, 1984 Ind. App. LEXIS 2910 (1984); Tolson v. State, 489 N.E.2d 42, 1986 Ind. LEXIS 1025 (1986); Mallery v. State, 499 N.E.2d 1100, 1986 Ind. LEXIS 1370 (1986); Conwell v. State, 542 N.E.2d 1024, 1989 Ind. App. LEXIS 834 (1989); Singer v. State, 674 N.E.2d 11, 1996 Ind. App. LEXIS 1605 (1996); Armstrong v. State, 742 N.E.2d 972, 2001 Ind. App. LEXIS 23 (2001); Ashley v. State, 757 N.E.2d 1037, 2001 Ind. App. LEXIS 1864 (2001); Williams v. State, 759 N.E.2d 661, 2001 Ind. App. LEXIS 2111 (2001); Haycraft v. State, 760 N.E.2d 203, 2001 Ind. App. LEXIS 2225 (2001); Lewis v. State, 759 N.E.2d 1077, 2001 Ind. App. LEXIS 1987 (2001); Rodriguez v. State, 785 N.E.2d 1169, 2003 Ind. App. LEXIS 558 (2003); Krumm v. State, 793 N.E.2d 1170, 2003 Ind. App. LEXIS 1529 (2003); Traylor v. State, 817 N.E.2d 611, 2004 Ind. App. LEXIS 2229 (2004); Anglemyer v. State, 845 N.E.2d 1087, 2006 Ind. App. LEXIS 662 (2006); Stringer v. State, 853 N.E.2d 543, 2006 Ind. App. LEXIS 1804 (2006); Windhorst v. State, 868 N.E.2d 504, 2007 Ind. LEXIS 489 (2007); Anglemyer v. State, 868 N.E.2d 482, 2007 Ind. LEXIS 490 (2007); Kemp v. State, 887 N.E.2d 102, 2008 Ind. App. LEXIS 1159 (2008).

RESEARCH REFERENCES

Collateral References.
Downward departure under state sentencing guidelines based on extraordinary family circumstances. 106 A.L.R.5th 377.

35-50-2-7. Class D felony.

(a) A person who commits a Class D felony shall be imprisoned for a fixed term of between six (6) months and three (3) years, with the advisory sentence being one and one-half (1 ½) years. In addition, the person may be fined not more than ten thousand dollars ($10,000).

(b) Notwithstanding subsection (a), if a person has committed a Class D felony, the court may enter judgment of conviction of a Class A misdemeanor and sentence accordingly. However, the court shall enter a judgment of conviction of a Class D felony if:

(1) the court finds that:

(A) the person has committed a prior, unrelated felony for which judgment was entered as a conviction of a Class A misdemeanor; and

(B) the prior felony was committed less than three (3) years before the second felony was committed;

(2) the offense is domestic battery as a Class D felony under IC 35-42-2-1.3; or

(3) the offense is possession of child pornography (IC 35-42-4-4(c)).

The court shall enter in the record, in detail, the reason for its action whenever it exercises the power to enter judgment of conviction of a Class A misdemeanor granted in this subsection.

History.
IC 35-50-2-7, as added by Acts 1976, P.L.148, § 8; 1977, P.L.340, § 120; 1982, P.L.204, § 40; P.L.334-1983, § 3; P.L.136-1987, § 7; P.L.167-1990, § 2; P.L.188-1999, § 9; P.L.98-2003, § 3; P.L.71-2005, § 10.

Cross References.
Compensation for victims of violent crimes, IC
5-2-6.1.

NOTES TO DECISIONS

ANALYSIS

Constitutionality.
—Added Years.
—Cruel and Unusual Punishment.
—Double Jeopardy.
—Equal Protection.
Aggravating Circumstances.
—Assertion of Innocence.
Alternative Sentencing Possibility.
Appellate Adjustment of Sentence.
Applicability.
Basic Sentence.
Comparable Offenses.
Determining Status of Offense.
—Ambiguous Sentence.
Discretion of Court.
—Aggravating and Mitigating Circumstances.
Effective of Reduction of Prior Felony Conviction
to Misdemeanor.
Harmless Error.
Home Detention.
Incompetent Defendants.
Instructions.
Jurisdiction.
Jury.
Minimum Sentence.
Modification of Sentence.
One-Year Sentence Improper.
Order of Sentencing.
Penalties Apportioned.
Penalty Fixed by Court.
Prior Criminal Record.
—Defendant Not Prosecuted.
—Failure to Advise Defendant of Effect.
Recommendation of Prosecutor.
Reduction to Misdemeanor.
Review.
Sentence Proper.

Constitutionality.
Sentence beyond statutory maximum for Class
B misdemeanor based on aggravating factors determined by judge was unconstitutional under
Blakely doctrine; accordingly, sentence was reversed and remanded for new sentencing hearing
where state could elect either to prove aggravating
circumstances before jury or accept statutory fixed
term. Smylie v. State, 823 N.E.2d 679, 2005 Ind.
LEXIS 199 (2005), cert. denied, 126 S. Ct. 545, 163
L. Ed. 2d 459, 2005 U.S. LEXIS 7865 (U.S. 2005),
superseded by statute as stated in, Anglemyer v.
State, 868 N.E.2d 482, 2007 Ind. LEXIS 490
(2007), superseded by statute as stated in, McMahon v. State, 856 N.E.2d 743, 2006 Ind. App.
LEXIS 2333 (2006).

—Added Years.
See note to IC 35-50-2-3, Boyd v. State, 396
N.E.2d 920, 1979 Ind. App. LEXIS 1430 (1979).

—Cruel and Unusual Punishment.
The wide range of penalties which may be imposed for the various classes of felonies in the new
criminal code does not invite discrimination and
cruel and unusual punishment. Rogers v. State,
272 Ind. 65, 396 N.E.2d 348, 1979 Ind. LEXIS 748
(1979).

—Double Jeopardy.
Recognizing that defendant's two attempted
criminal deviate conduct convictions and defendant's two sexual battery convictions constituted
same offense for purposes of double jeopardy, trial
court merged two attempted criminal deviate conduct convictions and two sexual battery convictions for sentencing purposes; however, trial
court's act of merging without also vacating the
convictions was error requiring remand to vacate
one attempted criminal deviate conduct conviction
and one sexual battery convictions. Morrison v.
State, 824 N.E.2d 734, 2005 Ind. App. LEXIS 518
(2005).

—Equal Protection.
This section providing for an increase in sentence for aggravating circumstances but not providing for lessening the sentence for mitigating
circumstances, does not violate the equal protection provisions of the constitutions. The court also
calls attention to the fact that subsection (b) of this
section authorizes the court to enter judgment for
a Class A misdemeanor which would carry a lesser
sentence. Collins v. State, 275 Ind. 86, 415 N.E.2d
46, 1981 Ind. LEXIS 657 (1981), cert. denied, 451
U.S. 991, 101 S. Ct. 2331, 68 L. Ed. 2d 851, 1981
U.S. LEXIS 2139 (1981).

Aggravating Circumstances.
Defendant's children-in-need-of-services
(CHINS) status and history is not a factor that can
be considered as an "aggravating circumstance."
Lane v. State, 551 N.E.2d 897, 1990 Ind. App.
LEXIS 375 (1990).
Enhancement of sentence was appropriate
based on aggravating circumstances of extreme
intoxication and repeated commission of alcohol-related offenses despite probation and short-term
imprisonment. Weida v. State, 693 N.E.2d 598,
1998 Ind. App. LEXIS 427 (1998).
Defendant was properly sentenced to the maximum term after pleading guilty to resisting law
enforcement and attempted residential entry,
where the trial court deemed defendant's violation
of a protective order, which was in effect with
respect to the person that was the target of defendant's attempted residential entry, a serious aggravating circumstance; further, the sentence was
not too harsh because the nature and circumstances of the crimes demonstrated a high level of
criminal purposefulness and moral culpability on

Aggravating Circumstances. (Cont'd)
defendant's part. Cox v. State, 792 N.E.2d 898, 2003 Ind. App. LEXIS 1410 (2003).

Defendant's right to jury trial was not violated by enhanced sentence where single aggravating circumstance, defendant's criminal record, alone was sufficient to enhance sentence and since jury is not required under Apprendi to find facts for enhancement if enhancement is based on criminal record; accordingly, it was unnecessary to consider whether trial court's consideration of other aggravating circumstances was improper. Williams v. State, 818 N.E.2d 970, 2004 Ind. App. LEXIS 2417 (2004), aff'd, 838 N.E.2d 1019, 2005 Ind. LEXIS 1110 (2005).

Where three aggravating factors used by trial court in imposing sentence, namely, that crime was committed in presence of person less than 18 years old, that there were many unarmed observers in extreme danger nearby, and that circumstances constituted worst type of criminal recklessness, were not found beyond reasonable doubt by jury, sentence beyond statutory presumptive term was improper. Heath v. State, 826 N.E.2d 650, 2005 Ind. LEXIS 426 (2005).

Where trial court erroneously imposed greater than presumptive terms for offenses of aggravated battery and criminal confinement without jury determination of aggravating factors as required by Sixth Amendment, reviewing court exercised its review and revise power under Ind. Const., art. 7, § 4 and AP. 7(B) to impose legal sentence. Williams v. State, 827 N.E.2d 1127, 2005 Ind. LEXIS 487 (2005).

Defendant by signing advisement and waiver of rights waived Apprendi rights, stipulated to facts in probable cause affidavit, and consented to judicial fact finding; accordingly, trial court in sentencing defendant for theft did not err in finding certain facts of crime to be aggravating factor and using that aggravating factor along with other aggravating factors to enhance presumptive sentence. Williams v. State, 836 N.E.2d 441, 2005 Ind. App. LEXIS 2035 (2005).

Defendant's 18-month sentence for obstruction of justice under IC 35-44-3-4(a)(4) was not an abuse of discretion because: (1) defendant presented no evidence supporting the special circumstances required to find an undue hardship on defendant's stepchildren due to defendant's incarceration; (2) the trial court considered defendant's lack of a criminal history as a mitigator; and (3) the trial court's finding of aggravators did not violate the Sixth Amendment as defendant received a presumptive sentence under IC 35-50-2-7. Roush v. State, 875 N.E.2d 801, 2007 Ind. App. LEXIS 2404 (2007).

—Assertion of Innocence.
Where there was no indication in the record that defendant's assertion of his innocence was in bad faith or amounted to disdain or recalcitrance, the trial court erred by enhancing defendant's sentence on that basis. Hollen v. State, 740 N.E.2d 149, 2000 Ind. App. LEXIS 2034 (2000), transfer granted, 753 N.E.2d 6, 2001 Ind. LEXIS 181 (2001), aff'd, 761 N.E.2d 398, 2002 Ind. LEXIS 48 (2002).

Alternative Sentencing Possibility.
Where the defendant enters a plea of guilty to a Class D felony, the trial judge advises him of the range of penalties appropriate to a Class D felony, but does not advise him of the alternative sentencing possibility pursuant to subsection (b), which allows penalties associated with a Class A misdemeanor to be levied, the defendant has not been adequately advised of the minimum possible sentence to which he was exposed upon entering a guilty plea. Shaw v. State, 456 N.E.2d 758, 1983 Ind. App. LEXIS 3662 (1983).

Appellate Adjustment of Sentence.
An appellate court will not adjust a sentence which is authorized by statute and which is not manifestly unreasonable in light of the nature of the offense and the character of the offender. A sentence is not manifestly unreasonable if any reasonable person could find the sentence to be appropriate to the particular offense and offender. Shanholt v. State, 448 N.E.2d 308, 1983 Ind. App. LEXIS 2861 (1983).

Defendant was improperly sentenced to 3 years' imprisonment for one count of child seduction because, in part, the trial court failed to consider defendant's lack of criminal history as a mitigator and further improperly considered defendant's position of trust with the victim, which was an element of the offense, as an aggravator; thus, the court reduced the sentence to a term of 1 years' imprisonment. Asher v. State, 790 N.E.2d 567, 2003 Ind. App. LEXIS 1108 (2003).

Applicability.
This section has no application to a sentence imposed under a prior law so as to change a felony conviction to a misdemeanor for the purposes of IC 35-50-2-8. Wise v. State, 272 Ind. 498, 400 N.E.2d 114, 1980 Ind. LEXIS 592 (1980).

Because IC 35-50-2-2 was a specific statute for suspended sentences and prevailed over the general sentencing parameters statute, IC 35-50-2-7, the trial court properly applied the specific statute in finding that the minimum non-suspendable part of defendant's sentence for his Class D felony conviction of operating while intoxicated with a prior conviction was one year rather than six months. Snider v. State, 753 N.E.2d 721, 2001 Ind. App. LEXIS 1323 (2001).

Basic Sentence.
The trial court does not err in sentencing the defendant to concurrent terms of ten years on child molesting and two years on incest, which are the statutory prescribed sentences. Newton v. State, 456 N.E.2d 736, 1983 Ind. App. LEXIS 3623 (1983).

Comparable Offenses.
Since perjury and obstruction of justice are offenses comparable to criminal contempt, in that they are Class D felonies, and the possible sentence for a Class D felony ranges from a minimum

Comparable Offenses. (Cont'd)
of six months to a maximum of three years, a trial court's sentence of eleven and one-half years for contempt of court was manifestly unreasonable, and remand for imposition of a sentence of three years was required. State v. MacWilliams (In re Gardner), 713 N.E.2d 346, 1999 Ind. App. LEXIS 1017 (1999).

Determining Status of Offense.
The trial court did not err in failing to determine the status of the offense as a Class A misdemeanor or a Class D felony prior to the start of the habitual offender proceeding. Sears v. State, 457 N.E.2d 192, 1983 Ind. LEXIS 1063 (1983).

—Ambiguous Sentence.
Where the sentence of a defendant, who was convicted of burglary, a Class D felony, and found to be an habitual offender, was reduced by the trial court from two years to one year, and it was ambiguous as to whether the court reduced the sentence due to mitigating factors or because it was treating the crime as a Class A misdemeanor, the case was remanded to the trial court for clarification, since the latter intention would require that the habitual offender conviction be expunged. Blatz v. State, 486 N.E.2d 990, 1985 Ind. LEXIS 1061 (1985).

Discretion of Court.
Under former IC 35-50-2-1.3(b), the trial court was not required to use an "advisory" sentence except in the three situations identified in IC 35-50-2-1.3(c), none of which applied to defendant. Therefore, the trial court was not required to impose the 18-month advisory sentence for a class D felony when sentencing defendant to a consecutive term. Robertson v. State, 871 N.E.2d 280, 2007 Ind. LEXIS 618 (2007).

—Aggravating and Mitigating Circumstances.
It is within the trial court's authority to determine the weight to be given aggravating and mitigating circumstances and to increase or decrease the sentence accordingly. Shanholt v. State, 448 N.E.2d 308, 1983 Ind. App. LEXIS 2861 (1983).
The four consecutive three-year sentences imposed by the trial court were not manifestly unreasonable since the court properly cited both aggravating and mitigating circumstances, concluding that the defendant's need for corrective and rehabilitative treatment in a penal facility outweighed the mitigating factor of his family's strong support. Ricketts v. State, 598 N.E.2d 597, 1992 Ind. App. LEXIS 1344 (1992).
Trial court had no obligation to accept as mitigating circumstances the factors submitted by defendant and properly considered defendant's prior criminal history to be an aggravating factor; that factor alone was sufficient to support defendant's enhanced sentence. Snyder v. State, 655 N.E.2d 1238, 1995 Ind. App. LEXIS 1176 (1995).
Even though defendant asserted certain factors he believed were mitigating, including his alcohol and drug use, the nonviolent nature of the crimes, and the likelihood that he would be deported which would eliminate the chances of further crimes, because the trial court is given the discretion to determine the weight to be given mitigating circumstances, the trial court did not err by not finding defendant's proposed mitigators significant. Mendoza v. State, 737 N.E.2d 784, 2000 Ind. App. LEXIS 1647 (2000).
Trial court did not err in imposing sentence upon defendant for defendant's home improvement fraud-related offenses pursuant to defendant's guilty pleas, because there was an aggravating factor of criminal history and defendant's proffered mitigating factors were properly rejected by a trial court where, in part, the trial court did not believe that defendant was merely a "bad businessman," defendant's last-minute guilty plea did not save judicial resources, and the claim of hardship to defendant's dependents was belied by the fact that defendant spent his money on gambling rather than on his dependents' support. Gray v. State, 790 N.E.2d 174, 2003 Ind. App. LEXIS 1061 (2003).
Trial court did not err in imposing a sentence upon defendant of 36 months in prison and 36 months of probation despite the fact that defendant did not have a criminal history, that defendant expressed remorse, that defendant pled guilty, and that incarceration would cause a hardship to defendant's family in a case where defendant pled guilty to confinement and sexual battery, both class D felonies; the victim's young age and defendant's violation of trust outweighed the mitigating factors. Bennett v. State, 862 N.E.2d 1281, 2007 Ind. App. LEXIS 530 (2007).
Determination of the appropriate habitual offender enhancement was within the range set forth in IC 35-50-2-8 and was left to the trial court's discretion and the relevant statutes did not impose a requirement that habitual offender enhancement had to be accompanied by a statement providing explanation for the length of the enhancement; thus, the trial court did not abuse its discretion by imposing a four-and-one-half-year habitual offender enhancement on one of defendant's intimidation convictions based on prior felonies. Montgomery v. State, 878 N.E.2d 262, 2007 Ind. App. LEXIS 2742 (2007).

Effective of Reduction of Prior Felony Conviction to Misdemeanor.
IC 35-50-2-2(b)(1) non-suspension rule still applied to defendant's sentence for a Class A felony conviction despite the fact that her earlier unrelated Class D felony conviction had been reduced to a misdemeanor after the sentencing on the Class A felony; when defendant was sentenced on the Class A felony, she had a prior unrelated Class D felony conviction, thus reduction of the Class D felony to a misdemeanor had only prospective operation, and trial court therefore had no authority to suspend the sentence on the Class A felony below the minimum at hearing on defendant's later motion to modify sentence. Gardiner v. State, 903 N.E.2d 557, 2009 Ind. App. LEXIS 641 (2009).

Harmless Error.
Any error by the trial court in offering to con-

Harmless Error. (Cont'd)
sider modification of the defendant's sentence if he made full restitution was harmless where the defendant did not accept the proposal and did not seek to modify his sentence based on the terms suggested by the court. Duren v. State, 720 N.E.2d 1198, 1999 Ind. App. LEXIS 2187 (1999).

Home Detention.
Because the minimum sentence for a Class D felony is six months under this section, and the minimum sentence for a Class C felony is two years, defendant could only be required to serve a maximum of two and one half years of his suspended sentences for a Class C felony and a Class D felony on home detention. Antcliff v. State, 688 N.E.2d 166, 1997 Ind. App. LEXIS 759 (1997).

Incompetent Defendants.
Even if defendant were to recover competency and then be tried and convicted of the charged offense, any incarceration she could receive would have to be reduced by the time spent in the state hospitals; thus, because the maximum term of incarceration for criminal recklessness as a Class D felony under IC 35-50-2-7 was three years, and because of the IC 35-50-6-3(a) credit time, defendant became immune from being sentenced to further confinement as of November 2006 by which time she had been confined for a total of 18 months. State v. Davis, 898 N.E.2d 281, 2008 Ind. LEXIS 1282 (2008).

Instructions.
Since jurors no longer fulfill any function regarding sentencing it was not error to refuse to instruct the jury as to the penalty for a Class D felony. Tinnin v. State, 275 Ind. 203, 416 N.E.2d 116, 1981 Ind. LEXIS 674 (1981).

Jurisdiction.
Where jurisdiction of court in criminal cases was limited to misdemeanors court had no jurisdiction to try a Class D felony even though the court imposed a sentence as for a misdemeanor. Childers v. State, 411 N.E.2d 157, 1980 Ind. App. LEXIS 1717 (1980).

Jury.
In Class D felony cases, such as theft, where the habitual offender status of the defendant is in issue, the defendant is entitled under IC 35-37-1-1 to a six, not a 12, person jury for all stages of the criminal case, including the felony sentencing hearing. Dyer v. State, 460 N.E.2d 511, 1984 Ind. LEXIS 768 (1984).

Minimum Sentence.
A defendant is properly advised of the minimum sentence for a Class D felony when informed of the possible misdemeanant sentencing under subsection (b). Wright v. State, 495 N.E.2d 804, 1986 Ind. App. LEXIS 2788 (1986).
IC 35-50-2-1 provides that the minimum sentence for a Class D felony is one year, but this section provides the court may reduce the one and one-half year presumptive sentence for a Class D

felony by up to one year, and because this section was most recently amended by the legislature, the minimum sentence for a Class D felony is six months. Antcliff v. State, 688 N.E.2d 166, 1997 Ind. App. LEXIS 759 (1997).

Modification of Sentence.
Although the trial court's offer to consider modifying the defendant's sentence if he made full restitution was improper, because restitution may not be ordered by a sentencing court without first inquiring into defendant's ability to pay, the issue was waived where the defendant discharged his counsel and indicated his interest in the court's proposal. Duren v. State, 720 N.E.2d 1198, 1999 Ind. App. LEXIS 2187 (1999).

One-Year Sentence Improper.
Trial court erred in ordering one year consecutive sentence for conviction of promoting professional gambling, since that offense is a Class D felony and carries a minimum two-year sentence. Atkins v. State, 437 N.E.2d 114, 1982 Ind. App. LEXIS 1296 (1982), cert. denied, 462 U.S. 1109, 103 S. Ct. 2460, 77 L. Ed. 2d 1337, 1983 U.S. LEXIS 448 (1983).

Order of Sentencing.
Trial court erred in failing to impose a sentence under this section for theft while giving only an "enhanced sentence" of 20 years upon a habitual offender finding, where the proper procedure would have been to sentence the defendant for theft and then to enhance the sentence. Carter v. State, 521 N.E.2d 669, 1988 Ind. LEXIS 100 (1988).
Trial court merged defendant's possession of cocaine conviction into his Class B felony dealing in cocaine conviction; therefore, to the extent that the trial court's sentencing statement read that defendant was convicted of and sentenced to 18 years for Class D felony possession of cocaine, when IC 35-50-2-7 specifically limited the penalty on Class D felonies to three years in prison, the matter had to be remanded for modification of the sentencing statement to reflect that defendant was convicted of and sentenced for only Class B felony dealing in cocaine. Washington v. State, — N.E.2d —, 2009 Ind. App. LEXIS 358 (2009).

Penalties Apportioned.
Sentencing under the current criminal code appropriately apportions penalties to the nature of the offense as required by Ind. Const., Art. 1, § 16. Wells v. State, 397 N.E.2d 1250, 1979 Ind. App. LEXIS 1481 (1979).

Penalty Fixed by Court.
Since under the statute the trial court is required to fix the penalty it was not error to refuse to give this section to the jury as an instruction. Inman v. State, 271 Ind. 491, 393 N.E.2d 767, 1979 Ind. LEXIS 707 (1979).

Prior Criminal Record.
It was proper for trial court to add two years for aggravating circumstances because of defendant's

Prior Criminal Record. (Cont'd)
prior criminal history. Evans v. State, 181 Ind. App. 687, 393 N.E.2d 246, 1979 Ind. App. LEXIS 1297 (1979).

It was not error for court to sentence defendant convicted of theft, a Class D felony, to a term of four years because of the rather extensive criminal record of the defendant. Gary v. State, 400 N.E.2d 215, 1980 Ind. App. LEXIS 1323 (1980).

—Defendant Not Prosecuted.
Court in finding aggravating circumstances could consider prior criminal activity although defendant was not prosecuted for such crimes. Bell v. State, 407 N.E.2d 1206, 1980 Ind. App. LEXIS 1592 (1980).

—Failure to Advise Defendant of Effect.
Aggravating circumstances may consist of defendant's prior criminal activity and therefore failure to advise defendant of the effect that prior convictions may have on his sentence prior to acceptance of his plea of guilty was reversible error. Bullock v. State, 406 N.E.2d 1220, 1980 Ind. App. LEXIS 1545 (1980).

Recommendation of Prosecutor.
The fact that prosecutor agreed with defendant that if he entered a plea of guilty he would not make a recommendation concerning sentencing and would make no objection if defendant asked for sentencing as a class A misdemeanor rather than a Class D felony, did not bind the court with respect to sentencing. Smith v. State, 181 Ind. App. 480, 392 N.E.2d 503, 1979 Ind. App. LEXIS 1269 (1979).

Reduction to Misdemeanor.
Under subsection (b), the trial court may enter a judgment of conviction for a Class A misdemeanor and sentence accordingly when the jury has found the defendant guilty of a Class D felony, but this statutory provision does not require the court to make this decision prior to the commencement of habitual offender proceedings. Rather, the court must state its reasons for the choice made whenever it exercises the power granted. Marsillett v. State, 495 N.E.2d 699, 1986 Ind. LEXIS 1206 (1986).

Where trial court, in addition to imposing term of imprisonment of 60 days, fined defendant $2,500 for felony offense of battery upon child causing injury, fine was inappropriate; trial court, in violation of IC 35-38-1-18(a), failed to hold indigency hearing, and failure of defendant to pay fine might jeopardize possibility that conviction would be reduced to Class A misdemeanor in future. Cooper v. State, 831 N.E.2d 1247, 2005 Ind. App. LEXIS 1422 (2005).

Defendant satisfied the first requirement of IC 35-38-1-1.5(a) because he pled guilty to operating a motor vehicle with a blood alcohol content greater than 0.08 with a previous conviction of operating while intoxicated, a Class D felony, he had not committed a prior felony that was reduced to a misdemeanor, and the offense was not one of domestic battery or possession of child pornogra-

phy; the additional conditions were met as well, and denial of defendant's motion to modify a Class D felony to a Class A misdemeanor was error because, under IC 35-38-1-1.5(d), once the trial court entered a conviction with an express provision to modify it and defendant completed the conditions imposed, the trial court was required to convert the conviction to a Class A misdemeanor. Leeth v. State, 868 N.E.2d 65, 2007 Ind. App. LEXIS 1259 (2007).

Evidence regarding plaintiff's second conviction for operating a vehicle while intoxicated might have been admissible as impeachment evidence under Fed. R. Evid. 609(a)(1) because that conviction was possibly a class D felony under Indiana law; however, pursuant to IC 35-50-2-7(b), plaintiff could have been convicted of a Class A misdemeanor instead, and conviction's probative value was significantly diminished under Fed. R. Evid. 609(b) because it was almost 10 years old; accordingly, conviction evidence should have been excluded under Fed. R. Evid. 403 because its prejudicial effect outweighed its probative value in plaintiff's slip-and-fall personal injury suit. Custer v. Schumacher Racing Corp., — F. Supp. 2d —, 2007 U.S. Dist. LEXIS 86877 (2007).

Review.
Appellate court will not adjust a sentence which is authorized by statute and which is not manifestly unreasonable in that no reasonable person could find it reasonable in light of nature of offense and character of offender. Atkins v. State, 437 N.E.2d 114, 1982 Ind. App. LEXIS 1296 (1982), cert. denied, 462 U.S. 1109, 103 S. Ct. 2460, 77 L. Ed. 2d 1337, 1983 U.S. LEXIS 448 (1983).

Sentence Proper.
Where defendant received one-year sentence for two Class D felonies, although this section, prior to the 1983 amendment, did not contemplate a one-year sentence for a Class D felony conviction, it was held that a defendant could not successfully claim prejudicial error because he received a lesser punishment than that prescribed by statute nor could he claim he was prejudiced because the commitment order reflected convictions for Class D felonies, as he was charged in both counts with Class D felonies and pled guilty to those charges. Harvey v. State, 498 N.E.2d 1231, 1986 Ind. LEXIS 1320 (1986).

Where defendant alleged that his four-year sentence, the maximum sentence for a conviction of a Class D felony, was excessive, but a review of the sentencing transcript showed that the trial court determined that defendant's lack of remorse and the fact that a short-term imprisonment would depreciate the seriousness of the crime were aggravating factors that persuaded the trial court to give him the maximum possible sentence, no error was found in the four-year sentence. Hatcher v. State, 510 N.E.2d 184, 1987 Ind. App. LEXIS 2854 (1987).

Where sentencing statement indicates a consideration of the facts of the subject crimes and the character of the defendant and adequately provides the reasons and logic supporting the en-

Sentence Proper. (Cont'd)

hanced sentence, it cannot be said no reasonable person could find the sentence appropriate to the particular offenses and offender, and thus, sentence of $10,000 fine and concurrent six and one-half years for burglary and three years for theft is not manifestly unreasonable. Herald v. State, 511 N.E.2d 5, 1987 Ind. App. LEXIS 2911 (1987).

After finding no mitigating circumstances and considering the defendant's status as a former attorney, the trial court did not commit reversible error by imposing a presumptive sentence of two years for theft of his clients' funds. Willis v. State, 512 N.E.2d 871, 1987 Ind. App. LEXIS 3061 (1987).

A sentence of 48 years for robbing the library at a children's hospital was upheld where defendant put three innocent children, two of whom had been diagnosed as terminally ill, in fear for their own safety and the safety of the people they loved; he worked at the hospital and knew the library was used by the children as a place to relax; and while he may have been under stress, his stress could not have been any greater than that of the persons he chose to rob. Harris v. State, 616 N.E.2d 25, 1993 Ind. App. LEXIS 702 (1993).

There was sufficient evidence to find that defendant knew of nursing home patient's propensities to engage in deviate sexual behavior when she took two girls, ages 11 and 12, to visit him and allegedly showed them how to perform oral sex on him, and a sentence of three years was not unreasonable considering that there was also a baby in the room at the time of the incident. Harrison v. State, 644 N.E.2d 888, 1994 Ind. App. LEXIS 1779 (1994).

Where trial court initially sentenced defendant to the presumptive 30 years' imprisonment for dealing in cocaine as a Class A felony and three years' imprisonment for failure to pay the controlled substance excise tax, and the court noted his extensive criminal history as an aggravating circumstance and the mitigating circumstances of his age and the total sentence, as its basis for the sentence given, the trial court's decision to impose an aggravated three-year sentence to be served concurrently with his sentences for dealing in cocaine was not manifestly unreasonable. Woods v. State, 654 N.E.2d 1153, 1995 Ind. LEXIS 114 (1995).

Where the defendant's sentence for dealing in marijuana and maintaining a common nuisance was within the statutorily authorized sentence, and where the trial court enumerated the factors it relied upon with regard to the nature of the offense and the offender, a sentence of one and one-half years on each count to be served concurrently, with six months suspended, was not manifestly unreasonable. Ladd v. State, 710 N.E.2d 188, 1999 Ind. App. LEXIS 425 (1999).

The trial court's sentence was reasonable where the court identified aggravating and mitigating factors, and it was clear from the record of the sentencing hearing and the sentencing order that the trial court thoughtfully considered and weighed all of the factors. Nantz v. State, 740 N.E.2d 1276, 2001 Ind. App. LEXIS 10 (2001).

Sentence of seven years to the Department of Correction for a Class D Felony with a habitual offender enhancement was proper. Watson v. State, 776 N.E.2d 914, 2002 Ind. App. LEXIS 1702 (2002).

Pursuant to IC 35-50-2-7, trial court properly enhanced defendant's sentence for conviction of pointing firearm, a Class D felony under IC 35-47-4-3, to maximum sentence of three years. Spears v. State, 811 N.E.2d 485, 2004 Ind. App. LEXIS 1331 (2004).

Eight-year sentence following guilty plea to operating vehicle while intoxicated causing serious injury and to being habitual traffic violator was valid even though, due to scrivener's error, plea agreement did not mention habitual traffic violator charge. Wells v. State, 836 N.E.2d 475, 2005 Ind. App. LEXIS 2034 (2005).

After defendant pleaded guilty to resisting law enforcement as a class D felony, battery as a class D felony, and intimidation as a class D felony, the trial court properly imposed a three-year sentence, based on its finding that defendant's acceptance of responsibility was a mitigating factor and that his extensive criminal history, which included felony convictions involving battery against police officers and resisting law enforcement, was an aggravating factor. The record did not clearly support a finding of undue hardship as a mitigating factor. Phillips v. State, 869 N.E.2d 512, 2007 Ind. App. LEXIS 1495 (2007).

Defendant was not entitled to a sentence no greater than the one-and-one-half year advisory sentence that IC 35-50-2-7 set for a Class D felony and, thus, imposition of a two-and-one-half year sentence on defendant's conviction for domestic battery as a Class D felony in violation IC 35-42-2-1.3 was not prohibited; defendant did not show that any exceptions applied that would prohibit imposition of a sentence higher than the advisory sentence. Freyn v. State, 884 N.E.2d 901, 2008 Ind. App. LEXIS 791 (2008).

Cited:

Stockton v. State, 180 Ind. App. 233, 388 N.E.2d 290, 1979 Ind. App. LEXIS 1108 (1979); Vicory v. State, 272 Ind. 683, 400 N.E.2d 1380, 1980 Ind. LEXIS 619 (1980); Pitts v. State, 410 N.E.2d 1387, 1980 Ind. App. LEXIS 1663 (1980); Bish v. State, 421 N.E.2d 608, 1981 Ind. LEXIS 758 (1981); Gilbert v. State, 426 N.E.2d 1333, 1981 Ind. App. LEXIS 1701 (1981); Funk v. State, 427 N.E.2d 1081, 1981 Ind. LEXIS 904 (1981); Ricketts v. State, 429 N.E.2d 289, 1981 Ind. App. LEXIS 1796 (1981); Hatton v. State, 439 N.E.2d 565, 1982 Ind. LEXIS 948 (1982); Abercrombie v. State, 441 N.E.2d 442, 1982 Ind. LEXIS 1005 (1982); Gross v. State, 444 N.E.2d 296, 1983 Ind. LEXIS 731 (1983); Busam v. State, 445 N.E.2d 118, 1983 Ind. App. LEXIS 2632 (1983); Eubank v. State, 456 N.E.2d 1012, 1983 Ind. LEXIS 1062 (1983); McMichael v. State, 471 N.E.2d 726, 1984 Ind. App. LEXIS 3105 (1984); Lucas v. State, 491 N.E.2d 1026, 1986 Ind. App. LEXIS 2548 (1986); Williams v. State, 493 N.E.2d 431, 1986 Ind. LEXIS 1146 (1986); Johnson v. State, 507 N.E.2d 980, 1987 Ind. LEXIS 926 (1987); Barker v. State, 508 N.E.2d

795, 1987 Ind. LEXIS 948 (1987); Tate v. State, 515 N.E.2d 1145, 1987 Ind. App. LEXIS 3250 (1987); Kail v. State, 528 N.E.2d 799, 1988 Ind. App. LEXIS 659 (1988); Auten v. State, 542 N.E.2d 215, 1989 Ind. App. LEXIS 777 (1989); Brown v. State, 613 N.E.2d 69, 1993 Ind. App. LEXIS 471 (1993); Meriweather v. State, 659 N.E.2d 133, 1995 Ind. App. LEXIS 1572 (1995); Singer v. State, 674 N.E.2d 11, 1996 Ind. App. LEXIS 1605 (1996); United States v. Jackson, 177 F.3d 628, 1999 U.S. App. LEXIS 8513 (7th Cir. Ind. 1999); Meagher v. State, 726 N.E.2d 260, 2000 Ind. LEXIS 245 (2000); Bailey v. State, 731 N.E.2d 447, 2000 Ind. App. LEXIS 893 (2000); Sanders v. State, 734 N.E.2d 646, 2000 Ind. App. LEXIS 1338 (2000); Armstrong v. State, 742 N.E.2d 972, 2001 Ind. App. LEXIS 23 (2001); In re Cheslek, 741 N.E.2d 1244, 2001 Ind. LEXIS 128 (2001); Allen v. State, 743 N.E.2d 1222, 2001 Ind. App. LEXIS 367 (2001); Lashley v. State, 745 N.E.2d 254, 2001 Ind. App. LEXIS 505 (2001); Haycraft v. State, 760 N.E.2d 203, 2001 Ind. App. LEXIS 2225 (2001); Stroud v. Lints, 760 N.E.2d 1176, 2002 Ind. App. LEXIS 27 (2002); Hollen v. State, 761 N.E.2d 398, 2002 Ind. LEXIS 48 (2002); Simmons v. State, 773 N.E.2d 823, 2002 Ind. App. LEXIS 1215 (2002); Bennett v. State, 787 N.E.2d 938, 2003 Ind. App. LEXIS 762 (2003); Cox v. State, 792 N.E.2d 878, 2003 Ind. App. LEXIS 1371 (2003); Jones v. State, 807 N.E.2d 58, 2004 Ind. App. LEXIS 752 (2004); Dixon v. State, 825 N.E.2d 1269, 2005 Ind. App. LEXIS 719 (2005); $ 100 v. State, 822 N.E.2d 1001, 2005 Ind. App. LEXIS 224 (2005); Stokes v. State, 828 N.E.2d 937, 2005 Ind. App. LEXIS 1056 (2005); McMahon v. State, 856 N.E.2d 743, 2006 Ind. App. LEXIS 2333 (2006); Warr v. State, 877 N.E.2d 817, 2007 Ind. App. LEXIS 2732 (2007); Anglemyer v. State, 868 N.E.2d 482, 2007 Ind. LEXIS 490 (2007); Kemp v. State, 887 N.E.2d 102, 2008 Ind. App. LEXIS 1159 (2008); Burke v. Bennett, 896 N.E.2d 505, 2008 Ind. App. LEXIS 2530 (2008); Lewis v. State, 898 N.E.2d 1286, 2009 Ind. App. LEXIS 15 (2009).

RESEARCH REFERENCES

Indiana Law Review.
Survey: Criminal Law and Procedure, 37 Ind. L. Rev. 1003 (2004).

Collateral References.
Downward departure under state sentencing guidelines based on extraordinary family circumstances. 106 A.L.R.5th 377.

35-50-2-7.1. [Repealed.]

Compiler's Notes.
This section, providing for sentencing defendants as habitual Class D offenders, was repealed by P.L.164-1993, § 14, effective July 1, 1993.

35-50-2-8. Habitual offenders.

(a) Except as otherwise provided in this section, the state may seek to have a person sentenced as a habitual offender for any felony by alleging, on a page separate from the rest of the charging instrument, that the person has accumulated two (2) prior unrelated felony convictions.

(b) The state may not seek to have a person sentenced as a habitual offender for a felony offense under this section if:

(1) the offense is a misdemeanor that is enhanced to a felony in the same proceeding as the habitual offender proceeding solely because the person had a prior unrelated conviction;

(2) the offense is an offense under IC 9-30-10-16 or IC 9-30-10-17; or

(3) all of the following apply:

(A) The offense is an offense under IC 16-42-19 or IC 35-48-4.

(B) The offense is not listed in section 2(b)(4) [IC 35-50-2-2(b)(4)] of this chapter.

(C) The total number of unrelated convictions that the person has for:

(i) dealing in or selling a legend drug under IC 16-42-19-27;

(ii) dealing in cocaine or a narcotic drug (IC 35-48-4-1);

(iii) dealing in a schedule I, II, III controlled substance (IC 35-48-4-2);

(iv) dealing in a schedule IV controlled substance (IC 35-48-4-3; and

(v) dealing in a schedule V controlled substance (IC 35-48-4-4);

does not exceed one (1).

(c) A person has accumulated two (2) prior unrelated felony convictions for purposes of this section only if:

(1) the second prior unrelated felony conviction was committed after sentencing for the first prior unrelated felony conviction; and

(2) the offense for which the state seeks to have the person sentenced as a habitual offender was committed after sentencing for the second prior unrelated felony conviction.

(d) A conviction does not count for purposes of this section as a prior unrelated felony conviction if:

(1) the conviction has been set aside;

(2) the conviction is one for which the person has been pardoned; or

(3) all of the following apply:

(A) The offense is an offense under IC 16-42-19 or IC 35-48-4.

(B) The offense is not listed in section 2(b)(4) of this chapter.

(C) The total number of unrelated convictions that the person has for:

(i) dealing in or selling a legend drug under IC 16-42-19-27;

(ii) dealing in cocaine or a narcotic drug (IC 35-48-4-1);

(iii) dealing in a schedule I, II, III controlled substance (IC 35-48-4-2);

(iv) dealing in a schedule IV controlled substance (IC 35-48-4-3; and

(v) dealing in a schedule V controlled substance (IC 35-48-4-4);

does not exceed one (1).

(e) The requirements in subsection (b) do not apply to a prior unrelated felony conviction that is used to support a sentence as a habitual offender. A prior unrelated felony conviction may be used under this section to support a sentence as a habitual offender even if the sentence for the prior unrelated offense was enhanced for any reason, including an enhancement because the person had been convicted of another offense. However, a prior unrelated felony conviction under IC 9-30-10-16, IC 9-30-10-17, IC 9-12-3-1 (repealed), or IC 9-12-3-2 (repealed) may not be used to support a sentence as a habitual offender.

(f) If the person was convicted of the felony in a jury trial, the jury shall reconvene for the sentencing hearing. If the trial was to the court or the judgment was entered on a guilty plea, the court alone shall conduct the sentencing hearing under IC 35-38-1-3.

(g) A person is a habitual offender if the jury (if the hearing is by jury) or the court (if the hearing is to the court alone) finds that the state has proved beyond a reasonable doubt that the person had accumulated two (2) prior unrelated felony convictions.

(h) The court shall sentence a person found to be a habitual offender to an additional fixed term that is not less than the advisory sentence for the underlying offense nor more than three (3) times the advisory sentence for the underlying offense. However, the additional sentence may not exceed thirty (30) years.

History.

IC 35-50-2-8, as added by Acts 1976, P.L.148, § 8; 1977, P.L.340, § 121; 1980, P.L.210, § 1; P.L.335-1983, § 1; P.L.328-1985, § 2; P.L.1-1990, § 353; P.L.164-1993, § 13; P.L.140-1994, § 14; P.L.305-1995, § 1; P.L.166-2001, § 3; P.L.291-2001, § 226; P.L.71-2005, § 11.

Compiler's Notes.

P.L.291-2001, § 228, effective May 11, 2001, provides:

"(a) This subsection applies only to a person whose community transition program commencement date is less than forty-five (45) days after the effective date of this SECTION solely as a result of the amendment of IC 11-8-1-5.6 by this act. The community transition program commencement date for a person described by this subsection is forty-five (45) days after the effective date of this SECTION.

"(b) IC 35-50-2-8(b)(3), as amended by this act, applies only if the last offense for which the state seeks to have the person sentenced as a habitual offender was committed after June 30, 2001. IC 35-50-2-10, as amended by this act, applies only if the last offense for which the state seeks to have the person sentenced as a habitual substance offender was committed after June 30, 2001. However, a prior unrelated conviction committed before, on, or after July 1, 2001, may be used to qualify an offender as a habitual offender under IC 35-50-2-8 or as a habitual substance offender under IC 35-50-2-10."

NOTES TO DECISIONS

Motor Vehicle Violations.
Notice.
—Adequate.
Number of Felonies.
Penal Institution.
Penalty for Prior Conviction.
Prejudice to Defendant.
—Not Shown.
Prior Convictions.
—Aggravating and Mitigating Circumstances.
—Collateral Attack.
—Constitutional Attack.
—Constitutional Validity.
—Dates of Commission.
—Escape Prosecution.
—Incarceration.
—Non-Violent Offenses.
—Presentence Reports.
—Set Aside.
—Special Verdict Forms.
—Third Prior Conviction.
—Under "Minor Statute."
—Unrelated Felony.
Probable Cause.
Proof of Habitual Offender Status.
—Burden of Proof.
—Cross Examination.
—Number of Convictions.
—Proof Required.
Proportionality.
Propriety of Charge.
Prosecutorial Discretion.
Records of Prior Trials.
—Prior Convictions Entered on Guilty Pleas.
Reduced Sentence.
—Discretion of Judge.
—Provision Not Retroactive.
—When Permitted.
Retrial.
—Vacation of Prior Conviction.
Retroactive Application.
Role of Court.
Sentence Under Old Statute.
Sentence Unreasonable.
Sentences Reasonable.
Sentencing Hearing.
—Evidence.
Separate Proceedings.
Successive Prosecutions.
Suspension of Sentence.
Third Prior Conviction.
—Striking Recent Felony.
Trial on Enhancement.
—Charge Enhancement and Habitual Offender.
Verdict.

In General.
   Habitual criminality is a state and not a crime. Goodman v. Kunkle, 72 F.2d 334, 1934 U.S. App. LEXIS 4542 (7th Cir. Ind. 1934), cert. denied, 293 U.S. 619, 55 S. Ct. 218, 79 L. Ed. 707, 1934 U.S. LEXIS 396 (1934).
   Habitual criminal statutes do not create or define a new or independent crime, but prescribe circumstances wherein one guilty of a specific crime may be more severely penalized because of his previous criminalities as they are alleged and

proved. Goodman v. Kunkle, 72 F.2d 334, 1934 U.S. App. LEXIS 4542 (7th Cir. Ind. 1934), cert. denied, 293 U.S. 619, 55 S. Ct. 218, 79 L. Ed. 707, 1934 U.S. LEXIS 396 (1934).
   The allegation and proof of former convictions by the accused are made for the single purpose of classifying the defendant as an habitual criminal, and for no other purpose. Metzger v. State, 214 Ind. 113, 13 N.E.2d 519, 1938 Ind. LEXIS 149 (1938).
   To authorize a sentence under the former statute, the previous convictions, sentences, and imprisonments had to be described specifically, and the jury had to find that the defendant was convicted, sentenced, and imprisoned in the instances described, and not otherwise. Midland v. State, 220 Ind. 668, 46 N.E.2d 200, 1943 Ind. LEXIS 278 (1943).
   The enactment of former IC 35-8-8-2 did not change the rules of evidence, nor increase the malignity of the crime, nor take the presumption of innocence away from a defendant, nor did it affect the rule as to the credibility of a defendant. Smith v. State, 227 Ind. 672, 87 N.E.2d 881, 1949 Ind. LEXIS 179 (1949).
   Before one could be sentenced under the former law, it had to be shown that he had previously been twice convicted, twice sentenced and twice imprisoned for felony, that the commission of the second offense was subsequent to his imprisonment upon conviction for the first and that the commission of principal offense was subsequent to his imprisonment upon conviction for the second. Cooper v. State, 259 Ind. 107, 284 N.E.2d 799, 1972 Ind. LEXIS 447 (1972).
   A life sentence was mandatory when two previous felony convictions, sentences, and imprisonments were alleged and proved, and defendant was convicted of a third felony. McCormick v. State, 262 Ind. 303, 317 N.E.2d 428, 1974 Ind. LEXIS 302 (1974).
   The enhanced penalty under the habitual criminal statute is imposed neither for the prior crimes nor for the status of habitual offender, but for the underlying crime involved in the current proceedings, and the habitual criminal statute to be applied is the one in effect at the time the underlying crime was committed, not the one in effect at the time of the commission of the prior criminal offenses. Collins v. State, 275 Ind. 86, 415 N.E.2d 46, 1981 Ind. LEXIS 657 (1981), cert. denied, 451 U.S. 991, 101 S. Ct. 2331, 68 L. Ed. 2d 851, 1981 U.S. LEXIS 2139 (1981).
   Fundamentally, the habitual criminal statute does not create a criminal offense. Smith v. State, 422 N.E.2d 1179, 1981 Ind. LEXIS 775 (1981).
   The purpose of this section is to more severely penalize those persons whom prior sanctions have failed to deter from committing felonies. Baker v. State, 425 N.E.2d 98, 1981 Ind. LEXIS 823 (1981); Graham v. State, 435 N.E.2d 560, 1982 Ind. LEXIS 825 (1982).
   Since habitual criminality is a vehicle for the enhancement of punishment upon the conviction of an additional, substantive crime, prior convictions used to establish the fact of habitual criminality at one trial can be used again after a subsequent

In General. (Cont'd)

felony conviction. This is based upon the reasoning that the use of the prior convictions is for a determination of status only and the additional punishment is imposed for each new crime, not for crimes for which the defendant has already been convicted and punished. Baker v. State, 425 N.E.2d 98, 1981 Ind. LEXIS 823 (1981).

It is clearly established that this section seeks to provide a fair procedure by which an individual convicted of a felony may receive an enhanced sentence. Turpin v. State, 435 N.E.2d 1, 1982 Ind. LEXIS 809 (1982).

To sustain conviction under this section, the state must show that the defendant had been previously twice convicted and twice sentenced for felonies, that commission of second offense was subsequent to his having been sentenced upon the first and that commission of principal offense upon which enhanced punishment is being sought was subsequent to his having been sentenced upon the second conviction. Graham v. State, 435 N.E.2d 560, 1982 Ind. LEXIS 825 (1982); Bray v. State, 547 N.E.2d 862, 1989 Ind. App. LEXIS 1284 (Ind. App. 1989).

A sentence upon a finding of habitual criminality is not imposed as "consecutive" to the sentence imposed for the underlying felony conviction; rather, the underlying felony sentence is enhanced by 30 years. Short v. State, 443 N.E.2d 298, 1982 Ind. LEXIS 1063 (1982).

Finding that defendant was an habitual offender allowed the trial court to enhance the sentence of the underlying felony, but did not allow the trial court to sentence the defendant simply for being an habitual offender because that is not a criminal offense in and of itself. St. Mociers v. State, 459 N.E.2d 26, 1984 Ind. LEXIS 747 (1984).

The enhanced penalty was imposed for the underlying crime charged in the current proceeding and did not impose punishment for a separate crime. Mc Brady v. State, 459 N.E.2d 719, 1984 Ind. LEXIS 755 (1984).

Habitual offender sentencing provision is neither a separate criminal charge nor an additional penalty for an earlier crime. The status of an habitual offender is not an offense or crime in itself but is a circumstance which calls for enhancement of sentence. Kalady v. State, 462 N.E.2d 1299, 1984 Ind. LEXIS 818 (1984).

At sentencing the trial court must specify the underlying felony to which an enhanced sentence for habitual criminality applies where there are two or more underlying felonies. Edwards v. State, 479 N.E.2d 541, 1985 Ind. LEXIS 868 (1985); Plummer v. State, 485 N.E.2d 1367, 1985 Ind. LEXIS 1054 (Ind. 1985).

Recidivism is a status, not a separate crime, which requires enhancement of an underlying sentence instead of the imposition of a consecutive sentence. Bowens v. State, 496 N.E.2d 769, 1986 Ind. LEXIS 1256 (1986).

Where the enhancement of a sentence under this section was found to be improper, it was not improper to enhance the original presumptive sentence based on the defendant's long criminal history and with no retaliatory motive present. Williams v. State, 494 N.E.2d 1001, 1986 Ind. App. LEXIS 2715 (1986), cert. denied, 481 U.S. 1054, 107 S. Ct. 2191, 95 L. Ed. 2d 846, 1987 U.S. LEXIS 2168 (1987).

Being a habitual offender is not a separate crime but rather a status requiring the trial judge to enhance a penalty already given. Petro v. State, 506 N.E.2d 467, 1987 Ind. LEXIS 891 (1987).

To sustain a sentence under the Habitual Offender Statute, the state must show that the defendant had been twice convicted and twice sentenced for felonies. The commission of the second offense must have been subsequent to the sentencing on the first offense, and the commission of the principal offense on which the enhanced punishment is being sought must be subsequent to the sentencing on the second conviction. Where there is no evidence in the record of the date of the commission of the offense to which the second prior conviction alleged in the information related because the state documented defendant's conviction through the commitment records of the department of correction and did not show when the offense was committed, this is fundamental error and the habitual offender determination will be vacated although the defendant did not raise the issue on appeal. Jordan v. State, 510 N.E.2d 655, 1987 Ind. LEXIS 993 (1987).

This section requires that the trial be bifurcated: that the jury first determine the defendant's guilt on the instant charge, and that they then reconvene to determine the defendant's status on the charge that he is an habitual offender. The habitual offender phase of the proceedings is not a separate trial but is a bifurcated continuation of the entire proceeding. Wine v. State, 539 N.E.2d 932, 1989 Ind. LEXIS 171 (1989).

The trial court's act of setting aside the habitual offender determination in reality constituted a refusal to enhance the defendant's sentence rather than a finding that the jury erred by determining the defendant an habitual offender. Abron v. State, 591 N.E.2d 634, 1992 Ind. App. LEXIS 793 (1992).

To establish that the defendant is a habitual offender, the State must prove beyond a reasonable doubt that the defendant has been previously convicted of two separate and unrelated felonies, and to be "unrelated," the commission of the second felony must be subsequent to the sentencing for the first, and the sentencing for the second felony must have preceded the commission of the current felony for which the enhanced sentence is being sought. Where the evidence did not establish the commission date of the second felony, the habitual offender enhancement was ordered vacated. Flint v. State, 750 N.E.2d 340, 2001 Ind. LEXIS 542 (2001).

Court properly used defendant's 1989 conviction of Class C felony battery to support both possession of firearm by serious violent felon conviction and habitual offender finding. Townsend v. State, 793 N.E.2d 1092, 2003 Ind. App. LEXIS 1526 (2003).

—Purpose.

The purpose of sentence enhancement under

In General. (Cont'd)

—Purpose. (Cont'd)
this section is to penalize more severely those persons whom prior sanctions have failed to deter from committing felonies. Marsillett v. State, 495 N.E.2d 699, 1986 Ind. LEXIS 1206 (1986).

The purpose of the habitual offender statute is to more severely penalize those persons whom prior sanctions have failed to deter from committing felonies and the additional punishment is imposed for each new crime and not for crimes for which a defendant has already been convicted and punished. Powers v. State, 539 N.E.2d 950, 1989 Ind. LEXIS 184 (1989).

—Sentence Under Old Statute.
This statute was not meant to be applied to indeterminate sentencing procedures which were in existence prior to October 1, 1977. Beavers v. State, 465 N.E.2d 1388, 1984 Ind. LEXIS 891 (1984).

Constitutionality.
The habitual criminal act (former IC 35-8-8-2) was constitutional. Goodman v. Daly, 201 Ind. 332, 165 N.E. 906, 1929 Ind. LEXIS 45 (1929); Gurecki v. State, 240 Ind. 177, 161 N.E.2d 610, 1959 Ind. LEXIS 266 (1959).

The former law did not deny equal protection of the law. Barr v. State, 205 Ind. 481, 187 N.E. 259, 1933 Ind. LEXIS 98 (1933).

Former IC 35-8-8-2 did not violate § 14 of Art. 1 of the Constitution prohibiting double jeopardy, nor did the admission in evidence of prior convictions contravene the Fifth Amendment to the U.S. Constitution which operates exclusively in restriction of federal power and has no application to the state. Hanks v. State, 225 Ind. 593, 76 N.E.2d 702, 1948 Ind. LEXIS 117 (1948). See, however, Lawrence v. State, 259 Ind. 306, 286 N.E.2d 830, 1972 Ind. LEXIS 478 (1972), holding evidence of prior convictions would violate due process clause unless there were separate proceedings.

The habitual criminal act did not violate the constitutional provision that no person shall be compelled to testify against himself. Smith v. State, 227 Ind. 672, 87 N.E.2d 881, 1949 Ind. LEXIS 179 (1949).

Punishment as an habitual criminal is not punishment for a status but punishment for the last crime committed and is therefore within the exception to the 13th Amendment of the U.S. Constitution permitting involuntary servitude as punishment for crime. United States ex rel. Smith v. Dowd, 271 F.2d 292, 1959 U.S. App. LEXIS 3250 (7th Cir. Ind. 1959), cert. denied, 362 U.S. 978, 80 S. Ct. 1063, 4 L. Ed. 2d 1013, 1960 U.S. LEXIS 1181 (1960).

Where a defendant was charged in the same proceeding with a separate felony and as habitual criminal, admission of evidence of defendant's prior crimes, which were not shown to be relevant to the felony charge, constituted a denial of defendant's rights under the due process of law clause of the 14th Amendment, United States Constitution, and the due course of law clause of Ind. Const., Art.

1, § 12. Lawrence v. State, 259 Ind. 306, 286 N.E.2d 830, 1972 Ind. LEXIS 478 (1972).

This section is not repugnant to Ind. Const., art. 1, § 18. Funk v. State, 427 N.E.2d 1081, 1981 Ind. LEXIS 904 (1981).

This section does not contravene Ind. Const., art. 3, § 1. Badelle v. State, 434 N.E.2d 872, 1982 Ind. LEXIS 815 (1982).

This section is not unconstitutional as an ex post facto law, or on grounds that it deprives defendant of a fair trial by requiring him to be tried on habitual count before same jury that heard evidence on substantive offense, or that prosecutor may arbitrarily enforce it by determining without adequate guidelines whom to prosecute. Yager v. State, 437 N.E.2d 454, 1982 Ind. LEXIS 874 (1982).

This section does not contravene U.S. Const., Amend. 8 or Ind. Const., Art. 1, § 18. Erickson v. State, 438 N.E.2d 269, 1982 Ind. LEXIS 911 (1982).

A combined sentence of 32 years for the Class D felony of stealing gasoline including an enhanced term of 30 years after a habitual offender finding as to prior unrelated Class D felonies, was not so disproportionate that no reasonable person could find it appropriate to the particular offense and offender. Hensley v. State, 497 N.E.2d 1053, 1986 Ind. LEXIS 1283 (1986).

The Indiana habitual offender statute does not provide for a second offense, but establishes a status of a defendant which provides for an enhanced sentence for the instant felony. Thus, it does not violate the federal constitutional proscriptions against bills of attainder or ex post facto laws. Keeby v. State, 511 N.E.2d 1005, 1987 Ind. LEXIS 1015 (1987).

—Bifurcated Trial.
In a bifurcated trial under this section the jury is not asked to find defendant guilty of another charge, but merely to find facts which would enhance defendant's sentence and therefore defendant is not denied right to trial by an impartial jury. Wise v. State, 272 Ind. 498, 400 N.E.2d 114, 1980 Ind. LEXIS 592 (1980); Ferguson v. State, 273 Ind. 468, 405 N.E.2d 902, 1980 Ind. LEXIS 695 (1980).

The bifurcated nature of the habitual offender proceeding has been determined to be necessary by the state Supreme Court in order to guarantee the accused's right to a fair trial on the underlying felony charge. Turpin v. State, 435 N.E.2d 1, 1982 Ind. LEXIS 809 (1982).

Where the same jury that heard the first phase of the defendant's habitual offender case heard the second phase of the case, and there was no doubt that the jury, while listening to the second phase of the case, had every right to consider all that it had heard in the first phase, this procedure did not deny defendant his Sixth Amendment right to a trial by jury. Brooke v. Duckworth, 824 F. Supp. 839, 1992 U.S. Dist. LEXIS 21481 (N.D. Ind. 1992), aff'd without op., 993 F.2d 1549, 1993 U.S. App. LEXIS 19557 (7th Cir. Ind. 1993).

—Cruel and Unusual Punishment.
A life sentence for an habitual criminal is not so disproportionate to the underlying offense as to

Constitutionality. (Cont'd)

—Cruel and Unusual Punishment. (Cont'd)
constitute cruel and unusual punishment. Parks v. State, 270 Ind. 689, 389 N.E.2d 286, 1979 Ind. LEXIS 593 (1979).

The habitual criminal statute does not impose cruel and unusual punishment. Norris v. State, 271 Ind. 568, 394 N.E.2d 144, 1979 Ind. LEXIS 720 (1979).

The imposition of a life sentence when the previous crimes did not involve violence did not amount to cruel and unusual punishment. Mitchell v. State, 272 Ind. 369, 398 N.E.2d 1254, 1979 Ind. LEXIS 814 (1979).

The additional 30-year sentence imposed on an habitual offender under this section does not constitute vindictive justice nor cruel and unusual punishment and is not unconstitutional. Wise v. State, 272 Ind. 498, 400 N.E.2d 114, 1980 Ind. LEXIS 592 (1980); Ferguson v. State, 273 Ind. 468, 405 N.E.2d 902, 1980 Ind. LEXIS 695 (1980).

Where underlying crimes of which defendant was convicted drew sentences of only five and two years respectively the 30-year sentence for being an habitual offender was not so grossly out of proportion to the severity of the crime as to violate Ind. Const., art. 1, § 16 or U.S. Const., Amend. 8. Comstock v. State, 273 Ind. 259, 406 N.E.2d 1164, 1980 Ind. LEXIS 661 (1980).

The penalty imposed by the habitual offender statute is not so grossly disproportionate to the offense committed as to constitute cruel and unusual punishment. Whitacre v. State, 274 Ind. 554, 412 N.E.2d 1202, 1980 Ind. LEXIS 827 (1980); Garland v. State, 444 N.E.2d 1180, 1983 Ind. LEXIS 750 (1983).

This section does not impose cruel and unusual punishment in contravention of Ind. Const., Art. 1, § 16 or U.S. Const., Amend. 8 or 14. Traylor v. State, 420 N.E.2d 887, 1981 Ind. LEXIS 748 (1981).

This section does not violate the proscription against cruel and unusual punishment by improperly vesting unlimited discretion in the prosecutor to determine whom and whom not to punish under the statute. Funk v. State, 427 N.E.2d 1081, 1981 Ind. LEXIS 904 (1981).

The habitual offender statute does not impose cruel and unusual punishment. State v. Williams, 430 N.E.2d 756, 1982 Ind. LEXIS 730 (1982), superseded by statute as stated in, Bauer v. State, 875 N.E.2d 744, 2007 Ind. App. LEXIS 2391 (2007).

Sentence of four years imprisonment enhanced by 30 years based on defendant's status as an habitual offender for conviction of illegal possession of a handgun, a Class D felony, did not constitute cruel and unusual punishment. Woods v. State, 471 N.E.2d 691, 1984 Ind. LEXIS 1058 (1984).

The Eighth Amendment right against greatly disproportionate sentences in relation to the severity of the crime was not violated when two sentences of two years each were imposed, to be served concurrently, for two convictions of burglary, plus a 30-year sentence on an habitual

offender count. Coble v. State, 476 N.E.2d 102, 1985 Ind. LEXIS 784 (1985).

A sentence of 36 years of imprisonment for burglary, as enhanced by an habitual offender determination, did not constitute cruel and unusual punishment, despite the defendant's criminal history allegedly being caused by alcohol addiction. Craig v. State, 481 N.E.2d 390, 1985 Ind. LEXIS 1083 (1985).

The enhanced sentence provided for the recidivist offender by the habitual offender statute does not constitute cruel and unusual punishment, even though the principal offense is burglary and may be characterized as nonviolent in nature. Beach v. State, 496 N.E.2d 43, 1986 Ind. LEXIS 1233 (1986).

Habitual offender finding did not constitute cruel and unusual punishment where the prior felonies, with one exception, were theft related and more than 25 years old. Hammers v. State, 502 N.E.2d 1339, 1987 Ind. LEXIS 821 (1987).

—Double Jeopardy.
The habitual offender procedures do not unconstitutionally subject the defendant to two trials. Ferguson v. State, 273 Ind. 468, 405 N.E.2d 902, 1980 Ind. LEXIS 695 (1980); Dorton v. State, 419 N.E.2d 1289, 1981 Ind. LEXIS 738 (1981).

An habitual criminal proceeding based on two prior felonies did not violate the prohibition against double jeopardy because of the fact that the court in sentencing defendant for the basic crime considered defendant's prior criminal history as one factor in finding the existence of aggravating circumstances resulting in a greater sentence. Ross v. State, 274 Ind. 588, 413 N.E.2d 252, 1980 Ind. LEXIS 816 (1980).

The fact that trial court considered prior crimes as well as other circumstances in finding aggravating circumstances for increase in penalty under IC 35-50-2-6 and added the additional penalty as an habitual offender based on prior offenses did not constitute double jeopardy. Griffin v. State, 275 Ind. 107, 415 N.E.2d 60, 1981 Ind. LEXIS 656 (1981).

The repeated use of prior convictions as a determinant of status does not constitute double jeopardy and thus does not invoke the doctrine of collateral estoppel. Baker v. State, 425 N.E.2d 98, 1981 Ind. LEXIS 823 (1981).

Because the habitual offender statute does not create new or separate offenses and the habitual offender proceedings does not deal with the underlying facts on the substantive charge, the use of prior convictions at more than one habitual offender proceeding does not constitute double jeopardy. Baker v. State, 425 N.E.2d 98, 1981 Ind. LEXIS 823 (1981).

If status of being an habitual criminal were to be considered a separate crime, conviction would be unconstitutional as double jeopardy. Pinkston v. State, 436 N.E.2d 306, 1982 Ind. LEXIS 846 (1982); Yager v. State, 437 N.E.2d 454, 1982 Ind. LEXIS 874 (1982).

This section only provides for an enhancement of a sentence imposed upon conviction for an underlying felony. To permit the adjudication of a defen-

Constitutionality. (Cont'd)

—Double Jeopardy. (Cont'd)

dant as an habitual offender to be interpreted as a finding of guilty of a separate crime would constitute violation of the double jeopardy clause of the United States Constitution. Dillon v. State, 448 N.E.2d 21, 1983 Ind. LEXIS 824 (1983).

Without subjecting the defendant to double jeopardy, the state may refile an habitual offender count along with refiling the underlying felony charges where the jury had previously found defendant not to be an habitual offender in a trial involving the same underlying felonies. Durham v. State, 464 N.E.2d 321, 1984 Ind. LEXIS 843 (1984).

Use of the same prior felony conviction to raise possession of a handgun from a Class A misdemeanor to a Class D felony under IC 35-47-2-1 and then to enhance the penalty under this section does not doubly punish defendant for the same past crime and thus does not constitute double jeopardy. Woods v. State, 471 N.E.2d 691, 1984 Ind. LEXIS 1058 (1984).

Where two independent juries considered a convicted defendant's prior criminal record in sentencing him for two unrelated thefts, enhancement of the defendant's second theft sentence by use of his prior felony convictions did not subject the defendant to double jeopardy and did not violate the principles of collateral estoppel. Baker v. Duckworth, 752 F.2d 302, 1985 U.S. App. LEXIS 27612 (7th Cir. Ind. 1985), cert. denied, 472 U.S. 1019, 105 S. Ct. 3483, 87 L. Ed. 2d 618, 1985 U.S. LEXIS 2422 (1985).

Enhancing the presumptive sentence for murder and then enhancing it further on the basis of an habitual offender determination does not violate the double jeopardy clause. Calhoun v. State, 484 N.E.2d 7, 1985 Ind. LEXIS 996 (1985).

The protections afforded by the double jeopardy clauses of the state and federal constitutions, including the collateral estoppel component, do not preclude the determination that defendant is a habitual offender following convictions for three felonies, where a prior jury declined to declare him a habitual offender based on conviction of a different group of three felonies, two of which were identical to the convictions considered in the later proceeding. Mers v. State, 496 N.E.2d 75, 1986 Ind. LEXIS 1239 (1986).

The habitual offender procedure does not involve double jeopardy because it merely provides a more severe penalty for the crime charged, rather than imposing punishment for a separate crime. Dullen v. State, 496 N.E.2d 381, 1986 Ind. LEXIS 1237 (1986).

The trial court does not commit reversible error when it allows defendant to be tried on the same habitual offender information for which he had been previously convicted. Washington v. State, 496 N.E.2d 392, 1986 Ind. LEXIS 1242 (1986).

Because the habitual offender statute does not create new or separate offenses and the habitual offender proceeding does not deal with the underlying facts on the substantive charge, the use of

prior convictions at more than one habitual offender proceeding does not constitute double jeopardy. Denton v. State, 496 N.E.2d 576, 1986 Ind. LEXIS 1252 (1986).

Habitual offender determinations are not findings of guilt of a separate offense and thus do not violate the double jeopardy clause. Kindred v. State, 521 N.E.2d 320, 1988 Ind. LEXIS 54 (1988), appeal dismissed, 639 N.E.2d 286, 1994 Ind. App. LEXIS 982 (Ind. App. 1994).

Where defendant argued that documents pertaining to his felony conviction for carrying a handgun without a permit were erroneously admitted into evidence, claiming they did not pertain to a prior "unrelated" felony because the handgun conviction would have been a misdemeanor were it not for an earlier burglary conviction and that made the handgun and burglary convictions related, which amounted to using the burglary conviction twice for a sentence enhancement, it was held that, in IC 35-47-2-1 on the handgun violation and this section on habitual offenders, the defendant's prior conduct placed him in a different status. That status is not an additional crime, but merely permits trial courts to enhance a given penalty by reason of the status of the offender, and such enhanced penalty does not constitute double jeopardy. Hampton v. State, 526 N.E.2d 1154, 1988 Ind. LEXIS 233 (1988).

The use of prior convictions to enhance a convict's sentence pursuant to a habitual offender statute does not violate the guaranty against double jeopardy because the convict is not twice tried or punished for the same offense. Hicks v. Duckworth, 708 F. Supp. 214, 1989 U.S. Dist. LEXIS 2384 (N.D. Ind. 1989), aff'd, 922 F.2d 409, 1991 U.S. App. LEXIS 265 (7th Cir. Ind. 1991).

The habitual offender statute does not create a separate offense or require consideration of the underlying facts on the substantive charge, and the double jeopardy clause did not bar redetermination of petitioner's habitual offender status. Denton v. Duckworth, 873 F.2d 144, 1989 U.S. App. LEXIS 5710 (7th Cir. Ind. 1989), cert. denied, 493 U.S. 941, 110 S. Ct. 341, 107 L. Ed. 2d 330, 1989 U.S. LEXIS 5095 (1989).

The habitual offender finding is not a separate punishment, but enhancement of the underlying conviction which allows for a longer term of imprisonment because previous contacts with the justice system have failed to provide any meaningful deterrence to the defendant. Mayo v. State, 681 N.E.2d 689, 1997 Ind. LEXIS 77 (1997).

Because defendant did not waive a double jeopardy argument by pleading guilty without a bargained-for benefit, and because the same underlying felony could not be used to support defendant's conviction under IC 35-47-4-5 for unlawful possession of a firearm by a serious violent felon and a habitual offender enhancement under IC 35-50-2-8, the sentencing defect could be remedied on remand. Graham v. State, 903 N.E.2d 538, 2009 Ind. App. LEXIS 643 (2009).

—Due Process.

The filing of an habitual criminal charge does

Constitutionality. (Cont'd)

—Due Process. (Cont'd)

not deny defendant due process of law. Norris v. State, 271 Ind. 568, 394 N.E.2d 144, 1979 Ind. LEXIS 720 (1979).

A defendant's prior habitual criminal history should not have been mentioned by the trial court to prospective jurors prior to voir dire, where it did not directly relate to an issue in the guilt phase of the trial. Leach v. State, 699 N.E.2d 641, 1998 Ind. LEXIS 235 (1998), amended, — N.E.2d —, 1998 Ind. LEXIS 507 (1998).

IC 35-50-2-8 did not violate due process by punishing defendant for his status; also, the trial court did not violate due process by requiring defendant to be present during the habitual offender phase of trial. Ziebell v. State, 788 N.E.2d 902, 2003 Ind. App. LEXIS 878 (2003).

While defendant voluntarily waived her right to jury trial on underlying charges, waiver was ineffective as to habitual offender information subsequently filed; she was never advised of right to jury trial as to habitual offender determination and never waived right after habitual offender information was filed. O'Connor v. State, 796 N.E.2d 1230, 2003 Ind. App. LEXIS 1914 (2003).

—Equal Protection.

This section does not violate equal protection clause of Fourteenth Amendment and Ind. Const., Art. 1, § 23. Ferguson v. State, 438 N.E.2d 286, 1982 Ind. LEXIS 901 (1982).

The habitual offender statute is not unconstitutional, in that it is arbitrarily and vindicatively asserted against certain defendants and not others and thereby results in unfair and disproportionate treatment to some offenders but not to others similarly situated. Hill v. State, 452 N.E.2d 932, 1983 Ind. LEXIS 935 (1983).

Mere showing that no females were sentenced as habitual offenders in Indiana prior to 1981 was insufficient to support defendant's equal protection claim. Kindred v. State, 540 N.E.2d 1161, 1989 Ind. LEXIS 193 (1989).

— —Record of Other Persons Charged with Felonies.

The defendant is not denied his constitutional right to present evidence because the trial judge denies his discovery request for the name, address, race, and gender of everyone charged with a felony in a particular county, during a period of several years, and who could have been charged under the habitual offender statute. Jones v. State, 449 N.E.2d 1060, 1983 Ind. LEXIS 864 (1983), overruled, 698 N.E.2d 732, 1998 Ind. LEXIS 96 (1998).

—Ex Post Facto Effect.

Where this statute went into effect before the crime with which defendant was charged it had no ex post facto effect. Hall v. State, 273 Ind. 507, 405 N.E.2d 530, 1980 Ind. LEXIS 689 (1980).

The habitual offender enhancement under this section was not forbidden for convictions subject to the former habitual traffic offender statute, IC 9-12, at the time of the plea agreement under then-existing law because *Stanek v. State,* 603 N.E.2d 152, 1992 Ind. LEXIS 252 (Ind. 1992) was not decided until four months after the plea agreement, so that when attempting to induce defendant to plead guilty, the prosecutorial threat to seek habitual offender enhancement under this section did not render the plea obtained invalid. Long v. State, 645 N.E.2d 1111, 1995 Ind. App. LEXIS 22 (1995).

—Ex Post Facto Laws.

This section is not unconstitutional as being an ex post facto law. Funk v. State, 427 N.E.2d 1081, 1981 Ind. LEXIS 904 (1981).

—Impartial Jury.

The right to an impartial jury and presumption of innocence are not violated by the habitual offender procedure because the jury determining habitual offender status was the same jury that convicted for the primary offense. Dullen v. State, 496 N.E.2d 381, 1986 Ind. LEXIS 1237 (1986).

—Right of Jury to Determine Law.

As the habitual offender statute is a means of sentencing and is not a determination of the law necessary to reach the verdict, it is not unconstitutional because it allegedly takes away the jury's right to determine the law. Jones v. State, 449 N.E.2d 1060, 1983 Ind. LEXIS 864 (1983), overruled, 698 N.E.2d 732, 1998 Ind. LEXIS 96 (1998).

—Separation of Powers.

As no standards are provided by law for the prosecutor's guidance in determining when any criminal charges should be prosecuted or to what extent they should be prosecuted, and as the legislature has the power to set the penalties and the range of available dispositions in criminal cases, the trial court's power extends only to choosing from legislatively granted sentencing alternatives, and thus the legislature's scheme for sentencing under the habitual offender statute does not violate separation of powers proscriptions. Havens v. State, 429 N.E.2d 618, 1981 Ind. LEXIS 967 (1981).

The habitual offender statute itself is not unconstitutional because it allegedly violates the separation of powers clause by allowing the prosecutor the discretion to charge someone as an habitual offender. Jones v. State, 449 N.E.2d 1060, 1983 Ind. LEXIS 864 (1983), overruled, 698 N.E.2d 732, 1998 Ind. LEXIS 96 (1998).

—Vindictive Justice.

Imposition of a 32-year sentence for the theft of $990 did not constitute vindictive justice, rather than reformation as required by Ind. Const., art. I, § 18, where the sentence had been enhanced under the habitual criminal statute. Marsillett v. State, 495 N.E.2d 699, 1986 Ind. LEXIS 1206 (1986).

Appeal.

Where no appeal had been taken from conviction under habitual criminal statute, constitutionality of such statute could not be raised for first time by habeas corpus. Dowd v. Grazer, 233 Ind. 68, 116 N.E.2d 108, 1953 Ind. LEXIS 287 (1953).

Appeal. (Cont'd)

If an appeal of the underlying felony is successful, the habitual offender determination and sentencing must also be reversed; without the former, the latter cannot stand. Rodgers v. State, 422 N.E.2d 1211, 1981 Ind. LEXIS 784 (1981).

Where the defendant did not in his original appeal question the adequacy of the trial court's statement of reasons for selecting a 25-year additional penalty to be imposed for an habitual offender finding, he could not raise the issue in this subsequent appeal. McDandal v. State, 615 N.E.2d 430, 1993 Ind. LEXIS 83 (1993).

Where defendant failed to request rehearing or transfer of the previous decision by the appellate court that he should be resentenced, this failure precluded further consideration of the matter. Boykin v. State, 622 N.E.2d 568, 1993 Ind. App. LEXIS 1273 (1993).

Defendant could not obtain relief from habitual offender finding without demonstrating that the prior convictions on which it was based did not meet the requirements of the statute. Lingler v. State, 644 N.E.2d 131, 1994 Ind. LEXIS 189 (1994).

—Dismissal Reversed.

The trial court was authorized to proceed with an habitual offender charge after a dismissal of the charge had been reversed on interlocutory appeal. Gibson v. State, 661 N.E.2d 865, 1996 Ind. App. LEXIS 141 (1996).

—Guilty Plea.

Because the state's success or failure in establishing the factual basis for defendant's guilty plea to the habitual offender charge can be determined from the record of the hearing, defendant should be allowed to directly appeal his guilty plea without regard to whether the issue he raises fits within one of the exceptions to the rule against direct appeals of guilty pleas. Tumulty v. State, 647 N.E.2d 361, 1995 Ind. App. LEXIS 169 (1995), vacated, 666 N.E.2d 394, 1996 Ind. LEXIS 56 (1996).

Arraignment.

It is appropriate procedure to conduct an arraignment on an habitual offender charge, but failure to conduct such an arraignment does not present grounds for reversal in the absence of prejudice. Foster v. State, 526 N.E.2d 696, 1988 Ind. LEXIS 221 (1988).

Burden of Proof.

The burden rests upon the state to prove beyond a reasonable doubt that the defendant has been twice previously convicted, sentenced and imprisoned in some penal institution for the commission of a felony. Smith v. State, 243 Ind. 74, 181 N.E.2d 520, 1962 Ind. LEXIS 133 (1962).

The test in the trial court is not a matter of establishing a prima facie case but rather one of proving beyond a reasonable doubt that the defendant has been previously twice convicted, sentenced and imprisoned in some penal institution for felonies. Smith v. State, 243 Ind. 74, 181 N.E.2d 520, 1962 Ind. LEXIS 133 (1962).

To show that there was an insufficient factual basis upon which to accept a plea of guilty to being an habitual offender, based upon the fact that the state failed to introduce proof of the dates of commission of the predicate offenses and therefore did not prove the sequential requirements of the habitual offender statute, it must be affirmatively demonstrated that the sequential requirement of the habitual offender statute was not present, and not merely that there was a technical deficiency at the guilty plea hearing. Long v. State, 645 N.E.2d 1111, 1995 Ind. App. LEXIS 22 (1995).

—Post Conviction Proceedings.

Defendant made no suggestion that the requisite prior felonies were not committed or were not committed in the appropriate statutory sequence, and it was his burden to do so if he wished to challenge the habitual offender determination by petition for post-conviction relief. Thomas v. State, 652 N.E.2d 550, 1995 Ind. App. LEXIS 776 (1995).

Calling Prior Defense Attorney.

Trial court did not abuse its discretion, during the habitual offender phase of trial, by allowing the state to call an attorney who represented defendant in a prior trial to identify defendant. Ziebell v. State, 788 N.E.2d 902, 2003 Ind. App. LEXIS 878 (2003).

Class D Felonies.

Although defendant was convicted of a Class D felony and under IC 35-50-2-7 the judge could have entered judgment for a Class A misdemeanor, defendant was not harmed by proceeding with the habitual offender portion of the trial prior to the entry of judgment when the court entered judgment for a Class D felony subsequent to the habitual criminal proceeding; however it might be different if after the recidivist hearing and after examining the presentence investigation report, the trial court would decide to enter judgment for a Class A misdemeanor, thereby unnecessarily subjecting the defendant to the habitual criminal phase of the trial. The Supreme Court stated that it would be the better practice in the future, in the case of a guilty verdict on a Class D felony, for the court, prior to the trial on the status question and after considering the presentence investigation report and arguments of counsel, to determine whether or not it will withhold judgment for a Class D felony and enter judgment for a Class A misdemeanor instead, and if the court decides to enter judgment for a Class D felony it should do so and reserve the imposition of sentence for the felony until after the trial on the habitual criminal charge. In the case of guilty verdicts for other felonies this problem would not be encountered, as the sentencing provisions for Class D felonies are unique. Collins v. State, 275 Ind. 86, 415 N.E.2d 46, 1981 Ind. LEXIS 657 (1981), cert. denied, 451 U.S. 991, 101 S. Ct. 2331, 68 L. Ed. 2d 851, 1981 U.S. LEXIS 2139 (1981); Wright v. State, 467 N.E.2d 22, 1984 Ind. LEXIS 907 (1984).

Former IC 35-50-2-7.1 did not apply to a defendant whose Class D felonies had been committed before the effective date of September 1, 1985.

Class D Felonies. (Cont'd)
Hensley v. State, 497 N.E.2d 1053, 1986 Ind. LEXIS 1283 (1986).

Former IC 35-50-2-7.1 did not apply to those cases in which the prior felonies relied upon to convict one of an habitual offender count were committed prior to September 1, 1985. In such cases, prosecution for habitual offender status had to occur under IC 35-50-2-8. Moncrief v. State, 525 N.E.2d 1286, 1988 Ind. App. LEXIS 527 (1988).

When the state charged a defendant as an habitual offender and listed as prior convictions several Indiana Class D felonies and several felonies from other states for which the penalty imposed was within the sentencing range for Indiana Class D felonies, former subsection (h) precluded a 30-year enhancement of sentence. Slocumb v. State, 573 N.E.2d 427, 1991 Ind. LEXIS 117 (1991).

Both the defendant's enhanced Class D felony and the prior Class D felonies must have been committed prior to September 1, 1985, in order for the defendant to have been sentenced under this section rather than the former Class D Habitual Offender Statute, former IC 35-50-2-7.1. Johnson v. State, 593 N.E.2d 1181, 1992 Ind. LEXIS 169 (1992).

A conviction could be sustained under former subsection (h) when any of the three convictions underlying the habitual offender charge, i.e., the two prior convictions and the present conviction, were greater than a Class D felony. Abron v. State, 591 N.E.2d 634, 1992 Ind. App. LEXIS 793 (1992); Cain v. State, 594 N.E.2d 835, 1992 Ind. App. LEXIS 1062 (1992).

Where defendant was sentenced to two years in prison for resisting law enforcement, a Class D felony, four year habitual offender enhancement of his sentence under IC 35-50-2-8(h) was not inappropriate where defendant engaged in high-speed chase on city streets, ran four stop signs, had six prior convictions and, while out on bond in current case, was arrested and convicted of criminal confinement. Goodall v. State, 809 N.E.2d 484, 2004 Ind. App. LEXIS 1052 (2004).

Defendant did not allege that any of the three Robertson exceptions applied that required a trial court to limit itself to imposing the advisory sentence when imposing a consecutive sentence, and, thus, the appellate court could uphold defendant's two-and-one-half year sentence for domestic battery, as a Class D felony, even though the advisory sentence for Class D felonies was one-and-one-half years; exceptions involved: (1) a consecutive sentence for nonviolent felony convictions arising out of a single episode of criminal conduct, according to IC 35-50-1-2; (2) a consecutive sentence imposed as an additional fixed term to a habitual offender, IC 35-50-2-8; or (3) a consecutive sentence imposed as an additional fixed term to a repeat sexual offender under IC 35-50-2-14, and since defendant could not show any of the exceptions applied, a sentence higher than the advisory sentence could be imposed. Freyn v. State, 884 N.E.2d 901, 2008 Ind. App. LEXIS 791 (2008).

Collateral Attacks.
The validity of a plea of guilty to the prior offenses could not be collaterally attacked in the habitual offender proceeding. Morris v. State, 273 Ind. 614, 406 N.E.2d 1187, 1980 Ind. LEXIS 715 (1980), superseded by statute as stated in, Havens v. State, 429 N.E.2d 618, 1981 Ind. LEXIS 967 (1981).

Collateral Estoppel.
Where defendant had previously been charged as an habitual offender based on the same two prior convictions but such previous habitual offender charge was dismissed because the state's exhibits did not show that a knowing and voluntary plea of guilty was made to such offenses, such fact did not prevent defendant from later being charged with being an habitual offender based on the same two prior convictions on the theory of collateral estoppel. Hall v. State, 273 Ind. 507, 405 N.E.2d 530, 1980 Ind. LEXIS 689 (1980).

The finding that a defendant is or is not an habitual offender is not an "ultimate issue of fact" in the sense that term plays in application of the doctrine of collateral estoppel. Baker v. State, 425 N.E.2d 98, 1981 Ind. LEXIS 823 (1981).

The state is not collaterally estopped from pursuing the habitual offender proceeding because one of the prior felonies alleged was alleged in an earlier habitual offender proceeding at which defendant was acquitted. Harrison v. State, 496 N.E.2d 49, 1986 Ind. LEXIS 1225 (1986).

The trial court does not err by excluding evidence that defendant was found not to be a habitual offender in an earlier proceeding which alleged the same two prior felony convictions as the present case. The previous habitual offender outcome was simply not relevant to the present case, because it merely established that the earlier jury declined to find that defendant, at that time, should be sentenced as a habitual offender in the context of the three felony convictions then existing. Mers v. State, 496 N.E.2d 75, 1986 Ind. LEXIS 1239 (1986).

Consolidated Trial.
In a consolidated trial, where it is clear that two separate crimes were committed involving two separate victims, sentencing defendant as an habitual offender in two separate causes was proper, as the habitual offender sentences were the enhancement of sentences in two separate crimes. Kelly v. State, 452 N.E.2d 907, 1983 Ind. LEXIS 926 (1983).

Construction with Other Laws.
Although IC 31-37-19-10 does not define "unrelated prior adjudications of delinquency," this language is similar to language in this section, and the court therefore could look to the habitual offender statute for guidance in its interpretation of the determinate sentence statute. W.T.J. v. State, 713 N.E.2d 938, 1999 Ind. App. LEXIS 1280 (1999).

In light of the statutory construction favoring more specific statutes as opposed to more general ones and because of the rule of lenity, a misdemeanor conviction under the handgun statute, once elevated to a felony due to a prior felony conviction, should not be enhanced again under

Construction with Other Laws. (Cont'd)
the general habitual offender statute. Ross v. State, 729 N.E.2d 113, 2000 Ind. LEXIS 484 (2000), superseded by statute as stated in, Mills v. State, 855 N.E.2d 296, 2006 Ind. App. LEXIS 2126 (2006).

Despite similar wording in the adult habitual offender statute, IC 35-50-2-8(c), the meaning of the phrase "unrelated prior adjudications of delinquency" in IC 31-37-19-10(a)(3) is that the earlier adjudications of delinquency are independent of the offense that is currently charged; "two unrelated prior adjudications of delinquency" in IC 31-37-19-10(a)(3) simply means that the earlier adjudications of delinquency are independent of the offense that is currently charged. N.D.F. v. State, 775 N.E.2d 1085, 2002 Ind. LEXIS 780 (2002).

By amending the IC 35-50-2-8 habitual substance offender statute to include offenses under IC 9-30-5, the Indiana General Assembly expressed its intention that a sentence enhancement under both IC 35-50-2-8 and the IC 9-30-5 operating while intoxicated statute were proper. Schnepp v. State, 768 N.E.2d 1002, 2002 Ind. App. LEXIS 802 (2002).

Aggravated battery statute, IC 35-42-2-1.5, was not a habitual offender statute, nor was it part of a progressively elevating sentence scheme; the trial court did not err in enhancing defendant's sentence under both the aggravated battery statute and by the general habitual offender statute, IC 35-50-2-8. Cushenberry v. State, 792 N.E.2d 571, 2003 Ind. App. LEXIS 1370 (2003).

Decision in Ross v. State, 729 N.E.2d 113, 2000 Ind. LEXIS 484 (Ind. 2000), holding that habitual offender charge could not be based on same prior convictions used to elevate misdemeanor offense to felony, was not retroactive, since it announced new rule of criminal procedure. Glasco v. State, 802 N.E.2d 973, 2004 Ind. App. LEXIS 166 (2004).

Construction with Other Sections.
Because the language mirrors the language contained in this section, decisions interpreting the habitual offender statute are applicable to issues raised under IC 35-50-2-10. Roell v. State, 655 N.E.2d 599, 1995 Ind. App. LEXIS 1171 (1995).

IC 35-45-4-2 and IC 35-50-2-8 compliment each other, and the prostitution statute is not a discreet, separate, and independent habitual offender statute; read together, they provide for a progressive scheme of punishment, and because they can be harmonized, both enhancement provisions may be simultaneously applied. State v. Dennis, 686 N.E.2d 901, 1997 Ind. App. LEXIS 1541 (1997).

Contradictory Verdict.
Where the jury, in the matter of the charge of being an habitual criminal, returned two verdicts, the first finding historical facts essential to constitute the status of habitual criminal, and the second stating that defendant was not guilty of being an habitual criminal, the second apparently contradictory verdict was properly treated as surplusage and judgment was properly rendered on the first. Rogers v. State, 226 Ind. 539, 82 N.E.2d 89, 1948

Ind. LEXIS 194 (1948), cert. denied, 336 U.S. 940, 69 S. Ct. 743, 93 L. Ed. 1098, 1949 U.S. LEXIS 2649 (1949).

Where jury found petitioner guilty of second-degree burglary and automobile banditry and that he had been twice before convicted of a felony — once in 1932 and once in 1928, its additional verdict that "we, the jury, find the defendant not guilty of being an habitual criminal" was beyond its province as the jury possessed no legislative power to repudiate or alter the habitual criminal act passed by the legislature. United States ex rel. Rogers v. Lane, 345 F.2d 357, 1965 U.S. App. LEXIS 5694 (7th Cir. Ind. 1965), cert. denied, 382 U.S. 991, 86 S. Ct. 570, 15 L. Ed. 2d 478, 1966 U.S. LEXIS 2660 (1966).

It was not error for the trial court to sentence petitioner as an habitual criminal where the jury found petitioner guilty of burglary and banditry and that he had been twice convicted of felonies in Indiana, although it further found "the defendant not guilty of being an habitual criminal." United States ex rel. Rogers v. Lane, 345 F.2d 357, 1965 U.S. App. LEXIS 5694 (7th Cir. Ind. 1965), cert. denied, 382 U.S. 991, 86 S. Ct. 570, 15 L. Ed. 2d 478, 1966 U.S. LEXIS 2660 (1966).

Conviction Improper.
Conviction as an habitual offender was improper where defendant was charged with four prior felony convictions and evidence was submitted as to all charges but defendant had not yet been sentenced for two of such prior convictions. Miller v. State, 275 Ind. 454, 417 N.E.2d 339, 1981 Ind. LEXIS 691 (1981).

Counting Convictions.
Where defendant was convicted, sentenced and imprisoned for second degree burglary, then paroled and while on parole was again convicted, sentenced and imprisoned, the fact that the parole board revoked his parole and held the new sentence in abeyance and made his second conviction occur before the first sentence was completed, did not prevent both convictions from being counted. Jameison v. State, 268 Ind. 599, 377 N.E.2d 404, 1978 Ind. LEXIS 712 (1978).

Sentencing as an habitual offender is improper where commission of requisite third felony was not subsequent to conviction and sentencing for second felony offense. Graham v. State, 435 N.E.2d 560, 1982 Ind. LEXIS 825 (1982).

Trial court erred when it permitted state in prosecution for burglary and theft to append felony conviction where defendant had not been convicted or sentenced for that offense prior to alleged commission of burglary and theft, and such error was not harmless where there were no special findings of fact to reveal rationale for conclusion that defendant qualified as an habitual offender. Wells v. State, 437 N.E.2d 1333, 1982 Ind. LEXIS 908 (1982).

The only times a prior conviction may not be used in an habitual offender proceeding is if it has been set aside or if it is one for which the person has been pardoned. This section makes no other

Counting Convictions. (Cont'd)
exceptions. Maisonet v. State, 448 N.E.2d 1052, 1983 Ind. LEXIS 836 (1983).

IC 35-50-2-8 required the state to prove that petitioner had been convicted of two prior felonies, and the fact that the use of 39 uncharged burglaries as evidence at trial was reversible error in petitioner's burglary and theft charges, but was not argued on direct appeal to reverse the habitual offender conviction showed ineffective assistance of appellate counsel; nevertheless, petitioner in all likelihood would not have been acquitted of the habitual offender charge if the argument had been made because it was undisputed that petitioner had been convicted of two prior felonies, and there were no exceptional circumstances to warrant that petitioner should not have been convicted as charged. Gibbs v. Van Natta, 329 F.3d 582, 2003 U.S. App. LEXIS 9797 (7th Cir. Ind. 2003).

Double use of a prior felony conviction as a sentence enhancement was not broadly prohibited under all circumstances, but only where it was twice used as a separate and discrete conviction to doubly enhance a sentence for one present conviction; although a misdemeanor enhanced to a felony may not have been further enhanced under the general habitual offender statute, such a conviction may itself serve as a predicate habitual offender felony, and a rape sentence was properly enhanced by a predicate felony which itself had been enhanced by another of habitual offender predicate felonies. Olatunji v. State, 788 N.E.2d 1268, 2003 Ind. App. LEXIS 904 (2003).

—Collateral Attacks.
The alleged invalidity of prior convictions cannot be collaterally attacked during the course of an habitual offender proceeding when the prior final judgments are regular on their face. Jones v. State, 425 N.E.2d 82, 1981 Ind. LEXIS 835 (1981).

—Nature of Prior Offenses.
Since the possible punishment for shoplifter at the time defendant pled guilty in 1974 could have been imprisonment in the state prison, the state correctly characterized this offense as a felony for purposes of the habitual offender statute. Baker v. State, 425 N.E.2d 98, 1981 Ind. LEXIS 823 (1981).

—Prior Conviction Set Aside.
The circuit court was required to vacate the 30-year portion of a sentence based upon habitual offender status where the defendant's successful prosecution of a post-conviction relief petition to set aside a prior conviction left the habitual offender finding without one of the necessary supporting prior convictions, notwithstanding the defendant's failure to challenge the prior conviction at the sentencing proceeding. Olinger v. State, 494 N.E.2d 310, 1986 Ind. LEXIS 1180 (1986).

Where defendant pled guilty to being habitual offender but post-conviction court vacated one of convictions upon which habitual offender status was based, defendant's guilty plea was properly set aside since under IC 35-50-2-8(b)(1) vacated conviction could not be counted. State v. Jones, 819 N.E.2d 877, 2004 Ind. App. LEXIS 2586 (2004).

Defenses.
It is defendant's burden to produce evidence in support of a defense that his prior convictions were invalid. Collins v. State, 275 Ind. 86, 415 N.E.2d 46, 1981 Ind. LEXIS 657 (1981), cert. denied, 451 U.S. 991, 101 S. Ct. 2331, 68 L. Ed. 2d 851, 1981 U.S. LEXIS 2139 (1981).

The exclusions mentioned in subsection (b) of this section are affirmative defenses to an habitual criminal charge. Williams v. State, 424 N.E.2d 1017, 1981 Ind. LEXIS 832 (1981).

The burden of proving a pardon or that a conviction had been set aside is upon the defendant to come forward with rather than on the state to prove the negative. Williams v. State, 424 N.E.2d 1017, 1981 Ind. LEXIS 832 (1981).

The legislature, in enacting this section, did not intend the question whether habitual offender penalties should attach would be resolved by evidence regarding defendant's general mental predilections toward the future commission of criminal acts. Instead, the legislature indicated the question should turn on defendant's record of criminal behavior. Underhill v. State, 428 N.E.2d 759, 1981 Ind. LEXIS 918 (1981).

Whether one of the charged prior convictions has been set aside or has resulted in a pardon is an affirmative defense to an habitual offender charge. Havens v. State, 429 N.E.2d 618, 1981 Ind. LEXIS 967 (1981).

Due Process.
Where defendant was aware, during the plea bargaining process, that his rejection of the state's offer might result in an amended information adding a recidivist charge, and where the habitual criminal count charged defendant with an offense for which he was properly subject to prosecution, as he had prior forgery convictions, defendant rejected the state's offer with full awareness of its terms and possible consequences, and the prosecutor's conduct did not violate defendant's right to due process. McMahan v. State, 269 Ind. 566, 382 N.E.2d 154, 1978 Ind. LEXIS 855 (1978).

Effect on Underlying Conviction.
Where a habitual offender conviction was vacated following a plea agreement, the sentence for the underlying conviction was altered, since the habitual offender statute provides only for enhancement of a sentence, and vacation of sentence for the underlying conviction was therefore required. Boykin v. State, 702 N.E.2d 1105, 1998 Ind. App. LEXIS 2101 (1998).

Enhanced Punishment.
The life sentence provided by the habitual criminal statute is an enhanced punishment for the underlying offense committed by those who have been twice previously convicted, sentenced and imprisoned for felonies and defendant cannot be sentenced for the underlying offense in addition to the life sentence. Swinehart v. State, 268 Ind. 460, 376 N.E.2d 486, 1978 Ind. LEXIS 691 (1978).

This section does not impose punishment for a separate crime but provides a more severe penalty

Enhanced Punishment. (Cont'd)
for the crime charged. Howard v. State, 268 Ind. 589, 377 N.E.2d 628, 1978 Ind. LEXIS 708 (1978), cert. denied, 439 U.S. 1049, 99 S. Ct. 727, 58 L. Ed. 2d 708, 1978 U.S. LEXIS 4247 (1978); Gibbens v. State, 434 N.E.2d 82, 1982 Ind. LEXIS 804 (1982); Yager v. State, 437 N.E.2d 454, 1982 Ind. LEXIS 874 (1982); Olinger v. State, 463 N.E.2d 1385, 1984 Ind. LEXIS 844 (Ind. 1984).

Habitual offender sentencing is an enhanced sentence imposed for the last crime committed and not an additional penalty for earlier crimes nor a separate criminal charge and therefore does not constitute double jeopardy. Wise v. State, 272 Ind. 498, 400 N.E.2d 114, 1980 Ind. LEXIS 592 (1980); Ferguson v. State, 273 Ind. 468, 405 N.E.2d 902, 1980 Ind. LEXIS 695 (1980); Johnson v. State, 432 N.E.2d 1358, 1982 Ind. LEXIS 778 (Ind. 1982).

The fact that one of the felonies upon which the habitual offender sentence was based would have been barred by the statute of limitations if tried at that time does not affect the sentence as an habitual offender since the enhanced sentence is imposed for the last crime and not for the earlier offense. Wise v. State, 272 Ind. 498, 400 N.E.2d 114, 1980 Ind. LEXIS 592 (1980); Ferguson v. State, 273 Ind. 468, 405 N.E.2d 902, 1980 Ind. LEXIS 695 (1980).

The habitual offender statute does not establish a new offense or separate crime but merely provides for the imposition of a greater sentence for the substantive crime charged. Hall v. State, 273 Ind. 507, 405 N.E.2d 530, 1980 Ind. LEXIS 689 (1980).

Under this section the imposition of enhanced punishment occurs only when the accused has already been convicted of other, clearly culpable conduct on three occasions. Smith v. State, 422 N.E.2d 1179, 1981 Ind. LEXIS 775 (1981).

The individual is subjected to the greater sentence under this section neither for the prior crimes nor for the status of habitual offender, but rather the enhanced sentence is imposed for the last crime committed. Baker v. State, 425 N.E.2d 98, 1981 Ind. LEXIS 823 (1981).

There was no merit to defendant's contention that the use of his prior convictions as the basis for the habitual offender count exposed him to double sentencing since these same two prior convictions were considered as aggravating circumstances to enhance the basic penalty on a theft conviction at a previous, unrelated trial. Baker v. State, 425 N.E.2d 98, 1981 Ind. LEXIS 823 (1981).

This section does not punish for a status but provides for an enhanced punishment because of the ineffectiveness of prior confinement and rehabilitative efforts. Funk v. State, 427 N.E.2d 1081, 1981 Ind. LEXIS 904 (1981).

The habitual offender statute is valid because the enhanced sentence is for the last crime committed and is neither a separate criminal charge nor an additional penalty for earlier crimes. Kelly v. State, 452 N.E.2d 907, 1983 Ind. LEXIS 926 (1983).

This section provides a mechanism for the enhancement of a sentence imposed upon the conviction on the underlying felony when it is proven the defendant has accumulated two prior unrelated felony convictions. This section does not name a crime in and of itself. State v. Hicks, 453 N.E.2d 1014, 1983 Ind. LEXIS 967 (1983).

The 30-year term of imprisonment provided for habitual offender findings is an enhancement of the sentence for the underlying felony and not a separate sentence which is to be served either consecutively or concurrently with another sentence. Wilson v. State, 465 N.E.2d 717, 1984 Ind. LEXIS 871 (1984).

Separate sentences for burglary and for being an habitual offender are improper, and a single sentence enhanced by reason of this section is required. Beavers v. State, 465 N.E.2d 1388, 1984 Ind. LEXIS 891 (1984).

A life sentence is not excessive when imposed after a defendant's third felony conviction, even if such felonies do not involve violence. Howard v. State, 467 N.E.2d 1, 1984 Ind. LEXIS 924 (1984) (decided under former IC 35-8-8-1).

A person found to be an habitual offender does not receive a separate sentence for that status. The proper procedure is to enhance one of the felonies for which he is being convicted by an extra 30 years because of the status of habitual offender. Lewis v. State, 512 N.E.2d 1092, 1987 Ind. LEXIS 1059 (1987).

Although defendant was not prejudiced by the admission of videotaped interviews with three of the child victims under IC 35-37-4-6 after all five of the children had testified at trial, because defendant's underlying conviction did not involve children or a sex offense, the trial court erred in sentencing defendant to a total executed time of 110 years in prison under IC 35-50-2-8(h). Tyler v. State, 903 N.E.2d 463, 2009 Ind. LEXIS 337 (2009).

—Basis for Enhancement.
Trial court did not err in first enhancing the presumptive sentence for murder based upon the habitual offender finding, then enhancing the sentence based upon the aggravating circumstances. James v. State, 643 N.E.2d 321, 1994 Ind. LEXIS 165 (1994).

—Consecutive Sentences.
A 30-year executed sentence consecutive to the sentence imposed upon the underlying felony for a finding that defendant was a habitual offender was erroneous and corrected to provide that original four-year sentence for underlying felony was enhanced to 34-year sentence. Wilburn v. State, 442 N.E.2d 1098, 1982 Ind. LEXIS 1065 (1982).

An order for separate sentences of five years for forgery and 30 years on an habitual offender determination, such sentences to run consecutively, was error, and the case was remanded for imposition of an enhanced sentence of 35 years for the forgery conviction. Wendling v. State, 465 N.E.2d 169, 1984 Ind. LEXIS 861 (1984).

A sentence of 5 years imprisonment upon a conviction for attempted burglary and to 30 years imprisonment on the habitual offender finding, said sentences to be served consecutively, is improper. The proper sentence would be a 5-year

Enhanced Punishment. (Cont'd)

—Consecutive Sentences. (Cont'd)
sentence enhanced by 30 years upon the habitual offender finding, for a sentence of 35 years for attempted burglary. Perry v. State, 471 N.E.2d 270, 1984 Ind. LEXIS 1052 (1984).

A separate, 30-year term of imprisonment for being an habitual offender was erroneous. The trial judge had to designate which of the two sentences for the two felony convictions would be enhanced. Carter v. State, 479 N.E.2d 1290, 1985 Ind. LEXIS 886 (1985); Pillow v. State, 479 N.E.2d 1301, 1985 Ind. LEXIS 882 (Ind. 1985).

It was error to impose a 30-year sentence to run consecutively with the sentences for two underlying felony convictions as the trial judge must enhance one of the underlying felony convictions rather than impose a consecutive sentence. Johnson v. State, 490 N.E.2d 333, 1986 Ind. LEXIS 1076 (1986).

This section provides the sentence imposed upon a habitual offender finding enhances the sentence for the underlying conviction; it does not impose a separate penalty. Geralds v. State, 494 N.E.2d 1287, 1986 Ind. LEXIS 1199 (1986).

The trial court erred in sentencing defendant upon the habitual offender determination to a term of 30 years to run consecutively to the sentences imposed for the primary offenses, since this section provides that the sentence imposed upon a finding of habitual offender shall enhance the sentence for the underlying conviction rather than impose a separate penalty. Dullen v. State, 496 N.E.2d 381, 1986 Ind. LEXIS 1237 (1986).

Sentencing court exceeded its legislative authorization when it imposed consecutive felony sentences, both of which were enhanced by 30 years, because of habitual offender status, at a single criminal trial. Starks v. State, 523 N.E.2d 735, 1988 Ind. LEXIS 129 (1988).

An aggregate sentence of 30 years for an underlying conviction of forgery with a presumptive sentence of five years and an habitual offender determination is improper. The proper sentence is the five-year presumptive sentence enhanced by 30 years for a total of 35 years. Golden v. State, 553 N.E.2d 1219, 1990 Ind. App. LEXIS 571 (1990).

Where defendant pled guilty to two counts of dealing marijuana and his sentences were enhanced for aggravating circumstances and were made to run consecutively, the trial court erred when it enhanced both sentences by reason of defendant's habitual offender standing which should have applied to only one of the convictions. Weaver v. State, 676 N.E.2d 22, 1997 Ind. App. LEXIS 5 (1997).

The trial court exceeded its legislative authorization when it imposed consecutive habitual offender sentence enhancements at a single criminal trial, since the habitual offender statutes are silent on the question of whether courts have the authority to require such sentences to run consecutively. McCotry v. State, 722 N.E.2d 1265, 2000 Ind. App. LEXIS 70 (2000).

In the absence of express statutory authorization for courts to require habitual offender sentences to run consecutively, when engaged in the process of meting out several sentences, there was no such authority. Ingram v. State, 761 N.E.2d 883, 2002 Ind. App. LEXIS 52 (2002).

—Determination of Status.
The habitual offender statute is not a separate crime but only a means of determining a defendant's status in order to decide whether to enhance the sentence on the underlying felony. Jones v. State, 449 N.E.2d 1060, 1983 Ind. LEXIS 864 (1983), overruled, 698 N.E.2d 732, 1998 Ind. LEXIS 96 (1998).

A corrected sentence properly treated the habitual offender finding as a status, not as a separate offense, and enhanced the conviction by thirty years accordingly. Woodson v. State, 515 N.E.2d 1108, 1987 Ind. LEXIS 1163 (1987).

—Convictions Ineligible for Enhancement.
Trial court erred by attaching defendant's habitual offender enhancement to conviction under IC 35-48-4-6 for possession of cocaine since that conviction was ineligible for enhancement under IC 35-50-2-8(b). Johnican v. State, 804 N.E.2d 211, 2004 Ind. App. LEXIS 324 (2004).

—Discretion of Prosecutor.
Where an offender can be charged with a habitual offender enhancement as either a habitual offender or a habitual substance offender, the prosecutor has discretion to bring enhancement charges under either provision. Hendrix v. State, 759 N.E.2d 1045, 2001 Ind. LEXIS 1104 (2001).

—Double Enhancement Improper.
Defendant's operating while intoxicated charge could not be elevated pursuant to IC 9-30-5-3 on the basis of a previous operating while intoxicated conviction where his sentence was also enhanced pursuant to this section as the result of his previous convictions for conspiracy to commit robbery and battery. Burp v. State, 672 N.E.2d 439, 1996 Ind. App. LEXIS 1444 (1996).

Defendant's four-year sentence for operating a motor vehicle after driving privileges are forfeited for life as a Class C felony could not be further enhanced under the general habitual offender statute. Wood v. State, 734 N.E.2d 296, 2000 Ind. App. LEXIS 1343 (2000).

Decision in Ross v. State, 729 N.E.2d 113, 2000 Ind. LEXIS 484 (Ind. 2000), holding that habitual offender charge could not be based on same prior convictions used to elevate misdemeanor offense to felony, was not retroactive, since it announced new rule of criminal procedure. Glasco v. State, 802 N.E.2d 973, 2004 Ind. App. LEXIS 166 (2004).

Ruling in Ross v. State, 729 N.E.2d 113, 2000 Ind. LEXIS 484, (Ind. 2000), that misdemeanor handgun charge enhanced to felony cannot be further enhanced by use of general habitual offender statute, is substantive rule and applies retroactively. Jacobs v. State, 835 N.E.2d 485, 2005 Ind. LEXIS 930 (2005).

Trial court erred in basing a defendant's Class C felony auto theft and habitual offender finding upon the same prior felony conviction where it had impermissibly imposed a double enhancement; un-

Enhanced Punishment. (Cont'd)

—Double Enhancement Improper. (Cont'd)
der judicial precedent interpreting IC 35-50-2-8, a double enhancement based upon the same offense, once for auto theft enhanced to a Class C felony and again for being a habitual offender, was impermissible. Goodman v. State, 863 N.E.2d 898, 2007 Ind. App. LEXIS 646 (2007).

In light of the Supreme Court of Indiana's clear position that, absent explicit legislative direction, a sentence imposed following conviction under a progressive penalty statute may not be increased further under either the general habitual offender statute or a specialized habitual offender statute, General Assembly's mere failure to specifically enumerate the double enhancement at issue as an exception under amended IC 35-50-2-8 did not therefore make it permissible. Goodman v. State, 863 N.E.2d 898, 2007 Ind. App. LEXIS 646 (2007).

—Habitual Offender.
Trial court did not abuse its discretion in imposing habitual offender enhancement of 30-years on count of unlawful possession of firearm by serious violent felon, a Class B felony, despite claim by defendant that enhancement was excessive given 20-year sentence on felony charge and that court failed to attach any significant weight to proffered mitigating circumstances. Lewis v. State, 800 N.E.2d 996, 2003 Ind. App. LEXIS 2410 (2003).

Ruling in Ross v. State, 729 N.E.2d 113, 2000 Ind. LEXIS 484, (Ind. 2000), that misdemeanor handgun charge enhanced to felony cannot be further enhanced by use of general habitual offender statute, is substantive rule and applies retroactively. Johnson v. State, 835 N.E.2d 492, 2005 Ind. LEXIS 928 (2005).

Defendant's failure to amend his appellate brief to petition for rehearing or to seek transfer after decision of Supreme Court of Indiana, which held that general habitual offender statute cannot be used to enhance sentence for handgun possession already enhanced from misdemeanor to felony, was not waiver of that issue on collateral review; however, state was not precluded from seeking resentencing under IC 35-50-2-8 since sentences were entered by trial court on more than one felony. State v. Jones, 835 N.E.2d 1002, 2005 Ind. LEXIS 929 (2005).

Sentence review under AP. 7(B) was available after a guilty plea, and sentences totalling 40 years resulting from two guilty pleas to Class B felonies and a habitual offender finding were not inappropriate under IC 35-50-2-5 and IC 35-50-2-8(h) where the nature of the offenses involved ongoing drug dealing and weapons violations, and the character of the offender showed that he was a serial criminal with an interest in financial gain through the sale of drugs. Weiss v. State, 848 N.E.2d 1070, 2006 Ind. LEXIS 473 (2006).

Defendant's proposed predicate offense of possession did not qualify under IC 35-50-2-8 as a prior unrelated felony conviction when defendant pleaded guilty to two counts of burglary as Class B felonies under IC 35-43-4-2. Stanley v. State, 849 N.E.2d 626, 2006 Ind. App. LEXIS 1103 (2006).

Trial court did not err in relying on the same criminal history to enhance defendant's conspiracy conviction and to support his habitual offender adjudication. Hollin v. State, 877 N.E.2d 462, 2007 Ind. LEXIS 1065 (2007).

Determination of the appropriate habitual offender enhancement was within the range set forth in IC 35-50-2-8 and was left to the trial court's discretion and the relevant statutes did not impose a requirement that habitual offender enhancement had to be accompanied by a statement providing explanation for the length of the enhancement; thus, the trial court did not abuse its discretion by imposing a four-and-one-half-year habitual offender enhancement on one of defendant's intimidation convictions based on prior felonies. Montgomery v. State, 878 N.E.2d 262, 2007 Ind. App. LEXIS 2742 (2007).

—Multiple Convictions.
When a defendant appeals a judgment imposing multiple felony convictions and obtains a reversal of a conviction enhanced by a habitual offender finding, the trial court on remand is not prohibited from revising the sentence for the surviving felony conviction to reflect the habitual offender enhancement. Greer v. State, 680 N.E.2d 526, 1997 Ind. LEXIS 46 (1997).

—Not Applicable.
Where defendant's license had been suspended for life, defendant sentence for a subsequent conviction of driving could not be enhanced under general habitual offender statute. Cardwell v. State, 666 N.E.2d 420, 1996 Ind. App. LEXIS 761 (1996).

Trial court imposed illegal sentence on defendant when it sentenced him for conviction under IC 9-30-10-17, habitual traffic offender statute, and further enhanced that sentence under IC 35-50-2-8, general habitual offender statute. Parrett v. State, 800 N.E.2d 620, 2003 Ind. App. LEXIS 2342 (2003).

—Reasons not Required.
There is no authority for the proposition that a trial court must set forth aggravating and mitigating circumstances explaining the particular habitual offender enhancement chosen by the court. Merritt v. State, 663 N.E.2d 1215, 1996 Ind. App. LEXIS 451 (1996).

—Separate Sentences.
Where trial court sentenced defendant for crime of receiving stolen property and separately sentenced him as habitual offender under IC 35-50-2-8, separate sentences were erroneous since habitual offender finding was merely sentence enhancement. Barnett v. State, 834 N.E.2d 169, 2005 Ind. App. LEXIS 1681 (2005).

—Specification of Crime.
The trial court must specify which of the underlying felonies is being enhanced by reason of the habitual offender determination. Collier v. State, 498 N.E.2d 1219, 1986 Ind. LEXIS 1319 (1986).

Where there are two or more underlying felony convictions, the trial court must specify which felony is being enhanced because of the habitual

Enhanced Punishment. (Cont'd)

—Specification of Crime. (Cont'd)
offender determination. Crank v. State, 502 N.E.2d 1355, 1987 Ind. App. LEXIS 2315 (1987).

If there is more than one underlying conviction, the court must specify which conviction it has enhanced. Smith v. State, 559 N.E.2d 338, 1990 Ind. App. LEXIS 1163 (1990).

The trial court erred in enhancing the sentence by 30 years without indicating which of the three separate primary felonies were enhanced by reason of the status as an habitual offender. Baker v. State, 562 N.E.2d 726, 1990 Ind. LEXIS 231 (1990).

—Upheld.
The trial court did not abuse its discretion when it refused to subtract 10 years from the fixed term of 30 years enhancement. Elliott v. State, 541 N.E.2d 942, 1989 Ind. LEXIS 243 (1989).

A 20 year habitual offender enhancement of defendant's conviction for dealing in cocaine was not manifestly unreasonable nor unconstitutionally disproportionate given that the enhancement was based upon prior convictions for robbery and aggravated assault and battery and given the gravity of the crime of dealing in cocaine. Young v. State, 620 N.E.2d 21, 1993 Ind. App. LEXIS 1013 (1993).

Where defendant's sentence for criminal deviate conduct was enhanced by 20 years by virtue of habitual offender finding, trial court did not abuse its discretion even where the court found the defendant's youth, affection for his daughter, good conduct in jail, and guilty plea to be mitigating factors. Tumulty v. State, 666 N.E.2d 394, 1996 Ind. LEXIS 56 (1996), superseded by statute as stated in, Collins v. State, 817 N.E.2d 230, 2004 Ind. LEXIS 989 (Ind. 2004).

No error occurred in denying defendant's motion for post-conviction relief in which defendant argued that the trial court should not have been able to use defendant's prior voluntary manslaughter conviction to both prove defendant's conviction for possession of a firearm by a serious violent felon and to enhance defendant's sentence for being a habitual offender; while defendant's contention was true, defendant waived that claim by not raising it at defendant's sentencing or on direct appeal, and, instead, pleading guilty and waiting to raise it in a motion for postconviction relief. Mills v. State, 868 N.E.2d 446, 2007 Ind. LEXIS 473 (2007).

Evidence of Other Convictions.
Prior convictions may be proved for the purpose of increased punishment under the habitual criminal act by certified transcripts of judgments, if defendant is identified as the person against whom the judgments were had. Kelley v. State, 204 Ind. 612, 185 N.E. 453, 1933 Ind. LEXIS 46 (1933).

Certified copy of the court's record of the proceedings and trial of the defendant, including a copy of the indictment, the names of the jurors, who tried the case, the verdict and judgment of the court, and a certified copy of the record of the

Indiana State Prison of the admission of the appellant upon the prior conviction was admissible at trial for subsequent offense. Barr v. State, 205 Ind. 481, 187 N.E. 259, 1933 Ind. LEXIS 98 (1933).

Charge and proof of prior convictions can have nothing to do with the proof and conviction of the offense with which defendant is charged. Sammons v. State, 210 Ind. 40, 199 N.E. 555, 1935 Ind. LEXIS 308 (1936).

In a prosecution for felony, in which the affidavit charged that the accused had previously been indicted, convicted, and imprisoned for two separate felonies, the state was required to produce duly authenticated copies of the charges of former convictions of the accused in order to entitle the introduction in evidence of orders of commitment of the accused upon conviction for the prior felonies charged to have been committed. Metzger v. State, 214 Ind. 113, 13 N.E.2d 519, 1938 Ind. LEXIS 149 (1938).

Former IC 35-8-8-2 which provided for the punishment of the accused as an habitual criminal when the affidavit or indictment alleged that accused had previously been indicted, convicted, and imprisoned for prior felonies, had to be strictly construed, and proof of the other offenses had to be considered separate and apart from the proof upon the offense charged and for which the accused was on trial. Metzger v. State, 214 Ind. 113, 13 N.E.2d 519, 1938 Ind. LEXIS 149 (1938).

Where defendant was charged with robbery and with being habitual criminal, and court erroneously allowed evidence to be admitted as to former convictions in Kentucky, all reference to habitual criminal charge before the jury was harmful to defendant in the trial of the robbery charge, and conviction thereon would be reversed. Shutt v. State, 233 Ind. 120, 117 N.E.2d 268, 1954 Ind. LEXIS 158 (1954).

Under former IC 35-8-8-2, the former conviction record of an alleged habitual criminal was shown for the single purpose of classifying the defendant as an habitual criminal, and for no other purpose and the jury had no right to consider such proof as bearing upon the charge for which the defendant was on trial, except insofar as he had been cross-examined concerning those convictions. Johnson v. State, 252 Ind. 79, 246 N.E.2d 181, 1969 Ind. LEXIS 327 (1969).

Where state put in evidence two prior felony convictions, it was error for the trial court to grant a motion for judgment on the evidence because record of prior conviction did not show that guilty plea was knowingly and voluntarily made, since the prior judgment could not be collaterally attacked, the remedy to attack the validity of the prior judgment being a challenge of such guilty plea under Post-Conviction Rule 1. State v. Dossett, 174 Ind. App. 501, 368 N.E.2d 259, 1977 Ind. App. LEXIS 1003 (1977).

The state is not barred from reusing prior felony convictions in support of an habitual offender charge where a prior habitual offender proceeding, based on the same prior felony convictions, had resulted in a verdict of acquittal. Baker v. State, 425 N.E.2d 98, 1981 Ind. LEXIS 823 (1981).

Subsection (e) of this section deems the date of

Evidence of Other Convictions. (Cont'd)
previous felony convictions relevant only insofar as the penalty to be assessed; it does not indicate that prior felony convictions are not proof of a defendant's habitual offender status. Underhill v. State, 428 N.E.2d 759, 1981 Ind. LEXIS 918 (1981).

The only issue before the trial court in a habitual offender proceeding is whether the defendant has been found guilty and sentenced for the prior offenses charged. Thomas v. State, 451 N.E.2d 651, 1983 Ind. LEXIS 910 (1983).

Trial court could not attach habitual offender finding to defendants's felony conviction for operating a motor vehicle after having been adjudicated an habitual traffic offender, as it was plainly excluded from IC 35-50-2-8(b)(2), the habitual offender statute. Puckett v. State, 843 N.E.2d 959, 2006 Ind. App. LEXIS 469 (2006).

Defendant was not entitled to a mistrial during the habitual offender phase of the trial because the state presented evidence of two prior judgments of conviction, which defendant admitted to during the guilt phase, and thus, inclusion of any additional non-felony offenses could not have prejudiced the jury's decision. Kyles v. State, 888 N.E.2d 809, 2008 Ind. App. LEXIS 1326 (2008).

—Admission of Other Relevant Information.
Although it is true that this section requires only that the state prove that the defendant has two prior unrelated felony convictions, relevant information connected with those convictions is not generally considered to be prejudicial to the defendant. Maisonet v. State, 448 N.E.2d 1052, 1983 Ind. LEXIS 836 (1983).

—Admitting Twice.
Where defendant claimed that the trial court improperly allowed the admission of three department of correction commitment papers on two separate occasions, as they originally were introduced during the testimony of the county clerk to establish that a Michael A. Luttrull had been convicted and sentenced for three prior felonies in the county and copies of the same commitment papers were among the certified department of correction records which the state later introduced while attempting to identify appellant through fingerprints as the same Michael A. Luttrull convicted of the prior felonies, it was held that while some of the documents were thus admitted twice, it was plain that doing so served a logical purpose, the trial court thus had the discretion to admit them, notwithstanding their cumulative nature, and it was unlikely that the jury would believe that defendant was convicted of six prior crimes, rather than three. Luttrull v. State, 499 N.E.2d 1139, 1986 Ind. LEXIS 1384 (1986).

—Authentication.
Documents used to prove prior convictions which were certified by the clerk of the court in which the prior conviction was obtained were properly authenticated. Griffin v. State, 275 Ind. 107, 415 N.E.2d 60, 1981 Ind. LEXIS 656 (1981).

Properly authenticated copies of court records are admissible in habitual offender proceedings, as an exception to the best evidence rule. Collins v. State, 453 N.E.2d 980, 1983 Ind. LEXIS 977 (1983).

Where defendant contended that the trial court erred in admitting a copy of an unsigned order book entry of defendant's sentencing for one of the prior felony convictions upon which the habitual offender finding was based, arguing that the exhibit was defective because of the lack of the judge's signature, but defendant did not contend that the exhibit failed to be properly authenticated or certified pursuant to former IC 34-1-17-7 (now see IC 34-37-1-8) or former IC 34-1-18-7 (now see IC 34-39-4-3), or to Rule TR. 44, but rather argued that the sentencing order itself was defective by reason of the absent signature; it was held that a collateral attack on the validity of previous convictions is not available to a defendant on an habitual criminal charge, and the trial court did not err in admitting the properly certified copy of the unsigned order book entry. Goliday v. State, 526 N.E.2d 1174, 1988 Ind. LEXIS 229 (1988).

A photostatic duplicate of a certification authenticating document copies does not provide certification necessary for proper authentication, and the document copies are not admissible. Kelly v. State, 561 N.E.2d 771, 1990 Ind. LEXIS 219 (1990).

Although the certifications of defendant's prior offenses at habitual offender proceedings were copies rather than originals, in violation of Evid. R. 902(1), this did not deprive defendant of a fair trial and did not result in fundamental error; defendant made no argument that the documents were not authentic, and conceded during the habitual offender closing argument that defendant had the prior robbery and theft convictions cited in the documents. Suggs v. State, 883 N.E.2d 1188, 2008 Ind. App. LEXIS 711 (2008).

—Certified Copies of Documents.
Certified copies of judgments or commitments containing the same or similar name as the defendant's may be introduced to prove the commission of prior felonies. However, there must be other supporting evidence, which includes circumstantial evidence to identify the defendant as being the same person named in the documents. Coker v. State, 455 N.E.2d 319, 1983 Ind. LEXIS 1009 (1983).

Certified copies of order book entries regarding cases in which the defendant has been convicted and sentenced for prior unrelated felonies, after an official record keeper has read and attested to the records, may be admitted into evidence in the habitual offender phase of the trial. Leavell v. State, 455 N.E.2d 1110, 1983 Ind. LEXIS 1014 (1983).

The trial court's certification of copies of microfilmed records stated that "they have the same legal efficacy as the original, as the same appears of record in my office." The certification, absent evidence that the microfilmed copies were not true and correct, provided sufficient reliability for them to be admitted in an habitual-offender proceeding. Carter v. State, 479 N.E.2d 1290, 1985 Ind. LEXIS 886 (1985).

Evidence of Other Convictions. (Cont'd)

—Certified Copies of Documents. (Cont'd)

Where, in an habitual offender proceeding, the prison records showing prior convictions were certified by the officer having their legal custody, a statement under seal attesting to the officer's authority was not required. Brackens v. State, 480 N.E.2d 536, 1985 Ind. LEXIS 887 (1985).

The certifications on one "page" of each of two challenged exhibits — a copy of an information for a burglary charge, and a copy of a judgment and sentence on a burglary charge—provided adequate certification for the entire exhibit for purposes of a habitual offender determination. Craig v. State, 481 N.E.2d 390, 1985 Ind. LEXIS 1083 (1985).

In an habitual offender proceeding, Department of Correction officials, designated as keepers of the records, signed and affixed department seals to commitment photograph, and fingerprint records, and the execution of the certification was acknowledged before a notary public having knowledge of the official capacity of the person making the acknowledgement. This was sufficient certification; there was no need for the superintendents of the correctional institutions involved to certify the records. Jones v. State, 482 N.E.2d 243, 1985 Ind. LEXIS 947 (1985).

The state is required to present certified records of the prior convictions alleged. Davis v. State, 493 N.E.2d 167, 1986 Ind. LEXIS 1157 (1986).

Where an information sheet was not listed on the certificate and therefore was not properly authenticated but it merely listed general data about defendant, such as his birthdate and address, which was evident in other admitted documents, the admission of the information sheet was harmless error. Luttrull v. State, 499 N.E.2d 1139, 1986 Ind. LEXIS 1384 (1986).

The introduction of properly authenticated commitment papers which contained photographs and a physical description of the defendant was sufficient evidence to support a habitual offender finding. Meredith v. State, 503 N.E.2d 880, 1987 Ind. LEXIS 826 (1987).

Certified copies of prison records are properly admissible as public records and may be used to establish the fact of defendant's prior felony convictions. Wilson v. State, 513 N.E.2d 653, 1987 Ind. LEXIS 1078 (1987).

While certified copies of judgments or commitments containing the same or similar name as the defendant may be introduced to prove the commission of prior felonies, there must be other supporting evidence to identify defendant as the same person named in the documents; this proof of identity may be in the form of circumstantial evidence, and a sufficient connection between the documents and the defendant is made if the evidence yields logical and reasonable inferences from which the trier of fact may determine it was indeed the defendant who was convicted of the two felonies alleged. Baxter v. State, 522 N.E.2d 362, 1988 Ind. LEXIS 108 (1988).

The documents were properly attested in compliance with TR 44(A)(1), which specifically states that no proof that the attesting officer has custody of the record is required. There was no error in the admission of these documents. Lewis v. State, 554 N.E.2d 1133, 1990 Ind. LEXIS 119 (1990).

Although the document bears the seal of the circuit court and a stamp indicating it was recorded in the official records book of Broward County, Florida, there was no attestation that would comply with either former IC 34-1-17-7 (now see IC 34-37-1-8) or TR 44(A)(1). However, this document was merely a judgment against the defendant for public defender fees, and its admission was harmless. Lewis v. State, 554 N.E.2d 1133, 1990 Ind. LEXIS 119 (1990).

—Convictions in Other States.

Official records of other state were properly admissible to show conviction for felony in such state. Morris v. State, 273 Ind. 614, 406 N.E.2d 1187, 1980 Ind. LEXIS 715 (1980), superseded by statute as stated in, Havens v. State, 429 N.E.2d 618, 1981 Ind. LEXIS 967 (1981).

Whether or not another state in which crime had been committed and in which defendant was convicted, classified such crime as a felony was not relevant for the purpose of establishing a prior felony conviction for purpose of habitual offender status in Indiana. Collins v. State, 275 Ind. 86, 415 N.E.2d 46, 1981 Ind. LEXIS 657 (1981), cert. denied, 451 U.S. 991, 101 S. Ct. 2331, 68 L. Ed. 2d 851, 1981 U.S. LEXIS 2139 (1981).

Where defendant was charged with the previous conviction of a felony in another state and the statute of such state was properly introduced in evidence and showed that the offense was a felony as defined by IC 35-50-2-1, it was sufficient to show that the prior conviction was for a felony. Collins v. State, 275 Ind. 86, 415 N.E.2d 46, 1981 Ind. LEXIS 657 (1981), cert. denied, 451 U.S. 991, 101 S. Ct. 2331, 68 L. Ed. 2d 851, 1981 U.S. LEXIS 2139 (1981).

Copies of out-of-state records of judgment and sentence certified to by the central administrator of the department of corrections, which had the originals of such records, were admissible in an habitual-offender proceeding, even though they were not certified by the clerk of the trial court. Carter v. State, 479 N.E.2d 1290, 1985 Ind. LEXIS 886 (1985).

A foreign state's classification of an offense as a felony or a misdemeanor is not relevant for purposes of establishing a prior felony conviction when determining habitual criminal status in Indiana. Beach v. State, 496 N.E.2d 43, 1986 Ind. LEXIS 1233 (1986).

Testimony of deputy sheriff of county in another state regarding defendant's prior convictions in that state, in which deputy made a courtroom identification of defendant, and documents concerning the prior convictions with the official seal of the out-of-state court affixed were sufficient proof that defendant had accumulated two prior unrelated felony convictions, the second of which was committed after his conviction and sentence on the first. Spencer v. State, 660 N.E.2d 359, 1996 Ind. App. LEXIS 20 (1996).

The defendant's conviction in Kentucky of Class

Evidence of Other Convictions. (Cont'd)

—Convictions in Other States. (Cont'd)
D felony with a sentence of one to five years met the definition of a felony under the habitual offender statute. Stewart v. State, 688 N.E.2d 1254, 1997 Ind. LEXIS 219 (1997).

Defendant's prior Illinois conviction for delivery of controlled substance and criminal drug conspiracy did not qualify as prior unrelated felony conviction under Indiana habitual offender statute. Lampitok v. State, 817 N.E.2d 630, 2004 Ind. App. LEXIS 2247 (2004).

Fact that the inmate's criminal history consisted of out-of-state convictions did not prevent the trial court from determining whether those convictions were subject to IC 35-50-2-8(d)(3), which excluded certain prior convictions from counting toward a habitual offender finding. Weiss v. State, 903 N.E.2d 557, 2009 Ind. App. LEXIS 729 (2009).

Fact that the inmate's criminal history consisted of out-of-state convictions did not prevent the trial court from determining whether those convictions were subject to IC 35-50-2-8(d)(3), which excluded certain prior convictions from counting toward a habitual offender finding. Weiss v. State, 903 N.E.2d 557, 2009 Ind. App. LEXIS 729 (2009).

— —Sufficiency.
Where the state relied on the defendant's plea of guilty to an out-of-state offense as one of the requisite prior convictions for an adjudication as an habitual offender, but where, under that state's law, the resulting suspended sentence and placement on probation did not constitute a "conviction," there was insufficient evidence to support his adjudication as an habitual offender. Bochner v. State, 715 N.E.2d 416, 1999 Ind. App. LEXIS 2419 (1999).

—Date of Offense.
There was insufficient evidence to support the defendant's habitual offender determination. The state only provided evidence of the time of the prior felony convictions and sentences, but did not present any evidence as to the dates of the commission of the prior felonies. As a result, there was no way to discern if the commission of the subsequent felonies occurred after the conviction and sentencing upon the felonies directly precedent, as is required. Clark v. State, 480 N.E.2d 555, 1985 Ind. LEXIS 907 (1985).

Evidence of the date the underlying offenses offered during the guilt phase is material, relevant, and appropriate to consider in resolving the issues in the habitual offender phase. Knuckles v. State, 549 N.E.2d 85, 1990 Ind. App. LEXIS 98 (1990).

Because of the profound impact of a determination of habitual offender status upon the length of sentence, the record must provide a rational basis upon which to conclude that the convictions are in their proper statutory sequence. Lee v. State, 550 N.E.2d 304, 1990 Ind. LEXIS 18 (1990).

Since the state presented evidence that the defendant was sentenced in October 1983 for one felony, and presented evidence that the defendant had been found guilty of a felony in another state in June 1986, but failed to present evidence of the date of the commission of that felony, the state failed to meet its burden of proving the necessary sequence of events to support an habitual offender enhancement. The state, in proving that a defendant has two prior unrelated felonies to support an habitual offender enhancement, must show that the second offense was committed after sentencing upon the first and that the principal offense upon which the enhanced punishment is being sought was committed after sentencing upon the second. Allen v. State, 596 N.E.2d 280, 1992 Ind. App. LEXIS 1134 (1992).

The facts alleged in the charging information and at the guilty plea hearing were insufficient to adjudge the defendant an habitual offender, and the guilty plea court erred when it accepted the defendant's guilty plea to being an habitual offender, since the habitual offender information set forth the dates the defendant was convicted of the two prior felonies, but it failed to show the dates he committed the prior felonies. Roe v. State, 598 N.E.2d 586, 1992 Ind. App. LEXIS 1351 (1992).

The charging document did not insufficiently allege the commission date of the predicate offense where the phrase "or about" was used. Webster v. State, 628 N.E.2d 1212, 1994 Ind. LEXIS 13 (1994), overruled, Richardson v. State, 717 N.E.2d 32, 1999 Ind. LEXIS 918 (1999).

The state need only prove the commission of the second offense was after sentencing for the first offense, and the current underlying offense was committed after sentencing for the second offense. Mayo v. State, 681 N.E.2d 689, 1997 Ind. LEXIS 77 (1997).

Where docket sheet and order book entry evidencing defendant's prior consecutive sentences were silent as to court's reason or statutory authority for consecutive sentences for prior convictions, jury could not infer court's reason from its silence and then make further inference regarding required statutory sequence of commission dates of convictions to find defendant an habitual offender. Spann v. State, 681 N.E.2d 223, 1997 Ind. App. LEXIS 545 (1997).

Where the only evidence in a habitual offender determination consisted of two commitment records, neither of which established the date the offenses were committed, the state did not prove beyond a reasonable doubt that the offenses occurred in the requisite sequence. Moore v. Parke, 148 F.3d 705, 1998 U.S. App. LEXIS 12804 (7th Cir. Ind. 1998).

Where there was no evidence on the record regarding the date of commission of the second offense upon which the finding of habitual offender was based, and no evidence from which the jury could infer that the defendant had committed the second offense after he was convicted and sentenced for the first offense, there was a "fundamental defect" which rendered the evidence insufficient to support a finding that the defendant was a habitual offender. Griffin v. State, 705 N.E.2d 580, 1998 Ind. App. LEXIS 1784 (1998).

—Evidence Sufficient.
Evidence was sufficient where certified docu-

Evidence of Other Convictions. (Cont'd)

—Evidence Sufficient. (Cont'd)
ments of defendant's prior conviction and his record at the penitentiary were introduced and the copy of the record at the penitentiary contained defendant's fingerprints. Duncan v. State, 274 Ind. 144, 409 N.E.2d 597, 1980 Ind. LEXIS 749 (1980).

Where a reasonable jury could have found that thumbprints and the same numerical sequence on documents relating to a prior conviction were sufficient to prove that the individual discussed in the documents was the defendant in the current case, that evidence was sufficient to support his habitual offender enhancement. Toney v. State, 715 N.E.2d 367, 1999 Ind. LEXIS 577 (1999).

Defendant, who was convicted of possession of weapon by serious violent felon, was then properly adjudicated habitual offender where proper evidence of two other prior felony convictions was introduced. Tate v. State, 835 N.E.2d 499, 2005 Ind. App. LEXIS 1904 (2005).

Since reasonable jury could have found that matching names, dates of birth and social security numbers in regard to prior convictions were sufficient to prove that defendant had committed other felonies, there was sufficient evidence to support habitual offender enhancement. Gentry v. State, 835 N.E.2d 569, 2005 Ind. App. LEXIS 1930 (2005).

Where defendant forced victim to have sexual intercourse with him and then forced victim to perform oral sex on him, defendant was properly convicted of two separate crimes, rape and criminal deviate conduct, and both crimes could be used for purposes of habitual offender statute. Firestone v. State, 838 N.E.2d 468, 2005 Ind. App. LEXIS 2259 (2005).

When defendant, who was charged in 2004 for conduct occurring in 2002 and 2004, had pleaded guilty to a felony in 1990 for acts that had occurred earlier that year, and had pleaded guilty in 1994 to a felony for acts that had occurred in 1991, the evidence was sufficient to establish that defendant had accumulated two prior, unrelated felonies that qualified him as a habitual offender. Ramsey v. State, 853 N.E.2d 491, 2006 Ind. App. LEXIS 1794 (2006).

Because there was fingerprint evidence linking defendant to the prior felonies, a reasonable fact finder could well have concluded beyond a reasonable doubt that he was the same person convicted of the two prior unrelated felonies as required by IC 35-50-2-8(a). Grant v. State, 870 N.E.2d 1049, 2007 Ind. App. LEXIS 1667 (2007).

—Federal Offenses.
Convictions not within the jurisdiction of the Indiana courts are admissible in a habitual offender determination, and this includes convictions to a federal institution. Denton v. State, 496 N.E.2d 576, 1986 Ind. LEXIS 1252 (1986).

—Form of Proof.
In order to prove prior felony convictions necessary to sustain an habitual offender finding under this section, it was not necessary to tender such proof in a form which strictly complied with former

IC 35-50-5A-1, relating to required contents of judgments. Clay v. State, 440 N.E.2d 466, 1982 Ind. LEXIS 963 (1982).

Where a police officer testified that the defendant committed the second offense after being convicted and sentenced on the first, but he did not state the exact date of commission, and also testified that he had personal knowledge of the proceeding of the second prior offense and that the second offense was committed after conviction and sentencing on the first, the evidence was sufficient to allow the jury to determine that the defendant was an habitual offender. State v. Brooke, 565 N.E.2d 754, 1991 Ind. LEXIS 2 (1991).

—Guilty Plea.
A conviction following a guilty plea is sufficient to support an habitual criminal finding. Blow v. State, 445 N.E.2d 1369, 1983 Ind. LEXIS 777 (1983).

The minimum requirements for a guilty plea to an habitual offender charge are met if the record shows either that the defendant admitted committing the two predicate felonies in the required sentencing/commission sequence or that the defendant was aware of the required sequence and, thus informed, admitted being an habitual offender. Tumulty v. State, 647 N.E.2d 361, 1995 Ind. App. LEXIS 169 (1995), vacated, 666 N.E.2d 394, 1996 Ind. LEXIS 56 (1996).

—Identification of Defendant.
Where there was no evidence to identify defendant as person who was convicted in another state, introduction by defendant of evidence that the person shown on such conviction was pardoned did not amount to an identification. Kelley v. State, 204 Ind. 612, 185 N.E. 453, 1933 Ind. LEXIS 46 (1933).

Testimony of police officer to admissions made by accused identifying accused as defendant against whom three prior convictions were obtained, held not to cure error in admitting incompetent hearsay evidence, including photographs bearing names alleged to be accused's aliases. Kelley v. State, 204 Ind. 612, 185 N.E. 453, 1933 Ind. LEXIS 46 (1933).

Where evidence showed that court and prison officials identified defendant as party convicted on felony charges and who had served sentences under such convictions, it was sufficient to prove prior convictions. Sammons v. State, 210 Ind. 40, 199 N.E. 555, 1935 Ind. LEXIS 308 (1936).

Where certified copies of prior prison records were introduced and such records contained defendant's fingerprints, signature and picture and showed defendant's age, weight, complexion, hair and eye color and a parole officer identified defendant prior to the introduction of such records, it was not necessary that a handwriting or fingerprint expert testify in order to connect defendant with such records. Brown v. State, 270 Ind. 399, 385 N.E.2d 1148, 1979 Ind. LEXIS 566 (1979).

Where certified copies of the informations charging the prior offenses were introduced, and certified copies of docket sheet entries showing the conviction in each cause were also introduced, and the investigating officers involved in such previous

Evidence of Other Convictions. (Cont'd)

—Identification of Defendant. (Cont'd)

offenses identified the defendant as the one charged in such previous offenses, evidence of identification was sufficient even though there was no showing that such officers were in court at the time of the previous convictions. Estep v. State, 271 Ind. 525, 394 N.E.2d 111, 1979 Ind. LEXIS 712 (1979), overruled, Jones v. State, 438 N.E.2d 972, 1982 Ind. LEXIS 928 (1982).

Where documents showing prior conviction contained pictures of defendant, a copy of the judgment finding defendant guilty, a copy of the sentence, and a form showing defendant's fingerprints together with defendant's signature, there was sufficient showing that defendant was the person previously convicted. Norris v. State, 271 Ind. 568, 394 N.E.2d 144, 1979 Ind. LEXIS 720 (1979).

Defendant was sufficiently connected to documents showing prior conviction where deputy sheriff who had executed probable cause affidavit identified defendant as the same individual as the one referred to in the affidavit. Griffin v. State, 275 Ind. 107, 415 N.E.2d 60, 1981 Ind. LEXIS 656 (1981).

Where defendant's fingerprints previously taken at state farm and department of corrections' diagnostic center were properly certified and admitted into evidence and were compared by expert witness to fingerprints taken in course of instant proceedings, it was not necessary that expert witness have been present when earlier prints were taken. Clay v. State, 440 N.E.2d 466, 1982 Ind. LEXIS 963 (1982).

Where defendant argued that certified copies of judgments and convictions alone are not sufficient to identify the defendant as the same person who is named in those documents, but a sheriff testified that he heard defendant admit to committing those prior felonies during a hearing and a transcript of that hearing was also produced, this evidence was sufficient to support the jury's finding that defendant was an habitual offender. Hadley v. State, 496 N.E.2d 67, 1986 Ind. LEXIS 1223 (1986).

Where the documents showing three burglary convictions in 1978 in Connecticut were accompanied by a photograph of defendant, it was clearly demonstrated that he was the same person involved in those convictions, and where as far as his 1982 conviction in Indiana, city policeman testified that he participated in defendant's arrest at that time, there was sufficient evidence to support the jury's finding that defendant was an habitual offender. Eckstein v. State, 526 N.E.2d 693, 1988 Ind. LEXIS 218 (1988).

Where defendant claimed an arrest report was not part of the court record because its certification was by the police department and not by the clerk of the courts, it was held that the arrest report supported the identification of defendant in the judgment of conviction in the court case and was relevant and material as it tended to prove defendant was the person charged, convicted, and sentenced for theft. Burton v. State, 526 N.E.2d 1163, 1988 Ind. LEXIS 232 (1988).

The jury could infer from the evidence that defendant and the Jesse A. Bell, Jr. named in the documentary evidence associated with the October 22, 1993 burglary were one and the same; the coincidence in time, place, and type of conviction shown by the documentary evidence and the police officer's testimony was sufficient to warrant a reasonable trier of fact to conclude beyond a reasonable doubt that appellant was convicted and sentenced for a Class C felony burglary committed October 22, 1983, and therefore, the state established that appellant had accumulated two prior felony convictions as required by this section. Bell v. State, 622 N.E.2d 450, 1993 Ind. LEXIS 143 (1993).

Match of fingerprints in state police central repository with fingerprints taken from defendant was sufficient evidence from which jury could conclude that defendant was convicted of prior rape. Palmer v. State, 679 N.E.2d 887, 1997 Ind. LEXIS 53 (1997).

—Inadmissible Evidence.

A definition of the word habitual from a dictionary is irrelevant to disprove whether defendant has been convicted of two prior felonies and thus inadmissible in a habitual offender proceeding. Thomas v. State, 451 N.E.2d 651, 1983 Ind. LEXIS 910 (1983).

Evidence regarding the severity of the sentence, defendant's positive character traits, opportunities for rehabilitation, and his work record were irrelevant and properly excluded in a habitual offender proceeding. Thomas v. State, 451 N.E.2d 651, 1983 Ind. LEXIS 910 (1983).

Trial court did not err in not allowing defendant to tell the jury during final argument about the 30 additional years which would be imposed if he were found to be an habitual offender. Leslie v. State, 558 N.E.2d 813, 1990 Ind. LEXIS 162 (1990).

Since the evidence supporting defendant's habitual determination was substantial, there was no reversible error in exhibits which indicated the defendant was charged with other felonies. Elmore v. State, 688 N.E.2d 213, 1997 Ind. App. LEXIS 1665 (1997).

—Incorporation From Earlier Phase.

Nothing in former IC 35-50-2-7.1 prohibited incorporating evidence submitted on an underlying misdemeanor charge and evidence of prior convictions for the same offense submitted to elevate the misdemeanor charge to a Class D felony to prove the habitual offender charge. Sowell v. State, 590 N.E.2d 1123, 1992 Ind. App. LEXIS 597 (1992), overruled, Shelton v. State, 602 N.E.2d 1017, 1992 Ind. LEXIS 251 (1992).

—Multiple Prior Convictions.

Proof of more than two former convictions was not harmful to defendant where it was offered for the single purpose of classifying defendant as an habitual criminal as alleged in the affidavit. Hanks v. State, 225 Ind. 593, 76 N.E.2d 702, 1948 Ind. LEXIS 117 (1948).

Evidence that defendant had prior conviction on lesser included offense of petit larceny under

Evidence of Other Convictions. (Cont'd)

—Multiple Prior Convictions. (Cont'd)
charge of robbery, and prior conviction for armed robbery, was sufficient to show defendant had been twice previously convicted and imprisoned for felonies, and any defect in proof of third prior conviction was moot because proof of such was mere surplusage. Jessup v. State, 256 Ind. 409, 269 N.E.2d 374, 1971 Ind. LEXIS 646 (1971).

Where defendant's last prior unrelated felony conviction occurred less than 10 years prior to commission of the underlying felony, the remoteness of a felony over 10 years' previous thereto was a matter for the jury, and not the judge, to weigh in its assessment of the habitual offender charge. Underhill v. State, 428 N.E.2d 759, 1981 Ind. LEXIS 918 (1981).

The only proof necessary for an habitual offender finding is that defendant had been previously convicted twice of unrelated felonies, and evidence of other convictions would be surplusage. McConnell v. State, 436 N.E.2d 1097, 1982 Ind. LEXIS 857 (1982).

Where the existence of two prior felony convictions is undisputed, the admission of other prior convictions is merely surplusage. Hensley v. State, 448 N.E.2d 665, 1983 Ind. LEXIS 835 (1983).

It is not reversible error to allege excess felonies, even though they are not subsequently proved. St. Mociers v. State, 459 N.E.2d 26, 1984 Ind. LEXIS 747 (1984).

Evidence that the defendant had been previously convicted of two unrelated felonies was sufficient to support a habitual offender determination. Johnson v. State, 699 N.E.2d 746, 1998 Ind. App. LEXIS 1589 (1998).

—Offenses Committed Against Police Officers.
The fact that a jury might view a charge of aiming a weapon at a deputy sheriff more harshly than they would if it had been aimed at an ordinary citizen does not make the evidence of such a prior conviction inadmissible nor does it make it unduly prejudicial. Ritchie v. State, 526 N.E.2d 699, 1988 Ind. LEXIS 216 (1988).

—Order Book Entries.
Order book entries are not required to prove defendant's prior conviction in an habitual criminal proceeding. Collins v. State, 275 Ind. 86, 415 N.E.2d 46, 1981 Ind. LEXIS 657 (1981), cert. denied, 451 U.S. 991, 101 S. Ct. 2331, 68 L. Ed. 2d 851, 1981 U.S. LEXIS 2139 (1981).

—Order of Proof.
The rule that the order of evidence is discretionary with the trial court is no different in a habitual offender trial. Pointer v. State, 499 N.E.2d 1087, 1986 Ind. LEXIS 1364 (1986).

In order to obtain post-conviction relief from this section, a petitioner must demonstrate that his various convictions did not in fact occur in the required order. Weatherford v. State, 619 N.E.2d 915, 1993 Ind. LEXIS 118 (1993).

—Original Charges.
A defendant has not been prejudiced by the introduction of documentary evidence which refers not only to the offenses of which he was convicted or "the predicate offenses," but also to the original charges which led to his conviction of the predicate offenses, where the state's documentary evidence clearly reflects the relationship between the original charges and the predicate felonies. Daniel v. State, 526 N.E.2d 1157, 1988 Ind. LEXIS 231 (1988).

—Parol Evidence.
Parol evidence standing alone is insufficient evidence of fact of prior convictions in absence of showing of unavailability of proper certified records. Morgan v. State, 440 N.E.2d 1087, 1982 Ind. LEXIS 989 (1982); Washington v. State, 441 N.E.2d 1355, 1982 Ind. LEXIS 1028 (1982).

Where state attempted to prove a theft conviction, in order to trigger the habitual offender statute, merely by oral testimony of the prosecuting attorney and without showing any official written court records showing a judgment of conviction, the finding of habitual criminality was vacated. Driver v. State, 467 N.E.2d 1186, 1984 Ind. LEXIS 935 (1984).

In an habitual offender proceeding, where there is documentary proof of the existence of the prior convictions, the identity and the sequence of events may be established by parol evidence. Powers v. State, 617 N.E.2d 545, 1993 Ind. LEXIS 99 (1993).

—Properly Admitted.
It was not error to admit exhibit consisting of information and commitment order to show prior conviction, although information charged dealing in a controlled substance while commitment order showed he was found guilty of possession, since possession was a lesser included offense and judge informed the jury of that. Collins v. State, 275 Ind. 86, 415 N.E.2d 46, 1981 Ind. LEXIS 657 (1981), cert. denied, 451 U.S. 991, 101 S. Ct. 2331, 68 L. Ed. 2d 851, 1981 U.S. LEXIS 2139 (1981).

Exhibits consisting of fingerprints, photographs, and a copy of commitment to department of corrections, properly certified by the director of records at the Indiana Reformatory, were properly admissible to show prior conviction. Gilmore v. State, 275 Ind. 134, 415 N.E.2d 70, 1981 Ind. LEXIS 668 (1981).

Where court, after examining exhibits to determine if they were properly certified, admitted them into evidence to prove prior convictions they were properly admitted even though court did not expressly state his reasons for allowing the exhibits into evidence and although defendant contended they were hearsay. Traylor v. State, 420 N.E.2d 887, 1981 Ind. LEXIS 748 (1981).

Allowing into evidence a document which showed that, in connection with one of the prior felony convictions, defendant had violated the terms of his probation and that his probation had been revoked was not error. Taylor v. State, 420 N.E.2d 1231, 1981 Ind. LEXIS 750 (1981).

—Reduced Charge.
Where the state attempted to introduce evidence that defendant had originally been charged with

Evidence of Other Convictions. (Cont'd)

—Reduced Charge. (Cont'd)
the commission of a crime while armed with a deadly weapon and that he had subsequently entered a plea of guilty to the lesser included offense of committing a crime of violence while armed with a firearm, but the trial court did not permit the state to present such evidence, in view of the fact that this conduct occurred during the habitual offender phase of the trial and the express purpose of that hearing was to inform the jury of appellant's past criminal conduct, it could not be said the mere mention of the fact that one of the convictions was a reduced charge would submit him to such grave peril that the trial court erred in denying his motion for a mistrial. Ritchie v. State, 526 N.E.2d 699, 1988 Ind. LEXIS 216 (1988).

—Remoteness.
Subsection (e) of this section deems the date of previous felony convictions relevant only insofar as the penalty to be assessed; it does not indicate that prior felony convictions are not proof of a defendant's habitual offender status. Underhill v. State, 428 N.E.2d 759, 1981 Ind. LEXIS 918 (1981).

Where defendant's last prior unrelated felony conviction occurred less than ten years prior to commission of the underlying felony, the remoteness of a felony over ten years' previous thereto was a matter for the jury, and not the judge, to weigh in its assessment of the habitual offender charge. Underhill v. State, 428 N.E.2d 759, 1981 Ind. LEXIS 918 (1981).

That the remoteness of prior convictions does not preclude their use in habitual offender proceedings is a matter of legislative policy. Darnell v. State, 435 N.E.2d 250, 1982 Ind. LEXIS 821 (1982).

—Representation by Counsel.
Where defendant was being tried as an habitual criminal offender and order book entries which were made part of the record clearly showed that defendant was represented by counsel at each of prior convictions it was sufficient to show representation by counsel at prior conviction. Parks v. State, 270 Ind. 689, 389 N.E.2d 286, 1979 Ind. LEXIS 593 (1979).

—Sufficiency.
Where one is charged with being an habitual criminal, based on crimes committed in other jurisdictions, it is sufficient to prove that the conviction was for offenses punishable with death or imprisonment in the state prison in the jurisdiction where conviction was had. Kelley v. State, 204 Ind. 612, 185 N.E. 453, 1933 Ind. LEXIS 46 (1933).

Accused's admissions of prior convictions in federal court and in another state, and as to serving time thereunder, were insufficient to authorize the imposition of life sentence under former IC 35-8-8-2. Kelley v. State, 204 Ind. 612, 185 N.E. 453, 1933 Ind. LEXIS 46 (1933).

The evidence on the essential element of the commission of former felonies and commitments in penal institutions was insufficient to sustain a conviction as an habitual criminal where a set of fingerprints was a part of each set of commitment papers which were introduced into evidence; however, no effort was made by the state to show that such fingerprints were those of the defendant and no other evidence was offered to show that defendant in this action was the same person as the defendant named in the other judgment and commitment papers. Smith v. State, 243 Ind. 74, 181 N.E.2d 520, 1962 Ind. LEXIS 133 (1962).

In order to sustain finding of habitual offender status, the court was not required to show prior incarceration. Havens v. State, 429 N.E.2d 618, 1981 Ind. LEXIS 967 (1981).

An information bearing a cause number and charging defendant with an offense, and a commitment order bearing the same cause number and specifically reciting that the trial court found defendant guilty of the offense, and ordered and adjudged defendant to serve two years in prison, adequately disclosed the prior conviction. Collins v. State, 275 Ind. 86, 415 N.E.2d 46, 1981 Ind. LEXIS 657 (1981), cert. denied, 451 U.S. 991, 101 S. Ct. 2331, 68 L. Ed. 2d 851, 1981 U.S. LEXIS 2139 (1981).

Parole officer's testimony that defendant once stated to him that he had been convicted in 1971 of automobile banditry, and documentation proving same, were sufficient proof of that offense for purposes of finding that defendant was an habitual criminal. Maier v. State, 437 N.E.2d 448, 1982 Ind. LEXIS 870 (1982).

There was sufficient evidence from which the trier of fact could have concluded the defendant had two prior felony convictions. Blackmon v. State, 455 N.E.2d 586, 1983 Ind. LEXIS 1007 (1983).

Evidence of prior convictions was sufficient to warrant finding as habitual offender. McAfee v. State, 459 N.E.2d 1186, 1984 Ind. LEXIS 758 (1984); McBrady v. State, 460 N.E.2d 1222, 1984 Ind. LEXIS 780 (1984); Wade v. State, 718 N.E.2d 1162, 1999 Ind. App. LEXIS 1929 (1999).

In light of the requirement that a person, to be an habitual offender, must be found to have been twice convicted and twice sentenced, there was insufficient evidence to support a finding beyond a reasonable doubt that the defendant was an habitual offender where the evidence that would have proven that the defendant was actually sentenced on the second of his two prior convictions was missing from the trial record. Williams v. Duckworth, 738 F.2d 828, 1984 U.S. App. LEXIS 21049 (7th Cir. Ind. 1984), cert. denied, 469 U.S. 1229, 105 S. Ct. 1229, 84 L. Ed. 2d 367, 1985 U.S. LEXIS 1118 (1985).

Evidence sufficiently supported an inference from which the jury could determine that defendant was the same person named in exhibits used to prove prior felony convictions. Gilliam v. State, 509 N.E.2d 815, 1987 Ind. LEXIS 970 (1987).

The evidence of prior convictions complies with the statutory sequential requirement where the information and commitment documents show on their face district and separate offenses, and evidence of the underlying offenses came out during the guilt phase of the trial. Knuckles v. State, 549 N.E.2d 85, 1990 Ind. App. LEXIS 98 (1990).

Evidence of Other Convictions. (Cont'd)

—Sufficiency. (Cont'd)

While the state may use the same prior convictions to support two habitual offender convictions, the felonies underlying those two habitual offender convictions must be distinct and unrelated. Golden v. State, 553 N.E.2d 1219, 1990 Ind. App. LEXIS 571 (1990).

Where the jury specifically found that four of the five convictions charged supported the habitual offender determination, error in the admission of one of the supporting felonies does not give rise to reversal. Smith v. State, 559 N.E.2d 338, 1990 Ind. App. LEXIS 1163 (1990).

Evidence was sufficient to support convictions for carrying a handgun without a license and being a habitual offender; fingerprint expert properly identified plaintiff in court and arrest reports and orders of convictions sufficiently linked defendant to prior offenses to show defendant was the person convicted of each crime. Sides v. State, 693 N.E.2d 1310, 1998 Ind. LEXIS 37 (1998), overruled, Jones v. State, 863 N.E.2d 333, 2007 Ind. App. LEXIS 573 (2007).

Decision finding defendant an habitual offender was reversed where the state presented no evidence regarding the date that either prior felony offense was committed. McManomy v. State, 751 N.E.2d 291, 2001 Ind. App. LEXIS 1076 (2001).

— —Discrepancy in Docket Sheets.

Where there is a discrepancy between the names of the judges indicated on the bench docket and on the docket sheet, this difference does not render the exhibit inadmissible in the consideration of habitual offender status because it merely reflects that one is the presiding judge and the other a former judge of the same court. Steelman v. State, 486 N.E.2d 523, 1985 Ind. LEXIS 1067 (1985).

—Testimony of Prior Counsel.

In habitual offender proceedings, prior counsel is permitted to testify as to the existence, nature, and date of a defendant's prior conviction, matters which are documented in the public record. Leavell v. State, 455 N.E.2d 1110, 1983 Ind. LEXIS 1014 (1983).

—Unalleged Convictions.

Evidence relative to proof of the prior conviction alleged is admissible even if that evidence also tends to prove an unalleged prior conviction. Denton v. State, 496 N.E.2d 576, 1986 Ind. LEXIS 1252 (1986).

—Use During Trial of Underlying Crime.

The mere fact that certain prior convictions would have to be proven in habitual offender proceedings was not ground to prohibit the cross-examination of defendant during the trial for the basic crime with respect to such prior convictions for the purpose of impeachment. Griffin v. State, 275 Ind. 107, 415 N.E.2d 60, 1981 Ind. LEXIS 656 (1981).

Where the determination of the fact of prior crimes is supported by direct evidence produced at the habitual offender phase of the trial, there is no undue prejudice to the defendant from the refusal to limit cross-examination of the defendant at the guilt or innocence phase of the trial as to his prior convictions. Denton v. State, 455 N.E.2d 905, 1983 Ind. LEXIS 1026 (1983).

When the defendant took the stand in his own defense during his trial on child molestation charges, he "opened the door" to evidence of his past convictions for theft and robbery, notwithstanding the pending habitual offender proceeding. Brackens v. State, 480 N.E.2d 536, 1985 Ind. LEXIS 887 (1985).

—Verdict.

Where jury's verdict specifically identifies the prior convictions on which its determination is based, and as long as at least two of the prior convictions were unrelated felonies, the habitual offender determination will be upheld. Stiles v. State, 686 N.E.2d 886, 1997 Ind. App. LEXIS 1500 (1997).

Failure to Enter Judgment for Underlying Felony.

It is not reversible error when the trial court fails to enter judgment for the underlying felony prior to commencing the second phase of the bifurcated proceeding. Collins v. State, 275 Ind. 86, 415 N.E.2d 46, 1981 Ind. LEXIS 657 (1981), cert. denied, 451 U.S. 991, 101 S. Ct. 2331, 68 L. Ed. 2d 851, 1981 U.S. LEXIS 2139 (1981).

While the better practice would be for the trial court to consider the presentence report and arguments of counsel before entering judgment for a Class D felony prior to the start of the habitual offender phase of the trial, there are no actual requirements which mandate this. Gross v. State, 444 N.E.2d 296, 1983 Ind. LEXIS 731 (1983).

Felony.

It is not necessary that imprisonment must be in the state prison in order for the offense to be characterized as a felony, but it is sufficient if the offender may be imprisoned in the state prison. Paneitz v. State, 246 Ind. 418, 204 N.E.2d 350, 1965 Ind. LEXIS 368 (1965), cert. denied, 382 U.S. 883, 86 S. Ct. 176, 15 L. Ed. 2d 123, 1965 U.S. LEXIS 500 (1965); In re Sobieski, 246 Ind. 222, 204 N.E.2d 353, 1965 Ind. LEXIS 344 (1965); Bernard v. State, 248 Ind. 688, 230 N.E.2d 536, 1967 Ind. LEXIS 498 (1967).

Whether an offense is a "felony" is purely a question of legislative categorization; it is not a question of fact for the jury, but a matter of law predetermined by the legislature and applied by the judiciary. Seward v. State, 453 N.E.2d 256, 1983 Ind. LEXIS 957 (1983); Cain v. State, 594 N.E.2d 835, 1992 Ind. App. LEXIS 1062 (1992).

Defendant was properly adjudged a habitual offender because the State provided the trial court with sufficient evidence to prove that defendant's Florida convictions were felonies. Hornbostel v. State, 757 N.E.2d 170, 2001 Ind. App. LEXIS 1812 (2001).

Felony Under Prior Law.

Even if the sentence imposed for prior crime

Felony Under Prior Law. (Cont'd)

could be construed as for a misdemeanor under IC 35-50-2-7 if such section had been in effect at the time of sentencing, since such section was not in effect at that time the conviction for a felony under the prior law was proper to use as the basis for an habitual offender charge. Wise v. State, 272 Ind. 498, 400 N.E.2d 114, 1980 Ind. LEXIS 592 (1980).

The fact that one of the prior felony convictions used in the habitual offender proceeding would have been a misdemeanor rather than a felony at the time of the habitual offender proceeding did not invalidate the habitual offender sentence since prior unrelated felony convictions are viewed as they existed at the time they occurred. Ross v. State, 274 Ind. 588, 413 N.E.2d 252, 1980 Ind. LEXIS 816 (1980); Maier v. State, 437 N.E.2d 448, 1982 Ind. LEXIS 870 (1982).

Prior conviction can be used in habitual criminal proceeding if range of penalty under statute at time of prior conviction provided for penalties in excess of a year and less than a year and penalty actually imposed was less than a year imprisonment. Dixon v. State, 437 N.E.2d 1318, 1982 Ind. LEXIS 892 (1982).

A conviction for theft under former IC 35-17-5-12 was a felony conviction and could properly serve as a basis for a little habitual offender determination (former IC 35-50-2-7.1). Dickson v. State, 624 N.E.2d 472, 1993 Ind. App. LEXIS 1020 (1993).

To determine the classification of pre-1977 felonies for habitual offender purposes under former IC 35-50-2-7.1, the present statutory classification scheme should be applied to pre-1977 felonies. Dickson v. State, 624 N.E.2d 472, 1993 Ind. App. LEXIS 1020 (1993).

Guilty but Mentally Ill.

It was not cruel and unusual punishment to find a defendant to be an habitual offender after first finding that he was guilty but mentally ill. Higgins v. State, 601 N.E.2d 342, 1992 Ind. LEXIS 227 (1992).

Guilty Plea.

—Plea Negotiations.

Where the habitual criminal count charged a defendant with an offense for which he was properly subject to prosecution before the failure of the plea negotiations, the filing of the habitual offender count after a breakdown of the plea negotiations was a justifiable exploitation of legitimate bargaining leverage. Baker v. State, 425 N.E.2d 98, 1981 Ind. LEXIS 823 (1981).

The threat of an habitual criminal charge, when supported by probable cause, is a legitimate bargaining tool by which the state may induce guilty pleas. Brown v. State, 453 N.E.2d 254, 1983 Ind. LEXIS 958 (1983).

The only instance in which a threatened habitual criminal charge will cause a guilty plea to be deemed void as involuntarily proffered is when the state could not have pursued the threatened charge for lack of probable cause. Brown v. State, 453 N.E.2d 254, 1983 Ind. LEXIS 958 (1983).

—Voluntariness.

The overall voluntariness of a plea of guilty is suspect where the plea is entered without any advisement to the defendant as to the effect of an adjudication he is an habitual offender on his sentencing, and such a case will be remanded and the defendant will be brought into court for a hearing at which he shall be advised of the effect of a successful habitual offender adjudication on his sentence for the underlying felony, and he shall be allowed upon motion to withdraw his plea of guilty without any further showing of necessity "to correct a manifest injustice" being required. State v. Hicks, 453 N.E.2d 1014, 1983 Ind. LEXIS 967 (1983).

Habitual Offender Hearing.

—In General.

The habitual offender proceeding is an evidentiary hearing in every sense, and the jury's decision therein is conclusive of whether the state satisfied its burden of proof; the habitual offender jury hearing is a jury trial within the meaning of IC 35-35-1-2. Snyder v. State, 654 N.E.2d 15, 1995 Ind. App. LEXIS 935 (1995), aff'd in part, 668 N.E.2d 1214, 1996 Ind. LEXIS 97 (1996).

Trial court did not err in admitting certain evidence at the habitual offender phase of defendant's trial since admission was harmless error. Beeks v. State, 839 N.E.2d 1271, 2005 Ind. App. LEXIS 2449 (2005).

—Role of Jury.

Where facts of prerequisite prior felony convictions are uncontroverted, the jury still has the unquestioned right to refuse to find defendant to be a habitual offender at law. Seay v. State, 698 N.E.2d 732, 1998 Ind. LEXIS 96 (1998).

State constitution does not require that jury be advised of penalty for being a habitual offender or be involved in deciding the amount of a penalty. Seay v. State, 698 N.E.2d 732, 1998 Ind. LEXIS 96 (1998).

—Waiver.

Regardless of whether the right to a jury trial in habitual offender proceedings is created solely by statute or is rooted in the United States or Indiana Constitutions, the safeguards and precautions attendant to the waiver of a jury trial apply to waiver of the habitual offender jury hearing. Snyder v. State, 654 N.E.2d 15, 1995 Ind. App. LEXIS 935 (1995), aff'd in part, 668 N.E.2d 1214, 1996 Ind. LEXIS 97 (1996).

Harmless Error.

A trial court's improper comments to prospective jurors regarding the defendant's habitual offender charge were harmless error beyond a reasonable doubt where other evidence presented at trial overwhelmingly established guilt. Leach v. State, 699 N.E.2d 641, 1998 Ind. LEXIS 235 (1998), amended, — N.E.2d —, 1998 Ind. LEXIS 507 (1998).

Indictment or Information.

To authorize a life sentence under former IC 35-8-8-2, the indictment had to describe specifi-

Indictment or Information. (Cont'd)
cally previous convictions, sentences, and imprisonments, and the jury had to find that defendant was convicted, sentenced, and imprisoned in instances described, and not otherwise. Kelley v. State, 204 Ind. 612, 185 N.E. 453, 1933 Ind. LEXIS 46 (1933).

Former convictions must be alleged in indictment and proved at trial of last offense. Barr v. State, 205 Ind. 481, 187 N.E. 259, 1933 Ind. LEXIS 98 (1933).

Charges of assault and battery with intent to kill and of being an habitual criminal may be contained in one indictment. Barr v. State, 205 Ind. 481, 187 N.E. 259, 1933 Ind. LEXIS 98 (1933).

An affidavit which attempted to charge prior convictions, sentences, and imprisonment, but which did not designate the place of imprisonment for one of the alleged convictions, failed to support a conviction of life imprisonment under former IC 35-8-8-2, since it was so uncertain as to be subject to a motion to quash. Midland v. State, 220 Ind. 668, 46 N.E.2d 200, 1943 Ind. LEXIS 278 (1943).

Where affidavit did not state court and county in which alleged convictions were obtained, it was not sufficient to charge defendant with being an habitual criminal. Shutt v. State, 233 Ind. 120, 117 N.E.2d 268, 1954 Ind. LEXIS 158 (1954).

Prior convictions need not be set out in any particular order or form in an indictment or information. McCormick v. State, 262 Ind. 303, 317 N.E.2d 428, 1974 Ind. LEXIS 302 (1974).

It was not error to amend information nine months after arraignment so as to add an habitual criminal count where defendant was given adequate time to prepare his defense and it did not prejudice the substantial rights of the defendant. Howard v. State, 268 Ind. 589, 377 N.E.2d 628, 1978 Ind. LEXIS 708 (1978), cert. denied, 439 U.S. 1049, 99 S. Ct. 727, 58 L. Ed. 2d 708, 1978 U.S. LEXIS 4247 (1978).

Count of an information charging defendant with being an habitual criminal could be amended as to the date of one of the convictions to conform to the evidence. Norris v. State, 271 Ind. 568, 394 N.E.2d 144, 1979 Ind. LEXIS 720 (1979).

It was not error to amend an information to include a count under the habitual criminal statute so long as defendant had adequate time to prepare his defense and his substantial rights were not otherwise harmed. Norris v. State, 271 Ind. 568, 394 N.E.2d 144, 1979 Ind. LEXIS 720 (1979).

Where information charging defendant with being an habitual offender stated that he was convicted of arson in "Hills County, New Hampshire" while evidence showed that he was convicted in Hillsborough County, New Hampshire, there was no fatal variance since Hills County in the information could be considered an abbreviation of Hillsborough County. Page v. State, 271 Ind. 670, 395 N.E.2d 235, 1979 Ind. LEXIS 733 (1979), overruled, Rhyne v. State, 446 N.E.2d 970, 1983 Ind. LEXIS 789 (Ind. 1983).

It was not error to permit amendment of information to change "Jefferson, Missouri," to "Jefferson City, Missouri" to show place of incarceration.

Morris v. State, 273 Ind. 614, 406 N.E.2d 1187, 1980 Ind. LEXIS 715 (1980), superseded by statute as stated in, Havens v. State, 429 N.E.2d 618, 1981 Ind. LEXIS 967 (1981).

State may not attempt to file one count information charging only habitual offender status, since the status is not a separate offense and relates only to length of sentence to be imposed upon underlying charge or charges, which provide basis for issuance of arrest warrant upon probable cause. Ferguson v. State, 438 N.E.2d 286, 1982 Ind. LEXIS 901 (1982).

Where defendant did not object to the filing of the habitual criminal charge the day before his trial began nor did he seek a continuance, he had thus waived the issue, and where he received documentation of his previous convictions and did not contend that any of the evidence presented at the habitual offender hearing was unknown to him, although he did claim that he did not have time to investigate these prior convictions to determine whether there were grounds for collateral attack, his assertions of prejudice were not sufficient to merit reversal of the habitual offender finding. Murphy v. State, 499 N.E.2d 1077, 1986 Ind. LEXIS 1373 (1986).

A habitual offender count does not allege a separate crime or change the theory of the case and is therefore a permissible amendment to the information after arraignment and plea on the principal offense so long as the defendant has adequate time to prepare a defense. Dixon v. State, 524 N.E.2d 2, 1988 Ind. LEXIS 146 (1988).

Where defendant claimed the habitual offender allegation must contain all of the procedural matters and safeguards of the original and underlying charges, it was held that there was nothing in this record to indicate that defendant challenged the habitual offender allegation at the time it was filed, but the sufficiency of an information must be challenged by motion to dismiss no later than 20 days prior to the omnibus date under IC 35-34-1-4(b)(1), and if this procedure is not followed, any error in regard to defects in the information is waived. Foster v. State, 526 N.E.2d 696, 1988 Ind. LEXIS 221 (1988).

Where defendant alleged the state should have been precluded from filing the habitual offender allegation regardless of when it was filed because the state was bound by a promise that it made to him during plea negotiations, but, prior to commencement of trial, at the hearing on his objections to the late filing, both the deputy prosecutor and defendant's trial counsel indicated that no plea agreement had been entered into by the parties and defendant admitted at that time that he had initially rejected the plea agreement, there was no error. Daniel v. State, 526 N.E.2d 1157, 1988 Ind. LEXIS 231 (1988).

Because defendant did not object at trial and because he failed to request a continuance pursuant to IC 35-34-1-5(c), he waived the issue of the state's late filing of the habitual offender allegation. Daniel v. State, 526 N.E.2d 1157, 1988 Ind. LEXIS 231 (1988).

Where the habitual offender count charged that defendant was convicted of "entering to commit a

Indictment or Information. (Cont'd)

felony," whereas the sentencing order contained the heading "first degree burglary" and the record reflected that defendant had pled guilty to the lesser offense of entering to commit a felony arising out of the original first degree burglary charge, the Supreme Court declined to find the inconsistency sufficient to impair either the admissibility of the sentencing order or the sufficiency of evidence supporting the habitual offender determination. Goliday v. State, 526 N.E.2d 1174, 1988 Ind. LEXIS 229 (1988).

—Amendment to Charge.

Where defendant was given adequate time to prepare his defense, an amendment adding an habitual offender count did not prejudice the substantial rights of the defendant. Gilmore v. State, 275 Ind. 134, 415 N.E.2d 70, 1981 Ind. LEXIS 668 (1981).

Fact that defendant was arraigned on amended habitual offender count just prior to the habitual offender proceeding did not prejudice defendant where it was obvious from the record that defendant was aware for nearly a year before trial that the state was charging him with being an habitual offender. Dorton v. State, 419 N.E.2d 1289, 1981 Ind. LEXIS 738 (1981).

The trial court erred in allowing the state to amend a burglary information by adding an habitual offender charge after the jury was selected, but as the defendant failed to show prejudice to his substantial rights by the court's denial of a motion for continuance, the error was harmless. Barnett v. State, 429 N.E.2d 625, 1981 Ind. LEXIS 960 (1981).

The state is not foreclosed from seeking sentence enhancement under this section because the allegation is not made at the time the original information or indictment alleging the underlying felony is filed since the state may file the habitual offender allegation as an amendment to the original charge. State v. Hicks, 453 N.E.2d 1014, 1983 Ind. LEXIS 967 (1983).

A defendant's right to be protected from double jeopardy is not prejudiced if he is prosecuted on an habitual offender amendment to the information after he pleads guilty to the underlying felony. State v. Hicks, 453 N.E.2d 1014, 1983 Ind. LEXIS 967 (1983).

Allowing an amendment to the information following a plea of guilty in order to allege that the defendant is an habitual offender does not prejudice his substantial rights on the ground that once the defendant has pleaded guilty to the original charge it has blossomed into a conviction and, hence, there is no longer a charging instrument of any legal effect to which the habitual offender allegation can attach. State v. Hicks, 453 N.E.2d 1014, 1983 Ind. LEXIS 967 (1983).

Amending the information to include a habitual offender count is a sentence enhancement and not a separate crime and does not change the theory of the case nor the identity of the offense. Perrault v. State, 490 N.E.2d 322, 1986 Ind. LEXIS 1051 (1986).

Lack of a formal motion to amend an informa-

tion for theft when adding an allegation of habitual offender did no prejudice to substantial rights, where the judge, the prosecutor, the defendant and defense counsel were all present when the written allegation of habitual offender was filed and a trial date considered. Nash v. State, 545 N.E.2d 566, 1989 Ind. LEXIS 320 (1989).

IC 35-34-1-5(e) is not an ameliorative sentencing amendment to which the doctrine of amelioration would apply, preventing the prosecution from filing a habitual offender charge where the omnibus charge was filed before the effective date of the amendment. Timberlake v. State, 679 N.E.2d 1337, 1997 Ind. App. LEXIS 519 (1997).

If the trial court found that the State knew of only one of defendant's prior felony convictions within the statutory time for amending the charging information, the trial court could have found good cause for a late amendment to include the habitual offender enhancement because the State had no reason to believe that defendant was an habitual offender; thus, the trial court's order allowing a belated habitual offender enhancement was affirmed. Watson v. State, 776 N.E.2d 914, 2002 Ind. App. LEXIS 1702 (2002).

— —Continuance.

While an amendment of an information to include an habitual offender count may be valid grounds for a continuance, where the defendant did not ask for a continuance when he first became aware of the amended charge but awaited the actual commencement of the trial and revealed neither a need for a continuance nor a justification for the delay in seeking it, it was properly denied. Ives v. State, 275 Ind. 535, 418 N.E.2d 220, 1981 Ind. LEXIS 710 (1981).

The addition of an habitual offender charge is permissible at any time so long as it does not prejudice the substantial rights of the defendant. A showing of such prejudice is required before a motion for continuance must be granted. Baxter v. State, 522 N.E.2d 362, 1988 Ind. LEXIS 108 (1988).

— —Notice.

Where an information containing a habitual offender count was filed during the defendant's trial and no objection was made at that time, the defendant was not denied due process of law for the failure of providing the defendant notice of the charge. Stanley v. State, 531 N.E.2d 484, 1988 Ind. LEXIS 347 (1988).

Where the trial court made no findings of good cause upon which to justify the addition of a habitual offender count three days before trial contrary to the requirements of IC 35-34-1-5(e) for amending the charging information, it was an abuse of discretion requiring reversal of the habitual offender conviction. Attebury v. State, 703 N.E.2d 175, 1998 Ind. App. LEXIS 2247 (1998), overruled in part, Williams v. State, 735 N.E.2d 785, 2000 Ind. LEXIS 935 (2000).

—Defective.

Trial court erred in denying defendant's motion to dismiss state's habitual offender charge where it was not sworn to as required by former IC 35-3.1-

Indictment or Information. (Cont'd)

—Defective. (Cont'd)

1-2 (now see IC 35-34-1-2), and where, in failing to parallel language of this section, the charge did not advise defendant of what he was charged with in order to enable him to prepare his defense. Anderson v. State, 439 N.E.2d 558, 1982 Ind. LEXIS 951 (1982).

—Formal Requisites.

Even though habitual criminal status is not a separate crime, the allegation that the defendant is a habitual criminal requires the same procedural safeguards of indictment or information, arraignment, etc., as are required of other criminal charges. Griffin v. State, 439 N.E.2d 160, 1982 Ind. LEXIS 934 (1982), overruled in part, Woodson v. State, 778 N.E.2d 475, 2002 Ind. App. LEXIS 1898 (2002).

While habitual offender charge is not a separate offense under the penal code, it is subject to rules governing charging of criminal offenses; and to invoke enhanced penalty state must charge prior unrelated convictions on page separate from rest of charging instrument. Anderson v. State, 439 N.E.2d 558, 1982 Ind. LEXIS 951 (1982); Parrish v. State, 453 N.E.2d 234, 1983 Ind. LEXIS 960 (Ind. 1983).

Where the habitual offender count was typed on a separate piece of paper attached to a page labeled "Amended Information" which recounted the four underlying offenses, as the habitual offender charge should always be attached to the original information on a separate page, the form of the habitual offender charge filed against defendant was proper. Murphy v. State, 499 N.E.2d 1077, 1986 Ind. LEXIS 1373 (1986).

—Multiple Prior Convictions.

It is unnecessary to allege and prove more than two previous convictions and imprisonments; and if four previous convictions are alleged, proof of two is sufficient. Sammons v. State, 210 Ind. 40, 199 N.E. 555, 1935 Ind. LEXIS 308 (1936).

Where an affidavit charging defendant with being an habitual criminal alleged three prior convictions, sentences and imprisonments for felony, the allegation as to the third conviction could be disregarded as surplusage. Hanks v. State, 225 Ind. 593, 76 N.E.2d 702, 1948 Ind. LEXIS 117 (1948).

—Notice.

An accused has the constitutional right to have notice and an opportunity to be heard regarding a recidivist charge. Barnett v. State, 429 N.E.2d 625, 1981 Ind. LEXIS 960 (1981).

There was no violation of right to prior notification of recidivist charge filed by amendment after jurors were selected but before jurors were sworn and before presentation of evidence on burglary count. Barnett v. State, 429 N.E.2d 625, 1981 Ind. LEXIS 960 (1981).

—Sufficient.

Information and accompanying affidavit together sufficiently apprised defendant of the na-

ture of the charge and enabled him to anticipate the proof and prepare his defense in advance of trial. Kindred v. State, 540 N.E.2d 1161, 1989 Ind. LEXIS 193 (1989).

Although the defendant's habitual offender status was charged on a page separate from the information, where it was sworn and signed by the prosecutor, and it described the prior offenses the State intended to prove, defendant had reasonable notice of the allegation of habitual offender to defend himself adequately. Perry v. State, 541 N.E.2d 913, 1989 Ind. LEXIS 237 (1989).

The information and affidavit of conviction property showed that defendant had been convicted of two prior felonies; the jury was entitled to know the nature of the prior offenses to determine if defendant was a habitual criminal. Warren v. State, 769 N.E.2d 170, 2002 Ind. LEXIS 522 (2002).

—Variance Between Information and Proof.

Variance between information on habitual offender charge, which indicated that one of defendant's prior convictions was for robbery, and proof introduced at trial, which showed that defendant's prior conviction was for armed robbery, was not fatal and did not require reversal of conviction where the date, court, and cause number alleged were all identical, defendant himself referred to his armed robbery conviction as a robbery conviction in a memorandum in support of his pretrial motion to dismiss, and defendant failed to show any unfairness caused by variance. Morgan v. State, 440 N.E.2d 1087, 1982 Ind. LEXIS 989 (1982).

Instructions.

Where the indictment or affidavit alleges former convictions of the accused, an instruction to the jury that it may consider evidence of former convictions for the purpose of determining the credibility of defendant is correct when applied to a former conviction upon which the accused had been examined, but incorrect as to a conviction as to which he had not been examined. Metzger v. State, 214 Ind. 113, 13 N.E.2d 519, 1938 Ind. LEXIS 149 (1938).

Where an affidavit charged that accused had been previously indicted, convicted, and imprisoned for two prior felonies, for the purpose of fixing the degree of the offense and the extent of the punishment to be inflicted, instructions that evidence of such former convictions, sentences, and imprisonment must be sufficient to satisfy the jury beyond a reasonable doubt, and limiting the jury to the consideration of the charges described in the affidavit, were not erroneous. Metzger v. State, 214 Ind. 113, 13 N.E.2d 519, 1938 Ind. LEXIS 149 (1938).

Where accused prosecuted for a felony is charged in the affidavit with having been previously indicted, convicted, and imprisoned for two prior felonies, it was not error for the court to instruct the jury that it must find beyond a reasonable doubt that the accused is the same person charged to have been previously convicted, sentenced, and

Instructions. (Cont'd)
imprisoned. Metzger v. State, 214 Ind. 113, 13 N.E.2d 519, 1938 Ind. LEXIS 149 (1938).

It is not error for trial court to refuse to instruct jury as to the penalty under the habitual offender statute. Comstock v. State, 273 Ind. 259, 406 N.E.2d 1164, 1980 Ind. LEXIS 661 (1980).

Since juries no longer fulfill any function regarding sentencing, it was not error that the court did not instruct jury as to the potential punishment for an habitual offender. Little v. State, 275 Ind. 78, 415 N.E.2d 44, 1981 Ind. LEXIS 659 (1981).

Instruction that judge was solely responsible for assessing penalty and that jury should not be aware of the penalty for an habitual offender was not error. Griffin v. State, 275 Ind. 107, 415 N.E.2d 60, 1981 Ind. LEXIS 656 (1981).

It was not error for trial court to instruct jury that the prior crimes that defendant was charged with having committed were felonies, since determination of whether the offense was a felony was a question of law for the court to determine and not a question of fact for the jury. Griffin v. State, 275 Ind. 107, 415 N.E.2d 60, 1981 Ind. LEXIS 656 (1981).

Where at the beginning of the criminal offender proceedings court read its preliminary instructions and after the close of the evidence and final arguments, which took only approximately two hours, court read a final instruction which merely referred to the prior instructions, such final instruction did not constitute fundamental error and defendant's failure to object waived any error. Muse v. State, 419 N.E.2d 1302, 1981 Ind. LEXIS 739 (1981).

Prohibition against instructing the jury that a 30-year sentence is imposed on a person found to be an habitual offender does not violate fundamental fairness. Harrington v. State, 421 N.E.2d 1113, 1981 Ind. LEXIS 769 (1981).

Because the defendant had already admitted to the jury that he had sustained prior convictions, because he had testified in an earlier phase of the trial, because such testimony touched upon the exact questions at stake in the habitual offender phase, and because of the limited scope of the habitual offender proceedings, there was no basis on which the jury could allegedly speculate on the defendant's reason for not testifying in the habitual offender phase, under these facts, an instruction concerning the defendant's failure to testify did not violate his right against self-incrimination. Smith v. State, 422 N.E.2d 1179, 1981 Ind. LEXIS 775 (1981).

It is error to instruct jury as to penalty involved upon conviction under habitual offender statute, since under present statutory scheme the jury is to play no role in sentencing defendants. Maier v. State, 437 N.E.2d 448, 1982 Ind. LEXIS 870 (1982); Erickson v. State, 438 N.E.2d 269, 1982 Ind. LEXIS 911 (1982).

It was proper to refuse requested instruction, in prosecution in which defendant was found to be an habitual offender, which implied that jury should consider matter of reformation of defendant, since reformation is not a matter for jury to be concerned with. Erickson v. State, 438 N.E.2d 269, 1982 Ind. LEXIS 911 (1982).

The trial court did not err in granting the state's motion in limine, which prohibited the defendant from informing the jury of the possible habitual offender charge and the sentence therefor. Hill v. State, 452 N.E.2d 932, 1983 Ind. LEXIS 935 (1983).

The jury fulfills no sentencing function in an habitual offender proceeding, sentencing is expressly and exclusively the responsibility of the judge, and the accused has no right to have the jury informed as to the potential penalties for an habitual offender. Beasley v. State, 452 N.E.2d 982, 1983 Ind. LEXIS 941 (1983).

The trial court's reference to the state's allegations of prior convictions as a "count or charge" in its preliminary instructions to the jury upon the habitual offender phase of the trial do not prejudice the defendant by inferring that he is being charged with an additional crime where the instructions clearly inform the jury of the issues they are to determine. Martin v. State, 453 N.E.2d 1001, 1983 Ind. LEXIS 969 (1983).

Where the trial court instructed the jury that they could find defendant to be an habitual offender if they found he was convicted of the underlying felonies, that instruction did not comply with this section, which requires that both commission and sentencing dates must be proven for an habitual offender finding, but that error was cured by the next instruction, which gave the definition of prior unrelated felony convictions. Thus, the charge as a whole properly informed the jury. Lucas v. State, 499 N.E.2d 1090, 1986 Ind. LEXIS 1365 (1986).

Where defendants asserted they were denied due process because the trial court failed to instruct the jury that they were required to find two prior unrelated felony convictions with commission sequential to conviction in order to find them guilty of the habitual offender count, arguing that an instruction containing an incorrect statement of the statutory law prejudicial to the defendant is fundamental error not waived by failure to tender instructions or to object specifically thereto, since the evidence clearly showed the proper sequence of conviction and sentence on the first prior felony before commission of the second prior felony, the jury could not have found that the sequence was other than proper for either defendant, and defendants failed to demonstrate prejudice and thus presented no reversible error. Burton v. State, 526 N.E.2d 1163, 1988 Ind. LEXIS 232 (1988).

The omission of a reference in the instructions to the inapplicability of convictions which had been set aside, or for which the defendant had been pardoned, is not error where the defendant presented no evidence that the prior convictions relied upon were invalid. King v. State, 531 N.E.2d 1154, 1988 Ind. LEXIS 358 (1988).

Instruction that defendant's conviction could be based solely on the uncorroborated testimony of the victims was error, because: (1) it unfairly highlighted the victims' testimony; (2) presented an appellate standard of review that was irrelevant to the jury's function; and (3) possibly con-

Instructions. (Cont'd)

fused the jury by using the technical term "uncorroborated," and, as the victims' testimony was uncorroborated, the error affected defendant's substantial right, requiring reversal and a new trial. Bayes v. State, 791 N.E.2d 263, 2003 Ind. App. LEXIS 1234 (2003).

Jury's finding that defendant was a habitual offender pursuant to IC 35-50-2-8 was proper because, although trial court refused defendant's requested instruction, that the jury had the right to refuse to find defendant a habitual offender even if it found that the prerequisite convictions occurred, which was a correct statement of the law, the substance of the instruction given by the trial court was the same; trial court's instruction emphasized that the jury "may" rather than "must" find defendant a habitual offender if the state proves the predicate convictions. Walden v. State, 895 N.E.2d 1182, 2008 Ind. LEXIS 1007 (2008).

—Independent Decision.

Jury instruction that if it found state had proved predicate felonies, it "should" find defendant to be habitual offender, invaded jury's prerogative by preventing it from making independent and separate decision on habitual offender status. Parker v. State, 698 N.E.2d 737, 1998 Ind. LEXIS 98 (1998).

Judgment.

It was error, 11 years after sentence for life under the former section to impose additional sentence for term of years. Witte v. State, 228 Ind. 153, 90 N.E.2d 802, 1950 Ind. LEXIS 120 (1950).

Where defendant entered plea of guilty as charged to crime of forgery and habitual criminal, fact that court did not enter sentence for forgery did not deprive it of jurisdiction to impose life sentence upon charge of habitual criminal, and conviction was not open to collateral attack by habeas corpus. Witte v. Dowd, 230 Ind. 485, 102 N.E.2d 630, 1951 Ind. LEXIS 237 (1951), cert. denied, 344 U.S. 841, 73 S. Ct. 54, 97 L. Ed. 654, 1952 U.S. LEXIS 1889 (1952).

Where trial court entered judgment under habitual criminal statute, but failed to sentence defendant for third offense, it did not have jurisdiction under petition for habeas corpus to vacate conviction under habitual criminal act after term, so that judgment stood unimpaired and was bar to further prosecution for same offense. State v. Gurecki, 233 Ind. 383, 119 N.E.2d 895, 1954 Ind. LEXIS 204 (1954).

Imposition of separate and distinct sentences, one imposing the normal penalty prescribed by law for the particular offense involved and the other imposing a further penalty of life imprisonment were required. McCormick v. State, 262 Ind. 303, 315 N.E.2d 360, 1974 Ind. LEXIS 301 (1974).

Judicial Responsibility.

Under this section, sentencing is expressly and exclusively the responsibility of the judge. Harrington v. State, 421 N.E.2d 1113, 1981 Ind. LEXIS 769 (1981).

There is no discretion reposed in the trial court

to depart from the demands of this statute. Turpin v. State, 435 N.E.2d 1, 1982 Ind. LEXIS 809 (1982).

The court has no sentencing discretion where, because of the form of the verdict, it is not possible for the judge to determine which two or more of the four prior felony convictions charged the jury attributed to defendant. Beasley v. State, 452 N.E.2d 982, 1983 Ind. LEXIS 941 (1983).

—Inability to Reduce Penalty.

An habitual offender penalty is not unreasonable because the trial court expresses regret at not being able to invoke subsection (e) of this section so as to reduce the penalty. Curry v. State, 453 N.E.2d 1006, 1983 Ind. LEXIS 970 (1983).

Jurisdiction.

A county court which is given jurisdiction of Class D felonies by statute also has jurisdiction of proceedings for habitual offenders. Pitts v. State, 410 N.E.2d 1387, 1980 Ind. App. LEXIS 1663 (1980).

Jury.

Fact that same jury which convicted defendant on principal charge also heard the habitual offender charge did not deny defendant's constitutional right to trial by an impartial jury. Dorton v. State, 419 N.E.2d 1289, 1981 Ind. LEXIS 738 (1981).

In the context of habitual offender proceedings, the jury serves no sentencing function. Owens v. State, 427 N.E.2d 880, 1981 Ind. LEXIS 891 (1981); Kalady v. State, 462 N.E.2d 1299, 1984 Ind. LEXIS 818 (1984).

The jury in habitual offender proceedings merely determines, based upon the evidence adduced, whether or not the defendant is an habitual offender as that term is defined by statute. Owens v. State, 427 N.E.2d 880, 1981 Ind. LEXIS 891 (1981).

A new jury, as opposed to the jury determining guilt on the underlying charge, is qualified to make the determinations necessary for a finding as to the habitual criminal status. Funk v. State, 427 N.E.2d 1081, 1981 Ind. LEXIS 904 (1981); Kalady v. State, 462 N.E.2d 1299, 1984 Ind. LEXIS 818 (1984).

Under this section, a defendant is not entitled to have the exact same jury, person for person, that determined his guilt of a specific charge, sit in the habitual offender proceeding. Havens v. State, 429 N.E.2d 618, 1981 Ind. LEXIS 967 (1981).

This section requires that the same jury which hears the evidence on the underlying offenses be the first to attempt to determine the habitual offender question; however, this section does not preclude a different jury from determining the issue after the first jury fails to reach an agreement. Murphy v. State, 499 N.E.2d 1077, 1986 Ind. LEXIS 1373 (1986).

Any discretion to be exercised is for the court alone at sentencing; it is not for the jury in making the habitual offender determination. Wolfe v. State, 562 N.E.2d 414, 1990 Ind. LEXIS 227 (1990).

Jury. (Cont'd)

—Guilty Plea.

Defendant who was not advised that he was waiving jury trial on habitual offender charge when he pled guilty to felonies, but did not claim he did not knowingly waive his right to trial on the felonies, would be given the opportunity for a jury trial on the habitual claim, but could not withdraw his pleas for felonies. Snyder v. State, 668 N.E.2d 1214, 1996 Ind. LEXIS 97 (1996).

Because defendant did not plead guilty, and on more than one occasion before the trial the defendant waived his right to a jury trial, the requirement that defendant be advised that he is waiving his right to a jury trial at the habitual offender phase of the trial was not at issue. Dixie v. State, 726 N.E.2d 257, 2000 Ind. LEXIS 244 (2000).

—Judge of Law and Facts.

The questions presented to the jury in a habitual offender proceeding are narrowly circumscribed, but nothing in the habitual offender statute suggests that the legislature intended for the jury's constitutional role to decide the law and the facts is to be diminished; instructions informing jurors they were not judges of the law were erroneous. Seay v. State, 673 N.E.2d 475, 1996 Ind. App. LEXIS 1511 (1996), transfer granted, 683 N.E.2d 580, 1997 Ind. LEXIS 321 (1997), aff'd, 698 N.E.2d 732, 1998 Ind. LEXIS 96 (1998).

Although a defendant who waives his right to jury trial in a habitual offender proceeding would forgo the possibility of jury nullification, because the jury is able to find a defendant not to be a habitual offender irrespective of the uncontroverted proof of prior felonies under Ind. Const., art. 1, § 19, nullification is not so likely to occur that a defendant must be informed of this consequence by the trial judge for his waiver to be considered to have been made knowingly. Gonzalez v. State, 757 N.E.2d 202, 2001 Ind. App. LEXIS 1850 (2001).

—New Trial on Habitual Offender Charge.

Where defendant was convicted by jury of theft and found to be an habitual offender and trial court granted new trial limited to habitual offender question, there was no error in denying defendant's motion to reconvene original jury to consider habitual offender question. Pitts v. State, 439 N.E.2d 1140, 1982 Ind. LEXIS 956 (1982).

The trial court did not err when it dismissed the first jury and impaneled a new jury to hear the habitual offender phase on the basis that it would have been inconvenient to have the first jury hear the habitual offender phase, especially as the defendant did not object to such procedure at the time the first jury was dismissed. Wade v. State, 718 N.E.2d 1162, 1999 Ind. App. LEXIS 1929 (1999).

—Number of Jurors.

Since six-member juries are constitutional and since the trial court correctly followed the applicable statutes while conducting defendant's bifurcated trial, there was no error in allowing a six-person jury to adjudge defendant to be an habitual

offender. Newland v. State, 459 N.E.2d 384, 1984 Ind. LEXIS 750 (1984).

In Class D felony cases, such as theft, where the habitual offender status of the defendant is in issue, the defendant is entitled under IC 35-37-1-1 to a six, not a 12, person jury for all stages of the criminal case, including the felony sentencing hearing. Dyer v. State, 460 N.E.2d 511, 1984 Ind. LEXIS 768 (1984).

—Reconvening.

Where after the rendition of the verdict, the defense counsel declines an opportunity to poll the jury and, immediately thereafter, without objection, the court informs the jury of the "second portion" of the trial, this is the accepted practice under this section and this does nothing which could harm the defendant or which deprives him of the bifurcation guaranteed by due process. Roarks v. State, 448 N.E.2d 1071, 1983 Ind. LEXIS 841 (1983).

—Verdict Form.

Providing the jury with a verdict form which asked them to decide whether defendant was or was not guilty of two underlying felonies, but which did not require the jury to specifically state whether he was or was not a habitual offender, was not fundamental error, where there was no substantial potential for harm. McCollum v. State, 582 N.E.2d 804, 1991 Ind. LEXIS 246 (1991).

—Voir Dire.

There was no constitutional error in trial court's denial of defendant's request, after return of guilty verdict on main charge, to conduct additional voir dire before commencement of second phase of trial concerning defendant's status as an habitual offender. Ross v. State, 442 N.E.2d 981, 1982 Ind. LEXIS 1036 (1982).

Where the defendant exercised only eight of his ten peremptory challenges at voir dire and then attempted to re-open voir dire after being convicted on the underlying felony of perjury, the trial court properly refused to allow additional voir dire before the habitual offender phase of the trial. Sears v. State, 457 N.E.2d 192, 1983 Ind. LEXIS 1063 (1983).

—Waiver.

Where habitual offender charges had not been filed when defendant signed jury waiver, and neither waiver nor trial court specified charges for which jury trial was waived, defendant did not voluntarily, intelligently, and knowingly waive jury trial on habitual offender count, and conviction on habitual offender charge was therefore reversed. Jones v. State, 810 N.E.2d 777, 2004 Ind. App. LEXIS 1161 (2004).

Legislative Intent.

The legislature, in enacting this section, did not intend that the question whether habitual offender penalties should attach would be resolved by evidence regarding defendant's general mental predilections toward the future commission of criminal acts. Instead, the legislature indicated that the question should turn on defendant's record of

Legislative Intent. (Cont'd)
criminal behavior. Underhill v. State, 428 N.E.2d 759, 1981 Ind. LEXIS 918 (1981).

—Amelioration.
This section is a truly ameliorative statute as it relates to Class C and Class D felonies, and the application of the general savings statute is unnecessary; the court could infer that the legislature's intent was to allow the application of the ameliorative provisions regarding Class C and Class D felonies to all to whom such application would be possible and constitutional. Bell v. State, 654 N.E.2d 856, 1995 Ind. App. LEXIS 1013 (1995).

Misdemeanors.
An underlying felony is essential to an habitual offender determination and to subsequent sentencing, and imposing an enhancement upon a misdemeanor conviction was contrary to law. Cooley v. State, 640 N.E.2d 433, 1994 Ind. App. LEXIS 1263 (1994).

Mistrial.
Where jury found defendant guilty of basic offense but could not agree in proceeding to determine if defendant was an habitual offender and court declared a mistrial it would be proper to have a new trial limited to the habitual offender question. State v. McMillan, 274 Ind. 167, 409 N.E.2d 612, 1980 Ind. LEXIS 762 (1980), cert. denied, 450 U.S. 1003, 101 S. Ct. 1714, 68 L. Ed. 2d 207, 1981 U.S. LEXIS 1418 (1981).

—Retrial.
A defendant may be retried on an habitual offender count in front of a new jury impaneled for that purpose following a declaration of a mistrial during the first habitual offender proceeding. Turpin v. State, 435 N.E.2d 1, 1982 Ind. LEXIS 809 (1982).

Motions.
Where defendant claimed that the state had not sought the leave of the court to amend the information to add the habitual offender count as required by IC 35-34-1-5(c), it was held that the state had implicitly moved to add the habitual offender count when it filed the amended information, which was not effective until the trial court accepted it, and therefore, there was no error. Murphy v. State, 499 N.E.2d 1077, 1986 Ind. LEXIS 1373 (1986).

Motor Vehicle Violations.
Statutory construction of this section together with former Article 12 Title 9, of the Motor Vehicle Code (former IC 9-12-3-2, see now IC 9-30-10-17) prior to the 1996 amendments to IC 35-50-2-10 which added subsection (a)(2), showed that the legislature did not intend that a conviction for a Class C felony under Article 12, a discrete, separate, and independent habitual offender statute, be subject to further enhancement under the general habitual offender statute. Stanek v. State, 603 N.E.2d 152, 1992 Ind. LEXIS 252 (1992), superseded by statute as stated in, Roberts v. State, 725 N.E.2d 441, 2000 Ind. App. LEXIS 310 (2000).

Notice.
Defendant was given sufficient notice to enable him to defend against recidivist charge where he was furnished a copy of his criminal record at omnibus hearing, was granted two days within which to file motion to dismiss the information, and did move to dismiss the habitual offender charge within the two days given him by trial court but the motion was denied, and did not then seek a continuance nor allege that he needed more time to investigate the charges or prepare a defense to them. McConnell v. State, 436 N.E.2d 1097, 1982 Ind. LEXIS 857 (1982).

The failure to formally charge defendant as an habitual offender and to so arraign him does not represent a fundamental error and a denial of due process, where the lack of formal notice did not deprive the defendant of actual notice, since the record shows evidence of the defendant's knowledge of the potential, and thus he was not denied a fair trial. Hutchinson v. State, 452 N.E.2d 955, 1983 Ind. LEXIS 931 (1983).

The failure of counsel to take action at the onset of the hearing with respect to the state's failure to amend the original information to include the "habitual" charge and to arraign defendant on the amended information not only shows their knowledge of the habitual allegation but also bars their subsequent objections. Hutchinson v. State, 452 N.E.2d 955, 1983 Ind. LEXIS 931 (1983).

—Adequate.
Where the court used the term "sentencing" instead of "habitual offender hearing," in the minute entry, the defendant had adequate notice. Gillie v. State, 465 N.E.2d 1380, 1984 Ind. LEXIS 880 (1984).

Number of Felonies.
The purpose of the habitual offender statute is to more severely penalize those persons whom prior sanctions have failed to deter from committing felonies and it is the number of felonies committed and not the value of property taken which is the essential element in the habitual offender determination. Maisonet v. State, 448 N.E.2d 1052, 1983 Ind. LEXIS 836 (1983).

Penal Institution.
The Indiana State Farm was a penal institution for the purposes of former IC 35-8-8-2. Bernard v. State, 248 Ind. 688, 230 N.E.2d 536, 1967 Ind. LEXIS 498 (1967).

Penalty for Prior Conviction.
For purposes of habitual offender status, the penalty actually imposed for a prior conviction was irrelevant. Donnersbach v. State, 444 N.E.2d 1184, 1983 Ind. LEXIS 747 (1983).

Prejudice to Defendant.

—Not Shown.
Evidence introduced during the bifurcated section of the trial in which the state had the burden of establishing that defendant in fact was a habitual offender could not have prejudiced the trial

Prejudice to Defendant. (Cont'd)

—Not Shown. (Cont'd)
on the charge which had been completed. Donahoo v. State, 640 N.E.2d 702, 1994 Ind. LEXIS 125 (1994).

Prior Convictions.
Defendant, who deliberately deceived the criminal court as to his age and accepted the benefit of a plea bargain substantially reducing the charge, was not allowed, eight years later, when faced with an enhanced sentence as an habitual offender, to assert his juvenile status for the first time, and have his conviction vacated. Twyman v. State, 452 N.E.2d 434, 1983 Ind. App. LEXIS 3253 (1983), vacated, 459 N.E.2d 705, 1984 Ind. LEXIS 737 (1984).

This section does not require that the sentences for any prior felony be completed in order that it be used in an habitual offender proceeding. Yeagley v. State, 467 N.E.2d 730, 1984 Ind. LEXIS 963 (1984).

Although IC 35-50-2-8(d)(3) refers to "dealing" offenses, it also lists specific statutes that make no distinction in terms of criminal liability between actual dealing and possession with intent to deliver; thus, the inmate's convictions for the offenses listed in IC 35-50-2-8(d)(3)(C) exceeded one and thus, the inmate's prior out-of-state convictions were properly counted as prior unrelated felony convictions, supporting the inmate's habitual offender admission. Weiss v. State, 903 N.E.2d 557, 2009 Ind. App. LEXIS 729 (2009).

Prior unrelated felony convictions used to convict defendant of the habitual offender enhancement were insufficient to satisfy the requirements of the habitual offender statute; state sought to enhance an offense under IC 35-48-4 with only one prior unrelated felony conviction enumerated in IC 35-50-2-8(b)(1)(3)(C), making the conviction unsupported by the charging information. Hape v. State, 903 N.E.2d 977, 2009 Ind. App. LEXIS 637 (2009).

—Aggravating and Mitigating Circumstances.
Aggravating and mitigating circumstances are to be considered as to the current charge only. It would not be proper for a court at a later date, in deciding a defendant's status as a habitual offender, to reevaluate the prior court's holdings and find there to be circumstances in mitigation of the prior conviction. Johnston v. State, 578 N.E.2d 656, 1991 Ind. LEXIS 186 (1991).

The trial court did not err in considering defendant's prior convictions as aggravating factors; a court may use the same prior conviction both to enhance a sentence and to support an habitual offender determination. Spivey v. State, 638 N.E.2d 1308, 1994 Ind. App. LEXIS 1091 (1994).

—Collateral Attack.
In habitual offender prosecution, court would not consider fundamental error doctrine in connection with defendant's collateral attack on prior conviction on ground that guilty plea was not voluntary where defendant had failed to preserve

error, if any, by proper in-trial objection or motion, and where error alleged was not that court erred in accepting guilty plea, but rather that it erred in subsequent denial of motion to withdraw it. Stone v. State, 437 N.E.2d 76, 1982 Ind. LEXIS 883 (1982).

No collateral attack can be made on an underlying conviction in a habitual offender proceeding when the conviction is "regular on its face." A conviction was regular on its face where the sentencing entry showed that the defendant was represented by counsel and changed his plea pursuant to plea negotiations, the judge questioned the defendant "to ascertain his understanding his rights," and, after this questioning, the court found "the defendant's plea of guilty to the charge of robbery is voluntarily made." Guajardo v. State, 496 N.E.2d 1300, 1986 Ind. LEXIS 1261 (1986).

Alleged invalidity of predicate felony convictions may not be challenged during habitual offender proceedings when the prior final judgments are constitutionally firm on their face. Collins v. State, 509 N.E.2d 827, 1987 Ind. LEXIS 969 (1987).

A collateral attack on the validity of a previous conviction is not available to a defendant on an habitual criminal charge. Gardner v. State, 641 N.E.2d 641, 1994 Ind. App. LEXIS 1435 (1994).

—Constitutional Attack.
An accused may challenge the predicate felony conviction in an habitual offender proceeding when the conviction is constitutionally invalid, that is, when: (1) the court records reflecting the proceedings which led to the prior conviction, on their face, raise a presumption that the conviction is constitutionally infirm; and (2) the apparent constitutional infirmity is of the type which undermines both the integrity and reliability of the determination of guilt. Edwards v. State, 479 N.E.2d 541, 1985 Ind. LEXIS 868 (1985).

To sustain a collateral attack on the underlying felonies alleged in an habitual offender proceeding, defendant must demonstrate that the documents used to prove the convictions, on their face, raise a presumption or that the convictions were constitutionally infirm, but a claim that the transcript of prior guilty plea hearings is nonexistent does not suffice for this purpose. Lucas v. State, 499 N.E.2d 1090, 1986 Ind. LEXIS 1365 (1986).

For a petitioner to use federal habeas corpus review to challenge past convictions after the custodial term for those convictions has expired, petitioner must establish that his current confinement violates the constitution because that sentence was enhanced on the basis of the prior convictions. Clay v. McBride, 946 F. Supp. 639, 1996 U.S. Dist. LEXIS 17280 (N.D. Ind. 1996).

—Constitutional Validity.
Due process requires that a defendant charged with being an habitual offender must be afforded the right to challenge the constitutional validity of the prior convictions upon the basis of which the state seeks to impose an enhanced penalty, but his failure to do so does not bar him from thereafter challenging such convictions. Haynes v. State, 436 N.E.2d 874, 1982 Ind. App. LEXIS 1281 (1982).

Prior Convictions. (Cont'd)

—Constitutional Validity. (Cont'd)

Even if the sentence is subject to collateral attack, a defendant may not enter a plea agreement calling for an illegal sentence, benefit from that sentence, and then later complain during habitual offender proceedings that it was an illegal sentence. Collins v. State, 509 N.E.2d 827, 1987 Ind. LEXIS 969 (1987).

The trial court did not err by refusing to allow a challenge to the constitutional validity of a predicate felony conviction during the habitual offender proceeding. The defendant argued that the earlier plea was not intelligently and voluntarily entered. But, since the transcript of the plea showed he consulted with counsel, he was relegated to a direct attack in his effort to set aside that conviction. Mills v. State, 512 N.E.2d 846, 1987 Ind. LEXIS 1054 (1987).

—Dates of Commission.

A habitual offender finding was vacated and the cause remanded for a new sentencing hearing, where there was no way to discern if defendant's prior convictions were in the requisite statutory sequence because the documents offered by the state did not indicate the dates on which the predicate felonies were committed. Timmons v. State, 500 N.E.2d 1212, 1986 Ind. LEXIS 1460 (1986).

To show a proper sequence to sustain a sentence under the habitual offender statute, the state must who the defendant had been twice convicted and twice sentenced for felonies, that the commission of the second offense was subsequent to his having been sentenced upon the first, and that the commission of the principal offense upon which the enhanced punishment is being sought was subsequent to his having been sentenced upon the second conviction. Moredock v. State, 514 N.E.2d 1247, 1987 Ind. LEXIS 1115 (1987).

One of the essential elements of a habitual offender finding is proof that the second predicate offense was committed subsequent to the date of sentencing for the first predicate offense. Smith v. State, 514 N.E.2d 1254, 1987 Ind. LEXIS 1107 (1987).

Where there was no evidence before the jury to prove that the commission of the second felony was after the date of sentencing on the first felony, there is insufficient proof for the habitual offender finding and it must be set aside. Youngblood v. State, 515 N.E.2d 522, 1987 Ind. LEXIS 1134 (1987).

Where the record lacks evidence of the date of commission of the offense to which the second conviction relates, the habitual offender determination cannot stand. Zavesky v. State, 515 N.E.2d 530, 1987 Ind. LEXIS 1127 (1987).

It was error to present evidence of an involuntary manslaughter conviction during the habitual offender phase of defendant's subsequent trial for murder, where the other two felonies alleged occurred between commission of the manslaughter and conviction. Fozzard v. State, 518 N.E.2d 789, 1988 Ind. LEXIS 35 (1988).

Where the record of the habitual offender proceeding clearly shows inadequate proof with regard to the chronological sequence of the underlying felonies, the Supreme Court considers such error to be fundamental. Williams v. State, 525 N.E.2d 1238, 1988 Ind. LEXIS 198 (1988).

The state is required to prove that the defendant committed the second prior felony after he was sentenced for the first offense, but the date the first offense was committed is irrelevant, and the state does not err in failing to prove the fact where the date of conviction of the first offense was proved. McConnell v. State, 526 N.E.2d 1214, 1988 Ind. App. LEXIS 584 (1988).

One of the essential elements of a habitual offender finding is proof that the second predicate offense was committed subsequent to the date of sentencing for the first predicate offense. Failure to prove this element requires that the habitual offender determinations be vacated. Henderson v. State, 534 N.E.2d 1105, 1989 Ind. LEXIS 62 (1989).

Failure or proof that a second predicate offense was committed subsequent to the date of sentencing for the first predicate offense will require that a habitual offender determination be vacated. Jaske v. State, 539 N.E.2d 14, 1989 Ind. LEXIS 165 (1989).

An inference that because defendant's prior convictions spanned nearly 20 years, they were committed in the sequence mandated by the statute, was not sufficient to support the imposition of an habitual offender status. McCovens v. State, 539 N.E.2d 26, 1989 Ind. LEXIS 168 (1989).

The defendant's habitual offender conviction was defective because there was no evidence in the record indicating when the prior offenses were committed; the evidence therefore did not satisfy the requirements of the statute. Williams v. State, 541 N.E.2d 921, 1989 Ind. LEXIS 241 (1989).

Although the state failed to prove when the defendant committed his first offense, the state satisfied subsection (b) when it proved the defendant was sentenced for the first offense before he committed the second offense, and that he was sentenced for the second offense before he committed the third offense. Steelman v. State, 602 N.E.2d 152, 1992 Ind. App. LEXIS 1593 (1992).

An indictment showing that an offense occurred on or about a date is sufficient to establish the commission date beyond a reasonable doubt; the date upon which an offense may have been committed may be found in the state's charging instruments. Gardner v. State, 641 N.E.2d 641, 1994 Ind. App. LEXIS 1435 (1994).

Where defendant showed that predicate convictions were not in proper order since earlier conviction was vacated after date of second conviction, post conviction relief was granted on habitual offender enhancement. Bryant v. State, 760 N.E.2d 1141, 2002 Ind. App. LEXIS 20 (2002).

—Escape Prosecution.

In a prosecution for escape, the crime for which the defendant was serving a prison term when he escaped is a prior unrelated felony which is avail-

Prior Convictions. (Cont'd)

—Escape Prosecution. (Cont'd)
able to support a habitual offender count. Harmer v. State, 455 N.E.2d 1139, 1983 Ind. LEXIS 1030 (1983).

—Incarceration.
This section does not require accused to have been imprisoned for prior felonies. Spivey v. State, 436 N.E.2d 61, 1982 Ind. LEXIS 837 (1982).

—Non-Violent Offenses.
Since a conviction for dealing or possession of an illegal drug does not count for habitual offender purposes if that crime was not classified a "crime of violence" under IC 35-50-2-2(b)(4) and the defendant has only one or no convictions for illegal drug dealing, the habitual offender enhancement was invalid as it was evident that an earlier conviction could not be used to support an habitual offender enhancement. Williams v. State, 834 N.E.2d 225, 2005 Ind. App. LEXIS 1757 (2005).

—Presentence Reports.
The nature of presentence reports filed in prior cases in which defendant was convicted is irrelevant to any of the issues presented in a habitual offender trial and, therefore, constitutes improper evidence to submit to the jury, but the submission of such reports to the jury does not present reversible error where there was overwhelming evidence other than the presentence reports that defendant committed two prior unrelated felonies and he fails to demonstrate any prejudice from the erroneous admission of these reports. Pointer v. State, 499 N.E.2d 1087, 1986 Ind. LEXIS 1364 (1986).

—Set Aside.
An habitual offender verdict which was based upon a predicate offense subsequently set aside for constitutional reasons must be vacated. Spivey v. State, 638 N.E.2d 1308, 1994 Ind. App. LEXIS 1091 (1994).

Any one of defendant's 13 prior felonies, all committed on different days, could have combined with his subsequent conviction to support a habitual offender determination, and vacation of one of those prior felonies was not grounds to reverse the habitual offender determination. Elmore v. State, 688 N.E.2d 213, 1997 Ind. App. LEXIS 1665 (1997).

—Special Verdict Forms.
In cases in which it is possible a defendant is subject to sentence enhancement under either this section or former IC 35-50-2-7.1, depending on which prior felonies the jury relies upon, a trial court commits error requiring remand by denying a request to use special verdict forms. Broshears v. State, 604 N.E.2d 639, 1992 Ind. App. LEXIS 1814 (1992), clarified, 609 N.E.2d 1, 609 N.E.2d 7, 1993 Ind. App. LEXIS 120 (1993), overruled, Seay v. State, 698 N.E.2d 732, 1998 Ind. LEXIS 96 (1998).

If the state decided to pursue an habitual offender charge on retrial, the defendant was entitled to special verdict forms if he asked for them and if it was possible he could be subject to either a "big" or "little" enhancement, depending on which prior convictions the jury relied. Broshears v. State, 609 N.E.2d 1, 609 N.E.2d 7, 1993 Ind. App. LEXIS 120 (1993).

—Third Prior Conviction.
Allegations of four prior felonies committed by appellant did not prejudice his right to a fair trial, as proof of three or more felony convictions is mere surplusage under requirements of this section. Minneman v. State, 441 N.E.2d 673, 1982 Ind. LEXIS 1011 (1982), cert. denied, 461 U.S. 933, 103 S. Ct. 2099, 77 L. Ed. 2d 307, 1983 U.S. LEXIS 4652 (1983).

Even though one of the defendant's three prior convictions had been set aside, failure of the jury to specify which of the two prior convictions it had relied upon to establish his habitual offender status did not render void his conviction as a habitual offender. Eldridge v. State, 498 N.E.2d 12, 1986 Ind. LEXIS 1290 (1986).

Where a person commits a third felony following his conviction for two prior unrelated felonies but is successful in setting aside one of the underlying felony convictions before being found a habitual offender in connection with the third felony, this section would clearly preclude the use of the vacated conviction as support for the habitual offender determination. Coble v. State, 500 N.E.2d 1221, 1986 Ind. LEXIS 1403 (1986).

—Under "Minor Statute."
Fact that record showed that defendant had been sentenced to 60 days for a prior conviction did not render record inadequate to prove felony conviction where record also showed that defendant had been charged with a felony but was convicted "under the minor statute," which gave courts discretion to sentence persons under 21 to less than one year for a felony conviction. Clay v. State, 440 N.E.2d 466, 1982 Ind. LEXIS 963 (1982).

—Unrelated Felony.
Term "unrelated felony" does not mean a felony of unlike kind, but rather means a felony not related to instant felony in sense that it is not connected to it as part of res gestae of instant crime. Erickson v. State, 438 N.E.2d 269, 1982 Ind. LEXIS 911 (1982).

A felony is not related to a prior felony merely by the fact that the victim from the present crime was the same victim of the prior crime committed by defendant. Yeagley v. State, 467 N.E.2d 730, 1984 Ind. LEXIS 963 (1984).

The phrase "unrelated felony" means that the predicate felony is not part of the res gestae of the principal offense, and that the second predicate felony was committed after conviction of the first predicate felony. Beach v. State, 496 N.E.2d 43, 1986 Ind. LEXIS 1233 (1986).

This section provides only two instances in which a prior conviction may not be used in the proceeding. These are: (1) A prior conviction that has been set aside; and (2) one for which the person has been pardoned. The legislature had not included remoteness of the prior conviction as disqualifying the prior conviction. Jackson v. State, 575 N.E.2d 617, 1991 Ind. LEXIS 136 (1991).

More than two prior unrelated felony convictions

Prior Convictions. (Cont'd)

—Unrelated Felony. (Cont'd)

may be proven in an habitual offender determination with the additional convictions considered to be "harmless surplusage." Where, however, one or more of the convictions are not qualified as felonies under the habitual offender statute, and the habitual offender finding is made by general verdict, the finding must be vacated. Waye v. State, 583 N.E.2d 733, 1991 Ind. LEXIS 255 (1991).

The requirement that the prior felonies be "unrelated" means that the commission of the second offense was subsequent to the conviction and sentence upon the first offense. Gardner v. State, 641 N.E.2d 641, 1994 Ind. App. LEXIS 1435 (1994).

To meet the requirement that the previous convictions be unrelated, the state must also show that the commission of the second offense was subsequent to the sentence upon the first offense. Roell v. State, 655 N.E.2d 599, 1995 Ind. App. LEXIS 1171 (1995).

Although IC 35-50-2-8(d)(3) refers to "dealing" offenses, it also lists specific statutes that make no distinction in terms of criminal liability between actual dealing and possession with intent to deliver; thus, the inmate's convictions for the offenses listed in IC 35-50-2-8(d)(3)(C) exceeded one and thus, the inmate's prior out-of-state convictions were properly counted as prior unrelated felony convictions, supporting the inmate's habitual offender admission. Weiss v. State, 903 N.E.2d 557, 2009 Ind. App. LEXIS 729 (2009).

Probable Cause.

Former IC 35-3.1-1-1(d) required probable cause determination of habitual offender status. Ferguson v. State, 438 N.E.2d 286, 1982 Ind. LEXIS 901 (1982).

Proof of Habitual Offender Status.

—Burden of Proof.

This section does not require the prosecution to plead and prove at the habitual offender stage of the trial the date the defendant was released from prison, parole, or probation on the last prior felony conviction in order to effectuate its provisions. The burden of the state in proving the status of habitual criminal is met solely by proof of convictions and sentences. Woods v. State, 456 N.E.2d 417, 1983 Ind. LEXIS 1051 (1983).

—Cross Examination.

Trial court was unduly restrictive of defendant's cross-examination of a fingerprint expert, and erred by failing to allow defendant to make an offer of proof; but defendant was not prejudiced, since this expert's testimony was not essential to prove defendant was a habitual offender, defendant having admitted to committing certain crimes, and the others having been proven by documentary evidence. Nelson v. State, 792 N.E.2d 588, 2003 Ind. App. LEXIS 1359 (2003).

—Number of Convictions.

To sustain a sentence under the habitual offender statute, the state must demonstrate that the defendant was twice convicted and twice sentenced. Roell v. State, 655 N.E.2d 599, 1995 Ind. App. LEXIS 1171 (1995).

—Proof Required.

In trial to establish defendant's status as an habitual offender, the state would have made its case by merely showing Idaho conviction for rape. The showing that the same cause contained three counts, one for oral sex and one for anal sex, was merely surplusage as far as the necessities of the state proof were concerned. Donahoo v. State, 640 N.E.2d 702, 1994 Ind. LEXIS 125 (1994).

This section does not require the state to reprove the underlying felony or felonies of which the jury has just convicted the defendant during the habitual offender phase of the proceedings. Payne v. State, 658 N.E.2d 635, 1995 Ind. App. LEXIS 1603 (1995).

Proportionality.

An enhancement of 30 years authorized by this section that is ultimately based upon a conviction for conduct that the legislature has classified as a misdemeanor, where there is no injury to person or property, such as driving under the influence, is entirely out of proportion to the gravity of the offense. Clark v. State, 561 N.E.2d 759, 1990 Ind. LEXIS 212 (1990).

Enhancement of the defendant's two-year sentence for driving while intoxicated, by adding 20 years under the habitual offender statute, was manifestly unreasonable, even though the defendant had a long history of nonviolent alcohol-related offenses, thefts, and burglaries. Best v. State, 566 N.E.2d 1027, 1991 Ind. LEXIS 17 (1991).

Propriety of Charge.

Where defendant had a long criminal record there was no merit in defendant's contention that habitual offender charge should have been dismissed because the sole purpose in filing the charge was to discourage defendant from taking the stand. Williams v. State, 275 Ind. 603, 419 N.E.2d 134, 1981 Ind. LEXIS 725 (1981).

It is not appropriate for a prosecutor to suggest that an habitual offender sentence should be attached to defendant because he might have faced more severe punishment than that given in the underlying trial. Russell v. State, 438 N.E.2d 741, 1982 Ind. LEXIS 923 (1982).

Prosecutorial Discretion.

Some selectivity by the prosecutor as to whether or not to charge a violation of a criminal statute is always permitted, so long as the election is not discriminatorily based on classifications of race, national origin, sex, religion, etc. Eaton v. State, 274 Ind. 73, 408 N.E.2d 1281, 1980 Ind. LEXIS 736 (1980).

The fact that it is within the discretion of the prosecutor as to whether to bring an habitual offender charge, does not violate due process. Eaton v. State, 274 Ind. 73, 408 N.E.2d 1281, 1980

Prosecutorial Discretion. (Cont'd)
Ind. LEXIS 736 (1980); Collins v. State, 275 Ind. 86, 415 N.E.2d 46, 1981 Ind. LEXIS 657 (1981), cert. denied, 451 U.S. 991, 101 S. Ct. 2331, 68 L. Ed. 2d 851, 1981 U.S. LEXIS 2139 (1981).

The prosecutor's discretionary use of the habitual offender statute in plea negotiations did not violate due process. Eaton v. State, 274 Ind. 73, 408 N.E.2d 1281, 1980 Ind. LEXIS 736 (1980).

The conscious exercise of some selectivity in enforcement is not in itself a federal constitutional violation; consequently, where the defendant did not assert that alleged selective enforcement of this section was based upon an unjustifiable standard such as race, religion, or other arbitrary classification, nor contend that this section is generally applied in arbitrary fashion or through some arbitrary classification, nor that this section was arbitrarily applied against him, nor that he was unjustly found to be an habitual offender, the defendant failed to show that the wide discretion granted to the prosecutor by this section is being, or has been applied in a manner which denied him equal protection of the law. Smith v. State, 422 N.E.2d 1179, 1981 Ind. LEXIS 775 (1981).

Defendant's contention that prosecutor's unwarranted threat to file habitual offender charge deceived him into pleading guilty was not sustained where there was no evidence to show that prosecutor ever made such a threat but that defendant's attorney told defendant that the prosecutor could file an habitual offender charge unless he pleaded guilty. Munger v. State, 420 N.E.2d 1380, 1981 Ind. App. LEXIS 1447 (1981).

The statutory discretion vested in prosecutors under this section to seek the recidivist penalty for habitual offenders does not violate the equal protection clause of the 14th Amendment. Collins v. Duckworth, 559 F. Supp. 541, 1983 U.S. Dist. LEXIS 18209 (N.D. Ind. 1983).

Records of Prior Trials.
Since an attack on the validity of prior convictions used to enhance defendant's punishment may be available in the case of a prior conviction that is constitutionally infirm, existing court records reflecting such prior trials should be made available to indigent defendants upon proper request. Morgan v. State, 440 N.E.2d 1087, 1982 Ind. LEXIS 989 (1982).

—Prior Convictions Entered on Guilty Pleas.
In habitual offender proceeding under this section, trial court properly denied defendant's request for transcripts of his previous "trials" where his prior convictions were entered upon guilty pleas and no trials were held. Morgan v. State, 440 N.E.2d 1087, 1982 Ind. LEXIS 989 (1982).

Reduced Sentence.
IC 35-50-2-2 pertains only to the suspended sentences for felonies generally. The statute which permits the trial court to reduce the fixed enhancement of 30 years upon an habitual offender determination is subsection (e) of this section. Marsillett v. State, 495 N.E.2d 699, 1986 Ind. LEXIS 1206 (1986).

Subsection (e) is clearly permissive. Reduction in sentence is left to the discretion of the trial court. Wilson v. State, 513 N.E.2d 653, 1987 Ind. LEXIS 1078 (1987).

Since the record indicated that the trial court might have sentenced the defendant differently upon the substantive charges and the habitual offender enhancement if it had realized that it had discretion to do so under subsection (e), remand for resentencing was required. Cain v. State, 599 N.E.2d 625, 1992 Ind. App. LEXIS 1468 (1992); Garrett v. State, 602 N.E.2d 139, 1992 Ind. LEXIS 247 (Ind. 1992), superseded by statute as stated in, Williams v. State, 771 N.E.2d 70, 2002 Ind. LEXIS 564 (2002).

—Discretion of Judge.
Although former subsection (e) allowed the court to subtract up to 10 years from the additional fixed term of 30 years where one of the prior felonies was a Class D felony, such a subtraction was discretionary with the trial judge. Where, although it had been several years since the prior convictions, the defendant had been discharged from his last sentence just six months prior to the instant offense, it was proper for the court not to use the permissive mitigation of the habitual offender enhancement. Stanley v. State, 515 N.E.2d 1117, 1987 Ind. LEXIS 1162 (1987).

Reduction of a sentence under subsection (e) is permissive, and is left to the discretion of the trial court. Cain v. State, 599 N.E.2d 625, 1992 Ind. App. LEXIS 1468 (1992).

Reduction of 30-year enhancement rests within discretion of trial judges who are presumed to be aware of and know the law, and where defendant did not prove judge did anything other than exercise discretion, sentence was upheld. Emerson v. State, 695 N.E.2d 912, 1998 Ind. LEXIS 75 (1998).

—Provision Not Retroactive.
The 1980 amendment which added subsection (e), effective April 1, 1980, did not apply to defendant's case where his trial was in February of 1980. Jones v. State, 425 N.E.2d 82, 1981 Ind. LEXIS 835 (1981).

—When Permitted.
The provision for sentence reduction in former subsection (e) was inapplicable where 10 years had not elapsed between defendant's most recent felony conviction and the commission of the present felony. Marsillett v. State, 495 N.E.2d 699, 1986 Ind. LEXIS 1206 (1986).

Retrial.
A defendant's retrial on a charge of being an habitual offender was not barred by double jeopardy where the state Supreme Court vacated the habitual offender conviction and remanded for a new hearing on the grounds of trial court error, not insufficient evidence. Washington v. Duckworth, 567 F. Supp. 513, 1983 U.S. Dist. LEXIS 14966 (N.D. Ind. 1983).

Where the defendant is found not to be an habitual criminal, but the conviction that triggers the invocation of the habitual criminal statute is set aside, any penalty associated with that convic-

Retrial. (Cont'd)
tion is also abandoned. Hence, there is no error in charging the defendant again with a violation of the habitual criminal statute upon retrial. Durham v. State, 458 N.E.2d 287, 1984 Ind. App. LEXIS 2218 (1984), vacated, 464 N.E.2d 321, 1984 Ind. LEXIS 843 (1984).

On a retrial of the defendant's habitual criminal status, it is not an abuse of discretion to admit a certified copy of defendant's underlying felony conviction. Denton v. State, 496 N.E.2d 576, 1986 Ind. LEXIS 1252 (1986).

The trial court does not err in allowing the state to file an amended habitual offender count alleging a prior unrelated felony conviction which was not alleged in the original charge. Denton v. State, 496 N.E.2d 576, 1986 Ind. LEXIS 1252 (1986).

It is not necessary for the State to independently prove the primary underlying felony to a second jury which has been subsequently assembled to hear the habitual offender evidence. Gilliam v. State, 563 N.E.2d 94, 1990 Ind. LEXIS 234 (1990).

—Vacation of Prior Conviction.
Where the state has successfully proven defendant's habitual offender status, the subsequent vacation of one of the prior felony convictions shown at the original proceeding creates no impediment to a retrial on the issue of his habitual offender status. Denton v. State, 496 N.E.2d 576, 1986 Ind. LEXIS 1252 (1986).

Retroactive Application.
Because the amendment to this section by P.L.164-1993, § 13, reduced the maximum sentence for Class C felonies, the court should have sentenced defendant pursuant to the statute in effect when he was sentenced, and not the statute in effect when the offense was committed, where the maximum sentence enhancement for a habitual offender conviction for that defendant would be reduced under the amended statute from 30 years to 12 years. Elkins v. State, 659 N.E.2d 563, 1995 Ind. App. LEXIS 1633 (1995).

Role of Court.
Once a jury has determined whether the defendant should receive an habitual offender enhancement, sentencing pursuant to habitual offender proceedings is expressly and exclusively the responsibility of the trial court. Broshears v. State, 604 N.E.2d 639, 1992 Ind. App. LEXIS 1814 (1992), clarified, 609 N.E.2d 1, 609 N.E.2d 7, 1993 Ind. App. LEXIS 120 (1993), overruled, Seay v. State, 698 N.E.2d 732, 1998 Ind. LEXIS 96 (1998).

Sentence Under Old Statute.
Where the third felony for which defendant was charged as being an habitual criminal was committed prior to October 1, 1977, although trial was after such date, defendant was properly sentenced under the old statute. Parks v. State, 270 Ind. 689, 389 N.E.2d 286, 1979 Ind. LEXIS 593 (1979).

The law in effect when the crime was committed controls sentencing; therefore, although IC 35-50-2-7.1 was repealed in 1993 and since then all habitual offender enhancements have been covered by this section, the trial court had to correct defendant's sentence applying former IC 35-50-2-7.1. Rowold v. State, 629 N.E.2d 1285, 1994 Ind. App. LEXIS 227 (1994).

Court did not err in sentencing defendant on the basis of the habitual offender statute in force at the time of the offense and his conviction rather than on the basis of the amended version in force at the time of defendant's sentencing. Lunsford v. State, 640 N.E.2d 59, 1994 Ind. App. LEXIS 1210 (Ind. App. 1994).

Where defendant's offense was committed in November of 1975, although his conviction and subsequent sentencing occurred after the new statute became effective, the old crime and penalty were expressly "saved" by the legislature. The legislature did not expressly state that the former punishment was too severe, and therefore, the provisions of the old statute were applicable, and to apply them was not unconstitutional and did not constitute vindictive justice. Weatherford v. State, 654 N.E.2d 899, 1995 Ind. App. LEXIS 1028 (1995).

Where sentencing judge stated additional thirty years was the "maximum time because the Court can impose up to three times the presumptive," his statement clearly illustrated he was sentencing defendant under the 1993 version of this section, which was error because the offenses occurred in 1992, and the case had to be remanded for reimposition of sentence under the earlier version of this section. Isaacs v. State, 673 N.E.2d 757, 1996 Ind. LEXIS 161 (1996).

Sentence Unreasonable.
Considering the nature of the offenses, the defendant's character as reflected by the trial court's sentencing findings, and the court's decision to impose the maximum fifty-year sentences for rape and criminal deviate conduct, the court's decision to impose a 30-year habitual enhancement by attaching it to one of the class A felony convictions was clearly and plainly unreasonable. The enhancement should be 10 years, implemented by attaching the enhancement to either criminal confinement as a class B felony or battery as a class C felony. Winn v. State, 748 N.E.2d 352, 2001 Ind. LEXIS 464 (2001).

Where defendant, who had been convicted of dealing in and conspiracy to deal in cocaine, sold only one gram, had been unarmed, and had never been convicted of a crime of violence as adult, his 90-year sentence, resulting from a habitual offender enhancement and imposition of consecutive sentences, was held excessive in light of defendant's character and the nature of the offense, and was reduced to 60 years. Nelson v. State, 792 N.E.2d 588, 2003 Ind. App. LEXIS 1359 (2003).

Forty year sentence for burglary with a habitual offender enhancement was inappropriate where there was no violence and marginal pecuniary loss, where defendant committed the burglary and theft while unarmed and while the victim was away from home, where the value of the stolen items was approximately $395, and where defendant's prior burglary conviction occurred more than 20 years

Sentence Unreasonable. (Cont'd)
before. Frye v. State, 837 N.E.2d 1012, 2005 Ind. LEXIS 1082 (2005).

When defendant received the 20-year maximum under IC 35-50-2-5 for conspiracy to commit burglary under IC 35-43-2-1(1)(B)(i) and IC 35-41-5-2(a) and a 20-year habitual offender enhancement under IC 35-50-2-8, the court revised his sentence to a 20-year aggregate under AP. 7(B) and Ind. Const., art. 7, § 4; since no one was at the burglarized home and neither defendant nor his companion was apparently armed, there was a decreased likelihood of violence, and, furthermore, although defendant, who was 18, had a long criminal history, most of his crimes were juvenile offenses and only one, cruelty to animals, involved violence. Hollin v. State, 877 N.E.2d 462, 2007 Ind. LEXIS 1065 (2007).

Sentences Reasonable.

Where defendants were charged with multiple burglaries, and one with being a habitual offender, and both received the maximum penalties for the crimes for which they were convicted, to be served consecutively, the sentences imposed were neither cruel and unusual nor manifestly unreasonable in view of their past criminal history and their apparent readiness to use deadly force although no injuries occurred. Lucas v. State, 499 N.E.2d 1090, 1986 Ind. LEXIS 1365 (1986).

A 110-year sentence imposed on a habitual offender convicted of dealing in cocaine was not disproportionate, excessive, and cruel and unusual in violation of the eighth amendment and the Indiana Bill of Rights. McCollum v. State, 582 N.E.2d 804, 1991 Ind. LEXIS 246 (1991).

Once defendant's sentence for murder had been enhanced based in part on his prior criminal history, it was not manifestly unreasonable for the judge to impose the full 30 years for an habitual offender determination. Binkley v. State, 654 N.E.2d 736, 1995 Ind. LEXIS 111 (1995).

Where master commissioner who originally sentenced defendant in 1990 lacked authority to enter judgment of conviction or to sentence him, and there was no final judgment entered, and the post-conviction judge deemed the master commissioner's sentence a nullity, and imposed a new sentence in 1994, approximately one year after the July 1, 1993 effective date of the amended habitual offender statute and the 1993 amendment was truly ameliorative as applied to Class C and Class D felonies, and as applied to defendant in particular, defendant should have been sentenced under the post-July 1, 1993 version of this section. Bell v. State, 654 N.E.2d 856, 1995 Ind. App. LEXIS 1013 (1995).

There was no abuse of discretion where the trial judge concluded that the "aggravating and mitigating circumstances balance" and imposed the presumptive sentence for the present crime, then added the applicable habitual offender enhancement. Tunstill v. State, 743 N.E.2d 1136, 2001 Ind. LEXIS 259 (2001).

Sentence of seven years to the Department of Correction for a Class D Felony with a habitual offender enhancement was proper. Watson v. State, 776 N.E.2d 914, 2002 Ind. App. LEXIS 1702 (2002).

Defendant committed the instant offense (which included a habitual offender enhancement under IC 35-50-2-8) while placed in a work release program following his prior criminal conviction and had to be returned to probation under IC 35-38-2.6-3(a); therefore, he had not been discharged from his incarceration, pursuant to IC 35-50-1-2(d), and thus trial court was required to order defendant's sentence to be served consecutively to his prior sentence. Breaston v. State, 893 N.E.2d 6, 2008 Ind. App. LEXIS 1940 (2008).

Sentencing Hearing.

An habitual offender proceeding is designated as a sentencing hearing and such proceedings are not necessarily governed by all the statutes and cases dealing with trial procedure. Muse v. State, 419 N.E.2d 1302, 1981 Ind. LEXIS 739 (1981).

The trial court violated subsection (c) in convening a jury to determine the defendant's habitual offender status after accepting the defendant's guilty plea on the underlying felony. However, as the error was not one of evidence insufficiency, the remedy was a retrial of the habitual offender charge rather than a reversal. Stone v. State, 599 N.E.2d 616, 1992 Ind. App. LEXIS 1442 (1992).

—Evidence.

Any evidence, which the defendant seeks to introduce in the habitual offender proceeding, must be relevant to the matters at issue. Owens v. State, 427 N.E.2d 880, 1981 Ind. LEXIS 891 (1981).

Defendant was not entitled to present the jury in an habitual offender proceeding with a presentence investigation report. Owens v. State, 427 N.E.2d 880, 1981 Ind. LEXIS 891 (1981).

Separate Proceedings.

To preserve defendant's right to due process the indictment or affidavit should be in two parts, one part containing the offense charged and the other part containing the prior convictions for the habitual criminal charge; the trial should then proceed as if there were no allegations of former convictions and if the finding is guilty the second part of the indictment should be read to the jury. Lawrence v. State, 259 Ind. 306, 286 N.E.2d 830, 1972 Ind. LEXIS 478 (1972).

Since 1972 ruling in *Lawrence v. State*, 259 Ind. 306, 286 N.E.2d 830, 1972 Ind. LEXIS 478 (1972) that there should be bifurcated proceedings for habitual criminal charges went to the fairness of the trial itself and was designed to eliminate a previously existing danger of convicting the innocent, such holding would be applicable where defendant was tried and convicted in 1954 for both automobile banditry and being an habitual criminal in which trial proof of his prior convictions was introduced to establish the elements of an habitual criminal at the same proceeding where the jury had to pass on the present felony charge. Enlow v. State, 261 Ind. 348, 303 N.E.2d 658, 1973 Ind. LEXIS 466 (1973).

Separate Proceedings. (Cont'd)

The requirement of a separate trial upon the issue of habitual criminality is not to be applied retroactively. McPhearson v. State, 262 Ind. 468, 318 N.E.2d 355, 1974 Ind. LEXIS 331 (1974); Paneitz v. State, 262 Ind. 473, 44 Ind. Dec. 379, 318 N.E.2d 353, 1974 Ind. LEXIS 332 (1974).

Successive Prosecutions.

The state is barred from seeking multiple, pyramiding habitual offender sentence enhancements by bringing successive prosecutions for charges which could have been consolidated for trial under IC 35-34-1-9. (Decided prior to the 1994 amendment to IC 35-50-1-2, affecting the court's discretion to impose consecutive sentences). Seay v. State, 550 N.E.2d 1284, 1990 Ind. LEXIS 30 (1990), superseded by statute as stated in, Davidson v. State, 763 N.E.2d 441, 2002 Ind. LEXIS 144 (2002), superseded by statute as stated in, Wilkerson v. State, 728 N.E.2d 239, 2000 Ind. App. LEXIS 771 (2000).

Suspension of Sentence.

When a criminal defendant receives an enhanced sentence under the habitual offender statute, such sentence may not be suspended. State v. Williams, 430 N.E.2d 756, 1982 Ind. LEXIS 730 (1982), superseded by statute as stated in, Bauer v. State, 875 N.E.2d 744, 2007 Ind. App. LEXIS 2391 (2007).

Although the habitual offender offense is not listed under IC 35-50-2-2 as a sentence that may not be suspended it is not suspendible. Atkins v. State, 550 N.E.2d 342, 1990 Ind. App. LEXIS 153 (1990).

Trial court erred in finding that the enhancement of defendant's sentence under the habitual substance offender statute could not be suspended, where defendant was being sentenced for his first felony conviction and his sentence for that conviction was properly suspendible. Collins v. State, 583 N.E.2d 761, 1991 Ind. App. LEXIS 2203 (1991).

The trial court erred in holding that it could not suspend part of defendant's sentence after finding that he was a habitual offender. While the trial court was required to order a habitual offender enhancement under IC 35-50-2-8 to be fully executed, it could suspend a portion of the sentence for the underlying conviction. Howard v. State, 873 N.E.2d 685, 2007 Ind. App. LEXIS 2138 (2007).

Third Prior Conviction.

Proof of a third prior conviction is mere surplusage and is not ground for reversal. Hall v. State, 273 Ind. 507, 405 N.E.2d 530, 1980 Ind. LEXIS 689 (1980).

Proof of a third felony conviction is mere surplusage. Collins v. State, 275 Ind. 86, 415 N.E.2d 46, 1981 Ind. LEXIS 657 (1981), cert. denied, 451 U.S. 991, 101 S. Ct. 2331, 68 L. Ed. 2d 851, 1981 U.S. LEXIS 2139 (1981).

Introducing evidence of a third prior conviction during the habitual offender proceeding is mere surplusage and harmless to the defendant under the requirements of the habitual offender statute.

Baker v. State, 425 N.E.2d 98, 1981 Ind. LEXIS 823 (1981).

It is necessary that the state bring forth only two prior unrelated felony convictions to establish the defendant as an habitual offender. Proof of three or more felony convictions is mere surplusage. Wilson v. State, 511 N.E.2d 1014, 1987 Ind. LEXIS 1020 (1987).

—Striking Recent Felony.

Where there is a surplus felony contained in the habitual offender charge, the defendant cannot pick and choose the sentence he would like to have stricken. Where the defendant has been convicted of a felony within 10 years of the present charge, the trial judge does not err in failing to withdraw this sentence from the jury's consideration in the habitual offender portion of the trial. Flick v. State, 455 N.E.2d 339, 1983 Ind. LEXIS 1000 (1983).

Trial on Enhancement.

—Charge Enhancement and Habitual Offender.

When the state charges a defendant with certain offenses which may be enhanced by virtue of prior convictions and also alleges that the defendant is an habitual offender, the trial need not proceed in three separate phases. Shelton v. State, 602 N.E.2d 1017, 1992 Ind. LEXIS 251 (1992).

Holding the charge enhancement and habitual offender determinations in the same phase of a trial does not offend any interest of the defendant in a fair trial. Shelton v. State, 602 N.E.2d 1017, 1992 Ind. LEXIS 251 (1992).

Combining the habitual offender and aggravating circumstances phase into one hearing did not deny defendant a fair trial. Defendant did not explain how the habitual offender evidence prejudiced him in the eyes of the jury, which had already convicted him of multiple felonies at that point, so no presumption of innocence remained to shield him. Ramsey v. State, 853 N.E.2d 491, 2006 Ind. App. LEXIS 1794 (2006).

Verdict.

In an habitual offender proceeding, the jury's use of the word "guilty" is technically incorrect, but does not constitute reversible error, as the addition of the word "guilty" in the verdict is mere surplusage. Bradford v. State, 453 N.E.2d 250, 1983 Ind. LEXIS 959 (1983).

Cited:

Harrison v. Indiana, 597 F.2d 115, 1979 U.S. App. LEXIS 14996 (7th Cir. Ind. 1979); State v. Holland, 273 Ind. 284, 403 N.E.2d 832, 1980 Ind. LEXIS 671 (1980); Bish v. State, 421 N.E.2d 608, 1981 Ind. LEXIS 758 (1981); Pennington v. State, 426 N.E.2d 408, 1981 Ind. LEXIS 865 (1981); Williams v. State, 426 N.E.2d 662, 1981 Ind. LEXIS 863 (1981); Field v. State, 426 N.E.2d 671, 1981 Ind. LEXIS 873 (1981); Whitlock v. State, 426 N.E.2d 1292, 1981 Ind. LEXIS 880 (1981); Harris v. State, 427 N.E.2d 658, 1981 Ind. LEXIS 892 (1981); Poston v. State, 429 N.E.2d 643, 1981 Ind. LEXIS 963 (1981); Nash v. State, 429 N.E.2d 666,

1981 Ind. App. LEXIS 1801 (1981); Williams v. State, 430 N.E.2d 759, 1982 Ind. LEXIS 732 (1982); Lyons v. State, 431 N.E.2d 78, 1982 Ind. LEXIS 744 (1982); Haynes v. State, 431 N.E.2d 83, 1982 Ind. LEXIS 737 (1982); Twyman v. State, 431 N.E.2d 778, 1982 Ind. LEXIS 763 (1982); Powers v. State, 431 N.E.2d 799, 1982 Ind. LEXIS 759 (1982); Smith v. State, 432 N.E.2d 1363, 1982 Ind. LEXIS 789 (1982); Jordan v. State, 435 N.E.2d 257, 1982 Ind. LEXIS 820 (1982); Foster v. State, 436 N.E.2d 783, 1982 Ind. LEXIS 859 (1982); Hatton v. State, 439 N.E.2d 565, 1982 Ind. LEXIS 948 (1982); Mickens v. State, 439 N.E.2d 591, 1982 Ind. LEXIS 942 (1982); Lee v. State, 439 N.E.2d 603, 1982 Ind. LEXIS 939 (1982); Allen v. State, 439 N.E.2d 615, 1982 Ind. LEXIS 936 (1982); Hernandez v. State, 439 N.E.2d 625, 1982 Ind. LEXIS 958 (1982); Sweet v. State, 439 N.E.2d 1144, 1982 Ind. LEXIS 954 (1982); Graham v. State, 441 N.E.2d 1348, 1982 Ind. LEXIS 1030 (1982); Glover v. State, 441 N.E.2d 1360, 1982 Ind. LEXIS 1029 (1982); Wells v. State, 441 N.E.2d 1366, 1982 Ind. LEXIS 1025 (1982); Dier v. State, 442 N.E.2d 1043, 1982 Ind. LEXIS 1051 (1982); Bray v. State, 443 N.E.2d 310, 1982 Ind. LEXIS 1070 (1982); Hudson v. State, 443 N.E.2d 834, 1983 Ind. LEXIS 725 (1983); Shaffer v. State, 443 N.E.2d 838, 1983 Ind. LEXIS 726 (1983); Poe v. State, 445 N.E.2d 94, 1983 Ind. LEXIS 759 (1983); Walker v. State, 445 N.E.2d 571, 1983 Ind. LEXIS 757 (1983); Hill v. State, 450 N.E.2d 64, 1983 Ind. LEXIS 870 (1983); McMillian v. State, 450 N.E.2d 996, 1983 Ind. LEXIS 876 (1983); Mack v. State, 457 N.E.2d 200, 1983 Ind. LEXIS 1069 (1983); Neeley v. State, 457 N.E.2d 532, 1983 Ind. LEXIS 1076 (1983); Compton v. State, 465 N.E.2d 711, 1984 Ind. LEXIS 875 (1984); Woodson v. State, 466 N.E.2d 432, 1984 Ind. LEXIS 911 (1984); Counceller v. State, 466 N.E.2d 456, 1984 Ind. LEXIS 916 (1984); Holliness v. State, 467 N.E.2d 4, 1984 Ind. LEXIS 926 (1984); Galmore v. State, 467 N.E.2d 1173, 1984 Ind. LEXIS 906 (1984); Smith v. State, 468 N.E.2d 512, 1984 Ind. LEXIS 941 (1984); Connell v. State, 470 N.E.2d 701, 1984 Ind. LEXIS 1017 (1984); Davis v. State, 472 N.E.2d 922, 1985 Ind. LEXIS 734 (1985); Smith v. State, 475 N.E.2d 1139, 1985 Ind. LEXIS 782 (1985); Coppock v. State, 480 N.E.2d 941, 1985 Ind. LEXIS 919 (1985); Richardson v. State, 481 N.E.2d 1310, 1985 Ind. LEXIS 936 (1985); Woodson v. State, 483 N.E.2d 62, 1985 Ind. LEXIS 979 (1985); Jackson v. State, 483 N.E.2d 1374, 1985 Ind. LEXIS 997 (1985); Foster v. State, 484 N.E.2d 965, 1985 Ind. LEXIS 1017 (1985); Martin v. State, 488 N.E.2d 1160, 1986 Ind. App. LEXIS 2310 (1986); Gibson v. State, 490 N.E.2d 297, 1986 Ind. LEXIS 1048 (1986); Turpin v. State, 490 N.E.2d 1109, 1986 Ind. LEXIS 1086 (1986); Ashley v. State, 493 N.E.2d 768, 1986 Ind. LEXIS 1174 (1986); Gilliam v. State, 494 N.E.2d 319, 1986 Ind. LEXIS 1187 (1986); Wendling v. State, 495 N.E.2d 192, 1986 Ind. LEXIS 1210 (1986); Gipson v. State, 495 N.E.2d 722, 1986 Ind. LEXIS 1218 (1986); Cavendish v. State, 496 N.E.2d 46, 1986 Ind. LEXIS 1227 (1986); Blue v. State, 504 N.E.2d 583, 1987 Ind. LEXIS 856 (1987); Carter v. State, 505 N.E.2d 798, 1987 Ind. LEXIS 871 (1987); Hutcherson v. State, 507 N.E.2d 969, 1987 Ind. LEXIS 927 (1987); Duff v. State, 508 N.E.2d 17, 1987 Ind. LEXIS 933 (1987); Vaxter v. State, 508 N.E.2d 809, 1987 Ind. LEXIS 949 (1987); Taylor v. State, 511 N.E.2d 1036, 1987 Ind. LEXIS 1031 (1987); Criss v. State, 512 N.E.2d 858, 1987 Ind. LEXIS 1061 (1987); Washington v. State, 517 N.E.2d 77, 1987 Ind. LEXIS 1199 (1987); Walker v. State, 527 N.E.2d 706, 1988 Ind. LEXIS 247 (1988); Caldwell v. State, 527 N.E.2d 711, 1988 Ind. LEXIS 244 (1988); Decker v. State, 528 N.E.2d 1119, 1988 Ind. LEXIS 285 (1988); Jones v. State, 531 N.E.2d 478, 1988 Ind. LEXIS 342 (1988); McCombs v. State, 536 N.E.2d 277, 1989 Ind. LEXIS 86 (1989); Adamov v. State, 536 N.E.2d 281, 1989 Ind. LEXIS 103 (1989); Sparks v. State, 537 N.E.2d 1179, 1989 Ind. LEXIS 140 (1989); Bernard v. State, 540 N.E.2d 23, 1989 Ind. LEXIS 183 (1989); Smith v. State, 543 N.E.2d 634, 1989 Ind. LEXIS 283 (1989); Cash v. State, 557 N.E.2d 1023, 1990 Ind. LEXIS 150 (1990); Reeves v. State, 564 N.E.2d 550, 1991 Ind. App. LEXIS 4 (1991); Slocumb v. State, 568 N.E.2d 1068, 1991 Ind. App. LEXIS 448 (1991); Jones v. State, 569 N.E.2d 975, 1991 Ind. App. LEXIS 599 (1991); Clay v. Bronnenberg, 950 F.2d 486, 1991 U.S. App. LEXIS 28874 (7th Cir. Ind. 1991); Wilson v. State, 583 N.E.2d 742, 1992 Ind. LEXIS 2 (1992); Smith v. State, 586 N.E.2d 890, 1992 Ind. App. LEXIS 152 (1992); Bauer v. State, 591 N.E.2d 564, 1992 Ind. App. LEXIS 1140 (1992); Higgason v. Clark, 984 F.2d 203, 1993 U.S. App. LEXIS 387 (7th Cir. Ind. 1993); Cuppett v. Duckworth, 8 F.3d 1132, 1993 U.S. App. LEXIS 26465 (7th Cir. Ind. 1993); Smith v. State, 636 N.E.2d 124, 1994 Ind. LEXIS 67 (1994); United States v. McKinley, 23 F.3d 181, 1994 U.S. App. LEXIS 9328 (7th Cir. Ind. 1994); Smith v. Farley, 25 F.3d 1363, 1994 U.S. App. LEXIS 10846 (7th Cir. Ind. 1994); Hazzard v. State, 642 N.E.2d 1368, 1994 Ind. LEXIS 151 (1994); Johnson v. State, 659 N.E.2d 116, 1995 Ind. LEXIS 190 (1995); Potter v. State, 666 N.E.2d 93, 1996 Ind. App. LEXIS 753 (1996); Tompkins v. State, 669 N.E.2d 394, 1996 Ind. LEXIS 85 (1996); Smith v. State, 670 N.E.2d 7, 1996 Ind. LEXIS 129 (1996); Williams v. State, 676 N.E.2d 1074, 1997 Ind. App. LEXIS 49 (1997); Moore v. Parke, 968 F. Supp. 1338, 1997 U.S. Dist. LEXIS 9408 (N.D. Ind. 1997); Hazzard v. State, 694 N.E.2d 283, 1998 Ind. LEXIS 56 (1998); Lee v. State, 694 N.E.2d 719, 1998 Ind. LEXIS 53 (1998); Allen v. State, 722 N.E.2d 1246, 2000 Ind. App. LEXIS 12 (2000); Price v. State, 725 N.E.2d 82, 2000 Ind. LEXIS 208 (2000); McGregor v. State, 725 N.E.2d 840, 2000 Ind. LEXIS 234 (2000); Farris v. State, 732 N.E.2d 230, 2000 Ind. App. LEXIS 1080 (2000); Ward v. State, 736 N.E.2d 265, 2000 Ind. App. LEXIS 1390 (2000); Williams v. State, 735 N.E.2d 785, 2000 Ind. LEXIS 935 (2000); Jackson v. State, 735 N.E.2d 1146, 2000 Ind. LEXIS 951 (2000); Burnett v. State, 736 N.E.2d 259, 2000 Ind. LEXIS 959 (2000); Garrett v. State, 737 N.E.2d 388, 2000 Ind. LEXIS 983 (2000); Carter v. State, 738 N.E.2d 665, 2000 Ind. LEXIS 1108 (2000); Hancock v. State, 737 N.E.2d 791, 2000 Ind. App. LEXIS 1714 (2000); Teer v. State, 738 N.E.2d 283, 2000 Ind. App. LEXIS 1832 (2000); Graham v. State, 738 N.E.2d 1096, 2000 Ind. App. LEXIS 1982 (2000);

Allen v. State, 743 N.E.2d 1222, 2001 Ind. App. LEXIS 367 (2001); State v. Bilbrey, 743 N.E.2d 796, 2001 Ind. App. LEXIS 370 (2001); Mitchell v. State, 745 N.E.2d 775, 2001 Ind. LEXIS 300 (2001); Smith v. State, 754 N.E.2d 502, 2001 Ind. LEXIS 830 (2001); State v. Downey, 770 N.E.2d 794, 2002 Ind. LEXIS 542 (2002); Jackson v. State, 785 N.E.2d 615, 2003 Ind. App. LEXIS 456 (2003); State v. Starks, 787 N.E.2d 885, 2003 Ind. App. LEXIS 629 (2003); O'Connor v. State, 789 N.E.2d 504, 2003 Ind. App. LEXIS 908 (2003); Gray v. State, 790 N.E.2d 174, 2003 Ind. App. LEXIS 1061 (2003); Douglas v. State, 800 N.E.2d 599, 2003 Ind. App. LEXIS 2340 (2003); Brown v. State, 825 N.E.2d 978, 2005 Ind. App. LEXIS 662 (2005); Tracy v. State, 837 N.E.2d 524, 2005 Ind. App. LEXIS 2164 (2005); Corbin v. State, 840 N.E.2d 424, 2006 Ind. App. LEXIS 31 (2006); Boney v. State, 880 N.E.2d 279, 2008 Ind. App. LEXIS 72 (2008); McCown v. State, 890 N.E.2d 752, 2008 Ind. App. LEXIS 1528 (2008).

RESEARCH REFERENCES

Indiana Law Review.
The Constitutional Infirmities of Indiana's Habitual Offender Statute, 13 Ind. L. Rev. 597 (1980).
Update — Criminal Law and Procedure, 26 Ind. L. Rev. 891 (1993).
Recent Developments in Criminal Law and Procedure, 27 Ind. L. Rev. 959 (1994).
Recent Developments in Indiana Criminal Law and Procedure, 28 Ind. L. Rev. 819 (1995).

Res Gestae.
Criminal Justice Notes, 35 Res Gestae 430 (1992).
Criminal Justice Notes: Jury instructions — habitual offender proceedings, 42 (No. 3) Res Gestae 16 (1998).

Criminal Justice Notes, 45 (No. 8) Res Gestae 35 (2002).
Criminal Justice Notes: Double enhancements: non-retroactivity. 47 (No. 7) Res Gestae 31 (2004).

Collateral References.
Chronological or procedural sequence of former convictions as affecting enhancement of penalty under habitual offender statutes. 7 A.L.R.5th 263.
Pardoned or expunged conviction as "prior offense" under state statute or regulation enhancing punishment for subsequent conviction. 97 A.L.R.5th 293.

35-50-2-8.5. Life imprisonment without parole — Prior felony convictions.

(a) The state may seek to have a person sentenced to life imprisonment without parole for any felony described in section 2(b)(4) [IC 35-50-2-2(b)(4)] of this chapter by alleging, on a page separate from the rest of the charging instrument, that the person has accumulated two (2) prior unrelated felony convictions described in section 2(b)(4) of this chapter.

(b) The state may seek to have a person sentenced to life imprisonment without parole for a Class A felony under IC 35-42-4 that is a sex offense against a child by alleging, on a page separate from the rest of the charging instrument, that the person has a prior unrelated Class A felony conviction under IC 35-42-4 that is a sex offense against a child.

(c) If the person was convicted of the felony in a jury trial, the jury shall reconvene to hear evidence on the life imprisonment without parole allegation. If the person was convicted of the felony by trial to the court without a jury or if the judgment was entered to guilty plea, the court alone shall hear evidence on the life imprisonment without parole allegation.

(d) A person is subject to life imprisonment without parole if the jury (in a case tried by a jury) or the court (in a case tried by the court or on a judgment entered on a guilty plea) finds that the state has proved beyond a reasonable doubt that the person:

(1) has accumulated two (2) prior unrelated convictions for offenses described in section 2(b)(4) of this chapter; or

(2) has a prior unrelated Class A felony conviction under IC 35-42-4 that is a sex offense against a child.

(e) The court may sentence a person found to be subject to life imprisonment without parole under this section to life imprisonment without parole.

History.
P.L.158-1994, § 6; P.L.53-2005, § 2.

Compiler's Notes.
P.L.53-2005, § 4, effective July 1, 2005, provides:

"IC 35-50-2-8.5, as amended by this act, applies only to offenses committed after June 30, 2005."

NOTES TO DECISIONS

Instructions.
Jury instruction that stated if the jury found the state had proved the predicate felonies, it "should" find defendant to be a habitual offender, invaded the jury's prerogative by preventing it from making independent and separate decision on habitual offender status. Parker v. State, 698 N.E.2d 737, 1998 Ind. LEXIS 98 (1998).

RESEARCH REFERENCES

Indiana Law Review.
Recent Developments in Indiana Criminal Law and Procedure, 28 Ind. L. Rev. 819 (1995).

35-50-2-9. Death sentences.

(a) The state may seek either a death sentence or a sentence of life imprisonment without parole for murder by alleging, on a page separate from the rest of the charging instrument, the existence of at least one (1) of the aggravating circumstances listed in subsection (b). In the sentencing hearing after a person is convicted of murder, the state must prove beyond a reasonable doubt the existence of at least one (1) of the aggravating circumstances alleged. However, the state may not proceed against a defendant under this section if a court determines at a pretrial hearing under IC 35-36-9 that the defendant is an individual with mental retardation.

(b) The aggravating circumstances are as follows:

(1) The defendant committed the murder by intentionally killing the victim while committing or attempting to commit any of the following:

(A) Arson (IC 35-43-1-1).

(B) Burglary (IC 35-43-2-1).

(C) Child molesting (IC 35-42-4-3).

(D) Criminal deviate conduct (IC 35-42-4-2).

(E) Kidnapping (IC 35-42-3-2).

(F) Rape (IC 35-42-4-1).

(G) Robbery (IC 35-42-5-1).

(H) Carjacking (IC 35-42-5-2).

(I) Criminal gang activity (IC 35-45-9-3).

(J) Dealing in cocaine or a narcotic drug (IC 35-48-4-1).

(2) The defendant committed the murder by the unlawful detonation of an explosive with intent to injure person or damage property.

(3) The defendant committed the murder by lying in wait.

(4) The defendant who committed the murder was hired to kill.

(5) The defendant committed the murder by hiring another person to kill.

(6) The victim of the murder was a corrections employee, probation officer, parole officer, community corrections worker, home detention officer, fireman, judge, or law enforcement officer, and either:

(A) the victim was acting in the course of duty; or

(B) the murder was motivated by an act the victim performed while acting in the course of duty.

(7) The defendant has been convicted of another murder.

(8) The defendant has committed another murder, at any time, regardless of whether the defendant has been convicted of that other murder.

(9) The defendant was:
   (A) under the custody of the department of correction;
   (B) under the custody of a county sheriff;
   (C) on probation after receiving a sentence for the commission of a felony; or
   (D) on parole;
at the time the murder was committed.

(10) The defendant dismembered the victim.

(11) The defendant burned, mutilated, or tortured the victim while the victim was alive.

(12) The victim of the murder was less than twelve (12) years of age.

(13) The victim was a victim of any of the following offenses for which the defendant was convicted:
   (A) Battery as a Class D felony or as a Class C felony under IC 35-42-2-1.
   (B) Kidnapping (IC 35-42-3-2).
   (C) Criminal confinement (IC 35-42-3-3).
   (D) A sex crime under IC 35-42-4.

(14) The victim of the murder was listed by the state or known by the defendant to be a witness against the defendant and the defendant committed the murder with the intent to prevent the person from testifying.

(15) The defendant committed the murder by intentionally discharging a firearm (as defined in IC 35-47-1-5):
   (A) into an inhabited dwelling; or
   (B) from a vehicle.

(16) The victim of the murder was pregnant and the murder resulted in the intentional killing of a fetus that has attained viability (as defined in IC 16-18-2-365).

(c) The mitigating circumstances that may be considered under this section are as follows:

(1) The defendant has no significant history of prior criminal conduct.

(2) The defendant was under the influence of extreme mental or emotional disturbance when the murder was committed.

(3) The victim was a participant in or consented to the defendant's conduct.

(4) The defendant was an accomplice in a murder committed by another person, and the defendant's participation was relatively minor.

(5) The defendant acted under the substantial domination of another person.

(6) The defendant's capacity to appreciate the criminality of the defendant's conduct or to conform that conduct to the requirements of law was substantially impaired as a result of mental disease or defect or of intoxication.

(7) The defendant was less than eighteen (18) years of age at the time the murder was committed.

(8) Any other circumstances appropriate for consideration.

(d) If the defendant was convicted of murder in a jury trial, the jury shall reconvene for the sentencing hearing. If the trial was to the court, or the judgment was entered on a guilty plea, the court alone shall conduct the sentencing hearing. The jury or the court may consider all the evidence introduced at the trial stage of the proceedings, together with new evidence presented at the sentencing hearing. The court shall instruct the jury concerning the statutory penalties for murder and any other offenses for which the defendant was convicted, the potential for consecutive or concurrent sentencing, and the availability of good time credit and clemency. The court shall instruct the jury that, in order for the jury to recommend to the court that the death penalty or life imprisonment without parole should be imposed, the jury must find at least one (1) aggravating circumstance beyond a reasonable doubt as described in subsection (*l*) and shall provide a special verdict form for each aggravating circumstance alleged. The defendant may present any additional evidence relevant to:

   (1) the aggravating circumstances alleged; or

   (2) any of the mitigating circumstances listed in subsection (c).

   (e) For a defendant sentenced after June 30, 2002, except as provided by IC 35-36-9, if the hearing is by jury, the jury shall recommend to the court whether the death penalty or life imprisonment without parole, or neither, should be imposed. The jury may recommend:

   (1) the death penalty; or

   (2) life imprisonment without parole;

only if it makes the findings described in subsection (*l*). If the jury reaches a sentencing recommendation, the court shall sentence the defendant accordingly. After a court pronounces sentence, a representative of the victim's family and friends may present a statement regarding the impact of the crime on family and friends. The impact statement may be submitted in writing or given orally by the representative. The statement shall be given in the presence of the defendant.

   (f) If a jury is unable to agree on a sentence recommendation after reasonable deliberations, the court shall discharge the jury and proceed as if the hearing had been to the court alone.

   (g) If the hearing is to the court alone, except as provided by IC 35-36-9, the court shall:

   (1) sentence the defendant to death; or

   (2) impose a term of life imprisonment without parole;

only if it makes the findings described in subsection (*l*).

   (h) If a court sentences a defendant to death, the court shall order the defendant's execution to be carried out not later than one (1) year and one (1) day after the date the defendant was convicted. The Supreme Court has exclusive jurisdiction to stay the execution of a death sentence. If the Supreme Court stays the execution of a death sentence, the Supreme Court shall order a new date for the defendant's execution.

   (i) If a person sentenced to death by a court files a petition for post-conviction relief, the court, not later than ninety (90) days after the date the petition is filed, shall set a date to hold a hearing to consider the petition. If a court does not, within the ninety (90) day period, set the date to hold the hearing to consider the petition, the court's failure to set the hearing date is not a basis for additional post-conviction relief. The attorney general shall answer the petition for post-conviction relief on behalf of the state. At the request of the attorney general, a prosecuting attorney shall assist the attorney general. The court shall enter written findings of fact and conclusions of law concerning the petition not later than ninety (90) days after the date the hearing concludes. However, if the court determines that the petition is without merit, the court may dismiss the petition within ninety (90) days without conducting a hearing under this subsection.

   (j) A death sentence is subject to automatic review by the Supreme Court. The review, which shall be heard under rules adopted by the Supreme Court, shall be given priority over all other cases. The Supreme Court's review must take into consideration all claims that the:

   (1) conviction or sentence was in violation of the:

     (A) Constitution of the State of Indiana; or

     (B) Constitution of the United States;

   (2) sentencing court was without jurisdiction to impose a sentence; and

   (3) sentence:

     (A) exceeds the maximum sentence authorized by law; or

     (B) is otherwise erroneous.

If the Supreme Court cannot complete its review by the date set by the sentencing court for the defendant's execution under subsection (h), the Supreme Court shall stay the execution of the death sentence and set a new date to carry out the defendant's execution.

(k) A person who has been sentenced to death and who has completed state post-conviction review proceedings may file a written petition with the Supreme Court seeking to present new evidence challenging the person's guilt or the appropriateness of the death sentence if the person serves notice on the attorney general. The Supreme Court shall determine, with or without a hearing, whether the person has presented previously undiscovered evidence that undermines confidence in the conviction or the death sentence. If necessary, the Supreme Court may remand the case to the trial court for an evidentiary hearing to consider the new evidence and its effect on the person's conviction and death sentence. The Supreme Court may not make a determination in the person's favor nor make a decision to remand the case to the trial court for an evidentiary hearing without first providing the attorney general with an opportunity to be heard on the matter.

(*l*) Before a sentence may be imposed under this section, the jury, in a proceeding under subsection (e), or the court, in a proceeding under subsection (g), must find that:

(1) the state has proved beyond a reasonable doubt that at least one (1) of the aggravating circumstances listed in subsection (b) exists; and

(2) any mitigating circumstances that exist are outweighed by the aggravating circumstance or circumstances.

History.
IC 35-50-2-9, as added by Acts 1977, P.L.340, § 122; P.L.336-1983, § 1; P.L.212-1986, § 1; P.L.320-1987, § 2; P.L.332-1987, § 2; P.L.138-1989, § 6; P.L.296-1989, § 2; P.L.1-1990, § 354; P.L.230-1993, § 5; P.L.250-1993, § 2; P.L.158-1994, § 7; P.L.306-1995, § 1; P.L.216-1996, § 25; P.L.228-1996, § 1; P.L.261-1997, § 7; P.L.80-2002, § 1; P.L.117-2002, § 2; P.L.1-2003, § 97; P.L.147-2003, § 1; P.L.1-2006, § 550; P.L.99-2007, § 213, emergency eff. May 2, 2007.

Cross References.
Compensation for victims of violent crimes, IC 5-2-6.1.
Pretrial Determination of Mental Retardation in Death Sentence Cases, IC 35-36-9.

NOTES TO DECISIONS

ANALYSIS

In General.
Constitutionality.
—Action by Court.
—Age of Offender.
—Appellate Review.
—Application to Accessories.
—Cruel and Unusual Punishment.
—Due Process.
—Equal Protection.
—Felony Murder.
—Mandatory Death Penalty.
—Mental Illness.
—Sentencer's Discretion.
—Shifting of Burden of Proof.
—Victim Impact Evidence.
—Vindictive Justice.
Accomplice Liability.
Actions of Prosecutor.
Aggravating Circumstances.
—Age of Victim.
—Commission of Other Murders.
—Commission of Specified Felony.
—Confession to Other Crimes.
—Defendant on Probation.
—Failure to Allege on Separate Page.
—Improper.
—Instructions.
—Lying in Wait.

— —Defined.
— —Found.
— —Not Found.
—Murder of Law Enforcement Officer.
—Perpetration of Rape.
—Pleading and Proof.
—Prior Criminal Activity.
—Sentence to Term of Years.
—Torture.
Appropriateness of Sentence.
—Upheld.
Attempted Burglaries.
Construction.
Course of Duty.
Double Jeopardy.
Evidence.
—Conflict.
—Exclusion Not Prejudicial.
—Method of Execution.
—Not Sufficient.
—Reasonable Inference.
—Relevance.
—Sufficient.
Exclusion of Jurors.
Guilty but Mentally Ill.
Guilty Plea.
—Denial of Intent.
—Indictment.
Ineffective Assistance of Counsel.
—Not Shown.

In General.

When the death penalty was assessed, the verdict need not have specified the manner of execution. Greenley v. State, 60 Ind. 141, 1877 Ind. LEXIS 334 (1877).

Under an earlier law, a jury was to be impaneled to assess the punishment in capital cases. Wartner v. State, 102 Ind. 51, 1 N.E. 65, 1885 Ind. LEXIS 9 (1885); Lowery v. Howard, 103 Ind. 440, 3 N.E. 124, 1885 Ind. LEXIS 542 (1885).

Constitutionality.

Where statute under which defendant was condemned to death contained no procedural safeguards of due process and was declared unconstitutional, the provision for death was invalid and could not be rendered valid by a judicially created procedure for due process since that was a legislative function. Bond v. State, 273 Ind. 233, 403 N.E.2d 812, 1980 Ind. LEXIS 665 (1980).

The fact that the prior death penalty statute was declared unconstitutional did not require reversal of convictions under such statute but where the death penalty was imposed under such unconstitutional statute the death sentence would be vacated and case remanded with instructions to impose life sentence. Norton v. State, 273 Ind. 635, 408 N.E.2d 514, 1980 Ind. LEXIS 719 (1980).

The statutory and procedural scheme for imposing the death sentence limit the imposition of such sentence in such manner as to assure that it will not be inflicted in an arbitrary or capricious manner and therefore the provisions for the sentence violate neither the federal nor state constitutions. Brewer v. State, 275 Ind. 338, 417 N.E.2d 889, 1981 Ind. LEXIS 684 (1981), cert. denied, 458 U.S. 1122, 102 S. Ct. 3510, 73 L. Ed. 2d 1384, 1982 U.S. LEXIS 2891 (1982); Dillon v. State, 454 N.E.2d 845, 1983 Ind. LEXIS 988 (1983), cert. denied, 465 U.S. 1109, 104 S. Ct. 1617, 80 L. Ed. 2d 145 (1984).

When the procedure prescribed by this section is properly followed the imposition of the death penalty is not unconstitutional. Judy v. State, 275 Ind. 145, 416 N.E.2d 95, 1981 Ind. LEXIS 665 (1981).

This section does not violate those sections of the Indiana Constitution prohibiting laws dependent upon authority other than provided by the constitution, prohibiting the suspension of the operation of laws, or prohibiting the promulgation of local or special laws for the punishment of crimes. Williams v. State, 430 N.E.2d 759, 1982 Ind. LEXIS 732 (1982), appeal dismissed, 459 U.S. 808, 103 S. Ct. 33, 74 L. Ed. 2d 47, 1982 U.S. LEXIS 3004 (1982).

This section is not unconstitutional per se, as being in derogation of either the United States Const., Amend. 8 or Ind. Const., Art. 1, § 16. Williams v. State, 430 N.E.2d 759, 1982 Ind. LEXIS 732 (1982), appeal dismissed, 459 U.S. 808, 103 S. Ct. 33, 74 L. Ed. 2d 47, 1982 U.S. LEXIS 3004 (1982).

Constitutionality. (Cont'd)

Discretion given to prosecuting attorneys under the death penalty statute to determine who will or who will not be charged with the death penalty does not violate the Indiana or United States Constitutions. Williams v. State, 430 N.E.2d 759, 1982 Ind. LEXIS 732 (1982), appeal dismissed, 459 U.S. 808, 103 S. Ct. 33, 74 L. Ed. 2d 47, 1982 U.S. LEXIS 3004 (1982).

There are no constitutional infirmities in the death penalty statute nor in the review that automatically follows the imposition of such sentence. Schiro v. State, 451 N.E.2d 1047, 1983 Ind. LEXIS 904 (1983), cert. denied, 464 U.S. 1003, 104 S. Ct. 510, 78 L. Ed. 2d 699 (1983).

This section does not constitute vindictive justice in violation of Ind. Const., Art. 1, § 18 and is not unconstitutional per se as being in derogation of the Eighth Amendment of the federal constitution. Dillon v. State, 454 N.E.2d 845, 1983 Ind. LEXIS 988 (1983), cert. denied, 465 U.S. 1109, 104 S. Ct. 1617, 80 L. Ed. 2d 145 (1984).

The death penalty does not per se violate the Eighth or Fourteenth Amendments. Resnover v. State, 460 N.E.2d 922, 1984 Ind. LEXIS 767 (1984), cert. denied, 469 U.S. 873, 105 S. Ct. 231, 83 L. Ed. 2d 160, 1984 U.S. LEXIS 370 (1984).

Indiana's death penalty statute establishes definite standards by which Indiana juries are given adequate and specific guidance. Resnover v. State, 460 N.E.2d 922, 1984 Ind. LEXIS 767 (1984), cert. denied, 469 U.S. 873, 105 S. Ct. 231, 83 L. Ed. 2d 160, 1984 U.S. LEXIS 370 (1984).

There is no constitutional provision prohibiting prosecutorial discretion in charging the death penalty. Resnover v. State, 460 N.E.2d 922, 1984 Ind. LEXIS 767 (1984), cert. denied, 469 U.S. 873, 105 S. Ct. 231, 83 L. Ed. 2d 160, 1984 U.S. LEXIS 370 (1984).

The lack of written jury findings does not make this section unconstitutional. Burris v. State, 465 N.E.2d 171, 1984 Ind. LEXIS 854 (1984), cert. denied, 469 U.S. 1132, 105 S. Ct. 816, 83 L. Ed. 2d 809 (1985), superseded by statute as stated in, Wrinkles v. State, 690 N.E.2d 1156, 1997 Ind. LEXIS 240 (1997).

Indiana's death statute and procedures meet all the constitutional requirements of proportionality review. Boyd v. State, 494 N.E.2d 284, 1986 Ind. LEXIS 1186 (1986), cert. denied, 479 U.S. 1046, 107 S. Ct. 910, 93 L. Ed. 2d 860, 1987 U.S. LEXIS 242 (1987).

Indiana's death penalty statute is not unconstitutional although it does not provide for a proportionality review of a sentence through comparison of a defendant's crime and penalty to those of others. The statutory requirement that the trial court weigh factors in mitigation and enter a specific record of its reasoning, automatically reviewed by the Supreme Court, is sufficiently tailored to ensure that the death penalty is not arbitrarily or disproportionately imposed. Van Cleave v. State, 517 N.E.2d 356, 1987 Ind. LEXIS 1196 (1987), cert. denied, 488 U.S. 1019, 109 S. Ct. 819, 102 L. Ed. 2d 808, 1989 U.S. LEXIS 56 (1989).

Allowing consideration of the aggravating circumstance of multiple related murders, while not permitting application of subsection (b)(8) when the additional murder is unrelated to the instant murder and has not been reduced to a conviction, does not deprive a defendant of equal protection. Townsend v. State, 533 N.E.2d 1215, 1989 Ind. LEXIS 37 (1989), cert. denied, 494 U.S. 1020, 110 S. Ct. 1327, 108 L. Ed. 2d 502, 1990 U.S. LEXIS 1248 (1990), cert. denied, McCollum v. Indiana, 496 U.S. 931, 110 S. Ct. 2633, 110 L. Ed. 2d 653, 1990 U.S. LEXIS 3063 (1990).

The Indiana death penalty scheme is not unconstitutional. Games v. State, 535 N.E.2d 530, 1989 Ind. LEXIS 406 (1989), cert. denied, 493 U.S. 874, 110 S. Ct. 205, 107 L. Ed. 2d 158, 1989 U.S. LEXIS 4557 (1989); Evans v. State, 563 N.E.2d 1251, 1990 Ind. LEXIS 253 (1990); Harrison v. State, 644 N.E.2d 1243, 1995 Ind. LEXIS 7 (1995), superseded by statute as stated in, Allen v. State, 737 N.E.2d 741, 2000 Ind. LEXIS 1075 (Ind. 2000), superseded by statute as stated in, Kroegher v. State, 774 N.E.2d 1029, 2002 Ind. App. LEXIS 1529 (2002).

This section requires the jury to find that the state proved the existence of at least one aggravating circumstance beyond a reasonable doubt and weigh the aggravating against mitigating circumstances that exist. It therefore adequately protects a capital defendant's right to be sentenced in a manner which is not arbitrary, freakish, or capricious. Canaan v. State, 541 N.E.2d 894, 1989 Ind. LEXIS 240 (1989), cert. denied, 498 U.S. 882, 111 S. Ct. 230, 112 L. Ed. 2d 185, 1990 U.S. LEXIS 4799 (1990).

Indiana's death penalty statute provides a categorical narrowing of persons eligible for the death penalty and an individualized determination on the basis of the character of the individual and the circumstances of the crime, in that the jury is allowed to consider any appropriate mitigating circumstance and the evidence introduced at the trial stage so that the death penalty statute does not fail to sufficiently narrow the class of persons eligible for the death penalty and is not unconstitutional. Huffman v. State, 543 N.E.2d 360, 1989 Ind. LEXIS 278 (1989), cert. denied, 497 U.S. 1011, 110 S. Ct. 3257, 111 L. Ed. 2d 767, 1990 U.S. LEXIS 3401 (1990), overruled, Street v. State, 567 N.E.2d 102, 1991 Ind. LEXIS 35 (1991).

The death penalty statute does not deny equal protection of the law to felony murderers. Minnick v. State, 544 N.E.2d 471, 1989 Ind. LEXIS 299 (1989).

This section on its face passes constitutional muster. Schiro v. Clark, 754 F. Supp. 646, 1990 U.S. Dist. LEXIS 17927 (N.D. Ind. 1990), aff'd, 963 F.2d 962, 1992 U.S. App. LEXIS 9889 (7th Cir. Ind. 1992).

The Indiana death penalty statute will not lead to arbitrary or discriminatory results generally; regardless of its rationale, a state may constitutionally establish pure judicial sentencing in capital cases or it may permit judicial sentencing upon a nonbinding, advisory recommendation from a jury, as Indiana has chosen to do. Schiro v. Clark, 963 F.2d 962, 1992 U.S. App. LEXIS 9889 (7th Cir. Ind. 1992), aff'd, 510 U.S. 222, 127 L. Ed. 2d 47, 114 S. Ct. 783, 1994 U.S. LEXIS 1135 (1994).

Constitutionality. (Cont'd)

Indiana's capital sentencing scheme did not unconstitutionally fail to provide sufficient guidance to the "sentencer" concerning who has the burden of proving whether aggravation outweighs mitigation; the statute is not constitutionally flawed for failing to require the sentencer to find that aggravating circumstances outweigh mitigating circumstances beyond a reasonable doubt. The determination of weight to be accorded between the aggravating and mitigating circumstances is not a "fact" to be proven but is a balancing process, and there is no question that under the statute the state is required to prove at least one aggravator beyond a reasonable doubt; however, it also is true that although some mitigating circumstances are an integral part of the state's case, during the sentencing process the defendant also is free to introduce any evidence which might be considered as mitigating. The comparison of those factors does not involve the process of proof beyond a reasonable doubt. Miller v. State, 623 N.E.2d 403, 1993 Ind. LEXIS 173 (1993).

This section does not mandate the jury to recommend the death penalty, but only gives them that option, which leaves room for the exercise of mercy, and there is no constitutional impairment in the statute in this regard. Miller v. State, 623 N.E.2d 403, 1993 Ind. LEXIS 173 (1993).

The Indiana capital sentencing statute was not unconstitutional as applied to the extent it required the sentencers to consider statutory mitigating circumstances whether they were relied upon by the defendant or were relevant to the case. It is difficult to conceive how a sentencer would feel they were required to consider irrelevant or unrelated mitigating circumstances. Even if a sentencer would run through the entire statutory list of mitigators and attempt to apply them to the case, it is difficult to see how this would harm a defendant. Miller v. State, 623 N.E.2d 403, 1993 Ind. LEXIS 173 (1993).

Where the jury was instructed that although they were the judges of the law they must apply the law as they find it, and they were not to disregard the law, such instruction was proper and the capital sentencing statute sufficiently guided the jury's discretion. Miller v. State, 623 N.E.2d 403, 1993 Ind. LEXIS 173 (1993).

The Indiana capital sentencing statute does not violate the Constitution in that it permits the judge to override a jury's recommendation. Miller v. State, 623 N.E.2d 403, 1993 Ind. LEXIS 173 (1993).

The capital sentencing statute is not unconstitutional because it minimizes the jury's sense of responsibility for its sentencing decision. Miller v. State, 623 N.E.2d 403, 1993 Ind. LEXIS 173 (1993).

The capital sentencing statute is not unconstitutional because the state is permitted to open and close final argument, as per IC 35-37-2-2. It is well-established procedure in this and most other jurisdictions that the party having the burden of proof opens and closes argument, and the sentencing in a death penalty case is no different than any other phase of that case or in fact of any other litigation as to the procedure to be followed concerning those having the burden of proof. Miller v. State, 623 N.E.2d 403, 1993 Ind. LEXIS 173 (1993).

The capital sentencing statute does not impermissibly create a presumption in favor of the imposition of capital punishment because the statute lists more aggravating factors than mitigating factors. The aggravators to be used in any given case are peculiar to that case, and there is no limitation on mitigators that may be submitted to the court. Miller v. State, 623 N.E.2d 403, 1993 Ind. LEXIS 173 (1993).

The capital sentencing statute is not unconstitutional because it vests in the prosecuting attorney unbridled discretion to file or not file a request for the death penalty. Miller v. State, 623 N.E.2d 403, 1993 Ind. LEXIS 173 (1993).

Death penalty is constitutional where state is required during penalty phase to prove beyond a reasonable doubt existence of at least one aggravating circumstance, jury is required to find aggravating factors outweigh mitigating ones, and court follows same process in deciding whether to follow jury's recommendation. Wrinkles v. State, 690 N.E.2d 1156, 1997 Ind. LEXIS 240 (1997), cert. denied, 525 U.S. 861, 119 S. Ct. 148, 142 L. Ed. 2d 121, 1998 U.S. LEXIS 5495 (1998).

Although IC 35-50-2-9 refers to aggravating factors, they serve the narrowing function required by the Eighth Amendment, and are not identical to the elements of a crime. West v. State, 755 N.E.2d 173, 2001 Ind. LEXIS 889 (2001).

Habeas petitioner was denied federal habeas corpus relief, where the appellate review of the death-sentence statute under which he was sentenced, IC 35-50-2-9(h) was not constitutionally deficient under the Eighth and Fourteenth Amendments to the United States Constitution; further, the Indiana Supreme Court reasonably concluded that the statute was not constitutionally deficient in providing adequate guidance to the jury regarding the balancing of aggravating and mitigating circumstances. Conner v. Anderson, 259 F. Supp. 2d 741, 2003 U.S. Dist. LEXIS 3036 (S.D. Ind. 2003), aff'd, 375 F.3d 643, 2004 U.S. App. LEXIS 15414 (7th Cir. Ind. 2004).

Amendment to death penalty statute, IC 35-50-2-9, which made jury's recommendation as to death penalty binding on judge rather than nonbinding, was procedural in nature for purposes of ex post facto doctrine and could therefore be applied to crimes committed before effective date of amendment. Ritchie v. State, 809 N.E.2d 258, 2004 Ind. LEXIS 476 (2004), cert. denied, 126 S. Ct. 42, 163 L. Ed. 2d 76, 2005 U.S. LEXIS 6128 (U.S. 2005).

Application of amended death penalty statute did not violate prohibition on ex post facto laws as applied to defendant since amended statute did not make criminal act that previously was not criminal, did not increase punishment for crime, and did not eliminate any available defenses or lesser punishment; statute simply shifted role of determining final sentence from judge to jury.

Constitutionality. (Cont'd)
Stroud v. State, 809 N.E.2d 274, 2004 Ind. LEXIS 473 (2004).

Fact that IC 35-50-2-9 does not require penalty-phase jury to find that aggravating circumstances outweigh mitigating circumstances beyond a reasonable doubt does not make statute unconstitutional under Sixth Amendment as interpreted by Apprendi and Ring. State v. Ben-Yisrayl, 809 N.E.2d 309, 2004 Ind. LEXIS 478 (2004), cert. denied, 126 S. Ct. 659, 163 L. Ed. 2d 533, 2005 U.S. LEXIS 8453 (U.S. 2005).

Trial court erred in concluding that death penalty statute, IC 35-50-2-9, is unconstitutional because it does not require jury to find that mitigating circumstances outweigh aggravating circumstances beyond a reasonable doubt. State v. Barker, 809 N.E.2d 312, 2004 Ind. LEXIS 477 (2004).

Argument that Indiana death penalty statute is unconstitutional because it does not require jury to find beyond reasonable doubt that aggravating factors outweigh mitigating factors before death or life imprisonment without parole may be imposed was rejected. Laux v. State, 821 N.E.2d 816, 2005 Ind. LEXIS 93 (2005).

Sentence of life imprisonment without parole for 1996 murder pursuant to 2002 amendment of IC 35-50-2-9(e), which did away with judge's discretion to deviate from jury's recommendation of death or life imprisonment without parole, did not violate defendant's constitutional rights. Houser v. State, 823 N.E.2d 693, 2005 Ind. LEXIS 198 (2005).

Indiana Supreme Court had previously upheld the life without parole statute, IC 35-50-2-9, in the face of Sixth Amendment challenges when, as here, defendant pleaded guilty; Blakely did not affect Indiana's death penalty statute since the jury's determination of whether the eligibility factors outweighed any mitigating factors was not a finding of fact and it did not increase the penalty of the crime. Covington v. State, 842 N.E.2d 345, 2006 Ind. LEXIS 127 (2006).

The breadth of the United States Supreme Court's decision in Kansas v. Marsh, 126 S. Ct. 2516, 165 L. Ed. 2d 429, 2006 U.S. LEXIS 5163 (2006), makes it apparent that any claim that the U.S. Constitution requires that aggravating circumstances outweigh mitigators beyond a reasonable doubt in death penalty cases is untenable. Kubsch v. State, 866 N.E.2d 726, 2007 Ind. LEXIS 360 (2007).

—Action by Court.
The United States Constitution does not require that only a jury can make the determination of the existence of circumstances to be used during the sentencing phase; therefore, subsection (f) of this section is constitutional. Roche v. State, 596 N.E.2d 896, 1992 Ind. LEXIS 191 (1992).

By foregoing the opportunity for a jury to make a recommendation on his sentence, defendant was not giving up a constitutional right that would require a separate advisement of his rights. Davis v. State, 675 N.E.2d 1097, 1996 Ind. LEXIS 194 (1996).

—Age of Offender.
Death sentence imposed on a 15-year-old murderer prior to the 1987 amendment of IC 35-50-2-3, which provided that 16, at the time of the offense, should be the minimum age for execution, was disproportionate to any other sentence for the same crime, and could therefore not be upheld. Cooper v. State, 540 N.E.2d 1216, 1989 Ind. LEXIS 216 (1989).

—Appellate Review.
This section's requirement that the Supreme Court specifically review the imposition of the death penalty provides for adequate appellate review and it is for this court to properly apply constitutional law in conducting such a review. The failure of this section to detail the nature of that constitutional review does not render this section unconstitutional. Conner v. State, 580 N.E.2d 214, 1991 Ind. LEXIS 197 (1991), cert. denied, 503 U.S. 946, 112 S. Ct. 1501, 117 L. Ed. 2d 640, 1992 U.S. LEXIS 1867 (1992).

The process of appellate review for Indiana capital sentences fully comports with constitutional requirements seeking to prevent the arbitrary and capricious imposition of the death penalty. Bivins v. State, 642 N.E.2d 928, 1994 Ind. LEXIS 146 (1994), amended, — N.E.2d —, 1995 Ind. LEXIS 34 (1995), cert. denied, 516 U.S. 1077, 133 L. Ed. 2d 734, 116 S. Ct. 783, 1996 U.S. LEXIS 547 (1996).

—Application to Accessories.
The death sentence may be constitutionally imposed upon one who is an accessory to murder. Brewer v. State, 275 Ind. 338, 417 N.E.2d 889, 1981 Ind. LEXIS 684 (1981), cert. denied, 458 U.S. 1122, 102 S. Ct. 3510, 73 L. Ed. 2d 1384, 1982 U.S. LEXIS 2891 (1982).

—Cruel and Unusual Punishment.
The death penalty is not unconstitutional as inflicting cruel and unusual punishment. Brewer v. State, 275 Ind. 338, 417 N.E.2d 889, 1981 Ind. LEXIS 684 (1981), cert. denied, 458 U.S. 1122, 102 S. Ct. 3510, 73 L. Ed. 2d 1384, 1982 U.S. LEXIS 2891 (1982).

A death sentence received by defendant for murder during commission of a robbery was not rendered cruel and unusual by the fact that an accomplice in the robbery thereafter received a sentence of 60 years on a plea of guilty before another judge. Brewer v. State, 275 Ind. 338, 417 N.E.2d 889, 1981 Ind. LEXIS 684 (1981), cert. denied, 458 U.S. 1122, 102 S. Ct. 3510, 73 L. Ed. 2d 1384, 1982 U.S. LEXIS 2891 (1982).

Indiana's death penalty is not cruel and unusual punishment. Resnover v. State, 460 N.E.2d 922, 1984 Ind. LEXIS 767 (1984), cert. denied, 469 U.S. 873, 105 S. Ct. 231, 83 L. Ed. 2d 160, 1984 U.S. LEXIS 370 (1984).

Imposition of the death penalty on a 15-year-old murderer was cruel and unusual punishment although the Indiana death penalty statute did not contain a minimum age at the time sentence was imposed. Cooper v. State, 540 N.E.2d 1216, 1989 Ind. LEXIS 216 (1989).

Imposition of the death penalty was not violative of guarantees against cruel and unusual punish-

Constitutionality. (Cont'd)

—Cruel and Unusual Punishment. (Cont'd)
ment or double jeopardy by virtue of the jury's consideration of two different aggravating factors that both related to rape of the victim, because one factor addressed defendant's character and the other addressed the victim's situation; furthermore, the jury in fact weighed only one factor, that the murder occurred in the course of perpetrating a rape, and found that it outweighed all the possible mitigators. Overstreet v. State, 783 N.E.2d 1140, 2003 Ind. LEXIS 167 (2003), cert. denied, 540 U.S. 1150, 124 S. Ct. 1145, 157 L. Ed. 2d 1044, 2004 U.S. LEXIS 704 (2004).

Indiana death penalty statute does not violate Sixth or Eighth Amendments of United States Constitution; statute's requirement that jury find at least one aggravating circumstance in order to recommend death penalty met requirements of Ring and Apprendi; furthermore, instruction to jury that its sentence recommendation was not binding did not unconstitutionally lead jury to feel less responsible than it should for sentencing decision. McManus v. State, 814 N.E.2d 253, 2004 Ind. LEXIS 780 (2004), cert. denied, 126 S. Ct. 53, 163 L. Ed. 2d 83, 2005 U.S. LEXIS 6178 (U.S. 2005).

—Due Process.
Subsection (b)(8) of this section listing the commission of another murder as an aggravating circumstance for which the death penalty may be imposed is unconstitutional as violating due process as applied to a case where the trial for such murder was still pending and the result would be a complete trial for both murders before the same jury. State v. McCormick, 272 Ind. 272, 397 N.E.2d 276, 1979 Ind. LEXIS 794 (1979).

When testimony which defendant gave at trial is used again at the sentencing hearing, there is no violation of any constitutional right since the issue of guilt or innocence has already been determined. Dillon v. State, 454 N.E.2d 845, 1983 Ind. LEXIS 988 (1983), cert. denied, 465 U.S. 1109, 104 S. Ct. 1617, 80 L. Ed. 2d 145 (1984).

Legislature's choice not to require penalty phase jury instructions stating either that reasonable doubt burden of proof applies to each element of aggravator, or that defendant is presumed innocent as to such crimes does not violate due process. Stevens v. State, 691 N.E.2d 412, 1997 Ind. LEXIS 242 (1997), cert. denied, 525 U.S. 1021, 119 S. Ct. 550, 142 L. Ed. 2d 457, 1998 U.S. LEXIS 7659 (1998).

Where the jury has found a defendant guilty of murder and the state seeks the death penalty, the court must find that the state proved beyond a reasonable doubt the existence of at least one aggravating circumstance listed in the death penalty statute, that the aggravating circumstance outweighed any mitigating circumstances, and the court must consider the jury's recommendation. The death penalty statute is not unconstitutional because it deprives the defendant the right of having the jury determine the existence of an aggravating circumstance beyond a reasonable

doubt. Saylor v. State, 765 N.E.2d 535, 2002 Ind. LEXIS 221 (2002); State v. Barker, 768 N.E.2d 425, 2002 Ind. LEXIS 341 (Ind. App. 2002).

—Equal Protection.
The death penalty statute applies equally to all criminal defendants charged with a capital crime, regardless of the recommendation of the jury, and does not violate the equal protection clause of U.S. Const., Amend. 14. Burris v. Parke, 948 F. Supp. 1310, 1996 U.S. Dist. LEXIS 19117 (N.D. Ind. 1996), aff'd, 116 F.3d 256, 1997 U.S. App. LEXIS 15031 (7th Cir. Ind. 1997).

—Felony Murder.
Because the state must prove beyond a reasonable doubt defendant possessed the specific intent to kill the victim in furtherance of committing a felony robbery, the class of death-eligible defendants is narrowed by the aggravating circumstance that defendant possessed the specific intent to kill, which is not a requirement for convicting defendant of felony murder; therefore, subdivision (b)(1)(G) is not unconstitutional. Burris v. Parke, 948 F. Supp. 1310, 1996 U.S. Dist. LEXIS 19117 (N.D. Ind. 1996), aff'd, 116 F.3d 256, 1997 U.S. App. LEXIS 15031 (7th Cir. Ind. 1997).

There is no culpability requirement for conviction of felony murder, and imposition of death penalty for knowing killing, as opposed to intentional killing, is constitutional. Wrinkles v. State, 690 N.E.2d 1156, 1997 Ind. LEXIS 240 (1997), cert. denied, 525 U.S. 861, 119 S. Ct. 148, 142 L. Ed. 2d 121, 1998 U.S. LEXIS 5495 (1998).

—Mandatory Death Penalty.
The imposition of a mandatory death penalty is contrary to constitutional considerations. Schiro v. State, 451 N.E.2d 1047, 1983 Ind. LEXIS 904 (1983), cert. denied, 464 U.S. 1003, 104 S. Ct. 510, 78 L. Ed. 2d 699 (1983).

This section is not unconstitutional because it does not require removal of any juror who says he will automatically vote to impose the death penalty following conviction. The statute does not permit an automatic recommendation of death. It mandates a procedure where juries must apply a high standard of proof of aggravation as a threshold matter and then weigh countervailing circumstances against it. It is highly unlikely that a trial court would permit a juror to serve who states that he or she could not follow the law. Burris v. State, 465 N.E.2d 171, 1984 Ind. LEXIS 854 (1984), cert. denied, 469 U.S. 1132, 105 S. Ct. 816, 83 L. Ed. 2d 809 (1985), superseded by statute as stated in, Wrinkles v. State, 690 N.E.2d 1156, 1997 Ind. LEXIS 240 (1997).

—Mental Illness.
Petitioner was not entitled to relief from death sentence imposed upon him for three murders based on his contention that murders were product of his mental illness; Indiana death penalty scheme took into account his mental health both at guilt phase and at sentencing phase, and at neither phase did petitioner show that he was either mentally ill at time of murders or that he was not

Constitutionality. (Cont'd)

—Mental Illness. (Cont'd)

presently competent to be executed. Baird v. State, 831 N.E.2d 109, 2005 Ind. LEXIS 665 (2005), cert. denied, 126 S. Ct. 312, 163 L. Ed. 2d 269, 2005 U.S. LEXIS 7142 (U.S. 2005).

Imposition of death penalty on petitioner conceded to have had delusions that others were conspiring against him was not violation of equal protection; mentally ill persons are not on same footing as mentally retarded persons. Matheney v. State, 833 N.E.2d 454, 2005 Ind. LEXIS 772 (2005).

—Sentencer's Discretion.

The Indiana capital sentencing scheme adequately channels the sentencer's discretion so as to prevent arbitrary results, which is satisfied by requiring the jury and judge to weigh aggravating and mitigating circumstances. Peterson v. State, 674 N.E.2d 528, 1996 Ind. LEXIS 167 (1996), cert. denied, 522 U.S. 1078, 118 S. Ct. 858, 139 L. Ed. 2d 757, 1998 U.S. LEXIS 520 (1998).

Additional sentencing option of life without parole affords the jury the opportunity to further narrow the class of defendants eligible for death penalty. Wrinkles v. State, 690 N.E.2d 1156, 1997 Ind. LEXIS 240 (1997), cert. denied, 525 U.S. 861, 119 S. Ct. 148, 142 L. Ed. 2d 121, 1998 U.S. LEXIS 5495 (1998).

Constitutional requirements of Ring and Apprendi were satisfied where, even though capital sentencing scheme at time of defendant's conviction allowed judge to find existence of aggravating circumstance to support death sentence or sentence of life without parole, jury returned verdict form stating: (1) that state proved beyond reasonable doubt that defendant committed murder by lying in wait and while defendant was on probation; (2) that aggravating circumstances outweighed mitigating circumstances; and (3) that jury recommended imposition of sentence of life imprisonment without parole. Washington v. State, 808 N.E.2d 617, 2004 Ind. LEXIS 461 (2004).

Defendant's sentence of life imprisonment imposed under IC 35-50-2-9 satisfied Ring and Apprendi where, although at time judge had discretion under statute to reject jury's recommendation, jury found beyond reasonable doubt statutory aggravating factor that increased defendant's penalty for murder, namely, that defendant intentionally discharged firearm into inhabited dwelling. Clark v. State, 808 N.E.2d 1183, 2004 Ind. LEXIS 460 (2004).

IC 35-50-2-9(f) is not unconstitutional as written and Ind. Const, art. 1, § 19, which is not applicable to sentencing, is inapplicable to penalty phase of capital cases; right to jury trial in Ind. Const., art. 1, § 19 does not extend to "weighing" of aggravating and mitigating circumstances, which is not a "fact" requiring jury determination under IC 35-50-2-9(f). State v. Barker, 826 N.E.2d 648, 2005 Ind. LEXIS 402 (2005), cert. denied, 126 S. Ct. 666, 163 L. Ed. 2d 537, 2005 U.S. LEXIS 8486 (U.S. 2005).

—Shifting of Burden of Proof.

The determination of the weight to be accorded the aggravating and mitigating circumstances is not a "fact" which must be proved beyond a reasonable doubt but is a balancing process; subsection (e) of this section does not shift the factual burden of proof in violation of the Eighth and Fourteenth Amendments. Bivins v. State, 642 N.E.2d 928, 1994 Ind. LEXIS 146 (1994), amended, — N.E.2d —, 1995 Ind. LEXIS 34 (1995), cert. denied, 516 U.S. 1077, 133 L. Ed. 2d 734, 116 S. Ct. 783, 1996 U.S. LEXIS 547 (1996).

—Victim Impact Evidence.

Brief testimony of murder victim's mother, limited by the trial court to evidence describing the victim's status in life, did not violate the United States Constitution, and state Supreme Court's finding that the introduction of the limited victim impact evidence was impermissible, though not reversible error, was not a ground for relief under federal law. Burris v. Parke, 948 F. Supp. 1310, 1996 U.S. Dist. LEXIS 19117 (N.D. Ind. 1996), aff'd, 116 F.3d 256, 1997 U.S. App. LEXIS 15031 (7th Cir. Ind. 1997).

Victim impact evidence of mother of murder victim was admissible in penalty phase where it was elicited on cross-examination and was relevant to statutory aggravating sentencing factor. Wrinkles v. State, 690 N.E.2d 1156, 1997 Ind. LEXIS 240 (1997), cert. denied, 525 U.S. 861, 119 S. Ct. 148, 142 L. Ed. 2d 121, 1998 U.S. LEXIS 5495 (1998).

—Vindictive Justice.

The Indiana death penalty does not violate the vindictive justice provision of the Indiana Constitution. Lowery v. State, 478 N.E.2d 1214, 1985 Ind. LEXIS 856 (1985), cert. denied, 475 U.S. 1098, 106 S. Ct. 1500, 89 L. Ed. 2d 900 (1986); Boyd v. State, 494 N.E.2d 284, 1986 Ind. LEXIS 1186 (1986), cert. denied, 479 U.S. 1046, 107 S. Ct. 910, 93 L. Ed. 2d 860, 1987 U.S. LEXIS 242 (1987).

Accomplice Liability.

Although vicarious liability for crimes perpetrated by one's confederates can justify one's conviction for those crimes, the imposition of death upon a vicariously guilty defendant must be based on his culpability, not on that of those who committed the robbery and killed the victims. Landress v. State, 600 N.E.2d 938, 1992 Ind. LEXIS 226 (1992).

Because there was no evidence that the defendant intended to participate in or facilitate a murder, to punish the defendant and her confederates alike by making the defendant vulnerable to the death penalty on account of her confederates' actions would have violated the eighth amendment. Landress v. State, 600 N.E.2d 938, 1992 Ind. LEXIS 226 (1992).

Concerted action that produces death can rise above simple accomplice liability and render the defendant eligible for death or life without parole even if someone else delivers the fatal blow. Ajabu v. State, 693 N.E.2d 921, 1998 Ind. LEXIS 19, 96 A.L.R.5th 669 (1998).

Actions of Prosecutor.

The prosecutor did not taint the jury's death sentence determination by repeatedly telling the jury that their decision regarding the death penalty was only advisory. Lowery v. State, 640 N.E.2d 1031, 1994 Ind. LEXIS 129 (1994), cert. denied, 516 U.S. 992, 116 S. Ct. 525, 133 L. Ed. 2d 432, 1995 U.S. LEXIS 7906 (1995).

There was no error in the sentencing court allowing the jury a momentary look at photographs of the deceased or in permitting the prosecutor's statement regarding murder, where the photographs were not victim impact evidence and where the prosecutor's statement that murder ends a life and all the things that make life meaningful was rather obvious. McIntyre v. State, 717 N.E.2d 114, 1999 Ind. LEXIS 880 (1999).

Aggravating Circumstances.

Defendant's claim that this section is invalid in that it does not require that the killer knew that the victim was a police officer has no merit, where the evidence overwhelmingly shows that the defendant knew that the victim was a police officer when he fired at him. Averhart v. State, 470 N.E.2d 666, 1984 Ind. LEXIS 1003 (1984), cert. denied, 471 U.S. 1030, 105 S. Ct. 2051, 85 L. Ed. 2d 323, 1985 U.S. LEXIS 2706 (1985).

When the death sentence is sought, courts must limit the aggravating circumstances eligible for consideration to those specified in the death penalty statute. Bivins v. State, 642 N.E.2d 928, 1994 Ind. LEXIS 146 (1994), amended, — N.E.2d —, 1995 Ind. LEXIS 34 (1995), cert. denied, 516 U.S. 1077, 133 L. Ed. 2d 734, 116 S. Ct. 783, 1996 U.S. LEXIS 547 (1996).

The aggravators to be weighed against mitigators in the death sentence process are only those expressly enumerated in the death sentence statute. Holmes v. State, 671 N.E.2d 841, 1996 Ind. LEXIS 100 (1996), cert. denied, 522 U.S. 849, 118 S. Ct. 137, 139 L. Ed. 2d 85, 1997 U.S. LEXIS 5167 (1997).

Where facts articulated in judge's sentencing statement were mostly restatements of culpable elements of aggravators, and where defendant's brief employed similar synonyms, there was no improper consideration of nonstatutory aggravators. Stevens v. State, 691 N.E.2d 412, 1997 Ind. LEXIS 242 (1997), cert. denied, 525 U.S. 1021, 119 S. Ct. 550, 142 L. Ed. 2d 457, 1998 U.S. LEXIS 7659 (1998).

Constitutional rule of construction that, in death penalty determinations, courts must limit the aggravating circumstances eligible for consideration to those specified in statute, does not apply on collateral review to those cases which have become final, including those on direct appeal before announcement of rule. Minnick v. State, 698 N.E.2d 745, 1998 Ind. LEXIS 102 (1998), cert. denied, 528 U.S. 1006, 120 S. Ct. 501, 145 L. Ed. 2d 387, 1999 U.S. LEXIS 7562 (1999).

—Age of Victim.

Death penalty statute involves weighing, not counting, of aggravating factors and there is no reason to believe that total aggravating weight given to victim's age by jury would necessarily increase because it is mentioned in more than one factor. Stevens v. State, 691 N.E.2d 412, 1997 Ind. LEXIS 242 (1997), cert. denied, 525 U.S. 1021, 119 S. Ct. 550, 142 L. Ed. 2d 457, 1998 U.S. LEXIS 7659 (1998).

When age aggravator is charged, state need only show beyond a reasonable doubt that victim was less than 12 years old, not that defendant was aware of age. Stevens v. State, 691 N.E.2d 412, 1997 Ind. LEXIS 242 (1997), cert. denied, 525 U.S. 1021, 119 S. Ct. 550, 142 L. Ed. 2d 457, 1998 U.S. LEXIS 7659 (1998).

—Commission of Other Murders.

Where jury found defendant guilty of four murders it could properly consider such other three murders as aggravating circumstances in deciding to recommend the death penalty. Judy v. State, 275 Ind. 145, 416 N.E.2d 95, 1981 Ind. LEXIS 665 (1981).

Subsection (b)(8) is constitutionally applied when more than one person was murdered in a "single episode" by a defendant acting under the influence of extreme emotional or mental distress. Moore v. State, 479 N.E.2d 1264, 1985 Ind. LEXIS 876 (1985), cert. denied, 474 U.S. 1026, 106 S. Ct. 583, 88 L. Ed. 2d 565, 1985 U.S. LEXIS 4839 (1985).

The aggravator in subsection (b)(7) contemplates the situation in which the defendant has committed a murder unrelated to the principal murder charged, for which he has already been tried and convicted in a separate proceeding. Hough v. State, 560 N.E.2d 511, 1990 Ind. LEXIS 184 (1990), corrected, — N.E.2d —, 1990 Ind. LEXIS 267 (1990).

For discussion of whether a conviction of murder occurring after the commission of the crime for which the death penalty is imposed can be used as an aggravating factor under subsection (b)(7), see dissenting opinion of Hough v. State, 560 N.E.2d 511, 1990 Ind. LEXIS 184 (1990), corrected, — N.E.2d —, 1990 Ind. LEXIS 267 (1990).

Subsection (b)(8) is considered in cases involving double or multiple murders for which the defendant is being tried in one proceeding. Hough v. State, 560 N.E.2d 511, 1990 Ind. LEXIS 184 (1990), corrected, — N.E.2d —, 1990 Ind. LEXIS 267 (1990).

A Texas murder conviction was properly considered as an aggravating circumstance in death penalty proceedings under Indiana law even though such conviction could not have been used in a Texas penalty enhancement proceeding. Lockhart v. State, 609 N.E.2d 1093, 1993 Ind. LEXIS 35 (1993).

The jury could properly give consideration to the "commission of another murder" aggravator, and the judge, after reading such aggravators in the death sentence allegations of the charge and after instructing the jury on such aggravator, did apply that same aggravator as had the jury, although he misspoke. Lowery v. State, 640 N.E.2d 1031, 1994 Ind. LEXIS 129 (1994), cert. denied, 516 U.S. 992, 116 S. Ct. 525, 133 L. Ed. 2d 432, 1995 U.S. LEXIS 7906 (1995).

Aggravating Circumstances. (Cont'd)

—Commission of Other Murders. (Cont'd)

The language of subsection (b)(8) in no way excludes multiple killings in one incident, and this aggravating circumstance is available in cases involving double or multiple murders. Williams v. State, 669 N.E.2d 1372, 1996 Ind. LEXIS 124 (1996), cert. denied, 520 U.S. 1232, 117 S. Ct. 1828, 137 L. Ed. 2d 1034, 1997 U.S. LEXIS 3161 (1997).

A prosecutor did not need to prove the order of killing to request the death penalty, but only to allege that the defendant committed another murder "at any time." McIntyre v. State, 717 N.E.2d 114, 1999 Ind. LEXIS 880 (1999).

—Commission of Specified Felony.

At a hearing concerning the imposition of the death penalty, incorporation of trial evidence on the underlying felonies of murder and felony-murder was sufficient to support the conclusion that the defendant intentionally killed the victim while committing or attempting to commit a robbery. Smith v. State, 475 N.E.2d 1139, 1985 Ind. LEXIS 782 (1985).

Where there is a close proximity in terms of time and distance between the underlying felony and the homicide, and there is no break in the chain of events from the inception of the felony to the time of the homicide, the two events are treated as one continuous transaction. Davis v. State, 477 N.E.2d 889, 1985 Ind. LEXIS 839 (1985), cert. denied, 474 U.S. 1014, 106 S. Ct. 546, 88 L. Ed. 2d 475, 1985 U.S. LEXIS 4703 (1985).

The substantially contemporaneous presence of the intent to kill and the intent to commit one of the serious enumerated felonies in subsection (b)(1) is the gravamen of this aggravating circumstance, and it serves to place the person convicted of murder as an initial matter in the class of those who are subject to the death sentence. It is not unconstitutional. Woods v. State, 547 N.E.2d 772, 1989 Ind. LEXIS 336 (1989), overruled in part, Laux v. State, 821 N.E.2d 816, 2005 Ind. LEXIS 93 (2005), overruled, Richardson v. State, 717 N.E.2d 32, 1999 Ind. LEXIS 918 (1999).

Proof of the aggravating felony is required in the sentencing phase; although charging the aggravating circumstance as felony murder rather than the felony alone is unnecessary, this manner of structuring the charge serves only to broaden the State's burden of proof, at no detriment to the defendant. Smedley v. State, 561 N.E.2d 776, 1990 Ind. LEXIS 214 (1990).

Where defendant was charged with and convicted of felony murder, the state was not required to prove intent to kill to obtain his conviction, and during the sentencing phase of the trial the state had the burden of proving beyond a reasonable doubt that the killing by arson was intentional if the arson as an aggravating circumstance was to be used to support a sentence of death. Harrison v. State, 659 N.E.2d 480, 1995 Ind. LEXIS 189 (1995), cert. denied, 519 U.S. 933, 117 S. Ct. 307, 136 L. Ed. 2d 224, 1996 U.S. LEXIS 6220 (1996).

If major participation is shown in a crime under subsection (b)(1), it is irrelevant whether defendant commits the crime by reason of the murder statute or by reason of the accomplice statute.

Ajabu v. State, 693 N.E.2d 921, 1998 Ind. LEXIS 19, 96 A.L.R.5th 669 (1998).

The trial judge's misstatement that he found the defendant committed murders while attempting to rob the victims was not error, even though the aggravating factor in the charge was that the murders were committed in the course of a burglary, where the evidence was clear that the defendant entered the property with intent to commit the felony of robbery. Lowery v. Anderson, 69 F. Supp. 2d 1078, 1999 U.S. Dist. LEXIS 20606 (S.D. Ind. 1999), aff'd, 225 F.3d 833, 2000 U.S. App. LEXIS 22173 (7th Cir. Ind. 2000).

—Confession to Other Crimes.

In a sentencing hearing for murder, the court did not err in admitting a "clean up" statement into evidence, i.e., a confession to other crimes used to clear police files, despite the fact that the state had improperly failed to disclose the information in discovery. The additional information did not alter the final decision to impose the death sentence. The state had already proven to the satisfaction of the court an alleged aggravating factor — an intentional killing during an attempted robbery — and the defendant's attempt to show in mitigation that he had no significant criminal history had already failed in light of other testimony about two felony convictions, several arrests, and a jail uprising. Van Cleave v. State, 517 N.E.2d 356, 1987 Ind. LEXIS 1196 (1987), cert. denied, 488 U.S. 1019, 109 S. Ct. 819, 102 L. Ed. 2d 808, 1989 U.S. LEXIS 56 (1989).

Where an inference of murder exists from independent circumstances, separate application of corpus delicti rule to child molestation aggravating factor would add little to ultimate reliability of confession, and confession will be fully admissible as direct evidence of factor. Stevens v. State, 691 N.E.2d 412, 1997 Ind. LEXIS 242 (1997), cert. denied, 525 U.S. 1021, 119 S. Ct. 550, 142 L. Ed. 2d 457, 1998 U.S. LEXIS 7659 (1998).

—Defendant on Probation.

Where the sentencing transcript did not clearly reveal whether the judge found that the defendant was on probation at the time of the murder or whether he meant that the defendant had previously been on probation, remand was required to clarify the timing of the defendant's probation and its relationship to the sentence imposed. Farber v. State, 703 N.E.2d 151, 1998 Ind. LEXIS 671 (1998).

—Failure to Allege on Separate Page.

Where the aggravating circumstance was the intentional murder in the perpetration of a robbery with which defendant was charged, failure of state to allege an aggravating circumstance on a page separate from the rest of the charging instrument did not prejudice the substantial rights of the defendant. Brewer v. State, 275 Ind. 338, 417 N.E.2d 889, 1981 Ind. LEXIS 684 (1981), cert. denied, 458 U.S. 1122, 102 S. Ct. 3510, 73 L. Ed. 2d 1384, 1982 U.S. LEXIS 2891 (1982).

—Improper.

It is inappropriate for prosecutor to advance

Aggravating Circumstances. (Cont'd)

—Improper. (Cont'd)

arguments regarding future dangerousness and failure to reform as reasons for imposing death penalty, since these are not aggravating factors under death penalty statute and penalty is imposed for what has been done, not what might be done in the future. Wisehart v. State, 693 N.E.2d 23, 1998 Ind. LEXIS 26 (1998), cert. denied, 526 U.S. 1040, 119 S. Ct. 1338, 143 L. Ed. 2d 502, 1999 U.S. LEXIS 2251 (1999).

Where defendant was charged with and pled guilty to "knowingly" killing victim, court improperly cited defendant's eligibility for death penalty as aggravating circumstance in support of enhanced sentence, since eligibility for death penalty requires "intentional" killing during robbery. Madden v. State, 697 N.E.2d 964, 1998 Ind. App. LEXIS 999 (1998).

The defendant was denied due process when the trial court employed as an aggravator that the defendant had committed another murder where that previous killing had not been reduced to conviction. Monegan v. State, 721 N.E.2d 243, 1999 Ind. LEXIS 1252 (1999).

Remand and resentencing was appropriate because the combination of the trial court's remarks in open court and written references in the sentencing statement to the innocence of the victims and the heinousness of the murders indicated that there was a significant possibility that the trial court may have relied upon non-statutory aggravating factors in deciding whether to impose the death penalty. Corcoran v. State, 739 N.E.2d 649, 2000 Ind. LEXIS 1142 (2000).

When imposing a sentence under IC 35-50-2-9 (2002), the trial court's statement of reasons: (i) must identify each mitigating and aggravating circumstance found; (ii) must include the specific facts and reasons which lead the court to find the existence of each such circumstance; (iii) must articulate that the mitigating and aggravating circumstances have been evaluated and balanced in determination of the sentence; and (iv) must set forth the trial court's personal conclusion that the sentence is appropriate punishment for this offender and this crime; accordingly, an amended sentencing order was remanded for failure to meet the requirements for a sentence of life without parole where the trial court cited the fact that the murder was intentional as an aggravating factor. Clark v. State, 808 N.E.2d 1183, 2004 Ind. LEXIS 460 (2004).

—Instructions.

The jury was adequately instructed about the aggravating factor that needed to be proved before a recommendation of death could be returned where the jury was informed in a final instruction that, before a recommendation of death could be returned, it first must find beyond a reasonable doubt that defendant intentionally killed the victim while defendant was committing a robbery, and preliminary instructions stated that the intentional murder during the course of robbery was the aggravating circumstance and defined "intention-

ally." Burris v. State, 465 N.E.2d 171, 1984 Ind. LEXIS 854 (1984), cert. denied, 469 U.S. 1132, 105 S. Ct. 816, 83 L. Ed. 2d 809 (1985), superseded by statute as stated in, Wrinkles v. State, 690 N.E.2d 1156, 1997 Ind. LEXIS 240 (1997).

Since this section does not require that the jury must be convinced of the existence of an aggravating circumstance "to a moral certainty," as well as beyond a reasonable doubt, the trial court properly struck that language from the defendant's tendered instruction. Bieghler v. State, 481 N.E.2d 78, 1985 Ind. LEXIS 920 (1985), cert. denied, 475 U.S. 1031, 106 S. Ct. 1241, 89 L. Ed. 2d 349, 1986 U.S. LEXIS 728 (1986).

Jury instructions regarding death penalty are not rendered defective where they do not explicitly recite one logical combination of mitigating and aggravating circumstances. Roche v. State, 690 N.E.2d 1115, 1997 Ind. LEXIS 238 (1997).

It was not error where some jury instructions referred to aggravating circumstances in plural, since those instructions were recitations of general principles, and instruction charging jury with what it should consider in making death penalty recommendation used singular. Wisehart v. State, 693 N.E.2d 23, 1998 Ind. LEXIS 26 (1998), cert. denied, 526 U.S. 1040, 119 S. Ct. 1338, 143 L. Ed. 2d 502, 1999 U.S. LEXIS 2251 (1999).

—Lying in Wait.

— —Defined.

The common-law definition of "lying in wait" applies in Indiana and the necessary elements include watching, waiting, and concealment from the person killed with the intent to kill or inflict bodily injury upon a person. Davis v. State, 477 N.E.2d 889, 1985 Ind. LEXIS 839 (1985), cert. denied, 474 U.S. 1014, 106 S. Ct. 546, 88 L. Ed. 2d 475, 1985 U.S. LEXIS 4703 (1985).

The elements of lying in wait include watching, waiting, and concealment from the person killed. Matheney v. State, 583 N.E.2d 1202, 1992 Ind. LEXIS 4 (1992), cert. denied, 504 U.S. 962, 112 S. Ct. 2320, 119 L. Ed. 2d 238, 1992 U.S. LEXIS 3376 (1992), overruled, Jackson v. State, 709 N.E.2d 326, 1999 Ind. LEXIS 270 (1999).

— —Found.

Where the defendant waited off to the side of a road near railroad tracks where he could not be observed, knowing that the victim would pass that way, the defendant's actions and preparations show that he had the necessary intent to kill or injure the victim and the defendant's subsequent molestation and killing of the child victim, committed within minutes of each other at the same location, was sufficient to support a finding that the murder was committed by lying in wait. Davis v. State, 477 N.E.2d 889, 1985 Ind. LEXIS 839 (1985), cert. denied, 474 U.S. 1014, 106 S. Ct. 546, 88 L. Ed. 2d 475, 1985 U.S. LEXIS 4703 (1985).

Evidence was sufficient to support aggravating circumstance of lying in wait where appellant, armed with a pistol, broke and entered house and concealed himself; when two women, man, and three children arrived, and settled into their routines, appellant appeared and unleashed deadly

Aggravating Circumstances. (Cont'd)

—Lying in Wait. (Cont'd)

— —Found. (Cont'd)

force against the man, shooting him in the stomach and disabling him, and while the others were kept at bay and helpless, appellant shot one of the women and again shot the man, killing them. Fleenor v. State, 622 N.E.2d 140, 1993 Ind. LEXIS 121 (1993), cert. denied, 513 U.S. 999, 115 S. Ct. 507, 130 L. Ed. 2d 415, 1994 U.S. LEXIS 8012 (1994).

Substantial evidence of probative value supported jury's finding of existence beyond reasonable doubt of aggravator of lying in wait in defendant's trial for stabbing death of his girlfriend; evidence established that: (1) defendant watched and waited for girlfriend in parking lot of her apartment complex; (2) although slightly illuminated, parking lot was dark; (3) defendant parked his car between two other cars; and (4) girlfriend was attacked immediately after defendant opened door to her car. Washington v. State, 808 N.E.2d 617, 2004 Ind. LEXIS 461 (2004).

— —Not Found.

Where the defendant concealed himself from view until a group of camping boys were asleep, but did not use concealment as a direct means to attack or gain control of the victim, but went openly to the tent where the victim slept and forced the victim to go with him by the use of a deadly weapon, there was not a sufficient connection between the concealment and the subsequent murder to support a finding that it was committed "by lying in wait." Davis v. State, 477 N.E.2d 889, 1985 Ind. LEXIS 839 (1985), cert. denied, 474 U.S. 1014, 106 S. Ct. 546, 88 L. Ed. 2d 475, 1985 U.S. LEXIS 4703 (1985).

While the defendant planned that crime be committed by lying in wait, and caused others to commit the crime as planned, she was not at the crime scene and did not make the required choice to participate in the attack upon the arrival of the victim. Consequently, while her conduct warranted conviction for murder as an accomplice or accessory, it did not place her in a category subject to the death sentencing process through the aggravating circumstance of committing a murder by lying in wait. Thacker v. State, 556 N.E.2d 1315, 1990 Ind. LEXIS 142 (1990).

—Murder of Law Enforcement Officer.

Subsection (b)(6) is constitutionally applied where the evidence clearly established that the defendant had the ability and timely opportunity to ascertain that his victim was a law enforcement officer acting in the course of his duty. Moore v. State, 479 N.E.2d 1264, 1985 Ind. LEXIS 876 (1985), cert. denied, 474 U.S. 1026, 106 S. Ct. 583, 88 L. Ed. 2d 565, 1985 U.S. LEXIS 4839 (1985).

Defendant could not be sentenced to death in the case of the murder of an unmarked, plainclothes law enforcement official without a finding that he, in fact, knew that his victim was a law enforcement official. Castor v. State, 587 N.E.2d 1281, 1992 Ind. LEXIS 72 (1992).

The jury was not misinstructed at the penalty hearing where the jury was instructed that it had to find that defendant knew his victim was a policeman; the instruction was adequate, and in any event, an error in the instruction could not have mattered where the same jury had just found defendant guilty beyond a reasonable doubt of conspiracy to murder a policeman and implicit in that finding was the further finding that the defendants knew that the man who knocked and cried "police" and shoved his way through the barricaded doorway was indeed a policeman. Smith v. Farley, 59 F.3d 659, 1995 U.S. App. LEXIS 16421 (7th Cir. Ind. 1995), cert. denied, 516 U.S. 1123, 116 S. Ct. 935, 133 L. Ed. 2d 861, 1996 U.S. LEXIS 1112 (1996).

Where the charged aggravating circumstance was that the victim was a police officer killed in the line of duty, the extensive testimony by the victim's police chief, his brother and his wife went far beyond the charged aggravator that victim was a police officer killed in the line of duty, and should not have been admitted. Lambert v. State, 675 N.E.2d 1060, 1996 Ind. LEXIS 189 (1996), cert. denied, 520 U.S. 1255, 117 S. Ct. 2417, 138 L. Ed. 2d 181, 1997 U.S. LEXIS 3465 (1997).

Trial court's finding of the aggravating circumstance of shooting a law enforcement officer in the line of duty was supported by sufficient evidence; specifically, there was probative evidence in the record from which the fact-finder could have found beyond a reasonable doubt that defendant knew the victim was a law enforcement officer. Moore v. State, 771 N.E.2d 46, 2002 Ind. LEXIS 563 (2002), cert. denied, 538 U.S. 1014, 123 S. Ct. 1931, 155 L. Ed. 2d 851, 2003 U.S. LEXIS 3506 (2003).

Sentence of life without parole was not error because, although defendant pled guilty but mentally ill to murdering policeman, trial court properly placed great weight on aggravator of murdering law enforcement officer and minimal weight to mitigators of defendant's mental illness and lack of criminal record. Salyers v. State, 862 N.E.2d 650, 2007 Ind. LEXIS 162 (2007).

—Perpetration of Rape.

Where jury found defendant guilty of murder while in the perpetration of rape, the circumstances of such killing constituted a valid aggravating factor for the jury to consider in deciding to recommend the death penalty. Judy v. State, 275 Ind. 145, 416 N.E.2d 95, 1981 Ind. LEXIS 665 (1981).

Where defendant was found guilty of killing victim while committing rape, and also sentenced to death for intentionally killing the victim while committing or attempting to commit rape, neither the double jeopardy clause nor collateral estoppel required vacation of his death sentence. Schiro v. Farley, 510 U.S. 222, 127 L. Ed. 2d 47, 114 S. Ct. 783, 1994 U.S. LEXIS 1135 (1994).

Testimony regarding findings from analysis of vaginal swabs taken from the victim, together with the circumstances in which the victim's body was found, was sufficient to support defendant's conviction of rape; this conviction was critical to the propriety of defendant's death sentence, because

Aggravating Circumstances. (Cont'd)

—Perpetration of Rape. (Cont'd)
the fact that the murder occurred during perpetration of a rape was the aggravating circumstance that resulted in its imposition. Overstreet v. State, 783 N.E.2d 1140, 2003 Ind. LEXIS 167 (2003), cert. denied, 540 U.S. 1150, 124 S. Ct. 1145, 157 L. Ed. 2d 1044, 2004 U.S. LEXIS 704 (2004).

—Pleading and Proof.
The trial court did not err in entering defendant's conviction for attempted murder and murder where it found additional aggravating circumstances, although such aggravating circumstances were not specifically enumerated and charged, as the defendant had specific notice of two aggravating circumstances which the state had alleged, and the state's burden to prove the existence of these two aggravating circumstances beyond a reasonable doubt did not change. Davis v. State, 477 N.E.2d 889, 1985 Ind. LEXIS 839 (1985), cert. denied, 474 U.S. 1014, 106 S. Ct. 546, 88 L. Ed. 2d 475, 1985 U.S. LEXIS 4703 (1985).

In seeking the death penalty under Indiana law, the state must allege and prove beyond a reasonable doubt the existence of at least one aggravating circumstances. Bivins v. State, 642 N.E.2d 928, 1994 Ind. LEXIS 146 (1994), amended, — N.E.2d —, 1995 Ind. LEXIS 34 (1995), cert. denied, 516 U.S. 1077, 133 L. Ed. 2d 734, 116 S. Ct. 783, 1996 U.S. LEXIS 547 (1996).

—Prior Criminal Activity.
The state may not use a prior unrelated crime such as a murder not yet reduced to conviction as a statutory aggravating factor in the death penalty phase. Rouster v. State, 600 N.E.2d 1342, 1992 Ind. LEXIS 233 (1992).

Although defendant waived his appellate claim by not objecting to the state's presentation of a written order from a previous case sentencing defendant for three counts of child molesting, presentation of the order and additional evidence that defendant was on parole after serving those sentences when he killed the victims was not error; absent objection, it was appropriate for the state to have used evidence of the convictions to help lay the foundation for proving that defendant was on parole and also to help establish the weight to be given to this aggravating circumstance. Bassett v. State, 895 N.E.2d 1201, 2008 Ind. LEXIS 1044 (2008).

—Sentence to Term of Years.
Where the defendant was eligible for either the death penalty or life without parole pursuant to IC 35-50-2-9, but was instead sentenced to a term of years, the trial court could consider the aggravating factors in IC 35-50-2-9 as well as the factors listed in IC 35-38-1-7.1. Davies v. State, 758 N.E.2d 981, 2001 Ind. App. LEXIS 2030 (2001).

—Torture.
The torture aggravator requires an appreciable period of pain or punishment intentionally inflicted and designed either to coerce the victim or for the torturer's sadistic indulgence; torture is the gratuitous infliction of substantial pain or suffering in excess of that associated with the commission of the charged crime. Nicholson v. State, 768 N.E.2d 443, 2002 Ind. LEXIS 462 (2002).

Aggravating circumstance of torture while attempting or committing child molestation was improperly applied to defendant since defendant did not attempt to coerce victim through torturous acts nor did he indulge in sadistic acts. Leone v. State, 797 N.E.2d 743, 2003 Ind. LEXIS 853 (2003).

Torture was properly considered as an aggravating circumstance under IC 35-50-2-9(b)(11) for a murder sentence where the evidence showed that defendant repeatedly tied a four-year-old victim to a booster chair, put duct tape over child's mouth, fed the child food that made the child sick, and made child sleep, tied to her chair, in an unheated room away from the family. Gauvin v. State, 883 N.E.2d 99, 2008 Ind. LEXIS 264 (2008).

Appropriateness of Sentence.
Death sentence was affirmed where defendant had been earlier convicted of murders in Ohio and the evidence demonstrated that he had enticed two young girls into a woods, bound them, stomped and strangled one of them to death, and repeatedly molested the other — all essentially as part of one episode. Coleman v. State, 558 N.E.2d 1059, 1990 Ind. LEXIS 171 (1990), cert. denied, 501 U.S. 1259, 111 S. Ct. 2912, 115 L. Ed. 2d 1075, 1991 U.S. LEXIS 3980 (1991).

Where the Supreme Court weighed the alcoholism and troubles during adolescence mitigating circumstances against the defendant's intentional killing in the course of a robbery, balancing the relatively low level of the mitigating circumstances against the proven substantial and serious aggravating circumstance, the proper and appropriate sentence for defendant was the death penalty. Bivins v. State, 642 N.E.2d 928, 1994 Ind. LEXIS 146 (1994), amended, — N.E.2d —, 1995 Ind. LEXIS 34 (1995), cert. denied, 516 U.S. 1077, 133 L. Ed. 2d 734, 116 S. Ct. 783, 1996 U.S. LEXIS 547 (1996).

Where there was no proper trial court finding that third aggravating circumstance charged by the state had been proven, because the properly proven aggravating circumstances outweighed the mitigating circumstances with respect to the death sentence imposed for the murder of one victim, those same aggravating circumstances outweighed those same mitigating circumstances with respect to the murder of the victim for which the third factor was charged, and the death penalty was proper for that murder. Harrison v. State, 659 N.E.2d 480, 1995 Ind. LEXIS 189 (1995), cert. denied, 519 U.S. 933, 117 S. Ct. 307, 136 L. Ed. 2d 224, 1996 U.S. LEXIS 6220 (1996).

Although the claims concerning severance, ineffective assistance of counsel, and trial court errors did not justify relief under 28 U.S.C.S. § 2254, relief was appropriate under that statute for defendant's claim regarding ineffective assistance of counsel on the issue of shackling. However, rather than require that defendant be retried when defendant had confessed to the crime, the court ordered defendant's death sentence changed to life

Appropriateness of Sentence. (Cont'd)
without parole. Roche v. Anderson, 132 F. Supp. 2d 688, 2001 U.S. Dist. LEXIS 1657 (N.D. Ind. 2001), aff'd in part, vacated in part, 291 F.3d 473, 2002 U.S. App. LEXIS 9974 (7th Cir. 2002).

Where the state proved beyond a reasonable doubt the subsection (b)(8) aggravating circumstance, and that the aggravating circumstance outweighed the non-statutory mitigating circumstances, the death penalty was appropriate and any residual doubt did not provide a basis for revising defendant's sentences to life without parole. Stephenson v. State, 742 N.E.2d 463, 2001 Ind. LEXIS 47 (2001), cert. denied, 534 U.S. 1105, 122 S. Ct. 905, 151 L. Ed. 2d 874, 2002 U.S. LEXIS 435 (2002).

Although defendant was sentenced using the "torture" aggravating circumstance that was not listed in the statute at the time the crime was committed, defendant's sentence of life imprisonment without parole was appropriate by reason of both the harmless error doctrine and independent appellate reweighing of aggravating and mitigating circumstances. Russell v. State, 743 N.E.2d 269, 2001 Ind. LEXIS 210 (2001).

Where defendant was sentenced to death in 1992 despite unanimous jury recommendation to the contrary and where Indiana law was changed in 2002 to require unanimous jury recommendation of death before death penalty could be imposed, defendant's death penalty was no longer deemed appropriate, and his sentence was revised to 100 years of imprisonment. Saylor v. State, 808 N.E.2d 646, 2004 Ind. LEXIS 464 (2004).

Trial court gave adequate consideration to mitigating circumstances in assigning defendant life without parole, IC 35-50-2-9, as the aggravators outweighed the mitigators and defendant's mental condition was properly given some, but not determinate, weight. Covington v. State, 842 N.E.2d 345, 2006 Ind. LEXIS 127 (2006).

Record did not provide evidence of any particularly strong, positive character attributes of the defendant. Giving due consideration to the trial court's decision, and in light of the nature of the offense shown by the defendant's brutal and savage slaying of a four-year-old child and her young mother, and the lack of demonstrated virtuous character in the defendant, the Supreme Court of Indiana declined to intervene in the jury's determination that the death sentence was appropriate. Baer v. State, 866 N.E.2d 752, 2007 Ind. LEXIS 363 (2007).

—Upheld.
The court properly concluded that the aggravating factor — an intentional killing during an attempted robbery — outweighed the mitigating factors — the defendant's home life which deteriorated in his early teens, his failed stint in the army from which he was honorably discharged, and the fact that thereafter he could not find a job. Van Cleave v. State, 517 N.E.2d 356, 1987 Ind. LEXIS 1196 (1987), cert. denied, 488 U.S. 1019, 109 S. Ct. 819, 102 L. Ed. 2d 808, 1989 U.S. LEXIS 56 (1989).

Evidence of the defendant's difficult childhood, emotional disturbance, having consumed some alcohol at the time of the offense, graduation from high school, service in the Marines, age, and caring relationship with his child and her mother, mitigating factors weighted in the low range, were outweighed by the aggravating circumstances that defendant murdered four people, aggravating circumstances of the highest range, so that the proper and appropriate sentence for the defendant was the death penalty. Peterson v. State, 674 N.E.2d 528, 1996 Ind. LEXIS 167 (1996), cert. denied, 522 U.S. 1078, 118 S. Ct. 858, 139 L. Ed. 2d 757, 1998 U.S. LEXIS 520 (1998).

On mandatory appeal to the Supreme Court of Indiana, the death sentence imposed against a defendant for the rape and murder of a 15-year-old girl was upheld. The Court refused to revisit the constitutionality of Indiana's death penalty statute; found that the defendant failed to establish any irregularities or any substantial non-compliance as a result of the trial court lacking a formal written and filed plan for selecting the petit jury pool; determined that the admission of evidence the police collected from his person following his arrest but before a search warrant was issued was proper as an authorized search incident to a lawful arrest as well as proper under the exigent circumstances exception; the Court agreed that the victim's autopsy photos were gruesome but each was accompanied by the testimony of a forensic pathologist explaining the nature of the medical procedures performed and were not erroneously admitted into evidence; and the Court found that the death sentence was appropriate in light of the horrendous crime committed and the proof of the aggravating factors of torture and mutilation that were established. Ward v. State, — N.E.2d —, 2009 Ind. LEXIS 343 (2009).

Attempted Burglaries.
The basic unfairness identified in *State v. McCormick, State v. McCormick,* 272 Ind. 272, 397 N.E.2d 276, 1979 Ind. LEXIS 794 (1979), is not present when the subsection (b)(1) aggravator, the intentional killing in the commission of an attempted burglary, is alleged. Lowery v. State, 640 N.E.2d 1031, 1994 Ind. LEXIS 129 (1994), cert. denied, 516 U.S. 992, 116 S. Ct. 525, 133 L. Ed. 2d 432, 1995 U.S. LEXIS 7906 (1995).

Construction.
Although appellant reasoned that the word "shall" in this section makes it mandatory for the court to impose the death penalty if aggravating circumstances are found, such an interpretation is strained; the court is allowed to sentence the defendant to death only if it finds the indicated factors. Burris v. State, 642 N.E.2d 961, 1994 Ind. LEXIS 145 (1994), cert. denied, 516 U.S. 922, 116 S. Ct. 319, 133 L. Ed. 2d 221, 1995 U.S. LEXIS 6919 (1995).

The word "may" in the death penalty statute does not violate the mandate that the sentencer must consider mitigating evidence. Benefiel v. State, 716 N.E.2d 906, 1999 Ind. LEXIS 859 (1999), cert. denied, 531 U.S. 830, 121 S. Ct. 83, 148 L. Ed. 2d 45, 2000 U.S. LEXIS 5249 (2000).

Former IC 35-30-2-9(a) contemplates the defini-

Construction. (Cont'd)
tion of "murder" as described in IC 35-42-1-1(1). Pittman v. State, 885 N.E.2d 1246, 2008 Ind. LEXIS 404 (2008).

Course of Duty.
Town marshal killed while attempting to arrest defendant for vandalizing a motor vehicle was acting in the course of duty as that phrase is used in subdivision (b)(6)(A), even though the marshal was effectuating the arrest outside his town limits. Spranger v. State, 498 N.E.2d 931, 1986 Ind. LEXIS 1304 (1986), cert. denied, 481 U.S. 1033, 107 S. Ct. 1965, 95 L. Ed. 2d 536, 1987 U.S. LEXIS 1912 (1987).

Double Jeopardy.
A reduction in the robbery conviction to a Class C felony and resentencing was required because the same evidence that supported defendant's murder conviction was also used to elevate defendant's robbery conviction to a Class A felony, and double jeopardy prohibits a defendant from being sentenced twice for committing a single act. Logan v. State, 729 N.E.2d 125, 2000 Ind. LEXIS 481 (2000).

Imposition of the death penalty was not violative of guarantees against cruel and unusual punishment or double jeopardy by virtue of the jury's consideration of two different aggravating factors that both related to rape of the victim, because one factor addressed defendant's character and the other addressed the victim's situation; furthermore, the jury in fact weighed only one factor, that the murder occurred in the course of perpetrating a rape, and found that it outweighed all the possible mitigators. Overstreet v. State, 783 N.E.2d 1140, 2003 Ind. LEXIS 167 (2003), cert. denied, 540 U.S. 1150, 124 S. Ct. 1145, 157 L. Ed. 2d 1044, 2004 U.S. LEXIS 704 (2004).

Where defendant was convicted of murder, felony murder and burglary for killing his former spouse, sentence of life imprisonment without possibility of parole under Indiana death penalty statute did not violate double jeopardy since felony murder conviction merged into murder conviction before sentencing and separate weighing of sentencing factors under death penalty statute did not amount to separate prosecution. Laux v. State, 821 N.E.2d 816, 2005 Ind. LEXIS 93 (2005).

Facts necessary to establish aggravating circumstances in IC 35-50-2-9(b)(1) served only to establish eligibility for penalties contained in that section and were not identical to elements of crime for which defendant was convicted, namely, burglary resulting in death. Houser v. State, 823 N.E.2d 693, 2005 Ind. LEXIS 198 (2005).

Evidence.
A defendant is not given carte blanche to introduce any evidence concerning the death penalty. The trial court may exclude as irrelevant evidence not bearing on the defendant's character, prior record, or the circumstances of his offense. Underwood v. State, 535 N.E.2d 507, 1989 Ind. LEXIS 58 (1989), cert. denied, 493 U.S. 900, 110 S. Ct. 257, 107 L. Ed. 2d 206, 1989 U.S. LEXIS 4707 (1989).

This section allows the jury to consider all the evidence which was introduced at the trial. Benefiel v. State, 578 N.E.2d 338, 1991 Ind. LEXIS 164 (1991), cert. denied, 504 U.S. 987, 112 S. Ct. 2971, 119 L. Ed. 2d 591, 1992 U.S. LEXIS 3599 (1992).

—Conflict.
Where evidence as to the provocation on the part of the deceased was in conflict reviewing court would not reduce conviction for murder in the first degree to voluntary manslaughter. Crisp v. State, 271 Ind. 534, 394 N.E.2d 115, 1979 Ind. LEXIS 714 (1979).

—Exclusion Not Prejudicial.
State trial court's decision to exclude as hearsay evidence in testimony of psychologist who testified for defendant during his sentencing trial, that defendant blamed himself for death of his primary caregiver, was improper, and counsel's performance in failing to object to that decision was constitutionally deficient, but defendant failed to establish exclusion of the evidence was prejudicial. Burris v. Parke, 948 F. Supp. 1310, 1996 U.S. Dist. LEXIS 19117 (N.D. Ind. 1996), aff'd, 116 F.3d 256, 1997 U.S. App. LEXIS 15031 (7th Cir. Ind. 1997).

—Method of Execution.
Method of execution was not required to be offered to the jury as a mitigating circumstance. Underwood v. State, 535 N.E.2d 507, 1989 Ind. LEXIS 58 (1989), cert. denied, 493 U.S. 900, 110 S. Ct. 257, 107 L. Ed. 2d 206, 1989 U.S. LEXIS 4707 (1989).

—Not Sufficient.
Defendant's death sentence was reversed where the state charged that defendant killed his wife while attempting to take her hostage and while "lying in wait," but the state failed to prove either of these "aggravating circumstances" specified by the legislature. Ingle v. State, 746 N.E.2d 927, 2001 Ind. LEXIS 393 (2001).

State had not established beyond a reasonable doubt that defendant killed a victim, who died from a single wound, where an expert testified that he could not determine what type of firearm was used, there was clear evidence that both defendant and another person were at the scene, and there was no evidence as to who shot the victim; imposition of life without parole based on the IC 35-50-2-9(b)(1) aggravator was not permitted under Indiana law. Pittman v. State, 885 N.E.2d 1246, 2008 Ind. LEXIS 404 (2008).

Life sentence was error where a jury did not find the IC 35-50-2-9(b)(3) aggravator and there was insufficient evidence to support the (b)(1) aggravator; the (b)(9) probation aggravator was not met by proof that defendant was guilty of felony murder and evidence did not show that he committted murder as defined in IC 35-42-1-1(1). Pittman v. State, 885 N.E.2d 1246, 2008 Ind. LEXIS 404 (2008).

—Reasonable Inference.
Premeditated malice is necessary for first-degree murder and even though a doctor witness testified that defendant was unable to act on a

Evidence. (Cont'd)

—Reasonable Inference. (Cont'd)
preconceived plan, jury could reject such testimony where there was other contradictory testimony and there was evidence of other facts from which the jury could reasonably infer that defendant formed the design in his mind before the killing. Beghan v. State, 271 Ind. 59, 390 N.E.2d 153, 1979 Ind. LEXIS 641 (1979).

—Relevance.
Where penalty phase jury is same as that which decided guilt there is no requirement that the state move to incorporate guilt phase evidence at the penalty phase, and this section specifically allows the jury to consider all guilt phase evidence for purposes of aggravating circumstances. Ben-Yisrayl v. State, 690 N.E.2d 1141, 1997 Ind. LEXIS 248 (1997), cert. denied, 525 U.S. 1108, 119 S. Ct. 877, 142 L. Ed. 2d 777, 1999 U.S. LEXIS 649 (1999).

—Sufficient.
Where evidence showed that victim was stabbed in Indiana and placed in trunk of automobile by defendant, that defendant stated that he was not dead and another stated "don't worry about it, he can't swim" and that defendant drove to Kentucky where he dumped victim in a ditch and shot him in the head when he saw he was still alive, such evidence was sufficient to support a premeditated murder conviction. Pollard v. State, 270 Ind. 599, 388 N.E.2d 496, 1979 Ind. LEXIS 611 (1979).

Where defendant threatened to kill victim earlier in the day, broke into his home, opened door into his bedroom, and grabbed gun which was lying on chair there was evidence to support jury's finding that killing was premeditated. Bonner v. State, 271 Ind. 388, 392 N.E.2d 1169, 1979 Ind. LEXIS 687 (1979).

Although defendant contended he did not know his companions intended to rob store until they were in store, where there was evidence that defendant knew his companions were armed, he knew that they left the motor running in the automobile when they went in the store, that he served as a lookout and entered the store and left the store with them, evidence was sufficient for jury to find that defendant had the intent to rob. Graham v. State, 271 Ind. 486, 393 N.E.2d 764, 1979 Ind. LEXIS 706 (1979).

Where there was abundant evidence of probative value that defendant shot deceased deliberately and for revenge there was sufficient evidence of malice. Walters v. State, 271 Ind. 598, 394 N.E.2d 154, 1979 Ind. LEXIS 725, 4 A.L.R.4th 609 (1979).

Death penalty was not arbitrarily or capriciously applied. Schiro v. State, 451 N.E.2d 1047, 1983 Ind. LEXIS 904 (1983), cert. denied, 464 U.S. 1003, 104 S. Ct. 510, 78 L. Ed. 2d 699 (1983); Burris v. State, 465 N.E.2d 171, 1984 Ind. LEXIS 854 (1984), cert. denied, 469 U.S. 1132, 105 S. Ct. 816, 83 L. Ed. 2d 809 (1985), superseded by statute as stated in, Wrinkles v. State, 690 N.E.2d 1156, 1997 Ind. LEXIS 240 (1997).

Evidence held sufficient to support conclusion that the sentence of death recommended by the jury and imposed by the trial court was not arbitrarily or capriciously arrived at, and was not manifestly unreasonable. Daniels v. State, 453 N.E.2d 160, 1983 Ind. LEXIS 940 (1983).

Record in a homicide prosecution clearly supported the conclusion that the imposition of the death sentence was determined by the nature of the offense and the character of the offender, where two of the statutory aggravating circumstances were proved beyond a reasonable doubt and both the jury and the judge found that these aggravating circumstances outweighed the mitigating circumstance of no prior criminal history. The sentence of death was not arbitrarily or capriciously arrived at and was not manifestly unreasonable. Dillon v. State, 454 N.E.2d 845, 1983 Ind. LEXIS 988 (1983), cert. denied, 465 U.S. 1109, 104 S. Ct. 1617, 80 L. Ed. 2d 145 (1984).

Evidence held sufficient to justify imposition of death penalty. Vandiver v. State, 480 N.E.2d 910, 1985 Ind. LEXIS 914 (1985); Wisehart v. State, 484 N.E.2d 949, 1985 Ind. LEXIS 1011 (Ind. 1985), cert. denied, 476 U.S. 1189, 106 S. Ct. 2929, 91 L. Ed. 2d 556 (1986).

Defendant's petition under IC 35-50-2-9(k) for review of his conviction and death sentence for multiple murders committed during robbery was denied since no new evidence was presented that cast doubt on verdict or sentence; new DNA blood evidence showing that blood on defendant's clothes was not from victim was immaterial because sufficient evidence outside of blood evidence existed to show defendant was heavily involved in robbery and actively participated in shooting. Williams v. State, 808 N.E.2d 652, 2004 Ind. LEXIS 472 (2004).

Exclusion of Jurors.
Objection that the exclusion of potential jurors due to their general objections to capital punishment was error became moot when the death penalty statute was declared unconstitutional unless appellant could show that jurors who were not opposed to death penalty tend to favor the prosecution in the determination of guilt or innocence. Norton v. State, 273 Ind. 635, 408 N.E.2d 514, 1980 Ind. LEXIS 719 (1980).

Guilty but Mentally Ill.
Trial court's imposition of the death penalty after accepting the plea of guilty but mentally ill to charges of murder, kidnapping and rape did not violate any statutory right to treatment or the eighth amendment prohibition against cruel and unusual punishment. Harris v. State, 499 N.E.2d 723, 1986 Ind. LEXIS 1357 (1986), cert. denied, 482 U.S. 909, 107 S. Ct. 2490, 96 L. Ed. 2d 382, 1987 U.S. LEXIS 2456 (1987).

Guilty Plea.

—Denial of Intent.
In a capital case, a trial court abuses its discretion when it fails to set aside a guilty plea when the defendant denies criminal intent at sentenc-

Guilty Plea. (Cont'd)

—Denial of Intent. (Cont'd)
ing. Patton v. State, 517 N.E.2d 374, 1987 Ind. LEXIS 1194 (1987).

—Indictment.
The state was not estopped or otherwise precluded from continuing its prosecution of defendant for the "offenses" of intimidation, battery and murder, after the state sought an indictment for a "violation" of the death penalty statute and the grand jury returned a no bill on whether to seek the death penalty; the court expressed doubt regarding whether the state had authority to seek an indictment under that statute. Owens v. State, 659 N.E.2d 466, 1995 Ind. LEXIS 181 (1995).

Ineffective Assistance of Counsel.
Defense counsel's almost complete lack of investigation into defendant's mental and family history, as well as his failure to argue mitigating factors to the jury, constituted ineffective assistance of counsel during the penalty phase of his trial for murder sufficient to undermine confidence in the outcome of the jury's death penalty recommendation. Brewer v. Aiken, 935 F.2d 850, 1991 U.S. App. LEXIS 12086 (7th Cir. Ind. 1991).

Elimination of the jury recommendation in a capital trial as a result of defendant pleading guilty is not "prejudice" of federal constitutional dimensions, demonstrating ineffective assistance of council. State v. Van Cleave, 674 N.E.2d 1293, 1996 Ind. LEXIS 173 (1996), cert. denied, 522 U.S. 1119, 118 S. Ct. 1060, 140 L. Ed. 2d 121, 1998 U.S. LEXIS 1027 (1998).

It was not ineffective assistance of counsel to fail to request an instruction on the intoxication defense as to aggravating circumstances in the sentencing phase of a murder trial, since such an instruction would have been refused by the court based on the considerable evidence that the defendant could communicate, deliberate, and act toward a chosen end. Williams v. State, 706 N.E.2d 149, 1999 Ind. LEXIS 67 (1999), cert. denied, 529 U.S. 1113, 120 S. Ct. 1970, 146 L. Ed. 2d 800, 2000 U.S. LEXIS 3248 (2000).

Defendant inmate was denied effective assistance of counsel under U.S. Const., Amend. 6 at death penalty phase of murder trial when his lawyers failed to discuss with him whether he should testify; accordingly, sentence was vacated and remanded for another sentencing hearing. Canaan v. McBride, 395 F.3d 376, 2005 U.S. App. LEXIS 404 (7th Cir. Ind. 2005).

Appellate counsel was not ineffective as (1) counsel was entitled to make a judgment call concerning which issues to raise on appeal and (2) even assuming that a failure to raise an AP. 7(B) challenge to the death sentence pursuant to the power to revise sentences under Ind. Const., art. 7, § 4 and IC 35-50-2-9 fell below an objective standard of reasonableness, appellant did not show a reasonable probability that such issue would have resulted in the revision of his sentence. Ritchie v. State, 875 N.E.2d 706, 2007 Ind. LEXIS 996 (2007).

—Not Shown.
Defendant failed to demonstrate that trial counsel's performance with respect to the investigation and presentation of mitigating circumstances in the penalty phase of his trial constituted ineffective assistance of counsel. Canaan v. State, 683 N.E.2d 227, 1997 Ind. LEXIS 86 (1997), cert. denied, 524 U.S. 906, 118 S. Ct. 2064, 141 L. Ed. 2d 141, 1998 U.S. LEXIS 3611 (1998).

Counsel's performance was not deficient where, through witnesses, he presented a reasonable basis for imposing a sentence other than death: aspects of plaintiff's background, character and record, and the circumstances of the crimes; while more mitigation evidence was uncovered at the post conviction hearing, counsel's performance at trial could not be deemed deficient. Johnson v. State, 693 N.E.2d 941, 1998 Ind. LEXIS 20 (1998).

Where trial counsel did not make an opening statement during the penalty phase, but did present substantial evidence of mitigating circumstances, incorporated by reference testimony from the guilt phase of the trial, and presented a brief closing argument in which he reminded the jury of its duty not to impose the death penalty if it did not find an intentional killing, and of its right to exercise mercy in sentencing the defendant, there was no ineffective assistance of counsel. Miller v. State, 702 N.E.2d 1053, 1998 Ind. LEXIS 611 (1998), cert. denied, 528 U.S. 1083, 120 S. Ct. 806, 145 L. Ed. 2d 679, 2000 U.S. LEXIS 231 (2000).

The defendant failed to demonstrate prejudice as a result of appellate counsel's failure to raise the issue of the trial court's not specifying at least one aggravating circumstance in support of the imposition of the death penalty, but instead listing factors relating to the murders of the victim's children, since, had the issue been raised on direct appeal, the case would merely have been remanded for an articulation of the statutory aggravators. Trueblood v. State, 715 N.E.2d 1242, 1999 Ind. LEXIS 734 (1999), cert. denied, 531 U.S. 858, 121 S. Ct. 143, 148 L. Ed. 2d 94, 2000 U.S. LEXIS 5649 (2000).

By presenting the information that counsel did on defendant's background, character, and record as part of a reasonable strategy to try to persuade the jury and the court not to impose death penalty, the performance of defendant's trial counsel during the penalty phase was not below the range expected of reasonable, professionally competent counsel. Bivins v. State, 735 N.E.2d 1116, 2000 Ind. LEXIS 937 (2000).

Information to Jury.
In proceeding to determine whether to impose the death sentence, it was not error for the court, in response to a question by the jury, to inform them as to provisions for parole if a death sentence was not imposed. Brewer v. State, 275 Ind. 338, 417 N.E.2d 889, 1981 Ind. LEXIS 684 (1981), cert. denied, 458 U.S. 1122, 102 S. Ct. 3510, 73 L. Ed. 2d 1384, 1982 U.S. LEXIS 2891 (1982).

Prosecutor who informed the jury that the responsibility for sentencing rested with the judge did not misrepresent the law or improperly condi-

Information to Jury. (Cont'd)
tion the jury at defendant's trial for murder. Burris v. State, 558 N.E.2d 1067, 1990 Ind. LEXIS 170 (1990).

The trial court erred by reading both the charging information and the death penalty information to all prospective jurors at voir dire, advising the jury of the death penalty information before the sentencing phase. Thompson v. State, 690 N.E.2d 224, 1997 Ind. LEXIS 234 (1997).

Intentional Killing.

Defendant's penalty phase conviction of a "knowing" killing in the guilt phase was not an implied acquittal of the greater offense of "intentional" murder, and thus it was proper and consistent with the guarantees of the prohibitions against double jeopardy to prove an "intentional" killing at the capital penalty phase. Fleenor v. State, 622 N.E.2d 140, 1993 Ind. LEXIS 121 (1993), cert. denied, 513 U.S. 999, 115 S. Ct. 507, 130 L. Ed. 2d 415, 1994 U.S. LEXIS 8012 (1994).

The subsection (b)(1) aggravating factor requires a finding of intentional killing. Ajabu v. State, 693 N.E.2d 921, 1998 Ind. LEXIS 19, 96 A.L.R.5th 669 (1998).

The trial court's finding of major participation in the killings was well documented and easily satisfied the actus reus requirement of subsection (b)(1) but did not establish that plaintiff acted intentionally within the meaning of the subsection (b)(1) aggravating circumstance. Ajabu v. State, 693 N.E.2d 921, 1998 Ind. LEXIS 19, 96 A.L.R.5th 669 (1998).

Where the trial court did not find that the defendant committed the murder by "intentionally killing the victim while committing or attempting to commit" robbery, but that the defendant "did intentionally commit the offense of robbery beyond reasonable doubt in the commission of" a murder, remand to the trial court was required to determine if the defendant intentionally killed in the course of a robbery and, if so, the imposition of life without parole could be imposed. Farber v. State, 703 N.E.2d 151, 1998 Ind. LEXIS 671 (1998).

Intentionally killing a victim while committing a robbery is a valid eligibility requirement under IC 35-50-2-9(b)(1)(G) and the court did not abuse its discretion in relying on this factor in sentencing defendant to life without parole. West v. State, 755 N.E.2d 173, 2001 Ind. LEXIS 889 (2001).

Jurisdictional Basis.

Although count for premeditated murder charged that victim was killed in Kentucky where it also charged that victim was stabbed in Indiana and then transported by defendant to Kentucky where he was killed by a shot through the head, the integral relationship between the assault, abduction, and murder of the victim provided an adequate jurisdictional basis for conviction of murder in Indiana. Pollard v. State, 270 Ind. 599, 388 N.E.2d 496, 1979 Ind. LEXIS 611 (1979).

Jury Instructions.

Defendant's death sentence was vacated for technical deficiencies in the imposition of sentence, where although there was a specific charge of aggravating circumstance (8), commission of another murder whether convicted or not, this aggravating circumstance was omitted from both the final instructions to the jury and from the trial court's findings supporting the death sentence. Thompson v. State, 492 N.E.2d 264, 1986 Ind. LEXIS 1125, 65 A.L.R.4th 805 (1986).

Where the instruction directed the jury to return a recommendation of death even if the jury felt the sentence was inappropriate, the erroneous instruction required a new sentencing hearing since the jury is not required to return a recommendation for the death penalty even if the state proves that the aggravating factors outweigh the mitigating circumstances under subsection (e). Williams v. State, 525 N.E.2d 1238, 1988 Ind. LEXIS 198 (1988).

The absence of instructions that the burden of proof applies to each element of the aggravating circumstances or that the defendant is presumed innocent as to circumstances in the penalty phase does not violate the due process clause. Bellmore v. State, 602 N.E.2d 111, 1992 Ind. LEXIS 240 (1992).

Court's instruction that if jury did not recommend the death penalty, the court must sentence defendant to a term of years, was erroneous, but did not prejudice the defendant or deny him due process and the error was harmless, where the jury failed to reach a unanimous recommendation on his sentence and the court correctly discharged the jury and proceeded as if sentencing had been by the court alone. Burris v. Parke, 948 F. Supp. 1310, 1996 U.S. Dist. LEXIS 19117 (N.D. Ind. 1996), aff'd, 116 F.3d 256, 1997 U.S. App. LEXIS 15031 (7th Cir. Ind. 1997).

It was harmless error for the trial court to read to the jury all of the aggravating circumstances listed in the death penalty statute at the outset of the penalty phase. Williams v. State, 669 N.E.2d 1372, 1996 Ind. LEXIS 124 (1996), cert. denied, 520 U.S. 1232, 117 S. Ct. 1828, 137 L. Ed. 2d 1034, 1997 U.S. LEXIS 3161 (1997).

Defendant who was charged with a crime that occurred prior to June 30, 1993, was not entitled to a jury instruction that a sentence of life imprisonment was an alternative to the death penalty. Saylor v. State, 686 N.E.2d 80, 1997 Ind. LEXIS 142 (1997), cert. denied, 525 U.S. 831, 119 S. Ct. 84, 142 L. Ed. 2d 66, 1998 U.S. LEXIS 5043 (1998).

A trial court may, in its discretion, instruct the jury on sentencing alternatives when there is reason to believe that the jury will engage in speculation over the extent of alternative penalties. Timberlake v. State, 690 N.E.2d 243, 1997 Ind. LEXIS 247 (1997), cert. denied, 525 U.S. 1073, 119 S. Ct. 808, 142 L. Ed. 2d 668, 1999 U.S. LEXIS 195 (1999).

The court correctly explained to the jury its role under the death penalty statute, when it explained that the determination of weights to be accorded to the aggravating and mitigating factors was a balancing process. Timberlake v. State, 690 N.E.2d 243, 1997 Ind. LEXIS 247 (1997), cert. denied, 525 U.S. 1073, 119 S. Ct. 808, 142 L. Ed. 2d 668, 1999 U.S. LEXIS 195 (1999).

Jury Instructions. (Cont'd)

By paraphrasing former subsection (e) in its instructions to the jury, the court did not mislead the jury to believe that defendant had the burden to prove, beyond a reasonable doubt, the existence of mitigating circumstances and that the jury had to unanimously find that defendant had met this burden before it could consider a circumstance as mitigating. Hough v. State, 690 N.E.2d 267, 1997 Ind. LEXIS 246 (1997), cert. denied, 525 U.S. 1021, 119 S. Ct. 550, 142 L. Ed. 2d 457, 1998 U.S. LEXIS 7658 (1998).

Court is not required to tell jury that they must start penalty phase deliberations with the presumption that no aggravating circumstances existed. Roche v. State, 690 N.E.2d 1115, 1997 Ind. LEXIS 238 (1997).

It is not error to inform jury its sentencing decision is a recommendation because this is a correct statement of law. Wrinkles v. State, 690 N.E.2d 1156, 1997 Ind. LEXIS 240 (1997), cert. denied, 525 U.S. 861, 119 S. Ct. 148, 142 L. Ed. 2d 121, 1998 U.S. LEXIS 5495 (1998).

Where court did not instruct jury on all statutory penalties for murder, it was not fundamental error when: (i) counsel's failure to object to absence of instruction may have been tactical; (ii) both state and defense referred to possibility of life sentence without parole in closing arguments; (iii) prior to the legislature requiring instruction on range of penalties, it was within court's discretion to refuse request for such instruction; and (iv) jury was instructed on option of recommendation of life without parole as alternative to death sentence. Wrinkles v. State, 690 N.E.2d 1156, 1997 Ind. LEXIS 240 (1997), cert. denied, 525 U.S. 861, 119 S. Ct. 148, 142 L. Ed. 2d 121, 1998 U.S. LEXIS 5495 (1998).

It is not beyond average lay juror to understand meaning of terms "mitigation" and "any other circumstances appropriate for consideration," and fact that statute does not require instruction on definitions is not unconstitutional. Wisehart v. State, 693 N.E.2d 23, 1998 Ind. LEXIS 26 (1998), cert. denied, 526 U.S. 1040, 119 S. Ct. 1338, 143 L. Ed. 2d 502, 1999 U.S. LEXIS 2251 (1999).

Where IC 35-50-2-3 provides that defendant may be sentenced to death or life imprisonment without parole, it was error not to instruct the jury on sentence options. Barker v. State, 695 N.E.2d 925, 1998 Ind. LEXIS 76 (1998).

Where the part of the defendant's tendered instruction that was refused by the trial court was not a statement of law, but a statement of historical practice surrounding clemency in the state, there was no error in modifying the tendered instruction. Dye v. State, 717 N.E.2d 5, 1999 Ind. LEXIS 868 (1999), cert. denied, 531 U.S. 957, 121 S. Ct. 379, 148 L. Ed. 2d 292, 2000 U.S. LEXIS 7046 (2000).

Since a trial court is not required to accept the jury's recommendation either for or against the death penalty, there was no error where the jury was informed that the responsibility for sentencing rests with the judge. Lowery v. Anderson, 69 F. Supp. 2d 1078, 1999 U.S. Dist. LEXIS 20606 (S.D. Ind. 1999), aff'd, 225 F.3d 833, 2000 U.S. App. LEXIS 22173 (7th Cir. Ind. 2000).

Since state law did not require the prosecution to charge the aggravator felony at the guilt phase, there was no error in the trial court failing to instruct the jury that the defendant was presumed innocent of an aggravating crime, where that aggravator was not presented as a separate criminal offense but as part of the state's case during the penalty phase. Lowery v. Anderson, 69 F. Supp. 2d 1078, 1999 U.S. Dist. LEXIS 20606 (S.D. Ind. 1999), aff'd, 225 F.3d 833, 2000 U.S. App. LEXIS 22173 (7th Cir. Ind. 2000).

Where the trial court did not give the jury a verdict form specifically advising that it could recommend the defendant be sentenced to a term of years even if the state carried its burden of proof, had the defendant requested such a verdict form, the trial court would have erred in failing to give it; however, because defendant did not object at trial to the verdict forms given by the trial court nor did he submit forms of his own, he waived his claim of error. Pope v. State, 737 N.E.2d 374, 2000 Ind. LEXIS 979 (2000).

Requirement in IC 35-50-2-9(d) that jury be told about possibility of executive clemency did not violate Eighth Amendment or California v. Ramos, 463 U.S. 992, 103 S. Ct. 3446, 77 L. Ed. 2d 1171, 1983 U.S. LEXIS 112 (1983), since executive clemency is so distinct from normal appellate processes that discussion of executive clemency would not lead jurors to believe they were not responsible for their decisions regarding death penalty. Pruitt v. State, 834 N.E.2d 90, 2005 Ind. LEXIS 822 (2005), cert. denied, 548 U.S. 910, 165 L. Ed. 2d 962, 126 S. Ct. 2936, 2006 U.S. LEXIS 5015 (2006).

Trial court order in murder case proposing preliminary jury instruction on determination of defendant's mental retardation was improper and was rejected by appellate court on interlocutory appeal because proposed instruction served no purpose other than to risk misleading jury by suggesting presumption of mental retardation since issue of retardation was inapplicable to murder case where state was not seeking death penalty. Miller v. State, 825 N.E.2d 884, 2005 Ind. App. LEXIS 642 (2005).

Jury Recommendation.

A jury recommendation against the death penalty is not binding upon the trial court. Schiro v. State, 451 N.E.2d 1047, 1983 Ind. LEXIS 904 (1983), cert. denied, 464 U.S. 1003, 104 S. Ct. 510, 78 L. Ed. 2d 699 (1983).

The jury plays an advisory role under subsection (e) of this section, thus the trial court may properly override its recommendation. Schiro v. State, 451 N.E.2d 1047, 1983 Ind. LEXIS 904 (1983), cert. denied, 464 U.S. 1003, 104 S. Ct. 510, 78 L. Ed. 2d 699 (1983).

Defendant was not placed in double jeopardy because the trial court ignored the jury's recommendation and sentenced him to death. Schiro v. State, 451 N.E.2d 1047, 1983 Ind. LEXIS 904 (1983), cert. denied, 464 U.S. 1003, 104 S. Ct. 510, 78 L. Ed. 2d 699 (1983).

The legislature would not have specifically re-

Jury Recommendation. (Cont'd)
quired the trial court to consider the jury's recommendation if that consideration amounted only to an order book entry noting the recommendation; the practical effect of the jury's recommendation in a death penalty case is significant. Williams v. State, 525 N.E.2d 1238, 1988 Ind. LEXIS 198 (1988).

A judge's imposition of the death penalty after the jury has recommended against it does not invoke the double jeopardy clause; the statute places the sentencing function on the trial judge, while the so-called verdict of the jury is advisory. Schiro v. Clark, 754 F. Supp. 646, 1990 U.S. Dist. LEXIS 17927 (N.D. Ind. 1990), aff'd, 963 F.2d 962, 1992 U.S. App. LEXIS 9889 (7th Cir. Ind. 1992).

—Constitutionality.
This section, which permits the trial court to make a judgment of death despite a jury recommendation to the contrary, is nonetheless constitutional. Bieghler v. State, 481 N.E.2d 78, 1985 Ind. LEXIS 920 (1985), cert. denied, 475 U.S. 1031, 106 S. Ct. 1241, 89 L. Ed. 2d 349, 1986 U.S. LEXIS 728 (1986).

The language of subsection (e), which provides for the jury to make a recommendation to the sentencing judge, leaving to the trial judge the option to follow or not follow the recommendation, is not an unconstitutional violation of a defendant's due process rights. Canaan v. State, 541 N.E.2d 894, 1989 Ind. LEXIS 240 (1989), cert. denied, 498 U.S. 882, 111 S. Ct. 230, 112 L. Ed. 2d 185, 1990 U.S. LEXIS 4799 (1990).

U.S. Const., Amend. 6, does not require a jury to make a determination on an aggravating circumstance alleged at sentencing if that circumstance is not an element of the crime for which the capital defendant is convicted. Burris v. Parke, 948 F. Supp. 1310, 1996 U.S. Dist. LEXIS 19117 (N.D. Ind. 1996), aff'd, 116 F.3d 256, 1997 U.S. App. LEXIS 15031 (7th Cir. Ind. 1997).

Since the jury, rather than the court, made the findings that defendant committed murder during the perpetration of a rape, the one aggravating circumstance that the jury further found to outweigh all mitigating circumstances, imposition of the death penalty on defendant did not violate the Sixth Amendment, even though the jurors did not use specific verdict forms. Overstreet v. State, 783 N.E.2d 1140, 2003 Ind. LEXIS 167 (2003), cert. denied, 540 U.S. 1150, 124 S. Ct. 1145, 157 L. Ed. 2d 1044, 2004 U.S. LEXIS 704 (2004).

Neither provision that judge was to determine pretrial whether defendant was mentally retarded for purposes of death penalty eligibility nor requirement that jury weigh aggravators and mitigators before making recommendation to judge violated right to jury trial; pretrial determination simply reduced pre-existing maximum sentence in event of finding of retardation, while jury's weighing of factors did not constitute fact finding to which reasonable doubt requirement applied; furthermore, use of jury's recommendation did not violate right to trial by jury because judge had to follow recommendation. Pruitt v. State, 834 N.E.2d

90, 2005 Ind. LEXIS 822 (2005), cert. denied, 548 U.S. 910, 165 L. Ed. 2d 962, 126 S. Ct. 2936, 2006 U.S. LEXIS 5015 (2006).

—Court's Sentencing Power.
Where the case is tried as a capital case, the state alleging the aggravating circumstance of "lying in wait," but in imposing the sentence the judge specifically adopts the jury's recommendation that the death penalty not be imposed, by so doing, he is not thereafter limited in considering the circumstances of the crime as favoring an enhanced sentence where there is nothing in the record to support the defendant's contention that the jury's recommendation upon the death penalty charge operates as an estoppel against the trial court's exercising its separate, discretionary, and statutorily granted sentencing power under 35-38-1-7(d). Vasquez v. State, 449 N.E.2d 284, 1983 Ind. LEXIS 845 (1983).

The jury decision on death sentence is merely a recommendation, and the trial court may impose the death sentence even if the jury recommends against it. Thompson v. State, 492 N.E.2d 264, 1986 Ind. LEXIS 1125, 65 A.L.R.4th 805 (1986).

After any jury recommendation pursuant to this section, the trial court, as trier of fact, must independently determine the existence of aggravators and mitigators, weigh them, consider the recommendation of the jury, and come to a separate conclusion as to whether or not to impose the death penalty. Kennedy v. State, 578 N.E.2d 633, 1991 Ind. LEXIS 166 (1991), cert. denied, 503 U.S. 921, 112 S. Ct. 1299, 117 L. Ed. 2d 521, 1992 U.S. LEXIS 1564 (1992).

Imposition of death penalty is appropriate where the court finds mitigating circumstances are outweighed by aggravating ones, the court gave consideration to jury's recommendation, and the court set forth its conclusion that sentence was appropriate. Wrinkles v. State, 690 N.E.2d 1156, 1997 Ind. LEXIS 240 (1997), cert. denied, 525 U.S. 861, 119 S. Ct. 148, 142 L. Ed. 2d 121, 1998 U.S. LEXIS 5495 (1998).

Subsection (k) of this section does not require juries to make a specific finding that the state has proved an aggravating circumstance beyond a reasonable doubt before trial courts are authorized to impose a sentence of death or life imprisonment without parole. Farber v. State, 729 N.E.2d 139, 2000 Ind. LEXIS 487 (2000).

— —Hung Jury.
State trial court is not required to consider or weigh in support of mitigation fact jury hung on its sentencing recommendation. Burris v. Parke, 948 F. Supp. 1310, 1996 U.S. Dist. LEXIS 19117 (N.D. Ind. 1996), aff'd, 116 F.3d 256, 1997 U.S. App. LEXIS 15031 (7th Cir. Ind. 1997).

— —Not Following Recommendation.
A trial judge can proceed to impose a penalty of death only when the charging aggravating circumstances have been proven beyond a reasonable doubt and when all the facts available to the court point so clearly to the imposition of the death penalty that the jury's recommendation against

Jury Recommendation. (Cont'd)

—Court's Sentencing Power. (Cont'd)

— —Not Following
  Recommendation. (Cont'd)
the death penalty is unreasonable. Kennedy v. State, 578 N.E.2d 633, 1991 Ind. LEXIS 166 (1991), cert. denied, 503 U.S. 921, 112 S. Ct. 1299, 117 L. Ed. 2d 521, 1992 U.S. LEXIS 1564 (1992).

Death penalty was set aside following review of post-conviction judgment, where the jury recommended against the death penalty and the record supported the conclusion the jury found the prosecution's claim for the death penalty based upon the existence of the intent to kill was unsubstantiated, the sentence of death imposed by the trial judge rested exclusively upon the trial judge's contrary determination that defendant had formed the specific intent to kill, and the unanimous rejection by the jury of the predicate for imposition of the death penalty was considered in tandem with the evidence in mitigation. Schiro v. State, 669 N.E.2d 1357, 1996 Ind. LEXIS 117 (1996).

Where jury failed to reach unanimous decision on prosecutions's request for death sentence, trial court nevertheless had authority to impose death sentence upon basis of aggravating circumstances. Holmes v. State, 820 N.E.2d 136, 2005 Ind. LEXIS 8 (2005).

—Divided Jury.

A recommendation for or against the death penalty must be unanimous, and in the event the jury is divided on the issue and can reach no unanimous recommendation, the jury's participation is at an end and sentencing by the court proceeds to a conclusion without the benefit of a recommendation. Holmes v. State, 671 N.E.2d 841, 1996 Ind. LEXIS 100 (1996), cert. denied, 522 U.S. 849, 118 S. Ct. 137, 139 L. Ed. 2d 85, 1997 U.S. LEXIS 5167 (1997).

This section does not require the jury to recommend against life imprisonment when it cannot reach an agreement on the recommendation of whether the defendant should receive life imprisonment without parole. Dunlop v. State, 724 N.E.2d 592, 2000 Ind. LEXIS 148 (2000).

—Duties of Court.

When the trial court has a jury recommendation against death before it, the single essential feature of this part of the sentencing process is that at the point of final decision, the court reflect upon the jury recommendation against imposing death; a judge who proceeds in this manner will have satisfied the requirement of due consideration of such jury recommendation. Roark v. State, 644 N.E.2d 565, 1994 Ind. LEXIS 201 (1994).

The requirement that the sentencing judge consider the jury recommendation need not apply in the absence of a unanimous juror viewpoint. Holmes v. State, 671 N.E.2d 841, 1996 Ind. LEXIS 100 (1996), cert. denied, 522 U.S. 849, 118 S. Ct. 137, 139 L. Ed. 2d 85, 1997 U.S. LEXIS 5167 (1997).

Although a jury makes a recommendation to the judge about whether or not to impose the death penalty, the judge is required only to give due consideration to that recommendation, is not required to follow it, and need not give it any particular weight. Fleenor v. Anderson, 171 F.3d 1096, 1999 U.S. App. LEXIS 5141 (7th Cir. Ind. 1999), cert. denied, 528 U.S. 891, 120 S. Ct. 215, 145 L. Ed. 2d 181, 1999 U.S. LEXIS 6088 (1999).

Defendant was not denied due process at a fair sentencing determination where the jury was told that its role was advisory and that the court makes the final sentencing determination, which was not an affirmative misstatement of law or fact that could have misled the jury. Lowery v. Anderson, 225 F.3d 833, 2000 U.S. App. LEXIS 22173 (7th Cir. Ind. 2000), cert. denied, 532 U.S. 959, 121 S. Ct. 1488, 149 L. Ed. 2d 375, 2001 U.S. LEXIS 2751 (2001).

When a jury makes the final sentencing determination, a Harrison-style order is out of place; any reasoning provided by a trial court's order would necessarily be that of the trial judge, not the jury; it is enough that by entering the sentence recommended by the jury, the trial court has made an independent determination according to the trial rules that there is sufficient evidence to support the jury's decision. Pittman v. State, 885 N.E.2d 1246, 2008 Ind. LEXIS 404 (2008).

Juvenile.

Since the youth of the offender may be considered as a possible mitigating factor, the death sentence may properly be imposed upon a juvenile. Thompson v. State, 492 N.E.2d 264, 1986 Ind. LEXIS 1125, 65 A.L.R.4th 805 (1986).

Lesser Included Offense.

Involuntary manslaughter is not a lesser included offense of felony murder. Rodriguez v. State, 270 Ind. 613, 388 N.E.2d 493, 1979 Ind. LEXIS 610 (1979).

Life Sentence Without Parole.

Those who receive a life sentence without parole are within the class of those eligible for death. The use of aggravating circumstances is not an end in itself but a means of narrowing the class of death-eligible persons and channelling the jury's discretion, thus reducing the risk of arbitrary and capricious sentencing of murderers. Stevens v. State, 691 N.E.2d 412, 1997 Ind. LEXIS 242 (1997), cert. denied, 525 U.S. 1021, 119 S. Ct. 550, 142 L. Ed. 2d 457, 1998 U.S. LEXIS 7659 (1998).

The trial court erred when weighing the aggravating and mitigating circumstances by not separating its findings concerning the life without parole sentence from those relating to the robbery sentence, because when either the death penalty or life without parole is sought courts must limit the aggravating circumstances eligible for consideration to those specified in the death penalty statute. Pope v. State, 737 N.E.2d 374, 2000 Ind. LEXIS 979 (2000).

A sentence of life imprisonment without parole is imposed under the same standards and is subject to the same requirements as the death penalty, and when the death sentence is sought, courts must limit the aggravating circumstances eligible

Life Sentence Without Parole. (Cont'd)
for consideration to those specified in the death penalty statute; therefore, a trial court may not consider non-statutory aggravating circumstances when imposing life in prison without parole. Holsinger v. State, 750 N.E.2d 354, 2001 Ind. LEXIS 593 (2001).

Because 2002 amendment to death penalty statute, which required judge to impose sentence recommended by jury, did not violate ex post facto prohibition, trial court was required to sentence defendant in accordance with jury's recommendation of life imprisonment without parole regardless of any additional evidence that might have been presented at judicial sentencing hearing; accordingly, trial court's denial of defendant's motion for continuance of final sentencing hearing did not harm defendant. Helsley v. State, 809 N.E.2d 292, 2004 Ind. LEXIS 471 (2004).

Trial court did not err in imposing life without parole sentence upon defendant for murder and dismemberment of his sister-in-law; single aggravating factor of dismemberment outweighed numerous mitigating factors. Losch v. State, 834 N.E.2d 1012, 2005 Ind. LEXIS 871 (2005).

Because an intentional killing is "murder" under both IC 35-42-1-1(1) and, if committed in the course of a burglary, under IC 35-42-1-1(2), defendant's conviction of felony murder with the additional finding of the IC 35-50-2-9(b)(1) aggravator supported a sentence of life without parole. Pittman v. State, 885 N.E.2d 1246, 2008 Ind. LEXIS 404 (2008).

—Statutory Authority.
Where a trial court relied on a version of the sentencing statute not in effect at the time of the murder to impose on the defendant a sentence of life imprisonment without parole, which statutorily was available at the time the murder was committed only as an alternative if the state sought a sentence of death, which the state had not done in this case, the sentence exceeded statutory authority and constituted fundamental error. Rhodes v. State, 698 N.E.2d 304, 1998 Ind. LEXIS 240 (1998).

Malice.

—Distinguished from Premeditation.
Although malice must be deliberated upon, premeditation may occur almost instantaneously. Chambers v. State, 271 Ind. 357, 392 N.E.2d 1156, 1979 Ind. LEXIS 683 (1979).

—Inferred.
Malice and a purpose to kill may be inferred from the use of a deadly weapon in a manner reasonably calculated to cause death or great bodily harm. Chambers v. State, 271 Ind. 357, 392 N.E.2d 1156, 1979 Ind. LEXIS 683 (1979).

Mentally Retarded Individual.
Sentence of a total of 195 years, including consecutive and habitual finding sentences, was manifestly unreasonable where court recorded no mitigating factors but record clearly showed defendant functioned with mental capacity of a child, having

been found mentally retarded under IC 35-36-9-2, and therefore was not eligible for life without parole. Young v. State, 696 N.E.2d 386, 1998 Ind. LEXIS 87 (1998).

Provisions of mental retardation statute were not available to defendant at time he committed crime for which he was convicted, and since act did not apply retroactively, sentence was proper under controlling law in effect at time of crime. Rhodes v. State, 698 N.E.2d 304, 1998 Ind. LEXIS 240 (1998).

The language of the public law amending the death penalty statute to exempt mentally retarded individuals from the death penalty did not specify retroactive application. Rondon v. State, 711 N.E.2d 506, 1999 Ind. LEXIS 345 (1999).

When the United States Supreme Court's Atkins decision is applied to Indiana's sentencing scheme, the mitigating circumstance of mental retardation necessarily outweighs any death-eligible aggravating circumstance. Allen v. State, — N.E.2d —, 2003 Ind. LEXIS 581 (2003).

Mitigating Circumstances.
The trial court is required to consider any relevant mitigating evidence during the penalty phase; however, a defendant is not given carte blanche to introduce any evidence concerning the death penalty. The trial court may exclude as irrelevant evidence not bearing on the defendant's character, prior record, or the circumstances of his offense. Huffman v. State, 543 N.E.2d 360, 1989 Ind. LEXIS 278 (1989), cert. denied, 497 U.S. 1011, 110 S. Ct. 3257, 111 L. Ed. 2d 767, 1990 U.S. LEXIS 3401 (1990), overruled, Street v. State, 567 N.E.2d 102, 1991 Ind. LEXIS 35 (1991).

The trial court can consider as a mitigating circumstance the mental condition of the defendant regardless of whether it might not have been so apparent as to merit a finding of not guilty of the commission of the crime. Benirschke v. State, 577 N.E.2d 576, 1991 Ind. LEXIS 153 (1991), cert. denied, 505 U.S. 1224, 112 S. Ct. 3042, 120 L. Ed. 2d 910, 1992 U.S. LEXIS 4671 (1992).

The trial court is not required to agree with defendant that each particular factor is a mitigating factor. Sims v. State, 585 N.E.2d 271, 1992 Ind. LEXIS 9 (1992).

The trial court's conclusion that the death penalty was appropriate must be set aside since it was arrived at without the required discrete and individualized consideration of the character of the offender necessary when the existence of the court's lone mitigating circumstance of having consumed alcohol is reviewed along with the uncontroverted evidence of parental neglect, abnormal behavior, psychiatric disorder, and that of immediate surrender to authorities. Evans v. State, 598 N.E.2d 516, 1992 Ind. LEXIS 204 (1992).

The trial court is not obligated to address every mitigating factor asserted by the defendant and explain why the court did not find it be mitigating. Timberlake v. State, 690 N.E.2d 243, 1997 Ind. LEXIS 247 (1997), cert. denied, 525 U.S. 1073, 119 S. Ct. 808, 142 L. Ed. 2d 668, 1999 U.S. LEXIS 195 (1999).

Mitigating Circumstances. (Cont'd)

Mitigating circumstances provisions of statute are not unconstitutionally vague, since catch-all mitigator properly allows jury to consider all relevant mitigating evidence presented. Wisehart v. State, 693 N.E.2d 23, 1998 Ind. LEXIS 26 (1998), cert. denied, 526 U.S. 1040, 119 S. Ct. 1338, 143 L. Ed. 2d 502, 1999 U.S. LEXIS 2251 (1999).

Legislature's choice to allow a death penalty defendant to present every conceivable mitigator does not dilute the significance or persuasiveness of a myriad of mitigating circumstances, absent any evidence that such dilution actually occurred, and claim that this section does not adequately channel discretion of judge and jury is unfounded. Minnick v. State, 698 N.E.2d 745, 1998 Ind. LEXIS 102 (1998), cert. denied, 528 U.S. 1006, 120 S. Ct. 501, 145 L. Ed. 2d 387, 1999 U.S. LEXIS 7562 (1999).

Where murder defendant argued, as mitigating factor, that because murder victim was a drug dealer, he implicitly consented to the risks of the trade, including death, the trial court's rejection of defendant's contention, and the imposition of a life sentence without parole was not an abuse of discretion. Highbaugh v. State, 773 N.E.2d 247, 2002 Ind. LEXIS 652 (2002).

—Duty to Consider.

A trial court is under no duty to deem mitigating every factor so alleged by the defendant simply because it is supported by some evidence in the record. Bivins v. State, 642 N.E.2d 928, 1994 Ind. LEXIS 146 (1994), amended, — N.E.2d —, 1995 Ind. LEXIS 34 (1995), cert. denied, 516 U.S. 1077, 133 L. Ed. 2d 734, 116 S. Ct. 783, 1996 U.S. LEXIS 547 (1996).

While failure to find existence of mitigating circumstances clearly supported by record may imply they were improperly overlooked, sentencing judge is not required to credit or discuss these factors in the same manner as the defense. Stevens v. State, 691 N.E.2d 412, 1997 Ind. LEXIS 242 (1997), cert. denied, 525 U.S. 1021, 119 S. Ct. 550, 142 L. Ed. 2d 457, 1998 U.S. LEXIS 7659 (1998).

Permissive language of preamble and of catch-all mitigator does not render optional jury's consideration of relevant proffered mitigating evidence. Wisehart v. State, 693 N.E.2d 23, 1998 Ind. LEXIS 26 (1998), cert. denied, 526 U.S. 1040, 119 S. Ct. 1338, 143 L. Ed. 2d 502, 1999 U.S. LEXIS 2251 (1999).

Trial court did not abuse its discretion when it rejected defendant's claim of extreme emotional disturbance at the time of the murder of a child but clearly considered defendant's severe emotional problems as a separate mitigating circumstance when considering defendant's sentence. Gauvin v. State, 883 N.E.2d 99, 2008 Ind. LEXIS 264 (2008).

—Evidence of Mental Retardation.

Mental retardation statute operates in conjunction with death penalty statute to prohibit execution or life imprisonment of mentally retarded defendant and to ensure that each defendant, whether or not mentally retarded under that statute, may present in mitigation during penalty phase whatever evidence of mental retardation is available. Rogers v. State, 698 N.E.2d 1172, 1998 Ind. LEXIS 252 (1998).

—Expert Witnesses.

The trial court abused its discretion by limiting defendant's mitigation expert to 25 hours of investigation, but the trial court's error did not require reversal of death sentence where the probable impact of additional evidence would not have affected the outcome of the jury's recommendation or the judge's sentencing decision. Williams v. State, 669 N.E.2d 1372, 1996 Ind. LEXIS 124 (1996), cert. denied, 520 U.S. 1232, 117 S. Ct. 1828, 137 L. Ed. 2d 1034, 1997 U.S. LEXIS 3161 (1997).

—Guilty Plea.

Although the legislature has not identified a defendant's decision to plead guilty as a statutory mitigating circumstance in either the death penalty statute nor the general sentencing statute, state courts have recognized that a guilty plea sometimes may be a significant mitigating circumstance. Trueblood v. State, 715 N.E.2d 1242, 1999 Ind. LEXIS 734 (1999), cert. denied, 531 U.S. 858, 121 S. Ct. 143, 148 L. Ed. 2d 94, 2000 U.S. LEXIS 5649 (2000).

—Intoxication.

Intoxication at the time of the offense, when proven to be of such a degree as to substantially impair the defendant's capacity to appreciate the criminality of his conduct or to conform his conduct to the requirements of the law, is a statutory mitigating circumstance which must be given mitigating weight in the process of determining the appropriateness of the death penalty. Johnson v. State, 584 N.E.2d 1092, 1992 Ind. LEXIS 14 (1992), cert. denied, 506 U.S. 853, 113 S. Ct. 155, 121 L. Ed. 2d 105, 1992 U.S. LEXIS 5137 (1992).

Where defendant was an alcoholic since childhood, had been drinking heavily before the crime, was arrested for public intoxication within an hour or two of the crime, had bloodshot eyes, smelled strongly of alcohol, and was violent and vociferous when confined, his intoxication was a mitigating circumstance to be considered in determining the death penalty. Johnson v. State, 584 N.E.2d 1092, 1992 Ind. LEXIS 14 (1992), cert. denied, 506 U.S. 853, 113 S. Ct. 155, 121 L. Ed. 2d 105, 1992 U.S. LEXIS 5137 (1992).

Disclosure immediately following murder that he committed the act to know what it felt like to kill was strongly probative evidence of the defendant's awareness of his conduct; the defendant's use of alcohol on the night of the crime did not substantially impair his ability to appreciate the criminality of his conduct. Bivins v. State, 642 N.E.2d 928, 1994 Ind. LEXIS 146 (1994), amended, — N.E.2d —, 1995 Ind. LEXIS 34 (1995), cert. denied, 516 U.S. 1077, 133 L. Ed. 2d 734, 116 S. Ct. 783, 1996 U.S. LEXIS 547 (1996).

An intoxication defense, although still available to defendants at death penalty sentencing because the state is required to prove its alleged aggravating factors beyond a reasonable doubt before the jury may consider them, cannot prevail if the evidence shows the defendant had the ability to perform tasks such as attempting to hide his

Mitigating Circumstances. (Cont'd)

—Intoxication. (Cont'd)
crime, giving instructions to others, or taking himself from place to place immediately following the crime. Rouster v. State, 705 N.E.2d 999, 1999 Ind. LEXIS 66 (1999).

—Jury Recommendation.
The failure of a jury to reach a recommendation should not be considered as a mitigating factor during the penalty phase. Roche v. State, 596 N.E.2d 896, 1992 Ind. LEXIS 191 (1992).

—Mental Disease or Defect.
If a defendant is unable to establish that he suffered from a mental disease or defect at the time of the crime, he cannot establish either an insanity defense or the death penalty mitigator; therefore, a finding that a defendant did not suffer from a mental disease or defect precludes the application of both, or either, of these statutes. Matheney v. Anderson, 253 F.3d 1025, 2001 U.S. App. LEXIS 13490 (7th Cir. Ind. 2001), cert. denied, 535 U.S. 1030, 122 S. Ct. 1635, 152 L. Ed. 2d 644, 2002 U.S. LEXIS 2806 (2002).

There is no practical difference between IC 35-50-2-9(c)(6) and IC 35-50-2-9(c)(2) in cases where there is no suggestion of mental defect, intoxication, severe emotional disturbance not produced by mental disease, or inability to understand criminality of act. Baird v. Davis, 388 F.3d 1110, 2004 U.S. App. LEXIS 23765 (7th Cir. Ind. 2004), cert. denied, 125 S. Ct. 1849, 161 L. Ed. 2d 739, 2005 U.S. LEXIS 3454 (U.S. 2005).

In imposing death penalty, state courts have discretion to determine in each case what weight to give mental disease that does not obliterate consciousness of wrongdoing. Baird v. Davis, 388 F.3d 1110, 2004 U.S. App. LEXIS 23765 (7th Cir. Ind. 2004), cert. denied, 125 S. Ct. 1849, 161 L. Ed. 2d 739, 2005 U.S. LEXIS 3454 (U.S. 2005).

Successive post-conviction relief petition in which petitioner argued that imposition of death penalty was cruel and unusual punishment because defendant was mentally ill was meritless because jury had explicitly declined, in guilt phase, to find petitioner guilty but mentally ill and, in penalty phase, to find mitigating circumstance of mental or emotional disturbance. Matheney v. State, 833 N.E.2d 454, 2005 Ind. LEXIS 772 (2005).

—Mental or Emotional Disturbance.
Trial court's denial of defendant's application for a defense psychologist to assist him during the penalty phase of trial was reversible error where defense counsel had been told by a psychologist that defendant "may have been under the influence of extreme mental or emotional disturbance when he committed the acts alleged in the information"; it was incumbent on the trial court to allow defendant appropriate resources to develop the opinion of this expert witness concerning this statutory mitigator. Castor v. State, 587 N.E.2d 1281, 1992 Ind. LEXIS 72 (1992).

Subsection (c) does not preclude consideration of non-extreme emotional disturbance or non-sub-stantial impairment. Benefiel v. State, 716 N.E.2d 906, 1999 Ind. LEXIS 859 (1999), cert. denied, 531 U.S. 830, 121 S. Ct. 83, 148 L. Ed. 2d 45, 2000 U.S. LEXIS 5249 (2000).

—No Significant History of Prior Criminal Conduct.
The state may offer evidence of independent crimes to disprove the lack of the mitigating factor of significant prior criminal conduct. Rouster v. State, 600 N.E.2d 1342, 1992 Ind. LEXIS 233 (1992).

Use of no significant history of prior criminal conduct as mitigating factor is not unconstitutionally vague. Wrinkles v. State, 690 N.E.2d 1156, 1997 Ind. LEXIS 240 (1997), cert. denied, 525 U.S. 861, 119 S. Ct. 148, 142 L. Ed. 2d 121, 1998 U.S. LEXIS 5495 (1998).

In the non-capital context, a single conviction or juvenile adjudication may negate the mitigating circumstance that a defendant has no history of delinquency or criminal activity, but the language of the death penalty statute suggests that something more is required to constitute a significant criminal history. Warlick v. State, 722 N.E.2d 809, 2000 Ind. LEXIS 53 (2000).

— —Not Found.
The trial court was justified in concluding that the defendant, sentenced to death for a multiple-victim shotgun slaying had a history of reacting to rejection or hostility by arming himself before confronting his adversaries, even though his conduct was disposed of with leniency or was not prosecuted. Moore v. State, 479 N.E.2d 1264, 1985 Ind. LEXIS 876 (1985), cert. denied, 474 U.S. 1026, 106 S. Ct. 583, 88 L. Ed. 2d 565, 1985 U.S. LEXIS 4839 (1985).

—Outweighed by Aggravating Circumstances.
Sentence of life imprisonment without parole under Indiana's death penalty statute was not manifestly unreasonable based on determination that extreme brutality of defendant's murder of former spouse outweighed mitigating factors of lack of criminal history, work ethic, educational achievement and remorse. Laux v. State, 821 N.E.2d 816, 2005 Ind. LEXIS 93 (2005).

Defendant's sentence of life without parole was reasonable and did not require revision under AP. 7(B) because the trial court properly found that the aggravating circumstance of killing a 10-year-old child weighed more heavily than proffered mitigators in that defendant did not live a relatively crime-free life and there was no clinical evidence regarding defendant's mental condition to show influence of extreme or emotional disturbance under IC 35-50-2-9(c)(2). Stockelman v. State, 868 N.E.2d 416, 2007 Ind. LEXIS 467 (2007).

—Presentation.
Society's interests in making sure defendants not deserving death did not receive the death sentence and in preventing defendants from using the death penalty statute as a means of state-assisted suicide did not justify appointment of special counsel to argue mitigating evidence in lieu

Mitigating Circumstances. (Cont'd)

—Presentation. (Cont'd)
of defendant presenting it personally. Smith v. State, 686 N.E.2d 1264, 1997 Ind. LEXIS 174 (1997).

—Rebuttal Evidence.
The death sentence statute permits the prosecution to introduce rebuttal evidence tending to disprove mitigating circumstances shown by the defendant's evidence. Woods v. State, 547 N.E.2d 772, 1989 Ind. LEXIS 336 (1989), overruled in part, Laux v. State, 821 N.E.2d 816, 2005 Ind. LEXIS 93 (2005), overruled, Richardson v. State, 717 N.E.2d 32, 1999 Ind. LEXIS 918 (1999).

Evidence of crimes committed after the offense for which the defendant is on trial is admissible in rebuttal of an assertion of absence of prior criminal history on the defendant's behalf. Brown v. State, 698 N.E.2d 1132, 1998 Ind. LEXIS 107 (1998), cert. denied, 526 U.S. 1056, 119 S. Ct. 1367, 143 L. Ed. 2d 527, 1999 U.S. LEXIS 2437 (1999).

—Refusal to Accept.
Trial court did not err in refusing to accept mitigating circumstances where evidence regarding the circumstances was at best conflicting. Saylor v. State, 686 N.E.2d 80, 1997 Ind. LEXIS 142 (1997), cert. denied, 525 U.S. 831, 119 S. Ct. 84, 142 L. Ed. 2d 66, 1998 U.S. LEXIS 5043 (1998).

—Testimony Disallowed.
Where appellant sought to offer testimony from a public defender concerning mitigating circumstances, and the public defender was prepared to testify about other cases in which the facts were similar to or, in her opinion, more grievous than those in appellant's case, but in which the death penalty was not requested or a plea bargain resulted, the trial court properly disallowed the testimony on the ground that a comparison of the cases based upon their naked facts was inappropriate because it failed to take into consideration the fact that the penalty assigned in each case was based upon a multitude of factors. Huffman v. State, 543 N.E.2d 360, 1989 Ind. LEXIS 278 (1989), cert. denied, 497 U.S. 1011, 110 S. Ct. 3257, 111 L. Ed. 2d 767, 1990 U.S. LEXIS 3401 (1990), overruled, Street v. State, 567 N.E.2d 102, 1991 Ind. LEXIS 35 (1991).

Newly Discovered Evidence.
In death penalty cases, the Supreme Court of Indiana is to evaluate claims of newly discovered evidence under the standard established in IC 35-50-2-9(k), which is whether the previously undiscovered evidence undermines confidence in the conviction or sentence. Stephenson v. State, 864 N.E.2d 1022, 2007 Ind. LEXIS 282 (2007).

Evidence that appellant's IQ score was elevated by an anti-psychotic drug was not previously undiscovered evidence pursuant to IC 35-50-2-9(k) because it was cumulative of a defense expert's testimony on this same issue during appellant's capital murder trial. Pruitt v. State, — N.E.2d —, 2009 Ind. LEXIS 338 (2009).

Trial counsel thoroughly investigated and pre-sented evidence regarding various aspects of appellant's social history, including appellant's mental health history, through both expert witness and lay witness testimony; in light of this evidence, appellant's narrative social history compiled for a post-conviction relief hearing was cumulative and therefore did not constitute previously undiscovered evidence pursuant to IC 35-50-2-9(k). Pruitt v. State, — N.E.2d —, 2009 Ind. LEXIS 338 (2009).

Petition for Consideration of New Evidence In Death Penalty.
State Supreme Court reviewed a petition for consideration of new evidence which an inmate who had been sentenced to death filed, pursuant to provisions including IC 35-50-2-9(k), and under Ind. R.P. Post-Conviction Remedies 1, § 12, but found that the inmate was not entitled to relief. Williams v. State, 793 N.E.2d 1019, 2003 Ind. LEXIS 614 (2003).

Plea Agreements.
Negotiated plea agreements for the death penalty do not violate Indiana Constitution, Article 1, § 18. Smith v. State, 686 N.E.2d 1264, 1997 Ind. LEXIS 174 (1997).

To approve a plea agreement calling for the death penalty, the trial court must make the findings specified in this section. Smith v. State, 686 N.E.2d 1264, 1997 Ind. LEXIS 174 (1997).

Indiana's death penalty and plea agreement statutes, read together, do not preclude negotiated plea agreements for the death penalty. Smith v. State, 686 N.E.2d 1264, 1997 Ind. LEXIS 174 (1997).

Procedure.

—Jury.
There is no error in submitting the question of sentencing recommendations to the same jury that heard the guilt phase of the trial. Smith v. State, 465 N.E.2d 1105, 1984 Ind. LEXIS 897 (1984).

In habitual offender cases, as in capital cases, the guilt phase of the trial is first held, then the jury is reassembled to determine whether appellant is an habitual offender; in such a situation it was entirely proper for the court upon remand to assemble a new jury for the habitual offender determination. Burris v. State, 642 N.E.2d 961, 1994 Ind. LEXIS 145 (1994), cert. denied, 516 U.S. 922, 116 S. Ct. 319, 133 L. Ed. 2d 221, 1995 U.S. LEXIS 6919 (1995).

Findings authorizing the imposition of the death penalty need not be made by a jury. Burris v. State, 642 N.E.2d 961, 1994 Ind. LEXIS 145 (1994), cert. denied, 516 U.S. 922, 116 S. Ct. 319, 133 L. Ed. 2d 221, 1995 U.S. LEXIS 6919 (1995).

As the 2002 amendment to the death penalty statute, which required trial courts to sentence defendants in accordance with the sentencing recommendation of the jury, was procedural, a third resentencing of inmate regarding a 1982 murder conviction had to be conducted under the post-2002 version of the statute; however, as the murder occurred in 1981, Pub. L. No. 250-1993, § 3 made life without parole unavailable as a sentence

Procedure. (Cont'd)

—Jury. (Cont'd)

option. State v. Azania, 875 N.E.2d 701, 2007 Ind. LEXIS 997 (2007).

—Sentencing Hearing.

The Sixth Amendment's right to confront adverse witnesses was not violated by the incorporation of evidence from the guilty plea hearing, including the presentence report, into the record of the sentencing hearing. The defendant was given the opportunity to rebut any and all of the matters contained in the report and, by pleading guilty, he waived his sixth amendment right. Moore v. State, 479 N.E.2d 1264, 1985 Ind. LEXIS 876 (1985), cert. denied, 474 U.S. 1026, 106 S. Ct. 583, 88 L. Ed. 2d 565, 1985 U.S. LEXIS 4839 (1985).

—Weight of Aggravating and Mitigating Circumstances.

It is constitutional to not require a finding that aggravating factors outweigh mitigating circumstances beyond a reasonable doubt. Moore v. State, 479 N.E.2d 1264, 1985 Ind. LEXIS 876 (1985), cert. denied, 474 U.S. 1026, 106 S. Ct. 583, 88 L. Ed. 2d 565, 1985 U.S. LEXIS 4839 (1985).

Several mitigating factors were outweighed by one aggravating factor to arrive at an appropriate sentence for defendant. Logan v. State, 729 N.E.2d 125, 2000 Ind. LEXIS 481 (2000).

TR. 59(J)(7) applies to verdicts, judgments and findings, but does not apply to jury's weighing of mitigating and aggravating factors under death penalty statute, IC 35-50-2-9. Ritchie v. State, 809 N.E.2d 258, 2004 Ind. LEXIS 476 (2004), cert. denied, 126 S. Ct. 42, 163 L. Ed. 2d 76, 2005 U.S. LEXIS 6128 (U.S. 2005).

Weighing of aggravating and mitigating factors by jury in death penalty case satisfies Sixth Amendment once jury finds existence of one statutory aggravator beyond a reasonable doubt; however, weighing process itself is not subject to reasonable doubt standard. Ritchie v. State, 809 N.E.2d 258, 2004 Ind. LEXIS 476 (2004), cert. denied, 126 S. Ct. 42, 163 L. Ed. 2d 76, 2005 U.S. LEXIS 6128 (U.S. 2005).

Prosecutorial Discretion.

That the prosecutor had been acquainted with the victims for about four years preceding their deaths, the victims were known to him through bar functions, and one was an attorney, who was the father of the judge of the local circuit court, were not facts warranting the conclusion that the exercise by the prosecutor of discretion to seek the death penalty was improper or should have been subjected to more stringent judicial oversight. Lowery v. State, 640 N.E.2d 1031, 1994 Ind. LEXIS 129 (1994), cert. denied, 516 U.S. 992, 116 S. Ct. 525, 133 L. Ed. 2d 432, 1995 U.S. LEXIS 7906 (1995).

Provision of IC 35-38-1-3 Applicable.

Provision of IC 35-50-1A-3 [now IC 35-38-1-3] that the sentencing judge include a statement of the reasons for selecting the sentence he imposes is applicable when a death sentence is to be imposed.

Brewer v. State, 275 Ind. 338, 417 N.E.2d 889, 1981 Ind. LEXIS 684 (1981), cert. denied, 458 U.S. 1122, 102 S. Ct. 3510, 73 L. Ed. 2d 1384, 1982 U.S. LEXIS 2891 (1982).

Rehabilitation.

A defendant is not entitled to present mitigating evidence of other death row inmates' rehabilitation as proof of his being amenable to rehabilitation. Spranger v. State, 498 N.E.2d 931, 1986 Ind. LEXIS 1304 (1986), cert. denied, 481 U.S. 1033, 107 S. Ct. 1965, 95 L. Ed. 2d 536, 1987 U.S. LEXIS 1912 (1987).

Remand for Statement of Reasons.

The Indiana Supreme Court's remand to the circuit court for a written entry reflecting the reasons for a death sentence did not violate the double jeopardy clause, since the remand was not because of insufficient evidence but was designed to give the Supreme Court a more explicit statement of the reasons for the sentence. Schiro v. Clark, 754 F. Supp. 646, 1990 U.S. Dist. LEXIS 17927 (N.D. Ind. 1990), aff'd, 963 F.2d 962, 1992 U.S. App. LEXIS 9889 (7th Cir. Ind. 1992).

Review.

—In General.

The procedures in the statutes, court rules and constitution of the state for the review of a death sentence by the Supreme Court meet the guidelines established by the Supreme Court of the United States. Brewer v. State, 275 Ind. 338, 417 N.E.2d 889, 1981 Ind. LEXIS 684 (1981), cert. denied, 458 U.S. 1122, 102 S. Ct. 3510, 73 L. Ed. 2d 1384, 1982 U.S. LEXIS 2891 (1982).

While a jury plays a very important and necessary role in the judicial system, a higher degree of scrutiny on appeal in situations where the trial court and jury disagree about the imposition of the death penalty will not be imposed. Schiro v. State, 451 N.E.2d 1047, 1983 Ind. LEXIS 904 (1983), cert. denied, 464 U.S. 1003, 104 S. Ct. 510, 78 L. Ed. 2d 699 (1983).

The death penalty statute guides the Supreme Court's review of death sentences by setting forth standards governing trial court imposition of death sentences. Harrison v. State, 644 N.E.2d 1243, 1995 Ind. LEXIS 7 (1995), superseded by statute as stated in, Allen v. State, 737 N.E.2d 741, 2000 Ind. LEXIS 1075 (Ind. 2000), superseded by statute as stated in, Kroegher v. State, 774 N.E.2d 1029, 2002 Ind. App. LEXIS 1529 (2002).

Upon finding a substantial irregularity in a trial court decision to impose the death penalty or life without parole, the Supreme Court can remand to the trial court for a clarification or new sentencing determination, affirm the sentence based upon a finding of harmless error, or independently reweigh the proper aggravating and mitigating circumstances at the appellate level. The sentence imposed by the trial court was determined to be appropriate by reason of both the harmless error doctrine and independent appellate reweighing. Long v. State, 743 N.E.2d 253, 2001 Ind. LEXIS 213 (2001).

Review. (Cont'd)

—In General. (Cont'd)

After the case was remanded because the trial court may have relied on non-statutory aggravators in its first sentencing order, the trial court fulfilled its obligation on remand by entering a revised sentencing order that showed it had only considered proven statutory aggravating factors in again imposing the death penalty on defendant for killing four people. Corcoran v. State, 774 N.E.2d 495, 2002 Ind. LEXIS 688 (2002).

—Constitutionality.

The appellate review that automatically follows the imposition of the death sentence fully satisfies the requirements imposed by the United States Supreme Court and does not violate the Eighth and Fourteenth Amendments. Burris v. State, 465 N.E.2d 171, 1984 Ind. LEXIS 854 (1984), cert. denied, 469 U.S. 1132, 105 S. Ct. 816, 83 L. Ed. 2d 809 (1985), superseded by statute as stated in, Wrinkles v. State, 690 N.E.2d 1156, 1997 Ind. LEXIS 240 (1997); Averhart v. State, 470 N.E.2d 666, 1984 Ind. LEXIS 1003 (1984), cert. denied, 471 U.S. 1030, 105 S. Ct. 2051, 85 L. Ed. 2d 323, 1985 U.S. LEXIS 2706 (1985).

The Eighth and Fourteenth Amendments do not require a state appellate court to compare the sentence in the case before it with the penalties imposed in similar cases if requested to do so by the prisoner. Smith v. State, 465 N.E.2d 1105, 1984 Ind. LEXIS 897 (1984).

This section provides for an adequate proportionality review and is not improper and unconstitutional on this ground. Moore v. State, 479 N.E.2d 1264, 1985 Ind. LEXIS 876 (1985), cert. denied, 474 U.S. 1026, 106 S. Ct. 583, 88 L. Ed. 2d 565, 1985 U.S. LEXIS 4839 (1985).

In a death penalty case, the interest that appellee has in life is curtailed by the procedures laid out in the death penalty statute, and there is no suspect class affected by the saving clause; accordingly, the appropriate level of scrutiny to apply is the rational basis analysis, which merely requires the classification to bear some rational relationship to a legitimate state interest or goal. State v. Alcorn, 638 N.E.2d 1242, 1994 Ind. LEXIS 96 (1994).

—Guilty Plea.

Where defendant could not demonstrate a reasonable probability of acquittal at trial, post-conviction court erred in setting aside conviction resulting from his guilty plea, where there was no evidence negating defendant's culpability for felony murder and the evidence confirming it was overwhelming, so that his felony murder conviction was reinstated, and the case was remanded for a new sentencing hearing. State v. Van Cleave, 674 N.E.2d 1293, 1996 Ind. LEXIS 173 (1996), cert. denied, 522 U.S. 1119, 118 S. Ct. 1060, 140 L. Ed. 2d 121, 1998 U.S. LEXIS 1027 (1998).

Defendant was not deprived of the right to a jury because defendant had pled guilty knowing that such a plea would deprive defendant of access to a jury. Moore v. State, 771 N.E.2d 46, 2002 Ind. LEXIS 563 (2002), cert. denied, 538 U.S. 1014, 123 S. Ct. 1931, 155 L. Ed. 2d 851, 2003 U.S. LEXIS 3506 (2003).

—Level of Scrutiny.

Supreme court automatically reviews every death sentence and applies a level of scrutiny more intensive than for other criminal penalties. Bivins v. State, 642 N.E.2d 928, 1994 Ind. LEXIS 146 (1994), amended, — N.E.2d —, 1995 Ind. LEXIS 34 (1995), cert. denied, 516 U.S. 1077, 133 L. Ed. 2d 734, 116 S. Ct. 783, 1996 U.S. LEXIS 547 (1996).

—Mitigating Circumstances.

Newly discovered evidence warrants relief only if evidence will probably produce different result, and evidence of mitigating circumstances that defendant's participation was relatively minor and that he acted under substantial domination of another, which was not supported by other evidence, did not reach that threshold. Wisehart v. State, 693 N.E.2d 23, 1998 Ind. LEXIS 26 (1998), cert. denied, 526 U.S. 1040, 119 S. Ct. 1338, 143 L. Ed. 2d 502, 1999 U.S. LEXIS 2251 (1999).

Inmate's application for habeas relief on grounds that Indiana Supreme Court, in affirming his sentence, failed to give proper consideration to his mental state as mitigating factor was rejected where inmate's brief did not suggest that court failed to consider or overlooked any part of IC 35-50-2-9(c)(6). Baird v. Davis, 388 F.3d 1110, 2004 U.S. App. LEXIS 23765 (7th Cir. Ind. 2004), cert. denied, 125 S. Ct. 1849, 161 L. Ed. 2d 739, 2005 U.S. LEXIS 3454 (U.S. 2005).

Trial court did not err in determining that the mitigating factors did not outweigh the two statutory aggravators, that the killing occurred during a robbery and while defendant was lying in wait. While, inter alia, defendant had no juvenile adjudication or prior adult criminal record, defendant admitted to drug use on numerous occasions and committed other crimes after the murder, such as using the victim's debit card and taking the victim's jewelry and car; in addition, there was no credible evidence that clearly linked defendant's impaired mental state to the commission of the murder or what defendant's mental state at the time of the crime was, and there was testimony that defendant was manipulative and glorified defendant's problems. Krempetz v. State, 872 N.E.2d 605, 2007 Ind. LEXIS 695 (2007).

—Preservation of Error.

With respect to trial evidentiary issues, review of a death penalty case is no different from the review of any other criminal appeal: In order to preserve error for appellate review, defendant must make proper trial objections. Thompson v. State, 492 N.E.2d 264, 1986 Ind. LEXIS 1125, 65 A.L.R.4th 805 (1986).

—Proportionality.

Proportionality review of death sentences is not constitutionally required. Thompson v. State, 492 N.E.2d 264, 1986 Ind. LEXIS 1125, 65 A.L.R.4th 805 (1986).

—Weight of Aggravating and Mitigating Circumstances.

During the sentencing hearing, where the trial

Review. (Cont'd)

—Weight of Aggravating and Mitigating Circumstances. (Cont'd)

court stated that the aggravating circumstance of intentionally killing the victim while committing robbery had been proven beyond a reasonable doubt, each mitigating factor listed in this section was discussed as to whether it applied to appellant's case, and appellant's drug and/or alcohol use was the only applicable mitigating factor, the trial court properly found the aggravating factor outweighed the mitigating factor. Huffman v. State, 543 N.E.2d 360, 1989 Ind. LEXIS 278 (1989), cert. denied, 497 U.S. 1011, 110 S. Ct. 3257, 111 L. Ed. 2d 767, 1990 U.S. LEXIS 3401 (1990), overruled, Street v. State, 567 N.E.2d 102, 1991 Ind. LEXIS 35 (1991).

Independent review of the sentencing process followed in a prosecution arising out of a rape-murder and of the trial judge's sentencing order; the review showed meticulous weighing of the jury's unanimous recommendation of death as well as a careful reconsideration of aggravating and mitigating circumstances. Overstreet v. State, 783 N.E.2d 1140, 2003 Ind. LEXIS 167 (2003), cert. denied, 540 U.S. 1150, 124 S. Ct. 1145, 157 L. Ed. 2d 1044, 2004 U.S. LEXIS 704 (2004).

Saving Clause.

Where, at the time of the alleged offense of murder with which appellee was charged, the sentence of life imprisonment without parole was not an available option under the statute, appellee's trial was governed by the law that was in effect when the crime was committed; the application of the more recently adopted saving clause did not violate any principle of reformation and neither was it an exercise of vindictive justice. State v. Alcorn, 638 N.E.2d 1242, 1994 Ind. LEXIS 96 (1994).

Sentence Reversed.

Counsel's failure to prepare for the penalty phase warranted reversal of defendant's death sentence. Smith v. State, 547 N.E.2d 817, 1989 Ind. LEXIS 366 (1989), corrected, 547 N.E.2d 817, 1990 Ind. LEXIS 31 (1990).

Sentence Upheld.

The court properly concluded that the aggravating factor — an intentional killing during an attempted robbery — outweighed the mitigating factors — the defendant's home life which deteriorated in his early teens, his failed stint in the army from which he was honorably discharged, and the fact that thereafter he could not find a job. Van Cleave v. State, 517 N.E.2d 356, 1987 Ind. LEXIS 1196 (1987), cert. denied, 488 U.S. 1019, 109 S. Ct. 819, 102 L. Ed. 2d 808, 1989 U.S. LEXIS 56 (1989).

Defendant's participation in the murder of and other criminal acts, including rape and deviate sexual conduct, upon the victim were clearly major and indicative of a reckless indifference of human life, so as to support imposition of the sentence of death. Lowery v. State, 547 N.E.2d 1046, 1989 Ind.

LEXIS 369 (1989), cert. denied, 498 U.S. 881, 111 S. Ct. 217, 112 L. Ed. 2d 176, 1990 U.S. LEXIS 4979 (1990).

Trial judge was warranted in finding that the aggravators outweighed the mitigators and in imposing the death penalty, where the court weighed substantial aggravating circumstances — the commission of a triple murder and the murder of young children — against the following mitigating factors: defendant had no significant history or prior criminal conduct, he was abused as a child, he at various times supported siblings and others financially and emotionally, and he might adjust well to long-term imprisonment. Trueblood v. State, 587 N.E.2d 105, 1992 Ind. LEXIS 40 (1992), cert. denied, 506 U.S. 897, 113 S. Ct. 278, 121 L. Ed. 2d 205, 1992 U.S. LEXIS 6214 (1992).

Where the judge duly considered the recommendation of the jury, found the state had proven at least one aggravating factor beyond a reasonable doubt, and weighed the specific, applicable mitigating and aggravating factors, his sentencing decision was based on the reasonable recommendation of the jury and on his own specific and clear findings, and there was no error. McIntyre v. State, 717 N.E.2d 114, 1999 Ind. LEXIS 880 (1999).

Defendant's petition under IC 35-50-2-9(k) for review of his conviction and death sentence for multiple murders committed during robbery was denied since no new evidence was presented that cast doubt on verdict or sentence; new DNA blood evidence showing that blood on defendant's clothes was not from victim was immaterial because sufficient evidence outside of blood evidence existed to show defendant was heavily involved in robbery and actively participated in shooting. Williams v. State, 808 N.E.2d 652, 2004 Ind. LEXIS 472 (2004).

Sentencing Order.

—Insufficient.

Sentencing order was insufficient for not complying with subsection (e) of this section by not setting forth specific facts and reasons which led the court to find the existence of each aggravating and mitigating circumstance, not establishing that the trial court found that the state proved beyond a reasonable doubt that at least one aggravating circumstance existed, not indicating that the trial court considered the jury's recommendation, and not containing the personal conclusion of the trial court that death was the appropriate punishment for this offender and this crime. Harrison v. State, 644 N.E.2d 1243, 1995 Ind. LEXIS 7 (1995), superseded by statute as stated in, Allen v. State, 737 N.E.2d 741, 2000 Ind. LEXIS 1075 (Ind. 2000), superseded by statute as stated in, Kroegher v. State, 774 N.E.2d 1029, 2002 Ind. App. LEXIS 1529 (2002).

While the sentencing order was insufficient to permit the meaningful appellate review required, the trial court conducted an extensive sentencing hearing in which it appeared to have recited on the record many of the findings required to be included in the written sentencing order; the trial court's oral statements at the sentencing hearing would

Sentencing Order. (Cont'd)

—Insufficient. (Cont'd)

not be incorporated into its sentencing order, but the trial court would be ordered to articulate more specifically its findings. Harrison v. State, 644 N.E.2d 1243, 1995 Ind. LEXIS 7 (1995), superseded by statute as stated in, Allen v. State, 737 N.E.2d 741, 2000 Ind. LEXIS 1075 (Ind. 2000), superseded by statute as stated in, Kroegher v. State, 774 N.E.2d 1029, 2002 Ind. App. LEXIS 1529 (2002).

—Jury Recommendation Not Followed.

Trial court's sentencing order, declining to follow the jury's recommendation that the death penalty not be imposed, and imposing the death penalty, demonstrated compliance with Indiana's death penalty law. Saylor v. State, 686 N.E.2d 80, 1997 Ind. LEXIS 142 (1997), cert. denied, 525 U.S. 831, 119 S. Ct. 84, 142 L. Ed. 2d 66, 1998 U.S. LEXIS 5043 (1998).

—Life Without Parole.

A literal reading of subsection (k), without reference to subsection (e), would elevate the jury's role in sentencing far above its long-standing role of making a nonbinding recommendation and would be in clear conflict with other subsections of this section; therefore, the jury's role in capital sentencing has been and is to make a nonbinding recommendation to the trial court. Farber v. State, 729 N.E.2d 139, 2000 Ind. LEXIS 487 (2000).

A sentence of life without parole is imposed under the same standards and is subject to the same requirements as a capital sentence, and the sentencing order in a capital case requires greater specificity than in other types of cases. Nicholson v. State, 734 N.E.2d 1047, 2000 Ind. LEXIS 898 (2000).

Where an elderly woman died from asphyxiation after defendant tied her to a bed with tissue paper stuffed in her mouth during a robbery, the trial court erred in imposing a life sentence without parole as the evidence at trial did not support the trial court's imposition of statutory aggravators for intentionally killing the victim while committing a robbery and torturing the victim while she was alive; furthermore, the State failed to allege criminal confinement. Nicholson v. State, 768 N.E.2d 443, 2002 Ind. LEXIS 462 (2002).

After conviction for murder, concurrent sentences of life imprisonment without parole were vacated and defendant was sentenced to consecutive 55-year terms where the legal requirements necessary for such a sentence were not satisfied; the order did not clearly establish that the trial court found that the State proved the existence of at least one aggravating circumstance beyond a reasonable doubt, the order did not set forth sufficient facts and reasons that led to a finding of particular aggravating and mitigating circumstances there was nothing in the sentencing order that indicated that the trial court considered the jury's recommendation, and the order did not contain the necessary personal conclusion of the trial court that life without parole was the appropriate punishment for this offender and this crime.

Brown v. State, 783 N.E.2d 1121, 2003 Ind. LEXIS 201 (2003).

—Sufficient.

Trial court's statement adequately established that it evaluated and balanced the mitigating and aggravating circumstances. Prowell v. State, 687 N.E.2d 563, 1997 Ind. LEXIS 182 (1997), cert. denied, 525 U.S. 841, 119 S. Ct. 104, 142 L. Ed. 2d 83, 1998 U.S. LEXIS 5186 (1998).

Where the trial court's sentencing order explicitly rejected the defendant's residual doubt argument, and where there was significant physical evidence connecting him to the murders, there was no basis for reversal of his conviction. Dye v. State, 717 N.E.2d 5, 1999 Ind. LEXIS 868 (1999), cert. denied, 531 U.S. 957, 121 S. Ct. 379, 148 L. Ed. 2d 292, 2000 U.S. LEXIS 7046 (2000).

—Specificity Required.

Remand for a new sentencing order was required because a sentencing order in a capital case requires greater specificity than in other cases, and the trial court did not comply with the requirements for specificity as set out in Harrison v. State, 644 N.E.2d 1243, 1995 Ind. LEXIS 7 (Ind. 1995). Rawley v. State, 724 N.E.2d 1087, 2000 Ind. LEXIS 151 (2000).

Defendant's life sentence without parole for murder conviction was affirmed even though trial court failed to set forth specific facts for concluding that state proved beyond reasonable doubt existence of aggravating circumstances; trial court's failure was harmless error where no mitigating circumstances were found, sufficient evidence supported aggravators of lying in wait and murder while on probation, and trial court expressly found that aggravating circumstances outweighed mitigating circumstances. Washington v. State, 808 N.E.2d 617, 2004 Ind. LEXIS 461 (2004).

—Victim Impact Evidence.

Because trial court's sentencing order did not refer to any evidence characterized by defendant as "victim impact evidence," any alleged error in admitting such evidence did not affect the sentence imposed. Prowell v. State, 687 N.E.2d 563, 1997 Ind. LEXIS 182 (1997), cert. denied, 525 U.S. 841, 119 S. Ct. 104, 142 L. Ed. 2d 83, 1998 U.S. LEXIS 5186 (1998).

Separate Offenses.

The crimes of kidnapping and premeditated murder are different offenses although arising from the same operative facts and separate sentences were appropriate. Pollard v. State, 270 Ind. 599, 388 N.E.2d 496, 1979 Ind. LEXIS 611 (1979).

Statements by Prosecutor.

Statements and comments of the trial prosecutor concerning: 1) the fear of the defendant which a witness had previously displayed; 2) the helpless, harmless, and productive natures of the victims; 3) defendant's own statements comparing himself to notorious killers; 4) blood pulsating from the head of one victim; 5) society's interest in convicting the guilty; 6) the presumption of innocence not being designed to protect the guilty; 7) his role of pros-

Statements by Prosecutor. (Cont'd)
ecutor as standing in for the victims'; 8) that defendant was given more due process than defendant gave the victims; and 9) the souls of the victims crying out for justice; were within the confines of the trial, and lacked those features which would seriously inflame the passions and emotions of the jury, and did not under all the circumstances place defendant in grave peril at either phase of the trial. Lowery v. State, 640 N.E.2d 1031, 1994 Ind. LEXIS 129 (1994), cert. denied, 516 U.S. 992, 116 S. Ct. 525, 133 L. Ed. 2d 432, 1995 U.S. LEXIS 7906 (1995).

Defendant sentenced to life without parole was entitled to a new sentencing hearing when the theme of the prosecutor's rebuttal remarks was that defendant deserved life without parole because he was an unsavory character; without the remarks, the jury might have concluded that violating probation for resisting law enforcement was not so serious an aggravator as to outweigh the claim that defendant had no prior history of criminal conduct and that a life sentence would pose a hardship on his three minor children. It was misconduct for a prosecutor to request a jury to return a death penalty or life without parole recommendation for any reason other than that the mitigating factors of IC 35-50-2-9 were outweighed by the aggravating factor or factors. Cooper v. State, 854 N.E.2d 831, 2006 Ind. LEXIS 887 (2006).

Trial Court's Role.
The sentencing court has a separate and independent role in assessing and weighing the aggravating and mitigating circumstances and in making the final determination whether to impose the death penalty. Williams v. State, 669 N.E.2d 1372, 1996 Ind. LEXIS 124 (1996), cert. denied, 520 U.S. 1232, 117 S. Ct. 1828, 137 L. Ed. 2d 1034, 1997 U.S. LEXIS 3161 (1997).

In the context of IC 35-50-2-9, a trial court may exercise its traditional TR. 50 and 59(J)(7) functions to find that there is insufficient evidence for a jury to find one or more aggravators. Pittman v. State, 885 N.E.2d 1246, 2008 Ind. LEXIS 404 (2008).

Waiver of Review.
While paragraph (h) of this section precludes waiver of review of the "sentencing" in a death penalty case, it does not preclude waiver of a review of a murder "conviction." Judy v. State, 275 Ind. 145, 416 N.E.2d 95, 1981 Ind. LEXIS 665 (1981).

On hearing before Supreme Court on defendant's request that he be permitted to waive his appeal, Supreme Court found that defendant had knowingly, voluntarily and intelligently waived his right to appeal his murder convictions and that defendant was fully competent to make such waiver. Judy v. State, 275 Ind. 145, 416 N.E.2d 95, 1981 Ind. LEXIS 665 (1981).

Upon the defendant's waiver of his right to appeal his murder conviction, the Supreme Court will limit its automatic review to: (1) Whether the procedure by which the death penalty was imposed comports with the dictates of this section; and (2)

whether death is an appropriate penalty according to the Rules for the Appellate Review of Sentences. Vandiver v. State, 480 N.E.2d 910, 1985 Ind. LEXIS 914 (1985).

This section requires automatic review by the Supreme Court of every death sentence. This review must occur whether a prisoner seeks it or not; it cannot be waived. Cooper v. State, 540 N.E.2d 1216, 1989 Ind. LEXIS 216 (1989).

Cited:
Lynk v. State, 271 Ind. 445, 393 N.E.2d 751, 1979 Ind. LEXIS 699 (1979); Ferguson v. State, 273 Ind. 468, 405 N.E.2d 902, 1980 Ind. LEXIS 695 (1980); Tapp v. State, 406 N.E.2d 296, 1980 Ind. App. LEXIS 1536 (1980); Suggs v. State, 428 N.E.2d 226, 1981 Ind. LEXIS 916 (1981); Dunaway v. State, 440 N.E.2d 682, 1982 Ind. LEXIS 992 (1982); Gibson v. State, 456 N.E.2d 1006, 1983 Ind. LEXIS 1059 (1983); Didio v. State, 471 N.E.2d 1117, 1984 Ind. LEXIS 1070 (1984); Dillon v. Duckworth, 751 F.2d 895, 1984 U.S. App. LEXIS 15559 (7th Cir. Ind. 1984); Rowan v. Owens, 752 F.2d 1186, 1984 U.S. App. LEXIS 15561 (7th Cir. Ind. 1984); Smith v. State, 474 N.E.2d 973, 1985 Ind. LEXIS 757 (1985); Schiro v. State, 479 N.E.2d 556, 1985 Ind. LEXIS 879 (1985); Mers v. State, 496 N.E.2d 75, 1986 Ind. LEXIS 1239 (1986); Brewer v. State, 496 N.E.2d 371, 1986 Ind. LEXIS 1220 (1986); Spranger v. State, 500 N.E.2d 1170, 1986 Ind. LEXIS 1473 (1986); Resnover v. State, 507 N.E.2d 1382, 1987 Ind. LEXIS 934 (1987); Fleenor v. State, 514 N.E.2d 80, 1987 Ind. LEXIS 1085 (1987); Ward v. State, 528 N.E.2d 52, 1988 Ind. LEXIS 255 (1988); Wallace v. State, 553 N.E.2d 456, 1990 Ind. LEXIS 65 (1990); Davidson v. State, 558 N.E.2d 1077, 1990 Ind. LEXIS 165 (1990); Resnover v. Pearson, 965 F.2d 1453, 1992 U.S. App. LEXIS 14492 (7th Cir. Ind. 1992); Smith v. Farley, 873 F. Supp. 1199, 1994 U.S. Dist. LEXIS 19154 (N.D. Ind. 1994); Matheney v. State, 688 N.E.2d 883, 1997 Ind. LEXIS 198 (1997); Bieghler v. State, 690 N.E.2d 188, 1997 Ind. LEXIS 231 (1997); Taylor v. State, 695 N.E.2d 117, 1998 Ind. LEXIS 71 (1998); Ben-Yisrayl v. State, 729 N.E.2d 102, 2000 Ind. LEXIS 483 (2000); Minnick v. Anderson, 151 F. Supp. 2d 1015, 2000 U.S. Dist. LEXIS 12573 (N.D. Ind. 2000); Azania v. State, 730 N.E.2d 646, 2000 Ind. LEXIS 533, 95 A.L.R.5th 775 (2000); Rastafari v. Anderson, 117 F. Supp. 2d 788, 2000 U.S. Dist. LEXIS 15681 (N.D. Ind. 2000); Wrinkles v. State, 749 N.E.2d 1179, 2001 Ind. LEXIS 596 (2001); Williams v. Davis, 301 F.3d 625, 2002 U.S. App. LEXIS 17982 (7th Cir. Ind. 2002); Gross v. State, 769 N.E.2d 1136, 2002 Ind. LEXIS 507 (2002); Mull v. Appellee, 770 N.E.2d 308, 2002 Ind. LEXIS 561 (2002); Canaan v. Davis, — F. Supp. 2d —, 2003 U.S. Dist. LEXIS 479 (S.D. Ind. 2003); Aki-Khuam v. Davis, 339 F.3d 521, 2003 U.S. App. LEXIS 15983 (7th Cir. Ind. 2003); Aki-Khuam v. Davis, 328 F.3d 366, 2003 U.S. App. LEXIS 8678 (7th Cir. Ind. 2003); Corcoran v. State, 827 N.E.2d 542, 2005 Ind. LEXIS 447 (2005); Crist v. South-West Lake Maxinkuckee Conservancy District, 875 N.E.2d 222, 2007 Ind. App. LEXIS 2372 (2007).

RESEARCH REFERENCES

Indiana Law Journal.
The Death Penalty Cases: Shaping Substantive Criminal Law, 58 Ind. L.J. 187 (1982).

Preliminary Screening of Prosecutorial Access to Death Qualified Juries: A Missing Constitutional Link, 62 Ind. L.J. 295 (1987).

The New Law of Murder, 69 Ind. L.J. 375 (1994).

Indiana Law Review.
Recent Developments in Criminal Law and Procedure, 27 Ind. L. Rev. 959 (1994).

Recent Developments in Indiana Criminal Law and Procedure, 28 Ind. L. Rev. 819 (1995).

Survey: Criminal Law and Procedure: Recent Developments in Indiana, 32 Ind. L. Rev. 789 (1999).

Indiana Appellate Procedure: A New Era Dawns in Appellate Procedure, 34 Ind. L. Rev. 741 (2001).

Survey: VII. Criminal Law and Procedure: Recent Developments in Indiana Criminal Law and Procedure. 36 Ind. L. Rev. 1003 (2003).

Survey: Criminal Law and Procedure, 37 Ind. L. Rev. 1003 (2004).

Survey: Criminal Law and Procedure: Recent Developments in Indiana Criminal Law and Procedure (October 1, 2003, to September 30, 2004), 38 Ind. L. Rev. 999 (2005).

Notre Dame Law Review.
The Case for Comparative Proportionality Review, 59 Notre Dame L. Rev. 1412 (1984).

The Evolving Meaning of the Fifth and Sixth Amendments: Sentencing Effects of Aggravating Factors As Elements of the Crime, 80 Notre Dame L. Rev. 403 (2004).

Res Gestae.
Criminal Justice Notes, 34 Res Gestae 138 (1990).

Criminal Justice Notes: The death penalty and mental illness, 46 (No. 5) Res Gestae 26 (2002).

Criminal Justice Notes: Death penalty — Mental retardation. 47 (No. 4) Res Gestae 42 (2003).

Criminal Justice Notes: Death penalty — DNA evidence. 47 (No. 4) Res Gestae 42 (2003).

Indiana Supreme Court Addresses Impact of Apprendi on Capital Sentencing Statute. 47 (No. 10) Res Gestae 22 (2004).

Criminal Justice Notes 4/08: Evidence of torture, 51 (No. 10) Res Gestae 38 (2008).

Valparaiso University Law Review.
The Indiana Death Penalty: An Exercise in Constitutional Futility, 15 Val. U.L. Rev. 409.

Victim Participation and Lex Talionis: Constitu-
tionality Under Section 18 of the Indiana Bill of Rights, 27 Val. U.L. Rev. 733 (1993).

Collateral References.
Sufficiency of evidence, for purposes of death penalty, to establish statutory aggravating circumstance that murder was heinous, cruel, depraved, or the like — post-*Gregg* cases. 63 A.L.R.4th 478.

Validity of rules and regulations concerning viewing of execution of death penalty. 107 A.L.R.5th 291.

Sufficiency of evidence, for purposes of death penalty, to establish statutory aggravating circumstance that murder was committed to avoid arrest or prosecution, to effect escape from custody, to hinder governmental function or enforcement of law, and the like — post-*Gregg* cases. 64 A.L.R.4th 755.

Sufficiency of evidence, for purposes of death penalty, to establish statutory aggravating circumstance that in committing murder, defendant created risk of death or injury to more than one person, to many persons, and the like — post-*Gregg* cases. 64 A.L.R.4th 837.

Sufficiency of evidence, for purposes of death penalty, to establish statutory aggravating circumstance that defendant was previously convicted of or committed other violent offense, had history of violent conduct, posed continuing threat to society, and the like — post-*Gregg* cases. 65 A.L.R.4th 838.

Sufficiency of evidence, for purposes of death penalty, to establish statutory aggravating circumstance that murder was committed for pecuniary gain, as consideration or in expectation of receiving something of monetary value, and the like — post-*Gregg* cases. 66 A.L.R.4th 417.

Sufficiency of evidence, for death penalty purposes, to establish statutory aggravating circumstance that murder was committed in course of committing, attempting, or fleeing from other offense, and the like — post-*Gregg* cases. 67 A.L.R.4th 887.

Sufficiency of evidence, for purposes of death penalty, to establish statutory aggravating circumstance that defendant committed murder while under sentence of imprisonment, in confinement or correctional custody, and the like — post-*Gregg* cases. 67 A.L.R.4th 942.

Application of death penalty to nonhomicide cases. 62 A.L.R.5th 121.

Victim impact evidence in capital sentencing hearings — post-*Payne v. Tennessee*. 79 A.L.R.5th 33.

Propriety of carrying out death sentences against mentally ill individuals. 111 A.L.R.5th 491.

35-50-2-10. Habitual controlled substance offenders.

(a) As used in this section:

(1) "Drug" means a drug or a controlled substance (as defined in IC 35-48-1).

(2) "Substance offense" means a Class A misdemeanor or a felony in which the possession, use, abuse, delivery, transportation, or manufacture of alcohol or

drugs is a material element of the crime. The term includes an offense under IC 9-30-5 and an offense under IC 9-11-2 (before its repeal).

(b) The state may seek to have a person sentenced as a habitual substance offender for any substance offense by alleging, on a page separate from the rest of the charging instrument, that the person has accumulated two (2) prior unrelated substance offense convictions.

(c) After a person has been convicted and sentenced for a substance offense committed after sentencing for a prior unrelated substance offense conviction, the person has accumulated two (2) prior unrelated substance offense convictions. However, a conviction does not count for purposes of this subsection if:

(1) it has been set aside; or

(2) it is a conviction for which the person has been pardoned.

(d) If the person was convicted of the substance offense in a jury trial, the jury shall reconvene for the sentencing hearing. If the trial was to the court, or the judgment was entered on a guilty plea, the court alone shall conduct the sentencing hearing, under IC 35-38-1-3.

(e) A person is a habitual substance offender if the jury (if the hearing is by jury) or the court (if the hearing is to the court alone) finds that the state has proved beyond a reasonable doubt that the person had accumulated two (2) prior unrelated substance offense convictions.

(f) The court shall sentence a person found to be a habitual substance offender to an additional fixed term of at least three (3) years but not more than eight (8) years imprisonment, to be added to the term of imprisonment imposed under IC 35-50-2 or IC 35-50-3. If the court finds that:

(1) three (3) years or more have elapsed since the date the person was discharged from probation, imprisonment, or parole (whichever is later) for the last prior unrelated substance offense conviction and the date the person committed the substance offense for which the person is being sentenced as a habitual substance offender; or

(2) all of the substance offenses for which the person has been convicted are substance offenses under IC 16-42-19 or IC 35-48-4, the person has not been convicted of a substance offense listed in section 2(b)(4) [IC 35-50-2-2(b)(4)] of this chapter, and the total number of convictions that the person has for:

(A) dealing in or selling a legend drug under IC 16-42-19-27;

(B) dealing in cocaine or a narcotic drug (IC 35-48-4-1);

(C) dealing in a schedule I, II, or III controlled substance (IC 35-48-4-2);

(D) dealing in a schedule IV controlled substance (IC 35-48-4-3); and

(E) dealing in a schedule V controlled substance (IC 35-48-4-4);

does not exceed one (1);

then the court may reduce the additional fixed term. However, the court may not reduce the additional fixed term to less than one (1) year.

(g) If a reduction of the additional year fixed term is authorized under subsection (f), the court may also consider the aggravating or circumstances in IC 35-38-1-7.1(a) and the mitigating circumstances in IC 35-38-1-7.1(b) to:

(1) decide the issue of granting a reduction; or

(2) determine the number of years, if any, to be subtracted under subsection (f).

History.

IC 35-50-2-10, as added by P.L.335-1983, § 2; P.L.327-1985, § 5; P.L.98-1988, § 11; P.L.1-1990, § 355; P.L.96-1996, § 8; P.L.97-1996, § 5; P.L.2-1997, § 77; P.L.291-2001, § 227; P.L.71-2005, § 12; P.L.213-2005, § 5; P.L.1-2006, § 551.

NOTES TO DECISIONS

In General.

This section is plainly penal in nature and must be construed against the state. Marshall v. State, 493 N.E.2d 1317 (Ind. App. 1986).

Amendment Not Timely.

Defendant had not waived his claim that the state violated IC 35-34-1-5 by amending the habitual substance offender charge outside the 30-day time limit when it discovered that a prior conviction did not qualify as a predicate offense under IC 35-50-2-10(a)(2); amendment of the indictment under IC 35-34-1-5 was one of substance, and under Fajardo, it should not have been made less than 30 days prior to the omnibus date; accordingly, trial court erred by permitting the state to make the amendment late. Fields v. State, 888 N.E.2d 304, 2008 Ind. App. LEXIS 1255 (2008).

Consecutive Sentences.

The trial court exceeded its legislative authorization when it imposed consecutive habitual offender sentence enhancements at a single criminal trial, since the habitual offender statutes are silent on the question of whether courts have the authority to require such sentences to run consecutively. McCotry v. State, 722 N.E.2d 1265, 2000 Ind. App. LEXIS 70 (2000)

Construction.

—Legislative Intent.

The language of this section, as amended, reflects the General Assembly's intent that double enhancements are appropriate. Roberts v. State, 725 N.E.2d 441, 2000 Ind. App. LEXIS 310 (2000)

Although defendant's misdemeanor charge for possession of marijuana was elevated to a felony, he could also be charged as a habitual offender under IC 35-50-2-10 since the legislature specifically included drug possession misdemeanors and felonies in the category of offenses that were subject to habitual substance offender enhancement. State v. Downey, 770 N.E.2d 794, 2002 Ind. LEXIS 542 (2002)

—With Habitual Violator of Traffic Laws Statute.

Effect is given to both habitual violator statutory schemes by extracting the offense of operating a motor vehicle while intoxicated from the scope of the general habitual substance offender statute and placing it within the exclusive dominion of the more specific habitual violator of traffic laws scheme. Freeman v. State, 658 N.E.2d 68, 1995 Ind. LEXIS 166 (1995)

—With Other Statutes.

Because the language mirrors the language contained in IC 35-50-2-8, the general habitual offender statute, decisions interpreting the habitual offender statute are applicable to issues raised under this section. Roell v. State, 655 N.E.2d 599, 1995 Ind. App. LEXIS 1171 (1995)

Prior to the 1996 amendments to IC 35-50-2-10 adding subsection (a)(2), IC 9-30-5-3 superseded IC 35-50-2-10 with respect to enhancing the sentence of one convicted for the second time of operating a vehicle while intoxicated. Freeman v. State, 658 N.E.2d 68, 1995 Ind. LEXIS 166 (1995)

IC 9-30-5 is a definite and specific statute. Prior to the 1996 amendments to IC 35-50-2-10 adding subsection (a)(2), it superseded the general habitual substance offender statute, IC 35-50-2-10, as effective before its 1996 amendments. Devore v. State, 657 N.E.2d 740, 1995 Ind. LEXIS 165 (1995)

Since the statutory definition of substance offense under this section was amended in 1996 to include an offense under the operating while intoxicated statute, it was proper to convict the defendant of both offenses. Weaver v. State, 702 N.E.2d 750, 1998 Ind. App. LEXIS 2090 (1998)

Under the version of this section in effect at the time the defendant committed the underlying offense in 1995, his sentence could only be enhanced under IC 9-30-5-3, and the trial court erred by also enhancing his sentence under the habitual substance offender statute. Settle v. State, 709 N.E.2d 34, 1999 Ind. App. LEXIS 603 (1999)

By including a conviction under IC 9-30-5-3 within the general habitual substance offender statute's definition of ""substance offense,"" the General Assembly evinced its intent that such convictions may also serve as a predicate offense in a general substance offender adjudication, and that a person may receive an enhanced conviction under IC 9-30-5-3 which may also be used as a predicate offense in a habitual substance offender determination. Roberts v. State, 725 N.E.2d 441, 2000 Ind. App. LEXIS 310 (2000)

Discovery.

Defendant was not denied due process by the

Discovery. (Cont'd)

state's failure to timely disclose evidence relating to an allegation that defendant was a habitual substance offender; because the failure appeared to be inadvertent, exclusion was not an appropriate remedy; furthermore, the evidence produced by the state as part of discovery at least put defendant on notice of the prior convictions on which the state intended to rely. Lindsey v. State, 877 N.E.2d 190, 2007 Ind. App. LEXIS 2725 (2007).

Effect of Amendments.

Once the 1996 amendments to the habitual substance offender statute took effect, prior operating while intoxicated convictions could be used as predicate offenses to support the enhancement of the underlying charge. Settle v. State, 709 N.E.2d 34, 1999 Ind. App. LEXIS 603 (1999)

Enhanced Sentence.

—In General.

An enhanced sentence imposed under the habitual substance offender statute may not be suspended. Devaney v. State, 578 N.E.2d 386, 1991 Ind. App. LEXIS 1565 (1991)

—Discretion of Court.

Court has discretion to determine which felony to enhance after a determination that the habitual offender enhancement statute applies. Hendrix v. State, 759 N.E.2d 1045, 2001 Ind. LEXIS 1104 (2001)

—Discretion of Prosecutor.

Where an offender could be charged with a habitual offender enhancement as either a habitual offender or a habitual substance offender, the prosecutor has discretion to bring enhancement charges under either provision. Hendrix v. State, 759 N.E.2d 1045, 2001 Ind. LEXIS 1104 (2001)

—Double Enhancement Improper.

Prior to the 1996 amendments to IC 35-50-2-10 adding subsection (a)(2), a defendant's sentence should not have been twice enhanced through IC 9-30-5 and IC 30-50-2-10, as effective before its 1996 amendments. Devore v. State, 657 N.E.2d 740, 1995 Ind. LEXIS 165 (1995)

—Double Enhancement Proper.

Given statutory amendment specifically authorizing double enhancement in cases of substance offense, there was no impermissible double enhancement in conviction of defendant for operating a vehicle while intoxicated as a Class D felony rather than a Class A misdemeanor, based upon the existence of prior conviction, and the imposition of a sentence as habitual substance offender based upon existence of two prior convictions. Weida v. State, 693 N.E.2d 598, 1998 Ind. App. LEXIS 427 (1998)

A trial court may enhance an operating while intoxicated offense to a Class D felony under IC 9-30-5-3, and that same conviction may then serve as a predicate offense for purposes of imposing an habitual substance offender enhancement under IC 35-50-2-10; therefore, the double enhancement

of defendant's sentence was proper. Roberts v. State, 725 N.E.2d 441, 2000 Ind. App. LEXIS 310 (2000)

—Improper.

Prior to the 1996 amendments to IC 35-50-2-10 adding subsection (a)(2), the trial court erred by twice enhancing defendant's penalty for operating a vehicle while intoxicated, first, when the court increased his penalty from a Class A misdemeanor to a Class D felony under the authority of IC 9-30-5-2 and IC 9-30-5-3 and, second, when it enhanced his term of imprisonment by finding him a habitual substance offender under IC 35-50-2-10, as effective before its 1996 amendments. Devore v. State, 657 N.E.2d 740, 1995 Ind. LEXIS 165 (1995)

Guilty plea by defendant in prior criminal action was insufficient to prove that judgment of conviction was entered on offense defendant had previously been charged with and therefore failed to support enhancement of conviction for operating while intoxicated causing death from Class C to Class B felony or to support habitual offender determination. Jaramillo v. State, 803 N.E.2d 243, 2004 Ind. App. LEXIS 211 (2004)

Trial court erred in sentencing defendant as a habitual substance offender by imposing an additional sentence for a violation of the habitual substance offender statute, IC 35-50-2-10, rather than enhancing defendant's substance offense conviction; furthermore, the trial court erred in suspending a portion of the habitual offender sentence. Reffett v. State, 844 N.E.2d 1072, 2006 Ind. App. LEXIS 599 (2006).

Trial court erred in treating the habitual substance offender finding as a separate conviction with a separate sentence. Bauer v. State, 875 N.E.2d 744, 2007 Ind. App. LEXIS 2391 (2007).

By using defendant's prior conviction to support his conviction as a Class D felony and to enhance the sentence based on a habitual substance offender finding, the trial court made an improper double enhancement. Beldon v. State, — N.E.2d —, 2009 Ind. App. LEXIS 833 (2009).

Sentence resulting from an improper double enhancement could be cured by entering a conviction for operating a vehicle while intoxicated as a Class A misdemeanor (which would not rely upon a prior conviction), and then adjusting the habitual substance offender enhancement of his sentence downward in accordance with IC 35-50-2-10, or by entering his conviction as a Class D felony but removing the habitual substance offender enhancement altogether. Beldon v. State, — N.E.2d —, 2009 Ind. App. LEXIS 833 (2009).

Use of same prior conviction as aggravator and as basis to enhance misdemeanor (IC 9-30-5-2) to felony (IC 9-30-5-3) was improper double enhancement under IC 35-50-2-10. Remedy was to enter misdemeanor conviction and adjust habitual substance offender enhancement downward, or enter felony conviction with no enhancement. Beldon v. State, — N.E.2d —, 2009 Ind. App. LEXIS 833 (2009).

Trial court's sentence of three years, with but 240 days suspended, for a conviction of operating a motor vehicle while intoxicated, as a Class D

Enhanced Sentence. (Cont'd)

—Improper. (Cont'd)

felony, was error; Class D felony served as the underlying offense for habitual substance offender adjudication, and pursuant to IC 35-50-2-10(f), the sentencing range for that felony was enhanced such that the new sentencing range was three and a half years to eleven years, but under IC 35-50-2-2(b), the trial court was permitted to only suspend that portion of the sentence in excess of three and a half years where the felony committed was an offense under IC 9-30-5-1 et seq. (operating while intoxicated) and the person who committed the offense had accumulated at least two prior unrelated convictions under IC 9-30-5-1 et seq.; therefore, because the trial court ordered that all but 240 days of defendant's sentence be suspended, that sentence was illegal. Young v. State, 901 N.E.2d 624, 2009 Ind. App. LEXIS 342 (2009).

—Prior Uncounseled Misdemeanors.

A prior misdemeanor conviction for operating while intoxicated could be considered to enhance a defendant's sentence for a subsequent operating while intoxicated offense under the habitual substance offender statute, though the defendant's prior misdemeanor conviction was uncounseled, so long as the prior uncounseled misdemeanor conviction did not result in a prison sentence. Morphew v. State, 672 N.E.2d 461, 1996 Ind. App. LEXIS 1452 (1996)

—Proper.

The general enhancement provision of this section applies in instances where the specific scheme provided by IC 9-30-5 is inapplicable, and trial court properly enhanced defendant's sentence pursuant to this section where IC 9-30-5-3 could not serve as the enhancement for the defendant's conviction because defendant's most recent conviction did not occur within five years of his prior conviction. Morphew v. State, 672 N.E.2d 461, 1996 Ind. App. LEXIS 1452 (1996)

Trial court did not err in denying defendant's post-conviction relief petition in which he sought to challenge the enhanced sentence imposed upon him for his conviction for Class A misdemeanor operating a motor vehicle while intoxicated in violation of IC 9-30-5-2; that offense was a substance offense under IC 35-50-2-10 and could be used as a predicate offense to support a habitual substance offender determination. King v. State, 848 N.E.2d 305, 2006 Ind. App. LEXIS 997 (2006).

When defendant was sentenced in accordance with a plea agreement, and defendant had received a significant benefit by having 7 out of 11 counts dropped, he could not complain that the sentence was illegal on grounds that it imposed consecutive habitual substance offender enhancements under IC 35-50-2-10. Borders v. State, 854 N.E.2d 888, 2006 Ind. App. LEXIS 1985 (2006).

Defendant's aggregate 52-year sentence for convictions of two counts of operating a vehicle while intoxicated (OWI) causing death, OWI causing serious bodily injury, and having a prior OWI conviction in the last five years was four years shorter than the maximum sentence possible, and

was not inappropriate; defendant's BAC was over three times the legal limit, he had cocaine in his system, and he was speeding in an area where pedestrians and traffic were common. Although neither of defendant's previous convictions involved offenses nearly as serious as the current offense, they involved the same illegal and dangerous conduct, driving while intoxicated. Pedraza v. State, 873 N.E.2d 1083, 2007 Ind. App. LEXIS 2182 (2007), transfer granted and vacated, 878 N.E.2d 218, 2007 Ind. LEXIS 1005 (2007).

Seven-year habitual substance offender enhancement under IC 35-50-2-10 to a one-year sentence for operating a vehicle while intoxicated was not disproportionate under Ind. Const., art. 1, § 16 where it was defendant's fifth operating-while-intoxicated conviction. Lindsey v. State, 877 N.E.2d 190, 2007 Ind. App. LEXIS 2725 (2007).

When defendant's one-year sentence for operating a vehicle while intoxicated was enhanced by seven years under IC 35-50-2-10, the Habitual Substance Offender statute, the resulting eight-year sentence was not inappropriate under AP. 7(B) given defendant's four prior operating-while-intoxicated convictions and an additional conviction involving alcohol. Lindsey v. State, 877 N.E.2d 190, 2007 Ind. App. LEXIS 2725 (2007).

Evidence.

—Identity.

The evidence was sufficient to support defendant's adjudication as an habitual substance offender where the state proved that he was the person who committed the 1989 offense through the use of documents showing the same name, date of birth and social security number. Devore v. State, 650 N.E.2d 37, 1995 Ind. App. LEXIS 426 (1995)

—Sufficient.

A conviction for operating a vehicle while intoxicated as a Class D felony requires a finding that the defendant had a previous conviction of operating a vehicle while intoxicated, and because defendant was convicted for operating a vehicle while intoxicated as a Class D felony, the court must have determined that the state presented sufficient evidence for it to reasonably conclude that defendant committed the 1992 offense after he had been placed on probation for a 1989 conviction in another county. Devore v. State, 650 N.E.2d 37, 1995 Ind. App. LEXIS 426 (1995)

Predicate Offenses.

As defined by IC 35-48-1-9, ""controlled substance"" does not include precursors listed in IC 35-48-4-14.5, but rather includes only those drugs, substances, or immediate precursors identified in statutes defining schedules of controlled substances; accordingly, under strict reading of IC 35-48-1-9, precursors listed in IC 35-48-4-14.5(a) are not ""controlled substances"" and thus not ""drugs"" for purpose of establishing predicate substance offense under IC 35-50-2-10, unless they are included in Schedules I, II, III, IV, or V. Murray v. State, 798 N.E.2d 895, 2003 Ind. App. LEXIS 2149 (2003)

Predicate Offenses. (Cont'd)

Possession of precursors for manufacture of methamphetamines does not constitute predicate ""substance offense"" for purposes of IC 35-50-2-10(b). Murray v. State, 798 N.E.2d 895, 2003 Ind. App. LEXIS 2149 (2003)

Prior Conviction as Aggravating Factor.

Use of a prior conviction to support a habitual substance offender finding or to elevate a criminal charge did not preclude a trial court from considering that same conviction as an aggravating factor. As such, the trial court did not abuse its discretion by considering defendant's criminal history as an aggravating factor. Beldon v. State, — N.E.2d —, 2009 Ind. App. LEXIS 833 (2009).

RESEARCH REFERENCES

Res Gestae.

Criminal Justice Notes: OWI causing death—insufficient evidence for enhancement; retrial. 47 (No. 8) Res Gestae 28 (2004).

Criminal Justice Notes 2/06: Habitual substance offender - evidence insufficient; conspiracy as "substance offense", 49 (No. 9) Res Gestae 36 (2006).

35-50-2-11. Use of firearm.

(a) As used in this section, "firearm" has the meaning set forth in IC 35-47-1-5.

(b) As used in this section, "offense" means:

(1) a felony under IC 35-42 that resulted in death or serious bodily injury;

(2) kidnapping; or

(3) criminal confinement as a Class B felony.

(c) The state may seek, on a page separate from the rest of a charging instrument, to have a person who allegedly committed an offense sentenced to an additional fixed term of imprisonment if the state can show beyond a reasonable doubt that the person knowingly or intentionally used a firearm in the commission of the offense.

(d) If the person was convicted of the offense in a jury trial, the jury shall reconvene to hear evidence in the enhancement hearing. If the trial was to the court, or the judgment was entered on a guilty plea, the court alone shall hear evidence in the enhancement hearing.

(e) If the jury (if the hearing is by jury) or the court (if the hearing is to the court alone) finds that the state has proved beyond a reasonable doubt that the person knowingly or intentionally used a firearm in the commission of the offense, the court may sentence the person to an additional fixed term of imprisonment of five (5) years.

History.

P.L.140-1994, § 15; P.L.203-1996, § 9; P.L.71-2005, § 13.

NOTES TO DECISIONS

ANALYSIS

Constitutionality.
Enhancement Improper.
Offenses Subject to Enhancement.
Procedure.

Constitutionality.

The application of the statute under which defendant's sentence was enhanced due to use of a firearm during a robbery did not offend due process. Parker v. State, 754 N.E.2d 614, 2001 Ind. App. LEXIS 1502 (2001).

Enhancement Improper.

Since use of gun elevated the class of a voluntary manslaughter charge, it was improper to enhance defendant's voluntary manslaughter sentence based on use of gun. Bradley v. State, 770 N.E.2d 382, 2002 Ind. App. LEXIS 967 (2002).

Offenses Subject to Enhancement.

Attempted murder was not an offense as defined in the sentencing enhancement statute, so the trial court's enhancement of defendant's sentence for use of firearm in the commission of an attempted murder was reversed. Crawford v. State, 755 N.E.2d 565, 2001 Ind. LEXIS 893 (2001).

Procedure.

It is clear that the legislature intended to require the state to seek an enhancement by first filing its allegation on a separate page of the charging instrument; thus, where the state did not comply with this requirement, the trial court erred by enhancing an otherwise maximum sentence

Procedure. (Cont'd)
imposed on a defendant. Sunday v. State, 720 N.E.2d 716, 1999 Ind. LEXIS 1167 (1999).

Cited:
Allen v. State, 722 N.E.2d 1246, 2000 Ind. App. LEXIS 12 (2000).

RESEARCH REFERENCES

Indiana Law Review.
Recent Developments in Indiana Criminal Law and Procedure, 28 Ind. L. Rev. 819 (1995).
Survey: Criminal Law and Procedure: Recent

Developments in Indiana Criminal Law and Procedure (October 1, 2003, to September 30, 2004), 38 Ind. L. Rev. 999 (2005).

35-50-2-12. Review of characteristics of offenders by Indiana criminal justice institute.

The Indiana criminal justice institute shall review characteristics of offenders committed to the department of correction over such period of time it deems appropriate and of the offenses committed by those offenders in order to ascertain norms used by the trial courts in sentencing. The Indiana criminal justice institute shall from time to time publish its findings in the Indiana Register and provide its findings to the legislative services agency and the judicial conference of Indiana.

History.
P.L.164-1994, § 4.

35-50-2-13. Enhanced sentence for using or possessing a firearm while dealing in a controlled substance.

(a) The state may seek, on a page separate from the rest of a charging instrument, to have a person who allegedly committed an offense of dealing in a controlled substance under IC 35-48-4-1 through IC 35-48-4-4 sentenced to an additional fixed term of imprisonment if the state can show beyond a reasonable doubt that the person knowingly or intentionally:
    (1) used a firearm; or
    (2) possessed a:
      (A) handgun in violation of IC 35-47-2-1;
      (B) sawed-off shotgun in violation of IC 35-47-5-4.1; or
      (C) machine gun in violation of IC 35-47-5-8;
    while committing the offense.

(b) If the person was convicted of the offense in a jury trial, the jury shall reconvene to hear evidence in the enhancement hearing. If the trial was to the court, or the judgment was entered on a guilty plea, the court alone shall hear evidence in the enhancement hearing.

(c) If the jury (if the hearing is by jury) or the court (if the hearing is to the court alone) finds that the state has proved beyond a reasonable doubt that the person knowingly or intentionally committed an offense as described in subsection (a), the court may sentence the person to an additional fixed term of imprisonment of not more than five (5) years, except as follows:
    (1) If the firearm is a sawed-off shotgun, the court may sentence the person to an additional fixed term of imprisonment of not more than ten (10) years.
    (2) If the firearm is a machine gun or is equipped with a firearm silencer or firearm muffler, the court may sentence the person to an additional fixed term of imprisonment of not more than twenty (20) years. The additional sentence under this subdivision is in addition to any additional sentence imposed under section 11 [IC 35-50-2-11] of this chapter for use of a firearm in the commission of an offense.

History.
P.L.148-1995, § 6; P.L.71-2005, § 14.

RESEARCH REFERENCES

Indiana Law Review.
Survey: Criminal Law and Procedure: Recent Developments in Indiana Criminal Law and Procedure (October 1, 2003, to September 30, 2004), 38 Ind. L. Rev. 999 (2005).

35-50-2-14. Repeat sexual offender.

(a) As used in this section, "sex offense" means a felony conviction:
   (1) under IC 35-42-4-1 through IC 35-42-4-9 or under IC 35-46-1-3;
   (2) for an attempt or conspiracy to commit an offense described in subdivision (1); or
   (3) for an offense under the laws of another jurisdiction, including a military court, that is substantially similar to an offense described in subdivision (1).

(b) The state may seek to have a person sentenced as a repeat sexual offender for a sex offense described in subsection (a)(1) or (a)(2) by alleging, on a page separate from the rest of the charging instrument, that the person has accumulated one (1) prior unrelated felony conviction for a sex offense described in subsection (a).

(c) After a person has been convicted and sentenced for a felony described in subsection (a)(1) or (a)(2) after having been sentenced for a prior unrelated sex offense described in subsection (a), the person has accumulated one (1) prior unrelated felony sex offense conviction. However, a conviction does not count for purposes of this subsection, if:
   (1) it has been set aside; or
   (2) it is a conviction for which the person has been pardoned.

(d) If the person was convicted of the sex offense in a jury trial, the jury shall reconvene to hear evidence in the enhancement hearing. If the trial was to the court, or the judgment was entered on a guilty plea, the court alone shall hear evidence in the enhancement hearing.

(e) A person is a repeat sexual offender if the jury (if the hearing is by jury) or the court (if the hearing is to the court alone) finds that the state has proved beyond a reasonable doubt that the person had accumulated one (1) prior unrelated felony sex offense conviction.

(f) The court may sentence a person found to be a repeat sexual offender to an additional fixed term that is the advisory sentence for the underlying offense. However, the additional sentence may not exceed ten (10) years.

History.
P.L.214-1999, § 4; P.L.71-2005, § 15; P.L.6-2006, § 9; P.L.140-2006, § 37; P.L.173-2006, § 37; P.L.125-2009, § 8, eff. July 1, 2009.

Compiler's Notes.
P.L.125-2009, § 10, effective July 1, 2009, provides:
"IC 35-42-4-7 and IC 35-50-2-14, both as amended by this act, apply only to crimes committed after June 30, 2009."

Amendments.
The 2009 amendment added (a); redesignated former (a) through (e) as (b) through (f); in (b), substituted ""described in subsection (a)(1) or (a)(2)"" for ""under IC 35-42-4-1 through IC 35-42-4-9 or IC 35-46-1-3, or for an offense committed in another jurisdiction that is substantially similar to a sex offense under IC 35-42-4-1 through IC 35-42-4-9 or IC 35-46-1-3"" and ""described in subsection (a)"" for ""under IC 35-42-4-1 through IC 35-42-4-9 or IC 35-46-1-3, or for an offense committed in another jurisdiction that is substantially similar to a sex offense under IC 35-42-4-1 through IC 35-42-4-9 or IC 35-46-1-3""; rewrote the first sentence of the introductory language of (c); substituted ""a conviction"" for ""one"" in (c)(2); added ""sex"" in the first sentence of (d); and substituted ""sex offense conviction"" for ""conviction under IC 35-42-4-1 through IC 35-42-4-9 or IC 35-46-1-3, or had accumulated one (1) prior unrelated conviction for an offense committed in another jurisdiction that is substantially similar to a sex offense under IC 35-42-4-1 through IC 35-42-4-9 or IC 35-46-1-3"" in (e).

Cross References.
Penalties for felonies, IC 35-50-1, IC 35-50-2, IC 35-50-5-2.

NOTES TO DECISIONS

Analysis

Constitutionality.
Illegal Sentence.
Sentence.

Constitutionality.

Right to have a jury determine the facts and the law regarding a defendant's repeat sexual offender status exists by virtue of Ind. Const. art. 1, § 19, and therefore, IC 35-50-2-14 is unconstitutional on its face. Smith v. State, 804 N.E.2d 1246, 2004 Ind. App. LEXIS 446 (2004), transfer granted, 812 N.E.2d 808, 2004 Ind. LEXIS 609 (2004), aff'd in part, superseded in part, 825 N.E.2d 783, 2005 Ind. LEXIS 385 (2005).

Ind. Const., art. 1, § 19 does not require jury to determine for sentence enhancement purposes repeat sexual offender status under Indiana Repeat Sexual Offender Statute, IC 35-50-2-14. Smith v. State, 825 N.E.2d 783, 2005 Ind. LEXIS 385 (2005).

Sixth and Fourteenth Amendments do not require jury to determine for sentence enhancement purposes defendant's repeat sexual offender status under Indiana Repeat Sexual Offender Statute, IC 35-50-2-14; Apprendi rule that any fact increasing penalty for crime beyond prescribed statutory maximum must be submitted to jury does not apply to determination of prior convictions. Smith v. State, 825 N.E.2d 783, 2005 Ind. LEXIS 385 (2005).

Illegal Sentence.

Sentence for child molesting and an enhancement based on being a repeat sexual offender was illegal because, after finding defendant to be a repeat sexual offender, the trial court was required to sentence defendant to an additional term of four years for the enhancement, not ten years. Primmer v. State, 857 N.E.2d 11, 2006 Ind. App. LEXIS 2374 (2006).

Defendant's appellate counsel provided ineffective assistance of counsel on direct appeal when appellate counsel failed to argue that: (1) trial counsel erred in eliciting an admission from defendant that defendant was a repeat sex offender; and (2) that defendant's enhanced sentence due to defendant's repeat sex offender status amounted to fundamental error; pursuant to IC 35-50-2-14, defendant's conviction for attempted rape did not qualify for repeat sex offender status and, thus, defendant should have been granted relief on defendant's petition for postconviction relief. Wright v. State, 881 N.E.2d 1018, 2008 Ind. App. LEXIS 373 (2008).

Sentence.

It was permissible for a trial court to consider the same prior offenses for both enhancement of the instant offense and to establish habitual offender status; an aggregate 20-year sentence for sexual misconduct with a minor and being a repeat sex offender was proper under circumstances in which, inter alia, defendant's prior molestation convictions and his conviction for vicarious sexual gratification directly related to his present offense, as they established a long history of sexual misconduct with children. Golden v. State, 862 N.E.2d 1212, 2007 Ind. App. LEXIS 522 (2007).

Defendant did not allege that any of the three Robertson exceptions applied that required a trial court to limit itself to imposing the advisory sentence when imposing a consecutive sentence, and, thus, the appellate court could uphold defendant's two-and-one-half year sentence for domestic battery, as a Class D felony, even though the advisory sentence for Class D felonies was one-and-one-half years; exceptions involved: (1) a consecutive sentence for nonviolent felony convictions arising out of a single episode of criminal conduct, according to IC 35-50-1-2; (2) a consecutive sentence imposed as an additional fixed term to a habitual offender, IC 35-50-2-8; or (3) a consecutive sentence imposed as an additional fixed term to a repeat sexual offender under IC 35-50-2-14, and since defendant could not show any of the exceptions applied, a sentence higher than the advisory sentence could be imposed. Freyn v. State, 884 N.E.2d 901, 2008 Ind. App. LEXIS 791 (2008).

Cited:

State v. Downey, 770 N.E.2d 794, 2002 Ind. LEXIS 542 (2002).

RESEARCH REFERENCES

Indiana Law Review.

Survey: Criminal Law and Procedure: Recent Developments in Indiana Criminal Law and Procedure (October 1, 2003, to September 30, 2004), 38 Ind. L. Rev. 999 (2005).

Survey: Constitutional Law: Indiana Constitutional Developments: Laches, Sentences, and Privacy, 39 Ind. L. Rev. 847 (2006).

Res Gestae.

Criminal Justice Notes 3/04: Repeat offender statute unconstitutional. 47 (No. 9) Res Gestae 37 (2004).

Criminal Justice Notes 4/05- 5/05: Constitutionality of Indiana's repeat sexual offender statute, 49 (No. 1) Res Gestae 40 (2005).

35-50-2-15. Sentencing enhancement for person committing felony offense while a member of, at the direction of, or in affiliation with a criminal gang — Expert testimony permitted.

(a) This section does not apply to an individual who is convicted of a felony offense under IC 35-45-9-3.

(b) The state may seek, on a page separate from the rest of a charging instrument, to have a person who allegedly committed a felony offense sentenced to an additional fixed term of imprisonment if the state can show beyond a reasonable doubt that the person knowingly or intentionally:

(1) was a member of a criminal gang while committing the offense; and

(2) committed the felony offense at the direction of or in affiliation with a criminal gang.

(c) If the person is convicted of the felony offense in a jury trial, the jury shall reconvene to hear evidence in the enhancement hearing. If the trial was to the court, or the judgment was entered on a guilty plea, the court alone shall hear evidence in the enhancement hearing.

(d) If the jury (if the hearing is by jury) or the court (if the hearing is to the court alone) finds that the state has proved beyond a reasonable doubt that the person knowingly or intentionally was a member of a criminal gang while committing the felony offense and committed the felony offense at the direction of or in affiliation with a criminal gang as described in subsection (b), the court shall:

(1) sentence the person to an additional fixed term of imprisonment equal to the sentence imposed for the underlying felony, if the person is sentenced for only one (1) felony; or

(2) sentence the person to an additional fixed term of imprisonment equal to the longest sentence imposed for the underlying felonies, if the person is being sentenced for more than one (1) felony.

(e) A sentence imposed under this section shall run consecutively to the underlying sentence.

(f) A term of imprisonment imposed under this section may not be suspended.

(g) For purposes of subsection (c), evidence that a person was a member of a criminal gang or committed a felony at the direction of or in affiliation with a criminal gang may include expert testimony pursuant to the Indiana Rules of Evidence that may be admitted to prove that particular conduct, status, and customs are indicative of criminal gang activity. The expert testimony may include the following:

(1) Characteristics of persons who are members of criminal gangs.

(2) Descriptions of rivalries between criminal gangs.

(3) Common practices and operations of criminal gangs.

(4) Behavior of criminal gangs.

(5) Terminology used by members of criminal gangs.

(6) Codes of conduct, including criminal conduct, of particular criminal gangs.

(7) Types of crimes that are likely to be committed by a particular criminal gang.

History.
P.L.109-2006, § 3.

35-50-2-16. Sentence enhancement in murder cases for causing termination of human pregnancy.

(a) The state may seek, on a page separate from the rest of the charging instrument, to have a person who allegedly committed or attempted to commit murder under IC 35-42-1-1(1) or IC 35-42-1-1(2) sentenced to an additional fixed term of imprisonment if the state can show beyond a reasonable doubt that the person, while committing or attempting to commit murder under IC 35-42-1-1(1) or IC 35-42-1-1(2), caused the termination of a human pregnancy.

(b) If the person is convicted of the murder or attempted murder in a jury trial, the jury shall reconvene to hear evidence in the enhancement hearing. If the trial was to the court, or the judgment was entered on a guilty plea, the court alone shall hear evidence in the enhancement hearing.

(c) If the jury (if the hearing is by jury) or the court (if the hearing is to the court alone) finds that the state has proved beyond a reasonable doubt that the person, while committing or attempting to commit murder under IC 35-42-1-1(1) or IC 35-42-1-1(2), caused the termination of a human pregnancy, the court shall sentence the person to an additional fixed term of imprisonment of not less than six (6) or more than twenty (20) years.

(d) A sentence imposed under this section runs consecutively to the underlying sentence.

(e) For purposes of this section, prosecution of the murder or attempted murder under IC 35-42-1-1(1) or IC 35-42-1-1(2) and the enhancement of the penalty for that crime does not require proof that:

(1) the person committing or attempting to commit the murder had knowledge or should have had knowledge that the victim was pregnant; or

(2) the defendant intended to cause the termination of a human pregnancy.

History.
P.L.40-2009, § 2, eff. July 1, 2009.

"IC 35-42-1-6, as amended by this act, and IC 35-50-2-16, as added by this act, apply only to a crime committed after June 30, 2009."

Compiler's Notes.
P.L.40-2009, § 3, effective July 1, 2009 provides:

CHAPTER 3

SENTENCES FOR MISDEMEANORS

35-50-3-1. Suspension — Probation.

(a) The court may suspend any part of a sentence for a misdemeanor.

(b) Except as provided in subsection (c), whenever the court suspends in whole or in part a sentence for a Class A, Class B, or Class C misdemeanor, it may place the person on probation under IC 35-38-2 for a fixed period of not more than one (1) year, notwithstanding the maximum term of imprisonment for the misdemeanor set forth in sections 2 through 4 [IC 35-50-3-2 through IC 35-50-3-4] of this chapter. However, the combined term of imprisonment and probation for a misdemeanor may not exceed one (1) year.

(c) Whenever the court suspends a sentence for a misdemeanor, if the court finds that the use or abuse of alcohol, drugs, or harmful substances is a contributing factor or a material element of the offense, the court may place the person on probation under IC 35-38-2 for a fixed period of not more than two (2) years. However, a court may not place a person on probation for a period of more than twelve (12) months in the absence of a report that substantiates the need for a period of probation that is longer than twelve (12) months for the purpose of completing a course of substance abuse treatment. A probation user's fee that exceeds fifty percent (50%) of the maximum probation user's fee allowed under IC 35-38-2-1 may not be required beyond the first twelve (12) months of probation.

History.
IC 35-50-3-1, as added by Acts 1976, P.L.148, § 8; 1977, P.L.340, § 123; P.L.5-1988, § 210;

P.L.135-1993, § 9; P.L.90-2001, § 1; P.L.1-2002, § 152.

NOTES TO DECISIONS

ANALYSIS

Maximum Term of Prison Sentence and Probation.
Revocation of Suspended Sentence.
Term of Probation.

Maximum Term of Prison Sentence and Probation.

In sentencing defendant convicted of a misdemeanor, the prison sentence, assessment of probation, or combination thereof cannot exceed the maximum term for conviction. Smith v. State, 621 N.E.2d 325, 1993 Ind. LEXIS 138 (1993).

Defendant's sentence, that included 365 days of jail time with 351 days suspended and credit for 7 days' time served coupled with 365 days of probation, exceeded the 1-year maximum term for conviction of a misdemeanor under IC 35-50-3-2 and was improper. Beck v. State, 790 N.E.2d 520, 2003 Ind. App. LEXIS 1100 (2003).

Where defendant was convicted of Class A misdemeanor of domestic battery and was sentenced to suspended sentence of 365 days in prison and additional 180 days of probation, combined term of imprisonment and probation exceeded one year in violation of IC 35-50-3-1(b). Copeland v. State, 802 N.E.2d 969, 2004 Ind. App. LEXIS 159 (2004).

IC 35-50-3-1 proscribes imposition of sentence, regardless of composition, in excess of one year; accordingly, sentencing agreement, which imposed 365 days in jail with all but 10 days suspended and with four days credit and which imposed 365 days probation, exceeded, in aggregate, considering incarceration and probation, statutorily prescribed maximum sentence. Collins v. State, 835 N.E.2d 1010, 2005 Ind. App. LEXIS 1941 (2005), clarified, 833 N.E.2d 1106, 2005 Ind. App. LEXIS 1564 (2005).

Since defendant's drunk driving offense involved abuse of alcohol, one-year limit of IC 35-50-3-1 did not apply, and sentence of one year imprisonment and one year of probation was therefore valid.

Datzek v. State, 838 N.E.2d 1149, 2005 Ind. App. LEXIS 2329 (2005).

Revocation of Suspended Sentence.

Where the trial court sentenced defendant on November 28, 1984, to 60 days in the county jail and suspended the sentence subject to his attending an alcohol program and subject to his having no alcohol-related arrests for one year, the court lost its ability to revoke the suspended sentence at the end of January 1985, and had no authority to revoke the suspended sentence on February 4, 1986. Sandy v. State, 501 N.E.2d 486, 1986 Ind. App. LEXIS 3271 (1986).

Term of Probation.

That part of the judgment which placed the defendant on probation beyond the one-year statutory limit was not authorized by law and had to be set aside, even though the defendant agreed to the probation. Hoage v. State, 479 N.E.2d 1362, 1985 Ind. App. LEXIS 2588 (1985), disapproved, Smith v. State, 621 N.E.2d 325, 1993 Ind. LEXIS 138 (1993).

A trial court does not have the authority to "extend" a defendant's term of probation beyond the maximum term of the defendant's sentence or sentences. Slayton v. State, 534 N.E.2d 1130, 1989 Ind. App. LEXIS 156 (1989).

This section permits the trial court to impose a term of probation of up to one year regardless of whether the term exceeds the suspended sentence. Smith v. State, 610 N.E.2d 265, 1993 Ind. App. LEXIS 171 (1993), aff'd in part, 621 N.E.2d 325, 1993 Ind. LEXIS 138 (1993).

Cited:

Rife v. State, 424 N.E.2d 188, 1981 Ind. App. LEXIS 1587 (1981); Wright v. State, 456 N.E.2d 733, 1983 Ind. App. LEXIS 3625 (1983); Johnson v. State, 659 N.E.2d 194, 1995 Ind. App. LEXIS 1627 (1995); Judge v. State, 659 N.E.2d 608, 1995 Ind. App. LEXIS 1630 (1995).

RESEARCH REFERENCES

Indiana Law Review.
Survey: Criminal Law and Procedure: Recent Developments in Indiana Criminal Law and Procedure, 35 Ind. L. Rev. 1347 (2002).

Res Gestae.
Criminal justice notes, 35 Res Gestae 225 (1993).

Collateral References.
Appealability of order suspending imposition or execution of sentence. 51 A.L.R.4th 939.

Propriety, in criminal case, of Federal District Court order restricting defendant's right to re-enter or stay in United States. 94 A.L.R. Fed. 619.

35-50-3-2. Class A misdemeanor.

A person who commits a Class A misdemeanor shall be imprisoned for a fixed term of not more than one (1) year; in addition, he may be fined not more than five thousand dollars ($5,000).

History.
IC 35-50-3-2, as added by Acts 1976, P.L.148, § 8; 1977, P.L.340, § 124.

Cross References.
Compensation for victims of violent crimes, IC 5-2-6.1.

NOTES TO DECISIONS

Charitable Contributions in Lieu of Fine.

Although there is no statutory provision that specifically authorizes a sentencing court to order a criminal defendant to make a charitable contribution in lieu of paying a fine, charitable contribution is an option in some cases. Charitable contribution options may not be proper when a plea agreement requires the defendant to contribute to a county "victim fund" in lieu of paying a fine, which has the practical effect of a "pay-off" in order to receive decisional favor, or when they conflict with penalties imposed by statute. Ratliff v. State, 596 N.E.2d 241, 1992 Ind. App. LEXIS 1117 (1992).

Since the defendants reached the plea agreements with the state in which they agreed to make donations to a charity of their choice, and both asked the court to accept their agreements even if the terms were improper, the defendants cannot complain about any error they invited; they chose the recipient of the donation, so there is no danger of it appearing the court accepted a "pay-off" to benefit a chosen entity. There is no statute that prohibits the charitable contribution option for Class A misdemeanors since imposing fines for Class A misdemeanors is discretionary. Ratliff v. State, 596 N.E.2d 241, 1992 Ind. App. LEXIS 1117 (1992).

Discretion of Court.

Sentencing is a decision within the trial court's discretion and will be reversed only upon a showing of manifest abuse of discretion. Hanic v. State, 406 N.E.2d 335, 1980 Ind. App. LEXIS 1516 (1980).

Sentence of 365 days with 351 suspended and credit for seven days time served was not the maximum punishment of 365 days of jail time that was allowed for misdemeanors and was not an abuse of discretion when imposed upon a first time offender. Beck v. State, 790 N.E.2d 520, 2003 Ind. App. LEXIS 1100 (2003).

Trial court did not abuse its discretion under IC 35-50-3-2 by failing to identify mitigating circumstances when sentencing defendant on five misdemeanor convictions, because IC 35-50-3-2 does not provide a presumptive or advisory sentence, but rather a maximum allowable sentence. Creekmore v. State, 853 N.E.2d 523, 2006 Ind. App. LEXIS 1803 (2006), clarified, 858 N.E.2d 230, 2006 Ind. App. LEXIS 2529 (2006).

Imposition of Fines and Costs.

Defendant's indigency status did not preclude trial court from imposing fine and costs under IC 35-50-3-2 and former IC 33-19-5-1; however, trial court lacked authority to stay execution of judgment imposing fine and costs until after defendant had served his sentence. McRoy v. State, 794 N.E.2d 539, 2003 Ind. App. LEXIS 1600 (2003), clarified, 798 N.E.2d 521, 2003 Ind. App. LEXIS 2108 (2003).

Maximum Term of Prison Sentence and Probation.

In sentencing defendant convicted of a misdemeanor, the prison sentence, assessment of probation, or combination thereof cannot exceed the maximum term for conviction. Smith v. State, 621 N.E.2d 325, 1993 Ind. LEXIS 138 (1993).

Where the defendant had served more than 365 days at the time of his sentencing for two convictions of driving while intoxicated, with only 154 days left to serve on the second of his two one-year sentences, the trial court erred in imposing a full year of probation for the second conviction, and remand was required for determination of a sentencing order that imposed terms of probation and imprisonment not in excess of one year for either of the convictions. Albright v. State, 708 N.E.2d 15, 1999 Ind. App. LEXIS 421 (1999).

Defendant's sentence, that included 365 days of jail time with 351 days suspended and credit for 7 days' time served coupled with 365 days of probation exceeded the 1-year maximum term for conviction of a misdemeanor and was improper. Beck v. State, 790 N.E.2d 520, 2003 Ind. App. LEXIS 1100 (2003).

No-Contact Order.

IC 35-50-3-2, which governed defendant's sentence for criminal recklessness, did not authorize extension of a no-contact order under IC 35-33-8-3.2(a)(4) as part of an executed sentence. Hamed v. State, 852 N.E.2d 619, 2006 Ind. App. LEXIS 1593 (2006).

Restitution.

Trial court was without power to impose restitution as part of sentence. Rife v. State, 424 N.E.2d 188, 1981 Ind. App. LEXIS 1587 (1981), superseded by statute as stated in, Smith v. State, 471 N.E.2d 1245, 1984 Ind. App. LEXIS 3182 (1984).

Sentence.

Defendant's sentence after he pleaded guilty to battery as a class A misdemeanor did not exceed the statutory maximum where the trial court judge ordered him to serve one year and perform 160 hours of community service; the community service was a condition of the trial court's recommendation that defendant serve his time in a work release program and did not constitute an additional sentence. Jester v. State, 746 N.E.2d 437, 2001 Ind. App. LEXIS 704 (2001).

Defendant was properly sentenced to the maximum term after pleading guilty to resisting law enforcement and attempted residential entry, where the trial court deemed defendant's violation

Sentence. (Cont'd)

of a protective order, which was in effect with respect to the person that was the target of defendant's attempted residential entry, a serious aggravating circumstance; further, the sentence was not too harsh because the nature and circumstances of the crimes demonstrated a high level of criminal purposefulness and moral culpability on defendant's part. Cox v. State, 792 N.E.2d 898, 2003 Ind. App. LEXIS 1410 (2003).

—Not Manifestly Unreasonable.

Sentence for prostitution found not manifestly unreasonable. Wright v. State, 456 N.E.2d 733, 1983 Ind. App. LEXIS 3625 (1983).

Cited:

Collins v. State, 275 Ind. 86, 415 N.E.2d 46, 1981 Ind. LEXIS 657 (1981); State v. Pickett, 423 N.E.2d 717, 1981 Ind. App. LEXIS 1538 (1981); Cronk v. State, 443 N.E.2d 882, 1983 Ind. App. LEXIS 2509 (1983); Micinski v. State, 479 N.E.2d 632, 1985

Ind. App. LEXIS 2530 (1985); Hoage v. State, 479 N.E.2d 1362, 1985 Ind. App. LEXIS 2588 (1985); Crandell v. State, 490 N.E.2d 377, 1986 Ind. App. LEXIS 2433 (1986); Summers v. State, 495 N.E.2d 799, 1986 Ind. App. LEXIS 2782 (1986); Burst v. State, 499 N.E.2d 1140, 1986 Ind. App. LEXIS 3217 (1986); Johnson v. State, 659 N.E.2d 194, 1995 Ind. App. LEXIS 1627 (1995); Judge v. State, 659 N.E.2d 608, 1995 Ind. App. LEXIS 1630 (1995); Armstrong v. State, 742 N.E.2d 972, 2001 Ind. App. LEXIS 23 (2001); Ratliff v. State, 741 N.E.2d 424, 2000 Ind. App. LEXIS 2185 (2000); Hollen v. State, 740 N.E.2d 149, 2000 Ind. App. LEXIS 2034 (2000); Haycraft v. State, 760 N.E.2d 203, 2001 Ind. App. LEXIS 2225 (2001); Hollen v. State, 761 N.E.2d 398, 2002 Ind. LEXIS 48 (2002); United States v. Brown, 235 F. Supp. 2d 931, 2002 U.S. Dist. LEXIS 24285 (S.D. Ind. 2002); Lawson v. Hill, 368 F.3d 955, 2004 U.S. App. LEXIS 10158 (7th Cir. Ind. 2004); Goldsberry v. State, 821 N.E.2d 447, 2005 Ind. App. LEXIS 118 (2005); United States v. Hagenow, 423 F.3d 638, 2005 U.S. App. LEXIS 18821 (7th Cir. Ind. 2005).

35-50-3-3. Class B misdemeanor.

A person who commits a Class B misdemeanor shall be imprisoned for a fixed term of not more than one hundred eighty (180) days; in addition, he may be fined not more than one thousand dollars ($1,000).

History.

IC 35-50-3-3, as added by Acts 1976, P.L.148, § 8; 1977, P.L.340, § 125.

NOTES TO DECISIONS

ANALYSIS

Ability to Pay.
Civil Damages.
Sentence Improper.
Sentence Proper.

Ability to Pay.

Order for defendant whose sentence was executed to make restitution to victim of his crime as part of his sentence by the authority of subsection (a) of this section was not subject to requirement of an inquiry into ability to pay as when restitution is ordered under IC 35-38-2-2.3(a)(5). Miller v. State, 648 N.E.2d 1208, 1995 Ind. App. LEXIS 354 (1995).

Although a trial court has the authority to order that one convicted of a felony or misdemeanor make restitution to the victim as part of his sentence or as a condition of probation, when a trial court orders restitution as a condition of probation, the amount of restitution cannot exceed an amount the defendant can or will be able to pay. Savage v. State, 650 N.E.2d 1156, 1995 Ind. App. LEXIS 568 (1995), superseded, 655 N.E.2d 1223, 1995 Ind. LEXIS 144 (1995).

Civil Damages.

Where the punitive damage award of $400,000 in a civil suit was substantially greater than the

$1,000 maximum criminal fine that could have been imposed upon the defendant had he been convicted of the Class B misdemeanor of battery, a new trial as to the punitive damage award was ordered. Fall v. Indiana Univ. Bd. of Trustees, 33 F. Supp. 2d 729, 1998 U.S. Dist. LEXIS 20794 (N.D. Ind. 1998).

Sentence Improper.

A sentence of imprisonment for one year for public intoxication was improper. Morgan v. State, 417 N.E.2d 1154, 1981 Ind. App. LEXIS 1314 (1981).

Sentence Proper.

Trial court did not err in sentencing defendant on his convictions on two counts of being a serious violent felon in possession of a firearm and a count of false informing to 20 years on each possession count, to be served consecutively, and 180 days suspended on the false informing count to be served concurrently to the sentences on the possession counts in a case where he purchased assault weapons that he gave to a known felon who could not possess them, the known felon was involved in a police chase in which the weapons were used to shoot a police officer to death and wound a bystander permanently, and defendant falsely reported that the weapons had been stolen; the sentence was justified in light of the nature of

Sentence Proper. (Cont'd)
the crime and defendant's character. Meadows v. State, 853 N.E.2d 1032, 2006 Ind. App. LEXIS 1888 (2006).

Cited:
State v. Kokomo Tube Co., 426 N.E.2d 1338, 1981 Ind. App. LEXIS 1681 (1981); Cronk v. State,

443 N.E.2d 882, 1983 Ind. App. LEXIS 2509 (1983); Johnson v. State, 648 N.E.2d 666, 1995 Ind. App. LEXIS 304 (1995); Johnson v. State, 659 N.E.2d 194, 1995 Ind. App. LEXIS 1627 (1995); Judge v. State, 659 N.E.2d 608, 1995 Ind. App. LEXIS 1630 (1995); United States v. Hagenow, 423 F.3d 638, 2005 U.S. App. LEXIS 18821 (7th Cir. Ind. 2005).

35-50-3-4. Class C misdemeanor.

A person who commits a Class C misdemeanor shall be imprisoned for a fixed term of not more than sixty (60) days; in addition, he may be fined not more than five hundred dollars ($500).

History.
IC 35-50-3-8, as added by Acts 1978, P.L.2, § 3554.

NOTES TO DECISIONS

Improper Penalty.
Confiscation of defendants' firearms and digging instruments following convictions under former IC 14-2-3-3 for possession of loaded firearms in a state

park and unlawfully cutting and removing ginseng roots in a state park was contrary to law. Vitaniemi v. State, 440 N.E.2d 5, 1982 Ind. App. LEXIS 1401 (1982).

CHAPTER 4

SENTENCES FOR INFRACTIONS

35-50-4-1 — 35-50-4-4. [Repealed.]

Compiler's Notes.
This chapter, concerning sentences for infrac-

tions, was repealed by Acts 1981, P.L.108, § 40. For present similar provisions, see IC 34-28-5.

CHAPTER 5

MISCELLANEOUS PENALTIES

35-50-5-1. [Repealed.]

Compiler's Notes.
This section, concerning penalty for bribery or official misconduct, was repealed by Acts 1980,

P.L.73, § 23. For present similar provisions, see IC 35-50-5-1.1.

35-50-5-1.1. Incapacity to hold public office — Removal from office.

(a) Whenever a person is convicted of a misdemeanor under IC 35-44-1, the court may include in the sentence an order rendering the person incapable of holding a public office of trust or profit for a fixed period of not more than ten (10) years.

(b) If any officer of a governmental entity is convicted of a misdemeanor under IC 35-44-1, the court may enter an order removing the officer from office.

(c) This subsection applies whenever:
  (1) the court enters an order under this section that applies to a person who is an officer of a governmental entity (as defined in IC 35-41-1-12); and
  (2) a vacancy occurs in the office held by the person as the result of the court's order.
The court must file a certified copy of the order with the person who is entitled under IC 5-8-6 to receive notice of the death of an individual holding the office. The person receiving the copy of the order must give notice of the order in the same manner as if the person had received a notice of the death of the officeholder under IC 5-8-6. The person required or permitted to fill the vacancy that results from a removal under this section must comply with IC 3-13 or IC 20, whichever applies, to fill the vacancy.

History.
  IC 35-50-5-1.1, as added by Acts 1980, P.L.73, § 3; P.L.4-1991, § 140; P.L.119-2005, § 35.

NOTES TO DECISIONS

Constitutionality.
  The existence of this section and former IC 3-7-1-15 did not nullify the statutes which allow the county election board to determine whether prospective candidates meet the qualifications to hold office. The statutes are not unconstitutional.

Wilson v. Montgomery County Election Bd., 642 N.E.2d 258, 1994 Ind. App. LEXIS 1498 (1994).

Cited:
  Turner v. City of Evansville, 729 N.E.2d 149, 2000 Ind. App. LEXIS 642 (2000).

35-50-5-2. Fine as alternative penalty for felony or misdemeanor.

In the alternative to the provisions concerning fines in this article, a person may be fined a sum equal to twice his pecuniary gain, or twice the pecuniary loss sustained by victims of the offense he committed.

History.
  IC 35-50-5-2, as added by Acts 1976, P.L.148, § 1; 1977, P.L.340, § 131.

35-50-5-3. Restitution orders.

(a) Except as provided in subsection (i) or (j), in addition to any sentence imposed under this article for a felony or misdemeanor, the court may, as a condition of probation or without placing the person on probation, order the person to make restitution to the victim of the crime, the victim's estate, or the family of a victim who is deceased. The court shall base its restitution order upon a consideration of:
  (1) property damages of the victim incurred as a result of the crime, based on the actual cost of repair (or replacement if repair is inappropriate);
  (2) medical and hospital costs incurred by the victim (before the date of sentencing) as a result of the crime;
  (3) the cost of medical laboratory tests to determine if the crime has caused the victim to contract a disease or other medical condition;
  (4) earnings lost by the victim (before the date of sentencing) as a result of the crime including earnings lost while the victim was hospitalized or participating in the investigation or trial of the crime; and
  (5) funeral, burial, or cremation costs incurred by the family or estate of a homicide victim as a result of the crime.
(b) A restitution order under subsection (a), or (i), or (j) is a judgment lien that:
  (1) attaches to the property of the person subject to the order;
  (2) may be perfected;

(3) may be enforced to satisfy any payment that is delinquent under the restitution order by the person in whose favor the order is issued or the person's assignee; and

(4) expires;

in the same manner as a judgment lien created in a civil proceeding.

(c) When a restitution order is issued under subsection (a), the issuing court may order the person to pay the restitution, or part of the restitution, directly to:

(1) the victim services division of the Indiana criminal justice institute in an amount not exceeding:

(A) the amount of the award, if any, paid to the victim under IC 5-2-6.1; and

(B) the cost of the reimbursements, if any, for emergency services provided to the victim under IC 16-10-1.5 (before its repeal) or IC 16-21-8; or

(2) a probation department that shall forward restitution or part of restitution to:

(A) a victim of a crime;

(B) a victim's estate; or

(C) the family of a victim who is deceased.

The victim services division of the Indiana criminal justice institute shall deposit the restitution it receives under this subsection in the violent crime victims compensation fund established by IC 5-2-6.1-40.

(d) When a restitution order is issued under subsection (a), (i), or (j), the issuing court shall send a certified copy of the order to the clerk of the circuit court in the county where the felony or misdemeanor charge was filed. The restitution order must include the following information:

(1) The name and address of the person that is to receive the restitution.

(2) The amount of restitution the person is to receive.

Upon receiving the order, the clerk shall enter and index the order in the circuit court judgment docket in the manner prescribed by IC 33-32-3-2. The clerk shall also notify the department of insurance of an order of restitution under subsection (i).

(e) An order of restitution under subsection (a), (i), or (j), does not bar a civil action for:

(1) damages that the court did not require the person to pay to the victim under the restitution order but arise from an injury or property damage that is the basis of restitution ordered by the court; and

(2) other damages suffered by the victim.

(f) Regardless of whether restitution is required under subsection (a) as a condition of probation or other sentence, the restitution order is not discharged by the completion of any probationary period or other sentence imposed for a felony or misdemeanor.

(g) A restitution order under subsection (a), (i), or (j), is not discharged by the liquidation of a person's estate by a receiver under IC 32-30-5 (or IC 34-48-1, IC 34-48-4, IC 34-48-5, IC 34-48-6, IC 34-1-12, or IC 34-2-7 before their repeal).

(h) The attorney general may pursue restitution ordered by the court under subsections (a) and (c) on behalf of the victim services division of the Indiana criminal justice institute established under IC 5-2-6-8.

(i) The court may order the person convicted of an offense under IC 35-43-9 to make restitution to the victim of the crime. The court shall base its restitution order upon a consideration of the amount of money that the convicted person converted, misappropriated, or received, or for which the convicted person conspired. The restitution order issued for a violation of IC 35-43-9 must comply with subsections (b), (d), (e), and (g), and is not discharged by the completion of any probationary period or other sentence imposed for a violation of IC 35-43-9.

(j) The court may order the person convicted of an offense under IC 35-43-5-3.5 to make restitution to the victim of the crime, the victim's estate, or the family of a victim who is deceased. The court shall base its restitution order upon a consideration of the amount of fraud or harm caused by the convicted person and any reasonable expenses (including lost wages) incurred by the victim in correcting the victim's credit report and addressing any other issues caused by the commission of the offense under IC 35-43-5-3.5. If, after a person is sentenced for an offense under IC 35-43-5-3.5, a victim, a victim's estate, or the family of a victim discovers or incurs additional expenses that result from the convicted person's commission of the offense under IC 35-43-5-3.5, the court may issue one (1) or more restitution orders to require the convicted person to make restitution, even if the court issued a restitution order at the time of sentencing. For purposes of entering a restitution order after sentencing, a court has continuing jurisdiction over a person convicted of an offense under IC 35-43-5-3.5 for five (5) years after the date of sentencing. Each restitution order issued for a violation of IC 35-43-5-3.5 must comply with subsections (b), (d), (e), and (g), and is not discharged by the completion of any probationary period or other sentence imposed for an offense under IC 35-43-5-3.5.

(k) The court shall order a person convicted of an offense under IC 35-42-3.5 to make restitution to the victim of the crime in an amount equal to the greater of the following:

(1) The gross income or value to the person of the victim's labor or services.

(2) The value of the victim's labor as guaranteed under the minimum wage and overtime provisions of:

(A) the federal Fair Labor Standards Act of 1938, as amended (29 U.S.C. 201-209); or

(B) IC 22-2-2 (Minimum Wage);

whichever is greater.

History.

IC 35-50-5-3, as added by P.L.337-1988, § 1; P.L.149-1988, § 6; P.L.240-1991(ss), § 99; P.L.2-1992, § 885; P.L.2-1993, § 194; P.L.47-1993, § 13; P.L.4-1994, § 21; P.L.300-1995, § 3; P.L.307-1995, § 1; P.L.1-1998, § 200; P.L.2-2002, § 105; P.L.88-2002, § 3; P.L.85-2004, § 54; P.L.98-2004, § 157; P.L.2-2005, § 129; P.L.125-2006, § 11; P.L.173-2006, § 54.

NOTES TO DECISIONS

Applicability of Section.

This section allows the trial court to order restitution, but where this was not law at the time of the offense (1980), the trial court erred in imposing restitution. Whitehead v. State, 511 N.E.2d 284, 1987 Ind. LEXIS 986, 71 A.L.R.4th 173 (1987), cert. denied, 484 U.S. 1031, 108 S. Ct. 761, 98 L. Ed. 2d 773, 1988 U.S. LEXIS 420 (1988).

Where the defendant was not convicted of reckless homicide, but rather of failing to stop at the scene of an accident, the deceased was not a victim of a crime as contemplated by this section and no funeral, burial, or cremation costs were incurred by the victim's estate because of the actions of the defendant. Utley v. State, 699 N.E.2d 723, 1998 Ind. App. LEXIS 1581 (1998).

Authority of Court.

A trial court has the authority to order a defendant to make restitution to the victim of a crime as a part of his sentence. McGuire v. State, 625 N.E.2d 1281, 1993 Ind. App. LEXIS 1515 (1993).

A trial court has the authority to order that one convicted of a crime make restitution to the victim as part of his sentence. Kotsopoulos v. State, 654 N.E.2d 44, 1995 Ind. App. LEXIS 968 (1995).

Authority of Court. (Cont'd)

Trial court's order, that a defendant who was convicted of criminal recklessness pay the air fare of the owner of a home which was damaged as a result of the crime, was not authorized by IC 35-50-5-3. Springer v. State, 779 N.E.2d 555, 2002 Ind. App. LEXIS 2006 (2002), transfer granted, 792 N.E.2d 39, 2003 Ind. LEXIS 171 (2003), aff'd in part, rev'd in part, 798 N.E.2d 431, 2003 Ind. LEXIS 944 (Ind. 2003).

Restitution order was improper because victim's execution of release in prior civil action prevented trial court from imposing restitution as condition of defendant's probation in subsequent criminal action. Haltom v. State, 808 N.E.2d 761, 2004 Ind. App. LEXIS 939 (2004), transfer granted, 822 N.E.2d 977, 2004 Ind. LEXIS 858 (2004), superseded, 832 N.E.2d 969, 2005 Ind. LEXIS 704 (2005), overruled, Myers v. State, 848 N.E.2d 1108, 2006 Ind. App. LEXIS 1102 (2006).

Trial court did not err in ordering defendant to pay restitution to victim of traffic accident arising out of defendant's alcohol-related driving offense despite fact that defendant's insurance company paid victim $100,000 and victim had in exchange signed release. Haltom v. State, 832 N.E.2d 969, 2005 Ind. LEXIS 704 (2005).

Defendant's sentence that included an order of restitution under IC 35-50-5-3 and to register as a sex offender under IC 5-2-12-5(a)(1) for convictions of child molestation under IC 35-42-4-3(a), (b) for having sex with and touching the breasts of a 13-year-old victim were proper when the scope of the framers' conception of U.S. Const., Amend. 6 did not embrace restitution orders; thus Blakely did not require a jury trial on the restitution order, and the same logic applied to the sex offender registry. Prickett v. State, 856 N.E.2d 1203, 2006 Ind. LEXIS 1027 (2006).

Trial court committed fundamental error when it entered a restitution order in defendant's case that contained no set amount, that specifically required unknown future expenses, that had no end date, and was not based on any evidence; order violated IC 35-50-5-3(a) and was an improper sentence, which meant that further proceedings were required to fashion a proper restitution order. Bennett v. State, 862 N.E.2d 1281, 2007 Ind. App. LEXIS 530 (2007).

Discretion of Court.

This section does not impose any burden relating to restitution upon the state; rather the trial court is vested with discretion to impose restitution as a condition of probation and to determine the terms thereof. Winter v. State, 587 N.E.2d 691, 1992 Ind. App. LEXIS 267 (1992).

There is no rational way to measure whether a restitution order and an eight-year sentence for battery is "more severe" than a previously imposed 10-year sentence for aggravated battery, and the trial court was within its discretion when it imposed such a sentence. Ault v. State, 705 N.E.2d 1078, 1999 Ind. App. LEXIS 168 (1999).

Enforcement.

Restitution order is a judgment lien that at-

taches to property of the subject person, and may be enforced in the same manner as a judgment lien created in a civil proceeding. Wininger v. Purdue Univ., 666 N.E.2d 455, 1996 Ind. App. LEXIS 773 (1996).

Restitution statute does not limit the property subject to the lien to real property, but rather gives a crime victim the right to enforce the lien by means of attachment of personal property or garnishment of wages. Wininger v. Purdue Univ., 666 N.E.2d 455, 1996 Ind. App. LEXIS 773 (1996).

Evidence.

Where the defendant failed to object to the submission of a ledger, the issue was waived on appeal, even though a restitution order based solely on that ledger would have been invalid because the ledger was shown to be inaccurate. Kellett v. State, 716 N.E.2d 975, 1999 Ind. App. LEXIS 1700 (1999).

Executed Sentence.

Restitution imposed upon a defendant with an executed sentence does not require an inquiry into the defendant's ability to pay by the trial court. Bitner v. State, 546 N.E.2d 117, 1989 Ind. App. LEXIS 1124 (1989).

Where restitution is ordered as part of an executed sentence, an inquiry into the defendant's ability to pay is not required, since restitution in such circumstances is merely a money judgment, and a defendant cannot be imprisoned for nonpayment. Ladd v. State, 710 N.E.2d 188, 1999 Ind. App. LEXIS 425 (1999).

Imprisonment.

Trial court erred when it threatened to imprison defendant if he failed to pay restitution to the victim of his crime, since it is well-established that an individual cannot be imprisoned for failing to pay a money judgment. Bitner v. State, 546 N.E.2d 117, 1989 Ind. App. LEXIS 1124 (1989).

Information to Jury.

Prosecutor who informed the jury that the responsibility for sentencing rested with the judge did not misrepresent the law or improperly condition the jury at defendant's trial for murder. Burris v. State, 558 N.E.2d 1067, 1990 Ind. LEXIS 170 (1990).

Payment to Third Party.

The restitution statute contemplates "medical costs incurred by the victim," and does not require that the victim directly receive the payment covering the cost of his care. Ault v. State, 705 N.E.2d 1078, 1999 Ind. App. LEXIS 168 (1999).

When defendant was sentenced for the Class C felony of battery, it was not error to order defendant to pay restitution to the hospital which provided defendant's victim with treatment for the injuries defendant caused because, under IC 35-50-5-3(a), the hospital could be considered a victim, for restitution purposes, as there was no evidence the victim had paid the hospital, and, to the extent he had, the hospital could reimburse

Payment to Third Party. (Cont'd)
him that amount. Mata v. State, 866 N.E.2d 346, 2007 Ind. App. LEXIS 1014 (2007).

Plea Agreements.
Strict adherence to plea agreement is essential, and trial court is precluded from imposing any sentence in addition to those agreed upon, including ordering restitution or reparation. Sinn v. State, 693 N.E.2d 78, 1998 Ind. App. LEXIS 331 (1998).

The trial court erred in granting the mother of a victim restitution for lost wages under IC 35-50-5-3 in defendant's prosecution for child molestation, because defendant's plea agreement did not specify restitution, and the trial court in essence increased the penalty by imposing a reparation condition after the plea agreement was accepted. Huddleston v. State, 756 N.E.2d 1054, 2001 Ind. App. LEXIS 1814 (2001), vacated, 764 N.E.2d 655, 2002 Ind. App. LEXIS 237 (Ind. Ct. App. 2002).

Restitution.
It was error for the trial court to render a conditional restitution order for prospective counseling expense, if any, for the victim; however, because defendant failed to object to the trial court's restitution order at sentencing, he waived review of this claim of error. Mitchell v. State, 730 N.E.2d 197, 2000 Ind. App. LEXIS 862 (2000).

Improper restitution order was fundamental error reviewable by appellate court even though defendant waived challenge to order by failing to object at earliest opportunity during sentencing hearing; order that defendant pay for any counseling costs that child-victim incurred as result of crime violated IC 35-50-5-3(a)(2) by failing to restrict counseling costs to those actually incurred as of date of sentencing. Ware v. State, 816 N.E.2d 1167, 2004 Ind. App. LEXIS 2182 (2004).

Because the appellate court was unable to determine whether the restitution provision was improper and resulted in fundamental error where the trial court ordered defendant to pay for 10-year-old victim's counseling, it remanded that portion of defendant's sentence to the trial court for clarification. Johnson v. State, 845 N.E.2d 147, 2006 Ind. App. LEXIS 598 (2006).

—Ability to Pay.
Defendant's challenge to a restitution error, which claimed that there was no inquiry made as to whether he had the ability to pay a restitution amount during a one year probationary period, failed because implicit in defendant's argument was the assumption that his obligation to make restitution terminated upon the end of his probationary term; expiration of defendant's probationary term did not terminate his obligation to pay restitution under IC 35-50-5-3(f). Pearson v. State, 883 N.E.2d 770, 2008 Ind. LEXIS 256 (2008).

—Amount.
The trial court erred in ordering restitution in an amount to be determined by the probation department. McGuire v. State, 625 N.E.2d 1281, 1993 Ind. App. LEXIS 1515 (1993).

Restitution must reflect actual loss incurred by a victim. Kotsopoulos v. State, 654 N.E.2d 44, 1995 Ind. App. LEXIS 968 (1995).

Defendant's sentence following his guilty plea for arson was not excessive, where he was ordered to pay $700,000 in restitution, based upon evidence at sentencing hearing that two to three million dollars would be needed to rebuild business damaged by defendant. Collins v. State, 676 N.E.2d 741, 1996 Ind. App. LEXIS 1735 (1996).

Because the amount printed on the face of the food stamps is competent evidence relating to their value, the trial court did not err by ordering defendant to pay the total face value of the stolen food stamps in restitution. Balls v. State, 725 N.E.2d 450, 2000 Ind. App. LEXIS 315 (2000).

While the trial court had the discretion to set the amount of restitution, it was constrained by principles of equal protection and fundamental fairness to set an amount within the juvenile's ability to pay because restitution was made a condition of probation; thus, the matter had to be remanded for the trial court to determine whether the juvenile had the ability to pay. M.L. v. State, 838 N.E.2d 525, 2005 Ind. App. LEXIS 2273 (2005).

Because the trial court ordered defendant to pay all of the money to the victim, who the court noted could be liable for subrogation of claims by his various insurers, an order to pay restitution greater than $24,458 to the victim personally constituted duplicated recovery as the remainder of victim's medical expenses were covered by insurance. Little v. State, 839 N.E.2d 807, 2005 Ind. App. LEXIS 2447 (2005).

Trial court properly ordered defendant to pay restitution, under IC 35-50-5-3, to his uncle's estate after defendant pleaded guilty to perjury regarding his disposition of estate funds. However, the order was remanded for the award to be offset by the amount that the estate recouped from defendant in a civil judgment regarding the matter. Myers v. State, 848 N.E.2d 1108, 2006 Ind. App. LEXIS 1102 (2006).

Restitution order was supported by evidence that the used product that buyer received was worth less than the new product defendant had agreed to send. Long v. State, 867 N.E.2d 606, 2007 Ind. App. LEXIS 1202 (2007).

There was no abuse of discretion in a trial court's imposition of an order of restitution on defendant pursuant to IC 35-50-5-3(a)(4) upon defendant's entry of guilty pleas to felony auto theft and misdemeanor criminal recklessness since estimated loss of rentals for the period that the rental vehicle was stolen was a fair measure of damages for restitution purposes; there was testimony regarding the amount of days that the vehicle was stolen, the average amount of days per week that the vehicle could have been rented, and the daily rental rate for the vehicle, from which the restitution award was calculated. Wittl v. State, 876 N.E.2d 1136, 2007 Ind. App. LEXIS 2675 (2007).

—Burial Expenses.
Survivors of murder victim may recover expenses for funeral and burial expenses resulting from defendant's acts, and it is not an abuse of

Restitution. (Cont'd)

—Burial Expenses. (Cont'd)
discretion for court to round expenses to nearest dollar or to include estimated amount for monument not yet erected. Roach v. State, 695 N.E.2d 934, 1998 Ind. LEXIS 79 (1998).

Since, prior to the amendment of this statute, restitution for funeral and burial expenses was not included within the plain and ordinary meaning of the statute, the trial court did not have the authority to order payment of these expenses. Roach v. State, 711 N.E.2d 1237, 1999 Ind. LEXIS 343 (1999).

When defendant was convicted of battery resulting in serious bodily injury, as a result of which the victim died, it was proper for the trial court to require defendant, as part of his sentence, to pay the victim's family the victim's funeral expenses. Martin v. State, 784 N.E.2d 997, 2003 Ind. App. LEXIS 363 (2003), overruled in part, Rutherford v. State, 866 N.E.2d 867, 2007 Ind. App. LEXIS 1086 (2007), overruled in part, Stewart v. State, 866 N.E.2d 858, 2007 Ind. App. LEXIS 1085 (2007).

—Child Support.
Although the trial court was vested with the authority to order defendant to make restitution to the victim's dependent children in care of the victim's ex-wife for the loss of child support, the trial court exceeded its authority when it ordered defendant to make restitution for the future loss of child support because subsection (a)(3) limits restitution to earnings lost before the date of sentencing. Creager v. State, 737 N.E.2d 771, 2000 Ind. App. LEXIS 1649 (2000).

—Cost of Litigation.
Where defense counsel specifically stated at the sentencing hearing, at which rules of evidence are relaxed for the purposes of sentencing, that he did not object to the admission of the deputy prosecuting attorney's affidavit as evidence of the costs of law enforcement and litigation, there was sufficient evidence to support the trial court's restitution order. Ladd v. State, 710 N.E.2d 188, 1999 Ind. App. LEXIS 425 (1999).

—Future Expenses.
The portion of the defendant's probation requiring him to pay for any counseling expenses his victims might incur was reversed, since the trial court, in formulating a restitution order, may consider only those expenses incurred by the victim prior to the date of sentencing, and in the instant case the victims had received no counseling. Carswell v. State, 721 N.E.2d 1255, 1999 Ind. App. LEXIS 2206 (1999).

—Improper.
Where defendant pled guilty to conspiracy to commit arson with intent to defraud, the trial court erred in ordering her to pay restitution to her insurer for the cost of its arson investigation. While the insurer incurred significant investigative expenses, there was no evidence it lost any revenue or income as required by IC 35-50-5-3. Henderson v. State, 848 N.E.2d 341, 2006 Ind. App. LEXIS 1003 (2006).

Trial court's restitution order was remanded where the defendant was erroneously ordered to pay restitution for damages incurred in a second burglary for which he was never accused. James v. State, 868 N.E.2d 543, 2007 Ind. App. LEXIS 1308 (2007).

Order of restitution in the form of counseling and any necessary help for the families for the victims of defendant's sexual molestation crimes was improper because restitution was authorized only for expenses incurred by victims before the date of sentencing; however, defendant was ordered to pay undetermined future expenses. Kline v. State, 875 N.E.2d 435, 2007 Ind. App. LEXIS 2377 (2007).

Trial court committed fundamental error in ordering defendant to pay restitution to a county's general fund as a condition of probation because there was no evidence that the state raised the issue; the state did not assert that the county was a victim entitled to restitution under IC 35-50-5-3, it made no offer to prove, presented no evidence, did not argue that defendant should be required to pay the county restitution as a condition of probation, and presented no evidence regarding the county's actual damages. Lohmiller v. State, 884 N.E.2d 903, 2008 Ind. App. LEXIS 792 (2008).

Pursuant to IC 1-1-4-1(1), a court only had the authority supplied by the plain language of a statute; since the plain language of the restitution statute, IC 35-50-5-3(a), only allowed for repair or replacement of property damaged in a crime, the trial court erred in directing defendant in a burglary case to reimburse the victims for the cost of installing and maintaining a home security system after the crime occurred because that was not property that was damaged in a crime. Rich v. State, 890 N.E.2d 44, 2008 Ind. App. LEXIS 1512 (2008).

—Lost Wages.
The trial court erred in granting the mother of a victim restitution for lost wages under IC 35-50-5-3 in defendant's prosecution for child molestation, because the mother failed to provided adequate proof of her claims. Huddleston v. State, 756 N.E.2d 1054, 2001 Ind. App. LEXIS 1814 (2001), vacated, 764 N.E.2d 655, 2002 Ind. App. LEXIS 237 (Ind. Ct. App. 2002).

Where defendant committed battery on her child, trial court improperly ordered her to pay restitution under IC 35-50-5-3(a) to child's father and stepmother since there was no evidence indicating that father's lost wages had anything to do with battery and there was no evidence that stepmother missed work as result of battery. Cooper v. State, 831 N.E.2d 1247, 2005 Ind. App. LEXIS 1422 (2005).

—Medical Expenses.
Only those medical expenses incurred by the victim before the date of sentencing may be included as restitution. Kotsopoulos v. State, 654 N.E.2d 44, 1995 Ind. App. LEXIS 968 (1995).

Only actual costs incurred by the victim before the date of sentencing may be considered for pur-

Restitution. (Cont'd)

—Medical Expenses. (Cont'd)
poses of a restitution order. Ault v. State, 705
N.E.2d 1078, 1999 Ind. App. LEXIS 168 (1999).

Where there was testimony that the parents of a
15-year-old victim of sexual misconduct, who received inpatient and outpatient psychiatric services, were responsible for $5,935.47 of the costs,
and defendant agreed that his bond could go towards restitution, the restitution order was proper
as there was sufficient evidence. Blixt v. State, 872
N.E.2d 149, 2007 Ind. App. LEXIS 1910 (2007).

—Ordered After Sentence Pronounced.
Trial court could have entered restitution order
when it originally sentenced defendant for theft
but the court could not enhance the sentence by
entering a restitution order after sentence was
pronounced. Wilson v. State, 688 N.E.2d 1293,
1997 Ind. App. LEXIS 1753 (1997).

—Reimposition as Condition of Probation.
Upon remand for a hearing on the propriety of a
prior restitution order, the trial court was not
precluded by principles of double jeopardy from
again imposing restitution as a condition of probation if it followed the appropriate procedures and
the order was supported by sufficient evidence.
Winter v. State, 587 N.E.2d 691, 1992 Ind. App.
LEXIS 267 (1992).

—Statute of Limitations.
Civil statute of limitations of IC 34-11-2-10 did
not apply to a criminal restitution case under IC
35-46-1-5, because criminal restitution under IC
35-50-5-3 was a portion of a sentence, and because
the criminal restitution statute did not incorporate
the civil statute of limitations, it did not apply.
McKenney v. State, 848 N.E.2d 1127, 2006 Ind.
App. LEXIS 1113 (2006).

—"Victim" Defined.
One who suffers harm as a result of criminal
wrongdoing, even if not the party directly against
whom the crime was committed, may appropriately be considered a "victim" for the purposes of
restitution. Reinbold v. State, 555 N.E.2d 463,
1990 Ind. LEXIS 126 (1990), overruled, Wright v.
State, 658 N.E.2d 563, 1995 Ind. LEXIS 162
(1995).

A state entity may be considered a "victim"
under the restitution statute, and drug task force
which lost money used by confidential informant to
execute drug purchases from defendant was entitled to restitution from defendant under this
section. Hendrickson v. State, 690 N.E.2d 765,
1998 Ind. App. LEXIS 32 (1998).

A state entity may be considered a "victim" for
purposes of restitution for property damages. Kopas v. State, 699 N.E.2d 1193, 1998 Ind. App.
LEXIS 1632 (1998).

Where there was no evidence that the Newton

County Prosecuting Attorney Council (NCPAC)
was damaged in any way by the defendant's operation of a vehicle under the influence of alcohol,
payment of costs to NCPAC under the restitution
statute was improper. Kopas v. State, 699 N.E.2d
1193, 1998 Ind. App. LEXIS 1632 (1998).

The state may be found to be a victim for
purposes of the restitution statute where Medicaid
has covered the medical expenses of a crime victim. Ault v. State, 705 N.E.2d 1078, 1999 Ind. App.
LEXIS 168 (1999).

IC 35-50-5-3(a) simply lists the considerations a
trial court must make in fashioning a restitution
order and does not limit a trial court's authority to
require a defendant to pay a victim's funeral
expenses to cases involving convictions for homicides, but, rather, restitution is properly ordered
payable to those shown to have suffered injury,
harm or loss as a direct and immediate result of
the criminal acts of defendant. Martin v. State, 784
N.E.2d 997, 2003 Ind. App. LEXIS 363 (2003),
overruled in part, Rutherford v. State, 866 N.E.2d
867, 2007 Ind. App. LEXIS 1086 (2007), overruled
in part, Stewart v. State, 866 N.E.2d 858, 2007 Ind.
App. LEXIS 1085 (2007).

Where defendant pled guilty to criminal confinement, fact that state was required to conduct
forensic examination as result of defendant's crime
did not make state "victim" entitled to restitution
under IC 35-50-5-3. Green v. State, 811 N.E.2d
874, 2004 Ind. App. LEXIS 1372 (2004).

Specifying Victim.
Trial court erred in ordering defendant to pay
restitution, where it could not be determined who
was the "victim" of his crime of possession of
marijuana, in view of the trial court's order, which
did not specify to whom he was to pay the restitution. Rumple v. State, 529 N.E.2d 861, 1988 Ind.
App. LEXIS 803 (1988).

Restitution has properly been ordered payable to
those shown to have suffered injury, harm or loss
as a direct and immediate result of the criminal
acts of a defendant. The survivors of murder victims, particularly their dependent children, could
certainly come within this class. Reinbold v. State,
555 N.E.2d 463, 1990 Ind. LEXIS 126 (1990),
overruled, Wright v. State, 658 N.E.2d 563, 1995
Ind. LEXIS 162 (1995).

Possession of marijuana is a victimless crime,
absent evidence to the contrary, and a restitution
order for payment to a "weed eradication fund"
would therefore be improper. Brock v. State, 558
N.E.2d 872, 1990 Ind. App. LEXIS 1086 (1990).

Cited:
Bailey v. State, 717 N.E.2d 1, 1999 Ind. LEXIS
828 (1999); Shane v. State, 769 N.E.2d 1195, 2002
Ind. App. LEXIS 955 (2002); Cherry v. State, 772
N.E.2d 433, 2002 Ind. App. LEXIS 1103 (2002);
Davis v. State, 772 N.E.2d 535, 2002 Ind. App.
LEXIS 1211 (2002).

RESEARCH REFERENCES

Notre Dame Law Review.
Where Offenders Pay For Their Crimes: Victim

Restitution and Its Constitutionality, 59 Notre
Dame L. Rev. 685 (1984).

Res Gestae.

Criminal Justice Notes 11/04: Erroneous restitution orders, 48 (No. 7) Res Gestae 41 (2005).

Criminal Justice Notes 7/08: Restitution - cost of victim's security system, 52 (No. 3) Res Gestae 35 (2008).

Collateral References.

Jurisdiction or power of juvenile court to order parent of juvenile to make restitution for juvenile's offense. 66 A.L.R.4th 985.

Measure and elements of restitution to which victim is entitled under state criminal statute. 15 A.L.R.5th 391.

Persons or entities entitled to restitution as "victim" under state criminal restitution statute. 92 A.L.R.5th 35.

35-50-5-4. Reimbursement plan.

(a) This section applies only:

(1) if the county in which a criminal proceeding was filed adopts an ordinance under IC 36-2-13-15; and

(2) to a person who is sentenced under this article for a felony or a misdemeanor.

(b) At the time the court imposes a sentence, the court may order the person to execute a reimbursement plan as directed by the court and make repayments under the plan to the county for the costs described in IC 36-2-13-15.

(c) The court shall fix an amount under this section that:

(1) may not exceed an amount the person can or will be able to pay;

(2) does not harm the person's ability to reasonably be self-supporting or to reasonably support any dependent of the person; and

(3) takes into consideration and gives priority to any other restitution, reparation, repayment, costs, fine, or child support obligations the person is required to pay.

(d) When an order is issued under this section, the issuing court shall send a certified copy of the order to the clerk of the circuit court in the county where the felony or misdemeanor charge was filed. Upon receiving the order, the clerk shall enter and index the order in the circuit court judgment docket in the manner prescribed by IC 33-32-3-2.

(e) An order under this section is not discharged:

(1) by the completion of a sentence imposed for a felony or misdemeanor; or

(2) by the liquidation of a person's estate by a receiver under IC 32-30-5 (or IC 34-48-1, IC 34-48-4, IC 34-48-5, and IC 34-48-6 before their repeal).

History.

P.L.123-1998, § 1; P.L.1-1999, § 79; P.L.2-2002, § 106; P.L.98-2004, § 158.

NOTES TO DECISIONS

Cited:

Everroad v. State, 730 N.E.2d 222, 2000 Ind. App. LEXIS 899 (2000).

RESEARCH REFERENCES

Indiana Law Review.

Survey: Criminal Law and Procedure: Recent Developments in Indiana, 32 Ind. L. Rev. 789 (1999).

CHAPTER 5A

COMMITMENT OF CONVICTED PERSON

35-50-5A-1 — 35-50-5A-4. [Repealed.]

Compiler's Notes.

This chapter, which was enacted as IC 35-4.1-5 and transferred to this position by the compiler, and concerned the commitment of convicted persons, was repealed by P.L.311-1983, § 49. For present similar provisions, see IC 35-38-3.

CHAPTER 6

RELEASE FROM IMPRISONMENT — GOOD TIME

35-50-6-1. Parole.

(a) Except as provided in subsection (d) or (e), when a person imprisoned for a felony completes the person's fixed term of imprisonment, less the credit time the person has earned with respect to that term, the person shall be:

(1) released on parole for not more than twenty-four (24) months, as determined by the parole board;

(2) discharged upon a finding by the committing court that the person was assigned to a community transition program and may be discharged without the requirement of parole; or

(3) released to the committing court if the sentence included a period of probation.

(b) This subsection does not apply to a person described in subsection (d), (e), or (f). A person released on parole remains on parole from the date of release until the person's fixed term expires, unless the person's parole is revoked or the person is discharged from that term by the parole board. In any event, if the person's parole is not revoked, the parole board shall discharge the person after the period set under subsection (a) or the expiration of the person's fixed term, whichever is shorter.

(c) A person whose parole is revoked shall be imprisoned for all or part of the remainder of the person's fixed term. However, the person shall again be released on parole when the person completes that remainder, less the credit time the person has earned since the revocation. The parole board may reinstate the person on parole at any time after the revocation.

(d) This subsection does not apply to a person who is a sexually violent predator under IC 35-38-1-7.5. When a sex offender (as defined in IC 11-8-8-4.5) completes the sex offender's fixed term of imprisonment, less credit time earned with respect to that term, the sex offender shall be placed on parole for not more than ten (10) years.

(e) This subsection applies to a person who:

(1) is a sexually violent predator under IC 35-38-1-7.5;

(2) has been convicted of murder (IC 35-42-1-1); or

(3) has been convicted of voluntary manslaughter (IC 35-42-1-3).

When a person described in this subsection completes the person's fixed term of imprisonment, less credit time earned with respect to that term, the person shall be placed on parole for the remainder of the person's life.

(f) This subsection applies to a parolee in another jurisdiction who is a person described in subsection (e) and whose parole supervision is transferred to Indiana from another jurisdiction. In accordance with IC 11-13-4-1(2) (Interstate Compact for Out-of-State Probationers and Parolees) and rules adopted under Article VII (d)(8) of the Interstate Compact for Adult Offender Supervision (IC 11-13-4.5), a parolee who is a person described in subsection (e) and whose parole supervision is transferred to Indiana is subject to the same conditions of parole as a person described in subsection (e) who was convicted in Indiana, including:

(1) lifetime parole (as described in subsection (e)); and

(2) the requirement that the person wear a monitoring device (as described in IC 35-38-2.5-3) that can transmit information twenty-four (24) hours each day regarding a person's precise location, if applicable.

(g) If a person being supervised on lifetime parole as described in subsection (e) is also required to be supervised by a court, a probation department, a community corrections program, a community transition program, or another similar program upon the person's release from imprisonment, the parole board may:

(1) supervise the person while the person is being supervised by the other supervising agency; or

(2) permit the other supervising agency to exercise all or part of the parole board's supervisory responsibility during the period in which the other supervising agency is required to supervise the person, if supervision by the other supervising agency will be, in the opinion of the parole board:

(A) at least as stringent; and

(B) at least as effective;

as supervision by the parole board.

(h) The parole board is not required to supervise a person on lifetime parole during any period in which the person is imprisoned. However, upon the person's release from imprisonment, the parole board shall recommence its supervision of a person on lifetime parole.

(i) If a court orders the parole board to place a sexually violent predator whose sentence does not include a commitment to the department of correction on lifetime parole under IC 35-38-1-29, the parole board shall place the sexually violent predator on lifetime parole and supervise the person in the same manner in which the parole board supervises a sexually violent predator on lifetime parole whose sentence includes a commitment to the department of correction.

History.

IC 35-50-6-1, as added by Acts 1976, P.L.148, § 8; 1977, P.L.340, § 132; 1979, P.L.120, § 11; 1981, P.L.298, § 7; P.L.240-1991(ss), § 100; P.L.11-1994, § 18; P.L.273-1999, § 215; P.L.90-2000, § 20; P.L.238-2001, § 22; P.L.116-2002, § 26; P.L.139-2006, § 6; P.L.140-2006, § 38; P.L.173-2006, § 38; P.L.1-2007, § 237, emergency eff. March 30, 2007; P.L.216-2007, § 51, emergency eff. July 1, 2007.

Compiler's Notes.

P.L.139-2006, § 10, effective July 1, 2006, provides:

"(a) The department of correction shall report to the legislative council before November 1 of each year concerning the department's implementation of lifetime parole and GPS monitoring for sex offenders. The report must include information relating to:

"(1) the expense of lifetime parole and GPS monitoring;

"(2) recidivism; and

"(3) any proposal to make the program of lifetime parole and GPS monitoring less expensive or more effective, or both.

"(b) The report described in subsection (a) must be in an electronic format under IC 5-14-6.

"(c) This SECTION expires November 2, 2010."

P.L.216-2007, § 57, effective July 1, 2007, provides:

"IC 35-38-1-29, as added by this act, and IC 11-8-8-17, IC 11-8-8-18, IC 35-42-4-3, IC 35-42-4-6, IC 35-42-4-9, IC 35-42-4-10, IC 35-42-4-11, IC 35-44-3-13, IC 35-50-6-1(e), and IC 35-50-6-1(i), all as amended by this act, apply only to offenses committed after June 30, 2007."

NOTES TO DECISIONS

ANALYSIS

In General.
Constitutionality.
Applicability of Former Law.
Construction.

Determinate Sentence.
Disproportionate Sentences Caused by Diminution.
Due Process.
Effect of Parole.

Effect of Plea Bargain Agreement.
Eligibility for Parole.
—Discharge of Sentence.
Good Time Credits.
Life Sentence.
Purpose.
Recommendations by Court.
Retroactivity.
Suspended Sentence.

In General.

Under former IC 11-7-6-2, the good-time law in effect at the time an offense was committed entered into the judgment as if written therein. Dowd v. Sims, 229 Ind. 54, 95 N.E.2d 628, 1950 Ind. LEXIS 99 (1950).

Constitutionality.

Former IC 11-7-6-2, which applied only to persons serving determinate sentences, was not unconstitutional as having been an improper classification because of the exclusion of persons serving indeterminate sentences, since it applied to all persons serving determinate sentences, and another method was provided by statute for rewarding good behavior of prisoners serving indeterminate sentences. Hinkle v. Dowd, 223 Ind. 91, 58 N.E.2d 342, 1944 Ind. LEXIS 194 (1944).

The fact that a person serving a five-year determinate or "flat" sentence with good-time off would be entitled to discharge after serving three years and nine months, while a person such as the defendant convicted of aggravated assault and battery, serving a one to five indeterminate sentence was not eligible for discharge after three years and nine months, but could only receive parole consideration, did not violate the equal protection clause of the 14th Amendment to the U.S. Constitution and Ind. Const., art. 1, § 23 because the measure in determining whether the penalty for one crime was greater than another was the maximum duration of penalty, not the possible duration of imprisonment. State v. Cooley, 162 Ind. App. 482, 319 N.E.2d 868, 1974 Ind. App. LEXIS 863 (1974).

Applicability of Former Law.

Former IC 11-7-6-1 did not apply to persons serving indeterminate sentences. Hinkle v. Dowd, 223 Ind. 91, 58 N.E.2d 342, 1944 Ind. LEXIS 194 (1944).

Former IC 11-7-6-2, preventing the accumulation of good-time by prisoner on parole, was inapplicable to prisoner paroled prior to passage thereof as being ex post facto. Dowd v. Sims, 229 Ind. 54, 95 N.E.2d 628, 1950 Ind. LEXIS 99 (1950).

Construction.

The trial court did not err in adopting the method of "good-time" credit computation urged by defendant-appellees, as such method allocated "good-time" credits in the same manner as did the statutory table in allowing such credits for the time which an inmate had actually served. Jenkins v. Stotts, 169 Ind. App. 273, 348 N.E.2d 57, 1976 Ind. App. LEXIS 917 (1976).

Where inmate, who was serving drug dealing sentence after parole revocation, was turned over to serve another sentence for several alcohol-related misdemeanors and felony battery, inmate was effectively discharged from rest of parole on drug dealing conviction, and IC 35-50-6-1 did not apply to case since inmate had not been released from prison prior to being turned over to serve new sentence. Meeker v. Ind. Parole Bd., 794 N.E.2d 1105, 2003 Ind. App. LEXIS 1592 (2003).

Where inmate was sentenced consecutively and released on parole before completing sentences and inmate then violated parole and was consequently ordered to serve balance of his sentences, inmate was not entitled to serve only shorter of two sentences; sentences were from single judgment rather than unrelated convictions and longer sentence was not discharged pursuant to IC 35-50-6-1 by parole board. Parker v. State, 822 N.E.2d 285, 2005 Ind. App. LEXIS 215 (2005).

When an inmate received an eight-year sentence for burglary, and a consecutive one-year sentence for failure to appear, his 24-month period of parole on his burglary conviction began running when he was discharged from incarceration for that sentence, even though he was serving a term for failure to appear, and he was not discharged from that period of parole by virtue of his consecutive incarceration; accordingly, when he violated parole within 24 months of the conclusion of his incarceration for burglary, it was proper to require him to serve the remainder of his burglary sentence, and he was not entitled to habeas corpus relief from that sentence. Mills v. State, 840 N.E.2d 354, 2006 Ind. App. LEXIS 13 (2006).

Determinate Sentence.

The word "determinate," as used in former IC 11-7-6-2, signified a definite or certain number of years fixed by the court. Hinkle v. Dowd, 223 Ind. 91, 58 N.E.2d 342, 1944 Ind. LEXIS 194 (1944).

Where an accused was convicted of forgery and sentenced for an indeterminate term of not less than two nor more than 14 years, and was thereafter released on parole but was returned to prison for violation thereof and given the remainder of his 14-year term, his sentence did not become a determinate one because of the action of the prison authorities, but remained an indeterminate sentence and was not governed by the "good-time law" (former IC 11-7-6-1 — IC 11-7-6-5) provided for prisoners having determinate sentences. Hinkle v. Howard, 225 Ind. 176, 73 N.E.2d 674, 1947 Ind. LEXIS 117 (1947).

Disproportionate Sentences Caused by Diminution.

Where indeterminate sentences of 10 to 20 years for the crime of robbery were imposed, there was no error as the measure in determining whether one penalty is greater than another is the maximum duration of the sentence and not the possible duration of imprisonment even though a person serving a determinate sentence of 10 to 20 years might be eligible for discharge earlier than the person serving the indeterminate sentence. Davis v. State, 156 Ind. App. 509, 156 Ind. App. 534, 297 N.E.2d 450, 1973 Ind. App. LEXIS 1159 (1973);

Disproportionate Sentences Caused by Diminution. (Cont'd)
Hamblen v. State, 157 Ind. App. 99, 299 N.E.2d 211, 1973 Ind. App. LEXIS 983 (1973).

Due Process.
Inmate is entitled to due process protection if disciplinary proceedings could result in loss of his of good-time credits, which would inevitably affect the duration of his sentence. Sweeney v. Parke, 113 F.3d 716, 1997 U.S. App. LEXIS 10732 (7th Cir. Ind. 1997).

Effect of Parole.
Under former IC 11-7-6-1, a prisoner who was sentenced for a determinate period of time and who was released on parole but subsequently returned to prison without his "good-time" earned pursuant to statute ever having been taken from him was entitled to the allowance of the full amount of good-time as provided by such statute, the same as if he had spent the entire time in prison. Boyd v. Howard, 224 Ind. 439, 68 N.E.2d 652, 1946 Ind. LEXIS 136 (1946).
Under former IC 11-7-1-3, a parole did not toll or suspend the running of the sentence, nor did it operate to shorten the term. Overlade v. Wells, 234 Ind. 436, 127 N.E.2d 686, 1955 Ind. LEXIS 162 (1955).
Where plaintiff was originally sentenced to one eight-year sentence with another two-year sentence to run consecutively to longer sentence, and plaintiff was paroled after he began serving shorter sentence, plaintiff was nevertheless also deemed to be on parole for longer sentence when released from custody; accordingly, when parole was revoked, original longer sentence was properly reinstated, and plaintiff's application for habeas corpus relief was properly denied. Hannis v. Deuth, 816 N.E.2d 872, 2004 Ind. App. LEXIS 2052 (2004).

Effect of Plea Bargain Agreement.
The fact that the acceptance of a plea bargain agreement by the trial judge forecloses subsequent judicial discretion by such judge to suspend the sentence does not affect the statutory discretion which is within the purview of the parole board or the department of corrections under this law. State ex rel. Goldsmith v. Marion County Superior Court, 275 Ind. 545, 419 N.E.2d 109, 1981 Ind. LEXIS 721 (1981).

Eligibility for Parole.

—Discharge of Sentence.
The credit time statute (IC 35-50-6-3) is only applied to determine when felons are eligible for parole. Where a prisoner is eligible for release, this does not mean that he has completed his sentence and is entitled to discharge. Subsection (a) of this section makes it clear that a felon is released to either parole or probation; he is not completely discharged. Page v. State, 517 N.E.2d 427, 1988 Ind. App. LEXIS 19 (1988).

Good Time Credits.
Although former IC 11-7-6-1 relating to good

time credits did not apply to a prisoner serving a life sentence, where a prisoner was serving both a life sentence and a 20-year sentence, such former IC 11-7-6-1 was applicable to the 20-year sentence. Lipps v. State, 271 Ind. 543, 394 N.E.2d 136, 1979 Ind. LEXIS 717 (1979).
Where, at time of sentencing former IC 11-7-6-1 was in effect, good time credits were to be figured on the basis of that section. Lipps v. State, 271 Ind. 543, 394 N.E.2d 136, 1979 Ind. LEXIS 717 (1979).
Credit time is applied only toward the date of release on parole for felons and does not diminish or otherwise impact the fixed term. Majors v. Broglin, 531 N.E.2d 189, 1988 Ind. LEXIS 338 (1988).
Parolee was not deprived of earned good time credits or any other credits when parole was revoked for violation of special conditions since parolees are deemed to be in legal custody throughout term of parole; parolee received benefit of credits when parole was granted. Harris v. State, 836 N.E.2d 267, 2005 Ind. App. LEXIS 1942 (2005).

Life Sentence.
The former section should not be construed to allow the granting of good time credits to prisoners serving life sentences. Jones v. Jenkins, 267 Ind. 619, 372 N.E.2d 1163, 1978 Ind. LEXIS 613 (1978).

Purpose.
Under former IC 11-7-6-1, the intent of the legislature, as gathered from the "good-time law" of 1933, was to grant to each and every minute inmate the opportunity to lessen the time of incarceration, and thus to improve the morale and well-being of each inmate in each institution. Dowd v. Johnston, 221 Ind. 398, 47 N.E.2d 976, 1943 Ind. LEXIS 200 (1943).

Recommendations by Court.
A recommendation of no parole by the court when sentencing defendant is merely a recommendation and not an order since the parole board of the department of corrections has the exclusive power to parole prisoners. Mott v. State, 273 Ind. 216, 402 N.E.2d 986, 1980 Ind. LEXIS 659 (1980).

Retroactivity.
A former similar law (IC 35-8-2.5-1 — IC 35-8-2.5-5, repealed), unless applied retroactively, denied equal protection under the Fourteenth Amendment and Ind. Const., art. 1, § 23, to persons convicted and sentenced prior to the effective date of the section since date of conviction and sentencing bore no relationship to the purpose and policy of the law. Brown v. State, 262 Ind. 629, 322 N.E.2d 708, 1975 Ind. LEXIS 245 (1975).

Suspended Sentence.
The legislature's reference to a "suspended sentence" in IC 35-38-2.6-4 means that any requirement that the offender actually serve executed time is suspended during a community corrections placement period. State v. Purcell, 721 N.E.2d 220, 1999 Ind. LEXIS 1189 (1999).

Cited:

Cottingham v. State, 424 N.E.2d 105, 1981 Ind. LEXIS 926 (1981); Greer v. State, 428 N.E.2d 787, 1981 Ind. LEXIS 937 (1981); Greer v. Duckworth, 555 F. Supp. 725, 1983 U.S. Dist. LEXIS 20021 (N.D. Ind. 1983); Mauricio v. Bronnenberg, 668 F. Supp. 1206, 1986 U.S. Dist. LEXIS 17169 (N.D. Ind. 1986); Boyd v. Broglin, 519 N.E.2d 541, 1988 Ind. LEXIS 81 (1988); Kuhfahl v. State, 710 N.E.2d 200, 1999 Ind. App. LEXIS 720 (1999); Renfroe v.

Parke, 736 N.E.2d 797, 2000 Ind. App. LEXIS 1661 (2000); Indiana Dep't of Corr. v. Bogus, 754 N.E.2d 27, 2001 Ind. App. LEXIS 1333 (2001); White v. Ind. Parole Bd., 266 F.3d 759, 2001 U.S. App. LEXIS 20912 (7th Cir. Ind. 2001); Harris v. State, 762 N.E.2d 163, 2002 Ind. App. LEXIS 131 (2002); Johnican v. State, 804 N.E.2d 211, 2004 Ind. App. LEXIS 324 (2004); Hart v. State, 889 N.E.2d 1266, 2008 Ind. App. LEXIS 1531 (2008).

RESEARCH REFERENCES

Indiana Law Review.

2006 Survey on Recent Developments in Indiana Law: Recent Developments in Indiana Criminal Law and Procedure, 40 Ind. L. Rev. 789 (2007).

Collateral References.

Validity of requirement that, as condition of probation, defendant submit to warrantless searches. 99 A.L.R.5th 557.

35-50-6-2. Release from imprisonment for a misdemeanor.

A person imprisoned for a misdemeanor shall be discharged when he completes his fixed term of imprisonment, less the credit time he has earned with respect to that term.

History.

IC 35-50-6-2, as added by Acts 1976, P.L.148, § 8; 1977, P.L.340, § 133.

NOTES TO DECISIONS

ANALYSIS

In General.
Life Sentence.

In General.

Comment by trial judge as to the effect of the good time statute at the beginning of the trial while error was not necessarily fatal. Johnson v. State, 173 Ind. App. 191, 362 N.E.2d 1185, 1977 Ind. App. LEXIS 845 (1977).

Where discharge notice was not issued when inmate, who was serving felony drug dealing sentence following parole revocation, was turned over to serve misdemeanor and felony alcohol related offenses, inmate was nevertheless effectively discharged from drug dealing conviction; discharge notice is required for misdemeanors under IC 35-50-6-2 but there is no similar requirement for

felonies. Meeker v. Ind. Parole Bd., 794 N.E.2d 1105, 2003 Ind. App. LEXIS 1592 (2003).

Life Sentence.

The ineligibility of prisoners serving life sentences for good time credits under former IC 11-7-6-1 was not a denial of equal protection. Jones v. Jenkins, 267 Ind. 619, 372 N.E.2d 1163, 1978 Ind. LEXIS 613 (1978).

Cited:

Wolfe v. State, 173 Ind. App. 27, 362 N.E.2d 188, 1977 Ind. App. LEXIS 821 (1977); Boyd v. Broglin, 519 N.E.2d 541, 1988 Ind. LEXIS 81 (1988); Antcliff v. State, 688 N.E.2d 166, 1997 Ind. App. LEXIS 759 (1997); Robinson v. State, 805 N.E.2d 783, 2004 Ind. LEXIS 229 (2004).

35-50-6-3. Credit time classification.

(a) A person assigned to Class I earns one (1) day of credit time for each day the person is imprisoned for a crime or confined awaiting trial or sentencing.

(b) A person assigned to Class II earns one (1) day of credit time for every two (2) days the person is imprisoned for a crime or confined awaiting trial or sentencing.

(c) A person assigned to Class III earns no credit time.

(d) A person assigned to Class IV earns one (1) day of credit time for every six (6) days the person is imprisoned for a crime or confined awaiting trial or sentencing.

History.

IC 35-50-6-3, as added by Acts 1976, P.L.148,

§ 8; 1977, P.L.340, § 134; P.L.80-2008, § 2, eff. July 1, 2008.

Compiler's Notes.

P.L.80-2008, § 6, effective July 1, 2008, provides:

"IC 35-41-1-5.5, as added by this act, and IC 35-50-6-3, IC 35-50-6-4, and IC 35-50-6-5, all as amended by this act, apply only to persons convicted after June 30, 2008."

NOTES TO DECISIONS

ANALYSIS

In General.
Accrual of Credit.
—Second Charge.
Additional Convictions in Interim.
Applicability.
Authority of Court.
Basis for Confinement.
—Psychiatric Hospital.
Community Corrections Programs.
Consecutive Sentences.
Drug Court.
Educational Credit Time.
Eligibility for Parole.
—Discharge of Sentence.
Federal Prisoners.
Good Time Credit.
Home Detention.
Multiple Offenses.
Presentence Commitment Credit.
—County Jail upon Return from Federal Prison.
—Out-of-State and Federal Prison.
Recommendations of Judge.
Resentencing Following Revocation of Parole.
Review.
Time Served Subsequent to Arrest.
—Extradition.
—Sentence to Which Credit Applies.
Voluntary Rehabilitation Program.

In General.

"Credit time" as used in this section is credit for good behavior or "good time credit," not credit for time served. Crow v. State, 797 N.E.2d 319, 2003 Ind. App. LEXIS 1969 (2003), transfer granted, superseded, 805 N.E.2d 780, 2004 Ind. LEXIS 231 (2004).

Accrual of Credit.

—Second Charge.

Where a defendant is in jail on one charge and a second charge is filed, credit on the second charge begins to accrue at the date of the arrest and not the date of filing. Dewees v. State, 444 N.E.2d 332, 1983 Ind. App. LEXIS 2568 (1983).

Additional Convictions in Interim.

Defendant should be given credit for all time served from the day of his arrest for that crime until the day of his sentence for that crime although he may have been tried and convicted of another offense between such times. Owen v. State, 272 Ind. 122, 396 N.E.2d 376, 1979 Ind. LEXIS 772 (1979).

Applicability.

IC 35-50-6-3 provides substantive rights and is not incorporated into the Juvenile Code by IC 31-32-1-1. Moreover, IC 35-50-6-3 concerns "good time credit," not credit for time served. J.D. v. State, 853 N.E.2d 945, 2006 Ind. LEXIS 817 (2006).

Because respondent was not "imprisoned for a crime," IC 35-50-6-3 and IC 35-50-6-4 did not apply to respondent's sentence for criminal contempt. Jones v. State, 847 N.E.2d 190, 2006 Ind. App. LEXIS 817 (2006).

Authority of Court.

A plain reading of former IC 35-8-2.5-5 indicated that the sentencing judge only had the authority to make recommendations with respect to good time allowances, and the trial judge could not enter a binding order. Garrett v. State, 411 N.E.2d 692, 1980 Ind. App. LEXIS 1733 (1980), disapproved, Sides v. State, 490 N.E.2d 318, 1986 Ind. LEXIS 1053 (1986).

The trial judge exceeded his authority where he denied good time credit for time served prior to sentencing, as the court could make only a recommendation regarding good time credit. Garrett v. State, 411 N.E.2d 692, 1980 Ind. App. LEXIS 1733 (1980), disapproved, Sides v. State, 490 N.E.2d 318, 1986 Ind. LEXIS 1053 (1986).

Basis for Confinement.

Determination of a defendant's pretrial credit is dependent upon pretrial confinement which is a result of the criminal charge for which sentence is being imposed. Willoughby v. State, 626 N.E.2d 601, 1993 Ind. App. LEXIS 1635 (1993).

A person imprisoned for a crime or confined awaiting trial or sentencing earns one day of credit time for each day he is imprisoned for a crime or confined awaiting trial or sentencing, but credit is to be applied only for time spent in confinement that is the result of the charge for which the defendant is being sentenced. Stephens v. State, 735 N.E.2d 278, 2000 Ind. App. LEXIS 1469 (2000).

—Psychiatric Hospital.

If defendant's stay in psychiatric hospital was another form of imprisonment as a consequence of her pending criminal charges, and if she was not free to leave hospital or face return to prison upon completion of her treatment, she would be entitled to credit for time spent in hospital. Wilson v. State, 679 N.E.2d 1333, 1997 Ind. App. LEXIS 513 (1997).

Even if defendant were to recover competency and then be tried and convicted of the charged offense, any incarceration she could receive would have to be reduced by the time spent in the state hospitals; thus, because the maximum term of incarceration for criminal recklessness as a Class D felony under IC 35-50-2-7 was three years, and

Basis for Confinement. (Cont'd)

—Psychiatric Hospital. (Cont'd)
because of the IC 35-50-6-3(a) credit time, defendant became immune from being sentenced to further confinement as of November 2006 by which time she had been confined for a total of 18 months. State v. Davis, 898 N.E.2d 281, 2008 Ind. LEXIS 1282 (2008).

Community Corrections Programs.
To extend IC 35-38-2.6-6(b) to mean that persons committed to community corrections programs should be deprived of earned credit time in accordance with IC 35-50-6 rather than rules adopted by the department of correction would be to operate outside the scope of the court's judicial authority and infringe on that which has been left solely to the prerogative of the legislature. Campbell v. State, 716 N.E.2d 577, 1999 Ind. App. LEXIS 1507 (1999).

Consecutive Sentences.
This section was satisfied by giving the defendant full credit for presentence confinement only on the first sentence of two consecutive sentences, and there is no basis for the proposition that the legislature could have contemplated "extra" or "double" credit to a convicted felon under these circumstances by also giving the defendant full credit for the same presentence confinement on the second sentence. Simms v. State, 421 N.E.2d 698, 1981 Ind. App. LEXIS 1469 (1981).

Credit is imposed against the aggregate sentences where consecutive sentences are imposed, and not against each individual sentence. Dewees v. State, 444 N.E.2d 332, 1983 Ind. App. LEXIS 2568 (1983).

Defendant, who escaped from jail while awaiting trial for murder, was not entitled to credit for pretrial incarceration on the escape charge, where she had been granted presentence confinement credit on her murder sentence, and the two sentences were to be served consecutively. Jorgensen v. State, 559 N.E.2d 616, 1990 Ind. App. LEXIS 1184 (1990).

Where a defendant is confined during the same time period for multiple offenses for which he is convicted and sentenced to consecutive terms, credit is applied against the aggregate sentence. Ragon v. State, 654 N.E.2d 906, 1995 Ind. App. LEXIS 1037 (1995).

Where defendant was required to serve consecutive sentences for multiple offenses because the second offense was committed while defendant was on bond, defendant was not entitled to have credit for time served applied against each separate sentence, but had to have credit applied to the aggregate sentence. Diedrich v. State, 744 N.E.2d 1004, 2001 Ind. App. LEXIS 413 (2001).

Drug Court.
By accepting a drug court agreement, defendant knowingly and voluntarily agreed to waive credit time; however, he was entitled to credit time under IC 35-50-6-3(a) for the days of imprisonment incurred prior to his signing the drug court agreement. House v. State, — N.E.2d —, 2009 Ind. App. LEXIS 285 (2009).

Defendant may waive credit time for any period of sanction imposed by the drug court by entering into a drug court agreement; express findings regarding the defendant's intention to waive his credit time in exchange for participating in the drug court are not required to show that the defendant knowingly and voluntarily agreed to the waiver. House v. State, — N.E.2d —, 2009 Ind. App. LEXIS 285 (2009).

Educational Credit Time.
Credit time awarded to prisoners who successfully complete educational programs during their stay behind bars should be applied to the term of years imposed by the sentencing court rather than subtracted from the earliest possible release date, after taking into account the maximum anticipated allotment of credit time from other sentence-reducing mechanisms before applying the educational credit. Miller v. Walker, 655 N.E.2d 47, 1995 Ind. LEXIS 116 (1995), modified, — N.E.2d —, 1995 Ind. LEXIS 121 (1995).

"Total" time includes, at a minimum, both educational credit time and "good time" credit, as used in the limitation on educational credit time in IC 35-50-6-3.3. State v. Eckhardt, 687 N.E.2d 374, 1997 Ind. App. LEXIS 1548 (1997).

Eligibility for Parole.

—Discharge of Sentence.
The credit time statute (this section) is only applied to determine when felons are eligible for parole. Where a prisoner is eligible for release, this does not mean that he has completed his sentence and is entitled to discharge. IC 35-50-6-1(a) makes it clear that a felon is released to either parole or probation; he is not completely discharged. Page v. State, 517 N.E.2d 427, 1988 Ind. App. LEXIS 19 (1988).

Federal Prisoners.
Where the defendant was incarcerated as a result of a federal conviction and not due to charges filed against him by the state, he was properly denied credit time against the sentences imposed for convictions arising from the state charges. Sweeney v. State, 704 N.E.2d 86, 1998 Ind. LEXIS 672 (1998), cert. denied, 527 U.S. 1035, 119 S. Ct. 2393, 144 L. Ed. 2d 793, 1999 U.S. LEXIS 4437 (1999).

Good Time Credit.
Where defendant was classified as class III for time credit purposes under IC 35-50-6-7, which made defendant ineligible for good time credit under IC 35-50-6-3(c), failure of trial court to explicitly state that defendant would be credited with zero days of good time credit was not error. Groves v. State, 823 N.E.2d 1229, 2005 Ind. App. LEXIS 431 (2005).

Home Detention.
Defendant was not entitled to good time credit

Home Detention. (Cont'd)
for pretrial home detention, because he would not be entitled to good time credit for post-conviction home detention under IC 35-38-2.6-6. Franklin v. State, 679 N.E.2d 510, 1997 Ind. App. LEXIS 433 (1997), transfer granted, 690 N.E.2d 1179 (Ind. 1997), superseded, 685 N.E.2d 1062, 1997 Ind. LEXIS 153 (1997). See also Franklin v. State, 685 N.E.2d 1062, 1997 Ind. LEXIS 153 (1997), overruled in part, State v. Purcell, 721 N.E.2d 220, 1999 Ind. LEXIS 1189 (1999).

Defendant was not eligible for credit for the time he served on pre-trial home detention. Franklin v. State, 685 N.E.2d 1062, 1997 Ind. LEXIS 153 (1997), overruled in part, State v. Purcell, 721 N.E.2d 220, 1999 Ind. LEXIS 1189 (1999).

Since credit time is earned only for each day of imprisonment for a crime or confinement awaiting trial or sentencing, the trial court did not err in denying the defendant credit for time spent in pre-trial home detention. Kuhfahl v. State, 710 N.E.2d 200, 1999 Ind. App. LEXIS 720 (1999), overruled, Dishroon v. State, 722 N.E.2d 385, 2000 Ind. App. LEXIS 58 (2000).

The trial court did not abuse its discretion when it denied defendant credit for time spent in pretrial home detention because time spent in pretrial home detention is not equivalent to pretrial time served in a prison or jail. Molden v. State, 750 N.E.2d 448, 2001 Ind. App. LEXIS 1130 (2001).

Trial court properly denied a defendant's motion for credit time after his daily reporting probation was revoked for having committed an additional crime and he was, therefore, ordered to serve the remainder of his sentence for his rape conviction, namely 10 years. The appellate court agreed with the trial court's determination that daily reporting to a probation officer did not amount to the type of freedom restrictions that deserved credit time and no statutory authority existed to support the defendant's request. Reed v. State, 844 N.E.2d 223, 2006 Ind. App. LEXIS 541 (2006).

When the original charges against defendant were dismissed and a different charge was filed based on the same conduct as the original charges, it was not error to deny defendant credit for time he spent on house arrest while awaiting trial on the dismissed charges. Because time spent at home did not place the same restrictions upon personal liberty as time spent in jail or prison, a trial court was within its discretion in denying a defendant credit for pretrial time served on home detention. James v. State, 872 N.E.2d 669, 2007 Ind. App. LEXIS 2000 (2007).

Multiple Offenses.
A defendant is entitled to full credit for time served for each offense for which he is sentenced, and defendant should have received credit for the time served from the day of his arrest until the date of his sentencing. Muff v. State, 647 N.E.2d 681, 1995 Ind. App. LEXIS 231 (1995).

Defendant was not entitled to a double award of credit time for the period during which he was detained on multiple charges. Ragon v. State, 654 N.E.2d 906, 1995 Ind. App. LEXIS 1037 (1995).

Jail credit is applied against the aggregate sentence where a defendant is convicted of multiple offenses and sentenced to consecutive terms. Shane v. State, 716 N.E.2d 391, 1999 Ind. LEXIS 799 (1999).

Where a person is incarcerated and awaiting trial on multiple charges and is sentenced to concurrent terms for those crimes, he is entitled by statute to receive credit time applied against each term. Peace v. State, 736 N.E.2d 1261, 2000 Ind. App. LEXIS 1709 (2000).

Presentence Commitment Credit.
Where defendant was arrested for escaping the Indiana State Reformatory while serving a sentence for robbery, pled guilty to the escape charge, received a four year sentence which was ordered to run consecutively to the robbery sentence he was still serving, but the trial court did not allow him any presentence commitment credit on his four-year escape sentence, since he received credit on the aggregate of the robbery sentence and the escape sentence by receiving credit on his robbery commitment, to additionally award him credit on the escape sentence would have been to award him double or extra credit, a result the legislature did not intend. Further, if he had been granted presentence credit against the sentence imposed for escape, the presentence credit portion of his sentence for escape would in effect have been served concurrently with his robbery sentence. Emerson v. State, 498 N.E.2d 1301, 1986 Ind. App. LEXIS 3082 (1986).

Defendant was entitled to Class I credit for time served in jail awaiting sentence after pleading guilty to six counts of theft; trial court was required under IC 35-38-3-2(b)(4) to include both credit for time served and credit for good behavior in defendant's judgment of conviction. Crow v. State, 797 N.E.2d 319, 2003 Ind. App. LEXIS 1969 (2003), transfer granted, superseded, 805 N.E.2d 780, 2004 Ind. LEXIS 231 (2004).

Since defendant's pretrial confinement was for probation violation, to which he later admitted guilt, rather than for charge pending at time of sentencing, to which he had not yet entered plea, defendant should have received credit for pretrial confinement in his sentence for probation violation; furthermore, although defendant asked trial court to "save" pretrial detention credit for pending charge, law precluded trial court from granting that request, and defendant did not therefore waive issue for appeal. Tate v. State, 813 N.E.2d 437, 2004 Ind. App. LEXIS 1638 (2004).

Defendant released on bond was not "confined awaiting trial" for purposes of pre-trial time credit statute. Murfitt v. State, 812 N.E.2d 809, 2004 Ind. App. LEXIS 1520 (2004).

—County Jail upon Return from Federal Prison.
Although the defendant was already serving time in federal prison for counterfeiting, upon being returned to Indiana, he should have been credited with the time spent in county jail since he was confined there as a result of a crime for which he was eventually convicted, and for which sen-

Presentence Commitment Credit. (Cont'd)

—County Jail upon Return from Federal Prison. (Cont'd)
tence was imposed. Bertucci v. State, 528 N.E.2d 90, 1988 Ind. App. LEXIS 730 (1988).

—Out-of-State and Federal Prison.
Since the defendant's pretrial confinement in Illinois and federal prison was for crimes unrelated to his Indiana charges, and was not a direct result of his Indiana charges, he should not have been granted pretrial credit for the time spent incarcerated in Illinois and federal prison. Bertucci v. State, 528 N.E.2d 90, 1988 Ind. App. LEXIS 730 (1988).

The defendant provided no evidence to show that either a January 28, 1984, Illinois detainer or an October 10, 1985, Illinois detainer served as a "hold" which would have caused Illinois to retain custody over the defendant even where no Illinois charges were pending, and therefore the defendant was not entitled to Indiana credit. Cohen v. State, 560 N.E.2d 1246, 1990 Ind. LEXIS 207 (1990).

Recommendations of Judge.
The trial judge could only make recommendations with respect to good time for time spent in confinement prior to sentencing but could not make an order that defendant not be given any good time allowance for such time spent in confinement prior to sentencing. Leavell v. State, 181 Ind. App. 69, 391 N.E.2d 246, 1979 Ind. App. LEXIS 1220 (1979).

Resentencing Following Revocation of Parole.
In revoking defendant's probation, because the court in Indiana was imposing sentence for the crime that defendant committed in Indiana, and it was not responsible for crediting time for a separate crime committed in Illinois, and it was not a party to the Illinois plea agreement, it did not have to credit defendant's Illinois sentence. Carneal v. State, 859 N.E.2d 1255, 2007 Ind. App. LEXIS 30 (2007).

Review.
A defendant who has not been awarded proper credit time under this section may seek review of this error at any time, because a defendant should not and cannot be incarcerated for any duration longer than that allowed by law. Weaver v. State, 725 N.E.2d 945, 2000 Ind. App. LEXIS 429 (2000).

Although defendant initially claimed based on an abstract of judgment that defendant was not granted all of the IC 35-50-6-3 sentence credit to which defendant was entitled, the SSC did not need to review the appellate court's rejection of the trial court's denial of defendant's IC 35-38-1-15 motion to correct an erroneous sentence; defendant conceded in one of defendant's SSC pleadings that the sentence credits actually had been correctly calculated and, thus, no dispute remained. Neff v. State, 888 N.E.2d 1249, 2008 Ind. LEXIS 485 (2008).

Defendant was presumptively entitled to 204 days of earned credit time in addition to defendant's 204 days of time already served, and did not have to resort to the state court system to receive credit as it was presumed that defendant was a Class I offender and was entitled to equal earned credit as that for time served under IC 35-50-6-3 since the trial court specified the credit for time served, but not the earned credit; however, in order to proceed in the state court system, defendant had to exhaust defendant's administrative remedies. Young v. State, 888 N.E.2d 1253, 2008 Ind. LEXIS 484 (2008).

Time Served Subsequent to Arrest.
Defendant was entitled to credit for the time served subsequent to his arrest. Bond v. State, 273 Ind. 233, 403 N.E.2d 812, 1980 Ind. LEXIS 665 (1980).

A defendant should be credited for the time he spent in confinement from the date of his arrest for such violation to the date of sentencing for such violation. Dolan v. State, 420 N.E.2d 1364, 1981 Ind. App. LEXIS 1446 (1981).

Under the plain language of this section, a person confined awaiting trial or sentencing is statutorily entitled to one day of credit for each day he is so confined; therefore, pre-sentence jail time credit is a matter of statutory right, not a matter of judicial discretion. Weaver v. State, 725 N.E.2d 945, 2000 Ind. App. LEXIS 429 (2000).

Trial court erred in not determining at time of sentencing whether defendant was entitled to good time credit for time served prior to sentencing; accordingly, denial of defendant's motion to correct sentence was reversed and case was remanded for determination of good time credit. Jackson v. State, 799 N.E.2d 551, 2003 Ind. App. LEXIS 2238 (2003), transfer granted, — N.E.2d —, 2004 Ind. LEXIS 254 (2004), superseded, 806 N.E.2d 773, 2004 Ind. LEXIS 234 (2004).

Although defendant was classified as class III for time credit purposes under IC 35-50-6-7, which made defendant ineligible for good time credit under IC 35-50-6-3(c), classification did not impact defendant's right to credit for time served prior to sentencing. Groves v. State, 823 N.E.2d 1229, 2005 Ind. App. LEXIS 431 (2005).

Defendant would have improperly received "double or extra credit" if the court permitted time served prior to sentencing to count against both his battery and his criminal deviate conduct sentences; defendant correctly received credit only against the aggregate of his battery and criminal deviate conduct sentences. Payne v. State, 838 N.E.2d 503, 2005 Ind. App. LEXIS 2267 (2005).

When the original charges against defendant were dismissed and a different charge was filed based on the same conduct as the original charges, defendant was entitled to credit for his pretrial incarceration on the original charges, as he was not being given credit for a wholly unrelated offense. James v. State, 872 N.E.2d 669, 2007 Ind. App. LEXIS 2000 (2007).

Trial court erred in not awarding defendant credit for a period of time served because defendant's credit time began to accrue the day on which defendant was arrested for the crime on which

Time Served Subsequent to Arrest. (Cont'd) defendant was ultimately sentenced. However, defendant was not entitled to credit for time served on factually unrelated charges that were dismissed. Brown v. State, — N.E.2d —, 2009 Ind. App. LEXIS 890 (2009).

—Extradition.
Defendant was entitled to credit for presentence time served in another state after charges in that state were dropped and while extradition to Indiana was pending. Nutt v. State, 451 N.E.2d 342, 1983 Ind. App. LEXIS 3129 (1983).

—Sentence to Which Credit Applies.
Although this section states a defendant is allowed credit for time confined awaiting trial or sentencing, the legislature clearly intended the credit to apply only to the sentence for the offense for which the presentence time was served. Dewees v. State, 444 N.E.2d 332, 1983 Ind. App. LEXIS 2568 (1983).

Where the time defendant spent confined after being served with an arrest warrant was the result of his illegal possession of a handgun, not his conviction for operating a vehicle while intoxicated (OWI), he was not entitled to credit time against the sentence imposed for his OWI conviction. Bischoff v. State, 704 N.E.2d 129, 1998 Ind. App. LEXIS 2020 (1998).

Voluntary Rehabilitation Program.
Voluntary rehabilitation programs do not constitute confinement within the meaning of the statute and thus do not qualify for good time credit. Dixon v. State, 685 N.E.2d 715, 1997 Ind. App. LEXIS 1267 (1997).

Cited:
Cottingham v. State, 424 N.E.2d 105, 1981 Ind. LEXIS 926 (1981); Badelle v. State, 434 N.E.2d 872, 1982 Ind. LEXIS 815 (1982); Bryant v. State, 446 N.E.2d 364, 1983 Ind. App. LEXIS 2722 (1983); Ramirez v. State, 455 N.E.2d 609, 1983 Ind. App. LEXIS 3503 (1983); Forbes v. Trigg, 976 F.2d 308, 1992 U.S. App. LEXIS 21815 (7th Cir. Ind. 1992); Johnson v. Trigg, 28 F.3d 639, 1994 U.S. App. LEXIS 16432 (7th Cir. Ind. 1994); Corn v. State, 659 N.E.2d 554, 1995 Ind. LEXIS 219 (1995); Davenport v. State, 689 N.E.2d 1226, 1997 Ind. LEXIS 232 (1997); Partlow v. Superintendent, 756 N.E.2d 978, 2001 Ind. App. LEXIS 1750 (2001); Williams v. State, 759 N.E.2d 661, 2001 Ind. App. LEXIS 2111 (2001); Jones v. State, 775 N.E.2d 322, 2002 Ind. App. LEXIS 1494 (2002); Bennett v. State, 787 N.E.2d 938, 2003 Ind. App. LEXIS 762 (2003); Robinson v. State, 805 N.E.2d 783, 2004 Ind. LEXIS 229 (2004).

RESEARCH REFERENCES

Res Gestae.
Criminal justice notes, 38 (No. 1) Res Gestae 38 (1994).

35-50-6-3.3. Additional credit time earned for completion of certain degrees, diplomas or certificates of completion — Limitations.

(a) In addition to any credit time a person earns under subsection (b) or section 3 [IC 35-50-6-3] of this chapter, a person earns credit time if the person:
(1) is in credit Class I;
(2) has demonstrated a pattern consistent with rehabilitation; and
(3) successfully completes requirements to obtain one (1) of the following:
(A) A general educational development (GED) diploma under IC 20-20-6, if the person has not previously obtained a high school diploma.
(B) A high school diploma, if the person has not previously obtained a general educational development (GED) diploma.
(C) An associate's degree from an approved postsecondary educational institution (as defined under IC 21-7-13-6(a)).
(D) A bachelor's degree from an approved postsecondary educational institution (as defined under IC 21-7-13-6(a)).
(b) In addition to any credit time that a person earns under subsection (a) or section 3 of this chapter, a person may earn credit time if, while confined by the department of correction, the person:
(1) is in credit Class I;
(2) demonstrates a pattern consistent with rehabilitation; and
(3) successfully completes requirements to obtain at least one (1) of the following:
(A) A certificate of completion of a career and technical education program approved by the department of correction.

(B) A certificate of completion of a substance abuse program approved by the department of correction.

(C) A certificate of completion of a literacy and basic life skills program approved by the department of correction.

(c) The department of correction shall establish admissions criteria and other requirements for programs available for earning credit time under subsection (b). A person may not earn credit time under both subsections (a) and (b) for the same program of study.

(d) The amount of credit time a person may earn under this section is the following:

(1) Six (6) months for completion of a state of Indiana general educational development (GED) diploma under IC 20-20-6.

(2) One (1) year for graduation from high school.

(3) One (1) year for completion of an associate's degree.

(4) Two (2) years for completion of a bachelor's degree.

(5) Not more than a total of six (6) months of credit, as determined by the department of correction, for the completion of one (1) or more career and technical education programs approved by the department of correction.

(6) Not more than a total of six (6) months of credit, as determined by the department of correction, for the completion of one (1) or more substance abuse programs approved by the department of correction.

(7) Not more than a total of six (6) months credit, as determined by the department of correction, for the completion of one (1) or more literacy and basic life skills programs approved by the department of correction.

However, a person who does not have a substance abuse problem that qualifies the person to earn credit in a substance abuse program may earn not more than a total of twelve (12) months of credit, as determined by the department of correction, for the completion of one (1) or more career and technical education programs approved by the department of correction. If a person earns more than six (6) months of credit for the completion of one (1) or more career and technical education programs, the person is ineligible to earn credit for the completion of one (1) or more substance abuse programs.

(e) Credit time earned by a person under this section is subtracted from the release date that would otherwise apply to the person after subtracting all other credit time earned by the person.

(f) A person does not earn credit time under subsection (a) unless the person completes at least a portion of the degree requirements after June 30, 1993.

(g) A person does not earn credit time under subsection (b) unless the person completes at least a portion of the program requirements after June 30, 1999.

(h) Credit time earned by a person under subsection (a) for a diploma or degree completed before July 1, 1999, shall be subtracted from:

(1) the release date that would otherwise apply to the person after subtracting all other credit time earned by the person, if the person has not been convicted of an offense described in subdivision (2); or

(2) the period of imprisonment imposed on the person by the sentencing court, if the person has been convicted of one (1) of the following crimes:

(A) Rape (IC 35-42-4-1).

(B) Criminal deviate conduct (IC 35-42-4-2).

(C) Child molesting (IC 35-42-4-3).

(D) Child exploitation (IC 35-42-4-4(b)).

(E) Vicarious sexual gratification (IC 35-42-4-5).

(F) Child solicitation (IC 35-42-4-6).

(G) Child seduction (IC 35-42-4-7).

(H) Sexual misconduct with a minor as a Class A felony, Class B felony, or Class C felony (IC 35-42-4-9).

(I) Incest (IC 35-46-1-3).

(J) Sexual battery (IC 35-42-4-8).

(K) Kidnapping (IC 35-42-3-2), if the victim is less than eighteen (18) years of age.

(L) Criminal confinement (IC 35-42-3-3), if the victim is less than eighteen (18) years of age.

(M) An attempt or a conspiracy to commit a crime listed in clauses (A) through (L).

(i) The maximum amount of credit time a person may earn under this section is the lesser of:

(1) four (4) years; or

(2) one-third (⅓) of the person's total applicable credit time.

(j) The amount of credit time earned under this section is reduced to the extent that application of the credit time would otherwise result in:

(1) postconviction release (as defined in IC 35-40-4-6); or

(2) assignment of the person to a community transition program; in less than forty-five (45) days after the person earns the credit time.

(k) A person may earn credit time for multiple degrees at the same education level under subsection (d) only in accordance with guidelines approved by the department of correction. The department of correction may approve guidelines for proper sequence of education degrees under subsection (d).

(*l*) A person may not earn credit time:

(1) for a general educational development (GED) diploma if the person has previously earned a high school diploma; or

(2) for a high school diploma if the person has previously earned a general educational development (GED) diploma.

History.
P.L.243-1993, § 2; P.L.148-1995, § 7; P.L.149-1995, § 17; P.L.183-1999, § 3; P.L.243-1999, § 3; P.L.14-2000, § 78; P.L.90-2000, § 21; P.L.164-2003, § 1; P.L.1-2005, § 229; P.L.2-2007, § 380, emergency eff. July 1, 2007; P.L.234-2007, § 171, emergency eff. July 1, 2007; P.L.80-2008, § 3, eff. July 1, 2008.

NOTES TO DECISIONS

ANALYSIS

In General.
Abuse of Discretion.
Behavior Consistent with Rehabilitation.
Calculation of Credit.
Disparate Treatment.
Educational Credit Time.
Exhaustion of Administrative Remedies.
Out-Of-State School.
Plea Agreements.
—Restrictions.
Receipt of Diploma.
Reduction of Sentence.
Right to Education Programs.
Sentence for Heinous Crime.
Subsequent Parole Violation.

In General.

This section is not ambiguous; the language employed by the legislature is simple and clear, and not susceptible to more than one meaning. Miller v. Walker, 642 N.E.2d 1000, 1994 Ind. App. LEXIS 1686 (1994), aff'd, 655 N.E.2d 47, 1995 Ind. LEXIS 116 (1995).

Deduction of the education credit reduces the actual days served in prison; this in turn, reduces the number of good time credit days that can be earned. Miller v. Walker, 642 N.E.2d 1000, 1994 Ind. App. LEXIS 1686 (1994), aff'd, 655 N.E.2d 47, 1995 Ind. LEXIS 116 (1995).

Defendant with disciplinary conviction was denied good time credit, since credit for inmates completing GED and substance abuse programs required that the inmate's record be free of disciplinary convictions while participating in programs. Diaz v. State, 753 N.E.2d 724, 2001 Ind. App. LEXIS 1357 (2001).

Defendant's motion for education time credit was actually a petition for post-conviction relief; the State was entitled to 30 days to respond to defendant's motion for education time credit, and where the trial court had denied the motion before the State had had a chance to respond, the order was reversed and the case was remanded. Wilson v. State, 785 N.E.2d 1152, 2003 Ind. App. LEXIS 525 (2003).

Abuse of Discretion.

Where a trial court stated that the defendant was entitled to educational credit, but sentenced the defendant to the maximum sentences allowed by statute, remand for resentencing was required.

Abuse of Discretion. (Cont'd)
Tumbleson v. State, 706 N.E.2d 217, 1999 Ind. App. LEXIS 172 (1999).

Behavior Consistent with Rehabilitation.
There is a subjective component involved in determining that a pattern of behavior consistent with rehabilitation entitled a defendant to educational credit, and merely completing the requirements for a degree does not confer automatic entitlement to the credit. Tumbleson v. State, 706 N.E.2d 217, 1999 Ind. App. LEXIS 172 (1999).

There is a subjective component involved in the granting of educational credit, i.e. a pattern of behavior consistent with rehabilitation, and merely completing the requirements for a degree does not automatically entitle a defendant to the credit; demonstrating a "pattern consistent with rehabilitation" means, at the least, that the inmate's record must remain free of disciplinary convictions while the inmate is participating in an educational or substance abuse program. Wilson v. State, 785 N.E.2d 1152, 2003 Ind. App. LEXIS 525 (2003).

Calculation of Credit.
Where defendant received a five year sentence with two years suspended, leaving a three year executed sentence remaining, the education credit was deducted from that sentence; in applying the education credit, it made no difference whether the education credit was deducted prior to figuring good time credit earned to that point, or deducted after subtracting the good time credit earned to that point. Miller v. Walker, 642 N.E.2d 1000, 1994 Ind. App. LEXIS 1686 (1994), aff'd, 655 N.E.2d 47, 1995 Ind. LEXIS 116 (1995).

"Total" time includes, at a minimum, both educational credit time and "good time" credit, as used in the limitation on educational credit time in this section. State v. Eckhardt, 687 N.E.2d 374, 1997 Ind. App. LEXIS 1548 (1997).

This section does not preclude a person from using multiple degrees of the same educational level to comprise his total credit time. Moshenek v. Anderson, 718 N.E.2d 811, 781 N.E.2d 811, 1999 Ind. App. LEXIS 1923 (1999).

In cases where an inmate has pre-1999 education credit, plus the maximum allowable post-1999 credit, nothing in the language of the educational credit time statute, IC 35-50-6-3.3, prevents the Indiana department of corrections from striking the pre-1999 credit in order to give an inmate the benefit of the full four years of his or her post-1999 educational credits; inmate was thus permitted to have the credits he earned prior to the amendment of the educational credit time statute change deducted from his total credits and receive the maximum allowable credit based solely on the post-amendment credits he earned. Cotton v. Ellsworth, 788 N.E.2d 867, 2003 Ind. App. LEXIS 836 (2003).

Inasmuch as at the time defendant committed an offense for which he was convicted and sentenced IC 35-50-6-3.3 allowed him to earn more than one associate's degree and earn one year's credit for each degree, application of a new statutory provision and the Department of Corrections'

policy to deny him credit for both degrees was a violation of his protections against ex post facto laws. Paul v. State, 888 N.E.2d 818, 2008 Ind. App. LEXIS 1327 (2008).

Disparate Treatment.
The disparate treatment caused by the different classification of jail prisoners from their counterparts in corrections department institutions did not amount to a violation of their constitutional rights, since there are important characteristics which distinguish the two groups, including the fact that jail prisoners generally have substantially shorter sentences, that their shorter sentences permit fewer of them sufficient time to complete programs, and that they constitute a small percentage of the total number of persons committed to the corrections department and are spread out in county jails all over the state. Cohn v. Strawhorn, 721 N.E.2d 342, 1999 Ind. App. LEXIS 2208 (1999).

Educational Credit Time.
Credit time awarded to prisoners who successfully complete educational programs during their stay behind bars should be applied to the term of years imposed by the sentencing court rather than subtracted from the earliest possible release date, after taking into account the maximum anticipated allotment of credit time from other sentence-reducing mechanisms before applying the educational credit. Miller v. Walker, 655 N.E.2d 47, 1995 Ind. LEXIS 116 (1995), modified, — N.E.2d —, 1995 Ind. LEXIS 121 (1995).

Where inmate had two disciplinary convictions in year before he received general education diploma (GED), fact that he did not receive disciplinary convictions during time he worked on GED did not compel finding of pattern of behavior consistent with rehabilitation; thus, denial of inmate's petition for post-conviction relief by way of educational credit was proper. Wilson v. State, 799 N.E.2d 51, 2003 Ind. App. LEXIS 2198 (2003).

In post-conviction petition by inmate seeking educational time credit pursuant to IC 35-50-6-3.3, inmate failed to show that he was entitled to relief by preponderance of evidence as required by P.C. 1(5); Indiana Department of Corrections, not trial court, is only entity with ability to determine whether inmate is entitled to credit since IC 35-50-6-3.3 requires showing that inmate has demonstrated pattern of behavior consistent with rehabilitation. Sander v. State, 816 N.E.2d 75, 2004 Ind. App. LEXIS 2000 (2004).

Trial court properly denied a petition by three prisoners, which asserted that they should have received six rather than three months sentence credit for completing vocational programs. IC 35-50-6-3.3(d)(5) explicitly allowed for up to six months credit at the discretion of the department of corrections, but does not require six months of credit. Fuller v. Meloy, 848 N.E.2d 1172, 2006 Ind. App. LEXIS 1118 (2006).

Appellate court had to dismiss the denial of the trial court, acting as a post-conviction court, of defendant's request for educational time credit; the denial in the first instance was by the state

Educational Credit Time. (Cont'd)
corrections department, and, thus, defendant was
required to exhaust all of his administrative remedies with the state corrections department,
through the procedure provided, before resorting
to the judicial system, as the judicial system,
including the trial court, did not have subject
matter jurisdiction to consider the matter until
that was done. Members v. State, 851 N.E.2d 979,
2006 Ind. App. LEXIS 1460 (2006).

Because there was no indication from the record
that a prisoner ever sought, let alone exhausted,
his administrative remedies from the proper authority in pursuing his claim for educational credit
time, the post-conviction court was without subject
matter jurisdiction to rule upon his petition. Watkins v. State, 869 N.E.2d 497, 2007 Ind. App.
LEXIS 1492 (2007).

Inmate could not obtain educational credit under IC 35-50-6-3.3 where the inmate did not show:
(1) that the petition was not an unapproved successive petition for post-conviction relief under
P.C. 1(12); (2) that the Indiana Department of
Correction's administrative grievance procedures
had been exhausted; (3) that the inmate had been
awarded a high school diploma; (4) the credentials
of the school that awarded it; and (5) that the
inmate met each requirement of IC 35-50-6-3.3.
Young v. State, 888 N.E.2d 1255, 2008 Ind. LEXIS
487 (2008).

Because defendant's initial grievance raised the
issue of educational credit time, and because defendant pursued an appeal from a classification
action, defendant exhausted his administrative
remedies; accordingly, because the trial court had
jurisdiction to review and determine defendant's
entitlement to the credit under IC 35-50-6-3.3(a), it
erred in denying his petition without a hearing.
Stevens v. State, 895 N.E.2d 418, 2008 Ind. App.
LEXIS 2442 (2008).

Exhaustion of Administrative Remedies.
Because the trial court did not determine
whether defendant had exhausted defendant's administrative remedies, pursuant to IC 35-50-6-
3.3(d), it erred in dismissing defendant's motion
for additional earned credit time for lack of subject
matter jurisdiction. Burks-Bey v. State, — N.E.2d
—, 2009 Ind. App. LEXIS 655 (2009).

Out-Of-State School.
Although petitioner had not been a paragon of
successful parole, that issue was separate and
distinct from the issues of credit for good behavior
and credit for educational self-improvement, and
the post-conviction court erroneously failed to recognize the application of subsection (b)(1) and the
credit earned by petitioner for educational self-
improvement. Renfroe v. Parke, 736 N.E.2d 797,
2000 Ind. App. LEXIS 1661 (2000).

Because this section specifically limits its applicability to degrees earned after July 1, 1993, where
the educational degrees that defendant had obtained were earned before July 1, 1993, the post-
conviction court could not use this section to reduce defendant's sentence. Poling v. State, 740
N.E.2d 872, 2000 Ind. App. LEXIS 2043 (2000),

overruled, Graves v. State, 823 N.E.2d 1193, 2005
Ind. LEXIS 205 (Ind. 2005).

The court correctly applied this section when
giving defendant credit for his GED because the
only amendment relevant to defendant's situation
was the addition of subsection (e), which allows
credit earned under this section to be subtracted
from the period of imprisonment imposed on the
person by the sentencing court. For other defendants, the result might necessarily differ according
to the version of the statute implicated by the facts
of the case. Renfroe v. State, 743 N.E.2d 299, 2001
Ind. App. LEXIS 61 (2001).

Credits awarded to prisoner who earned college
degrees advanced the date he became eligible for
parole but did not reduce the length of his sentence, and the prisoner could be required to serve
the total period remaining on his 20-year sentence
after his parole was revoked. Indiana Dep't of Corr.
v. Bogus, 754 N.E.2d 27, 2001 Ind. App. LEXIS
1333 (2001).

Prisoner was not precluded from using multiple
degrees at the same educational level to reach his
total credit time. Partlow v. Superintendent, 756
N.E.2d 978, 2001 Ind. App. LEXIS 1750 (2001).

Under the clear and unambiguous language of
IC 35-50-6-3.3(d), an inmate may not receive more
than a total of six months of credit time toward his
sentence for all vocational programs he completes.
Denney v. State, 773 N.E.2d 300, 2002 Ind. App.
LEXIS 1287 (2002).

IC 35-50-6-3.3(a) provides that only three requirements must be established in order to earn
credit time: (1) the person is in credit class I; (2)
has demonstrated a pattern consistent with rehabilitation; and (3) successfully completes a general
educational development diploma; IC 35-50-6-
3.3(i) is a limit to credit time, not a requirement to
be established in order to receive credit time.
Wilson v. State, 785 N.E.2d 1152, 2003 Ind. App.
LEXIS 525 (2003).

Under IC 35-50-6-3.3, a defendant is entitled to
educational credit time for a high school diploma
granted by an out-of-state high school as long as
the standards of instruction for earning that diploma are substantially similar to those in Indiana. McGee v. State, 790 N.E.2d 1067, 2003 Ind.
App. LEXIS 1204 (2003).

Inmate was not entitled under IC 35-50-6-3.3 to
credit on his murder sentence for obtaining his
high school from an out-of-state school because he
failed to present evidence sufficient to establish
that the school had the same standard of instruction as Indiana schools. Glass v. Wrigley, 899
N.E.2d 652, 2008 Ind. App. LEXIS 2630 (2008).

Out-of-state school did not meet the requirement
that its standard of instruction be substantially
similar to that of schools in Indiana where the
school did not require proctoring of its exams
during courses and did not include a final examination equivalent to the ISTEP+ exam required
under IC 20-32-4-1. Glass v. Wrigley, 899 N.E.2d
652, 2008 Ind. App. LEXIS 2630 (2008).

Plea Agreements.
Guilty plea court did not have authority pursu-

Plea Agreements. (Cont'd)
ant to former IC 35-38-1-23 to modify sentence of defendant who pled guilty pursuant to plea agreement which contained agreed upon sentence unless plea agreement specifically reserved right to do so for the court. Thompson v. State, 617 N.E.2d 576, 1993 Ind. App. LEXIS 889 (1993).

Under former IC 35-38-1-23 , the prospect of future sentence modification may be contemplated by the parties in their plea bargaining, and specifically provided for in the plea agreement. Pannarale v. State, 638 N.E.2d 1247, 1994 Ind. LEXIS 111 (1994).

—Restrictions.
Where the trial judge could have sentenced defendant to fewer years of incarceration when he initially passed sentence, he could subsequently reduce the 10-year sentence actually imposed; when he accepted the plea agreement and sentenced defendant to prison, the only restriction imposed on the judge by the plea agreement was an upper limit on the sentence of 10 years. Pannarale v. State, 638 N.E.2d 1247, 1994 Ind. LEXIS 111 (1994).

Receipt of Diploma.
Receiving a diploma does not constitute "completing a portion of a degree" within the meaning of this section, and therefore prisoner who received associate's degree on July 23, 1993, was not entitled to a one-year reduction in sentence pursuant to subsection (c) of this section. Miller v. Bryant, 644 N.E.2d 188, 1994 Ind. App. LEXIS 1708 (1994).

Reduction of Sentence.
A defendant who entered a plea agreement with the state did not have the right to reduction of the executed portion of his sentence under former IC 35-38-1-23, where the plea was accepted by the court prior to the legislative enactment of the statute and where the written plea agreement did not address the statute. Schippers v. State, 622 N.E.2d 993, 1993 Ind. App. LEXIS 1287 (1993).

The rationale expressed in *Goldsmith v. Marion County Superior Court,* 275 Ind. 545, 419 N.E.2d 109, 1981 Ind. LEXIS 721 (1981), that a plea

agreement is contractual in nature and permitting modification of its terms defeats the essential purpose of the agreement, is equally applicable to this section (former IC 35-38-1-23) as it is to the shock probation statute (IC 35-38-1-17). Schippers v. State, 622 N.E.2d 993, 1993 Ind. App. LEXIS 1287 (1993).

Right to Education Programs.
Denial of educational programs, because of transfer to a different cellhouse, might deprive prisoner of the opportunity to earn good time credits under this section, but did not deprive him of a liberty interest because it was not inevitable he would complete an educational program and earn good time credits if he had been given the opportunity. Higgason v. Farley, 83 F.3d 807, 1996 U.S. App. LEXIS 1354 (7th Cir. Ind. 1996).

The denial of access to educational programs to earn good time credits does not infringe on an inmate's protected liberty interest under the Fourteenth Amendment. Zimmerman v. Tribble, 226 F.3d 568, 2000 U.S. App. LEXIS 20683 (7th Cir. Ind. 2000).

Sentence for Heinous Crime.
The court did not abuse its discretion in denying a petition for modification under former IC 35-38-1-23 (see this section for similar provisions), notwithstanding a determination that the defendant had done well in prison and deserved praise, where his crime, i.e., the molestation of his step-daughter, was heinous. Myers v. State, 718 N.E.2d 783, 1999 Ind. App. LEXIS 1881 (1999).

Subsequent Parole Violation.
The plain language of the phrase "has demonstrated a pattern consistent with rehabilitation" limits the time period for evaluation of the inmate's behavior to that period before he receives his diploma or degree, and a subsequent parole or probation violation does not deny him the credit time already earned. Rodgers v. State, 705 N.E.2d 1039, 1999 Ind. App. LEXIS 152 (1999).

Cited:
State v. Eckhardt, 687 N.E.2d 374, 1997 Ind. App. LEXIS 1548 (1997).

RESEARCH REFERENCES

Indiana Law Review.
Update — Criminal Law and Procedure, 26 Ind. L. Rev. 891 (1993).

Res Gestae.
Criminal justice notes, 38 (No. 4) Res Gestae 40 (1994).

Criminal justice notes, 38 (No. 8) Res Gestae 48 (1995).

Criminal Justice Notes 7/07:Credit time for completion of substance abuse - must exhaust administrative remedies, 51 (No. 3) Res Gestae 40 (2007).

35-50-6-4. Initial assignment to credit time classification.

(a) A person who is not a credit restricted felon and who is imprisoned for a crime or imprisoned awaiting trial or sentencing is initially assigned to Class I.

(b) A person who is a credit restricted felon and who is imprisoned for a crime or imprisoned awaiting trial or sentencing is initially assigned to Class IV. A credit restricted felon may not be assigned to Class I or Class II.

(c) A person who is not assigned to Class IV may be reassigned to Class II or Class III if the person violates any of the following:

(1) A rule of the department of correction.

(2) A rule of the penal facility in which the person is imprisoned.

(3) A rule or condition of a community transition program.

However, a violation of a condition of parole or probation may not be the basis for reassignment. Before a person may be reassigned to a lower credit time class, the person must be granted a hearing to determine the person's guilt or innocence and, if found guilty, whether reassignment is an appropriate disciplinary action for the violation. The person may waive the right to the hearing.

(d) A person who is assigned to Class IV may be reassigned to Class III if the person violates any of the following:

(1) A rule of the department of correction.

(2) A rule of the penal facility in which the person is imprisoned.

(3) A rule or condition of a community transition program.

However, a violation of a condition of parole or probation may not be the basis for reassignment. Before a person may be reassigned to Class III, the person must be granted a hearing to determine the person's guilt or innocence and, if found guilty, whether reassignment is an appropriate disciplinary action for the violation. The person may waive the right to the hearing.

(e) In connection with the hearing granted under subsection (c) or (d), the person is entitled to:

(1) have not less than twenty-four (24) hours advance written notice of the date, time, and place of the hearing, and of the alleged misconduct and the rule the misconduct is alleged to have violated;

(2) have reasonable time to prepare for the hearing;

(3) have an impartial decisionmaker;

(4) appear and speak in the person's own behalf;

(5) call witnesses and present evidence;

(6) confront and cross-examine each witness, unless the hearing authority finds that to do so would subject a witness to a substantial risk of harm;

(7) have the assistance of a lay advocate (the department may require that the advocate be an employee of, or a fellow prisoner in, the same facility or program);

(8) have a written statement of the findings of fact, the evidence relied upon, and the reasons for the action taken;

(9) have immunity if the person's testimony or any evidence derived from the person's testimony is used in any criminal proceedings; and

(10) have the person's record expunged of any reference to the charge if the person is found not guilty or if a finding of guilt is later overturned.

Any finding of guilt must be supported by a preponderance of the evidence presented at the hearing.

(f) A person may be reassigned from Class III to Class I, Class II, or Class IV, or from Class II to Class I. A person's assignment to Class III or Class II shall be reviewed at least once every six (6) months to determine if the person should be reassigned to a higher credit time class. A credit restricted felon may not be reassigned to Class I or Class II.

History.

IC 35-50-6-4, as added by Acts 1976, P.L.148, § 8; 1977, P.L.340, § 135; 1979, P.L.120, § 12; P.L.90-2000, § 22; P.L.80-2008, § 4, eff. July 1, 2008.

Compiler's Notes.

P.L.80-2008, § 6, effective July 1, 2008, provides:

"IC 35-41-1-5.5, as added by this act, and IC 35-50-6-3, IC 35-50-6-4, and IC 35-50-6-5, all as amended by this act, apply only to persons convicted after June 30, 2008."

NOTES TO DECISIONS

In General.

Good time credits are still not constitutionally required; "liberty" still attaches only when the credits are actually given. Cottingham v. State, 424 N.E.2d 105, 1981 Ind. LEXIS 926 (1981).

Legislature invested the department of correction, not the trial court, with the responsibility of determining, denying, or restoring credit time. Trial court properly set aside its order directing the department of correction to award good time credit time to defendant as the trial court did not have the statutory authority to direct that credit time be awarded. Kindred v. State, 771 N.E.2d 760, 2002 Ind. App. LEXIS 1143 (2002), overruled in part, Robinson v. State, 799 N.E.2d 1202, 2003 Ind. App. LEXIS 2292 (Ind. Ct. App. 2003).

Credit time determinations were entrusted not to the courts but to the administrators of the department of corrections, regardless of whether the context was pre-sentence or post-sentence incarceration; a court only had the authority to make recommendations regarding credit time. Robinson v. State, 789 N.E.2d 965, 2003 Ind. App. LEXIS 960 (2003), transfer granted, — N.E.2d —, 2003 Ind. LEXIS 582 (2003), superseded, 805 N.E.2d 783, 2004 Ind. LEXIS 229 (2004).

Accrual of Credit.

—Second Charge.

Where a defendant is in jail on one charge and a second charge is filed, credit on the second charge begins to accrue at the date of the arrest and not the date of filing. Dewees v. State, 444 N.E.2d 332, 1983 Ind. App. LEXIS 2568 (1983).

Applicability.

Because respondent was not "imprisoned for a crime," IC 35-50-6-3 and IC 35-50-6-4 did not apply to respondent's sentence for criminal contempt. Jones v. State, 847 N.E.2d 190, 2006 Ind. App. LEXIS 817 (2006).

Consecutive Sentences.

Although inmate may have been in class I when one sentence expired, when the new sentence commenced he was a new prisoner and it was proper to automatically place him in class II at the commencement of the second sentence. Dunn v. Jenkins, 268 Ind. 478, 377 N.E.2d 868, 1978 Ind. LEXIS 694 (1978).

Credit is imposed against the aggregate sentences where consecutive sentences are imposed, and not against each individual sentence. Dewees v. State, 444 N.E.2d 332, 1983 Ind. App. LEXIS 2568 (1983).

Defendant, who escaped from jail while awaiting trial for murder, was not entitled to credit for pretrial incarceration on the escape charge, where she had been granted presentence confinement credit on her murder sentence, and the two sentences were to be served consecutively. Jorgensen v. State, 559 N.E.2d 616, 1990 Ind. App. LEXIS 1184 (1990).

Where defendant was required to serve consecutive sentences for multiple offenses because the second offense was committed while defendant was on bond, defendant was not entitled to have credit for time served applied against each separate sentence, but had to have credit applied to the aggregate sentence. Diedrich v. State, 744 N.E.2d 1004, 2001 Ind. App. LEXIS 413 (2001).

Correction of Error.

Where both defendants were apprehended at the same time and tried simultaneously but there was a two-day discrepancy between the two in the time served allowance on their sentences the cause was remanded for correction of the time served. Collins v. State, 266 Ind. 430, 364 N.E.2d 750, 1977 Ind. LEXIS 413 (1977).

Daily Reporting Probation.

Trial court properly denied a defendant's motion for credit time after his daily reporting probation was revoked for having committed an additional crime and he was, therefore, ordered to serve the remainder of his sentence for his rape conviction, namely 10 years. The appellate court agreed with the trial court's determination that daily reporting to a probation officer did not amount to the type of freedom restrictions that deserved credit time and no statutory authority existed to support the defendant's request. Reed v. State, 844 N.E.2d 223, 2006 Ind. App. LEXIS 541 (2006).

Due Process.

This right is created by statute and the legislature is given wide latitude in designing and implementing a good time scheme; but when rights of this nature are affected so that an individual is likely to suffer a "grievous loss" then due process mandates that minimum procedural safeguards be

Due Process. (Cont'd)
insured. Dunn v. Jenkins, 268 Ind. 478, 377 N.E.2d 868, 1978 Ind. LEXIS 694 (1978).

While under former IC 11-7-6.1-4 an inmate had a substantial interest in being initially classified into earning class II, there was no denial of any constitutional right where, at the time that section went into effect, some inmates were classified in class III or IV although there was no administrative hearing where the classification committee reviewed each inmate's packet and based its determination of that inmate's new classification solely on his established institutional record. Dunn v. Jenkins, 268 Ind. 478, 377 N.E.2d 868, 1978 Ind. LEXIS 694 (1978).

The trial court erred where it denied a defendant credit time for violating the terms of his release on bond, but not for any conduct while incarcerated, and where the court did not provide the defendant with a hearing regarding the appropriateness of reassigning him to a lower credit time class. Tumbleson v. State, 706 N.E.2d 217, 1999 Ind. App. LEXIS 172 (1999).

Defendant's 28 U.S.C.S. § 2254 habeas corpus petition was denied because his claims were procedurally defaulted and his claims otherwise lacked substantive merit, as he had received all the process that was due him under IC 35-50-6-4 and IC 35-50-6-5, and the federal constitution in connection with a prison disciplinary proceeding that resulted in the loss of earned good-time credits: (1) defendant was found guilty of possessing or using an unauthorized substance and failure to submit a urine sample after marijuana was found in his cell; (2) defendant's habeas claims were procedurally defaulted because he had not asserted them in the administrative appeal that he filed challenging the prison conduct board's decision; and (3) defendant had received all of the process that was due him under state and federal law because he had received timely advance notice of the charges against him, he was given the opportunity to appear and challenge the charges, the conduct board explained its decision, and there was "some evidence" to support that decision. Milligan v. Meloy, — F. Supp. 2d —, 2007 U.S. Dist. LEXIS 30571 (S.D. Ind. 2007).

—Disciplinary Proceedings.
The terms of the sentence imposed upon the defendant — including the right to be incarcerated at a particular institution, the right to be on work release status and to maintain his current, private employment, and the right to be released from jail for treatment — gave the defendant a liberty interest protected by the Fourteenth Amendment. As such, the defendant was entitled to the following minimum due process requirements for prison disciplinary proceedings: (1) The right to have a reasonable time to prepare for the hearing; (2) the right to call witnesses and present evidence; (3) the right to confront and cross-examine each witness, so long as there was no potential for havoc and where the hearing did not become unmanageably long; (4) the right to counsel; (5) the right to have a written statement of the findings of fact, the evidence relied upon, and the reasons for the action taken; and (6) the right to have a meaningful review of the hearing. Smith v. Stoner, 594 F. Supp. 1091, 1984 U.S. Dist. LEXIS 23818 (N.D. Ind. 1984).

Equal Protection.
A statute which provided for good time but which excepted those inmates under sentence of death or life imprisonment did not violate the equal protection clause of the U.S. Const., Amend. 14 or Ind. Const., Art. 1, § 23. Jennings v. State, 270 Ind. 699, 389 N.E.2d 283, 1979 Ind. LEXIS 621 (1979).

Imprisoned Awaiting Trial.

—Home Detention.
Defendant was not entitled to good time credit for pretrial home detention, because he would not be entitled to good time credit for post-conviction home detention under IC 35-38-2.6-6. Franklin v. State, 679 N.E.2d 510, 1997 Ind. App. LEXIS 433 (1997), transfer granted, 690 N.E.2d 1179 (Ind. 1997), superseded, 685 N.E.2d 1062, 1997 Ind. LEXIS 153 (1997). See also Franklin v. State, 685 N.E.2d 1062, 1997 Ind. LEXIS 153 (1997), overruled in part, State v. Purcell, 721 N.E.2d 220, 1999 Ind. LEXIS 1189 (1999).

Multiple Sentences.
Full credit should be allowed against each sentence where defendant was awaiting two trials on different crimes during the same period, and was convicted and sentenced separately on each. Franks v. State, 262 Ind. 649, 323 N.E.2d 221, 1975 Ind. LEXIS 248 (1975).

Where, between the time defendant was released on bond and his trial and conviction, he was incarcerated on a separate federal charge, such period of incarceration was not a result of the criminal charge for which sentence is imposed or as a result of the conduct on which such charge is based and he was not entitled to credit therefor against his sentence. Smith v. State, 165 Ind. App. 37, 330 N.E.2d 384, 1975 Ind. App. LEXIS 1212 (1975).

Former IC 35-8-2.5-1 — IC 35-8-2.5-5 allowed credit only for that time served on account of the criminal charge for which the sentence was imposed, not for time served on another separate criminal charge. Dunn v. State, 171 Ind. App. 206, 355 N.E.2d 870, 1976 Ind. App. LEXIS 1077 (1976).

Trial court did not err in denying defendant credit time for the days spent awaiting trial for jail takeover, where defendant was serving a sentence on an unrelated charge when the jail takeover occurred and he was sentenced to a term consecutive to the prior sentence. Corn v. State, 659 N.E.2d 554, 1995 Ind. LEXIS 219 (1995).

Prospective Application.
The equal protection clause does not require this section to be applied retroactively. Cottingham v. State, 424 N.E.2d 105, 1981 Ind. LEXIS 926 (1981).

Time Prior to Sentencing.

Defendant was entitled to credit for the full period in which he remained incarcerated from time of arrest through sentencing. Lee v. State, 156 Ind. App. 569, 297 N.E.2d 890, 1973 Ind. App. LEXIS 1167 (1973).

Accused, whose murder conviction was reversed, but who pleaded guilty and was sentenced to life imprisonment at a second trial, must be given full credit for time spent in detention prior to the first trial and time served after the first conviction as the constitutional guarantees against multiple punishments for the same offense required that the accused be given full credit for any time already served in imposing sentence for the new conviction. Pruett v. State, 263 Ind. 405, 332 N.E.2d 212, 1975 Ind. LEXIS 321 (1975).

Where the trial court erred in denying defendant's motion to correct an erroneous sentence regarding defendant's conviction for attempted murder, and it was unclear whether defendant was properly credited for both defendant's time served and credit time, remand was required to determine the amount of time defendant actually served prior to sentencing. Robinson v. State, 783 N.E.2d 1206, 2003 Ind. App. LEXIS 297 (2003), op. withdrawn,
2003 Ind. App. LEXIS 963 (Ind. Ct. App. May 9, 2003), op. replaced, 789 N.E.2d 965, 2003 Ind. App. LEXIS 960 (2003).

Time Served Outside State.

Former IC 35-8-2.5-1 — IC 35-8-2.5-5 did not provide credit for time served in another state for a totally different offense which occurred in the other state. Cooley v. State, 172 Ind. App. 199, 360 N.E.2d 29, 1977 Ind. App. LEXIS 748 (1977).

Cited:

Simms v. State, 421 N.E.2d 698, 1981 Ind. App. LEXIS 1469 (1981); Bates v. State, 426 N.E.2d 404, 1981 Ind. LEXIS 866 (1981); Harper v. Gibson, 666 F. Supp. 1252, 1987 U.S. Dist. LEXIS 7792 (N.D. Ind. 1987); Boyd v. Broglin, 519 N.E.2d 541, 1988 Ind. LEXIS 81 (1988); Johnson v. Trigg, 28 F.3d 639, 1994 U.S. App. LEXIS 16432 (7th Cir. Ind. 1994); State v. Eckhardt, 687 N.E.2d 374, 1997 Ind. App. LEXIS 1548 (1997); Robinson v. State, 805 N.E.2d 783, 2004 Ind. LEXIS 229 (2004); Portee v. State, 806 N.E.2d 358, 2004 Ind. App. LEXIS 676 (2004).

RESEARCH REFERENCES

Res Gestae.
Criminal justice notes, 38 (No. 1) Res Gestae 38 (1994).

Criminal Justice Notes 3/04: Credit time cleared up. 47 (No. 9) Res Gestae 37 (2004).

35-50-6-5. Violations — Deprivation of credit time — Hearing — Restoration.

(a) A person may, with respect to the same transaction, be deprived of any part of the credit time the person has earned for any of the following:

(1) A violation of one (1) or more rules of the department of correction.

(2) If the person is not committed to the department, a violation of one (1) or more rules of the penal facility in which the person is imprisoned.

(3) A violation of one (1) or more rules or conditions of a community transition program.

(4) If a court determines that a civil claim brought by the person in a state or an administrative court is frivolous, unreasonable, or groundless.

(5) If the person is a sex offender (as defined in IC 11-8-8-5) and refuses to register before being released from the department as required under IC 11-8-8-7.

(6) If the person is a sex offender (as defined in IC 11-8-8-5) and refuses to participate in a sex offender treatment program specifically offered to the sex offender by the department of correction while the person is serving a period of incarceration with the department of correction.

However, the violation of a condition of parole or probation may not be the basis for deprivation. Whenever a person is deprived of credit time, the person may also be reassigned to Class II (if the person is not a credit restricted felon) or Class III.

(b) Before a person may be deprived of earned credit time, the person must be granted a hearing to determine the person's guilt or innocence and, if found guilty, whether deprivation of earned credit time is an appropriate disciplinary action for the violation. In connection with the hearing, the person is entitled to the procedural safeguards listed in section 4(e) [IC 35-50-6-4(e)] of this chapter. The person may waive the person's right to the hearing.

(c) Any part of the credit time of which a person is deprived under this section may be restored.

History.

IC 35-50-6-5, as added by Acts 1976, P.L.148, § 8; 1977, P.L.340, § 136; 1979, P.L.120, § 13; P.L.146-1995, § 6; P.L.90-2000, § 23; P.L.140-2006, § 39; P.L.173-2006, § 39; P.L.80-2008, § 5, eff. July 1, 2008.

Compiler's Notes.

P.L.80-2008, § 6, effective July 1, 2008, provides:

"IC 35-41-1-5.5, as added by this act, and IC 35-50-6-3, IC 35-50-6-4, and IC 35-50-6-5, all as amended by this act, apply only to persons convicted after June 30, 2008."

NOTES TO DECISIONS

ANALYSIS

Constitutionality.
Administrative Responsibility.
Applicability.
Frivolous Actions.
"Good Time" Credit.
Infractions of Rules.
Object of Law.
Pretrial Detainees.

Constitutionality.

IC 35-50-6-5(a)(4) is not void for vagueness, is not constitutionally overbroad, does not violate substantive due process principles, and does not violate the federal Equal Protection Clause. Parks v. Madison County, 783 N.E.2d 711, 2002 Ind. App. LEXIS 2197 (2002).

Administrative Responsibility.

The legislature did not intend to invest the trial court with the responsibility of denying or restoring credit time, but provided that the deprivation or restoration of credit time is a discretionary matter entrusted, not to the courts, but to the administrators of the Department of Correction. Campbell v. State, 714 N.E.2d 678, 1999 Ind. App. LEXIS 1064 (1999), overruled in part, Robinson v. State, 805 N.E.2d 783, 2004 Ind. LEXIS 229 (2004).

The trial court was without authority under IC 35-50-6-5 to require defendant, as a condition of receiving good time credit, to hang a picture of the two victims killed by the drunk driver to whom he served 10 double drinks over a period of 130 minutes. Irwin v. State, 744 N.E.2d 565, 2001 Ind. App. LEXIS 493 (2001).

Credit time determinations were entrusted not to the courts but to the administrators of the department of corrections, regardless of whether the context was pre-sentence or post-sentence incarceration; a court only had the authority to make recommendations regarding credit time. Robinson v. State, 789 N.E.2d 965, 2003 Ind. App. LEXIS 960 (2003), transfer granted, — N.E.2d —, 2003 Ind. LEXIS 582 (2003), superseded, 805 N.E.2d 783, 2004 Ind. LEXIS 229 (2004).

Applicability.

Definitions of the terms "frivolous," "unreasonable," and "groundless" as used in IC 34-52-1-1(b)(1) are applicable as well to those terms as used in IC 35-50-6-5(a)(4). Parks v. Madison County, 783 N.E.2d 711, 2002 Ind. App. LEXIS 2197 (2002).

Frivolous Actions.

Where a prisoner filed several civil rights suits against a judge, a prosecutor, and others, the trial court did not err in finding that the prisoner's claims were frivolous. Parks v. Madison County, 783 N.E.2d 711, 2002 Ind. App. LEXIS 2197 (2002).

Inmate's claims against a judge so clearly fell within the doctrine of judicial immunity that the inmate could not have rationally argued that his complaint had merit; further, since the inmate had extensive experience with the legal system, he was subject to deprivation of earned credit time under IC 35-50-6-5(a)(4). Sumbry v. Boklund, 836 N.E.2d 430, 2005 Ind. LEXIS 989 (2005).

"Good Time" Credit.

The violation of parole or probation may not be the basis for the deprivation of "good time" credit, because, in order to receive such credit, a person must be imprisoned. Rodgers v. State, 705 N.E.2d 1039, 1999 Ind. App. LEXIS 152 (1999).

Denial of a motion to correct erroneous sentence was proper since court's failure to record defendant's credit time earned/good time credit in abstract of judgment did not render sentence facially erroneous. Hatchett v. State, 794 N.E.2d 544, 2003 Ind. App. LEXIS 1595 (2003), overruled in part, Robinson v. State, 805 N.E.2d 783, 2004 Ind. LEXIS 229 (2004).

IC 35-50-6-5(c) permits restoration of good time credit but does not stipulate policy for doing so. Diaz v. Mitchell, — F. Supp. 2d —, 2005 U.S. Dist. LEXIS 6860 (N.D. Ind. 2005).

Parolee was not deprived of earned good time credits or any other credits when parole was revoked for violation of special conditions since parolees are deemed to be in legal custody throughout term of parole; parolee received benefit of credits when parole was granted. Harris v. State, 836 N.E.2d 267, 2005 Ind. App. LEXIS 1942 (2005).

Infractions of Rules.

Under former IC 11-7-5-1, where prisoner was

Infractions of Rules. (Cont'd)
deprived of accrued "good-time" by disciplinary board due to trafficking, it was error for circuit court to order prisoner released on basis of such "good-time," since it did not begin to accrue again until after he was placed in administrative segregation. Hudkins v. Baromich, 256 Ind. 183, 267 N.E.2d 382, 1971 Ind. LEXIS 610 (1971).

Under former IC 11-7-5-1, when an inmate committed an infraction of the rules and regulations of the institution, his accumulation of good-time started anew at the lowest rate of three days for the first month. Hudkins v. Baromich, 256 Ind. 183, 269 N.E.2d 867, 1971 Ind. LEXIS 611 (1971).

Defendant's 28 U.S.C.S. § 2254 habeas corpus petition was denied because his claims were procedurally defaulted and his claims otherwise lacked substantive merit, as he had received all the process that was due him under IC 35-50-6-4 and IC 35-50-6-5, and the federal constitution in connection with a prison disciplinary proceeding that resulted in the loss of earned good-time credits: (1) defendant was found guilty of possessing or using an unauthorized substance and failure to submit a urine sample after marijuana was found in his cell; (2) defendant's habeas claims were procedurally defaulted because he had not asserted them in the administrative appeal that he filed challenging the prison conduct board's decision; and (3) defendant had received all of the process that was due him under state and federal law because he had received timely advance notice of the charges against him, he was given the opportunity to appear and challenge the charges, the conduct board explained its decision, and there was "some evidence" to support that decision. Milligan v. Meloy, — F. Supp. 2d —, 2007 U.S. Dist. LEXIS 30571 (S.D. Ind. 2007).

Object of Law.
The objective of former IC 11-7-5-1 was to give prison authorities control over the prisoners and induce the prisoners to behave well. Hudkins v. Baromich, 256 Ind. 183, 269 N.E.2d 867, 1971 Ind. LEXIS 611 (1971).

Pretrial Detainees.
Prior to the effective date of subsection (a) which was April 1, 1980, there was no authority for depriving pretrial detainees of good time credit. Bates v. State, 426 N.E.2d 404, 1981 Ind. LEXIS 866 (1981).

Cited:
Smith v. Stoner, 594 F. Supp. 1091, 1984 U.S. Dist. LEXIS 23818 (N.D. Ind. 1984); Boyd v. Broglin, 519 N.E.2d 541, 1988 Ind. LEXIS 81 (1988); Isby v. Bayh, 75 F.3d 1191, 1996 U.S. App. LEXIS 1549 (7th Cir. Ind. 1996); Martin v. Heffelfinger, 744 N.E.2d 555, 2001 Ind. App. LEXIS 465 (2001); Robinson v. State, 805 N.E.2d 783, 2004 Ind. LEXIS 229 (2004); Parks v. State, 789 N.E.2d 40, 2003 Ind. App. LEXIS 895 (2003).

35-50-6-5.5. Reassignment to lower class or deprivation of credit time — Review.

A person who has been reassigned to a lower credit time class or has been deprived of earned credit time may appeal the decision to the commissioner of the department of correction or the sheriff.

History.
IC 35-50-6-5.5, as added by Acts 1979, P.L.120, § 14; P.L.204-1986, § 3.

NOTES TO DECISIONS

ANALYSIS

Due Process.
Refusal to Release.

Due Process.
The terms of the sentence imposed upon the defendant — including the right to be incarcerated at a particular institution, the right to be on work release status and to maintain his current, private employment, and the right to be released from jail for treatment — gave the defendant a liberty interest protected by the Fourteenth Amendment. As such, the defendant was entitled to the following minimum due process requirements for prison disciplinary proceedings: (1) the right to have a reasonable time to prepare for the hearing; (2) the right to call witnesses and present evidence; (3) the right to confront and cross-examine each witness, so long as there was no potential for havoc and where the hearing did not become unmanageably long; (4) the right to counsel; (5) the right to have a written statement of the findings of fact, the evidence relied upon, and the reasons for the action taken; and (6) the right to have a meaningful review of the hearing. Smith v. Stoner, 594 F. Supp. 1091, 1984 U.S. Dist. LEXIS 23818 (N.D. Ind. 1984).

Refusal to Release.
Under former IC 11-7-1-3, the action of the board of managers of the Indiana Reformatory in refusing to release a prisoner before the maximum term of his sentence had expired could not be reviewed by the courts. Terry v. Byers, 161 Ind. 360, 68 N.E. 596, 1903 Ind. LEXIS 175 (1903).

Cited:
Harper v. Gibson, 666 F. Supp. 1252, 1987 U.S.

Dist. LEXIS 7792 (N.D. Ind. 1987); Feagin v. Broglin, 693 F. Supp. 736, 1988 U.S. Dist. LEXIS 9723 (N.D. Ind. 1988).

35-50-6-6. Degree of security not a factor in assignment of credit time — Effect of revocation of parole.

(a) A person imprisoned for a crime earns credit time irrespective of the degree of security to which he is assigned. Except as set forth under IC 35-38-2.5-5, a person does not earn credit time while on parole or probation.

(b) A person imprisoned upon revocation of parole is initially assigned to the same credit time class to which he was assigned at the time he was released on parole.

(c) A person who, upon revocation of parole, is imprisoned on an intermittent basis does not earn credit time for the days he spends on parole outside the institution.

History.
IC 35-50-6-6, as added by Acts 1976, P.L.148, § 8; 1977, P.L.340, § 137; 1979, P.L.120, § 15; P.L.166-2001, § 4.

NOTES TO DECISIONS

ANALYSIS

Credit Time.
Effective Date.
Home Detention.
Probation.

Credit Time.
When the words "credit time" appear in a statute, the legislature is referring to good time credit. Dishroon v. State, 722 N.E.2d 385, 2000 Ind. App. LEXIS 58 (2000).

Trial court properly denied a defendant's motion for credit time after his daily reporting probation was revoked for having committed an additional crime and he was, therefore, ordered to serve the remainder of his sentence for his rape conviction, namely 10 years. The appellate court agreed with the trial court's determination that daily reporting to a probation officer did not amount to the type of freedom restrictions that deserved credit time and no statutory authority existed to support the defendant's request. Reed v. State, 844 N.E.2d 223, 2006 Ind. App. LEXIS 541 (2006).

Effective Date.
The amendment of Acts 1976, P.L.148 by Acts 1977, P.L.340, so as to postpone the effective date from July 1, 1977 to October 1, 1977, was proper. Lohm v. State, 177 Ind. App. 488, 380 N.E.2d 561, 1978 Ind. App. LEXIS 1019 (1978).

Home Detention.
Since home detention is a benefit to defendants, the refusal to grant credit time for time served on home detention does not amount to cruel and unusual punishment. Collins v. State, 639 N.E.2d 653, 1994 Ind. App. LEXIS 1093 (1994), overruled, Dishroon v. State, 722 N.E.2d 385, 2000 Ind. App. LEXIS 58 (2000).

Person placed on home detention as condition of probation is not entitled to credit time. Wharff v. State, 691 N.E.2d 205, 1998 Ind. App. LEXIS 18 (1998), overruled, Dishroon v. State, 722 N.E.2d 385, 2000 Ind. App. LEXIS 58 (2000).

Although the defendant was not entitled to good time credit for the time he served in home detention while on probation, because his liberty was restricted he was entitled to one day credit for each day that he actually served at home. Dishroon v. State, 722 N.E.2d 385, 2000 Ind. App. LEXIS 58 (2000).

Probation.
Where defendant was on probation but was not in custody, and was in no way confined nor was his liberty restricted while he was released on his own recognizance, defendant was not entitled to credit for the time he spent on probation. Via v. State, 738 N.E.2d 684, 2000 Ind. App. LEXIS 1836 (2000).

Defendant was not entitled to credit against his sentence for time spent in a drug rehabilitation facility that was ordered as part of his probation when he violated probation and was ordered to serve out his sentence. Oswalt v. State, 749 N.E.2d 612, 2001 Ind. App. LEXIS 897 (2001).

Cited:
Boyd v. Broglin, 519 N.E.2d 541, 1988 Ind. LEXIS 81 (1988); Burton v. State, 547 N.E.2d 882, 1989 Ind. App. LEXIS 1286 (1989).

35-50-6-7. Reassignment and suspension of credit time due to misconduct.

(a) A person under the control of a county detention facility or the department of correction who:

(1) Has been charged with a new crime while confined; or

(2) Has allegedly violated a rule of the department or county facility;

may be immediately assigned to Class III and may have all earned credit time suspended pending disposition of the allegation.

(b) A person assigned to Class III under subsection (a) shall be denied release on parole or discharge until:

(1) He is in the actual custody of the department or the county detention facility to which he was sentenced; and

(2) He is granted a hearing concerning the allegations.

The department or sheriff may waive the hearing if the person is restored to his former credit time class and receives all previously earned credit time and any credit time that he would have earned if he had not been assigned to Class III.

(c) A person who is assigned to Class III under subsection (a) and later found not guilty of the alleged misconduct shall have all earned credit time restored and shall be reassigned to the same credit time class that he was in before his assignment to Class III. In addition, the person shall be credited with any credit time that he would have earned if he had not been assigned to Class III.

History.
IC 35-50-6-7, as added by P.L.338-1983, § 1.

NOTES TO DECISIONS

ANALYSIS

Credit for Time Served.
Good Time Credit.

Credit for Time Served.
Although defendant was classified as class III for time credit purposes under IC 35-50-6-7, which made defendant ineligible for good time credit under IC 35-50-6-3(c), classification did not impact defendant's right to credit for time served prior to sentencing. Groves v. State, 823 N.E.2d 1229, 2005 Ind. App. LEXIS 431 (2005).

Good Time Credit.
Where defendant at initial hearing on felony charge threatened to kill victim, which resulted in additional charge of intimidation against defendant, defendant was properly classified for credit time purposes as class III pursuant to IC 35-50-6-7 because he was charged with new crime while confined. Groves v. State, 823 N.E.2d 1229, 2005 Ind. App. LEXIS 431 (2005).

Where defendant was classified as class III for time credit purposes under IC 35-50-6-7, which made defendant ineligible for good time credit under IC 35-50-6-3(c), failure of trial court to explicitly state that defendant would be credited with zero days of good time credit was not error. Groves v. State, 823 N.E.2d 1229, 2005 Ind. App. LEXIS 431 (2005).

35-50-6-8. Person serving life sentence without parole does not earn credit time.

A person serving a sentence of life imprisonment without parole does not earn credit time under this chapter.

History.
P.L.53-2005, § 3.

CHAPTER 7

PROBATION ORDERS

35-50-7-1. Applicability of chapter.

This chapter applies when a person is placed on probation after being convicted of an offense.

History.
P.L.216-1996, § 26.

35-50-7-2. Orders prohibiting person from entering certain areas or property.

The court that places a person on probation following conviction may issue an order, reasonable in scope, under this chapter that prohibits the person from entering the:
(1) area or property where an offense was committed by the person; and
(2) area immediately surrounding the area or property where an offense was committed by the person.

History.
P.L.216-1996, § 26.

35-50-7-3. Description of property.

An order issued under this chapter must describe the area or property that the person is prohibited from entering with sufficient specificity to:
(1) allow the person to guide the person's conduct accordingly; and
(2) enable a law enforcement officer to enforce the order.

History.
P.L.216-1996, § 26.

35-50-7-4. Restrictions on and supervision of return to residential premises.

A court that issues an order under this chapter may:
(1) allow a person to return to the person's residential premises to pick up personal belongings and effects;
(2) restrict the time and duration of the person's return; and
(3) provide for supervision of the person's return by a law enforcement officer.

History.
P.L.216-1996, § 26.

35-50-7-5. Copy of order to be given to person concerned.

A person shall be given a copy of an order issued under this chapter concerning the person and shall acknowledge the receipt of the order in writing.

History.
P.L.216-1996, § 26.

35-50-7-6. Notice of order.

The court shall provide notice of an order issued under this chapter to:
(1) the law enforcement agency that arrested the person; and
(2) the prosecuting attorney.

History.
P.L.216-1996, § 26.

35-50-7-7. Notification of stay, modification, or vacation of order.

A court shall immediately notify all appropriate law enforcement agencies when an order issued under this chapter is stayed, modified, or vacated.

History.
P.L.216-1996, § 26.

35-50-7-8. Evidence considered.

In determining whether to issue an order under this chapter, the court may consider evidence regarding whether the order would:
(1) cause undue hardship to innocent persons; and
(2) constitute a serious injustice that overrides the need to protect the rights, safety, and health of other tenants and residents of the property or area affected by the order.

History.
P.L.216-1996, § 26.

35-50-7-9. Violation — Penalty.

A person who knowingly or intentionally violates an order issued by a court under this chapter commits a Class C misdemeanor.

History.   **Cross References.**
P.L.216-1996, § 26.   Penalties for misdemeanors, IC 35-50-1, IC 35-50-3, IC 35-50-5-2.

CHAPTER 8

PRIMARY OR SECONDARY SCHOOL STUDENT DELINQUENCY AND CRIMINAL CONVICTION INFORMATION

Section

35-50-8-1. Judge to notify school officers of student's conviction or adjudication.

(a) If an individual is enrolled in a primary or secondary school, including a public or nonpublic school, and:
(1) is convicted of:
(A) a Class A felony;
(B) a Class B felony;
(C) a Class C felony; or
(D) at least two (2) Class D felonies; or
(2) has been adjudicated as a delinquent child for:
(A) an act that would be:
(i) a Class A felony;
(ii) a Class B felony; or
(iii) a Class C felony; or
(B) acts that would be at least two (2) Class D felonies;
if committed by an adult;
the judge who presided over the trial, accepted the plea agreement, or adjudicated the child a delinquent child shall give written notification of the conviction or

adjudication to the chief administrative officer of the primary or secondary school, including a public or nonpublic school, or, if the individual is enrolled in a public school, the superintendent of the school district in which the individual is enrolled.

(b) Notification under subsection (a) must occur within seven (7) days after the conclusion of the trial, the date a plea agreement is accepted, or the date the child is adjudicated a delinquent child.

(c) The notification sent to a school or school district under subsection (a) must include only:

(1) the felony for which the individual was convicted or that the individual would have committed if the individual were an adult; and

(2) the individual's sentence or juvenile law disposition.

(d) If the court later modifies the individual's sentence or juvenile law disposition after giving notice under this section, the court shall notify the school or the school district in which the individual is enrolled of the sentence or disposition modification.

History.
P.L.67-2007, § 7, eff. July 1, 2007.

Index

CHINESE THROWING STAR.
Manufacture, sale or possession, §35-47-5-12.

CIGARETTES AND TOBACCO PRODUCTS.
Coin machines.
Sale or distribution of tobacco by use of, §35-46-1-11.5.
Criminal law and procedure.
Coin machines.
Sale or distribution of tobacco by use of, §35-46-1-11.5.
Definition of tobacco, §35-46-1-1.7.
Persons under 18 years of age prohibited from entering retail stores that have as primary purpose sale of tobacco products, §35-46-1-11.7.
Purchase or acceptance of tobacco by persons under eighteen years of age, §35-46-1-10.5.
Sale or distribution to persons under eighteen years of age, §35-46-1-10.
Definition of tobacco, §35-46-1-1.7.
Notice concerning prohibition on sale, §35-46-1-11.
Retail establishments, §35-46-1-10.2.
Use of coin machines, §35-46-1-11.5.
Schools.
Tobacco business.
Operation within two hundred feet of school, §35-46-1-11.2.
Tobacco business.
Defined, §35-46-1-1.
Operation within two hundred feet of school, §35-46-1-11.2.
Defenses.
Sale or distribution of tobacco to persons under eighteen years of age, §§35-46-1-10, 35-46-1-10.2.
Minors.
Definition of tobacco, §35-46-1-1.7.
Persons under 18 years of age prohibited from entering retail store that has as primary purpose sale of tobacco products, §35-46-1-11.7.
Purchase or acceptance of tobacco by persons under eighteen years of age, §35-46-1-10.5.
Sale or distribution of tobacco to persons under eighteen years of age, §35-46-1-10.
Definition of tobacco, §35-46-1-1.7.
Notice concerning prohibition on sale, §35-46-1-11.
Retail establishments, §35-46-1-10.2.
Use of coin machines, §35-46-1-11.5.
Sales.
Self-service display other than coin-operated machine.
Sale by retail establishment through.
Prohibited, §35-46-1-11.8.
Schools.
Operation of tobacco business within two hundred feet of school, §35-46-1-11.2.
Self-service display other than coin-operated machine.
Sale by retail establishment through.
Prohibited, §35-46-1-11.8.
Throwing burning material from moving vehicle, §35-45-3-3.

CITIZENS BAND RADIO.
Obscene messages prohibited, §35-45-2-2.

CIVIL DISORDERS.
Riots, §§35-45-1-1, 35-45-1-2.

CIVIL RIGHTS.
Criminal law and procedure, §35-46-2-1.
Discrimination in jury selection, §35-46-2-2.
Housing discrimination, §35-46-2-1.
Jury selection.
Discrimination, §35-46-2-2.
Misdemeanors.
Violations, §35-46-2-1.
Violations.
Discrimination in jury selection, §35-46-2-2.
Generally, §35-46-2-1.

CLONING, §§35-46-5-2, 35-46-5-3.

COCAINE.
Definition, §35-48-1-7.

COCKFIGHTS.
Definitions.
Animal fighting contests, §35-46-3-4.
Felonies.
Attending animal fighting contest, §35-46-3-10.
Possession of animal for purpose of contest, §35-46-3-8.
Prohibition of animal fighting contests, §35-46-3-9.
Misdemeanors.
Attending animal fighting contest, §35-46-3-10.

CODE GRABBING DEVICES.
Defined, §35-45-12-1.
Possession or use, §35-45-12-2.

CODEINE.
Controlled substances.
Schedule II, §35-48-2-6.
Schedule III.
Narcotic drugs, §35-48-2-8.

COMBATIVE FIGHTING, §§35-45-18-1 to 35-45-18-3.
Defined, §35-45-18-1.
Participation unlawful, §35-45-18-2.
Promoting or organizing unlawful, §35-45-18-3.

COMPUTERS AND SOFTWARE.
Spam.
Blocking by interactive computer services, §§35-45-5-4.6, 35-45-5-4.7.

CONCURRENT SENTENCES, §35-50-1-2.

CONFIDENTIALITY OF INFORMATION.
Burn injury reporting, §35-47-7-3.
Controlled substances.
Central repository for controlled substances data.
INSPECT program, §35-48-7-11.1.

CONFLICTS OF INTEREST.
Felonies, §35-44-1-3.
Local government.
Criminal offense, §35-44-1-3.
Public officers and employees.
Conduct constituting, §35-44-1-3.

CONSECUTIVE SENTENCES, §35-50-1-2.

DRUGS AND CONTROLLED SUBSTANCES
—Cont'd

Infractions.
Paraphernalia.
Dealing in paraphernalia, §35-48-4-8.5.
Machine guns.
Use or possession while dealing in controlled substances, §35-50-2-13.
Manufacture.
Defined, §35-48-1-18.
Methamphetamine.
Environmental cleanup costs, assessment, §35-48-4-17.
Offenses relating to manufacture, §35-48-4-14.
Manufacturers.
Methamphetamine.
Environmental cleanup costs, assessment, §35-48-4-17.
Substances represented to be controlled substance, §35-48-4-4.6.
Marijuana.
Dealing in, §35-48-4-10.
Defined, §35-48-1-19.
Schedule I, §35-48-2-4.
Methamphetamine, dealing in, §35-48-4-1.1.
Methamphetamine manufacture.
Environmental cleanup costs, assessment, §35-48-4-17.
Misdemeanors.
Central repository for controlled substances data.
Violations of chapter, §35-48-7-14.
Nuisances.
Taking a minor or endangered adult into a place where drugs are present, manufactured or sold, §35-48-4-13.3.
Visiting or maintaining a common nuisance, §35-48-4-13.
Paraphernalia.
Possession of paraphernalia, §35-48-4-8.3.
Reckless dealing in paraphernalia, §35-48-4-8.5.
Possession of substance represented to be controlled substance, §35-48-4-4.6.
Registration.
Offenses relating to registration, §35-48-4-14.
Motor vehicles.
Registration and license plates.
Suspension of registration, §35-48-4-15.
Narcotic drugs.
Dealing in, §35-48-4-1.
Defined, §35-48-1-20.
Schedule III, §35-48-2-8.
Schedule IV, §35-48-2-10.
Schedule V, §35-48-2-12.
Nomenclature, §35-48-2-2.
Nuisances.
Taking a minor or endangered adult into a place where drugs are present, manufactured or sold, §35-48-4-13.3.
Visiting or maintaining a common nuisance, §35-48-4-13.
Obesity.
Prescribing controlled substances to control obesity, §35-48-3-11.

DRUGS AND CONTROLLED SUBSTANCES
—Cont'd

Opiate.
Defined, §35-48-1-21.
Schedule I, §35-48-2-4.
Schedule II, §35-48-2-6.
Opium poppy.
Defined, §35-48-1-22.
Poppy straw.
Defined, §35-48-1-23.
Schedule II, §35-48-2-6.
Order forms.
Generally, §35-48-3-8.
Violations of provisions, §35-48-4-14.
Paraphernalia.
Dealing in paraphernalia, §35-48-4-8.5.
Conduct constituting, §35-48-4-8.5.
Reckless dealing in paraphernalia, §35-48-4-8.5.
Felonies.
Dealing in paraphernalia, §35-48-4-8.5.
Manufacturing of paraphernalia, §35-48-4-8.1.
Possession of paraphernalia, §35-48-4-8.3.
Manufacturing.
Conduct constituting, §35-48-4-8.1.
Misdemeanors.
Possession of paraphernalia, §35-48-4-8.3.
Reckless dealing in paraphernalia, §35-48-4-8.5.
Possession, §35-48-4-8.3.
Reckless dealing in paraphernalia, §35-48-4-8.5.
Parks.
Certain offenses occurring on or near parks, §§35-48-4-0.5 to 35-48-4-4, 35-48-4-6, 35-48-4-6.1, 35-48-4-7, 35-48-4-10.
Phenylpropanolamine.
Possession, §35-48-4-14.5.
Poppy straw.
Defined, §35-48-1-23.
Possession, §35-48-4-7.
First offense.
Conditional discharge, §35-48-4-12.
Hashish, §35-48-4-11.
Hash oil, §35-48-4-11.
Marijuana, §35-48-4-11.
Methamphetamine, §35-48-4-6.1.
Narcotic drugs, §35-48-4-6.
Paraphernalia, §35-48-4-8.3.
Practitioner.
Defined, §35-48-1-24.
Prescriptions, §§35-48-1-25, 35-48-3-9.
Production.
Defined, §35-48-1-26.
Pseudoephedrine.
Possession, §35-48-4-14.5.
Storage and reporting requirements, §35-48-4-14.7.
Registration of manufacturers and distributors.
Criteria, §35-48-3-4.
Denial.
Grounds, §35-48-3-5.
Order to show cause, §35-48-3-6.
Procedure, §§35-48-3-5, 35-48-3-6.
Exceptions to requirement, §35-48-3-3.

FIREARMS AND OTHER WEAPONS —Cont'd
Handguns —Cont'd
Sale of handguns —Cont'd
Photographic identification required,
§35-47-2.5-5.
Prohibited acts.
Dealers, §35-47-2.5-13.
False statements, §35-47-2.5-12.
Resale of guns, §§35-47-2.5-14,
35-47-2.5-15.
Residence.
Documentation of residence, §35-47-2.5-5.
Sale or transfer.
Alcohol abusers.
Prohibited, §35-47-2-7.
Drug abusers.
Prohibited, §35-47-2-7.
False information.
Use in obtaining handgun, §35-47-2-17.
Felons.
Prohibited, §35-47-2-7.
Loans secured by handgun prohibited,
§35-47-4-2.
Mentally incompetent persons.
Prohibited, §35-47-2-7.
Persons to whom sale regulations apply,
§35-47-2-8.
Prohibited sales or transfers, §35-47-2-7.
Use of false or altered license, §35-47-2-22.
Waiting period, §35-47-2-8.
Violations of chapter, §35-47-2-23.
Burden of proof, §35-47-2-24.
Wholesale.
Defined, §35-47-1-13.
Interstate firearms sales, §35-47-5-6.
Knives.
School property or school buses, possession,
§35-47-5-2.5.
Switchblade knives.
Prohibited, §35-47-5-2.
Wounds.
Report of certain wounds, §35-47-7-1.
Exceptions, §35-47-7-2.
Laser pointers, §§35-47-4.5-1 to 35-47-4.5-4.
Law enforcement officers.
Retired officers identification for carrying
firearms, §§35-47-15-1 to 35-47-15-6.
Annual photographic identification,
§35-47-15-4.
Definitions, §§35-47-15-1 to 35-47-15-3.
Training and qualifications, evidence,
§35-47-15-5.
Immunity for agency providing evidence,
§35-47-15-6.
Local regulations.
Ammunition, §35-47-11-2.
Applicability of provisions, §35-47-11-1.
Emergency ordinance.
Adoption for disaster, §35-47-11-3.
Adoption procedure, §35-47-11-4.
Expiration, §35-47-11-5.
Restriction on firearms for seventy-two
hours, §35-47-11-6.
Time of taking effect, §35-47-11-5.
Ownership, sale, transfer, etc., §35-47-11-2.
Machine guns.
Controlled substances.
Use or possession while dealing, §35-50-2-13.

FIREARMS AND OTHER WEAPONS —Cont'd
Machine guns —Cont'd
Operation or discharge.
Prohibited, §35-47-5-9.
Exemptions, §35-47-5-10.
Ownership or possession.
Prohibited, §35-47-5-8.
Exceptions, §35-47-5-10.
Pointing at another, §35-47-4-3.
Mass destruction, weapons of.
Money laundering to support, §35-45-15-5.
Terroristic mischief, §35-47-12-3.
Undisclosed transport of dangerous device,
§35-47-6-1.1.
Use to carry out terrorism, §35-47-12-1.
Use to damage crops or livestock, §35-47-12-2.
Minors.
Dangerous possession of firearm, §35-47-10-5.
Providing firearm by adult to child,
§35-47-10-6.
Misdemeanors.
Chinese throwing star.
Manufacture, sale or possession, §35-47-5-12.
Handguns.
Pointing at another, §35-47-4-3.
Violations of chapter, §35-47-2-23.
Intoxicated persons.
Sale or delivery of weapon to intoxicated
persons, §35-47-4-1.
Laser pointers.
Directing light at public safety officer,
§35-47-4.5-4.
Pointing of firearm, §35-47-4-3.
Pointing firearm at another, §35-47-4-3.
Possession of certain firearms.
School property and school buses, §§35-47-9-1,
35-47-9-2.
Prisons and prisoners.
Possession, §35-44-3-9.5.
Proper person.
Defined, §35-47-1-7.
Proper reasons.
Defined, §35-47-1-8.
Retail.
Defined, §35-47-1-9.
Riots.
Rioting while armed with deadly weapon,
§35-45-1-2.
Sales.
Interstate firearm sales, §35-47-5-6.
Searches and seizures.
Seizure and retention of firearms, procedures,
§§35-47-14-1 to 35-47-14-9.
Dangerous individual, defined, §35-47-14-1.
Destruction or permanent disposal,
§35-47-14-9.
Hearings, §35-47-14-5.
Burden of proof, §35-47-14-6.
Determinations, §35-47-14-6.
Return of firearm, §§35-47-14-6, 35-47-14-7.
Petition, §35-47-14-8.
Warrants, §35-47-14-2.
Filing, §35-47-14-4.
Sentencing.
Use of firearms, §35-50-2-11.
Seriously violent felon.
Possession of firearms by, §35-47-4-5.

HOUSING.
Discrimination, §35-46-2-1.

HUMANE SOCIETIES.
Controlled substances.
Limited permits, §35-48-3-2.
Drugs.
Limited controlled substances permit,
§35-48-3-2.

HUMAN ORGANS.
Unlawful transfer, §35-46-5-1.

HUSBAND AND WIFE.
Battery.
Domestic battery.
Firearms.
Possession by domestic batterers,
§35-47-4-6.
Restoration of right, §35-47-4-7.
Domestic battery.
Firearms.
Possession by domestic batterers, §35-47-4-6.
Restoration of right, §35-47-4-7.
Nonsupport of a child, §35-46-1-6.

I

IMPERSONATION.
Firefighter, §35-44-4-7.
Law enforcement officers, §35-44-2-3.
Public officers and employees, §35-44-2-3.

IMPOUNDMENT OF ANIMALS, §35-46-3-6.

INCEST.
Defenses.
Valid marriage, §35-46-1-3.
Elements of offense, §35-46-1-3.
Felony, §35-46-1-3.
First cousin marriages, §35-46-1-3.
Marriage.
Defenses.
Valid marriage, §35-46-1-3.

INDECENCY.
Public indecency, §35-45-4-1.
Public nudity, §35-45-4-1.5.

INDECENT EXPOSURE, §35-45-4-1.
Public nudity, §35-45-4-1.5.

INFRACTIONS.
Cigarettes.
Self-service display other than coin-operated
machine.
Sale by retail establishment through,
§35-46-1-11.8.
Throwing burning material from moving
vehicle, §35-45-3-3.
Contact lenses.
Dispensing without prescription, §35-45-20-2.
Controlled substances.
Paraphernalia.
Dealing in paraphernalia, §35-48-4-8.5.
Emergency incident area.
Refusal to leave.
Firefighter not dispatched, §35-44-4-6.

INFRACTIONS —Cont'd
**Exploitation of dependent or endangered
adult.**
Failure to report battery, neglect or
exploitation of endangered adult,
§35-46-1-13.
Retaliation against person making report
concerning endangered individual,
§35-46-1-13.
Explosives.
Permit for regulated explosives magazine.
Violations, §35-47.5-4-6.
Littering, §35-45-3-2.
Throwing burning material from moving
vehicle, §35-45-3-3.

INJURIES.
Reports.
Burn injury reporting.
Confidentiality of information, §35-47-7-3.
Requirements, §35-47-7-3.
Firework or pyrotechnic injury reports,
§35-47-7-7.
Wounds caused by certain weapons, §35-47-7-1.
Exceptions, §35-47-7-2.
Wounds caused by manufacture of destructive
devices, §§35-47.5-4-7, 35-47-7-5.

INSPECTIONS.
Explosives.
Inspection of manufacturing plants,
§35-47.5-4-1.
Inspection of storage locations, §35-47.5-4-3.

INSPECT PROGRAM.
**Indiana scheduled prescription electronic
collection and tracking program.**
Confidentiality of information, §35-48-7-11.1.
Controlled substances data fund, §35-48-7-13.1.
Definition of INSPECT, §35-48-7-5.2.
Required actions, §35-48-7-10.1.
Rulemaking to implement, §35-48-7-12.1.

INSURANCE.
Explosives.
Insurance requirements, §35-47.5-4-2.

INTERNET.
Online motion picture piracy, §§35-46-8-1 to
35-46-8-5.

INTIMIDATION.
Conduct constituting, §35-45-2-1.
Criminal gang intimidation, §35-45-9-4.
Definitions.
Threat, §35-45-2-1.
Felonies.
Criminal gang intimidation, §35-45-9-4.
Misdemeanor, §35-45-2-1.

INVASION OF PRIVACY, §35-46-1-15.1.
**Notice of release of or hearings for persons
convicted of,** §35-46-1-18.
Time limit for providing notice, §35-46-1-19.
Persons convicted of.
Maintaining of confidential information
relating to, §35-46-1-16.
Restrictions on access to information,
§35-46-1-17.

PRISONS AND PRISONERS —Cont'd
Weapons.
Possession, §35-44-3-9.5.

PRIVACY.
Invasion of privacy, §§35-46-1-15.1 to 35-46-1-19.
Notice of release of or hearings for persons convicted of, §35-46-1-18.
Time limit for providing notice, §35-46-1-19.
Person convicted of.
Maintaining of confidential information relating to, §35-46-1-16.
Restrictions on access to information, §35-46-1-17.

PRIVILEGES.
Burn injury reporting.
Confidentiality of burn injury reporting information, §35-47-7-3.

PROBATION.
Conditions of probation.
Restitution or reparation to victim.
Requiring as condition of probation, §35-50-5-3.
Evidence.
Considerations by court in deciding issuance of orders, §35-50-7-8.
Felony.
Suspension of sentence for, §35-50-2-2.
Misdemeanor.
Suspension of sentence for, §35-50-3-1.
Notice.
Orders, §35-50-7-6.
Stay, modification or vacation, §35-50-7-7.
Orders, §§35-50-7-1 to 35-50-7-9.
Applicability of chapters, §35-50-7-1.
Copy to be given to persons concerned, §35-50-7-5.
Evidence considered in determining issuance, §35-50-7-8.
Notice of order, §35-50-7-6.
Notice of stay, modification or vacation, §35-50-7-7.
Penalty for violations, §35-50-7-9.
Prohibiting person from entering certain areas or property, §35-50-7-2.
Description of property, §35-50-7-3.
Return to residential premises.
Restrictions on and supervision of return, §35-50-7-4.
Restitution.
Conditions of probation.
Requiring restitution as condition.
Restitution orders, §35-50-5-3.
Suspension of sentence for felony, §35-50-2-2.
Suspension of sentence for misdemeanor, §35-50-3-1.

PROFESSIONAL LICENSING AGENCY.
Indiana scheduled prescription electronic collection and tracking (INSPECT) program.
Confidentiality of information, §35-48-7-11.1.
Controlled substances data fund, §35-48-7-13.1.
Definition of INSPECT, §35-48-7-5.2.
Required actions, §35-48-7-10.1.

PROFESSIONAL LICENSING AGENCY —Cont'd
Indiana scheduled prescription electronic collection and tracking (INSPECT) program —Cont'd
Rulemaking to implement, §35-48-7-12.1.

PROFITEERING.
Public service, §35-44-1-7.

PROSECUTING ATTORNEYS.
Gambling.
Operators of illegal activity.
Notice specifying gambling illegal activity, §35-45-5-4.5.

PROSTITUTION.
Conduct constituting, §35-45-4-2.
Felonies, §35-45-4-2.
Patronizing prostitute, §35-45-4-3.
Misdemeanors, §35-45-4-2.
Patronizing prostitute, §35-45-4-3.
Patronizing prostitute.
Conduct constituting, §35-45-4-3.
Promoting prostitution.
Conduct constituting, §35-45-4-4.

PROTECTIVE ORDERS.
Criminal law and procedure.
Violation, §35-46-1-15.1.
Foreign protection orders.
Enforcement by law enforcement officers, §35-46-1-20.
Law enforcement officers.
Enforcement of foreign protective order, §35-46-1-20.

PSEUDOEPHEDRINE.
Possession, §35-48-4-14.5.
Storage and reporting requirements, §35-48-4-14.7.

PSYCHEDELIC SUBSTANCES.
Controlled substances.
Schedule I.
Hallucinogenic substances, §35-48-2-4.
Schedule II.
Hallucinogenic substances, §35-48-2-6.

PUBLIC INDECENCY.
Conduct constituting, §35-45-4-1.

PUBLIC NUDITY, §35-45-4-1.5.

PUBLIC OFFICERS AND EMPLOYEES.
Bribery.
Conduct constituting, §35-44-1-1.
Penalty, §35-50-5-1.1.
Conflicts of interest.
Conduct constituting, §35-44-1-3.
Criminal law and procedure.
Official misconduct, §35-44-1-2.
Profiteering from public service, §35-44-1-7.
Ghost employment, §35-44-2-4.
Impersonation, §35-44-2-3.
Misconduct.
Official misconduct.
Conduct constituting, §35-44-1-2.
Official misconduct.
Conduct constituting, §35-44-1-2.